A History of Asia

FIFTH EDITION

Rhoads Murphey

Professor Emeritus of History
University of Michigan

PEARSON
Longman

New York Boston San Francisco
London Toronto Sydney Tokyo Singapore Madrid
Mexico City Munich Paris Cape Town Hong Kong Montreal

To my lifelong teacher and friend, John Fairbank, who died on September 14, 1991, before I had the chance to present him with this book, so much of which stems from his inspiration and example.

Senior Acquisitions Editor: Janet Lanphier
Executive Marketing Manager: Sue Westmoreland
Media and Supplements Editor: Kristi Olson
Production Manager: Donna DeBenedictis
Project Coordination, Text Design, and Electronic Page Makeup: Nesbitt Graphics, Inc.
Cover Designer/Senior Design Manager: Nancy Danahy
Cover Image: Twelve-symbol robe. Kesi in various shades of blue and white. Chinese, early 19th century. Victoria and Albert Museum, London, Great Britain. Photo Credit: Victoria and Albert Museum, London/Art Resource, NY.
Photo Researcher: Linda Sykes
Senior Manufacturing Buyer: Alfred C. Dorsey
Printer and Binder: Hamilton Printing Company
Cover Printer: The Lehigh Press, Inc.

Library of Congress Cataloging-in-Publication Data

Murphey, Rhoads, 1919–
 A history of Asia / Rhoads Murphey.—5th ed.
  p. cm.
 Includes bibliographical references and index.
 ISBN 0-321-34054-X
 1. Asia—History. I. Title.
 DS33.M87 2005
 950—dc22

                     2005019545

Please visit us at http://www.ablongman.com

ISBN 0-321-34054-X

1 2 3 4 5 6 7 8 9 10—HT—08 07 06 05

Brief Contents

Detailed Contents

INTRODUCTION Monsoon Asia as a Unit of Study 1

CHAPTER 1 Prehistoric Asia 10

CHAPTER 2 Asian Religions and Their Cultures 21

CHAPTER 3 The Traditional Societies of Asia 43

CHAPTER **9**   **Early, Classical, and Medieval Japan and Korea 162**

CHAPTER **10**   **Mughal India and Central Asia 185**

CHAPTER **11**   **New Imperial Splendor in China: The Ming Dynasty 206**

CHAPTER **12**   **The West Arrives in Asia 229**

CHAPTER **13**   **Manchu China and Tokugawa Japan 249**

Contents by Country or Region

List of Maps

List of Documents

Preface

There has long been a need for a history of Asia, but that need has become more pressing as courses dealing with it, and enrollments in them, have multiplied. This book is designed primarily for students taking courses in Asian history, but students taking courses in world history or non-Western history will also find it useful. To most people, "Asia" means primarily the areas and cultures east of Persia (Iran) and south of the former Soviet Union, which are the focus of this book. This vast and varied part of the world, containing roughly half the world's people since about 3000 B.C.E. until the present, is sometimes called "monsoon Asia," the generally warm and wet parts of the continent, sharply distinct from the desert landscape of the Middle East or the cold areas of the former Soviet Union. Its permissive climate is, of course, responsible for the size and density of its population, in contrast with the far emptier areas of western and northern Asia. So defined, it stretches from the Khyber Pass on the border between Pakistan and Afghanistan, through India, mainland and island Southeast Asia, to China, Korea, and Japan.

Each of these separate regions has long contained distinctively different peoples and cultures, but nearly all achieved a high level of sophistication 2,000 years ago or more. Given the great age of these Asian civilizations and the size of their populations from early times, more people have lived in Asia than in the rest of the world combined. Together they thus represent the largest, richest, and most varied chapter in the history of the human experience. Any attempt to deal with world history must make a major place for Asia, but the history of Asia is important and rewarding in itself.

Introduction to Major Asian Civilizations

This book is designed either to stand alone or be supplemented by readings from those listed at the end of each chapter or from primary materials (in addition to those quoted in the text). Chapters are of approximately equal length. The book itself can, thus, serve as the text for a one-semester course, a two-quarter course, or a full-year course, or it can be integrated into a larger world course. Chapter 3 offers a comparative analysis of traditional Asian societies including some comparisons with the Western tradition. With Chapter 12, the modern West begins to impinge on the great Asian traditions, and in subsequent chapters Western pressures and Asian responses play an increasing role, from colonialism, semicolonialism, and wars of conquest to World War II and the coming of Asian independence and revolution. A final chapter considers major themes in Asian development at the start of the twenty-first century, including its unprecedentedly high economic growth rate, the reasons for this, and the rise of Asia to a position of leadership in the contemporary world.

Nearly all texts in Asian history concentrate on one of the four major civilizations; only a few cover the closely interrelated histories of China and Japan, sometimes including minor coverage of Korea, which in this book is given relatively greater attention, as is often-neglected Vietnam. Each of the four major Asian civilizations has its own corps of specialists, and most of them rarely stray far from their center of expertise. But there is a strong argument for studying Asian history as a whole, perhaps especially on the part of undergraduates, but to the benefit of specialists as well. This book is explicitly comparative, as well as offering a balanced history of each major tradition from its beginnings to the present day. Chapter 21 returns to the theme of Asian universals and cross-cultural comparisons. The book as a whole draws on the most recent scholarship and reflects the author's professional involvement with Asia and its history over more than forty years, including long periods of research, observation, and residence there. It is written for beginning students with no previous background in Asian history, introducing them to its major features in clear, simple language.

Focus on Social and Cultural History

A major development in the writing of history during the past twenty years or more has been the increased attention to social and cultural history and the effort to re-create as much as possible the lives of ordinary people. This book is especially strong in its attention to such matters, although for the early periods in Asia, as elsewhere, we have only a little information on which to draw. Nevertheless, every chapter includes as much as can be derived about social and cultural trends and about the everyday life of the common people, in addition to major political and economic events and developments. A further feature is the coverage of all the major Asian religions (Chapter 2) and its consideration of how each religious tradition fit in with and reflected the societies where it flourished. The emphasis on sociocultural developments is especially clearly brought out in the book's wealth of photographic illustrations. Maps in nearly every chapter further illustrate the stage on which the events described took place. An additional feature of this book is its recurrent emphasis on the geographic basis of each Asian civilization, and the role of the environment in the evolution of each. Finally, particular attention is paid in every chapter to the changing role of women, both individually in the case of women who rose to prominence in various fields, and collectively in terms of the changing status of women in each Asian society.

Features and Primary Source Materials

Not only to add vividness but also to pursue many of the points mentioned above, most chapters also include an urban portrait of a city during the time of the chapter's coverage, with special attention to the lives of ordinary people, and a biographical portrait with the same objectives; many of the latter are of prominent women, but all help to make history come alive. Nearly every chapter includes boxed quotations from relevant primary sources that further contribute to putting the reader into the scene in a participatory way as well as providing a sample of the kinds of documents with which historians work. Finally, at the end of every chapter except the last is a list of relevant Web sites and an extensive set of suggestions for further readings, selected mainly from the most recent scholarship on each chapter's subject but including also classical or standard works, and usually providing a range of differing interpretations.

The writing of history, like that in any discipline, is continually changing, as our own perceptions of the past change and as each new generation looks for different things in the past. This book reflects those changes, and presents the history of Asia as most professionals in the field view it today. Its currency, and its coverage of recent events, is a strong asset. Asian history is a rapidly growing field, and it is time for a text that covers it for beginning students, as a whole rather than as the history of individual countries, as we have long had for Western history. It is at least as rich, as old or older, and as important in the global scene, by any combination of measures. The world of the twenty-first century seems likely to be dominated by Asia, even more than in its traditional and glorious past. We need to understand far more about it, and the best way to achieve that, including an understanding of the present and future, is to study its history.

Changes in the Fifth Edition

The text has again been reviewed carefully, and the material brought up to date as of 2005. Thanks to the suggestions of readers, nine new boxed feature essays, written by Southeast Asian historian Kenneth Hall, have been added to this edition. Titled "Reading Across Cultures," they emphasize cross-cultural comparisons and provide expanded treatment of Southeast Asia. They also introduce students to major themes that recur in Asian and world history.

Other new features include chronologies at the beginning of most chapters, a set of discussion questions at the end of each chapter, and the listing of many new Web sites. In addition to the material in Reading Across Cultures. the treatment of Southeast Asia has been expanded throughout the text and also by the addition of a new Chapter 7, which focuses on early and medieval Southeast Asia.

Instructor Supplements

Instructor's Manual/Test Bank
ISBN: 0-321-35742-6
Prepared by Christopher Gerteis of Coastal Carolina University, this instructor supplement includes chapter outlines, essay and discussion questions, classroom discussion questions, and multiple-choice questions.

PowerPoint Presentation
Prepared by Christopher Gerteis of Coastal Carolina University, the PowerPoints contain lecture notes and images from every chapter of the text. Available by download only via the Instructor Resource Center at *www.ablongman.com/irc*.

Acknowledgments

No one really writes alone, and I have been enabled to undertake this doubtless presumptuous task by a host of other scholars, some my friends and colleagues at Michigan and elsewhere, many others whom I have known only through what they have written. My debt to all of these people is incalculable, and I can never hope to repay it. Without in any way regarding it as adequate, I want nevertheless to thank specifically a few of my colleagues and friends who have taken the trouble to read parts, and in a few cases most, of the book in manuscript, have shared their comments with me, and have saved me from many errors: Professors Dilip Basu, Michael Cullinane, Karl deSchweinitz, Roger Hackett, Karl Hutterer, Victor Lieberman, Thomas Trautmann, and Philip Woodruff. James Chan read the entire manuscript and provided valuable comments and corrections.

I am also grateful to the readers to whom the publisher sent the manuscript for their most helpful comments: Kenneth R. Hall, Ball State University; Yonglin Jiang, Oklahoma State University; Daniel Meissner, Marquette University; Wing-Kai To, Bridgewater State College; and William Wie, University of Colorado.

Let me also thank the many readers whose comments were so helpful in preparing previous editions: Anita Andrew, Northern Illinois University; E. Taylor Atkins, Northern Illinois University; Sue Chung, University of Nevada, Las Vegas; Ned Davis, University of Hawaii at Manoa; Howard Didsbury, Kean College of New Jersey; Ron Edgerton, University of Northern Colorado; Edward Glatfelter, Utah State University; Jeff Hanes, University of Illinois at Urbana-Champaign; Yong Ho, China Institute; Lisa Hollander, Jefferson College; George Hopkins, Western Illinois University; William F. King, Mt. San Antonio Community College; Justin Libby, Indiana University Purdue University; Sumiko Otsubo, Creighton University; Mingte Pan, SUNY Oswego; Loretta Pang, Kapiolani Community College; Wesley Sasaki-Uemura, University of Utah; Douglas P. Sjoquist, Lansing Community College; Tracy Steele, Sam Houston State University; Chin H. Suk, York College of Pennsylvania; and C. K. Yoon, James Madison University. It should go without saying that errors, infelicities, or imbalances that remain are entirely my own responsibility.

Equally important, I am indebted to all of my fellow Asianists at many universities and colleges in this country and abroad from whom I have learned so much over many years through association and interchange as well as through reading their work. They have been and remain my teachers, but I also owe a special debt to my original teachers: John Fairbank, Edwin Reischauer, Daniel Ingalls, Rupert Emerson, and Norman Brown, each of whom began my apprenticeship in the most exciting ways and from whom I am still learning. To that list of teachers I would add the kind, cheerful, helpful, understanding, wonderful people of China, India, Korea, Japan, and Southeast Asia, among whom I have lived and worked at various times for many years all told, and without whom I could never have attempted such a book or a career in Asian studies at all. They have been my first and greatest teachers, and they have also given me a love for them and their world, which is what brought me to Asian studies to begin with and which has continued to sustain me. One cannot begin to understand without sympathy, and that they have given me in overflowing measure.

All of these, my teachers and friends, have not only inspired me in this overambitious endeavor but have made it, quite honestly, a pleasure. My wife Eleanor has also helped to make it so with her encouragement, her often insightful critical readings of what I wrote, and her cheerful support throughout. I can never discharge my debt to all those who have helped me, but I will be richly rewarded if they, and the readers of this book, find it acceptable, and for those new to the field, an invitation to a further voyage of discovery, to find at least some of the excitement my many teachers around the world have given me in the riches of Asia.

RHOADS MURPHEY

Author's Note to the Reader

No single-volume attempt to write the history of Asia can be more than the briefest introduction. I hope that all who read it will take it as an invitation to explore further. Space limits have made it necessary to foreshorten the treatment of every major aspect of Asian history and to do less than justice to all of them. I have nevertheless tried within these constraints to apportion space more or less in relation to the size, populousness, and level of development of each culture or country at each period. It has been necessary to adjust to the additional consideration that, especially for the earlier periods, we do not have adequate sources for many areas, by comparison with others that are consequently somewhat more fully treated. Thus, for example, Japan before about 1500, Korea before about 1850, and most of Southeast Asia before about 1800 are not treated here as extensively as India and, especially, China, where we have so much more material and many more centuries of literate development on which to draw. It is perhaps some consolation that none of these areas contained more than a small fraction of India's or China's populations, and that what development took place there owed a great deal to the Chinese and/or Indian models and their diffusion. All of these considerations, except perhaps the last, are even more relevant for Central Asia.

Periodization is a perennial problem for all historians, and the same is true for period labels. I have had to be both sweeping and arbitrary in this book, given its temporal and areal scope. Medieval is a European term and has many connotations for European history. It does not carry those associations for Asia, but one must use some term in so general a treatment to cover the period between "ancient" or "classical" and "modern." *Medieval* means simply "middle era" or "middle period," and I have used it here strictly in that sense, as being simpler and clearer than any alternatives but without implying that European patterns or preconceptions are intended. When one writes about anything beyond the recent past, there is another and more vital problem: We know far too little of the lives of most people, especially the nonliterate who were the great majority everywhere until recently and who thus have left us only indirect evidence about themselves. For much of the past we have records primarily of the lives and doings of the elites and the rise and fall of states and kingdoms, monuments and battles, kings and conquests. Here and there we can catch a glimpse of the lives of ordinary people, and I have tried to draw on some of this material where possible, including what popular literature has survived, festivals, folk religion, and guesses about mass welfare, but I am well aware that I can give only an incomplete picture. The record of major events is important too, and given the limitations of any one-volume treatment, they necessarily take up most of these pages.

About the Author

Born in Philadelphia, Rhoads Murphey, a specialist in Chinese history and in geography, received his doctorate from Harvard University in 1950. Before joining the faculty of the University of Michigan in 1964, he taught at the University of Washington; he has also been a visiting professor at Taiwan University and Tokyo University. From 1954 to 1956 he was the director of the Conference of Diplomats in Asia. The University of Michigan granted him a Distinguished Service Award in 1974. Formerly president of the Association for Asian Studies, Murphey has served as editor of the *Journal of Asian Studies, Michigan Papers in Chinese Studies*, and the Association for Asian Studies' *Monographs*. The Social Science Research Council, the Ford Foundation, the Guggenheim Foundation, the National Endowment for the Humanities, and the American Council of Learned Societies have awarded him fellowships. A prolific author, Murphey's books include *Shanghai: Key to Modern China* (1953), *An Introduction to Geography* (4th ed., 1978), *A New China Policy* (with others, 1965), *Approaches to Modern Chinese History* (with others, 1967), *The Scope of Geography* (3d ed., 1982), *The Treaty Ports and China's Modernization* (1970), *China Meets the West: The Treaty Ports* (1975), and *The Fading of the Maoist Vision* (1980). *The Outsiders: Westerners in India and China* (1977) won the Best-Book-of-the-Year award from the University of Michigan Press. At Michigan he was for many years director of the Program in Asian Studies.

A Note on the Spelling of Asian Names and Words

Nearly all Asian languages are written with symbols different from our Western alphabet. Chinese, Japanese, and Korean are written with ideographic characters, plus a phonetic syllabary for Japanese and different scripts for Korean and Vietnamese. Most other Asian languages have their own scripts, symbols, diacritical marks, and alphabets, which differ from ours. There can, thus, be no single "correct spelling" in Western symbols for Asian words or names, including personal names and place names—only established conventions. Unfortunately, conventions in this respect differ widely and in many cases reflect preferences or forms related to different Western languages.

Chinese presents the biggest problem, since there are a great many different conventions in use. Most American newspapers and some books and journals now use the romanization system called *Pinyin*, approved by the Chinese government, which renders with greater phonetic accuracy, as Beijing and Guangzhou, the two cities previously known as Peking and Canton.

The usage in this book follows the Pinyin system because it has become widely used. Readers will encounter both Wade-Giles and Pinyin spellings, plus others, in other books, papers, and journals, and some familiarity with both conventions is thus necessary (see the facing table).

In general, readers should realize and remember that English spellings of names from other languages (such as Munich for München, Vienna for Wien, Danube for Donau, and Rome for Roma), especially in Asia, can be only approximations and may differ confusingly from one Western source or map to another.

Wade-Giles/Pinyin Equivalents

Wade-Giles	Pinyin	Wade-Giles	Pinyin	Wade-Giles	Pinyin	Wade-Giles	Pinyin
		ch'en	chen			p'ien	pian
		ch'eng	cheng				
cha	zha	ch'i	qi	j	r		
chai	zhai	ch'ia	qia	jih	ri	shih	shi
chan	zhan	ch'iang	qiang	jo	ruo	so	suo
chang	zhang	ch'iao	qiao	jung	rong		
chao	zhao	ch'ieh	qie			ssu, szu	si
che	zhe	ch'ien	qian	k	g	sung	song
chen	zhen	ch'i	chi	ko	ge		
cheng	zheng	ch'in	qin	kuei	gui	t	d
chi	ji	ch'ing	qing	kung	gong	tieh	die
chia	jia	ch'iu	qiu	k'	k	tien	dian
chiao	jiao	ch'iung	qiong	k'o	ke	to	duo
chieh	jie	ch'o	chuo	k'ung	kong	tung	dong
chien	jian	ch'ou	chou				
chih	zhi	ch'u	chu			t'	t
chin	jin	ch'ü	qu	lieh	lie	t'ieh	tie
ching	jing	ch'uai	chuai	lien	lian	t'ien	tian
chiu	jiu	ch'uan	quan	lo	luo	t'o	tuo
cho	zhuo	ch'uang	chuang	lüeh	lüe	tung	tong
chou	zhou	ch'üeg	que	lung	long	ts, tz	z
chu	zhu	ch'ui	chui			tso	zuo
chü	ju	ch'un	chun	mieh	mie	tsung	zong
chua	zhua	ch'ün	qun	mien	mian	tzu	zi
chuai	zhuai	ch'unh	chong				
chuan	zhuan					ts', tz'	c
chüan	juan			nieh	nie	ts'o	cuo
chuang	zhuang	erh	er	nien	nian	ts'ung	cong
chüeh	jue			no	nuo	tz'u	ci
chui	zhui	ho	he	nüeh	nüe		
chun	zhun	hung	hong	nung	nong		
chün	jun						
chung	zhong	hs	x	o	e	yeh	ye
		hsieh	xie			yen	yan
ch'a	cha	hsien	xian	p	b	yu	you
ch'ai	chai	hsiung	xiong	pieh	bie	yü	yu
ch'an	chan	hsü	xu	pien	bian	yüan	yuan
ch'ang	chang	hsüan	xuan			yüeh	yue
ch'ao	chao	hsüeh	xue	p'	p	yün	yun
ch'e	che	hsün	xun	p'ieh	piep	yung	yong

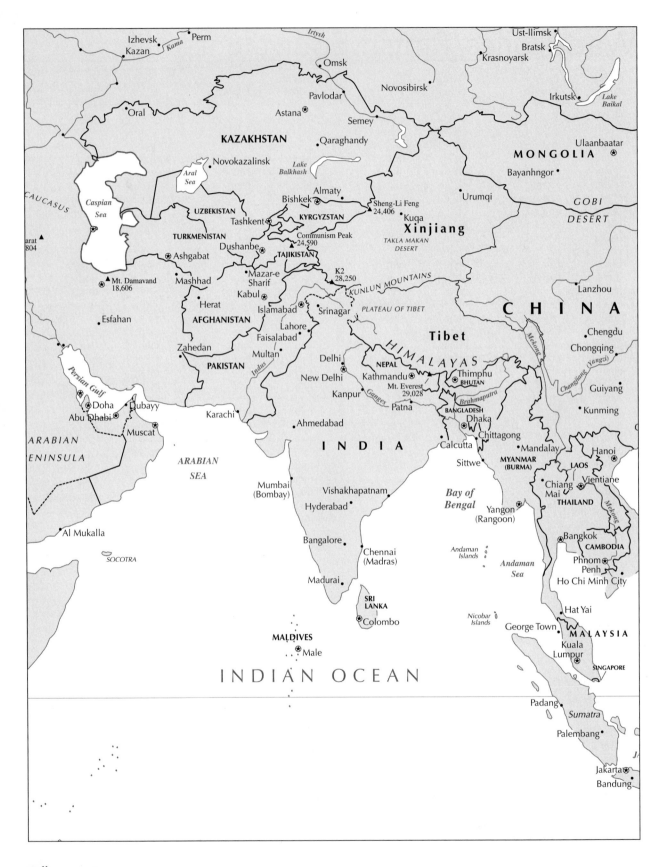

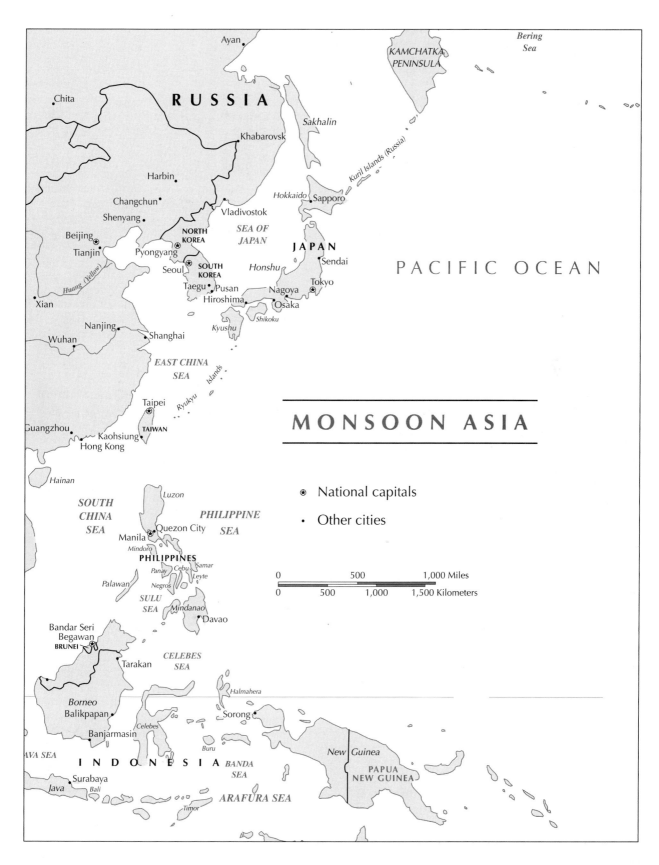

MONSOON ASIA

- ⊛ National capitals
- · Other cities

| 0 | | 500 | | 1,000 Miles |

| 0 | 500 | 1,000 | 1,500 Kilometers |

Chronology

India	China	Korea-Japan	Southeast Asia	Other Civilizations
4000 B.C.E.				
Indus culture, 3000–2000 B.C.E.	Yangshao, c. 3000–c. 2000 B.C.E. Longshan, c. 2500–c. 1800 B.C.E.	Jomon culture in Japan to c. 300 B.C.E.	Early bronze and agriculture	Sumer and Egypt, 4000 B.C.E.
2000 B.C.E.				
Aryan migrations, 1700–1200 B.C.E.	Xia (?) Shang, c. 1600–1050 B.C.E.	Chinese civilization spreads to Korea	Javanese (?) sailors to Africa	Hammurabi's code, 1750 B.C.E. Hysos invasion of Egypt Trojan War
1000 B.C.E.				
Vedic culture, 1000–500 B.C.E. The Buddha, c. 563–c. 480 B.C.E. Magadha, 500 B.C.E. Maurya, 322–180 B.C.E. Ashoka, r. 269–232 B.C.E.	Zhou conquest, 1027 B.C.E. Confucius, c. 551–479 B.C.E. Warring states Qin conquest, 221 B.C.E.	Yayoi culture in Japan, c. 300 B.C.E.– 250 C.E.	Nam Viet	Homer, Socrates, Plato Greek city states Aristotle, Alexander Rise of Roman power Julius Caesar
C.E.				
Kushans, c. 100 B.C.E.–C.E. Guptas, c. 320–c. 550 Harsha, 606–648 Southern Kingdoms: Chola, Pandya, Pallava Tamils invade Ceylon Arabs in Sindh	Han dynasty, 206 B.C.E.–220 C.E. Northern Wei and "Six Dynasties"; spread of Buddhism Suri, 581–617 Tang, 618–907 Northern Song, 960–1127 Southern Song, 1127–1279 Su Shi, Zhu Xi	Paekche, Koguryo and Silla in Korea Tomb period, 250–550 in Japan Yamato state, c. 550–c. 710 Nara period, 710–784 Heian, 794–1185 Lady Murasaki Koryo in Korea, 935–1200	China conquers Nam Viet Early states: Funan, Champa Northern Vietnam free from China Tang retake N. Vietnam, Song let it go Pagan kingdom in Burma, 850–1280s	Jesus Christ Roman Empire in Mediterranean and Western Europe Fall of Rome by 410 Muhammed, 570–632 Abbasid caliphate Byzantine Empire Charlemagne, 768–814
1000				
Mahmud of Ghazni and Muslim invaders in N. Delhi sultanate, 1206–1526 Ala ud din, r. 1296–1316 Tughluks and Lodis Vijayanagara, 1336–1565	Mongol conquest, Yuan dynasty, 1279–1368 Ming, 1368–1644 Zheng He's fleets Water margins, golden lotus	Mongol conquest of Korea, Yi, 1392–1910 Kamakura in Japan, 1185–1339 Ashikaga, 1336–1570 Nobunaga and Hideyoshi	Ankor Thom and Wat, c. 900–c. 1200, Khmer glory and decline Rise of Thai state Borobodur, Sri Vijaya, Majapahit, 800–1400	Mayas in Central America Aztecs in Mexico Incas in Peru Crusades, 1096–1204 Tamerlane, 1136–1405

Ithaka

As you set out for Ithaka
hope your road is a long one,
full of adventure, full of discovery.
Laistrygonians, Cyclops,
angry Poseidon—don't be afraid of them:
you'll never find things like that on your way
as long as you keep your thoughts raised high,
as long as a rare excitement
stirs your spirit and your body.
Laistrygonians, Cyclops,
wild Poseidon—you won't encounter them
unless you bring them along inside your soul,
unless your soul sets them up in front of you.
Hope your road is a long one.
May there be many summer mornings when,
with what pleasure, what joy,
you enter harbors you're seeing for the first time;
may you stop at Phoenician trading stations
to buy fine things,
mother of pearl and coral, amber and ebony,
sensual perfume of every kind—
as many sensual perfumes as you can;
and may you visit many Egyptian cities
to learn and go on learning from their scholars.
Keep Ithaka always in your mind.
Arriving there is what you're destined for.
But don't hurry the journey at all.
Better if it lasts for years,
so you're old by the time you reach the island,
wealthy with all you've gained on the way,
not expecting Ithaka to make you rich.
Ithaka gave you the marvelous journey.
Without her you wouldn't have set out.
She has nothing left to give you now.
And if you find her poor, Ithaka won't have fooled you.
Wise as you will have become, so full of experience,
you'll have understood by then what these Ithakas mean.

C. P. Cavafy

Introduction: Monsoon Asia as a Unit of Study

Half the world lies in Asia east of Afghanistan and south of the former Soviet Union: half of its people and far more than half of its historical experience, for these are the oldest living civilized traditions. India and China developed sophisticated cultures and technologies long before Europe and led the world for more than 2,000 years, economically and politically as well as culturally and technologically. Korea, Japan, and Southeast Asia evolved their own high civilizations during the many centuries after the fall of Rome while Europe endured the barbarian invasions, the so-called Dark Ages, and the long medieval period. The great Asian traditions and the vigorously growing modern states and economies of Asia offer the student a rich and varied record of human experience, in literature, philosophy, and the arts, in statecraft and empire building, in the varied lives of their people, but perhaps most of all in the many different approaches to universal human conditions and problems. India, China, and Southeast Asia, well over one and a half times the size of all of Europe, are all equally rich in their cultural variety. Japan, though smaller, offers still another set of experiences, additionally fascinating because of Japanese success in meeting the modern West on its own terms.

Each of these major civilizations deserves study, and increasingly, their histories are part of the college and university curriculum. But they also need to be seen as part of the larger Asian whole, just as we study, for example, France within Europe and European history as a composite of the history of its parts. This book provides the beginning student with an introduction to Asian history through the histories of its major civilized traditions. As the treatment progresses, successive chapters relate them to each other and to Western history, until the two great traditions of West and East begin to merge in the age of European expansion at the beginning of the sixteenth century. Knowledge of Asia is vital to understanding the world in which we live, a world where Asia is more and more deeply woven into our lives. But the richness and depth of the Asian experience are perhaps even more important rewards awaiting the student who begins with this book.

Geography

The continent of Asia begins by convention at Suez, the Bosporus at Istanbul, and the Ural Mountains in the former Soviet Union; it is, thus, the eastern four-fifths of the single landmass of Eurasia, encompassing over 17 million square miles and by far the largest of the continents. But these conventional lines do not mark any major or abrupt change in landscape or culture, especially not along the principal line of the Urals. This range is relatively low and easily crossed; on both sides of it the northern coniferous forest that covers much of northern Europe and most of northern Asia continues with few breaks, an area of sparse population, little rainfall, and great seasonal temperature extremes.

The southern third of the former Soviet Union east of the line of the Urals is similarly an extension of what lies to the west, an area of aridity that merges eastward into the sparsely populated desert whose traditional nomadic or oasis cultures still contrast sharply with Russian culture and with those of India, Southeast Asia, China, and Japan. Much of this arid desert area of Central Asia was conquered by Muslim invaders beginning in the eighth century C.E., further establishing the area's similarity with the Arab lands to the west and with adjoining Iran. Most of the inhabitants of Central Asia are of Turkish origin; some of the Turkish groups moved steadily westward and, by the fifteenth century, had conquered Anatolia, modern Turkey.

The southern and eastern rim of Asia is a very different place, both physically and culturally. Rainfall is generally adequate despite occasional dry years in some areas, and temperatures are more moderate, under the

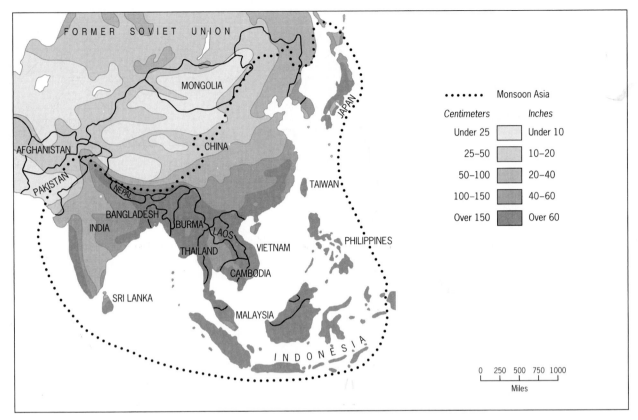

Precipitation in Monsoon Asia

Note the patterns: heaviest rainfall near the sea and along the Himalayan front.

influence of the sea. Except in the northern fringes, winters are relatively mild, for the same reason. This is the area called "monsoon Asia," set off from the rest of Asia by high mountain ranges along most of its landward borders, which help to keep the climatic influence of the sea out of Central Asia. The word *monsoon* is of Arab origin and originally meant "season" or "seasonal wind." In summer the huge landmass of Eurasia, whose center is farther from the sea than any part of the globe, heats up rapidly and generates a mass of hot air. As it rises, cooler air, which in its passage across the water picks up moisture, is drawn in from the surrounding oceans. On reaching the land, these maritime air masses release their moisture as rain, especially where they encounter hills or mountains, which force them to rise and hence cool them enough to produce condensation.

There is thus a pattern of relatively heavy summer rainfall along the southeastern crescent of Eurasia, on the oceanic side of the mountains that divide it from Central Asia. In winter the flow of air is reversed. The center of Eurasia, relatively little affected by the moderating influences of the sea, cools rapidly, and by December a mass of cold, heavy air begins to dominate the area. The sea remains relatively warm, storing the summer's heat, and winds blow out from the cold center toward the sea with its warm, rising air. In the northern parts of monsoon Asia, these outblowing winter winds can produce low temperatures but little or no rainfall, because they originate in dry Central Asia. By May or June, depending on the area, Central Asia has begun to heat up again, and moist maritime air masses are drawn in once more, bringing the monsoonal rains.

The oversimplified description above basically fits what usually happens, but the mechanisms of the monsoon are in fact far more complex. It is said that "Every schoolboy understands the workings of the monsoon, but the Indian Meteorological Service is still puzzled by it." The arrival and duration of the monsoon in spring or summer are notoriously unreliable, varying widely from year to year in many areas and producing floods in one

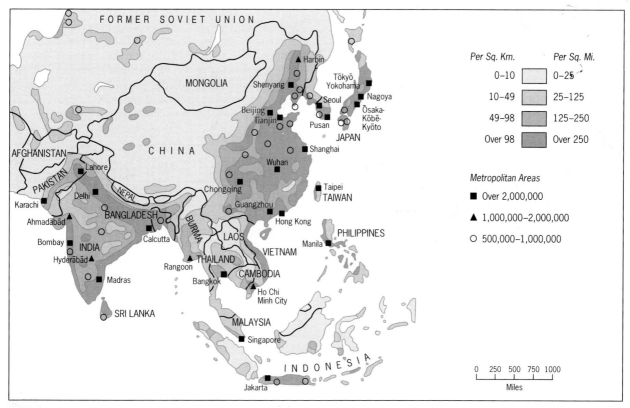

Population Density, Monsoon Asia

Note the coincidence of heavy rainfall and dense population. The major exceptions are
northeastern China, where level land takes precedence, and the islands of Indonesia (except for
Java), where mountains and jungle exclude dense settlement.

year and droughts in another. The islands of Southeast Asia also derive rain from the winter monsoon, because by the time it reaches them it has passed over large stretches of sea and picked up considerable moisture. The same is true to a lesser extent for Japan.

Population Densities

The general adequacy of rainfall and the generally mild winters under the protection of mountain ranges to landward have provided a basis for the sharpest of all distinctions between what is appropriately called *monsoon* Asia and the rest of the continent: half of the world's people live here, as they have during all of recorded history (although monsoon Asia's preponderance was even greater until a century or two ago), while most of the rest of Asia is one of the most thinly settled areas of the world (see the map above). The hilly or mountainous parts of monsoon Asia, including much of Southeast Asia, west China, Korea, and Japan, are in fact rather thinly peopled, while in the lowlands population densities reach the highest levels in the world.

It is hardly surprising that monsoon Asia developed a highly distinctive set of cultures, based from the beginning on productive agricultural systems in this generally warm, wet area, which also contains extensive plains, river valleys, and deltas. The first Asian civilizations arose on an agricultural base in the great river valleys, and agriculture remains the dominant employment and the major source of production in almost all of monsoon Asia outside Japan. It was agricultural wealth that supported the successive empires and brilliant cultures of traditional monsoon Asia, and that kept its people as a whole almost certainly better off materially than people anywhere else. It was richer than Europe until recently, probably sometime in the eighteenth century, as European observers noted from the time of Marco Polo on.

The expansion of the Chinese state and empire beginning under the Han dynasty in the second century B.C.E. progressively incorporated under Chinese control a number of areas that do not fit very closely with the above generalizations about monsoon Asia. Given the absence of effective political or military rivals to the west and north, the Chinese state first conquered Xinjiang, sometimes called Chinese Turkestan, a largely desert area still inhabited mainly by Turkic peoples, and then added much of arid Mongolia to protect itself against nomadic raids. Later Chinese expansion with the same motives conquered the huge Himalayan area of Tibet, although its tiny population remained overwhelmingly Tibetan. Finally, in the seventeenth century, an originally nomadic group, the Manchus, conquered China and added their Manchurian homeland to the empire. Manchuria is monsoonal in the sense that it gets most of its sparse rainfall in summer as part of the monsoonal pattern, but it has a long and bitterly cold winter, and much of it is marginal for agriculture. Most of Mongolia and Xinjiang are too dry for farming and belong both climatically and culturally to Central Asia. Tibet is an alpine desert, too dry, too cold, and too high to permit agriculture except in a few tiny areas.

Taken together, these marginal regions compose over half of China's area; Tibet, Xinjiang, and Mongolia are each nearly the size of western Europe, but they contain much less than 1 percent of China's population, and even Manchuria contains less than 10 percent. Most of China's people, and the roots and body of Chinese civilization, have always been located in the eastern and southern parts of the country, where agriculture has strong advantages. The empire expanded into the outer areas mentioned above in the absence of major topographic barriers (except for Tibet) but reached its limits roughly along the line formed by the main chain of the Himalayas and its northern extensions, which form the western and northwestern boundaries of Tibet and Xinjiang; other mountain ranges helped to limit Chinese expansion into northern Mongolia. But the people of these areas have until very recently remained predominantly non-Chinese, as Tibet still is.

The other major area that lies at best on the margins of monsoon Asia in physical terms, Pakistan, has from earliest times been inhabited by people who belonged to the major stream of Indian culture, and indeed this area saw the birth of civilization on the subcontinent. Much of Pakistan is desert or near-desert, but irrigation since late Neolithic times, especially along the Indus River and its tributaries, has made possible a productive agricultural system and a dense population. Despite its marginality in climatic terms, most of Pakistan gets its limited rainfall in summer as part of the monsoonal system, of which it lies on the fringes, as does northwest-

ern China. The high and steep mountain ranges that form the western and northwestern borders of Pakistan have always drawn a relatively sharp line between the peoples and cultures of the Indian subcontinent and those to the west in the Persian and Arab world of the Middle East. Like the distinction between the monsoon realm and the rest of Asia as a whole, that line is perhaps clearest of all in terms of population density.

Common Cultural Patterns

Apart from that all-important characteristic of monsoon Asia—the area east of Afghanistan and south of what is now the former Soviet Union that stands out so sharply on any map of population density—it has other common features that make it an appropriate unit of study. Even the monsoon part of Asia is a very large area, nearly twice the size of all of Europe to the Urals, and it is divided by mountains and seas into many subregions with different cultures, in many cases also inhabited by ethnically different people. The four major subregions of monsoon Asia—India, China, Southeast Asia, and Japan—are divided from each other in all of these ways and each is further subdivided, to varying degrees, into internal regions. But there is a broad range of institutions, ideas, values, conditions, and solutions that have long been distinctively Asian, common to each of the four major parts of monsoon Asia, different at least in degree from those elsewhere, and evolving in Asia in distinctive ways.

These include, among many others, the basic importance of the extended family and kin network and its multiple roles; the respect for and importance attached to learning, for its own sake and as the path to worldly success; the veneration of age and its real or fancied wisdom and authority; the traditional subjugation and submissive roles of women, at least in the public sphere (although Southeast Asia and southern India are qualified exceptions); the hierarchical structuring of society; the awareness of and importance attached to the traditional past; the primacy of group welfare over individual interest; and many more distinctively Asian cultural traits common to all parts of monsoon Asia.

Agriculture

Except for Japan, and there only since the 1920s, most of Asia has traditionally been and remains primarily an agrarian-based economy. Asian agriculture, including that of Japan today, has always been distinctive for its labor intensiveness, still in most areas primarily human labor, including that involved in the construction and maintenance of irrigation systems. This too goes back to the origins of the great Asian civilizations, which

Rice paddies in south-central Thailand. This scene is typical of warm, wet Asia and of its great river valleys and plains, which are highly productive agriculturally. (R. Murphey)

arose on the basis of agricultural surpluses produced by labor-intensive, largely hand cultivation supported by irrigation. From the beginning, Asian per-acre crop yields have been higher than anywhere else in the world. With the addition of manuring in later periods and chemical fertilization more recently, they are still the highest in the world, especially in Japan. High yields have always supported large populations in monsoon Asia, concentrated in the plains, river valleys, and deltas, where level land and fertile alluvial (river silt) soils have also maximized output in this region of generally warm temperatures, long growing seasons, and normally adequate rainfall.

Since approximately the first millennium B.C.E. or even earlier, monsoon Asia has contained the largest and most productive agricultural areas in the world. As one consequence, population densities per square mile have also remained high throughout this period, especially on cultivated land, and higher than anywhere else until the present. This was to some degree a chicken-and-egg situation. Productive land supported a growing population, which generated a need for more food but also provided the labor required to increase yields still further. This has been the consistent pattern of the agrarian and population history of each of the major regions of monsoon Asia over the past 4,000 years.

Social Hierarchy

Very high population densities have had much to do with the equally consistent nature of Asian societies, especially their emphases on group effort and group welfare, their mistrust of individualism, and their dependence on clearly stated and sanctioned rules for behavior. Individuals have always been subject to group direction and subordinate to group interest. They were fitted into the larger structure of societies that were hierarchically organized; each individual has always had his or her defined place and prescribed role. Individual happiness and welfare, like those of the societies as a whole, have always been seen as resting on such a structure. Most of these societies remain patriarchal and male dominant, although there are regional variations; the primary institution has always been the family, where the oldest member rules, sometimes a female but usually a male. The chief virtue extolled by all Asian societies is respect and deference to one's elders and to all others of higher status. Age and learning are equated with wisdom, an understandable idea in any agricultural society, where accumulated experience is the best guide to life's problems, and where the few learned men are looked up to by the mass of illiterates.

It has always seemed strange to Asians that others elsewhere do not share to the same degree their own deference to age and to learning—and that they do not put the same high value on education as both the most effective and the most prestigious way for any individual to succeed in life. But individual success is also seen as bringing both credit and material benefit to the family, and family obligation remains an unusually powerful drive for most Asians. Even in the traditional past, it was possible for those born in humble circumstances to rise in the world by acquiring education, an effort that could be successful only with close family support and much family sacrifice. Those who achieved success, and all those in authority or with education, were expected to set a good example for others. Indeed, society was seen as being held together by the model behavior of those at the top, from the emperor and his officials to the scholars, priests, and other leaders to the heads of families.

The family, the basic cement of all Asian societies, commonly involved three generations living together: parents, surviving grandparents, and children. But its network of loyalties and obligations extended further to include to varying degrees cousins, uncles, aunts, mature siblings, and in-laws. It was a ready-made system of mutual support, often necessary in hard times but seen as a structure that benefited everyone at all times and was hence given the highest value. There were of course strains within it, and within the societies as a whole, especially in the generally subordinate role of women, younger children, and others at the bottom. No society anywhere has ever achieved perfect solutions to all human problems, but these Asian societies seem to have been more successful than most, if only because they have lasted, in fundamentally similar form in these terms, far longer than any others elsewhere.

Except for Southeast Asia, a notable distinction, when women married they became members of their husband's family and moved to his house and village. New brides were often subjected to tyranny from their mothers-in-law, but when they had borne a son, all-important for continuation of the husband's family line, they acquired some status, and in time could tyrannize their sons' new wives. This system was the norm in China, Japan, Korea, Vietnam, and India, or rather it became so as these civilizations matured. It seems reasonably clear that in prehistoric times and before the beginning of written records (quite late in Japan), all these cultures had been matriarchal, with women dominant. That seems to have been the case for the Indus civilization of India, before the Aryan invasion, and strong traces of matriarchy persist even now in Dravidian south India. In Japan it is no accident that their chief deity was a woman, Ametarasu, or the sun goddess. Southeast Asia, including Vietnam even after the conquest by the Qin and Han dynasties, remained a world apart and is still so, with women dominant and playing a major role in, for example, trade; there men had to pay, as they still do, a bride price for wives, whereas the rest of monsoon Asia required dowries for the women.

Individual privacy was largely absent, given the dense population, the family structure, and the pattern common to most of monsoon Asia whereby even in rural areas houses were grouped together in villages rather than scattered over the landscape on separate farms, as in much of the Western world. Asian farms were small, averaging less than five acres in most areas, still smaller in the most densely settled parts. Their high productivity as a result of intensive cultivation meant that a family could normally support itself on a relatively tiny plot or plots. These were grouped around each village, housing 20 to 50 families on average who walked the short distance to and from their fields morning and evening, all but the very young and the very old. One was almost never out of sight or sound of others, and learned early to adjust, to defer to elders and superiors, to work together in the common interest, and in general to accept living very closely with, virtually on top of, other people, realizing that clear and agreed-on rules for behavior were and are essential. Marriage partners had to be sought in another village or town; most of one's fellow villagers were likely to be relatives of some degree, and in any case did not offer the widening of the kin network and its mutual support advantages conferred by marriage into another village. In other respects, one village or town was, and remains, much like another, and most people were, and are today outside Japan, villagers or farmers.

The chief Asian crop, rice, is the most productive of all cereals under the care that Asian farmers gave it, irrigated in specially constructed *paddies,* weeded, fertilized, and harvested largely by hand. Rice was probably native to, and first cultivated in, mainland Southeast Asia, but it spread relatively early to adjacent China, and somewhat later to India, Korea, and Japan, until by the first few centuries of the first millennium it dominated Asian agriculture. Rice has demanding requirements, especially for water, but where it can be grown it can support, and must employ, large numbers of people. In the drier areas such as north India and north China, wheat largely replaced rice as the dominant cereal, but it too could produce good yields under intensive cultivation. More marginal areas could grow millet, sorghum, or barley. There was little place for animals, except for draft purposes including ploughing and transport, although pigs, chickens, and ducks were raised as scavengers. Cereals produced far more food per acre than could be obtained by grazing animals or feeding them on crops, and there was continual pressure to have the land yield as much food as possible to support the dense populations. Monsoon Asia has accordingly been called "the vegetable civilization," centered on cereals and other plants (including a variety of vegetables), minimizing meat in the diet, and building primarily in wood, thatch, straw, and mud, with metal used only for tools and weapons, and stone largely reserved for monumental religious or official structures.

In all of these ways, monsoon Asia is a legitimate unit of study, an area with more basic commonality than differences. There is of course a wide range of differences in languages and other cultural traits, how people have lived and still live, earned their livings, and interacted with one another, the institutions they constructed, the basic values they still follow. But they have differed, and differ still, amazingly little from one part of monsoon Asia to another, given its very large size and its huge populations, separated from one another by seas and mountains, and growing up without regular or extensive contact with one another until their cultures and societies

South China landscape, Sichuan. This agricultural scene is typical of much of monsoon Asia, where the principal crop is irrigated rice. The rice is grown in fields (paddies) that are finely engineered to hold water within their low embankments, letting it trickle down from higher up the slope to each paddy in turn for constant irrigation. The water level is raised as the crops grow, and then is drained in the few weeks before harvest. The gentler hillsides are terraced, as in this picture, to create a staircase of nearly level irrigated fields. The heavy labor required to maintain this system is repaid by high crop yields. (R. Murphey)

were reasonably well formed. The states and empires of monsoon Asia were built consistently on their common peasant base of intensive, high-yield agriculture, which provided the great bulk of revenues, the manpower for armies, and the highly structured social base directed and manipulated by officials and by learned men, whose values were largely echoed by most of those far greater numbers ranked below them, a few of whom occasionally joined the ranks of the elite through education. The village worlds were largely self-governing and self-regulating, thanks to the family system, the kin network, and the basic social institutions common to the area as a whole, but they formed the essential foundation for the building and maintenance of empires.

Trade took place far beyond the intervillage level, linking distant provinces or subregions and reaching overseas between the four major areas of Asia and beyond. But until very recent times, and then only in Japan, it never rivaled the basic importance of agriculture as a means of employment or a source of wealth. Each Asian area produced rich merchants, who often supported a brilliant urban culture. But nowhere, with few and brief exceptions until modern times, did merchants acquire political power or high formal status. All of these Asian societies continued to be dominated by the pool of educated men and others whose membership in the elite derived from learning in one form or another, supplemented by ownership of land and the management of the productive agricultural system that underlay everything. In these terms, too, there are few differences between one major Asian culture and another. On such grounds one may indeed argue that

monsoon Asia has been and remains at least as much a cultural and historical unit as Europe, almost half its size, despite Asia's far wider variations in language and ethnic mixtures, its far longer recorded history, and its immensely greater population.

The Study of Monsoon Asia

European societies and European history have their own undoubted unity, despite regional and temporal differences, and we commonly study them as a whole, including their variations and changes from area to area and period to period. The same kind of approach is at least equally valid for monsoon Asia, although it is less often pursued. The primary reason is that we as Westerners still know much less about Asia or its history than we know about Europe. As Western knowledge of and attention to Asia have increased, especially since the end of World War II, our efforts have perhaps understandably been concentrated on learning Asian languages so that we can read their texts and records, and then on using such materials to study the histories and cultures of each major region separately. This is necessary since knowledge of Chinese, for example, is of marginal help in studying India, as knowledge of Sanskrit or Hindi is of little use in studying Japan. The sheer size of Asia, its great regional variety, and its uniquely long and rich history, or histories, further discourage most scholars, or even students, from trying to tackle the whole problem, often even at an introductory level.

Lowland Taiwan: intensive hand labor in the permissive climate of warm, wet Asia. Rice, the most productive crop of Asia, is commonly weeded laboriously by hand, as these four are doing. The effort is repaid by very high yields. (Getty Images)

But as we enter the twenty-first century, Asia increasingly looms as over half the human world. Its societies and economies are rapidly changing and are acquiring a major position in world affairs in all respects. Western study of Asia has matured enough to have produced a still-growing body of published work on the history of each major Asian area. It is both essential and possible to study Asia as a whole. Not to do so leaves us unprepared for the world of the new century, and at the same time prevents us from benefiting from the insights that almost any comparative approach to the several parts of Asia offers. Before we can usefully compare, it is first necessary to learn something of what happened in the history of each major area. This book not only attempts to do that for each part of Asia but also looks at parallels, differences, and interactions among them and between Asia and the Western world in both ancient or traditional and modern times.

Since World War II, the United States has produced more scholarly and popular books on Asia than any other country. Our universities are the world's leading centers of Asian studies. Yet as a people, Americans are woefully ignorant of Asia, as they are of the world as a whole, clearly more so than the people of any other developed country and of many of the developing ones. Some Americans know a little about Europe, the origin of many of our people and much of our culture, but there is far less general knowledge or even adequate awareness of Asia, on the other side of the globe. Yet since about 1970 by far the largest share of U.S. trade, and the most rapidly increasing, has been with Asia. Several of its nations have the highest economic growth rates in the world, and several have become major powers in world affairs. Asian Americans are a fast growing segment of our own population.

Most important, the Asian cultural and historical experience is well over half of the human experience, now and in the past. We impoverish ourselves if we remain ignorant of it—and we expose ourselves to possible disaster if we try to play a global role in the modern world, where Asia is increasingly the major player, without some knowledge of its cultures and civilizations. Perhaps especially for Asia with its long history and the importance its modern inhabitants attach to that, we cannot understand the present or plan for the future without a knowledge of the past. These are all important practical reasons for studying Asian history. But perhaps the best reason for studying anything is that it enriches the life of the student. This book aims to widen its readers' horizons and to make each of them richer with their learning about Asia.

Questions

1. What are monsoons, and what are their impact on Asian society and culture? What are Asia's monsoon seasons?

2. What distinguishes "monsoon Asia" from the remainder of Asia? What are the consequent differences between the two? How does this especially have an impact on Chinese civilization?

3. What is the "exception" that the text makes in referencing south Indian and Southeast Asian civilizations?

4. What are the societal consequences of an irrigation wet-rice society?

5. Where did the most populous early Asian societies form, and why?

6. What is a "vegetable civilization"? What are its consequences?

7. What are the common features among monsoon Asia's societies and cultures?

Suggested Web Sites

Asian Studies World Wide Web Virtual Library

http://coombs.anu.edu.au/WWWVL-AsianStudies.html

A large-scale, collaborative project providing an up-to-date guide to the networked scholarly documents, resources, and information systems concerned with social science research in Asia.

Library of Congress Country Studies

http://lcweb2.loc.gov/cs/cshome.html

A continuing series of books prepared by the Federal Research Division of the Library of Congress, presently containing studies of 101 countries. Each site offers a chronology of important events, country profile, geographic, and demographic studies, as well as information on religion, ethnicity, education, agriculture, foreign relations, along with an extensive bibliography of English-language publications.

Time Magazine, Asia

http://www.time.com/time/asia/index.html

The latest and previous issues of *Time* magazine in Asia; contains good information on contemporary topics, with a focus on Asian political, economic, and social issues, explored at more depth than found in the American edition of the magazine.

CIA World Factbook

www.cia.gov/cia/publications/factbook/geos/my.html

A handy source of current and concise information on countries throughout Asia, beginning with up-to-date histories, followed by the names of current leaders, surveys of local productivity, and other relevant information that would be especially useful to government officials, bankers, investors, or businesspeople.

Lonely Planet Guidebooks

http://www.lonelyplanet.com/destinations

The entry portal for all Lonely Planet guidebooks, which are among the best in the marketplace. They provide useful geographical, historical, and cultural information as well as practical information for the world traveler.

The following Web sites are also good sources on specific countries:

Bangladesh: http://independent-bangladesh.com/
(especially good on local affairs)

Brunei: http://www.brunei.bn/news/bb/front.htm
(current affairs of the country and region)

China: http://insidechina.com/
(English-language version of *China Today*)
http://www.semp.com/
(*South China Morning Post*, based in Hong Kong)
http://www.straitstimes.asia1.com/
(China and the larger region from Singapore)

India: http://www.hinduonline.com/
(online version of the *Hindu*, India's leading paper)

Indonesia: http://www.thejakartapost.com
(major English-language daily)

Japan: http://www.asahi.com/english/english.html
(online version of the *Asahi News*)
http://www.japantimes.co.jp/
(Japan's most widely read English daily)

Malaysia: http://thestar.com.my/
(widely read Malaysian English-language daily)

Nepal: http://www.nepalnews.com/
(originates from Kathmandu)

North Korea: http://www.kena.co.jp/
(from government Central News Agency via Japan)

Pakistan: http://www.dawn.com/daily
(most popular English-language daily in Pakistan)

Philippines: http://www.philstar.com
(the *Philippines Star* from Manila)

South Korea: http://www.yonhapnews.co.kr/services/2000000000.html
(Seoul-based news)

Sri Lanka: http://www.dailynews.lk/
(major Sri Lanka English-language daily)

Thailand: http://www.bangkokpost.com/
(major Thai English-language daily)

Vietnam: http://www.saigon-news.com/
(the *Saigon Daily Times*)

1

Prehistoric Asia

This chapter summarizes the beginnings of the human species in Asia, the long Paleolithic period or Old Stone Age, the Neolithic revolution, the origins of agriculture in the Near East and in Southeast Asia, the beginnings of civilization in Southeast Asia, China, Korea, and Japan, and the close connection between Korea and early Japan.

Early and Paleolithic Cultures

The direct ancestors of the human species seem clearly to have evolved first in East Africa some 3 million years ago. After another million years or perhaps more, these creatures, known as *Homo erectus,* slightly smaller than modern humans but walking erect, using fire, and making crude stone tools, had spread to Asia and Europe. The earliest Asian finds of *Homo erectus* were made in Java (now in Indonesia) in 1891, and near Beijing in 1921, labeled respectively "Java Man" and "Beijing Man." Both original finds were dated approximately 500,000 B.C.E., although subsequent discoveries in Java have now pushed the date of "Java Man" back to 900,000 B.C.E. and other finds suggest that this species was reasonably widespread in Asia by 1.5 million years ago. More recently remains of *Homo erectus* have been found in Yunnan in southwest China dated about a million years ago, and near Xi'an in the northwest dated about 600,000 B.C.E. *Homo erectus* merged with later humanoid species after about 300,000 B.C.E. Given the span of time and the mixing of peoples since, it is not reasonable to think of these creatures as early Asians rather than simply as ancestors of modern people in general. They fashioned handheld stone axes with a cutting edge, probably used for chopping, scraping, and digging, and may have been cannibals, or at least have ritually eaten the brains and bone marrow of their own dead.

The hand axes they produced were remarkably uniform and look much the same at sites scattered over most of Asia, Africa, and Europe as far as Britain. After about 150,000 B.C.E. a new species, called *Homo neanderthalis* (from the Neander River valley in Germany

where one of the first finds was made) rose to dominance over the Old World of Eurasia and Africa.

In the course of the last glaciation, between approximately 70,000 and 20,000 B.C.E. *Homo neanderthalis,* the chief successor to *Homo erectus,* was gradually displaced or superseded by modern humans, whom we call *Homo sapiens;* since that time *Homo sapiens* has been the only human inhabitant of the globe. Physical differences among the various branches of *Homo sapiens* are relatively slight; they are most marked in shades of skin color and a few other superficial and external features such as hair color and texture, amount of body hair, and minor facial features. Since few of these minor attributes are discernible for long after death, we do not know when the present small racial distinctions emerged. It is probable that people who lived or remained in hot, sunny climates retained what was probably the original human skin color—dark, as a protection against strong sunlight—while those who migrated into, or were overtaken by, colder or cloudier climates slowly evolved lighter skin colors in order to maximize the beneficial effects of sunlight on the body, especially as a source of vitamin D.

Until very recently, Africa, Asia, and Europe—the units of the Old World divided only by the narrowest of water barriers (the Bosporus and the Gulf of Suez) and hence sometimes called "the world island"—were nevertheless largely isolated from each other by great distances and by intervening deserts and mountains. Since about 200,000 B.C.E. the minor physical differences we now observe between humans of European, African, and Asian origins slowly began to emerge. These differences, including those of the many subgroups, such as the Inuit (Eskimos) and American Indians, originally from eastern Asia, resulted from interbreeding as well as from isolated regional differences. Physical evolution is an extremely slow process on any human time scale, and there are no discernible physical differences between contemporary members of each of these major racial groups and those who lived when recorded history begins. Well-preserved bodies from the Egypt of 2500 B.C.E. for example, or from Han dynasty China of the first century C.E. are indistinguishable from modern

 CHRONOLOGY

1 million B.C.E.	■ Java Man
	■ Beijing Man
10,000 B.C.E.	■ Origins of agriculture in the Near East and Southeast Asia
8000–300 B.C.E.	■ Jomon culture in Japan
5000–1000 B.C.E.	■ Southern Mongoloid agriculturalist migrations into Southeast Asia replacing and assimilating Austrolo-Melanesian hunter–gatherers
4000 B.C.E.	■ Urbanization in Sumer (Mesopotamia) and in Egypt
3000 B.C.E.	■ Urbanization in the Indus River system
	■ Dravidian culture in South Asia, earliest temple culture
	■ Malayo-Polynesian migrations
	■ Emergence of Malay coastal cultures
	■ Maritime contact between Southeast Asia and Madagascar
	■ Development of Austroasiatic (Mon-Khmer, Vietnamese), Tai-Kadai, Tibeto-Burman, and Austronesian languages (Chamic, Malayo-Polynesian)

2800 B.C.E.	■ Legendary birth of Vietnam
2500–2000 B.C.E.	■ Longshan and Yangshao pottery cultures in China
2000 B.C.E.	■ Urban centers in China
	■ Bronze culture in Southeast Asia
1600–1400 B.C.E.	■ Aryans to India
1600–1050 B.C.E.	■ Shang dynasty
	■ Chinese civilization in Korea
600 B.C.E.–200 C.E.	■ Dong-son bronze drum culture (northern Vietnam, Cambodia, Thailand, Malayasia, and Indonesia)
	■ Nan Yueh civilization in Vietnam and south China
500 B.C.E.	■ Iron use in Malaysia and island Southeast Asia
300 B.C.E.–300 C.E.	■ Yayoi (Japan)
200 B.C.E.	■ Southeast Asia–based sailors (*Kunlun*) in Chinese ports
100 B.C.E.	■ Malayo–Polynesian-speaking people settle in Madagascar

Egyptians or Chinese, or for the most part from any contemporary people, including what evidence remains of skin and hair color, tooth and bone structure, vital organs, brain capacity, and so on. The same would almost certainly be true for the people of 10,000 B.C.E. or even much earlier.

We need not concern ourselves here in any detail with the almost equally slow early evolution of culture—how people lived and what they created—during the thousands of years of the Paleolithic period (the Old Stone Age). This lasted from about 1 million years ago or more to about 25,000 B.C.E. During this time people gradually learned to use fire, build shelters or make use of caves, and fashion garments out of skins or furs; slowly they improved their stone tools and increased the effectiveness of their hunting, developing stone-tipped spears. Soon after 30,000 B.C.E., however, the pace of change began to quicken, probably hastened by the last phase of glacial ice advance and its subsequent retreat. Magnificent paintings on cave walls in northern Spain and southern France, then near the edge of the glacial ice sheet, dating from 28,000 to 10,000 B.C.E., attest to the

skill and artistic imagination of the people who created them and suggest a highly developed social organization. Rock and cave paintings from the latter part of this same period in North Africa, the Middle East, and monsoon Asia suggest similar developments. By or well before this time, *Homo sapiens* had migrated from the Old World to the Americas and to Australia. The earliest New World finds are dated about 20,000 B.C.E., but there is good reason to believe that people had crossed the narrow Bering Strait between northeasternmost Asia and what is now Alaska, perhaps on the glacial ice, by about 40,000 B.C.E. or even earlier, and had reached Australia across what may then have been a nearly complete land bridge from the Asian mainland by about the same time.

With the last retreat of the ice in Europe and Asia, beginning about 20,000 B.C.E. but reaching its present limits only by about 3000 B.C.E., forests slowly replaced the ice sheets and the treeless tundra along their margins. The game, such as the woolly mammoth, that the Paleolithic people had hunted also moved northward or became extinct. Basic changes in the environment required basic human adjustment, as had been necessary when the ice sheets were advancing. Some groups developed new techniques, including the bow and arrow, for hunting in the forest; others moved to coastal sites and lived primarily on fish and shellfish, creating new or improved tools such as needles for sewing and fishhooks, now made of bone. But far more significant and rapid changes were beginning to take place in drier areas, centered in the region we now call the Near East, or Southwest Asia.

The Neolithic Revolution

The term *Neolithic* is to some degree a misnomer, since it means literally "New Stone Age," referring to the rapid improvement and new variety in finely made stone tools. But although stone tools continued to be made in great quantities, bone and clay were of increasing importance, and toward the end of the period tools and weapons began to be made of metal. The term *revolution* is more appropriately applied to the beginnings of agriculture. This made possible for the first time large permanent settlements, a great increase in population, the accumulation of surpluses, the consequent need for writing (in part to keep records), and the growth of the first true cities, from which our word *civilization* comes, via its Latin, Greek, and Sanskrit roots. In the few thousand years between about 10,000 B.C.E. and about 4000 B.C.E.—an extremely short space of time compared with the almost imperceptible pace of change during Paleolithic times—most of the elements of what we call modern civilization emerged.

By 3000 B.C.E. early cities in Mesopotamia and the Indus Valley had bureaucrats, tax collectors, priests, metalworkers, scribes, schools, housing and traffic problems, and almost all of the features of our own times. As the Old Testament Book of Ecclesiastes put it about 200 B.C.E., a view that we can echo today: "There is no new thing under the sun. Is there anything whereof it may be said, See, this is new? It hath been already of old time, which was before us."[1] That is in fact a very Asian view. The changes of which we are so conscious in our own times are extremely recent and center on new technology beginning with the steam engine a mere two centuries ago and accelerating rapidly in the second half of the present century. But people, human society, and their problems have not changed much since the building of the first cities some 5,000 years ago.

The Neolithic revolution in agriculture and town building transformed the lives of everyone involved. The change came about over several thousand years, probably first in the Near East and then spreading to other parts of the Old World; similar developments in eastern Asia and much later in Mexico and Peru proba-

bly began independently. *Neolithic* refers to a stage of development. It came later in western Europe and most of the rest of the world; isolated areas like Australia or the tropical rain forests were still in the Paleolithic period when they were invaded by modern Europeans after the eighteenth century.

Archaeological evidence suggests two main areas as the earliest cradles of settled agriculture: the uplands of Southwest Asia surrounding the Tigris-Euphrates lowland of Mesopotamia, and the coastal or near-coastal areas of mainland Southeast Asia. There is clear evidence of early settlement in southern Anatolia (now in modern Turkey), Palestine and Syria, northern Iraq, and western Iran. In these semiarid areas with some winter rainfall grew steppe grasses that included the wild ancestors of wheat and barley. Early Neolithic stone-toothed sickles, dated to about 10,000 B.C.E. have been found here and have a sheen from cutting such grasses with their grain heads. Dating from a little later, small hoards of stored grains have been found. It must have been a long process of adaptation from gathering such grasses or grains in the wild to planting them, perhaps originally by accident, in fields that then could be prepared and tended until harvest. Fields growing only the desired grain could obviously yield far more than could be gathered in the wild, but they did require care and hence a permanent settlement of farmers at a given site, usually one where a supply of water was available. Soon after 10,000 B.C.E. stone mortars appeared, indicating that the grain was milled (ground into flour) and that it helped to support a population already beginning to grow beyond what could be sustained by hunting and gathering.

By about 7000 B.C.E. there were large and numerous storage pits for grain, and early clay pots for the same purpose and for carrying or storing water. By this time cultivated wheat, barley, and peas had clearly evolved into more productive forms than their wild ancestors, probably through purposeful selection by the cultivators. Sheep, goats, and dogs were domesticated instead of being used as hunting prey or hunting assistants. A thousand years later cattle and pigs had joined the list of domesticates. There is a reasonably clear record of this evolution at a number of Near Eastern sites including Jericho in southern Palestine, Cayonu and Catal Huyuk in southern Anatolia, Jarmo in northern Iraq, Hassuna and Ali Kosh in western Iran, and many others.

By about 4000 B.C.E. or slightly earlier, agricultural techniques were far enough advanced and populations large enough to permit an expansion into the different environment of the Tigris-Euphrates lowland, and somewhat later to the Indus Valley in what is now Pakistan, the latter based on models transmitted via early agricultural settlements in eastern Iran and Afghanistan. Most of these areas, including Mesopotamia, were desert or near-desert, with a few scattered oases in Iran, but the river floodplains, given their fertile alluvial soils and long growing seasons of high temperatures, were potentially highly productive if they could be provided with water by controlled irrigation. The Tigris-Euphrates and Indus rivers are fed by rains and snowmelt in their mountain source areas and hence are subject to seasonal flooding. The destructive aspects of these floods had to be controlled to permit permanent agriculture. There were also problems of drainage to be solved, especially in the lower course of the Tigris-Euphrates, where the two rivers meet and empty into the Persian Gulf together through what was originally a vast, swampy delta.

Techniques of irrigation also had to be developed at about the same time in lower Egypt. Soon after 4000 B.C.E. villages began to grow into small cities at the conjunction of the Tigris and Euphrates and in the lower Nile. Lower Nile sites have since been buried under silt, and we do not know their names or locations; but in Mesopotamia, perhaps slightly earlier than in Egypt, these first true cities included Ur, Nippur, Uruk, and Eridu. Their names are recorded in the world's first written texts, which have been preserved on clay tablets.

The Neolithic revolution was completed with the development of metalworking and the production of bronze tools and, unfortunately, weapons. Copper was the first metal to be worked, in both the Old and New Worlds, because it sometimes occurs at or near the surface in nearly pure form and can be beaten into a more or less rigid shape without refining or smelting, although it will not hold an edge and was used primarily for ornaments. In Mesopotamia by about 4000 B.C.E. successive experiments mixing copper with tin and lead in varying proportions produced bronze, which was stronger and would take and keep an edge. But it needs to be remembered that it was agricultural surpluses that made possible the division of labor. Some people were able to pursue nonfarm occupations, and there was more leisure time for experimentation and for the perfecting of artisan techniques, including the smelting and working of metal. The need for better tools for farming, clearing trees, and building towns and cities provided further incentives.

Perhaps through the medium of trade, agricultural and irrigation techniques spread east from Mesopotamia and western Iran, and by at least 3500 B.C.E. both were fully developed at sites in eastern Iran, Afghanistan, Baluchistan, and the fringes of the Indus Valley, although early protoagricultural villages have recently been dated to about 7500 B.C.E. By or before 3000 B.C.E. irrigated agriculture was fully established on the floodplain of the Indus and its major tributaries, where the first true cities of monsoon Asia arose, growing out of Neolithic villages and towns. The major Indus crop

Pottery from Baluchistan, c. 3500 B.C.E.

was wheat, probably derived from Southwest Asia in its later cultivated form rather than its wild form. The story of the Indus civilization is given in Chapter 4, which begins the account of recorded history as opposed to prehistory—that is, the history of the Indian subcontinent from approximately 3000 B.C.E. to about 650 C.E.

Agricultural Origins in Southeast Asia

Rice was almost certainly native to Southeast Asia, as a swamp plant around the shores of the Bay of Bengal or in the valleys of the great rivers of the Indo-Chinese Peninsula. It may be the accident of which sites have been excavated so far in Southeast Asia that suggests a clustering of early agriculture in northern and central Thailand and northern Vietnam. Subsequent work may fill out the pattern suggested of agricultural beginnings in the upland fringes of river valleys, with perhaps also sites on or near the coast, where gathering and early cultivation could be supplemented by fishing and by collecting from fixed shellfish beds. It is plausible that this area of unbroken growing season and ample rainfall, where both rice and several tropical root and tree crops were native in wild form, should have seen the first transition from gathering cultures to those that planted and tended fields.

Early developments in Southeast Asia probably centered on root crops, easily cultivated in this tropical climate by setting cuttings in the ground. Taro and yams are still grown this way all over Southeast Asia and offer plentiful output for minimal labor. But there is as yet no hard evidence for early beginnings, let alone reliable dating. Rice was probably also first domesticated somewhere in this area, but there too the evidence is elusive and incomplete. All organic material rapidly decays in the humid, warm climate, and except for occasional bits of charcoal from fires, little but stone, metal, and perhaps some bone survive even for as long as 1,000 years.

What evidence we have suggests that by about 8000 B.C.E., or probably about as early as in the Near East, a late Neolithic culture called *Hoabinhian* had evolved in what is now northern Vietnam. Stone tools and other remains left by this culture suggest a move already made from gathering to the beginnings of agriculture, with fixed permanent settlements, some of which also depended on shellfish beds. At later and better-known sites in northern Thailand, there are severe dating problems, given the perishability of organic materials in this wet area, and the estimates for the beginnings of settled rice agriculture and the first bronze implements range from 4500 B.C.E. to as late as 2000 B.C.E. There is also some debate over whether the few identifiable food remains represent wild or cultivated forms, including rice, which is present as impressions in hardened clay pots in the earliest layers. Remains of chickens and pigs, bronze tools and weapons, and the presence of a large cemetery at one of the sites certainly suggest agriculture to support so large and technically advanced a population.

Sites elsewhere in Southeast Asia, and in closely related south China, may yield firmer evidence. Rice agriculture may be as old in parts of south China as anywhere in Southeast Asia. The extremely fertile volcanic soil of the island of Java and of parts of nearby Sumatra (both now in Indonesia) may well have supported early agricultural beginnings. Pigs (as opposed to the more widely occurring wild boar) and chickens (originally jungle fowl) are native to mainland Southeast Asia and were almost certainly first domesticated there. They spread from Southeast Asia westward to India, Mesopotamia, and Europe and northward to China, Korea, and Japan, together with the water buffalo, also native to and first domesticated in Southeast Asia.

Other evidence suggests that millet may have been the first cereal actually cultivated in Southeast Asia. Rice could be gathered wild, to supplement the more easily grown and more productive root crops in the tropics. Millet was not native, but was introduced, from northwest China or from Central Asia, and, hence, could be grown only on a tended basis. As an originally arid-climate or steppe grass, like wheat, millet was better suited to uplands or to elevated sites than to the floodplains. This may help to explain why the earliest Southeast Asian agricultural sites thus far found are of that sort. It was apparently not until about 1000 B.C.E., with the development of controlled irrigation, flood management, and the rise of rice as the dominant crop, that farmers began to occupy and increasingly to concentrate in the lower river valleys and deltas, which since then have been the major agricultural areas. Much earlier, wild rice may have invaded root crop fields as a weed and then been domesticated when its potential was realized. Until then taro, a root crop, may have dominated the agricultural system, because it is a water-loving plant probably domesticated first in upland areas where shallow depressions fill with water each rainy season.

There is understandably little evidence about gender roles before the start of written records, but in monsoon Asia, as elsewhere, societies were likely matriarchal to begin with and were displaced by patriarchal systems (except for Southeast Asia) only when warfare became common and physical strength was important. Women were probably the pioneer farmers, sowing and tending crops while the men were out hunting and gathering. In Southeast Asia, the original matriarchal pattern has been preserved until the present.

Peoples and Early Kingdoms of Southeast Asia

Most of the modern inhabitants of Southeast Asia came originally from what is now China, mainly from the south, perhaps including Tibet, with minor and later additions from India. The migrations began many thousands of years ago, probably before the Neolithic period, and migrants probably interbred with what may have been still earlier inhabitants of Southeast Asia as well as with other strains, probably including Negrito groups and others from farther south. Ethnically and culturally, however, there is a clear line of demarcation between the Philippines and Indonesia west of New Guinea on the one hand, and the Pacific and Australasian world on the other. The latter include New Guinea, the Solomon Islands, Australia, New Zealand,

and the many tiny islands of the South Pacific eastward from there—Melanesia, Micronesia, and Polynesia, the latter reaching as far as the Hawaiian Islands (until their recent overwhelming by American people and culture). Southeast Asia thus ends as a cultural region at the Moluccas, the easternmost islands of Indonesia, although in the 1950s Indonesia took over western New Guinea as part of its territory.

While scholars are not clear about the precise source area, the Philippines, Indonesia, and the Malay Peninsula on the mainland were probably settled by successive groups of migrants who are called Malays and who belong to a common culture and language family. For the most part, the Malays of Malaysia and Indonesia speak the same language, with regional differences, and the many languages of the Philippines are all in that same group. Ethnically and physically, these Malay people are all broadly similar. Malays were probably the earlier dominant inhabitants of all of mainland Southeast Asia as well, but they were displaced southward by later migrations of different peoples from south and southwest China, who became dominant in Burma, Thailand, Vietnam, Laos, and Cambodia. We cannot date either the Malay migrations or those that later followed them, except to say that both began long before the beginnings of written records and before the emergence of a Chinese state.

Mainland Southeast Asia received a series of migrants from the north over a long period who became almost the sole inhabitants of Burma, Thailand, Vietnam, Laos, and Cambodia, all of whom speak languages related to Chinese and Tibetan but unrelated to Malay or the languages of India, although Burmese and Thai are written in an Indian-derived script. Migrations probably had begun by 2500 B.C.E. or earlier and continued in scattered spurts involving different people, into the thirteenth century C.E.

However, there may well have been some movement of peoples even earlier from mainland Southeast Asia northward into China. Culturally as well as environmentally, south China was far more closely linked to adjacent Southeast Asia than to environmentally very different north China until the first Chinese empire united most of the present country into a single state in 221 B.C.E. Northern Vietnam was in fact part of an early kingdom that included much of southeastern China and whose culture and language were strikingly different from those of the early kingdoms in north China (see Chapter 5). Chickens, pigs, rice, and water buffalo moved north from their origins in mainland Southeast Asia to Neolithic south China, within what was until quite late a single culture region. In any case, traditional Chinese agriculture is inconceivable without any one of these basic elements derived from the south; some people and other aspects of culture may well have moved north with them.

There is relatively easy access between northern Vietnam and southeast China, by river and across a low mountain range, and until about the third century C.E. there was little or no distinction between the two areas in people, language, and culture.

Burma and Thailand were progressively settled by somewhat different groups coming originally from mountainous south China, but interaction across the present political borders continued until recently. As already indicated, agriculture and bronze technology developed very early in mainland Southeast Asia and adjacent south China. The technology also spread throughout what is now Indonesia, but we have no evidence of true cities in this period. Writing, the other element of what we call civilization, came to all of Southeast Asia except northern Vietnam from India beginning about the second century B.C.E. as part of the larger spread of Buddhism, Hinduism, and other aspects of Indian culture, and also through the medium of trade (see Chapter 4). Northern Vietnam's close ties with China ensured that the Chinese system of writing and many other aspects of Chinese culture became dominant there. By the time we have evidence of the first Southeast Asian states or kingdoms they already seem thoroughly Indianized or, in northern Vietnam, Sinicized (based on the Chinese pattern). But in basic social culture, as opposed to the more sophisticated levels of literature, statecraft, elite art, and revealed religion, Southeast Asia retained its far older and distinctive regional character, including such things as the higher status of women, the nature of village organization, patterns of inheritance, the hierarchy of values, popular art forms, folk religion, and so on.

Prehistoric China

The emergence of civilization in China is most clearly documented archaeologically for the north China plain of the Yellow River (or Huang He). But because of the probable earlier origins of agriculture and bronze technology in Southeast Asia, and the close cultural and ethnic connections between that area and south China before the rise of the Chinese empire, it seems clear that developments in south-central China may have been even earlier than in the north. Rice, pigs, chickens, water buffalos, and bronze would easily have moved northward from their Southeast Asian origins, following first the several north-flowing tributaries of the Yangzi River from the northern edge of the Guangzhou area. The latter was culturally closely linked

The Bronze Age: bronze figure of a warrior from the Dong-Son culture of northern Vietnam, c. 400 B.C.E. (Giraudon/Art Resource, NY)

to, and from about the third century B.C.E. or before, politically a part of what is now northern Vietnam, the old kingdom of Nan Yue (Nam Viet, or Viet Nam, in Vietnamese) with twin capitals at Hanoi and Guangzhou and sharing a common language, identity, and way of life.

Archaeological evidence is much less complete for south China than for north China, for the same reasons that explain its scarcity for Southeast Asia: high humidity, ample rainfall, and high temperatures, which rapidly break down organic remains. But the south has also been much less investigated archaeologically than the north, and future finds may well alter the present picture. Already sites excavated since 1949 have revealed traces of advanced farming, bronze-making, and town-building cultures at several places in south and central China, as far as the northern edges of the Yangzi Valley, that are about as old as their culturally different equivalents found in north China. There are severe dating problems, but the estimates for the oldest of these sites range from 5500 to 4500 B.C.E. Their occupants grew a domesticated form of rice and kept pigs and water buffa-

los. Excavated sites in the south are too few as yet to demonstrate what may well have been still earlier developments in domesticated root crops, if indeed any evidence remains.

China north of mountain-girt Sichuan Province and north of the lower Yangzi Valley, essentially the floodplain of the Yellow River and its tributaries, is by contrast a semiarid area of precarious and limited rainfall and with a long, cold winter. In these terms it is not all that different from the early cradle of agriculture in Southwest Asia, where wild forms of wheat and barley were first domesticated. The great agricultural advantage of north China has always been its highly fertile soil, often found in semiarid areas, in this case deep deposits of wind-laid dust called *loess,* much of it also picked up and redeposited by rivers. It is very easily cultivated and of almost inexhaustible fertility if adequate water is available. The largely treeless plain, open for agriculture and for transport of surpluses and other goods, offered the same advantages as the Nile, Tigris-Euphrates, and Indus valleys, although the heavily silted Yellow River was less useful for navigation.

Neolithic cultures in north China were probably producing pottery as early as or perhaps earlier than in Southwest Asia; pottery fragments from Japan have been dated to about 8000 B.C.E., and it is unlikely that development there was earlier than on the mainland. Pottery suggests the need for storing surpluses and, hence, at least the beginnings of agriculture, but the emergence of farming, here as elsewhere, was no doubt a long, slow transition from earlier gathering and hunting. The dominant, and perhaps the only, early crop plant in north China was millet, like wheat a drought-tolerant steppe grass. It was probably native to the area and domesticated there in two varieties by at least 4500 B.C.E., or perhaps as early as 5000. Dependence on millet suggests that agriculture in the north was an independent development rather than a diffusion from either the south or from Southwest Asia.

A major early northern site has been excavated at Banpo near modern Xi'an, which was well established as a small village by at least 4000 B.C.E. Its people grew millet and kept sheep, goats, and pigs, supplementing their diet with river fish and game. Rice and water buffalo probably did not spread widely to the north until about 1500 B.C.E., after their basic usefulness had long been demonstrated farther south. It was the heavy water demands of rice, rather than the cold winter and shorter growing season, that retarded its spread northward. The first form of rice domesticated from its wild ancestor was, however, a warm-climate plant, and as its cultivation spread northward different varieties were developed that were better suited to colder temperatures and shorter growing seasons. These were the varieties later diffused to Korea, and from there to Japan.

Banpo and most of the many other early northern sites are in the loess uplands well away from the main floodplain of the Yellow River. As elsewhere, it was only after the rise of some form of water control that the major farming centers moved into river valleys and deltas. This seems to have begun in north China by about 2000 B.C.E. but did not acquire full momentum for another millennium. By that time, about 1000 B.C.E., wheat had replaced the earlier dominance of millet in the north and was supplemented by barley and rice. Rice could now be irrigated from river water or floods and from shallow wells. Wheat and barley are not native to East Asia and must, therefore, have been diffused from Southwest Asia some time between 4000 and 1000 B.C.E., joining an agricultural system that was already there and that had probably emerged independently.

The Banpo people belonged to an early stage of what is called the Painted Pottery culture, or *Yangshao,* taking its name from a village in Henan Province where the major find was made. It lasted as late as 1500 B.C.E., after which it merged with other late Neolithic cultures to form the first literate and city-building, metal-using civilization, the Shang dynasty. Painted pottery was covered with intricate geometric designs, in red or black; it included a wide range of sizes and shapes and was baked in a kiln, although it was made without the potter's wheel. The culture's original domain extended from Gansu in the northwest eastward into Henan, where it overlapped with another late Neolithic culture called Black Pottery, or *Longshan,* from the major type site in Shandong Province, whose domain reached westward from the sea. Central and south China during this period were occupied by other Neolithic cultures, as indicated above, each producing distinctively different types of pots. Black Pottery ware was of fine quality and often elegant in design, wheel-made and kiln-fired at temperatures over 1,000 degrees centigrade. Neither it nor the Painted Pottery ware shows any connection with Mesopotamian or Indus pottery. Both these late Neolithic Chinese cultures still used stone tools, including finely worked and polished arrowheads and some smaller bone tools such as needles and fishhooks.

By about 2000 B.C.E. the Longshan or Black Pottery culture, perhaps by that time merged in part with the Painted Pottery culture, was building larger and larger villages, now better called towns, and producing the first north China bronze ornaments and weapons, probably for mainly ceremonial use since no bronze tools have yet been found from this period. Many of their settlements were surrounded by thick walls made of successive layers of stamped earth, a technique that was to continue for many centuries of subsequent recorded Chinese history. The later Longshan sites included bronze foundries and produced fine black pottery whose quality and shapes closely resemble those of the first historically authenticated dynasty, the Shang, which rose to power about 1600 B.C.E. Indeed, the Shang built one of their early capitals on the foundations of the late Longshan town at Ao, near modern Zhengzhou in Henan, on the floodplain of the Yellow River.

A further practice that links late Longshan culture to the Shang is the use of animal bones for divination purposes, the so-called oracle bones. Interpretations were based on the cracks made in the bones when they were heated in a fire. Questions, sometimes requests, were then inscribed, probably in part as a record. There is thus a clear line of succession from late Neolithic cultures in north China to the beginning of recorded history, with the Shang as the first literate, city-building Chinese civilization, according to present evidence. We can only speculate that similarly advanced development may well have taken place as early or earlier in the Yangzi Valley and/or the south, and that the relatively sudden emergence of the Shang on the Yellow River plain may have owed much to innovations farther south. What does seem clear is that the rise of civilization in both north and south China owed little if anything to early developments in Southwest Asia, Mesopotamia, or the Indus Valley. China does not seem to have been in contact with those areas or to have received anything from them until considerably later, when wheat, barley, alfalfa, donkeys, the horse, and the spoked chariot were diffused to China between about 1800 and 600 B.C.E. The story of the Shang Dynasty, and the spread of a unified Chinese state southward, is picked up again in Chapter 5.

Korea and Japan

Millet-based agriculture, accompanied by domesticated pigs, sheep, and goats, spread from north China to Korea by about 2000 B.C.E., although some evidence of questionable date suggests millet cultivation in the Han River valley near Seoul as early as 5000 B.C.E. Rice and bronze entered later, via north China, possibly aided by the flow of refugees from the fall of the Shang Dynasty, about 1100 B.C.E. The development of rice varieties adapted to a colder climate probably continued in Korea by purposeful selection. The ancestors of the Korean people migrated there from the north via Manchuria, probably from an original homeland in what is now Siberia and the northeastern Commonwealth of Independent States, a migration that continued well into historic times. The clearest evidence for this is the Korean spoken language, unrelated to Chinese and part of the language family of northeast Asia called Altaic.

The early Koreans were tribal peoples with a fishing, hunting, and gathering culture but producing technically advanced pottery and later, after the emergence of agriculture, building large above-ground tomb chambers of stone blocks, often mounded over with earth. As their culture began to merge into farming, permanent villages and towns arose and bronze weapons and ornaments appeared, probably derived from north China. Korean tradition dates the founding of a Korean state to 2333 B.C.E. by a ruler who was the son of the divine creator and a female bear in human form, but this is almost certainly far too early, if indeed it can be taken seriously at all. Another myth has it that a royal refugee from the fall of the Shang founded the state of Choson (an old name for Korea). That too seems improbable, though more plausible, and in any case fits with the transfer of much of Shang culture and technology to Korea during the first millennium B.C.E.

By the third century B.C.E. iron technology had also spread from China to Korea. The Chinese border kingdom of Yan with its capital near modern Beijing apparently also had some control over southern Manchuria and northern Korea. In the second century an unsuccessful rebel against the Han dynasty fled to Korea and established, about 194 B.C.E., a Sinicized state that controlled the northern half of the peninsula. It too was called Choson, with its capital at Pyongyang, still the capital of North Korea. The Han emperor Wu Di (see Chapter 5) conquered Choson in 109–108 B.C.E. and added further territory in central Korea under his control. Before the fall of the Han dynasty in 220 C.E. most of the Chinese garrisons had been withdrawn, and from 220 C.E. onward Korea remained an independent state, or states, since it was long divided into rival kingdoms.

Although remnants of the Chinese colonies planted under the Han survived in the north and continued to transmit Chinese cultural influences, by the fourth century C.E. they were overwhelmed by Korean insurgents or tribal groups, much as the Roman settlements in Britain and northern Europe were largely extinguished somewhat later by the rise of Germanic, Gallic, and British tribes. Nevertheless, as in Europe but to a much greater extent, influences from what was acknowledged to be a superior civilization continued throughout the later periods of Korean history. Unlike Rome, China successively rebuilt its empire and restored the vigor of its brilliant culture under the Tang, Song, Ming, and Qing dynasties from the seventh to the eighteenth centuries. Successive Korean states explicitly sought to adopt many elements of Chinese culture and continued to admire it as a model while maintaining their political independence. Three rival Korean kingdoms emerged after the end of Han Chinese control; their history and those of subsequent Korean states are given in Chapter 9.

As an island country—four main islands and many smaller ones 120 miles off the coast of Korea at the nearest point—Japan has preserved a separate identity, and its culture has remained a distinctive variant of anything on the mainland. Isolation and insularity not only kept Japan free from foreign control until the U.S. occupation from 1945 to 1952 but also helped to retard its early civilized development. Like the Koreans, the present-day Japanese people can be traced back to migrants from Northeast Asia or Siberia; these migrants spoke an Altaic language related to Korean but not to Chinese. Their distinction from the Koreans was, however, minimal until well after they entered Japan, sometime between 300 B.C.E. and 200 C.E. in successive waves, a movement about which we know very little. Other and unrelated groups already inhabiting the Japanese islands were absorbed by intermarriage, and the few survivors of the Japanese invasion were slowly driven northward.

At a much earlier date it is probable that there were also some movements of people into Japan from south China, the Malay areas of Southeast Asia, and perhaps from the South Pacific, as well as cultural influences, although these are hard to trace. Paleolithic cultures were widespread in Japan at least 40,000 years ago, differing little from those of the Asian mainland. By about 6000 B.C.E. according to present archaeological evidence, a great variety of early Neolithic cultures had arisen in Japan, of which the best known is called Jomon. We know too little about this period to be precise, but it seems likely that the Jomon people themselves were quite diverse and often in conflict. Some groups may have begun to practice a rudimentary agriculture about 300 B.C.E. Most of the Jomon people made cord-marked pottery, lived in sunken pit shelters, and engaged in hunting, gathering, and fishing. They seem, in other words, to have been as advanced as the Banpo people of north China and possibly a little earlier in achieving such a level. But the Jomon people were only very indirectly and partially the ancestors of the Japanese, who as pointed out were much later invaders from northern Asia, via Korea, although they probably merged in part with people already in Japan.

In any case, the Jomon culture was progressively displaced beginning in the third century B.C.E. by an early agricultural Neolithic culture called Yayoi. The Yayoi used the potter's wheel, cultivated rice, practiced irrigation, and had begun to use bronze and iron, all of these things diffused from earlier developments in China and entering Japan from Korea. A few Chinese coins and polished bronze mirrors found at Yayoi sites show that there was trade between the two areas. Like the Longshan, Yayoi bronze objects seem to have been ornamental or ceremonial; the few weapons that have been found are too thin to have been used in combat. By the third century C.E. the Yayoi began to construct large earthen

Pottery figure from the Jomon period in Japan, c. 500 B.C.E. The pottery is still relatively crude and is not wheel-made. The impressions were made by rolling twisted cords of different types onto the clay while it was still wet and then firing. Similar cord-marked vessels were made in the Neolithic period in the rest of Asia. (The Granger Collection, New York)

mounds over the tombs of prominent men, a practice presumably derived from Korea; indeed much of Yayoi culture, and its people, may most accurately be seen as provincial Korean.

By the fifth century iron swords and iron armor appeared. These were similar to or identical with Korean equivalents, as were the jeweled crowns and other ornaments found in some of the tombs. Houses were now raised off the ground, agriculture was becoming more productive with the help of iron tools, and pottery had become harder and more highly fired, unlike the cruder earthenware containers and stylized clay figures of earlier Yayoi. Now inhabited by people whom we may legitimately call Japanese, Honshu and Kyushu had reached the technological levels achieved by the Shang in China

some 2,000 years before, and by Korea perhaps 1,000 years thereafter. Japan still lacked writing, and we have no evidence of genuine cities or of the emergence of a true state.

Early Asian Commercial and Cultural Networking

Japan's adaptations of Chinese civilization, as well as Southeast Asia's localizations of Indian and Chinese civilizations, reflect societal interactions among Asia's earliest societies that were foundational to the transitions from the prehistoric to the historical eras of Asia's history. The interregional trade routes were the means by which the ideas of India spread to China, where they had a profound impact on the rethinking of China's Confucian traditions during the Tang dynasty, and it was this Chinese synthesis of the Indian and Chinese intellectual traditions that was passed on to Korea and Japan and became foundational to their political developments in the seventh century.

The fall of the Han dynasty between 190 and 225 C.E. increased the Chinese gentry's need for a maritime link between East and West to supply them with exotic goods. The first century also marked a great age of Buddhism in Asia. By the sixth century Buddhism would become especially important to the Chinese, and Southeast Asia assumed a key intermediary role between South Asia, the source of Buddhism, and China. Chinese monks traveled to India by sea with stopovers in Buddhist pilgrimage centers in Vietnam, Java, and Sumatra to acquire deeper understanding of their faith, and Indian monks journeyed to China to share their knowledge with Chinese patrons. There was an economic as well as an intellectual dimension to this Buddhist networking, as the Chinese sought religious artifacts and ritual objects as well as religious texts, all of which would, in their minds, allow them to legitimately perform Buddhist rituals in China.

During this earliest phase of Buddhist diplomatic networking in the Tang and Song eras, China localized the South Asian Buddhist tradition. By the fifteenth-century Ming era China no longer claimed the Indian heritage of its Buddhism, focusing instead on its own Buddhist practices, schools, and teachings, and developing its own Buddhist scholarship rather than feeling the need to disseminate the latest Buddhist texts of India. The increasingly ethnocentric Chinese minimized the role of their Buddhist communication with India and Southeast Asia, and no longer stressed the old sense of a spiritual bond with these other Buddhist realms. Instead, they took greater interest in commercial rather than religious exchanges with the southern neighbors.

Questions

1. What is the "Neolithic Revolution" and what are its distinguishing features? Why are pottery fragments important in telling us about earliest societies?

2. Although Southeast Asia is a distinct culture, it continues to share much with both China and India. How did this blending occur? What made Southeast Asia distinct from its Asian neighbors? What did it share with them? How did Southeast Asia potentially contribute to the development of Chinese civilization?

3. What role did the secondary and continuing migrations of populations by land and by sea into already settled regions assume in the further development of Asia's civilizations?

4. Why did China's initial center of civilization develop in north China? What role did the Yellow River assume in these developments?

5. What were Korea's and Japan's earliest contacts? What were their consequences?

6. What were the characteristics of Japan's Jomon culture?

Note

1. Eccles. 1:9–10.

Suggested Web Sites

Ancient, Prehistoric, and Early Peoples of Asia

http://www.china10k.com/english/history/
Highlights evidence of primitive humans in China, including chronological charts, maps, poems, and photos for prehistoric China.

http://www.ancientman.com/asia/asia.htm
Provides links with a vast number of sites on everything pertaining to prehistoric and ancient peoples of Asia.

http://ancienteastasia.org/
Good articles on the archaeology of China, Japan, and Korea.

Ancient Korea

**http://www2.hawaii.edu/korea/bibliography/
three_kingdoms-general.htm**
A bibliographic reference site on Korean history, archaeology, society, and culture.

Ancient Art

http://witcombe.sbc.edu/ARTHLinks3.html
A handy link to the significant sites that address Asian art and architecture.

Suggestions for Further Reading

Agarwal, D. P. *The Archeology of India.* New Delhi: Select Books, 1984.

Aikens, M. C., and Higuchi, T. *The Prehistory of Japan.* New York: Academic Press, 1982.

Ayyangar, P. T. S. *The Stone Age in India.* New Delhi: Asian Educational Services, 1982.

Barnes, G. L. *Prehistoric Yamato.* Ann Arbor, MI: Center for Japanese Studies, 1988.

Bellwood, P. *Prehistory of the Indo-Malaysian Archipelago.* New York: Academic Press, 1985.

Chang, K. C. *The Archeology of Ancient China,* 4th ed. New Haven: Yale University Press, 1987.

Chard, C. S. *Northeast Asia in Prehistory.* Madison: University of Wisconsin Press, 1974.

Higham, C. *The Archeology of Mainland Southeast Asia.* Cambridge: Cambridge University Press, 1989.

———. *The Bronze Age of Southeast Asia.* Cambridge: Cambridge University Press, 1996.

Keightly, D. N., ed. *The Origins of Chinese Civilization.* Berkeley: University of California Press, 1983.

Kennedy, A. R., and Possehl, G. L. *Studies in the Archeology and Paleoanthropology of South Asia.* New Delhi: Oxford University Press, 1984.

Kim, J. H. *The Prehistory of Korea.* Honolulu: University of Hawaii Press, 1978.

Kohl, P., ed. *The Bronze Age Civilization of Central Asia.* Armonk, NY: M. E. Sharpe, 1981.

———. *Central Asia: Paleolithic Beginnings to the Iron Age.* Paris: Éditions Recherchés sur les Civilizations, 1984.

Loewe, M., and Shaunghessy, T., eds. *The Cambridge History of Ancient China.* New York: Cambridge University Press, 2000.

Masson, V. M., and Sairanidi, V. *Central Asia Before the Achaemenids.* New York: Praeger, 1972.

Nelson, S. *The Archeology of Korea.* New York: Cambridge University Press, 1993.

Pearson, R. J., ed. *Windows on the Japanese Past: Archeology and Prehistory.* Ann Arbor, MI: Center for Japanese Studies, 1986.

Possehl, G. L. *Harappan Civilization.* Oxford: Oxford University Press, 1987.

2

Asian Religions and Their Cultures

This chapter considers Hinduism (an exclusively Indian religion), Jainism, Buddhism and its divisions, Confucianism, Daoism, Judaism in Asia, Islam in Asia, and Shinto (exclusive to Japan). It closes with some considerations on Asian religions as a whole and on the contrasts between them and the Western Judeo-Christian tradition.

All of the world's major religions are Asian in origin, including Christianity and Judaism, which moved westward to Europe and the New World. They, plus Hinduism, Buddhism, Confucianism, Daoism, and Islam, are many hundreds or thousands of years old, but together they still affect the lives of most of the world's people. Most Communist states substituted another kind of belief system, but in China, the biggest of them, much of both Confucianism and traditional folk religion survive, while even in Russia and eastern Europe religion is far from dead, and indeed is currently undergoing a revival.

Hinduism

Hinduism, probably the oldest of all the main world religions, remains vigorous, with more than 800 million followers today. India is the most religiously oriented of all major cultures. Hinduism—literally, "Indianism"—is hard to define, and the religious element is hard to separate from more general cultural practice. The caste system is the best illustration. It is a Hindu practice, but it is also observed by South Asian Muslims, Christians, and Buddhists* (in Sri Lanka). Thus, it is clearly separable from Hinduism as a nonreligious system that has evolved as a means of imposing some

social order on an often-disrupted society. (Caste as a system of social organization is discussed in Chapter 3.)

The functional units of caste were and remain "subcastes," or *jatis,* usually connected with occupation, marrying only fellow jati members, and forbidden to share food or water with other jatis. Caste can still be transcended by religious devotion, which again emphasizes its nonreligious nature. The *sadhu,* or Hindu holy man, has always been beyond caste. Holy men and other mystics have long been a prominent aspect of Indian civilization, more so than in any other major culture. Caste has remained a source of group identity and strength, but is rapidly losing force as India becomes increasingly industrialized, urbanized, and secularized, although it still plays an important part in the lives of most villagers, who are the majority of the population.

Hindu Beliefs and Writings

Hinduism is often called a way of life, which is true but not very helpful. There is no founder or single doctrinal text, like the Koran, the New Testament, or the Buddha's sayings. Hinduism developed in part from the religions of the Indus civilization, which included the cult of Shiva, still the dominant Hindu god. The Aryans brought their own tribal gods, including the war god Indra and the fire god Agni (compare Latin *ignis,* "fire," and English *ignite*), but by the time the first texts, the Vedas, were written down, many centuries later, Vedic religion was already a mixture of Harappan, Aryan, and Dravidian (southern Indian) elements. The Dravidian element probably included the god Krishna, one of many manifestations in human form of Vishnu the creator; Krishna represents gentleness and compassion and is always shown and spoken of as "the dark one," colored blue or even black—hence the guess at Dravidian origin.

The Vedas are the world's oldest religious texts still used in worship. They were composed cumulatively between about 1500 and 600 B.C.E., first orally and later

---

*The Indian world of South Asia, often called the Indian Subcontinent, includes the modern states of Pakistan, India, Nepal, Bangladesh, and Sri Lanka.

CHRONOLOGY

1600–1500 B.C.E. ■ Aryans enter India; Vedic religious tradition begins

1000 B.C.E. ■ Brahmanical religious tradition in India

550–400 B.C.E. ■ Buddha; Confucius; Laozi; Mahavira; *Upanishads*

372–289 B.C.E. ■ Mencius

100 B.C.E. ■ Therevada and Mahayana Buddhism

c. 100–300 C.E. ■ Classical Hinduism; Bhakti; *Bhagavad Gita*

622 C.E. ■ Mohammed's Hejira (origin of Islam)

written down as a set of hymns, spells, rituals, and mystic poems used at sacrifices. The last of the Vedas chronologically, the Upanishads of the seventh century B.C.E., deal mainly with the nature of the universe and the place of humans in it. They involve a sophisticated

A modern *sadhu*, or holy man, who has renounced the world and lives by begging for his food. He stands in front of a temple frieze in south India. (Stella Snead, New York)

metaphysics that is characteristically Indian but a far cry from earlier Aryan anthropomorphic gods. Asceticism and mysticism are seen in the Upanishads as the chief paths for humans to realize wisdom and eternal truth.

The Upanishads deal also with good and evil, law, morality, and human duty and are often seen as the core of classical Hinduism. But Hinduism's main ethical text is the much later Bhagavad Gita (second century C.E.), which tells the story of Prince Arjuna, who is faced with a rebellion led by disloyal friends, relatives, and teachers, people he has loved and respected. His cause is just, but he cannot bring himself to fight and kill those so close to him. He stands in his chariot awaiting battle and talks to his charioteer, who turns out to be Krishna. Krishna tells him that bodily death does not mean the death of the soul and is thus unimportant. For any individual's life, what is important is duty, and action in accordance with duty, but without attachment, personal desires, or ambition. Each person has his or her own duty or role in society, and morality lies in faithfulness to that prescribed role.

This is the concept of *dharma,* the selfless execution of one's earthly duties, which came to be applied also to the faithful following of caste rules. Arjuna was a ruler and, hence, had to follow the ruler's dharma, which included the duty to fight to uphold his rightful power. Other roles in society have their own different dharmas, including (later) those of lower castes to serve and defer to those above them, and the rules associated with students, wives, parents, and so on. *Karma* is the consequences of one's actions; faithfulness to one's dharma produces good karma. Thus, moral behavior brings rewards, and bad behavior yields bad karma. There is much universal human wisdom in this, but it also clearly supports the status quo, as well as condoning violence in certain cases. It has accordingly been much criticized, even by leading Hindus, and is in many ways inconsistent with other parts of Hinduism, especially the religious commitment to *ahimsa,* or nonviolence and reverence for all life. Mahatma Gandhi saw no conflict between the Gita and ahimsa and took the story of Arjuna simply as emphasizing duty.

Hinduism has cumulatively incorporated varied ideas, texts, and practices and combines what may seem excessive emphasis on ritual with much genuine spirituality. But the notions of dharma and karma have remained basic to Hinduism, as have the traditions of meditation and asceticism, and have helped create the tolerance for which Hinduism is noted. All faiths and all ascetic disciplines—all religions and all pursuits of divine truth—have the same goal, and divine truth is universal; the paths to it are rightly varied, as dharma is rightly different for everyone. Gandhi said about Christian missionaries that he did not object to their preaching but did wish they would be more faithful to their professed dharma, that is, true Christians.

Reincarnation

The probable Harappan belief in reincarnation and the immortality of the soul had reappeared by late Vedic times and became a further basic part of Hinduism. The karma produced by one's mortal life determines the next rebirth of that soul, in a person of higher or lower status or in an animal or insect. Special piety, meditation, asceticism, and understanding of eternal truth can bring escape from the cycle of birth and rebirth; the soul of such a one is liberated from that cycle and achieves *moksha,* not a bodily Heaven but a blissful spiritual rejoining with the godhead or with creation. Mortal life can include a vision of eternity, of the undying power of creation, of God as love, through the mortal body's immortal soul, which is born again, or reincarnated.

Belief in reincarnation heightened the Hindu feeling of reverence for all life. One's relative or ancestor might have been reborn as a horse or a spider. From Harappan times cattle were especially revered, for their basic usefulness and for the obvious symbolism of creation and motherhood offered by the cow, with her prominent milk production. Bulls and oxen are natural symbols of patient strength and of virility (as in Mediterranean cultures), and cows are gentle creatures with large, lustrous eyes. But to Hinduism, all life is sacred, all one, and all creatures are part of the great chain of being that manifests the divine. Accordingly, pious Hindus are vegetarians, and all but the lowest castes particularly avoid eating beef. Milk, curds, clarified butter (*ghee*), and yoghurt were used ritually in religious ceremonies.

By late Vedic times (c. 600 B.C.E.) the Hindu pantheon was dominated by a trinity of Vishnu, Shiva, and Brahma, all supreme deities and all creators. But there developed also a bewildering variety of consorts, divine incarnations, and lesser gods, each with his or her own cult, as Hinduism continued to incorporate regional and folk religious figures and traditions: among many others, Ganesh, the benevolent, elephant-headed son of Shiva and his consort Parvati; Hanuman, the monkey god, symbolizing loyalty and strength; Sarasvati, goddess of wisdom and learning; Krishna, Lakshmi, consort or wife of Vishnu and goddess of wealth and worldly success; and Kali or Durga, a mother goddess, consort or female equivalent to the grimmer aspects of Shiva, sometimes called the goddess of death and disease but also, like Shiva, a figure prayed to for help, especially by women.

Shiva became the most commonly worshipped god, seen as both creator and destroyer, god of the harvest, of fertility, the cosmic dance of creation, and the chief god of yogis (practitioners of yoga and meditation). He is still celebrated as the lord of both death and life and the genius of procreation. He is paralleled by similar figures in many other religions, including Christ, who represents both death (the crucifixion) and eternal life. In other religions human sacrifice was also used as a means for the renewal of life; the sacrificial victim gives life to and for others or enriches it. Hinduism recognizes this concept, as it accepts death as a natural part of life, and celebrates it in the figures of Shiva and Kali.

Like Buddhism and Zoroastrianism, Hinduism accepted the presence of evil and suffering in the world to a greater extent than other religions and recognized that people—themselves a mixture of good and evil, love and hate, pain and joy, pettiness and nobility, selfishness and altruism—must come to terms with their own nature and with the nature of the cosmos. The major Hindu gods and goddesses, thus, represent both aspects, destroyers as well as creators, makers of suffering as well as of bliss, true representations of the world as it is. Nevertheless most devout Hindus, and especially literate ones, have always been basically monotheistic, stressing the oneness of creation and the majesty of a single creative principle, above the level of a humanlike god figure. Access to the creative power or truth of the cosmos was possible without cults or intermediaries through devotion, meditation, and mystical understanding of eternal truth. As the Hindu proverb put it, "God is one, but wise people know it by many names." Jainism and Sikhism, reformist offshoots of Hinduism (respectively, in the sixth century B.C.E. and late fifteenth century C.E.) centered on monotheism, as did the teachings of the Buddha, derived from the Hinduism into which he was born, where universal truth was given no anthropomorphic identity, as it is not in pure Hinduism. The same can be said about pure Christianity, as opposed to the worship of saints and other cults in folk Christianity.

Hinduism never developed fixed or uniform rituals comparable with those of Christianity or Judaism. Pious Hindus recite specified prayers daily before the simple altar found in nearly all Hindu homes. They may make frequent offerings of prayer, food, and flowers at one of the many temples throughout India, which are tended by people who are called priests. But there is no set formal service, no established ordination or clergy, and no special holy day set aside for worship, like the Christian Sunday, the Jewish Sabbath, or the Muslim Friday. Brahmins, the highest caste and the exclusive keepers and reciters of the sacred rituals, mainly texts from Sanskrit Vedas and epics, are the only people who perform the rituals for death, marriage, coming of age, and intercession with the divine. These are certainly priestly functions, but such people are not seen as necessary intermediaries with God for laypersons. All Hindu Brahmins are not priests, and although Hindu priests may tend temples and receive offerings, they are a far more informally constituted group than in Christianity or Judaism.

Creation:
Hindu Views

These selections are designed to show the evolution of Hinduism from Vedic times. Compare the first selection, from the Rig Veda, with the biblical accounts in Genesis and the Gospel of John.

> Let me proclaim the valiant deeds of Indra,
> The first he did, the wielder of the thunder,
> When he slew the dragon and let loose the waters,
> And pierced the bellies of the mountains. . . .
>
> When, Indra, you slew the firstborn of dragons,
> And frustrated the arts of the sorcerers,
> Creating sun and heaven and dawn,
> You found no enemy to withstand you. . . .
>
> At first there was only darkness wrapped in darkness.
> All this was only unillumined water.
> That One which came to be, enclosed in nothing,
> Arose at last, born of the power of heat. . . .
>
> But who knows, and who can say
> Whence it all came, and how creation happened?
> The gods themselves are later than creation,
> So who knows truly whence it has arisen?

From the Upanishads:

> "Fetch me a fruit of the banyan tree"
> "Here is one, sir"
> "Break it"
> "I have broken it, sir"
> "What do you see?"

There are a number of Hindu festivals, most of which are as much cultural as religious, such as the autumn Diwali, or Festival of Lights, and the spring festival of Holi. There is an ancient tradition of religious pilgrimage to famous temples and sacred sites. To observe contemporary Indian festivals or pilgrimages is to catch a glimpse of something like Chaucer's England or medieval Europe, a time in the West when religion was prominent in the minds of most people. The Kumba Mela religious festival held at Allahabad on the central Ganges every 12 years drew 30 million pilgrims in 2001. Nevertheless, the secularization that overtook the West at the beginning of the Renaissance can be seen today in modern India, spurred on by urbanization, industrialization, the technological revolution, and the rise of the nation-state. For increasing numbers of urban professional Indians religion is less important than other, more worldly guides. Although such peoples are still a minority of the total population, they tend to be the same

groups that have also discarded caste or pay little or no attention to it. Most of the leaders of modern India have adopted a secular outlook. Even Gandhi preached against caste discrimination and explicitly against the harsh treatment of Untouchables.

Nevertheless, Hinduism is deeply rooted in the Indian tradition, and it remains the basic guide for over 800 million people, probably more so than for most of the adherents of any other religion, although such things are hard to measure. But despite its strong elements of spirituality, Hinduism has also long recognized the importance to human life of achieving material well-being (*artha*), the responsibility of individuals to provide for their families, and the importance of interpersonal love and of sex (*kama*). Such matters are basic parts of human nature and hence accepted as good. Hinduism in effect rejects nothing that God has made but celebrates and enshrines all of life, including its creation through sex, while making much less distinction than in

"Tiny seeds, sir"
"Break one"
"I have broken it, sir"
"What do you see?"
"Nothing, sir"
"My son, what you do not perceive is the essence,
and in that essence the mighty banyan tree exists. . . .
That is the true, that is the self, and you are that self."

The snarer, who rules alone in his might,
He who governs the world in his power,
Is always one and the same,
Though all else rise and decay. . . .
He stands behind all beings, he made all worlds. . . .
He lives in the innermost heart of all.

The good is one thing and the pleasant another.
Both, with their different ends, control a man.
But it is well with him who chooses the good,
While he who chooses the pleasant misses his mark.

From the Bhagavad Gita:

He who thinks this is the slayer, and this the slain,
Does not understand. It neither slays nor is slain.
It is never born and never dies, nor does it cease to be.
Unborn, eternal, abiding, and ancient,
It is not slain when the body is slain. . . .

There is more joy in doing one's own duty badly
Than in doing another man's duty well.
It is joy to die in doing one's duty,
But doing another man's duty brings dread.

Source: A. L. Basham, *The Wonder That Was India,* 3d ed. (London: Macmillan, 1968), pp. 248, 250–251, 252–253, 254, 341, 400.

the West between the sacred and the profane; all are part of creation, which is divine.

Hinduism's acknowledgment of the bad as well as the good things of life may perhaps have made things easier or psychologically healthier for its followers, who accept the tragedies and sufferings of life without feeling that they are somehow being punished or picked on, as well as enjoying life's blessings. In any case happiness and suffering are both largely unavoidable parts of every existence, and it may be better to acknowledge this than to attempt to deny or gloss over the bad parts, including the death of the body and the existence of evil, pain, suffering, and cruelty. Religion seems always to have been basic for most Indians, in the way that it was for most medieval Europeans, and to have provided comfort and assurance as all religion aims to do. Nearly all religions accept the immortality of the soul; the Hindu belief in reincarnation and moksha merely carries that one step further.

Buddhism in India and Its Spread Eastward

The preoccupation of the Hindu Upanishads with eternal truth reflected in part a troubled world of those times, the period preceding the rise of empire. A new hybrid India was emerging, including the appearance of larger states, and with them an increase in the scale of warfare. The age of heroic chivalry and of aristocratic privilege was yielding to one of power politics. Many people understandably sought solace or escape from harsh reality through otherworldly quests, including avenues of release from the sufferings of everyday life. The founders of Buddhism and Jainism, roughly contemporary figures in the sixth century B.C.E., pursued such a path and also reacted against the growing ritualization of Hinduism and its dominance by the

---

The Divine Couple and the Human Family

In both southern India and Southeast Asia there was continuity between preexisting recognitions of the female divine and acceptance of Vedic male divinity. This is not only shown in the noted popularity of depicting the male divine accompanied by his female counterpart, but also in continuing exclusive worship of a female deity. In most cases the female divine was approached as the devotee's potential intercessionary with a male divine, in the same way that the cults of the Virgin Mary and the female saints in the Catholic tradition emphasize their interventionary capacities. Such notions of the female counterpart, as well as a softening of the image of the distant and omnipotent male Absolute Divine, were founded in the Indian Bhakti ("devotional") Hindu literature that developed in southern India during the tenth century (see Chapter 6) but that had its roots in classical north Indian Sanskrit literature. Such devotional appeals to a beneficent and forgiving deity (Visnu and Shiva and their associated deities) were an alternative to the sacrificial tradition of the Vedas and the intellectualism of the Upanishads.

The themes of a male and female divine partnership are developed in the literary and iconographic portrayals of Siva's divine partner Uma, or Parvati. While the Lord Siva is near perfection, his consort Uma has human frailties, both physical and character flaws. The implication is that Siva is too pure to be approached directly by the common worshipper, unlike his consort Uma, who has the humanlike imperfections of the earthbound devotee.

The Uma literature illustrates the consequences of human imperfection, self-serving intentions, and uncontained anger in the creation of the demonic. In these tales Uma has the undisciplined, feminine, and unpredictable human personality traits generally ascribed to women in South Asian tradition. Uma personifies feminine forces in general; she might cause problems for humankind as well as for the gods. However, due to her divinity, and despite her humanlike imperfections, she might equally intervene to restore order, to redeem humankind from curses, and even to rescue her husband Siva from his own misadventures. In such a way the divine male cannot exist without his consort, in the same way that the human husband and wife become as one. This sacred bond between human spouses was foundational to a family's success and, subsequently, that of the wider society.

---

priestly caste of Brahmins. Both urged independent access to truth through meditation and self-denial without the aid of priests or ritual, and both taught the equality of all in these terms, rejecting caste distinctions and the hierarchy they represented. But Buddhism and Jainism developed out of the Hindu tradition and share the Hindu beliefs in dharma, karma, *samsara* (reincarnation), moksha (*nirvana,* or union with the godhead), devotion, and nonviolence or reverence for life. Both rejected the folk panoply of Hindu gods but reaffirmed Hinduism's basic monotheism, its nonpersonalized worship of the infinite and the great chain of being.

Jainism

The man called Mahavira ("Great Hero," c. 546–468 B.C.E.) founded Jainism as an ascetic faith, and he himself went naked and finally starved himself to death. Jainism reasserted the Hindu veneration of all living

things. Even now pious Jains wear face masks to avoid inhaling insects and do not engage in agriculture for fear of harming organisms in the soil. They have instead gone into business and grown wealthy, the majority living in Gujarat, the traditional home of merchants.

A CLOSER LOOK

Gautama Buddha

The founder of Buddhism was born about 563 B.C.E. in the Himalayan foothill region of Nepal, the son of a minor king (*raja;* compare the English word "royal") of the Sakya clan. His family name was Gautama and his given name Siddartha, but he was also later called by some Sakyamuni ("Sage of the Sakyas"), as well as Gautama and Prince Siddartha. Until he was 29 years old, he led a conventional life for a prince, filled with earthly pleasures. At 19 he married a beautiful princess, and in due time they had a son, or so says the pious legend elaborated in great detail after his death, as with so many other religious figures. We know that he became an ascetic as an adult, wandered and taught for many years, acquired a number of disciples, founded a religious order, and died at about the age of 80, somewhere between 485 and 480 B.C.E. This is all we know of his life for certain. The later embroidered story of his life, replete with miraculous tales, is important as it has influenced the lives of so many millions of successive generations of Asians, from India eastward.

According to this story (in its briefest form), Prince Siddartha, filled with nameless discontent, wandered one day away from his walled palace and met in quick succession an old man broken by age, a sick man covered with boils and shivering with fever, a corpse being carried to the cremation ground (Hindus have always burned their dead), and a wandering sadhu (holy man) with his begging bowl and simple yellow robe, but with peacefulness and inner joy in his face. Overwhelmed by this vision of the sufferings of mortal life, the emptiness of worldly pleasure, and the promise of ascetic devotion, he shortly thereafter left his palace, abandoned his wife and son, and became a wandering beggar seeking after the truth and owning nothing but a crude wooden bowl (to beg the bare essentials of food) and a rag of clothing. For several years he wandered, wasted from fasting, until he determined to solve the riddle of suffering through intense meditation under a great

tree. After 49 days, during which he was tempted by Mara, the prince of demons, with promises of riches, power, and sensual pleasures, all of which he ignored, he knew the truth and attained enlightenment. From this moment, he was known as the Buddha, or the Enlightened One. Soon after, he preached his first sermon, near Banaras (Varanasi) in the central Ganges Valley, and spent the rest of his life as an itinerant preacher with a band of disciples.

The Four Noble Truths, announced in that first sermon, formed the basis for the new faith: (1) life is filled with pain, sorrow, frustration, impermanence, and dissatisfaction (dukkha); (2) all this is caused by desire, by wanting, and by the urge for existence; (3) to end suffering and sorrow, one must end desire, become desireless; and (4) desirelessness can be gained by the eightfold path of "right conduct."

Faithful followers of the path outlined in the first sermon may attain nirvana, or release from the sufferings of worldly existence by avoiding the cycle of rebirth, and achieve blissful reabsorption of their souls into the spiritual infinite, as the Buddha did on his death. Such devotion and such insight into truth through meditation are, however, rare, and although the Buddha did not say so, Buddhism incorporated the Hindu concept of karma: less dutiful individuals were reborn in successive existences in forms appropriate to their behavior in their most recent incarnations. The "right conduct" of the eightfold path was defined as

Buddhist Teachings

Many of the teachings attributed to the Buddha are almost certainly later additions or commentaries. Here are two rather striking passages from such Buddhist scriptures, whose closeness to the Christian Gospels is remarkable.

> A man buries a treasure in a deep pit, thinking: "It will be useful in time of need, or if the king is displeased with me, or if I am robbed, or fall into debt, or if food is scarce, or bad luck befalls me." But all this treasure may not profit the owner at all, for he may forget where he hid it, or goblins may steal it, or his enemies or even his kinsmen may take it when he is not on his guard. But by charity, goodness, restraint, and self-control man and woman alike can store up a well-hidden treasure—a treasure which cannot be given to others and which robbers cannot steal. A wise man should do good; that is the treasure which will not leave him.

> Brethren, you have no mother or father to care for you. If you do not care for one another, who else will do so? Brethren, he who would care for me should care for the sick.

Source: A. L. Basham, The *Wonder That Was India,* 3d ed. (London: Macmillan, 1968, p. 284).

The great stupa (temple) at Sanchi in central India. Begun by Ashoka in the third century B.C.E., it was enlarged during the century after his death, when the outer ring and gateways were added. The stupa form represents the universe and the great bowl of the sky. The small three-tiered structure on top became the basis for the pagoda form as Mahayana Buddhism spread from India to China, Korea, and Japan. (Government of India Tourist Office)

kindness to all living things, purity of heart, truthfulness, charity, and avoidance of fault finding, envy, hatred, and violence. To these were added specific commandments not to kill, steal, commit adultery, lie, speak evil, gossip, flatter, or otherwise wander from the Path. Accounts of the Buddha's own teachings were recorded in a collection of texts called the Tripitaka ("three baskets"), and there was a growing literature of moral tales about the life of Buddha and related events, as well as commentaries on the teachings, all comparable in many ways with the New Testament. The worship of relics, such as alleged teeth or hair of the Buddha, also became part of Buddhist practice, as in later Christianity.

As with Christianity, Buddhism remained for its first several centuries a minority religion, but the difficult discipline of the original teachings was softened somewhat so as to accommodate more followers. The conversion of the Emperor Ashoka (ruled c. 269–c. 232 B.C.E.) helped to transform Buddhism into a mass religion and began its spread from India, first to Ceylon and Southeast Asia and later via Central Asia to China, Korea, and Japan. Within India, Buddhism survived for many centuries, although its following slowly declined from a peak about 100 C.E. For many, the distinction from Hinduism was gradually blurred, and in general one may say that, except for the several monastic orders and some lay devotees, Buddhism was slowly reabsorbed into Hinduism. Many Hindus saw Buddhism's rejection of the sensory world as "life denying" and returned to their own religion's affirmation of life. The remaining Buddhist centers and monasteries in the central Ganges heartland of the faith were destroyed and the few survivors driven into exile by the Muslim slaughter of the twelfth century, when Buddhism was largely extinguished in the land of its birth.

Theravada and Mahayana Buddhism

Soon after Ashoka's time Buddhism divided into two major schools, known as Theravada or Hinayana ("the lesser vehicle") and Mahayana ("the greater vehicle"). Theravada Buddhism remained closer to the original faith, although it too was necessarily popularized to some extent. As it spread, it came to include more scope for the doctrine of good works as a means of acquiring "merit." Good works could even offset bad conduct in the building of karma; for example, one could give money to finance a temple and make up for the bad karma that may have been created by unethically acquired money or in other wanderings from the Path. Theravada was the form of Buddhism transmitted to Southeast Asia, where especially in Burma, Thailand, Cambodia, and Laos (plus Sri Lanka), it has remained the dominant religion and is still taken very seriously by most of the people of those countries; nearly all young men traditionally spent two years in a Buddhist monastery, as many still do, with shaven heads, a yellow robe, and a begging bowl; as adults, they and most others pay far more than lip service to the Theravada version of the Path.

Mahayana Buddhism developed a little later, during the Kushan period in India between about 100 and 200 C.E. What had begun as a spiritual discipline for a few became a mass religion for all, popularized, humanized, and provided with a variety of supports, including the worship of relics. The Buddha himself was made into a supernatural god, and there were also innumerable other Buddhas called *bodhisattvas,* saints who out of compassion delayed their entrance into nirvana in order to help those still on earth to attain deliverance. Faith in and worship of a bodhisattva also offered comfort to those who believed they needed divine help for any purpose. This in turn promoted the worship of images, including those of the original Buddha, and the development of elaborate rituals and cults. Such worship by itself could produce salvation and also solve worldly problems.

Bodhisattvas became the chief gods of Mahayana Buddhism. The figure called the Buddha Amitabha was originally a bodhisattva and was worshipped in China as E-mi-tuo-fu, in Japan as Amida Buddha, the principal savior of the Western Paradise. Another bodhisattva, the compassionate Avalokitesvara, came to be worshipped by Mahayana Buddhists as a female goddess of mercy, called in China Guanyin and in Japan Kannon. She was much prayed to, especially by women, for help in the present world rather than for release from it, as the classical Buddhist doctrine emphasized. Like Theravada, Mahayana Buddhism also came to stress the redemptive power of charity and good works, both to help others and to contribute to one's own salvation. None of these later developments had much to do with the Buddha's original teachings, but they did relate Buddhism to everyday life and to everyday people and their needs rather than rejecting this-worldly concerns. Especially in Japanese Buddhism, salvation in some sects might be won simply by faith and devotion or by reciting the Buddha's or bodhisattva's name. Lamaistic Buddhism in Tibet saw similar developments, including belief in the power of relics and the use of prayer flags and prayer wheels on which a simple incantation was written; it was believed that each time the wheel was turned or the winds fluttered the flag, the prayer ascended to heaven and won merit for the one who had turned the wheel or placed the flag. This, plus the worship of many anthropomorphic gods and the doctrine of good works, made the asceticism, self-denial, and "desirelessness" of the original teachings of the historical Buddha less necessary. That was, in any case, a difficult road for most

people, and as Buddhism won more converts it was transformed almost unrecognizably.

Some forms of Mahayana Buddhism acquired a magic overlay: bodhisattvas and their attendants flew through the air; worshippers could obtain sanctity merely by repeating ritual phrases or worshipping supposed relics of the Buddha. The Mahayana school also developed details of a bodily heaven to which the faithful would go, filled with recognizable pleasures and wholly different from nirvana. To match it, there was a gruesome hell, presided over by a host of demons, where the wicked or unworthy suffered an imaginative variety of hideous tortures. One may again compare all this with

The great bronze Buddha at Kamakura, near Tokyo, completed in 1252 and originally housed in its own temple but now in the open and still visited by millions of tourists, daytrippers, and worshippers every year. It was built with the help of funds raised from the common people of the Kamakura domains and shows the compassionate benevolence of the Buddha, or Amida Buddha as the Japanese say. (Cameramann International, Ltd.)

the changes in Christianity from its origins to its medieval form. As with Christianity also, the popularization of Buddhism, especially in the Mahayana school, led to a flourishing of artistic representation in painting, sculpture, and architecture: endless and often profoundly beautiful paintings and statues of the Buddha and his attendants and temples in great variety. The latter included the pagoda form in the Mahayana countries and the *dagoba* in Theravada lands.

It was Mahayana Buddhism that was transmitted to China, Tibet, Korea, and Japan because it had by that time become the dominant form in India. Its spread into China via Central Asia in the later Han dynasty and its popularity after the fall of the Han will be noted in Chapter 5. From China it spread to Tibet and Korea, and from there to Japan by about 500 C.E. A number of Mahayana monastic orders and sects that originally developed in China, including the contemplative and mystical school of Chan Buddhism, were diffused to both countries. In Japan, *Chan* became *Zen,* and other schools and monastic orders of Buddhism also flourished. The growth of Japanese Buddhism was greatly accelerated during the period of direct Japanese contact with, and borrowing from, Tang dynasty China (eighth century C.E.), when many Japanese Buddhist monks visited China.

In Japan and Korea too, Buddhist art flourished in a variety of forms. Later in the Tang dynasty, about 840 C.E., the imperial state, concerned about and jealous of the growing wealth and power of Buddhist temples and monasteries, confiscated much of it and suppressed Buddhism except as a small minority religion within a dominantly Confucian context. That was to be its fate for the rest of Chinese history, but in Japan Buddhism remained proportionately far more important, as it still is. Buddhism is, nominally, the major religion, but in fact most Japanese pay little attention to its precepts or discipline and are either wholly secular or very casual followers of any religious creed.

Confucianism

Many would argue that Confucianism is not a religion but merely a set of ethical rules, a moral philosophy. It is true that it specifically avoids any concern with theology, the afterlife, or otherworldly matters. Most Chinese, Korean, Vietnamese, and Japanese Confucianists have apparently found it appropriate to supplement their religious diets with bits of Buddhism, Daoism, or Shinto (traditional Japanese animism or nature worship), which provide what Confucianism leaves out. Perhaps it does not matter whether one calls Confucianism religion or philosophy; it is the creed by

which millions of successive generations of East Asians, something like a third of the world, have lived for over 2,000 years. Confucianism has probably had more impact on belief and behavior than any of the great religions, in the sense that most East Asians accept and follow the teachings of the sage more thoroughly than followers of the ethical teachings of any other system of belief. Confucian teachings contain much common sense about human relations, but they are a good deal more than that, reflecting and shaping a highly distinctive set of values, norms, and sociopolitical patterns. Confucianism has its temples too, monuments to the doctrine, though it lacks a prescribed ritual or organized priesthood; for those things, Confucianists turn elsewhere, as indicated, but do not thereby cease to be true and diligent followers of the sage's teachings.

Confucius and Mencius

Confucius (551–c. 479 B.C.E.) was the son of a minor official in one of the smaller states of eastern China long before the first imperial unification. He became a teacher, and later a sometime adviser, to various local rulers. He never had a definite official post, and he had no real political clout. Like Plato, he looked for a ruler who might be shaped by his advice, but also like Plato, he never really found one. Several of his students became his disciples, though never as organized as in Plato's Academy; after his death they and their students began to write down his teachings and to expand on them. His most famous later follower and commentator was Mencius (c. 372–c. 289 B.C.E.). Confucius and Mencius lived in the chaotic Warring States period and sought means for restoring order and social harmony through individual morality, a parallel to the origins of Buddhism and Jainism.

The Confucian View

Society in East Asia has always been profoundly hierarchical, and the social order was seen as a series of status groups and graded roles, from the ruler at the top through officials, scholars, and gentlemen to the father of the family, all with authority over those below them but also with responsibility to set a good example. The key element was "right relationships," carefully defined for each association: father-son, subject-ruler, husband-wife, elder brother-younger brother, and so on. Confucius and Mencius provided what became doctrinal support for such a system. It left small place for the individual as such but at the same time stressed the vital importance of self-cultivation and education as the only true assurance of morality, or "virtuous behavior." To paraphrase Plato, "Education makes people good, and

A portrait of Confucius. This Qing dynasty rubbing was made over 2,000 years after the death of the sage, of whom there are no contemporary portraits. (The Granger Collection, New York)

good people act nobly." According to Confucianism, people are born naturally good and naturally inclined to virtue but need education and the virtuous example of superiors to stay that way. Confucius emphasized "human-heartedness," benevolence, respect for superiors, filial loyalty, "right relations," and learning as cures for chaos and as the formula for achieving the "great harmony" that was his chief objective.

Force and law are no substitutes for or guarantees of individual virtue or social harmony, and indeed they were seen as ineffective as well as unnecessary in a properly run society. People must *want* to do right, and that can be achieved only by internalizing morality. When force or punishment has to be used, the social system has broken down. Confucianism is a highly pragmatic, this-worldly, and positive view of humanity and society; it provided little scope for metaphysical speculation, for the supernatural, or for concepts like sin or salvation. And although Confucius and Mencius were certainly conservatives, supporters of a hierarchical social order, their doctrine also allowed for individual ability and dedication, based on the conviction that everyone is born with the seeds of virtue. By self-cultivation and by following virtuous examples, anyone can become a sage. No priests are necessary, only self-development.

This concept was later incorporated in the imperial examination system and the selection of officials from the ranks of the educated, regardless of their social origins. Confucianism also reaffirmed the right of the people to rebel against immoral or unjust rulers who had forfeited the mandate of Heaven by their lapse from virtue; loyalty to superiors was a basic Confucian tenet, but loyalty to moral principle could win out, although this often presented individuals with a severe dilemma: for example, fathers, however unjust, were rarely defied.

In general, Confucianism reflected the basically positive as well as practical Chinese view of the world, where the greatest of all blessings was the enjoyment of a long life, or, more accurately, "the enjoyment of living." This included the particularly Chinese emphases on the pleasures of good food, the production of children, and the attainment of a ripe old age surrounded by one's descendants. These are still notably Chinese values, and the culture built around them has attracted the admiration of successive generations of Western observers, who approach it from the perspective of their own more somber and more theological religious and social tradition with its overtones of original sin, guilt, retribution, and divine judgment. Confucianism was more human-centered and, like Hinduism, more life-celebrating. Hard work, achievement, and material prosperity and its enjoyment were valued and pursued, but the enjoyment of leisure, of nature, and of what Confucianists called "self-cultivation" were also important goals, far more than in the West. The educated elite obviously had more opportunities for such pursuits, including the chance to write about them and, thus, to provide us with evidence of their values.

Although most peasants had a life of toil, they too enjoyed to the full what leisure they could manage, especially in winter with its succession of festivals, including the two-week celebration of Chinese New Year. Those who were fortunate enough to accumulate a bit more than was necessary for survival quickly adopted the lifestyle of the gentry. Rather than continuing to work their land or to amass more wealth, most of them rented it out to tenants and lived on the rents even at a modest level. Most landlords owned very small amounts of land by Western standards, living on the income from 8 or 10 acres, and did not strive to become richer or to branch out into other enterprises, except for some money lending.

Natural calamities like floods, droughts, or earthquakes were commonly taken as portents of Heaven's displeasure at the unvirtuous behavior of rulers and as pretexts for rebellion, especially since they disturbed the Confucian sense of order and harmony, the greatest social goals. The natural world was seen as the model for the human world, both running by regular rules. Nature

 ## Sayings of Confucius

Sayings attributed to Confucius and printed in the Analects are usually brief and pithy. Here are some examples.

- Learning without thought is useless. Thought without learning is dangerous.
- Shall I teach you the meaning of knowledge? When you know a thing to recognize that you know it, and when you do not know to recognize that you do not know, that is knowledge.
- Not yet understanding life, how can one understand death?
- The gentleman is concerned about what is right, the petty man about what is profitable.
- Do not do to others what you yourself would not like.
- The gentleman's quality is like wind, the common people's like grass; when the wind blows, the grass bends.
- If one leads them with administrative measures and uses punishments to make them conform, the people will be evasive; but if one leads them with virtue, they will come up to expectations.

Source: Rhoads Murphey, after James Legge.

was a nurturing power, not a hostile one, grander and more to be admired than human works, something to which people should harmoniously adjust rather than attempt to conquer. But as Confucius said, "Heaven does not speak"; it merely shows us a model of order and harmony to emulate.

The occasional references to Heaven as an impersonal force superior to humankind are about as far as Confucius went beyond the human world. When disciples asked about the suprahuman world or about life after death, he merely said we had enough to do in understanding and managing human affairs without troubling about other matters. Although he did not explicitly say so, he did approve of what is rather misleadingly called "ancestor worship." In folk religion, ancestors were prayed to as if they could intervene as helpers. Formal Confucianism merely extended respect for one's elders to those who had gone before, valuing them as models and performing regular rituals in small household shrines to keep their memory alive. It was the duty of the eldest son to perform rituals on the death of his father, through successive generations, keeping the ancestral chain intact and thus ensuring family continuity. Mencius underlined this by saying that of all sins against filiality, the greatest was to have no descendants, by which he meant male descendants, since women left their parental family at marriage and became members of their husband's family. This attitude still plagues current Chinese efforts to reduce the birthrate, since it

clearly favors sons and may influence the parents of girls to keep trying for a boy.

In the twelfth century C.E., many centuries after Confucius and Mencius, the Confucian philosopher Zhuxi (1130–1200) went somewhat further in speculating about the nature of the universe, where he saw the working of abstract principles (rather like those of Plato) and a Supreme Ultimate, or impersonal cosmic force. From his time on it is appropriate to speak of neo-Confucianism, which also stresses self-cultivation and the goal of every person to become a sage. Like classical Confucianism before it, neo-Confucianism spread to Korea, Vietnam, and Japan, where it became the dominant philosophy, especially for the educated.

Because Confucianism never developed a formal priesthood or set rituals, some analysts believe that it is not a religion, although the same can be said to a somewhat lesser degree of Hinduism, Buddhism, and Islam. Faithful Confucianists did build temples in nearly every city and town in China and northern Vietnam, as well as many in Korea and some in Japan. These were cared for by people who were called priests, who did conduct what may be called services, usually in honor of the ancestors or of illustrious local figures of the past. Such services are carried out for the sage himself at the large temple complex erected at his birthplace in Shandong province. After Confucianism became, in effect, the state religion during the Han dynasty, the emperor of China presided over annual rituals at the imperial capital

Confucian temple, Yunnan Province, China, 1944. This is a modern photograph, but the building's style is traditional. (R. Murphey)

to intercede with Heaven for good harvests, to pray for rain, an end to floods, pestilence, or civil chaos, or to commemorate the imperial ancestors. Emperors sometimes also issued penitential edicts acknowledging their lack of virtue as a ruler, real or fancied, in order to persuade Heaven to restore prosperity or the broken harmony of society. This stemmed from the Confucian precept that if things went wrong lower down it was the result of the bad example or lack of moral leadership of the "superior men."

Some analysts have attributed the rapid economic growth rates of modern Japan, Korea, Hong Kong, Singapore, and more recently mainland China to their common heritage of Confucianism, with its stress on collective effort, hard work, education, and the dedication of individuals to the interests of the larger group: family, work unit, or even state. Such an analysis does fit the circumstances and achievements of these societies, as it also helps to explain the long-lasting success of imperial China. Confucianism in general strikes an interesting balance between providing scope for individual self-development or cultivation, and hence achievement, on the one hand, and on the other the subjection of the individual to the greater good of the family and society. Individualism and freedom, basic positive values to Americans, have in East Asia the chief connotation of selfishness and lack of rules ("don't fence me in," as we would put it). The result of both is chaos and anarchy, from which everyone suffers. Every society evolves its own balance between individual license and the need to protect the group interest and to preserve order through rules. Confucianism persisted because it worked as the creed of probably the world's most successful society over so long a time.

Daoism

The second major moral or religious philosophy of traditional China was Daoism. The Dao ("the Way") is hard to define because one of the basic axioms of Daoism is silence, even inaction. The observable, rational, human world is not what matters; only the far greater cosmic world of nature matters. It is from the cosmos one must seek guidance, but this is not the realm of words. The chief text of Daoism, the Daode Jing ("Classic of the Way"), is a cryptic collection of mystical remarks whose meaning even in Chinese is unclear, let alone their meaning in the many hundreds of Western translations. The famous opening line is typical, varyingly translated as "The name that can be named is not the eternal name," or "The Way that can be spoken of is not the true Way, which is inconstant," implying (one supposes) that truth cannot be put into words or, if at all, only through riddle and paradox. Much of its content is attributed to a contemporary of Confucius known simply as Laozi, "The Old One," although the present text is not older than the third century B.C.E. and was probably compiled by several hands. Laozi is said to have debated with Confucius and to have disappeared in old age, traveling westward, where he somehow became an immortal.

On one point the Daode Jing is clear: "Those who understand don't talk; those who talk don't understand." This may well have been aimed at the Confucians, but although Daoist figures did occasionally speak or write, it was usually in riddles or in parallels with nature, all making the point that worldly strivings, and especially government, are both futile and wrong. Their message is to relax, go with the flow, stop trying to "improve" things (as the Confucians were always doing), and model yourself on water, flowing around obstructions, adapting to what is, and seeking the lowest places. Whatever is, is natural and hence good.

The other major figure of Daoism is the philosopher Zhuangzi (died c. 329 B.C.E.), whose recorded essays further pursued the relativism, mysticism, and amorality already associated with the school and who still intrigues us with his stories. One of the most delightful tells of how he dreamed he was a butterfly and when he woke could not be sure if he was himself or if he was the butterfly, now dreaming he was Zhuangzi.

Daoism grew into a religion as it merged with folk beliefs, earlier animism and worship of natural forces, belief in the supernatural, and a variety of mystical practices. Daoist priests, temples, and monastic orders developed (however inconsistent with the earlier message), and the originally rather esoteric philosophy became a mass religion. Later Daoists, especially after the Han dynasty, practiced magic and alchemy and pursued the search for elixirs of immortality. Such activities put them in bad repute with proper Confucians, as did their habit of irresponsible hedonism or pleasure seeking. However, the Daoist search for medicinal herbs and their varied experimentation contributed importantly to the growth of Chinese medicine and other technologies. In this they deviated from their supposed founder's injunctions to accept nature without questioning and began instead to probe for its secrets.

As it acquired a mass following, Daoism also developed a pantheon of gods and immortals offering help to people in trouble and also easing the way to a Daoist version of the Buddhist Heaven. But as already suggested, Confucianists often found Daoism attractive even though they might scorn its superstition. It was aptly said that most Chinese were Confucian when things went well (or when they were in office), and Daoist when things went badly and in retirement or old age—workday Confucians and weekend Daoists. Confucianism's activism and social reformism were complemented by Daoism's passivism and laissez-faire philosophy. This dualism appealed also to older Chinese notions of harmonious balance in all

Scholar Viewing the Moon, Chinese, Ming dynasty, fifteenth to sixteenth century, ink and color on silk. This work reflects the Chinese interest in the beauty and wonder of the natural world, which is also the Daoist message. (The Seattle Art Museum, Eugene Fuller Memorial Collection)

things and the principles of yin and yang, where yang is strong, assertive, active, intellectual, bright, and male, and yin is soft, gentle, passive, dark, intuitive, and female. Daoists and Confucianists alike agreed that both nature and humans must approximate a balance of yin and yang elements, and agreed also in seeing nature as a model for man. But where Confucians sought to shape the world through education, Daoists urged acceptance of things as they are, confident that human meddling could not improve on cosmic truth, compared with which it was in any case microscopically petty.

Judaism in Asia

The Indian west coast had long been in regular trade contact with Mesopotamia and, from Alexander's time, with the Mediterranean world. After the Romans destroyed the temple in Jerusalem in 70 C.E. as part of their sack of the city, and the Jews were dispersed abroad (known as the Diaspora), small Jewish colonies were founded on the west coast of southern India, especially in the port city of Cochin. (During approximately the same period a Christian church was also founded in southern India, probably by the apostle Thomas.)

Over time the Jews at Cochin intermarried with Indians, and by early British times (seventeenth century) or before they were no longer physically distinct, although they retained their religious identity and their Hebrew rituals. They were fully accepted by Hindus, both because of general Hindu tolerance of other faiths and because of the Jewish devotion to religion and to the study of sacred texts, values that were a fundamental part of Hindu culture as well. But the Jewish community was never very large—perhaps 1,000 to begin with and growing thereafter mainly through intermarriage with and conversion of Indians, many of them probably from the lowest castes. Low-caste Indians saw Judaism, like Christianity, as a means of evading at least some of caste prejudice and hence a path of upward mobility. Over the centuries the Jews of Cochin became in most respects just another of India's many religious groups, however interesting historically. By about 1980 most of those who still thought of themselves as Jews had emigrated to Israel or elsewhere.

Another Jewish colony was established in the cosmopolitan setting of Tang dynasty China at least by the end of the seventh century C.E.; it was described in Chinese records as one of the many foreign groups in the capital at Chang'an. Jews may have migrated to China earlier, but we do not know when or by what route. (There was also a colony of Nestorian Christians in Chang'an at the same time, people who had left the Mediterranean area before, or had been expelled after, their version of Christian doctrine had been condemned by the Byzantine church in 431 C.E., although they may have come from Persia [Iran].) Both groups are described in ample detail, and faithful artistic representations also survive showing their facial features, clothing, and even their religious texts. The Nestorians seem soon to have died out or to have been absorbed into Chinese culture, but the Jewish group won the favor of a Song dynasty emperor, who like many Chinese respected them for their emphases on learning and on written texts. Indeed, the Chinese called them "people of the book."

Early in the eleventh century, the emperor gave them a grant of land and other privileges in the Song capital, Kaifeng, where they built a synagogue and apparently flourished. From the mid-twelfth century China was overwhelmed by the Mongol invasion, and Kaifeng in particular was totally devastated. We have no records of the fate of the Jewish community in that general holocaust, but some survivors and a rebuilt synagogue were still in Kaifeng when Jesuit missionaries arrived in China in the seventeenth century. With the enforced opening of China after 1850, missionaries eager to rediscover the Jews of China went to Kaifeng, only to find that the synagogue and its records had been swept away in a flood and the supposed Jews were indistinguishable from Chinese. A few old men remembered some phrases of Hebrew but had forgotten their meaning. Clearly the Jews had intermarried with Chinese, had long ago abandoned Jewish dietary rules, and had been absorbed into Chinese culture while retaining a faint trace of their earlier origins. The many centuries of isolation from other Jewish communities beyond the mountains and the deserts of Central Asia, as well as the attractiveness and weight of Chinese culture, had eroded the Jewish attachment to separate identity.

Islam in Asia

Islam is the youngest of the great world religions. The founder of Islam, Mohammed (also spelled Muhammad), was born into a prosperous merchant family at Mecca in Arabia about 570 C.E.. As a young man he entered the family business and served for a time as a camel driver and trader, but he became distressed about the social injustice and corruption that he found in Mecca. When his preaching against these evils attracted few supporters, he moved some 200 miles north to the town of Medina in 622, a journey known as the Hejira, which is still used to mark the first year of the Muslim era, or "year of the prophet." Mohammed's preaching centered on the affirmation of one god, as opposed to the many nature spirits of the animistic tribal religion of his own and earlier times in Arabia. At his new base in Medina he established a religious community and further developed his teachings.

From this period there emerged the Koran, the principal sacred text of Islam, probably completed after Mohammed's death in 632 C.E. Mohammed and his followers believed that the Koran was inspired by god and therefore represented the direct word of Allah and communicated directly to Mohammed, his messenger. As such, not a word could be changed, at least not for the first few centuries. However, from the beginning the text was accompanied by commentaries explaining and interpreting the supposedly divinely dictated text, a practice that continued in subsequent centuries and

The Dao

The Daode Jing is hard to fathom, but many of its passages are appealing as a kind of mystic text. Here are some samples.

- There was an ever-flowing something that existed prior to heaven and earth. Silent and shapeless, it stands by itself and does not change. So may it be the mother of heaven and earth.
- The Way is void, yet inexhaustible when tapped.
- Always make the people innocent of knowledge, and desireless, so those with knowledge dare not, and refrain from wrongdoing. Of old, the followers of the Dao did not teach people cleverness. A people difficult to rule is because they are too clever.
- Emptying one's heart in pursuit of the Void, that is the exhaustion of all inquiries.
- Men should be bland, like melting ice, pure and peaceful like a block of uncarved wood.

Two centuries after Laozi, Zhuangzi's essays deal with happiness and pain, life and death, with a perspective typical of Daoism.

> I received life because the time had come. I will lose it because the order of things passes on. Be content with this time and dwell in this order, and then neither sorrow nor joy can touch you. . . . The inaction of heaven is its purity; the inaction of earth is its peace. . . . How do I know that loving life is not a delusion? How do I know that in hating death I am not like a man who, having left home in his youth, has forgotten the way back? . . . Man's life between heaven and earth is like the passing of a white colt glimpsed through a crack in the wall: whoosh!, and that's the end.

Source: The excerpt from the Daode Jing was translated by Chao Fu-san; the excerpt from Zhuangzi's essay was translated by Burton Watson in *Early Chinese Literature* (New York: Columbia University Press, 1962), pp. 163, 164.

their cumulative versions. The version compiled in the thirteenth century remains the standard for modern orthodox Muslims.

Although it originated in Arabia and still dominates the Middle East as a whole and parts of Africa, Islam was carried to India and from there to Malaya, Indonesia, and the southern Philippines, as well as into northwestern China via Central Asia. Since about the eighteenth century Indonesia has in fact been, at least nominally (since there is also a substantial non-Muslim population), the largest Muslim country in the world, followed by India (even though Muslims remain a large minority there), Bangladesh, and Pakistan, in that order, all dwarfing any of the countries of the Middle East. There are many more Muslims east of Afghanistan than in all the rest of the world put together. Islam came to India first as an eastward extension of the great wave of conquest following the death of Mohammed and was then spread further east by Indian and other converts along trade routes, primarily by sea to insular Southeast Asia.

Overland merchant converts from Central Asia brought the new faith to northwest China.

The content of the Koran, written in classical Arabic, shows considerable adoption of earlier Jewish and Christian beliefs, including its basic tenet of monotheism. From Christianity Mohammed also adopted beliefs in the resurrection of the physical body, a heavenly afterlife, and a Last Judgment in which the damned are consigned to a flaming Hell. Humans can avoid Allah's wrath by virtuous living and by showing compassion for others, especially the poor. But the chief means to salvation and entry into paradise is through prayer, supplemented by good works and the giving of alms.

Muslims are enjoined to worship Allah but also to fear and to live in awe of him. His word may also reach the faithful through both divine and human messengers: angels and prophets. These include the originally Christian angel Gabriel and a string of prophets before Mohammed: Adam, Moses, Alexander the Great (a remark-

Holy War

The Koran speaks of jihad, *or holy war, as follows:*

Fight in the way of God against those who fight against you, but do not commit aggression. . . . Slay them wheresoever you find them, and expel them from whence they have expelled you, for sedition is more grievous than slaying. . . . Fight against them until sedition is no more and allegiance is rendered to God alone; but if they make an end, then no aggression save against the evildoers.

When the sacred months are over, kill those who ascribe partners to God [worship more than one deity] wheresoever ye find them; seize them, encompass them, and ambush them; then if they repent, observe prayer, and pay the alms, let them go their way.

Fight against those who believe not in God nor in the Last Day, who prohibit not what God and his Apostles have prohibited, and who refuse all allegiance to the True Faith from among those who have received the Book, until they humbly pay tribute out of hand.

Source: H. A. R. Gibb, *Mohammedanism* (New York: Oxford University Press, 1962), p. 67.

able choice!), and Jesus. Mohammed himself was held to be the last of the prophets, although unlike Jesus he was not accorded any divinity in his own person. His mortal life and teachings provide a sufficient example for the faithful, who are called to prayer five times every day by a reciter, or *muezzin,* a ritual followed throughout the Islamic world. The muezzin usually climbs to the top of a slender tower from which he calls the faithful to prayer; all other activities cease while the worshippers

kneel, bow in the direction of Mecca, and recite their prayers. There is only a short interval, in the dark hours of the night, between the last prayers of one day and the first of the next, before dawn.

Although there is no priesthood, men (never women) learned in the Koran and its commentaries are recognized as *mullahs* and commonly turned to for advice or leadership. The faithful must fast and avoid even water during daylight hours throughout the lunar month of Ramadan (celebrated in successive months in successive years until the lunar cycle is complete). During their lifetime the faithful must also make a pilgrimage, or *hajj,* to Mecca and Medina, the sacred places of Islam. Gambling, money lending, the taking of interest, all alcohol, and the eating of pork are forbidden, although slavery and polygamy are permitted. Women have an explicitly inferior status, can be set aside at will by their husbands, must cover their bodies and faces outside their own domestic quarters (to which they are in practice largely confined), and are subject to their fathers, brothers, and husbands in all things. The Koran also sanctions "holy war" *(jihad)* against unbelievers, and the killing of infidels, although like all religions Islam's basic message is one of charity, peace, and love. Jihad may be waged by four means: the heart, the tongue, the hand, and, only when those fail, the sword.

In the century following the death of Mohammed in 632, Islamic forces swept across North Africa and the Middle East. The Islamicized Moors of North Africa conquered Spain and were finally turned back in their

A page from the Koran, written in one of the many Arabic scripts. The text reads: "And pardon us and grant us protection and have mercy on us, thou art our patron, so help us against the unbelieving people." (The Metropolitan Museum of Art, Rogers Fund, 1937. ([37.99.2] Photograph, all rights reserved, The Metropolitan Museum of Art.)

advance into France at a battle near Tours in 732. In the next century, Arabs and their converts completed their conquest of the Middle East and swept on by a mixture of warfare and conversion through Persia (Iran) and Afghanistan to the frontiers of monsoon Asia. In the course of this whirlwind expansion, most of the Turkic peoples of Central Asia were converted to the new faith and subsequently pursued their own conquest and jihad. Beginning in the tenth century, the Turks and their Afghan allies brought Islam to India. Although these invaders never became more than a tiny portion of the Indian population, they won some converts by force. Others converted because they found the Islamic emphasis on the equality of all people (except women) before Allah an attractive alternative to the hierarchical ordering of groups characteristic of East Asian society.

Arab merchants, who had long been trading with Asia by sea, helped to spread Islam to Malaya and insular Southeast Asia, but this long process seems to have been furthered more importantly by Indian merchant converts, whose role in the trade with Southeast Asia was larger as well as older. Mainland Southeast Asia remained devoted to Theravada Buddhism (or to Confucianism in northern Vietnam), except for peninsular Malaya, which has always been more closely integrated with insular Southeast Asia. In China, Islam won substantial numbers of converts only among the marginal people of the northwest and southwest frontiers. Although in time Chinese Muslims totaled many millions, they remained a tiny fraction of the Chinese population, and eventually most of them found it convenient to modify many of the Islamic strictures, including the five daily prayers, the hajj, the strict observance of Ramadan, and the dietary prohibitions. Most of them married Chinese women and their descendants became almost indistinguishable from Chinese, except in their avoidance of pork. Most Chinese kept to the Confucian–Daoist way described earlier and continued to reject any theological religion, especially of foreign origin, as Islam, Buddhism, and Christianity all were. (Buddhism was largely rejected after the ninth century—see Chapter 8.)

The mystic version of Islam, Sufism, developed first at Baghdad in the eighth and ninth centuries and later spread through the Muslim world. Sufism taught that individuals could find salvation only through meditation and prayer and by cutting their ties with society, living like a Hindu sadhu. Sufis studied the Koran and followed other spiritual exercises but drew their inspiration primarily from their own efforts to understand pure truth through meditation. They aimed to acquire an intimacy with Allah and a vision of his creation. The name *Sufi* derived from the white woolen cloak worn by devotees, rather like the gown used by Christian monks. Sufism grew especially in India, where the old tradition of

mysticism, denial of the material world, and meditation offered congenial ground. The blind Muslim poet Kabir of Benares (1440–1518) was a Sufi and inspired many thousands to follow his example. The emperor Akbar of Mughal India (1542–1605) became a Sufi. But the message of Sufism was not denominational, and it appealed to many people of other religions besides Islam. The Sufi was largely free of doctrine, but in India especially, Sufi orders were founded with formal ceremonies of initiation and a hierarchy of disciples and spiritual directors. Sufis could be found in many walks of life: scholars, rulers, teachers, and wandering holy men. They sought direct, intuitive experience of the divine reality and prayed for divine grace. In some ways they served as a link between different cultures, adapting the demands of Islam and the injunctions of the Koran to different cultural contexts as Islam moved into and through South Asia and Southeast Asia. Some Sufis came to be venerated as saints after their deaths, and their tombs were the goal of pilgrimages.

Mohammed's successors quarreled among themselves, and this gave rise to a split between those who called themselves Sunni, or "followers of custom," and a breakaway group called Shi'ite. The differences between them in doctrine and practice were relatively slight, but the Shi'ites maintained that the text of the Koran is incomplete and that a pious Muslim can perform the pilgrimage to Mecca by hiring a proxy or by visiting the tomb of one of the many Shi'ite saints. Most Muslims in monsoon Asia were Sunni, while the Persians (Iranians) were Shi'ite, a source of conflict between Iran and Mughal India. But all Muslims were taught that Mohammed was the last of the prophets accepted by Islam, and that only he had the complete message of Allah. Islam is thus held to be the only full and perfect religion, the consummation of all others, including Judaism and Christianity, whose prophets it accepts. Islam's creed is simple and is repeated at each of the five daily prayers: "There is no God but Allah, and Mohammed is his prophet."

Shinto

Ritual practices in early Japan, centered around the worship of nature, were later called Shinto, "the way of the gods," primarily to distinguish them from Buddhist practices when Buddhism reached Japan. Shinto, probably a consolidation of local nature-worship cults, has remained in contemporary Japan as a particularly Japanese religion, with its own priesthood and temples. It is an interesting survival of what is still readily recognizable as a primitive animistic cult or cults typical of most preliterate societies but overlaid or extinguished elsewhere long ago. Shinto has never been an organized body of thought or even what we might call a religion. It never developed a clear moral code or coherent philosophy but did preserve early notions of ritual purity. Physical dirt, death, childbirth, illness, menstruation, and sexual intercourse were all seen as polluting and had to be ceremonially cleansed or exorcised by a priest. Priests also acted as diviners and mediums, like the shamans of Korea.

Shinto attributes divinity not only to the forces of nature but to its manifestations, such as mountains, big trees, waterfalls, or unusual rocks, all of which are said to contain *kami*, or a divine spirit. Earlier fertility cults, or aspects of them, were also incorporated, including a rice god and phallic symbols. Modern Japanese society is still notable for its insistence on cleanliness, at least at home and in what is referred to as "private space," if not always in "public space." Water, especially running water, is still seen as pure and purifying—hence the tiny spring (sometimes artificial) and pool with dipper provided in the forecourt of every temple and shrine (not just Shinto ones), where the worshipper or tourist can cleanse him/herself before entering the sacred area proper. This is a very Shinto notion, and it is possible that the Japanese fondness for bathing, especially for hot baths as the proper close to a day, may go back to early Shinto or pre-Shinto origins. This is still more plausible when one considers the great number of natural hot springs in this volcanic country, still much visited and used for bathing, and the obvious power of nature that they represent, a kind of opening into the navel of the earth where titanic forces were generated, as in volcanic eruptions, which of course are closely linked to hot springs.

All over Japan one can still see beautiful Shinto shrines, beautiful not only because they celebrate nature and because they are located in natural beauty spots but also because of their classically simple architectural style. Most of the shrines are surrounded by tall trees, others are tiny things the size of a large birdhouse, with natural bark-covered roofs, dotted in the mountains, far from human habitation. The most famous shrine-temple is at Ise, on the peninsula that stretches south from the Kyoto area. Ise is the chief center of the Sun Goddess cult, and the shrine's graceful simple lines are designed to fit in without a discordant note to the trees and nearby stream. It was probably built some time in the sixth century C.E. but is lovingly rebuilt every 20 years on precisely the same pattern and, thus, gives us a glimpse of what early Japanese temple architecture must have been like. In the approaches to every temple and many shrines is a *torii*, or simple open gateway, to signal sacred ground ahead. Worship at Shinto shrines and temples is equally simple: clapping the hands to attract the god's attention, bowing, and usually leaving a small gift

as sacrifice. At the same time, shrines and temples are often the sites of festivals with a carnival atmosphere, booths selling food, large and sometimes noisy crowds, and various amusements, accompanied by a good deal of drinking and high jinks. The persistence of Shinto can be seen not only as an assertion of Japanese distinctiveness despite the massive wave of Chinese and later Western influences but also as a celebration of the outstandingly beautiful Japanese landscape.

Asian Religions: Some Reflections

Most East Asians have always been eclectic in religion, weaving into their beliefs and practices elements from different religious traditions. Confucianism and Daoism are dominant everywhere except in Japan where Buddhism or Shinto share attention with Confucianism. These complementary parts form a whole, representing the religion of nearly a third of the world. Each part of the combination has its undeniable appeal, and it is not hard to see why most people followed both or a combination of all three, depending on their circumstances or even moods. Christian missionaries found the religious ground already thoroughly occupied in Asia, by Hinduism, Buddhism, Confucianism, Daoism, Shinto, and Islam, all old and sophisticated religions with a long literate and philosophical tradition. Although Jews and Christians were represented by small branches in southern India from Roman times, and even in Tang China, the later missionary effort never made much headway in an Asia already richly supplied with religions that had long been part of each major culture.

Hinduism remained largely peculiar to India and in many ways simply the main channel of Indian culture, including its nonreligious aspects. The same tended to be true for Confucianism in China, which was little altered by being spread to Korea, Vietnam, and Japan. Since these other areas admired and accepted so much of Chinese culture and left it largely unchanged, Confucianism, more perhaps a moral than a religious system, became a part of their own cultures as well. Confucianism thus became a transcultural or transnational institution, while Hinduism remained virtually synonymous with Indianism. Buddhism divided early into two separate schools, Theravada and Mahayana, and as it spread eastward from India brought some aspects of Indian culture with it, including art forms, and developed some characteristics reflecting each of the different cultures that adopted it.

Of all the great religions originating in Asia, only Christianity, Buddhism, and Islam claimed to be universal creeds for all people everywhere, and only Christianity and Islam included organized efforts at conversion, both by force or conquest and by preaching. Yet both also carried large elements of the cultures where they were most deeply rooted: western European civilization and its values for Christianity, Arabic language and culture for Islam. Although both religions originated in western Asia, the great majority of Asians were content with their own far older and more sophisticated religious traditions, and there were few openings for what were seen as alien faiths, promoted by resented outsiders.

All of the religions originating in monsoon Asia, from Hinduism through Buddhism and Confucianism to Daoism and Shinto, recognize that there is evil in the world, and even evil people, but none of them ever developed the sharp dichotomy (or dualism) between good and evil that is characteristic of Zoroastrianism, Judaism, Christianity, and Islam. In the Indian and Chinese view, all of creation is the work of God (or Heaven, the creative principle), which thus necessarily includes both good and bad, or what is seen by humans as good and bad. Consequently, there was no conception of original sin inherent in individuals, no Garden of Eden or early innocence from which people then fell into error and suffered punishment because they had broken God's rules. Evil was understood as part of God's created world, not as some human aberration. The Christian idea of sin had little meaning in Asia. As has often been said, "Eden was preserved in the East."

Bad behavior was acknowledged and might be punished in this world and the next, but the basic presumption was that people were born and remained intrinsically good, not with built-in inclinations to "sin." Their misbehavior was seen as a failure of society, which God created imperfect, and of the individual's straying from the teaching and model of her or his elders or superiors, as in Confucianism, or from the established rules of her or his dharma in Hinduism and Buddhism, as made clear by priests and sages. People were seen not as morally lost when they strayed from the path but as always redeemable through education or through renewed efforts at right behavior, aided by piety and meditation. Return to virtue, or "merit," might also be won by good deeds, including charity, or simply by leading, in the Christian words, "a godly, righteous, and sober life," but never by having one's sins magically forgiven by priestly or other ritual, since sins were never seen or even acknowledged in such a light. Nor was faith or the acceptance of any creed ever seen as paramount, if important at all; people were judged by their actions.

One further distinction between all of these eastern Asian religions on the one hand and Christianity, Judaism, and Islam on the other is their acceptance of the natural world as good, as part of a divine creation that is greater and more powerful than humankind but, like humans, is a part of the cosmos. People occupy a humbler place in God's creation, and it behooves them, therefore, to adjust, while seeking the image of God in nature, rather than in themselves. The sages and holy men who sought wisdom and the understanding of God or of the cosmos sought it in nature, in the mountains far from human distractions. There was no conception of the natural world as an enemy to be fought against or overcome, a concept found especially in later Christianity. Nature is instead seen as a nurturing mother or an inspiring model. Adapting to it and understanding it are the keys both to earthly success and to spiritual and moral truth.

Such a thread runs deeply through Hinduism, Buddhism, Confucianism, Daoism, and Shinto; this concept is far weaker, absent, or explicitly opposite in Judaism, Christianity, and Islam, as in the Book of Genesis with its call to the human world to "have dominion" over all the world of nature, or in the nineteenth- and twentieth-century Western drive for "the conquest of nature." One might perhaps argue that Judaism, out of which Christianity grew in part, and later Islam, were conceived in a harsher environment than the great religions of Asia farther east, where it may be easier to see nature as beneficent and nurturing and people as prospering through adjusting to, accepting, and admiring it. Whatever the reasons, Asia west of India followed a different religious path.

Judaism and Islam specifically devalue women, as does Pauline Christianity, although to a lesser degree. It must be remembered, however, that, in all probability, women were the leading religious figures in prehistoric times, as attested by the numerous statues of the earth goddess found at so many Paleolithic and Neolithic sites. Women were worshipped as fertility figures, and the earth goddess figures are shown with swollen bellies and large breasts. It may have been some time before it was realized that male insemination was necessary for pregnancy. In any case, the chief religious figures were for long women, priestesses and keepers of the sacred places, as is still the case in India, as it was in classical Greece. Women were believed to have greater spiritual powers and greater intuition. A little of this was preserved in the cult of the Virgin Mary and the many other female saints of the Catholic Church. The religion brought into India by the Aryan migrants reflected their warlike culture, and its blending with the preexisting religion of the Indus people still reflects that, although male figures, like Shiva, are accompanied by female counterparts such as Parvati, Kali, and Durga. Confucianism was a later development and it reflects what had by then become a patriarchal society. Buddhism, Daoism, and Shinto make only little distinction between male and female, but Buddhism does have its female deities, most importantly Kuan Yin (Kannon in Japan), to whom women pray for intercession.

Questions

1. Even though all major religions originated in Asia, including Christianity and Islam, those that have remained dominant in Asia show clear difference from the Christianity and Judaism dominant in the West. How does the phrase "Eden was preserved in the East" reflect these differences?

2. Western religious tradition tended toward humanistic rationalism since roughly 1500, which contrasts with much of the Asian religious tradition that is often thought of as commitment to myth. What is meant by this distinction, and what are its consequences relative to Western views of the Asian religiosity?

3. What are the fundamental differences between Theravada and Mahayana Buddhism; Daoism and Confucianism; Hinduism and Buddhism; Buddhism and Confucianism; Shinto and Buddhism; Islam and Hinduism; Sunni/Shi'ite and Sufi Islam?

4. Is Confucianism a true religion or is it better thought of as a moral code?

5. What do Sufi Islam and Bhakti Hinduism have in common? What were the features of Sufi Islam, in contrast to the Shi'ite and Sunni traditions, which initially made it the most appealing version of Islam, and the basis of early conversions among already well-established Asian societies? (See Chapter 6 where Sufism is considered.)

6. What role do female divines assume in Asian religious tradition?

Suggested Web Sites

Hinduism

http://www.uni-giessen.de/-gk1415/hinduism.htm
A detailed site about Hinduism from the *Gazetteer of India;* provides valuable information ranging from a general introduction to schools of thought and movements of reform, with sublinks.

http://www.fordham.edu/halsall/india/indiasbook.html
A detailed *Indian History Sourcebook*, with good references to various aspects of Indian history, religion, and civilization.

http://religion-cults.com/eastern.htm
Useful short articles that address the basic beliefs and practices of the various Asian religions.

http://religiousmovements.lib.virginia.edu/nrms
A detailed presentation of religious movements, with cross-references to additional Web sites.

http://plato.stanford.edu/contents.html
Entry to the *Stanford Encyclopedia of Philosophy*, which has detailed discussions of the various Asian religious traditions, including extensive bibliographies of suggested follow-up readings.

Buddhism

http://www.ciolek.com/WWWVL-Buddhism.html
One-stop access to the leading information facilities in the fields of Buddhism and Buddhist studies.

Daoism and Shinto

**http://www.fordham.edu/halsall/eastasia/eastasiasbook
.html**
Access to the *East Asia Sourcebook*, which has extensive coverage of the various religious traditions of East Asia.

Suggestions for Further Reading

Basham, A. L., ed. *The Origins and Development of Classical Hinduism.* Boston: Beacon Press, 1989.

Brown, W. N. *Man in the Universe: Some Continuities in Indian Thought.* Berkeley: University of California Press, 1970.

Callicot, J. B., and Ames, R. T., eds. *Nature in Asia: Traditions of Thought.* Albany: SUNY Press, 1989.

Chamberlayne, J. II. *China and Its Religious Inheritance.* London: Allen and Unwin, 1993.

Cheng, C. Y. *New Dimensions of Confucian and Neo-Confucian Philosophy.* Albany: SUNY Press, 1991.

Cragg, K., and Speight, R. M. *The House of Islam,* 3d ed. Belmont, CA: Wadsworth, 1988.

Creel, H. G. *What Is Taoism?* Chicago: University of Chicago Press, 1970.

Dean, K. *Taoist Ritual and Popular Cults of Southeast China.* Princeton: Princeton University Press, 1995.

Earhart, H. B. *Japanese Religion,* 3d ed. Belmont, CA: Wadsworth, 1988.

Gernet, J. *Buddhism in Chinese Society.* New York: Columbia University Press, 1995.

Gombrich, R. F. *Theravada Buddhism: A Social History.* London: Routledge, 1988.

Graham, A. C. *Disputers of the Tao.* La Salle, IL: Open Court, 1989.

Hardy, F. *The Religious Culture of India.* Cambridge: Cambridge University Press, 1994.

Herman, A. L. *A Brief Introduction to Hinduism.* Boulder, CO: Westview, 1991.

Hopkins, T. J. *The Hindu Religious Tradition.* Belmont, CA: Wadsworth, 1987.

Irving, T. B. *The World of Islam.* New York: Amana Books, 1985.

Israeli, R., ed. *Islam in Southeast and East Asia.* Boulder, CO: Westview, 1984.

Kirkland, R. *Taoism: The Enduring Tradition.* London: Routledge, 2004.

Kitagawa, J. M., ed. *The Religious Traditions of Asia.* New York: Macmillan, 1989.

Klostermaier, K. K. *A Survey of Hinduism.* Albany: SUNY Press, 1989.

Kohn, L. *Laughing at the Tao.* Princeton: Princeton University Press, 1995.

Lipner, J. J. *Hindus.* New York: Routledge, 1993.

Liu, X. *Classifying the Zhuangzi.* Seattle: University of Washington Press, 2004.

Mair, V. H. *Tao Te Ching.* New York: Bantam Doubleday, 1991.

Martin, R. C. *Islam: A Cultural Perspective.* Englewood Cliffs, NJ: Prentice-Hall, 1982.

———, ed. *Approaches to Islam.* Tucson: University of Arizona Press, 1985.

Michaels, A. *Hinduism.* Princeton: Princeton University Press, 2003.

Morgan, K. W. *Reaching for the Moon: Asian Religious Paths.* Chambersburg, PA: Anima, 1991.

Palmer, M. et al. *The Book of Chuang Tzu.* Harmondsworth, England Penguin Books, 1996.

Peerenboom, R. P. *Law and Morality in Ancient China.* Albany: SUNY Press, 1993.

Renard, A. S. *Seven Doors to Islam.* Berkeley: University of California Press, 1996.

Roald, A. S. *Women in Islam.* New York: Routledge, 2001.

Robinet, I. *Taoism.* Seattle: University of Washington Press, 1998.

Robinson, R. H., and Johnson, W. L. *The Buddhist Religion,* 3d ed. Belmont, CA: Wadsworth, 1988.

Schimmel, A. *Islam in the Indian Subcontinent.* Leiden, Netherlands: Brill, 1980.

Schwartz, B. I. *The World of Thought in Early China.* Cambridge: Harvard University Press, 1985.

Sharma, A., ed. *Women in World Religions.* Albany: SUNY Press, 1987.

Shun, K. L. *Mencius and Early Chinese History.* Stanford, CA: Stanford University Press, 1997.

Smart, N. *Religions of Asia.* Englewood Cliffs, NJ: Prentice-Hall, 1993.

Taylor, R. L. *The Religious Dimensions of Confucianism.* Albany: SUNY Press, 1991.

Thompson, L. G. *Chinese Religion,* 4th ed. Belmont, CA: Wadsworth, 1988.

Waley, A. *Three Ways of Thought in Ancient China.* New York: Doubleday, 1956.

Williams, P. *Mahayana Buddhism.* New York: Routledge, 1989.

Yu, D. C. *History of Chinese Daoism.* Lanham, MD: University Press of America, 2001.

3

The Traditional
Societies of Asia

This chapter surveys the traditional societies of Asia and finds, despite the differences among them, many similarities, especially in their emphasis on hierarchical ranking (as in the Indian caste system but also markedly in East Asia), the primacy of the family and of larger groups beyond it within the context of group solidarity and group effort, and patterns of marriage and child rearing. It then considers the status of women, sexual customs, the importance of education and learning, material welfare, attitudes toward nature and human life, and the role of law.

As is still true today to a large extent, traditional Asian societies showed a remarkable similarity in their emphasis on hierarchical status groupings based primarily on age, gender, and occupation or social role. They also stressed, and still stress, the subordination of individual interests to the common interest of the group: family, village, caste, guild, or other occupational unit. Individuals advanced or lost status as members of groups, as the groups advanced, prospered, or declined, or as the individuals grew older. Much of the achievement of traditional Asia is attributable to this acceptance of the need to work together in pursuit of common goals.

People were discouraged from trying to operate on their own, and certainly from attempting to challenge, subvert, get around, or change the group-oriented social system. The system rewarded those who worked within it and provided both material and emotional security. In fact there were few attempts to change it until modern times. Those who tried to "rock the boat" or to avoid behaving like "team players" were often seen as troublemakers or even dangerous radicals, threatening group solidarity and welfare or even the entire social order, whose preservation was the primary goal. Individualism and individual expression, so highly valued in the modern West, were seen as antisocial, disruptive, selfish, and destructive of the group interest (which of course they often are), except to a degree in Southeast Asia. Deviants were, thus, often ostracized or punished but in any case condemned.

Given the relative stability and the impressive accomplishments of traditional Asian societies, it must be acknowledged that their social systems and values worked well however different they were from modern Western norms. As the traditional Chinese proverb, revived by the Communist government after 1949, put it, "When there is water in the big river, the little streams will be full also." In other words, individuals benefited best from devoting themselves to strengthening the group enterprise, which in turn rewarded them. The alternative, having people follow their own inclinations or ambitions, was seen as leading to disorder or even chaos, considered the greatest of all catastrophes and one from which everyone suffered. Put another way, it is said that Asian societies operated on the principle that "the acknowledgment of limits leads to happiness." Modern Western ideas of freedom had little place in traditional Asian societies. Freedom is not easy to define in English, or in American usage, although the word is used a great deal. The closest equivalent in many Asian languages is "absence of rules," perhaps one version of the traditional American "Don't fence me in," or "Don't tread on me." But to the traditional Asian mind (and to a considerable extent even now), absence of rules had primarily bad connotations and was associated with chaos and disorder as well as with the weakening or destruction of the achievements for all that group effort could produce.

One measure of the success of this traditional social system was its survival, essentially unchanged, for some 2,000 years in India and China and only slightly less long in the rest of Asia. Even contemporary Japan, despite its considerable degree of Westernization, including its political and legal systems, and its spectacular material success through industrialization and technological progress, still fits most of the just mentioned generalizations about social norms; indeed, its modern success is often attributed to group effort within a hierarchically organized society. Contemporary China and Korea, with their own modern successes (and their reluctance to accept Western-style "freedoms"), have followed a similar path. The same is true to varying degrees of most of Southeast Asia, although there individuals and personal achievement were more recognized. India was profoundly influenced by the long period of British colonial control, and its political, legal, and economic systems are closer to modern Western models, but its larger society, including the family and the village (where most Indians still live) retains many of the traditional norms described previously. In contemporary Asia as a whole, authority, power, and patronage still tend to be controlled by heads of groups: family, village, work or administrative units, corporations, and even states.

The longevity of traditional social systems suggests that they delivered rewards and satisfaction to most people most of the time. When political orders collapsed in the past, or when new rulers took over, the traditional values and social systems were usually reasserted and basic change in those respects was seldom attempted. The authority of those with superior status, including family heads and elders, was seldom questioned, still less defied; people were supposed to follow their directions, a pattern still widely observable in contemporary Asia. This heritage continues to make Asian versions of what we call democracy distinctive at least in its social forms, and different from the patterns and attitudes of the modern West. Individuals could advance through education, and this was stressed more than in any non-Asian society. But in doing so they became members of the small elite groups of educated men (rarely women) that tended to work as a unit, rather like a guild. The clearest illustration of this is the scholar-gentry group of China.

The traditional social system particularly disadvantaged women, except in Southeast Asia, and the young (including younger brothers), as well as tending to stifle individual initiative. No social system is perfect, and none satisfy all legitimate claims or needs. In Asia the emphasis on the group may have been related to the need for directed, cooperative effort in the highly intensive agricultural system (including the need for irrigation) that dominated the economy, and to the relatively small place of manufacturing or long-distance trade. The subjugation of women may have been related to the physical demands of agriculture, although peasant women took full part in agricultural labor and other manual tasks, as they still do. In later centuries, as urbanization and nonagricultural occupations grew, women were often less useful as labor, and perhaps consequently still more subjugated.

More important was the perceived need for sons. Women were valued mainly as mothers or potential mothers. In most of Asia, wives became (and still become) members of their husbands' families and could not provide support for their own parents. Thus sons were essential to care for parents, especially in their old age, and to carry on the family line. Nevertheless most families were small, averaging only a little over two children; mortality was high, and only the well-to-do could support greater numbers. The pressure for sons still weakens efforts to reduce family size in India and China as death rates have fallen, since parents tend to keep trying until they can produce at least one son, or preferably two—and also retards the efforts to improve the status of women.

Social Hierarchies

Traditional Asian civilizations were hierarchically based, marked not only by the uniquely Indian institution of caste but by the status groupings associated with kingship, feudal-style relations, occupation, age, gender, and levels of literacy and learning. The emphasis on achieving status through learning remains a distinctive aspect of Indian, Chinese, Korean, and Japanese societies to the present day. The importance attached to education and learning, both for prestige and for advancement, was and is greater in most of Asia than elsewhere, but education beyond primary or intermediate grades still does not include most Asians outside Japan, and it was even more restricted in the past. In most traditional Asian societies, it was a relatively tiny elite who acquired full literacy and advanced learning, and through them, superior status, authority, and power. For most Asians an individual's place in the social hierarchy is still the most important single determinant of how he or she must behave, and the proper observance of hierarchical rules the most basic means of preserving social and political harmony. Southeast Asia has remained fundamentally different from China, Korea, India, and Japan, perhaps because of the influences of Buddhism and Islam, both of which stress equality, but mainly because of the indigenous nature of Southeast Asian society, which helps to explain why these two religions were accepted there. Kingship and the hierarchies related to it were, however, common in Southeast Asia too.

Caste and the Social Order in India

In contrast to the merit-based system of China founded on examinations, and its variants in Vietnam, Korea, and Japan, caste was decreed by birth and affected nearly all South Asians including those living in what are now Pakistan, India, Nepal, Bangladesh, and Sri Lanka.

Caste evolved as a sociocultural rather than religious practice, but with some religious concepts woven in. Because it is still practiced by South Asian Muslims, Christians, and Buddhists (in Sri Lanka and Nepal), it is clearly separable from Hinduism as a system evolving later than Hinduism and as a means of ordering an otherwise disordered society. South Asia (India) suffered more or less chronic political chaos after the end of the Gupta period, or after about 650 C.E. No strong central, let alone national, state emerged. India's religious diversity after the forcible advent of Islam, and its great linguistic variety, made the cultural scene still more diverse or even confused and conflicted. Caste provided a system of social organization that was otherwise largely lacking and gave each individual a sense of belonging in the form of membership in a larger group beyond the basic nexus of the family. Caste operated also as a mutual benefit society, helping caste members who were in material trouble, settling disputes, and working as a common interest group on behalf of the welfare of all members, including efforts to upgrade the caste's relative status, help in arranging marriage partners, and response to other basic needs.

Ritual pollution and purity became the essence of caste definition, drawing boundaries of intergroup interaction, but its operative units were and are subcastes, or *jatis*, commonly linked to occupation: potters, weavers, farmers, etc. Each jati was and is endogamous (restricting marriage to fellow jati members) and members are forbidden to eat with or accept food or water from any members of other jatis. Caste cannot be changed, any more than one can change the place where one was born. Individuals might improve or degrade their status as their caste group rose or fell in the hierarchy.

Those outside the original four *varnas* (priests, warriors, merchants, farmers—see Chapter 4) came to be regarded as outcasts, and in later centuries "untouchables," since their touch or even their shadow could defile. Their occupations were defiling in themselves—they performed the essential services of cleaning and sweeping and disposing of the dead bodies of animals and people, including the tanning of leather from hides and the making of leather goods. Most of the untouchables also ate meat, even beef, forbidden to higher-caste Hindus or Buddhists, and lived in squalid, segregated ghettoes. In Buddhist Japan a comparable group emerged, the *eta*, who were also considered untouchable and for the same reasons, although the Japanese did not adopt the rest of the caste system and may even have been unaware of it.

But caste distinctions seem not to have been observed rigidly until relatively late in Indian history, well after the time of Harsha (seventh century C.E.). Escape from caste was always possible through religious devo-

A learned *sadhu*, or holy man, who through ascetic devotion and learning has risen beyond caste or sectarian religion. (Stella Snead, New York)

tion, again underlining caste's nonreligious nature. The ascetic sadhu, or holy man, was, regardless of his earthly origins, beyond caste and honored by all. Such figures and other mystics were and remain, like priests (Brahmins), far more numerous in India than elsewhere. For many centuries all South Asians have known what jati they were born into, but it is not really part of their religion, perhaps no more than genealogy, social class, or occupation are for Christians.

Caste has remained a highly flexible system. Although individuals are born into a given subcaste, by sustained group effort any jati might raise its status, often by adopting the religious, dietary, and other practices of higher-status groups and by asserting higher status. This process is called "Sanskritization," from the use of Sanskrit rituals associated with the Brahmins. In addition, the power of group action can be a potent weapon, especially in politics. This is particularly characteristic of Asian societies, where the individual is important primarily as a member of a group, whether family, clan, caste, guild, or regional or linguistic division.

Caste also served the need for some form of hierarchical order in a region of complex divisions. As fresh invaders, new religions, and new cultures and peoples came into India, no single culture, language, religion, or state emerged as permanently dominant. In this bewildering context, caste provided a sense of group identity, a means of support and defense, and a cultural vehicle as well, since each caste was necessarily local and shared a common language. Occupational associations for most subcastes meant that they also functioned as the equivalent of guilds and mutual-support groups. Caste was less a matter of religious than of social ordering, and the hierarchy it involved was perhaps less important than the day-to-day supporting functions it served, while at the same time it made social mobility possible for group members.

Brahmins have always been as widely distributed as Hinduism, but nearly all other caste groups (jatis) remain limited to much smaller areas speaking a common regional language and sharing a common local culture. This often meant an area with a radius of little more than 50 or 75 miles, beyond which one entered or merged with a different dialectical, linguistic, or cultural region. As in all premodern societies, most people moved about very little from where they were born. India was not different in these terms from the rest of Asia, or from medieval Europe, except that more Indians took part in periodic religious pilgrimages to sacred sites, sometimes at considerable distances from their native places. People traveled in groups, not only for better security and for company but also because they often could not communicate with pilgrims from other areas, and they camped at the pilgrimage site in the same groups, preparing meals and interacting only with one another.

Social Hierarchy in East Asia

Despite the uniqueness of caste, Indian society conformed in other respects to the dominant Asian social model, of which China is the principal example. China was the original model for the rest of East Asia and remained overwhelmingly its largest and most populous unit. Under the empire in China, which lasted from the third century B.C.E. to 1911, power, responsibility, and status formed a pyramidal structure, with the emperor at the top as a truly absolute monarch. Below him were appointed officials in a series of grades: councilors, provincial governors, and generals, down to the district magistrates in some 2,000 counties, all of whom were selected from the ranks of the scholar-gentry who had passed the third level of the imperial examinations.

But this was not merely a political pyramid, and it did not act alone. The emperor and his officials had as their highest duty the setting of a good example, of "virtuous conduct." They were seen, and saw themselves, as fathers to the people, since the family was the basis of social order in Asia to an even greater extent than in most other societies. In theory, if the emperor and his officials behaved properly and responsibly, others in the social hierarchy would do so as well. In practice, social order, or in Confucian parlance, the "Great Harmony," was preserved primarily by the family system; this operated in much the same way in the rest of Asia. The family was the state in microcosm. Younger people deferred to their elders, as did wives to their husbands and social "inferiors" to their "superiors." This was the Confucian formula for happiness and social harmony, which spread with the rest of Confucianism to Korea, Vietnam, and Japan. But it was in most respects paralleled by Indian social mores. For all Asians, age was equated with wisdom and authority.

Southeast Asia

The hierarchical structure of society was less pronounced in Southeast Asia, sometimes attributed to the egalitarian emphasis of both Buddhism and Islam, but even before these religions spread to the area the traditional society appears to have been more open, less rigidly stratified, and with far more opportunity or even equality for women. However, age and learning were respected in Southeast Asia too, although status or authority was usually associated with kingship, religious piety, or achievement. Southeast Asian women played important economic roles, as they still do, especially in trading and the management of family business. Women had different functions from men, but these included rice cultivation, handicraft production, and marketing. Perhaps their chief distinction from men was the bearing of children, which tended to attribute magical and ritual powers to them.

In part for these reasons, daughters were valued far more highly than in the rest of Asia or in Europe; indeed, they were regarded as an economic asset. Southeast Asians commonly practiced bilateral kinship, in which inheritance might pass through either the male or female ancestors. At marriage, money and property were transferred from a husband's to his wife's family, whereas in most of the rest of Asia a bride had to be given with a dowry, often a heavy burden to her parents who were at the same time losing her help. Many Southeast Asian grooms had to pay a "bride-price," a kind of reverse dowry. Southeast Asian married couples often moved to the wife's village or family rather than the other way around as in the rest of Asia, and property was held by the couple jointly. Property was frequently inherited equally by all the children whatever their sex, again a departure from other Asian practice where the eldest son inherited all or most. In many parts of Southeast Asia women retained their own names and identities and sometimes passed them on to their children; property also could descend through the female line. Women took an active and often initiating part in courtship and lovemaking, and in that sphere seem to have been fully the equals of men, if not dominant. Divorce was relatively easy for both partners, far more so than in the rest of Asia, but monogamy was the standard, except for rulers. Women could initiate divorce, and remarriage by divorced women was relatively easy, again unlike the rest of Asia.

Early European observers of Southeast Asia in the sixteenth century, whose own early modern cultures were often rather prudish about sex and frowned on premarital sexual activity, were shocked at the behavior of Southeast Asians. Portuguese described the Malays as "fond of music and given to love," while all Southeast Asians were said to be "very lasciviously given, both men and women." Dutch observers did note, however, that Southeast Asian women were "very constant when married, but very loose when single," and that it was "thought to be an obstacle and an impediment to marriage for a girl to be a virgin." The relative economic freedom of women and their income-earning ability, mainly in trade, made it easier for them to leave an unsatisfactory marriage. This seems to have made both spouses try harder to make the marriage work.

What was called "temporary marriage" often took the place of prostitution as a means of providing foreign traders with female companions, an arrangement that apparently brought no shame on the woman and may even have increased her appeal as a marriage partner, in part because she was well paid for her services. Husbands, including "temporary" husbands, generally treated their wives with respect. An early English observer in 1606, on seeing a Chinese beat his Vietnamese wife (although they were living in Java) commented that this would never have been tolerated if his wife had been a local woman, "for the Javans will hardly suffer them to beat their women."[1] There was deep prejudice against political power for women in most of mainland Asia (East and South plus Burma, Thailand, and Vietnam), but in Indonesia and the Philippines there were

occasional women rulers, and in a few areas most rulers were female. Women were also often used as diplomatic and commercial negotiators because they were seen as more reasonable and less bound by male codes of aggression or "honor."

The Family

With the exception of Southeast Asia, the paternalistic family was a hierarchical structure in which group welfare took precedence over individual preferences. The father was like a little emperor, not only with absolute power but also with absolute responsibility. Filial obedience was the cardinal Asian virtue; loyalty and obligation to parents and elders was rigid and inflexible, but it produced a tight-knit unit. In family relations age was the major determinant. Three generations commonly lived under one roof, and the grandfather was thus the dominant figure, although his place might be taken after his death by his widow. Younger sons were subject to their older brothers, wives and sisters to their husbands and brothers, and all to the eldest male. Individual initiative other than by the patriarch was not tolerated; the welfare of the family as interpreted by him came first and all decisions were accordingly made by the elder members. It was the duty of each family to care for its older members, as well as to be ruled by them. The larger society had no adequate mechanisms for taking care of the elderly, so they died in the households where they were born, or in total penury in the few cases where they had no surviving children.

Family continuity also had a semireligious aspect, not only in the context of Chinese, Korean, Vietnamese, and Japanese "ancestor worship" but also in India as well. The oldest surviving son had the responsibility in all of these cultures to conduct funeral services for his parents and annual and periodic rituals thereafter, theoretically forever, so as to ensure the well-being of the departed spirits and their continued help from the hereafter. In China and India each generation's eldest son might thus be responsible for rituals on behalf of past generations of ancestors, by name, over many preceding centuries. In Vietnam, Korea, and Japan similar practices developed, although continuity with the ancestral past was less extensive and rituals usually did not name ancestors for more than a few generations back. But the general Asian belief in the basic importance of family and generational continuity and in the permanence of family and personal identity was a further expression of the central role of the family as the anchor for all individuals and their place

Security and continuity: the family. Rajasthani grandmother and her grandson hope for the future. (Stella Snead, New York)

in the temporal and spiritual worlds. It also underlined and gave a critical aspect to the importance of producing sons who could continue the family line and perform the rituals for those who had died, functions that were seen as essential for both the dead and the living.

A new Asian bride was the servant of the husband's family and was often victimized by a tyrannical mother-in-law. More so than in the West, Asian girls could be married against their wishes and had little or no right of refusal—except by committing suicide. An entire genre of Asian stories was devoted to this theme. In a typical story, a bride was carried in an enclosed cart or sedan chair to her new husband's family; when the curtains were opened, an unwilling bride would sometimes be found to have killed herself. Marriage was seen as a business arrangement between families, not as an individual choice or a love match. In later centuries the custom of foot-binding became widespread in China, inflicting dreadful pain on growing girls and emphasizing their role as erotic playthings. About the same period, the practice of *purdah*, the veiling and sequestering of women, spread with the Muslim conquerors even through Hindu northern India.

Few Asians questioned the family hierarchy. The family operated as a collective entity; each member was both socially and legally responsible for the behavior of all other members. Collective responsibility, family pride, and the shame of family disgrace are still credited for the relatively low rate of crime in much of Asia. Government from higher levels was far less necessary.

Asian societies have been called self-regulating, and to a very large extent that was true. The price of this was the sacrifice of individual initiative, independence, and self-fulfillment so prized by the modern West and now increasingly attractive in many parts of modern Asia.

Individuals moved through life only as members of families, as did members of larger groups such as castes, clans, or guilds. Yet there was a surprising amount of vertical mobility in Chinese society. Judging from the numerous biographies of successful examination candidates, as many as a third of the gentry group in each generation represented new blood. The Chinese had a proverb like our own: "Rags to riches in three generations," and new entrants into the gentry group were matched by those suffering downward mobility—"riches to rags"—about whom there are also numerous stories. Downward mobility was often hastened by the corrupting effects of wealth and its sapping of the ethic of hard work in favor of luxurious and idle living. In Asian countries families and sometimes villages, clans, or guilds squeezed their resources to support promising boys through the lengthy education needed for entry to the scholarly ranks, in effect as their representative and as one who could bring prestige and profit. Many Asian-American families and students continue this tradition, at least for a generation or two, including the realization that education, like anything else worth having, cannot be achieved without hard work.

The larger society offered few support mechanisms. Without a family or descendants to care for them, the sick, the poor, and the elderly could not survive. In the Hindu and Buddhist countries, minimal shelter and food were available to all at temples, as they still are, but in most of Asia the production of offspring, especially sons, was the overriding goal for simple self-preservation. Those who did well in life were bound to help not only siblings but also uncles, aunts, cousins, and *their* families.

The bonds of obligation and collective responsibility reached throughout the extended family, which included all paternal and maternal relatives, or at least those with whom a given nuclear family was in touch. It was thus fortunately uncommon for individuals to be *wholly* without some family connection and consequent claim for support, although for those whose relatives were too poor to offer much help—which was not so uncommon—life was often a losing struggle. Most Asian societies retain even now a complex variety of name designations for each of these kin relationships. One still does not refer merely to one's brother, sister, uncle, aunt, or grandmother, but to elder or younger brother, first, second, or third paternal uncle, maternal grandfather, and so on. This extended network of relationships not only put a heavy burden on individuals but also provided mutual support. Those unfortunate enough to have no surviving children, spouses, or close relatives, especially true of widows, were often totally destitute and frequently starved or eked out a miserable existence by begging.

Marriage

Marriages were almost always arranged by agreement between the two families concerned. Dowries were commonly part of the marriage contract outside Southeast Asia, especially in India; in Southeast Asia the male's family commonly paid a "bride-price." Part of a woman's dowry, again especially in India, was often, however, in the form of jewelry that remained her own and that could serve as a kind of security against hard times. The average age at marriage was lower than in the medieval or early modern West (and lower than it has since become in Asia): approximately 21 for males and 17 for females in traditional China, 16 and 14 respectively in India, and 20 and 16 in Japan and Southeast Asia.

Except for most of Southeast Asia and a small region of South India, most marriage was and remains patrilocal; that is, the bride, who was almost invariably recruited from another village to avoid inbreeding, left her family and became a member of her husband's family. Under this patrilocal arrangement, she was the lowest-status member until she had borne a son. She might visit her parents occasionally, but she was lost to them as a family member or helper and cost them heavily in dowry. Girls were often loved as much as boys, but on practical grounds they were of far less value, although girls did much of the household work. Sons were essential for family continuity and security. Because life was an uncertain business and death rates were high, especially in the early years of life, most families tried to produce more than one son. Girls, on the other hand, might be sold in hard times as servants or concubines in rich households. The childless family was truly bankrupt and might even pay relatively large sums to acquire a son by adoption. A wife who failed to produce a son after a reasonable amount of time was commonly returned to her parents as useless, for the prime purpose of marriage was perpetuation of the male line. It was not known until recently that the sex of a child is determined by the father or that childlessness may result from male as well as from female sterility, so the woman was always blamed. In time, however, most women became willing and even enthusiastic members of their husbands' families, passing on these attitudes to their children. Eventually they might sometimes achieve considerable power.

Marriage was seen by all as a contract between families for the furthering of their interests. Virtually all marriages were arranged by the families, usually through a go-between. Go-betweens were often older widows who surveyed the assortment of suitable partners in the area. They made it their business to keep informed, to investigate the characters of prospective partners and their family circumstances, and to do at least the preliminary negotiations. The small fee they charged was often their primary income. Bride and groom had usually not met before their wedding. Sometimes they might be allowed to express preferences, although these might be overruled in the family interest. Compatibility was rarely considered, and love marriages were extremely rare, although affection might grow in time.

Divorce was rare in Asia outside the Southeast, but though difficult, was still possible. Remarriage was even more difficult if not impossible, and that knowledge probably helped people try harder to make their marriages work. It doubtless helped too that romantic expectation levels were not as high as in the modern West. People were trained to put individual wants second to family interest. There is abundant evidence from biographies, memoirs, popular literature, and legal records that most marriages were successful within these terms, and that husbands and wives valued and even loved one another and worked together in the family unit to reproduce the dominant social pattern.

Child Rearing

In India and East Asia children were taught to obey, boys as well as girls, but until about the age of seven boys were especially indulged, as were infants of both sexes. Given the pressing need for sons, boys were clearly favored, but children in general were welcomed and loved and much fuss was made over them. They were often not formally named until they were about a year old and their survival was more assured; to give them names earlier was often thought to be tempting fate. Parents sometimes made loud public complaints, for the folk religion gods to hear, about how ugly or ill-favored their child was, hoping that this might preserve it from the early death that excessive pride or pleasure in it could invite. Girls were trained early to accept their lowly place in the hierarchy of the family and of the larger society, and there seems to have been little or no possibility of rebellion.

Some modern psychological studies have in fact shown that females, at least in the modern West, are far less inclined than males to think and act hierarchically or to accept such ranking as appropriate, but we lack comparable modern studies from Asia. Women's much lower level of literacy also tended to mean that their voices remained unheard, including whatever objections they may have had in the past to their general subjugation. However, boys were not free of what we would

Wives in India

Wives in India were supposed to be dutiful and cheerful, but they were also highly valued, as this passage from the Mahabharata suggests.

> The wife is half the man, the best of friends.
> The root of the three ends of life,
> And of all that will help him in the other world.
>
> With a wife man does mighty deeds. . . .
> With a wife man finds courage.
> A wife is the safest refuge.
>
> A man aflame with sorrow in his soul,
> Or sick with disease, finds comfort in his wife
> As a man parched with heat finds relief in water.
>
> Even a man in the grip of rage will not be harsh to a woman,
> Remembering that on her depend the joys of love, happiness, and virtue.
> For woman is the everlasting field in which the self is born.

Source: A. L. Basham, *The Wonder That Was India,* 3d ed. (London: Macmillan, 1968), pp. 181–182.

call oppression, especially at the hands of their fathers, older brothers, and other male relatives. The great indulgence that boys were accustomed to often came to an abrupt end when they were seven years old. Some autobiographies suggest that this was commonly a traumatic time for the male child, no longer waited on and coddled but subjected to an often harsh discipline, especially in Japan and China.

Nevertheless, the early years of life were made as easy and pleasant as possible, and by the modern consensus that is the critical period for the development of an individual. Babies were commonly nursed by their mothers until they were at least two or three and were carried everywhere, first on their mother's back in a sling and later in her arms or those of an older sister. Babies and young children were handled, played with, touched, and kept close to mother, father, or siblings until they were about five or six, and were given lots of love. Fathers often looked after the babies and young children. With such a start on life, it may be that the seven-year-old had become emotionally secure enough to withstand the trauma of adulthood training.

In any case, Western observers (and many modern Asians) find that the Asian adult male, especially an oldest son, remains heavily dependent on others throughout his life. He not only tends readily to accept the hierarchy of society and his place in it but also assumes that people will take care of him—especially his wife but also society in general, his superiors, his friends, and so on. This extreme dependency has been most remarked on in Japanese and Indian adult males, who, some observers have said, never grow up or remain in practical terms helpless, expecting their wives, or others, to do almost everything for them except perform their specific professional or occupational roles. Of course there is a range of such behavior in all societies, and dependent adult males are far from unknown in our own society. But this trait does seem to be related to Indian and East Asian child-rearing practices. While we can of course observe it best in contemporary terms, there is plenty of evidence to suggest that the patterns described above have a very long history and were part of traditional Asian societies.

The Status of Women

Although many women might have been powers within their families, their role in general was highly subordinate. There is no question that theirs was a male-dominated world (except to a degree in Southeast Asia), and that their chief claim to status was as breeders of sons. Females were subject first to their fathers and brothers, then to their husbands and to their husbands' male relatives. Most Asian widows, again outside the Southeast and parts of South India, were not supposed to remarry or even to have male friends. Given the high death rate and the unpredictable fortunes of life, many women—often no more than girls—were thus condemned to celibacy, loneliness, and penury for most of their lives. "Chaste widows" were praised, and though some managed a little life of their own, most conformed to the expected model and suffered. The suicide of widows was not uncommon in China but was carried to its extreme in India, where it was often the expected practice for the higher castes. Hindu funeral practice includes the burning of the corpse; a surviving widow was supposed to throw herself on her husband's funeral pyre, a ritual known as *sati* (suttee). Perhaps as many as a fifth of childless Indian upper-caste widows actually sacrificed themselves in this way.

The almost equally inhuman equivalent in China was foot-binding, apparently first practiced in the Song dynasty (960–1279), and like sati limited to the upper classes. Unfortunately, it spread in later centuries and became accepted as a necessary torture if a girl was to obtain a good husband. It is hard for us to understand the foot fetishism that gave rise to this practice, but the so-called lily foot came to be praised as a sexual object, and much was written about its erotic charms. While the girls were still young and their bones were supple, their feet were tightly wrapped and prevented from growing or distorted until the arch was broken and the toes bent under. The victims were effectively crippled and could walk only in a painful hobble; they became mere playthings for men, especially for the well-to-do, and their freedom of action was further limited.

As in the West, in hard times female infants were sometimes killed at or soon after birth so that the rest of the family could survive. Female babies were also sold as servants or potential concubines. The selling of children seems especially heartless, but such a girl might have a better life as a slave-servant or concubine in a wealthy household than starving to death with her own family. Women were rarely permitted any formal education, and although some acquired it, they were primarily instructed by their mothers and mothers-in-law in how to be good, subservient wives, mothers, and daughters-in-law.

Power within the family brought women rewards that were especially important in this family-centered society. Their key role in ensuring family continuity brought much satisfaction. In most families women, as the chief raisers of children, shaped the future. More directly, they managed most families' finances, as they still do in Asia. Some women achieved public prominence as writers, reigning empresses, and powers behind the throne

Memorial arch to a virtuous widow, at the approaches to a Chinese town, 1944. The inscription at the top reads: "Chaste and filial." (R. Murphey)

as imperial consorts or concubines. In India, China, and Southeast Asia a few women became rulers in their own right, but only in India could one find women who were brilliant generals and cavalry fighters, such as the Rani of Jhansi. Admittedly these were a tiny handful within Asia as a whole.

But the crucial role of women in what mattered most—the family, its well-being, and its perpetuation—was recognized within clear status limits. Among the peasantry, the overwhelming mass of the population, women played a crucial role in agricultural labor and were usually the major workers in cottage industry, producing handicraft goods for sale or barter. In reality, for most people, women were as important as men, even though their public rewards were far less and they suffered from discrimination. Upper-class women lived a generally idle life and commonly turned their children over to nurses or tutors.

Southeast Asia has traditionally been freer of sex discrimination than India, China, Korea, or Japan, and most of its regional cultures included some matrilocal marriage, female control and inheritance of property, and female dominance within the family. Property usually descended through the female line, and children often carried their mother's family name. In the rest of

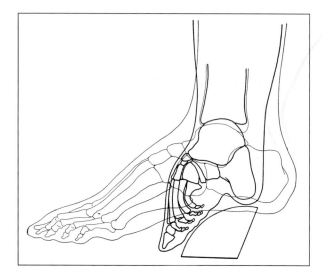

Diagram of a bound foot, superimposed on a normal foot. (From John K. Fairbank, Edwin O. Reischauer, and Albert M. Craig. *East Asia: Tradition and Transformation,* Revised Edition. Copyright © 1989 by Houghton Mifflin Co. Used with permission.)

Asia the traditional patterns just described were formed many centuries ago and persisted largely unchanged until the present century. Of course, there were women of strong character—as many as men—and many outside Southeast Asia did become dominant within their husbands' families. Publicly they were supposed to behave submissively, but inside the household it was often different, especially for older women who had produced grown sons or whose husbands were weaker people.

In the Islamic areas (mainly north and northwest India and what is now Pakistan and Bangladesh), women were discouraged from participating in activities outside the home by the conviction that females should be secluded as well as veiled. The latter practice was also an obvious practical way of enforcing anonymity on them when they did appear in public. Women who engaged in trade or educational pursuits were rare exceptions outside Southeast Asia, where the orthodox Muslim restrictions on women did not apply, even in the Islamic areas of Malaya, Indonesia, and the southern Philippines. Elsewhere the women's primary task was to marry and raise children, especially boys, and they were regarded as the property of their husbands, a view reinforced by the Koran. The Koran was used explicitly to legitimize the subordination of women. This point was succinctly stated by a seventeenth-century Iranian theologian, who asserted that a wife's principal spiritual duty was subservience to her husband: "A wife must obey her husband, never disobey his commands, never leave the house without his permission." As early as the 1200s Islamic society was characterized by a separate social life for men and women.

Sexual Customs

Asian women outside Southeast Asia were expected to be modest and chaste. Upper-class women seldom appeared in public, and any open display of affection with their spouses was taboo, as it still tends to be. At the same time, the elite Asian cultures are famous for their erotic literature and art and for the development of a courtesan (prostitute) tradition older than in any other living civilization. The *geisha* tradition of Japan and its original, the "sing-song" or "flower-boat" women of China, are well known, as is the cult of ritual sex among Indian temple priestesses and the orgies of Tantric Buddhism. In India, too, courtesans were often highly educated and accomplished. Explicit portrayals of sex appear in Indian art, and the classic Indian sex manual, the *Kamasutra*, is world-famous. But this behavior was reserved for the privileged few. Asian courtesans were, however, also patronized by the elite as witty and learned conversationalists, and even poetesses, steeped in the classics and able to match wits and learning with their patrons or to cap a classical quotation with a brilliant extempore invention.

In contrast to the Judeo-Christian West, India, Tibet, and parts of Southeast Asia had a religious tradition in which sex was used as ritual, in some ways rather like the ancient cult of Dionysus in classical Greece. Representations of sex in Indian sculpture and painting use gods and goddesses as subjects, not ordinary mortals, and celebrate the divine life force, creation. Tantric Buddhist and some Hindu temple sex rites had the same purpose.

All of this—the pleasures of the elite dallying with their concubines, sing-song girls, erotic pictures and stories, and the joys of Islamic rulers in their harems—was far beyond the experience of most people. For the great mass of the population, sex was a brief and often furtive pleasure after dark (which brought only a minimum of privacy), and centered on procreation. Most people lived close together, and most households included three generations, sharing at most two small rooms. Privacy was nonexistent, and one was almost never out of sight or sound of other people. In Japan, and especially in most of Southeast Asia, premarital sexual experience was tolerated or even encouraged. Especially in parts of South-

 ## Women Traders

> *Early European and Chinese traders to Southeast Asia were continually surprised to find that their counterparts often were women. Here is a collection of their comments on this phenomenon.*[1]
>
> - In Cambodia it is the women who take charge of trade (Zhou 1297:20).
> - It is their [Siamese] custom that all affairs are managed by their wives . . . all trading transactions great and small (Ma Huan 1433:104).
> - The women of Siam are the only merchants in buying goods, and some of them trade very considerably (Hamilton 1727:96).
> - The money-changers are here [Aceh], as at Tonkin, most women (Dampier 1699:92, also 47).
> - In Cochin-China [Vietnam] every man is a soldier. The commercial operations are performed by women (White 1824:261; also Chapman, quoted Yu 1978:102).
> - Women in the Birman country . . . manage the more important mercantile concerns of their husbands (Symes 1827 I:255).
> - It is the women [of Maluku] who negotiate, do business, buy and sell (Galo 1544:75).
> - [In Melaka] women hold a market at night (Hwang Chung 1537:128; cf. Pires 1515:274).
> - It is usual for the husband to entrust his pecuniary affairs entirely to his wife. The women alone attend the markets, and conduct all the business of buying and selling. It is proverbial to say the Javanese men are fools in money concerns (Raffles 1817 I:353).
>
> *Source:* A. Reid, *Southeast Asia in the Age of Commerce: The Lands Below the Winds* (New Haven: Yale University Press, 1988), p. 164. Copyright © 1988. Reprinted by permission of Yale University Press.

east Asia, virgins were not considered attractive as brides, although most marriages were monogamous once entered into, and sexual infidelity after marriage by either partner was condemned and often punished. Elsewhere in Asia any bride discovered not to be a virgin was commonly rejected, and even males were supposed to avoid sex before marriage. There was, as in the West, a double standard after marriage, again outside of Southeast Asia. Wives were strictly forbidden to commit adultery and were often very harshly punished for it, while male sexual infidelity was often tolerated. In practice, as pointed out, philandering and visits to sing-song girls or other prostitutes was largely limited to the elite, who could afford such indulgences and also could afford additional wives and concubines.

In most of Asia homosexuality was considered shameful and those who were caught at it were condemned or punished, in part because it was held to be unnatural and could not produce offspring, the prime goal of marriage or even of society as a whole. To Confucians, having no descendants was the ultimate disloyalty to one's parents. Homosexuality was, however, more common and more tolerated among the *samurai* of Japan, many of whom remained unmarried, and periodically rulers and the upper classes in all countries.

Education, Literacy, and the Printed Word

 Asians, far more than Europeans, accepted and followed Plato's dictum that education makes men good, and good men act nobly. Education was thus the path to authority and power, where the learned man was assumed to act responsibly in the public interest. Respect for learning was universal in Asia. Written texts in particular or even scraps of paper with writing on them were to be reverently treated and preserved. This was partly due to the importance of the philosophical, moral, and religious texts that played so great a part in each Asian cultural tradition, but partly also because literacy and learning were the surest and most prestigious paths

A *samurai* (note the sword) relaxes with geishas in a teahouse. (*Perspective Picture of Cooling-off in the Evening at Ryogoku Bridge* [detail] by Okumura Masanobu, Japanese, 1686–1764 Woodblock print, c. 1735–1740, 44.6 x 56.5 cm. Clarence Buckingham Collection, 1932.1355. Photograph © 2003 The Art Institute of Chicago. All rights reserved.)

to worldly success. Even in the medieval and early modern warrior-dominated society of Japan, the Confucian tradition helped to assure the same attitudes; many of the samurai acquired classical learning and became "gentlemen warriors."

In the cultures where religion was more centrally important than in China, especially in India and Buddhist Southeast Asia, literacy and learning also led to an honored status for priests and monks; they were above even the ruler in the status hierarchy, as Koranic scholars often were in the Muslim areas. The Indian Brahmin combined the role of scholar and priest, while in Buddhist countries the monkhood calling has remained the most honorable of all. Scholars, priests, and monks were exempt from manual labor, and legal punishments for them were less severe than for others. Lip service was paid to the worth and importance of peasant labor and agriculture, but the rewards and status went to those who had risen above the necessity of physical work. In Asia even kings and emperors deferred to the learned holy man or to the upright scholar.

Freedom from manual labor for the educated was marked by dress, lifestyle, and the deference of others. Sumptuary laws prohibited the lower orders (including merchants) from wearing the finer clothes or the robes of gentry, samurai, monks, or priests. Indian Brahmins were invested at puberty with the sacred thread, worn over the chest, in an elaborate Sanskrit ritual that asserted their special status as "the twice born." It was the duty of the rest of society to support monks and priests by regular donations and alms and to finance their temples and rituals. Their activities were also connected with ordinary life, including weddings, namings of children, funerals, and religious festivals. Officials, drawn from the ranks of the learned, also wore distinctive clothing and enjoyed special privileges, including exemption from corporal punishment. Especially in China, they were treated with respect by the masses in deference to their awesome authority as the direct representatives of the emperor. The Chinese gentry, from whom officials were selected, wore the long, blue scholar's gown, which touched the ground and hung from the arms with loose, floppy sleeves. Since no physical exertion could be performed in such a garment, it was in effect a badge of their freedom from manual labor. The scholar-gentry also frequently let their fingernails grow to extreme lengths, sometimes protecting them with special covers, to make the same point.

There were three grades of gentry, reflecting the three levels of the examination system. Only those who had passed the third level could be selected as officials, but those in the two lower grades were also recognized as educated men and followed gentry lifestyles and dress. Many of them served as teachers of the next gen-

Court scene, attributed to Ku Kaizhi (344–406 C.E.). An instructor is writing down directions for her pupils, ladies of the court who, in China, as elsewhere in Asia, were expected to be literate and accomplished in several arts. (© Copyright The British Museum)

eration of candidates, running both private and government-financed schools where Chinese boys learned their characters and worked their way through the Confucian classics under stern discipline. Most gentry did not become officials but were an unofficial local elite, serving as teachers, arbiters of disputes, and managers of local enterprises, deferred to by all below them.

Merchants also needed at least a degree of literacy in all Asian cultures, especially since they had to deal with the state and the official bureaucracy as well as keep records and accounts and communicate over long distances. Some of them also acquired a good deal of classical education, and certainly they read poetry and fiction, both classical and popular. We have no accurate means of measuring literacy in traditional Asian societies. It may have been as high as a quarter of the population or higher, far in advance of Europe until the late eighteenth century at least in terms of the most basic ability to read and write. Literacy was much higher in Japan after about 1600, and by 1800 probably reached 50 percent for males, while in Burma and Thailand male literacy (primarily among Buddhist monks) was at least 40 percent. But even a literacy rate of 25 percent would be remarkable, considering the difficulty of learning Chinese characters, which were also the chief basis of the Japanese, Korean, and Vietnamese written languages.

The gentry group in China, and comparable elites in other Asian societies, probably never constituted more than about 2 percent of the population. To these one must add merchants and petty traders (who often had at least some degree of literacy), clerks and scribes, and some village elders. Despite the fact that they did not attend the regular schools, women sometimes acquired literacy from their brothers or fathers or occasionally on their own. The best evidence is probably the respectable number of female Asian authors, including the famous Lady Murasaki, Japanese author of the world's earliest psychological novel, *The Tale of Genji*. Court ladies such as Lady Murasaki had the leisure to learn to read and write. Literacy was expected of them, as were accomplishments in music, painting, and dance. In the Buddhist countries of Southeast Asia the monkhood claimed virtually all young men for at least two years and at any one time may have included, with older monks, 10 or 15 percent of the population, nearly all of whom were literate. In India the Brahmins, as sole performers of ritual and keepers of the Great Tradition, had to be literate.

Paper and printing were both invented in China, the former by the first century C.E. under the Han, the latter by early Tang times (eighth century). Movable type appeared in the Song by about 1030 C.E. and shortly thereafter in Korea. These inventions spread rapidly to Japan, though more slowly to India, Southeast Asia, the Islamic areas, and the West. The importance of sacred texts and commentaries for Hinduism, Buddhism, and Islam meant that even before printing, large numbers of copies were made by scribes. As in the West, the spread of printing greatly increased the reading public. The most important result was the increased circulation of literature, first in China and then progressively in other parts of Asia. This included copies of the classics, philosophical and religious texts, epic tales, such as the Indian *Mahabharata* and the *Ramayana*, and similar epics and accounts of heroic deeds from the classic traditions of China, Japan, and Korea.

Literature for a mass audience was being printed by Tang times in China (c. 600–900 C.E.) and soon thereafter in the rest of Asia, including plays, short stories, poetry, and the first novels. Well before the Tang period in China, in the splendor of Guptan India (300–500 C.E.), the court poet and playwright Kalidasa had created a brilliant series of dramas. With the spread of printing, his plays and poems were made available to a mass audience. Throughout Asia, printing also meant that what had long been present as an oral tradition of storytelling and drama took on new life. Much of it has been lost or is available only in much later printed versions, but from Tang times on there was a vigorous popular literature in the vernacular, less lofty and more down-to-earth than the classics. Stories and plays about universal human foibles—akin to Chaucer's *Canterbury Tales* in the West—were read avidly by a growing number of people, including scholars to whom such works were supposedly prohibited and who hid them under their pillows. In China there were even detective stories, accounts of difficult cases solved by clever magistrates. India produced similar tales, and some of the works of Kalidasa are in this genre. Accounts of adventure and intrigue flourished throughout Asia.

Material Welfare

It is impossible to measure levels of well-being for most periods in the past. We can only roughly calculate living standards, using such evidence as travelers' accounts, estimates of population and production, trade figures, glimpses of lifestyles, famine records, and remedial measures. Before the modern period these records are fullest for China, where we have a wealth of official and local documents and an extensive literature. Generally, most Chinese seem to have been materially better off in diet, housing, and clothing than most people elsewhere in the world until perhaps as late as the mid-nineteenth century. But the only real defense against absolute poverty was the family system in Asia, which provided its own mutual-assistance network.

The greatest problem was recurrent famine, resulting from drought, flooding, or locusts. North China and northwest India were especially prone to periodic drought, sometimes worsened by floods when the monsoonal rains finally arrived, too late to save the crops, or when there was an unusually wet season. The monsoonal climate is notoriously variable from year to year, both in the amount of rainfall and in its timing. Northern China and inland north India lie close to the edges of the main monsoonal airflows and were particularly hard-hit by this variability. Nevertheless, both became densely settled by an agricultural population that had increased to the point where it could just be sustained in good years. Drought was not regular in its occurrence, but on average both areas experienced it in roughly a third of the years, with catastrophic drought or flooding something like one year in thirty, when literally millions of peasants starved to death.

The British historian R. H. Tawney described the Chinese peasant as living metaphorically up to his neck in water so that he might be drowned by the slightest rip-

ple. Drought was worse and more frequent in the areas farthest from the sea. Famine relief, including some tax relief and the distribution of stored grain at controlled prices, was not always available, and even when it was could offer at best inadequate help. Most of the rest of Asia (except for well-watered Japan and most of insular Southeast Asia) experienced periodic drought on a usually smaller scale. In drought-stricken areas, traditional irrigation systems also dried up or were inadequate, and in any case most of the cultivated areas in the north were not irrigated but depended on the unreliable rainfall. Variability was highest in the driest areas, fitting the biblical prescription: "For unto everyone that hath shall be given, and he shall have abundance, but from him that hath not shall be taken away, even that which he hath."[2]

Most Chinese peasants tried to keep a pig or two and some chickens, which could live by scavenging; in the wetter areas of the south, the diet included ducks and lake, river, or sea fish. Eggs could supplement the diet, but meat was often sold or eaten only at festival times. Traditional Japan was largely vegetarian, in keeping with Buddhist ideas, but because most of the population hugged the coast, fish was a major source of protein. Korean practice was similar to China's, as was Vietnam's, but in both areas there was greater availability of fish given the population concentration near the coast. Some of the Buddhist areas of Southeast Asia were also largely vegetarian, although there too fish and eggs were often eaten. Pious Hindus in India and the higher castes, perhaps one-third of the population, ate no meat; many avoided even eggs or fish, but consumed a variety of milk products including yoghurt, butter, and cheese, as well as lentils and other legumes as a source of protein. (Adult East Asians are genetically disadvantaged in the digestion of milk and milk products and have traditionally avoided them in all forms, in part also because of its association with the culturally despised nomads of Central Asia.) In the Muslim areas mutton replaced pork, but it too was eaten largely by the rich few. In general, Asians depended overwhelmingly on grains: rice, wheat in the drier areas, and sorghum, millet, and buckwheat. Beans, peas, cabbage, squash, eggplant, peppers, and other vegetables were grown on the side or in kitchen gardens. The overall diet was often short of protein but was probably better nutritionally and in total amount than the average European peasant or laborer's diet until modern times. Chickens, originally native to Southeast Asia, were a useful protein source in all of the nonvegetarian areas.

Food is an especially prominent part of culture in most agricultural or peasant societies, but perhaps especially so in Asia. France and Italy are well-known Western examples, related to their traditional and recent agricultural or peasant past, and China and India are equally well-known examples from Asia. Where the food supply is periodically uncertain, as in all societies of the past, eating is understandably an important part of life, and food is a symbol of prosperity and hospitality. In Asia a diet dominated by cereals—rice or wheat—could be enlivened by seasonings and by cooking what little protein was available with tasty sauces. Traditional Southeast Asian food was prepared much like Indian and Chinese food, and like them included a variety of spices. In at least nominally Buddhist, and hence vegetarian, traditional Japan, fish in some variety replaced meat, but like meat, it was used often as a seasoning or dressing on the rice, as was seaweed and fresh or pickled vegetables. The strong Japanese aesthetic sense also tended to emphasize colors, shapes, visual arrangements, and combinations in food, which stressed subtle taste contrasts.

Chinese and Indian food are perhaps now so well known in the West that they need no special description, but in both, as in Southeast Asian food, rice or wheat (noodles, chapattis, or unleavened wheaten cakes) served as the base with which small amounts of meat, eggs, fish, or vegetables were served in various piquant or hot sauces. It is hard to realize that the hot red peppers or chilies now so prominent a part of much Indian and Chinese food came originally from the New World. They were introduced into Asian cuisine by the Spanish via Manila in the late sixteenth century.

Food was the centerpiece of most festivals, birth ceremonies, weddings, and other special occasions and the predominant vehicle of entertaining. At such times, more elaborate dishes were produced; some of them might take days to prepare and would include meat, fowl, eggs, fish, or other materials rarely seen in daily fare. The food served in Indian, Chinese, Southeast Asian, or Japanese restaurants in the West is of this sort—feast food—and should not be taken as representative of what most people ate, or eat even now, most of the time. Nevertheless, most Asian households prided themselves on the excellence and flavorfulness of the food they could cook for a special occasion, often spending many hours and much of their meager resources preparing it.

Food was, and remains, basic to Asian culture to a degree not found in most other cultures, perhaps with the exceptions of France and Italy. The emphasis was not so much on eating to live but on living to eat, particularly on any special occasions—and there were as many of those as a family could afford, including simply visits by family members. It is certainly true that the food was outstandingly good by any judgment, the outcome of a very long tradition in which food was seen as important and where standards were high. Royalty and the elites had especially elaborate and expensive dishes, of course, but the common people ate well too whenever

they could afford it; this was not often for most people, and never for the very poor, but when there was an occasion, even the food for commoners tended to live up to the best Asian tradition.

Malnutrition, periodic famine, and endemic and epidemic disease were responsible for the low life expectancy. However, those who survived the first five years could expect to live longer in most of Asia than in Europe until modern times, although accurate figures are lacking. The great bulk of the population, close to 90 percent, lived in rural areas in small village clusters rather than in isolated farmsteads, where the villages might contain between 50 and 200 people. Houses were extremely simple, mud or wattle huts with thatched roofs. Living quarters were often only a single room for the family, and sometimes work animals were sheltered in an attached lean-to. In the towns people were often victims of polluted water, the chief carrier of epidemics, and of crowded living conditions. Cholera, typhoid, typhus, malaria, various forms of dysentery, and smallpox were major epidemic or endemic diseases, and there occurred occasional outbursts of bubonic plague. Infant mortality was especially high, and death was a familiar fact of life.

The larger Asian society had pitifully inadequate means beyond the family level to intervene on behalf of the poor. In China the imperial bureaucracy ameliorated severe hardship to some degree by remitting taxes, controlling floods, keeping order, and storing grain for distribution in lean years at uninflated prices, a policy called the "ever-normal granary system." Such efforts flagged or failed when the dynasty was weak or collapsed—perhaps a third of the time—and even in strong periods the state could not cope with a major catastrophe. In India and Southeast Asia, and to a lesser degree in the Buddhist areas of Korea and Japan, temples provided some refuge for the destitute, but this too was inadequate. In general, the family system of mutual support could keep most people from total destitution most of the time, but no means were adequate to deal with the recurrent large-scale disasters to which all premodern societies were subject, such as drought-induced famine, flooding, or long periods of civil disorder.

Values

One of the striking differences between Asia and the West is in their attitudes toward the natural world and the role of humankind within it. Partly as a reflection of Judeo-Christian doctrine, the West has tended to see human beings as kings of the universe, while Asians saw nature as grander, more powerful, and more to be admired, emulated, and listened to than whatever humans can construct. This view was characteristic not only of Daoism and Shinto (although particularly strongly expressed there) but of all Asian religions and of the societies that produced and practiced them. But nature was seen for the most part as a benevolent and nurturing force, not as an enemy or an object for mastery, as often in the West, where the biblical injunction enthroned humankind as lord of all creation:

> And God said, "Let us make man in our image, after our likeness, and let him have dominion over the fish of the sea and over the fowl of the air and over cattle and over all the earth, and over every creeping thing that creepeth upon the earth. . . . Be fruitful and multiply and replenish the earth and subdue it, and have dominion over the fish of the sea and over the fowl of the air and over every living thing that moveth upon the earth."[3]

The Asian view was that humans should fit into and adjust to the greater natural world, of which they were a comparatively insignificant part; this was seen not only as philosophically right but also as the best way to prosper, especially considering the fundamental importance of agriculture in all Asian civilizations. There was no thought of "conquering" nature, still less of destroying aspects of the environment through abuse. Population pressures did increasingly cause the removal of most of the original forests of China and India, with disastrous modern consequences, but at least this was done originally in order to clear the land for farming, which was seen as making nature more productive.

Natural irregularities or disasters, such as floods, droughts, volcanic eruptions, or epidemics, unseasonable weather of all sorts, and especially earthquakes and eclipses, were seen as portents, signs of Heaven's displeasure, to which people had to respond by acts of piety or appeasing ritual. In China on many such occasions, the emperor would issue a penitential edict, laying the blame on himself as "lacking in virtue" and promising to set a better example for his people. One reason for this was that natural disasters were often seen as foretelling the end of a dynasty that had lost Heaven's favor. Peasants everywhere erected simple shelters or small temples to the local earth god, to which they prayed for good harvests or for an end to drought, flood, or other natural catastrophes. But nature was in general seen as beneficent, not only to be propitiated when necessary but also to be revered and admired. The elite spent as much time as they could observing and admiring nature, writing about its beauties and its moods, and even building pavilions from which they could view especially beautiful natural landscapes or the changing seasons. Nature is the most common subject of Asian painting, usually shown as a peaceful, contemplative, or inspiring scene rather than as something wild or threatening, as it was so often portrayed in the West.

The positive and respectful Asian attitude toward nature was probably related to their perception of nature's bounty. Monsoon Asia was very much more productive agriculturally than any other part of the world. By comparison, Europe was much less prosperous, especially after the fall of Rome, and suffered from cold and shortage of sunshine north of the Alps and Pyrenees. Agriculture was the predominant source of wealth, outstandingly so in Asia, and human prosperity was seen as directly stemming from monsoon Asia's fortunate endowment of a generally warm, wet climate, a long growing season, and fertile alluvial or volcanic soils. Nature's awesome power and its vagaries—its extremes of weather or periods of drought—were also clear and hence to be respected; human beings had to adjust to the natural order and invoke its favor, but for the most part nature was seen as nurturing rather than threatening. Gods and goddesses often personified or symbolized natural forces in ways that combined awe and respect with support.

Hard work and worldly accomplishment were highly valued and were seen as the foundation of society, but leisure and its enjoyment were equally valued. There was an ascetic and mystical tradition in every Asian culture, especially prominent in India, but most Asians were not ascetics and enjoyed life's pleasures. Most people in Asia saw the enjoyment of leisure and its uses as an end or good in itself. The drive to accumulate yielded for most people at a relatively early stage to the counterattractions of the enjoyment of leisure. In the early modern and modern West, accumulation tended to become an end in itself for many. R. H. Tawney has in fact labeled the early modern West, from the time of the Reformation, as "the acquisitive society." On the other hand the German sociologist Max Weber, based on his studies of India and China and what he knew of Japan and Southeast Asia, remarked (in paraphrase here) that to those Asians who had surmounted the urgent demands of the struggle for existence, the opportunity of earning more was less attractive than that of working less.

These were values voiced only by the literate elite, but they appear to have been shared by many of the peasants, laborers, and artisans whenever they could afford to do so. Frequent festivals and pilgrimages dotted the yearly calendar. Some of these festivals might last for days and were occasions for rest, feasting, dance, music, theater, visiting, and general enjoyment. The medieval fairs and festivals of Europe were similar, but what has been called the Protestant work ethic tended to become dominant in Europe after about 1600. Each

Asian tradition had its annual sequence of festivals, such as the two-week-long celebration of Chinese New Year (observed also in Korea, Japan, and Vietnam), the Indian observance of Diwali in fall and Holi in spring, Southeast Asian gamelan and theater performances, and a host of other regular festivals. During these festivals little or no work was done and people gave themselves up to ritual and enjoyment. Such recurrent occasions involved the active or passive participation of the entire population and were not limited to the elite, although royal weddings or coronations provided additional opportunities for mass recreation.

Law, Crime, and Punishment

In general terms, Asian thought made no place for the Judeo-Christian concept of sin, let alone "original sin," hence the image that, as has been proverbially said, "Eden was preserved in the East." Correction of deviant behavior and, if possible, reform through reeducation or renewed piety were stressed more than retribution or punishment, although these were certainly used and frequently harsh. The incidence of crime or social deviance was almost certainly less in Asia than in other areas, thanks to the self-regulating mechanism of the family and the deterrent power of the shame that individual misbehavior might bring on the group. It is sometimes said that while Western societies emphasized sin and guilt, the East stressed the unacceptability of antisocial behavior and used shame to enforce moral codes. Guilt and shame are of course similar, and interrelated, but guilt tends to be more permanently internalized, while shame can to a degree be expiated or washed away by punishment, retribution, and compensatory behavior. In addition to the social stigma of misbehavior, public shaming was commonly used as an official punishment. Criminals were publicly exhibited or executed and were often paraded through the streets carrying placards or wearing labels indicating their offenses.

Banditry was a common response by those reduced to absolute poverty. Banditry was especially frequent in periods of political disorder and, hence, virtually endemic in parts of India, while its incidence rose and fell in China with the changing effectiveness of the imperial government and the levels of peasant distress. Bandits operated most successfully on the fringes of state-controlled areas or in frontier zones between provincial jurisdictions, areas that were often mountainous or forested. In Southeast Asia, south coastal China, and coastal Korea and Japan banditry took the form of piracy. These were areas that combined local poverty or overpopulation with opportunity: rich coastal or ocean trade routes passing nearby, local forests for shipbuilding, and ample small harbors along indented coastlines far from state power centers, which made evasion or concealment easier. Pirates and bandits often further increased the poverty of those on whom they preyed. Although their prime targets were the rich and the trade routes, these were often better protected than the common people and their villages.

Some bandit groups turned into rebels who built on the support of the disaffected majority to overthrow the government and found a new order that could better serve mass welfare. A large share of popular fiction dealt with the adventures of bandit groups, often depicted as Robin Hood–type figures but in any case regarded as heroes rather than criminals. Criminals operated in towns and cities too, and in the larger cities, especially major trade centers, a genuine criminal underworld existed, as well as highly organized beggars' guilds. Controlling urban crime was often difficult because people were packed into overcrowded alleys, streets, and shanties in warrenlike districts.

The incidence of banditry or piracy was often taken as a barometer of the vigor and justice of the political and social order, as well as a measure of economic hardship. It was certainly related to all of these factors, perhaps especially to economic hardship; people in general often interpreted increased banditry or piracy as a sign that the sociopolitical system was breaking down, the greatest of all disasters, and in China that the ruling dynasty had lost the "mandate of Heaven." Of course natural disasters, commonly blamed on unvirtuous rulers, were often followed by a rise in banditry in the areas most affected. Many bandit groups and most rebellions adopted a religious and magic mystique. They followed secret rites, usually Buddhist, the obvious antidote to establishment Confucianism. Dissent often began within secret societies, which had their own rituals and underground organizations; as secret societies joined or emerged into banditry or rebellion, this aspect of their origins was retained, including blood oaths of loyalty and rituals purporting to give their members invulnerability to the enemy. Bandit and rebel groups in India similarly used secret societies and religious inspiration.

Criminals were tried and laws and punishments were enforced by civil courts run by the state and presided over by magistrates, rulers or their representatives, community elders, or learned men. In Asia, there was no prior assumption of guilt or innocence; judgment was made and sentences were arrived at on the basis of evidence, including the testimony of witnesses. Except for Burma, Asians had no lawyers standing between people and the law; plaintiffs and defendants spoke for themselves. In China and most of the rest of Asia, those charged with criminal behavior could be found guilty and punished only if they confessed their guilt. If they refused to do so despite the weight of evidence against them, they were often tortured to extract a confession.

It should be noted that torture was also used in medieval and early modern Europe, sometimes to extract a confession, sometimes simply as punishment. Trial by ordeal was also used in Asia, as in Europe, where the accused might prove his or her innocence by surviving a prolonged immersion under water or by grasping red-hot metal. Asian law, like its European counterpart, was designed to awe all who appeared before its majesty. Plaintiffs, defendants, and witnesses knelt before the magistrate or judge, and could be whipped if they were not suitably reverential—another expression of a strongly hierarchical and authoritarian society. Apart from that, flogging was a common punishment—except for insular Southeast Asia where a blow on the body was regarded as a mortal insult, and most minor crimes were punished by fines; those unable to pay became the slaves of their victims. In many of the Islamic areas, Koranic law was followed; this law, for example, called for amputation of the right hand as a punishment for theft. In China, the accused were sometimes made to kneel on broken glass or on heated chains.

Punishment for major crimes was almost invariably in Asia, as in Europe, death, commonly by beheading or strangulation. For especially dreadful crimes such as parricide (killing of one's parents), treason, rebellion, or other forms of filial or political disloyalty, more gruesome punishments were used: dismemberment, the pulling apart of limbs from the body by horses, the Chinese "death of a thousand cuts," or in India and parts of Southeast Asia, impalement or trampling by elephants, equivalent to dismemberment by "drawing and quartering" as used in Europe. Punishments were seen as deterrents to would-be criminals and as bringing shame on their families or groups. The heads of executed criminals were exhibited on poles until they rotted, a practice used in Europe until late in the eighteenth century. For all Confucianists, most Indians, and many Southeast Asians, the body was thought to be held in trust from one's parents, and to have damage inflicted on it was regarded as unfilial, thus increasing the shame of any penal disfiguration or dismemberment, including, of course, beheading. (This attitude tended to prevent autopsies or the development of anatomical and other medical knowledge that might have been gained through the dissection of corpses, as well as strongly discouraging surgery.)

For lesser offenses, East Asian and some Southeast Asian criminals were displayed in painfully small cages so they could not sit, lie, or stand up, or were mutilated by having ears or noses cut off or tongues cut out, practices also widely used in India and in Europe. In China a

Chinese punishment for minor offenses. The heavy collar, the *cangue,* was a burden to support and prevented the criminal from reaching his mouth, so that he would starve if not fed by others. His crime is recorded on the inscription, but all that shows here is the official title and seal of the imperial magistrate at Shanghai in 1872. Public humiliation was an important part of any punishment in China, as it still is. (Photo by John Thomson. Harvard Yenching Library, Harvard University)

common punishment was being forced to wear a heavy wooden collar shaped in such a way that the criminal could not feed himself and had to depend on the pity of others, to his greater shame. Prisons were, again as in Europe, dreadful places where inmates might starve if they were not brought food by relatives. For what we might call misdemeanors, Asian law tended to stress reeducation and reform (which produced the quite inappropriate label of "brain washing" as applied to Communist Chinese practice; this was simply reeducation and reform, following long-established Asian practice). Criminality, or at least misbehavior, was seen as potentially correctable, especially with family help, and as a failure of society. Strayed individuals were to be redeemed by reeducation wherever possible and by the model behavior of their "betters."

People naturally worried about falling afoul of the machinery of the law and the courts, especially in criminal cases. Two important points need to be made. First, probably about 90 percent of all disputes and minor crimes—and probably most crimes of all sorts—never reached the courts because they were settled or recompensed through family, village, gentry or other unofficial elite or local networks. Second, modern Western scholars conclude that justice probably was achieved, by such means and by the full panoply of the law and courts, more consistently than in the West and perhaps as successfully even as in our own times, when legal justice is far from perfect. The Asian record in this respect is creditable. Most magistrates and other dispensers of justice were diligent with evidence, judicious, and concerned to see justice done, not only to avoid the censure that could ruin their careers but also because of the sense of responsibility that they bore.

But there was, as often in the West, a double standard of justice; it tended to be harder on the poor, whose crimes generally stemmed from poverty, than on their social superiors. Punishments for lesser crimes were also lighter for those of higher status, or for "white-collar criminals," an injustice still characteristic of modern Western law. Laws were made and administered by elite groups, whose interest in the preservation of their privileged status and property were often at least as great as their devotion to justice. Nevertheless, dishonest, disloyal, or ineffective officials were often severely punished and even exiled or executed, although such punishments might often result from a change of rulers or from arbitrary and sometimes unfair censure.

As one surveys premodern Asian societies—and as one reads the many accounts of European travelers to Asia in the sixteenth and seventeenth centuries, who commonly compared what they observed there with what they knew of their own societies at home—one is strongly inclined to conclude that Asian societies were far better ordered than any elsewhere. This was at least in part because of their hierarchical structure and emphasis on group identity and shared responsibility, most of all within the extended family but throughout the society as a whole. Individual "freedom" in our modern terms was virtually unknown, but there were counterbalancing rewards of security, protection, and the accomplishments that group effort could win.

It is impossible to measure happiness, individually or collectively, but the longevity of these traditional Asian social systems suggests that they gave some satisfaction to most people most of the time. They tended to preserve the harmony so valued by Asian social philosophers. Of course there were tensions and personal and intergroup conflicts, as anywhere, but most of these were resolved without recourse to formal law. Clearly, women and the younger generation suffered from these traditional mores, but apart from the distressing pattern of bride suicide, there is not much evidence that most

women saw their role as miserable, especially once they had become established family members and had produced sons, whose care and upbringing was so largely in their hands. As mothers-in-law to their sons' wives, they acquired additional power and sometimes became dominant figures within the family.

Except for Southeast Asia, and to an extent Japan, women had little or no sexual freedom, had almost no chance for divorce, and usually could not remarry even if their husbands died. But most seem to have accepted these burdens without major recorded protest. A few elite women acquired literacy, and a small number became famous writers, especially in Japan, but with few exceptions they were denied political power except indirectly through their husbands, male relatives, or sons. Economically, especially in Southeast Asia, they often played an important role as household or family business managers.

There was an extensive literature, especially after the invention of papermaking and printing spread from China. Most literature was written by the elite and often consisted of retold classical stories, but some of it was clearly designed for a mass audience and dealt with day-to-day human problems and human foibles. The elites were somewhat differently organized or structured in the different Asian societies, but in all of them learning was the major key to status; however, power was seen as bringing with it special responsibility. The unofficial elite of literate or learned men also served as teachers and as local elders or authorities who played a major role in the settling of local disputes.

The Asian stress on education, and the dominant status of the educated man, clearly helped to produce power holders who were often men of some vision, perspective, humanity, and responsibility; of course, this was never wholly true, human nature and the corruption of power being what they are everywhere. As in all societies, especially before modern times, most people were poor by modern Western standards and were exposed to periodic disaster or death through droughts, floods, famines, and epidemics. Levels of material welfare varied widely from area to area and from period to period, but most Asians, including the lower orders, seem to have been better off materially most of the time than most premodern Europeans.

All Asian societies were fundamentally concerned with order or harmony in society and in the greater world of nature, which they often took as a model. They valued leisure as much as or more than work. Most of their frequent festivals marked seasonal points in the agricultural cycle and were often based on lunar observations. The stress on order and the importance of shame and the group ethic tended to limit crime, but criminals were often harshly punished. The official administration of law was sometimes severe but aimed to discover the truth and to punish only the guilty. For lesser crimes, the aim was reform or redemption through reeducation and the example of superiors.

People are much the same everywhere and in all cultures and periods. Asian societies developed distinctive philosophical ideas and systems of social organization, but they were derived from and applied to the management of universal human problems of poverty, conflict, greed, envy, jealousy, the corruption of power and wealth, and the rest of the failings of human society everywhere. The long record of Asian societies suggests that their particular solutions to these problems were successful most of the time and compare favorably with the solutions evolved by other societies, including the modern West.

Questions

1. Why did the Indian caste system develop? What was its appeal among South Asians?

2. Why do Indians, Chinese, Koreans, and Japanese stress the importance of the birth of sons? Why is this less an issue in Southeast Asia?

3. Why did Asian societies widely discriminate against women? How representative is the relatively late development of the practice of foot-binding in China?

4. What were the differences between the literate or text-based religions and continuing rural beliefs and practices?

5. Why are Asian families often considered to be the greatest threat to the modern Asian nation-state? Why did the People's Republic of China initially attempt to eliminate the traditional Chinese family system? How can Asian families be major contributors to development, as in the case of Japan?

6. How are issues of poverty, social order, education, corruption, wealth, and conflict dealt with among traditional Asian societies?

7. What roles have banditry and piracy assumed in Asian societies?

Notes

1. All quotations from A. Reid, *Southeast Asia in the Age of Commerce: The Lands Below the Winds.* (New Haven: Yale University Press, 1988), pp. 160 ff.
2. Matt. 25:29.
3. Gen. 1:26–28.

Suggested Web Sites

Indian Caste System

http://www.indianchild.com/caste_system_in_india.htm
Good introductory explanation of the South Asian caste system, with links to follow-up reference sites.

East and Southeast Asian Culture

http://newton.uor.edu/Departments&Programs/ AsianStudiesDept/china-culture.html
The *East and Southeast Asian Annotated Directory of Internet Sources,* a treasure trove of Internet links that cover the diversity of Southeast and East Asian societies and cultures.

Suggestions for Further Reading

Birch, C. *Stories from a Ming Collection.* London: Bodley Head, 1958.

Bodde, D., and Morris, C. *Law in Imperial China.* The Hague: J. G. Brill, 1967.

Brandaner, P., and Huang, C. C. *Imperial Rulership and Cultural Change in Traditional China.* Seattle: University of Washington Press, 1994.

Buxbaum, D., ed. *Chinese Family Law and Social Change.* Seattle: University of Washington Press, 1978.

Chang, C. L. *The Chinese Gentry.* Seattle: University of Washington Press, 1955.

Chang, H. C., ed. *Chinese Popular Fiction and Drama.* New York: Columbia University Press, 1973.

Ch'u, T.-t. *Law and Society in Traditional China.* Paris: Mouton, 1961.

Cohn, B. S. *India: The Social Anthropology of a Civilization.* Englewood Cliffs, NJ: Prentice-Hall, 1971.

Dumont, L. *Homo Hierarchicus: An Essay on the Caste System,* trans. Mark Sainsbury. Chicago: University of Chicago Press, 1970.

Ebrey, P. *Confucian and Family Rituals in Imperial China.* Princeton: Princeton University Press, 1992.

Elman, B., and Woodside, A. *Education and Society in Late Imperial China.* Berkeley: University of California Press, 1993.

Freedman, M., ed. *Family and Kinship in Chinese Society.* Stanford, CA: Stanford University Press, 1970.

Goody, J. *The Oriental, the Ancient, and the Primitive: Marriage and the Family in the Preindustrial Societies of Eurasia.* Cambridge, England: Cambridge University Press, 1990.

Hinsch, B. *Passions of the Cut Sleeve: The Male Homosexual Tradition in China.* Berkeley: University of California Press, 1990.

———. *Women in Early Imperial China.* Lanham, MD: Rowan and Littlefield, 2003.

Ho, P.-t. *The Ladder of Success in Imperial China.* New York: Columbia University Press, 1964.

Kalidasa. *Shakuntala and Other Writings,* trans. A. W. Ryder. New York: Dutton, 1959.

Kolenda, P. *Caste in Contemporary India.* Menlo Park, CA: Benjamin Cummings, 1978.

Lannoy, R. *The Speaking Tree: Indian Culture and Society.* New York: Oxford University Press, 1971.

Le May, R. S. *The Culture of Southeast Asia.* London: Allen and Unwin, 1954.

Leslie, C., and Young, A. *Paths to Asian Medical Knowledge.* Berkeley: University of California Press, 1992.

Mandelbaum, D. G. *Society in India: Continuity and Change.* 2 vols. Berkeley: University of California Press, 1970.

Mann, S. and Cheng, Y. *Under Confucian Eyes: Writings on Gender in Chinese History.* Berkeley: University of California Press, 2001.

McKnight, B. *The Quality of Mercy: Amnesties and Traditional Chinese Justice.* Honolulu: University Press of Hawaii, 1981.

Naquin, S., and Rawski, E. S. *Chinese Society in the Eighteenth Century.* New Haven: Yale University Press, 1988.

Rawksi, E. S. *Agricultural Change and the Peasant Economy of South China.* Cambridge: Harvard University Press, 1972.

————. *Education and Popular Literacy in Ch'ing China.* Ann Arbor: University of Michigan Press, 1979.

Rozman, G., ed. *The Confucian Heritage and its Modern Adaptation.* Princeton: Princeton University Press, 1993.

Wakeman, F., ed. *Conflict and Control in Late Imperial China.* Berkeley: University of California Press, 1975.

Watt, J. R. *The District Magistrate in Late Imperial China.* New York: Columbia University Press, 1972.

4

The Civilization of Ancient India

This chapter covers the origins of civilization in India with the rise of the Indus culture about 3000 B.C.E., the coming of the Aryans from Central Asia, the growth of the Vedic culture from about 1000 to about 500 B.C.E., and the Mauryan empire from 322 B.C.E. to about 250 B.C.E., after the death of emperor Ashoka. Invasions by Greeks and Kushans followed, and there was also a largely separate development of civilization in south India and Ceylon (Sri Lanka). The Gupta empire from about 320 C.E. to about 550 C.E. restored political unity in the north. Discussions on women in ancient India and Indian achievements in mathmatics, science, and medicine conclude the chapter.

Of all world civilizations, India's is the oldest still in continuous existence.* If one defines civilization as involving a writing system, metalworking, and some concentration of settlement in cities where most of the inhabitants are not farmers, the earliest such developments seem to have occurred in Mesopotamia by about 4000 B.C.E. and about the same time in Egypt. Civilization in these terms had emerged by about 3000 B.C.E. in India, and by about 2000 B.C.E. in China. Mesopotamian and Egyptian civilizations came to an end by Roman times and were later superseded by the Arab conquest. The present cultures of these areas have little or no connection with ancient Sumer or the time of the pharaohs, leaving India as the oldest survivor.

Although a literate urban culture was in existence in India by 3000 B.C.E. and lasted until about 2000 B.C.E., we know relatively little about it. We cannot yet decipher the texts or symbols its people inscribed on clay tablets, and the evidence we have is only the very large cities they built, now in ruins and only partly excavated. After the collapse of what is called the Indus civiliza-

tion, north India was invaded, over many centuries, by a Central Asian people who called themselves Aryans. They gradually became the dominant group in the north, although they intermarried with the indigenous people. When Alexander the Great invaded India in 326 B.C.E. many regional kingdoms had arisen. After Alexander withdrew, these were welded together into an empire by the Maurya dynasty (c. 322–c. 180 B.C.E.), which unified most of the north. A new group of invaders reunified the north under the Kushan dynasty from 100 B.C.E. to about 200 C.E. In the following century, the indigenous Gupta dynasty restored most of the Mauryan accomplishments in the north from 320 to 550 C.E., while the south remained divided among flourishing rival kingdoms. Gupta rule collapsed about 550, as did the short-lived northern empire of Harsha by 648, and India as a whole became a complex pattern of separate states once more.

Origins of Civilization in India

   Agriculture had evolved much earlier than the emergence of Indian civilization, probably in a number of widely separated places where the development was independent, including tropical Southeast Asia, westernmost Asia (what is now eastern Turkey, Syria, and northern Iraq), Africa, and, by the first millennium B.C.E., Central and South America. In Africa and the Americas the early and independent evolution of farming did not lead to the appearance of a fully developed system of writing or of metalworking until much later, although particularly in the Americas large cities were ultimately built by agricultural societies that in other terms were technically still in the Stone Age. Agriculture in permanent fields, as opposed to a gathering culture, requires a permanent settlement. Villages or even small towns of this sort inhabited by farmers began to emerge soon after 10,000 B.C.E. in westernmost Asia.

---

*The Indian subcontinent, as it is called, is about the size of Europe less Russia. It includes the present states of Pakistan, India, Nepal, Bangladesh, and Sri Lanka. Before the contemporary period, it is often referred to simply as "India."

CHRONOLOGY

Our word *civilization* is derived from the Latin word *civitas* for "city" and implies a larger settlement where most people are no longer farmers; it includes clerks, scribes, officials, artisans, metalworkers, shopkeepers, traders, and other specializations that mark the division of labor and distinguish a city from a village or town. Archaeological and documentary evidence for such developments is most complete for Asia, although it is now increasing for Africa and the Americas and may in time change the present picture somewhat. But it seems clear that civilization in these terms evolved along the lines just indicated.

It was not far from Sumer to India and the way was relatively easy: by ship along the sheltered coasts of the Persian Gulf and thence still following the coast to the mouth of the Indus River. The route by land across Iran and Baluchistan ran through desert with few oases, but it was used too. Neolithic developments in agriculture and the beginnings of large, settled villages or towns were taking place at several locations along this land route and in the upland Baluchistan borderlands west of the Indus during the fifth millennium B.C.E. Although

these developments were probably independent of Sumer, they may have benefited from early Sumerian achievements. Agriculture had also appeared on the Indus floodplain by the sixth and fifth millennia and may thus have developed independently there. By about 3000 B.C.E. true cities had arisen in the Indus Valley, much as early agriculture in the highlands around Mesopotamia later spread onto the riverine lowlands. As in Mesopotamia, the floodplain presented new challenges to early agriculturists: how to control river flooding, manipulate irrigation, and drain swampy land. The long experience with an evolving set of agricultural techniques ultimately made it possible to exploit the potentially rich agricultural resources of the lowlands. Consistent agricultural surpluses provided the basis for real cities, as opposed to towns. They had populations that were literate, used metal, stored surplus food, had a division of labor, and exhibited great sophistication in the arts, in building, and in town planning.

The Indus Civilization

The chief urban centers so far discovered are Kalibangan in modern Rajasthan (probably the oldest city site yet found in India). Harappa in what is now the Pakistani part of Punjab, and Mohenjo Daro on the lower course of the Indus. All three, plus nearly 200 smaller town or village sites from the same period, scattered over an immense area from the Indus Valley east to the upper Ganges and south to near modern Bombay, show similar forms of settlements, pottery, seals (for marking pieces of property), and artwork. Weights and measures at all these sites were uniform, further emphasizing the unity of Harappan culture. This vast culture complex, covering by far the largest area of any of the ancient civilizations anywhere, is called the Indus civilization. It clearly had a close relationship to the river and its tributaries, a situation very like that in Sumer and in Egypt. Like the Nile and the Tigris-Euphrates rivers, the Indus is an exotic river, that is, one that originates in a well-watered area. Rising with its tributaries in the Himalayas, the source of snowmelt and the heavy monsoonal rains of summer, it flows across lowland Punjab and arid Rajasthan into the desert of Sind to reach the sea near modern Karachi. All of this lowland area is dry, and the lower half of the Indus Valley is virtually desert, as in Sumer and Egypt, so agriculture is dependent on irrigation. Annual river floods provided both water and highly fertile, easily worked alluvium, or silt. Combined with a long growing season of high temperatures and unbroken sunshine, this was the same set of agricultural advantages that helped to explain the early prominence of Egypt and Sumer after the management and use of floodwater had been mastered. The river also offered

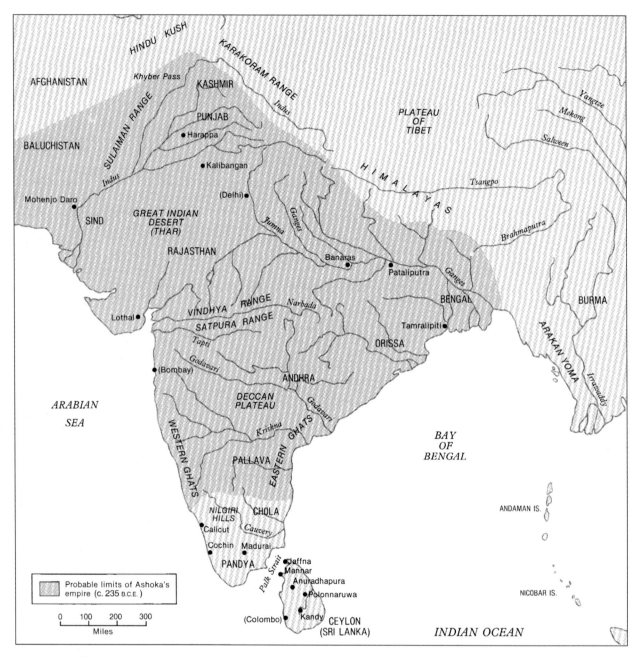

Ancient India

Note how the Vindhya and the Satpura range, buttressed by the Narbada and Tapti rivers, tend to divide northern and southern India, with the latter also protected by the uplifted Deccan Plateau. On the northern border, the Hindu Kush, Sulaiman, and Himalaya ranges form a formidable barrier. The ancient city sites are all closely related to the Indus River and its tributaries: Kalibangan, Harappa, and Mohenjo Daro. After the collapse of the Indus civilization, settlement came to center in the Ganges Valley, where the Maurya dynasty arose.

cheap, easy transport for bulky goods such as grain or building materials and, together with the treeless and level plain, created the transport access that is essential for exchange and hence for the division of labor.

Relations with Sumer

We know much less about the Indus civilization and its cities than about Sumer or ancient Egypt, in part because the Indus script has not yet been deciphered despite more than a generation of effort by cryptologists and linguists. The texts we have are incised on clay tablets and seals, as in Sumer, and contain over 300 different symbols. They may help provide some clue to who the writers were. There is some linguistic evidence that they were part ancestors of the present inhabitants of southern India, although some scholars suspect a closer link with the peoples of Iran. But the Indus script has no resemblance at all to anything from Sumer, and especially not to cuneiform. That in itself is convincing evidence that the Indus civilization was not an offshoot of earlier Mesopotamian developments but an independent creation. By at least 3200 B.C.E., almost certainly before the beginnings of city-based civilization in India, cuneiform had replaced earlier pictographs in Sumer. Its clear superiority as a form of writing ensured its rapid spread. If the Indus civilization had been an outgrowth of Sumer, it would surely have used cuneiform, or at least shown some connection with earlier Sumerian writing systems.

The art of the Indus people, and their remarkable city planning, are also completely distinctive and show no relation to Sumerian equivalents. The seals that they used are very similar to those of earlier and contemporary Mesopotamia, and we know that from at least 2500 B.C.E. there was trade between them. Objects from India at this period have been found in Sumer, and Sumerian objects in India. It seems likely that because seals were probably used primarily to mark property or goods, they were adopted by the Indus people in the course of their trade with Sumer. But in all other respects, their civilization was distinctively their own.

When exactly Indus civilization emerged is difficult to determine, beyond the rough guess of approximately 3000 B.C.E. The city sites, including the three major ones at Kalibangan, Harappa, and Mohenjo Daro, were necessarily close to the Indus or its tributaries and the local water table is high. The lowest (earliest) levels are now below the modern water table and thus present severe problems for the archaeologist. There have been major changes in stream courses also since these cities were built some 5,000 years ago. Flooding and silt deposition have carried away, buried, or drowned most of the earliest levels of evidence. As in the Nile Delta and for similar reasons, we can no longer see beginnings that may be considerably earlier than we can now prove. The earliest objects that have been dated cluster around 2500 B.C.E., but they come necessarily from upper site levels and from a period when the urban culture was already well advanced. Especially in the emerging phase of civilization, development is relatively slow. One must assume that it began many centuries before 2500, during which it evolved, built the first city levels, and acquired the form and quality evident by 2500. The guess at 3000 B.C.E. is a convenient though arbitrary round number.

We do not know what the builders of these cities called themselves or their settlements. The place names we use for them are modern—Mohenjo Daro means "place of the dead." The Greeks called the land they encountered in Alexander's time "India," which is derived from Sanskrit *Sindu,* the Aryan name of the river and by association the river's valley and the land beyond it. *Hind,* the Persian and modern Indian name for their country, is of course the same root, as is *Hindu, Hinduism, Hindustan* (*stan* means "country"), and the province of *Sind* (or *Sindh*) in the lower Indus Valley. The first external account of India is by the Persians in the time of Cyrus the Great (reigned 550–530 B.C.E.), who added the northwest briefly to his empire; they rendered *Sind* or *Sindus* as *Hind* or *Hindush,* establishing a form that has persisted.

Trade with Sumer took place both overland and through the port of Lothal on the coast below the mouth of the Indus, where the remains of large stone docks and warehouses have been found. These were associated with a city that was clearly part of Harappan culture (a convenient shorter label for the Indus civilization). A site along the route between them, on Bahrain Island, has yielded objects from both Sumer and India and seems to have supported a major trade center where many routes to and from Sumer met. Sumerian texts speak of a place called Dilmun, which was probably Bahrain, a few days' sail southward from the mouth of their river, where were found goods from a place they called Meluha, to the east: ivory, peacocks, monkeys, precious stones, incense, and spices, the "apes, ivory, and peacocks" of the Bible. Meluha must have been India, but it is not clear whether people from Sumer went there or whether the Indus people, or some intermediary, carried their cargoes to Dilmun.

The Cities of the Indus

Perhaps the most remarkable thing about this civilization was the planned layout of its cities, including wells, a piped water supply, bathrooms, and waste pipes or drains in nearly every house. There is no parallel for these developments anywhere in the ancient world, and indeed one must leap to the late nineteenth century in western Europe and North America to find such

Dancing girl in bronze, from Mohenjo Daro, c. 2500 B.C.E. The figure is stylized, even abstract, but powerfully conveys the spirit and movement of the dance. (National Museum of India)

achievements on a similar scale. The rivers that nourished these cities were the source of their municipal water supply, led by gravity from upstream, a technique later used by the Mughal emperors for their palaces in Delhi and Agra. The importance attached by the Indus people to personal use of water already suggests the distinctively Indian emphasis both on bathing or washing and on ritual purity. Religious figures found are varied, but they include many that suggest an early representation of the Indian god Shiva, Creator and Destroyer, god of the harvest, of the cycle of birth, life, death, and rebirth, and also the primal yogi,* represented even then

seated with arms folded and gaze fixed on eternity. Figures of a mother goddess, phallic images, and the worship of cattle are other elements that provide a link with classical and modern Indian civilization. Some scholars have suggested that the distinctively Indian idea of reincarnation and the endless wheel of life were Harappan beliefs. Indeed, the roots of most of traditional and modern Indian culture, including not only religion but also many other aspects, can be found or guessed at in what we can piece together from the Indus culture.

The houses in these cities were remarkably uniform, suggesting an absence of great divisions in the society, and were arranged along regular streets in a semigrid pattern. There were a few larger buildings, including in most of the cities a large public bath, perhaps appropriately the largest single structure, and others that were probably municipal granaries or storehouses. The art

---

*One who practices yoga, the Hindu philosophy that entails a strict spiritual and physical discipline in order to attain unity with the Universal Spirit.

these still-unknown people have left behind is strikingly varied and of high quality. Its variety may suggest that it was produced over a very long time, during which styles changed, as anywhere else in the world over 1,000 years: abstract, realistic, idealized, and so on. One of the most appealing forms is the enormous number of clay and wooden children's toys, including tiny carts pulled by tiny oxen or little monkeys that could be made to climb a string. This suggests a relatively prosperous society that could afford such nonessential production—a tribute to the productivity of its irrigated agriculture—and one whose values seem admirable. Complementing the picture, very few weapons or other indications of warfare have been found at these sites. It seems to have been a notably peaceful and humane civilization as well as organized and sophisticated. Cotton, indigenous to India, was woven into cloth earlier here than anywhere

else. This distinctively Indian innovation spread much later to the rest of the world. The animal sculpture and bas-relief, including the figures on many of the seals, were superbly done and include very large numbers of bovines, mainly the familiar humpbacked cattle, which suggests that cattle were already venerated, as ever since in India. This and other evidence leads one to believe that already by Harappan times the reverence for life and the quest for nonviolent solutions that mark the consistent Indian stress on the great chain of being and the oneness of creation had emerged.

The chief Indus food crop was wheat, probably derived originally from areas to the west, augmented by barley, peas, beans, oil seeds, fruits, and vegetables and by dairy products from domesticated cattle and sheep. Tools were made of bronze, stone, and wood, but in later centuries iron began to appear and was used, for example, in

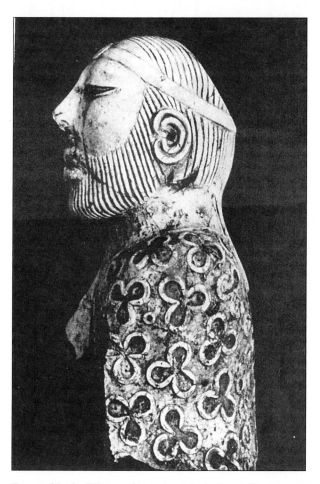
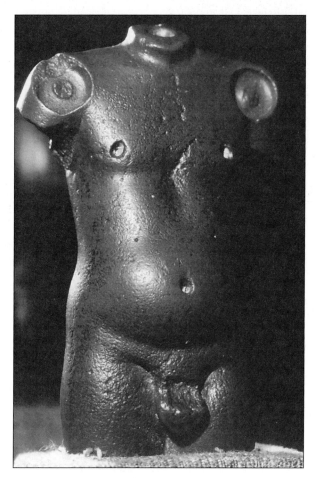

Two strikingly different objects from the Indus civilization, a priestlike figure from Mohenjo Daro and a torso from Harappa. The highly stylized "priest" suggests comparison with Minoan (Cretan) art, the torso with classical Greece. That both came from the Indus civilization may suggest that they were produced at different periods and reflect stylistic changes over time. (Left: Stella Snead/ Archaeological Survey of India; right: Borromeo/Art Resource, NY)

axle pins for wheeled carts. Rice appeared as a minor crop only toward the end of the Indus period, imported from its Southeast Asian origins as a crop plant via contact with the Ganges Valley. Sugarcane is native to India and was first cultivated there, but more is now grown in the better-watered Ganges Valley. In the Indus region, riverine location not only was essential for irrigation but also made for recurrent problems from irregular and occasionally disastrous flooding. The remains of successive dikes speak of efforts to protect even the cities themselves against floods and major course changes, not always successfully. There was no building stone in this flat and semiarid or desert region, and the cities were built of brick, as in Sumer, some of it sun-baked and some kiln-fired, using fuel from riverside tree stands (which must soon have been exhausted), or brought down the rivers from the better-forested hills and mountains upstream. The ruins of Harappa were first investigated in the 1850s by a British military engineer whose sharp eye noticed the strange dimensions of the bricks and other fragments brought to him by Indian contractors for railway ballast and the equally strange markings on some of them, samples of the Indus script, which he traced back to the site of Harappa and realized were the remains of a civilization.

Humped bull. The Indian veneration of cattle had its origins in the Indus civilization. (Jehangir Gazdar/Woodfin Camp & Associates)

Decline and Fall

Toward the end of the third millennium B.C.E. the Indus civilization began to decay. We can only guess at the reasons, but there is clear evidence of progressive shrinking of the area under cultivation or irrigation, and of the urban area occupied. The port of Lothal was abandoned by about 1900 B.C.E., and the other major centers probably supported only a fraction of their earlier populations, huddled in a small part of the decaying city. There is also evidence of violence at some of these sites: ashes and unburied or headless corpses, victims perhaps of bandit raids now that the cities were so largely defenseless against plunder. Any civilization that had already lasted for many centuries might be expected to show signs of decay. But the Indus people encountered some specific problems resulting from their desert or semiarid environment, problems that may rather quickly have become overwhelming. Continued irrigation of any arid area leads to the progressive buildup of salts and alkalines left behind by the evaporating water and not washed away adequately by rainfall. Irrigation also raises the water table, which may drown crop roots. When accumulated salts and alkalines reach levels toxic to plants or when the root zone is flooded, agriculture may rather suddenly come to an end. We have modern experience with both problems in many arid irrigated areas, including the drier parts of the United States.

In the Indus Valley, large parts of the areas cultivated in ancient times appear to have been abandoned for these reasons, as the telltale white deposits on the ancient surface indicate. In addition, recurrent flooding and course changes not only menaced the cities directly but also indirectly undermined their agricultural base by destroying or choking with silt the irrigation channels that fed the fields. Course changes perhaps resulting from earthquakes, to which the area is prone, could also deprive a city or an irrigated area of its water. All of this is characteristic of the behavior of exotic rivers, rising in the mountains and then flowing across a treeless desert. There is no evidence that the climate changed, as has often been asserted despite clear evidence to the contrary, but plenty to suggest that the agricultural surpluses that had built the cities and nourished their culture shrank and then disappeared, leaving only a remnant population living on a relatively primitive level in the ruins of the once-great cities on what they could still wring from the remaining but far less productive fields, plus hunting and gathering. In this reduced state, they were less and less able to defend themselves against raiders. The Aryan migrants, arriving later, could never have seen the Indus civilization in its prime and are thus unlikely causes for its decline. The people who built it, or their descendants, probably dispersed eastward into the Ganges Valley and southward into peninsular India, taking their culture and technology with them.

The Aryans

Aryan is, strictly speaking, a linguistic term, but it has been used (and widely misused) to mean a people or, even more inappropriately, a race. In the centuries after about 1600 B.C.E. a series of migration waves moved out from South-Central Asia, including what is now Iran, to richer areas both eastward and westward. One such group was probably the seaborne invaders of Greece, arriving after 1000 B.C.E.; another, the Kassites who invaded and conquered Sumer about 1750 B.C.E.; and another, the Hittites, who occupied northern Anatolia about 1900 B.C.E. Still another group moved eastward through passes in the Hindu Kush range into India sometime after about 1800 B.C.E. and called themselves Aryans. They spoke an early form of Sanskrit but were still preliterate, preurban, seminomadic tenders of cattle, sheep, and goats who also lived in part from hunting, from plough agriculture of wheat and barley, and from raiding more highly developed agricultural settlements and trade centers or routes. What little we know about them comes from their ritual hymns, the Vedas, and from later epic poems, the *Mahabharata* and the *Ramayana,* tales of heroic deeds and warfare written down many centuries later in Sanskrit, the classical language of India. By that time the Aryans had acquired literacy, plus the arts of agriculture, city building, and other aspects of civilization, presumably from contact and intermarriage with the more highly developed people already in India.

Vedic period culture (c. 1000–c. 500 B.C.E.) was, like its people, a combination of originally Aryan, Harappan, and other indigenous Indian strains. Sanskrit is the oldest written language among the ancestors of modern European languages, and it is also the direct ancestor of the languages of modern northern India.* The connection was not realized until the pioneering research of a British judge in Bengal in the late eighteenth century, Sir William Jones, who established the clear link among all the Indo-European tongues—between Greek, Latin, Celtic, Persian, and Sanskrit, as well as their modern derivatives—all originally stemming from the great migration of linguistically related peoples both eastward and westward from South-Central Asia beginning around 2000 B.C.E. Later research has shown that the common ancestor of the Indo-European languages was probably in western Asia about 4000 B.C.E. and that the daughter languages diverged from it as different migrations went both east and west.

Aryan Domination

The Aryans had a telling advantage, despite their more primitive culture: by the time they reached India they had acquired not only metal-tipped weapons but a light, fast war chariot with spoked wheels drawn by two or more horses, equivalent to the Greek war chariots of Homer's time, with a driver and an archer or spear thrower. Their culture glorified war, and they made a disproportionate military impact on a more peaceful Indian population. The Kassites, Hittites, Hyksos invaders of Egypt, and Dorian or Mycenean Greeks made a similar impact with the same tactics. The Vedas and epics tell the story of Aryan victories over "alien" peoples, whose cities they besieged and conquered, led often by their warrior God Indra riding in his chariot with his great war bow. Like most history written by the victors, the Vedas and epics portray the Aryans as godlike heroes and the conquered as "irreligious" inferior people. The archaeological record of the Indus civilization abundantly disproves such propaganda, but in language the Aryans triumphed, presumably because, though a minority numerically, they became the ruling class. *Arya* means "noble" or "pure" in Sanskrit; the same root word appears in the Greek *arios* ("good quality") and in the names of Iran and Eire (Ireland), all illustrating the Indo-European connection.

We do not know exactly when the institution of caste first appeared, the division of Indian society into ranked status groups who could marry or eat only with each other. One possibility, however, is that it evolved later out of distinctions made in Vedic times between a conquering group of Aryans, insecure because of its numerical weakness, and a conquered people, although such distinctions must in time have been submerged by intermarriage and cultural hybridization. In any case, caste distinctions and rules, including bans on intermarriage, seem not to have been widely observed until much later, perhaps as late as the fifth century C.E. (More detail on caste is given in Chapters 2 and 3.) The Aryans brought with them their male and warlike gods and their male-dominated culture, which slowly blended with the female goddesses and matrilinear culture of early India. By about 1000 B.C.E. these warlike Aryan-speaking groups had conquered or absorbed most of India north of the Vindhya Range, which divides and protects the peninsular south and the Deccan Plateau from the Ganges and Indus valleys of the north. Their language never prevailed in the south, which still speaks mainly four non-Indo-European languages collectively known as Dravidian, each with its own extensive and ancient

---

*Many Sanskrit words are easily recognizable as the roots of Latin and related English words. Some examples include *nava,* "ship"; *deva,* "god"; and *dua* "two," which have given us *naval, divine* or *deity,* and *dual.*

literature. The south has also tended to resist what it still refers to as "Aryan" pressures or influences, but in fact interactions with the "Aryan" north have been a heavily traveled two-way street for thousands of years now, in religion, art, literature, philosophy, and many other aspects of culture. There is a clear north-south distinction in Indian culture, but Indian civilization is a generic whole. We can only guess at what the south was like in Vedic times. The great epic poems, the *Ramayana* and the *Mahabharata,* speak of the south and of Ceylon (now Sri Lanka) as inhabited by savages and demons with whom the Vedic heroes were at war, in keeping with their pejorative descriptions of the people they conquered in the north. But although there were probably battles and raids, the south, protected by distance and mountains, remained beyond Aryan control except where coastal plains at the western and eastern ends of the Vindhyas allowed easier access. Ceylon was, however, invaded by sea and settled by an Aryan-speaking group in the sixth century B.C.E. and, soon thereafter, or possibly earlier, also by Dravidians from southern India.

Vedic Culture

It is during the Vedic period, c. 1000–c. 500 B.C.E., that the basis of traditional Indian culture and most of its details evolved. We know little of that process or of actual events. The Vedas and the epics are concerned with romantic adventure involving gods and demons or with philosophical and religious matters rather than with accounts of worldly events or daily life. We know only that these centuries saw the maturation of a highly sophisticated culture, no longer simply Aryan or Aryan-dominated but Indian, which we can see in worldly terms for the first time in any detail through the eyes of Greek observers after 326 B.C.E., when Alexander the Great invaded northwestern India. They show us a culture remarkable not only for its absorption in philosophy and metaphysics but also for its achievements in more mundane respects. The later classical West, like the Chinese, acknowledged India as the home of the most advanced knowledge and practice of medicine; of mathematics, including the numbering system we still use, incorrectly called "Arabic"—the Arabs got it from India; and of iron and steel metalworking. Indian steel was later to be transmitted to the West, also through the Arabs, as "Damascus" or "Toledo," though the steel itself was Indian. Indian medicine, known as Ayurveda (*Ayur,* "longevity," and *veda,* "knowledge," related to our word "wit"), enriched both Greek and Chinese knowledge and was widely disseminated, although it also benefited from Greek and Chinese medical practices.

These and other elements of Indian science had something to do with Vedic period assumptions about the universe and the physical world. Like some of the Greek philosophers, but even more consistently, Vedic India thought in terms of universal laws affecting all things—a supreme principle or indwelling essence, an order of nature that they called *Rta.* Unlike the Greek conception, this order existed above and before even the gods and determined all observable and nonobservable phenomena. Modern science and technology are not conceivable without such an assumption. The Greeks were on the right track in those terms, but the Indians anticipated and probably influenced them. Later European thinking veered off on other tracks, at least until the Renaissance resumed the Greek path. Given Indian and Chinese early developments in science, the final and much later European leap is somewhat ironic, even though when it came it necessarily built on earlier Indian and Chinese as well as Greek foundations.

The Rise of Empire: Mauryan India

By about 500 B.C.E. kingdoms had emerged in the Ganges Valley, already established as India's primary center of population, productivity, cities, and commerce. This was the area traditionally known as Hindustan, which stretched from Delhi in the upper valley to Bengal near the river's mouth. Population had multiplied many times since the fall of the Indus civilization, and agriculture had spread from the Indus Valley into the Ganges, a potentially more productive area watered far more plentifully by monsoonal rains and with the advantage of rich alluvial soils and a long growing season. In Harappan times the Ganges Valley was still heavily forested and probably only thinly settled by hunter-gatherers. With the increasing use of iron tools after about 1000 B.C.E. and the rise in population, the forest was progressively cleared and most of Hindustan was settled and cultivated. Growing numbers and surplus production provided the basis for the emergence of territorial states with revenue bases, officials, cities, roads, and armies.

The Invasion of Alexander the Great

When Alexander, fresh from his conquest of the Persian Empire and anxious to add what the Persians had earlier controlled in northwestern India, burst through the northwestern passes in 326 B.C.E. (providing thereby the first certain date in Indian history), India was composed of many rival states covering both the north and the south. He encountered and defeated some of them in the Indus Valley and Punjab and heard accounts of others. Alexander's campaign against Porus, king of West Punjab, with his large army and his battalions of war elephants, was the most difficult of his career. When the proud but wounded and defeated Porus was brought before him, Alexander asked how he wished to be treated. Though barely able to stand, Porus boldly replied: "As befits me—like a king!" Alexander was so impressed that he gave him back his kingdom as an ally, a pact that Porus kept to his death. Alexander's invasion was undertaken with a strong sense of mission, to unite East and West and to create a cosmopolitan fusion of cultures, a plan he had already begun to carry out by merging Greek, Persian, and Medean elements and by taking a wife and a male companion from Persia. He encouraged his 10,000 Greek and Macedonian soldiers to take Indian wives, in keeping with his larger vision, although like most soldiers far from home, his men probably needed little urging. Greek genes were also infused into the already hybrid Indian population from the Greek-ruled kingdoms in the northwest, which survived for some three centuries after this time. Even now, blond hair and blue eyes occasionally turn up in the population of northwestern India, although they are probably more likely to have come from subsequent invaders from Persia, Central Asia, or even Britain.

Nevertheless, the Greek impact is symbolic of the continuous link between India and the West, not only in common linguistic roots but in physical and cultural terms too. Hellenic-style art continued to be produced by the Greek kingdoms in the northwest, such as Bactria and Ghandara, and influenced the evolution of Buddhist art in India. Indian philosophical ideas circulated more widely in the West as a result of the link that Alexander's invasion strengthened, although they clearly influenced classical Greece, including philosophy, mathematics, and medicine. Alexander was himself a widely curious person. Realizing the Indian penchant for philosophy, he summoned Indian scholars to instruct and debate with him and recorded much of what he learned and observed for his own teacher, Aristotle. One Indian sage whom he summoned refused at first to come, saying that Alexander's evident preoccupation with conquest and empire could leave little place for philosophy. Alexander had him brought in, and the two men apparently impressed each other enough that they became friends and companions until Alexander's untimely death in 323 B.C.E. Before his homesick and rebellious troops obliged him to turn back, far short of his goal of descending the Ganges to the Bay of Bengal, he made several alliances (as with Porus), set up several Hellenic kingdoms in the northwest, and received a number of Indian princes, among them the young

Advice to Indian Princes

The Arthashastra, in addition to its advice to princes on how to seize and hold power and to outwit rivals by often unscrupulous means, stresses the responsibilities of the king to take care of his people.

> The king's pious vow is readiness in action,
> his sacrifice the discharge of his duty. . . .
> In the happiness of his subjects, his welfare.
> The king's good is not that which pleases him,
> but that which pleases his subjects.
>
> Therefore the king should be ever active,
> and should strive for prosperity,
> for prosperity depends on effort,
> and failure on the reverse. . . .
>
> A single wheel cannot turn,
> and so government is possible only with assistance.
> Therefore a king should appoint councillors
> and listen to their advice.

Source: A. L. Basham, *The Wonder That Was India,* 3d ed. (London: Macmillan, 1968), p. 89.

Chandragupta Maurya, who was to found the first Indian empire and the Maurya dynasty.

The Maurya Dynasty

By 322 B.C.E. Chandragupta had emerged as head of an empire that included the whole of Hindustan and most of the northwest, with its capital on the Ganges at Pataliputra, near modern Patna in what is now the state of Bihar. The age of heroic chivalry, as recorded in the Vedas and the epics, was long passed, and the time of ruthless power politics had arrived. One may also guess this from the *Arthashastra,* a book attributed to Chandragupta's prime minister, Kautilya. This is one of the earliest samples we have of what was to become a genre, a handbook for rulers with advice on how to seize, hold, and manipulate power, of which the most famous in the West is Machiavelli's *The Prince.* The *Arthashastra* also deals with the wise and humane administration of justice, but the text we have was composed by many hands over several centuries after Kautilya's time, although he may well have been the author of a now-lost original. In any case, empire building is a rough game everywhere, and such a manual fits the circumstances of the time. About a century later across the Himalayas, it is paralleled very closely by a similar text, *The Book of Lord Shang,* and the doctrines of Li Si, prime minister to China's first imperial unifier, Qin Shih Huangdi, as warring states there too were welded into an empire by conquest.

In both India and China in the sixth century B.C.E. warfare and political rivalries had begun to break up the institutions and values of an earlier age. This period saw the emergence of new philosophical and religious efforts to restore the social order (Confucianism in China) or to provide an escape from worldly strife through contemplation, mysticism, and otherworldly salvation (Daoism in China, Buddhism and the Hindu revival in India). These religious and philosophical developments are dealt with in Chapter 2. In India, we know very little about actual political forms or events during the centuries before the rise of the Mauryan Empire. The documents we have are, as indicated earlier, concerned almost exclusively with heroic deeds or metaphysical and religious matters. Politics and the rise and fall of kingdoms, by their nature ephemeral and transitory, were perhaps considered not important enough to record by comparison with the eternal quest for the mysteries of man and the universe, the consistent Indian emphasis. We know the names of some of the states immediately preceding the Mauryan conquest, including the kingdom of Magadha in the central Ganges Valley, which

seems to have been Chandragupta's original base. But even for Mauryan India we are dependent for actual descriptions largely on Greek sources, including surviving fragments of *The Book of Megasthenes.* Megasthenes was posted by Alexander's successor Seleucus Nicator to Chandragupta's court at Pataliputra.

Pataliputra and the Glory of Mauryan India

The book itself is lost, but later Greek and Latin writers drew on *The Book of Megasthenes* extensively. It is the earliest description we have of India by an outsider. In Megasthenes' time and for some two centuries or more after, Pataliputra was probably the largest and most sophisticated city and center of culture in the world, rivaled in its later days perhaps only by the Han dynasty capital at Chang'an (see Chapter 5) and larger than anything in the West, as the Greek accounts state. It may have been larger than imperial Rome at its height and was said to be 22 miles on each side within its wooden walls. It was the seat of a famous university and library, to which scholars came, reputedly, from all over the civilized world, a city of magnificent palaces, temples, gardens, and parks. Megasthenes describes a highly organized bureaucratic system that controlled the economic and social as well as political life of Mauryan India, complete with a secret service to spy on potential dissidents, suspected criminals, and corrupt or ineffective officials. But he clearly admired Chandragupta for his conscientious administration of justice and for his imperial style. The emperor presided personally over regular sessions at court where cases were heard and petitions presented, and ruled on disputes in similar fashion on his travels around the empire. His enormous palace at Pataliputra was a splendid complex, and visitors were awed by its magnificence and by the throngs of courtiers, councilors, and guests at state receptions.

Pataliputra was surrounded by a huge wall with 570 towers and 64 gates. All mines and forests were owned and managed by the state, and there were large state farms and state granaries, shipyards, and factories for spinning and weaving cotton cloth, all supervised by appropriate government departments. To guard against corruption and favoritism, departments were supposed to be headed by more than one chief, and officials were to be transferred often. Even prostitution was controlled by the state. Megasthenes describes Mauryan India as a place of great wealth and prosperity and remarks on the bustling trade and rich merchants. By this time, if not before, there was already an extensive seaborne trade as well, perhaps extending to Southeast

Ashoka's Goals

Ashoka had edicts inscribed on rocks and pillars at widely scattered locations all over India stating official policy and giving instructions and advice. In one he recounts his own conversion and outlines his new goals.

When the king, of gracious mien and Beloved of the Gods, had been consecrated eight years, Kalinga was conquered. 150,000 people were taken captive, 100,000 were killed and many more died. Just after the taking of Kalinga, the Beloved of the Gods began to follow righteousness, to love righteousness, to give instruction in righteousness. When an unconquered country is conquered, people are killed. . . . That the Beloved of the Gods finds very pitiful and grievous. . . . If anyone does him wrong it will be forgiven as far as it can be forgiven. The Beloved of the Gods even reasons with the forest tribes in his empire and seeks to reform them. . . . The Beloved of the Gods considers that the greatest of all victories is the victory of righteousness.

Source: A. L. Basham, *The Wonder That Was India*, 3d ed. (London: Macmillan, 1968), pp. 53–54.

Asia, and a large seaport city in Bengal, Tamralipiti, close to the mouth of the Ganges not far from modern Calcutta. Roads were essential to hold the empire together, and by Mauryan times the main trunk road of India had been built from Tamralipiti along the Ganges Valley to Pataliputra, Banaras, Delhi, through Punjab, and on to the borders of Afghanistan. Other routes branched southward, on to the mouth of the Indus, linking together all the chief cities of Hindustan. The road system was apparently well maintained, marked with milestones, provided with wells and rest houses at regular intervals, and planted with trees to provide shade. Megasthenes says that famine was unknown, although it seems more likely merely that he did not hear of it during his years there. Until the recent development of cheap bulk transport, famine was endemic everywhere in the world whenever drought, floods, unseasonable frosts, or insect plagues made for crop shortages, and northern India is especially prone to drought, given the fickleness of the monsoon rains.

A CLOSER LOOK

The Emperor Ashoka, "Beloved of the Gods"

Chandragupta died about 297 B.C.E.; we do not know the exact year, and one legend has it that he wearied of affairs of state and became a wandering ascetic, in the Indian tradition, for the last few years of his life. The empire was further expanded and consolidated by his son Bindusara, who maintained the Greek connection and exchanged gifts with Antiochus I, the Seleucid king of Syria. But the greatest Mauryan ruler was Chandragupta's grandson Ashoka, one of the great kings of world history. Here, however, is another reminder of the traditional Indian lack of interest in political history. Ashoka was perhaps the greatest Indian ruler ever, and yet he was all but forgotten until his rediscovery by British antiquarians and archaeologists in the later nineteenth century, thanks to Ashoka's habit of inscribing his name and imperial edicts on rocks and pillars, which he set up all over his immense empire. He came to the throne about 269 B.C.E. and spent the first several years of his rule in military campaigns to round out the empire by incorporating the south. According to his own rock-cut inscriptions, Ashoka saw and was grieved by the carnage that his lust for more power had brought. His campaign against the Kalingas of Orissa and northern Andhra in the northern Deccan Plateau was apparently a turning point. After the campaign he foreswore further territorial aggression in favor of what he called "the conquest of righteousness." Ashoka was converted to the teachings of the Buddha, who had died four centuries earlier, and vowed to spend the rest of his life, and his great imperial power and prestige, in spreading those noble truths.

The beautifully carved stones and pillars that presumably marked his empire extend far into the south, well beyond Andhra, and may suggest that he added to his military conquests those of the spirit. We do not

Perhaps the best-known samples of Mauryan art are the pillars erected by the emperor Ashoka, usually bearing Buddhist edicts and surmounted by sculpted figures. This triad of royal lions in stone, still used as an official symbol of India, formed the capital of one of Ashoka's columns and effectively captures the splendor of Mauryan India. The base is a Buddhist symbol, a stylized lotus; the lotus grows in mud and slime but produces an ethereal white blossom, thus representing the Buddha's message of the triumph of the soul over earthly ties. (Stella Snead/Archaeological Survey of India)

know to what extent the south was ruled from Pataliputra during his time, although a Mauryan governor was appointed for the southern provinces. Ashoka clearly felt a sense of mission, not only to spread Buddhism but also to set an example of righteousness in government that could persuade others elsewhere to follow it—a more humane form of imperialism. He declared that all people everywhere were his children ("brothers and sisters" might perhaps have been less pretentious!), and he softened the harsher aspects of Chandragupta's police-state methods of control. He advocated the ancient Indian ideal of nonviolence (adopted also by the Buddha), urged pilgrimages as a substitute for hunting, and encouraged the spread of vegetarianism. But he kept his army, law courts, and systems of punishment, including execution for major crimes, and remained an emperor in every sense, with his feet firmly in the world of politics, even though his mind reached out to higher and more worthy goals. Nevertheless, his reign was remarkable for its humanity and its vision. The modern Republic of India appropriately adopted for its state seal the sculptured lions from the capital of one of Ashoka's pillars. Ashoka also sent explicitly Buddhist missions to Ceylon, and missionaries later went to Burma and Java. They converted the first two countries almost entirely to that faith, which they still hold, while establishing Buddhism as a new religion in much of the rest of Southeast Asia. Indian traders and adventurers, as well as priests and scholars, also carried Indian high culture in art, literature, written language, and statecraft to Southeast Asia. This cultural diffusion from India marked the beginning of literate civilization, in the Indian mode, in much of that extensive region, an origin still evident in many respects.

Kushans and Greeks

Soon after Ashoka's death about 232 B.C.E., the Mauryan Empire seems to have disintegrated into civil war among provincial governors, although the Mauryan name continued through several successive rulers at Pataliputra. By about 180 B.C.E. India had returned to its more normal patterns of separate regional kingdoms. The northwest was again invaded by Greeks, descendants of groups left behind by Alexander. Northern India was subsequently invaded by new groups of outsiders, the Sakas (Scythians) from West-Central Asia, and other originally nomadic peoples from East-Central Asia who were driven from their pasture lands by the ancestors of the Mongols and by the rise of the first Chinese empire, the Qin, in the late third century. One such group at about 100 B.C.E. crossed the passes into Kashmir and down onto the Indian Plain, where they defeated the Greek, Saka, and Indian kingdoms and welded most of the north into a new empire, the Kushan dynasty. The Kushans restored much of the former Mauryan grandeur, ruling also from Pataliputra, but they too declined after some three centuries, and by about 200 C.E. the north was once again, like the south, a regional patchwork. The Kushans adopted and promoted Buddhism and disseminated it to their former homelands in Central Asia, from which it later reached China. In other respects, like nearly all invaders or conquerors of India, they became thoroughly Indianized, not only through their adoption of the other aspects of Indian culture and language but also through widespread intermarriage, adding still further to the hybrid character of the population. The most obvious and enduring legacy of the Kushans is probably the magnificent Buddhist sculpture produced under their rule and patronage. It is interesting also for its clear traces of Greek and Hellenistic artistic influences still important in India in the time of the Kushans, deriving both from the remaining Greek-style kingdoms in the northwest and from direct contact with the Hellenic world by sea.

Throughout the centuries after Alexander, Greek traders and travelers visited India on a regular basis. Greek ships carried Indian goods to the Mediterranean: spices, precious stones, incense, brasswork, fine cotton textiles, ivory, peacocks, monkeys, and even larger wild animals. Indian philosophers visited Mediterranean and Levantine cities, perhaps making some contribution to the Western intellectual heritage from a culture where religion and concern for the individual's relationship to God and to eternity have always been of prime importance. In return, there seems little reason to doubt the claim of Indian Christians that their early church was begun by Thomas the Apostle, who probably reached India and founded there what may well be hence the world's oldest Christian community. The trip from Suez—or from Alexandria, where we know the apostles preached—was routine in the first century C.E. India was connected to the Greco-Roman world, and it would

Yakshis, the goddess of living waters. The genius of Indian sculpture was already established in Harappan times but was further developed in subsequent centuries and millennia. This goddess figure is a fine sample of the grace and voluptuousness that, even under alien Kushan rule in the second century C.E., Indian sculptors were able to create in stone, as they did later under the Guptas. The small figures at the top are drawing lots for marriage. A husband is in the birdcage, held by the love goddess, and signifying "I've caught him!" as her sweet smile also says. (Indian Museum, Calcutta)

be strange if none of the apostles had included it in carrying out the command recorded in Mark 16:15: "Go ye into all the world and preach the gospel to every creature." To this day, a large proportion of Indian Christians, clustered in the southwest near the ports the Greeks and Romans used, carry the surname Thomas.

Our most important source for this period of Indian history is a Greek handbook for traders and travelers to India called the *Periplus of the Erythrean Sea,* dated about 80 C.E., which gives sailing directions, information on prices and sources for Indian goods, and brief descriptions of Indian culture. Large hoards of Roman coins, to pay for India's exports, and Roman pottery have been found at many ports along the west coast, from Mannar in Ceylon through Cochin and Calicut to the Bombay area and now-abandoned ports south of the Indus mouth.

Standing Buddha from Gandhara, a Greek-ruled kingdom of the second and first centuries B.C.E. in the northwest. Notice the close similarity in style to Hellenic sculpture, including the conventional representation of the folds of the garment and the generally realistic portrayal. (Lahore Museum, Pakistan)

Southern India and the City of Madurai

The south was protected against pressures from successive states or empires in the north by the Deccan Plateau and its fringing mountains, the Vindhya and Satpura ranges, punctuated by the Narbada (Narmada) and Tapti rivers as further barriers. There was also fierce southern resistance to the repeated attempts at conquest from the north. We know very little about this lower half of India before the time of Ashoka. By then it was clear that southern cultures and states, although divided into rival groups, were fully as rich and sophisticated as those of the Aryan-influenced north. They shared what was by the third or second century B.C.E. a common Indian civilization, including Hinduism, philosophy, values, art forms, and material culture. The three largest political states of the south were Chola, Pandya, and Pallava, which vied with each other for regional dominance but were never able to unite the whole area under the control of any one of them. Each maintained extensive trade relations by sea, mainly with Southeast Asia, and the cultural, economic, religious, and political lives of each centered in their respective capitals, which were dominated by temple complexes. Of these, probably the largest and best-preserved was the Pandya capital of Madurai.

The fullest and most detailed account of any ancient Indian city is included in an early Tamil poem of the third century C.E. called *The Garland of Madurai,* which may be summarized in part as follows:

The poet enters the city by its great gate, the posts of which are carved with the images of the goddess Lakshmi. It is a festival day, and the city is gay with flags; some, presented by the king to commemorate brave deeds, fly over the houses of captains; others wave over the shops which sell toddy [a fermented drink made from the blossom of the palm tree]. The streets are broad rivers of people of every race, buying and selling in the market place or singing to the music of wandering minstrels.

The drum beats and a royal procession passes down the street, with elephants leading and the sound of conchs [shell trumpets]. An unruly elephant breaks his chain and tosses like a ship in an angry sea until he is brought under control. Chariots follow, with prancing horses and fierce footmen. Stall keepers ply their trade, selling sweet cakes, garlands of flowers, scented powder, and rolls of betel nut [to chew]. Old women go from house to house selling nosegays and trinkets. Noblemen drive through the streets in their chariots, their gold-sheathed swords flashing, wearing brightly dyed garments and wreaths of flowers. The jewels of the perfumed women watching from balconies and turrets flash in the sun.

People flock to the temples to worship to the sound of music, laying flowers before the images. Craftsmen work in their shops, bangle-makers, goldsmiths, cloth weavers, coppersmiths, flower sellers, wood carvers, and painters. Food shops are busily selling mangoes, sugar candy, cooked rice, and chunks of cooked meat. [Note that at this period, only some of the more pious Hindus were strict vegetarians.] In the evening, the city's prostitutes entertain their patrons with dancing and singing to the accompaniment of the lute. The streets are filled with music. Drunken villagers, in town for the festival, reel about in the streets. Respectable women visit the temples in the evening with their children and friends, carrying lighted lamps as offerings. They dance in the temple courts, which resound with their singing and chatter.

At last the city sleeps . . . all but the ghosts and goblins who haunt the dark and the housebreakers, armed with rope ladders, swords, and chisels. But the watchmen are also vigilant, and the city passes the night in peace. Morning comes with the sounds of brahmins intoning their sacred verses. The wandering bands renew their singing, and the shopkeepers open their booths. The toddy-sellers ply their trade for thirsty early morning travelers. The drunkards stagger to their feet. All over the city the sound is heard of doors opening. Women sweep the faded flowers of the festival from their courtyards. The busy everyday life of the city is resumed.[1]

This gives a vivid picture of what urban life must really have been like; with few adjustments, it could serve as a description of a festival day in a small Indian city even now.

Ceylon

The island of Ceylon (called Sri Lanka since 1975, reviving an ancient name for the country) lies within view of the tip of southern India, only some 20 miles across the shallow Palk Strait via a disconnected chain of islands. Nevertheless the two countries have always been separate politically, and Ceylon developed a distinctive culture and sense of separate identity even though it remained, understandably, a part of greater Indian culture. Sometime in the sixth century B.C.E. a Sanskrit- or Aryan-speaking prince named Vijaya came to Ceylon by sea from northwestern India with a large band of followers and established a kingdom. It is likely that Indian merchants had visited Ceylon earlier and perhaps settled there, but we have no record of such earlier contact. The followers of Vijaya called themselves Sinhala ("lion people") and became the dominant inhabitants of Ceylon as the Sinhalese (Singhalese). This is also the name of their Indo-European language, which is related to those of northern India. They

Tamil Love Poetry

Southern India was producing superb poetry very early, although most of what has survived dates only from about the third century C.E. Here is a sample from that period, a young man's praise of his sweetheart's cooking.

At every post before the house
is tied the gentle calf of a crooked-horn buffalo.
There dwells my sweetheart, curving and lovely,
languid of gaze, with big round earrings
and little rings on her tiny fingers.

She has cut the leaves of the garden plantain
and split them in pieces down the stalk
to serve as platters for the meal.
Her eyes are filled with the smoke of cooking.
Her brow, fair as the crescent moon,
is covered with drops of sweat.

She wipes it away with the hem of her garment
and stands in the kitchen and thinks of me.
Come in then if you want a good meal!
You'll see her smile and show her tiny
sharp teeth, whom I long to kiss.

Source: A. L. Basham, *The Wonder That Was India,* 3d ed. (London: Macmillan, 1968), p. 467.

brought with them not only the literacy, writing forms, and religion of late Vedic northern India but much of the rest of its culture and technology, including the knowledge of irrigation and the cultivation of rice. They were probably joined shortly by a second wave of settlement from Bengal, which merged with them. The Sinhalese soon displaced the earlier and far less technically developed Neolithic inhabitants of the island, the Veddas, a few survivors of whom still live in the remoter jungles, although in the earlier centuries there was considerable intermarriage.

By the first century B.C.E. and in subsequent centuries the Sinhalese constructed an extensive system of irrigated rice agriculture, centered in the northern half of the island with its capital at Anuradhapura and a secondary urban center at Polonnaruwa. This area was part of the so-called Dry Zone of Ceylon, where permanent field agriculture is impossible without irrigation but where fertile soils, level land, and an unbroken growing season of strong sun and high temperatures can produce high crop yields if water is available. Considerable rain falls there in a brief period of three months during the northeast monsoon of winter, leaving the rest of the year mainly dry. The Sinhalese kingdom constructed large reservoirs called *tanks* to catch the winter rain and stream runoff and then to distribute it to rice fields through an intricate system of canals. Dams also diverted water from the few year-round streams that flowed through the area. The population of the Dry Zone grew substantially, and Anuradhapura at its height about the tenth century C.E. may have contained 100,000 people or more, while Ceylon as a whole may have reached as much as 3 or 4 million. It was only with such a large population, controlled by the state through *corvée* (conscript labor), that the massive irrigation works could be built and maintained, and the many large palaces and temples at Anuradhapura constructed. Nowhere else in the premodern world was there such a dense concentration of irrigation facilities at such a high technical level, but it was dependent on maintaining state control over mass labor.

Ceylon was the first area beyond India to which Buddhism spread. The pious legend is that Ananda, a disciple of the Buddha, brought the message himself in the Buddha's own lifetime, but Buddhism probably did not extend beyond northern India, and almost certainly not to Ceylon, until Ashoka's time in the third century B.C.E., when missionaries were specifically dispatched to Ceylon and Burma. The Sinhalese rapidly accepted and have retained Buddhism. They produced beautiful works of sculpture and architecture in the Buddhist-Indian tradition, including the world's largest mound temples or stupas and colossal statues of the Buddha and his disciples. The great stupa at Anuradhapura is bigger than all but one of the pyramids of ancient Egypt; it is

The great stupa—a Buddhist mound temple—at Anuradhapura; it was restored in the twentieth century, but there are many others like it nearby. (R. Murphey)

surrounded for miles by others nearly as big and by a host of beautiful and monumental stone buildings and large baths. All of this gorgeous display suggests large and consistent surpluses from the agricultural system to pay for the costs of construction and art and an economy that could spare labor for such purposes. The classical Sinhalese chronicles, compiled and preserved by Buddhist monks, deal mainly with the pious acts of successive kings, especially their building or endowing of temples, but indirectly they reflect a prosperous and generally controlled society.

Given the short and easy journey from southern India to Ceylon, continuous interaction probably began before the fifth century B.C.E. By or before the Christian era, the northern tip of Ceylon had been settled by people from the Dravidian Tamil-speaking area of southern India, who practiced their own form of irrigated agriculture based mainly on wells. They became the dominant inhabitants of the Jaffna Peninsula and the immediately adjacent parts of the north but retained their cultural ties with southern India as well as their Hinduism. Immigration from southern India continued for several centuries, and there was some intermarriage with the Sinhalese. These two groups of Indian immigrants, Sinhalese and Tamils, coexisted for most of Ceylon's history, until their differences were made into a violent political issue in the 1950s.

The Sinhala kingdom based on Anuradhapura periodically controlled the Tamil areas of the north but had to protect itself against intermittent raiding from the far larger Tamil kingdoms in southern India. These raids often stimulated or increased internal dissension when rival Sinhalese claimants to the throne made common cause with the invaders, especially after about the sixth century C.E. The Chola Empire, which arose in the early centuries of the Christian era in southern India, launched a particularly destructive invasion of Ceylon in the eleventh century that sacked Anuradhapura in 1017. The Sinhalese capital was moved to Polonnaruwa, from which base the local forces finally drove the Cholas out of the country by 1070. In the following century King Parakrama Bahu (r. 1153–1186) unified the whole of Ceylon under his control from his capital at Polonnaruwa, invaded southern India and Burma, and constructed huge, new irrigation works and public buildings that made his capital almost as impressive as

Anuradhapura had been. But his death was followed by civil war and new and especially destructive invasions from southern India, which, by the thirteenth century, led to the virtual abandonment of the Dry Zone, whose vital irrigation works could no longer be maintained. The much reduced population clustered from then on in the protection of the hills and mountains of southeastern Ceylon, centered around the medieval capital of Kandy, and later in the lowlands around the port of Colombo.

The Guptas and the Empire of Harsha

There was to be one more imperial revival of the Mauryan model in India, the Gupta dynasty, which ruled the north from about 320 to about 550 C.E.. Pataliputra was again the imperial capital and seems again to have played the role of cultural center for surrounding areas. Contact with the West appears to have shrunk or disappeared by this time; Roman vigor had ebbed, and the eastern Roman Empire based in Constantinople went on the defensive and was largely cut off from India by the rise of the Sassanid dynasty in Persia. However,

The art of ancient Ceylon: divine nymphs dropping flowers on the earth, from a mural painting of the fifth century C.E. on the rock face of the fortress of Sigiriya in the southern Dry Zone, and preserved there better than most Indian paintings of the same period, which it closely resembles. (Stella Snead/ Archaeological Survey of India)

there was still extensive trade and cultural exchange with Southeast Asia, although most of it probably took place from the southern Indian kingdoms of Chola, Pandya, and Pallava and from ports on the southeast coast, beyond Guptan imperial control but part of greater Indian culture. As for earlier periods, and given the traditional Indian lack of interest in recording their worldly history, we are dependent on foreign observers for much of what we know about the Gupta period. The chief source is the diary of Fa Xian, a Chinese Buddhist monk who made the long and arduous journey to India via Central Asia and the Himalayas to seek true copies of the Buddhist sutras (scriptures) and who lived and traveled there for six years in the early 400s. A typical literate Chinese, he carefully recorded what he observed at Pataliputra and elsewhere. He gives us a picture of a rich and sophisticated society and its culturally brilliant capital as of the early fifth century, when it was probably at its height.

Life and Culture in the Guptan Period

Fa Xian noted the peacefulness of Guptan India and the mildness of its government. His journal remarks that crime was rare and that one could travel from one end of the empire to another without harm and with no need for travel documents. He made special note of the free hospitals for treatment of the sick, supported by private donations. He also says that all "respectable" people (by which he probably means those of high caste) were vegetarians, a trend that seems to have picked up momentum since the time of Ashoka, but that the lower orders ate meat and hence were regarded as sources of "pollution," an aspect of caste that he was the first outsider to describe. He describes Buddhism as still flourishing but apparently in the process of being reabsorbed into the Hinduism from which it had originally sprung. In general, his account shows us a prosperous, tranquil, and smoothly operating society, which probably contrasted with the China of his time, still suffering from the chaos after the fall of the Han dynasty and well before the re-unification and new splendor of the Tang revival.

The Gupta period was the golden age of Sanskrit literature, including poetry and drama, and of classical Indian sculpture and monumental building, although unfortunately only fragments of the art have survived the troubled centuries since. This cultural flowering was equally vigorous in the south, beyond Gupta control, and in both south and north seems to have taken the form of a renaissance of much of the Mauryan grandeur of the past. Kalidasa, widely acclaimed as India's greatest poet and playwright, lived and worked in the late fourth and early fifth centuries, near the peak of Gupta

Standing bronze Buddha, Mathurā. Gupta, Phopnar, 6th century. C.E. (National Museum of India, New Delhi, India/ Bridgeman Art Library)

vigor and a further expression of the cultural brilliance of the age. Many of his works have survived, with fragments of some others, perhaps because they were so widely copied. They still make fresh and enchanting reading—moving commentaries on the foibles of human existence—and indeed bear comparison with Shakespeare's plays and poems.

The Collapse of the Guptas

By about 550 C.E. the Gupta power was destroyed by new invaders, the so-called White Huns (probably Iranians or Turks from Central Asia), one more group in the long succession of ethnically and culturally different outsiders drawn to India by its wealth and sophistication and then woven into the hybrid Indian fabric. Like earlier and later invaders, they came from the west, through the only easy entrance into the subcontinent, the passes that punctuate the northwest frontier. As the linguistic tie still reminds us, India's relations were and remained overwhelmingly with the West since at least Harappan times and, except for the sea connection with Southeast Asia, hardly at all with the East and with China, the other major cultural center of Asia. Buddhism did move from India, first into Central Asia and then into China by Han times, but it seems to have carried very little of Indian culture with it except for some art forms, while almost nothing of Chinese culture seems to have penetrated into India. Cotton, native to India, spread to China only some 3,000 years after the Indus people first wove it into cloth. Trade between the two societies, the other common vehicle of cultural exchange, was minimal and indirect. The reason is clear from a glance at a map: the world's highest mountains lie between India and China, and behind them the desert or alpine wastelands of Xinjiang and Tibet. It is in fact a very long and exceptionally difficult way between the centers of Indian and Chinese civilizations, from the plains of Hindustan to the lower Yellow and Yangzi river valleys. The shorter route from eastern India through Burma and into mountainous southwest China (still a long way from the Chinese center) has proved even more difficult, with its combination of mountains, deep gorges, and rain forest, and has never carried more than a trickle of faint and indirect contact.

With the collapse of the Gupta Empire, India reverted once more to its regional structures. The new invaders from Central Asia did not succeed in building their own empire, and for a time there was political chaos, but the first half of the seventh century saw a final indigenous effort at unification. This was the reign of Harsha (606–648), who in a series of campaigns joined the separate kingdoms of the north together and presided over a notable reflowering of Sanskrit literature and art. Harsha also encouraged Buddhism, and the Chinese Buddhist monk Xuanzang visited his court, leaving a valuable account of it and of the contemporary India through which he traveled. His journal gives an admiring picture of Harsha as a charismatic, energetic, and able administrator and an impressive emperor of his domain, through which he made repeated tours to supervise its government. Like earlier and later Indian emperors, he held court wherever he went, to hear complaints and dispense justice. Like them, he lived in luxury and pomp but loved literature and philosophy and was a generous patron; he even found time to write plays himself. By this time, Xuanzang's account shows Buddhism declining and Hinduism again dominant, but, perhaps because of the newness and brevity of Harsha's rule, law and order were not as well kept as in Guptan times. Xuanzang reports banditry and was himself robbed twice on his travels. Harsha's empire was so much his own creation that when he died in 648, leaving no heirs, it disintegrated into factional fighting.

Women in Ancient India

Medieval and early modern India tended to fit the popular stereotype applied to most traditional Asian societies: heavy male dominance and female subservience or even servitude. That had been changing quickly throughout twentieth-century Asia and was, like most stereotypes, not totally accurate even for the past. In particular, it overlooks the major part nearly all women played in the basic Asian institution of the family—a private as opposed to public role, but often critically important—and overlooks also the many women writers and performers of other public roles, including political power. However, ancient India was substantially different from the later period of Indian history in this respect. There is much evidence to show that early Indian society, especially in the south, was matriarchal; women held important economic and social power; property, status, and family names often descended through the female line. Survivals of this ancient pattern remain in parts of southern India today. From Vedic times, the Aryan north was more clearly patriarchal, and women were conventionally seen as subject to their parents, husbands, and male relatives. But they had some control over personal property, and some women even owned businesses. Women could not serve as priests but were free to become nuns, several of whom were notable poets and scholars. The *Upanishads,* treatises dating from about the seventh century B.C.E., tell the story of an exceptionally learned woman, Gargi Vacaknavi, who took an active part in discussions with the sage Yajnavalkya and outdistanced all her male counterparts. Other women attended lectures by sages and mastered the Vedas. Goddesses were as important as gods in Vedic religion, and a goddess's name was commonly recited before that of a god, a practice that still persists.

By the Mauryan era, however, the scope for women in religious and intellectual pursuits seems to have been reduced. Convention shifted to an emphasis on marriage

In Praise of Women

A passage in the Mahabharata extols the virtues of a wife.

> The wife is half the man, the best of friends,
> the root of the three ends of life,
> and of all that will help him in the other world.
> With a wife a man does mighty deeds,
> with a wife a man finds courage.
> A wife is the safest refuge;
> a man aflame with sorrow in his soul or sick with disease
> finds comfort in his wife as a man parched with heat
> finds relief in water.
> Even a man in the grip of rage will not be harsh to a woman,
> remembering that on her depend the joys of love, happiness, and virtue.
> For a woman is the everlasting field
> in which the self is born.

Some centuries later the Laws of Manu, written about the second century C.E., reflect the growing emphasis on the domesticity and dependency of women.

> She should always be cheerful, and skillful in her domestic duties with her
> household vessels well cleaned and her hand tight on the pursestrings. In
> season and out of season her lord, who wed her with sacred rites, ever
> gives happiness to his wife, both here and in the other world. Though he
> be uncouth and prone to pleasure, though he have no good points at all,
> the virtuous wife should ever worship her lord as a god.

Source: A. L. Basham, *The Wonder That Was India,* 3d ed. (London: Macmillan, 1968), pp. 181–182.

and the care of the family as the proper female role, although many upper-class women continued to be educated privately or independently, and several wrote poetry and drama that were widely read. Others learned music—both performance and composition—dancing, and painting. In early Vedic times (we know too little about society in Harappan times to speculate about it), unmarried men and women seem to have mixed freely. By the time of the *Arthashastra* (third century B.C.E.) upper-class women were more circumscribed by convention, although widows were still free to marry. By late Gupta times (sixth century C.E.) restrictions on women had increased, and widows could no longer remarry. Women were to be cherished, but protected—and restricted—a trend that apparently had begun under Mauryan rule, at least in the north. In the south, women have remained freer and less submissive.

The freest women in ancient India were probably the courtesans (high-class prostitutes). In many traditional societies, including India, they were usually well educated and well versed in the classics, the arts of music, dance, poetry and its composition, flower arranging, the composition of riddles and other mental puzzles, and even fencing. There were lower grades of prostitutes, but the standard was generally high. As in China, Japan, and the classical West, such women were often praised for their learning and quick verbal wit, sometimes even more than for their beauty. Even the Buddha is said to have chosen to dine with a famous courtesan rather than with the city fathers, no doubt duller company. Many of the courtesans were celebrated poets, but most of them were considered especially sensitive and as having "great souls."

Another group of women were hereditary dancers in the service of temples; most of them also served as prostitutes, but in any case they never married, having dedicated themselves to the god. Dance was a particularly important religious ritual in India, as well as a beautiful art form. The god Shiva was thought to have created the world through his cosmic dance and to dance on the harvest floor as the spirit of life and of creation. From at least the Gupta period, classical Indian dance came to be associated with the temple dancers, servants of the god but a special class of women of whom some were also prostitutes. They were honored and admired for their art but socially discriminated against, and because of this association, other women were discouraged from dancing until recent years, when the classical dance forms have seen a national revival and have once again become respectable.

The custom of *sati* (suttee), wives burning themselves to death on their husband's funeral pyre, does not seem to have been the fate of most widows at any period in Indian history. Although it was known in ancient India, as it was in Sumer and in ancient China, it appears to have been uncommon; when it was practiced, it was mainly as part of the custom of burning or burying all the followers, retainers, horses, and prized possessions of a dead ruler or aristocrat with him. *Sati* was relatively rare until late Gupta times, when widow remarriage had begun to be strongly discouraged or prohibited, as it had not been before. It became more common thereafter, although it was supposed to be voluntary, as a mark of exceptional fidelity. Social and family pressure, plus the emptiness and often the material hardship especially of a young widow's life, doubtless added other incentives. *Sati* horrified early Western observers, and the British suppressed it in the nineteenth century, but it was not characteristic of ancient India. Many ancient and even medieval Indian writers and poets condemned it, and in the end the Hindu renaissance and reform movement of the nineteenth century turned Indian opinion against it.

The Indian Heritage

The building and maintaining of empires exacts a heavy human cost everywhere. India's return to its more normal regionalism with the collapse of the Gupta Empire and the death of Harsha was hardly a tragedy, but it leaves the historian, whose data are only fragmentary, to try to deal with a confused tapestry that, like India's history and culture as a whole, has many threads. The revival of regional kingdoms did, however, encourage the continued development of the rich regional cultures that make up the Indian fabric. Given India's size and diversity, it is not surprising that the subcontinent has only very briefly been united into a single empire, although even under Ashoka and under the British some areas remained outside imperial control. We are accustomed to thinking of Europe as properly composed of a large number of separate states and cultures, despite the heritage of common Roman rule over much of it for some four centuries and despite its common membership in the Greek, Roman, and Christian traditions. India too has long shared common traditions, including the universal spread of Hinduism, and like Europe has experienced successive efforts at unification by conquest. But the strength of separate regional cultures and states remained at least as great as in Europe, reinforced by different languages, literatures, and political rivalries. India's more recent success in building a modern state, or rather the three states of Pakistan, India, and Bangladesh, contrasts with the continued political division of Europe but still overlies regional differences that remain important and legitimate, each with its own proud tradition reaching back before Ashoka. In these terms, there is nothing improper or backward about regional separation, for India or for Europe, and especially in an area the size and variety of the subcontinent. India, like Europe, would be the poorer without its array of different cultural and regional traditions. Their separate contributions in literature, philosophy, and the arts in the centuries of political disunity after the death of Harsha continued to enrich the varied tapestry of Indian civilization. But the political picture we have of those centuries is confusing, frequently changing, and plagued by a severe shortage of information.

Ancient and classical India as a whole had a deep respect for learning and for education, beginning with literacy and mathematics and continuing to philosophy and the study of the Vedas. But education was a privilege enjoyed only by the upper classes, and after the Vedic age for the most part only by males, as in nearly all premodern societies. As mentioned earlier, courtesans were highly educated and widely read as well as accomplished dancers, singers, musicians, and poets; their role was to entertain their patrons in the fullest sense of the word. However, most people were peasant villagers, uninvolved with any of these upper-class matters, but with their own active communal lives. The several Greek and Chinese travelers to classical India who have left accounts describe the rural scene as productive and prosperous and compare it and the lot of villagers favorably with their own homelands. India during these centuries may have been less burdened by mass poverty or by communal tensions than it is now, but we have no way to measure that. Contemporary accounts from that period can, of course, make judgments only in terms of what they knew of conditions elsewhere. Our modern perspectives are different. But the classical accounts we have nearly all stress the relatively high level of material well-being, the orderliness of the society, and its impressive achievements in science, technology, philosophy, and the arts. It is a tradition of which modern Indians are justly proud.

From the modern perspective, classical India seems especially noteworthy for its scientific accomplishments. Earlier beginnings in mathematics were further developed by Gupta times to a high level of sophistication, including a rudimentary algebra and a numeration system using nine digits and a zero, exactly as we use them now and far more efficient than the cumbersome Roman numerals. The Arabs, who transmitted it to the West, called mathematics "the Indian art" (*Hindisat*). Later European science would have been impossible without it. Medieval Indian mathematicians after Harsha's time developed the concepts of negative and positive quantities, worked out square and cube roots, solved quadratic and other equations, understood the mathematical implications of zero and infinity, worked out the value of pi to nine decimal places, and made important steps in trigonometry, sine functions, spherical geometry, and calculus. By the sixth century C.E. Indian astronomers had anticipated Copernicus nearly 1,000 years later in describing a solar-centered planetary system and a rotating Earth in orbit around the sun, knowledge that was absorbed by the Arabs later. The game of chess was invented in India and spread from there westward. Earlier Indian scientists anticipated the classical Greeks in developing an atomic theory of elements, basic to twentieth-century Western science, by the sixth century B.C.E., an imaginative leap into what would become basic modern physics. Traditional Indian medicine had a very extensive pharmacopoeia and used a variety of herbal remedies and drugs only much later discovered and used in the West. Physicians appear to have understood the function of the spinal cord and the nervous system, and successful surgery included cesarean section, complicated bone setting, plastic surgery, and the repair of damaged limbs. Indian surgery remained ahead of Europe until the eighteenth century. In many of the kingdoms or empires, the poor were given free medical care. Vaccination against smallpox was first used in Guptan India, well over 1,000 years before the West. Doctors were highly respected, and the textbook of the famous physician Caraka in the late first century C.E. includes a passage reminiscent of Hippocrates, the classical Greek physician:

> If you want success in your practice . . . you must pray every day on rising and going to bed for the welfare of all beings . . . and strive with all your soul for the health of the sick. You must not betray your patients, even at the cost of your own life. . . . You must be pleasant of speech . . . and thoughtful, always striving to improve your knowledge.
>
> When you go to the home of a patient you should direct your words, mind, intellect, and senses nowhere but to your patient and his treatment. . . . Nothing that happens in the house of the sick man must be told outside, nor must the patient's condition be told to anyone who might do harm by that knowledge.[2]

It is more than possible that the political turmoil of invasions and internal struggles did not greatly affect the lives of most people most of the time. Perhaps it is not terribly important that we have inadequate information to follow in any detail the variety of empires, kingdoms, rivalries, and confusing political changes. What we do have is enough to show us a sophisticated civilization, a remarkably humane set of values, and enough glimpses of the life of the common people to make ancient and classical India indeed a great tradition, one of the major achievements of the human experience. The great British Indologist A. L. Basham says that slavery was less than in any ancient society, and that ancient India was distinguished for its humanity, "a cheerful land which emphasized kindliness and gentleness."[3]

This chapter began by summarizing the origins, flowering, and decline of the Indus civilization from roughly 3000 B.C.E. to about 2000 B.C.E., with its major urban centers at Kalibangan, Harappa, and Mohenjo Daro. The migration of Aryan-speaking peoples from Central Asia into north India after about 1600 B.C.E. produced what is called Vedic culture, which became dominant in most of the north. Regional kingdoms had emerged by about 500 B.C.E., some of which Alexander encountered when he invaded the northwest in 326 B.C.E. By 322 the Mauryan Empire emerged under Chandragupta Maurya and unified most of the north from the imperial capital at Pataliputra in the central Ganges Valley. Chandragupta's grandson Ashoka ruled as emperor from about 269 to c. 232 B.C.E. and extended the empire southward. Troubled by the slaughter occasioned by his conquests, he converted to the nonviolent faith of Buddhism and devoted the rest of his reign to spreading its message. The Mauryan power faded after his death, and both north and south India reverted to regional rule. New Greek and Scythian invaders in the north yielded to another dynasty of conquest, the Kushans, from about 100 B.C.E. to about 200 C.E., while the south and Ceylon supported separate flourishing kingdoms and built impressive architectural monuments. The Gupta dynasty restored much of the Mauryan grandeur in the north from about 320 to 550 C.E., based again at Pataliputra, and Harsha from 606 to 648 reunited the Guptan Empire. After Harsha's death India resumed its more normal political pattern of separate regional kingdoms, where art, learning, philosophy, and commerce continued to flourish.

The Gupta Legacy in the Bay of Bengal Region

After the Gupta realm fragmented into regional units, for the next thousand years an assortment of Hindu, Buddhist, and Muslim groups sought to reestablish political unity across the Gangetic Plain. Among these, the Gupta state stood as a standard of achievement. Gupta successors in the Bengal region of northeastern India patronized Mahayana Buddhism. Under the Pala monarchs (750–1199 C.E.), Nalanda, on the northwestern edge of the Ganges delta, become the preeminent center of Buddhist scholarship and attracted students and pilgrims from all over Asia. Not only was Pala Bengal the home of the diverse Mahayana schools of that age, but it also served as the incubator for an emergent Tantric Hindu-Buddhist tradition, which stressed a highly personalized, often magical, interaction with the powers of the divine.

From the sixth century the kings in southern India consolidated their positions by force or alliance, and then encouraged their subjects to join them in the worship of powerful Hindu deities. Southern India's kings patronized Brahmins, built impressive urban centers, endowed temples, financed artistic expression, and sponsored elaborate court rituals, artistic performance, and exhibitions of scholarship that were basic to the further development of southern Indian culture as well as to the emergence of the area's ports as paramount international ports of trade. In the same era Ceylon Theravada Buddhist sects established branch temples and monasteries in newly settled zones, and supervised the construction of the local irrigation networks that were foundational to the emergence of Sinhalese kingdoms. The Ceylon Buddhist Sangha would become the source for the subsequent spread of Theravada Buddhism into mainland Southeast Asia, where kings also turned to the Buddhist Sangha ("monastic community") in recognition of their ritual and management potential.

These patterns of cultural appropriation in the Bay of Bengal region became more pronounced with the increase in the volume of trade and the proliferation of wealth and societal prosperity. Above all, these regional evolutions in the post-Gupta age show that this was not an era of regional localizations and stagnations as in northern India, but instead demonstrate that there were ways to organize international commerce, cultural exchange, and societal development other than through the rigid political centralizations and royal autocracies that were characteristic of other regions of the globe c. 1500. (For later periods of Indian history, see Chapters 6, 9, 14, 15, 16, 17, 20, and 21.)

Questions

1. Was there a relationship between the Indus Valley civilization and that of Sumer in Mesopotamia? What are the similarities and differences between the two cultures?

2. What are the similarities between Indus Valley society and culture and post-Aryan Indian civilization, especially as demonstrated in southern India's Dravidian culture?

3. It used to be popular to debate "flood theory" and "invasion theory" in explaining the decline and fall of the Indus Valley civilization. Invasion theory especially tried to connect the fall of the Indus Valley societies to invading Aryan warriors. What is the cited evidence against such a conclusion?

4. Why was the Mauryan king Ashoka successful in his rule over India's diverse populations?

5. How has the repeated conquest of northern India by foreign warriors contributed to the South Asian world view? Is this similar to China's view of its periodic "barbarian" invaders, and their consequent impact on China's society and culture?

6. What is the cited evidence that India was in regular contact with the West following the invasion of Alexander the Great, in the Mauryan and post-Mauryan eras? What was the nature of these contacts, and what was their result—from both an Indian and a Western perspective? What effect did the West have on Indian civilization and what impact did India have on the West?

7. Why is the Gupta era frequently regarded as India's "classical age?" What were the contributions of the Gupta era to Asian civilizations, both in India and beyond?

Notes

1. A. L. Basham, *The Wonder That Was India,* 3d ed. (New York: Grove Press, 1959), pp. 203–204.
2. Ibid., p. 500.
3. Ibid., p. 9.

Suggested Web Sites

Ancient Indian History and Culture

http://www.harappa.com/har/har0.html
All one could ever want and more on Indus Valley civilization. More than 1,000 illustrations and excellent descriptive narratives.

http://www.wsu.edu:8080/~dee/(use resource link)
Washington State University world civilization web site, which also includes resource links to Buddhism and Japan. Good selections that introduce India's early history and culture through the Gupta age; includes a bibliography, glossary of terms, historical atlas, and Internet links.

http://www.fordham.edu/halsall/india/indiasbook.html
Excellent sourcebook on India's history and civilization

Suggestions for Further Reading

India

Allchin, B., and Allchin, R. *The Rise of Civilization in India and Pakistan.* Cambridge: Cambridge University Press, 1982.

Auboyer, J. *Daily Life in Ancient India.* London: Weidenfeld and Nicolson, 1965.

Basham, A. L. *The Wonder That Was India,* 4th ed. London: Macmillan, 1968.

Begley, V. and de Puma, R. D., eds. *Rome and India.* Madison: University of Wisconsin Press, 1992.

Bryant, E. *The Quest for the Origins of Vedic Culture.* New York: Oxford University Press, 2001.

Buck, W. *Ramayana.* Berkeley: University of California Press, 1976.

Chakravarti, R. P. *Knowledge and Liberation in Classical Indian Thought.* New York: St Martin's, 2001.

Dutt, A. K., and Selb, M. *Atlas of South Asia.* Boulder, CO: Westview, 1987.

Fa Hsien. *Travels of Fa-hsien.* Trans. H. A. Giles. London: Trubner, 1956.

Gokhale, B. G. *Asoka Maurya.* New York: Twayne, 1966.

Jacobson, G. J. *The Wheel of Civilization.* Princeton: Princeton University Press, 2003.

Kalidasa. *The Cloud Messenger.* Trans. F. Edgerton and E. Edgerton. Ann Arbor: University of Michigan Press, 1964.

Kautilya. *The Arthashastra.* Trans. R. P. Kangle. Bombay: University of Bombay Press, 1969.

Kosambi, D. D. *Ancient India: A History of Its Culture and Civilization.* New York: Pantheon, 1966.

Liu, Xinru. *Ancient China and Ancient India: Trade and Religious Exchange.* New York: Oxford University Press, 1988.

Miller, B. S., ed. and trans. *Theater of Memory: The Plays of Kalidasa.* New York: Columbia University Press, 1984.

———, trans. *The Bhagavadgita.* New York: Columbia University Press, 1986.

Moharty, J. N. *Classical Indian Philosophy.* Lanham, MD: Rowan and Littlefield, 2000.

Nilakana, S. *A History of South India,* 4th ed. Madras: Oxford University Press, 1976.

Possehl, G. L., ed. *Ancient Cities of the Indus.* Durham, N.C.: Carolina Academic Press, 1979.

———. *The Indus Civilization.* Lanham, MD: Rowan and Littlefield, 2002.

Rapson, E. J., ed. *The Cambridge History of India,* vol. 1. Cambridge: Cambridge University Press, 1982.

Singhal, D. P. *A History of the Indian People.* London: Methuen, 1983.

Smith, B. *Classifying the Universe: The Ancient Indian Varna System and the Origins of Caste.* New York: Oxford University Press, 1995.

Thapar, R. *Asoka and the Decline of the Mauryas.* London: Oxford University Press, 1961.

———. *A History of India,* vol. 1. Baltimore: Penguin Books, 1966.

Van Buitenen, J. A. B., trans. *The Bhagavadgita and the Mahabharata.* Chicago: University of Chicago Press, 1981.

Warmington, E. H. *Commerce Between the Roman Empire and India.* Cambridge: Cambridge University Press, 1928.

Woodcock, G. *The Greeks in India.* London: Faber, 1966.

Ceylon

de Silva, K. M. *A History of Sri Lanka.* Delhi: Oxford University Press, 1981.

Murphey, R. "The Ruin of Ancient Ceylon," *Journal of Asian Studies,* vol. 16 (1957): 181–200.

5

The Civilization of Ancient China

This chapter summarizes the beginnings of civilization in China, by about 2000 B.C.E., the rise of the Shang dynasty (c. 1600–1050 B.C.E.), the Zhou dynasty (c. 1050–256 B.C.E.), Confucius the Sage, the period of the Warring States, from about 600 to 221 B.C.E., and the conquest by the Qin in 221 B.C.E. and the nature of its empire, the first to rule all of China. It was replaced after only a brief reign by the Han dynasty (202 B.C.E.–220 C.E.), which conquered southern Manchuria, Korea, Vietnam, and Xinjiang under the emperor Wu Di. Han rise, culture, and collapse, cities in ancient China, and Han achievements in science and technology conclude the chapter.

Chinese civilization arose largely independent of contact with or influences from other areas and early developed its own distinctive form and style. China was effectively isolated by high mountains and deserts along its northwestern, western, and southwestern borders and by the friction of distance across the great breadth of arid Central Asia. Northward lay the desert and steppe of Mongolia and the subarctic lands of Siberia and northern Manchuria. In part because of its isolation until recent centuries, the Chinese civilized tradition was more continuous, coherent, and slow to change over a longer period than any other in history.

Interaction was much easier with areas to the east, and the model of Chinese civilization spread later to Korea, Vietnam, and Japan, where it still forms a basic part of the literate cultures of those areas. East Asia as a whole is accordingly sometimes called the *Sinic* culture (from the Latin word for China, or Chinese), one that also inherited most of the traditional Chinese agricultural system as well as its systems of writing, philosophy, literature, political and social institutions, and art forms. This diffusion took place, however, only 2,000 years or more after Chinese civilization first began, and after the establishment of the first empire in the third century B.C.E. The empire discarded some elements developed in earlier centuries and added others, to create

the model of imperial Chinese culture that subsequently spread to the rest of East Asia. But long before the beginning of the Christian era in the West, China had already produced one of the world's major civilized traditions, and the model of the Han dynasty (202 B.C.E.–220 C.E.) was to be reaffirmed by successive Chinese dynasties for the next 2,000 years.

The Origins of China

We cannot fix a precise date for the emergence of city-based, literate, metal-using civilization in China. As everywhere else, it happened over a long period of transition out of Neolithic beginnings. By about 2000 B.C.E., however, the late Neolithic culture we call Longshan, or Black Pottery, had begun to build walled settlements larger than villages, to make bronze tools, weapons, and ornaments, and to use a pictographic and ideographic script clearly recognizable as the ancestor of written Chinese. Their towns or cities included large groups of non-farmers—scribes, metallurgists, artisans, and perhaps officials—and already the Longshan people had learned the art of silk making, long an exclusive Chinese skill and trademark. Approximately four centuries later, about 1600 B.C.E., the first authenticated Chinese dynasty, the Shang, was established in the same area around or near the great bend of the Yellow River, where the major Longshan settlements had also clustered, on the North China Plain. The Shang probably consolidated or arose from a combination of the previously distinct Longshan and Yangshao (Painted Pottery) cultures, but they and other late Neolithic cultures may well have begun to merge considerably earlier, perhaps to form the dynasty of Xia, recorded as such by traditional Chinese texts but not yet confirmed archaeologically.

Whether the Xia was a real state and dynasty or not, the name was certainly used, and the Shang could not

CHRONOLOGY

1600–1050 B.C.E.	■ Shang dynasty
1050–256 B.C.E.	■ Zhou dynasty
600–221 B.C.E.	■ Warring states in northern China; Nam Yueh civilization in northern Vietnam and southern China
221–202 B.C.E.	■ Qin dynasty
221 B.C.E.–939 C.E.	■ Intermittent Chinese administration of Vietnam
202 B.C.E.–220 C.E.	■ Han dynasty
141–87 B.C.E.	■ Han Wu Di; Silk Road develops
100 B.C.E.–589 C.E.	■ Spread of Buddhism into China
9–23 C.E.	■ Wang Mang interregnum

have appeared without a predecessor. The existence of the Shang was also discounted by modern historians, despite its mention in the traditional texts giving the names of kings, as for the Xia, until archaeological discoveries in the 1920s began to reveal its capitals and inscriptions that listed Shang kings exactly as the traditional texts had them. Xia may still be a convenient label for late Longshan-Yangshao culture in the last stages of its evolution. By about 2000 B.C.E. Longshan towns were large and were surrounded by pounded earth walls with heavy gates, clearly no longer farmers' villages and possibly organized into some form of kingdom or kingdoms. What may have been a capital from this period, near modern Zhengzhou, perhaps of the Xia and referred to in the traditional histories as Yangcheng, had a rammed earth wall 20 feet high and a mile square, with two bronze foundries outside the walls.

Longshan settlements with a similar material culture extended eastward to the sea and southward into the Yangzi Valley and the south coast. The traditional Chinese texts give the names of five pre-Xia "emperors" who are recognizable as mythological culture heroes, credited with the "inventions" of fire, agriculture, animal domestication, calendrics, writing, and flood control. The last of these, the great Yu, is said to have founded the Xia dynasty, which may tentatively be dated 2000–1600 B.C.E., but we know almost nothing more about it. The earliest texts we have were written down many centuries later.

By Shang times, in any case, many of the elements of a distinctively Chinese culture are present. There has been a long debate about how much, if anything, Shang or its Chinese predecessors may have owed to earlier achievements further west, by diffusion from Mesopotamia or India. There seems no question that wheat, and later donkeys, alfalfa, grapes, and some elements of mathematics were carried to China from western Asia, but well after 2000 B.C.E. The light, spokewheeled war chariot, an important Shang war weapon, seems also to have come in by about 1500, perhaps related to the Aryan migration into India. Rice, water buffalo, chickens, and pigs, also not native to northern China, came considerably earlier from their Southeast Asian origins via southern China. Indeed China owed far more to diffusion from the south than from the west, especially if one considers the basic place in its economy that came to be occupied by these originally southern imports.

In Neolithic times, southern China was culturally, as it is physically, closer to adjacent Southeast Asia than to dry, cold northern China. Recent archaeological finds in the lower Yangzi Valley and south of the great river suggest that the beginnings of civilization may have emerged there as early as or earlier than in the better-surveyed and better-preserved north. The first East Asian bronzes, and the first evidence of rice cultivation so far discovered, came from what is now northern Thailand and Vietnam. Presumably, bronze-making spread from there relatively easily into neighboring southern China, probably long before Shang times, together with pigs, chickens, and water buffalo, although all of these things were present in the north by early Shang. By that time there seems already to have been a good deal of cultural mixing between northern and southern China, although the people were ethnically distinct, as were their languages and emerging scripts.

The chief crop of Shang China and for many centuries later was not wheat but millet, probably an indigenous grain. There is no aspect of Shang culture that suggests any connection with Mesopotamia or India, including Shang art and two other basic and conclusive elements, writing and bronze technology. Both were developed earlier in Sumer and then in India, but the earliest Chinese writing resembles neither. It seems highly unlikely that the Chinese would not have adopted or adapted cuneiform instead of the far more cumbersome ideographic characters if they had been in touch with Mesopotamia or had imported ideas or techniques from there. As for bronze, Shang China stands alone in the technical perfection and beauty of its bronze work, sharply distinct from that of any other ancient culture and showing in China a long history of experimental progress, using varying proportions of copper, tin, lead, and zinc until the optimum mix was achieved. The farther one goes from the Shang centers, the cruder the bronze artifacts become; there is no trail leading from Sumer or Harappa. For these and other reasons it seems clear that Chinese civilization, like Indian, was an independent innovation that was already well formed before it came into effective contact with other or older centers of equal sophistication. This is also consistent with the Paleolithic and early Neolithic records, where the stone tools of China remained distinct in type from those produced in the area from India westward through Central Asia to Europe. Chinese civilization evolved largely on its own, after the much earlier diffusion of some agricultural elements from the south.

The Shang Dynasty

The Shang ruled from several successive walled capitals, first near modern Luoyang, then near modern Zhengzhou (both close to the Yellow River), and finally at Anyang at a city they called Yin. We do not know the extent of the Shang political domain, but cultural remains suggest it was limited to the central Yellow River floodplain, although the Shang had, or claimed, vassals to the west, east, northeast, and possibly the south, who shared much of Shang material culture. By this time wheat was beginning to share prominence with millet, and rice was also grown, though mainly in the Yangzi Valley and the south. Hunting remained a subsidiary source of food in addition to domesticated cattle, pigs, and poultry. The Shang kept slaves, mainly war captives from among less highly developed or subjugated groups on the Shang borders, and slaves may have been an important part of the agricultural workforce. They were also used extensively to build the cities and palaces, and perhaps as troops.

Especially at Anyang, monumental building was impressive, and the city may have covered at its peak as much as 10 square miles, with nearly a dozen elaborate royal tombs, complete with a variety of grave furniture. The tombs provide evidence of a surplus production that could support extravagant display, including richly decorated chariots with bronze fittings and caparisoned horses to draw them; the horses had been harnessed, backed into the underground tombs down a ramp, and killed. Royal or aristocratic dead were accompanied in their burials not only by things of use and value but by tens or even hundreds of followers, buried as human sacrifices to serve in the afterlife, and probably also as a mark of the dead man's status. Bronze vessels and weapons of great beauty and technical perfection attest to the high quality of Shang technology.

We have no written texts as such, but there are a great number of Shang inscriptions, most of them incised on the flat shoulder bones of cattle or on tortoise shells, and used for divination purposes. A text, usually in the form of a question, was inscribed on bone or shell after heating in a fire or with a hot iron rod until it

Shang bronzes are technically sophisticated and are dominated by ritual vessels in a variety of forms. This piece (c. 1100 B.C.E.), with its removable lid, probably served as a pitcher for pouring ceremonial wine. Like other Shang bronze objects, it shows a mythical beast in abstract form and is covered with abstract designs. (Courtesy of the Freer Gallery of Art, Smithsonian Institution, Washington, D.C. [61.33])

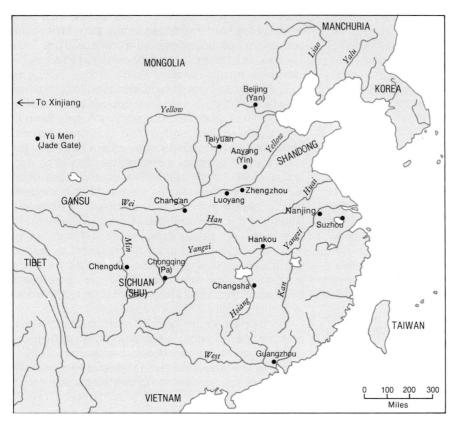

China and Korea in Han Times

cracked; the cracks supposedly provided an oracular answer to the question, probably better seen as a wish or a ritual to influence a favorable outcome. Others of the so-called oracle bone inscriptions, like the divination texts using characters close enough to classical Chinese that most can be read, provide lists of the Shang kings and brief accounts of royal activities.

Altogether this inscriptional material gives a picture of a hereditary aristocratic society in which warfare against surrounding groups was chronic; archers used a powerful compound bow, there were ranks of spearmen, and nobles and their drivers rode in their light, fast war chariots similar to the chariots of the Indo-Europeans. The royal hunt remained important and was usually a very large affair in which hundreds took part and thousands of animals perished. The inscriptions make it clear that the spirits of royal and perhaps all aristocratic ancestors demanded respectful service from the living and could intercede for them with a supreme deity—the roots of traditional Chinese "ancestor worship." Slaves were not thought to have souls or spirits and, thus, could safely be killed; the Shang

aristocrats seem not to have thought about what might happen to them if they became war captives themselves. Although those at the top lived in great luxury, the houses of the common people seem to have been quite crude, often simple pit dwellings, certainly not in a class with those of the Indus civilization. Many of the divination questions ask about the weather and suggest that the northern China climate then, as now, was semiarid and prone to both drought and river flooding, but there is little evidence of any large-scale irrigation, apart from what one may assume was the possible use of floodwater. Northern China was not as dry as the Indus Valley, and the agriculture there seems to have been primarily rain-fed except perhaps in small areas adjacent to the river or on a small scale from local wells in long dry spells. Millet is highly drought-tolerant and can produce good yields where other crops might fail. The great agricultural advantage of northern China was its highly fertile loess soil (wind-laid alluvium), which is also easily worked, and the level expanse of the largely treeless plain, allowing easy transport and exchange.

The Zhou Dynasty

Relations between the Shang and their vassals were uneasy, and chronic warfare with other groups on the margins strained Shang resources, as did the extravagant demands of royal building and display, much of it extorted from slave laborers and artisans. The last Shang king is said to have been a physical giant and a monster of depravity who, among other cruelties, made drinking cups of the skulls of his vanquished enemies. The dynasty ended in a great slave revolt about 1050 B.C.E., which was joined by one of the Shang vassals, the Zhou, (pronounced like "Joe"), who guarded the western frontier in the Wei Valley with their capital near modern Xi'an. Originally, the Zhou were probably a barbarian group taken over by the Shang, tough frontiersmen who seem to have been awaiting their chance to take over the whole kingdom. By about 1050 B.C.E. when they finally succeeded, together with the slave rebels, in defeating the last Shang king and sacking Anyang (where the Shang king died in the flames of his own palace), the Zhou had acquired most of Shang culture and technology. Their conquest was not merely a plundering expedition but a succession to a new dynasty that continued the cultural and technical evolution already begun. The victorious Zhou, now fully literate, gave their own account of the excesses and oppression of the Shang as justification for their conquest and first voiced what was to become a standard Chinese justification for political change: "The iniquity of Shang is full; Heaven commands me to destroy it." In other words, the Shang had lost the "mandate (approval) of Heaven" by their misgovernment, and it was the duty of responsible people to overthrow them.

The Zhou set up their new capital in the Wei Valley, their old base. They continued and extended the Shang system of feudatory vassals (dependent allies) whereby surrounding groups and areas, soon to begin emerging as states, were linked to the Zhou king by oaths of loyalty that acknowledged him as sovereign. The parallel with medieval European feudalism is not exact in details, but the basic system and the reasons for it were the same: a central kingdom with pretensions but without the means, at this early stage of statecraft, to control or administer any large area beyond its own immediate territory that made agreements with local chieftains in a feudal-style compact that extended the authority of the central state, at least in name. In addition, there was a need for joint defense against surrounding enemies or raiders. The Zhou appear to have subdued a much larger area than they inherited from the Shang, from the Wei Valley to the sea, north into southern Manchuria, and south into the Yangzi Valley. Mutual interest among evolving kingdoms, or dukedoms, as the Zhou called them, using much the same terms as in medieval Europe, and their hierarchical aristocracy with titles such as marquis, earl, etc., may also have led them to join together in the defense of the "civilized" area against the outer barbarians and to keep order internally.

For a time this system seems to have worked reasonably well, based also on what appears to have been an institution like serfdom by which most land was cultivated under the ownership of hereditary lords, and perhaps with some irrigation from shallow wells in a center plot, later labeled the "well field system." As in medieval Europe, serfs were bound to the land and could not leave, virtually the property or chattels of their lords. At both the royal Zhou court and increasingly at the courts of other dependent states there was an unbroken evolution of technological and artistic development, built on the original Shang foundations. Bronze remained the chief metal, and magnificent ritual vessels, often of great size, increasingly bore long texts recording events or decrees.

Although most writing was by now done with brush and ink on silk or on strips of bamboo, none of these perishable texts has survived, and we are dependent on much later copies, possibly substantially altered versions. It is generally assumed, however, that the central body of the Chinese classics originated in early Zhou, including the *Book of Changes* (*Yi-Jing,* a cryptic handbook for diviners), the *Book of Songs,* the *Book of Rituals,* and collections of historical documents, among them the texts that give the story of the five culture-hero emperors and the Xia dynasty, as well as a now-confirmed account of the Shang and of the Zhou conquest. Already the Chinese were writing history and attaching characteristic importance to the keeping of records.

But fundamental changes were at work that were to disrupt and then destroy the entire Zhou structure. As technology improved, iron was slowly becoming cheaper and more plentiful. It began to be available for agricultural implements, including iron-tipped plows, which the Chinese developed over 1,000 years before the West. Helped by better tools, irrigation was spreading, especially important in semiarid northern China, and more and more land was being brought under cultivation. Iron axes speeded the attack on remaining forests in the hilly margins of the north and in the Yangzi Valley. Spurred by rising agricultural output, the population began to grow much more rapidly, perhaps to 20 million by the mid-Zhou period, whereas the Shang had ruled perhaps 4 million. Except for recurrent years of drought, population did not apparently outrun food supply and surpluses were common, the basis for increasing trade.

New agricultural productivity freed increasing numbers from farm labor to serve as artisans, transport workers, soldiers, officials, scholars, and merchants. Increasingly, towns, now more important as centers of trade than of royal or feudal control and dominated by merchants, began to dot the plain and the richer lands to the south in the Yangzi Valley, where easier transport by water further stimulated the growth of trade and of urban centers. Fixed and hereditary serfdom and the domination of a landed aristocracy came to seem less and less suited to the changing conditions, a situation that may have been in some ways similar to that in the later periods of medieval European feudalism. At the same time, many of the original Zhou vassals were evolving toward separate statedom, each with its distinctive and regional culture. After some four centuries of Zhou rule, the political, social, and economic structures began to show strains, and eventually it disintegrated.

Warring States

In 771 B.C.E.* the royal capital in the Wei Valley was sacked by a barbarian group from the north and the Zhou king was killed. His son was installed as king the next year, but in a new and better protected capital at Luoyang, in the hope that a control point closer to the center of the royal domain would be more secure and more effective in holding the kingdom together. It was a vain hope. To guard the northwest borders, the old Zhou base in the Wei Valley was given as a fief (a grant of land) to a loyal noble of Qin clan; five centuries later, the Qin were to sweep away the crumbled remnants of Zhou rule to found the first empire.

By 770 B.C.E., with the shift to Luoyang, royal authority over the surrounding dependencies had dwindled and vassals had become rival states: Qin to the west, Jin to the north, Yan to the northeast in the area around modern Beijing, Qi to the east in Shandong, Chu to the south in the central Yangzi Valley, and a number of smaller states including Shu in Sichuan and Lu in Shandong, where Confucius was born and served for a time as an adviser. It is still too early to speak of any of them, even of the Zhou, as "China"; each was culturally, linguistically, and politically distinct, and there were probably also some racial differences. China as we know it emerged only under the empire of Qin in the third century B.C.E. The Qin Empire put its own overpowering stamp on what was to become the dominant Chinese

style in statecraft and social organization for the ensuing two millennia. Our name *China* comes, appropriately enough, from the Qin, the creator of an imperial Chinese identity for the first time.

Until then, there was no dominant strand within the varied assortment of people, cultures, and states that occupied what is now China. They warred constantly among themselves and against the still more different groups around the edges of the cultivated area but still well within the borders of modern China proper. Technology probably passed relatively easily and quickly from group to group, and by mid-Zhou most seem to have shared more or less common achievements in metallurgy, agriculture and irrigation, and other arts. But in spoken and written language, in many aspects of culture, and in political identity they were as different as, say, the evolving states of late medieval Europe.

The state of Chu provides a good example. Its location straddling the central Yangzi Valley made it probably the most productive of the rival states as well as the largest; its agriculture benefited from the more adequate and reliable rainfall and longer growing season of central China as well as from greater ease of irrigation. But it was different in character too, in particular in the size and importance of its merchant group and the role of water-borne trade and towns in its economy. Chu had evolved far beyond the earlier Shang pattern, where power was held by hereditary landowning nobility and where agriculture worked by slaves or serfs was virtually the sole source of wealth. And unlike the northern states Chu was also a naval power; it had fleets on the Yangzi and its tributaries and adjacent lakes and even larger numbers of trading junks (riverboats). Nevertheless, Chu was ultimately defeated by a coalition of northern states in 632 B.C.E. and again in 301 B.C.E.; although it continued to exist, its power and further growth were greatly reduced while those of the other states rose. This may have been one of those contests that change the course of history, giving the future to a peasant-based authoritarian empire rather than to a state where trade and merchants were prominent. A China that followed the Chu pattern would have been very different from what was established by the final victory of the Qin, whose shape is described in more detail later in this chapter.

With increasing agricultural yields and total output, it was now possible to field large armies of men who could be spared from agriculture at least for parts of the year and could be fed on surpluses. Warfare became larger in scale and more ruthless, and its character changed from that of earlier chivalric contests of honor between aristocrats to one of more wholesale conquest and fights for survival. The crossbow with a trigger mechanism, developed by this time, greatly increased firepower,

---

*By this time traditional Chinese dates, almost certainly inaccurate for earlier periods, are fully reliable and are confirmed by other evidence. The earliest surviving books come from the ninth century B.C.E., and by the eighth century the Zhou were recording eclipses of the sun, which in fact did occur exactly when their records state.

range, and accuracy, and by the fourth century B.C.E. foot soldiers were supported by armed cavalry. Such developments combined to undermine the earlier dominance of hereditary aristocrats, their chariots, and their personal retinues.

What was happening in China paralleled the Indian pattern a century or so before, as described in Chapter 4, where a chivalric age gave way to interstate power struggles and the emergence of the Mauryan Empire, based on the spread of iron, improvements in agriculture, and a population boom. As in India, bronze and copper coins minted by the state became common in this period in China, trade and cities grew rapidly, roads were built, standing armies proliferated, and the bureaucratic apparatus of the state began to appear. All of this offered a range of new opportunities for able commoners. For many it was a positive and welcome change, but for others the passing of the old order and the great disruptions and sufferings of warfare offered only chaos

and moral confusion. Confucius, who lived at the beginning of the Warring States period, made it clear that his prescriptions were an effort to reestablish order and what he referred to as "harmony," following the values of an earlier "golden age."

A CLOSER LOOK

Confucius, the Sage

Confucius was born about 551 B.C.E. in one of the smaller states that arose out of the Zhou domain in Shandong Province and died about 479. He was, thus, roughly contemporary with the Buddha and died only a few years before the birth of Socrates. His family name was Kong, and Chinese refer to him as Kongfuzi, "Master Kong"), which modern Europeans Latinized as Confucius. The Kong family appear to have been rather

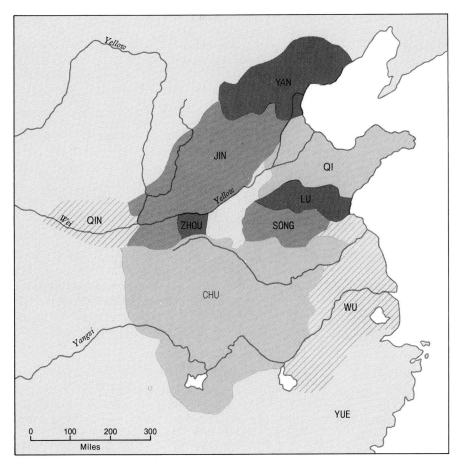

China in the Sixth Century B.C.E.

Reflections on Social Reform

The philosopher Mozi, who was born in the fifth century B.C.E. soon after Confucius, was less of a traditionalist and more interested in reforming society.

It is the sage's business to regulate the world; he must thus know whence disorder comes in order to be capable of regulating it. . . . The origin is the lack of mutual love. . . . All the disorders of the world have this cause and this alone. . . . If mutual love prevailed universally throughout the world, no state would attack another state; no family would trouble another family; thieves and brigands would not exist; princes and subjects, fathers and sons, would all be filial and good. Thus the world would be well governed. . . . Where do ills come from? They come from hatred of others, from violence toward others. . . . The love which makes distinctions among persons causes all the ills of the world. . . . This universal love is very advantageous, and far more easy to practice than you imagine. If it is not put into practice, that is because the rulers take no pleasure in it. If the rulers took pleasure in it, I believe that men would throw themselves into it. . . . Nothing on earth could stop them. . . . To kill a man is called an unjust thing; it is a crime deserving death. To kill ten men is ten times more unjust, to kill a hundred men a hundred times more unjust. Today every prince in the world knows that this must be punished; they declare it unjust. Yet the greatest of injustices, the making of war, they do not punish. On the contrary, they glorify it and declare it just! Truly they do not know how unjust they are.

Source: After H. Maspero, *La Chine Antique* (Paris: Presses Universitaires de France, 1927), pp. 253–254.

low-ranking aristocrats in reduced circumstances but were able to arrange for their son's education. This was still more than three centuries before the establishment of the imperial examinations, and Confucius made a career out of teaching, periodically serving as consultant or counselor to various feudal lords. To his pupils he taught not only literacy and the classics but his own philosophy of life and government. Some of his pupils won high-level jobs in state administration, but Confucius himself was never very successful in such terms, and at the end of his life apparently thought of himself as a failure. In fact, he was the founder of probably the most successful philosophical, moral, and ethical system in human history, measured by the number of people in China, Korea, Japan, and Vietnam who followed his precepts for more than 2,500 years and who are still profoundly influenced by them.

We have nothing that the sage himself wrote and not very much information about him or his teachings. All we know for sure comes from a collection of discourses, or sayings, known as the *Analects,* which were put together in a rather unsystematic way after his death by his disciples and are hence probably not wholly accurate. Later commentaries expanded on the meaning and application of his teachings.

The picture we have of the man himself and of his ideas from the *Analects,* while incomplete at best, is of a thoughtful but also very human person. He complained that he could never seem to get the right kinds of students or the kinds of appointments for which he yearned. And he is rather transparent in discussing his lack of success: "I don't mind not being in office; I am more concerned about being qualified for it. I don't mind not having recognition; I strive to be worthy of recognition." Yet he complained about being treated "like a gourd fit only to be hung on the wall and never put to use." He seems to have been so anxious to get a post as adviser that he even considered working for rebel groups, believing that, given any kind of opportunity, he could remake men and states in line with his philosophy—an attitude that Plato was to share a century later. But he also had a good sense of the ridiculous and could even enjoy jokes on himself.

The basic message of all his teachings is that people can be molded and elevated by education and by the virtuous example of superiors. "Civilized" people so

Mencius on Good Government

Mencius, the first great follower of Confucius, lived from 372 to 289 B.C.E. and wrote down his own moral precepts and anecdotes. On benevolent government, he recorded the following advice to a certain king of one of the Warring States.

> Dogs and pigs in your realm feed on the food of your subjects, but you do not restrain them. People are starving on your roads, but you do not open your granaries. When people die as a result, you say, "It is not my fault; it is a bad year." How is this different from stabbing a man to death and saying, "It is not my fault; it is the sword." If your majesty would stop putting blame on the year, people from throughout the empire would come to you.

Source: After C. O. Hucker, *China's Imperial Past* (Stanford, CA: Stanford University Press, 1975), p. 81.

formed will *want* to do what is morally right, rather than merely expedient, and hence, will preserve the "harmony" of society, which is what distinguishes humans from animals. Force and threats are ineffective controls; only internalized values can produce correct behavior. Behavior should also be modeled on that of higher-status people, beginning within the family and extending to the ruler, who thus must match power with responsibility and uprightness. For all relationships, "Do not do unto others what you yourself would not like."

Confucianism is a prescription for benevolence in human affairs and in government, but it is also essentially conservative, placing stress on order. Nevertheless, the focus on benevolence meant that bad government should rightly be rejected, despite the threat to order, a point that the *Analects* repeats in several contexts. The Confucian model is the upright man who unswervingly pursues the right moral course whatever the consequences, even at the expense of his own self-interest. Master Kong's life seems to have conformed to the model he preached. Perhaps he was too outspoken, like Socrates, to win the favor of the powerful men of his day. But his teachings and his example have far outlived the petty politics of the age in which he lived.

The Qin Conquest

Qin, originally one of the poorest, smallest, and most remote of the Zhou dependencies, seemed easily outclassed by the other contending states. Its succes-

sion of able rulers made virtues of its relative poverty, peasant base, and frontier location. It stressed the importance of hard work, frugality, and discipline and emphasized agriculture and peasant soldiers instead of trade, merchants, or intellectuals, blending these elements to create military power. Its tough armies defeated those of rival states in a long series of campaigns that were kept away from the mountain-ringed Qin home base in the Wei Valley but were often devastating to the more fragile economies of its enemies with their dependence on trade. Opponents saw the menace of rising Qin power too late to unite against it and were picked off one by one. Qin generals and statesmen were masters of strategy and tactics and used diplomacy, propaganda, treachery, espionage, and various forms of psychological warfare adroitly.

A series of victorious campaigns during the 230s and 220s culminated in the final defeat of all the other states in 221 B.C.E. Northern China and the Yangzi Valley were united politically for the first time, and the Qin ruler, who now took the title of emperor (Huang Di) as Qin Shi Huang Di, applied to his new empire as a whole the systems that had built Qin power. Further conquests after 221 began the long Chinese absorption of the south, beginning with the acquisition of the kingdom of Yue centered in the Guangzhou Delta and the route to it southward from the Yangzi, together with Yue territory in what is now northern Vietnam. Throughout the new domain, as in the former state of Qin, primogeniture (whereby the eldest son inherits all of the father's property and status) was abolished, as was slavery except for minor domestic servants. The former feudal and land-tenure arrangements were abolished. Land became privately owned and was freely bought and sold. The state levied a tax on all

The Great Wall was probably Qin Shi Huang Di's most famous, or infamous, project. Here it is shown west of Beijing snaking along the mountain ridges separating northeastern China from Mongolia. The wall was built wide enough to allow two war chariots to pass abreast. The sections of it that remain standing now date from its most recent wholesale reconstruction under the Ming dynasty in the fifteenth century. (Danielle Hayes/Bruce Coleman Inc.)

land in the form of a share of the crop. A new uniform law code was applied to all subjects without discrimination, ending many centuries of aristocratic privilege, a reform that clearly appealed to most people. Currency, weights, measures, and forms of writing, previously widely varied among what had been separate cultures and states, were also unified by imperial fiat to follow the Qin mode, a change essential for empire. An imperial system of roads and canals was begun, and a splendid new capital called Xianyang was built near modern Xi'an in the Wei Valley. Even axle lengths for carts were standardized so that all carts would fit the same ruts.

Probably the most spectacular and best known of the new public works projects was the Great Wall, which Qin Shi Huang Di ordered consolidated from a series of much earlier walls along the northern steppe border and reconstructed as a uniform barrier with regularly spaced watchtowers. It and subsequent reconstructions (the remains currently visible date from the Ming rebuilding in the fifteenth century C.E.) constitute probably the largest single works project in human history. The Great Wall was made possible by the new mobility of labor, which could be freed from farming at least seasonally. Reportedly, 1 million men died in building the wall, conscripts working as corvée labor (work performed as part of state tax, equivalent to military conscription). Ironically, the wall was never very effective in its supposed purpose of preventing nomadic incursions; end runs around it and intrigues that opened the gates made it often quite permeable. It was seldom easy to distin-

guish friend from foe, harmless traders or travelers from troublemakers or invaders, or potential invaders. But it did serve as a symbolic affirmation of empire and as a statement of territorial and sovereign limits. "Good fences make good neighbors," the Chinese might have said, to which the Mongols and their predecessors might have replied, also quoting Robert Frost (however anachronistically), "Something there is which doesn't love a wall." The new and powerful state control over mass labor tempted the emperor, with his megalomaniacal tendencies, to plan more and more projects of monumental scope, including the road system, the new canals (useful for transporting troops and their supplies as well as for irrigation), and his own magnificent palace and tomb, in addition to fresh conquests.

Qin Authoritarianism

Agriculture was stressed as the basis of the economy and the state, with hardy peasants available in the off-seasons for corvée or for the army. Trade and merchants were regarded as parasitic and as potentially dangerous power rivals to the state, hence in part the removal of primogeniture, which also reduced the threat from landed power. But the chief target of the Qin system was intellectuals, people who ask questions, consider alternatives, or point out deficiencies. China al-

Qin Shi Huang Di was buried in a huge underground tomb near modern Xi'an with an army of life-size clay figures to guard the approaches. Excavations in the 1970s brought them to light again after more than 2,000 years; each figure is a faithful representation of a real individual. (Erich Lessing/Art Resource, New York)

ready had a long tradition of scholars, philosophers, and moralists, of whom Confucius and Mencius (his later disciple) were honored examples. The Qin saw such people, perhaps accurately, as troublemakers and boat-rockers. It was an openly totalitarian state, and its sense of mission made it additionally intolerant of any dissent.

Qin Shi Huang Di persecuted intellectuals, buried several hundred scholars alive for questioning his policies, and ordered the burning of all books that could promote undesirable thoughts, which meant most books other than practical manuals and the official Qin chronicles. The documents destroyed included invaluable material accumulated from earlier periods. There was to be no admiration of the past, no criticism of the present, and no recommendations for the future, except the state's. These policies, especially the burning of the books, were profoundly contrary to the Chinese rever-

ence for the written word and the preservation of records. They earned the emperor the condemnation of all subsequent Chinese scholars and historians. Certainly he was a cruel tyrant, inhumane, even depraved in his lust for absolute power. But his methods, harsh though they were, built an empire out of disunity and established most of the bases of the Chinese state for all subsequent periods, including the present.

Much of his policies were in fact the work of his prime minister, Li Si, whose career closely paralleled that of Kautilya in Mauryan India and who is credited with founding a new school of philosophy called Legalism, which embodied the Qin policies of tight state control over everything. Control was augmented by a greatly expanded state bureaucracy and by rigid supervision of all education. Only those values that supported the state design were inculcated, and practical skills were stressed over critical inquiry. As in Mauryan India, there was a highly developed police system and a secret service to ferret out and punish dissidents. Another potential source of ferment, travel, within the realm or abroad, was forbidden except by special permit.

Empire building, anywhere and in any form, is a disagreeable business, and one may question its usefulness in any case. Are people better off forcefully unified in an empire, at tremendous cost in lives, than if they had been left to their own regional cultures and states? Unfortunately, empire building seems to be a common human failing, as is inhumanity in the name of religion. Both have the appeal, at least for some, of a grand idea, or simply of pride, for which costs are not counted. China, once unified, even by such methods, was to cling to the idea of imperial unity ever after. Each subsequent period of disunity following the fall of a dynasty was regarded as a time of failure, and each ended in the rebuilding of the empire. But one must acknowledge also the appeal of the new order that the Qin represented. By its time most people were clearly ready to break with their feudal past, and to move toward a system based on achievement rather than birth. The Qin believed firmly that their new order was progress; they had a visionary conviction that they were creating a better society. The parallels with Communist China were striking, and indeed Qin Shi Huang Di was praised as a model during the Cultural Revolution in the late 1960s. Sacrifice for an inspiring national goal has its own appeal; the end is seen to justify the means, including treachery, cruelty, and inhumanity toward the people, who are nevertheless seen as supposedly the beneficiaries of the new order.

Lord Shang, an earlier Qin official and the true progenitor of the Legalist school, summarized state policy in classic totalitarian terms:

> Punish severely the light crimes. . . . If light offenses do not occur, serious ones have no chance of coming. This is said to be "ruling the people in a state of law and order. . . ."
>
> A state where uniformity of purpose has been established for ten years will be strong for a hundred years; for a hundred years it will be strong for a thousand years . . . and will attain supremacy. . . .
>
> The things which people desire are innumerable, but that from which they benefit is one and the same. Unless the people are made one, there is no way to make them attain their desire. Therefore they are unified, and their strength is consolidated. . . .
>
> If you establish what people delight in, they will suffer from what they dislike, but if you establish what they dislike, they will be happy in what they enjoy.[1]

In other words, in unity is strength, but the state knows best what is good for people. The major figure of the school of Legalism is the philosopher Han Feizi (died 233 B.C.E.), who also stressed the need for severe laws and harsh punishments, the only means to establish *order,*

under the direction of the ruler. People are naturally selfish, and they must be held mutually responsible for each other's actions. Visitors to Qin from other states before 221 B.C.E. remarked on the positive and confident atmosphere they found there, and the conviction that the Qin represented "progress" and a model that would prevail.

Nevertheless, there was merit in the new equality under the law and new opportunities for advancement; and ambitious projects have an allure that draws people to support them, perhaps especially those associated with empire building. The best illustration of the more constructive aspects of the Qin is the figure of Li Bing, appointed provincial governor of the former state of Shu (Sichuan) and also famed as a hydraulic engineer associated with many of the big Qin projects, including control works on the Yellow River. It was Li Bing who announced the best formula for minimizing the floods that had already made the Yellow River notorious: "Dig the bed deep, and keep the banks low." This helped to prevent the buildup of silt in the river's bed, which in time raised it above the level of the surrounding country and greatly worsened the destructive consequences of floods that could not forever be retained within the dikes along the river's banks. Li Bing's sound advice was finally acted on effectively only under the present Communist government after 1949. Li Bing is credited with designing and constructing the famous irrigation works at Guanxian in western Sichuan, diverting the Min River where it emerges from the mountains and enters the wide plain around the capital city of Chengdu. His irrigation works, much visited by tourists, still stand, together with his statue and that of his son, who completed the project, overlooking them, and are reputed to have saved millions of people on the Chengdu Plain from drought and famine ever since. Like all big projects, they took enormous labor and hardship, mainly from conscript workers under iron discipline. According to the great Han dynasty historian Simaqian, writing a century later, Li Bing toward the end of his life said:

> People can be depended on to enjoy the results, but they must not be consulted about the beginnings. Now the elder ones and their descendants dislike people like me, but hundreds of years later let them think what I have said and done.

Li Bing's memory is still honored, while that of his emperor is reviled.

The Han Dynasty

Qin Shi Huang Di died in 210 B.C.E., leaving the throne to his eldest son, but Li Si and other counselors suppressed the news of his death for fear of uprisings and then installed the second son as their puppet. But the harshness of Qin rule had left the country in turmoil, exhausted the people, drained the treasury, and alienated the educated upper classes. Without their cooperation, the regime was in trouble. The empire was in fact already collapsing into rebellion, and several army commanders deserted. In 206 B.C.E. rebel armies occupied the capital and burned the emperor's splendid new palace. Rival forces contended for power in the ensuing struggle, and large groups of soldiers, workers, and former officials roamed the country. By 202 B.C.E. a new rebel leader, Liu Bang, emerged out of this chaos. He founded a new dynasty, which he named the Han. Under Han rule China took both the territorial and the political and social shapes it was to retain until the present century. The Chinese still call themselves "people of Han," in distinction from Mongols, Tibetans, other domestic minorities, and more distant foreigners, a label that they carry with much pride as the heirs of a great tradition of culture and empire first established in its classic form by the Han. Han dynasty imperial success, and that of later dynasties, depended, however, on retention of many of the techniques of control used by the Qin. The administration of an empire the size of all of Europe, and with a population of probably about 60 million people by Han times, could not have been managed otherwise.

Beginning with the Han, the harsher aspects of the Qin Legalist approach were softened by both common sense and the more humane morality of Confucianism. Liu Bang, who took the title Han Gao Zi ("High Progenitor") as the first emperor, emphasized the Confucian precept that government exists to serve the people and that unjust rulers should forfeit both the mandate of Heaven and the support of the ruled. He abolished the hated controls on travel, education, and thought, lowered taxes, and encouraged learning so as to build a pool of educated men whose talents, in the Confucian mode, could be called on to serve the state. However, conscription for the army and forced labor for public works such as road and canal building were retained, as was the administrative division of the empire into *hsien xian,* ("counties"), each under the control of an imperial magistrate. The imperial state superimposed its model in all things, including currency, weights, measures, script, and orthodox thought, on a vast and regionally diverse area that had long been politically and culturally varied. Under beneficent rule, this was a system that could be made to work successfully and could command general support. Early Han was a time of great prosperity and enthusiasm for the new order.

Expansion Under Han Wu Di

Power corrupts everyone everywhere, however, and the new power of the Han Empire, on Qin foundations and with the boost of new economic and population growth, tempted successive emperors to further conquests and imperial glory. Liu Bang's son and grandson continued his frugal and benevolent model as rulers, but the bitter memories of Qin had faded by the time of the emperor Wu Di (141–87 B.C.E.). He first tightened imperial control, removed the remaining power of the lords created by Liu Bang for faithful service, imposed state regulations on trade and merchants, and set new taxes and new state controls on salt, iron, and the supply of grain. The last measure, which came to be known as the "ever-normal granary system," was intended to prevent famine by state collection of grain in good years or surplus areas for sale at low, controlled prices when lean years came. It was a good idea and was practiced with some success also by subsequent dynasties but, like Li Bing's projects, was not always popular with the local producers, let alone the merchants.

Having put the imperial house in order and increased state revenues and state power, Wu Di began in 111 B.C.E. an ambitious program of new conquests, first in the southeast against Yue in the Fujian and Guangzhou areas, which had broken away after the fall of the Qin. The Yue kingdom had included the related people and culture of what is now northern Vietnam, and this was again added to the Chinese Empire. Thus began the long struggle of the Vietnamese to reassert and maintain their separate identity despite their absorption of much of Chinese literate culture. In Han times, the southern people and culture of Yue were regarded as foreign and were in fact very different from those of the north; more than traces of these differences remain

Bronze casting continued its development under the Han. This magnificent horse from the second century C.E. shows the sophistication of Han technology and art. (The Granger Collection, New York)

even now, including the Cantonese language and cuisine, but the south has been an integral part of China for 2,000 years and has been largely remade in the greater Chinese image. The people and culture of Vietnam were still more different and regained their independence from China after the fall of Han.

Turning north in 109–108 B.C.E., Wu Di's armies conquered southern Manchuria and northern Korea for the empire, while other campaigns established a looser control over the still non-Chinese populations of Yunnan and Guizhou in the southwest. Southern Manchuria was to remain off and on Chinese territory and in any case solidly a part of the Chinese system, with large, originally military colonies planted there by Wu Di. These became agricultural settlements in the fertile valley of the Liao River.

Similar garrisons were established in northern Korea, and there was heavy Chinese influence from Han times on. But the Koreans, like the Vietnamese, remained anxious to reclaim their national identity and independence. As in Vietnam, Korea had already generated its own civilization and cultural style and was linguistically and ethnically distinct from China despite massive Chinese cultural influence. After the Han collapse in 220 C.E. both areas broke away from Chinese control—Korea as a nominally tributary state, and Vietnam to endure later Chinese reconquest under the Tang and then successive wars of independence until modern times, with a heavy legacy of mutual mistrust reflecting the past 2,000 years. The Vietnamese record of repeated nationalist success in expelling the seemingly overpowering forces of imperial China should have been enough to dissuade the United States from its own misadventure there; ignorance of history imposes a high price.

China's northern and northwestern frontiers had been and were to remain a chronic problem for other reasons. The Great Wall had been built to solve this problem, but it could not prevent infiltrations by the horse-riding nomads who occupied the steppe border zone and who periodically harried Chinese agricultural areas and trade routes. The major route for international trade was the famous Silk Road through the Gansu Corridor and along the northern and southern edges of the Tarim Desert in Xinjiang (Chinese Turkestan), where there are widely spaced oases fed by streams from the surrounding mountains. The two routes met at Kashgar at the western end of the Tarim and then crossed the Pamirs into Central Asia, where the trade passed into other hands on its long way to the Levant and eventually to Rome. Silk was the main export, a Chinese monopoly since Longshan times and in great demand in the West, especially in luxury-loving imperial Rome. The Romans were obliged to pay for it largely in gold, a drain that Pliny and other Roman historians believed weakened the economy and contributed to Rome's ultimate fall. It was profitable to China, and Wu Di's pride in his new imperial power made him less willing to accept nomad interruptions of the trade and raids on Chinese territory.

The chief nomad group at this period was the Xiongnu, a Turkic people whose mounted mobility and cavalry tactics gave them the kind of military effectiveness later used by the Mongol leader Chinghis Khan. The Han generals complained that the Xiongnu "move on swift horses and in their breasts beat the hearts of beasts. They shift from place to place like a flock of birds. Thus it is difficult to corner them and bring them under control." One can understand the Han frustration, but in a series of major campaigns Wu Di defeated them, drove them at least for a time out of most of Inner Mongolia, Gansu, and Xinjiang, and then planted Chinese military colonies and garrisons in those areas and along the Silk Road, which is still marked by ruined Han watchtowers. Xinjiang and inner Mongolia were to fall away from Chinese control in later periods whenever the central state was weak but were reclaimed by most subsequent strong dynasties as part of the empire. Non-Han groups like the Xiongnu and the Mongols remained the major steppe inhabitants until the present century. Another Turkic people, the Uighurs, became the dominant oasis farmers in otherwise desert Xinjiang. The Uighurs later embraced Islam and helped to transmit it to China proper, where there are still a number of Chinese Muslims concentrated in the northwest.

China and Rome

Wu Di sent an ambassador westward in 139 B.C.E., a courtier named Zhang Qian, to try to make an alliance with other nomads against the Xiongnu and to scout out the country more generally. He was captured instead by the Xiongnu but escaped after 10 years. Eventually, in 126 B.C.E. he returned to the Han capital at Chang'an, "Long Peace," in the Wei Valley, where the Qin had ruled, with firsthand accounts of Central Asia, including bits of information about India and routes to it, and about a great empire far to the west, where the silk went. This was China's first news of Rome, but they were never to learn much more. Travelers who said they had been to Rome turned up much later at the Han court with their own tales, including a group of jugglers in 120 C.E. and some merchants in 166 C.E., both of whose visits were recorded in the Han annals. The Romans knew China only as the source of silk and called it, accordingly, Seres, the Latin word for silk.

Wu Di was tempted by Zhang Qian's report to move on Central Asia and add it to his conquests, partly out of pure vainglory, partly to secure supplies of the excellent horses to be found there, which he wanted for the imperial stables and his cavalry. If he or his successors had done so, the Chinese and Roman empires, or their for-

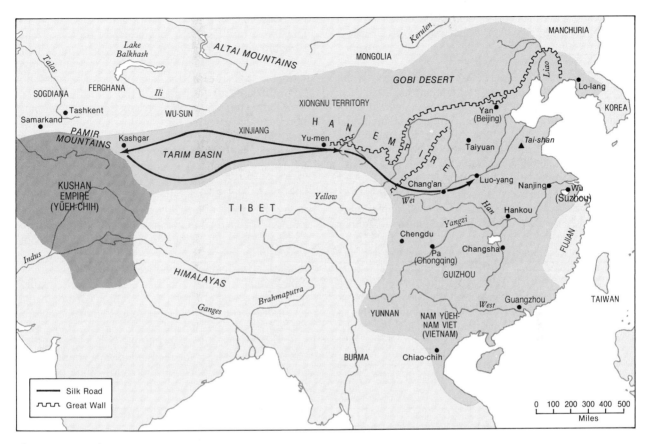

The Han Empire

This was close to the extent of the modern state, including Xinjiang and inner Mongolia, although the modern state excludes northern Vietnam.

ward troops, might have met and perhaps learned from each other. In the first century C.E. with the Han still in power and still occasionally probing westward, Rome was at the same time campaigning against the Parthian kingdom in Persia (Iran). If the Romans had conquered Parthia, they might have at least encountered Han patrols, or they might have followed the Silk Road, which they knew about, from Central Asia to the borders of China. But both armies were very far from home. Moreover, the Parthians and other Central Asian groups were formidable opponents and were anxious to retain their profitable middleman role in the silk trade rather than allowing the two empires to meet. Han envoys reached the Parthians but were advised to return home, advice that they followed.

Each empire thus remained largely in ignorance of the other except for travelers' tales, although both were of comparable size, sophistication, power, and achievements. China might have developed a different and more open attitude to the rest of the world on the basis

of some experience with another empire and culture, Roman or Indian, at their own level of sophistication. Like the Chinese Empire, both Rome and Mauryan India were builders of roads, walls, and planned cities, synthesizers of varied cultures under an expansionist and cosmopolitan system, and contenders with "barbarians" along the fringes of their empires. Of the three, the Han Empire was the largest and probably the most populous and richest, although its level of cultural and technical sophistication was probably matched by both ancient India and Rome.

Wu Di's endless campaigns and his impositions on the people exhausted the country's patience and resources. One of his earlier reforms had been the establishment of imperial censors whose job it was to keep officials, even the emperor, faithful to their duty to serve the people. The censors finally convinced Wu Di that he had neglected this basic precept and persuaded him to issue a famous penitential edict apologizing for his excesses and promising to be a better ruler, more deserving of the mandate of Heaven—and less likely to be overthrown by rebellion, which was already brewing. The institution of the censorate remained a regulatory feature of all subsequent dynasties.

Wu Di's immediate successors, while largely abandoning further conquests, continued to press the Xiongnu as a defensive strategy and even sent an expeditionary force across the Pamirs into the Samarkand region in pursuit. There, in 42 B.C.E., on the banks of the Talas River near Tashkent in Central Asia, they defeated a Xiongnu coalition that included some mercenary troops, who, from the Chinese description, may have been Roman auxiliaries. These people had learned the Roman *testudo* formation with shields overlapping over their heads to ward off arrows and spears—another near-miss at a direct encounter with Rome. Han armies in Central Asia, having marched across deserts and high mountains, were further from their capital than regular Roman troops ever were from Rome. But this was the high point of Han power, and the empire that Wu Di welded together was not to be significantly enlarged in subsequent centuries, except for the much later incorporation of Tibet (and the loss of Korea and Vietnam).

Wider Trade Patterns

Contacts across Eurasia had been important during and since the prehistoric period. Sumer may have contributed something to the origins of Indian civilization (and vice versa) and perhaps indirectly to the emergence of Chinese civilization. Given the multiplicity and often the mutual hostility of the various cultural groups in Central Asia during the ancient and medieval periods, the passage of goods and ideas through this area, in either direction, was necessarily slow and difficult. There was certainly trade from China and India to western Asia, Greece, and Rome. From at least 600 B.C.E. there was also sea trade, bringing Indian and southeast Asian spices to the Mediterranean and Europe. But except for the visits of Greek and Roman traders to the coasts of India, and perhaps of Romans as far east as Malaya (where Roman trade goods have been found), plus the travels of a few Indian philosophers to Greece and Rome and the invasion of India by Alexander, there was no direct contact between Eastern and Western civilization from then until the time of Marco Polo in the thirteenth century. Arab ships traded by sea, and a chain of various Central Asian peoples transmitted ideas as well as goods across Eurasia, but the transmission was incomplete, and understandably some of the ideas were lost or garbled in the process.

Commerce between China and the rest of Eurasia almost certainly developed later than India's trade with Mesopotamia, and there is no evidence of Chinese exports westward until the beginning of the silk route, probably during the Zhou dynasty. Chinese merchants took the silk only as far as Xinjiang, handing it over there to a long series of Central Asian traders who passed it along through the thousands of miles to the shores of the Mediterranean, where Syrian, Greek, and Roman merchants picked it up for transport farther west. This trade continued after the fall of the Han dynasty and was later augmented by the export of porcelain and lacquer goods, all high-value commodities that could bear the very heavy costs of such long-distance transport. The camel caravans carrying them were also exposed to frequent raids from other Central Asian groups along the route, risks that further increased the prices charged for Chinese exports when they finally reached their destinations. By the eleventh century much of the Chinese export trade was being carried westward by sea to India, while Indian exports westward—fine cotton textiles, spices, gems, and other goods—continued from the earliest times through the Middle Ages to move mainly by ship from ports on the Indian west coast. There must have been some return flow of trade by sea from India to China, but apart from the mention of what sound like Indian merchants in ports on the south China coast, we know very little about it.

Han Culture

The first two centuries of Han rule were also a time of great cultural flowering in poetry, painting, music, philosophy, literature, and the writing of history. Confucianism was more firmly established as the official orthodoxy and state ideology, and the famous Chinese imperial civil service system recruited men of talent, schooled in classical Confucian learning, to hold office through competitive examination regardless of their birth. Liu Bang, the founder of the Han, had been born a peasant, and the new stress was on ability and education rather than on inherited status. This approach was to remain a source of strength and effectiveness for the state for the next 2,000 years and was rightly admired by the modern Western heirs of Plato. Officeholding by the scholar-gentry, who were enriched each generation by new blood rising from peasant or commoner ranks and entering the elite through the imperial examinations, became the most prestigious of all occupations. That in turn helped to ensure that able people went into the administration and preserved the political arena and government service generally from much of the corruption, mediocrity, and ineffectiveness that have plagued political systems everywhere and at every period.

China was far from free of such problems or from other imperfections, but each new dynasty reestablished the system begun under the Han and on the whole probably managed the task of government better than most other states, perhaps including most modern ones. One may thank Confucius for this, with his stress on duty, learning, "human-heartedness," and virtue. Chinese society chose that way among many others and periodically reaffirmed what had been the minor teachings of an obscure consultant to a small feudal lord in the sixth century B.C.E., long before there was any thought of empire. Great landed-gentry families remained and were periodically nuclei of power, together with court aristocrats, eunuchs,* and ambitious generals—a pattern familiar from imperial Rome, Persia (Iran), and elsewhere. In China, the original Han ideal endured through the rise and fall of successive dynasties and, with all its imperfections, built a long and proud tradition of power combined with service that is still very much alive in China. The People's Republic is the conscious heir of greatness.

Han rule was briefly broken by a palace coup of the empress's nephew Wang Mang, who made himself emperor from 9 to 23 C.E.. As a model Confucian ruler, Wang Mang tried to curb the resurgent power of merchants and of the landowning gentry. He also extended new state controls over the economy, all in an effort to reestablish the egalitarianism he claimed to derive from the sage's teaching. His reforms included the abolition of private estates, which had increasingly avoided paying taxes, and the nationalization of land. Such policies bitterly alienated the rich and powerful, and Wang Mang was murdered by a new rebel group called the Red Eyebrows, who were supported both by distressed peasants suffering from a drought-induced famine and by merchant and gentry groups.

Landowning and its abuses were problems for all ancient and medieval empires and were to remain a plague for every Chinese dynasty. Ownership of land meant power, and the abolition of primogeniture did not always prevent powerful families from accumulating large blocks of land. Big landowners not only built up wealth but also threatened the supremacy of the state by their growing political power. By manipulating political influence locally, usually as members themselves of the gentry group with its official and unofficial connections, they managed to reduce or avoid paying state taxes on their lands or got them off the tax rolls entirely, a major problem for most dynasties. Their tenants, the peasants who farmed their land, were often cruelly exploited and hence driven to rebellion. Reformers in government pe-

Pottery figure titled *Balladeer*, part of the grave furniture from a Han dynasty tomb in Sichuan. The afterlife was clearly supposed to be a happy time, replete with worldly pleasures. This figure beautifully captures the human quality of Han folk culture. (Innervisions)

riodically tried to correct these abuses, as in Wang Mang's abortive reforms and many similar efforts in later centuries, but the imperial state was never able to overcome completely the power of landed families.

In 25 C.E. the Han was reestablished, though under new rulers and with a new capital at Luoyang, following the earlier model of the Zhou and for the same reasons. It is thus known as the Eastern or Later Han, while the Chang'an period from 202 B.C.E. to 9 C.E. is called Western or Former Han. The new rulers, a succession of strong and conscientious emperors, restored the power, prosperity, and cultural vigor of Wu Di's time. Learning, philosophy, and the arts flourished once more and elite society reached new levels of affluence, elegance, and sophistication. Peace was reestablished along all the imperial frontiers by reconquest, and in 97 C.E. a Han army marched all the way to the Caspian Sea. Scouts were sent further west, reaching either the Persian Gulf or the Black Sea before returning, another missed encounter

---

Eunuchs are men castrated as youths and hence without heirs. They were often used as courtiers who could not intrigue on behalf of their sons. However, they often formed power cliques of their own and seldom used power responsibly.

Raised ceramic tile from a Han dynasty tomb showing a festive scene with jugglers, dancers, and musicians. (Werner Forman/Art Resource, New York)

with imperial Rome, then too at the height of its power and conquests. In 89 C.E. a Han army invaded Mongolia and again defeated the Xiongnu, probably contributing to the start of their subsequent migration westward and their ultimate role, merged by then with other Central Asian groups, as invaders of Europe under the name of the Huns. Xinjiang, northern Vietnam, northern Korea, southern Manchuria, and Inner Mongolia were all reincorporated into the empire; trade flourished, and China gloried in its confidently reasserted power and cultural leadership.

The Later Han produced some of the most famous generals in Chinese history, especially those who had repeated successes against the nomads on the northwest frontier. One of the best known of these was Ban Chao, whose brother and sister were joint authors of a well-known history of the Han dynasty. Ban Chao is said to have asserted that "only he who penetrates into the tiger's lair can carry off the cubs." In 73 C.E. he was sent with a detachment of troops to pacify the area south of Xinjiang. Surrounded by enemy troops, tribal groups with whom he was attempting to negotiate, he planned and carried out a daring night attack. He sent part of his forces behind the enemy lines to beat drums and simulate an attack, while the remainder built a huge fire in front of the barbarian fortress. The barbarians were completely surprised; many were killed as

they rushed out, and many more died in the flames. The barbarian chief surrendered and renewed his oath of vassalage to China.

After the first century, landlord power and oppression grew again; Wang Mang had been right to try to curb them. There were growing peasant revolts, and imperial relatives and powerful families jockeyed for position or influence. The elite, especially those at court surrounding weak emperors, indulged themselves in luxurious living heedless of the problems around them—all echoes of the problems Rome was facing at the same time. Palace intrigues grew out of control, and eunuch groups acquired more and more power. Generals in the provinces became rival warlords after suppressing peasant revolts. The entire imperial structure was crumbling, and in 220 C.E. the last Han emperor abdicated.

The power, wealth, and expansion of Han China were based in part on trade with Mongolia, Korea, Central Asia, Vietnam, and northern India as well as on the productivity and trade of newly conquered southern China. The incorporation of these areas within the empire (except for India and Central Asia) gave it secure frontiers, defended by mountain and desert barriers, beyond which there was little incentive to expand further. But control over all of these regions beyond China proper was lost with the collapse of the imperial structure. By this time nearly all of the Chinese originally settled in Xinjiang as garrison troops had withdrawn, leaving their watchtowers and fortified bases along the Silk Road to crumble away, like the Great Wall, in succeeding centuries. The loss of trade and revenue contributed to the fall of the dynasty, but the primary cause was self-destructive indulgence and faction fighting at court, as well as local and provincial rivalries. No empire, especially not one based on conquest, has lasted more than a few centuries at best. Regional and provincial counterpressures, and efforts by conquered peoples to reassert their independence, have joined with decay at the center to destroy every empire. The difference in China is that each new group that came to power founded a new dynasty and strove to rebuild the empire the Han had first established.

We know relatively little about the role of women in ancient and classical China, except that the advent of Confucianism tended to relegate them to a subordinate status. Nevertheless, there were some notable exceptions, perhaps most importantly the power of successive Han empresses and their families, including the many Empress Dowagers who, like women who became heads of their families after the deaths of their husbands, wielded virtually absolute power. Female figures also appeared in Chinese cosmology, especially the Queen Mother of the West, who presided over the realm of the setting sun and, hence, of the afterlife, in large part a Daoist conception. Even more eminent, by Chinese standards of value, was Ban Zhao, sister of the historian Ban Gu, who collaborated with him on an equal basis in writing the great *History of the Han Dynasty,* completed about 82 C.E.

The Collapse of the Han Order

A new dynasty called Wei was proclaimed, but it was impossible to hold the empire together, and rival dynasties soon emerged. In ensuing years the north was progressively overrun by barbarians, Xiongnu and other steppe nomadic groups, who sacked both Chang'an and Luoyang by the early fourth century. The north disintegrated into a bewildering series of minor rival kingdoms under barbarian control, while the south was similarly divided into rival Chinese states. The period from the fall of the Han in 220 C.E. to the ultimate reunification of China in 589 C.E. is sometimes rather misleadingly called the Six Dynasties (there were many more than six); it was a long interval of disunity, invasion, disruption, intrigue, and warfare that lasted nearly four centuries, shattered the imperial image, and left most Chinese disheartened. Much of the former high culture survived, especially in the arts, and little of it was forgotten by educated Chinese, but it was seen as a time of troubles. Except among the elite, many of whom fled south, many people suffered.

These centuries suggest comparison with what began only a little later in the breakup of the Roman empire and the barbarian invasions of southern Europe. In China too, the period was thought of as a Dark Age, and as in Europe there was a loss of confidence and the spread of a new mass religion of otherworldly salvation, Christianity in the West, Buddhism in China. The Wei, founded by an originally barbarian group, were vigorous promoters of Buddhism and left behind a rich legacy of Buddhist art, although their control was limited to the north. But the imperial idea continued to appeal to Chinese pride, and in time it was to be reestablished in a new birth of unification, power, and glory, the Tang.

A CLOSER LOOK

Cities in Ancient China

The Shang capitals, and their immediate Longshan predecessors, were primarily cosmic, ceremonial centers, symbols of royal authority. The late Longshan city on the site of modern Zhengzhou and the Shang capitals there, at Luoyang and at Anyang were massively walled and gated. The walls enclosed royal palaces and tombs, royal residences, some quarters for priests, slaves or kept artisans, and military guards, but much of the enclosed area was not built on. Most nonroyal inhabitants, and most of the workers, lived in village-like settlements outside the walls that, unlike the walled area, were not apparently planned. By at least late Shang, the Chinese character and the spoken word for "city" were the same as those for "wall," and this has remained so to the present. Cities were in other words designed as statements of authority; the wall was a symbol of state or (later) imperial power, and distinguished cities from unplanned villages or market towns. Apart from the capitals, imperial and provincial, most cities first arose as county seats, the lowest rung of national administration and, from Han times, the base of an imperial magistrate.

Chinese cities were built predominantly of wood and, thus, very little evidence remains from this early period to show what they or their buildings may have looked like. By Zhou times we do at least have some written documents that describe the precise planning of all walled cities and their ritual or symbolic importance, including their exact north-south orientation and the arrangement and dimensions of the royal or imperial buildings within the walls. Religious cults such as ancestor worship and the worship of what the Chinese called Heaven, or the Supreme Deity, were represented in every walled city by specific and carefully placed temples.

By the time of the Han dynasty, there had been nearly 2,000 years of urban experience in China; much of it was reflected in the Han capital at Chang'an. The

Han Civilization in Vietnam

Han era outposts in Vietnam at the beginning of the first millennium were primarily commercial centers. During the early first century interregnum, Han ruling-class refugees reinforced the local Han officials, and new patterns of Chinese rule emerged. Chinese administrators now had to pay for their expanded administration, and saw the local agrarian economy as a potential stable tax base. They began to promote greater productive efficiency as well as the extension of agriculture into previously uncultivated lands. To support their objectives, they encouraged transition to a formal patriarchal society as a way to increase the role of Vietnamese men in agricultural production as well as to discourage locally preferred male hunting and gathering, which produced no taxable surplus. The male role in agriculture, or the lack thereof, and the apparent female control of cultivation were difficult for Chinese administrators to accept. Han officials tried to combat male hostility by ordering all men aged 20 to 50 to marry; would-be elites were expected to pay for Chinese-style marriage ceremonies. Family-based productive units were registered, and stable kin groups were now made accountable for tax payments.

Han bureaucrats viewed traditional Vietnamese landholding patterns, which were based on communal usage rather than family ownership, as incompatible with their goals to create revenue systems based on private ownership. Han soldiers were settled in newly built walled outposts to govern new administrative prefectures and districts, and to negate the attempts of the old Lac aristocracy to stand in their way. Soldier-farmers supervised the digging of local ditches, to irrigate the fields surrounding the frontier population clusters. It was Han policy to keep these soldiers in place and self-sustaining, as they settled in and became part of the local social fabric.

Han rule resulted in a merging of Chinese and Vietnamese societies, as a powerful Han-Viet landlord class came into existence as government tax demands forced peasants to sell land to rich officials and become tenant farmers on the officials' private estates or as Han soldiers were given communal lands in return for their service. As the Han dynasty fell in the third century C.E., the Han-Viet elite took greater interest in seaborne trade as a secondary source of income.

---

site was carefully chosen by Liu Bang, the first Han emperor, but it was not until the reign of his successor, in 192 B.C.E., that the city walls were begun, 52 feet thick at the base and 27 feet high, made of pounded earth and over 3 miles long on each of the four sides. The walls enclosed imperial palaces, tombs, and temples to the ancestors among other temples, but as with the Shang, the Zhou, and the Qin, much of the walled area was not built on, although it remained important symbolically. The government regulated and supervised market areas inside as well as outside the walls, and the city was divided into 160 wards. Straight, broad avenues led from each of the major gates at the main compass points, but there was apparently a less planned growth of lanes and alleys in each of the quarters. The ideal city form was a square, which Han dynasty Chang'an approximated, with three gates on each of the four sides, one major central gate and two lesser ones.

The Han now ruled an immense territory, much of it newly conquered, especially in the south. The imperial stamp on these new lands was achieved primarily through the building of walled cities. Once the original inhabitants had been subdued and the land cleared, settled, and farmed, garrison towns or fortresses gave way to or were made over as walled county seats from which the imperial magistrate could keep order, dispense justice, and supervise the collection of taxes and the exactions of corvée and military conscription. In the hilly south such cities often had to accommodate to the terrain and sometimes altered the square shape somewhat, but the imperial model was apparent in all of them, including their official buildings, temples, military barracks, and appointed and regulated market areas inside and outside the walls. One can in fact chart the southward spread of Han occupation and the growth of Chinese-style agricultural settlement by noting the successive establishment of new, walled county seats. They appeared first along the rivers leading south from the Yangzi and then spread progressively inland from the rivers. Cities were linked with each other and with the imperial and provincial capitals by the imperial road system begun under the Qin and greatly extended under the Han.

Han Achievements

China by Han times was highly developed technologically as well as culturally. Little has survived of Chang'an and Luoyang to tell us much about them, but what accounts we have suggest that they rivaled imperial Rome in size and splendor. It is symptomatic of this vast bureaucratic empire, whose culture also put a high value on education and learning, that paper was first made there, by or before 100 C.E., more than 1,000 years before the knowledge of papermaking spread to Europe. Another Han innovation was an early form of porcelain, one more Chinese gift to the world known everywhere simply as "china." Water-powered mills were invented in Han China, as was the prototype of the modern horse collar and breast strap, which made it possible for draft animals to pull much heavier loads more efficiently and without being choked. Lacquer had made its appearance by Wu Di's time, and samples of fine lacquerware have been found in Han tombs. Han dynasty alchemists invented the technique of distillation, not discovered in Europe until the twelfth century C.E. Ships were built with watertight compartments, multiple masts, and sternpost rudders, and magnetic compasses were in use 1,000 years before Europe. Metallurgy, already well advanced, was given a further boost by the invention of a double-acting piston bellows, something not achieved in the West until the seventeenth century C.E. The wheelbarrow had made its appearance by late Han, better balanced than its later Western copy since the single wheel was placed in the middle instead of at one end, thus enabling a much greater weight to be transported with less effort. The square-pallet chain pump, for moving or raising water, and the suspension bridge were also Han innovations. The circulation of the blood was also first discovered in Han China, despite the conventional Western claim for its discovery by William Harvey in the seventeenth century.

By the first century B.C.E., the tube seed drill was in use, ahead of Europe by nearly 2,000 years and greatly increasing yields. Steel, probably diffused from India, was in use by the second century B.C.E. and was used among other things for suspension bridges. Why China did not move from this impressive technology to theoretical science is a puzzle. Confucian China was highly this-worldly, and the technological achievements were just a catalog of empiricism, the work of gifted artisans, who remained quite separate from those (fewer) who dealt in theory. But there was no tradition of experimentation, as in the West, essential to modern science.

Probably the greatest literary achievement of the Han was in the writing of history, a consistent Chinese emphasis on preserving the record of the past. Many Zhou records destroyed by Qin Shi Huang Di were reconstructed by Han scholars from memory, and the texts we have date largely from this period. New pride in empire and tradition produced the man called China's Grand Historian, Sima Qian (died c. 85 B.C.E.). His massive *Historical Records* put together materials from earlier texts in an effort to provide an accurate record of events since before the Shang and added summary essays on geography, culture, the economy, and biographies of important people. A century later Ban Gu (died 92 C.E.) compiled a similarly comprehensive *History of the Han Dynasty,* which became the model for the standard histories commissioned by each subsequent dynasty, another respect in which the Han set the pattern for later centuries.

Han writers set a high standard for historical scholarship that many Western scholars believe was not equaled elsewhere until the eighteenth century in the West. Here is another point of comparison between Han China and imperial Rome, where the writing of history also reached a high standard and reflected a similar pride in accomplishment and the tradition that had led to it. The Roman ideal remained appealing to the European mind and still underlies much of the modern West, but in China the state system, the imperial model, and most of the other institutions and forms first established under the Han endured to shape the course of the next 2,000 years.

The rise of civilization in China can be traced through the Shang, about 1600 B.C.E., its conquest by the Zhou, about 1050 B.C.E., the Warring States period in the last centuries of nominal Zhou rule, the Qin Empire from 221 to 206 B.C.E., and the rise, flourishing, and decline of the Han from 202 B.C.E. to 220 C.E.. The pattern of subsequent Chinese history was largely set by the achievement of the Han Empire, much of it based in turn on the teachings of Confucius, who lived in the sixth century B.C.E. From local beginnings on the North China Plain under the Shang, the Chinese state and empire had grown by the end of the Han to incorporate most of the area within the borders of modern China. During the same centuries the traditional model of Chinese civilization was established, a model that was largely adhered to for the next 20 centuries. (For later periods of Chinese history see Chapters 8, 11, 13, 15, 16, 17, 18 and 21.)

Questions

1. What does the Shang era contribute to the Chinese dynastic tradition? What changes in Chinese society took placed during the Zhou era that followed?

2. How do Confucius and Mencius reflect the circumstances of their times? How does China in this era compare with the consolidation of political power in India a century or so before, as described in the previous chapter? Were there similar results? Why or why not?

3. What were the Qin solutions to the divided political landscape of China? Why did the Qin dynasty have such a brief reign? What was the legacy of the Qin to China's future?

4. What was the difference between Qin Legalism and the teachings of Confucius and Mencius? How was Qin Legalism softened under the Han?

5. Han Wu Di is often viewed as China's greatest emperor. Is this warranted? What were his accomplishments, and what was his legacy to China's future?

6. What might have changed had the Han and imperial Rome met?

7. What were the reasons for Wang Mang's interregnum from 9 to 23 C.E. as this rebellion addressed problems in Han society? Were these problems adequately resolved by Wang Mang or by later Han rulers, or did they remain throughout China's history? Why and how did the Han successfully reassert their authority? Why did the Han ultimately fall?

8. How did Han governance in Vietnam reflect the strengths and weaknesses of the Chinese dynastic system?

Note

1. J. J. L. Duyvendak, trans., *The Book of Lord Shang* (London: Arthur Probsthain, 1928), pp. 193–194, 203, 209, 211, 229.

Suggested Web Sites

Early History of China

http://www~chaos.umd.edu/history/

An overview of chronology, texts, and images of Chinese history from 2000 B.C.E. to the present.

Confucius

http://www.confucius.org/main.htm

Comprehensive information from the Confucius Publishing Company. Includes a biography of Confucius, full text of the *Analects* and a photograph archive. Presented in many different languages.

China: Dynasties Timeline

http://emuseum.mnsu.edu/prehistory/china/index.html

Comprehensive information and maps, as well as a timeline of ancient China offered by Minnesota State University-Mankato.

Ancient China

http://www.crystalinks.com/china.html

An impressive site, including artifacts, philosophy, inventions, and script on ancient China.

http://www.ancient-china.net/

An extensive interactive site that addresses Chinese dynastic history through the Qin.

Suggestions for Further Reading

Ames, R. T., ed. *Wandering at Ease in the Zhuangzi.* Albany: SUNY Press, 2001.

Bigley, P. *Ancient Szechuan.* Princeton: Princeton University Press, 2001.

Birrell, A. *Popular Songs and Ballads of Han China.* Honolulu: University of Hawaii Press, 1993.

Bodde, D. *China's First Unifier.* Hong Kong: Hong Kong University Press, 1967.

Chang, K. C. *The Archeology of Ancient China,* 4th ed. New Haven: Yale University Press, 1987.

Creel, H. G. *The Origins of Statecraft in China.* Chicago: University of Chicago Press, 1970.

Crump, J. *Legends of the Warring States.* Ann Arbor: University of Michigan Press, 1998.

Dawson, R., ed. *The Legacy of China.* Oxford: Clarendon Press, 1964.

De Bary, W. T., ed. *Sources of Chinese Tradition.* New York: Columbia University Press, 1960.

De Crespigny, R. *Northern Frontier Policies and Strategies of the Later Han Empire.* Canberra: Australian National University Press, 1985.

Di Cosmo, N. *Ancient China and Its Enemies.* Cambridge, England: Cambridge University Press, 2004.

Gernet, J. *A History of Chinese Civilization,* trans. J. R. Foster. Cambridge: Cambridge University Press, 1996.

Hinsch, B., *Women in Early Imperial China.* Lanham, MD: Rowan and Littlefield, 2004.

Hsu, C. Y. *Ancient China in Transition: An Analysis of Social Mobility.* Stanford, CA: Stanford University Press, 1965.

Hsu, C. Y., and Linduff, K. M. *Western Chou Civilization.* New Haven: Yale University Press, 1988.

Keightley, D. *The Origins of Chinese Civilization.* Berkeley: University of California, 1983.

———.*The Ancestral Landscape in Late Shang China.* Berkeley: University of California Press, 2000.

Li, C. *Anyang.* Seattle: University of Washington Press, 1976.

Loewe, M. *Everyday Life in Early Imperial China.* New York: Putnam, 1968.

Needham, J. *Science in Traditional China.* Cambridge: Harvard University Press, 1981.

Owen, S. *Remembrances: The Experience of the Past in Classical Chinese Literature.* Cambridge: Harvard University Press, 1986.

Peerenboom, R. P. *Law and Morality in Ancient China.* Albany: SUNY Press, 1993.

Powers, M. *Art and Political Expression in Early China.* New Haven: Yale University Press, 1992.

Puett, M.J. *To Become a God.* Cambridge: Harvard University Press, 2002.

Raphals, L. *Sharing the Light: Representations of Women and Virtue in Early China.* Albany: SUNY Press, 2000.

Rubin, V. A. *Individual and State in Ancient China.* New York: Columbia University Press, 1976.

Schwarz, B. I. *The World of Thought in Ancient China.* Cambridge: Harvard University Press, 1985.

Sivin, N. *Science in Ancient China.* Aldershot, England: Variorum Press, 1995.

Sullivan, M. *The Arts of China.* Berkeley: University of California Press, 1977.

Twitchett, D., ed. *The Cambridge History of China,* vol. 1: *Ch'in and Han.* Cambridge: Cambridge University Press, 1986.

Wang, Z. *Han Civilization.* New Haven: Yale University Press, 1982.

Watson, B. *Courtier and Commoner in Ancient China.* New York: Columbia University Press, 1977.

Watson, W. *Ancient China: Discoveries of Post-Liberation Archeology.* London: British Broadcasting Corporation, 1974.

Yu, Y. S. *Trade and Expansion in Han China.* Berkeley: University of California Press, 1967.

6

Medieval India

This chapter covers developments in India after the fall of the Gupta Empire and the death of Harsha in 648 C.E., the coming of Islam, the Delhi Sultanate and its successors (1206–1526 C.E.), and the separate kingdoms of south India.

From the mid-tenth century, about three centuries after the collapse of the Guptas and the death of Harsha, northern India endured a long period of disunion, conflict, and renewed invasions from Central Asia, culminating in 1526 with the establishment of the Mughal Empire and a new flowering of unity and cultural brilliance. The medieval centuries of disorder and conquest, comparable in some ways to the so-called Dark Ages in Europe after the fall of Rome and resulting from similar causes, were, however, far from a period of universal disaster. Invasion and disruption involved only the northern half of the subcontinent, and for relatively short periods. Most people in most parts of India went on with their lives in the usual way most of the time.

These centuries also saw the vigorous continuation of the Indian artistic tradition that had been patronized by the Guptas and by Harsha, including the construction of a great many magnificent temples and their attendant sculpture, especially in the south. Trade flourished, particularly with Southeast Asia; wealthy merchants patronized temple complexes and the arts in the rich urban culture of medieval India, and great literature continued to be produced. For much of the north, however, invasion, conquest, and warfare brought periodic misery for many during these troubled centuries.

Early Islamic Influence in Northern India

The new invaders of the north were part of the explosive expansion of Islam, and they brought with them an often harsh and intolerant version of the new religion. But they also brought Islamic, and in particular Persian, culture including many literate and educated Iranians, who served as scribes for the largely illiterate conquerors as well as administrators, artists, writers, and other elites. India, with its wealth, numbers, and sophistication, was an irresistible target, and both Hinduism and Buddhism were seen as pagan creeds, to be conquered by the faith of the Prophet. The invaders' early motives and ruthless behavior were closely similar to those of the sixteenth-century Portuguese and Spanish invaders of Asia and Latin America in their search for plunder, such as gold and spices, and for converts to Catholic Christianity. For the fervent new Muslim converts who invaded India from Central Asia, Hinduism, with its "idolatry" and pantheism (many gods), its tolerance, and its lack of precise scriptural creed, was viewed as sacrilege and an evil to be eliminated. Their attitude to the closely related faith and practice of Buddhism was much the same. Probably the chief original motive for their invasion of India was, however, simple plunder. Many of these Central Asian groups contented themselves at first with pillaging India's wealth and slaughtering "infidel" victims before withdrawing across the passes with their loot.

In time, however, Muslim kingdoms with a largely Persian courtly culture were established in much of northern India, which had far more to attract and support them than their dry, barren, and mountainous homelands in Central Asia. And in time this new infusion of alien vigor blended with older strands of the Indian fabric.

Following the Muslim conquest of northern India by the thirteenth century, the new religion was also carried to insular Southeast Asia by Indian converts and other India-based Muslim traders, as well as by Islamic clerics who set out to proselytize non-Muslim populations—much as Indian Brahmins and Buddhist monks had in an earlier age. These and other aspects of Indian civilization were, however, overlaid on a well-developed, preexisting base whose character was distinctly different.

CHRONOLOGY

180 B.C. E.–1300 C. E.	■ Cholas, Pandyas, Pallavas in southern India
	■ Ajanta caves 5th–8th centuries C. E.
1000–1200 C. E.	■ Muslim raids into northern India
1206–1325 C. E.	■ Delhi Sultanate
r. 1296–1316 C. E.	■ Ala-ud-din Khalji
1314 C. E.	■ Defeat of the Monguls
1325–1526 C. E.	■ Tughluks
1336–1565 C. E.	■ Vijayanagara
1489–1526 C. E.	■ Lodis

The Islamic Advance into Northern India

India at first lay beyond the wave of the seventh-century Islamic conquests that engulfed most of the Middle East and North Africa, but Arab traders continued to bring back samples of Indian wealth. Sind, the lower half of the Indus Valley, was conquered by Arab forces in the eighth century, primarily as a rival trade base. But the major advance came nearly three centuries later, from the newly converted Turks of Central Asia, who had been driven westward and into Afghanistan by earlier Chinese expansion under the Han and the Tang.

The Turkish leader Mahmud of Ghazni (971–1030), known as the "Sword of Islam," mounted 17 plundering expeditions between 1001 and 1027 from his eastern Afghan base at Ghazni into the adjacent upper Indus and western Punjab, destroying Hindu temples, sacking rich cities, killing or forcibly converting the inhabitants, and then returning to Ghazni with jewels, gold, silver, women, elephants, and slaves. His remote, mountain-ringed capital became by the eleventh century a great center of Islamic culture, thanks in part to stolen Indian riches. Plunder and slaughter in the name of God did not make a good impression for Islam on most Indians, but the austere new religion with its offer of certainty and the equality of all (except women) did appeal to some, as wherever it spread in other countries. And India began to appeal as a base to Mahmud's successors and to rival Central Asian Turkish groups.

True to their nomadic heritage, their military effectiveness depended importantly on their mastery of cavalry tactics and their use of short, powerful compound bows of laminated wood, horn, and sinew that they could fire from a gallop on horseback. The Rajputs of Rajasthan, on the flank of the Islamic invasion route, fought relentlessly from their desert strongholds and fortified cities against these Turco-Afghan armies, which the more peaceful inhabitants of Hindustan were less able to resist. Some of the Rajputs had Central Asian origins too, some centuries earlier, and hence shared an originally nomadic tradition of mounted mobile warfare, but all Rajputs were part of a military culture of great tenacity, nurtured in the desert of Rajasthan. They were never completely overcome, but most of the rest of the north, seriously weakened by continued political division and internal conflict, was progressively conquered.

By the end of the twelfth century Punjab and most of Hindustan (the valley of the Ganges) had been incorporated into a Turco-Afghan empire with its capital at Delhi. Delhi controlled an easy crossing place on the Jumna (Jamuna) River where a range of hills stretched southwest and provided protection. Northward and westward were the barriers respectively of the Himalayas and the Thar Desert of Rajasthan. Eastward the broad Ganges Valley led into the heart of Hindustan, but for access to it and for routes southward, Delhi had first to be secured, as all invaders from the northwest, the repeated route of entry via the Punjab, were obliged to do. Bengal was overrun in 1202, and in 1206 the Delhi sultanate was formally inaugurated. As a series of successive Islamic dynasties, it was to dominate most of northern India for the next 320 years, until the rise of the Mughal Empire as a new dynasty of conquest in 1526.

Bengal had prospered as a separate kingdom after the fall of the Gupta order. It remained the chief Indian center of Buddhism, including a great university and monastery at Nalanda, where some 10,000 monks lived and studied, and similar Hindu centers of learning and piety, as at Banaras. Both religions and their followers were targets for the Muslim invaders. Tens of thousands of monks and other Hindus and Buddhists were slaughtered and the universities and monasteries destroyed. This catastrophe marked the effective end of Buddhism in the land of its birth. The few surviving Buddhists fled from the slaughter to Nepal and Tibet. Hindu monuments also suffered, for their sculpture as well as their faith violated Islamic principles forbidding the artistic representation of divine creation, including the human form.

Unfortunately for its people, northern India remained hopelessly divided among rival kingdoms, most of them small and nearly all of them in chronic conflict with one another. In total, their armies were huge, but they seem never to have considered a united or even partially united stand against the invaders who, like Alexander before them, defeated the few armies sent against them one by one. Even after Mahmud and his successors had established their rule over most of the north, little opposition was organized against them or against their repeated efforts to spread their conquests southward into central India and the Deccan.

Medieval India

India seems as if it should be a natural unit, surrounded as it is by mountains enclosing great river valleys and floodplains, but in fact it is divided into many separate linguistic, cultural, and even political regions.

The Delhi Sultanate

Successive Turco-Afghan rulers were more accepting, if not of Hinduism and its artistic traditions, then of Hindus, who remained the vast majority of the Indian population. Even these ruthless conquerors realized in time that it was impossible to kill or convert all Indians. But Hindus were treated as decidedly second-class citizens and forced to pay a special tax as "infidels" if they refused, as most did, to convert. This was an improvement on the atrocities of the earlier raiders, who followed the dictum, "Islam or death"; in fact, it was more in keeping with the original Islamic practice of rec-

Approaches to the Khyber Pass near the eastern border of Afghanistan. The mountain barrier around India is formidable but is penetrable via several passes. Through them have come a long succession of invaders, including the Turco-Afghan conquerors of northern India. (R. Murphey)

ognizing in other established religions a special, if inferior, status. As for Christians and Jews, "protected peoples of the book," these non-Muslims were given a degree of protection and were called *dhimmis*.

There was no shortage of Hindu religious texts, and it was not hard in time to accept Hinduism as a sophisticated religion, not simply as "paganism." With more knowledge it was also recognized that Hinduism was basically monotheistic, like Islam, and could not be judged only on the basis of the many gods of Indian folk religion. This distinction was comparable to that between textual Christianity and folk practice involving many saints and local cults, as, for example, in Latin America. The head tax (*jizya*) paid by protected non-Muslims (dhimmis) was heavy—about 6 percent of an individual's total net worth annually—but it bought a degree of freedom to practice one's own religion, however scorned by those in political power. Together with this softening of the earlier total intolerance of Hindus and Hinduism, the later Delhi sultans agreed to leave many of the original Hindu Indian local rulers and petty rajas in control of their domains. The sultanate, thus, slowly became more of an Indian order and less of an alien conquest that used India as object rather than subject. It came in time to depend increasingly on the support of India's indigenous people, and under the best of its rulers, to try to govern rather than merely to exploit.

The stronger rulers of the Delhi sultanate continued to make raids and plundering expeditions into the mountain-protected Deccan, south of the Ganges Plain of Hindustan, but they never won a permanent position there or elsewhere in the south. The landscape strongly favored the Hindu defenders, beginning with the double range of mountains that mark the northern edge of the

Deccan—the Vindhyas and the Satpura—and further strengthened as barriers by the Narbada and Tapti rivers, which run between the two ranges.

The Deccan itself is heavily dissected, and in many areas cut up into steep ravines and river valleys, with easily defended hills or smaller mountains in almost every part. It has seen many bloody campaigns but never a complete or permanent victory for any of the successive invaders from the north, including both the Delhi sultanate and the Mughal dynasty as well as the Guptas, Mauryas, and Aryans long before. The seemingly endless campaigns have instead sapped the resources of the invaders and contributed importantly to the ultimate downfall of their states. The chief and most consistent Hindu defenders against the Muslim attackers were the warlike Marathas of Maharashtra, the arid northwestern quarter of the Deccan. They were protected by their plateau base and its mountain fringes and, like the Rajputs, had a proud martial tradition of resisting northern invasions, which they were in a good strategic position to block or harry from the flank.

The Delhi sultanate was also weakened by internal power struggles and by political intrigues, in a pattern they brought with them from Central Asia, and which also plagued their Ottoman Turkish cousins later in their far larger empire. Most of the Delhi sultans were absolute rulers who tolerated no dissent and demanded total submission; most of them consequently provoked chronic revolts and plots against themselves, and many died by assassination, poisoning, or in the dust of a coup or a civil war, after coming to power and maintaining it by the same means at the expense of other rivals. There was no clearly agreed-upon method of succession, and the death of each sultan was the occasion for fighting and intrigue among rivals for power.

Hindu-Muslim Conflict

Barani, the fourteenth-century Arab historian, was severely critical of Muslim intolerance in India and their persecution of Hindus but gave his own answer to Hindu assertions of the superiority of their culture.

> We Muslims, of course, stand entirely on the other side of the questions, considering all men as equal, except in piety, and this is the greatest obstacle which prevents any approach or understanding between Hindus and Muslims.

The modern historian Rawlinson repeats the traditional poem of a Rajput lady whose husband had fallen in battle against the Muslim invaders, epitomizing the fierce Rajput defense of Hindu India.

> "Son, tell me ere I go, how bore himself my Lord?"
> "As a reaper of the harvest of battle! I followed his steps as a humble gleaner of his sword. On the bed of honor he spread a carpet of the slain, whereon, with a barbarian for his pillow, he sleeps ringed by his foes. Oh mother, who can tell his deeds? He left no foe to dread or admire him."

Source: H. G. Rawlinson, *India: A Short Cultural History* (New York: Praeger, 1965), pp. 202, 218, 228.

Their armies, like those of the Ottomans and other Turkish states, owed their strength in large part to *mamelukes,* usually Turks bought in their youth as slaves and then demandingly trained as full-time professional fighters, as few armies were anywhere until recent times. They were an outstandingly disciplined force, but like many lifetime mercenaries they were not above an interest in power and in its rewards. Military commanders at the head of mameluke troops could be and often were formidable political contenders. The ruthlessness and often extreme cruelty of many of the sultans provided frequent motives for revolt, as did their minority position within Hindu India and the resentment provoked by any alien invader.

In general, the sultanate succeeded only partially and for brief periods in becoming an effective administration for the areas it controlled in the north. The records we have tell us about power rivalries, intrigues at court, tax policies, coups, civil wars, and the abortive efforts to invade the south, but we have little concrete evidence of how much these petty affairs of state affected the lives of most ordinary people. Political power was highly concentrated in Delhi, leaving much of the sultanate's domains under local rulers with a good deal of autonomy in practice. It seems likely that, after the first half century or so of ruthless plunder, conquest, slaughter, and intolerance, most people in northern India were left largely to themselves as long as they paid both land taxes and the jizya.

The main impact of the sultanate on India was probably to implant a deep mistrust of politics, government

in general, and Islam in particular, where it was used as the basis of state policy. Few monuments remain from this generally oppressive period in north Indian history. In broader cultural terms, these centuries did, however, see a fusion of originally Hindu elements with the Iranian influences brought in with the Turkish conquerors. Like the Mughals who followed them, they were the agents of a largely Persian culture, whose richness and variety in time found ready acceptance among many Indians. What we now think of as "traditional" Indian poetry, music, architecture, painting, the languages of northern India and their literatures, all in fact derived their present forms from this fusion. Islam and Hindu-Muslim differences proved to be neither a bar to such cultural hybridization nor a source of conflict, except where it was made an issue in political and military matters. Religion was far less important than other aspects of culture, and proved no barrier to cultural mixing.

But as a government or administration, or as a patron of culture, the Delhi sultanate wins no prizes, despite a few of its later abler and larger-minded rulers (see A Closer Look that follows). Islam was progressively Indianized and over the centuries after 1206 it won some converts on its own merits and through the agency of a long line of Islamic mystics (*sufis*) whose vision was broad enough to appeal to the long-standing Indian involvement with religious truth, which in its pure form is universal, as Hindu and Muslim mystics and philosophers agreed.

A CLOSER LOOK

Notable Sultans: Ala-ud-din Khalji

The power of the Delhi sultans was severely tested by the Mongol invasion of the early fourteenth century. By this time the Turco-Afghan invaders had been partly Indianized, like so many conquerors before them, and depended more on the support of the indigenous people. It was fortunate that a capable ruler was on the throne of Delhi. Ala-ud-din Khalji (reigned 1296–1316), augmented his forces, including mameluke troops, to meet this gruesome challenge, and drove the Mongol horsemen back into Afghanistan—one of the very few cases of a Mongol defeat. Ala-ud-din had usurped the throne by having his uncle murdered, after raiding into the Deccan and bringing back loot, which he used to buy the loyalty of those around his uncle, Sultan Jalal-ud-din. Ala-ud-din paid his army officers in cash and kept tight personal control over his forces. He could neither read nor write and had no tolerance for intellectuals, sophisticated courtiers, or other elites. He abolished all regular stipends and grants to the Muslim nobles, eliminating their political influence and leaving them wholly dependent on him. He outlawed wine parties, which were in any case against Muslim doctrine, as possible breeders of plots against him.

His power base was fueled by a land tax, which he raised to 50 percent of the value of each crop, and by new taxes on milk cows and houses. The 50-percent crop tax tended especially to impoverish Hindus, since they were the farmers. Barani, the fourteenth-century Arab historian of India, quoted Ala-ud-din as saying:

> I am an unlettered man, but I have seen a great deal. Be assured that Hindus will never become submissive and obedient until they have been reduced to poverty. I have therefore given orders that just enough shall be left them of grain, milk, and curds from year to year, but that they must not accumulate hoards or property.

Hindus were also forbidden to possess any weapons or ride horses. Loyalty and conformance with his decrees were further ensured by a network of spies, harsh penalties, and intricate court intrigues. He also imposed wage and price controls in Delhi and prohibited the private hoarding of gold and silver, while at the same time requiring all merchants to be licensed and their profits restricted as well as taxed. Peasants had to sell their crops only to licensed merchants and at set prices and could retain only fixed amounts for their own use. These measures kept most prices low enough to permit soldiers and workers to live adequately on their pay, at least within the Delhi area, though merchants and peasants everywhere resented them bitterly. But the controls and taxes made it possible for Ala-ud-din to field an army that could meet and repulse the Mongol invasion.

With the Mongols defeated, Ala-ud-din resumed his plundering raids in the Deccan, overcoming even some of the Rajputs and penetrating briefly as far as Pandyan territory further south. But with his death in 1316 not only these efforts but also his own family line came to an end; his first son was murdered by his own soldiers, and a second son abandoned all efforts at maintaining the controls established by his father and gave himself up to pleasures at court. Ala-ud-din was ruthlessly cruel and oppressive and was understandably feared and hated. His system died with him, but during his lifetime it and his own fierce determination and arbitrary power made it possible for Hindustan to avoid the fate of being sacked and pillaged by the Mongols. His

The Mongols: An Eyewitness Account

Even the Turco-Afghan rulers of the Delhi sultanate were appalled by the Mongols, whose invasion of India they managed to repel. Here is a description of the Mongols by a Turkish eyewitness.

> Their eyes were so narrow and piercing that they might have bored a hole in a brazen vessel. Their stink was more horrible than their color. Their faces were set on their bodies as if they had no neck. Their cheeks resembled soft leather bottles, full of wrinkles and knots. Their noses extended from cheek to cheek and their mouths from cheek bone to cheek bone. Their nostrils resembled rotten graves, and from them the hair descended as far as the lips.

Source: H. G. Rawlinson, *India: A Short Cultural History* (New York: Praeger, 1965), p. 224.

Islamic Ideals

The Key to Paradise, *a guide to the good Muslim life, was compiled in the fourteenth century as an aid to newly converted Indians.*

> The Prophet said that whoever says every day at daybreak in the name of God the Merciful and the Compassionate, "There is no god but Allah and Muhammad is his Prophet," him God most high will honor with seven favors. First, He will open his spirit to Islam; second, He will soften the bitterness of death; third, He will illuminate his grave; fourth, He will show the recording angels his best aspects; fifth, He will give the list of his deeds with His right hand; sixth, He will tilt the balance of his account in his favor; and seventh, He will pass him over the eternal bridge which spans the fire of hell into Paradise like a flash of lightning. . . . Keep your lips moist by repeating God's name. . . . The servant of God should make the Qur'an [Koran] his guide and his protection. On the day of judgment, the Qur'an will precede him and lead him toward Paradise. Whoever does not stay diligently close to the Qur'an but lags behind, the angel will come forth and striking him on his side will carry him off to hell. One's rank in Paradise depends upon the extent of one's recitation of the Qur'an. Everyone who knows how to read a small amount of the Qur'an will enjoy a high position in Paradise, and the more one knows how to read it, the higher one's status in Paradise. . . . The Prophet said that on the night of his ascent to heaven he was shown the sins of his people. He did not see any greater sin than that of him who did not know and did not read the Qur'an.

Source: W. T. de Bary, ed., *Sources of Indian Traditions,* vol. 1 (New York: Columbia University Press, 1964), pp. 386–387.

economic controls in particular were remarkable, especially for any premodern state, but they rested on absolute power and grinding taxation, both bound to provoke resistance and ultimately to destroy them. He had bought and murdered his way to the throne with the help of the plunder brought back from his Deccan raids, but he and his successors failed to hold any part of the south or to again tap its wealth. They could maintain their authoritarian rule in the north only by bleeding the agricultural system, which was the base of the economy—a prescription for disaster.

The Tughluks

With the collapse of Ala-ud-din's order, a new Muslim dynasty succeeded to power in the Dehli sultanate, the Tughluks, whose founder was the son of a Turkish court slave and a Hindu woman, perhaps a symbol of the changes since the sultanate was first established. His son and successor, Muhammad Tughluk (reigned 1325–1351), came to the throne when a pavilion he had

erected for his father collapsed and killed the father. Muhammad's reign of strict piety and renewed efforts at carrying Islam southward may be seen as an attempt at expiation of his sense of guilt. He ordered everyone to observe the Koranic ordinances for ritual, prayers, and Islamic doctrine and forced large numbers of troops and officials to man his drive into the Deccan, where he briefly established a secondary capital.

The endless campaigns, and taxes to support them, provoked growing rebellion as well as southern resistance. From 1335 to 1342 northern India endured a seven-year drought and famine, one of the worst in its history, but Muhammad was too busy fighting, collecting taxes, and promoting strict Islam to respond, and there was no organized effort by the state to provide tax relief or food distribution. Well over 1 million people died, and revolts became even more widespread in the north as well as in the south, and even in Delhi itself. Bengal broke away and declared its independence in 1338, retaining it for the next three centuries.

Muhammad was killed fighting a rebellion in Sind in 1351, and his cousin Firuz Tughluk claimed the throne,

The Bhakti Synthesis

Kabir, the blind Muslim weaver-poet of the fifteenth century, is the best-known representative of the Hindu-Muslim fusion in the bhakti movement.

> O servant, where dost thou seek me? Lo, I am beside thee.
> I am neither in the temple nor in the mosque,
> Not in rites and ceremonies nor in yoga and renunciation.
> If thou art a true seeker thou shalt at once see Me;
> Thou shalt meet Me in a moment of time.
> It is needless to ask of a saint the caste to which he belongs,
> For the priest, the warrior, the tradesman and all the other castes
> Are all alike seeking God. The barber has sought God,
> The washerwoman, and the carpenter.
> Hindus and Muslims alike have achieved that end,
> Where there remains no mark of distinction.
> O Lord, who will serve Thee?
> Every supplicant offers his worship to the God of his own creation;
> None seek Him, the perfect, the Indivisible Lord.
> Kabir says, "O brother, he who has seen the radiance of love, he is saved."
> When I was forgetful, my true guru showed me the way.
> Then I left off all rites and ceremonies, I bathed no more in the holy water.
> I do not ring the temple bell, I do not set the idol on its throne
> Or worship the image with flowers.
> The man who is kind and who practices righteousness, who remains passive
> Amidst the affairs of the world, who considers all creatures on earth
> As his own self, he attains the Immortal Being;
> The true God is ever with him; he attains the true Name whose words are pure,
> And who is free from pride and conceit.
> Look within your heart, for there you will find the true God of all.

Source: W. T. de Bary, ed., *Sources of Indian Traditions,* vol. 1 (New York: Columbia University Press, 1964), pp. 355–357.

which he held until his death in 1388. Firuz proved a more constructive ruler, who largely abandoned the earlier efforts at conquest and warfare and concentrated instead on the rebuilding of Delhi, with splendid new gardens, mosques, hospitals, and colleges for the study of Islam. He also supported the construction of new irrigation schemes, including dams and reservoirs, which brought new land into production. Although a Muslim zealot like Muhammad, he cut back the sultanate's system of spies and informers, abolished torture, and tried to improve the material welfare of his subjects. But his Islamic orthodoxy and intolerance, his insistence on payment of the jizya tax by all infidels, and his clear message that Hindus were at best second-class citizens in time alienated most of the people, who were, after all, predominantly Hindu. Soon after his death the sultanate's domains broke up into warring factions.

This chaos in northern India invited, as so often before, a catastrophic invasion, this time by the Central Asian armies of Tamerlane (1336–1405), a Turkish leader who had already ravaged much of Central Asia and the Middle East (see Chapter 10). After plundering the Punjab, he entered Delhi in 1398 and systematically slaughtered the inhabitants; the survivors were taken away as slaves or forced to carry his booty. Famine and pestilence followed in his wake. The Delhi sultanate never fully recovered from this devastating blow, and its political fragmentation accelerated. Gujarat declared its independence in 1401 and flourished under its own rulers, especially in the Gujarati capital of Ahmedabad. Gujarat had always depended on its maritime trade, which extended westward across the Arabian Sea and the Indian Ocean and eastward to Southeast Asia, and this trade now increased still more. Many Gujaratis, including their rulers, had converted to Islam, which

The Qutb Minar. Begun in 1199 by Sultan Qutb-ud-din Aibak, completed by Sultan Il-tumish (r. 1211–1236), and repaired by Firuz Tughluk, it was built to celebrate the victory of the new rulers of Delhi and also as a minaret to the adjacent mosque, largely destroyed not long afterward. The tower, 73 meters high and beautifully decorated in each segment, is one of the few monuments preserved in reasonable condition from the centuries of the Delhi sultanate. (R. Murphey)

proved useful in trade connections both westward and eastward. With their commercial profits they built luxurious new palaces and mosques in Ahmedabad and brought new prosperity to Gujarat as a whole.

Sikander Lodi

In what remained of the Delhi sultanate, an Afghan clan, the Lodis, took the throne in 1450 and produced an able ruler, Sikander (reigned 1489–1517). His origin is indicative of the ongoing Indianization of an originally alien order, as his mother was Hindu; he himself was both a poet and a patron of what was fast becoming a hybrid culture, and he encouraged scholarship and the compilation of books on medicine and music. Though a

highly orthodox Muslim, he fell in love with a Hindu princess, and his reign saw the continued blending of the mystical traditions of Islam, represented by sufis, with the equivalent tradition in Hinduism—the best and most effective formula for the success of Islam in a country already devoted to religion. Sikandar himself did not succumb to Sufism, and perhaps to prove his orthodoxy, given his Hindu mother and Hindu leanings in other respects, unfortunately continued the Muslim policy of destroying temples and other Hindu religious art.

In the troubled time after 1000 C.E., with its shifting and periodically disastrous political changes, punctuated by invasion and bloody warfare, it is understandable that people turned even more fervently to religion. Beginning in the relatively peaceful south in the tenth century, a new movement within Hinduism known as *bhakti* ("devotion") spread north and by the fourteenth century had reached Bengal, where at the ancient sacred city of Banaras on the Ganges a latter-day disciple, Ramananda, preached the bhakti message of divine love. Its universal appeal as well as its solace, and its emphasis on the simple love of God and the abandonment of sectarian or rival causes attracted a mass following in all parts of India, including many Muslims. This was the sufi message also, and Muslim sufis helped to spread the bhakti movement while they also increased the appeal of a more humane and at the same time more mystical Islam. It was celebrated by a long series of poet-saints in both its southern origins and its later northern spread. Probably the most beloved of all the bhakti advocates was the blind and illiterate Muslim weaver-poet Kabir of Banaras (1440–1518), a disciple of Ramananda whose moving poetry on the bhakti theme has inspired many millions since his time.

The modern India historian D. P. Singhal sums up the history of the Delhi sultanate as follows:

> The history of the sultanate of Delhi is full of dynasties which were short-lived and weak. Of the thirty-five sultans belonging to the five dynasties who sat on the throne of Delhi during a period of 300 years, nineteen were assassinated by Muslim rebels. It is almost a catalogue of kings, courts, and conquests, but it was the richest of all the Islamic states during the period. An important feature of the period was the Hindu-Muslim cultural fusion. It was not an authentic Islamic state; it charged more than the one-fifth land tax prescribed by Muslim law, and also interest. Kingship was hereditary and not elected. The sultans were unlimited despots. Even agriculture did not flourish; no attempt was made to better the lot of the cultivators. . . . Rebellions and military expeditions were common and their political fortunes varied. The Turco-Afghan rulers lacked national support and a sound administration based on tradition, so essential for any government to survive and flourish. There was no well defined, well regulated administrative machinery under their rule. The authority of the central government, which was dominated by the ruler and

military aristocracy, hardly extended beyond the capital, court, and fort. The rest of the country was in the hands of ambitious provincial governors who, having sent tribute or presents to Delhi, felt free to continue their autocratic rule. Their rule in turn rarely extended beyond their own courts. . . . The disintegration which began toward the close of the reign of Muhammad Tughluk was completed by [Tamerlane's] invasion and the following anarchy. The recovery of northern India under the Lodi kings was too brief to alter the picture materially.[1]

Southern India

Most of India remained in fact in indigenous hands during these centuries, including the ancient kingdoms of Pallava, Pandya, and Chola, whose rule, cultures, and literary and artistic traditions continued largely unbroken. In much of the Deccan and the south, however, with the exception of the Chola kingdom, central state control was relatively loose, and the Hindu monarchies were organized on a semifeudal basis. Lands were held by lords as fiefs in return for military assistance, payments in kind, and periodic attendance at court, a system similar to that in Zhou dynasty China and medieval Europe. Rulers also granted tax-free estates as rewards for service. In India, as in medieval Europe, the tax burden was made heavier by grants of

tax-free domains to religious orders, monasteries, and temples. These were often in fact the richest groups in the country, and they also received large voluntary donations, especially from merchants anxious to demonstrate their piety.

The chief cities of medieval India, as of Europe, were mainly religious centers, grouped around a complex of temples, although supported by profits from trade, farming, and artisan production. The great Indian tradition of monumental architecture and sculpture flourished especially in the south during these centuries. The major southern kingdoms alternated in their efforts to dominate all of the south, but trade continued between southern India and Southeast Asia. Commercial ties served, as they had since Mauryan times, as a channel for Indian influence in the parts of Southeast Asia close to the sea. There was also some settlement by Indian colonists, who brought both Hinduism and Buddhism as well as other aspects of Indian culture.

Preoccupation with the violent political scene in the medieval north, for which we have more detailed records, should not obscure the unbroken continuance and further evolution of indigenous Indian civilization in the south, largely undisturbed by the northern turmoil. The south remained politically divided and periodically involved in warfare among contending states, but such problems were chronic in most societies of the time elsewhere, as in Europe. The medieval southern Indian

Some of the caves at Ellora, showing a sample of the sculptures cut out of the rock. (Government of India Tourist Office)

record of temple building alone, including many immense and outstandingly beautiful complexes, tells a more positive tale of wealth derived from agriculture and extensive overseas and domestic trade, of an orderly society and government, for most of the time within each kingdom, which could foster prosperity, and of the continued Indian emphasis on religion and its earthly manifestations in worship. Much of the urban culture was supported by merchants, and this too provides some evidence of the scope and wealth of commerce, including the maritime trade with Southeast Asia from a series of ports on the southeast coast.

Temple Builders and Rival Kingdoms

The history of southern India during these centuries is in fact recorded largely in the building of temples and their records and inscriptions. Through them we know the outlines of rival and successive kingdoms, their conquests, rise, and decline, and the names of rulers and rich donors. Perhaps the greatest temple builders were the Pallavas of the western and central Deccan from the fourth to the tenth centuries, but all of the southern Indian kingdoms built temples. It was an age of faith, like the European Middle Ages, and as in Europe, Indian builders worked in stone, although many of the temples were hewn out of solid rock and consist of a series of adjoining caves, ornately decorated and with ceilings supported by carved stone pillars.

The best known and most extensive of these rock-cut temples is the complex of 27 caves at Ajanta in the central Deccan, built by the Vakataka Kingdom, which stretch in a crescent shape across an entire mountainside, and the nearby 34 similar cave temples at Ellora, constructed in the fifth and the sixth to eighth centuries, respectively. The Ajanta caves were later partly buried by a landslide and were rediscovered in the early nineteenth century in excellent condition by British amateur archaeologists, who marveled at the beautifully ornate friezes, sculptures, bas-reliefs, monumental figures of elephants, gods, and goddesses, and wall paintings.

The Pallavas and other southern dynasties who also patronized the arts built a great number of other temples. Many of them were freestanding, including the enormous complex at Madurai built by the Pandyan kingdom, those at Tanjore built by the Cholas, and similar clusters in other southern Indian cities, in a variety of styles.

Revenues from trade and productive agriculture, as well as donations from the pious, not only helped to make this extensive building possible but also supported political power and imperial ambition. In that competition the Cholas were the most successful in the extent of their conquests, from their base in what is now the state of Tamilnadu (southeastern peninsular India).

Classical Hindu temple architecture in southern India, preserved from the Muslim onslaught on the north. (Adam Woolfitt/Corbis)

Their economic strength depended in part on their organized success in constructing a system of excavated tanks or reservoirs to hold the monsoon rains and then in distributing water to fields via canals during the long dry periods. Originally a feudatory dependency of the Pallavas, the Cholas emerged as the dominant power in southern India by the tenth century and even absorbed much of the earlier Pandyan kingdom, including its capital at Madurai. They further developed the Pallava style of temple building. The revived Pandyan kingdom continued the tradition when it supplanted the Cholas after the thirteenth century, and in the seventeenth century it completed the Madurai temple complex in the form we see today.

Throughout the classical and medieval periods, temples were the scenes of frequent festivals that included music, drama, elaborate processions, and dance. These forms of religious worship were also often combined with markets, as in the fairs of medieval Europe, and offered attractions for secular as well as religious interests. Pilgrimages to temple centers were popular, with the same mixture of devotion or piety and social entertainment, complete with storytellers and itinerant actors

Hindu Devotion

Here are some samples of Hindu bhakti devotional literature of medieval southern India.

I am false, my heart is false, my love is false, but I, this sinner, can win Thee if I weep before Thee, O Lord, Thou who art sweet like honey, nectar, and the juice of sugar cane. Please bless me so that I might reach Thee. . . . Melting in the mind, now standing, now sitting, now lying, and now getting up, dancing in all sorts of ways, gaining the vision of the Form of the Lord shining like the rosy sky, when will I stand united with and entered into that exquisite Gem? . . . Without any other attachment, I cherished with my mind only Thine holy feet; I have been born with Thy grace and I have attained the state whereby I will have no rebirth. O benevolent Lord, worshipped and praised by the learned! Even if I forget you, let my tongue go on muttering your praise. . . . Lighting in my heart the bright lamp of knowledge, I sought and captured Him. Softly the lord of Miracles too entered my heart and stayed neuter. He is not to be seen. He neither is nor is not. When He is sought He will take the form in which He is sought, and again He will not come in such a form. How can one describe the nature of the Lord? . . . The name of the Lord will bless one with high birth and affluence; it will obliterate all the sufferings of the devotees; it will endow one with the heavenly state; it will bring success and all good things; it will perform for one more beautiful acts than one's own mother. . . . The lamb brought to the slaughterhouse eats the leaf garland with which it is decorated. The frog caught in the mouth of the snake desires to swallow the fly flying near its mouth. So is our life. . . . He who knows only the sacred books is not wise. He only is wise who trusts in God.

Source: W. T. de Bary, ed., *Sources of Indian Traditions,* vol. 1 (New York: Columbia University Press, 1964), pp. 349–352.

and jugglers plus vendors of food, trinkets, and religious objects. Chaucer's *Canterbury Tales* could equally well have been set in medieval southern India, and in fact pilgrimages and religious festivals of much the same sort remain an important feature of modern Indian culture.

The Cholas

What gave the Cholas additional power for expansion during their centuries of dominance was their profitable involvement in maritime trade and their navy. Chola armies conquered most of the south, from the central Deccan to the tip of the peninsula. The Chola navy was the greatest maritime force of the surrounding oceans. It even defeated the fleet of the Southeast Asian empire of Sri Vijaya in 1025, intervening again in 1068 to defend the Malayan dependencies it had acquired.

With the help of their navy, the Cholas also invaded the northern half of Ceylon (Sri Lanka) and occupied it for over 50 years in the eleventh century, until they were driven out by a great revival of Sinhalese power, which lasted until the thirteenth century. The Sinhalese capital was moved from its classical site at Anuradhapura to a new monumental capital at Polonnaruwa, and its armies in turn briefly invaded the Tamil country of the Cholas and temporarily occupied Madurai in the later twelfth century. The Sinhalese took advantage of a Pandyan revolt against the Cholas, which in itself was symptomatic of the overall decline of Chola power and the resurgence of rival south Indian kingdoms. By the thirteenth century Chola power had faded and the south resumed its more normal political fragmentation, although a reduced Chola kingdom remained and continued to patronize Tamil culture and to prosper economically. The kingdom's administration was remarkable for the role played by village and district councils, which were under central supervision but retained a large measure of local autonomy.

The Indian art of bronze casting and the further flowering of sculpture reached new levels of perfection in medieval southern India, especially in the Chola domains. The famous and exquisite figure of the dancing, many-armed Shiva was cast in eleventh-century Chola, and the form was widely copied by other Indian artists. Other pieces from this period have the same grace and beauty. These artistic accomplishments bespeak the wealth and confidence of the times, and make one want to know more. But until recent times most Indians, unlike Greeks, Romans, Chinese, and later, Europeans, have thought that, except for some of their literature, accounts of the everyday world were not important enough to record. Apart from inscriptions and temple records, we have few accounts of day-to-day life. Indian writers concentrated on religion, philosophy, and literature. In comparison with the eternal questions, politics and material details seemed of little consequence.

Vijayanagara: Empire of Victory

Continued raids into the Deccan by the Delhi sultanate, beginning in the thirteenth century, helped to stimulate the rise of a new Hindu kingdom in 1336, the empire of Vijayanagara ("city of victory"). Having organized to resist the sultanate's incursions southward and the pressures of their Muslim associates in the northern Deccan, the founders of Vijayanagara went on to unify most of the peninsular south under their rule. Their capital, which bore the same name as their empire, impressed European travelers in the fifteenth and early sixteenth centuries as the most splendid in India at that time and larger and more populous than contemporary Rome. The city was dependent on a huge excavated tank or reservoir and was adorned with numerous magnificent temples. A textbook on government written by the last great Vijayanagara king, Krishna Deva Raya (reigned 1509–1529), a latter-day Arthashastra, suggests part of the reason for the empire's success in its advice on how to deal with minority subjects: "If the king grows angry with them, he cannot wholly destroy them, but if he wins their affection by kindness and charity they serve him by invading the enemies' territory and plundering his forts."[2] The Portuguese traveler Domingos Paes visited Vijayanagara in Krishna Deva Raya's time and described him as follows:

> He is the most feared and perfect king that could possibly be, cheerful of disposition and very merry. . . . He is a great ruler and a man of much justice. . . . He is by rank a greater lord than any, by reason of what he possesses in armies and territories, but he has nothing compared to what a man like him ought to have, so gallant and perfect is he in all things.[3]

Thirty-six years after the king's death, in a great battle in 1565, a coalition of the Islamic sultanates of the northern Deccan, with the help of the new Mughal conquerors of northern India, defeated Vijayanagara,

Nataraja, Shiva as King of the Dance. With one foot crushing the demon dwarf, he is poised in the cosmic dance of life, holding in one hand the drum of awakening and in another the fire of creation as well as destruction. With still another hand he gives the gesture whose meaning is "fear not." Southern India, Chola period, 11th century. Bronze, height 111.5 cm. (© The Cleveland Museum of Art, 2002. Purchase from the J. H. Wade Fund, 1930.331.)

sacked and destroyed its capital city, and ended its period of greatness.

There is no doubt that the coming of Islam greatly depressed the status of women in India. Since the south and Ceylon (Sri Lanka) remained free of Islam, women there retained much more of their traditional freedom and status, if not nearly equal status they had enjoyed in classical times. The Muslim custom of *purdah,* or the veiling of women in public, unfortunately spread even to Hindus in the north, but the south remained free of it.

From the late tenth century to the foundation of the Mughal dynasty in 1526 India was divided and in conflict politically as waves of invaders from the northwest brought in both a new religion, Islam, and a new cultural infusion. It was nevertheless a period of great artistic creativity, especially in the south, and though the records we have tell mainly of battles, kings, and conquests, they tell also of monumental building, a flourishing of the arts, and a growing and profitable trade. Surpluses helped to support these creations as well as the political structures and armies of numerous states.

In northern India, Sikandar's successor, Ibrahim (reigned 1517–1526), was a far less compelling figure than his father had been and was confronted by revolts in many parts of the remaining sultanate territories. The

Rajput confederacy grew as a rival power that threatened to extinguish the sultanate altogether. Lahore, chief city of Punjab, was in rebellion, and its governor unwisely invited in a new group of Central Asian Turks to strengthen his hand against Sultan Ibrahim. This was the army of Babur (1483–1530), known as "the Tiger," claiming descent from Tamerlane through his father and from Chinghis Khan through his mother. For 20 years, as his own account of his life tells us, he had "never ceased to think of the conquest of Hindustan." India's wealth, and its political divisions, chronically tempted Afghans, Turks, and others to plunder and conquest. Babur's outnumbered but brilliantly generaled forces defeated those of Ibrahim at Panipat, northwest of Delhi, in 1526, and in the next year similarly vanquished the Rajput Confederacy, now plagued by internal divisions. Northern India was again under alien domination, but the Mughal dynasty that Babur founded was to reach new levels of splendor and imperial achievement.

Questions

1. The Delhi sultanate can be portrayed as parasitical—as in the quotation that concludes the discussion of the sultanate era in the text. According to this view, the Delhi sultans and their armies were a Muslim Turko-Afghan warrior elite who lived in fortified urban centers, from which they extracted protection fees from surrounding local Hindu producers. Is this characterization justified?

2. Why was Delhi selected as the political center of Muslim authority in India? Why was northern India unable to mount a successful defense against the Turko-Afghan warriors? How could this be viewed as a negative commentary on India's Hindu society and culture, which the British could cite as legitimating their colonial Raj?

3. Who were the Rajputs and Marathas and how do they negate this image of the "typical Hindu"?

4. How did the Islamic Qur'an provide religious justification for the forced conversion of India's Hindu populations by the Delhi sultans? How did this contribute to the character of Muslim rule over Hindus?

5. Who were the *mamelukes*, and what was their significance in the Turkish military system?

6. What was the role of temples in the southern Indian Cola state?

7. Explain Why Muslim rule did not significantly penetrate into southern India. Were Vijayanagara's rulers and their political system the Hindu equivalent of the Delhi sultanate?

Notes

1. D. P. Singhal, *A History of the Indian People* (London: Methuen, 1983), pp. 173—174.
2. A. L. Basham, *The Wonder That Was India,* 3d ed. (London: Macmillan, 1968), p. 198.
3. Ibid., p. 76.

Suggested Web Sites

Medieval India

http://www.indiaheritage.com/history/medieval/medieval .htm
Text and illustrations of medieval Indian leaders, with links to culture, creative arts, and religion.

http://www.webindia123.com/history/MEDIEVAL/ delhisultanate/slave_dynasty.htm
Good coverage of the different eras of Muslim rule in India prior to the Mughals. The Web site also includes similar coverage of early Indian history.

Suggestions for Further Reading

Ali, D. *Courtly Culture and Political Life in Early Medieval India.* Cambridge, England: Cambridge University Press, 2004.

Auboyer, J. *Daily Life in Ancient India.* New York: Macmillan, 1965.

Basham, A. L. *The Wonder That Was India,* 3d ed. London: Macmillan, 1968.

Eaton, R. M. *The Rise of Islam and the Bengal Frontier.* Berkeley: University of California Press, 1993.

Ikram, S. M. *Muslim Civilization in India.* New York: Columbia University Press, 1964.

Jackson, P. *The Delhi Sultanate.* Cambridge, England: Cambridge University Press, 1999.

Ricklefs, M. C. *A History of Modern Indonesia.* Bloomington: Indiana University Press, 1981.

Sar Desai, D. R. *Southeast Asia Past and Present,* 3d ed. Boulder, Colo.: Westview, 1997.

Shaffer, L. N. *Maritime Southeast Asia, 300 B.C. to A.D. 1528.* Armonk, New York: M. E. Sharpe, 1993.

Sharma, P. V. *Indian Medicine in the Classical Age.* Varanasi: Chowkamba, 1972.

Singhal, D. P. *A History of the Indian People,* 3d ed. Boulder, CO: Westview, 1989.

Stein, B. *Peasant, State, and Society in Medieval South India.* Berkeley: University of California Press, 1980.

———.*Vijayanagara.* Cambridge, England: Cambridge University Press, 1989.

Thapar, R. *A History of India,* vol. 1. Baltimore: Penguin Books, 1969.

Yazdani, G., ed. *The Early History of the Deccan.* London: Oxford University Press, 1960.

7

Early and Medieval Southeast Asia

The region known as Southeast Asia includes Burma (Myanmar since 1987), Siam (Thailand since 1932), Laos, Cambodia, Vietnam, Malaysia, Singapore (not until 1819), what is now Indonesia, and the Philippines. This chapter surveys the start of civilization in this large and fragmented area and the rise of many separate kingdoms there. But first let us set the stage.

The Setting

Southeast Asia is in effect a series of peninsulas where settlement has long been concentrated in the great river valleys that run through them: the Irrawaddy in Burma, the Chao Praya in Siam, the Red River of northern Vietnam, and the Mekong in Cambodia and southern Vietnam. The thin tail of Malaya has no large rivers, but it is geographically important; its west coast faces the Straits of Melaka, long the main route from India eastward, since the way around Sumatra, the western edge of the Melaka Straits, is plagued by reefs and has no good harbors, especially during the monsoon season. The rest of Southeast Asia is composed of two extensive island chains, or archipelagos: what is now Indonesia and the Philippines. The region enjoys uniform high temperatures except at the few high altitudes, and ample monsoonal rainfall at all seasons except for in the so-called Dry Zone of central Burma and a small area of Java plus small parts of the Philippines. Although Java is not the largest island of Indonesia, it has always been the main center of population. The island is deeply covered by weathered volcanic soils that are periodically renewed (as evident from the still smoking volcanoes on many horizons), thus making this one of the most productive agricultural areas in the world. It is not surprising that it was probably one of the first sites of the origins of agriculture. The same volcanic soil extends into many parts of the Philippines. There is also rich alluvial soil in the valleys and deltas of the great rivers in Burma, Siam, Cambodia, and Vietnam. The banana is native to Southeast Asia, as are breadfruit, taro, yams, squash, beans, and a variety of fruits. Environmentally, it is like a Garden of Eden.

Origin of Peoples

Nearly all of the people of Southeast Asia came originally from China. Malays, now dominant in Malaya and insular Southeast Asia, were pushed south from the rest of the mainland well before the start of recorded history, by later migrants from China, through Burma, Siam, Cambodia, Laos, and Vietnam. Their spoken languages thus belong to the Sino-Tibetan family rather than to the Malay. All except Vietnam, right next to China, received their literate culture, including writing, from India as well as Buddhism, Hinduism, art, architecture, dance, and forms of state. In Vietnam, Chinese forms of all these aspects became dominant.

The first kingdoms in Southeast Asia appear to have been based more on trade than on agriculture, perhaps by or before the first century B.C.E. By the second century C.E. such states had developed along the shores of the Melaka Straits, although during that period the trade did not pass through the straits themselves but instead made a portage across the Isthmus of Kra to the north; ships then sailed from the Malay Peninsula along the coastline of the Gulf of Thailand to ports along the coast of Vietnam. In time the richer agricultural base of the great river valleys came to support more powerful states: the Vietnamese in the Red River valley centered on a populated predecessor to Hanoi on the northern edge of the Red River delta, and the kingdoms the Chinese called Linyi and Funan in central and southern Vietnam and the Mekong Delta. Chinese records show all three well established by the third century C.E., but

CHRONOLOGY

200 B.C.E.–500 C.E.	■ Funan; Linyi
500	■ Champa; earliest Khmer (Chenla) states
600–1350	■ Srivijaya
760–860	■ Sailendra Buddhist kings in Java (Borobudur built 778–824)
802–850	■ Jayavarman II unites Khmers
889–1431	■ Angkor-centered Khmer state
849–1287	■ Pagan
939	■ Dai Viet founded
960–1225	■ Ly dynasty in Vietnam
c. 1120	■ Angkor Wat
c. 1180	■ Angkor Thom
1225–1400	■ Tran dynasty in Vietnam
c. 1240	■ Sukothai
1257–1301	■ Mongol invasions of Southeast Asia
1293–1528	■ Majapahit Java
c. 1300	■ First Islamic state in Southeast Asia (Samudra-Pasai)
1351–1767	■ Ayudhya-based Siam state
1402–1511	■ Melaka sultanate
1407–1428	■ Ming fail to reconquer Vietnam
1428–1527	■ Le dynasty in Vietnam
c. 1430	■ Khmer state centered at Phnom Penh
1471	■ Champa falls to Vietnamese
1540–1802	■ Trinh, Mac, and Nguyen partitions of Vietnam
1555–1752	■ Toungoo dynasty in Burma
1580–1830	■ Mataram Java
1752–present	■ Chakrit dynasty in Siam
1752–1886	■ Konbaung dynasty in Burma

Funan was the most prosperous among these. It prospered until the late fifth century, when the Champa kingdom, which controlled the river systems of the Vietnamese coastline between the Mekong Delta and Vietnamese territory to the north, took its place. Funan spread its control into Cambodia and southern Siam until displaced by the new Khmer states in the seventh

and eighth centuries. By or before the third century C.E. Indianized kingdoms were founded in the Irrawaddy Valley; the first for which we have records centered on the Mon urban center near the southern Burmese coast, which by the ninth century had a degree of authority over the Irrawaddy Valley. It was a Mahayana Buddhist monarchy, which developed out of the initial introduction of Buddhism to Burma during the time of Emperor Ashoka (see Chapter 4) and built many large Buddhist temples or *dagobas*, funded by a productive rice agriculture.

Thais had been trickling down from southwest China for some centuries, increasing to a flood after the Mongols conquered their Yunnan homeland (although many Thais continue today to live in western Yunnan) in the thirteenth century. The Thai kingdom in Southeast Asia was founded in the lower valley of the Chao Praya River by the fourteenth century. Malaya was thinly settled until recently, somewhat mountainous and covered with dense rain forest and supported no literate tradition, dominated on its west coast by trading empires based in Sumatra or Java. The earliest recorded Indonesian state was the trade empire of Srivijaya initially based in Sumatran Palembang. The Java-based Sailendra dynasty ruled over central Java in the eighth and ninth centuries, but Java had developed its own culture long before its Indianization beginning in the second century B.C.E. This included the *gamelan*, an orchestra of bells, gongs, and drums; *wayang*, a puppet shadow theater; *batik*, cotton cloth dyed after it was marked with wax in complex patterns; and bark cloth. Southeast Asian spices were important in world trade from early times, as were batik and bark cloth. Describing Java in the late thirteenth century, Marco Polo called it the world's richest country. The people of the Philippines, speaking many Malay-related languages, were divided into numerous separate tribes, isolated by mountains, forests, and the many islands of the country.

In Vietnam, the old Chinese-style state of Yue was conquered by the first Chinese empire, the Qin, in the third century B.C.E. (see Chapter 5), again by the Han dynasty, free from the collapse of the Han until the rise of the Tang nearly five centuries later, and after the end of the Tang Vietnam regained and maintained its independence despite repeated Chinese efforts to reconquer it. Dinh Bo Lin rose to power in c. 960 C.E., with his capital located at Hoa-lu, in the hills at the southern edge of the Red River Delta. After 1099 the capital was moved to the site of modern Hanoi, then called Thang-long, where aristocratic leaders proclaimed the Ly dynasty under Ly Cong Uan. His son and successor Ly Phat Ma (r. 1028–1054) is remembered as one of Vietnam's greatest kings. He published a new book of laws, now lost, and increased the king's powers. Amazingly, Vietnam repelled even the Mongols, who three times

Volcanic mountains, rural central Java. Volcanos are the source of Java's rich soil and agricultural productivity but also cause severe destruction when they periodically erupt. In recognition of both potentials, volcanic mountains have been the focus of traditional religion, which associates them with animistic, ancestral, Hindu, and Buddhist deities. (Kenneth Hall)

captured Hanoi and three times were driven out! If anyone in Washington had known anything of Vietnamese history, they might not have attempted their losing misadventure there forty years ago. But by the early thirteenth century the country was embroiled in civil war, until in 1225 the Tran family founded a new dynasty, the Le, and subsequently began the long southward advance of the Vietnamese, who overran Champa in 1471 and had fully annexed Champa's former territories by 1700. Melaka was established as a new Muslim sultanate by the early 1400s, and remained Southeast Asia's foremost trade center, with a population of about 100,000, until it was conquered by the Portuguese in 1511. Thang-long (Hanoi) had about the same total, as did Ayudhya, the Thai capital—until its sack by the Burmese in 1767, and possibly Pegu in lower Burma. Other cities of nearly the same early sixteenth-century population included Makassar in Celebes (Sulawesi) and Aceh at the northern tip of Sumatra.

The Eastward Spread of Islam

Buddhism and trade provided the initial links between India and Southeast Asia in the classical and early medieval periods, and both served as vehicles for the spread of Hinduism and other aspects of Indian civilization. But Arab traders had been active in inter-Asian trade well before the time of Mohammed and had extended their commercial networks throughout most of maritime Southeast Asia and as far east as the China coast. It seems, however, to have been largely Indian converts to Islam after the founding of the Delhi sultanate who were primarily responsible for carrying the new religion to insular Southeast Asia, following the long-established trade routes by sea, where they had long played a more important role than the Arabs. This included Indian merchants from Gujarat on the northwest coast and its major ports of Surat and Cambay, which had probably been India's principal base for overseas trade, at least since Mauryan times, including the trade with the Hellenic and Roman world, and probably also its largest group of merchants, entrepreneurs, and bankers.

These enterprises continued under the Delhi sultanate, which for some two centuries ruled Gujarat and saw the conversion of some of its inhabitants to Islam. Merchants anxious for official favor, a common commercial concern, probably chose conversion for their own financial benefit. In Southeast Asia, it would seem that while there was resistance to conversion by Arabs, the long tradition of learning from Indian civilization meant that Islam was more readily accepted from Indian

Conversions to Islam

There is no single Southeast Asian Islamic tradition. As Islam spread throughout the region, it was adapted to local cultures. Indian seamen who had converted to Islam spread the new religion eastward along the maritime trade routes, while Islamic clerics who accompanied the Muslim merchants converted the local populations. Political, commercial, and military elites were the first to convert to Islam. Eventually, rulers encouraged—or obliged—their subjects to accept and convert to Islam to legitimize and strengthen their own authority, to win favor with Muslim traders and thus increase their realm's overall economic welfare, or to link subordinates to the sultan through participation in new Islamic court rituals.

In Southeast Asia, Islamic scholars transmitted Islamic thought and beliefs to newly converted societies, but they adapted the new religion in ways that supported their patrons, the rulers of Southeast Asia's first Islamic states. The earliest Islamic scholars in the region found the mysticism of Sufi Islam especially compatible with indigenous religious values, and thus promoted a modified version of Sufism—one that blended Islamic and local values—to win converts.

Islam reached Malaya by the end of the fourteenth century and spread throughout the region over the course of the fifteenth century. Malay literature highlights the actions of individuals preparing to become Islamic rulers. The majority of the Malay realm adhered to the locally modified Islamic statecraft that developed in the fifteenth-century Melaka court. One minority group, however, accepted the more legalistic and conservative traditions of Middle Eastern Sufism that developed in the Aceh court, which controlled the lucrative pepper trade of north Sumatra, over the sixteenth and seventeenth centuries.

The form of Islam that took hold in Java placed less emphasis on Islamic doctrine or the authenticity of local connections to Muhammad or Mecca. Rather, the Javanese were more interested in Islamic mysticism and ritual. Java's conversion to Islam is attributed to the intervention of divinely empowered saints, or *wali sanga*, who allied with Java's sovereigns to unite the natural and supernatural worlds.

Throughout Southeast Asia, Islamic thought, practice, and ritual adapted to local circumstances and cultures. However, Southeast Asia's Islamic societies did not develop in isolation, as Southeast Asia–based Islamic clerics regularly participated in the theological debates among leading Islamic scholars in Mecca and other major religious centers in the Middle East. Initially conversion to Islam may have been a token gesture undertaken for economic benefits. Viewed in a more positive light, however, conversion may have been due to genuine commitment.

---

hands. In any case, both Indian and Arab traders spread Islam eastward along the sea routes, as earlier Indian merchants had spread Hinduism and Buddhism. Burma, Siam (Thailand), Cambodia, and Laos on the mainland remained dedicated to Buddhism, but the coastal areas of peninsular Malaya as well as insular Indonesia and the southernmost Philippines, where trading fleets had easier access, were largely converted to Islam over many centuries.

Local merchants in many of these Southeast Asian kingdoms also adopted Islam as an advantage in dealing with Muslim traders from India. In several cases local rulers were converted or chose Islam, perhaps for similar reasons, and their subjects were obliged to do likewise. Insular Southeast Asia became a patchwork of Islamic sultanates. By the late fourteenth century Indian

and Arab Muslims largely controlled the trade of this enormous area and made converts first in Sumatra and Malaya, closest by sea to India, and in coastal ports through the far-flung archipelago. Melaka, on the west coast of Malaya, where it dominated the routes through the Melaka Straits, became a great center of commerce and a spearhead for the advance of Islam eastward. Nearly all trade eastward from India has always passed through the strait as the shortest and safest route, avoiding the treacherous southwest coast of Sumatra and the difficult Sunda Strait between Sumatra and Java.

In the course of the fifteenth century the new religion incorporated most of Malaya, north coastal Java, and coastal parts of the rest of the archipelago, including Mindanao, the southernmost large island of the Philippines, where in fact it seems to have arrived as early as anywhere in Southeast Asia. Islam's further spread was checked in part by the almost simultaneous arrival of the Spanish in the Philippines and of the Portuguese and Dutch in Indonesia, although away from the coast, inland Java remained Hindu and Buddhist for another century or so, even under some nominally Muslim rulers.

By the sixteenth century only a few small and isolated areas of Indonesia outside Java retained their original animism or tribal religion, while the island of Bali, east of Java, remained Hindu, as it still is. The very different context of Southeast Asian culture, however, softened some of the more rigid aspect of Islam. This was particularly the case with regard to the treatment of women, where Southeast Asia has always been distinctive in its closer approach to gender equality than any other major culture. At the same time Islam brought, as in India, a new emphasis on the equality of all before God. In India, the Islamic practice of purdah (literally, "curtain"), whereby women must not be seen by men outside the family and must cover themselves completely when outside the house, spread also to Hindus in many parts of the north ruled by Muslim conquerors. In Southeast Asia, with its far more open society and its tradition of female equality, this custom was rejected.

The longstanding dominance, or perhaps better prominence, of women prevailed over the strictures of the prophet, and women continued to be prominent in trade and diplomacy, while men had to pay a bride price for their wives. As in parts of southern India, it was often women who entered the professions, their husbands necessarily following them as they sought positions. Premarital sex tended to be encouraged in Southeast Asia, although postmarital infidelity was punished, and women in general remained about as free and equal as anywhere in the world.

Many other Koranic injunctions were modified in practice, including dietary prohibitions, strict fasting during Ramadan, and rigid observance of the rule to pray facing Mecca five times a day. Indonesia has for some time been by far the world's largest Muslim country, but Indonesian (and much of Malaysian) Islam is recognizably different from that found in Saudi Arabia, Iraq, or Iran.

Indianized Southeast Asia

Like southern India's rulers, emergent Southeast Asian political elite also found north Indian culture useful as a means to enhance their status above that of their dependents. Since the time of Ashoka and the first Buddhist missions (see Chapter 4), there had been a close connection between India and Southeast Asia. It is possible that Indian influences on that extensive region began before Ashoka, but the earliest data for Southeast Asian kingdoms comes from the centuries after his reign and show a political, literate, and religious or philosophical culture already Indianized.

Indian and Chinese influences continued to operate on Southeast Asia until the present. But the widespread and highly varied region—from Burma to Thailand, Laos, Cambodia, Vietnam, Malaysia, Indonesia, and the Philippines—has retained, despite differences among its components, its own clearly recognizable social and cultural forms, preserved and evolved from their separate origins before the coming of Indian and Chinese elements. Briefly, only "high culture"—writing and various literary, artistic, political, and religious forms—came in from India and China. The social base and most other aspects of culture were less affected and indeed helped to shape many aspects of the borrowed culture. This section deals with the civilization of Southeast Asia after the fall of the Gupta Empire in India.

Indian forms of dance, music, literature, art, and dramatic versions of the great Hindu epics, the *Mahabharata* and the *Ramayana*, continued to dominate the culture of insular Southeast Asia, as they still do. Meanwhile Chinese traders became more active and more numerous from the tenth century, especially in the eastern half of the area, and founded permanent settlements of merchants in the major port cities in the Philippines and Java. Peninsular Malaya at this period was very thinly settled, and although Malay-related languages and culture were widespread throughout the archipelago, Malays remained a small group on the mainland. The traditional Buddhist monarchies of Burma, Siam, and Cambodia, centered in the productive cores of their economies in the mainland deltas and lower valleys of the great rivers, were more self-contained. They too built magnificent temple complexes in the Indian-Buddhist style, such as those at the later abandoned Cambodian capital of Angkor built by the Khmer Empire, which flourished from the ninth to the twelfth century.

The people of Burma and Siam include large infusions of stock originally from south China, where many of their close ethnic relatives still live. The spoken languages of both countries are distantly related to Chinese but are written with an Indian-derived script. Over many centuries the majority of the inhabitants of Siam, the Thais, probably moved down into the delta from an original homeland that straddled the mountainous border zones of China. The origins of the people of northern Burma, and to a lesser extend of the lowland Burmans, are similar. However, the civilization of both countries has been profoundly shaped by the Indian models that spread to them from Ashoka's time on,

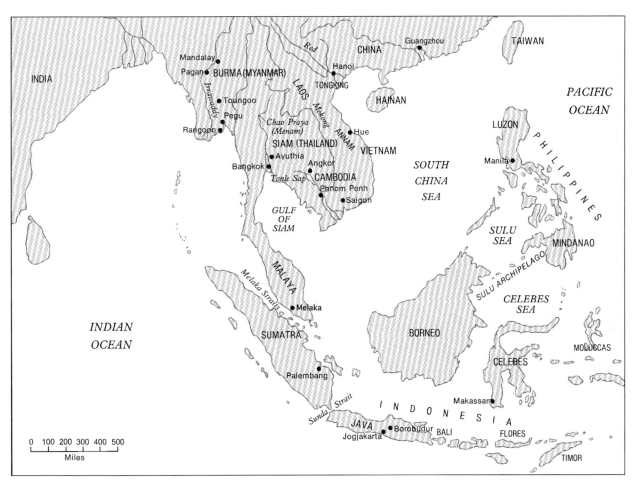

Southeast Asia

The area is broken up by mountains and sea and even now supports ten different states. Linguistic and cultural diversity is in fact far greater.

including not only Buddhism but also Indian systems of writing, art, literature, symbols, ideas, kingship, and government.

Cambodia, Laos, and Vietnam

As previously discussed, the Khmer people probably came originally from southern China and are ethnically related to other populations who migrated into neighboring Burma at the same time. They followed a migration route down the Mekong River into what is now Cambodia, probably by or before 100 B.C.E. but before they had any lasting contact with Chinese or Indian civilizations. In Cambodia the first wave of Khmer migrants seem to have been the founders of the kingdom of Funan, described in Han Chinese records, which by that time had been partly Indianized in its literate and political culture. By the third century C.E. Funan seems to have controlled what is now southern Vietnam, east and central Thailand, northern Malaya, and southernmost Burma. Its large fleet dominated the sea lanes and carried much of the trade moving eastward from India and to China, of which it became a tributary state. In fact Funan was probably several small, loosely integrated kingdoms, which were overthrown by a later-arriving group of Khmers in the seventh century. By the ninth century the center of the Khmer domain had centered on the northern edge of Cambodia's Great Lake (Tonle Sap), where its rulers began to build a magnificent capital city and temple complex at Angkor, which for the next several centuries was the most important center of culture and political power in mainland Southeast Asia.

A CLOSER LOOK

Angkor: City of Monumental Splendor

The Khmer king Yasovarman I (r. 889–900), who began the building of the new capital, designed it with the help of Brahmans invited from India to legitimize his claim to divine kingship as a manifestation of Shiva. This plan of the city reflected the structure of the world according to Hindu cosmology. It was surrounded by a wall and a moat, as the universe was thought to be encircled by rock and ocean. In the exact middle of the city, on an artificial mound, stood a pyramidal temple representing the sacred Mount Meru in the high Himalayas, where Shiva was said to be perpetually meditating for the eternal maintenance of the cosmic order. Numerous other temples were grouped on and around the mound, which was regarded as the center of the universe. The king declared himself Ruler of the Universe. This title, together with other symbols, titles, and attendant rituals, were passed on to successive Khmer kings.

The final and complete form of Hindu Angkor was built at the beginning of the twelfth century at Angkor Wat (*wat* means "temple") by Suryavarman II (r. 1113–1150), but following its desecration by Champa invaders in 1175, Jayavarman VII (r. 1181–1218) constructed a spectacular new Mahayana Buddhist temple complex adjacent to the royal city at neighboring Angkor Thom. While new Buddhist elements were added; worship of earlier Hindu deities remained, and the Khmers seem to have accepted both religious traditions and their symbols. Lingering controversy over Jayavarman's assertive rule following his death, the continuing threat of another Cham attack, and the subsequent financial drain of state revenues to maintain an army and to rebuild the state's infrastructure all contributed to the decline and conquest of the empire only a few decades later. Both ritual sites were largely abandoned after a Thai invasion in 1431; Angkor Thom was left in ruins but Angkor Wat was better preserved since it was not so central a target. Today, it remains one of the chief monuments of early Southeast Asian art and architecture, reflecting the glory of the Khmer empire at its height.

The whole urban complex was a symbol of the union between king and god and of harmony between human and divine worlds. It was intended to ensure prosperity for the kingdom and its people as well as the authority of the ruler. Water, a further symbol of life-giving nurture, was led from the Mekong to keep the moat full as part of a much larger system of irrigation. The city formed a square about 2 miles on each side, enclosed within its walls and moat, and was entered by five huge monumental gates. Inside were the large royal palace as well as the temple complex, but little evidence remains of other buildings inside and outside the walls where the court, officials, clerks, engineers, workers, artisans, and other inhabitants of the city were housed. We know from surviving inscriptions that there was a large and highly organized bureaucracy, including those responsible for the irrigation works.

The city, and Cambodia as a whole, may have had a larger population then than now. The Mekong floodplain's fertile alluvial soil was made still more productive by an intricate hydraulic network of canals, dams,

The temple complex at Angkor Wat in Cambodia, dating from the twelfth century. (John Elk III/Stock, Boston)

and dikes both for irrigation and to prevent flooding. Fish from the nearby Tonle Sap, a lake in the middle Mekong Valley, added to the food supply. The monsoon rains were heavily concentrated in a short summer season, when the Tonle Sap tended to overflow, leaving much of the rest of the year too dry. Flood-prevention works, storage tanks, and reservoirs were carefully engineered, and canals were built to direct water to rice fields while protecting them from too much water. Canals were also used to transport the stone used to build Angkor Thom and Angkor Wat.

The construction and maintenance of these extensive works required enormous amounts of planning and controlled labor. As the authority of the Khmer kings began to weaken and the country suffered from invasion, culminating in the Thai capture of Angkor in 1431, dams, tanks, and canals could not be maintained. Without the productive agriculture they made possible, the economic base was severely reduced. The collapse of the Khmer kingdom suggests comparison with the fall of the Sinhalese kingdom in the dry zone of Ceylon two centuries earlier. In 1434, the capital was moved to Phnom Penh on the lower Mekong; the Khmer Empire never recovered its former power and glory, while jungle invaded the ruins of Angkor Thom and Angkor Wat. They were revealed again when French explorers stumbled on them in the later nineteenth century, and the French colonial government later cleared the sites, where tourists may still go to marvel at their splendor.

The southern part of the landlocked and mountainous state of Laos had been included in the Khmer Empire during its centuries of power. It then came under Thai domination until the whole of Laos was absorbed by French colonialism at the end of the nineteenth century. The dominant Laotian inhabitants are related to the Thais and Burmese and, like them, migrated originally from southern China, but their language and culture are distinctive. The three small Lao states had to contend with Thai, Burmese, and Vietnamese pressures and attacks. Buddhism spread to Laos from Mon and Khmer sources and was followed with faithful devotion, but Laos was chronically squeezed between expansionist states on all sides.

Vietnam: Expansion to the South

The northern part of Vietnam, known as Tongking, in the productive basin of the Red River with its capital at Hanoi, had been part of the pre-Han south China kingdom of Nan Yue, or Nam Viet, which included the Guangdong area and was then incorporated in the Han and Tang empires. It thus acquired a heavy overlay of Chinese civilization, including written language and artistic, philosophical, and political forms, the only Southeast Asian state to become Sinified rather than Indianized. But below the elite level, Vietnamese culture remained distinctively Southeast Asian and determined to maintain its separate identity.

Goddesses (Apsaras) from a frieze at Angkor Wat. Despite its clear Indian origins (see Yakshis, p. 77), Southeast Asian art diverged early into its own styles, as these beautiful and unmistakably Cambodian figures from the thirteenth century suggest. (Marie Mattson/Black Star. Stockphoto.com)

Vietnam regained its independence after the fall of the Tang dynasty, although it had to repel efforts at reconquest by the Mongols, the Ming, and the Manchus. During these centuries, however, the Vietnamese were engaged in their own expansion southward, down the narrow coastal plain of Annam and eventually into the agriculturally rich delta of the Mekong in what is now southern Vietnam, a process that took nearly 1,000 years to complete. Southward movement took place at the expense of the Indianized Champa kingdom in Annam, and then of the Khmers, who originally controlled the Mekong Delta and the surrounding plain.

In this long struggle, the Vietnamese drew strength from a fervent nationalism originally engendered by their efforts to resist and finally to throw off Chinese control, a 2,000-year ordeal of chronic war that probably contributed to Vietnamese aggressiveness. But their growing empire was managed very much on Chinese bureaucratic lines, and their later rulers even adopted the title of emperor, although they prudently accepted the status of tributary to China. Like the Koreans and the Japanese, the Vietnamese freely sought Chinese culture while resisting Chinese political control. By the early nineteenth century their empire included essentially all of the modern state, including territories conquered or detached from Cambodia and Laos, and its chief capital was Hue in central Vietnam. The northern and southern areas were ruled from subsidiary capitals at Hanoi and Saigon. The delta of Tongking in the north around Hanoi and of the Mekong around Saigon, as well as the coastal plain of Annam joining them, were fertile and became highly productive under a Chinese-style system of intensive irrigated agriculture. This lent further strength to the state, helping it to maintain control over the mountainous western borderlands inhabited by a variety of non-Vietnamese tribal minorities in addition to Laotians and Khmers.

Medieval Pagan and Thai Ayudhya

Burmans became the dominant inhabitants of Burma only after 800 C.E., and the Thais of Thailand after about 1300, each displacing earlier groups who had followed the same route in their southward migration from China and possibly Tibet over several centuries. These earlier inhabitants were either assimilated or remain as minorities, pushed up into the hills in most cases, a problem particularly severe in Burma and still a source of chronic tension. The Burmans and Thais occupied the far more productive lowlands and floodplains of the Irrawaddy in Burma and the Chao Praya (Menam) in Thailand (called Siam until 1932), where

they founded successive capitals. Indian cultural influences were welcomed, especially since they came without political objectives, ambitions, or strings. Local rulers invited Indian administrative advisers and priests as well as philosophers, artists, and musicians. Trade was an important source of revenue along the sea routes described above, but in the great river valleys of the mainland, agriculture and its revenues were the heart of the economy and the chief support of the state. The early medieval capital of Burma was at Pagan, founded about 850 in the central Irrawaddy Valley, which by 1057 had incorporated the Irrawaddy Basin and an upland perimeter within its boundaries.

Included in the new empire were several minority groups. Some of these were in fact culturally more advanced, especially those in the south, which had been the beneficiaries of earlier Indian influence by sea. Most important among these were the Mons, whose more sophisticated culture and political experience with originally Indian forms led to their domination of the court and culture at Pagan until the late twelfth century and their prominent role in Burma's overseas trade from their delta base in the south. It was via the Mons that Theravada Buddhism spread to the Burmans, together with the rest of the Mon legacy of Indian civilization. But the Pagan kingdom was utterly destroyed by the Mongol invasion of the 1280s. New waves of migrants and raiders poured into Burma, and rival kingdoms struggled against each other for control after the Mongols had withdrawn. A new Burmese dynasty, Toungoo, emerged in the early sixteenth century in the southwest. By 1555, after prolonged civil wars, Toungoo had brought most of the country again under one rule.

Successive kingdoms in Burma were strongly Buddhist after the initial conversion assisted by the Mons, and kings competed, as in Thailand, in building temples and endowing religious enterprises. This supposed piety did not prevent them from engaging in internal military struggles, efforts at territorial expansion, and brutal campaigns against alleged heretics, followers of Buddhist sects that were considered unorthodox. From the sixteenth century there was also chronic warfare between Burma and Siam. But despite the gross denial by monarchs and armies of the Buddha's teaching of reverence for life, most people in both countries were more genuinely committed to Buddhism as a culture as well as a path to personal salvation.

The Toungoo dynasty was vigorously expansionist, mainly at the expense of the Thias. The rising importance of maritime trade, in which lower Burma played a growing role under the newly reunited order, provided increased revenues to fuel conquests, and the locus of political authority shifted toward the coast. Improved guns brought in by the Portuguese gave new and often devastating firepower to Burmese expansionism. But the Toungoo order proved fragile and overextended. Its capital, now at Pegu in lower Burma, fell to rebellion and invasion in 1599, and successive Toungoo rulers abandoned their claims to Thai territory, although Thai-Burmese warfare continued intermittently.

By 1635 a restored Toungoo state transferred the Burmese capital to Ava, some 300 miles up the Irrawaddy, from where it ruled until 1752. It was succeeded by the Konbaung or Alaungpaya dynasty, with its base also in the central dry zone of Burma and its capital at Mandalay on the Irrawaddy. Toungoo and Konbaung armies again invaded Siam repeatedly, but the rise of a stronger Thai state by the end of the eighteenth century turned Burmese attention westward. Their expansionist campaigns conquered the previously independent state of Arakan on the west coast and penetrated into Assam, which brought them into conflict with the English East India Company. Burmese efforts to form an alliance with the French were unable to forestall three successive British military campaigns. The first, from 1824 to 1826, confirmed British control of Assam and Arakan and installed a British resident at the court of Mandalay; the second, in 1852, resulted in British annexation of lower Burma, including the port of Rangoon; and the third, in 1886, led to the annexation of the rest of the country and ended the Burmese monarchy and the Konbaung dynasty.

Meanwhile, the Thais had formed a state that grew in power and began to impinge on and eventually take over much of the earlier Khmer Empire, which was decaying by about 1250, and in 1431 captured the Khmer capital at Angkor. Thais had probably spilled southward across the present border of southern China before 1200, but the trickle became a flood after the Mongol conquest of their Yunnan homeland in the late thirteenth century. By the fourteenth century they were the dominant inhabitants of the Chao Praya Basin. They pushed south and east against the Khmers, from whom they adopted Indian art forms, writing, and political systems while accepting Buddhism from Burma and from the earlier Mon inhabitants of the Chao Praya Basin. The Thai capital was established in the mid-fourteenth century at Ayudhya on the edge of the delta, then close to the Khmer frontier of Thai expansion and with easy access to the Gulf of Siam for trade and foreign contacts as well as to the Mon area of lower Burma.

Ayudhya consolidated its hold on the delta and continued the Thai push southward into the thinly settled Malay peninsula and eastward into Khmer Cambodia. Thais were also a major part of the invasion that sacked the Toungoo capital at Pegu in lower Burma in 1599, but in the following two or three centuries successive Burmese armies generally had the upper hand in their wars with the Thais and finally sacked Ayudya in 1767, leaving the once-splendid capital in total ruins. After a period of disorder and confusion, a new Thai dynasty, the Chakri, emerged in 1782 with a new capital at Bangkok, the same dynasty that rules present-day Thailand. Bangkok, near the seaward edge of the delta, was originally a place of marshes and tidal creeks on the Chao Praya, and the site was chosen in part because of the protection it offered against Burmese raids. With the rapid growth of maritime trade in the nineteenth century, Bangkok became a major port and a major economic support of the state as well as by far its largest city.

Malaya, Indonesia, and the Philippines

Malay-style culture and the Malay language family are dominant not only in the Malay Peninsula but also in most of insular Southeast Asia, especially the coastal areas easily accessible by sea. The peninsula itself, however, has never supported a very large population, especially compared to the larger and more productive areas of Indonesia and the Philippines, and probably did not reach half a million until the late nineteenth century. Its mountainous and rain-forested landscape contained no extensive river valleys or productive agricultural plains, and settlement was most concentrated on the coast, where small ports were engaged in the trade of the archipelago. There is no evidence of a highly developed indigenous civilization until the fifteenth-century rise of Melaka, which itself was part of a larger system in greater Malay Southeast Asia. During the medieval period most of Malaya was first controlled by the Indonesian trading empire of Sri Vijaya, with its capital on nearby Sumatra, and later by the Thai state. Malaya was not politically unified until it was brought under twentieth-century British colonial control, and its principal growth dates only from the tin and rubber booms of the same period.

In Indonesia, the central island of Java, with its richly productive volcanic soils, has consistently remained the heart of this sprawling island country. Rival agriculturally based kingdoms arose in Java, while larger empires based on maritime trade grew to control and profit from the sea lanes. Much earlier, probably in the second millennium B.C.E., sailors from Indonesia in their double-out-rigger vessels had ventured as far as East Africa, introducing cinnamon there and in Ceylon en route and leaving their language and genes in the island of Madagascar off the African coast. The first and most enduring of the medieval trading empires was that of Sri Vijaya, with its capital at Palembang on Sumatra, from which it could dominate the Melaka Straits, the crucial passage between east and west. Srivijaya held power over most of the archipelago's maritime trade from the seventh to the eleventh century, until the

READING ACROSS CULTURES

Borobudur

When the Chinese Buddhist pilgrim Fa Hsien (Fa Xian) visited Java around 414, he found it inhabited by followers of the Brahmanical religious tradition, with few—if any—adherents to Buddhism. This situation would change dramatically by the Sailendra period (c. 750–860), which marks one of the cultural high points of Java's patronage of Buddhism. Merchants and clerics who traveled the international sea route between India and China first introduced Hindu-Buddhist culture to peoples of the Indonesian archipelago. Local rulers, like Java's Sailendra kings, elevated this new culture to a central place in the religious life of their subjects. Borobudur, an immense Buddhist temple complex, is the most significant monument of the Sailendra period. It depicts the Sailendra monarch's personal pilgrimage to become a bodhisattva, an enlightened being who compassionately delayed his own entrance to nirvana in order to assist his subjects in their pursuit of salvation.

A place of instruction as well as worship, Borobudur is a symbolic representation of the cosmology of Mahayana Buddhism. In both form and structure, the complex is a microcosm of the universe. Its ten levels—from its 403-square foot base, above which rise five stories of square galleries, followed by three terraces of concentric circles, finally to the summit 150 feet above the base—represent the path of life that a pilgrim must follow to reach enlightenment. The journey from base to summit is a three-mile walk. The base is decorated with friezes of "ugly ones," humans bound to earth and the cycles of rebirth by their greed, envy, and ignorance. This realm, known as the World of Desire, symbolizes the Buddhist conception of hell. Here the individual is a slave to earthly desires and suffers from unfulfilled longings.

Completing the circuit of the base, the pilgrim begins ascending the next levels, walking clockwise through the corridors of five square galleries, called the World of Form, which correspond to the realm of earth. The galleries are decorated with 1,460 pictorial and 1,212 ornamental panels depicting episodes from the life of the historical Buddha and his previous incarnations. In all, 27,000 square feet of the stone surface are carved in high relief. More than 400 statues of the Buddha, seated in the lotus position, also adorn these galleries. High walls along the corridors prevent the pilgrim from looking out while right angles of the passageways limit the view ahead.

The eighth-century Buddhist stupa at Borobudur in central Java, chief remaining monument to the Indianization of Southeast Asia before the arrival of Islam. (Brian Brake/Photo Researchers)

Above the five square galleries are three levels of circular terraces, the World of Formlessness. On these levels sit 72 bell-shaped, trellised stupas, each housing a statue of the meditating Buddha. Here no walls impede the pilgrim's view of the world outside, nor do right angles prevent the view ahead. Neither are there carvings, reliefs, friezes, or other decorations representing the earthly world. The pilgrim has left behind the earthly attachments represented by the carvings in the square lower terraces to prepare for total devotion to the Buddhas on the circular terraces. The bell-shaped stupa at the summit points toward heaven, or the realm of enlightenment known as nirvana. Here the pilgrim ascends beyond all material form to achieve the spiritual state of "nothingness" (anatman) symbolized by the sealed stupa on the barren plain at the top of the monument.

Borobudur is considered the highest expression of early Javanese artistic expression. Its bas-reliefs depict the pantheon of Buddhas and bodhisattvas in the classical style of Gupta India, but there are distinctive Javanese characteristics. The characters of the Borobudur bas-reliefs are more relaxed, playful, and self-confident than those of fourth-through sixth-century Gupta India carvings. Each of the 304 Buddhas in the niches above the lower galleries displays a hand gesture (mudra) in accord with the iconographic rules of Mahayana Buddhism, with each gesture corresponding to one of five directions. The Buddhas facing north display the hand gesture symbolizing an absence of fear. The hand gesture of those facing east calls the earth to witness; those facing south have the gesture of bestowing blessings; and the Buddhas facing west show the gesture of meditation. The sixty-four Buddhas on the topmost gallery wall face center and display the gesture of teaching. Clearly, local Javanese artists adapted Indian models to conform to Javanese tradition in the Borobudur reliefs, which portray the Indic textual legends in a Javanese style and setting. Art historians acknowledge that Sailendra-era monuments surpass those of India, where the philosophical and cosmological concepts were originally formulated and the literature that inspired the bas-reliefs at Borobudur was composed.

Chola navy from Southern India plundered its ports in 1025. Reconstituted at a new Jambi center in the late eleventh century, it would continue to exist as a major Straits port-polity to the thirteenth century, when Srivijya's rulers eventually shifted their base to Melaka. Mahayana Buddhism spread early to Srivijaya, and Palembang became a major center of Buddhist learning. Meanwhile in central Java the Sailendra dynasty in the eighth century built a land-based state on prosperous agricultural revenues, which were also used to construct one of the world's great architectural monuments, the immense Buddhist temple at Borobudur, competed by about 825.

Borobudur, like Angkor, was a symbolic representation of the sacred Mount Meru, built up in a series of nine terraces some 3 miles in circumference and including about 400 statues of the Buddha. Indian artists and sculptors were probably involved, along with Javenese artisans. Other Javenese states built many similar temples, which also combined Buddhist and Hindu iconography and ideas, as at Angkor.

Majapahit Kingdom, which lasted between 1293 and 1528, marked the culmination in the development of the Hindu-Buddhist states of island Southeast Asia. Its kings came to possess a degree of central control in eastern Java that went beyond previous precedent, and they created a state center that established varying degrees of hegemony over central Java and an overseas empire almost three times the size of what had been Srivijaya's, a realm that included all the islands that now form Indonesia, and more. Majapahit subsequently acquired, at the opposite end of the hemisphere, an expanding market of great significance, that of Western Europe, which was beginning to consume quantities of Indonesian spices.

Chinese goods and copper cash flowed into Majapahit Java; Mediterranean gold also moved through the Middle East and India to Java, along with major export items from these regions. Copper coins (either Chinese or similar to China's) had become the local currency not only in Java but in Sumatra's ports as well.

During the fifteenth century, Majapahit faced aggressive competition from the new trading state of Melaka and newly Islamicized ports on the north coast of Java, which soon wrested from it control of the strait and nibbled away its control of the maritime trade eastward and of Majapaphit client states in the archipelago. Islam had earlier spread to northern Sumatra along the trade routes from India, and the rulers of Melaka and the north coast of Java adopted the new religion as a means of enhancing their commercial connections, through which they made further converts. In 1513, a coalition of Javanese coastal communities attacked the core area of the Majapahit realm; in 1528 the court finally fell, and thereafter all those who had been Majapahit's followers would kneel and pray toward Mecca, the sacred center of Islam on the Arabian peninsula.

The Mongols demanded submission and tribute from the king of east Java, Kertanagra, who had made an alliance with Champa against the Mongols. When Kertanagra sent the Mongol emissaries back to Peking with their faces mutilated, Kubilai Khan launched a punitive expedition in 1292 with 1,000 ships and 20,000 men. They found Java embroiled in a civil war and the fleet away in Sumatra. Kertanagra was dead but the Sri Vijaya heir agreed to become a Mongol vassal if the Mongols would help him against his enemies. By the time the fleet returned, the rebellion had been put down, and Javanese naval and land forces defeated and expelled the Mongols. The Javanese ruler had survived the rebellion by fleeing to a village named Majapahit. Now restored to power, he put his new capital there, in east Java, and gave its name to the new empire. For a time Majapahit brought most of the archipelago under its control, and its military success was accompanied by a cultural and literary renaissance.

The recorded history of the Philippines begins only with the Spanish conquest, or with Magellan's voyage in 1521, in which he claimed the islands for Spain, although a settlement was not made on Luzon, the main island, until 1565. The Philippines are even more fragmented, into some 7,000 islands, than is Indonesia, with only some 3,000. Although speakers of Malay-related languages have long been dominant, other and probably earlier cultural groups remained in relative isolation, especially in the mountainous and heavily forested parts of the larger islands. Differences of dialect, language, and culture divided the inhabitants of most of the islands, and until recent times they lived in largely separate worlds despite a degree of interisland trading. No recognizable state emerged in any area before Spanish times, and there was no well-established or widely used form of writing, although Indian writing systems and some aspects of the Hindu tradition did make a faint impact in the course of the far-flung extension of Indian civilization into Southeast Asia.

There was also trade contact from China, probably from Han times, but little cultural evidence remains from that early period, apart from Chinese coins and pottery shards. Islam penetrated most of Mindanao in the south, but until the Spanish occupation the religious pattern of the rest of the Philippines was dominated by a great variety of local animistic cults. In the absence of any text-based religious tradition, the lack of anything approaching Filipino national coherence or identity made for ready conversion to Islam and to Christianity and contributed to the relative ease of the Spanish conquest and control. Four centuries of Spanish control left the Philippines in many ways culturally, socially, and politically closer to Latin America than to Asia.

Under Spanish colonialism, from the late eighteenth century, trade in sugar, *abaca* (Manila hemp), and tobacco boomed, tripling in value from 1825 to 1850. British and American merchants were prominent in the main trade center at Manila.

Southeast Asia was divided and engaged in chronic warfare, but these centuries saw the building of majestic temples and the flowering of the arts, supported as in India in part from profits earned in extensive maritime trade as well as from taxes on highly productive agricultural land in the great river valleys and deltas of the mainland and on the rich volcanic soils of Java. Religion in Southeast Asia too was periodically a source of conflict, as Buddhism developed new sects and Islam spread eastward from India and ultimately absorbed much of insular Southeast Asia in the wake of a trade dominated by Muslim merchants.

Buddhist Burma and Siam (Thailand) were periodically at war with each other, but both built impressive capitals and rested on the productive rice agriculture of their central river valleys, as did the Khmer empire of Cambodia. Vietnam, free of China by the tenth century, expanded southward to its present borders. Malaya was thinly settled and isolated, but in Java (Indonesia) successive kingdoms flourished, including Sumatra-based Sri Vijaya, while another kingdom, the Sailendras, in central Java built the massive Buddhist temple at Borobudur.

Southeast Asian Kingdoms 1300–1850			
Burma	**Thailand**	**Vietnam**	**Indonesia**
Pagan 850–1285	Ayudhya 1351–1767	Tran 1225–1400	Sri Vijaya 7th–13th centuries
Toungoo 1550–1752	Chakri, at Bangkok 1782–present	Le 1428–1527	Mejapahit 1292–1526
Konbaugh, at Mandalay 1752–1886		Mac 1527–1592	Spreading Dutch control, 1619–1949
		Le 1592–1788	

Melaka and the Entry of the West

In the fifteenth century, the sultanate of Melaka provided a singular trade emporium at the intersection of the Bay of Bengal, South China Sea, and Java Sea regional networks. Melaka's rise to prominence in the fifteenth century depended on the complexity of the multi-centered trade in the Indian Ocean, and the practicality at that time of establishing a single Indian Ocean port as a clearinghouse. It was appropriate that this central emporium was in Southeast Asia, because that area was then the pivotal center of Asian trade, as the source of the most demanded commodities; the most important consumer marketplace for imported textiles and ceramics; and the common center for the exchange of the variety of commodities that derived from China and the Middle East.

In the words of the early fifteenth-century Portuguese scribe Tome Pires, Southeast Asia was "at the end of the monsoon, where you find what you want, and sometimes more than you are looking for."[1] When Europeans came to Southeast Asia in the early sixteenth century, they saw Melaka as more than a marketplace. It was a symbol of the wealth and luxury of Asia. They were eager to circumvent the monopoly of Venice and the Ottoman Empire on the priceless spice trade, and the great wealth and luxury available in this trading had enticed them halfway around the world in their tiny, uncomfortable ships. Thus, when the Portuguese entered the Indian Ocean in the early 1500s, their objective was to seize Melaka, which they rightfully considered to be the dominant center of contemporary Asian trade (see Chapter 12).

What the Portuguese did not understand was that Melaka was no more than an agreed upon marketplace for the commodities of other centers, and when they seized Melaka the sedentary and migratory merchant communities responded by shifting their trade to other equally acceptable and mutually interchangeable regional ports. International merchants entered partnerships with the leaders of newly emerging Islamic and Buddhist states that capitalized on the benefits of an alliance between rulers and merchants—in much the same way that contemporary Western European monarchs (e.g., in Tudor England and the Netherlands) did.

Questions

1. How did geography determine the rise of early political and societal centers in Southeast Asia?

2. To what extent is the literate culture of Southeast Asia imported from India and China?

3. How would you characterize the rise and fall of Angkor? What was the significance of Angkor Wat and Angkor Thom in the Angkor political system?

4. How did the political systems of the Angkor and Majapahit kings compare with those of their contemporaries in medieval Europe, India, and China?

5. What role did Southeast Asia assume in the early Indian Ocean trade networks, and what were the consequences both to Southeast Asia as well as the remainder of Asia? What was the normal relationship between China and Southeast Asia (with the exception of Vietnam) as reflected in the Mongol naval expedition to Java in the late thirteenth century—as well as in the Tang-era poem in the next chapter? What products did Southeast Asia have that attracted the later sixteenth-century voyages of the Portuguese and Spanish?

6. What was the initial appeal of Islam in Southeast Asia and how did its spread there differ from its introduction to South Asia?

7. The Philippines were largely characterized by tribal societies that were isolated from other regional developments prior to the coming of the Spanish in the early sixteenth century. Why didn't all of the Philippines convert to Islam?

Notes

1. Armando Cortesao, trans., *The Suma Oriental of Tome Pires,* vol. 2. (London: 1944), p. 228.

Suggested Web Sites

http://www.hartford-hwp.com/archives/54/index.html
Political, economic, labor environment, and cultural history documents. Features sections on the history of Laos, Myanmar (Burma), Cambodia, Thailand, Malaysia, Indonesia, East Timor, Singapore, the Philippines, and Vietnam.

http://www.archaeolink.com/
ancient%20southeast%20asian%20civilizations.htm
Explores the archaeological remains of early Cambodia, Thailand, Vietnam, and Korea, with links.

http://www.borobudur.tv/history_1.htm

http://rubens.anu.edu.au/htdocs/bycountry/Indonesia/
borobudur/
Devoted to Borobudur, with links to explore early Indonesian history and culture.

http://www.eastjava.com
Include good introductions to the various east Java temple sites, as well as a brief summary of Java's history during the pre-1500 era.

http://www.angkor-net.de/english/
Angkor-West_Baray-e.shtml

Provides the opportunity for an interactive exploration of the major Angkor sites.

Suggestions for Further Reading

Andaya, B., and Andaya, L. *A History of Malaysia.* New York: St. Martin's Press, 1982.

Aung-Thwin, M. *Pagan: The Origins of Modern Burma.* Honolulu: University of Hawaii Press, 1985.

Briggs, L. *The Ancient Khmer Empire.* Philadelphia: American Philosophical Society, 1951.

Chandler, D. P. *A History of Cambodia.* Boulder, CO.: Westview, 1983.

Coedes, G. *The Indianized States of Southeast Asia,* ed. W. F. Vella. Honolulu: East-West Center Press, 1968.

Gesick, L., ed. *Centers, Symbols, and Hierarchies: Essays on the Classical States of Southeast Asia.* New Haven: Yale University Press, 1983.

Groslier, B. P., and Arthaud, J. *Angkor: Art and Civilization.* New York: Praeger, 1966.

Hall, K. R. *Maritime Trade and State Development in Early Southeast Asia.* Honolulu: University of Hawaii Press, 1985.

Higham, C. *The Civilization of Angkor.* Berkeley: University of California Press, 2004.

Lieberman, V., *Business Administrative Cycles: Anarchy and Conquest, 1580–1760.* Princeton: Princeton University Press, 1984.

———. *Strange Parallels: Southeast Asia in a Global Context, c. 800–1830.* New York: Cambridge University Press, 2003.

Miller, H. *A Short History of Malaya.* New York: Praeger, 1965.

Osborne, M. *Southeast Asia: An Illustrated Introductory History.* London: Allen and Unwin, 1997.

Reid, A. *Southeast Asia in the Age of Commerce, 1450–1680.* New Haven: Yale University Press, 1988.

Richards, D. S. *Islam and the Trade of Asia.* Philadelphia: University of Pennsylvania Press, 1970.

Ricklefs, M. C. *A History of Modern Indonesia.* Bloomington: Indiana University Press, 1981.

Sar Desai, D. R. *Southeast Asia Past and Present,* 3d ed. Boulder, CO: Westview, 1997.

Shaffer, L. N. *Maritime Southeast Asia, 300 B.C. to A.D. 1528.* Armonk, NY: M. E. Sharpe, 1993.

Tarling, N., ed. *The Cambridge History of Southeast Asia,* vol. 1. Cambridge, England: Cambridge University Press, 1992.

Taylor, K. W. *The Birth of Vietnam.* Berkeley: University of California Press, 1983.

Thapar, R. *A History of India,* vol. 1. Baltimore: Penguin Books, 1969.

Van Leur, J. C. *Indonesian Trade and Society.* The Hague: W. van Hoeve, 1955.

Vlekke, B. *Nusantara: A History of Indonesia.* The Hague: W. van Hoeve, 1960.

Wolters, O. L. *Early Indonesian Commerce: The Origins of Srivijaya.* Ithaca, NY: Cornell University Press, 1967.

Woodside, A. *Vietnam and the Chinese Model.* Cambridge: Harvard University Press, 1988.

Wyatt, D. *Thailand: A Short History.* New Haven: Yale University Press, 1984.

Yazdani, G., ed. *The Early History of the Deccan.* London: Oxford University Press, 1960.

8

China: A Golden Age

This chapter surveys what many Chinese consider the greatest period in their history: the empire of the Tang dynasty (618–907 C.E.). The splendor of the Tang from its capital at Chang'an (modern Xi'an) included great poetry and art as well as the expansion of Chinese control once more into Central Asia. It was succeeded by a new period of brilliance under the Song dynasty (960–1279); although the Song were ultimately defeated by the Mongols, their power lasted over 300 years and they saw notable achievements in painting, literature, and technology, in many ways like early modern Europe. The Mongols took 40 years to complete their conquest of China, but their rule there lasted only about 70 years, until they were expelled by Chinese rebellion. Marco Polo visited under the Yuan or Mongol dynasty (1279–1368) and described what he saw. The chapter concludes with a survey of traditional Chinese culture.

Reunification in China

For nearly four centuries after the fall of the Han dynasty in 220 C.E. China was divided into many separate kingdoms, with much of the north under barbarian control. Buddhism flourished, perhaps as a response to the troubled times, and was promoted also by the Sinicized barbarian rulers of the north. The chief such kingdom, known as the Northern Wei, controlled most of north China from 386 to 534. It built a number of splendid Buddhist cave temples with both small and immense statues of the Buddha and his devotees. Their style, though Chinese, reveals the Indian origins of Buddhism, as do the many pagodas also built at this period, a temple form evolved from the earlier Indian stupa. The Chinese cultural and political tradition was carried on in indigenous hands by a succession of rival dynasties

vying for supremacy in the south, which was enriched by a flood of wealthy and educated refugees from the north. Nanjing was the chief southern capital and major urban center, but none of the southern dynasties or kingdoms were able either to unify the region or to provide strong government. Literature, philosophy, and the arts continued vigorously with no real break, and Buddhism also became popular in the south. This was the period both of Indian Buddhist missions to China and of Chinese pilgrim visits to India. In China there were also new technological achievements, including gunpowder, further advances in medicine, refinements in the use of a magnetized needle for indicating direction (the forerunner of the compass), and the use of coal as fuel.

Most Chinese wanted to see the Han model of greatness restored, but first the country had to be reunified, and the imperial machine rebuilt. This was primarily the work of the short-lived Sui dynasty, which in 589 again welded contending Chinese states together by conquest. The Sui base was the same Wei Valley from which the Qin had erupted, and like the Qin they built roads and canals as the necessary infrastructure of empire, radiating out from their capital at Chang'an. The second Sui emperor, Yang Di (r. 604–618), heady with new power, is often compared to Qin Shi Huang Di. His style was similar, and he too rebuilt the Great Wall, at a cost of a further million lives, and reconquered northern Vietnam and much of Xinjiang and Mongolia, although his campaign in Korea was defeated by fierce resistance.

Yang Di built a magnificent new capital at Luoyang, following the model of the Zhou and the Han, but at heavy expense. Perhaps his most notable project was the building of the Grand Canal, from Hangzhou in the south to Kaifeng in the north to bring rice from the productive Yangzi Delta to feed troops and officials in semiarid north China. But his megalomaniacal behavior caused great suffering to his exhausted troops, forced laborers, taxpayers, and tyrannized officials. Rebellion spread, as in the last years of the Qin, and

CHRONOLOGY

386–534	▪ Northern Wei; southern kingdoms
589–618	▪ Sui dynasty
618–907	▪ Tang dynasty
c. 767–c. 960	▪ Protectorate of An Nam
960–1137	▪ Northern Song
1137–1279	▪ Southern Song
1279–c. 1350	▪ Yuan (Mongol) dynasty

Yang Di was assassinated by a courtier in 618 after only 14 years on the throne. A frontier general swept away the pretensions of the Sui heir and proclaimed a new dynasty, the Tang. The new dynasty lasted nearly 300 years, but it owed its success in large part to the empire building of the Sui, as the Han had rested on foundations laid by the Qin.

The Splendor of the Tang

Under Tang rule China achieved a new highpoint in prosperity, cultural sophistication and greatness, and imperial power. The cosmopolitan Tang capital at Chang'an, where the Han had ruled, was the world's largest city, with about 2 million inhabitants. The imperial civil service and examinations were reestablished, and learning and the arts flourished. The Tang is still seen as the greatest period of Chinese poetry, especially in the work of Li Bo (701–762) and Du Fu (712–770).

Some 1,800 samples of Li Bo's 20,000 poems survive, including these lines:

Beside my bed the bright moonbeams glimmer
Almost like frost on the floor.
Rising up, I gaze at the mountains bathed in moonlight;
Lying back, I think of my old home.

• • •

A girl picking lotuses beside the stream—
At the sound of my oars she turns;
She vanishes giggling among the flowers,
And, all pretense, declines to come out.

• • •

Amid the flowers with a jug of wine
The world is like a great empty dream.
Why should one toil away one's life?
That is why I spend my days drinking . . .
Lustily singing, I wait for the bright moon.

• • •

I drink alone with none to share
Raising up my cup, I welcome the moon . . .
We frolic in revels suited to the spring.

The legend, almost certainly untrue but appealing, is that Li Bo drunkenly leaned out of a boat to embrace the reflection of the moon and drowned, happy in his illusion.

The poet Li Bo (701–762), perhaps the most appealing Tang figure. His poetry is still learned and quoted by successive generations of Chinese. (Courtesy of the Tokyo National Museum. DNParchives.com)

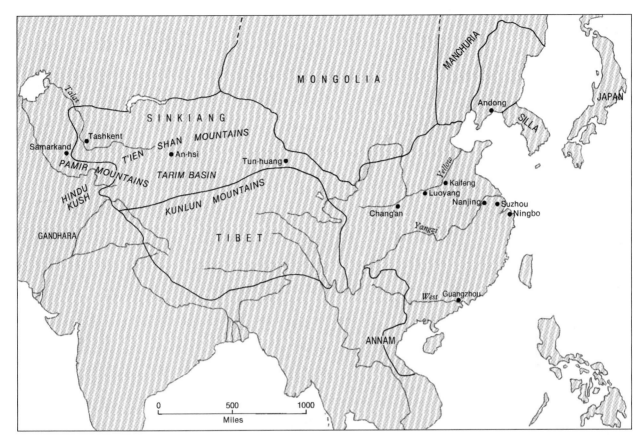

China Under the Tang

The Tang reclaimed the territory ruled by the Han and added to it. The Tang also saw a great increase in the Chinese settlement of the south at the expense of the indigenous inhabitants.

Du Fu was a more sober poet than Li Bo, but equally admired. Here are some samples of his lines:

Frontier war drums disrupt everyone's travels.
At the border in autumn a solitary goose honks.
Tonight the hoar frost will be white . . .
I am lucky to have brothers, but all are scattered . . .
The letters I write never reach them.
How terrible that the fighting cannot stop.

• • •

Distant Annam* sends the court a red parrot,
Gaudy as a peach blossom and as talkative as we are.
But learning and eloquence are given the same treatment—
The cage of imprisonment. Is one ever free?

• • •

The capital is captured, but hills and streams remain.
With spring in the city the grass and trees grow fast.
Bewailing the times, the flowers droop as if in tears.

---

*Annam is central Vietnam, beyond the empire's direct rule but, as implied here, tributary.

Saddened as I am with parting, the birds make my heart
*   flutter.*
Army beacons have flamed for three months.
A letter from home now would be worth a king's ransom.
In my anxiety I have scratched my white hairs even shorter.
What a jumble! Even hairpins cannot help me.

Du Fu's poetry, concerned as it is with human troubles, reminds us that the rebuilding of empire exacted a price, for all its glory. Most of the Han-ruled territories were reclaimed by conquest after they had fallen away at the end of the Sui, including northern Vietnam, but Tibet (a new interest), Xinjang, Mongolia, and southern Manchuria were wisely left as tributary regions, after their non-Han inhabitants had been defeated in a brilliant series of campaigns by the emperor Tang Tai Zong (r. 626–649). Korea again fought the Chinese armies to a standstill but accepted tributary status. Much of the mountainous southwest, home of the Thai and other groups, remained non-Han in population and outside imperial rule. Tai Zong is remembered as a model ruler, fostering education and encouraging conscientious officials. In his cosmopolitan time, Buddhism was still tolerated and widely popular.

The gradual Sinification of the originally non-Han or barbarian south, below the Yangzi valley, continued apace under imperial momentum. By the late Tang most of the empire's revenue came from the more productive south, including the Yangzi valley, and most Chinese lived in that area. The north, where empire was born, suffered as always from recurrent drought, erosion, and siltation of the vital irrigation works, but now the south, progressively cleared of its earlier forests, more than made up the difference. Agricultural techniques were slowly adapted to the wetter and hillier conditions and the far longer growing season. The growing use of human manure (night soil) improved the less fertile southern soils outside the alluvial river valleys; the continued increase of population thus provided its own rise in agricultural yields. Many northerners had fled south after the fall of the Han dynasty; now they and their descendants were joined by new streams seeking greater economic opportunity than in the overcrowded and often marginal north. Imperial tradition, and defense of the troublesome northwest frontiers, kept the capital in the north, but the south was flourishing.

Renewed contacts with more distant lands westward revealed, as in Han times, no other civilization that could rival the Celestial Empire. The Son of Heaven, as the emperor was called, was seen as the lord of "all under heaven," meaning the four corners of the known world, within which China was clearly the zenith of power and sophistication. Did not all other people the Chinese encountered acknowledge this, by tribute, praise, and imitation of Chinese culture, the sincerest form of flattery? In fact, even beyond the world the Chinese knew, they had no equal, in any terms. Rome was long gone, and the Abbasid caliphate with its capital at Baghdad was no match for the Tang or its great successor, the Song. A coalition of Arabs and western Turks did repulse a Tang expeditionary force, far from its base in Central Asia at the battle of the Talas River near Samarkand in 751. But the battle is perhaps more significant in that some captured Chinese transmitted the recently developed Tang art of printing to the West, and that of papermaking, widespread in China from the late first century C.E. after its invention a century earlier. From about 700 C.E., printing was done from carved wooden blocks a page at a time, but by 1030 C.E. the Chinese, and only slightly later the Koreans, had developed movable-type printing, with individual characters made of wood, ceramics, or metal, all long before its later spread into fifteenth-century Europe.

Paper and printing were typical creations of the Chinese genius, with their love of written records and of learning, literature, and painting. They were also two of China's most basic gifts to the later-developing West,

The Tang emperor Tai Zong (r. 626–649), an able man and brilliant field commander but also an astute administrator. His campaigns reestablished Chinese control over Xinjiang and northern Vietnam, conquered Tibet, and even extended imperial rule into Central Asia. Tai Zong also restored and extended the imperial bureaucratic system of the Han. (The Granger Collection, New York)

along with cast iron, the crossbow, gunpowder, the compass, the use of coal as fuel, the waterwheel, paper currency, the wheelbarrow, wallpaper, and porcelain, to mention only a few. Fully perfected porcelain had appeared by Tang times and from it were made objects of exquisite beauty never matched elsewhere, although the process finally made its way to Europe in the eighteenth century. Porcelain joined silk and, later, tea as China's chief exports to a cruder world abroad.

The secret of silk making had been smuggled out of China, supposedly by two monks in the time of the eastern Roman emperor Justinian (r. 527–565) in the form of cocoons concealed in hollow walking sticks. But later Western silk production in Italy and France never equaled the Chinese quality, which still remains an export staple, although in the nineteenth century the Chinese lost ground to more uniform Japanese and later Korean silk. Tea, largely unknown in Han times, was introduced from Southeast Asia as a medicine and an aid to meditation and began to be drunk more widely in fifth-century China. It became the basic Chinese drink during the Tang, grown in the misty hills of the south, another Chinese monopoly that later drew Western traders. Seeds and cuttings of the tea plant were smuggled out of China by the English East India Company in 1843 to start plantation production in India and Ceylon, and tea became the world's most popular drink.

A CLOSER LOOK

Chang'an in an Age of Imperial Splendor

The splendor of the Tang and its empire was symbolized in its capital at Chang'an, where the Han and the Qin had also ruled. It was the eastern terminus of trade routes linking China with Central Asia and lands beyond; it also presided over the largest empire the world had yet seen, exceeding even the Han and Roman empires. People from all over Asia—Turks, Indians, Persians, Syrians, Vietnamese, Koreans, Japanese, Jews, Arabs, and even Nestorian Christians and Byzantines—thronged its streets and added to its cosmopolitan quality. It was probably also the largest wholly planned city ever built, covering some 30 square miles and including within its massive walls about 1 million people. The imperial census also recorded nearly another million people living in the urban area outside the walls.

Like all Chinese administrative centers, Chang'an was laid out on a checkerboard pattern, with broad avenues running east-west and north-south to great gates at the cardinal compass points. These were closed at night, and the main avenues leading to them divided the city into major quarters, further subdivided by other principal streets into 110 blocks, each constituting an administrative unit, with its own internal pattern of alleyways. The emperor's palace faced south down a 500-foot-wide central thoroughfare to the south gate, the one used by most visitors and all official envoys and messen-

gers. This arrangement was designed to awe and impress all who came to Chang'an with the power and greatness of the empire. Kaifeng and Beijing were later designed similarly and for the same purpose.

Within the city, people lived in rectangular wards, each surrounded by walls whose gates were closed at night. The West Market and the East Market, supervised by the government, occupied larger blocks to serve their respective halves of the city. There and elsewhere in the city, in open spaces and appointed theaters, foreign and Chinese players, acrobats, and magicians performed dramas, operas, skits, and other amusements. Women of fashion paraded their fancy clothing and coiffures. For men and women alike, one of the most popular pastimes was polo, adopted from Persia; Tang paintings showing polo matches survive, making it clear that women played too. As later in India, the wealthy prided themselves on their stable of good polo ponies and their elegant turnout for matches.

Artists and sculptors also found horses popular subjects; despite their apparent mass production, Tang paintings and clay figurines of horses are still full of life and movement. Another favorite subject for art was the endless variety of foreigners in this cosmopolitan center, depicted faithfully in both paintings and figurines so that one can easily recognize which people are being represented by their dress and physical features.

Tang culture was worldly, elegant, and urbane, but Buddhism was still in vogue and in official favor. Buddhist temples and pagodas also gave Chinese architects an outlet for their talents, and the first half of the Tang was a golden age of temple architecture and sculpture, the latter showing clear artistic as well as religious influences from the Indian home of Buddhism. A cosmopolitan center for all of Asia, Chang'an was also, like China, the cultural model for the rest of East Asia. Official tributary embassies, and less formal visitors and merchants or adventurers, came repeatedly from Korea, Japan, and lesser states to the south and west to bask in the glories of Chang'an and to take back with them as much as they could for the building of their own versions of Tang civilization. Persian Zoroastrians, Muslims, Jews, Indian Buddhists and Hindus, and Nestorian Christians from the eastern Mediterranean, representing thus nearly all of the great world religions, were among the city's permanent residents, all welcomed in this center of world culture and all leaving behind some evidence of their presence. Chang'an flourished for two and a half centuries, from the early seventh to the mid-ninth, when the capital, like the empire, fell into chaos. But from 618 to about 860 it shone with a cosmopolitan brilliance perhaps never equaled anywhere.

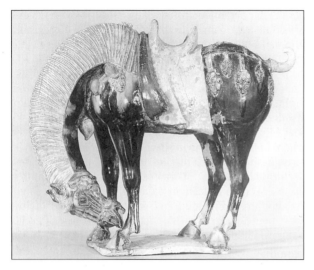

A sample of perhaps the best-known Tang art form, in glazed pottery. Horses, like this one, camels, and hundreds of other figures, were turned out in great quantity, but each figure is of superb quality. Tomb figure, buff earthenware with sancai (three-color) lead glazes and molded decorations, Tang dynasty, first half 8th century, 62.9 × 78 cm. Gift of Russell Tyson, 1943.1136. 3/4 view. (Photograph © 2002 The Art Institute of Chicago. All rights reserved.)

Cultural Brilliance and Political Decay

Relatively little Tang painting has survived, apart from a few tomb walls, but we have many accounts of the great painters of the time and of fiction writers of whose work we have only the tiniest sample. What has survived in great abundance is the magnificent glazed-pottery figures used to furnish tombs and adorn houses and palaces, probably the best-known aspect of Tang art. Learning and the arts enjoyed a further blooming under the encouragement of the emperor Xuan Zong (r. 712–756) and at his elegant but efficient court. But in his old age Xuan Zong became infatuated with a son's concubine, the beautiful Yang Guifei; she and her relatives and protégées gained increasing control of the empire, but ran it badly. Rebels sacked the capital in 755. Xuan Zong fled south with Lady Yang, but his resentful guards strangled her as the cause of all the empire's troubles, and Xuan Zong abdicated in sorrow. The rebellion was finally put down and order restored.

Half a century earlier, a beautiful concubine of the first and second Tang emperors named Wu Zhao was made a consort and empress by Tai Zong's son and successor, Gao Zong, whom she soon came to dominate.

After his death in 683, she ruled alone or through puppets and then proclaimed herself emper*or* of a new dynasty, the only female emperor in Chinese history. She struck at the old aristocracy, her chief opposition (one can imagine their reactions to her!), and actually ordered many of them executed. She drew support from the Buddhist establishment, which she strongly favored and which declared her a reincarnation of the Bodhisattva Maitreya, the Buddhist messiah. Wu Zhao had become a Buddhist nun after Tai Zong's death in 650 but grew restless without greater scope for her talents. Empress Wu, as she is called, was denounced by Chinese historians, although this has clear sexist overtones; she was a strong and effective if ruthless ruler, obviously opposed to the Confucian establishment, and promoted its "enemy," the alien faith of Buddhism. To be a woman in addition was just too much, and in 705 she was deposed in a palace coup.

Although there were to be no more outstanding rulers after Xuan Zong, the power of court factions and great families grew, the economy thrived, and culture flourished. There was a Confucian revival, and partly as a result the state, jealous of Buddhist wealth and power, moved in the 840s against Buddhist temples, monasteries, and monks. Most temple and monastic properties and tax-free estates, which had grown to immense size, were confiscated by the state, and most monasteries destroyed, a move reminiscent of Henry VIII of England seven centuries later and with the same motives—the need to regain control over lost revenues. Chinese Buddhism never recovered from this blow and remained thereafter a mainly minority religion in a Confucian and Daoist society. Buddhism was also resented as a rival faith by many Chinese, especially orthodox Confucianists and dedicated Daoists, because of its alien origins, as Christianity was to be later. Its association with the Empress Wu did not help.

At the dynasty's midpoint, a number of regional commanders who had built their own local power bases began to contend for power. One of them, An Lushan, a man of Turkish descent, went on to full rebellion and even captured Chang'an in 755; it was his troops who drove Xuan Zong and Lady Yang southward, to her death and his abdication. An Lushan was murdered by his own son in 757, and order was restored by loyal armies by 762, but the rebellion shook the dynasty to its roots. It was never the same again, becoming more and more dependent on foreign or barbarian troops, as An had been—echoing late imperial Rome! Regional commanders continued to build their power, and a series of rebellions broke out after 875, originally prompted by a great drought in the north but spreading among disaffected subjects all over the country whom the Tang no longer served well. Rival generals or their puppets succeeded one another as emperor after 884, but in 907 the dynasty dissolved. After a confused period from 907 to 960, a young general proclaimed a new dynasty, the Song, which was to last more than three centuries.

The Song Achievement

In many ways, the Song is the most exciting period in Chinese history. Later generations of Chinese historians have criticized it because it failed to stem the tide of barbarian invasion and was ultimately overwhelmed by the hated Mongols. But it lasted from 960 to 1279, longer than the roughly 300-year average for dynasties, and presided over a period of unprecedented growth, innovation, and cultural flowering. For a long time the Song policy of defending their essential territories and appeasing neighboring barbarian groups with money payments worked well. It made sense to give up the exhausting Han and Tang effort to hold Xinjiang, Tibet, Mongolia, Manchuria, Vietnam, and even the more marginal arid fringes of northern China. These areas were all unprofitable from the Chinese point of view; they never repaid, in any form but pride, the immense costs of controlling them. Most of them were arid or mountainous wastelands thinly settled by restless nomads who took every chance to rebel and who were very effective militarily.

Vietnam and Korea had been chronic drains on China's wealth and military strength; both were determined to fight relentlessly against Chinese control but were willing to accept a mainly nominal tributary status, which protected Chinese pride and avoided bloody struggles. The Song wisely concentrated on the productive center of Han Chinese settlements south of the Great Wall and even made a truce, with gifts, to accept barbarian control of what is now the Beijing area and a similar arrangement with another barbarian group for the arid northwestern province of Gansu. Little of value was lost by these agreements, and the remarkable flowering of Song China had much to do with its abandonment of greater imperial ambitions. What remained under Chinese control was still roughly the size of non-Russian Europe and, with a population of some 100 million, was by far the largest, most productive, and most highly developed state in the world.

The Song capital was built at Kaifeng, near the great bend of the Yellow River. In addition to its administrative functions, it became a huge commercial center and also a center of manufacturing, served in all respects by the Grand Canal, which continued to bring rice and other goods from the prosperous south. There was a particularly notable boom in iron and steel production and metal industries, using coal as fuel. China in the eleventh century probably produced more iron, steel, and metal goods than the whole of Europe until the mid-eighteenth century and similarly preceded Europe by seven centuries in smelting and heating with coal. Kaifeng was better located to administer and draw supplies from the Yangzi valley and the south than Chang'an, whose frontier pacification role was in any case no longer so necessary. The Song army was large, mobile, equipped with iron and steel weapons, and well able for some time to defend the state's new borders. Kaifeng probably exceeded 1 million inhabitants, with merchants and artisans now proportionally more important than in the past, although there were also clouds of officials, soldiers, providers, servants, and hangers-on.

The early Song emperors prudently eliminated the power of the court eunuchs and the great landed families and rebuilt the scholar-officialdom as the core of administration. Civil servants recruited through examination had no power base of their own but did have a long tradition of public service and could even check the abuses of the powerful. To further ensure their loyalty to the empire, their local postings were changed every three years, and they never served in their native places, lest they become too identified with the interests of any one area. In each county and at each higher level the emperor appointed both a civil administrator—a magistrate or governor—and a military official, each with his own staff, who with other officials such as tax collectors and the imperial censors or inspectors had overlapping jurisdiction and could check on each other. It was an efficient system that ensured good administration most of the time. The growing spread of mass printing promoted literacy and education and opened wider opportunities for commoners to enter the elite group of the scholar-gentry from whom officials were recruited or to prosper in trade.

The Tang are credited with first developing recruitment of officials through examination beyond its Han origins, but such people filled, at most, a quarter of the posts. Under the Song, this system, one of the chief glories of imperial China, reached its peak. Upper-level officials could recommend people for junior posts, but most high positions were filled by those who had passed all three levels of the examinations: the prefectural and provincial levels and a final interview with the emperor. On passing the first level, one acquired gentry status and an extensive education in the Confucian classics, which some then used as teachers to upcoming generations of aspirants. Officials were regularly rated for merit—mainly honesty and efficiency—and were also watched by the imperial censors, who frequently toured local districts, sometimes unannounced or incognito. Able men from any background could rise to office through the examinations, although, of course, the sons of the rich and well-connected had an advantage through their leisure for education. In the Song, successful

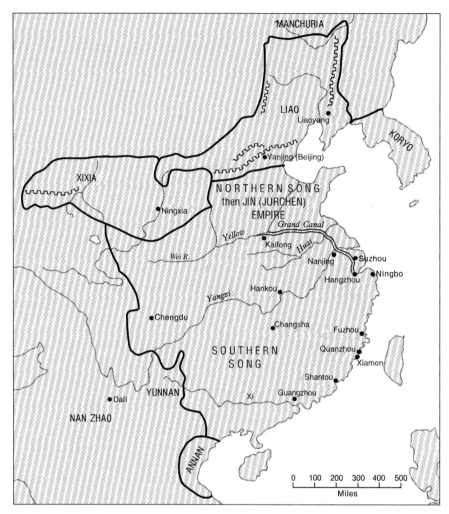

China and Korea in 1050

Note the shrinking of the empire under the Song, the loss of Vietnam and much of the north and northwest.

candidates included a third or more from nongentry families, a remarkable degree of upward mobility in any premodern society or even in many modern ones.

It was in many ways a golden age of good government, prosperity, and creativity. Paper promissory notes and letters of credit, followed by mass government issue of paper currency, served the growth of commerce. Government officials distributed printed pamphlets and promoted improved techniques in agriculture: irrigation, fertilization, ingenious new metal tools and protomachines, and new, improved crop strains. Painting had a glorious development, often patronized by rich urban merchants as well as by the Song court. Literature also flourished, boosted by the spread of cheap printing. Fic-

tional tales proliferated, some now in the vernacular. The most famous Song literary figure is the poet-painter-official Su Shi, also known as Su Dongpo (1037–1101), perhaps the best known of China's long tradition of poetic nature lovers. It was a confident, creative time.

Su Shi was, like so many of the scholar-gentry, a painter as well as a poet. In several of his poems he tries to merge the two media, inviting readers to step into the scene and lose themselves in a mind-emptying union with the great world of nature. He also used dust as a symbol both for official life (dead files, lifelessness, etc., as in our own culture) and for the capital on the dusty plains of the north, where he served for many years as an official.

Life along the river near Kaifeng at spring festival time. This scene comes from a long scroll that begins with the rural areas and moves through suburbs into the capital, giving a vivid picture of the bustling life in and around Kaifeng, at the time the largest city in the world. The painting (in English, Spring on the River), by Zhang Zeduan, was done in the early twelfth century. (Werner Forman/Art Resource, NY)

Foggy water curls and winds around the brook road;
Layered blue hills make a ring where the brook runs east.
On a white moonlit shore a long-legged heron roosts.
And this is a place where no dust comes.
An old man of the stream looks, says to himself:
"What is your little reason for wanting so much to be a
*   bureaucrat?*
You have plenty of wine and land;
Go on home, enjoy your share of leisure!"

• • •

A boat, light as a leaf, two oars squeaking frighten wild geese.
Water reflects the clear sky, the limpid waves are calm.
Fish wriggle in the weedy mirror, herons dot misty foreshores.
Across the sandy brook swift, the frost brook cold, the moon
*   brook bright.*
Layer upon layer like a painting, bend after bend like a
*   screen.*
Remember old Yan Ling long ago—"Lord," "Minister"—a
*   dream,*
Now gone, vain fames.
Only the far hills are long, the cloudy hills tumbled, the dawn
*   hills green.*

• • •

Drunk, abob in a light boat, wafted into the thick of flowers,
Fooled by the sensory world, I hadn't meant to stop here.
Far misty water, thousand miles' slanted evening sunlight,
Numberless hills, riot of green like rain—
I don't remember how I came.

Wang Anshi: Reform and Retreat

In 1068 a new, young emperor, Shen Zong, appointed the head of a reformist faction, Wang Anshi, as chief councilor. Wang tried to rearrange the whole sphere of government policies, especially in military and financial matters. Wang has earned a reputation as a socialist through his policies of government control over the economy, but the system by his time was in growing crisis; he did his best to check the decline and restore the dynasty's financial solvency, which suffered from the old problem of the avoidance of taxes by the rich and landowners. Wang tried to control prices and to cut out usurious moneylenders by offering government loans to poor peasants at lower rates. He set up a state trading organization to break the monopoly of the big merchants. Taxes were readjusted based on the productivity of the land, and all personal property was assessed for taxation. These were all reasonable measures but they aroused, not surprisingly, the bitter opposition of those with vested interest, including, of course, the conservative bureaucracy.

A major military weakness of the Song was their difficulty in maintaining cavalry units because they had lost control over the chief horse-breeding areas in the north and northwest—and to steppe tribes whose cavalry was

The "Ever-Normal Granary" System

Bo Juyi (722–846), one of China's greatest poets, was also a Tang official. While serving as an imperial censor in 808 he wrote a memorial criticizing the "ever-normal granary" system.

I have heard that because of the good harvest this year the authorities have asked for an imperial order to carry out Grain Harmonization so that cheap grain may be bought and the farmers benefitted. As far as I can see, such purchases mean only loss to the farmers. . . . In recent years prefectures and districts were allowed to assess each household for a certain amount of grain, and to fix the terms and the date of delivery. If there was any delay, the punitive measures of imprisonment and flogging were even worse than those usually involved in the collection of taxes. Though this was called Grain Harmonization, in reality it hurt the farmers. . . . If your majesty would consider converting the taxes payable in cash into taxes payable in kind, the farmers would neither suffer loss by selling their grain at a cheap price, nor would they have the problem of re-selling bales of cloth and silk. The profit would go to the farmers, the credit to the emperor. Are the advantages of that commutation in kind not evident? . . . I lived for some time in a small hamlet where I belonged to a household which had to contribute its share to Grain Harmonization. I myself was treated with great harshness; it was truly unbearable. Not long ago, as an official in the metropolitan district, I had responsibility for the administration of Grain Harmonization. I saw with my own eyes how delinquent people were flogged, and I could not stand the sight of it. In the past I have always wanted to write about how people suffered from this plague [but] since I was a petty and unimportant official in the countryside, I had no opportunity to approach your majesty. Now I have the honor of being promoted to serve your majesty and of being listed among the officials who offer criticism and advice. [If] my arguments are not strong enough to convince . . . order one of your trustworthy attendants to inquire incognito among the farmers. . . . Then your majesty will see that my words are anything but rash and superficial statements.

Source: W. T. de Bary, ed., *Sources of Chinese Traditions* (New York: Columbia University Press, 1960), pp. 423–425.

their chief and very effective weapon. Wang tried to buy horses for distribution to peasant families north of the Yangzi valley, with the understanding that they would be available when needed as part of the imperial cavalry. He also tried to get each district to provide quotas of trained militia to help strengthen the quality of the army. He expanded the number of government schools, to offer education and a chance at officeholding to those who could not afford the private academies, and urged that the imperial examinations include practical problems of administration and tests of aptitude rather than so heavily concentrating on memorization of the classics. This too was a step forward, but of course it drew the resistance of the

Confucian bureaucracy, men who had risen by the old system and were wedded to it. The conservative group at court forced Wang out in 1076; he was recalled in 1078, but when the emperor Shen Zong died in 1085, Wang was dismissed and his reforms canceled or destroyed.

Along the northern frontier, the Tang had been obliged to accept control of 16 border prefectures based on what later became Beijing by a Mongol offshoot, the Qidans, who went on to take over much of southern Manchuria, where they established a dynasty called Liao, from 947 to 1125. The Song were obliged to confirm this, and paid the Qidan-Liao what amounted to an annual tribute. It is probably from the name Qidan that

 The Confucian Revival

The Song poet, official, and historian Ouyang Xiu (1007–1070) was one of several leading figures who promoted the revival of Confucianism and criticized Buddhism as alien.

> Buddha was a barbarian who was far removed from China and lived long ago. In the age of Yao, Shun, and the Three Dynasties [the golden age of China's remote past], kingly rule was practiced, government and the teachings of rites and righteousness flourished. . . . But after the Three Dynasties had fallen into decay, when kingly rule ceased and rites and righteousness were neglected, Buddhism came to China [taking] advantage of this time of decay and neglect to come and plague us. . . . If we will but remedy this decay, revive what has fallen into disuse, and restore kingly rule in its brilliance and rites and righteousness in their fullness, then although Buddhism continues to exist, it will have no hold upon our people. . . . Buddhism has plagued the world for a thousand years. . . . The people are drunk with it, and it has seeped into their bones and marrow so that it cannot be vanquished by mouth and tongue. . . . There is nothing so effective in overcoming it as practicing what is fundamental. . . . When the way of Confucius [is] made clear, the other schools will cease. This is the effect of practicing what is fundamental in order to overcome Buddhism. . . . These days a tall warrior clad in armor and bearing a spear may surpass in bravery a great army, yet when he sees the Buddha he bows low and when he hears the doctrines of the Buddha he is sincerely awed and persuaded. Why? Because though he is indeed strong and full of vigor, in his heart he is confused and has nothing to cling to. . . . If a single scholar who understands rites and righteousness can keep from submitting to these doctrines, then we have but to make the whole world understand rites and righteousness and these doctrines will, as a natural consequence, be wiped out.

Source: W. T. de Bary, ed., *Sources of Chinese Traditions* (New York: Columbia University Press, 1960), pp. 442–445.

the Russian name for China, Khitai, was derived, and the later name of Marco Polo's time, Cathay. In the northwest, a Tibetan group of Tanguts established their own independent state in the Gansu area, and in 1038 assumed the Chinese-style dynastic title of Xixia. Repeated Song efforts to defeat them failed, and from 1044 the Song also paid them an annual tribute, although the Xixia were wiped out by the 1220s as part of the great Mongol conquests.

Barbarians in the North, Innovation in the South

Still more trouble was brewing on the northern frontiers. One among the several barbarian groups, the Jurchen, ancestors of the Manchus, spilled over from their home-

land in southern Manchuria, and, in alliance with the Song, they defeated in 1122 the Qidan who had ruled the northeastern border area, returning it to Chinese control. The warlike Jurchen were not overly impressed by the army of their Song allies, and the Song foolishly treated them as inferiors. The Jurchen advanced southward, besieged Kaifeng, and sacked the city in 1127 after the Chinese failed to pay them an extravagant indemnity. The war continued for a decade, with Jurchen armies briefly penetrating south of the Yangzi. But the Song armies regrouped and drove them back into northern China, finally concluding a treaty that left the Jurchen in control of the area north of the Yangzi valley, with the Song as a tribute-paying vassal. Now called the Southern Song, the dynasty built a new capital at Hangzhou at the southern edge of the Yangzi delta. They had lost the north, but now they could concentrate

Advice to a Chinese Emperor

The Song official Sima Guang (1019–1086) was also part of the Confucian revival and wrote a monumental general history of China. Here is part of one of his memorials to the emperor, urging the abolition of Wang Anshi's reforms.

Human inclinations being what they are, who does not love wealth and high rank, and who does not fear punishment and misfortune? Seeing how the wind blew and following with the current, the officials and gentry vied in proposing schemes, striving to be clever and unusual. They supported what was harmful and rejected what was beneficial. In name they loved the people; in fact they injured the people. The crop loans, local service exemptions, marketing controls, credit and loan system, and other measures were introduced. They aimed at the accumulation of wealth and pressed the people mercilessly. The distress they caused still makes for difficulties today. Besides, there were frontier officials who played fast and loose, hoping to exploit their luck. They spoke big and uttered barefaced lies, waged war unjustifiably, and needlessly disturbed the barbarians on our borders. . . . Officials who liked to create new schemes which they might take advantage of to advance themselves . . . changed the regulations governing the tea, salt, iron, and other monopolies and increased the taxes on families, on business, and so forth, in order to meet military expenses. . . . They misled the late emperor, and saw to it that they themselves derived all the profit from these schemes. . . .

Now the evils of the new laws are known to everyone in the empire, high or low, wise or ignorant. Yet there are still some measures which are harmful to the people and hurtful to the state. These matters are of immediate and urgent importance, and should be abolished. Your servant will report on them in separate memorials, hoping that it may please your sage will to grant us an early decision and act upon them. . . . The best plan is to select and keep those new laws which are of advantage to the people, while abolishing all those which are harmful. This will let the people of the land know unmistakably that the court loves them with a paternal affection.

Source: W. T. de Bary, ed., *Sources of Chinese Traditions* (New York: Columbia University Press, 1960), pp. 487–489.

---

on China's heartland, the Yangzi valley and the south. Another century of brilliance and innovation ensued, with only brief loss of momentum.

The Southern Song Period

Cut off from normal overland trade routes through the northwest, the Song turned in earnest to developing sea routes to Southeast Asia and India. Permanent colonies of Chinese merchants grew in many Southeast Asian trade centers. Ports on China's south-east coast, from Hangzhou south, flourished, including large numbers of resident foreigners, mostly Arabs, who lived in special quarters under their own headmen. Foreign accounts agree that these were the world's largest port cities of the time. Taxes on maritime trade provided a fifth of the imperial revenue, something that was unheard of in the past.

There was a striking advance in the size and design of oceangoing ships, some of which could carry over 600 people as well as cargo, far larger than any else-where until modern times. The earlier Chinese invention of the compass was a vital navigational aid, and these ships also used multiple masts (important for

Piracy in Southeast Asia

Until Europeans introduced into Asia the concept of piracy as a criminal activity, Asians regarded acts of piracy as standard and legitimate political or commercial practices. For example, revenue for the local regimes along the Strait of Melaka and Vietnam coastlines came from commercial monopolies and port-polities (states based in a coastal or river-mouth emporium) that drew foreign traders. Raiding, or *merompak*, was a frequent occurrence in these areas. It served as a means of commercial competition, political warfare, and tax collection, as well as a way for young chiefs to establish their power.

A warrior chief might, for example, unite a group of sailors and set up a port-polity at a strategic location where he could control the river mouths and sea lanes. In exchange for port fees, he offered a friendly port and safe passage. The enterprising chief was in essence selling protection from his band of raiders, who might otherwise seize the cargoes of those who refused the chief's guarantee of safe passage. Raiders might also take prisoner those seeking passage and force them to join their band or sell them as slaves in marketplaces elsewhere.

Early records of the international trade routes are filled with warnings about the dangers of the Southeast Asia passageway. The Chinese tried to reduce the danger by offering preferential trade status to those port-polities that would guarantee ships safe passage to China's ports. In return for their preferred trade status, the port-polities were required to make regular presentations of tribute at the Chinese court.

The system, however, never worked perfectly. As overseas trade became ever more important to China during the second millennium C.E., the Mongol rulers of China tried to deal directly with the recurring threat to international shipping by launching naval expeditions against the pirates of the southern Vietnam coast in the 1280s.

By the late thirteenth century, the Javanese ruler Kertanagara controlled the passageway through the Strait of Melaka. The Mongol ruler Kubilai Khan sent an envoy to Java to demand that a member of the Javanese royal family go to China to present tribute at the Beijing court.

From the Chinese perspective, presenting tribute at the Chinese court represented a great honor for Kertanagara's family. Kertanagara, however, refused the Chinese demand and persecuted Kubilai Khan's envoy. Chinese sources imply that the envoy was sent home with the Javanese ruler's brand on his head; Javanese sources assert that the envoy's decapitated head was returned to the Chinese court. In response, Kubilai Khan launched a punitive, but ultimately unsuccessful, expedition against the Javanese in 1292.

During the Ming era, the eunuch admiral Zheng He launched seven enormous naval expeditions. With his fleet of huge ships—400 feet long and capable of carrying 500 tons of cargo—Zheng He sailed throughout Southeast Asia, along the east and west coasts of India, through the Persian Gulf, finally traveling as far as East Africa. The legacy of Zheng He's exploits was a stable international trade network centered in the Strait of Melaka passageway. From this same era, however, along the Vietnam coastline, so-called wokou pirates—a combination of displaced Chinese, Koreans, and Japanese as well as Malays, Chams, and Bugis sailors based in the eastern Indonesian archipelago—continued to threaten ships sailing along the coast.

As the British and Dutch colonial empires began to expand in Southeast Asia in the nineteenth century, the political and commercial practices of local Asian raiders came to be regarded as criminal activities in direct opposition to Western beliefs in free trade, antislavery, and legality. When in 1819 the British established their trade base at Singapore and declared it a free port, they put an end to the trading system that had been controlled by the local Johor chiefs and their followers by cutting them out of their traditional share of the trade revenues. Yet, as the old Straits political system ended, the volume of international trade increased, thus creating more opportunity for raiding and other acts of piracy.

The arrival of steamships and British naval vessels in the Strait of Melaka and along the Borneo coast destroyed the rival port-polities of native traders. By 1837, Singapore had become part of the British Empire and embarked on its own punitive expeditions against coastal enclaves with "piratical" reputations. The increasing dominance of the square-rigged European and Chinese trading vessels further contributed to the decline of piracy, as the speed of these new ships allowed them to escape the slower craft of local pirates.

manageability as well as speed), separate watertight compartments (not known elsewhere until much later), and, equally important, the sternpost rudder instead of the awkward and unseaworthy steering oar. In all of these respects Song ships and their Han dynasty predecessors predated modern ships by many centuries. Ironically, they helped make it possible much later for Europeans to make the sea voyage to Asia using the compass, rudder, and masts—plus gunpowder, of course—originally developed by China and to record their conquests and profits on Chinese-invented paper.

Domestically, commerce and urbanization also flourished. The Yangzi delta and the southeast coast had long been China's commercial center, with the help of high productivity and easy movement of goods by river, sea, and canal. The proliferation of cities included for the first time several as big as or bigger than the capital and many only slightly smaller. Suzhou and Fuzhou each had well over 1 million people, and according to Marco Polo there were six large cities in the 300 miles between them. An immense network of canals and navigable creeks covered the Yangzi and Guangdong deltas, serving a system of large and small cities inhabited increasingly by merchants managing a huge and highly varied trade. Hangzhou, the new capital, with its additional administrative role, may have reached a population size of 1.5 million, larger than cities became anywhere until the age of railways; water transport made this possible for Hangzhou and other big cities, including Pataliputra, Rome, Chang'an, Istanbul, Edo (Tokyo), and eighteenth-century London. Chinese medicine became still more sophisticated, including the use of smallpox vaccination learned from Guptan India and usually attributed by provincial Westerners to the Englishman Edward Jenner in 1798.

We know a good deal about Hangzhou, both from voluminous Chinese sources and from the accounts of several foreigners who visited it, including Marco Polo, who actually saw it only later, toward the end of the thirteenth century under Mongol rule after its great period had long passed. Nevertheless he marveled at its size and wealth and called it the greatest city in the world, by comparison with which even Venice, his hometown and then probably the pinnacle of European urbanism, was, he says, a poor village. The great Arab traveler Ibn Battuta, 50 years later in the fourteenth century, says that even then Hangzhou was three days' journey in length and subdivided into six towns, each larger than anything in the West. His rough contemporary, the traveling Italian friar John of Marignolli, called Hangzhou "the first, the biggest, the richest, the most populous, and altogether the most marvelous city that exists on the face of the earth."

These were all men who knew the world; even allowing for the usual hyperbole of travelers' tales, they were

Song landscape painting by Ma Yuan, late twelfth century. Chinese painters have always been fascinated by mountains and by nature that is unblemished by, or towers over, human activity. In nearly all such paintings, however, there are tiny human figures, as here near the bottom of the painting, emphasizing the harmony between people and nature, with humans appropriately in a minor role, accepting and drawing wisdom from the far greater and more majestic natural world. Landscape painting had its greatest flowering under the Song dynasty and its brief successor, the Yuan (Mongol) dynasty. *Bare Willows and Distant Mountains,* Southern Song Dynasty, end of 12th century, Chinese, active 1190–1235, Round fan mounted as album leaf; ink and light color on silk, 9 3/8 × 9 1/2 in. (23.8 × 24.2 cm), Special Chinese and Japanese Fund, 14.61. (Courtesy, Museum of Fine Arts, Boston. Reproduced with permission. Copyright © 2002 Museum of Fine Arts, Boston. All rights reserved.)

right about Hangzhou. Its rich merchant and scholar-official community and its increasingly literate population of shopkeepers, artisans, and the upwardly mobile supported a new bloom of painting, literature, drama, music, and opera, while for the unlettered, public storytellers in the ancient Chinese oral tradition abounded. Southern Song (and the Yuan or Mongol dynasty that followed it) is the great period of Chinese landscape painting, a celebration of the beauties of the misty mountains, streams and lakes, bamboo thickets, and green hills of the south.

Unfortunately, it was in the great Song period that the practice of foot binding first appears. Binding the feet of young girls, supposedly to make them more attractive to men, was limited then to a few of the upper classes; it did not spread widely until much later. Foot fetishism is hard for us to understand, but the idea was that a woman's foot, considered a sex object, should be tiny, a so-called "lily foot." Tight binding prevented the foot from growing normally. It broke the arch over time and caused great pain. This made walking difficult, in fact reducing it to a hobble, but fit in with the view of some that women should be kept at home anyhow, as a toy for men. Foot binding was one of the first targets of reform in modern China and has long been gone, although one can still occasionally see an old woman hobbling because her feet were once bound.

Certainly the outstanding female figure of the Tang was the Empress Wu, or Wu Zhao, who made herself an absolute ruler, flying in the face of Chinese tradition and, thus, alienating especially the Confucians, who became dominant at court and in the bureaucracy. Their prejudice against her has deeply colored Chinese accounts of this period, but she was clearly a very able person. As for other women in the Tang, Song, and Yuan periods, there is the remarkable figure of Li Qingzhao, China's leading woman poet, who never even mentions foot binding, although this dreadful practice began under the Song, when she lived. Her attractive descriptions of married life are probably more typical of the elite, of whom she was one; many elite women were fully literate, like Li, and so were many of the courtesans. The Song also saw a revival of Confucianism, which most Chinese women seem to have accepted happily enough, despite its overtones of male supremacy.

Innovation and Technological Development

Just as in goverment and the arts, the Southern Song period was also an exciting time of technological innovation and even of what seem like the first steps toward the emergence of modern science. The philosopher Zhu Xi (1130–1200), the founder of what is labeled Neo-Confucianism, was in many ways like Leonardo da Vinci, interested in and competent at a wide range of practical subjects as well as philosophy. This was in the pattern of the Confucian scholar-gentry, but Zhu Xi and some of his contemporaries carried what the sage called "the investigation of things" still further, into the area of what one is tempted to call scientific inquiry. Zhu Xi's journals record, for example, his observation that uplifted rock strata far above current sea level contained marine fossils. Like da Vinci in Renaissance Italy but three centuries earlier, he made the correct deduction and wrote the first statement of the geomorphological theory of uplift. Zhu Xi argued that through the Confucian discipline of self-cultivation, every man could be his own philosopher and sage, a doctrine similar to Plato's.

In agriculture, manufacturing, and transport there was rapid development, on earlier foundations, of a great variety of new tools and machines: for cultivation and threshing, for water lifting (pumps), for carding, spinning, and weaving textile fibers, and for windlasses, inclined planes, canal locks, and refinements in traction for water and land carriers. Water clocks were widespread, as were water-powered mills, to grind grain and to perform some manufacturing functions. It all looks reminiscent of eighteenth-century Europe: commercialization, urbanization, a widening market (including overseas), rising demand, and hence both the incentive and the capital to pursue mechanical invention and other measures to increase production.

Would these developments have led to a true industrial revolution in thirteenth-century China, with all its profound consequences? We will never know, because the Mongol onslaught cut them off, and later dynasties failed to replicate the details of the Song pattern. The great English historian of early modern Europe, R. H. Tawney, warns us against "giving the appearance of inevitableness by dragging into prominence the forces which have triumphed and thrusting into the background those which they have swallowed up."[1] It is tempting to think that if the Song had had just a little longer—or if Chinghis (Ghengis) Khan had died young (as he nearly did many times)—China might have continued to lead the world unbrokenly, and the rise of modern Europe might never have happened as it did. Nothing is "inevitable," and historians dislike the word. The seeds of the present and future are of course there in the past, but they seldom dominate it; each period has its own perspectives and does not see itself simply as a prelude to the future—nor should we. We know what has happened since, but we must avoid the temptation to see the past only in that light and try to understand it in its own terms.

The Mongol Conquest and the Yuan Dynasty

The Mongols overran Southern Song because they were formidable fighters, and because of some serious Song errors. Chinghis (Ghengis) Khan (1155–1227) first attacked the Jurchen territories in the north and then the other non-Chinese groups in the northwest. In 1232 the Song made an alliance with the Mongols to crush the remnants of the Jurchen and within two years reoccupied Kaifeng and Luoyang. A year later they were desperately defending northern China against an insatiable Mongol army, other wings of which had already conquered Korea (that tough nut),

Central Asia, the Near East, and eastern Europe. He who sups with the Devil needs a long spoon!

For 40 years the fighting raged in the north, where the heavily fortified Chinese cities were both defended and attacked with the help of explosive weapons. Gunpowder had been used much earlier in China for fireworks and for warfare too as an explosive and "fire powder." Fire arrows using naphtha as fuel and part propellant were known in early Han, and by the tenth century fire lances, spear-tipped bamboo tubes filled with a gunpowder propellant, were in use. In the struggle between the Chinese and the Mongols, cast-metal barrels using gunpowder to propel a tight-fitting projectile appeared, marking the first certain occurrence of cannon in warfare. The devastating new technology, especially helpful in sieges, quickly spread to Europe and was in use there by the early fourteenth century.

The Song were fatally weakened by divided counsels and inconsistent, often faulty, strategies, worsened by factionalism at court, and by a general undervaluing of the military by the traditional Confucian bureaucracy. Earlier, the Song army had driven the rampaging Jurchen north of the Yangzi under the gifted general Yue Fei, one of the martyrs of Chinese military history. Despite his successes in the field, he was adamantly opposed by a counterfaction of conservatives at the new court at Hangzhou and died in prison in 1142 after he was dismissed and jailed. Yue Fei is still celebrated as a hero betrayed, and he was clearly the outstanding general of the Song. The long, expensive, and fruitless campaigns against the Xixia drained Song resources but seem not to have taught them enough, although their long resistance to the Mongols does them some credit. Factionalism among conservative groups who resisted all innovation was in any case a major factor in the ultimate Song defeat.

By 1273 the Mongols had triumphed. They soon poured into the south, where Hangzhou surrendered in 1276. Resistance continued in the Guangzhou area until 1279, when the Song fleet was defeated in a great sea battle. During much of the long struggle it was touch and go, but the Mongols made few mistakes and the Song made many. One false move against an enemy like the Mongols was usually all it took, and in fact the Song put up a far more effective and far longer resistance to the Mongols than did any of their many other continental opponents except the Delhi sultanate of Ala-ud-din Khalji and his mameluke troops. (The Mongol seaborne expeditions to Japan and Java left them at a serious disadvantage; their fleet was twice scattered by major storms at critical points, and their invasion attempts were abandoned.)

The Mongols could never have conquered China without the help of Chinese technicians, including siege engineers, gun founders, artillery experts, and naval specialists. Chinghis died in 1227, but he had already planned the conquest of Song China, which was completed by his grandson Kubilai (r. 1260–1294), who fixed his capital at Beijing as early as 1264 and adopted the dynastic title of Yuan. Korea, northern Vietnam, and the previously non-Chinese southwest were also conquered; southern Vietnam, Siam, Burma, and Tibet were forced to accept tributary status. The Mongol conquest of China's southwest included the defeat of the Thai kingdom of Nan Zhao based at Dali in western Yunnan and forced a major wave of Thais out of their homeland southward into Siam to join earlier migrants (see Chapter 7).

China, for all its size, was only a small part of the vast Mongol Empire. It is astounding that such a vast area was conquered by a people who probably numbered only about 1 million in all, together with a few allies from other tribes of steppe nomads. The simple answer is that they were uniquely tough warriors, almost literally born in the saddle, used to extreme privation and exposure, and welded into a formidable fighting force by the magnetic leadership of Chinghis Khan, who consolidated the many warring Mongol and related tribes into a single weapon. Chinghis was born clutching a clot of blood

"The sad thing, if it catches us, is that no one will know that we invented the motorcar in 1227."

This cartoon, adapted from one in the *New Yorker* magazine for May 29, 1978, speaks for itself. (© The New Yorker Collection 1978 Warren Miller from cartoonbank.com. All rights reserved.)

in his tiny fist. The Mongols in his time were shamanists (animists and believers in magic), and his mother hurriedly called a soothsayer, who declared, "This child will rule the world."

The Mongols' great military advantage was mobility. Their brilliant use of cavalry tactics, controlled by the ingenious use of signal flags, plus their powerful but short compound reflex bow (like a Cupid's bow), which they could load and fire from a gallop, maximized their striking force. They could cover 100 miles a day in forced marches, unencumbered by a baggage train since they carried their spartan rations of parched grain and mare's milk in their saddlebags. When pressed, they knew how to open a vein in the necks of their wiry steppe ponies (usually spare mounts) and drink some blood, closing it again so horse and rider could continue. Through Kubilai's time, the Mongols rarely lost an engagement and even more rarely a campaign. Those who resisted were commonly butchered to a man, and their women and children raped, slaughtered, or enslaved.

The terror of the Mongol record demoralized their opponents, who described them as inhuman monsters. They were certainly expert practitioners of psychological warfare and even employed spies or agents to spread horrifying stories of their irresistible force and their ruthlessness toward any resisters. Chinghis, as a true steppe nomad, especially hated cities and city dwellers and made a series of horrible examples of them, often leaving no one alive. Chinghis is said to have remarked that "the greatest pleasure is to vanquish one's enemies . . . to rob them of their wealth, and to see those dear to them bathed in tears, to ride their horses and clasp to your bosom their wives and daughters."[2] The Mongols loved the violence and pride of conquest but had little understanding of or interest in administration, and their empire began to fall apart within a few years of its acquisition.

Their rule in China, the Yuan dynasty (1279–1350), lasted a little longer only because by that time they had become considerably Sinified and also realized that they could not possibly manage China without employing many thousands of Chinese. They also used many foreigners whom they thought they could better trust, including the Venetian Marco Polo, who served as a minor Mongol official in China from 1275 to 1292. He and his contemporaries got to China at this period because for the brief years of the Mongol empire a single control was imposed on most of Eurasia, and one could travel more or less safely across it. The Polos carried a special heavy silver pass from the Mongol khan (ruler), which guaranteed them food, lodging, and security along the way. Marco Polo's famous journal, like all medieval tales, includes some supernatural stories, and it was dismissed by many because it speaks in such extravagant terms about the size and splendor of Yuan China. Indeed he soon became known as "Il Millione," someone who told tall tales of millions of this and that. But when his confessor came to him on his deathbed and urged him to take back all those lies, Marco is said to have replied, "I have not told the half of what I saw."

Yuan China

The Mongols ran China largely through Chinese officials, plus a few Sinified Mongols and foreigners. The Chinese bureaucratic system was retained, leaving the military entirely in Mongol hands. For the short period of Mongol rule (only about 70 years, since they had lost control of most of the country by 1350 and were destroyed also by fighting between different Mongol clans and leaders), Chinese culture continued its growth on Song foundations, once the country had recovered from the immense devastation of the Mongol conquest. In particular, the glories of Song landscape painting were restored and extended by a new group of great Chinese artists, and there was a notable new flowering of drama and of vernacular literature. The Yuan period drama was rather like opera; it included orchestral music, singing, and dance. Scenery was replaced by a variety of conventional gestures and stylized movements, somewhat like Elizabethan theater in England, and like it too, most female characters were played by men. The novel was developed first by storytellers, who created tales of love and adventure. Their prompt books became the basis for later written novels.

The Chinese were discriminated against and forbidden to have weapons. Taxation was very heavy, and laborers were forced to work on big state projects without pay. In time, after Kubilai ascended the throne and until his death in 1294, Mongol rule from their new capital at Beijing became somewhat looser. But they rebuilt the Grand Canal and extended it to feed Beijing with forced labor, at a heavy cost in lives and revenue. They set up a new, efficient postal system and again issued paper money, both of which astonished Marco Polo, as did the burning of "black rocks" (coal) to heat houses and as a metallurgical fuel.

Kubilai was an able ruler of his new empire but concentrated on China and became almost entirely Chinese culturally. Marco Polo gives a flattering portrait of his sagacity, majesty, and benevolence, which was probably as accurate as his more general accounts of Yuan China. But Kubilai was followed on the throne by less and less able figures, and after about 1310 there was what amounted to civil war. Smouldering Chinese resentment and hatred of their conquerors flared into widespread

 ## Escapist Poetry

The Yuan dynasty was a hard time for most Chinese. Here is a series of short poems by Chinese of that period.

Chao Tianzi

Be unread, To get ahead
Be illiterate and benefit!
Nowadays, to gain men's praise just act inadequate.
Heaven won't discriminate, Between the wicked and the great,
Nor have we ever had Rules to tell the good from bad.
Men cheat the good, They scorn the poor.
The well-read trip On their scholarship.
So practice no caligraphy, Great Learning or epigraphy!
Intelligence and competence Now count for less than copper pence.

Yujiao Zhi

Among the hills, Beneath the forest shade,
A thatched hut, sheltered window, made For elegant solitude.
The pine's blue, Bamboo's deep green,
Combine to make a scene For artists' brush.
Nearby threads of smoke From hearths of huts unseen—
And I drift through my pleasant dream As blossoms fall through air—
Insipid as chewing wax, That bustling world out there,
To a heart that's proof against desire, What matters a head of whitened hair?

Qiao Ji

State honor rolls will lack my name, As will biographies for men of fame.
I have from time to time Found sagehood in a cup of wine;
Now and then, Some verse of mine
Has contained one brilliant line Enlightening as zen.
Drunken Sage of lake and stream, With a Doctorate in Sunset Skies,
I've laughed at all of those who strained At great official enterprise.

Ma Zhiyuan

Gold in piles, Jade in heaps—Then there comes a single day Old Death sweeps them all away!
What use are they? The cloudless hour The day benign, Salute with carven cup and amber wine;
With swaying waists, With flashing teeth and eyes—Ah, there's where pleasure truly lies.

Source: Translated by J. Crump.

revolts by the 1330s, and by 1350 Mongol control of the Yangzi valley was lost, while factions of their once-united front fought one another in the north. A peasant rebel leader welded together the Chinese forces, chased the remaining Mongols back into the steppe beyond the Great Wall, and in 1368 announced the founding of a new dynasty, the Ming, which was to restore Chinese pride and grandeur.

Chinese Culture and the Empire

By the late Tang period, Chinese culture had largely acquired the form that it was to retain until the present. With the Chinese occupation and Sinification of most of the south, begun under the Han dynasty, extended in the Tang and Song periods, and completed at least as conquest by the Yuan in the southwest, the state largely assumed its present form. Tibet was more permanently incorporated later, by the Qing or Manchu dynasty in the eighteenth century, which also added their Manchurian homeland to the empire. By Song times, the institutions of government and society had also evolved, especially with the firmer establishment of the scholar-bureaucracy and the gentry groups in the outlines and most of the details that persisted until the twentieth century. Civil administration was divided among six ministries; in addition, there was the censorate and a military administration, which was under ultimate civil control. At the top of the pyramid was the emperor, assisted by high officials. The empire was divided into provinces within the Great Wall, 18 of them by the seventeenth century, each under a governor and subdivided into prefectures and counties, the last under the control of imperial magistrates.

There was an immense flow of paper to and from the capital, transmitted along an empirewide network of paved roads and canals. Most decisions ultimately had to be made or approved by the emperor, which often created a bottleneck at the top. An equally important limitation was the small number of officials of all ranks, probably no more than 30,000, to govern an area the size of Europe and with a population of about 100 million by Song times, rising to 400 million by the nineteenth century. This thin layer of imperial administration was, however, indirectly augmented by unofficial but effective gentry leadership and management at all levels, including the vast rural areas, which in practice were beyond the power of the county magistrate to manage.

Still more important in the ordering of society was the family, that basic Asian institution that in practice not only controlled people's lives but settled most disputes and ensured harmony also by virtuous example. Government controls were thus far less necessary, and indeed a peasant proverb runs, "Work when the sun rises, rest when the sun sets. The emperor is far away." Dynasties rose and fell, but the fundamental order of Chinese society persisted.

Chinese history readily divides into dynastic periods and into what is called the dynastic cycle. Most dynasties lasted about three centuries, sometimes preceded by a brief whirlwind period of empire building such as the Qin or the Sui. The first century of a new dynasty would be marked by political, economic, and cultural vigor, expansion, efficiency, and confidence; the second would build on or consolidate what the first had achieved; and in the third vigor and efficiency would begin to wane, corruption would mount, banditry and rebellion would multiply, and the dynasty would ultimately fall. A new group coming to power from among the rebels would rarely attempt to change the system, only its management and supervision.

Culture was continuous, even during the political chaos following the fall of the Han. By Tang times most of the elements of contemporary Chinese culture were present. Especially with the rise in importance of the south, rice was now the dominant element in the diet. This was supplemented or replaced in the more arid parts of the north by wheaten noodles (perhaps brought back to Venice by Marco Polo in the thirteenth century as the origin of spaghetti) and steamed bread, or, for poorer people, by millet. Food was eaten with chopsticks, a model adopted early by Korea and Japan, while the rest of the world ate with its fingers. Given the size and density of population and the consequent pressure on land, poultry, eggs, meat, and fish were relatively scarce and the diet was largely rice or wheat with a variety of vegetables, including beans and bean products like curd (doufu—in the Japanese version, tofu) as a source of protein. Oxen or water buffalo were needed for ploughing but were usually eaten only when they died naturally. Pigs, chickens, ducks, and fish, however, could scavenge for food.

The Chinese cuisine is justly famous, including as it does such a wide variety of ingredients (the Chinese have few dietary inhibitions), flavors, and sauces. What foods went on the rice—vegetable or animal—was sliced small so that their flavors were maximized and distributed and also so that they could cook very quickly over a hot but brief fire. There was a progressive shortage of fuel as increasing population cut down the forests and people were reduced to twigs, branches, and dried grass for cooking. The universal utensil was the thin, cast-iron, saucer-shaped pot (wok in Cantonese), still in use, which heated quickly but held the heat and distributed it evenly—the techniques we now call "stir frying."

The Chinese landscape became more and more converted into an artificial one of irrigated and terraced rice paddies, fish and duck ponds, villages, and market towns where the peasants sold their surplus produce or exchanged it for salt, cloth, tools, or other necessities not produced in all villages. From Tang times, teahouses became the common centers for socializing, relaxation, and gossip and for negotiating business or marriage contracts. Fortune-tellers, scribes, booksellers, itinerant peddlers, actors, and storytellers enlivened the market towns and cities, and periodic markets with similar accompaniments were held on a smaller scale in most villages.

All this made it less necessary for people to travel far from their native places, and most never went beyond the nearest market town. Beyond it they would have found for the most part only more villages and towns like those they knew, except perhaps for the provincial capital, and of course the imperial capital. In the south most goods and people in the lowlands moved by waterways; in the dry north they were carried by pack animals, carts, and human porters, which also operated in the mountainous parts of the south. The wheelbarrow and the flexible bamboo carrying pole were Chinese inventions that greatly enhanced the ability to transport heavy weights, balanced as they were by each design and hence enabling porters to wheel or trot all day with loads far exceeding their unaided capacity. All these and many other aspects of Chinese culture have remained essentially unchanged until today, as has the deep Chinese sense of history and of the great tradition to which they are heir.

Questions

1. In what ways did the Sui recapitulate the Qin as they reasserted dynastic control over China?

2. How do the Du Fu and Li Bo poetry selections reflect Tang era society and culture? Is there a difference between these selections and that of the Song poet Su Shi and the Yuan-era selections that appear later in the chapter? How do these poems reflect either Confucian or Buddhist influence as well as the differing concerns of Chinese literati during each of these eras?

3. The Tang era is portrayed as China's "cosmopolitan age." How did life at the Tang capital of Chang'an support this characterization? What was the impact of Tang achievement on the future of China?

4. During the Tang dynasty, China's rulers repeatedly tried to address the proper relationship between Buddhism and Confucianism. What are some examples of the fortunes of Buddhism under the various Tang rulers? Why was Buddhism perceived as a threat to traditional Chinese political order? In what ways did Buddhism ultimately change Chinese culture, especially as it had an impact on what became known as Neo-Confucianism?

5. Some cite the Song dynasty as the prime example of misguided Chinese leadership. Others regard it as China's golden age. What evidence does either side use in support of their argument? How does this debate focus on inconsistencies—or even a bipolarity—in the administration of the Chinese dynastic system? Why do some argue that had Song rule continued, especially under the Southern Song, China could have had its own Industrial Revolution?

6. How did Mongol/Yuan rule of China have a lasting impact on Chinese civilization?

7. What were the changing Chinese relationships with the international trade routes under the Tang, Song, and Yuan dynasties? Why did this happen and with what lasting impact on Chinese civilization? How did these policies contribute to the development of overseas Chinese communities (the Chinese diaspora)? Could this networking, as well as the continuing interest in the Southern Seas under their successors the Ming, have led to greater regional cooperation and subsequent development, to the point that Asia could have remained dominant rather than giving way to the European West?

Notes

1. R. H. Tawney, *The Agrarian Problem in the Sixteenth Century* (London: Longman, Green, 1912), p. 177.
2. J. Chambers, *The Devil's Horsemen* (London: Weidenfield and Nicolson, 1979), p. 6.

Suggested Web Sites

Imperial China

http.//www.~chaos.umd.edu/history/imperial2.html
Textual site exploring the imperial era.

Tang Poems

http://www.etext.lib.virginia.edu/chinese/frame.htm
A site offering 300 Tang poems from China's golden age of literature.

Tang Dynasty

http://travelchinaguide.com/intro/history/tang.htm

http://www.emuseum.mnsu.edu/prehistory/china/
    classical_imperial_china/tang.html
Engaging sites presenting images and textual information on the rulers and society of the Tang dynasty (618–907).

Song Dynasty

http://www.wsu.edu:8000/~dee/CHEMIRE/SUNG.HTM

http://www.travelchinaguide.com/intro/history/song.htm
Fascinating sites documenting the agricultural and commercial revolution, and Confucian revival during the Song dynasty (960–1279).

Mongol Empire: Yuan Dynasty

http://www.wsu.edu/~dee/CHEMPIRE/YUAN.HTM

http://www-chaos.umd.edu/history/imperial3.html

http://emuseum.mnsu.edu/prehistory/china/
    later_imperial_china/yuan.html
Sites retelling China's struggle during the Yuan dynasty (1279–1350) when the Mongols ruled China.

Suggestions for Further Reading

China

Adshead, S., *Tang China*. London: Palgrave Macmillan, 2005

Allen, T. T. *Mongol Imperialism*. Berkeley: University of California Press, 1987.

Benn, C., *China's Golden Age*. Oxford University Press, 2004.

Carter, T. F., and Goodrich, L. C. *The Invention of Printing in China and Its Spread Westward*. New York: Ronald Press, 1955.

Chaffee, J. W. *The Thorny Gates of Learning: A Social History of Examinations in Sung China*. Albany: State University of New York Press, 1995.

Chiv-Dake, J. *To Rebuild the Empire*. Albany: State University of New York Press, 2001.

Dawson, R. S. *Imperial China*. London: Oxford University Press, 1972.

De Crespigny, R. *Under the Brilliant Emperor: Imperial Authority in T'ang China*. Canberra: Australian National University Press, 1985.

Dien, A. E., ed. *State and Society in Medieval China*. Stanford: Stanford University Press, 1990.

Ebrey, P. *The Inner Quarters: Women in the Sung*. Berkeley: University of California Press, 1993.

Franke, H. *China Under Mongol Rule*. Aldershot, England: Vanoram Press, 1994.

Franke, H. *The Cambridge History of China*, vol. 6, *Alien Regimes*. Cambridge, England: Cambridge University Press, 1995.

Gardener, D. K. *Zhu Xi's Reading of the Analects*. New York: Columbia University Press, 2003.

Gernet, J. *Daily Life in China on the Eve of the Mongol Invasion*, trans. H. M. Wright. London: Macmillan, 1962.

Hoang, A. *Genghis Khan*. New York: St. Martin's, 2001.

Hymes, R. *Statesmen and Gentlemen: Elites of the Southern Sung*. Cambridge, England: Cambridge University Press, 1986.

———. *Way and Byway*. Berkeley: University of California Press, 2002.

Keswick, M. *The Chinese Garden*. Cambridge: Harvard University Press, 2002.

Lee, T. H. ed. *The New and the Multiple: Sung Sense of the Past* New Haven: Yale University Press, 2003.

Lo, W. W. *An Introduction to the Civil Service of Sung China*. Honolulu: University of Hawaii Press, 1987.

McKnight, B. *Law and Order in Sung China*. Cambridge, England: Cambridge University Press, 1993.

McMullen, D. L. *State and Scholars in T'ang China*. Cambridge, England: Cambridge University Press, 1987.

Meskill, J. *An Introduction to Chinese Civilization*. Boston: Heath, 1973.

Morgan, D. *The Mongols*. Oxford, England: Blackwell, 1986.

Murck, A. *Poetry and Painting in Song China*. Cambridge: Harvard University Press, 2002.

Olschki, L. *Marco Polo's Asia*. Berkeley: University of California Press, 1960.

Philip, E. D. *The Mongols*. New York: Scribner, 1969.

Rossabi, M. *Khubilai Khan: His Life and Times*. Berkeley: University of California Press, 1988.

Schafer, E. *The Golden Peaches of Samarkand: A Study of T'ang Exotics*. Berkeley: University of California Press, 1963.

———. *Pacing the Void*. Trumbull, CT: Weatherhill, 2004.

Spuler, B. *History of the Mongols*. Berkeley: University of California Press, 1972.

Tillman, H., and West, S. *China Under Jurchen Rule*. Albany: State University of New York Press, 1996.

Twitchett, D. *Printing and Publishing in Medieval China*. New York: Bell, 1983.

Twitchett, D., and Franke, H. *The Cambridge History of China*, vol. 6. Cambridge: Cambridge University Press, 1995.

Waley, A. *The Poetry and Career of Li Po*. London: Allen and Unwin, 1960.

Watson, R. *Po Chu-i*. New York: Columbia University Press, 2000.

Weinstein, S. *Buddhism Under the T'ang*. Cambridge, England: Cambridge University Press, 1988.

Xiang, V. C. *Sui-Tang Chang'an*. Ann Arbor: University of Michigan Press, 2000.

Yu, C. F. *Kuan Yin*. New York: Columbia University Press, 2001.

Yu, F. F. *The Chinese Transformation of Avalokitesvara*. New York: Columbia University Press, 2000.

9

Early, Classical, and Medieval Japan and Korea

This chapter introduces Japan and the relatively late beginnings of civilization there, with literacy only by about the ninth century C.E. Early Japan owed much to the prior development of civilization in Korea, and the two were closely tied. Tribal clans in Japan called *uji* were consolidated under some central control by Prince Shotoku in the seventh century C.E., who began the long effort to import Chinese culture by sending Japanese missions there. By the eighth century the first real Japanese state, on the Yamato plain between modern Osaka and Kyoto, built a Chinese-style capital at Nara and toward the end of the century moved it to a new site at Kyoto, then called Heian. Heian court culture was elegant and refined but largely limited to the capital, where Lady Murasaki wrote *The Tale of Genji*. Buddhism spread widely, but aristocratic families such as the Fujiwara built up private estates and diluted the authority of Heian, which was finally overthrown in 1185 by a warrior clan of the Minamoto family. The Minamotos based their control at Kamakura, now a suburb of Tokyo, under a *shogun*, who was technically the emperor's military chief but from this time on the real ruler. This was part of the rise of the military and the dominance of *samurai* or warriors, in a Japan chronically torn by fighting. Kamakura was defeated by another warrior group, the Ashikaga, who returned the capital to Kyoto from 1338 to its collapse by about 1570. But the Ashikaga saw a flourishing of culture in art and literature.

Korean culture had developed even before the Han conquest. With the Han's fall in 220, C.E. Korea regained its freedom, although divided into three rival kingdoms until it became unified under the Silla in 669. The Koryo succeeded the Silla in 995, and the Mongols, in turn, destroyed Koryo power, but a new dynasty, the Yi, arose in 1392 and presided over a brilliant period before its control weakened with its growing age.

Japan

Composed of four main islands (and many smaller ones) off the southern tip of Korea at the nearest point, Japan had been protected by its insularity from turmoil on the mainland and, to a degree, also isolated from the process of development. The Straits of Tsushima between Korea and Japan are about 120 miles wide, and although Japan has been periodically involved in interaction with the mainland, the connection has never been as close as between Britain and Europe, separated by only some 21 miles across the Straits of Dover. Nor has the connection been as varied, since East Asia remained dominated by the culturally monolithic civilization of China as opposed to the multiplicity of cultural and ethnographic strands of Europe. Japan has had the advantage of a clearly separate identity and of cultural and linguistic homogeneity resulting from insularity and from its relatively small size, about that of an average Chinese province. The Japanese have been able to make their own choices at most periods about what they wanted to adopt from abroad; what came in was what the Japanese wanted to have.

Overall, Japan is smaller than France or California and larger than the British Isles, but it is mainly covered by mountains. Settlement thus has remained heavily concentrated on the narrow coastal plain, mainly between modern Tokyo and Osaka, in a series of disconnected basins over an area roughly equivalent to the coastal corridor between Boston and Washington in the

CHRONOLOGY

Japan

200 B.C.E.–200 C.E.	■ Japanese ethnicities reach Japan via Korea; Yayoi Tomb culture
c. 400–c. 650 C.E.	■ Uji clans develop; Yamato state develops
c. 552	■ Buddhism to Japan
c. 600-622	■ Prince Shotoku; Soga-dominated court missions to China
604	■ Seventeen Article Constitution
645	■ Taika Reforms and Fujiwara (Nakatomi)-dominated court at Naniwa (Osaka)
710–784	■ Nara Period
784–1185	■ Heian Court Period
	■ Lady Murasaki (c. 978–c. 1015)
784–1868	■ Kyoto (Heian) capital
1185–1333	■ Kamakura shogunate
1180–1600	■ Age of the samurai
1268 and 1274	■ Mongol invasions repulsed
1333–c. 1570	■ Ashikaga shogunate
1467–1568	■ Onin Wars

Korea

c. 200 B.C.E.	■ Chinese-style state near Pyongyang
109 B.C.E.	■ Han conquers northern Korea
c. 250–669 C.E.	■ Paekche, Silla, Koguryo regional kingdoms
935–1392	■ Koryo
1218–1350	■ Mongol conquest and occupation
1392–1895	■ Yi dynasty
1592–1598	■ Hideyoshi's invasion

United States. In practice, this makes Japan an even smaller country, since so much of it (in the mountains) is thinly populated. Hokkaido, the northernmost island, was effectively occupied by the Japanese very late, mainly after the World War I. Mountains retarded Japanese economic development and political unification, as in Korea, and political unification came very late, in 1600, after many centuries of disunity and chronic fighting among rival, regionally based groups. Agriculture

too has been hampered by the shortage of level land, and even now only some 17 percent of the total land area is cultivated, a situation similar to Korea's.

Japan's great agricultural advantage is its mild maritime climate, the gift of the surrounding sea, which keeps it humid, mild in winter, and largely free of the droughts that plague northern China. Coastal sea routes have also helped to link settled areas and carry trade, while the sea provides fish and other seafood that have always formed an important part of the diet, especially convenient since the bulk of the population lives close to the sea. Soils in Japan are of relatively low natural fertility but they have been improved by centuries of use and fertilization. This area of the world is a volcanic archipelago, and most soils are the product of weathered lava and ash. Sometimes, as in Java, this is the basis of high fertility, but in Japan the product of vulcanism is mainly acidic rather than basic, and most soils are also rather thin. Mountains are steep and come down to or close to the sea, so that nowhere are there extensive plains where alluvium can build up, as in China. Rivers are short and swift, carrying most of their silt loads into the sea rather than depositing them along their lower courses or deltas.

Largely for this reason, Japan has become the largest user of chemical fertilizers in the world, and it has been able to support a quadrupling of its population since the eighteenth century despite the disadvantages of its agricultural base and without disproportionately heavy food imports. In the modern period the Japanese have achieved the highest rice yields in the world through a combination of intense fertilization and the development of improved crop strains. All of this rested on Japan's remarkable success in industrialization and technological development, primarily since 1870. The modern image of Japan as industrially and technically advanced is accurate, but it represents a fundamental change that has come about mainly in the last century and, hence, is not an appropriate picture of Japan for most of its history.

The origins of the Japanese people are summarized in Chapter 1, so it is unnecessary to present that information here. As pointed out in that chapter, agriculture seems to have come relatively late to Japan, perhaps in the course of the migration of the people we may call Japanese from somewhere in northeastern Asia, via Korea. The Neolithic Yayoi culture that emerged about the third century B.C.E., cultivators of rice and users of first bronze and then iron, may well have been stimulated if not created by these immigrants from the mainland, bringing with them these aspects of new technology through contact with Chinese civilization in the course of their movement through Korea. We know that there was trade, perhaps indirect via Korea, between the Yayoi people and China, judging from Chinese coins and

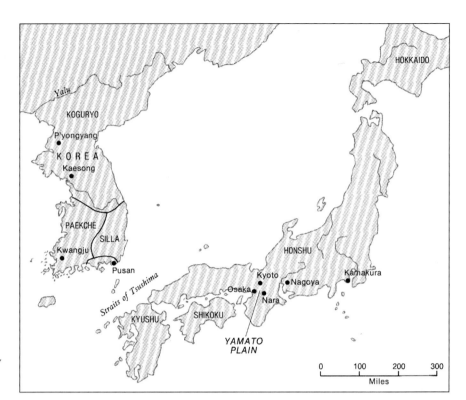

**Korea and Japan,
c. 500–1000**

It is easy to see why there were
such close connections between
the two countries. For a time
Japanese society was dominated by
Korean aristocrats. Later Japan
largely went its own way.

polished bronze mirrors that have been found at some
Yayoi sites.

Ties with Korea and the Tomb Builders

The connection with Korea was clearly a close
one. The later Yayoi built large above-ground tombs covered with earthen mounds very much like those built in
Korea slightly earlier. They also used both bronze and
iron weapons (the latter appearing in the third century
C.E.) that closely resemble those made in Korea, as do
late Yayoi jeweled ornaments. By this time one may certainly call the people Japanese, but, as mentioned in
Chapter 1, it may be equally accurate to think of them as
provincial Koreans or Korean cousins. The Yayoi people
made pottery on a potter's wheel rather than the coil-
made pottery of Jomon, the culture that preceded it and
that seems to have spread over the whole of Japan including Hokkaido, or at least Jomon sites have been
found there as well as in Okinawa in the Ryuku Islands.
The potter's wheel presumably entered from China via
Korea, along with bronze, iron, and rice. With the coming of rice agriculture, population increased substantially and there was probably some surplus, as evidenced by the large tombs built from the third century
C.E. and the many bronze bells, some of them quite large
and similar to Korean forms but already distinctively
Japanese. Yayoi culture from the third to the sixth centuries C.E. is labeled the tomb period; some of the
tombs, or the mounds erected over them, were built in
an interesting keyhole shape. Pottery figures found
arranged around these tombs, perhaps as guardians, include those of people, warriors, animals, and houses,
and are known as *haniwa*. They are certainly attractive,
but still seem rather primitive.

The tombs, presumably built for aristocrats, show
strong similarities to Korean forms, as do Yayoi
weapons, helmets, and armor. Remains of this tomb culture have been found in the Tokyo area and in the
southwestern island of Kyushu, although the original
and chief center was the area between Kyoto and
Osaka, soon to be known as Yamato. People now lived
in wood and thatch houses supported off the ground on
pilings or stilts rather than the pit dwellings of Jomon
times, and there were similar structures for storing
grain. The first Chinese written account of Japan, the
Account of the Three Kingdoms, compiled about 290 C.E.,
described Japan as a sort of appendage to Korea (hence

the title of the work, which clearly refers to Korea), talked about routes from Korea to Japan, and said that the Japanese were a law-abiding people (likely to attract Chinese approval) who depended on agriculture and fishing and observed strict social differences that were marked by tattooing. But at this period neither Korea nor Japan were in any sense unified as nations, nor was there any "conquest" of Japan by Koreans but rather a movement of culture from one to the other and probably some migration. Japan was said to be divided into a hundred "countries" of a few hundred households each—"clans" is probably a better word—some ruled by kings and some by queens. Thus, in Japan too, the original social pattern seems to have been matriarchal, merging at this period into a patriarchy of male dominance. The haniwa figures include some that seem to represent female shamans, who probably played an important role. The Chinese *Account of the Three Kingdoms* tells us that the Japanese were much involved with divination and ritual, and it speaks of an unmarried queen who, as a kind of high priestess, ruled over several "kingdoms," or clans and was considered important enough to have one of the largest tombs and mounds erected for her on her death.

Mythical Histories

The first Japanese written records are much later, and are not reliable or even consistent regarding this early period. These are the *Kojiki (Record of Ancient Matters)* of 712 C.E. and the *Nihon shoki,* or *Nihongi,* of 720 C.E. (*Nihon* is still the Japanese word for their country). Their purpose seems to have been to give the contemporary ruling family a long history comparable to China's (from whom the Japanese were then eagerly adopting its literate civilization), put together from various contradictory myths. These begin with creation myths about a divine brother and sister, Izanagi and Izanami, who between them created the Japanese islands—in one version as the drops from the goddess's spear—and also gave birth to the sun goddess, Amaterasu. According to the myth, Amaterasu's grandson, Ninigi, descended to the earth and brought with him three imperial regalia, still the symbols of imperial authority in Japan: a bronze mirror (symbol of the sun), an iron sword, and a necklace made of curved jewels somewhat in the shape of bear claws. All three closely resemble regalia found in Korean tombs of early Silla date, again suggesting the close tie between Korea and early Japan. The myths recount how Ninigi's grandson moved up from Kyushu, conquered the lowland area around Nara known as the Kinai region, and founded the Japanese state there on the Yamato Plain—but in 660 B.C.E., when it seems reasonably clear that the people whom we call Japanese had

not yet entered the country and were not to begin doing so for another three centuries or more!

Ninigi's grandson, the conqueror of Kinai, is called the first "emperor," and is given a Chinese-style title as Jimmu, the "Divine Warrior." We do know that by the fifth century C.E. the emerging state in the Kinai region, which also called itself Yamato, had extended its control into Kyushu and northward in Honshu, the main island, to the vicinity of modern Tokyo. In the same period, the Japanese won (or continued to maintain?) a coastal foothold in southeastern Korea, a colony that the *Kojiki* refers to as the work of the priestess-queen Himiko, whose name means "Sun Princess," although the Kojiki's dates for this are far too early. When the people we may call the Japanese entered the islands the dominant occupants, at least of Honshu, were an unrelated people called the Ainu, apparently a branch of Caucasians whose physical characteristics differed markedly from the Japanese (including larger amounts of facial and body hair, so much so that they were often referred to as the "hairy Ainu").

As Japanese occupation and conquest moved northward and eastward from Kyushu, their first center since it was closest to Korea, they did so at the expense of the Ainu, and perhaps of other groups as well about whom we know little. Japan had been settled by people, presumably from somewhere in Asia, since at least 100,000 B.C.E., and these people had first to be conquered, enslaved, absorbed, or driven eastward and northward. For a long time the boundary with the Ainu was along Lake Biwa, just north of Kyoto. Gradually the Japanese prevailed, although there was a good deal of intermarriage or interbreeding, evidenced in the modern population by people with more facial and body hair than those in China. Indeed, the Chinese in their superior attitude toward all other people called the Japanese "hairy sea dwarfs," since they were also shorter than the Chinese norm (possibly the result of a low-protein diet) and were more aggressive and effective seagoers as well as pirates. The earliest Chinese name for the Japanese was *wa,* which simply means "dwarf." The Ainu remained dominant in northern Honshu well into historical times, and now exist as a tiny and dwindling group on reservations in the northernmost island of Hokkaido.

By about 200 C.E., iron tools and weapons were being made in Japan rather than being imported and, thus, became far more widespread. This doubtless helped to increase agricultural productivity still more, and with it population totals, giving the Japanese a further advantage in their contest with the Ainu, who were in any case technologically less developed. Japanese pottery improved in the tomb period beyond the Yayoi stage, and in particular was more thoroughly fired and hence more practical for everyday use. Close interaction continued with Korea, and in a genealogical list of 815 C.E. over a third of the Japanese nobility claimed Korean descent, clearly a mark of superiority. Many Korean artisans, metallurgists, other technologists, and scribes (the Japanese were still preliterate) lived in Japan, as well as Korean nobles and perhaps even rulers. There were also invasions and raids in both directions, including some Japanese efforts to hold or expand their small coastal base in southeastern Korea, until by about 400 such violent interactions faded. By this time, Chinese accounts and various Japanese traditions begin to coincide factually and on at least rough dates, although true Japanese historical records in any detail do not begin for another 400 years, after the time of the mythical and mixed accounts given in the *Kojiki* and *Nihongi* in the early eighth century.

The Uji

The Japan we can begin to see somewhat more clearly by the fifth century, long after the fall of the Han, was still a tribal society, divided into a number of clans called *uji,* each of which was ruled by hereditary chiefs and worshipped the clan's ancestor. The lower orders were farmers, fishermen, potters, and some who seem to have been diviners, although we do not know how many by this time were women. Some uji expanded at the expense of others, but in any case they were the hundred "countries" referred to in the Chinese accounts. The Yamato state seems to have emerged as a consolidation of various uji groups in the area, headed by the Yamato uji, although it may be a bit inaccurate to refer to it as a "state," despite its continued conquest or absorption of other uji clans. It did try to organize the uji through the creation of ranks, the largest of which were *Omi* and *Muraji,* respectively lesser branches of the ruling family of Yamato, referred to as the "sun line," an unrelated but important uji. Headmen were appointed for each, eventually called government ministers. Already there had begun the depiction of the ruler, later the emperor, as descending from the sun goddess Amaterasu and, hence, himself divine.

Both uji and Yamato rulers combined religious and political functions, as did the Chinese emperor. The Chinese emperors, however, never claimed divinity but acted merely as the performers of state rituals while serving overwhelmingly a political function, a sort of temporal head of Confucianism that was itself a very this-worldly affair. The early Japanese rulers served also in effect as priests, and were very active in building or recognizing and ranking a great number of local shrines to Amaterasu. This had by now merged with early Japanese animism, the worship of nature and natural forces. Such worship is characteristic of all early societies everywhere, but in Japan it was retained, or

merged with the worship of the mythical Amaterasu as the sun goddess, rather than being displaced, as everywhere else, by a textually based religion of greater sophistication. The Japanese landscape is exceptionally beautiful, which may help to explain why the Japanese identified with it so personally, but Japan also has its dramatic and awesome reminders of the power of nature: active volcanoes, occasional tidal waves, frequent earthquakes, and the yearly visitation of typhoons in late summer and fall, which can do enormous damage. Mountains, waterfalls, large trees, and even rocks were thought to contain or to embody a divine spirit, or *kami.* Emperors were of course kami too, as were some notable uji rulers. At many natural beauty spots, plentiful in Japan, shrines were built to the local kami. Nature in Japan was seen as productive, as in China, although such a perception long antedated the influx of Chinese influence. To celebrate or worship this beneficent force, there were phallic cults, a common focus of the belief in the central importance of fertility, and also shrines to the god of rice.

These practices, centered around the worship of nature, were later called *Shinto,* "the way of the gods," primarily to distinguish them from Buddhism when Buddhism reached Japan. Shinto has remained a particularly Japanese religion, with its own priesthood and temples, even into contemporary times.

The Link with China

By the middle of the sixth century (officially in 552) Buddhism had reached Japan from Korea, although the Japanese were aware of it through their continued close contact with Korea and their foothold in the south there in the Kaya League. Kaya was absorbed by Silla in 562, and thereafter the Japanese had no territorial base in Korea, although the flow of Koreans into Japan continued until the early ninth century, not as conquerors (nor had the Japanese been in Kaya) but as closely related people who moved across the straits, probably in both directions, and as allies or associates rather than as invaders. Buddhism was at first opposed by many as an alien religion, but was championed by the Soga uji, which vanquished many of its rival uji in a war over the succession in 587 and then established Buddhism at the Yamato court, where it seems to have appealed to many as a powerful new magic. Buddhism served as a vehicle for Chinese influence, and Japanese began to adopt many aspects of Chinese civilization, in a move that was over the next two centuries to transform the country. The rise of the Sui dynasty in China and the subsequent reunification under the Tang offered a powerful model, just when the old uji system and its clan-based values and limited organizational force or control over even local areas was proving inadequate to the needs of an emerging state.

With the Soga dominant at the Yamato court this process was accelerated. It is noteworthy that the Soga chief installed his niece on the throne, a late assertion of the old matriarchal system, and appointed her nephew, Prince Shotoku, as regent. In 604 Shotoku issued a document later dubbed the "Seventeen Article Constitution," which promoted the supremacy of the ruler, the establishment of an officialdom on the Chinese pattern, based on ability, the central power of government, and a set of court ranks for officials. Shotoku's "constitution" also decreed reverence for Buddhism by all Japanese, but at the same time praised Confucian virtues, a combination that was to endure in Japan into modern times. The hereditary ranks of the uji were slowly replaced by the new official ranks as the chief marks of status. These new designations were divided into senior, junior, upper, and lower groups (in keeping with the Japanese passion for graded hierarchy), altogether making some 26 divisions.

Shotoku was the first Japanese ruler to send large-scale official embassies to China—in 607, 608, and again in 614—although some had been sent in earlier centuries. Later these became still larger and, by the next century, included five or six hundred men in four ships, which by that time, as a result of friction with Korea and civil war there, had to go by sea, some 500 miles of open ocean on which there were many founderings and shipwrecks. Despite the risks, the Japanese were determined to tap the riches of Chinese civilization at their source and to bring back to Japan everything they could learn or transplant. Students, scholars, and Buddhist monks rather than traders were the dominant members of these embassies, and their numbers included even painters and musicians. The missions generally lasted for one year, but many men stayed on for another year or more and returned to Japan with later returning embassies. Over time this constituted one of the greatest transfers of culture in world history, with the added distinction that it was all by official plan and management.

Taika, Nara, and Heian

After Prince Shotoku died (in or about 622), the surviving uji head provoked a revolt in 645 against the high-handed administration of the Soga and their aggressive promotion of Buddhism, which was resented by many who saw it as an alien rival to Shinto. The victorious rebels installed a new "emperor," Tenchi (then a youth), supported and advised by a rising aristocrat who took the new family name of Fujiwara (formerly Nakatomi).

The traditional Japanese style. Tatami (grass mats), sliding rice paper doors, tea, and a garden view—the recipe for tranquility. (Sumitano Industries)

Their leader, Fujiwara Kamatari, was to found a long line of nobility that would play a major role at the Japanese court for many subsequent centuries. The two allies, Tenchi and Fujiwara Kamatari, began a major movement of reform designed to sweep away what remained of earlier forms of government and to replace them on a wholesale basis with Chinese forms, assisted by returnees from earlier embassies to China. To aid this restructuring, which is called the Taika Reforms, five more embassies were sent to China between 653 and 669.

Taika, meaning "great change" in Japanese, was adopted as the name of the new period of Chinese style and was decreed as having begun with the success of the rebels against Soga in 645. One of the first great changes was the laying out of a new capital on the Chinese model at Naniwa (now within the modern city of Osaka), complete with government ministries and on a checkerboard pattern but without the walls around all Chinese cities. A census was carried out in 670 (although the population totals it reported are not clear), and on that basis a Chinese form of taxation was established. A Chinese-style law code was issued, and efforts were made to impose a uniform centralized rule. Not long thereafter, following the death of Tenchi, the capital was moved in 710 to Nara, farther from the sea (see the map on page 164), known at the time as Heijo, farther north on the Yamato Plain. The law code had been reissued with some changes in 702, and for the next 75 years while Nara remained the capital there were even greater efforts to replicate the Chinese pattern.

Nara was built as a direct copy of Chang'an, the Tang capital, and was the first real city in Japan. It was laid out on the same checkerboard pattern as Chang'an but was about a quarter of its size, though it included an imperial palace facing south and many large Buddhist temples. Here too there were no walls, as at Naniwa, and even at this reduced size Nara's plan was never filled in; about half of it was never built. Japan was still a small country, even tinier at that period before the spread of Japanese settlement and the apparatus of the state much beyond the Yamato area. Nara seems to have been dominated, both physically and politically, by its many Buddhist monasteries and temples, some of which still remain. In 784 a new emperor, Kammu (r. 781–806), decided to move the capital from Nara, first just a few miles northward, perhaps to escape the Buddhist domination of Nara, but in any case he promoted rival Buddhist sects. This was not followed through, and in 794 Kammu began the building of a new city called Heian (modern Kyoto) at the northern end of the plain just south of Lake Biwa. It was larger than Nara but on the same Chinese plan and also lacked walls. The original checkerboard layout is still apparent in modern Kyoto, which remained the capital of Japan and the seat of the emperor until 1868.

The emperor's role was modeled on that in China, a figure who combined all power over a centralized state. He had been given a Chinese-style title from the time of Prince Shotoku: *Tenno* ("heavenly ruler," like the "son of Heaven" in China). In fact the Japanese emperor, at least after Kammu's time (he seems to have been a forceful person), played mainly a ceremonial and symbolic role, as he still does. This was partly because, as a divinity, he could not be expected to involve himself in the rough and tumble of everyday politics, but primarily because real power came increasingly to be wielded by great aristocratic families at court. The emperors were also busy with their ritual function as the head figure of the Shinto cult, and perhaps in keeping with their exalted position far above the noise and dust of *realpolitik,* most of them came to retire early. One of the consequences of the Sinification of Japan, especially in its political forms, was the end of female power and rulers, which had clearly been important in the past but which now clashed with Confucian notions and Chinese precedents. There was one reigning empress, who favored Buddhism, like the Tang empress Wu a century or less earlier, and during her reign a Buddhist monk who had influence with her tried to take over the throne. This may have prejudiced people against her, but, in any case, on the death of the empress in 770 the monk was exiled and no female rulers appeared again in subsequent Japanese history.

In other respects the Japanese altered the Chinese model of government wherever they saw it as necessary to fit Japan's quite different society and its far smaller size. Once again the entire area occupied by the Japanese was divided into provinces and districts, although the provinces were far smaller than in China. As in the Tang, there was a Grand Council of State, and below it eight (rather than six) ministries or boards, including one to supervise the imperial household and another in charge of the Shinto cult and its many shrines. At the court in Heian there was an effort to replicate the behavior and rituals of the Tang court, including its court music and dance forms, long since gone in China but still preserved in unchanged form at the Japanese court even now. One of the fascinations of Japan lies in its transplantation and preservation of a great deal of Tang culture, including its architecture and even the famous "Japanese" tea ceremony, taken lock, stock, and barrel from Tang China at this period, complete with the rather bitter and sludgy green tea, the beautiful bowls, and the elaborate ritual around which it is built. In these and many other respects, anyone who wants to get a glimpse of what Tang China was like must go to Japan.

Officials at the local level in Heian times, and for a long time thereafter, were not, as in China, imperially appointed magistrates but local leaders, comparable to headmen. Nevertheless land was thought to belong to the central state, and peasants paid taxes based on the land they owned, primarily in the form of rice but also in textiles (where they could be produced), and in corvée labor, as in China. The hereditary aristocracy dominated the local areas and provided troops as needed: themselves with their weapons and, later, horses, and their retainers or followers. Otherwise it was a Chinese-style system, although it seems likely that much of it was on paper rather than followed in practice. It would not be reasonable to expect that such sweeping changes could be carried out overnight, or that the Chinese model could be made to fit Japan in every respect. Although the power of the central state clearly did increase, at the local level it seems likely that much of the earlier uji values, forms, and social organization persisted and were only slowly absorbed into the new state.

The regular flow of tax revenues strengthened the central government, and between the late eighth and early ninth century its control expanded to encompass all of Kyushu and pushed Japanese control eastward and northward against the Ainu, whose power was finally broken in northern Honshu, although the area north of modern Tokyo was effectively settled by Japanese only slowly. They had begun their occupation in northern Kyushu, almost semitropical, and northern Honshu was cold and snowy. Japanese culture had adjusted to a mild winter climate and hot summers: houses that could be easily opened to breezes, minimal heating, and loose-fitting clothing; it is possible that some elements in the population had come originally from tropical or subtrop-

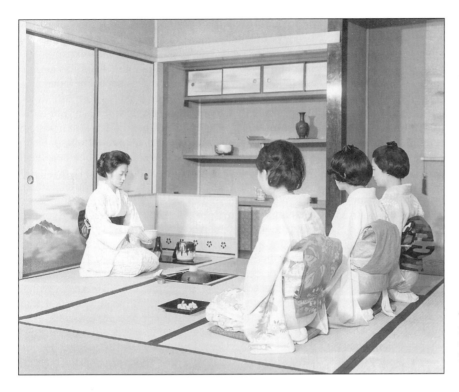

The tea ceremony is the ceremonial form of serving tea according to strict rules that regulate the manner in which tea is prepared and drunk. (Consulate General of Japan)

ical southern China, and southern Kyushu was truly subtropical.

In Nara and Heian times, despite the growth of the central state, Japan was still not only small but poor, especially by comparison with China, and economically retarded. The elegant court life of Heian, which is what we know most about because it was literate, is far from representative of the way most people lived. As in Korea, barter was still the principal basis of trade, such as it was, and government issue of copper coins in 708, in imitation of the Chinese model, made little impact. One of the chief achievements of the Tang and subsequent dynasties, the bureaucracy based on merit as measured by the imperial examinations, was briefly toyed with, but all official posts and all political power, even at the lower levels, remained with the hereditary aristocracy. As in Korea, and in further imitation of China, a government university was established, but rather than offering education as a means of social mobility it educated only the sons of the court nobility. Peasants do seem to have escaped from the serfdom of the uji system and became taxpayers to the central government, but this was not necessarily accompanied by any major improvement in their economic well-being. And it would again be logical to assume that the old uji aristocracy did not abdicate all their former power and wealth. Their aristocratic status continued to be recognized, as "outer" ranks, and they

probably retained much of their wealth as well as their superior position over the peasantry. Since they no longer were the chief powers, however, they did not begin to match in their local areas the splendors of Heian and its sophisticated culture.

Chinese and Buddhist Art

Buddhism continued to act as a vehicle for Chinese culture, including Buddhist art. This gave a new opportunity for the expression of the Japanese artistic genius. Craftsmen worked mainly in wood, where in China many had worked in stone, but because of the Japanese faithfulness in preservation (and because most images were housed in roofed temples) a great deal of the Buddhist art of this period still survives. Bronze and lacquer were other media used by the Japanese to perfection, as fine as anything in China or Korea and closely resembling these earlier forms, but already by Heian times distinctively Japanese. This is equally true of architecture, both in palaces and in temples, on Chinese lines but beautifully done. Here too one can see still preserved many buildings in the Tang style built in the seventh and eighth centuries, including the temple and monastery complex begun by Prince Shotoku at Horyuji not far from Nara and then rebuilt a few decades later, probably the oldest wooden buildings in the world and as close as one can get to Tang period architecture. Inside the buildings are Buddhist images and wall paintings from this period that are an aesthetic treat. Only a little later in age is the great Todaiji temple at Nara itself, built to ensure good fortune for the new imperial state and imperial and aristocratic families. Subsequent emperors were patrons of Buddhism and endowed many temples and monasteries and ordered the mass printing of Buddhist charms. Inside the Todaiji is an enormous bronze figure of the Buddha dedicated in 752, still one of the largest in the world. A nearby storehouse (*Shosoin*) contains imperial treasures from the eighth century: rugs, paintings, screens, weapons, and musical instruments, many of them imported from Tang China.

Buddhism and Literacy

By the ninth century Buddhism, promoted by the court, had spread throughout Japan and tombs were no longer built. Following Buddhist and Indian practice, Japanese began to burn their dead, although the ashes often were given a burial or an enshrinement in an urn. Diet gradually became vegetarian, in keeping with Buddhist ideas against the taking of life, although fish continued to be eaten and provided a vital source of protein. Since practically all of the Japanese population lived near the sea on the narrow coastal plain, fish were widely available, either fresh or dried and salted, as was dried seaweed, which continues to be an important element in Japanese food. The few who lived in the mountains often could not obtain, or afford, fish, and probably continued to eat some local game; birds were referred to as "mountain fish," but for the most part the mountain people too observed the Buddhist ban on meat. Buddhism offered, as Shinto did not, doctrines on the afterlife, text-based rituals and theology, the promise of salvation, and an emphasis (in this Mahayana version imported from China and Korea) on good works as the means of acquiring merit and thus increasing one's chances of higher status in the next life. Shinto cults were tolerated and came to be regarded as minor and local versions of Buddhist deities. The sun goddess, Amaterasu, was eventually identified as Vairocana, the universal Buddha, and she is the one represented in the large bronze figure in the Todaiji. Since Shinto had no theology and little in the way of doctrine, it offered no real contest for Buddhism, and most Japanese continued to follow both, a little like the persistence of Daoism in China in the face of both Confucianism and Buddhism. Indeed, Daoism and Shinto had much in common, especially in their admiration of nature and their feeling about it as the best guide for human existence.

Japanese monks returning from visits to China brought with them many of the Buddhist sects that had arisen there. The Shingon sect, brought to Japan in 806 by the monk Kobo Daishi, used magic formulas and incantations, which had a broad mass appeal in Japan as it had in China. Kobo founded a monastery on Mt. Koya, near Nara, most of which still exists and is a reminder of the grand scale of Buddhist building in that period. Many stories and myths were generated about Kobo and his wanderings and achievements, and he became a popular religious hero. In 805 the Tien Tai (Tendai in Japanese) sect was brought to Japan by another returning monk, Dengyo Daishi, who established the sect's headquarters in the mountains northeast of Kyoto at Enryakuji, near the top of Mt. Hiei, where one can still visit the extensive area and buildings, although none date from this period in their present form. Tendai was a highly eclectic faith, taking elements from many sects as well as echoes of Daoism and even Hinduism, which were reconciled by the simple and easy assertion that each belonged to different levels of truth, or as the Hindus later put it, "There are many ways to moksha (nirvana)." A later Enryakuji abbot was the monk Ennin, who went to China and whose travel diary is such a rich source on Tang China. Tendai became the dominant sect in Japan in part because Ennin combined its teachings with those of the more esoteric Shingon sect.

The coming of Buddhism accelerated the spread and use of Chinese characters, not only for Buddhist texts but for other purposes as well. Along with the characters, though most were given a Japanese sound, came many thousands of Chinese words, which remain in the language still. Some of them, such as the word for "three"—*san* in both languages—are quite straightforward; others are less directly equivalent but easily recognizable. To begin with, as in Korea, Japanese used Chinese characters for all their writing, and produced an extensive literature in Chinese, foreign and difficult language though it was. This of course put a premium on education, which was virtually equated with knowledge of Chinese, and further strengthened the position of the upper classes, the only people who had the time and education to master it. The adoption of characters, along with so much of the rest of Chinese culture, also stimulated the first Japanese writing of history, beginning with the *Kojiki* in 712. It was a mark of respectability and civilization to keep records, as the Chinese did, and to compile accounts of the past. The *Nihongi* in 720 was followed in the ninth century by five further histories on the Chinese model. The Japanese also began in the eighth century to produce equivalents of the Chinese local gazetteers called *fudoki,* accounts of local geography, history, economy, legends, politics, and notable features. As in China, calligraphy was regarded as the highest form of art and as the mark of an educated person. Poetry and prose were written both in characters and in Japanese phonetic syllables (kana). Another echo of China was the development of short poems, mainly about nature and its reflection in human affairs, or lack thereof, much like many of the Chinese originals. This short form in the Heian period was called *tanka,* and in a later version is perhaps the form of Japanese literature best known in the West, the *haiku.*

The Heian period is usually dated as running from 794 to 1185, and, even more than the briefer Nara period before it, saw a new flood of Chinese influence that remade most of at least the upper levels of society and many of the forms of government. But with the last century of the Tang, China was falling into chaos, and the glories of Chang'an were no longer so attractive a model. At the same time, the very different Japanese circumstances and traditional forms began to reassert themselves. Embassies to China were discontinued; although individual monks and traders continued to go in smaller numbers, China was no longer a magnet. Within Japan, the political system founded so squarely on Chinese lines began to encounter the same problems as the Chinese original had done as each dynasty grew old in office.

The Heian aristocracy included the descendants of uji rulers with their large landholdings, and the new or higher aristocracy often were given land grants in recognition of their rank or special services. Much land was also granted to Buddhist monasteries and the major Shinto shrines. These paid no taxes, and many of the aristocracy managed to avoid or at least to minimize them. With the slow rise in population (we have no accurate numbers for this period), much new land, which had to be cleared and then drained or irrigated, was opened for rice cultivation. Some of the land was reclaimed from the sea or from lakes, but it all cost money. The court encouraged this, reasonably enough and allowed those who brought new land into cultivation to keep it under their ownership, at first for one generation but soon thereafter on a permanent basis. The only groups who could afford the heavy expense of the original development were of course the small upper classes, and so there developed a situation very like that in the declining years of most Chinese dynasties: more and more land slipping off the tax rolls and becoming concentrated in the hands of the rich.

The Shoen System

The growing concentration of land in the hands of the rich fit the long-established patterns of Japanese society, dominated by a small hereditary aristocracy that held all

power as well as most wealth. Private estates (*shoen*) began to emerge, which more and more acquired some of the aspects of small local states. Powerful families at court, like the Fujiwara, patronized and protected the shoen ruling families, and in some cases became estate owners themselves. Estate owners began to assert their virtual independence from the central government, declaring themselves immune to government inspection or jurisdiction. The shoen were not large single blocks of land like the European manor but often discrete pieces of farmland that might be scattered around a wider area while being run as a unit, and almost always under the ownership of an aristocratic family, with court patronage and protection. They in turn hired local managers but left the job of farming to small peasant farmers and workers attached to them. One interesting aspect of this system, which seems in other respects retrograde, is its provision for income from the estate and inheritance of it to go to women as well as to men. Perhaps this was a modest revival of earlier Japanese forms, as indicated above, but it also reflected the decline of the Chinese-style state, its imposition of Chinese social forms, and thus the reversion in this period to something closer to the original Japanese patterns.

Over time the shoen came to occupy the great bulk of the agricultural land; although most were not very large, there were thousands of them and they dominated not only the landscape but the entire society and polity, as their owners became the chief local and even regional powers. Even in the remaining state-owned lands, perhaps about half of the total, aristocrats who served there as officials became in many ways similar to the shoen owners, and in time their positions also became hereditary. By the twelfth century, Japan was falling apart in terms of effective central rule. All of this reflected the declining power of the central state, although its power had never been very effective outside the immediate capital area. As time went on, more and more power was exercised primarily by the great aristocratic families and by the large Buddhist monasteries, both in the capital area and in the provinces. The emperor increasingly became a figurehead, as he was to be for nearly all the rest of Japanese history. In this longish period the Fujiwara family dominated court politics and, in 901, even exiled to Kyushu an emperor who had dared to appoint an official of whom they disapproved. In 1069 another emperor attempted to establish a land-records office with the aim of confiscating estates that had come into being in the preceding 20 years, but the Fujiwara blocked this obviously overdue effort at reform. Another emperor, Shirakawa, was somewhat more successful in challenging the Fujiwara after he formally retired in 1086 by working through lesser and non-Fujiwara aristocrats. But by his time the central government had been fatally weakened, in large part because it had lost most of its earlier revenues. The Fujiwara were split into factions and there was widespread general violence, even in the capital itself.

Heian Culture

Despite political disintegration, economic and cultural development in Japan continued, as it did in China under similar circumstances. The political scene in both countries was only one aspect of society, and in both a relatively superficial one. Even in the chaotic centuries after the fall of the Han, Chinese culture and economic and technological growth continued. In Japan, the shoen system was perhaps in fact more conducive to regional development than the earlier effort at central control had been, and clearly it was based in and tended to further the interests of local areas, including those far from the capital. It was in this period, between the ninth and twelfth centuries, that the plains area around what was to become modern Tokyo was effectively occupied and put to use for an increasingly intensive agricultural system. Honshu farther north, the area later known as Tohoku, was first filled in by Japanese settlement and made productive where it could be, producing a great deal of local wealth in the hands of aristocratic families, including branches of the Fujiwara. At the same time, the Chinese cultural model spread from the capital at Heian, where it had been cultivated like a hothouse plant, to the rest of Japan. Heian court culture became even more refined, centering on intellectual and aesthetic self-cultivation in the Chinese mode. Court nobles, who by now had no real political role but did have income from their estates, pursued an exaggerated form of the Chinese elite lifestyle, composing classical-style poems at wine parties and taking enormous pains with their refined manners *(li)* and their clothing, which was suited to each formal or ritual occasion.

Clothing offered an opportunity for the characteristically Japanese aesthetic sensitivity, with its combinations of colors and textures. By all odds the most famous of the literary works of this period is *The Tale of Genji,* written by a court lady, Murasaki Shikibu. In it there are many scenes in which clothing is described in loving detail, and in one such scene a high-born lady is sighted in her carriage. She casually but artfully shows a bit of her forearm on the sill of the carriage window; the successive layers of her clothing thus revealed are noted instantly by the gentlemen who are watching, who comment on the superb taste displayed by the combinations of texture and color in this tiny sample and conclude that this is indeed a lady worth knowing and worth conquering. Much of the *Genji,* and other literature of the time, deals with amorous affairs among the court aristocrats, in a setting where such dalliance was clearly acceptable socially and where marriage was not seen as confining.

Most of the surviving literary output from this period is in fact the work of female authors. In addition to Lady Murasaki, there were a number of other court ladies who wrote both poetry and prose. Probably the best known of them is Lady Sei Shonagon, whose *Pillow Book,* written about 1000 C.E., is a collection of comments on court life, by turns witty and caustic. Several other court women wrote novels, and most of them kept diaries, in which they included poems that reflect on the changing moods of the seasons and on the foibles of humanity. Court ladies were apparently less conventional than the men and freer to express themselves. The absence of harems and of extensive concubinage in Japan also left them a wider scope than in China. It is indeed remarkable that women writers dominated the literary output of Heian Japan, but this provides little clue to the more general status of women outside the exalted circles of court life. The aristocratic women who lived there generally were idle otherwise but were highly educated, unlike women in the rest of Japanese society, a kind of rarified and small inner group. Nevertheless, their output is impressive and their literary prominence is unmatched by any premodern society anywhere.

A CLOSER LOOK

Murasaki Shikibu (Lady Murasaki)

Lady Murasaki's birth date is not known precisely, though it was probably about 978 C.E., and we are also unsure of the date of her death, probably about 1015 C.E. We do not know her real name, since in Heian Japan it was considered improper to record the personal names of aristocratic women outside of the imperial family. It is known that she came from a junior branch of the great Fujiwara clan, and that her father was a provincial governor. The name Murasaki may derive from that of a major figure in her novel, *The Tale of Genji,* or from its meaning of "purple," a pun on the *Fuji* of Fujiwara, which means "wisteria." "Shikibu" refers only to an office held by her father.

Lady Murasaki's journal is our only source of information about her life. It is casual about dates, but records that she was a highly precocious child and became literate early:

> My father was anxious to make a good Chinese scholar of [my brother], and often came to hear him read his

lessons. . . . So quick was I at picking up the language that I was soon able to prompt my brother. . . . After this I was careful to conceal the fact that I could write a single Chinese character.[1]

But she acquired a wide knowledge of both Chinese and Japanese works and also became a talented calligrapher, painter, and musician, achievements suitable to an aristocratic girl. At about age 21 she was married to a much older man, a distant Fujiwara cousin, and bore a daughter. The next year her husband died, and in her grief she considered becoming a Buddhist nun but turned instead to reflection on the problem of human happiness, especially for women. Around that time, approximately the year 1001, she began work on her masterpiece, *The Tale of Genji,* which was probably nearly finished when, some six years later, she became a lady-in-waiting at the imperial court.

Like the *Genji,* her journal describes the refined and colorful life at court, as well as its less glamorous aspects of rivalries and intrigues. Both are the subject of her great novel, which combines a romantic as well as psychological approach with realistic detail and subtle insight into human behavior. It is still praised as the chief masterpiece of all Japanese literature. Her people are real despite the highly mannered world in which they lived, and through her journal we also have a picture of her as an extraordinarily alive, imaginative, and even compelling person. A collection of her poems has also survived and further mark her as an accomplished stylist.

Genji deals with the life of a prince and his seemingly endless affairs with various court ladies, including careful attention to the details of manners, dress, and court politics—not perhaps the most rewarding of subjects, but in the author's hands they become so. Although the hero is idealized, this is far more than a conventional romantic tale, including the subtle portrayal of Genji as he grows older. Toward the end of her own journal, Lady Murasaki gives us a candid glimpse of herself: People think, she wrote, that "I am very vain, reserved, unsociable . . . wrapped up in the study of ancient stories, living in a poetical world all my own. . . . But when they get to know me, they find that I am kind and gentle."[2] Perhaps she was all these things. But whatever her personal character, she was a gifted and inspired writer.

Art and Gardens

During the Heian, or Fujiwara, period, from 794 to 1185, the graphic arts continued to follow a more clearly Chinese path, including the prominence of calligraphy and the painting of scrolls and many-paneled screens (*shoji*).

But Japanese art had already begun to distinguish itself from its original Chinese model with its greater attention to simple line drawing of flat surfaces, often telling a story. Palace architecture became less massive than the earlier copies of Tang palaces had been, lighter and with more open pavilions, now usually set in artfully re-created "natural" surroundings of carefully designed ponds, gardens, and trees that greatly enhance the buildings' appeal and express the particular Japanese appreciation of nature. We know little of domestic architecture at this period, but the emphasis on openness apparent in Heian temple and palace architecture already suggests the later evolution of the traditional Japanese house, with its sliding panels that could be opened to the summer breezes and to reveal a garden and/or pond, sometimes very small but designed as a microcosm of the greater natural world. That is perhaps a good example of the Japanese adaptation of an originally Chinese style, as is the Japanese garden. The Japanese are justly famous as gardeners, but nearly all of the plants used were originally developed in China, including what became the imperial flower, chrysanthemum, the showy tree peonies that the Japanese, like the Chinese, loved to paint, camellias, flowering fruit trees, and many others. Even the Japanese art of *bonsai,* the artificial dwarfing of trees and shrubs grown in pots or tubs through careful and repeated pruning, was originally Chinese; the intent of course was to keep these microcosms of nature down to manageable size so that they could decorate living space or a tiny garden and still serve as reminders, miniaturized samples of a larger world, like the Japanese garden as a whole.

The garden style of Japan, where carefully placed trees and shrubs rather than tended flower beds dominate and are usually grouped around a pond, was originally derived from Tang China, like so much else of Japanese culture, but we can see its Chinese origins only in the Song, and even there, in any living form, probably in a much later version. Gardens of course are always changing as plants and trees are replaced over time, but garden styles change too, and what we can see of Chinese gardens now makes them look quite different from contemporary Japanese gardens, although one can certainly see the connection, including the often purposeful retention of a dead tree, partly to complete the picture of nature and partly to serve as a contrast to the living forms. The gardens originally laid out in the Song in the city of Suzhou west of Shanghai have probably been preserved closer to their original form than other Chinese gardens, although there have doubtless been changes there too. In the Suzhou gardens, grouped around a pond and with many open pavilions and galleries for viewing at different seasons, one is much closer to the modern Japanese garden style, and indeed it is possible

Traditional Japanese stone garden, Ryoanji Temple, Kyoto. (Michael Yamashita)

that much of the latter was originally based on the Song rather than the Tang model, about which we unfortunately know very little and of which there are no surviving examples except for a few plantings or preserved growth around temples. But it is in China, referred to as "the mother of gardens," that one must look for the sources of this, like so many aspects of Japanese culture, which we tend to think of now as particularly Japanese. The Japanese have indeed made it their own, like their graphic arts, ceramics, literary and political forms, the institution of the emperor, the writing of history, even the tea ceremony, all taken directly from China and woven into Japanese culture, although in each case (some more than others) these imports were refashioned to suit Japanese tastes and circumstances.

Kana and Monastic Armies

One of the early assertions or expressions of separate Japanese identity was the development of a system of phonetic symbols to transcribe the sounds of the Japanese spoken language, unrelated to Chinese. Although Chinese characters continued to be used, and are still used by educated Japanese, more and more texts came to be written in this syllabary, known as *kana*. At first the Japanese sounds were in effect spelled out by using the characters' phonetic sound, but during the ninth century, with the borrowing from Chinese civilization still at its height, the phonetic elements of Chinese characters were simplified into a new set of symbols. This was relatively easy for Japanese, even though it is not monosyllabic like Chinese, since each sound syllable is distinct and each is fully pronounced. Most poems came to be written in kana, since sound is such an important element of poetry, although in many other texts, and sometimes in poetry, kana was mixed with characters, as it still is, especially to write words borrowed from Chinese. Cumbersome as this sounds (and of course it meant learning both systems), it made writing much easier and more authentically Japanese. Lady Sei Shonagon's *Pillow Book* and Lady Murasaki's *Tale of Genji* were both written primarily in kana, although both authors were also fully literate in Chinese.

As Buddhism (also of course introduced from China by both Chinese and Japanese monks) spread more widely beyond court circles and merged with Shinto, Pure Land Buddhism, imported in the ninth century, became the most popular sect. Like the original message of the Buddha himself, it focused on the doctrine of rebirth and, hence, escape from what it asserted was a "degenerate age" into the Pure Land Paradise presided over by the Buddha Amida. It was, thus, a form of belief in magic, which had a wide appeal to the uneducated. At court the more elaborate rituals of Tendai and Shingon remained favored. In Japan at large, great Buddhist monasteries grew up to rival those in the capital area, and the various sects became armed rivals. The monasteries drew revenues from the lands they owned and became powers that also rivaled the declining central state and the rising shoen. Many monasteries developed armed bands, and then genuine armies, originally to protect their lands but later to engage in large-scale warfare with rival sects and their armies. By the end of the eleventh century these nominally Buddhist armies became the major military powers in Japan and even threatened the capital, a sad sequel to the teachings of the original Buddha and his doctrine of nonviolence.

Heian court culture was no doubt delightful, but its elegance and refinement were far removed from the real world of most of Japan. The Fujiwara had tried to hold the country together through links with other aristocratic families and through extensive patronage, but it is hardly surprising that in time this indirect means of control proved inadequate. The shoen and the Buddhist monasteries increasingly became the real powers, and some of the shoen were owned by families who also built up their own armies to rule lands they had originally guarded for court-based families or had acquired through patronage. Some of these armies, together with the new group of warriors called *samurai,* a hereditary aristocratic group who were both educated and trained in the arts of war—"gentlemen warriors," as they have been called—had developed out of the frontier wars as Japanese settlement spread north beyond the Yamato area. Monastic armies also sometimes intervened in factional conflicts and, thus, became power brokers. By the end of the Heian period, contending armies dominated politics. The new rising class of warriors were called *bushi,* from which is derived *bushido,* "the way of the warrior," which became a dominant code stressing bravery, indifference to pain and exhaustion, and determination to win against all odds.

Pressures on the Environment

As in China, decay at the center did not necessarily mean that the country as a whole suffered economically, although the rise in violence and disorder was certainly harmful or fatal to many. We have no real population figures for this period, but by 1000 C.E. the total population is estimated to have been about 5 million. This represents a considerable increase from the even rougher estimate of about 2 million or perhaps a bit more as of about 550 C.E., and indicates that cultivation was spreading over larger areas. As mentioned ear-

lier, the soils of Japan are mainly thin and poor and are easily eroded. Efforts at fertilization seem to have been limited largely to the use of green manure—leaves, grass, weeds, and branches cut in the surrounding woodlands. The use of human manure, or night soil, seems not to have begun until later (although this is unclear), but the intensiveness of farming, especially the spreading use of controlled irrigation, certainly contributed to steady increases in the total food supply, enough to feed the increase in population and perhaps a bit more. But Japan remained poor and underdeveloped in comparison with China, and perhaps even with Korea, and its population totals are unimpressive by such measures.

Nevertheless, as population grew, pressures on the environment increased. These were most evident, and potentially most serious, in the progressive cutting of the forests, primarily for building material but also to clear land for agriculture. Given the thin soils and steep slopes of Japan, good forest cover is essential to prevent or limit erosion and to prevent the siltation of irrigation systems on the limited area of lowlands. The influx of Chinese influences on a large scale, beginning in the eighth century, led to the building first of Naniwa, then of Nara, and finally of Heian (Kyoto), which created an enormous new demand for wood, increased still further as population rose and needed housing. At the same time, and even more in succeeding centuries, the many very large Buddhist temples and monastery complexes consumed cumulatively even larger amounts of wood. The use of iron tools after about 200 C.E. speeded the assault on the forests and also brought new demands for wood and charcoal for smelting. The beginnings of shipbuilding brought further uses for wood, but the major forest depredations were caused by the building of the two successive capitals at Nara and Heian and the Buddhist temples and monasteries. Since all building was done in wood, fires were frequent and often uncontrolled and, hence, necessitated frequent rebuilding.

By the time of the building of Nara, accessible timber in the southwestern part of the Yamato area was largely gone and trees had to be hauled from relatively far away. In the eighth century the rulers, now called emperors, thought it appropriate to build two capitals, one for the reigning emperor and another for the heir. The building of Heian, on a much larger scale than Nara, could draw on still largely untapped forests nearby to the northwest and around Lake Biwa. Hundreds of thousands of workers were employed in the construction and in the felling and hauling of timbers. But for all the scale of building at Heian, Buddhist and Shinto construction was probably larger still, including the buildings at Horyuji, the Shinto shrine at Ise, and hundreds of others. The monumental scale of much of this construction ate deeply into remaining accessible forest stands, beginning with the building of the great Buddhist temple at Nara, the Todaiji. Like the palaces, most temples required frequent rebuilding as well as repair. By the tenth century, all of the accessible forests of and around the Yamato area had been cut, and inroads begun into mountainous areas despite the high costs of getting the trees to where they were needed. It is possible that the slow deterioration of Heian was at least partly the result of the difficulty in obtaining wood for construction.

One consequence of this difficulty was the development of a less extravagant form of building, including domestic architecture, which emphasized open walls that could be closed by sliding screens covered with translucent rice paper. Some roofs began to be covered with tile instead of wood, far more durable and also fire-resistant, although many roofs began to be made of bark. Floors were covered by rush or grass mats, *tatami,* which could be laid over rough boards and which produced an attractive surface as well as welcome insulation and a degree of springiness, important since Japanese have always slept on the floor. This is of course the nature of the traditional Japanese house as one can still see it and as it is represented in art from the past. Houses also became smaller, and the building of large palaces largely came to an end in the course of the ninth century.

By the ninth century timber for shipbuilding had become so scarce that an imperial order of 882 tried to prevent tree felling in the area where the most suitable ship timbers grew (except for shipbuilding purposes). As another indication of the growing scarcity of wood, the kind most favored for the thousands of large statues that adorned Buddhist temples had apparently become so scarce in the course of the eighth century that sculptors began to work instead in other less suitable woods. By the eleventh century, with the unavailability of large logs, sculptors began to build their images out of separate pieces of wood joined together.

Successive emperors tried to control cutting and to keep peasants out of imperial woodland, as the shoen owners and the great monasteries tried to keep any but their own loggers or collectors out of their lands. It seems to have been realized that good forest cover was essential for the stability of rivers and streams. An imperial order of 821 declared as follows:

> The fundamental principle for securing water is found in the combination of rivers and trees. The vegetation on mountains should always be lush.[3]

As the chief center of political control moved northeastward, to Kamakura near Tokyo, some of the originally forested areas in and around the Yamato Plain did recover somewhat through natural regrowth, and Japan was saved the disastrous consequences of the deforestation that continued in China without a break. Japan's mild, moist climate, where trees grow rapidly, was an important asset, ensuring that forests would recover when human pressures lessened. But the seemingly unbroken mantle of forest that covers Japan's mountains today is the result primarily of determined conservation and reforestation programs undertaken since the late 1940s.

The Kamakura Period

Fujiwara rule ended in 1185, when one of the warrior lineages, the Minamoto clan, set up a rival capital in its then frontier base at Kamakura (now a southern suburb of Tokyo). The refined court culture of Heian was now supplemented by a less cultivated but far more politically effective system based on military power and the security offered by the emerging group of samurai. The samurai were not simply warriors but were educated hereditary aristocrats who eventually served as administrators as much as fighting men. Heian culture continued through them and through other educated aristocrats and in time influenced even Kamakura. But the rise of new noble families and their samurai armies led to the emergence of Japanese feudalism, a close parallel to that of medieval Europe but very different from the imperial civil bureaucracy and meritocracy of China.

The emperor, still residing in Kyoto, became increasingly a figurehead, and real power rested with whoever could grasp and hold the office of *shogun,* the emperor's chief military commander and agent—first the Fujiwara and then the Minamoto and other military clans. The shogun in turn presided over a feudal hierarchy of lords bound to him in loyalty assured by oaths, periodic homage, certain payments, and promises of military support. In return, the shogun confirmed the nobles' hereditary rights to their lands. As in medieval Europe, this was a symptom of limited central state power, an arrangement of mutual convenience; but it was also inherently unstable as ambitious or upstart vassals sought to improve their positions or rebel against the shogun's authority. Military power was now what counted, but it was seldom unified under any single control for long. Each noble vassal maintained his own group of samurai and his own army; the martial virtues of bravery, endurance, and loyalty were stressed, but loyalty could not always be ensured, either to local lords or to shoguns. The patterns that emerged in the Kamakura shogunate (1185–1333) were in many respects to dominate Japan until the nineteenth century.

In 1268 Kubilai Khan demanded the submission of the Japanese, and when his order was refused the Mongols forced the recently conquered Koreans to build and man a fleet for the invasion of Japan, where they arrived

Samurai armor from the Kamakura Period. (The Metropolitan Museum of Art, Fletcher Fund, 1928. [28.60.1] Photograph, all rights reserved, The Metropolitan Museum of Art.)

in 1274. Soon after the first landings a great storm wrecked many of their ships and forced their withdrawal. The Japanese executed subsequent Mongol envoys, and in 1281 a far larger expedition of both subject Koreans and Chinese arrived, only to be swept away by an even greater storm, one of the late summer typhoons common along the coasts of East Asia. The Japanese can perhaps be forgiven for attributing this double deliver-

ance to a "divine wind," the *kamikaze*. However, the costs of meeting the terrible Mongol threat and of the preparation that went on against a feared and expected third expedition drained Kamakura resources and diverted large numbers of people from productive occupations. With the weakening of Kamakura power, political divisions and open revolts multiplied. In 1333 an unusually active emperor, Go-Daigo, whom the dominant faction at Kamakura had tried to depose, gathered support and attracted dissidents from the crumbling Kamakura structure. One of his commanders burned Kamakura and ended its power. But another of his supporters, from the rival Ashikaga clan, turned against him, put a different member of the imperial line on the throne, and in 1338 had himself declared shogun.

The constant fighting in the age of the warrior after the collapse of Heian left less and less place for women, despite Japan's origin as a matriarchal society. Even in Heian times women were prominent at court, but that was only the tiniest fraction of the population. As the centuries of fighting wore on, women were more and more reduced to a subservient role of caring for and supporting their husbands, whom they might only rarely see while they returned for brief visits from the wars. This was essentially the foundation of the submissive place of most modern Japanese women.

Despite the clear matriarchal origins of Japanese culture and the divine figure of the sun goddess Ameratsu, or the myth of Izanagi and Izanami, or the remarkable prominence of women writers during the Heian period, the rise of the warrior culture that followed the fall of Heian brought in a strongly male-dominant culture, with women reduced to an essentially subservient role, as wives and mothers. This brought with it also a heavy preference for sons, to carry on the family line, as in China, and the unfortunate spread of female infanticide with it. Literature and art came to be monopolized by men, and even women tended to extol the virtues of *bushido*, the way of the warrior. Trends in Korea were closely similar, and for similar reasons. In both countries women became largely an oppressed group, with the possible exception of the *geisha*, high-class prostitutes.

Ashikaga Japan

The Ashikaga shoguns, who established themselves in Kyoto, were never able to build effective central control. A rival faction supporting another member of the imperial family remained in power in southwestern Honshu and could not be dislodged; Kyushu continued under the control of still another group or groups. Civil war became endemic, and as one consequence feudal lords beyond the limited central control supported

The Golden Pavilion in Kyoto: Japanese adaptation of a Chinese original, with careful attention to the blending of architecture with landscaping. This beautiful building dates from 1397, in the Ashikaga period, but has had to be restored several times after fires. (Cameramann International, Ltd.)

what developed into highly profitable piracy along the coasts of China, which got the Ashikaga in chronic trouble with the Ming dynasty. They tried to suppress piracy, but their power to do so was totally inadequate. For a time the Ming felt obliged to abandon large stretches of their own coast and pull settlements back to more easily protected sites up rivers and estuaries. Until the end of the fifteenth century political chaos in Japan was chronic, despite the country's small size and the even smaller dimensions of its principal settled areas. By 1467 effective Askikaga rule was ended, and much of Kyoto had been destroyed, although the emasculated shogunate continued in name. Rival Buddhist sects and their monasteries continued to fight bloody wars against each other with armed monks as troops. Peasant revolts and bitter conflicts among petty feudal lords continued to mar the landscape.

Yet despite the growing political disorder, especially after about 1450, the last century of the Ashikaga saw a remarkable flowering of culture. In part this was the result of a conscious fusion of aristocratic Heian traditions with those of the newer samurai culture. Millions also found solace in popular new Buddhist sects, including Zen and the popular evangelical and egalitarian Shin and Nichiren sects, all originally from China but adapted to varying Japanese tastes and styles. Zen (Chinese *Chan*) was a contemplative and mystical approach that concentrated on eternal truth and self-cultivation rather than on the pointless turmoil of political life. Based on disciplined meditation and oneness with universal creation, Zen appealed nevertheless to the aristocratic warrior class of samurai; it also stressed unity with nature, a traditional Japanese interest.

Less detached but clearly related to a turning away from the dusty arenas of worldly strife, or as an alternative to them, were the further blossoming of temple and palace architecture. Buildings were consciously and ingeniously integrated with their peaceful natural settings; landscape gardening and nature painting, much of it in the Southern Song mode, also flourished. The literature of the period commented on the shifting fortunes of politics and the foibles of those grasping for power or gloried in the simple beauty of nature and the joys of untroubled rural life. The shogunate patronized Zen, as it supported art and literature, thus continuing the Heian tradition.

Even more specifically Japanese was the Ashikaga evolution of the tea ceremony as a graceful, soothing, contemplative, and highly aesthetic ritual. Although its origins too were in Tang China, it became and remains a distinctively Japanese assertion of cultural identity and personal serenity. Delicate teahouses set in a naturally landscaped garden in unobtrusive elegance provided brief havens of tranquility and aesthetic enjoyment for samurai and other members of the elite, who characteristically took additional pleasure from the simple, exquisite beauty of the teacups. It was all a thoroughly Japanese counterpart to the bloody and often ruthless life of the times.

Finally, the Ashikaga era saw the birth and flowering of another distinctively Japanese form, the *Noh* drama, a subtle Zen-inspired blending of dance, spoken lines, and theater where costumes, makeup, and refined gestures can communicate rich meaning, emotion, and passion. Every step and every movement are precisely measured in a state of controlled tension, a slow-moving con-

Troubled Times in Japan

Political conflict in Ashikaga Japan had its echoes in literature but did not prevent contin-
ued cultural growth. This period saw the development of the haiku poetic form, evolved
from an originally Chinese model but becoming in time a distinctively Japanese mode, still
much used. Here are some samples, roughly a century apart but both reflecting troubled
times.

Nijo Toshimoto (1320–1398)

In the hills the cries of deer,
In the fields the chirping insects.
In everything
What sadness is apparent
This autumn evening.

Shinkei (1407–1475)

The clouds still possess
Some semblance of order:
They bring the world rain.

Sogi, a pupil of Shinkei (1421–1502)

To live in the world
Is sad enough without this rain
Pounding on my shelter.

Source: J. W. Hall, ed., *Japan in the Muromachi Age* (Berkeley: University of California Press, 1977),
pp. 254, 257.

---

centrated experience of understatement, but with a heavy freight of feeling and disciplined expression.

Despite the turmoil of the age, artisan production, including, appropriately enough, the making of fine swords, developed still further, and with the arrival of the Portuguese early in the sixteenth century trade was stimulated and Portuguese armed ships largely eliminated Japanese pirates.

The Ashikaga shogunate dissolved even more completely into civil war in the 1570s, and Japan was torn by rival clans and their armies until the end of the century.

Maritime Contacts Between Medieval Japan and the Continent

During the Ashikaga shogunate, Japan gained an international reputation for its piracy. Japanese and Korean buccaneers were based in Japan's southern (western) islands. From 1350 to 1400, they not only preyed on merchant vessels in East Asian waters but also were a menace to Chinese and Korean coastal communities. Indeed, in Korea they became so bold that they sacked the capital area and were a significant factor in the fall of the Koryo dynasty in 1392.

When the Ming dynasty came to power, the Ashikaga shogun Yoshimitsu reestablished a tributary relationship with China, which Japan had not acknowledged for almost six centuries (Japan's last official embassy was in 838). This opened official trade between China and Japan, in part because the Ashikaga shoguns hoped to curtail the rampant piracy that was causing serious diplomatic problems, but also because they needed the revenues that the trade would bring, since they could not depend on sufficient collections of land taxes to fund their government's expenses.

In 1392, the new Yi dynasty rulers in Korea were also intent upon ending the pirate menace, and they saw the opening of official trade with Japan as one way to do it. After 1443, this trade between Japan and Korea was managed by one samurai house, the So, who controlled the island of Tsushima (and its previous pirate lair), which lies in the strait between Japan and Korea. From around 1400, piracy in Japanese waters was checked for about sixty years, until the Onin Wars destroyed centralized order. By the early fifteenth century, Japan's trade with China was monopolized by the Ouchi, a family of samurai in partnership with previous pirates who were based at the southern tip of Honshu and controlled the Straits of Shimonoseki. When the Ouchi were attacked and overthrown in 1551, all semblance of order was lost, and piracy once again became a serious problem. In the Inland Sea, competing samurai lords (*daimyo*) sponsored rival pirate bands. In 1592, after order was restored, these pirates participated in the Japanese assault on China, which the Japanese claimed to be their retribution for the Mongol's invasion attempts of 1274 and 1281. By this time Japan's own maritime trade had developed and Japan-based sailors were sailing directly to Southeast Asia. Thereafter piracy tended to concentrate further to the south, around the Philippines and in the South China Sea (see Chapter 10).

Korea

Korean culture, though adopting much from China, added its own innovations and retained a strong sense of separate identity, together with a fierce determination to preserve its political independence. The Korean Peninsula, set off from the mainland, is further marked by mountains along its northwestern base adjacent to Manchuria and by the gorge of the Yalu River, which marks the boundary. The Korean people probably came originally from eastern Siberia and northern Manchuria, as their spoken language, unrelated to Chinese, suggests. They brought with them or evolved their own culture, already well formed before they were exposed to heavy Chinese influence at the time of the Han occupation in the late second century B.C.E. Rice, wheat, metals, written characters, paper, printing, lacquer, porcelain, and other innovations spread to Korea after they appeared in China.

As in Vietnam, literate Chinese-style culture in Korea was an upper-level overlay on an already developed cultural base that remained distinctive. A Chinese-style state arose in the north around Pyongyang in the century before Han Wu Di's conquest. After the fall of the Han in 220 C.E. and the withdrawal of the Chinese military colonies, Korea regained its independence and was thenceforward ruled by Koreans (except for the brief Mongol interlude) until the Japanese takeover in 1910, although Chinese influences continued and indeed were freely sought.

Paekche, Silla, and Koguryo

Three Korean kingdoms arose after 220 with the Han garrisons gone: Paekche in the southwest, Silla in the southeast, and Koguryo in the north, the largest and the closest to China and the Han legacy in Korea. Confucianism, Chinese law, and Chinese forms of government, literature, and art spread rapidly, followed by Buddhism as it grew in China. But Korea's long tradition of a hereditary aristocracy within a hierarchically ordered society of privilege prevented the adoption of China's more open official system of meritocracy based on examinations. Like the Japanese, the Koreans also departed from the Chinese pattern in providing an important place for a military aristocracy.

In 669, with help from the Tang, Silla succeeded in conquering Koguryo, after having earlier demolished Paekche. With its now-united strength and new sense of Korean nationalism, Silla repelled the Tang efforts at reconquest, a remarkable feat given the power and proximity of Tang China. As a formal vassal of the Tang, Silla presided over a golden age of creativity and continued adaptation of Chinese-style elite culture. Tang cultural splendor was an appealing model, as were other Chinese ideas, institutions, and technology. Korean ceramics had a magnificent development, fully the equal of anything in China, particularly in a consistent Korean tradition of excellence in pottery and fine porcelain. This included the beautiful celadon-ware with its subtle milky-green, jade-colored glaze, a secret formula admired and envied by the Chinese but extinguished by the Mongol conquest of the thirteenth century and never recovered. Silla Korea went beyond Chinese characters and began a system of phonetic transcription, derived from the sound of characters but designed to write spoken Korean, which by the fifteenth century was further refined into the *han'gul* syllabary.

Silla control weakened by the tenth century and was taken over by a usurper in 935, who named his new united state Koryo, an abbreviation of Koguryo and the origin of the name Korea. The Koryo capital at Kaesong, just north of Seoul, was built faithfully on the planned imperial model of Tang Chang'an and incorporated most of the Chinese system of government. Interest in Buddhism and its texts as well as the example of the Song stimulated a virtual explosion of woodblock printing in the eleventh century in which Koreans continued the technological development of the art, and magnificent celadon pieces were again produced. Koryo rule dissolved into civil war on the eve of the Mongol invasion, an unfortunate circumstance for Korean resistance to the armies of Chinghis Khan. The Mongols easily overran the peninsula in 1218 against only scattered opposition. The Mongols exacted heavy tribute and imposed an iron rule, including forcing Koreans to aid them in

A masterpiece of Korean art in bronze from the Silla period, sixth or seventh century C.E. This seated figure is Maitreya, Buddha of the future. (National Museum of Korea, Seoul)

their later expeditions against Japan. Fortunately, their occupation lasted only until the 1350s when the Mongol Empire collapsed, and in 1392 a new dynasty arose, the Yi, which was to preside over a united Korea until 1910.

Yi Korea

Yi dynasty Korea continued the adaptation of Chinese civilization to a greater extent than any of its predecessors, including now the imperial examination system and Confucian bureaucracy. But though Confucian ideology prospered, in practice officeholding was still dominated by hereditary aristocrats. The Yi capital at Seoul and the eight provinces into which the country was divided all followed the Chinese model, and Yi rulers continued to accept the formal status of a Chinese tributary state, a relationship that both parties spoke of amicably as that between "younger brother and elder brother." Buddhism declined almost completely, while Confucianism and Chinese-style painting and calligraphy flourished. A group called the *yangban,* originally landowners, acquired most of the functions and status of the Chinese gentry as an educated elite but remained a hereditary class, providing both civil and military officials, unlike the Chinese model.

Korean economic development was retarded by the mountainous landscape, which is divided into separate, small basins as in Japan, and by a long, harsh winter, especially in the north. Only about one-seventh of the total land area could be cultivated, and easy exchange and the resulting concentrated urban growth and trade were also disadvantaged. But although most Koreans remained materially poorer than most Chinese, elite culture, technology, and the arts prospered in distinctively Korean styles, including the still-superb ceramics. Korean dress, house types, diet, lifestyles, marriage and inheritance customs, and the volatile, earthy, robust, spontaneous Korean temperament remained their own as well. Food was flavored by the peppery pickled cabbage called *kimch'i,* as it still is. The indigenous cultural fabric of Korea was basic and showed through the Chinese overlay. There was no risk that Korea would simply be absorbed into Chinese culture, and Koreans remained proud of their independence and of their own sophisticated cultural tradition.

The first century or so of Yi rule was a brilliant period in Korean and East Asian history. In the fifteenth century there was a new explosion of printing, now vigorously supported by a Confucian state that put a high value on texts and learning. To aid this effort Koreans further perfected the art of metal movable type, which was used among other things to reproduce the libraries burned by the Mongols and the wooden plates from which those books had been made. Eight other ambitious printing projects were carried out between 1403 and 1484. This was the first extensive use of movable type anywhere in the world. The technique originated in eleventh-century Song China and was further developed in Korea a century or so later; this innovation belatedly stimulated the European beginnings of movable-type

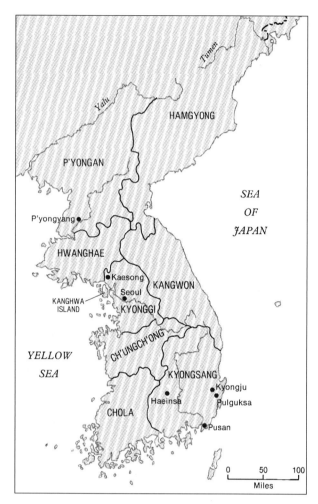

Korea During the Yi Dynasty

There has been relatively minor change in the provincial divisions of Korea since the time of the Yi dynasty and no change in its external boundaries. In 1945 the country was divided between a Communist North and a supposedly democratic South, but this split is totally out of keeping with the unity of Korean culture.

The vigor of the Yi order was slowly weakened by bureaucratic factionalism, which the throne never really overcame. Factionalism already had a long and disruptive history in Korea, dating from the time of the three early kingdoms, and it progressively eroded the effectiveness and authority of the Yi state. No strong rulers emerged after the early sixteenth century, and toward its end a divided and enfeebled Korea had to face the invasion of the Japanese warlord Hideyoshi. From 1592 to 1598 his army overran and ravaged the country, until the Korean people, aided by "elder brother" Ming China, drove the invaders back almost to the coast, where the contest was stalemated. The gifted Korean admiral Yi Sun-sin then repeatedly defeated Japanese naval detachments and disrupted their supply lines with his ingenious "turtle ships." These ships were armed fore and aft with metal prows shaped like beaks and covered with overlapping plates of iron and copper to make them almost invulnerable. They could ram and sink any ship by moving either forward or backward, powered by rowers under the projection of the outer "turtle shell"—the first armored warships.

The invasion was abandoned when Hideyoshi died in 1598, but Korea never fully recovered from its devastation. The Yi dynasty continued its decline, picked away at by perennial faction fighting, although it still patronized learning and the arts and supported major new printing projects. There was considerable economic growth, and population probably doubled between 1600 and 1800, based now on improved agriculture and on a rising commercial sector. Merchants began to buy their way to yangban status, as did prosperous farmers; Korea was following the path of Song, Ming, and Manchu China, and of Tokugawa Japan. But its political and administrative health was poor, and ultimately invited Japanese intervention after 1894.

Japanese civilization, having been largely created on the Chinese model and with Korean help, in time asserted its own separate cultural identity and produced a graceful elite culture combined with chronic political division and conflict. Japanese feudalism and the role of the samurai evolved after the Heian period (794–1185) under the Kamakura and Ashikaga shogunates (1185–1568), but such methods were unable to unify the country or end the endemic civil war until the emergence of the Tokugawa clan in 1600. Despite political turmoil, Japan also produced great art, literature, and architecture and a refined culture for the upper classes. It should be stressed that "borrowing" does not mean merely "echoing." Koreans and Japanese made what they took from China their own and went on to modify or further develop it, each in their own distinctive ways, while retaining their own indigenous culture as the basic fabric.

printing in the time of Gutenberg (1400–1468). The fifteenth century in Korea also saw important new developments in mathematics and in the manufacture of astronomical instruments.

More closely related to printing and the Confucian emphasis on learning was the roughly contemporary perfection of the earlier invented *han'gul* system, combining an alphabet and a syllabary, not only for writing Korean but also to give the Korean pronunciation of Chinese characters. Characters continued to be used for official documents and elite literature, as in Japan, but the development and popularity of han'gul was an affirmation of Korea's proud and confident distinctiveness.

Korean culture, which arose before the Han conquest, retained its distinctiveness but borrowed heavily from Chinese civilization at the elite level and went on to create new innovations in ceramics, movable-type printing, and institutions adapted from a Chinese original. Korea was first unified by the Silla dynasty (669–995) and then under the Koryo dynasty, until it was destroyed by the Mongol invasion in 1218. Yi dynasty Korea (1392–1910) saw a new burst of cultural and technological brilliance, but its vigor was slowly eroded by factionalism, and its last centuries, although still culturally creative, lapsed into administrative ineffectiveness and factionalism.

Questions

1. How have mountains had an impact on the historical development of both Korea and Japan?

2. How do the *Kojiki* and *Nihongi* reflect early Japanese society and culture?

3. What did Chinese civilization offer to Japan, as Prince Shotoku began to innovate at the Japanese court? How does Japan's localization of the Chinese tradition differ from Chinese practice?

4. Why was the Japanese court moved from Nara to Heian (Kyoto)? Specifically, how did this relate to the problems Buddhism presented to Japan's elite? How did Buddhism develop in Japan thereafter, and what was its impact on Japanese culture?

5. How do the writings of Lady Murasaki reflect both the best and the worst of early Japanese court culture? How does what she describes relate to the development of *shoen* and the collapse of the Heian order?

6. What are the differences between the Kamakura and Ashikaga shogunates? What did each contribute to Japanese civilization?

7. Why did the Koreans try to reproduce Chinese culture so faithfully? How did their efforts compare with those of their Japanese neighbors? How were they also selective in their localizations of the Chinese system?

Notes

1. M. Shikibu, *The Tale of Genji*, trans. A. Waley (New York: Doubleday, 1955), p. ix.
2. Ibid., p. xxi.
3. Quoted in Conrad Totman, *The Green Archipelago* (Berkeley: University of California Press, 1989), p. 29.

Suggested Web Sites

Japan

www.womeninworldhistory.com/heroine9.html
Information on the life and times of Lady Murasaki, the author of *The Tale of Genji*.

http://www.wsu.edu/~dee/FEUJAPAN/CONTENTS.HTM
Extensive source detailing feudal Japan, accompanied by readings and figures related to early Japan.

Korea

http://www.areastudies.org/documents/asia002.html
A seventeen-page article reexamining the early archaeological remains in Korea, with bibliographical references.

**http://www.archaeolink.com/
ancient%20southeast%20asian%20civilizations.htm**
One segment of this Web site provides links to explore the early history and culture of Korea.

Suggestions for Further Reading

Japan

Berry, M. E. *Hideyoshi*. Cambridge: Harvard University Press, 1986.
———. *The Culture of Civil War in Kyoto*. Berkeley: University of California Press, 1994.
Brown, D., Yamamura, K., eds. *The Cambridge History of Japan*. vols. 1 and 2. Cambridge, England: Cambridge University Press, 1992.
Butler, G. *Emperor and Aristocracy in Japan, 1467–1680*. Cambridge: Harvard University Press, 2003.
Conlan, T. D. *State of War in Fourteenth-Century Japan*. Ann Arbor, MI: Center for Japanese Studies, 2004.
Davis, N. *Japanese Religion and Society*. Albany: SUNY Press, 1992.
Dunn, C. J. *Everyday Life in Traditional Japan*. London: Batsford, 1969.
Duus, P. *Feudalism in Japan*. New York: McGraw-Hill, 1993.
Elison, E., and Smith, B., eds. *Warlords, Artists, and Commoners: Japan in the Sixteenth Century*. Honolulu: University of Hawaii Press, 1981.
Farris, W. W. *Population, Disease, and Land in Early Japan*. Cambridge: Harvard University Press, 1985.
Frederic, L. *Daily Life in Japan at the Time of the Samurai*. Rutland, VT: Tuttle, 1973.
Friday, K. F. *Samurai, Warfare, and the State in Early Medieval Japan*. New York: Routledge, 2004.
Habu, J. *Ancient Jomon of Japan*. Cambridge, England: Cambridge University Press, 2005.
Hall, J. W., ed. *Japan Before Tokugawa*. Princeton: Princeton University Press, 1986.
Hanley, S. *Everyday Things in Premodern Japan*. Berkeley: University of California Press, 1997.
Hirota, P., ed. *Toward a Contemporary Understanding of Pure Land Buddhism*. Albany: SUNY Press, 2000.
Jansen, M., ed. *Warrior Rule in Japan*. Cambridge, England: Cambridge University Press, 1995.

Kasulis, T., *Shinto*. Honolulu: University of Hawaii Press, 2005.

Keene, D. *No: The Classical Theatre of Japan*. Stanford: Stanford University Press, 1966.

Kierstead, T. *The Geography of Power in Medieval Japan*. Princeton: Princeton University Press, 1997.

King, W. L. *Zen and the Way of the Sword*. New York: Oxford University Press, 1993.

Mass, J. P. *Warrior Government in Early Medieval Japan*. New Haven: Yale University Press, 1974.

———, ed. *The Origins of Japan's Medieval World*. Stanford: Stanford University Press, 1997.

Morris, I. *The World of the Shining Prince*. Oxford: Oxford University Press, 1964.

Parker, J. D. *Zen Buddhist Landscape Arts of Early Muromachi Japan*. Albany: SUNY Press, 2000.

Sanyri, P. F. *The World Turned Upside Down: Medieval Japanese Society*. New York: Columbia University Press, 2001.

Shively, D. H., ed. *The Cambridge History of Japan*, vol. 2. Cambridge, England: Cambridge University Press, 1999.

Tiedemann, A. E., ed. *An Introduction to Japanese Civilization*. New York: Columbia University Press, 1974.

Totman, C. *Japan Before Perry: A Short History*. Berkeley: University of California Press, 1981.

Trumbull, S. *Samurai Warlords*. Poole, Dorset, England: Firebird Books, 1992.

Walker, B. *The Conquest of Ainu Lands*. Berkeley: University of California Press, 2001.

Korea

Deunchler, M. *The Confucian Transformation of Korea*. Cambridge: Harvard University Press, 1993.

Duncan, J. B. *The Origins of the Choson Dynasty*. Vancouver: University of British Columbia Press, 2000.

Hang, W. *Ancient Korean and Japanese History*. Seoul: Kudara International, 1995.

Henthorn, G. *History of Korea*. Glencoe, IL: Free Press, 1971.

Lee, K. B. *A New History of Korea*, trans. E. Wagner. Cambridge: Harvard University Press, 1985.

Pai, H. *Constructing Korean Origins*. Cambridge: Harvard University Press, 2000.

Peterson, M. *Korean Adoption and Inheritance*. Ithaca, NY: Cornell University Press, 1995.

Tenant, R. *A History of Korea*. New York: Columbia University Press, 1996.

10

Mughal India and Central Asia

This chapter deals with the Mughal dynasty, which ruled India from 1526 to the early eighteenth century. Babur, "The Tiger," invaded India from his base in Afghanistan and founded the dynasty. His grandson Akbar (1542–1605) was one of India's greatest rulers and tried to build a fusion between Turkish, Persian, and Indian cultures. His successors on the throne were less dedicated and more absorbed in the pleasures of the court; his grandson Shah Jahan (r. 1627–1657) built the Taj Mahal at Agra and a splendid new capital at Delhi. Aurangzeb (or Alamgir), who succeeded Shah Jahan, was an Islamic zealot whose attempt to conquer the Hindu south failed but sparked revolt from the Sikhs of Punjab, the Rajputs of Rajasthan, and the Marathas of Maharashtra. At his death in 1707, India collapsed into a chaos of fighting, in which the British slowly enlarged their coastal footholds.

Central Asia had been closely involved with India since at least the time of the Aryan migrations, and the Mughals were thus in a long chain of Central Asian peoples who have moved into the subcontinent. This section briefly surveys Central Asia and its nomadic cultures, whose mounted warriors confronted both India and China.

The Mughals in India

After Tamerlane's bloody invasion of 1398, the Delhi sultanate never regained its earlier control, and the north remained fragmented. An Afghan clan, the Lodis, seized power in Delhi in 1451 but could not extend their rule beyond the neighboring Punjab. Their continued temple razing and oppression of Hindus sparked rebellions that could not be put down, erupting eastward in the central Ganges Valley, westward among the Rajputs of Rajasthan (who were still defending Hindu India), and finally in Punjab itself.

Babur and the New Dynasty

A rebel governor in Punjab asked for help from the Central Asian leader Babur (1483–1530), known already as "The Tiger" and by this time established also as ruler of most of Afghanistan. Babur claimed descent on his father's side from Tamerlane and on his mother's from Chinghis Khan. Like many other Central Asian Turks, he had acquired a great deal of Persian culture and was a gifted poet in Persian. In 1526, Babur's tough, mounted Turco-Afghan troops defeated the numerically superior Lodi forces and their war elephants at the battle of Panipat in Punjab, some 70 miles northwest of Delhi. The next year Babur routed the Rajput army which tried to eject him, and in 1529 he crushed the Delhi sultanate's last effort to regain power. Babur was master of the north, proclaiming the Mughal dynasty (the name is derived, via Persian, from *Mongol*), which was to restore imperial grandeur in northern India for nearly two centuries.

The greatness of the Mughal period rested on a fortunate combination of able, imaginative rulers, especially the emperor Akbar (1542–1605), and the new infusion of Persian culture into northern India. Under Akbar and his immediate successors, Persian, the official language of court, government, and law, merged with the earlier language of the Delhi-Agra area to form modern Hindi, now the largest single language of India, and Urdu, its close equivalent, now the official language of Pakistan. Persian artistic and literary forms blended with earlier traditions in the north and enriched all of

CHRONOLOGY

1526 ■	Babur's victory at Panipat initiates Mughal rule
1508–1556 ■	Hamayun
1542–1605 ■	Akbar
1573 ■	Surat becomes the Mughal's official port-of-trade
1605–1627 ■	Jahangir
1627–1658 ■	Shah Jahan
1658–1707 ■	Aurangzeb
1664 ■	Shivaji sacks Surat; international traders move to Bombay
1660–1800 ■	Sikhs, Rajputs, Marathas
1739 ■	Nadir Shah invades India from Persia and takes the Peacock Throne

Indian culture. The Mughals reestablished firm central control in the north. Within their empire, agriculture and commerce flourished again. Steady revenues and an efficient imperial administration enabled the building of a network of imperial roads to link the empire together. This was no small task, given India's previous centuries of disunity and regional separatism, as well as its size.

The total population within the empire was probably over 100 million, on a par with China's but most likely larger than Europe's. To symbolize their power and wealth, the Mughal emperors built magnificent new capitals at both Delhi and Agra, some 100 miles to the south. This area, between the Jumna and Ganges rivers, had long been the strategic key to Hindustan, the Ganges Valley, and routes southward, as described in Chapter 6. Successive Delhis had risen and fallen on this strategic site, controlling, with Agra as its satellite, the heart of repeated imperial efforts. Like sentinels, both cities were built on the west bank of the Jumna, which flows into the Ganges below Agra after running parallel to it like a defensive moat from well north of Delhi.

Each city was now dominated by a great walled fort containing the palace and audience halls. Inside and outside the walls the Mughals also constructed great mosques, gardens, tombs (such as the Taj Mahal at Agra), and other monumental buildings in the Persian style, which they further developed and made distinctively Indian. Literature, music, and the graphic arts flourished under imperial patronage at both capitals, which were the seat of government alternately, at the pleasure of the emperor. Strong imperial rule was often oppressive, but it helped to ensure an unprecedented period of unity and prosperity in which most Indians shared. Hindus too could feel pride in the new imperial grandeur, for they were given an important role in it.

Akbar's Achievement

Akbar's success in building a truly Indian empire rather than just another alien conquest was the chief foundation of Mughal greatness, but he had first to establish his rule. Babur died prematurely in 1530, after offering his life to God in exchange for that of his son Humayun, who was deathly ill. But Humayun (1508–1556) was a weakling who was finally driven out of India in 1540 by one of Babur's Afghan generals and forced to take

Babur in Battle

In his Memoirs Babur wrote that for 20 years he had "never ceased to think of the conquest of Hindustan." After he had been invited to aid the rebel governor of Lahore in 1526 against the Delhi sultanate, he commented:

I placed my foot in the stirrup of resolution and my hands on the reins of confidence in God, and marched against Sultan Ibrahim . . . whose army in the field was said to amount to a hundred thousand men and who had nearly a thousand elephants. [Babur had about 10,000, but these included superb horsemen from central Asia, and he also used cannons lashed together to fire broadsides against the enemy's elephants.] The sun had mounted spear-high when the onset began, and the battle lasted till midday, when the enemy was completely broken and routed. By the grace and mercy of Almighty God this difficult affair was made easy to me, and that mighty army, in the space of half a day, was laid in the dust.

Source: From *A New History of India, Sixth Edition* by Stanley Wolpert, copyright © 1997 by Oxford University Press, Inc. Used by permission of Oxford University Press, Inc.

refuge in Iran. A year after he returned in 1555 at the head of a Persian army to reclaim his father's conquests, he fell on the stone steps of his private astronomical observatory and library, light-headed from opium, and died early in 1556, leaving the job to his 13-year-old son, Akbar, who had been born in exile in 1542.

Immediately challenged upon his accession, Akbar with his army defeated yet another Hindu effort to drive out the invaders, again at Panipat, and in 1562, at age 20, Akbar assumed full charge of the empire from his advisers. In the same year he married a Rajput princess, beginning what was to be a lifelong campaign to blend the many strands of India's ancient cultural, regional, and religious heritage, building both an empire and a new culture that was as nearly all-Indian as he could make it, uniting elements under firm Mughal control.

He saw himself as an Indian ruler, not as a foreign despot, and understood from the beginning that his and his dynasty's success must depend on commanding the support and participation of all Indians, varied and often antagonistic as they were. But he could be ruthless if his power was challenged. When the chief Rajput faction resisted his diplomacy, he sacked their capital in 1568 and massacred the surviving defenders. By 1570 all but a small remnant of the Rajputs had sworn allegiance to him; in return, he made a Rajput whose military skills he knew well one of his chief generals; other Rajputs thereafter also had a strong role in the imperial army. This political wisdom solved what would otherwise have been his major and perhaps most unworkable military problem. Rajputs became his comrades rather than his implacable enemies. To further mark his religious toleration, he chose for the four wives allowed to rulers by the Koran two Hindus (including his Rajput bride), one Christian, and one Muslim, thus, symbolically embracing India's religious variety.

With his new Rajput allies, Akbar invaded wealthy Gujarat, capturing Surat, the chief seaport of the west coast, in 1573. In 1576 he completed the conquest of Bengal in the east, and by 1581 had added most of Afghanistan to his empire. For many years his armies raided the northern Deccan but were never able to win permanent control, a goal that also eluded his successors. But India and Afghanistan under Akbar and his successors remained until the end of the seventeenth century one of the greatest empires in history, both in size and wealth and in effective administration and cultural splendor. It was divided into 15 provinces, each under a governor but with a separate set of officials responsible for revenue collection. Provinces were subdivided into districts, where representatives of the governor kept order and dispensed justice. Revenue demands were smaller than under the Delhi sultans, and the large number of Hindus employed in the revenue service, as well as at its head, helped to keep taxes from becoming exploitive or unfair. Hindu law

was applied in disputes between Hindus. Revenue collectors were ordered to remit taxes in districts that had had a poor harvest.

One reform that endeared Akbar to his subjects was his abolition of two hated taxes: on Hindu pilgrims traveling to sacred sites and on all Hindus as infidels (the *jizya,* or poll tax), both of which had been collected by Muslim rulers for centuries. He abolished the enslaving of war prisoners and their families and forbade forcible conversion to Islam, a bitter issue since the first Muslim invasions of the tenth century and the rule of the Delhi sultanate. Hindus were welcome at court, and their advice was regularly sought. Akbar patronized Persian and Urdu art and literature but also appointed a court poet for Hindi and encouraged Hindu literature and art more generally. Most of the greatest court painters were Hindus, producing beautiful portraits, miniatures, and naturalistic bird, animal, and flower paintings. Orthodox Muslims challenged this defiance of the Islamic ban on the depiction of natural, especially human or animal, forms, but Akbar replied that he could not believe God, "the giver of life," would disapprove of the beauty he had made, which was portrayed in true art.

Like the other Mughal emperors after him, Akbar loved gardens. Nearly all Mughal buildings, including palaces, forts, and tombs, were surrounded by magnificent blendings of green lawns, gaily colored beds of flowers, and flowering trees for shade. The ingenious use of water in fountains, pools, and fluted channels enhanced the atmosphere of coolness, restfulness, and verdure, especially striking in the hot, dry surroundings of the plains of northern India. Akbar took a personal interest in the planning and care of the imperial gardens and is shown by court painters supervising the planting of flower beds and tending his roses.

Akbar was widely curious and loved to discuss philosophy and religion with all comers, including Portuguese Jesuits as well as Hindu Brahmins. He had the Christian gospels translated into Persian and attended mass. But just as he came to reject the dogma of Islam as the only true religion, he could not accept the exclusive truth of any one faith, except a universal faith in an all-powerful creation. In later life he increasingly became a sufi, or Islamic mystic, blending ideas from many religions and symbolizing his mission to merge the best of all the Indian traditions with those the Mughals brought into India. He was a deeply religious person, but his departures from orthodox Islam shocked many Muslim leaders and provoked a revolt against him in 1581. He suppressed it by force and then in deference to Hindu values forbade the slaughter of cattle and became a vegetarian, even giving up hunting, of which he had been very fond. Akbar founded a new faith that he hoped could unite his varied subjects in the common love of God, without need for a sectarian priesthood, but it did not survive him. If he had been followed

The Court of Akbar

One of the many accounts of Akbar and the India of his time is that of the Jesuit Antonio Monserrate, who visited the court from 1580 to 1583. Here are some excerpts from his Commentary.

This Prince is of a stature and type of countenance well fitted to his royal dignity, so that one could easily recognize even at first glance that he is the king. . . . His forehead is broad and open, his eyes so bright and flashing that they seem like a sea shimmering in the sunlight. . . . He creates an opportunity almost every day for any of the common people or of the nobles to see him and converse with him. It is remarkable how great an effect this courtesy and affability has in attaching to him the minds of his subjects. . . . He has an acute insight, and shows much wise foresight both in avoiding dangers and in seizing favorable opportunities for carrying out his designs. . . . Unlike the palaces built by other Indian kings, his are lofty [and] their total circuit is so large that it easily embraces four great royal dwellings. . . . Not a little is added to the beauty of the palaces by charming pigeon cotes. . . . The pigeons are cared for by eunuchs and servant maids. Their evolutions are controlled at will, when they are flying, by means of certain signals, just as those of a well trained soldiery. . . . It will seem little short of miraculous when I affirm that when sent out they dance, turn somersaults all together in the air, fly in orderly rhythm, and return to their starting point, all at the sound of a whistle. [Akbar's] empire is wonderfully rich and fertile both for cultivation and pasture, and has a great trade both in exports and imports. . . . Indian towns appear very pleasant from afar; they are adorned with many towers and high buildings in a very beautiful manner. But when one enters them, one finds that the narrowness, aimless crookedness, and ill planning of the streets deprive these cities of all beauty. . . . The common people live in lowly huts and tiny cottages, and hence if a traveller has seen one of these cities, he has seen them all.

Source: D. Lach and Carole Flaumenhaft. *Asia on the Eve of Europe's Expansion* (Englewood Cliffs, NJ: Prentice-Hall, 1965), pp. 63–69.

---

by successors like him, his dream of a united India free of strife might have moved closer to realization.

A CLOSER LOOK

Akbar, the Man

Akbar is a fascinating figure, and much has been written about him. He was a contemporary of Elizabeth I of England, Henry IV of France, Shah Abbas of Iran, and the Ming emperor Wan-li. Europeans who had met them all agreed that as both a human being and a ruler he towered over his contemporaries. He had not only great strength of intelligence, character, and will but also the good sense to realize that compromise and co-operation work better than force. He was full of energy and imagination but highly sensitive and often prey to melancholy and fits of depression. He seems to have been an epileptic, like many other famous men, including Julius Caesar and Napoleon, and to have been illiterate, astonishing as that appears. As a child he preferred hunting and other sports to lessons, but he had a phenomenal memory, like many unlettered people, and was a great listener. From adolescence he appointed courtiers to read to him several hours a day; he had over 24,000 manuscripts in his library, and the learned men who debated with him often found him better "read" than themselves. He had a broadly inquiring mind, but a complicated one; the Jesuits at his court, who came to know him well, could never fully understand it or predict what he might say or do. He kept his dignity with all but had the knack of making the humblest petitioner feel at ease, and he charmed everyone who met him, high and low.

He was remarkably versatile, not only in his interests but with many skills. He was an accomplished polo player, metalworker, draftsman (many of his beautiful drawings have survived), and musician. He even invented a lighted polo ball so that the game could be played at night and a gun with a new mechanism that could fire multiple rounds. But his main preoccupation shifted to religion, especially after he had completed his major conquests, and he spent many nights alone in prayer and meditation, seeking truth. In 1575 he built a Hall of Worship, to which he invited the widest range of philosophers and theologians for periodic discussions, first from Islamic schools of thought and then from all religions he could gather, including individual holy men, ascetics and mystics, Hindu sadhus and Muslim sufis, Jesuit priests and Iranian fire worshippers. In time, these seminars on religion were held regularly every Thursday evening, while Akbar continued his own private devotions at sunrise, noon, sunset, and midnight. Although he hoped earnestly that his new mystic religion, founded in 1581 to unite all people, would attract a mass following, it was typical of him never to force it on anyone.

Akbar was too intellectually alive and too religiously devout to lapse into the life of extravagant luxury that surrounded him at court, but he was no purist or prude. He enjoyed the food and wine, the sherbet (the word is Turkish) brought to him daily by runners from the snowy Himalayas, the dancing girls, the music and plays, and the flourishing literature and art that he so generously patronized. He was, in other words, a truly regal monarch, but a most unusual one in the range of his vision and understanding. It was too much to ask for a succession of others like him, but India was never again to be served by even one ruler of his quality until the first prime minister of its modern independence, Jawaharlal Nehru.

Akbar was still without an heir after six years of marriage. He sought help from a sufi saint who lived at a place called Sikri, some 20 miles west of Agra. A year later his first son was born, and in gratitude Akbar built a magnificent new, red-sandstone capital, which he called Fatehpur Sikri, next to the saint's humble cottage. Here he had fresh scope to blend Indian, Persian, Islamic, and Mughal themes in architecture, drawing also on traditional Hindu architecture in the south. But the water supply in this arid area proved inadequate and Fatehpur Sikri had to be abandoned after only 15 years. The deserted stone city still stands much as Akbar left it, a monument to his vision that still can move those who visit it.

The last four years of his life were clouded by the rebellion of his eldest son, whose birth had been such a

Akbar in his older years, a portrait that suggests his absorption in religion and philosophy. (By permission of the British Library)

joyous occasion. The Mughals were never able to work out satisfactorily the problem of succession. From this time on, each emperor was plotted against in his old age by his many sons, who also tore the empire apart by their fighting until the most ruthless had disposed of his rivals. It was a pattern inherited from the Mughal's Central Asian origins, and it blighted their otherwise great achievements while also draining the country's resources. In 1605 Akbar reasserted his authority, only to die of poison administered by his rebellious son, who took the throne that year with the title Jahangir ("world seizer").

Jahangir and Shah Jahan

Jahangir's Persian wife, Nur Jahan, a power in her own right, further entrenched Persian culture at the court and throughout the north. The administrative system inherited from Akbar continued to run smoothly, and revenues flowed in to pay for the brilliance of the court. Jahangir and Nur Jahan preferred Agra to Delhi and further adorned it with new palaces, gardens, and tombs. Court life took on a more luxurious splendor; Jahangir was no mystic like his father. He and his courtiers delighted in silks and perfumes, jewel-decked costumes, wine, song, and the pleasures of the harem.

Akbar's planned capital at Fatehpur Sikri, near Agra. The buildings are designed open to the breezes, with wide courtyards between them, and with water flowing under the floors of the sleeping rooms to cool them. In one of the courtyards shown here, marked off as a giant pachisi (parcheesi) board, the game was played with court ladies as live pieces whose moves were directed by players throwing dice. (R. Murphey)

There were state processions with elephants covered with silk and jewels, troupes of dancing girls, and month-long festivities to celebrate the marriages of Jahangir's many sons.

The painting of this era became more naturalistic, and the orthodox Islamic prohibition against representing human or animal forms gave way to older Indian traditions, including nearly nude figures and embracing couples in classic Rajput and earlier Hindu styles as well as portraits of the emperor, often in his beloved gardens. For all their use of Persian language, culture, and art forms, the Mughals had become Indian rulers and were increasingly seen as such by most Indians. They were following a traditional Maharaja lifestyle, and their pretensions to divine authority were familiar to their subjects; like luxurious living, they were expected for royalty.

A resurgent Iran under Shah Abbas (1587–1629) began to challenge Mughal control and conquered most of Afghanistan, but Jahangir was too busy with his gardens, wine, and harems to lead his army over the mountains. He had given his son, the future Shah Jahan, command of the army, but Shah Jahan refused to leave the capital because he was already plotting to seize the throne, having previously poisoned his elder brother. He knew that his real enemy was Nur Jahan, who appointed her own father and brother to the highest offices and entirely manipulated Jahangir, hoping to occupy the throne herself. Entranced by her beauty and wit, Jahangir had named her Nur Jahan, meaning "light of the world," but she became empress in all but name soon after he married her. She arranged the marriage of her brother's daughter, Mumtaz Mahal, to Shah Jahan as an extension of her power into the future.

But Shah Jahan openly rebelled in 1623, and when Jahangir died late in 1627, he put to death all of his closest relatives and pensioned off Nur Jahan. He declared himself "emperor of the world," which is the meaning of his regnal name, and marked his coronation with three weeks of extravagant ceremonies. He ruled for three decades, the most lavish of all the Mughal reigns, especially in his passion for monumental architecture inlaid with precious stones. Court life under Shah Jahan was sumptuous, in the pattern set by his father, but he was even more attached to his harem, where 5,000 concubines awaited his pleasure. Nevertheless, he was genuinely devoted to his wife, Mumtaz Mahal, who bore him 14 children. When she died in childbirth in 1631 at age 39, he was desolated. "Empire has no sweetness, life has no relish for me now," he said when told of her death.

To honor her memory he built what is probably the most famous structure in the world, the Taj Mahal at Agra, which took 20,000 workmen over 20 years to complete. Designed by two Persian architects, it beautifully blends Iranian and Indian themes and Indian craftsmanship, the characteristically Mughal emphasis on water and gardens, and the use of Rajput canopies around the base of the dome. Before it was finished, Shah Jahan had begun a new capital city at Delhi, site of so many capitals before, modeled on Akbar's Red Fort at Agra and built of the same red sandstone, with massive walls and battlements but even larger. Inside were beautiful gardens, palaces, audience halls, harems, barracks, stables, and storehouses, and outside he built India's largest mosque, the Jama Masjid. Both still stand, little altered, and still dominate Old Delhi, sometimes known by its Mughal name, Shah Jahanabad ("Shah Jahan's City"). Monumental building and the

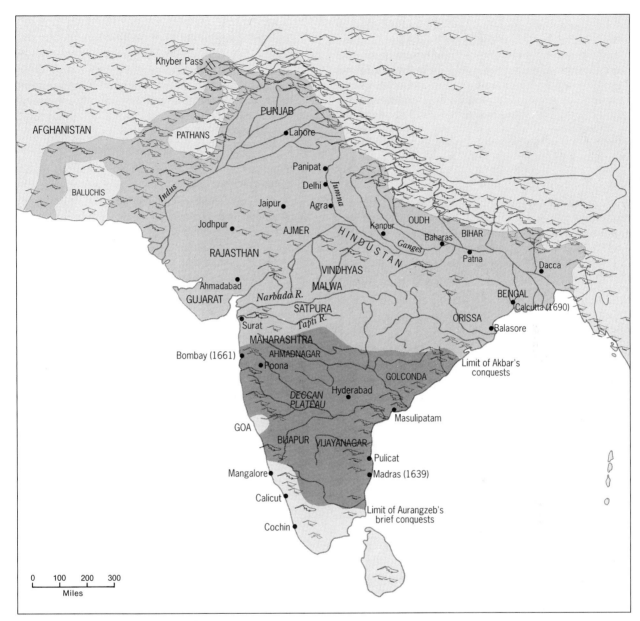

India at the Height of Mughal Power

The darkened area shows the maximum extent of Aurangzeb's conquests, but they lasted for only a few years as southern forces, aided by Rajput, Mahratha, and Sikh attacks destroyed his position. Also shown are the early English trading bases, with dates for the founding of each.

opulent court were not his only extravagances. He ordered campaigns to reclaim Afghanistan and restore Mughal rule in Central Asia. Both failed but exhausted the treasury. From his Red Fort palace on his Peacock Throne, encrusted with the largest jewels ever found, the emperor doubled Akbar's revenue demands, and the empire groaned.

Meanwhile his many sons were already conspiring against each other, impatient to succeed the ailing emperor. His favorite son, Dara, a philosopher and mystic like his great-grandfather Akbar, might have made a fine ruler, but a younger son, Aurangzeb (or Alamgir) was insatiably ambitious. From 1657 there was open warfare among rival brothers. Aurangzeb imprisoned his father,

No photograph can do full justice to the Taj Mahal, whose great bulk seems to float weightlessly above the pool that holds its reflection. Mughal cupolas and domes are matched by minarets (the four slender towers on each side) in the Islamic tradition, while the central archway beneath the dome is reminiscent of the Persian models on which it was based. Inscriptions from the Koran and beautiful inlaid floral patterns cover much of the outer and inner walls, worked on for over 20 years by craftsmen from as far away as China and Italy. The entire structure is of glistening white marble. (R. Murphey)

Shah Jahan, in the dungeon of Agra's Red Fort while he completed his gruesome work, and then sent the old emperor the head of his son Dara. The aged Shah Jahan could just see through the barred window of his cell a glimpse of his beloved Taj Mahal. Hearing that this gave the old man a little comfort, Aurangzeb is said to have had his father's eyes put out.

The Reign of Aurangzeb: Repression and Revolt

This cold-blooded zealot ascended the throne in 1658. By poison, intrigue, or assassination he had eliminated a dozen of his own brothers and half-brothers, as well as uncounted others. He gave as the reason for this slaughter his own devotion to orthodox Islam and the more lax or tolerant views of his many rivals. But Aurangzeb was also a brilliant and single-minded ruler and administrator and a cunning statesman. Sunni Muslims revered him as much as Hindus hated him. He is said to have had no friends, only servile admirers and bitter enemies.

Civil war on top of Shah Jahan's extravagances had emptied the treasury, but Aurangzeb increased his revenue demands still further and at the same time extended his own puritanical tastes to the running of court and empire. He stopped all court luxuries, especially the wine, song, and dance forbidden by the Koran, and ended all monumental construction. He also appointed censors of public morals to enforce rigid Islamic law, ordered everyone to pray at stated intervals every day, tried to abolish gambling and drinking, and began a lifelong campaign to demolish all surviving Hindu monuments and temples. Unfortunately, he largely succeeded in the north and the only surviving samples of pre-Mughal architecture are in the south, where Aurangzeb never prevailed. Hindus were forbidden to carry arms, forced conversion was resumed for many, and all Hindu festivals or public expression outlawed. Aurangzeb knew the Koran by heart and copied it out twice in his own hand. But his piety and his zealous praying do not seem to have guided him toward anything but dogmatic orthodoxy and gross inhumanity in pursuit of it. To increase the revenue needed to maintain his army and to pay for new conquests in the name of Allah, he reimposed the hated jizya tax on Hindus, levied a new tax on Hindu pilgrims, and doubled the taxes on Hindu merchants. When crowds gathered outside the Red Fort in Delhi to protest, he ordered the imperial elephants to crush them to death.

Within a few years, there were widespread revolts, which merely increased Aurangzeb's pressure for more revenue to raise armies to put them down. For many years he did so successfully, thanks to his superior generalship and to the fear-induced loyalty of most of his court and army. When revolt failed, or the risks of defying Aurangzeb or his tax collectors seemed too great, growing numbers of peasants abandoned their homes and fields to become bandits or join dissident groups or armies elsewhere, including explicitly Hindu forces such as the Sikhs of Punjab (particularly brutalized by Aurangzeb), the formerly loyal Rajputs, and the Marathas.

Relentless in suppressing rebellion, Aurangzeb was also determined to extend his empire into the south. The last half of his wearily long reign was consumed in bloody but ultimately unsuccessful campaigns into the Deccan, while at the same time his forces tried to stem the rising tide of Sikh, Rajput, Afghan, Bengali, and Maratha revolt. His brief conquests in the south, won at terrible cost in money and lives, quickly evaporated.

Interior of the Delhi Red Fort from an audience hall, showing the pearl mosque for the use of the court. An inscription on the wall reads, "If there is a paradise on earth, it is this." (R. Murphey)

From their mountain fortresses in the northwestern Deccan, the Hindu Marathas became increasingly powerful and took the field to harry Mughal forces retreating from the south near the end of Aurangzeb's reign. His campaigns exhausted the country and left it split among contending powers, sharing an implacable hatred of Mughal rule but divided by their own differences and rivalries. India was never to recover from this legacy of religious strife and factionalism.

Sects and Rebels: Rajputs, Sikhs, and Marathas

Three groups stood out against Aurangzeb's intolerance and military conquests and as his most effective opponents: the Rajputs, the Sikhs, and the Marathas. Unfortunately for them, they never made common cause, as they also failed to do later against the expanding East India Company. Aurangzeb broke the alliance that Akbar had prudently made with the Rajputs and eliminated their previously prominent role in the Mughal army. Throughout most of his reign they were in revolt, maintaining their reputation as courageous fighters and never effectively being suppressed. The proximity of their base and its fortresses in Rajasthan to the center of Mughal power in the Delhi-Agra region made them highly vulnerable, and they suffered repeated annihilation campaigns. But Rajput resistance survived and hung onto the margins of Rajasthan as a permanent thorn in Aurangzeb's side, precisely the danger that Akbar had so wisely turned to his advantage by making the Rajputs his collaborators. Each campaign against them bred new bitterness and new determination to fight. Aurangzeb's bigotry and conquering ambition called forth resistance in the name of India and of Hinduism against a Mughal order now seen afresh as alien and hateful, a sad sequel to Akbar's vision and achievement of a multiracial, multicultural, and multireligious India, in which all groups could be partners in a common enterprise under Mughal leadership and could share pride in the empire. Throughout their history the Rajputs had been quick to spring to the defense of Hindu India, and now they took the field again, convinced of the rightness of their all-India cause.

As an outgrowth of the bhakti movement (see Chapter 6) late in the fifteenth century, the Sikhs of Punjab emerged as a religious group with its own separate identity. As elsewhere in India where bhakti ideals spread, a series of nonsectarian saint-reformers preached a puritanical form of life and freedom from priestly domination, discarding the more dogmatic and hierarchical aspects of Hinduism but retaining its devotion to nonviolence. The founder of Sikhism, Guru Nanak (1469–1538), tried at first to work out a compromise between Hinduism and Islam and then to purify Hinduism. He was a contemporary of Martin Luther (1483–1546) but less contentious and less of a theologian. He preached the bhakti message of a universal, loving God, to whom everyone has access without the need for priests or rituals. Perhaps his best-known saying is "Man will be saved by his works alone; God will not ask a man his tribe or sect, but what he has done. There is no Hindu and no Muslim. All are children of God."[1]

His disciple and successor Guru Angad (active 1530–1552) began the compilation of the Sikh holy book, the Granth Sahib, recording all he had learned from Guru Nanak and adding devotional reflections. Successive Sikh gurus continued opposition to caste and to all forms of discrimination. Sikh leaders met with Akbar, who listened to them with interest and granted them a site for their chief temple in Amritsar, near Lahore. The origins of Sikhism were thus wholly peaceful, but in the sixteenth century some Sikhs were drawn into support for one of Jahangir's rebellious sons, hoping that he would be more tolerant of non-Muslims. When the rebellion failed and Jahangir had the Sikh leader executed in 1606, the Sikhs began to develop a defensive military emphasis in order to maintain their own identity and their territorial base in Punjab.

By 1650 their numbers had greatly increased, and they began to see themselves as a separate state. Sikh gurus urged their followers to eat meat not only in distinction from high-caste Hindus but also to give them strength. Martial skills, bravery, and physical strength began to be cultivated as Sikh hallmarks. Shah Jahan left them largely alone, preoccupied as he was with his ambitious building projects and the luxurious pleasures of his harem and court. But when the Sikhs understandably supported his favored son Dara's bid for the throne, they became Aurangzeb's enemies. His persecutions of them and his efforts to eliminate them as both a power and a community predictably strengthened their commitment and led to their further militarization in self-defense. Aurangzeb cruelly tortured to death the ninth Sikh guru, Teg Bahadur, in 1675 when he refused to embrace Islam and ignored the guru's warning against the still tiny but foreboding European threat to India.

Teg Bahadur's son and successor, Guru Govind Singh (r. 1675–1708), first organized the Sikhs into a real political power and a great military fraternity. He urged them all to adopt the surname Singh ("lion") as he had done, to swear never to cut their hair (which came to be worn knotted up in a turban) or their beards, and to avoid tobacco and alcohol. The practices of *purdah* (the veiling and seclusion of women) and *sati* (the burning of widows) were rejected in part not only because they were Muslim and Hindu customs but also because they were seen as inhuman. Sikh women were freer, more nearly coequals to men, than in most other Indian religions. Govind Singh's four sons were captured by Aurangzeb and tortured to death, steadfastly refusing to convert to Islam.

When Govind Singh himself died in 1708, the line of ten guru leaders ended and the Sikhs were thereafter ruled by political rather than religious leaders. Many Punjabis and others from neighboring areas adopted Sikhism. A former Rajput, Banda Bairagi, ravaged the Mughal forces as leader of the Sikhs until he was betrayed, captured, and executed in 1716. Nadir Shah's invasion from Iran in 1739 finally eliminated Mughal power and gave the Sikhs new opportunity to extend their domination of Punjab. During the remainder of the eighteenth century the Sikh kingdom became still stronger and stood finally as the last major obstacle to British rule, overcome only in 1849 after two campaigns against them.

The Marathas were probably the most formidable and effective enemies of the Mughals, and for some two centuries played a major all-India role. For a time it seemed as if they would become the dominant power in the subcontinent and would found a new Indian empire. Their home base was well protected by mountains, the Western Ghats, just back from the coast behind Bombay; by the Deccan Plateau east of the Ghats broken by numerous hills and defended outcrops; and by the central Indian mountain ranges of the Vindhyas and their spurs to the north and east, ideally suited to guerrilla warfare. The Marathas gloried in their hardiness, which they attributed to the relative barrenness of their mountain-girt homeland, rather like the Ghurkas of Nepal or the Scots, and like them had a proud military tradition (Maharashtra means "Great Country").

The greatest Maratha leader was Shivaji (1627–1680), who rose to prominence just as Hindus, embittered by Aurangzeb's oppression, were ready to take up arms against him. Shivaji combined his zealous Hinduism with his martial background and determination to free India of the alien Mughal tyranny. From the beginning of Aurangzeb's reign, Shivaji and his commando cavalry raided Mughal territory. The Mughal general sent against him captured Poona, the Maratha capital, in 1663, but was routed by Shivaji in a daring night attack. A few months later in 1664 Shivaji attacked Surat in Gujarat, then the richest port in India, and carried off immense booty. A second major Mughal campaign against him ended in negotiations after some of Shivaji's feuding adversaries deserted to the Mughal cause. Shivaji visited Agra, expecting to be offered a high post, but when he complained that Aurangzeb's offer was not good enough he was imprisoned. He smuggled himself out concealed in a basket and rebuilt his forces and resources for what he now saw as the inevitable conflict.

When Aurangzeb ordered all Hindu temples and schools demolished and all Hindu public teaching and practice suppressed, Shivaji renewed his raids in 1670, and over the next ten years more than doubled the territory under his control, rivaling the Mughal territory as an enemy state with which to be reckoned. This achievement inspired the Marathas with renewed pride, and Shivaji remains their greatest hero to this day. Unlike his successors, he was not only a brilliant military strategist and tactician but also an effective organizer and political administrator. He ruled with a council of ministers, made Marathi and Sanskrit the court languages, and banned the use of Urdu and Persian. For nearly 20 years he defied a series of Mughal armies, a considerable accomplishment in itself. Aurangzeb called him "the mountain rat"; "My armies have been employed against him for nineteen years," he said, "and nevertheless his state has always been increasing."

But Shivaji did not live to see the death of Aurangzeb and the collapse of the Mughal power, and the son who succeeded him neglected the army and the state and spent his time enjoying the luxuries of court life. He was defeated and captured by the Mughals, who executed him and many other Maratha chiefs in 1689. Shivaji's grandson, the next Maratha ruler, defected to the Mughals and was made one of their high officials, but other Marathas renewed the struggle. A younger descendant of Shivaji reorganized the army and resumed his grandfather's devastating raids. In 1699, after his own generals had failed to put them down, Aurangzeb himself marched against the Marathas, but without success. By 1702 the Mughals were on the defensive. The Marathas were now led by Tara Bai, the remarkable wife of the ruler who had died in 1700, although she ruled in name through her son, Shivaji III. She rode a horse with fearless skill and led the Maratha cavalry charges, which were their chief weapon.

After Aurangzeb's death and the collapse of his over-ambitious crusade, the Marathas were torn by civil war, a continuation of the feuding that was also part of their tradition, again like the Scots. Successive leaders after 1712 resumed campaigns to the north, south, and east, extending their territory close to Delhi, conquering most of the peninsular south, and raiding even into Bengal. The Maratha Confederacy, as it was called, had become by far the greatest power in India, but it lacked the firm hand and administrative skills of Shivaji and was chronically troubled by factionalism. The Maratha army was used as much to raid and plunder as to fight major engagements, and raids or conquests were seldom followed up by responsible government of the captured areas.

In 1761 the army marched north to meet an Afghan invasion on the historic field of Panipat, northwest of Delhi, and was totally defeated with heavy losses. Their short-lived "empire" was dissolved, and their power never recovered. The real beneficiaries were the English, since the Marathas had been the only major defenders of India against foreign invaders and the only group with the potential to reunite the country. Internal feuding among themselves, lack of commitment to responsible administration, a predatory pattern that repelled support, and the strain of chronic fighting against the Mughals left them unequal to that enormous task. India itself was exhausted by unending warfare. The Mughals, Marathas, Sikhs, and Rajputs merely bloodied and drained each other and the country as a whole rather than taking any united stand.

The Mughals and India

By the beginning of the eighteenth century, the order and prosperity that had flourished under Akbar and his immediate successors had been fatally weakened. Akbar's carefully designed revenue system, under Hindu management, had been eroded by the excessive granting of tax-collecting rights for large areas, known as *jagirs,* to those whom the throne wanted or needed to pay off. Especially under Aurangzeb, Mughal attention was concentrated on military conquest, which meant not only mounting demands for revenue but also decreasing attention to normal administration and supervision. Hindu revenue officials were eliminated; holders of jagirs (*jagirdars*) became more and more independent, and more and more rapacious in extracting everything they could from an oppressed peasantry and merchant group, retaining for their own pockets any balance beyond the official government tax rates. The same was true for the group known as *zamindars,* who were also granted tax-collection rights for smaller local areas and used these rights to enrich themselves, often acquiring the ownership of land from peasants who were unable to pay the tax.

This demise of Akbar's system was a disaster for the well-being of most of the agricultural sector, the predominant basis of the economy and the major tax base. The Mughals had built an imperial road system, but it was used mainly for the movement of troops and supplies. Even so, it was not well maintained and became impassable in many sections, especially given the torrential rains of the annual monsoon. More important, Mughal economic policy concentrated heavily on obtaining revenue and far too little on maintaining or enhancing the system's ability to generate production or even to pay taxes. The state did almost nothing to increase irrigation, so badly needed in most of India, or to promote other agricultural improvements. Neglect of agriculture meant neglect of most of the country and its people.

Even before Aurangzeb, whatever wealth was left over after paying the staggering costs of military campaigns was used primarily for gorgeous display at the capital and the court and for monumental building. The Mughals were at war on a major basis for much more than half of the years between Babur's victory at Panipat in 1526 and Aurangzeb's death in 1707, and fighting continued into the 1750s. Even a prosperous and well-run system would have been fatally weakened by such an outpouring of treasure to no constructive result and by the large-scale devastation of the countryside over two centuries. (German development is said to have been set back 100 years by the Thirty Years War of 1618–1648.) The Indian economy was progressively drained, and almost nothing was put back into it, while even administration was increasingly neglected.

A CLOSER LOOK

Commerce at the Mughal Port of Surat

Ahmedabad, the capital of pre-Mughal Gujarat, served as the economic center for the collection and distribution of Gujarati cotton, which was transported overland to Surat, the dominant Mughal-era international port. Surat also served as the Indian base for pilgrimage to

Shah Jahan's Red Fort in Delhi, massively built of red sandstone, with the characteristic Mughal towers and domes. (Lindsay Hebberd/ Woodfin Camp & Associates)

Mecca. Surat's prosperity ultimately depended on Mughal protection and the commitment of Mughal rulers to allow it to run its affairs free of the state's intervention, but as the Mughal state's commercial partners.

Surat's hereditary merchant plutocracy, known collectively as the *mahajan* ("great men"), controlled local financial, commercial, and artisan activities, and their agents dominated the surrounding agricultural hinterland, ensuring a steady flow of raw cotton, indigo (a valuable blue-black textile dye), tobacco, foodstuffs, and craft products to Surat's merchant houses. Grain merchant/moneylenders controlled the resident laborers and artisans, who were organized into caste groups and craft guilds.

The elite of the community were the *sarafi,* commercial financiers, who represented family firms of Jains, Parsis, and Hindu Banias. In addition to transacting their own commercial affairs, sarafi and their broker representatives exchanged money, acted as paymasters, financed Mughal authorities and other merchants, provided insurance, and served as trustees for religious and charitable enterprises. Sarafi issued *hundi,* bills which were promissory notes guaranteeing payment over distance. These were discounted to cover interest, insurance, and the cost of the transmission of the monetary payment. Since the major sarafi houses had well-established branches or representatives in the major trade centers of India and Asia, they could send messages to their local agents instructing them to make payment or to invest the transferred sum in a specified business venture. This system eliminated the danger of transferring large sums of coinage or bullion and also avoided the loss of exchange value experienced between one monetary region and another.

At the top of Surat's merchant hierarchy was the *nagarsheth,* a chief merchant-prince who negotiated on the mahajan community's behalf with the Mughal government as well as foreign traders by establishing the terms by which they might participate in Surat's marketplace and predetermining the value of their merchandise. Major foreign merchants were assimilated as special members of the resident elite and were allowed the same rights and privileges as the merchant-princes as long as they lived by the community's rules.

Court life at Delhi and Agra was sumptuous and brilliant but expensive. Officials knew that their money and property would revert to the emperor when they died, and consequently they spent it freely in lavish conspicuous consumption, with stables full of Arabian horses and harems filled with dancing girls. Massive entertainments and banquets, complete with music, dance, and poetry readings, filled much of their time. Courtiers and the upper classes dressed in magnificent silk outfits or fine Kashmir wool in the brief northern winter, while the peasants wore coarse sackcloth woven from jute or locally made cottons. Indian cotton cloth won extensive overseas markets in the rest of Asia and much of Africa as well as in Europe; weavers benefited, but the state's tax collectors benefited still more.

For all the brilliant splendor of court life, however, science and technology were largely neglected after Akbar. What learning there was centered on the Koran and on the cultivation of the arts. There were no changes or improvements in the arts of production, and by the seventeenth century India had fallen behind Europe in science and technology and probably in the productivity of both agriculture and manufacturing, while at the same time bleeding from virtually continuous warfare. It is significant that while Shah Jahan was building the Taj Mahal at staggering expense, India suffered probably the worst famine in its history, from 1630 to 1632; between 1702 and 1703, in another famine that was nearly as bad, over 2 million people died while Aurangzeb was campaigning in the Deccan with a huge army and supply corps. The Mughals put peasant welfare low on their list of priorities, and Indians were overwhelmingly peasants.

Aurangzeb moved south in 1683, and for the rest of his life he ruled the empire and directed his military campaign from a new capital he established in the Deccan. Annual losses were estimated at 100,000 men and over 300,000 transport animals, mainly requisitioned from the peasantry. Continued Maratha raids sapped his forces, in addition to fierce southern resistance. After 1705 he seems to have spent most of his time reading and copying the Koran, preparing himself for death. Until then, he had refused to recognize the destructiveness of his policies. At least one anonymous letter reached him after he had restored the poll tax on Hindus; the letter read in part: "Your subjects are trampled underfoot; every province of your empire is impoverished; depopulation spreads and problems accumulate. . . . If your majesty places any faith in those books called divine, you will be instructed there that God is the God of all mankind, not the God of Muslims alone."[2] In 1705, he confessed to his son: "I came alone and I go as a stranger. I do not know who I am, or what I have been doing. I have sinned terribly and I do not know what punishment awaits me."[3] The Mughals had come full circle from the inspiring vision of Akbar to the nightmare of Aurangzeb. The effective power of the Mughals ended with Aurangzeb's death in 1707. India slowly dissolved into civil war, banditry, intergroup rivalry, and mounting chaos, a context that provided the English traders, present on the fringes for well over a century, with a path to ultimate power.

Aurangzeb's long reign spanned nearly 50 years, from 1658 to 1707. He was thus a contemporary of the Manchu emperor Kang Xi in China (Chapter 13), Louis XIV of France, the "Glorious Revolution" in England, Frederick I of Prussia, and Peter the Great of Russia. During these years Europe began its modern development of strong centralized states, continued its commercial and colonial expansion overseas, and rode a wave of unprecedented economic growth that was reflected in

Central India, in the Vindhya mountains. Terrain like this kept successive northern-based efforts, including Aurangzeb's, from conquering or holding the south. (R. Murphey)

the beginnings of major population increases. Manchu China in Aurangzeb's time also saw a boom period of prosperity and vigorous economic growth, with major increases in trade and at least a doubling of agricultural output and population. The modern agricultural revolution was beginning at the same time in Europe, and the foundations were laid for the later Industrial Revolution. European science and technology leaped ahead of the rest of the world with the pioneering discoveries of scientists like Isaac Newton and Robert Boyle, early figures in the European Age of Reason and the Enlightenment. Europe developed in these years a lead that was to widen greatly in subsequent centuries.

If Akbar's open-minded curiosity and zeal for learning and experimentation had prevailed into Aurangzeb's time, India might have taken part in or at least benefited from these important advances. The early European visitors to India had, like Marco Polo, been drawn to and impressed by its wealth and sophistication. In Akbar's time there seems little question that India was at least on a par with Europe and China technologically, economically, and politically. But Jahangir and Shah Jahan were preoccupied with the pleasures of the court, monumental building, and intrigue, and Aurangzeb was a single-minded zealot who cared nothing for the material welfare of his people and bled the empire to finance his wars. Instead of scholars, as at Akbar's court, Aurangzeb surrounded himself with sycophants, servile yes-men who dared not disagree or suggest alternatives and who flattered the emperor into thinking that he and his empire led the world. He did not deign to correspond with other monarchs, as Akbar had done, or to take an interest in anything but his endless military campaigns in the name of Islam, to impose his tyrannical rule over all of India, a goal he never achieved. By the time of his death, much of India was economically and politically a shambles, and technological development was nonexistent. This was to prove a fatal combination of weaknesses, resulting in a situation of virtual anarchy where the now far more effective and technologically advanced Europeans were able to establish footholds from which their power in India would grow.

The custom of *purdah*, the veiling of women in public now became nearly universal in the north, even for Hindus, while the south remained free. However, among the Rajputs, and even more the Sikhs, women were also free of such restrictions and often played an active public role. Among the nomads of central Asia, despite their generally warlike culture, although women did not take part in fighting, women were never veiled and took a more active part in the life of the tribe. The Marathas, fighting in defense of Hindu India against the tyranny of Aurangzeb, were led after the death of Shivaji by the Tara Bai, a fearless female cavalry commander who rode astride like a man and struck terror into the hearts of the Mughal opponents.

Central Asia

Like China but to an even greater degree, India was chronically involved with invasion and conquest from the great Central Asian steppe area. Although there were many short-lived dynasties of conquest in China, only the Mongols and the Manchus conquered more than a small part of the north. India, however, suffered repeated invasions by steppe nomads, beginning with the Aryans from Central Asia and Iran, various Persian groups at different periods, a Mongol invasion, and, beginning in the tenth century C.E., successive waves of primarily Turkish invaders from Central Asia (including Afghanistan), which progressively conquered most of the north. Turco-Afghan conquests culminated in the Mughal Empire, which also brought in a fresh wave of Persian influence and culture. Both China and India

have also been closely involved with Tibet, to which Buddhism and trade spread from India, as they also did from China, and in which both countries have maintained a proprietary interest, although only China since the Manchu dynasty has established direct political control over Tibet.

The history of both countries cannot be fully understood without some knowledge of Central Asia and its people. The relative poverty of the steppe economy chronically tempted the nomads to raid and invade the rich agricultural areas of adjacent China and India. Despite their small numbers, their use of horse cavalry tactics made them formidable militarily. In addition, trade routes across the Central Asian steppes were of major importance, for this was where most contact between India and China took place; nearly all of it was indirect and depended on Central Asian intermediaries, as in the transmission of Buddhism and its associated art forms from India to China. Finally, Central Asia and its people and history are important for themselves, and no history of Asia would be complete without some attention to them. These Central Asian people were preliterate (until a few acquired literacy from surrounding cultures), and hence most of their history is recorded only in terms of their interactions with the sedentary cultures around them, most importantly China and India. What we know about them is based largely on the descriptions of outsiders.

The world's largest area of semiarid steppe and true desert covers the middle of the Eurasian continent, from the Ukraine and what is now Turkey across the southern half of the former Soviet Union, most of Iran, Afghanistan, and what is now Pakistan, the Mongolian People's Republic, and most of China north of the central Liao Valley of Manchuria and east of about 75° east longitude. On climatic and vegetational grounds, Tibet belongs in the same category of steppe-desert, although its physical environment is conditioned by high altitude. Throughout most of this vast Eurasian area, permanent field agriculture is possible only in a few favored spots where water is available as supplemental irrigation, as in the few widely scattered oases.

Nomadic Lifestyle

Traditionally, nearly all of this immense region has been occupied by a variety of peoples, most importantly Turkish and Mongol, who supported themselves primarily by nomadic pastoralism, using animals to extract sustenance from grazing on the steppe and living in turn on their milk and meat. Many of the pastoral nomads of Central Asia scorned all agriculture and those who practiced it. This view seems to have been most true of the Mongols, who associated all farming with their traditionally despised Chinese enemies and regarded settled agriculture and all sedentary lifestyles as equivalent to slavery, preferring the free life of the open steppes—and the relative anarchy that often resulted from individual and group resistance to direction or control, even in cooperative efforts for the common good.

The typical pastoral nomad grouping was the tribe, and although many tribes might share a common language, racial stock, and culture, the normal form of interaction among them was rivalry, competition, and periodic warfare. Turks, Mongols, and other tribes sometimes operated together against other nomad groups or, as in the cases of the Seljuk and Ottoman Turks, the Mongols of Chinghis Khan's time, and the Manchus under Nurhachi's leadership (see Chapter 11), banded together in pursuit of wider conquest. Most conflicts, however, took place between much smaller tribal groups and commonly centered on disputes over

grazing rights. Grass was the indispensable and finite resource of all pastoral nomads, the means for sustaining the herds on which they lived. Each pastoral tribe worked out over time a more or less fixed pattern of movement whereby individual pasturage areas would be grazed only as frequently as was compatible with the maintenance of a permanent yield.

Because of such land-use patterns, any one part of a tribe's claimed grazing areas as part of their seasonal, annual, or multiannual rotation would be out of use for long periods of time, sometimes for several years, while the tribe and its herds might be literally hundreds of miles away. Such absence inevitably invited poaching by other tribes and resulted in chronic small-scale warfare, since the preservation of claims to grazing rights was truly a matter of life or death for the tribe and its herds. As with arid and semiarid areas

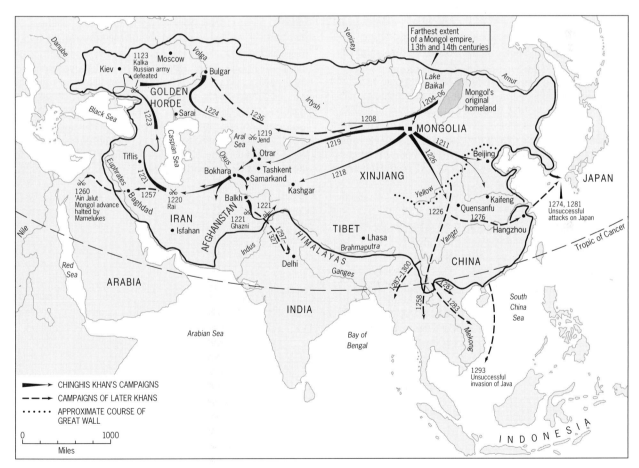

Central Asia and the Mongol Empire

The vast extent of the Mongol conquests is to some extent misleading since they lasted only for a few years, destroyed largely by fighting among the Mongol clans. But for a brief interval most of Eurasia was under their control, and the Pax Tartarica, as it was called, enabled Marco Polo and several other Europeans to reach China.

everywhere, rainfall may vary as much as 40 percent from year to year. The severe limitations of the environment, the low productivity of pastoral nomadism, and the chronic intertribal fighting kept the human populations at very low levels. The Mongol tribes consolidated by Chinghis Khan in the twelfth century appear to have amounted to at most 1 million people, about the same total as in the early twentieth century, in an overall area almost as large as western Europe. The population figures are similar for Tibet, only slightly smaller in size and similarly dependent largely on pastoral nomadism. Turkish tribes probably totaled only a little more.

The animals that made the pastoral nomadic way of life possible were primarily sheep and goats, native to the Central Asian steppe and very little altered from their wild forms. They were often hybrid mixtures that, like these species everywhere, were able to survive on far sparser and less nutritious or luxuriant pasturage than would be needed to sustain cattle. Given their grazing habits, however, especially their close cropping, they would quickly exhaust the pasturage and had to be moved on before they destroyed its capacity to recover.

Horses and camels were kept for riding and as carriers. It was earlier farming communities rather than pastoral nomads that first trained the horse to pull loads, using some sort of harness, perhaps as early as the third millennium B.C.E. Probably only much later did farming communities train the horse for riding. The emergence of pastoral nomadism is observable indirectly through its interactions with the sedentary agrarian communities on the margins of Central Asia—China, India, Sumer, Babylonia, and Egypt—in the course of the second and first millennia B.C.E. By about 2000 B.C.E., with the migration of early Indo-European groups both eastward and westward from their area of origin in Central Asia, perhaps in what is now Iran, pastoral nomadic peoples invaded westward into Sumer and Egypt and eastward as the Aryans who entered India. By the time of their invasions they were using the light, fast war chariot with charioteer and warrior, drawn by one or two horses, a weapon that struck terror into the opposing armies.

The role of the horse for the nomads was primarily as an aid in herding and driving their animals in their cyclical search for pasture. Sheep move very slowly but can be hastened by a mounted rider, who can also mount mobile guard against predators and scout the route ahead. The pastoral nomads became masters of horse riding and horse breeding and brought the art of horsemanship to its peak of perfection. Males (and rarely, females) spent most of their waking hours from an early age in the saddle; horses were almost as valuable or vital as the flocks they tended. The so-called Mongol horse, or steppe pony, made up for its small size by extreme hardiness, especially since it was very little bred away from its wild origins on the eastern steppe by mixtures with other subspecies. It could survive on a lower quality and quantity of grass, and its shaggy coat and general endurance helped it to withstand the harsh winters of extreme cold and high winds characteristic of its native habitat. The invention of the breast strap beginning about the fourth century B.C.E.

The Mongols in Battle

Marco Polo gave this description of battle with the Mongols.

> They never mix with the enemy, but keep hovering about him, discharging their arrows first from one side and then from the other, occasionally pretending to fly, and during their flight shooting arrows backwards at their pursuers, killing men and horses. . . . In this sort of warfare the adversary imagines that he has gained a victory, when in fact he has lost the battle; for the Tartars, observing the mischief they have done him, wheel about and, renewing the fight, overpower his remaining troops and make them prisoners in spite of their utmost exertions. Their horses are so well broken-in to quick changes of movement that upon the signal given, they instantly turn in any direction; and by these rapid maneuvers many victories have been obtained.

Source: M. Komroff, ed., *The Travels of Marco Polo* (Garden City, NY: Doubleday, 1930), p. 95.

and of the horse collar soon after the fifth century C.E., both in China, greatly increased the animal's usefulness for draft purposes, but the major spurt in horse-riding technology came with the invention of the stirrup in Zhou dynasty China, and probably independently by Central Asian Turks and/or the Kushan invaders of India in the first century B.C.E. The stirrup enabled the rider to load, aim, and fire at a gallop, to stand and fire sideways or even backward, the so-called Parthian shot. They also mastered the technique of firing volleys on command by wheeling companies of mounted archers.

Mounted archery became the principal military weapon of the nomads, used with great skill and with devastating effect by warriors who were also consummate horsemen. The bow was adapted for use on horseback by making it in so-called compound form, a double reflex in the shape of a Cupid's bow, which made it much shorter and hence more manageable on horseback but without any significant loss of firepower, range, or accuracy. Like the original domestication of the horse and its training for draft and riding, the compound bow was an invention of the sedentary peoples, appearing in China as early as the second millennium B.C.E. The bows were composites of laminated wood, horn, and sinew, materials readily available to the nomads.

Throughout Central Asia the camel was also used, not in general for herding but for carrying and for travel. Camels were native to Central Asia and wonderfully adapted to its harsh environment. They are, of course, known for their ability to live without water or food for extended periods by drawing on and oxidizing fat stored in their humps, but they can also subsist at least for a time on thorny, tough, or bitter vegetation and on brackish water that is rejected even by goats. Their soft, splayed feet enable them to walk more easily in loose or deep sand. The camel also has a secondary transparent eyelid so that it can see in the frequent dust or sandstorms without being blinded. This was the dominant carrier of trade within and across Central Asia, for which its qualities and its larger carrying capacity fit it far better than the horse. The Arabs and Turks also used camels as military cavalry, although such use was less common with the nomads of eastern Eurasia. Camel meat and milk occasionally were added to the diet, and their hides were used or sold, but they were not kept primarily for such purposes.

The Steppe and the Sown

The Chinese persisted in their efforts to extend agriculture out into their steppe borderlands, often in defiance of what the environment, unaided by modern techniques of irrigation, could in the long run sustain. Along

In the steppes and mountains of Central Asia. A barren landscape, suited to camels but not to dense or productive populations. It is easy to see why so many Central Asian groups were tempted to invade India or China. This scene is in Afghanistan. (R. Murphey)

many of the borders of Central Asia, the environmental zone between areas where agriculture is possible and those where it cannot be permanently successful under conditions of traditional technology is in fact quite broad. Across the zone the contest between pastoral nomadism and sedentary agriculture has flowed back and forth over the millennia since the emergence of nomadism. It has been resolved resoundingly in favor of agriculture, backed by the support structures of the modern state, only in the course of the past century and with the advent of new technology: railways, roads, power equipment, dams, pumps, canals, new agronomic techniques, and the enhanced power of national and international markets.

It was of course through this traditionally contested zone that the Great Wall of China was built, not primarily as a military barrier—in any case it proved all too permeable—but as a line of demarcation between the steppe and the sown, between the territory of the nomadic pastoralist and that of the imperial Chinese state. Inside the wall, Chinese jurisdiction and Chinese standards held sway; outside it, Chinese authority rapidly waned, and those who went beyond the wall did so at their own risk. It is not surprising that there were in fact a series of walls, begun some centuries before Qin Shi Huang Di's consolidation of the late third century B.C.E., which attempted to mark such a line in what is better seen as a zone. Settlements and walls farther out, built in years of good rainfall, were progressively abandoned as rainfall patterns reasserted their long-term average and left Chinese farming colonies that had been unwisely extended too far to wither, or to be abandoned. The remaining Great Wall, extensively rebuilt under the Ming in the fifteenth century C.E., represents a reasonable average of the shifting line marking the practicable limits of permanent agriculture without extensive irrigation based on modern technology. India's wall was the towering and largely unbroken mountain ranges—Hindu Kush, Sulaiman, Karakoram, and Himalaya—that form the subcontinent's northern and northwestern borders.

Relations between the pastoral nomads and the sedentary peoples around them were seldom cordial and usually mutually hostile. The nomads tried for the most part to minimize their dependence on trade or barter, but they had to look to the agricultural areas for most of their supplies of grain, salt, metal and metal goods (though some nomadic groups occasionally mined, smelted, and made their own, or employed foreign smiths or metallurgists to do so), and later tea and porcelain. To pay for what they needed, the nomads bartered wool, hides, horses, camels, other livestock, and sometimes furs. The surrounding sedentary empires had an almost inexhaustible appetite for horses, predominantly for military purposes; they were never able to breed enough themselves, whereas the steppe was the natural breeding ground.

Nomad Warriors

It was tempting to the nomads—Turks, Arabs, or Mongols—with their ability to move and to strike quickly, to simply take what they needed from the agricultural areas along their borders, or to raid the trade caravans that ran through their domains, carrying high-value goods like silk, gold, or lacquer that could in turn be bartered for more mundane necessities. Within their steppe-desert world were also the scattered oases, some of them relatively large but all highly productive and with markets crowded with a wide variety of goods. There, too, the nomads could often obtain what they wanted by lightning raids. Hit-and-run attacks on the settled farming communities on the edge of the steppe and along the trade routes that ran through it brought them into chronic conflict with the sedentary empires around them. In this contest the nomads usually had the upper hand.

Their great weapon was their mobility, and hence unpredictability, through the striking power of their mounted warriors. Mobility and horsemanship were their basic way of life, and after the invention of the stirrup and the perfection of their cavalry tactics they were often irresistible in the short, sharp engagements that they could plan for times and places of their own choosing. The vastly superior forces of the sedentary empires, with their dependence on supply trains and on grain or fodder and water for their heavier and more numerous horses and soldiers, were at a crippling disadvantage out on the steppe. The nomads defended themselves against counterattacks, punitive expeditions, or efforts to subdue them by drawing their opponents' armies far out onto the grasslands away from their supply bases and then surrounding them or cutting them off. Successive Chinese armies, greatly superior in numbers and striking power, were annihilated in this way, from the time of the Xiongnu battles against the Han into the mid-Qing dynasty of the eighteenth century, when the Mongol power was finally destroyed in the campaigns of Qian Long (see Chapter 13). Shah Jahan's efforts to reconquer Afghanistan and the former Mughal domains in Central Asia met a similar fate.

The nomads produced their own bows and arrows, often made by each warrior for himself, and they often did not have (and hence were not encumbered by) swords or spears. Each cavalry charge could be planned and manipulated so that horses and men moved in response to signal flags and hence could be adjusted in their maneuvers as the battle developed.

Each rider could discharge a volley of four or five arrows at short range and at high velocity while moving at high speed. They would then wheel away in unison and reload their stock of arrows, return for another charge, and then retreat to their own lines, passing on the way a fresh contingent of their companions with full quivers. The nomads would often seek to draw their opponents out in pursuit and would then turn in their saddles and shoot their pursuers or lead them into an ambush or to the nomads' own lines, where freshly mounted and armed warriors could confront them or cut them off. In any such battle of rapid movement, the nomads had the advantage, but most of their conquests were short-lived, and in time they tended to be absorbed into the far greater mass of Indian or Chinese civilizations.

Inner Mongolia has been absorbed by the modern Chinese state, as has Manchuria, and in both areas Han Chinese have become the overwhelming majority of the population. Xinjiang was repeatedly conquered by China, but its Turkish inhabitants (Uighurs, Kazaks, Khirghiz) remained dominant until the influx of Chinese settlement after 1949. After a long history of raiding and counterraiding, revolt and reconquest, and of the encroachment of Chinese agricultural settlement in the eastern approaches, Tibet was finally subdued by the Qing dynasty in the eighteenth century but nevertheless retained into the 1950s its traditional culture and Lamaistic Buddhist theocratic government. Until then,

for example, half the adult male population were Buddhist monks living in vast monasteries; but the economic level of the population was low. Tibetan revolts against the efforts of the new Communist government of China to reclaim its imperial heritage led to brutal Chinese repression, which still continues. Though they are clearly a separate people, Tibetans have been overwhelmed by the modern Chinese state, so much more powerful than in the past, as have the Mongols, Manchus, and Turkic people of Xinjiang. Their modern fate parallels that of other Central Asian peoples farther west, who have been overwhelmed by the modern Russian state. This also parallels U.S. history, as the American Indians and their cultures were conquered and absorbed by the rise of the United States.

By the late seventeenth century the Safavids of Iran as well as the Mughals were in chaos. The Safavid dynasty collapsed in 1736. In India the Mughals after the death of Aurangzeb in 1707 were increasingly reduced to impotence and ruled only nominally over a progressively shrinking part of northern India. After the death of the emperor Akbar in 1605, his successors were more preoccupied with court life than with affairs of state. Aurangzeb (1658–1707) drained India in endless warfare in the name of Islam. So weak was India that in 1739 an Iranian army not only defeated the Mughal emperor but stole the Peacock Throne (later captured by the Ottomans and taken to Istanbul). Thus, the sixteenth-

The Potala Palace in Lhasa, Tibet, the residence of the Dalai Lama until 1959. (Sovfoto/Eastfoto)

century flowering of western and south-Central Asia had turned to decline, and in India's case to genuine disaster, by the eighteenth century.

The French traveler François Bernier, who visited India in Aurangzeb's time, reported that the emperor complained to him, after belatedly realizing the potential strength of the Europeans, that his tutor had told him, "The whole of Feringustan [Europe] was no more than some inconsiderable island, that its kings resembled petty rajahs, and that the potentates of Hindustan eclipsed the glory of all other kings."[4] This may not have been, for all its sycophant overtones, a grossly inaccurate description, but it did of course help to blind Indians to the danger posed by the Western presence. Their innate sense of cultural superiority was to remain both an obstacle to rational adjustment to changed circumstances and a prop for their wounded egos. Bernier's contemporary, the Italian traveler in India Nicolo Manucci, recorded his impression that Indians believed Europeans "have no polite manners, that they are ignorant, wanting in ordered life, and very dirty."[5] This too had considerable truth in it, especially the last point, which shocked Indians, given their scrupulous attention to daily washing and toothbrushing, habits that did not become European practice until well into the nineteenth century. Crude and dirty or not, the Europeans were fast becoming the most effective groups in India, given the ruin of the Mughals and the disorganization of the Marathas or other possible Indian orders. The way was open for the rise of a British-dominated India.

Questions

1. How did the differing administrative styles and values of Akbar and Aurangzeb have different political results?

2. How did the Afghan Mughals reflect their Central Asian roots? How was this both an advantage and disadvantage as they ruled India? How was this specifically demonstrated in repeated Mughal succession crises and their consequences?

3. In what ways did Mughal architecture deviate as well as remain consistent with Islamic standards?

4. Why were the Rajputs, Sikhs, and Marathas effective against Aurangzeb?

5. What Mughal economic policies were detrimental to their subject populations. How did this contribute to the Europeans passing India's level of technology and economic productivity?

6. How did the Mughal obsession with conquest in the Deccan demonstrate the dangers of unrestrained military expenditure, on the local quality of life as well as the ability of political elite to maintain their authority?

7. How did commerce at the Mughal port of Surat reflect the strengths and weaknesses of the Asian economic system in the sixteenth and seventeenth centuries?

Notes

1. D. P. Singhal, *A History of the Indian People* (London: Methuen, 1983), p. 206.

2. J. Sarkar, *History of Aurangzeb*, vol. 3 (Bombay: Orient Longman, 1972), p. 34.

3. W. Hansen, *The Peacock Throne* (New York: Holt, Rinehart and Winston, 1972), p. 485.

4. R. Murphey, *The Outsiders: The Western Experience in India and China* (Ann Arbor: University of Michigan Press, 1977), p. 54.

5. Ibid.

Suggested Web Sites

The Mughal Empire and Mughal Monarchs

http://www.sscnet.ucla.edu/southasia/History/Mughals/ mughals.html

http://rubens.anu.edu.au/student.projects/tajmahal/ mughal.html

http://www.wsu.edu:8080/~dee/MUGHAL/ MUGHAL.HTM

http://www.edwebproject.org/india/mughals.html
Maps, portraits, and information on the lives of the Mughal rulers and the cultural history of India during the Mughal Empire.

Central Asia

http://vlib.iue.it/history/asia/central_asia.html
Dedicated to the countries of Central Asia, with comprehensive links to view maps, images, documents, and literature from Central Asia.

http://www.oxuscom.com/cahist1.htm

http://www.oxuscom.com/cahist2.htm
Chronologies of Central Asian history from earliest times to the present.

http://spotlightongames.com/background/emw.html
Detailed eighteen-page timeline of Central Asia during the Tang dynasty.

http://oxuscom.com/timursam.htm
Discussion (with photos) of the major architecture in Samarkand during the Timurid dynasty.

Suggestions for Further Reading

Mughal India

Bernier, F. *Travels in the Mughal Empire*, trans. A. Constable. London: Pickering, 1934.

Blake, S. P. *Shajahanabad: The Sovereign City in Mughal India*. Cambridge, England: Cambridge University Press, 1991.

Cole, D., and Sambhi, P. S. *The Sikhs*. London: Routledge, 1978.

Findly, E. B. *Nur Jahan*. New York: Oxford University Press, 1993.

Gascoigne, B. *The Great Moghuls*. New York: Harper and Row, 1972.

Goalen, P. *From Mughal Empire to British Raj*. Cambridge, England: Cambridge University Press, 1993.

Gordon, S. *The Marathas*. Cambridge, England: Cambridge University Press, 1993.

Habib, I. *The Agrarian System of Mughal India, 1556–1707*. New York: Asia Publishing House, 1963.

Habib, I., et al. *The Cambridge Economic History of India*, vol. 1: 1200–1750. Cambridge, England: Cambridge University Press, 1982.

Hintze, A. *The Mughal Empire and Its Decline*. Cambridge, England: Cambridge University Press, 1998.

Laine, J. W., *Shivaji*. Oxford: Oxford University Press, 2003.

McLeod, W. H. *The Sikhs*. New York: Columbia University Press, 1989.

Prawdin, M. *Builders of the Mughal Empire*. New York: Allen and Unwin, 1963.

Richards, J. F. *The Mughal Empire*. Cambridge, England: Cambridge University Press, 1993.

Sakar, J. *A Short History of Aurangzeb*. Calcutta: M. C. Sarkar, 1962.

Shalat, J. M. *Akbar*. Bombay: Bharatiya Bidya Bhavan, 1964.

Singhal, D. P. *A History of the Indian People*. London: Methuen, 1983.

Subrahmanyam, S. *The Political Economy of Commerce: Southern India 1500–1650*. Cambridge, England: Cambridge University Press, 1990.

Central Asia

Adshead, S. *Central Asia in World History*. New York: St. Martin's, 1993.

Barfield, T. J. *The Perilous Frontier: Nomadic Empires and China*. Oxford: Blackwell, 1989.

Beckwith, C. I. *The Tibetan Empire in Central Asia*. Princeton: Princeton University Press, 1987.

Di Cosmo, N. *Warfare in Inner Asia*. Boston: Brill, 2002.

Jagchid, S., and Symons, V. J. *Peace, War, and Trade Along the Great Wall*. Bloomington: Indiana University Press, 1990.

Khazanow, A. M. *Nomads and the Outside World*. Cambridge, England: Cambridge University Press, 1984.

Kwanten, L. *Imperial Nomads: A History of Central Asia*. Philadelphia: University of Pennsylvania Press, 1979.

Litvinsky, A., ed. *Crossroads of Civilization*. New York: St. Martin's, 1993.

Manz, B. F. *The Rise and Rule of Tamerlane*. Cambridge, England: Cambridge University Press, 1990.

Mcleod, W. H., *Sikhs and Sikhism*. Oxford: Oxford University Press, 2004.

Morgan, D. *The Mongols*. Oxford: Blackwell, 1986.

Philips, E. D. *The Royal Hordes: Nomad Peoples of the Steppe*. London: Thames and Hudson, 1965.

Richardson, H. E. *Tibet and Its History*, 2d ed. New York: Random House, 1990.

Rossabi, M. *China and Inner Asia*. New York: Pica Press, 1975.

Sinor, D., ed. *The Cambridge History of Central Asia*. Cambridge, England: Cambridge University Press, 1990.

Trippet, F. *The First Horsemen*. New York: Time-Life Books, 1974.

11

New Imperial Splendor in China: The Ming Dynasty

With the expulsion of the Mongols in the mid-fourteenth century, the Chinese imperial tradition was reasserted with the founding of the Ming dynasty in 1368. Pride in regained power and wealth led to the building of magnificent new capitals, first at Nanjing and then at Beijing, as well as to the resumption of the tributary system whereby lesser Asian states sent regular missions to China, acknowledging its superiority and prostrating themselves before the Son of Heaven. Ming armies reconquered much of the empire of the Tang and the Song, and early in the dynasty a series of seven naval expeditions toured Southeast Asia, India, the Persian Gulf, and as far as the east coast of Africa, acquiring new tributaries, trading in Chinese products, and bringing back curiosities from afar. The growing commercialization of the economy, aided from the sixteenth century by imports of silver from the Spanish New World, greatly stimulated urban growth and a rich merchant culture. Literature, philosophy, and the arts flourished, and popular culture also expanded into vernacular writing, opera, plays, and woodblock prints.

For at least its first two centuries Ming administration was effective and the country was prosperous. But the dynasty became increasingly conservative and traditional. It was plagued by court intrigues, and a series of weak emperors sapped its vigor. Popular unrest mounted as government became less and less able to provide an equitable order or to move with the times. Rebels took Beijing and then were replaced by a new set of alien conquerors, the Manchus from Manchuria, who inaugurated the Qing dynasty in 1644. Manchu rule nevertheless rested consciously and purposefully on the Ming heritage, and most of the trends that began under the Ming continued with little break once order was restored.

The Founding of the Ming

By the early 1300s Mongol control of China was weakening under the ineffective successors of Kubilai Khan (died 1294). Mongol power was enfeebled by chronic feuding within the imperial clan and pressures from rival clans, and by 1330 there was open civil war. Beginning in 1333 successive drought-induced famines wracked northern China, worsened by unchecked flooding in the Yellow River where the dikes had been neglected. Most Chinese interpreted these natural disasters as portents of divine displeasure and the loss of the mandate of Heaven by the Yuan dynasty, a response typical of the declining years of all previous dynasties but further fed in this case by bitter Chinese hatred of the alien Mongols and their oppressive rule.

Banditry and rebellion spread rapidly in nearly every province, and rebel leaders vied for Heaven's mandate in efforts to eliminate their rivals. Many rebel groups were aided by or belonged to secret societies, which recruited supporters from among poor peasants and drew on anti-Mongol sentiment. The most important of these was the White Lotus, a Buddhist sect originating in the Southern Song period that consistently opposed the ruling dynasty and hence had to remain secret, with its own private rituals. The White Lotus, which was most active in the Yangzi Valley, persisted underground or in association with banditry and rebellion until the twentieth century. Another Buddhist secret society that dated back to the Song was the Red Turbans, so called for their distinctive headdress; they played a major role in the lower Yellow River plain.

One of the rebel leaders, Zhu Yuanzhang (1328–1398), rose to a commanding position in the 1350s and went on

to found a new dynasty. His forces swept the Yangzi Valley by the end of the decade, set up a government at Nanjing in 1356, and in 1368 captured Beijing, proclaiming the Ming ("brilliant") dynasty, which was to last until 1644. The Ming achievement in rebuilding the empire and restoring Chinese pride ushered in a period of unprecedented economic and cultural growth, on Song foundations but going far beyond where the Song had left off. The population probably rose by at least 50 percent by the end of the dynasty, stimulated by major improvements in agricultural technology promoted by the state. There was also rapid commercialization of the economy as a whole, an accompanying rise in the number and size of cities, and perhaps a doubling of total trade.

A CLOSER LOOK

Hongwu: The Rebel Emperor

Zhu Yuanzhang, the victorious rebel leader who became the first Ming emperor, took the name Hongwu ("great military power"); he is known mainly by this name and by his official dynastic title Ming Taizu ("Great Progenitor"). Life had been hard for him up to that point. Like Liu Bang, the founder of the Han dynasty, he had been born a peasant, in 1328. Orphaned early in life he entered a Buddhist monastery, where he became literate, and at age 25 joined a rebel band, where his native ability soon brought him to the top. As emperor his strong personality and high intelligence made a deep and lasting impression on the first two centuries of the Ming, whose foundations he largely built. He was an indefatigable worker, concerned with all the details of administering his new empire, but he had few close associates or friends and led an austere

lifestyle that reflected his difficult and impoverished youth. He was notoriously frugal and often a pinchpenny in his disapproval of expenditures proposed by others. Having risen to power over rebel rivals, he became paranoid about supposed plots against him and was given to violent rages of temper during which he often ordered harsh punishments or tortures for suspected disloyalty or trivial offenses.

Irritated by continued Japanese piracy along the China coast, Hongwu also wrote to the Ashikaga shogun (see Chapter 9): "You stupid eastern barbarians! Living so far across the sea . . . you are haughty and disloyal; you permit your subjects to do evil." The Japanese replied, two years later, in a more Confucian mode, but doubtless partly tongue in cheek: "Heaven and earth are vast. They are not monopolized by one ruler."[1] Hong Wu's reaction, perhaps fortunately, is not recorded. In his last will, he wrote of himself: "For 31 years I have labored to discharge Heaven's will, tormented by worries and fears, without relaxing for a day."[2] One wonders if he thought that the winning of the Dragon Throne had really been worth it!

Hongwu increasingly concentrated power in his own hands, trusting no one, and in 1380 abolished the Imperial Secretariat, which had been the main central administrative body under dynasties of the past, after suppressing a plot for which he blamed his chief minister. The emperor's role thus became even more autocratic, although Hongwu necessarily continued to use what were called the "grand secretaries" to assist with the immense paperwork of the bureaucracy: memorials (petitions and recommendations to the throne), imperial edicts in reply, reports of various kinds, and tax records.

This group was later more regularly established as the Grand Secretariat, a kind of cabinet, but in Hongwu's time he supervised everything and made or approved all decisions. He was concerned about the power of the eunuchs, remembering the trouble they had often caused in earlier dynasties, and erected a tablet in the palace that read, "Eunuchs must have nothing to do with administration."[3] He greatly reduced their numbers, forbade them to handle documents, insisted that they remain illiterate, and got rid of those who so far forgot themselves as to offer comments on government matters. Some eunuchs were considered necessary as guards and attendants for the imperial harem, which the emperor was thought to need so as to ensure male heirs. In time the eunuchs were to reemerge as closely connected and scheming insiders at court, until in later Ming they were once more a scourge of good government.

One policy of Hongwu's that shocked the Confucians was his resumption of the Mongol practice of having officials publicly beaten when they had

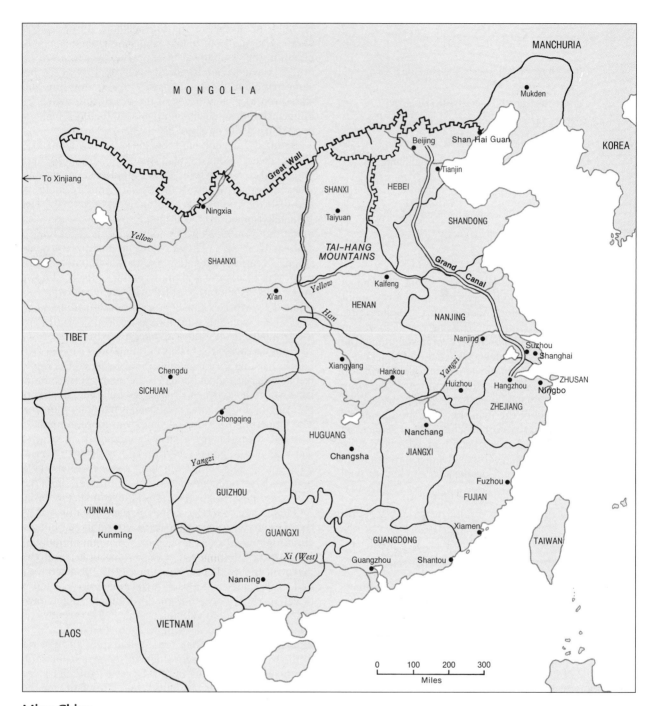

Ming China

Note the new Great Wall, rebuilt by the Ming, and the restored Grand Canal. The arrangement and naming of provinces differ somewhat from the contemporary forms.

The emperor Hongwu (1328–1398), also known more formally as Taizu ("Great Progenitor"), in a caricature by an unknown fifteenth-century artist, one of a series of caricatures of notable emperors. Hongwu's rather piglike face, commented on by many of his contemporaries, was pockmarked from smallpox, which had nearly killed him as a young man. The caricature conveys Hongwu's forceful personality. (National Palace Museum, Taipei, Taiwan)

throughout the empire and along the frontiers. While some of his policies seemed extreme to many and his personality forbidding or fearsome, rather than benevolent according to the Confucian ideal, Hongwu was a strong emperor whose work provided the Ming with a momentum of imperial power and effectiveness that lasted far beyond his time. His concentration of power in the emperor's personal hands worked well when the emperor was as able and dedicated as he was. When weaker and less conscientious men occupied the throne, the empire was in trouble, as was to happen disastrously in the last decades of Ming rule. To be successful, despotism had to be enlightened; the late Ming emperors were no match for Hongwu.

When Hongwu died in 1398 the provinces within the Great Wall were secure and Chinese power was again dominant in eastern Xinjiang, Inner Mongolia, and southern Manchuria. Vietnam, Tibet, Korea, and Japan accepted tributary status. Hongwu built a splendid new capital at Nanjing with a city wall 60 feet high and 20 miles around, the longest city wall in the world, intended like most Chinese city walls more as a symbolic affirmation of imperial power than for defense. Indeed, the Chinese word for city also means "wall," to distinguish it from a mere town. Beijing was passed over to begin with as a capital because of its association with the Mongols and its location on the northern fringe of the country, far from major trade routes and unable to feed itself in this semiarid area on the edge of Mongolia. The Yangzi Valley had long been the economic heart of the empire, and it made sense to put the capital there.

The second Ming emperor, Yongle (r. 1403–1424), was also an able and conscientious administrator. Continued prosperity, plus the new southern emphasis of the Ming, stimulated the further expansion of trade, including its maritime extensions. Commerce and city life grew rapidly. Ports on the southeast coast acquired new importance as links with the colonies of overseas Chinese in Java, the Philippines, Vietnam, and elsewhere in Southeast Asia.

displeased him. Confucian doctrine held that corporal punishment was only for the ignorant masses; the "superior man" was to be exempt because one could reason with him and expect him to mend his ways by following the virtuous example of those above him. Hongwu was a tough ruler and demanded complete submission despite his praise for the Confucian classics, which he saw as a prop for the state. But as a peasant by birth, he never lost his envy and distrust of intellectuals. He also reorganized the army around a new system of elite guard units stationed at strategic points

The Ming Tributary System

To mark the resurgence of empire after the brief Mongol eclipse, the traditional tributary system was enlarged and made more formal. This was mainly a device to feed the Chinese ego, but it also helped to keep peace along the extensive borders and to assert Chinese overlordship. In theory, Chinese political and cultural superiority was a magnet for all lesser peoples or states, who would willingly acknowledge its greatness and model themselves on it, "yearning for civilization," as the official Chinese phrase put it. In practice, there was just enough truth in this to warrant saying it. Although, of course, non-Chinese states and cultures had their own pride and their own sense of superiority, like all peoples, all of them also freely recognized that Chinese civilization was more advanced than their own and had a great deal to offer them, in trade, culture, and technology. The Chinese capital and other cities were exciting and profitable places to visit, and near neighbors such as Korea or Vietnam, and later Burma, Laos, Tibet, and even Mongolia, had reason to fear Chinese military power and hence to accept tributary status. Recognizing China's supremacy cost them little; as long as they did not try to challenge it, they were left to manage their own affairs.

The required ritual obeisance to the Son of Heaven was probably not seen as humiliating but in keeping with the way in which they had to deal with their own monarchs at home, and in any case the proper way to behave before any exalted person. Once that was completed, they could learn and profit and return home without feeling they had given anything away, since their own states were in fact fully sovereign. Tributary states sent regular missions every few years to the imperial capital, where they kneeled before the Son of Heaven in a series of prescribed prostrations known as the *ketou* (later Westernized as *kowtow*, literally "bang head," on the floor, as a token of respect). They presented a long list of "gifts" and in return were given "presents," which were often greater in value and amount. The missions were in part really a polite cloak for trade, combining mutual benefit with diplomacy and the prestige of association with the Celestial Empire. It also fed the Chinese bias about themselves as the only imperium, the only true civilization, the center of the world, compared with which all other people were mere barbarians. This was a long-standing attitude since at least Han times, when the tribute system that reflected it included over 50 Central Asian "barbarian" states.

At its height, first under the Ming and later in early Qing, the tributary system involved over 40 states, including Korea, Vietnam, Tibet, Japan, Java, the Philippines, Burma, Siam, Ceylon, Malacca, and a number of others, in addition to many Central Asian kingdoms. The renewed Chinese interest in the wider world was a feature of the first few decades of the Ming, although the tributary system continued into the nineteenth century. The last half or more of Ming rule was, in contrast, a period of retrenchment, preoccupation with the defense of the land frontiers, and cultural conservatism. Such a shift fits the pattern of the dynastic cycle discussed in Chapter 8. All dynasties tended to be open-minded, cosmopolitan, and expansionist in their first century, complacent in their second century, and overwhelmed by problems in their third and last century,

when the effectiveness and vigor of the imperial government deteriorated, corruption mounted, and rebellion spread. The Ming were no exception to this recurrent pattern, and the memory of the Mongol conquest tended in any case to make them xenophobic, conservative in their determination to reaffirm the great tradition of the Chinese past, and inward-centered. All this was understandable and probably benefited the country, at least in the short run, as much as or more than foreign adventuring. China was a huge and productive world in itself. Until late in the 1500s things continued to go well, and general prosperity kept most people content.

Japanese and Korean pirate raids at places all along the coast did worry the Ming and not only because of what the pirates stole or destroyed. The raids demonstrated that the Chinese government could not keep order locally or defend its people. The raids were regarded as equivalent to rebellion, and the government also knew that a good many renegade Chinese were involved, masquerading as Koreans or Japanese or in league with them. After much pressure from the Chinese court, the Ashikaga shogunate in Japan, formally a Ming tributary, suppressed some of the Japanese pirate activity and sent some captured pirates to Beijing for execution. A Ming document addressed to the Ashikaga in 1436 acknowledged this and went on to say, in the customary language of the tributary system and with its pretentious assumptions:

> Since our Empire owns the world, there is no country on this or other sides of the seas which does not submit to us. The sage Emperors who followed one another had the same regard and uniform benevolence for all countries far and near. You, Japan, are our Eastern frontier, and for generations you have performed tributary duties. The longer the time, the more respectful you have become.[4]

Ming Maritime Expeditions

What distinguished the early Ming, but fit the pattern of early Han, Tang, and Song, was the outreach of imperial pride, especially in their remarkable maritime expeditions. Using the nautical technology inherited from the Song, the eunuch admiral Zheng He mounted seven naval expeditions of Chinese fleets between 1405 and 1433, with up to 60 vessels. They toured much of Southeast Asia, the east and west coasts of India (including Calicut, where 90 years later Vasco da Gama was to make his Asian landfall), Ceylon, the Persian Gulf and the Straits of Hormuz, Aden, Jidda (from where seven Chinese went to Mecca), and East Africa. Some ships may have gone as far as the Cape of Good

Hope or even around it. They brought back giraffes, zebras, and ostriches to amaze the court and tributary agreements with gifts from a host of new states. When the king of Ceylon was considered not deferential enough, he was arrested and taken back to Nanjing, and Yongle appointed a new king in his place.

Zheng He's many-decked ships carried up to 500 troops but also cargoes of export goods, mainly silks and porcelains, and brought back foreign luxuries such as spices and tropical woods. The economic motive for these huge ventures may have been important, and many of the ships had large, private cabins for merchants. But the chief aim was probably political, to show the flag and command respect for the empire, as well as to enroll still more states as tributaries.

Some of the ships were larger than anything previously built in the world, 400 feet long and of 500 tons burden, with four decks. They were reported nevertheless to be faster sailers than the Portuguese caravels or Spanish galleons of a century or two later, especially with a favorable wind. They were designed in accordance with the well-known monsoonal wind patterns of Asia and the Indian Ocean. Properly timed voyages could count on going with the wind for about half the year almost anywhere in that vast region and then returning with the opposite monsoon in the other half of the year.

Zheng He's ships, like those of the Song, were built with double hulls and up to a dozen separate watertight compartments. Despite their far-flung voyages and their many encounters with storms and unknown coasts, few were ever lost. They were provided with detailed sailing directions, at least for the waters nearer home, as well as compasses.

Such exploits of seamanship and exploration were unprecedented in the world. Their grand scale and imperial pretension, as well perhaps as their commercial ambition, were an expression of new imperial pride and vigor. But they contributed little to the economy, except temporary employment for shipbuilders and crew, and made no lasting impression on the Chinese mind, except to further confirm their sense of superiority as the only civilized empire.

A Ming Naval Expedition

The following is part of a text engraved on a stone tablet in 1432, commemorating the expeditions of Zheng He.

The Imperial Ming dynasty in unifying seas and continents . . . even goes beyond the Han and the Tang. The countries beyond the horizon and from the ends of the earth have all become subjects. . . . Thus the barbarians from beyond the seas . . . have come to audience bearing precious objects. . . . The Emperor has ordered us, Zheng He . . . to make manifest the transforming power of the Imperial virtue and to treat distant people with kindness . . . We have seven times received the commission of ambassadors [and have visited] altogether more than thirty countries large and small. We have traversed immense water spaces and have beheld huge waves like mountains rising sky-high, and we have set eyes on barbarian regions far away hidden in a blue transparency of light vapors, while our sails loftily unfurled like clouds day and night continued their course, traversing those savage waves as if we were treading a public thoroughfare. . . . We have received the high favor of a gracious commission of our Sacred Lord, to carry to the distant barbarians the benefits of his auspicious example. . . . Therefore we have recorded the years and months of the voyages. [Here follows a detailed record of places visited and things done on each of the seven voyages.] We have anchored in this port awaiting a north wind to take the sea . . . and have thus recorded an inscription in stone . . . erected by the principal envoys, the Grand Eunuchs Zheng He and Wang Jinghong, and the assistant envoys.

Source: J. J. L. Duyvendak, "The True Dates of the Chinese Maritime Expeditions in the Early Fifteenth Century," *Toung Pao,* vol. 24 (1938): 349–355.

The expeditions were very expensive and were stopped after 1433, perhaps mainly for that reason, although abuses and corruption in procuring shipbuilding materials and in contracts with shipyards also attracted official criticism. Zheng He was a Muslim as well as a eunuch, and this may have generated prejudice against him in the orthodox and highly Confucian court. Yongle may have believed that he had made his imperial point, and it is unlikely that trade profits covered the costs. Another factor was his decision to move the primary capital to Beijing in 1421 (Nanjing was kept as a secondary capital) to better command the chronically troubled northern frontier, where there was an attempted revival of Mongol power, as well as to bring the Ming into line with what was by now the hallowed tradition of a northern capital. The monumental building of Beijing also competed with the shipyards for shrinking sources of timber and construction workers, as well as for treasury allocations.

But the abandonment of the maritime expeditions, like the move to Beijing, was a symptom of the Ming's basic conservatism once the first half century had passed. There were understandable fears of a Mongol resurgence and deep concern about the Central Asian conquests of the Turkish leader Tamerlane (1336–1405), who, they had reason to fear, was planning to invade China. His death ended that threat, but the Mongols were still active. Yongle personally led five expeditions out into the steppe to combat the Mongol revival and remained preoccupied with his northern defenses, for which there was ample precedent in Chinese history. Newly reorganized Mongol tribes continued to harass the border areas and raid across the frontier until the mid-seventeenth century. The Ming also promoted the spread of Lamaistic Buddhism to the Mongols in an effort to pacify them, a strategy that seems in the end to have been more effective than military confrontation.

The cost of the anti-Mongol campaigns on top of the building of Beijing was a strain, and the extravagant oceanic adventures were a logical item for retrenchment. Zheng He's voyages had been supported by his fellow eunuchs at court, who were strongly opposed by the Confucian scholar-officials; their antagonism was in fact so great that they tried to suppress any mention of the naval expeditions in the official record.

China's relations by sea had always been given a far lower priority than her land frontiers, and this ancient pattern was now reasserted. The expeditions discov-

Magnificent paintings of nature continued under the Ming in the now long-established Chinese tradition. This lovely spray of white magnolia is part of a larger painting by the master Wen Zhengming (1470–1559). (The Metropolitan Museum of Art, New York, Bequest of John M. Crawford, Jr., 1988. [1989.363.64] Photograph, all rights reserved, The Metropolitan Museum of Art.)

ered nothing worth the effort, and conquest was never part of the plan. Nevertheless, the scale of Zheng He's voyages remains impressive. While the Portuguese were just beginning to feel their way cautiously along the West African coast in sight of land, Chinese fleets of far larger ships dominated the Indian Ocean and the western Pacific and traded in most of the ports. They did not try to cross the Pacific or continue westward to Europe, which they were clearly capable of doing,* only because to their knowledge there was nothing in either direction to make such a voyage worthwhile.

If they had reached Europe, they probably would have been no more impressed by it than by what they saw in Southeast Asia, India, the Persian Gulf, or Africa, nor any more than they were to be a century later by the early European arrivals in China, still to their way of thinking crude barbarians. Fifteenth-century North America would have seemed to them too primitive even to mention. As with some earlier Chinese innovations in science and technology, these maritime achievements were not followed up. The conquest of the seas, global expansion, and a sea-based commercial revolution were left to the poorer and less complacent Europeans, who from both their own and the Chinese point of view had more to gain thereby—and less to concern them or to take pride in at home. The chief early goal of the European expansion overseas was in fact China, whose riches and sophistication had attracted Europe's mind and ambitions since the Roman imports of Chinese silk, that symbol of luxury and wealth.

Prosperity and Conservatism

Meanwhile the Ming turned inward from their new capital at Beijing, rebuilding the Great Wall and its watchtowers in the form it still has today and promoting the development of their own home base. Such domestic concerns had always been the center of Chinese attention. Since Shang times they had called their country the Middle Kingdom, meaning not only that it was the center of the world but that it combined the advantages of a golden mean, avoiding the extremes of desert, jungle, mountains, or cold around its borders. In whatever direction one went from China, the physical environment deteriorated: north (too cold), south (too hot and jungly), west (too mountainous or dry), or east into a vast and, in cultural or economic terms, empty ocean.

The Chinese attributed the lack of civilization they noted in all "barbarians" to their far less favorable geographic environment (in which there was of course some truth) as well as to their distance from the only center of enlightenment.

China was indeed the most productive area of comparable size anywhere in the world, especially its great river valleys and floodplains. The empire was bigger than all of Europe in size, more populous, and with a far greater volume of trade. The Chinese saw their interests best served by further embellishing their home base rather than by pursuing less rewarding foreign contacts. As the Italian Jesuit missionary Matteo Ricci reported early in the seventeenth century, "Everything which the people need for their well-being and sustenance . . . is abundantly produced within the borders of the kingdom."[5] Domestic and interprovincial trade between provinces the size of many European states was far greater than foreign trade and served the world's largest market. Revenues now went increasingly to nourishing the domestic scene and glorifying its rulers.

There was thus a growing turn to conservatism even before the end of the Ming's first century. Partly this reflected a determination to reestablish the traditional Chinese way in all things after the Mongol humiliation, but it also stemmed from enhanced prosperity. With everything going so well, there was less incentive to seek change or be innovative, at least in terms of official policy. The emperors who followed Yongle were less and less able or imaginative and tended to leave policy and administration to the intrinsically conservative Confucian bureaucracy, once again entrenched in power. The imperial censors were revived (they had been understandably reluctant to speak out under Hongwu!) to keep officials honest and responsible and to keep the capital informed of actual or potential problems. On the whole, this tried-and-true system worked well for another century. In time it became increasingly rigid and less able to respond to change or the need for change, but until the last decades of the Ming, as with other dynasties, it was an impressive form of government that kept order and ensured justice to an admirable degree.

Nor did official conservatism and Confucian-based anticommercialism prevent the basic changes at work in the economy. As for every Chinese dynasty, agriculture was regarded as the predominant source of wealth and as something to be officially promoted. Under Hongwu there was a major reconstruction effort to rebuild agriculture in the extensive areas devastated by the Mongols and the rebellions against them. Many thousands of reservoirs and canals were built or repaired, and depopulated areas resettled by mass transfers of people. Many thousands of acres of farmland were newly reclaimed. There was also a major campaign of reforestation. There were many new government projects to

---

*In fact there is some evidence that they may have reached the California coast—anchors of Chinese design and appropriate age have been found recently in shallow water off Santa Barbara.

extend irrigation, build new canals and paved roads, stock public granaries, and construct flood-prevention works.

Rice yields rose with the use of new, more productive, and earlier-ripening varieties introduced from Southeast Asia and actively promoted by the state. New irrigation and better manuring, as well as new land brought under cultivation to feed the growing population, produced a major rise in total output and a marked improvement in average material well-being. In the sixteenth century new crops, most importantly maize (corn), sweet and white potatoes, and peanuts reached China from Spanish America via the trade connection with the Philippines. All of these imported plants increased output still further since they did not need irrigation, and for the most part they did not replace rice or wheat but fit into the system using hilly or sandy areas little cultivated before.

The Ming government and most of its Confucian magistrates cared about the welfare of their people, at least until the final collapse, and even reformed the tax system to make it less burdensome for peasants, although the bulk of imperial revenue now again came from taxes on land and grain, plus the official monopoly taxes on salt, tea, and such foreign trade as was officially recognized. Regular labor service was also required of all districts and households for public works of general usefulness, including the building and maintaining of irrigation and flood-prevention systems and the imperial road network. The roughly 2,000 local magistrates, forbidden to serve in their native provinces lest they show favoritism, were necessarily but effectively assisted by a large staff and also by local degree-holding gentry. Local gentry were often the major factors in keeping order and ensuring that official policy and projects were carried out. Imperial censors traveling on circuit from the capital watched for irregularities and reported directly to the emperor. A newly comprehensive code of administrative and criminal law was published in 1397.

Food crops were still considered of prime importance, but there was a boom in commercial crops also, encouraged by the state, such as mulberry (for silkworms) and cotton. Silk was produced principally in the densely populated Yangzi Delta area, where its dependence on intensive hand labor could rest on family members as a household enterprise, especially women and older children. The Guangdong area, equally densely populated, and the similarly populous Red Basin of Sichuan, were other important silk-making regions. All three were close to major urban markets and to navigable waterways to distribute their output at low cost throughout the empire. Under the Ming cotton became for the first time, after its earlier diffusion from India, the predominant fabric of daily clothing for most people. It was cheaper and more durable than silk and displaced coarser or more laboriously made hemp and linen. Silk remained a luxury item for the wealthy, more numerous than ever before, but cotton became a far larger crop, grown and woven mainly in the lower Yangzi, eastern northern China, and central China, adding to the income of farmers and providing new employment for weavers and merchants. It was a peaceful, confident, prosperous time for most people, and Ming culture reflected it.

Commerce and Culture

For all the ambitiously revived system of imperial bureaucracy, it remained a thin and superficial layer at the top, administered by a relative handful of officials—about 2,300 outside the capital—which barely touched most aspects of daily life in this vast country with a population by now well over 150 million. Commerce was officially disparaged, except for its taxation, but the most significant changes taking place in Ming China were in the expanding commercialization of the economy. Zheng He's expeditions were past, but trade with most of the places he had visited continued to increase, especially with eastern Southeast Asia. Although the largest trade was domestic, new supplies of silver and silver coins came into China to pay for the exports of silk, tea, porcelain, lacquerware, and other goods and heightened the pace of commercialization and monetization. More and more production was undertaken for sale, in agriculture and in manufacturing. Most of it was consumed in the rapidly growing cities, but some found its way to Korea, Japan, Java, the Philippines, and farther abroad.

Some of the silver flowing back came from Japan, but increasingly it came from the new Spanish base at Manila by the end of the sixteenth century, where it was brought from the mines in Peru and Mexico. Spanish-minted silver dollars began to circulate widely in the China market. By about 1450 silver coins, bars, and smaller ingots had driven out paper money; it was abandoned as people came to prefer silver, which by then was plentiful, to a paper currency that could not be exchanged for metal; after its value deteriorated beyond recall, it was given up. Taxes began to be commuted from a share of the grain harvest and periods of labor on public-works projects to cash payments in silver. A sweeping reform in the sixteenth and early seventeenth centuries known as the "single lash of the whip" attempted, with considerable success, to simplify the tax system. The reform lumped what had previously been a great variety of exactions into a few categories and collected them at fixed dates in silver, a major step toward modern revenue systems. At least for a time, this greatly reduced both the confusion and the corruption or evasion that had bedeviled the former system. It also increased the government's net income.

Merchant guilds acquired new though unofficial power in many Chinese cities, especially in the lower Yangzi and the southeast coast, the country's most urbanized and commercialized areas. Guilds controlled much nonagricultural production, marketing, and long-distance trade, informally and often through family or native-place networks, and very effectively. Merchants were still considered parasitic rather than productive and were formally subject to officials and periodically to special government exactions. But they had their own less formal official connections, usually through a degree-holding or officeholding gentry member of an extended family, as protection, access to favors, and indeed the only secure basis for commercial success in this bureaucratic society. Despite the Confucian disdain for their activity, at least on the surface, many merchants grew rich in this expanding economy. Some were able to buy gentry rank, although those who purchased rank were almost never permitted to hold office. In any case, their money enabled them to live in the style of the scholar-gentry, as literate connoisseurs of sophisticated art and literature in their great townhouses in the fashionable quarters.

After about 1520, capital investment increasingly moved away from the ownership and rental of land and into commercial enterprises: trade and artisan production. Prices for land continued to fall, and coastal piracy did not apparently discourage the increase of maritime trade as charges rose to cover those risks, although the biggest growth was in domestic commerce. In agriculture too, commercial or industrial crops such as cotton, indigo (for dyeing fabrics), and vegetable oil for illumination became more important. Handicraft production of tools, furniture, paper, porcelain, and art objects for wider sale grew rapidly, and large, specialized workshops became common, distributing finished products to a regional or even national market. Some of them employed several hundred workers—another step toward industrialization.

A major cluster of porcelain workshops at Jingdezhen in the central Yangzi Valley made magnificent pieces for the imperial household and the court as well as for the domestic market as a whole and for export. Iron and steel were made in many places, especially in southern Hebei, in what amounted to factories. Large cotton mills producing cloth in major urban centers in the lower Yangzi Valley and the highly commercialized delta area sold their output nationwide. There were 50,000 workers in 30 papermaking factories in Jiangxi Province alone at the end of the sixteenth century. Skilled workers were in great demand and were recruited over a very wide area. A national labor market

developed, with the equivalent of hiring halls in major regional centers. Silk, porcelain, and tea especially, among other products, were exported in growing volume and with great profit. For example, Chinese silk sold in Japan at five or six times its price in the domestic market, and it continued to be sold in the West at even higher prices.

As would happen two centuries later in Europe, growing commercialization, a widening market, and rising demand for goods provided incentives for improving and speeding up production and the development of new technology to turn out more goods. In the last century of the Ming, a number of technical handbooks and treatises were published that show impressive progress in production technology. Some of the new techniques are reminiscent of those that appeared in eighteenth-century Europe, where the increase in trade and demand helped lead to technological innovation, rising output, and the beginnings of the Industrial Revolution. In Ming China, such innovations included mechanical looms with three or four shuttle winders for producing larger amounts of silk or cotton cloth in less time and without increasing labor requirements. New techniques emerged for the printing of woodblocks in three, four, and five colors to feed the booming market for books and prints, and further improvements were made in movable type. An alloy of copper and lead was developed that made the type sharper and more durable so that it could be used for many more copies, and could be reused many more times. New procedures were even worked out for the manufacture of specially refined grades of sugar to suit the tastes and pocketbooks of the greatly increased numbers of the wealthy.

Suspension bridges using iron chains carried the booming trade over rivers. Originally developed during the Han and Tang dynasties, they were widespread under the Ming and greatly impressed the early European observers, although they were not successfully copied in Europe until the eighteenth century. The use of a mast and sail on wheelbarrows, important carriers of trade and raw materials on a local scale, especially on the North China Plain with its wide expanses of level and treeless areas and strong winds, also attracted European attention. They were soon copied by the Dutch. The wheelbarrow itself had been invented in Han China and sails added soon thereafter.

A huge network of rivers and canals linked most places from the Yangzi Valley south by cheap water transport. The Jesuit Matteo Ricci's journal comments on the immense traffic by water and the great numbers of people who lived on their boats, concluding that there were as many boats in China as in all the rest of the world put together. In agriculture, building on Song foundations, new machines were developed under the Ming for cultivating the soil, for irrigation, and even for mechanical sowing, planting, and harvesting. Productive New World crops continued to add to total agricultural output. After Hongwu and Yongle, Ming population figures were increasingly unreliable—another symptom of the decline in governmental efficiency—but total population probably increased to something like 230 million by the end of the dynasty.

To serve the needs of an increasingly commercialized economy, guilds of moneychangers and bankers became more important, and some of them developed a national network, with representatives in most major cities and at the capital. Techniques for transferring money through the equivalent of letters of credit, referred to as "flying money," had been used in the Song dynasty but were further refined and greatly expanded in the second half of the Ming, as were other aspects of banking and the financing of trade. These developments, too, suggest comparison with what was happening in Europe along similar lines. The Marxist historians of China in the 1970s identified these trends in the Ming as "early sprouts of capitalism," a description that seems quite reasonable despite the official downgrading of trade and merchants and the state regulation of commerce. Many of the richest merchants in fact grew wealthy through managing what were officially state enterprises or monopolies: supplies for the army, the shipment of rice to feed the capital, and the trade in salt.

Patronage and Literature

Wealthy merchants patronized literature and the arts, decorated their houses lavishly with art objects, and supported an elegant urban culture. Vernacular literature, which had had its major beginnings under the Song, took on new dimensions and variety, appealing now to a growing mass of urban readers. Ming painting was in general less imaginative or innovative than that of the Song and tended to rework older themes and styles, but later Ming produced its own great painters, especially gifted in their exquisite representations of birds and flowers. Ceramics reached a new level of perfection, and beautiful pieces were part of every rich merchant household. This was the period of the famous Ming blue-and-white porcelain, samples and copies of which were prominent among Chinese exports to the West.

Yongle commissioned an immense encyclopedia of all knowledge, on which 3,000 scholars worked for five years. It was followed later in the fifteenth century by a great medical encyclopedia and others devoted to geography, botany, ethics, and art. The medical volumes, completed in 1578, listed over 10,000 drugs and prescriptions, most of them unknown in the West, and recorded the use of inoculation to prevent smallpox, far in advance of this discovery in eighteenth-century Europe. A handbook of industrial technology printed in 1637, just before the dynasty collapsed, described methods and tools or machines in the production of rice, salt, porcelain, metals, coal, weaving, ships, canal locks, paper, weapons, and many other fruits of Chinese industry and ingenuity. Science and technology in Ming China still led the world.

In the more popular realm, the theater flourished, but the major advance of Ming literature was in long, popular novels and other stories of adventure and romance. They still make excellent reading and give a vivid picture of the life of the times. Perhaps the best known now is titled *Water Margins* (translated by Pearl Buck as *All Men Are Brothers*), which tells the story of an outlaw band and its efforts to correct the wrongs done by unjust officials. Bandits of the Robin Hood variety had the same romantic appeal in China as in the West, and their life as "men of the greenwood" (a phrase identical to that used in medieval England), meaning of course the forest where they had their protected bases, was idealized. Many centuries later, Mao Zedong said that *Water Margins* (the title came from the marshes that surrounded the outlaws' base) was his favorite book, and of course it did glorify those attempting to defy, and if possible replace, the existing government. Another still widely read Ming novel, *The Golden Lotus,* an often-pornographic satire about the amorous adventures of a druggist with servants, neighbors, and other people's wives, seems as fresh as today's best-sellers.

Most of the characters in *The Golden Lotus* are members of the leisure class, servants, or concubines in a wealthy household. The novel is generally interpreted as a critical portrayal of decadence, but since the characters are mainly well educated, including the concubines, it includes scenes in which they recite or improvise classical-style poems or songs. Here is one of them:

It is evening.
The storm has passed over the southern hall,
Red petals are floating on the surface of the pool.
Slowly the gentle thunder rolls away.
The rain is over and the clouds disperse;
The fragrance of waterlilies comes to us over the distance.
The new moon is a crescent
Fresh from the perfumed bath, decked for the evening;
Over the darkening courtyard it wanes
Yet will not go to rest.
In the shade of the willow the young cicada bursts into song,
Fireflies hover over the ancestral halls.
Listen. Whence comes this song of Ling?
The painted boat is late returning,
The jade chords sink lower and lower;
The gentlefolk are silent:
A vision of delight!
Let us rise and take each other by the hand
And dress our hair.
The moon lights up the silken curtains,
But there are no sleepers there.
The mandarin duck tumbles the lotus leaves

On the gently rippling water
Sprinkling them with drops like pearls.
They give out fragrance,
And a perfumed breeze moves softly over the flower beds
Beside the summer-house.
How can our spirits fail to be refreshed?
Why crave for the islands of the blest, the home of fairies?
Yet when the west wind blows again, Autumn will come with
*   it.*[6]

Popular Culture

By the sixteenth century there was a large and growing number of people who were literate or semiliterate but who were not members of any elite or of the very small numbers of official Confucian-style gentry, who probably never exceeded at most 2 percent of the population. These nonelite literates and semiliterates lived in the vast Chinese world that was little touched by the imperial system and its canons, most of them outside the big cities and the circles of the rich merchant elites. Popular literature, stories, novels, and plays produced by and for them probably exceeded in volume and in circulation the more proper output in the orthodox classical mode, extensive and varied as that was. Much of it was also read in private by the elite, who would hide any "undignified" book under the pillow if someone entered the room. For us today, too, most of it is more fun than the restrained, polished, or formal material that the scholarly gentry were supposed to read and write.

In addition, as part of popular culture, there were numerous puppet shows, shadow plays, mystery and detective stories (four or five centuries before they appeared in the West), operas, ballads, the oral tradition of itinerant storytellers, and a wealth of inexpensive woodblock prints, many of them dealing with aspects of daily life, others with mythology or folk religion. Opera, which combined drama, music, dance forms, singing, and gorgeous costumes, could also appeal to illiterates, still the majority (although Ming and Qing China may well have been the world's most literate societies, like the Song before them), as could storytellers, balladeers, and the various forms of plays. Performances in all of these media were offered everywhere, even in small towns, by itinerant groups. Storytellers would often be accompanied by musicians or would provide their own music; they would end each recital at a moment of suspense: "Come back next time if you want to hear the next episode," or "Pay now if you want to know how it all came out!"

Over 300 different local or regional genres of opera have been identified, intended mainly for nonelite audiences. Many operas, plays, and stories centered on the adventures of heroes and villains of the rich Chinese past, not always historically accurate in every detail but always entertaining, appealing to the deep and consistent Chinese interest in their own history. Most of the common people learned their history from opera, theater, and storytellers, and they learned a great deal of it. The connection with folk religion was close, including folk versions of Buddhism and Daoism as well as local animist cults and deities, and many of the operas, plays, and stories focused on it. Operas were commonly per-

Love of unsullied nature remained a prominent theme for Ming painters. Like the white magnolia for spring, white lotus for summer represented purity, regeneration, and tranquility, as in this peaceful scroll by Chen Xun, who lived from 1483 to 1544. (The Nelson-Atkins Museum of Art, Kansas City, Missouri (Purchase: Nelson Trust 31-135/34.)

formed at festivals celebrating a local god or as part of temple rituals, and many operas and shadow plays had an explicitly religious or ritual content, like the medieval miracle plays of Europe. Still others satirized daily life: henpecked husbands, jilted or faithless lovers, grasping merchants, corrupt officials, overprotective or authoritarian parents, tyrannical landlords, and so on—set in villages or towns rather than in the more sophisticated and urbane world of the cities.

They formed in effect a countertradition to the elite culture and expressed strong sympathy for the powerless, the oppressed, and the underdogs, including especially women, who were often the major figures. They show a contempt for wealth without compassion, for power without responsibility, and for all forms of hypocrisy, opportunism, and moral compromise. Of course, such failings are endemic in all societies, including our own, but especially common among the elite, even in a Confucian China, many of whose supposed values are in fact faithfully mirrored in the popular literature. In this extensive genre, as later in the Qing dynasty, individuals are, however, valued and respected for their achievements and their moral virtue regardless of their social position, unlike the hierarchical ordering of individuals that Confucian doctrine came to support. Through this rich and varied literature we can catch far more than a glimpse of what has been called the "little tradition," present in all societies and often at odds with or showing a very different perspective on the great tradition. It was, of course, already old in China, but with the expansion of printing and literacy under the Ming, these various literary and artistic forms began to be recorded on a much greater scale. It has a universal flavor and many parallels in the popular culture of most other societies around the world, past and present. But it also reveals the basic good sense, the humor, and the appealing human qualities of the common people of Ming China.

Elite Culture and Traditionalism

In monumental architecture the Ming created new glories in their capitals at Nanjing and Beijing and in temples in every city and many towns, a further indication of prosperity. But in general, and particularly after their first century, the Ming looked to the past for guidance. This accounted for their interest in encyclopedias, collecting the wisdom and experience of previous generations as guardians of tradition. Most Ming scholars and philosophers were traditionalists, mistrusting speculation or innovation. There were exceptions, of course, but orthodoxy tended to dominate thought, as it did the imperial examinations. As one Ming writer put it: "Since the time of Zhu Xi [the Song Confucianist] the

truth has been made clear. No more writing is needed. We have only to practice."[7] There were nevertheless some important developments in philosophy, especially in the thought of Wang Yangming (1472–1529), a scholar-official who went beyond the Neo-Confucianism of Zhu Xi in urging both a meditative and intuitive self-cultivation, much influenced by Buddhism, and an activist moral role in society. Wang's most famous aphorism stresses the organic connection between knowledge and behavior: "Knowledge is the beginning of conduct; conduct is the completion of knowledge"—a maxim still much admired by Confucianists in China, Korea, and Japan and one that makes excellent sense to any thoughtful person.

Before Wang's time, Hongwu had issued six brief imperial edicts that were posted in all villages and towns in 1397, a year before his death. They ordered people to be filial, to respect elders and ancestors, to teach their children to do the same, and to peacefully pursue their livelihoods. Local gentry, those not in office but functioning as local elites and keepers of order and morality, helped to see that these prescriptions were carried out. The revived orthodox Confucian denigration of trade and merchants and their subordination to officialdom helped to strengthen official disinterest in commerce. Foreign trade was left largely in private hands or was managed by powerful eunuchs at court, which further devalued it in Confucian eyes.

Grain had to be hauled north from the Yangzi Valley to feed the cloud of officials, garrison troops, and commoners as well as the elite of Beijing. Japanese and Korean piracy prompted Yongle to restore the Grand Canal, which had silted up and fallen into disrepair, and to abandon the coastal route by sea after 1415. Fifteen locks were constructed and the canal dredged. The cost was high, but the canal helped to stimulate further increases in interregional trade and in artisan and other consumer goods production to supply a now-enlarged market. It also stimulated the growth of cities along its route. Suzhou, in the Yangzi Delta just west of Shanghai, was until the nineteenth century the major city and port of that productive area after Nanjing. It became a national financial and commercial center near the canal's southern end and was noted for its fine silk goods, distributed to the wealthy all over China, but especially in fashionable Beijing. Cotton cloth, lacquerware, magnificent porcelain pieces, iron cooking pots from Guangzhou, and a long list of other goods were distributed, mainly by water routes, to an increasingly national market. Hankou (now part of the city of Wuhan) on the central Yangzi grew as a major junction of rivers and a national distribution center as well as a major market in itself. Private Chinese merchants went to Southeast Asia in great numbers and managed an increasing overseas trade from bases on the southeast China coast such as

Street people of the Ming: beggars and hawkers, painted by Zhou Chen (active c. 1500–1535). (Chinese, c. 1450–after 1536, Ming dynasty. *Beggars and Street Characters* [detail], 1516. Handscroll, ink and color on paper, overall 31.9 × 244.5 cm. © The Cleveland Museum of Art, 2002, John L. Severance Fund, 1964.94)

Guangzhou, Xiamen, Shantou, and Fuzhou, despite official discouragement. Tianjin, the port of Beijing, grew also as the chief port for trade with Korea. Other booming cities included Chengdu, the capital of agriculturally rich Sichuan with its many rivers, and Changsha, the capital of Hunan on the Xiang River, a tributary of the Yangzi flowing through the productive lowlands of Central China known as "China's rice bowl."

But increasingly conservative official attitudes were reflected in the Ming imprint on the imperial examination system. In 1487 a set form was established for the writing of examination papers in eight categories using no more than 700 characters altogether, following a prescribed style of polished commentary on the Confucian and Neo-Confucian classics. This was the famous "eight-legged essay," which clearly and probably intentionally inhibited individual thought or innovation and encouraged a past-centered orthodoxy. Government-supported schools at the county and prefectural levels, originally established by Hongwu, offered classical education to able boys, the best of whom were brought to the capital for further study and for training as apprentice officials. On an earlier Song model, private academies and tutors for the sons of the wealthy (daughters were given no such formal education) passed on the distilled wisdom of the past to those fortunate enough to attend and shaped their instruction to prepare aspiring youths to conform to what the examinations now required.

Candidates had to pass preliminary examinations at the *xian* (county) level. Success there enabled the student to compete in exams at the prefectural city, where he could obtain the lowest principal degree, the *xiucai* or shengyuan. That constituted admission to the gentry class, with, among other things, exemption from labor service and corporal punishment. The second level of exams was held in each provincial capital; it lasted several days during which time each candidate was walled into a tiny separate cell and provided with food and water. Only about one in a hundred passed, earning the degree of *juren* and the right to compete in the final exam every three years at the imperial capital. Success there brought the designation *jinshi* and then a final test interview with the emperor himself, who could appoint those he chose to an official post. The lowest degree, *xiucai,* could be purchased, especially as the dynasty declined and needed money, but such buyers—merchants or landlords—did not serve as officials. The sale of these degrees also served to some extent as a concession to wealthy families who might otherwise have become discontented or restive, a kind of co-optation.

Both the state-financed schools and the private academies multiplied after Hongwu's time. But although learning and the examinations became more rigidly orthodox, the basic Confucian message of responsibility and human-heartedness continued to be stressed, with its conviction that human nature is fundamentally good and moldable by education and the virtuous example of superiors. The ultimate deterioration and collapse of the Ming, and in 1911 of the entire imperial system, should not obscure its positive aspects, especially during its many centuries of relative vigor. Even up to the last years of the Ming, corruption and ineffectiveness at court were not much reflected in the continued operation of the system elsewhere in the country, which rested far more on the basic Chinese social fabric of family, gentry, and Confucian principles than on the management or intervention of the few imperial officials.

The lives and values of most people had their own momentum. "The emperor is far away," as the traditional saying went, expressing a wealth of meaning. Local freedom and good order had little to do with imperial politics and much to do with the traditional Chinese system of the self-regulating society. Local gentry directed and raised money for public works, especially irrigation, roads, canals, bridges, and ferries. Often they organized and funded schools and academies, orphanages, care for old people, and relief measures in hard times or after floods. Many of them compiled the local histories or gazeteers that are still a mine of information about local conditions, events, and notable local people. This was all done as part of Confucian morality, and without pay or official appointment. When all went well, perhaps half or more of the time during the 2,000 years of dynastic rule, the local gentry were thus a major supplement to government and an important cement for society.

A CLOSER LOOK

Imperial Beijing: Axis of the Ming World

When Yongle decided to move the capital back to the north, Beijing was the obvious choice, primarily for its nearness to the most threatened frontiers. It is only about 40 miles from the mountains that surround and protect the city on the west, north, and northeast. The Great Wall runs through the mountains, crossing a narrow lowland strip of coastal plain east of the city leading to Manchuria called Shan Hai Guan ("mountain sea gate"). Passes to the northwest lead directly into Mongolia. Both areas were accurately seen by now as the chief trouble spots along the frontier, and it was mainly to guard against them that the Great Wall was rebuilt, at tremendous cost.

The Xiongnu menace that had plagued the Han had been replaced by that of the Mongols farther east, and by the early signs of what was to become the next alien conquering group, the Manchus of Manchuria. The gradual west-to-east progression of China's capital from Zhou, Qin, Han, and Tang Chang'an to Luoyang, the Song move to Kaifeng and Hangzhou, and now the Ming choice of Beijing reflected these changes. The location of the capital was also affected by the growth of the south, the drought and agricultural deterioration of the northwest, and the provision of canals to bring food from the surplus areas of the Yangzi to feed successive northern capitals.

The new Beijing was designed to make a statement of imperial power and majesty. The pre-1850 center of the city today is largely a Ming creation, replacing what was left of the Mongol capital but on a much larger scale. The main outer city walls were 40 feet high and nearly 15 miles around, forming a rectangle pierced by nine gates with watchtowers and outer gates to further deter attackers, check permit papers, and awe all those who entered. Inside was the Imperial City, within its own walls, 5 miles in circumference.

Wild Geese and Tree Peonies in Moonlight, a painting on silk by Lu Ji (active in the late fifteenth and early sixteenth centuries). Mists drift across the moon in this poetic and decorative but deeply restful painting, where the detailed plumage of the geese is balanced by the simple and naturalistic brush strokes of the tall grasses. (National Palace Museum, Taipei, Taiwan)

These enclosed in turn the red inner walls of the Forbidden City, which contained the palace and was surrounded by a moat 2 miles around. Successive courtyards inside the Forbidden City, dominated by throne halls for different purposes, were set on terraces of white marble and with gleaming gold-tiled roofs. These led along a north-south axis to the palace. Outside the Forbidden City (so called because it was closed to all except those with official business), a similar succession of elegant stone-paved courtyards, terraces, and audience halls led to the main gates. The outermost walls enclosed gardens, artificial lakes, and even an artificial hill.

The orientation of the city as a whole was based on astronomical principles and followed throughout a north-south axis to reflect and draw authority from the supreme correctness of the universe. The whole plan and all its details were designed to awe and impress all who approached or entered its series of walls and courtyards. It still has that effect and, partly for that reason, a section has been restored by the People's Republic of China as the centerpiece of their capital. The Ming design was accepted and further embellished by their successors, the Qing, as serving their similar purposes admirably. That part of Beijing remains one of the best preserved and impressively planned capitals anywhere. Its splendid courtyards, the gracefulness and yet strength of architectural and roof lines in all of its buildings, and the lavish use of colored glazed tiles make it aesthetically as well as symbolically overwhelming.

A less planned city grew up outside the walls, where most of the common people lived, and it soon housed most of Beijing's residents. The total population, inside and outside the walls, was probably a little over 1 million under both the Ming and the Qing, fed in part with rice brought from the Yangzi Valley by the Grand Canal. Some space was left clear immediately around the outer walls, for better defense, and there were large military barracks. A maze of streets, alleys, and small courtyards covered most of the extramural area, including the small, walled compounds with their tiny gardens and living space for extended families, for which Beijing became famous and some of which can still be seen. The majestic Imperial and Forbidden cities were formally ordered on a grand scale, in sharp contrast to the unplanned alleys and irregular streets of the city around them, but above all Beijing was—and remains—an imperial statement in wood, stone, brick, and tile that dominated the entire urban area physically as well as symbolically.

Complacency and Decline

Beijing was built in the days of power and pride, but as the decades went by, complacency replaced new achievements and was less and less appropriate to a number of growing problems. Japanese and Korean pirate attacks on the coast proved impossible to control, and the government's ultimate response was to order the removal of all settlement 30 miles inland and officially forbid maritime trade, although the ban was widely ignored. Guns had been in use for centuries, but

The Imperial Palace, Beijing. (R. Murphey)

China had begun to fall behind advances in Western gunnery. When, late in the fifteenth century, a touring censor asked a garrison to demonstrate their obviously long-neglected cannons, the commander said, "What, fire those things? Why, they might kill somebody!"[8] This may be an unfair example, however humanly appealing, and during most of the dynasty the Ming armies were reasonably effective in keeping the long peace at home and on the frontiers, maintaining an order that encouraged economic prosperity. But the failure to control raids by supposed "tributaries" was worrying.

Now China also had to deal with Westerners. The Portuguese reached the south China coast by 1514, but their aggressive and barbarous behavior led to their expulsion from Guangzhou in 1522, where their envoy died in prison. To the Chinese, they were just another lot of unruly pirates, like the Dutch who followed them later, and their numbers and ships small enough to be brushed off. The Chinese also found them hairy, misshapen, and very smelly, and although a few military commanders noted that their guns were superior to

China's, no one in the government could take them seriously, still less learn anything from them.

The Jesuit missionary effort of the sixteenth-century Counter-Reformation in Europe soon had its eye on China as an immense potential harvest of souls (as all missionaries were to do until the present century) and sent a series of missioners there beginning with Matteo Ricci in 1582 (see Chapter 12). He and his successors, notably Adam Schall von Bell and Ferdinand Verbiest, were learned men with a good working knowledge of the rapidly developing science and technology of post-Renaissance Europe. Complacent Chinese pride kept China from learning from the Jesuits what would have been most useful: new European advances in mathematics, geography (their own picture of the world was still woefully incomplete and inaccurate), mechanics, metal-

lurgy, anatomy, surveying, techniques and instruments for precise measuring and weighing, and even gunnery.

The court was instead fascinated by the clocks and clockwork gadgets or toys that the Jesuits brought and used to ingratiate themselves, while their real potential contribution was passed over. Von Bell, a trained astronomer and mathematician, was able to figure out and explain the use of some remarkable astronomical instruments built under the Yuan dynasty in Beijing; by late Ming the Chinese had lost the secret of these instruments. Their own astronomers had noticed that their calculations no longer accurately predicted the movements of the heavenly bodies, but instead of questioning their assumptions and methods, they concluded that "the heavens were out of order." All these were symptoms of an increasing tendency to ignore new ideas or

Folk Wisdom:
Maxims from the Chinese

A wise man adapts himself to circumstances, as water shapes itself to the vessel that contains it.

Misfortunes issue out where diseases enter in—at the mouth.

The error of one moment becomes the sorrow of a whole life.

The gem cannot be polished without friction, nor man perfected without trials.

A wise man forgets old grudges.

A mouse can drink no more than its fill from a river. [Enough is as good as a feast.]

Who swallows quick can chew little. [Applied to learning.]

What cannot be told had better not be done.

The torment of envy is like a grain of sand in the eye.

Dig a well before you are thirsty.

Better be a dog in peace than a man in anarchy.

To win a cat and lose a cow—the consequences of litigation.

Forbearance is a domestic jewel.

Kindness is more binding than a loan.

Those who cannot sometimes be unheeding or deaf are not fit to rule.

Parents' affection is best shown by teaching their children industry and self-denial.

A truly great man never puts away the simplicity of a child.

To obtain one leads to wishing for two—enough is always something more than a man possesses.

If the upper beam be crooked, the lower will be awry. [The example of superiors.]

One lash to a good horse, one word to a wise man.

The man who combats himself will be happier than he who contends with others.

Let every man sweep the snow from before his own door, and not busy himself about the frost on his neighbour's tiles.

A man need only correct himself with the same rigor that he reprehends in others; and excuse others with the same indulgence he shows to himself.

Source: J. R. Davis, ed., *The Chinese*, vol. 2 (London, Charles Knight, 1845), pp. 235–240.
Note: Text in brackets added to explain maxims in modern terms.

troublesome problems, such as foreigners, or to gloss over them with confident-sounding pronouncements.

At the capital, there was a clear decline in administrative effectiveness by the end of the sixteenth century. The court was filled with intriguing factions, including the eunuchs. This was to become a curse of the imperial system. Hongwu had created a pattern of secrecy, harsh authoritarianism, plotting, and counterplotting. Because they had no heirs, eunuchs were often trusted, given the care of imperial sons, and had ready access to the emperor and to powerful wives and concubines. They were also given command of the palace guard and often won high military posts as commanders or served as imperial inspectors in the provinces. They controlled the workshops that made luxury products for the court and supervised the tribute sent from the provinces and foreign countries. Eunuchs were also often appointed as heads of official missions abroad.

All this gave them limitless opportunities for graft, which they used to enrich themselves. Eunuchs also came to control the fearsome secret police and used their power to blackmail and corrupt as well. This was a burden on the treasury as funds were siphoned off from normal revenues. Another serious drain was the huge allowances paid to the endless relatives of the imperial family and the nobility, altogether many thousands of people and their dependents. By the late sixteenth century these allowances alone consumed over half of the revenues of two provinces, which provides some measure of their gargantuan scope. The heavy expenses of the expedition to Korea to expel the invasion of the Japanese warlord Hideyoshi (see Chapter 9) drained financial resources still further. Subsidies to Mongol and other Central Asian princes, to keep them quiet and to deter them from new uprisings or raids on Chinese territory, increased financial strain. The already high taxes were raised still more, and there were both urban and rural revolts. The burden fell disproportionately on the poor, because many families with money and connections had managed to get their names off the tax registers. Peasants also had to perform heavy labor service, including the rebuilding of the Grand Canal and the Great Wall. Many became so desperate that they just melted away into the countryside or the towns or became bandits.

Strong rulers, such as Hongwu, could check these abuses and control the eunuchs, but under weaker emperors eunuchs often became the real powers, and they did not use their power responsibly. Hongwu had warned his ministers: "Anyone using eunuchs as his eyes and ears will be blind and deaf." After Yongle there was a succession of undistinguished emperors, most of whom kept to the pleasures of their palaces and left the running of the empire to the eunuchs and bureaucrats. This was a disastrous pattern in a system where author-

A sample of the famous Ming blue-and-white porcelain. (Giraudon/Art Resource, NY)

ity and responsibility had been so heavily centralized in the person of the emperor.

Banditry and piracy mushroomed, largely a response not only to growing poverty, as always, but also to the still-growing trade, especially with Japan. Japanese often alternated as traders and as pirates, or "privateers," like their rough contemporaries Drake and Hawkins in Elizabethan England. When the government in 1530 canceled permission for the official Japanese trading missions to Ningbo (on the coast south of Shanghai), piracy and smuggling multiplied. Pirates and smugglers had their major base for the central coast in the Zhusan Islands off the mouth of the Yangzi River, conveniently near Ningbo, then the dominant maritime trade center for populous and highly commercialized central China. Other pirate and smuggling bases were scattered along the much-indented coast of the south in the innumerable small harbors there, shifting from one to another as government pressures or other circumstances required.

This coast, from the Yangzi southward, was almost impossible to patrol adequately, and it had a long history of piracy. Mountains come down to the sea in most of this area, which meant that there were limited opportunities for agriculture or trade on land, but ample forest cover for concealment and to provide timber for ships. Like the shores of much of the Mediterranean, the Dalmatian coast of the Adriatic, or the Caribbean, it combined motives and bases for piracy with tempting opportunity: a golden stream of seaborne trade passing just offshore. In fact, piracy along the south China coast was not finally put down until after 1950, and smuggling continues there still.

As an early twentieth-century report by the Chinese Maritime Customs put it, speaking of the south coast, "Piracy and smuggling are in the blood of the people." When hard-pressed by the authorities of law and order, pirates and smugglers from Xiamen or Shantou southward could cross the border into nearby Vietnam, where they could find sanctuaries, supplies, and Vietnamese colleagues. Hainan Island off the coast opposite the border was long notorious as a pirate and smuggling base for desperadoes from both countries, and even the People's Republic has had trouble preventing large-scale smuggling there. The people of the south China coast were China's principal seafarers in any case, and many earned their livings by fishing and trading. The fleets of Zheng He were built there in those harbors, from local timbers in yards on this coast, and their sailors were recruited there. As the power of the central government weakened under the later Ming, including its naval strength and efficiency, and as poverty worsened after the fifteenth century, piracy and smuggling grew once again out of control. By late Ming, most of the pirates were not Japanese or Korean but Chinese.

There was a great and briefly successful effort at reform led by an outstanding minister, Zhang Zuzheng, who became grand secretary from 1573 to 1582. The emperor Wanli had ascended the throne as a boy in 1572 and was guided for some time by Zhang Zuzheng, who as a distinguished Confucian scholar stressed the need for economy, justice, and responsibility. Zhang tried to increase the now shrinking imperial revenue by once more reforming the tax system to get exempted lands and families that had slipped off the rolls after the earlier tax reform back on again. He also tried to limit the special privileges and extravagant expenses of the court and the imperial family and to rebuild the authority of the censors to report on and check abuses. But after Zhang's death in 1582, Wanli abandoned all pretense at responsibility and indulged in more extravagance and pleasures while leaving the court eunuchs to run the empire. He avoided even seeing his own ministers for many years and refused to make appointments, conduct any business, or take note of or react to any abuses.

Unfortunately, he lived and reigned until 1620, and the 15-year-old who succeeded him on the throne was mentally deficient and spent most of his time tinkering with carpentry in the palace. He gave over control of the government to an old friend of his childhood nurse, a eunuch named Wei who had been a butler to his mother. Wei then almost certainly poisoned the emperor, although it was never proved; by then people were reluctant to challenge him. Wei put together a small eunuch army to control the palace and set up a spy network all over the empire. Earlier he had been a wastrel and built up huge gambling debts. He had himself castrated, confident that as a eunuch he could get a job in the palace. Although he was illiterate, and despite his poisoning of the boy emperor, he was given an official position by the new emperor. By unscrupulous plotting and force he eliminated all of his enemies—most of the Confucianists at court—filled their places with his opportunist supporters, and extorted new taxes to pay for his luxurious lifestyle. There was a general persecution of intellectuals as "conspirators," and many hundreds were executed. Most of the academies were closed. Half the government offices were left vacant, and petitions went unanswered. There was of course Confucian resistance, and a group of scholars calling themselves the Dong Lin, from the name of a famous academy, attempted a moral crusade against these evils. Wei responded with terror tactics after the Dong Lin leader accused him of murders, the forced abortion of the empress, and 24 other "high crimes." In the end, Wei's unscrupulous power won out and most of the Dong Lin scholars were disgraced, jailed, or beaten to death by the time of Wei's own death in 1628 at the hand of an assassin.

It was late for reform, and the eunuch stranglehold was now too strong to break. But as already pointed out, factionalism, corruption, heedlessness, irresponsibility, and moral rot at the capital did not mean that the same problems dominated the rest of the country, which went on under its own momentum until the very end, although with less vigor or success in the last years. Eunuch power at court undercut and then virtually eliminated the power and even the role of the imperial censors. Many were killed when they dared to speak up. By the 1630s most of the country had lost its former confidence in the imperial order and the smooth working of the traditional system. Palace eunuchs went on making most policy, or not making it, after Wei's death. The state treasury had been exhausted by the heavy expense of assisting the Koreans to repel Hideyoshi's invasion (see Chapter 9) and never fully recovered, with disastrous results for the efficient operation of all state systems. Inflation greatly worsened the problem. There were major droughts and famine in Shaanxi Province in the northwest in 1627 and 1628 and spreading revolts, soon covering most of the north.

An Earthquake at Beijing, 1626

The Chinese interpreted earthquakes and other natural disasters as symbols of Heaven's displeasure. When they coincided with popular discontent and dynastic decline, they were seen as warnings. Here is a description of an earthquake in 1626 at Beijing, in the last corrupt years of the Ming. The partisans referred to were palace eunuchs.

Just when the . . . partisans were secretly plotting in the palace, there was a sudden earthquake. A roof ornament over the place where they were sitting fell without any apparent reason and two eunuchs were crushed to death. In a moment there was a sound like thunder rising from the northwest. It shook heaven and earth, and black clouds flowed over confusedly. Peoples' dwellings were destroyed to such an extent that for several miles nothing remained. Great stones hurtled down from the sky like rain. Men and women died by the tens of thousands [a phrase which in Chinese means "a great many"]. Donkeys, horses, chickens, and dogs all had broken or cracked limbs. People with smashed skulls or broken noses were strewn about—the streets were full of them. Gunpowder that had been stored in the Imperial Arsenal exploded. This alarmed elephants, and the elephants ran about wildly, trampling to death an incalculable number of people. The court astrologer reported his interpretation of these events as follows: "In the earth there is tumultuous noise. This is an evil omen of calamity in the world. When noise gushes forth from within the earth, the city must be destroyed. . . . The reason why the earth growls is that throughout the empire troops arise to attack one another, and that palace women and eunuchs have brought about great disorder."

Source: C. O. Hucker in D. Lach, *Asia on the Eve of Europe's Expansion* (Englewood Cliffs, N.J.: Prentice-Hall, 1965), p. 133.

Officials and local magistrates had to cope with a much larger population, one that was increasingly troubled by discontent, banditry, and even rebellion. Their salaries were increased and special allowances were given to discourage them from diverting official funds or taking bribes, but none of this made up for inflation or for the far heavier demands, which necessitated their hiring larger and larger staffs to assist them. These "aides," although essential, were not official employees and their wages were not provided by the state, leaving magistrates and other officials to meet the costs out of their own inadequate salaries and allowances. The inevitable result was increased corruption and bribery, since the greatest of all traditional Confucian virtues was responsibility for one's own family. More and more, the rest of Confucian morality disappeared as individuals and families strove simply to survive.

The Ming army did not distinguish itself in Korea. It drove the Japanese back but then was ambushed near Seoul, the Korean capital; the rest of the campaign was largely a stalemate until Hideyoshi providentially died and his army promptly returned to Japan. A few years later, Matteo Ricci found the Ming army unimpressive: "All those under arms lead a despicable life, for they have not embraced this profession out of love of their country or love of honor but as men in the service of a provider of employment."[9] Ricci added that the army's horses were poor, worn-out things that fled in panic at the mere whinnying of the steppe horses of their opponents. By this time the Chinese saying was common: "Good iron is not used for nails, or good men for soldiers."

Much of the Ming army by this time was composed of ex-prisoners, drifters, former bandits, and idlers. Its size had doubled since the beginning of the dynasty, but its effectiveness had sharply declined. Military contracts had become an open and expanding field for graft and corruption, and the quality of equipment and other supplies had greatly deteriorated, as had military morale and leadership. One of the reasons for the failure to drive the Japanese out of Korea was what had become the inferiority of most Chinese weapons, including swords, spears, and guns. The Japanese had quickly noted and copied the Portuguese improvements in cannons, and the development of an early version of the rifle, the harquebus, a cumbersome muzzle-loading weapon too heavy to hold and fire accurately and hence usually propped up on some support but devastating in close combat. But the Ming cannon were superior, and that made a huge difference.

At the capital under the dissolute emperor Wanli, and progressively elsewhere in the empire, there was a similar decline in effectiveness and morale. Despite Zhang Zhuzheng's brief reforms, corruption had again removed much land and other wealth from the tax rolls, and the new taxes imposed by the eunuch Wei and his successors, together with continuing population increases, created widespread economic hardship and a rapid growth of tenancy, lawlessness, and local famine. Banditry, local revolts, and secret rebel societies, always a barometer of impending collapse, multiplied. There was open talk that the Ming had forfeited the mandate of Heaven.

The now incompetent and demoralized government, almost without a head, had to face two major revolts. The famine in Shaanxi Province in the northwest in 1628 led to arbitrary government economies instead of the needed relief. A postal clerk named Li Zicheng was laid off and joined his uncle who was already a bandit in the mountains. Li and his forces raided widely among three or four adjoining provinces, attracted more followers, set up a government, distributed food to famine victims, appointed officials, and proclaimed a new dynasty. Early in 1644 he advanced on Beijing, meeting only weak resistance. The last Ming emperor, deserted by his officials and driven to despair by news that the city had already fallen, hanged himself in the palace garden where he had lived a life of ease and irresponsibility, after failing to kill his oldest daughter with a sword.

A rival rebel leader named Zhang had meanwhile been raiding and plundering over much of north China with hit-and-run tactics that the Ming armies were unable to cope with. In 1644 he invaded Sichuan, set up a government, and moved to claim the throne himself. His power plays and his terror tactics, however, lost him the support of the gentry, whom he saw as rivals for power, and without them on his side his cause was lost. But the Ming had really defeated themselves by ignoring the basic functions of any government—namely, to govern and to serve their subjects.

The repression of women, which was part of the traditional legacy of Chinese civilization, continued under the Ming, and we have records of very few exceptions. The evil custom of foot-binding, which had begun on a small scale under the Song, became more widespread, causing untold suffering to young girls as their feet were constrained by tight bindings so that the arch of the foot was broken. This was an effort to produce the so-called "lily" foot, an erotic turn-on for men, and to ensure that the girl could find a good husband. In Ming times this custom was largely confined to the upper classes, although it later spread to most of the population of the north, while the south remained, in part, free of it. Yet the Ming novel *Golden Lotus*, and many of the stories of the time, reveled in open promiscuity and pornography.

The Manchu Conquest

Beyond the Great Wall in Manchuria, a non-Chinese steppe people, the Manchus, descendants of the Jurchen who had conquered the Northern Song, had risen to power despite earlier Ming efforts to keep them divided and subdued. A strong leader, Nurhachi (1559–1626), united several previously separate tribes and founded a Chinese-style state, taking the title of emperor and promoting the adoption of the entire Confucian system and its philosophy. His capital was established at Mukden (now called Shenyang) in southern Manchuria, where his two sons, also capable people, succeeded him and continued the Sinification of the Manchu state and culture.

By 1644 the Manchus were politically and culturally largely indistinguishable from the Chinese, except for their spoken language, and they controlled the whole of Manchuria as far south as Shan Hai Guan. Their administration and army included large numbers of Chinese, who accurately saw them as a coming power and as a far more effective state than the Ming had by then become. The Manchus made vassals of the Mongols of Inner Mongolia and of the Koreans, after expeditions had conquered both. They were consciously building their power to take over China, and in 1644 they had their opportunity.

A Ming general, Wu Sangui, confronted with the rebel forces of Li Zicheng, who now occupied Beijing, invited the Manchu armies waiting on the border at Shan Hai Guan to help him defeat the rebels. Having done so handily, the Manchus remained to found the Qing dynasty, rewarding a number of Chinese collaborators with grants of land. Some of these collaborators later rebelled but were suppressed in heavy fighting. Finally, in 1683, the new dynasty conquered the offshore island of Taiwan (Formosa), which had clung to the defeated Ming cause, a situation with parallels in the twentieth century. It thus took nearly another 40 years after 1644 before all Chinese resistance to this new conquest was eliminated by another originally steppe people. But unlike Mongol rule, it ushered in a long period of domestic peace and unprecedented prosperity.

The Manchus called their new dynasty Qing, a title adopted by Nurhachi's son and continued by his grandson, Kangxi (r. 1661–1722), who was only six years old in 1644 and thus "ruled" through a regent until 1661, when he ascended the throne. *Qing* means "pure," and the name was intended to add legitimacy to an alien, even barbarian, rule. But the Manchus had learned their Chinese lessons well. They honored and continued the Ming tradition, and with it the Chinese imperial tradition, and could legitimately say that they were liberators restoring China's glorious past. While this made them, like the Ming, conservative stewards rather than innovators and in time helped to harden them against any change, they too presided over a brilliant period in Chinese history for their first two centuries. Qing was the China most Westerners first knew well. Although the Qing was then in its declining years in the nineteenth century, Westerners still found it impressive, built on a long foundation of imperial greatness before it.

The Ming dynasty ended in ineptness and disgrace, but the more positive aspects of its achievements were valued and preserved by its successors. Having begun with great vigor and success, the Ming went on to administer effectively for two centuries or more a new wave of prosperity, cultural growth, commercial and urban development, and the further refinement of sophisticated taste. Popular culture, aided by cheap printing, enjoyed a notable boom, and in the larger cities rich merchants patronized and participated in elite culture. Although the dramatic maritime expeditions of Zheng He were abandoned, private Chinese trade multiplied with Southeast Asia, and domestic commerce thrived. Agriculture was made more productive, in part under state direction, and the population increased substantially. Ming Beijing still stands as a monument to the dynasty's wealth and power. But the highly centralized system of government begun under Hongwu helped to sap administrative effectiveness under later and weaker emperors, while power came increasingly into the hands of court eunuchs with disastrous results. The Ming ceased to serve their subjects, the country was torn with revolt, and in the end was easy prey for the far better organized Manchus, who had learned the Confucian lessons that the Ming had forgotten.

Questions

1. Why did so many rebel groups adopt a non-Confucian religion?

2. In what ways did the Ming modify the Chinese administrative system?

3. Why did the Ming court decide to end its maritime voyages after China had asserted its dominance over the Asian seas?

4. What were the characteristics of Ming elite culture? How did Ming elite culture differ from that of the Song era?

5. What are the benefits and deficiencies of the rigid examination system implemented by the Ming?

6. Describe the Chinese economy in Ming times. Some have argued that there were ample foundations for capitalist development, especially in the late Ming era. What is the evidence to support such a characterization? What restrained its further development?

7. In what ways was there considerable local autonomy during Ming times, as regional elite and political authorities openly ignored the court's official policies? In what other ways can it be argued that, although the Ming tried to centralize their authority and standardize Chinese culture, Chinese civilization was still substantially decentralized? How is this specifically demonstrated in the development of Chinese popular culture?

Notes

1. J. K. Fairbank, E. O. Reischauer, and A. Craig, *East Asia: Tradition and Transformation* (Boston: Houghton Mifflin, 1978), p. 197.
2. Ibid., p. 182.
3. Ibid., p. 182.
4. W. Bingham, H. Conroy, and F. Ikle, *A History of Asia,* vol. 1 (Boston: Allyn and Bacon, 1964), p. 459.
5. M. Ricci, *China in the Sixteenth Century: The Journals of Matthew Ricci, 1583–1610,* trans. L. J. Gallagher (New York: Random House, 1953), p. 10.
6. After W. McNaughton, *Chinese Literature: An Anthology* (Tokyo: Charles Tuttle, 1959), pp. 697–698.
7. C. O. Hucker, *China's Imperial Past* (Stanford: Stanford University Press, 1975), p. 373.
8. C. O. Hucker, *China to 1850* (Stanford: Stanford University Press, 1980), p. 139.
9. J. Gernet, *A History of Chinese Civilization,* trans. J. R. Foster (Cambridge, England: Cambridge University Press, 1985), p. 431.

Suggested Web Sites

Imperial China: The Ming

http://www.fordham.edu/halsal/eastasia/ eastasiasbook.html
Maps and images pertaining to the Ming dynasty, 1368–1644; a part of the Internet East Asian History Sourcebook.

http://asianart.com/splendors/
A beautiful collection of early Chinese art treasures.

http://loki.stockton.edu/~gilmorew/consorti/2feasia.htm

http://mnsu.edu/emuseum/prehistory/china/ later_imperial_china/ming.html

http://www.wsu.edu:8080/~dee/MING/MING.HTM

**http://bergen.org/AAST/Projects/ChinaHistory/
MING.HTM**
Descriptions of China under the Ming.

Suggestions for Further Reading

Berliner, N. *Chinese Folk Art.* Boston: Little, Brown, 1986.

Birch, C. *Stories from a Ming Collection.* New York: Grove Press, 1958.

Boxer, C. R., ed. *South China in the Sixteenth Century.* London: Hakluyt Society, 1953.

Brook, T. *The Chinese State in Ming Society.* New York/London: RoutledgeCurzon, 2005.

———. *The Confusions of Pleasure: Commerce and Culture in Ming China.* Berkeley: University of California Press, 1998.

Cass, V. *Dangerous Women.* Lanham, MD.: Rowan and Littlefield, 2003.

Chang, S. H. *History and Legend: Ideas and Images in the Ming Historical Novels.* Ann Arbor: University of Michigan Press, 1990.

De Bary, W. T., et al. *Self and Society in Ming Thought.* New York: Columbia University Press, 1970.

Duyvendak, J. J. L. *China's Discovery of Africa.* London: Probsthain, 1949.

Eberhard, W. *Moral and Social Values of the Chinese.* Taipei: Chengwen Publishing, 1971.

Fairbank, J. K. *The Chinese World Order: Traditional China's Foreign Relations.* Cambridge: Harvard University Press, 1968.

Farmer, E. L. *Early Ming Government: The Evolution of Dual Capitals.* Cambridge: Harvard University Press, 1976.

Hayden, G. *Crime and Punishment in Medieval Chinese Drama.* Cambridge: Harvard University Press, 1978.

Hsia, C. T. *The Classic Chinese Novel.* New York: Columbia University Press, 1968.

Huang, R. *Taxation and Government Finance in Sixteenth Century Ming China.* Cambridge: Harvard University Press, 1974.

Hucker, C. O., ed. *Chinese Government in Ming Times.* New York: Columbia University Press, 1969.

Idema, W. L. *Chinese Vernacular Fiction.* Leiden: Brill, 1974.

Johnson, A., Nathan, A., and Rawski, E., eds. *Popular Culture in Late Imperial China.* Berkeley: University of California Press, 1985.

Ko, D. *Every Step a Lotus.* Berkeley: University of California Press, 2002.

Lach, D. F. *China in the Eyes of Europe: The Sixteenth Century.* Chicago: University of Chicago Press, 1968.

Meyer, J. F. *The Dragons of Tienanmen: Beijing as a Sacred City.* Columbia: University of South Carolina Press, 1991.

Mote, F. W. *Imperial China.* Cambridge: Harvard University Press, 1999.

Mote, F. W., and Twitchett, D., eds. *The Cambridge History,* vol. 7, *The Ming.* Cambridge, England: Cambridge University Press, 1987.

Parsons, J. B. *The Peasant Rebellions of the Late Ming Dynasty.* Tucson: University of Arizona Press, 1970.

Rawski, E. S. *Agricultural Change and the Peasant Economy of South China.* Cambridge: Harvard University Press, 1974.

Ricci, M. *China in the Sixteenth Century: The Journals of Matthew Ricci, 1583–1610,* trans. L. J. Gallagher. New York: Random House, 1953.

Rossabi, M. *China Among Equals.* Berkeley: University of California Press, 1983.

Roy, D. T., Transl. *The Plum in the Golden Vase: Chin Ping Mei.* Princeton: Princeton University Press, 2002.

So, K. W. *Japanese Piracy in Ming China During the Sixteenth Century.* East Lansing: Michigan State University Press, 1975.

Struve, L. *The Southern Ming.* New Haven: Yale University Press, 1984.

Tong, J. W. *Disorder Under Heaven: Collective Violence in the Ming.* Stanford: Stanford University Press, 1991.

Tsai, S. H. *The Eunuchs in the Ming Dynasty.* Albany: SUNY Press, 1995.

———. *Perfect Happiness: The Ming Emperor Yongle.* Seattle: University of Washington Press, 2001.

Van Gulik, R. *The Chinese Bell Murders.* Chicago: University of Chicago Press, 1984; and other detective novels set in the Ming and closely modeled on Ming originals.

12

The West Arrives in Asia

Chapter 12 surveys the long isolation of Asia from the West, the beginnings and circumstances of European expansion at the end of the Middle Ages, the Portuguese pioneers of the sea route to Asia around Africa, the nature of the Portuguese trade empire, and the Spanish in the Philippines. Catholic and Jesuit efforts at conversion to Christianity are then considered, including the Jesuits in China, missionary adventures in "Japan's Christian Century," and finally the Dutch and English in Asia, their rivalry, and English attitudes toward Asia as depicted in Shakespeare's play *The Tempest*.

Independent Development

 Although Marco Polo's journal of his spectacular trip to China and India late in the thirteenth century was widely read, Europe and monsoon Asia, the two major poles of world civilization, remained largely isolated from each other until the fifteenth century. The chief exception was India, but its early contact with the Greco-Roman world of the Mediterranean was largely broken after about the fourth century C.E. with the decline of the Roman order. From the seventh century the Arab and Islamic conquest of the Middle East and Central Asia also imposed a formidable barrier. European civilization arose out of the Roman collapse without any but the dimmest awareness of what lay beyond the Arab realms and without the benefit of Asia's far older and more sophisticated model of civilization. The Arabs transmitted westward a few samples of Asian science and technology: Indian mathematics and numeration system, Indian medicine and steel-making technology, Chinese silk, paper, and printing. But medieval Europeans tended to call all of these "Arabic" and either never knew or ignored their Asian origins, especially after the end of direct Roman connections with India and the interposition

of an Arab monopoly on the trade with India and China, by sea, and by land across Central Asia.

From classical times, trade was proportionally more important in Europe than in Asia. Europeans were well aware of a wider and far more varied world than their own, including the Arab-Persian-Turkish world as well as the peoples and cultures of North Africa. European traders from the time of the early Greeks periodically sought to explore and do business with these adjacent areas, so easily linked to their own shores by easy sail across the narrow and usually calm Mediterranean and by relatively easy land routes eastward.

Asians were in general more complacent, proud of their own rich and sophisticated civilizations, whereas Europeans realized early that their own domestic base and, by the Middle Ages, their level of development lagged behind. They knew that wealth could be won through trade abroad. This was an important motive for the Crusades and led, among other things, to a Venetian near-monopoly of trade and great prosperity. Venice went into official mourning on hearing the news of Vasco da Gama's triumphal return from India to Lisbon in 1499, realizing that this meant the end of their monopoly. The Atlantic was now the start of the route to Asia; that meant Portuguese, Dutch, and later English ports, merchants, and ships designed for the open sea—and the eclipse of Venice by its Italian rival, Genoa, the home of Christopher Columbus and Italy's premier port for trade with the Atlantic and hence with the world overseas.

The Portuguese in Asia

 Christopher Columbus, though a Genoese, sailed under the Spanish flag; his objective was Polo's Cathay, which he believed could be reached by sailing westward on a round earth. Until his death he thought

CHRONOLOGY

that the coasts and islands he encountered in the New World were outposts of Asia, perhaps the islands of "Cipangu" (Japan). But the Spanish entered the competition relatively late, delayed in large part by their long effort to eject the Moors, which was finally successful only in 1492. In the end, it was the Portuguese, not Columbus, who pioneered the direct sea route to the East.

Portugal's position on the open Atlantic and the long Portuguese tradition of seafaring and fishing in its stormy waters gave the Portuguese an advantage in this enterprise. Cape St. Vincent, at the southwestern tip of Portugal, is the last outpost of Europe, the jumping-off place for any routes around Africa, which the Portuguese realized early was the way to go. Portugal had never been an important commercial center. It was a relatively poor, mountainous, and backward country, but it knew the open sea, as Mediterranean sailors like the Venetians with their oared galleys did not.

The Portuguese, like the Dutch, had long since necessarily developed more seaworthy craft and had begun to build small ships with benefits from some of the Arab experience riding the monsoon winds in the Indian Ocean, especially the large triangular lateen sail. The Portuguese combined it with an adjustable square sail and then with a kind of jib, making it possible to move better on an angle off the wind instead of only with it. This was the origin of the Portuguese caravel. By the thirteenth century Arab traders had brought the Chinese invention of the compass to Europe. It was adopted early by the Portuguese together with multiple masts and the sternpost rudder, which replaced the awkward and unseaworthy steering oar and was developed first in Han and then in Song China.

Navigation was still crude, and European ships hugged the coasts, using the astrolabe and quadrant to determine their course. These early navigational instruments were arrangements of crosspieces on a disc used to sight the elevation of the sun or the stars and thus to give a rough approximation of latitude. The Portuguese until the late fifteenth century made few open sea voyages out of sight of land, unlike the great Chinese naval expeditions or trading voyages and the Arab and Indian vessels plying the Indian Ocean and the seas between India, China, and Southeast Asia. In their slow progress down the African coast the Portuguese commonly landed every few days and hung their primitive instruments on a tree or staff rather than trying to use them on a rolling or pitching deck. They did, however, begin to make increasingly detailed charts as they followed the coast southward, paving the way for later progress.

By the late fourteenth century, after the Chinese inventions of gunpowder and cannons had spread to Europe, the Portuguese and the Dutch began slow improvements in naval warfare, developing guns designed for use at sea and taking advantage of the greater maneuverability of their vessels with their combinations of sails. Guns were now used to destroy enemy ships or fortifications on shore and replaced the traditional method of ramming or grappling and boarding to enable hand-to-hand fighting, as the Greeks, Romans, and Venetians had done, although Venetians and Turks were also early users of cannon at sea.* But Europeans made their way to Asia with the help of a variety of originally Asian nautical and military technology—and came to record their conquests, profits, and colonial management on Chinese-invented paper.

---

*Turks and Persians never used the sea for trade with monsoon Asia.

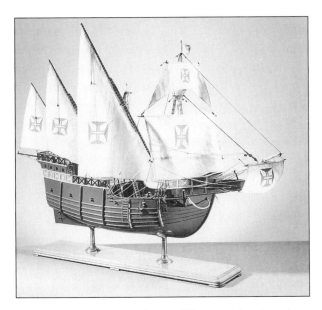

This model of a four-masted caravel illustrates the triangular lateen sails combined with square sails for sailing with the wind. (© National Maritime Museum, London)

Motives for Expansion

The Portuguese had played only a minor role in the Crusades and a European push eastward, partly because they did not have a major commercial interest at that time, but they were fervent Roman Catholics and saw themselves as defenders of the faith. They too had been conquered by the Islamic Moors, and Islamic North Africa lay just across the Gibraltar Straits. All Muslims were seen as the archenemy—and also as blocking the routes to the East and fattening on their control of the trade with Asia. Since early medieval times there had been tales of a Christian ruler, Prester ("priest") John, somewhere east of Europe, who had withstood the Arab onslaught and would make a valuable ally against the common foe. Indeed, the pope of the time gave Marco Polo letters to be delivered to Prester John, thought by some to be Kubilai Khan. More immediately, Muslim traders based in North Africa also controlled the trade in slaves, gold, ivory, drugs, and spices from West Africa by land across the Sahara; this provided the major incentive for the first Portuguese venture abroad, their capture in 1415 of the Moorish city of Ceuta on the Atlantic coast of North Africa west of Gibraltar. This was the beginning of the long Portuguese push down the African Atlantic coast that occupied most of the remainder of the century.

Until his death in 1460, Prince Henry the Navigator (born 1394), younger son of King John I of Portugal, directed and inspired this campaign. Henry sent successive expeditions down the African coast, collected and recorded what they learned, and built up an academy of cartographers and students of exploration and navigation at Sagres on Cape St. Vincent, on a bluff in sight of the sea. Henry's captains built forts and trading stations as they pressed southward, and by the end of the century had replaced the Muslim traders as the dominant commercial power in much of West Africa, importing slaves, gold, ivory, and other trade goods directly to Europe by sea.

Voyages of Exploration

After Prince Henry's death Portuguese explorers continued their progress southward, and in 1487 Bartholomeu Dias finally sailed around the tip of Africa, which he named the Cape of Good Hope. By this time Portuguese interest in trade with Africa had taken second place to their determination to tap the far richer trade of Asia. An expedition of four ships was prepared under Vasco da Gama; it set sail from Lisbon in 1497 with India as its objective. Both da Gama and Columbus had been inspired by Marco Polo's journal and carried copies of it with them. Europeans were still a bit vague about the location of Cathay, "the Indies," or the Spice Islands, as well as the distances and differences between them or between Europe and monsoon Asia. For this reason, though Columbus thought he had reached the margins of Cathay, he called the people he encountered there Indians.

Arab, Indian, and Chinese ships had long been trading across the Indian Ocean to East Africa. After rounding the Cape in the track of Dias, Vasco da Gama arrived at Malindi (now in Kenya) in East Africa early in 1498. He commandeered an Indian Gujarati pilot who had made the voyage many times before to guide him to the port of Calicut on the southwest coast of India. With such help, he reached there easily in May of 1498, after a voyage of nearly a year from Lisbon. The Indian merchants and local rulers realized immediately that the Portuguese represented a threat to their own position in the spice trade and soon found them to be ruthless competitors. When the authorities at Calicut tried to stall him in his requests for trade, da Gama bombarded the town and took Indian hostages. In the end he got his cargo of spices, which on his return to Lisbon in 1499 were said to have brought a 3,000 percent profit and to have paid the full costs of his expedition 600 times over. By 1503 the price of pepper in Lisbon was about a fifth of its price in Venice. Portugal's part in the European discovery of the New World was an incident of the second expedition to India in 1500, when Pedro Cabral's ship was blown off course westward in a great storm off West Africa. His ship reached Brazil, which he claimed for the Portuguese crown.

The Portuguese Commercial Empire

In 1502 da Gama returned to Calicut, which he again bombarded, and then defeated or destroyed Indian and Arab ships sent against him. The Portuguese explored the whole of the Indian west coast and Ceylon, and in 1510 settled on Goa as their principal Asian base, from which they enforced their monopolistic control of all trade westward. It was already clear that the West's new power at sea could win them the upper hand, at least along the coastal areas within range of their guns. Chinese and Indian ships had carried cannon for some time, most of them larger and heavier than those of the Portuguese, and their ships were generally much bigger. But they were also less easily maneuvered, especially in changing wind conditions, and their guns were usually fixed so that they could not be aimed. In repeated encounters after 1498, Western ships resoundingly defeated Indian and Chinese ships, and by the early years of the sixteenth century they had won control of the sea lanes as well as of strategically located trade bases. Even the dreaded Asian pirates were usually no match for them. Soon after the Portuguese arrival, Asian shipbuilders on the Indian west coast began to adopt a Western-looking rig in the hope of scaring off pirates. They sometimes added dummy gun ports for the same purpose.

Meanwhile another Portuguese sailor, Ferdinand Magellan (1480–1521), in the service of Spain, tried to reach Asia as Columbus had done, by sailing westward. He negotiated the stormy and dangerous straits at the tip of South America that still bear his name and sailed across the Pacific to the Philippines, where he and 40 of his men were killed after he had first claimed the islands for Spain. The survivors took the two remaining ships to the Moluccas and loaded a cargo of cloves. Piloted by Juan Sebastian del Cano, a skeleton crew of only 18 men returned to Spain after great hardships. They sailed across the Indian Ocean and around Africa rather than daring again the dangerous passage through the Straits of Magellan. This was the first circumnavigation of the globe; it took some three years and cost the lives of most of those who took part. On the long passage across the Pacific the crew suffered terribly from scurvy and were forced to eat rats, hides, and sawdust, a fate that befell mariners on long voyages for several centuries thereafter.

By the 1520s, the Portuguese, spreading their control rapidly eastward from India and Ceylon, had won a strong position in the East Indies (what is now Indonesia), and in 1529 the Spanish sold their claims to the Moluccas to Portugal. Spain retained the Philippines,

A traditional Chinese junk. These vessels were seaworthy and fast sailers with the monsoonal winds; many were large and had far greater cargo capacity than European ships until the eighteenth or nineteenth centuries. Like the Ming fleets of Zheng He, they were built with separate watertight compartments. (Collections of The New York Public Library, Astor, Lenox, and Tilden Foundations)

and Manila was made the colonial capital in 1571, after earlier Spanish bases and settlements elsewhere in the archipelago had been established. Spain's colonial conquests in the Americas took its major attention, but the Philippines nevertheless became the first major Western colonial territory in Asia and the longest lasting of all large colonial dominions, since Philippine independence was not won until 1946. Latin America threw off Spanish control by the mid-nineteenth century, as did Portuguese Brazil. The tiny Portuguese bases in Asia, which lasted as colonial property even longer (Goa remained Portuguese from 1510 to 1961, Macao from the 1540s technically to 1999), are hardly in the same class.

In this context, the outstanding exception to the general East and South Asian subjugation and devaluing of women was Southeast Asia. There the traditional culture continued to make women equal or even dominant over men, controlling most trade and diplomacy. The bride price that men had to pay to obtain wives amply illustrates the relationship between them, in sharp contrast to the dowry system in the rest of Asia. Women in Southeast Asia often took the initiative in love-making, and premarital sex was encouraged. The system of "temporary or substitute wives," which provided European colonialists or traders with wives for a time, was a further expression of gender equality. (See document on page 238.)

The Spanish in the Philippines

Manila prospered as an interisland entrepôt as well as the colonial capital and provided an important link between Spanish America and Asia, primarily through trade with China. The Manila galleon, as it was called, carried annual shipments of Mexican and Peruvian silver from Acapulco to Manila, much of which went on to China to pay for exports of silk, porcelain, and lacquer back to both New and Old Spain. New World silver flowed into the China market, with major consequences for the economy of the Ming and Qing (1644–1911) periods and their growing commercialization, as well as into Japan. Productive New World crops previously unknown in Asia, especially maize (Indian corn) and potatoes, also entered Asia via Manila and helped to support the subsequent major increase in China's population. Spanish control of the Philippines was relatively loose and did not extend effectively into the more remote or mountainous areas, especially on the larger islands like Luzon (where Manila lies on an extensive bay) or Mindanao in the south.

But it was accompanied by a determined missionary effort to win the inhabitants to Catholic Christianity, which by the later periods of Spanish domination had converted most Filipinos except for some of the mountain tribes and the remaining Muslim groups in southern Mindanao. The Philippines became the only Asian area where Christian missions had any substantial success, owing largely to the absence there of any literate or sophisticated indigenous religious tradition, unlike India, China, Korea, Japan, or the rest of Southeast Asia. When the Spanish arrived, Islam had just begun to penetrate Mindanao, but most of the archipelago remained at an essentially tribal level culturally, practicing a great variety of animistic beliefs and without written texts or philosophical and theological traditions. Spanish also became the language in which educated Filipinos communicated with each other, since there was previously no common language and great regional linguistic variety. The missionary effort included schools, and a new educated elite began to emerge; among them in time the seeds of nationalism would grow, as elsewhere in Western-dominated Asia.

Trading Bases in Asia

Portuguese and later Dutch settlements in Africa were incidental to the drive into Asia, but they served as way stations and provisioning bases along the sea route. Although the Portuguese began the slave trade from West Africa, including to Brazil, and sought a few other African goods such as gold, they did not penetrate inland and their coastal bases were few and scattered. The Asian objective of their effort was emphasized by the names they gave to their two principal African bases: Algoa Bay ("to Goa," now Port Elizabeth in South Africa) and Delagoa Bay ("from Goa," now Maputo in

Portuguese Slavers

Especially after the great period of their trade dominance in Asia had passed, the Portuguese increasingly became pirates—and slavers, as this sixteenth-century text makes clear.

> The Arakan [north coastal Burma] pirates, who were both Portuguese and native, used constantly to come by water and plunder Bengal. They carried off such people as they could seize, pierced the palms of their hands, passed thin slips of cane through the holes, and shut them huddled together under the decks of their ships. Every morning they flung down some uncooked rice, as we do for fowl. . . . Many noblemen and women of family had to undergo the disgrace of slavery or concubinage. . . . Not a house was left inhabited on either side of the rivers. . . . The sailors of the Bengal flotilla were so terrified of the pirates that if a hundred armed boats of the former sighted four of the latter their crews thought themselves lucky if they could save themselves by flight.

Source: M. Collis, *The Land of the Great Image* (New York: Knopf, 1943), p. 85. The author is quoting the sixteenth-century Mughal historian Shiab-ud-din Talish.

The Manila Galleon Trade

The Spanish conquest of Peru in the 1530s provided Spain with immense quantities of silver that it used to purchase directly the luxuries of the East, thus eliminating its dependence on Portuguese intermediaries. Since the Chinese government would not allow Spain to establish a permanent settlement on the China coast, Spain was forced to find a suitable harbor elsewhere. When Spain seized Manila on the island of Luzon in 1570, it was already a prosperous port with a well-established commercial community of Chinese and Southeast Asian merchants. These Manila-based traders had become wealthy as marketers of products from the eastern Indonesian archipelago, but they also traded regularly with Japan, Vietnam, and Thailand.

The Manila galleon was a heavy, square-rigged, three- to five-masted sailing ship that from the sixteenth through the eighteenth centuries sailed between Manila in the Philippines and Acapulco in New Spain (present-day Mexico). In 1573 the first Manila galleon carried Chinese silks, satins, porcelains, and Southeast Asian spices to Acapulco, returning to Manila

with Spanish silver from the Americas. For the next 250 years, Manila was the hub of a commercial circuit in which Asian products were exchanged for New World silver.

A navigational route from Manila to Acapulco and back had been discovered in 1565. The voyage westward from Acapulco to Manila was a relatively easy eight to ten weeks with the wind, catching the Japan Current down the coast of America. The return voyage, however, was much longer—between four and six months—and far more dangerous, as it required a more northerly route and went against the Pacific Ocean wind currents. A galleon leaving Manila departed between April and July. Sometimes up to 75 percent of the crew members died from disease or malnutrition before the galleon reached Acapulco; a 30 to 40 percent loss of crew was usual. To improve the odds of survival on the voyage from Manila, the Spanish settled the California coast in order to provision galleons before they made their way south to Acapulco.

The voyage, though risky, produced high profits. The Atlantic Ocean trade normally returned a 15 percent profit, but it was not unusual to realize a 30 to 50 percent interest on an investment in the Manila galleon trade. Between 1570 and 1780 an estimated 4,000 to 5,000 tons of silver were exported to Manila. In 1597, the bullion shipped from Acapulco to Manila reached an

---

Mozambique). The names reflected the dominant wind patterns that determined the best routes by sail across the Indian Ocean to and from Goa, the administrative center of Portugal's Asian enterprise.

But for over two centuries after Europeans had made contact with Asia by sea, they remained insignificant on the Asian scene, a handful of people dismissed by Asians as crude barbarians. At sea and along the Asian coasts they had the upper hand, but their power on land extended little beyond the range of their naval guns, and they were completely outclassed in power on land by the great Asian empires or more local states. The Portuguese and later the Dutch built a strong position in the spice trade and were rivals for the monopoly of its export to Europe, but within Asian commerce as a whole, even its seaborne component, their role was minor. They bought spices and a few other goods in preexisting markets at established ports, such as Calicut, where they had already been collected by Asian traders, and then hauled them to Europe. The Portuguese never, and

the Dutch only much later, had any involvement in production, and both continued to compete as traders with numerous Chinese, Indian, Southeast Asian, and Arab entrepreneurs, who did the bulk of the assembly. Only in the transporting of Asian goods to Europe did they have a monopoly. There the Portuguese in time faced intense competition from the Dutch and English.

As if to emphasize their role as ocean carriers with their improved ships for long voyages, the Portuguese developed a highly profitable trade between China and Japan, carrying Chinese silks and porcelains and some Southeast Asian spices from the Guangzhou area to Nagasaki in southwestern Japan, bringing back Japanese silver and copper for China. They, and later the English, also found profit in hauling Southeast Asian and Chinese goods to India and exchanging them for the Indian cottons that had an even larger and more eager market in Europe.

Recognizing their weakness on land or in trade competition with Asian and Arab merchants, Europeans

astounding 12 million pesos. So much silver was shipped to Manila and so many Asian products were returned that Spanish merchants in Seville, who had been granted a monopoly on the New World import and export trade, forced the Spanish government to limit the value and volume of the annual Manila galleon trade. Official regulations of the galleon trade were meant to guarantee sufficient profit in order to subsidize Manila's Spanish population and government while also protecting the interests of Spanish merchants. Despite these regulations, the volume of the galleon trade always far exceeded the official limits. When the Englishman George Anson captured the Manila galleon *Covadonga* in 1746, he found over 1 million pesos on board, much of it hidden to escape customs payments.

Restrictions on the volume of the galleon trade inhibited Spain's interest in developing trading relationships with other Asian states. Not until the British occupied Manila in 1762—and subsequently plundered it—did the residents of Manila's Spanish community venture into Luzon's interior to cultivate crops for export. Since the Spanish elite were content to remain in Manila, Filipinos and *mestizos* (people of mixed race) managed the transport of produce from the interior to the ports, and together with the Spanish friars established landed estates on which they began to raise cash crops for export.

Cargo space in the Manila galleon was divided into shares of fixed size that were controlled by the Spanish community in Manila. Few of these Spaniards in Manila were merchants themselves. Instead, they sold their cargo space to Chinese merchants or depended on Chinese trade partners who secured cargoes and traded on their behalf. The Spanish Church was also a major participant in the trade, often supplying most of the capital to purchase Chinese goods and outfit the galleon and frequently subsidizing Manila's Spanish community between the galleon's annual visits. Spanish residents of Manila were so dependent on the galleon trade that the loss or capture of a galleon could bring the community to financial ruin.

The Manila galleon trade brought together Spanish, Chinese, and local Filipino residents, linking them through both commercial and marriage alliances. By the end of the nineteenth century, the mestizo offspring of these marriage alliances would challenge Spanish rule and claim authority in Manila, in a new partnership with United States colonists.

---

built on their strength at sea by occupying and fortifying coastal footholds at key points along the sea routes. Ideally, these were in areas on the fringes of the great Asian empires or where the local power was weak or could be persuaded to grant privileges in return for favors. The latter often included Western naval help against pirates, rebels, or small rival states. The Portuguese seized Goa on the Indian west coast in 1510 and soon made it into their major Asian base. The small area around the city was not then part of any powerful Indian state. The Portuguese saw that they had little hope of controlling the larger ports farther south, such as Calicut, although they did establish some smaller bases elsewhere on the Malabar coast in the west. From Goa, however, their ships could patrol the entire coast and essentially control Indian Ocean trade. Goa was a logical choice as the administrative center of the extensive Portuguese trade network farther east, and it prospered so much on the profits of that trade that it became known as "Golden Goa."

A commercial empire that stretched another 6,000 miles east by sea, through all of Southeast Asia (except the Philippines) and on to China and Japan required other bases too. The most obvious control points over the sea lanes eastward from India were Colombo in Ceylon (now Sri Lanka) and Melaka in Malaya. The Palk Strait between India and Ceylon was too shallow for shipping, and the route around Sumatra and through the Sunda Strait between Sumatra and Java added extra miles and was plagued by reefs and currents, with no safe harbors along the Sumatran west coast. Traffic to and from East Asia was therefore funneled through the Straits of Melaka. The Portuguese seized the town of Melaka, commanding the straits, in 1511, but Malaya at that period was thinly settled and relatively unproductive. Melaka's role was primarily strategic, and drew the Portuguese because they rightfully saw it as that era's critical intermediary in the China trade as well as the paramount international marketplace for insular Southeast Asia's spices. Colombo, which the Portuguese also fortified after

The harbor of Goa, with craft much the same as those used in the fifteenth and sixteenth centuries. (R. Murphey)

establishing themselves there about 1515, was able to draw on the nearby production of cinnamon, predominantly a Ceylonese product produced from the bark of a rain forest tree, and thus played a commercial role as well.

For trade with China and Japan, the Portuguese somewhat later established their chief base at Macao, at the seaward edge of the Guangzhou delta. There they could be a little freer of the restrictions imposed on foreign merchants at Guangzhou by the Ming government and be tolerated by the Chinese authorities, enough to permit modest fortifications and a small, permanent settlement. From the Chinese point of view, these unruly and barbaric foreigners were better shunted off to such a remote neck of land and closed off by a wall (which still stands) where they could not make trouble or corrupt the Chinese and where they could govern themselves according to their own strange customs. In the sixteenth century the Ming were still close to the height of their power and effectively excluded all foreigners except for tribute missions and a handful of traders at the fringes. There was no comparable territorial base in Indonesia, where in any case there was no large state at this time. The Portuguese dominated the spice trade and excluded rival Europeans by intimidation of local sultans, alliances or treaties with others, and a scattered string of forts as far east as Ternate and Amboina in the Moluccas.

The shape and nature of the Portuguese commercial empire are clearly defined by its emphasis on strategically located ports, most of them already long in existence, and on domination of the sea lanes. They controlled no territory beyond the immediate area of the few ports named and traded in the hundreds of other ports in competition with Asian and Arab traders. Even so, their effort was overextended, and by the latter part of the sixteenth century they could no longer maintain what control they had earlier established. Their home base was tiny as well as poor; it could not provide either manpower or funds to sustain the effort required to maintain their overseas stations against competition. As the century ended they were rapidly being ousted by the Dutch in Southeast Asia and were soon to be eliminated as serious competitors in the rest of the Asian trade by the other rising European power, the English.

Many Portuguese stayed on, picking up crumbs of trade and operating as pirates. As in Africa, they had from early days married local women, and from the seventeenth century virtually all of them in Asia were Eurasians, though commonly carrying Portuguese names and retaining the Catholic faith to which they had been converted. To this day Portuguese names such as Fernando or de Souza are common in coastal south India, Sri Lanka, Melaka, dotted throughout the Indonesian archipelago, and in Macao. As Portuguese power faded, their bases were no longer a threat, so Portugal retained formal sovereignty over Goa until it was forcibly reclaimed by India in 1961. Amazingly enough, the fiction of Portuguese control was maintained for Macao until 1999, an arrangement that suited the convenience of the Chinese government.

"Christians and Spices"

Conversion to Roman Catholicism was a major motive of the Portuguese and Spanish drive overseas from the beginning. They saw it as a new Crusade. Like all the Spanish and Portuguese explorers, da Gama, and Cortez in Mexico, carried missionary priests as well as soldiers in their ships and saw their

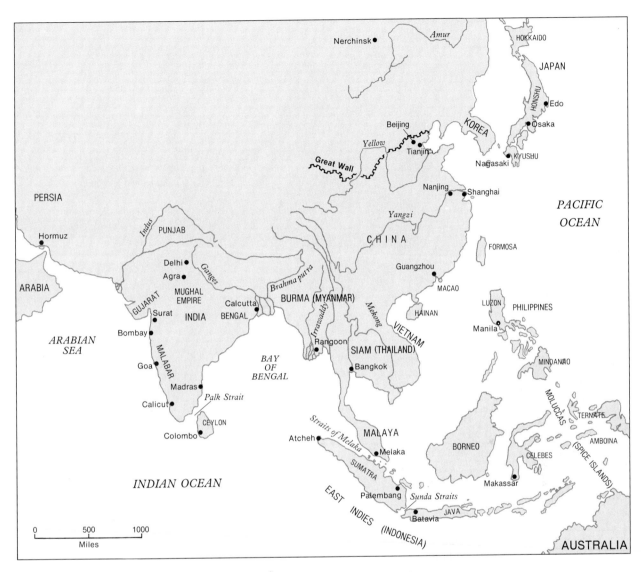

Asia in the Age of Early European Expansion

Note the Straits of Melaka as the shortest route east from India, which in turn was naturally the first Asian area to be reached by the Europeans by sea.

goal as winning souls (or killing heathens) as much as winning trade profits. When da Gama reached Calicut, according to a widely repeated story, he is said to have replied to questions about what he sought, "Christians and spices," a neat summary of the two aims of both the Iberian states abroad. The Portuguese did encounter the Christians of southern India but soon dismissed them contemptuously as "heretics." They freely slaughtered Hindus and Muslims, both of whom they saw as enemies. The Portuguese and Spanish were, after all, the heirs of the Roman Catholic Inquisition and its persecution or execution of all alleged heretics and infidels. Such people and their beliefs were seen as the work of Satan, and those who had the

truth had a sacred duty to destroy them and to spread the "true word."

Affonso de Albuquerque (1453–1515), named viceroy of the Indies in 1508 and the chief architect of the Portuguese commercial empire in Asia, wrote of his plan to capture Melaka in 1511:

The first aim is the great service which we shall perform to our Lord in casting the Moors out of this country and quenching the fire of the sect of Mohammed. . . . And the other is the service we shall render to the king . . . in taking this city, because it is the source of all the spiceries and drugs which the Moors carry every year. . . . For I hold it certain that if we take this trade of Malacca (Melaka) away

Portuguese-founded church in Kerala, southern India. The architecture clearly marks its Western origin. (R. Murphey)

from them, Cairo and Mecca will be entirely ruined, and Venice will receive no spiceries unless her merchants go and buy them in Portugal.[1]

When Albuquerque took Melaka, he massacred all the Muslims but tried to make allies or friends of the few other inhabitants. In Malaya and Indonesia, by now dominantly Muslim, these were not attitudes or policies calculated to ingratiate the Portuguese. Their cruel practice of conversion by torture, their pitiless extortion, and their slaughter of "heathen" Hindus and Buddhists as well as their ancient Muslim foes earned them hatred. The Portuguese record during their brief century of power in Asia is at least as horrendous as that of

Convenience Marriage

An early Dutch traveler to the Malay Peninsula remarked on the Southeast Asian practice of "temporary marriage" to accommodate foreign visitors:

When foreigners come there from other lands to do business . . . men come and ask them whether they do not desire a woman; these young women and girls themselves also come and present themselves, from whom they may choose the one most agreeable to them, provided they agree what he shall pay for certain months. Once they agree about the money (which does not amount to much for so great a convenience), she comes to his house and serves him by day as his maidservant and by night as his wedded wife. He is then not able to consort with other women or he will be in grave trouble with his "wife", while she is similarly forbidden to converse with other men, but the marriage lasts as long as he keeps his residence there. . . . When he wants to depart he gives her whatever is promised, and so they leave each other in friendship, and she may then look for another man as she wishes, in all propriety and without scandal.

Source: A. Reid, *Southeast Asia in the Age of Commerce: The Lands Below the Winds.* (New Haven, CT: Yale University Press, 1981), p. 155.

the Spanish in the New World, and their decline was regretted by none.

By the early 1500s, with the beginnings of the Protestant Reformation in Europe and widespread criticisms of the Roman Catholic church, the Catholic European powers mounted a counteroffensive, a movement that came to be known as the Counter-Reformation. This was designed to regain ground lost to the Protestants and included renewed efforts to spread Catholicism abroad. In 1534 Ignatius Loyola founded the Society of Jesus, also called the Order of the Jesuits, dedicated to reaffirming and teaching the Roman Catholic faith and to winning new converts. Asia became the major target because of its huge population and because of the Western conviction that Hinduism, Buddhism, and Confucianism were not legitimate or adequate religions at all and hence should easily yield to the superior message of Christianity. Islam remained the archenemy against which European Christendom had been at war for centuries. Thus, a new urgency was added to Portuguese and Spanish efforts in Asia, one that profoundly colored their impact.

The Chinese remained aloof from these Western maritime and commercial rivalries and kept European traders at arm's length at Guangzhou, where they were not even permitted to enter the city but did their business outside the walls during the six-month trading season and then were obliged to depart until the next year. Successive Portuguese, Dutch, and English efforts to break these restrictions by trading elsewhere on the China coast were repelled, as Europeans did not have the means to challenge the Dragon Throne. The sixteenth-century missionary effort to penetrate China was more successful, at least for a time. For the Jesuits, as for all later missionary groups, China was the chief goal, if only because of its immense population, its sophisticated culture, and the knowledge that it lacked an indigenous religion of salvation. Successive Jesuit efforts to enter the country failed after Francis Xavier died off the south China coast in 1552, still cherishing the dream of converting China's millions.

A CLOSER LOOK

Matteo Ricci: Missionary to the Ming Court

The pioneer of the Jesuit effort in China was Matteo Ricci. He was born at Ancona in 1552, where he soon demonstrated his scholastic ability and magnetic personality. At the age of 16 he went to Rome to study law, and at 19 he entered the Society of Jesus, where he distinguished himself in mathematics and geography. In 1577 he determined to pursue his career in the East and arrived in Goa the following year. After finishing his religious training, he taught in the college there until 1582,

when he was called to Macao to prepare himself for the challenge of China. There he began diligent study of written and spoken Chinese and in 1583 became the first Jesuit to enter China, although at first only as a "guest" in Guangdong Province near Guangzhou. There he continued his study of the Confucian classics and in 1589 built a church in Chinese architectural style. By this time he had discovered that priests of any kind were associated with the now-despised Buddhists, and he, therefore, adopted the dress as well as the manner and education of a Confucian scholar.

Ricci was a compelling person, tall and vigorous with flashing blue eyes, a curly beard (which assured the Chinese of his sagacity), and a resonant voice. What impressed them most, however, was his remarkable learning, combining as it did most of contemporary Western achievements, including cartography, and a thorough mastery of the classical Chinese corpus. He also had a phenomenal, almost photographic, memory and made use of a variety of mnemonic devices to assist it. This was a tremendous help to a

Matteo Ricci with his most prominent convert, Li Paulus, who translated European works on astronomy from Latin into Chinese. Li Paulus is wearing the winged cap of a high Chinese official, which he was, and Ricci the gown of a Chinese scholar. (Rare Book Division, The New York Public Library, Astor, Lenox, and Tilden Foundations)

scholar, especially for learning Chinese characters. Ricci was accordingly much sought after by Chinese who wanted to succeed in the imperial examinations or wanted their sons to do so. This enhanced his acceptability, as did his success in dissociating himself entirely from the Portuguese traders at Macao. In 1595 he and his missionary colleagues were permitted to move north to the Yangzi valley and in 1601 to establish their permanent base at Beijing.

The reigning emperor, Ming Wanli, had become incompetent and concerned only with pleasures; the court was corrupt and full of scheming factions. Ricci finally caught the emperor's fancy by presenting him with two clocks and a clavichord, a precursor of the piano. When asked to demonstrate it, he composed some "edifying" madrigals for his majesty to sing. Later he was given a special imperial stipend and accepted at court as an outstanding and useful scholar. As the first missionary to China and one who fully understood how the hierarchical Chinese society worked, Ricci concentrated on the well placed. To avoid alienating them and to make Christianity more understandable and appealing, he represented it as a system of ethics similar to and compatible with Confucianism, leaving out such potentially upsetting parts as the crucifixion, the virgin birth, and equality of all persons. He also avoided discussion of Christian theology.

This abbreviated version of the faith got the Jesuits in trouble with Rome later on, but it made excellent sense if the aim was to interest the Chinese. Ricci avoided preaching or overt efforts at conversion, and when he died in 1610 he was buried at Beijing in a special plot granted by the emperor. He and his colleagues won few converts, but they saw their role as preparing the ground for a later assault by easing the Chinese into accepting the less controversial parts of Christianity and by masquerading as Confucian scholars. With his sharp mind, vast erudition, and winning personality, Ricci was an ideal person for such a role, but interest in him as a scholar never led to an equivalent interest in the religion he came to China to plant.

Such success as Ricci and his successors achieved was largely the result of their use of some of the new fruits of the European Renaissance as a lure, especially early clocks, improvements in the calendar, maps of the world, astronomy, and glass prisms. Such things intrigued the Chinese and ingratiated the Jesuits at court as learned men. By now they had necessarily learned not only the Chinese language and the Confucian classics but the full deportment of the Confucian scholar as the vital credential for acceptance. They also understood that in this hierarchical society the key to missionary success was to convert those at the top, especially the emperor, and that preaching to the masses would only label them as troublemakers. Aided by their Confucian guise as men of learning and their use-

ful Renaissance knowledge and interesting inventions, they made some converts among the gentry and court officials, but though they interested successive emperors, they never converted many Chinese. Western technology was more appealing than Western religion; this has remained true into our own times.

In the end, the Jesuit effort was undermined by the pope, who refused to permit their softening of Catholic doctrine or the acceptance of some Confucian rites in order to avoid offending potential converts. The controversy simmered for years, but the ground had been cut out from under the Jesuits, and they were ultimately expelled in the early eighteenth century. Meanwhile, their accounts of China became an important source of Western knowledge and contributed to the European Enlightenment view that China was a state of philosopher-kings. European admiration of China and India, and what people like the French philosophers Voltaire and Montesquieu wrote about it, influenced the American heirs of the Enlightenment, who framed our republic in the Jeffersonian vision of an educated citizenry. During much of this period there was a Western craze for things Chinese: paintings, furniture, gardens, flowered wallpaper, as well as the Confucian order.

The Russian Advance in Asia

Russian expansion across Siberia was slow but involved permanent Russian occupation and domination of these vast territories and their technologically less developed peoples, whose numbers were also small. By 1637 the Russians had reached the Pacific north of what is now Vladivostok, but they were behind the western Europeans in making direct connection with China. Early Russian explorers followed the major Siberian rivers, but these flow northward into the Arctic. Gradually a network of fortified garrisons and trading posts spread eastward. When the Amur River was reached, it was eagerly used as an easier route leading to more productive areas and to the sea. Russian presence in the Amur Valley came to Chinese attention when northern Manchurian tribes, tributary vassals of the Qing dynasty, appealed for help. Mongol groups were also trading with the Russians, which additionally alarmed the Chinese. Two successive Russian embassies to Beijing, in 1654 and 1676, requesting trade privileges, refused to perform the required prostrations before the emperor and were sent away. By the 1680s, the Qing, now having consolidated their power within China, began to establish new routes and military colonies in the Amur region and put naval ships on the river itself. The Russians were quickly chased out, and a large Qing army besieged the one remaining Russian fortress. The Russians now agreed to negotiate and sent an ambassador to their major post at Nerchinsk, on an upper Amur tributary but still within Siberia.

The treaty concluded there in 1689 confirmed the Amur region as Chinese and obliged the Russians to destroy their remaining fortress but accepted limited Russian trade rights by camel caravan to Beijing, in part because the Chinese court wanted to maintain the supply of fine Russian furs from Siberia. A later treaty in 1727 excluded Russia from Mongolia and further delimited the boundary between Russia and China, leaving the Russians only Siberia. The Qing emperor Kangxi would not deal directly with "barbarians," still less go to them, so he sent as his representatives two Jesuits from the court whom he deemed appropriate agents for the management of such affairs. Nevertheless, the Treaty of Nerchinsk treated both sides as essentially equal sovereign states. It was the only such treaty agreed to by China with a Western state until the nineteenth century, when China was forced to abandon the pretense of political superiority and accept inferior status. Until 1842, the various "sea barbarians" could be treated as savages, though Russia as a rival and adjacent land power had to be dealt with differently. Fear of Russia and its ambitions remained a fixture in the Chinese mind and was later intensified by Russian expansion into Manchuria.

Japan's Christian Century

The Japanese, as a small, remote, and, in their own view, less-developed people, were far more open than the Chinese or the Indians to new ideas, even of foreign origin. Where Chinese, and often Indians, with their immense cultural pride and self-confidence, tended to dismiss anything foreign as crude and undesirable, the Japanese remained curious and sought opportunities to learn, as they had done from Tang China. The sixteenth century, sometimes called "Japan's Christian Century," saw significant numbers of Christian converts as well as a flourishing trade with Europeans, centered in Nagasaki but also at Osaka, Edo (Tokyo), and other ports. After missionary work in Goa and the East Indies, Francis Xavier spent two years (1549–1551) in Japan preaching, teaching, and disputing with Buddhist monks.

But Christians were soon branded as troublemakers. Rival Catholic religious orders contended with one another, often violently, as did the Portuguese, Spanish, Dutch, and English. Their ships and arms were often used in domestic Japanese factional fighting and intrigue, and Christianity was also seen as corrupting the Confucian loyalty of the Japanese and making converts potential subversives. Portuguese missionaries in Japan

were told that if Christianity was, as they asserted, the only true religion, it would have been adopted by the Chinese long ago. This convinced the Jesuits that the Chinese were key to the rest of East Asia, but, as just indicated, their efforts at conversion failed. In Japan, the contending missionaries were increasingly seen as disruptive. Christianity was suppressed by 1640, thousands of converts were crucified, and all foreigners were expelled. The Japanese were forbidden to go abroad, and contact with the world beyond China was limited to one Dutch ship a year, allowed to trade only on an island in Nagasaki Harbor.

The first burst of Western activity in Asia thus ended with only minor success. It was the Europeans who sought out the East, because Europe—poor and backward by comparison with the riches of Asia—was eager for contact. In terms of power the Europeans were no match for the great Asian empires or even for lesser states, and they had nothing desirable to offer in trade with the more sophisticated economies of the East. This was to inhibit European contacts for several more centuries. The Europeans had to be content with a few tiny and insecure footholds on the coast, where they competed with Asian and Arab merchants. Sometimes they were thrown out at the whim of the Asian states and their goods confiscated.

Only at sea were the Europeans powerful—hence in part the Dutch success in controlling most of the trade of insular Southeast Asia—and there they tended to cancel each other out as rivals. Their chief commercial advantage was in the carrying trade, where their ships made them competitive but where they served mainly Asian markets. Although Portuguese power subsequently faded in the face of Dutch and English competition, often forcing the Portuguese into piracy, the Asians continued to acknowledge Western superiority at sea. As the first British consul at Shanghai was to remark over three centuries later in 1843: "By our ships our power can be seen, and if necessary, felt."[2] This was to remain the major basis of Western success in Asia throughout the centuries from 1498 to the end of colonialism in the ashes of World War II.

In the early period, Asians saw Westerners (except the Jesuits) as clever with ships and guns but ignorant, dirty, contentious, drunken, uncivilized, and treacherous—all understandable descriptions of the European adventurers of the time. The habit of regular bathing did not come to Europe until well into the nineteenth century, with the advent of piped water and more adequate domestic heating. The smell of the Westerners who arrived in Asia during the first three centuries of their contact, after several months cooped up on board their tiny ships, disgusted the far cleaner Asians, especially Indians and Japanese with their practice of scrupulous daily bathing and Indian daily toothbrushing. Westerners were also generally bearded, unkempt, and

Western traders arriving at Nagasaki. A contemporary painting of the seventeenth century. (Courtesy of the Tokyo National Museum. DNParchives.com)

ill-mannered, brawling with each other and with rival Western nationals.

The Chinese, noticing their greater amount of body hair, smell, and strange features as well as their wild behavior, reasoned that they must be more closely descended from apes. They were certainly by Asian standards an unimpressive, impetuous lot of ruffians, adventurers and pirates by their own accounts, as well as religious bigots. The only qualities that made them viable in a far more civilized Asia were their naval skills and their ruthlessness. Nevertheless, and to Asia's later cost, they were largely ignored. That seemed reasonable enough in the splendid and confident context of Mughal India, Ming and Qing China, and Tokugawa Japan (1600–1869), and it remained so for another two or three centuries. But one after the other, the Asian political orders declined, while by the late eighteenth century, Europe began to ride the wave of new industrial, economic, and technological power.

The Dutch in Asia

The union of Portugal and Spain in 1580 did not materially strengthen what was now their joint effort in the East, but it did highlight the enmity and rivalry between them as Catholic powers and the rising Protestant states of the Netherlands and England. All of the Iberian positions overseas became attractive targets, and Portuguese profits were newly tempting. The Dutch were the first to pick up this challenge effectively in Asia. At this period the Netherlands was a more important center of trade and shipping than was England, and Dutch ships had the upper hand in the English Channel. There were more of them, backed by merchant capital earned in trade, and in the course of the sixteenth century they became larger and more powerful, as well as more maneuverable, than the Portuguese caravels. Dutch seamen had traveled east on Portuguese ships and learned what they needed to know about sailing to Asia and about trading there: what and where to buy and sell most profitably.

The Dutchman Jan Huyghen van Linschoten sailed on a Portuguese ship to Goa and spent some six years there from 1583 to 1589 in the service of the Portuguese archbishop. After his return to Holland he published in 1595–1596 an *Itinerario,* a geographical description of the world as he knew it, his observations in Asia, and a set of sailing directions for reaching most of the major Asian ports. This was exactly what the Dutch (and the English, who soon translated the book) needed. The Dutch had earlier made determined efforts to find a northeast passage around Russia but found (as the English were to do) that this was not possible. Now a better path east lay open, and the Dutch also knew that the Portuguese trade empire was overextended and weakening. A Dutch fleet under Cornelis de Houtman sailed to Asia in 1595, using van Linschoten's sailing directions, and this was followed by a series of trading expeditions financed by various Dutch syndicates.

They found the Portuguese generally disliked, especially in Southeast Asia, and they quickly broke the Portuguese spice monopoly. Their ships and sailors were better and could accomplish cheaper and quicker passages to and from Europe. The first real battle between Dutch and Portuguese ships off Bantam in western Java in 1601 led to a decisive Dutch victory; even though the Portuguese ships and men outnumbered them, the Portuguese guns were inferior and their ships were less able at maneuvering. As the seventeenth century opened, Dutch ships already outnumbered the Portuguese in Asia and had established their own semimonopoly of the spice trade, concentrating their Asian effort on what is now Indonesia and adjacent Malaya. They also ousted the Portuguese from Ceylon beginning in the 1640s and captured Melaka in 1641, both of them strategic points whose passing to Dutch control signaled the end of the Portuguese position and the rise of Dutch power.

Unlike the Portuguese, the Dutch concentrated on trade and avoided all missionary efforts or religious conflict. But they were a hard lot and enforced their new monopoly ruthlessly against both Asian and European rivals. The several rival Dutch companies organized for trading to Asia were amalgamated into one national organization in 1602, the Dutch East India Company, to which the government gave a monopoly of all trade with the East. It was empowered to make war or treaties, seize foreign ships, build forts, establish colonies, and coin money—all under loose government supervision from home. The new company's chief rivals were now the English, whom the Dutch ultimately drove out of their new domain in what is now Indonesia. Their monopoly was far more effective than that of the Portuguese had been, and they had better means to maintain it by force. English ships were driven off by gunfire, and a small group of 10 English merchants who had begun to buy spices in the Moluccas, at Amboina, were accused of conspiracy, tortured to extract confessions, and then executed in 1623. This was the final blow to English hopes in the islands of the East Indies, and thereafter they concentrated their efforts on India. The Dutch retained some trading posts on the Indian east coast and Bengal, in mainland Southeast Asia, and in Formosa (Taiwan) and had a small part in the trade with Guangzhou and Nagasaki (in Japan), but their major focus was the East Indies, especially the productive island of Java.

Dutch success was due in part to their highly able governor-general Jan Pieterzoon Coen, appointed in 1618, who fixed the naval and administrative capital of the Dutch East Indies at Batavia (now Jakarta) in western Java, where it could guard the Sunda Straits. Dutch ships patrolled the waters and ports of Southeast Asia south of the Philippines and excluded Western competitors, while recognizing that the long-established trade of Asia would remain largely in Asian and Arab hands. They realized that greater profits could be won by taking whatever part in it they could win competitively and by hauling Asian goods, mainly spices, to the European market. Governor-general Coen did for the Dutch what Albuquerque had done for the Portuguese, but with far greater and longer-lasting effect. He turned what had been a network of trading posts into a chain of strongholds and ruled this new commercial empire with an iron hand.

The Dutch drove hard bargains and eliminated rivals wherever they could. Many of the local rulers began to regret their earlier willingness to exchange the Portuguese for the Dutch, but Coen and his successors gave them little choice. On their own company ships, the standard punishment for fighting among the crew was to nail to the mast one hand of the man judged guilty; thirst in the hot sun might eventually drive him to tear his hand loose, unless he was taken down sooner. For a second offense the punishment was keelhauling: tying one end of a rope to the man's feet and the other to his hands while the crew pulled on the rope so as to pass him under the ship's keel, a procedure that not many survived.

The Dutch acquired territory in Asia slowly and reluctantly; they were interested in profits only and resented the labor and cost of administration or involvement in local politics. But if they were to protect their bases and forts and to enforce their monopoly, they realized in time that some of their attention and resources would have to be diverted from making money to safeguarding it. The vicinity of Batavia came under direct Dutch rule, as did the other major ports. Slowly their grip on western Java, Ceylon, and the Moluccas strengthened, first by treaties with local rulers, then by joining one side against the others, and finally, by the eighteenth century taking over more or less full control. Many Dutch-controlled territories in the East Indies were ostensibly headed by a native regent or were managed as protectorates or allies, with a Dutch resident appointed as the ruler behind the scenes.

Trade profits were augmented by tribute exacted from the local states, as well as by forced deliveries of commodities at artificially low prices. The Dutch introduced coffee growing to Java in the late seventeenth century; while they initially compelled the Javanese to grow it, western Java's peasants soon responded to the new marketing opportunity by converting their fields to coffee production at their own initiative. By the eighteenth century it became the island's largest export to Europe. They also encouraged the production of sugar and indigo, and both became highly profitable exports. Almost as much as the Portuguese, however, the Dutch in Asia freely married local women, although such wives were often discriminated against, as were their children. The Chinese, with their commercial experience, were welcomed by the Dutch but lived in their own areas at each port and under the administration of their own headmen, as had been the case for most foreigners throughout Asian history.

The Dutch East India Company slowly began to regulate production in order to maintain prices and to impose their direct control on the areas that produced the most valuable crops. Indonesians in the areas ruled directly by the Dutch were subject to forced labor, most often for construction and harbor-improvement projects. Spices remained crucially important to the company, and the island of Amboina in the Moluccas and the Banda Islands were wholly Dutch-run. Production was adjusted to market demand, and in some years trees were actually cut down to avoid surpluses that might depress prices. Production of other crops was "encouraged" by various pressures, including later the imposition of taxes that obliged subsistence growers of rice to grow sugar or other cash crops in order to pay the taxes. Crops could be sold only to the company. Indigenous traders and shipbuilders were driven out by Chinese and Dutch competition, and the Javanese especially became largely a group of cultivators and laborers. It was their misfortune that by the sixteenth century the Muslim conquest had undermined the earlier Hindu-Buddhist civilization of Java. The whole archipelago, as well as Java itself, was divided into a great number of small rival kingdoms that were easily outmaneuvered and in the end subdued by the determined, highly organized, and persistent Dutch.

The English in Asia

Like the Dutch, the English first tried to find a northeast passage, and a company was formed in London in 1553 to open up trade with "Cathay" by that route. They sent an expedition of three ships under Sir Hugh Willoughby and Richard Chancellor. Willoughby and his men died on the north coast of Scandinavia in their two ships, but Chancellor went on to Russia and obtained a formal trade agreement from the czar, Ivan IV. Subsequent efforts to find a sea route to the East around Russia and northwest around North America all failed, but Francis Drake's return from his circumnavigation of the globe in 1580 and his successful penetration of the Moluccas (after an earlier landing at San Francisco) rekindled English interest in the southern route. In

1583 Ralph Newberry and Ralph Fitch sailed to Syria and thence went overland to the head of the Persian Gulf, where they found a Portuguese ship to take them to Goa, the first Englishmen to reach India. Newberry died there, but Fitch traveled widely in the subcontinent for over two years and then shipped on to Burma and Melaka before returning to England, via the Persian Gulf and Syria, in 1591.

Soon after his return he wrote an account of his travels that in some ways paralleled Linschoten's *Itinerario,* although it was less accurate or detailed and included a good deal of hearsay. But its descriptions of Asian wealth whetted English appetites still further and contributed to the founding of the English East India Company in 1600. Meanwhile, Thomas Cavendish duplicated Drake's circumnavigation and his successful raiding of Spanish and Portuguese ships in the Pacific from 1586 to 1588. In 1589, the year after England's victory over the Spanish Armada, a group of London merchants began to seek support for an ambitious trading venture to the East using da Gama's route around Africa. "Great benefit," they said "will redound to our country, as well as for the annoying of the Spaniards and Portugalls (now our enemies) as also for the selling of our commodities."[3] Continued seizure by English freebooters like Drake and Cavendish of Portuguese and Spanish ships loaded with valuable Asian cargoes provided new reminders of the profits to be won and fired the English imagination, as did the successful Dutch expedition of 1595–1597 under Houtman.

Especially with the defeat of the Spanish Armada and the surge of national feeling and ambition, the last decade of Queen Elizabeth's reign (r. 1558–1603) saw an almost feverish interest in extending English shipping and trade overseas, as their old rivals the Dutch were already doing so successfully, following the Portuguese lead. English ships were already beginning to get the upper hand against the larger and far less maneuverable Spanish and Portuguese galleons and caravels, and they were pulling up equal to the earlier-developed Dutch. The relatively small Dutch home base now began to tell against them in the competition with England with its far larger, rapidly developing, and expansionist economy and population, including the eager merchants of London and Bristol.

This was also the time of William Shakespeare (1564–1616), whose last play, *The Tempest,* written about 1614, reflects the wide contemporary English interest in the new overseas discoveries. *The Tempest* also foreshadows to an almost uncanny degree what were much later to become the dominant European attitudes toward Asians as "inferior" people fit only to serve the conquering Westerners. In fact, although Elizabethan and Shakespearean England exuded confidence and pride, the handful of Westerners in Asia remained awed by

Eastern power and wealth and were confined to precarious, tiny footholds on the fringes of the great Asian empires until the late eighteenth century in India and Java and the mid-nineteenth century in the rest of Asia. Most of them acknowledged that the Asian civilizations were superior to their own. But racial and cultural differences have nearly always been occasions for prejudice when different peoples have confronted each other.

Shakespeare seems to have understood that (see also, for example, *Othello* and *The Merchant of Venice*) and somehow to have anticipated the attitudes that became prominent in the Western mind two centuries or more after his death. He clearly had read and heard accounts of the new discoveries of exotic lands and people and set *The Tempest* on an isolated island where Prospero, an exiled duke, had been shipwrecked with his daughter Miranda. There, by his special powers of magic (new Western technology?), Prospero made the only two native inhabitants his servants: Caliban, a brutish "savage," and Ariel, an elfin wood spirit. These two characters seem to personify the later Western image of Asia as "uncivilized" (that is, different) but also, as in Ariel, graceful, intuitive, and charming, even "childlike." Nearly three centuries later Rudyard Kipling probably had Caliban and Ariel in mind when he put it even more explicitly in *The White Man's Burden,* written for the Americans in 1899 as they took over colonial administration of the Philippines from the defeated Spanish (see Chapter 15). Kipling offers them the advice of an older colonial power and details what to expect in trying to govern "your new-caught sullen peoples, half devil and half child."[4]

Such attitudes were still far in the future, despite Shakespeare's accurate vision, when, on the last day of December 1600, Queen Elizabeth signed a royal charter to a group of London merchants organized into an East India Company for trading with all of Asia. For all the enthusiasm for overseas exploration and trade, England was still primarily a country of farmers, and the scale of its enterprise in Asia was for some time relatively small. The Dutch had little trouble in repelling English efforts to break their monopoly in the East Indies, but the English hung on as minor players at some of the mainland Southeast Asian ports, and in India after primary Dutch attention shifted to the more profitable East Indies. But in 1597 the Dutch foolishly doubled the price they charged the London brokers for pepper, which helped to persuade Elizabeth to lend royal support to an English East India Company. Interestingly enough, the new Company excluded as members any "gentlemen"—that is, hereditary aristocrats, most of whom owned land and represented the old England rather than the new order, which was to become increasingly dominated by commerce and later manufacturing.

The new Company's first two expeditions, both aimed at the spice trade of the East Indies, were only moderately successful, thanks in large part to Dutch efforts to prevent their trading where they would have preferred to do business. Meanwhile the London merchant John Midnall traveled overland to India from the Near East via Persia and Afghanistan, arriving at Agra in 1603 while Emperor Akbar was still on the throne. He had an audience with Akbar in which he asked for English trade privileges like those granted to the Portuguese. He believed that the Jesuits then at the court were speaking against him, and against the English as troublemakers, but Midnall's journal says that he won Akbar over and was given what he asked for. Nothing seems to have come of this, since the first English ship to reach India was William Hawkins's *Hector* in 1608, sailing for the Company.

Hawkins tried establishing trading rights at Surat, but the Portuguese there attacked his goods and tried to drive him away. He traveled to Agra for an audience with Emperor Jahangir, who said he would grant all his requests if Hawkins remained at court as an ambassador from King James I, from whom he had brought a letter. The Jesuits, still at court, and the Portuguese in both Surat and Goa continued to urge that the English be excluded, and Jahangir withdrew his earlier promise. Hawkins departed for England but died on the voyage home. The next Company expedition to India in 1611 was also refused permission to trade at Surat, and they were obliged to do the best they could at Bantam in Java, but the Dutch continued to make things as difficult as possible for outsiders in their new domain, as they had for earlier ventures of the English Company.

Another opportunity, previously ignored, now began to seem more attractive: buying Indian cottons on the Coromandel (southeast) coast of India, beyond Mughal control, and selling them in mainland Southeast Asia, China, and Japan, where they were in great demand and where the Dutch monopolistic control did not operate. The Portuguese and then the Dutch had been doing this for some time and had established trading posts at several points along the Coromandel coast for that purpose. Both groups tried to chase off the English, but the latter managed from time to time to buy cottons and sell them profitably at Patani on the east coast of the Malay Peninsula and even at Ayudia, then the Thai capital. The first such Company expedition was in 1612, but after several years it was judged more profitable to concentrate operations on the Coromandel coast, especially at the port of Masulipatam north of what was later to become Madras.

Efforts to trade in China were largely blocked by the Chinese authorities at Guangzhou and by the Portuguese at Macao. Even the determined Dutch had little or no success in their repeated attempts to break through this system. The English captain John Weddell fought his way up the river to Guangzhou in 1637 and took back some English merchants who had been imprisoned there but was denied permission to trade as well as harried by the Portuguese at Macao. Much the same fate befell subsequent English ventures to China, including an effort in the 1670s to succeed the Dutch in Taiwan after their expulsion by the Ming loyalist Koxinga in 1661, but by 1683 the Qing dynasty had conquered Taiwan and all foreigners were told to trade at Guangzhou. By the early eighteenth century, trade by Westerners slowly became easier at Guangzhou, but the English did not get permission to establish a regular trade base there until 1762—a story told in more detail in Chapter 15.

Meanwhile, there was a brief English adventure in Japan. Will Adams, an English shipmaster and pilot, was appointed pilot-major to a fleet of Dutch ships bound for the East Indies in 1598. They were scattered in successive storms, and only the ship captained by Adams appears to have survived the passage around Cape Horn, arriving in Kyushu in southwestern Japan in the spring of 1600. Foreigners and their ships were still uncommon, and Adams was summoned to Osaka by Tokugawa Ieyasu, who was about to become the effective ruler of the entire country. Again the Jesuits and the Portuguese, already well-entrenched in Japan, tried to persuade Ieyasu to execute Adams as an intruder. He did spend some time in prison and was then ordered to bring his ship around to Edo (now Tokyo), where Ieyasu was beginning his rule as shogun. After the Japanese had carefully studied it, the ship was confiscated and Adams and his Dutch crew forbidden to leave the country without permission. Adams settled down in Japan, learned the language, and married a Japanese woman. At Ieyasu's orders he built a couple of small, Western-style vessels and in return was granted an estate near Edo.

Adams's story made its way back to London via Holland, and the English East India Company, anxious not to be outdone by the Dutch (for whom Adams had after all been working), sent three ships in 1611 with a letter from King James I requesting trade privileges. Two ships loaded spices in Southeast Asia and returned home, but the third reached Hirado, on an island off the westernmost tip of Japan some 50 miles from Nagasaki, in 1613, where a trading warehouse was provided. Adams came down from Edo to talk with his compatriots and accompanied them to Ieyasu, who gave them full permission to trade. When the ship sailed home later that year, seven Englishmen were left at Hirado to promote trade. Adams decided to remain in Japan, although Ieyasu had given him permission to leave, and in 1620 he died there. The English trade begun in 1613 lasted only about a decade and never became very profitable, partly because of continued Portuguese and Dutch resentment and competition (including their own imports of Indian cottons). After the death of Ieyasu in 1616 there were increasing pressures against foreigners, culminating in their complete expulsion, but the English Company was not impressed with trade prospects there and withdrew its people and enterprises in 1623.

The English in Seventeenth-Century India

These various efforts elsewhere in Asia tended to confirm the English Company's belief that their prospects were safest and best in India. A further letter was sent from James I with Thomas Best in the Red Dragon accompanied by a smaller vessel, the Hosiander, which reached Surat in 1612. Best expected, from the earlier English experiences, that he would have trouble trading at Surat, especially since word had reached there of the piracy by earlier English ships against Indian vessels in the Indian Ocean. Apparently this had helped to convince the Mughal and Gujarati authorities that they could not afford to antagonize the English, whose ships could so easily defeat their own. Indian trade to the Red Sea and the pilgrim traffic by Indian Muslims to Mecca were vitally important. The Mughal governor of Gujarat agreed to permit the English to trade there and promised the emperor's formal assent later. Within a month four Portuguese galleons, accompanied by twenty-five smaller vessels, arrived from Goa with the express purpose of destroying the English ships and their effort. In a series of engagements, Best's two small merchant ships completely defeated the Portuguese fleet of war vessels. Much of the action was visible from the shore, and the point was not lost on the Indians. Two months later the emperor's formal document giving permission to trade arrived at Surat.

Best was enthusiastic about the prospects, including the market for English goods. His agent at Surat delivered King James' letter to Jahangir at Agra, but once again the Jesuits there intervened to prevent the emperor from having further serious dealings with the English, while the Portuguese at Surat and Goa continued to intrigue against them. In 1615 another Portuguese armada sailed north from Goa, but it was repelled by four English ships that had just arrived two months earlier at Surat. They then loaded a cargo of Indian cottons and indigo, some of which was sold in Sumatra in exchange for spices, and the ships returned to England with a handsome profit. But the Dutch power in the East Indies proved greater and more implacable an obstacle to English trade than the inconsistent and periodically friendly Mughals in India. Local Indian rulers, especially in the areas beyond Mughal control, were also often accommodating, and the English effort shifted more and more toward India.

With all of this in mind, the English East India Company persuaded James I to send yet another letter to Jahangir, to be carried by Sir Thomas Roe, special ambassador to the Mughal court. He reached Surat in the fall of 1615 with a fleet of four ships and was received by the emperor in January 1616. He remained at Jahangir's court for two years, pressing for a formal trade treaty, but the Mughals, like the Chinese rulers, were unwilling to deal with any foreigners as equals, and matters of trade were beneath their notice. To them, the foreigners had very little to offer, either in trade goods or in more general interchange, and they were regarded as unruly, crude, and troublesome. Roe hinted at English assistance against the Portuguese, who were often a problem to the Mughals, but also asked for permission to trade and set up warehouses in eastern India, specifically in Bengal, where he knew the finest of the Indian cottons came from. Eventually, Jahangir agreed to English rights of residence and storage at Surat and limited trade privileges there. But Roe knew that goods were assembled at Surat from all over India, mainly by a series of local merchant networks, and that Bengal was, as all the Westerners agreed, the chief storehouse of Indian wealth and trade prospects. Portuguese and some Dutch traders were already established there, and as Roe reported:

> The number of Portugalls residing there is a good argument for us to seek it; it is a sign that there is good doing. An abbey was ever a token of a rich soil, and stores of crows of plenty of carrion. . . . We must fire them out and maintain our trade at the pike's end.[5]

These were appropriate sentiments for an Englishman of his time, but it was to be many years before an English trading post was established in Bengal, as detailed in Chapter 14.

The first century and a half of the Western experience in Asia was in general a period of only limited success, and it would have been hard to foresee even as late as 1700 or 1750, let alone in 1650, that in the nineteenth century the tiny groups of Western traders and their few scattered trading posts would yield to full-scale colonial empires or to the kind of Western dominance imposed on Siam, China, and Japan. Until then, Westerners were present in Asia only on the fringes and at the pleasure, or mercy, of the great Asian empires or local states. Europeans did not have the means to challenge these states, nor did such an idea occur to them. They were there to make money as merchants, not to take on administrative responsibility for territory and people. Profitable commerce came first and last. If this meant flattering, bribing, or prostrating themselves before Asian rulers or other important men, they were quick to do so. Whatever was good for business was what these Western traders wanted. They wished to avoid whatever was dangerous (annoying their Asian hosts or getting involved in local politics except where it paid off) or unprofitable (acquiring territory and the consequent headaches and expense).

But as the eighteenth century entered its second half, great changes were at work in Europe that would produce strong new nation-states with overseas ambitions. A series of technological and scientific breakthroughs set the Industrial Revolution in motion. Europe was thus to acquire major new power as well as wealth, and in the course of the nineteenth century it was progressively enabled to overwhelm Asia.

Questions

1. What, why, and when did the Europeans arrive in Asia? What was the state of Asia's political, social, and economic development at that time? What does the phrase "gunpowder empire" imply about European aggression—and how did this differ from the normal characteristics of Indian Ocean trade?

2. What did Asia contribute to the European knowledge base and economic situation? What European behaviors shaped the views of Asians toward the West?

3. Why did the Europeans treat China and Japan differently from the Indonesians?

4. What were the characteristics of the Portuguese empire during the sixteenth century? The Portuguese intended to impose their monopoly of Asia's maritime trade. Why were they unable to do so? Why did their larger imperial enterprise ultimately fail, while they were able to retain their bases in Goa, Macao, and East Timur well after their European competitors had relinquished their centers of authority?

5. What was the Jesuit impact on China and Japan? What were the reasons for their initial successes, as also their consequent failures? What was the Church's relationship with the early Spanish enterprise in the Philippines? What impact did the Jesuit accounts have on European society? In the next chapter, the text asserts that "China seemed close to the Platonic ideal, a state ruled by philosopher-kings." What were the consequences of this view relative to initial European contact with China? Was this view justified? How would this change over time?

6. Why were the Dutch ultimately more successful in their Asian enterprise than their Portuguese predecessors? What was the focal point of their initial Asian interests, and why? What was their initial relationship with the local political systems?

7. Why did the English East India Company have only limited success in the seventeenth century?

Notes

1. G. F. Hudson, *Europe and China* (London: Arnold, 1931), p. 201.
2. R. Murphey, *The Outsiders: The Western Experience in India and China* (Ann Arbor: University of Michigan Press, 1977), p. 21.
3. W. Foster, *England's Quest for Eastern Trade* (London: A. and C. Black, 1966), pp. 127–128.
4. J. N. das Gupta, *India in the Seventeenth Century* (Calcutta: Spink, 1916), p. 212.
5. Ibid.

Suggested Web Sites

The Western Intrusion in India

http://www.fordham.edu/halsail/india/indiasbook.html
Lengthy documents retelling the Western intrusion.

http://www.bl.uk/whatson/exhibitions/trading/ world1.html
British Library exhibit on the world in 1600, including the trading places of the East India Company in Asia, 1600–1834.

Dutch and Portuguese Colonial History

http://www.geocities.com/Athens/Styx/6497
Information, annotated bibliographies, and maps of the Dutch and Portuguese colonies. Includes information on historical remains and the Portuguese language heritage in former colonies; brief history of the Portuguese in Ceylon with a list of governors and photos of the Dutch cemetery in Cochin.

European Expansion

http://www.ualberta.ca/~janes/Marworld.htm
Background and links to various sites introducing the history of European expansion, including its political and economic motivations.

Suggestions for Further Reading

Andrews, K. R. *Trade, Plunder and Settlement: Maritime Enterprise and the Genesis of the British Empire, 1480–1630.* Cambridge, England: Cambridge University Press, 1987.

Arasaratnam, S. *Merchants, Companies, and Commerce on the Coromandel Coast, 1650–1740.* Delhi: Oxford University Press, 1986.

Boxer, C. R. *The Dutch Seaborne Empire, 1600–1800.* London: Knopf, 1965.

————. *The Portuguese Seaborne Empire, 1415–1825.* New York: Knopf, 1969.

Bruijn, J. R., et al. *Dutch-Asiatic Shipping in the Seventeenth and Eighteenth Centuries.* The Hague: Mouton, 1987.

Chaudhuri, K. N. *The Trading World of Asia and the English East India Company, 1600–1760.* Cambridge, England: Cambridge University Press, 1978.

Cipolla, C. M. *Guns and Sails in the Early Phase of European Expansion, 1400–1700.* London: Collins, 1965.

Crosby, A. W. *Ecological Imperialism: The Biological Expansion of Europe, 900–1200.* Cambridge, England: Cambridge University Press, 1986.

Diffie, B. W., and Winius, G. D. *Foundations of the Portuguese Empire, 1415–1580.* Minneapolis: University of Minnesota Press, 1977.

Furber, H. *Rival Empires of Trade in the Orient, 1600–1800.* Minneapolis: University of Minneapolis Press, 1976.

Honour, H. *Chinoiserie: The Vision of Cathay.* New York: Harper, 1973.

Kling, B. B., and Pearson, M. N., eds. *Europeans in Asia Before Dominion.* Honolulu: University Press of Hawaii, 1979.

Masselman, G. *The Cradle of Colonialism.* New Haven, CT: Yale University Press, 1963.

Meilink-Roelofsz, M. A. P. *Asian Trade and European Influence in the Indonesian Archipelago, Between 1500 and About 1630.* Berkeley: University of California Press, 1993.

Moran, J. F. *The Japanese and the Jesuits.* New York: Routledge, 1992.

Mungello, D. E. *Jesuit Accommodation and the Origins of Sinology.* Honolulu: University of Hawaii Press, 1989.

————. *The Great Encounter of China and the West.* Lanham, MD: Rowan and Littlefield, 2005.

Parry, J. H. *The Age of Reconnaissance,* 2d ed. Berkeley: University of California Press, 1981.

————. *The Discovery of the Sea,* 2d ed. Berkeley: University of California Press, 1981.

————. *The Establishment of European Hegemony, 1415–1715.* New York: Harper Row, 1961.

————, ed. *The European Reconnaissance: Selected Documents.* New York: Walker, 1968.

Pearson, M. N. *Merchants and Rulers in Gujarat: The Response to the Portuguese in the Sixteenth Century.* Berkeley: University of California Press, 1976.

————. *The Portuguese in India.* Cambridge, England: Cambridge University Press, 1988.

Ricci, M. *China in the Sixteenth Century: The Journals of Matthew Ricci, 1583–1610,* trans. L. J. Gallagher. New York: Random House, 1953.

Ronan, C. R., and Oh, B. C. *East Meets West: The Jesuits in China.* Chicago: Loyola University Press, 1988.

Schurz, W. L. *The Manila Galleon.* New York: Dutton, 1959.

Souza, G. B. *The Survival of Empire: Portuguese Trade and Society in China and the South China Sea, 1630–1754.* Cambridge, England: Cambridge University Press, 1986.

Spence, J. D. *The Memory Palace of Matteo Ricci.* New York: Viking, 1984.

Subrhmanyan, S. *The Portuguese Empire in Asia, 1500–1770.* New York: Longman, 1993.

Tracy, J. E., ed. *The Rise of Merchant Empires.* Cambridge, England: Cambridge University Press, 1990.

13

Manchu China and Tokugawa Japan

This chapter begins with an account of the Qing or Manchu dynasty in China and the prosperity and population increase that took place under its rule. Two outstanding emperors, Kangxi (1654–1722) and Qianlong (1711–1799), gave the dynasty a strong start, and the empire reached its greatest extent up to that time. But continued population increases without corresponding production increases from advancing technology progressively weakened China and left it unable to deal with new pressures from the Westerners, culminating in the first Anglo-Chinese (or Opium) war of 1839–1842, in which China was humiliatingly defeated.

In Japan, the civil war that marked the last years of the Ashikaga shogunate brought a victory for the warlord Hideyoshi, but on his death in 1598 he was replaced by Tokugawa Ieyasu (1542–1616), who founded the Tokugawa shogunate that ruled Japan from Edo (modern Tokyo) until 1869. The Tokugawa imposed strong central control over all of Japan for the first time. By 1638 all foreigners were expelled, including the troublesome missionaries, and Christian converts were killed or forced to recant. One or two Dutch ships a year were allowed to trade at Nagasaki so that the Japanese remained aware of developments elsewhere. But the increase in domestic trade and the rise of merchants strained the feudal system; in the end the Americans forced Japan to open its doors in 1853, leading to the collapse of the Tokugawa.

On the eve of the modern world, China and Japan both emerged, in their separate ways, from periods of decay, rebellion, and civil war to found vigorous new orders. In China this development occurred with the advent of the Qing or Manchu dynasty, which took power in 1644 and ruled the empire until 1911. Under Manchu rule, China became once again the greatest power in the world and its richest and most sophisti-

cated society. Despite their earlier nomadic origins in northern Manchuria and their role as alien conquerors, the Manchus quickly adopted Chinese culture. This began even before 1644 as they built their power base in southern Manchuria, which had long been part of the Chinese system. They called their new dynasty Qing, meaning "pure," in an effort to give legitimacy to their rule; in fact they governed China completely in the Chinese mode and with widespread Chinese collaboration.

Under the Qing, China prospered. The commercialization and urbanization begun under the Song and the Ming developed still further, while agriculture also became far more productive, with total output at least doubling. But population growth, in itself a sign of prosperity, began to exceed production, and in the nineteenth century the Qing regime also slowly lost its effectiveness. Peasant poverty bred rebellion, and China was at the same time unable to resist foreign pressures for trade concessions. Between 1839 and 1842, the Chinese were humiliatingly defeated by the British in the so-called Opium War. China entered a steep decline, while Western fortunes and power rose even more steeply.

In Japan, centuries of conflict among rival clans degenerated into open civil war in the sixteenth century. But in 1600 a strong new centralized government, the Tokugawa shogunate, emerged to unify Japan for the first time, replacing the weak rule of the Ashikaga shoguns. Under strict Tokugawa control, Japan enjoyed over two centuries of order, prosperity, and economic growth. But control rested on a revived system of feudal ties, and as the economy matured and a new merchant class became more prominent, pressures for change increased. Foreign demands for trade concessions, as in China, finally broke down Japan's self-imposed isolation

CHRONOLOGY

China

1644	Manchu conquest of China
1682	Manchu conquest of Taiwan
1654–1722	Kangxi
1711–1799	Qianlong
1793	Maccartney embassy
1839–1842	First Opium War
1842	"Unequal" treaty of Nanjing

Japan

1534–1598	Daimyos Oda Nobunga (Nagoya), Toyotomi Hideyoshi (Osaka), and Tokugawa Ieyasu (Edo)
1587–1638	Periodic ban and persecutions of Christians
1600	Battle of Sekigahara
1600–1868	Tokugawa shogunate
1638–1640	Expulsion of Westerners and bans on all Japanese travel overseas; designation of Nagasaki as the only legal port for foreign trade
1650–1868	Edo-centered government
1760–1849	Hokusai
1853	Perry "opens" Japan
1854	Treaty of Kanagawa
1868	Meiji Restoration

in 1853; this revealed Japan's weakness and at the same time fed domestic discontent with the Tokugawa rulers. The shogunate was ended in 1868 by what is called the Meiji Restoration; although it did ostensibly restore the emperor, it is more accurately seen as a nonviolent revolution that brought to power a new group of radical reformers who set Japan on a course of rapid modernization, while China continued to flounder under a deteriorating Qing government.

China Under the Manchus

Scattered groups of Ming loyalists and others, including a rebellion by some of the original Chinese collaborators with the Manchus who had been granted fiefs in the south, fought against the new conquerors until the 1680s. Once resistance had been crushed, how-

ever, the new dynasty made a genuine effort to win not only Chinese support but actual partnership, a far more successful approach than that of the alien Mongol dynasty of conquest four centuries earlier. With Chinese collaboration on a large scale, the Qing gave the empire good government, order, and tranquility under which it prospered as never before.

Like the Mongols, the Manchus, totaling only some 1 percent of the empire, or a little over 1 million people, could not hope to rule without Chinese collaborators, who filled about 90 percent of all official posts throughout the dynasty. Manchu aristocrats kept the top military positions, but the army, militia, and police were predominantly Chinese, as were many generals. Provincial administration was headed by two-man teams of Chinese and Manchu governors working in tandem—and, of course, checking on each other. The gentry, who provided unofficial leadership and authority at all local levels, remained almost entirely Chinese. The gentry continued to supply from their ranks of men educated in the Confucian classics nearly all of the officials through the imperial examination system, which was retained and expanded by the Manchus. At the capital, Beijing, the Grand Secretariat, the various ministries, and the imperial censorate were staffed equally by Chinese and by Manchus. Qing China was far more Chinese than Manchu.

But the Manchus succeeded also because they had become, even before 1644, as Chinese in culture as their "subjects"—indeed, they had been an outlying part of the Chinese Empire. They came from an area where pastoral nomadism in northern Manchuria merged with Chinese-style intensive agriculture in the Liao valley, where the Chinese cultural model in all respects was at least as old as the Han dynasty. To protect their homeland and their identity, they tried to prevent further Chinese emigration to Manchuria and to keep northern Manchuria as an imperial hunting preserve.

In their administration of China, they continued the now long-established imperial structure and its institutions. The emperor appointed all officials down to the level of the county magistrates and presided over a mobile body of civil and military servants who owed direct loyalty to the throne. He was accessible to all his officials, who could send confidential memoranda (known as "memorials") to the emperor alone, and to which he would reply in confidence to the sender only. The emperor had to approve all policy matters, sign all death sentences, and hear all appeals.

It was a top-heavy structure, but on the whole it worked well for the first two centuries under strong emperors. Each official had his own extensive unofficial staff to help with the otherwise unmanageable burden of administrative routine and paperwork. But even so, it was a thinly spread system—about 30,000 imperially appointed officials, including by far the biggest cluster in

Beijing and secondary clusters in the 18 provincial capitals, for a population that rose from some 200 million to over 400 million. Most of China, still over 90 percent rural, continued to govern itself through the Confucian system of the "self-regulating society." But there was a huge amount of imperial administrative business too. Communication was essential among the widely scattered provinces and districts of this enormous empire, considerably larger than the modern United States and far more populous, and between each of them and the capital, where most important decisions had to be made or approved. The Qing established some 2,000 postal stations along the main and feeder routes of the imperial road system, many of which were paved and which extended into Manchuria, Mongolia, Xinjiang, and Tibet. Less urgent communications and shipments traveled by water wherever possible—most of the populated areas from the Yangzi Valley southward—but for emergency messages or documents mounted couriers using relays of fast horses could cover 250 miles a day or more. This still meant at least a week of travel from Guangzhou to Beijing, but it was almost certainly faster than anything in the West, rivaled only by the Roman courier system for parts of their empire at its height.

We know more about Qing China than about any previous period, partly because its recency means that far more of the documentation is still available. But we also have a great many foreign accounts, especially after the late eighteenth century, including early Jesuit descriptions. The Europeans were fascinated by China, and they can give us a perspective, and a comparative dimension, lacking for earlier periods. Their accounts help to establish a picture of Manchu China as the largest, richest, best governed, and most highly developed country in the world of its time. European thinkers of the Enlightenment, including Leibniz and later Voltaire and Quesnay, were much influenced by what they knew of Qing China. They were struck in particular by its emphasis on morality (as opposed to revealed religion) and on selection for office of those who were best educated—or best "humanized" in the Confucian tradition—through competitive examination. China, they thought, thus avoided the evils they ascribed in Europe to a hereditary nobility and a tyranny of the landed aristocracy. To them, China seemed close to the Platonic ideal never achieved in the West, a state ruled by philosopher-kings.

The Qing compiled a vast new law code, dealing mainly with criminal offenses; most civil disputes continued to be handled locally through family, clan, and gentry networks. It also impressed European philosophers and legal scholars, particularly the application of law on the basis of Confucian ethics. Admiration of China led to a European vogue for Chinese art, architecture, gardens, porcelains, and even furniture and wallpaper (another item in the long list of Chinese innovations), all of which became the height of fashion for the upper classes, especially in France and England. The foreign perspective on China began to change in the nineteenth century as China declined and the West began its steep rise. But the change in attitudes was slow, and traces of the original admiration remained for those of a more open mind, less blinded by the disease of Victorian imperialist arrogance.

Prosperity and Population Increases

The first 150 years of Qing rule were an especially brilliant period, marked by the long reigns of two exceptionally able and dedicated emperors, Kangxi (r. 1661–1722) and Qianlong (r. 1735–1796). As a consequence of the order and prosperity they established, population began an increase that was to continue until after 1900, probably tripling from approximately 1650. But until late in the eighteenth century production and the growth of commerce more than kept pace. Even by the 1840s and 1850s, when per capita incomes had probably been declining for two generations or more, British observers agreed that most people were materially better off than most Europeans. A particularly well-informed traveler and resident in China writing in 1853 provided a one-sentence summary of many such accounts by saying "In no country in the world is there less real misery and want than in China."[1] One must remember that he wrote from the perspective of the industrializing England of Charles Dickens and knew the bad working and living conditions for most Westerners at that time. But his judgment was probably accurate about China and is confirmed by other contemporary Western observers.

The massive growth of population, and of production to match it until late in the eighteenth century, is a good measure of the orderly beneficence of Qing rule and the confident spirit of the times. Government officials diligently promoted improvements in agriculture, new irrigation and flood-prevention works, roads, and canals. More new land was brought under cultivation to feed the rising population and more new irrigation projects were constructed than in the whole of previous Chinese history put together. The Qing period also saw the completion of Chinese agricultural occupation of the cultivable areas of the south and southwest, at the expense of the remaining non-Han inhabitants, in essentially the same pattern as today. Much of the new tilled land was in the hilly south, where terracing was often pushed to extremes, driving the indigenous people into still more mountainous areas, especially in the southwest. Large new acreage was also brought under the plow in the

China Proper Under the Qing

The dynasty also controlled Xinjiang, Manchuria, and, after the 1780s, Tibet. The surrounding countries were "tributaries," including Burma, Siam, Korea, Vietnam, and Japan.

semiarid margins of northern China. Yields everywhere rose with new irrigation, more fertilization, better seeds, and more intensive cultivation.

Merchants were also allowed a larger scope under the Qing even than under the Ming. Trade with Southeast Asia grew still further, as did permanent settle-

ments of Chinese merchants there. Foreign trade as a whole seems clearly to have been larger than Europe's. Domestic commerce, larger still, and urbanization reached new levels and remained far more important than overseas connections. Merchant guilds proliferated in all of the growing Chinese cities and often acquired great social and political influence. Rich merchants with official connections built up huge fortunes and patronized literature, theater, and the arts. Fleets of junks (Chinese-style ships) plied the coast and the great inland waterways, and urban markets teemed with people and goods. General prosperity helped to ensure domestic peace. Silver continued to flow in to pay for China's exports, including now tea and silk to the West, and there was a large favorable trade balance. Cloth and handicraft production boomed as subsistence yielded to more division of labor and to increasing market forces.

Along with silver, other New World goods entered the China market through the Spanish link to Manila; the most important were new and highly productive crops from the Americas, including sweet potatoes, white potatoes, maize (corn), peanuts, and tobacco. These were all unknown in Asia before, and in many cases they supplemented the agricultural system without displacing the traditional staples of rice, wheat, and other more drought-tolerant cereals such as millet and sorghum grown in the drier parts of the north. Potatoes could be raised in sandy soils unsuited to cereals, white potatoes in the colder areas and sweet potatoes in the south. Both produce more food energy per unit of land than any cereal crop. Corn yielded well on slopes too steep for irrigated rice. Peanuts and tobacco filled other gaps and added substantially to total food resources or to the list of cash crops, like cotton.

Early ripening rice introduced from Southeast Asia in the Song and Ming was further developed under the Qing, and the period from sowing to harvest was progressively reduced. In the long growing season of the south, this meant that more areas could produce two crops of rice a year, and some could even manage three. The practice of transplanting rice seedlings from special nursery beds to spaced rows in large irrigated paddies first became universal in the Qing. This greatly increased yields, as well as further shortening the time to harvest.

Food and nonfood crops were now treated with the kind of care a gardener uses for individual plants; they were fertilized by hand and hand-weeded at frequent intervals, and irrigation levels were precisely adjusted to the height and needs of each crop as the season advanced. The use of night soil (human manure) now also became universal, and the amounts increased as the population rose, providing both the source and the need for more intensive fertilization. Rice yields probably more than doubled by a combination of all these methods, and the total output rose additionally as the result of double and triple cropping and newly cultivated land. Improvements in rice agriculture, China's major crop since Han times, as well as new irrigation and other intensification of the traditional system, were probably the chief source of food increases. Rising population totals provided the incentive and the means for greater intensification, but it was a process pushed also by the Qing administration and its local magistrates as well as by local gentry. The irrigation system for rice was a finely engineered affair, permitting the altering of water levels as needed and the draining of the paddies in the last few weeks before harvest. It all required immense amounts of labor, but it paid handsomely in increased yields, and a prosperous China continued to provide the additional hands needed.

These changes, improvements, and additions to an existing highly productive agricultural system help to explain how an already huge and dense population could double or triple in two centuries and still maintain or even enhance its food and income levels. Agriculture remained the heart of the economy and the major

Adam Smith on China

The founder of classical Western economics and advocate of the free market, Adam Smith, commented on China in his Wealth of Nations, *published in 1776 and based on the accounts of Europeans who had been there.*

> The great extent of the empire of China, the vast multitude of its inhabitants, the variety of climate and consequently of productions in its various provinces, and the easy communication by means of water carriage between the greater part of them, render the home market of that country of so great extent as to be alone sufficient to support very great manufactures, and to admit of very considerable subdivisions of labor. The home market of China is perhaps in extent not much inferior to the market of all the different countries of Europe put together.

Source: A. Smith, *The Wealth of Nations,* vol. 2 (New York: Dutton, 1954), p. 217.

source of state revenue, but its surpluses created a growing margin for both subsistence and commercial exchange. The population figures compiled by the Qing were, like those of earlier dynasties, not designed as total head counts, but were based on local reports by village headmen enumerating households and adult males fit for military service. Land and its owners and output were also recorded for tax purposes, and for a time, as in previous centuries, there was a head tax. Since everyone knew that these figures were used for calculating taxes and for conscription or corvée labor, there was an understandable tendency for local headmen and households to understate the true numbers.

Early in the dynasty it was announced that the head tax would never be raised, and it was later merged with the land tax and with taxes in the form of a share of the crop. At the same time the Qing made it plain that reports of population increase were welcome evidence of the prosperity resulting from their reign. Reports showing little or no gain would reflect on the effectiveness of the local magistrate. For these and other reasons having to do with the imprecision, inconsistency, and incompleteness of the count (which often but not always excluded women, servants, infants, migrants, and non-Han people), Qing population figures must be used cautiously. However, the long-term trend is clear. From roughly 150 million, clearly an undercount, in the late seventeenth century, the population had reached 400 million or possibly 450 million by 1850, and 500 million by 1900. The official figures, almost certainly an undercount to begin with and possibly an overcount after about 1750, show 142 million in 1741 and 432 million in 1851. It was strong evidence that all was well, but in time it became a burden that the system could no longer carry successfully and that produced spreading poverty and disorder.

Kangxi and Qianlong

The emperor Kangxi, completely Chinese in culture and even a poet in that language (the Manchus also retained their own language), encouraged literature, art, printing, scholarship, and artisan production. He revived and enlarged the Imperial Potteries, which turned out great quantities of beautiful porcelain, originally for the palace and court and later for rich merchants and even for export. A patron of learning, Kangxi himself studied Latin, mathematics, and Western science with Jesuit tutors at his court and corresponded with European monarchs. Toward the end of his reign he lost patience with the sectarian quarreling of the Catholic missionaries and was incensed that a pope in "barbarian" Rome should presume to tell the few Chinese Christian converts what they should and should not believe. But he remained in-

Official court painting of the emperor Kangxi (1661–1722) wearing the imperial dragon robes, by an unknown artist. (The Metropolitan Museum of Art, Rogers Fund, 1942. [42.141.2] Photograph, all rights reserved, The Metropolitan Museum of Art.)

terested in a wide variety of things and is described by his Jesuit tutors as insatiably curious, as other Jesuits had earlier described the Mughal emperor Akbar.

Kangxi was a conscientious and able administrator of boundless energy who tried to ensure honesty in government and harmonious partnership among Chinese and Manchu officials. He went on six major state tours around the empire and showed a great interest in local affairs. He commissioned an ambitious new encyclopedia of all learning, updated and greatly expanded from Yongle's compilation under the Ming. At 5,000 volumes, it is probably the largest such work ever written anywhere. The huge dictionary of the Chinese language that he also commissioned and that still bears his name remains the most exhaustive and authoritative guide to classical Chinese up to his own time. He also supervised the compilation of a voluminous administrative geography of the empire. He encouraged the further spread of private academies for the sons of the gentry, and state-supported schools for worthy but poorer boys, both of which multiplied far beyond what they had been in the Ming, to spread classical learning and open the way to office for those who mastered it. Older scholars and retired officials were sent around the empire at government expense to lecture to the populace on morality and virtue.

Kangxi was equally effective in military affairs. He supervised the reconquest of Taiwan, restored Chinese control over Mongolia and eastern Xinjiang, and in 1720 mounted an expedition to put down civil war in Tibet, where he then established firm Chinese authority. His armies had earlier chased the expanding Russians out of the Amur region of northern Manchuria. He then negotiated the Treaty of Nerchinsk in 1689 with the czar's representatives, confirming Chinese sovereignty in the Amur Valley and southward. This was China's first significant engagement and its first treaty with a Western power. It was a contest in which the Qing clearly emerged as the winners, successfully defending China's traditionally threatened landward frontiers. The Russian negotiators were kept on the frontier and not received in Beijing; Nerchinsk was a minor border post and relatively minor Chinese officials were sent to deal with them, assisted by Jesuit interpreters.

Far less attention was paid to the sea barbarians—the Portuguese, Dutch, English, and others—already attempting to trade at Guangzhou and to extend their efforts farther north along the coast. The Westerners were regarded as troublesome but were put in the same category as bandits or pirates. They were certainly not to be seen as representatives of civilized states with whom China should have any dealings. These differing responses reflected the long-established Chinese concern about their continental borders, the source of so much trouble in the past, where any challenge to their authority had to be met and subdued. Their lack of concern about the maritime frontier, which had never presented any major problem for them in the past, was ultimately to prove critical. Their

Why China Downgraded Science

Jean Baptiste du Halde published in 1738 A Description of the Empire of China, *based on earlier Jesuit accounts. In that volume he wrote:*

> The great and only road to riches, honour, and employments is the study of the jing (the classical canon). History, the laws, and morality, and to learn what they call wen-chang, that is to write in a polite manner, in terms well chosen and suitable to the subject. By this means they become Doctors (jin-shi), having passed the third level of the examinations; soon after they are sure to have a government post. Even those who return to their provinces to wait for posts are in great consideration with the mandarins of the place; they protect their families against all vexations and enjoy a great many privileges. But as nothing like this is to be hoped for by those who apply themselves to the speculative sciences, and as the study of them is not the road to honours and riches, it is no wonder that these sorts of abstract sciences should be neglected by the Chinese.

Source: from J. B. du Halde, *A Description of the Empire of China,* vol. 2. (London: E. Cave, 1738).

defenses, their front doors, and their military priorities faced the other way.

Qianlong, Kangxi's grandson, succeeded him in 1735. He might have reigned officially even longer, but filial piety, that most hallowed of Chinese virtues, prompted him to formally retire in 1796 after 60 years so as not to stay on the throne longer than his grandfather. However, he remained the real power until his death in 1799 at the age of 89. Less austere and more extroverted than Kangxi, his grand manner has often been compared to that of Louis XIV of France. But comparison with Louis XIV does Qianlong less than justice. Until his last years he was a diligent and humane ruler who continued his grandfather's administrative and patronage model in all respects. Not wanting to seem to rival Kangxi, instead of an encyclopedia he commissioned a collection and reprinting of an immense library of classical works in over 36,000 volumes. But he also ordered the destruction of over 2,300 books that he thought were seditious or unorthodox, a censorship and literary inquisition that deeply marred his otherwise admirable record of support for learning.

Qianlong was, of all Chinese emperors, probably the greatest patron of art. He built up in the imperial palace a stupendous collection of paintings and other works of art from all past periods as well as his own. Most of it is still intact, and Qianlong also spent huge sums on refurbishing, embellishing, and adding to the imperial buildings inherited from the Ming.

Militarily, he was an aggressive and able leader. Despite Kangxi's expeditions against them, the Mongols had remained troublesome. Qianlong completely and permanently destroyed their power in a series of campaigns in the 1750s, after which he reincorporated the whole of Xinjiang into the empire and gave it its present name, which means "new dominions." A revolt in Tibet shortly afterward led to a Qing occupation that fixed Chinese control there even more tightly. Punitive expeditions invaded Nepal, northern Burma, and northern Vietnam and compelled tributary acknowledgment of Chinese overlordship.

Until the 1780s Qianlong, like those before him on the Dragon Throne, dealt personally with an immense mass of official documents and wrote his own comments on them. One of the Grand Council secretaries remarked "Ten or more of my comrades would take turns every five or six days on early morning duty, and even so would feel fatigued. How did the Emperor do it day after day?"[2] But as Qianlong grew older he became more luxury-loving and surrounded himself with servile yes-men. For most of his life an astonishingly hard worker, in old age he left matters increasingly in the hands of his favorites. His chief favorite, the unscrupulous courtier He Shen, built up a clique of corrupt henchmen and truly plundered the empire. When he en-

tered the palace in 1775 as a handsome young bodyguard of 25, He Shen had impressed the emperor, then 65 years old. Within a year he had risen to become grand councilor. At his fall after Qianlong's death, the private wealth He Shen had extorted was said to be worth some $1.5 billion, an almost inconceivable sum for that time and probably a world record for corrupt officials. From this exalted post and with the emperor's support he concentrated all power in his own hands, holding in time as many as 20 different positions simultaneously. He betrothed his son to the emperor's daughter and clearly intended to take over the dynasty.

He Shen's rise was symptomatic of Qianlong's growing senility. But it also showed the deterioration of the administrative system as a whole with no responsible figure on the throne, the chief liability of the top-heavy imperial structure. With He Shen in charge and giving most of his attention to building his own fortune, the efficient running of the empire was neglected, including the army. This had a good deal to do with the inconclusive sparring action against a major rebellion of the White Lotus sect that erupted in 1796. The rebels were finally put down only after He Shen's fall under the new emperor, Jia Qing, who reigned officially from 1796 to 1820. He did not acquire any real power until Qianlong died in 1799, when he quickly moved against He Shen.

He Shen's career also illustrates the importance of personal connections in imperial China, a tradition still vigorous in China today. With Qianlong's death, his connections were destroyed and he was soon stripped of his power and wealth.

Corruption, connections, and nepotism were aspects of China, and of all Asia, that Westerners criticized as being more widespread than in their own political and economic systems. Westerners at least were embarrassed by it at home; Asians supported it as proper. Family loyalties and the ties of friendship were the highest goods. Anyone with wealth or power who did not use it to help relatives and friends was morally deficient. The family was the basic cement of society, and its support system of mutual aid was blessed by Confucius and by Chinese morality as a whole. The family was a microcosm of the empire where the emperor was properly the nurturing father of his people, and all his officials right down the pyramid were enjoined to behave similarly. The connections of friendship were also part of the sanctified "five relationships" and took precedence over other considerations. Political office was relatively poorly paid, and it was expected that officials would use their position to provide for their families and friends by diverting funds or contracts and receiving "presents." People of rank were expected to live well, in keeping with the dignity of their position. Even now one hears repeated the traditional

Qing glory: the Altar of Heaven, just outside the Forbidden City in Beijing, originally a Ming structure but rebuilt by the Qing. Here the emperor conducted annual rites to intercede with Heaven for good harvests. The temple roofs are covered with magnificent colored and glazed tiles. (Northwest Orient Airlines)

saying, "Become an official and get rich." He Shen broke the rules only by grossly overdoing it.

The Later Qing: Decline and Inertia

By the 1750s the dynasty was already well into its second century. The eighteenth century saw the pinnacle of Qing glory, prosperity, and harmony, but even before the death of Qianlong, decline had begun. Prosperity remained for most and with it a major output of art and literature. This included new vernacular novels such as *Dream of the Red Chamber,* which prophetically deals with the decline and degeneracy of a once-great family and is still widely read. Except for the disastrous interval of He Shen, government remained well organized and efficient. But despite the still-rising population, there was only a small increase in the number of official posts, perhaps 25 percent as against a doubling and later a tripling of total numbers. This had an obvious negative effect on governmental effectiveness and was also bad for morale. A prestigious career in the bureaucracy, once a reasonable ambition for able scholars, became harder and harder to obtain. At the same time, the imperial examinations became still more rigidified exercises in old-fashioned orthodoxy and the memorization of "correct" texts. These were to be regurgitated and commented on in the infamous eight-legged

essays (see Chapter 11), allowing no scope for imagination or initiative. "Men of talent," as they had been called since the Han, were often weeded out. The examination failure rate climbed rapidly, as the system lacked the flexibility to accommodate the ever-greater numbers of aspirants.

Disappointed examination candidates, and others who passed but were not called to office, became a larger and larger group of able and ambitious but frustrated men. Educated, unemployed, and frustrated intellectuals are a worrying problem in all societies. In China the problem was only made worse by the earlier Qing efforts to expand education and to open it to larger sections of the population. Learning had always been the key to advancement. Now it was far from necessarily so. The system had hardened just when flexibility was most needed. Instead of preserving the Great Harmony, it bred discontent. Degrees, and occasionally even offices, once attainable only by examination, began to be sold. Failed candidates and disappointed office seekers provided the leadership for dissident and ultimately rebellious groups, whose numbers increased rapidly after about 1785.

The lack of firm leadership and virtuous example under He Shen and after the death of the emperor Jiaqing in 1820 aggravated the burdens of overworked officials. They now had to manage districts whose populations had more than doubled. A magistrate of the

Song dynasty 500 years earlier was responsible for an average of about 80,000 people in his county. By the end of the eighteenth century the average county, still administered by a single magistrate and his staff, numbered about 250,000; many were larger, and the average rose to about 300,000 in the nineteenth century. Local gentry, landlords, merchant guilds, and sometimes dissident or even criminal groups began to fill the vacuum. There was increasing anti-Manchu sentiment, for the Qing was after all an alien dynasty of conquest.

By the last quarter of the eighteenth century population growth had probably outrun increases in production. Per capita incomes stabilized and then began slowly to fall. The poorest areas suffered first, and there was a rise in local banditry. By the end of the century there were open rebellions, which increasingly marred the remainder of Qing rule. The secret society of the White Lotus, revived from its quiescence since the fall of the Mongols and the Ming, reemerged in a major upris-

By mid-Qing (mid-eighteenth century), this had become a common sight in any Chinese town or city; the problems posed by the mushrooming population were unmistakable. This is a late nineteenth-century photograph of a crowd of famine refugees in a mission courtyard. (Keystone View Company)

ing in 1796. Its reappearance tended to suggest to many Chinese that once again the ruling dynasty was in trouble and perhaps was losing the mandate of Heaven. The secret, semi-Buddhist rituals of the White Lotus and its promise to overthrow the Qing attracted many followers, drawing on the now-widespread peasant distress. The rebels defied the imperial army until 1804 from their mountain strongholds in the upper Yangzi Valley along the borders of three provinces. The enormous expense of suppressing the White Lotus bled the treasury and fed corruption in the military and its procurement. The unnecessarily long campaign also revealed the decline in the effectiveness of the army, which in the end, even after the fall of He Shen, had to depend on the help of some 300,000 local militia.

New Barbarian Pressures

These problems were just beginning to appear as the Qing approached its third century. Even into the nineteenth century the problems remained manageable, and the traditional system continued to impress European observers, now in far greater numbers than ever before. China was still able to overawe Westerners who tried to deal with the Dragon Throne as an equal or to obtain trading privileges. Like all foreigners, they had from the beginning been fitted into the forms of the tributary system, the only way China knew how to deal with outsiders. At Guangzhou, the only port where Westerners were permitted to trade, they were not allowed to stay beyond the trading season of about six months and were forbidden to bring in firearms or women, to enter the city proper, or to trade elsewhere on the China coast. They were obliged to deal only with the official monopoly that controlled all foreign trade, a restraint that they found galling given their image of China as a vast market filled with a variety of merchants. The Westerners were viewed as barbarians, but wilder and more uncouth than most, as potential troublemakers and perverters of Chinese morality. It was believed that they should be kept on the fringes of the empire and walled off from normal contact with its people.

Various attempts by the English and Dutch to trade elsewhere or with other merchants were rebuffed. In 1755 the English trader James Flint had sailed into several ports north of Guangzhou, including Shanghai and Tianjin, in an effort to establish trade there. He was jailed and then deported, but the emperor ordered execution for the Chinese who had served as his interpreter and scribe. By the 1790s the restrictions at Guangzhou seemed intolerable, especially to the British, then in their own view the greatest mercantile and naval power in the world and tired of being treated like minor savages.

In 1793 George III of England sent an embassy to Qianlong led by a British nobleman, Viscount Macartney, to request wider trading rights and to deal with China as an equal nation. He brought with him as presents samples of British manufactures to convince the Chinese of the benefits of trade with the West. The articles he brought were not yet highly developed enough to impress the Chinese; they included samples of the contemporary pottery of Josiah Wedgewood, hardly likely to appeal to the inventors of porcelain. The Chinese could still make most of the things Macartney brought better and cheaper and saw no need for his samples. The whole mission was a comedy of errors on both sides, since both were still profoundly ignorant of one another and lacked any standard of comparison. The Chinese interpreted the visit and the presents as a standard tribute mission, although from an especially distant (they had only the dimmest of notions where England was) and hence backward group of barbarians, too far from China to have picked up any civilization. Chinese politeness obliged them to accept the presents, but with the kind of indulgence that a kindly parent might feel for the work of children.

They expected Macartney to perform the *ke tou* (kowtow), or ritual submission, as all tribute missions including kings did before the Son of Heaven. Macartney, as a typical pompous Georgian aristocrat in his satin knee breeches and also suffering from gout, refused. He offered instead to bend one knee slightly, as to his own sovereign, rather than prostrating himself and banging his head on the floor as the Chinese ritual prescribed. Macartney said that he was "sure the Chinese would see that superiority which Englishmen, wherever they go, cannot conceal." One can almost hear him saying it! As a result, he never had a proper audience with Qianlong, although he was kept waiting in Beijing for over a month, and all his requests were refused. Qianlong sent him a letter for George III that was a masterpiece of crushing condescension, imperial Chinese style:

> I have already noted your respectful spirit of submission. . . . I do not forget the lonely remoteness of your island, cut off from the world by intervening wastes of sea. . . . [But] our Celestial Empire possesses all things in abundance. We have no need for barbarian products.[3]

One can imagine the reaction of George III and Macartney.

In 1793 it was still possible for China to get away with such haughty behavior, and it was true that China was happily self-sufficient. A Dutch embassy of 1795 that also asked for better trade conditions was similarly rejected, even though the Dutch, less concerned with power or dignity than with profits, vigorously performed the *ke tou* several times as they lined up at court with other representatives from barbarian countries sending tributary missions. A later British embassy under Lord Amherst in 1816 had a similarly humiliating experience. Amherst had the bad luck to turn up just when the British in India were fighting the Gurkhas of Nepal, a Chinese tributary since 1792, and was ordered out of the country by the emperor without an audience.

Foreign trade remained bottled up at Guangzhou under the same restrictions, increasingly frustrating to Western traders. They were now beginning to feel the new strength and pride that industrialization at home was starting to give them. Nevertheless, the accounts of China given by members of the Macartney and Amherst parties as they traveled south from Beijing to Guangzhou, nursing their rage at the way they had been treated, were still strongly positive. They found it prosperous, orderly, and agriculturally productive, with immense trade flows and numerous large cities and bustling markets. Here are a few samples from the diary kept by a member of the Amherst mission in 1816:

> Tranquility seemed to prevail, nothing but contentment and good humor. . . . It is remarkable that in so populous a country there should be so little begging. . . . Contentment and the enjoyment of the necessities of life [suggest that] the government cannot be a very bad one. . . . The lower orders of Chinese seem to me more neat and clean than any Europeans of the same class. . . . Even torn, soiled, or threadbare clothing is uncommon. . . . All the military stations are neatly whitewashed and painted and kept in perfect repair, and instead of mud cabins the houses of peasants are built in a neat manner with brick. The temples are also handsome and numerous.[4]

Qing Glory and Technological Backwardness

China may have declined from its eighteenth-century peak, but it was far from being in ruins. Although the emperors after Qianlong fell somewhat short of his or Kangxi's brilliance, they were conscientious and honest. The corruption that had marred Qianlong's last years was greatly reduced, his scheming favorites disposed of, and a renewed atmosphere of responsibility and service established. The official salt monopoly, which had become semiparalyzed by corruption, was totally reformed in the 1830s. This was one of many pieces of evidence that even the imperial bureaucracy still had resilience and the power to correct weaknesses.

At its best Qing art remained magnificent, but much of later Qing painting, decoration, and ceramics lacks originality, and toward the end it often became overly ornate. Like the scholarship and philosophy of the time, it is technically superb but concentrates on reproducing traditional themes without the exuberance or imagination of earlier periods. Urban culture continued to thrive as merchant wealth spread more widely, and city dwellers could read the new vernacular literature, enjoy the art of the time, and attend plays. It remained a sophisticated society as well as a prosperous one and still generally confident, even complacent. Imperial slights to barbarian upstarts like the British were in keeping with what most Chinese thought.

But all was not well domestically. The state really had no adequate long-run means to respond to the inexorable pressures of increasing population. Decline was slow at first. China was immense, and its society and economy, largely independent of state management except for the official monopolies, took time to decay. Signs of trouble here and there did not mean that the whole system was rotten—not yet, at least. Nor did governmental or military inefficiency or corruption among some officials mean that the whole administration was in trouble. Most of the Chinese world lay outside the political sphere in any case and continued to flourish after political decay was far advanced. Government was a thin layer. Both foreign and Chinese critics were often misled by signs of political weakness into wrongly assuming that the whole country was falling apart.

The basic problem was rural poverty in some areas, as population rose faster than production. Traditional agricultural technology, already developed to a peak of

As population increased and demand for food rose, agriculture was pushed up onto steeper and steeper slopes, as in this photograph from the southwestern province of Yunnan. Terracing required immense labor but could create only tiny strips of level land, and water for irrigation was a major problem. Terracing was necessary because by the late Qing period all gentler slopes had been occupied, while the population continued to rise. This is an extreme example, but such terraces were not uncommon. (R. Murphey)

efficiency, had reached its limit, as had usable land. Further growth in production of any sort could be won only with new technology. China was now rapidly falling behind the West and showed no signs of realizing this or any readiness to try new ways. There was little interest in the now-superior technology of Europe, especially not in the disruption that must inevitably accompany its spread. China continued to protect itself against such things and against any ideas or innovations of foreign origin. It strove to preserve the Great Harmony; it was complacently and even narcissistically proud of its glorious tradition and mistrusting of anything that might threaten it. There might have been a different sort of response from a new and vigorous dynasty, but the Qing was now old, rigid, and fearful of change. As alien conquerors, they were also nervous about departing in any way from their self-appointed role as the proponents and guardians of the ancient Chinese way in all things.

The still-growing commercialization of the economy and the rise of urban-based merchants were not accompanied by the developments that these same trends had produced in Europe. Individual or family wealth came not so much from increasing production as from acquiring a greater share of what already existed, through official connections or by managing the state monopolies. Merchants and their guilds never became an independent group of entrepreneurs or sought to change the system to their advantage, as their European opposite numbers did. In the Chinese view, they prospered by working within the existing system and had few incentives to try to alter it. For longer-term investment, land was the preferred option since it was secure and also offered social prestige. Capital earned in trade went into land, to money lending at usurious rates (always a symptom of capital shortages), or into luxurious living; only rarely did it go into enterprises that could increase productivity, such as manufacturing or new technology.

Leisure and gracious living in gentry style were more valued in China than in the modern West, and there was less interest in further accumulation for its own sake. The gentry and the scholar-officials dominated Qing China as they had since at least the Han dynasty, leaving little separate scope for merchants, who were officially looked down on as parasites and who depended on their gentry or official connections to succeed. They neither could nor wanted to challenge the Confucian bureaucracy and were instead content to use it for their own ends. All of this discouraged or prevented the rise of capitalism and the kinds of new enterprise and investment that were such a basic part of the commercial and industrial revolutions in the modern West. But it made perfectly good sense in the Chinese context.

In science and technology China had been an outstanding pioneer. Iron-chain suspension bridges, canal locks, the beginnings of mechanical threshers, water-powered mills, looms, clocks, and even the crankshaft, connecting rods, and piston rods for converting rotary to longitudinal motion and back, all originated in Han, Song or post-Song China and were still spreading under the Qing. In the eighteenth century China seemed again to be on the threshold of new technological and economic change. The achievements just mentioned are closely similar to what was worked out in eighteenth-century Europe. Until some time in the later seventeenth or early eighteenth century China remained ahead of the West in most respects. It had invented printing, paper, gunpowder, the compass, and so on, all later adopted and adapted by the West. But Chinese accomplishments were primarily a catalog of cumulative empirical discoveries, as in medicine and pharmacology and their adaptations, rather than the result of systematic or sustained scientific inquiry. Confucianism made little place for abstract theorizing or speculation about what was not directly perceivable. Learning concentrated on the Confucian classics and on records of the past as the proper guide for the present and future.

The tradition of the learned man as a gentleman also created a deep division between those who "labored with their minds," as Mencius put it, and those who worked with their hands. Chinese artisans were highly skilled and ingenious but rarely engaged in theory or experiments, and most were not even literate. Scholars saw all manual work as beneath them, even experimental work. It was the joining of theory, design, experiment, and practice that produced the achievements of modern Western science and technology. This did not happen in China, which rested on its already high level of development.

It seems easier to understand why China did not move into capitalism or push on from its early successes in science and technology than to understand why Europe did. The West's abrupt break with its own past and the explosion of modern science are harder to explain. China was too successful by Qing times to conceive of possible improvements or to seek change. To a poorer and less developed Europe, change and new enterprise were more compelling, as the means to "progress." In any case, by the nineteenth century China had fallen critically behind the West and was also ruled by a dynasty old in office and suffering from the common dynastic pattern of complacency and loss of efficiency. The timing was bad, since it coincided with the rapid rise of Western power. The weakened government faced two unprecedented problems: a population bigger than ever before and now sliding into economic distress and the threat posed by militant Westerners. Neither was ever adequately dealt with.

Corruption is endemic in all systems; its seriousness is only a matter of degree. As the nineteenth century wore on in China, it became a growing cancer sapping the vigor of the whole country. Confucian morality began to yield to an attitude of "devil take the hindmost." People and families with good connections had their lands and fortunes progressively removed from the tax rolls, as in the last century of all previous dynasties. This, of course, put a heavier burden on the decreasing number who still had to provide the state's revenue, mainly peasants. The strain on their already marginal position led many of them into banditry and rebellion. In all of these respects, late Qing China was especially unprepared to meet the challenge of an aggressive, industrializing West. It was hard also to readjust Chinese perspectives, which had always seen the landward frontiers as the major area of threat. China was slow to recognize that external danger now came from the sea and along the coast, or to take these new, hairy sea barbarians seriously. Their pressures continued to be treated as China had always treated local piracy or banditry, not as a basic challenge to the entire system.

The Opium War

Opium imports rose dramatically after about 1810, and by the 1820s the favorable balance of trade that China had enjoyed in the seventeenth and eighteenth centuries was reversed as more and more silver flowed out of the country to pay for it. Most of the opium was grown in India, though some came from Turkey and Iran. The English East India Company encouraged its cultivation as a cash crop to pay for its purchases of tea and silk in Guangzhou.

Opium had been imported from Persia and was later grown in China for many centuries. It was widely used for medicinal purposes but began to be smoked as an addictive drug on a large scale only in the late eighteenth century. Chinese addicts and their merchants and middlemen created the market for imported opium, which was thought to be superior to the domestic supply that had earlier provided the major source.

Although the imperial government declared opium smoking and trade a capital offense, the profits of the trade were high for both Chinese and foreigners and the ban was ineffective. No foreign pressures were necessary. Westerners, including Americans as well as European traders, some of whom bought their opium in Turkey and Iran, merely delivered it to Chinese smugglers on the coast, who then distributed it throughout the country through a vast network of dealers. It was in

short a Chinese problem, although foreign traders can hardly be exonerated. Most of the fortunes won by early American traders to China rested on opium. Its spreading use in China was a symptom both of the growing despair of the disadvantaged and of the degeneracy of a once proud and vigorous system, including many of its now self-indulgent upper classes.

Meanwhile, opium provided the occasion for the first military confrontation with these new sea barbarians in the first Anglo-Chinese war of 1839–1842, the so-called Opium War. Nearly 50 years had passed since Qianlong's rebuff of Macartney and his refusal of all of the British requests. British patience was wearing thin, and new power from industrialization was ready to seek a different solution. Opium was the immediate issue that sparked the outbreak of hostilities, but much larger matters were involved. Britain and other Western trading nations wanted freer trading opportunities with the huge Chinese market, as well as direct access and recognition, as equals, by its government. They saw China as rigidly out of step with a modern world where free trade and "normal" international relations were the common ground of all "civilized" nations. They could no longer tolerate being looked down on or ignored and excluded, and they now had the means to do something about it. China's resistance to such demands was taken as proof of its backwardness; Westerners were inspired in part also by their sense of mission to use force if necessary to bring China into the modern world, for its own benefit as well as their own. Chinese and Western arrogance, though resting on somewhat different grounds, were approximately equal, and in 1839 they met head on.

An imperial commissioner, Lin Zexu, was sent to Guangzhou in 1839 to stop the illegal and damaging traffic in opium. Lin ordered the stocks of the drug stored there destroyed, most of which was technically the property of British merchants. Although they had no right to keep opium on Chinese soil under Chinese law, the British used the incident as a pretext to declare war. A small mobile force sent mainly from India soon destroyed the antiquated Chinese navy, shore batteries, and coastal forces. With the arrival of reinforcements, it attacked Guangzhou, occupied other ports northward on the coast including Shanghai, and finally sailed up the Yangzi River to Nanjing to force the still-stalling Chinese government to negotiate a treaty that would grant what the British wanted. Distances, supply problems, and the unwillingness of the Chinese government to face facts made the war go on in fits and starts for over three years. It was a disconnected series of separate actions, each one ending in a Chinese rout and demonstrating the overwhelming superiority of Western military technology. The Chinese finally capitulated in the Treaty of Nanjing, signed in 1842 on board a British

The Opium War: the British steam-powered paddle wheeler *Nemesis* destroying a Chinese fleet in a battle on January 7, 1841, near Guangzhou. *Nemesis*, aptly named, was one of the first iron-hulled steam vessels; it was designed with a shallow draft so that it could attack inland shipping. Its guns had far greater range and accuracy than those of the Chinese ships or shore batteries, and its easy success made it a symbol of Western naval and military superiority. (Hulton/Archive/Getty Images)

naval vessel. This was the first of a long series that the Chinese came to call "the unequal treaties." Western imperialism had come to China.

Reunification and the Tokugawa Shogunate in Japan

Late medieval Japan under the Ashikaga shogunate was marked by the rise of regional feudal lords and their armies, as summarized in Chapter 9. Ashikaga rule from Kyoto became increasingly ineffective in the sixteenth century. Although the shogunate was never in control of more than central Japan, areas beyond the immediate vicinity of Kyoto became more and more independent under their own daimyo (feudal lords), each with an army of samurai and based in impressive forti-fied castles. Fighting between them became chronic, and with the final collapse of the Ashikaga in 1573, Japan dissolved into civil war.

Japan was still a small, poor, relatively backward country on the edge of the major Asian stage, divided between warring clans. The settled area was the size of a Chinese province, and the total population numbered only about 15 million. The court and urban culture of Kyoto with their extreme refinement were luxurious, and technologically Ashikaga Japan had made much progress and even surpassed its Chinese teacher in some fields, including steelmaking and the production of fine swords, a major Japanese export to the rest of East Asia.

Trade was in fact extensive; by the fifteenth century Japanese shipping dominated the East China Sea, and domestic networks had also grown. Japan's small size and population, as well as its weak central government, made it relatively easier to develop a national commercial system and a strong and semi-independent merchant group, unlike China or India. Foreign trade was also proportionately more important than in China or India and more like the experience of European countries. But Japan was still split into many contending feudal units, and the rural areas—most of the country—were a world apart from Kyoto or Osaka culture, lagging far behind technically and economically as well as in sophistication. The political chaos of the late sixteenth century tore Japan apart once more, but it was to emerge from these troubles to find a new national unity and new development under Tokugawa rule.

Tokugawa Japan

Note the tiny size of Japan, and especially its settled area along the Pacific Coast, by comparison with China. (Hokkaido, the northernmost island, was not significantly settled by Japanese until the twentieth century). Japan is mainly mountains and they are extremely thinly settled.

It was the rising power of the daimyo that destroyed the Ashikaga. The continued growth of their feudal domains, each more and more like a state in miniature, needed only some form of leadership to turn Japan into a national political unit. That was essentially the nature of the Tokugawa solution. The Tokugawa founders started out as daimyo like any of the others. Over about a generation, a series of three exceptionally able leaders progressively conquered all their daimyo rivals. They superimposed their own dominance on what was still a largely unchanged feudal system. The subject daimyo ran their areas to a great extent on their own in return for formal submission to the Tokugawa shogun and periodic attendance at his court. Tokugawa central authority was far stronger and extended over a much larger area than any government in previous Japanese history. Despite its feudal trappings it was in many respects in a class with the emerging national states of contemporary Europe. Samurai served not only as military officers but as administrators. The flourishing merchant group provided revenue to add to land or agricultural taxes and also transported troops and supplies.

The Era of the Warlords

The process of unification began even before the formal end of the Ashikaga shogunate when Oda Nobunaga (1534–1582), a powerful daimyo who ruled the area around Nagoya, seized Kyoto in 1568 and became supreme in central Japan. He later captured the great temple-castle of Osaka, until then the independent seat of the militant Shin Buddhist sect. He was murdered by a vassal in 1582, but his place was taken by his chief general, Toyotomi Hideyoshi (1536–1598), who, though born a peasant, rose to the top through his ability and driving ambition. Hideyoshi soon eliminated the remaining faction of Nobunaga's family, subdued its vassals, and rebuilt the castle at Osaka as the base of his military government. In a campaign westward, he crushed the major daimyo power of the Satsuma clan in the island of Kyushu. In 1590 all of eastern and northern Honshu submitted to him after he had defeated the chief daimyo in the Edo (Tokyo) area. Hideyoshi scorned the title of shogun and ruled instead as a dictator, although warlord is probably a more appropriate title.

With a large unified army of professional fighters forged in a century of incessant warfare, Hideyoshi looked abroad for more worlds to conquer. His abortive invasion of Korea and his death in 1598 are recounted in Chapter 9. His place was soon taken by one of his lead-

 ## Hideyoshi Writes to His Wife

Hideyoshi wrote to his wife while he was besieging a daimyo castle in the spring of 1590.

Now we have got the enemy like birds in a cage, and there is no danger, so please set your mind at rest. I long for the Young Lord [his son], but I feel that for the sake of the future, and because I want to have the country at peace, I must give up my longing. So please set your mind at rest. I am looking after my health. . . . There is nothing to worry about. . . . Since as I have thus declared it will be a long siege, I wish to send for Yodo [his concubine]. I wish you to tell her and make arrangements for her journey, and tell her that next to you she is the one who pleases me best. . . . I was very glad to get your messages. We have got up to within two or three hundred yards and put a double ditch around the castle and shall not let a single man escape. All the men of the eight eastern provinces are shut up inside. . . . Though I am getting old, I must think of the future and do what is best for the country. So now I mean to do glorious deeds and I am ready for a long siege, with provisions and gold and silver in plenty, so as to return in triumph and leave a great name behind me. I desire you to understand this and to tell it to everybody.

Source: G. B. Sansom, *Japan: A Short Cultural History,* rev. ed. (New York: Appleton-Century-Crofts, 1962), p. 410.

---

ing vassal-allies, Tokugawa Ieyasu (1542–1616).* Ieyasu had already built a castle headquarters at Edo, where he had served as Hideyoshi's deputy. In 1600 he won a great victory in the battle of Sekigahara, near Nagoya in central Japan, over a coalition of rivals. This established his power as Hideyoshi's successor, and he completed his supremacy by capturing Osaka castle in 1615. Hideyoshi forced all nonsamurai to surrender their swords and ensured that all commoners would be kept down, unable to challenge him. His famous "sword hunt" in which houses were searched and swords confiscated reestablished rigid class lines, and new laws prohibited farmers or common soldiers from becoming merchants. Hideyoshi saw the changes of his time as a threat and tried to control them. Thus, the new Tokugawa order had its roots in the earlier work of Nobunaga and Hideyoshi.

---

*Japanese names, like Chinese, are customarily given with surname or family name first and personal name second. Somewhat inconsistently, Nobunaga, Hideyoshi, and Ieyasu are, however, commonly referred to by their personal names only, presumably because they are so well known as key figures—as Americans recognize "Marse Tom" or "Old Abe."

Tokugawa Rule

Ieyasu wanted to build a strong, centrally controlled political system. He and his able Tokugawa successors largely achieved this and created relative stability and peace for the next 250 years. They did so by enforcing a set of rigid controls on society as well as on political behavior and by repressing change. Tokugawa feudalism was even more hidebound than that of earlier eras, and the shoguns also tried to control "dangerous thought" with the help of a fearsomely efficient secret police. They themselves administered the central core of the country, from the Edo area to Kyoto, Osaka, and the peninsula south of Osaka, placing members of their own clan in key centers: Mito (northeast of Edo), Nagoya, and Wakayama (south of Osaka).

This was, then as now, the economic heart of Japan, containing most of the commercial towns and cities. Other loyal allies and early supporters of Ieyasu were given fiefs in the rest of this central area. Beyond it, to the north and to the west, the Tokugawa bound other daimyo to them by feudal ties, helping to ensure their loyalty by requiring them to leave members of their own families in Edo as hostages, including wives and sons. Daimyo had to keep a permanent residence in Edo and to spend time alternately there and in their distant fiefs, but armies were not permitted to leave their fiefs. This was the *Sankin Kotai* system, or "alternate residence." The heavy expense of this required travel, with their large retinues, and of maintaining two residences, which were usually luxurious, put the daimyo increasingly into debt with merchants, whose unofficial power thus slowly rose.

As in feudal Europe, marriage ties were used to cement loyalty, but the special feature of the Tokugawa control system was the requirement for all daimyo to leave their wives and immediate heirs in Edo as hostages, and to personally attend the shogun's court there in alternate years. The expenses of the journey, with an extensive retinue, and of maintaining two luxurious households and estates, at their home bases and in Edo, were heavy, taking over half of their incomes. Money had increasingly to be borrowed from merchants, or acquired through marriage with their daughters, thus increasing merchant power. This tie with Edo tended to increase cultural unity in Japan; even remote areas followed the cultural lead of Edo. Daimyo processions to and from Edo, especially along the coastal road from and to Kyoto (still the seat of the emperor), also served to spread an increasingly national culture, as well as stimulate trade along the route, known as the Tokaido. Daimyo processions, including the overnight stops along the route, became favorite subjects for Japanese artists.

A close eye was kept on construction or repair of daimyo castles, which were not permitted to become potential bases for rival military power, as they had been in previous centuries. The shogunate created a new group of officials who acted as censors, in the Chinese pattern, and the secret police watched for any threats to Tokugawa rule. At Edo, a new castle was built as the shogun's headquarters, a vast fortress inside massive walls and moats arranged in a series of concentric rings about two miles across. The innermost ring, with its moat and walls, remains as the imperial palace in the center of downtown Tokyo today. The emperor was left in place with his court at Kyoto, and the ancient fiction of imperial divinity and supremacy preserved. Technically, the shogun was only the emperor's military chief of staff; in reality, he was the acknowledged ruler of Japan.

By the time Ieyasu died in 1616, having prudently transferred power to his son so as to avoid disputes over the succession, the new, but at the same time traditionally feudal, order was firmly established. A new post of prime minister was created, assisted by a council of state, in part to ensure that the system would not weaken or collapse under a less effective shogun. In time, a relatively complex central administration grew up, with posts filled first largely by able members of the Tokugawa clan or from the families of loyal daimyo and later from the expanding group of gentry in the central area.

Merchant groups and other commoners had begun to acquire new power and even some independence as

Daimyo castle, Nagoya. This is a typical example of the fortresses built during the last troubled decades of the Ashikaga and in the early Tokugawa period by local lords who then were conquered or swore allegiance to the Tokugawa shogunate. The massive wall was surrounded by a moat. Such castles could usually be taken only by a long siege, leading to the surrender of the starving defenders. (Wim Swann)

Ashikaga rule deteriorated. At the same time, the economy grew. Large-scale trade centered in the Osaka area. The neighboring commercial center of Sakai, now part of greater Osaka, was actually a self-governing city run by merchants with their own army, like a Renaissance Italian mercantile city-state. The Tokugawa suppressed the rising political power of the middle and lower classes as a threat to their central authority. Merchants were restricted and supervised in their activities and made subservient to the new aristocratic order. Sakai's walls were demolished, its armies dissolved, and its government absorbed into the Tokugawa system.

The same order was brought into the countryside. Large armies were no longer necessary, and armed peasants available as daimyo troops were a potential menace. Peasants were again made to surrender their swords and other weapons to the government, and the hereditary warrior class of samurai was left in complete charge of military affairs. Swords became the badge of the samurai, a mark of aristocratic birth and status that came to symbolize their dual role as "gentlemen warriors" and as administrators. Firearms, which the Japanese knew of both from the Chinese and from the Portuguese and Dutch, were also seen as potentially disruptive and as making disorder or rebellion easier. They too were successfully outlawed, and Japan was free of them for more than two centuries, since foreigners were also excluded. Swords became even more an exclusive hallmark of the aristocracy, not easily challenged by unarmed peasants.

Peasants and artisans were essential producers, although of low status, but merchants, despite their obvious accomplishments, literacy, often cultivation, and wealth, were seen as parasites and put into the lowest social order of all. This reflected classic Confucian values. Japan had retained Confucianism especially within the aristocratic class, and it was revived and strengthened under Tokugawa rule as suiting admirably their feudal and hierarchical system and their stress on loyalty. Merchants were forbidden to wear the fine clothes or materials of the upper classes, to ride in sedan chairs, or to omit the groveling and subservient bowing also required of peasants and artisans to samurai or other aristocrats whom they encountered. Those who did not bow low enough might have their heads chopped off by samurai guards.

The Expulsion of Foreigners

The Portuguese had reached Japan by 1543, and for nearly a century they and later the Spanish and Dutch carried on an extensive export-import trade. Catholic missionaries came too and began to make numerous converts. Japan was more curious about and open to Westerners than China, having long understood the value of learning from others. But the Tokugawa grew irritated by the factional bickering among the different missionary orders and by the allegiance converts had to give to a distant and alien pope. The combination of missionaries and traders as agents or forerunners of foreign influence or even colonial expansion was disturbing to the smooth order the Tokugawa had worked so hard to establish. Hideyoshi had welcomed Christian missionaries and foreign traders, but he too came to see them as disruptive and banned missionaries in 1587 and in 1597 began active persecution by crucifying nine Catholic priests and seventeen Japanese converts as an example. In the years after Ieyasu's death in 1616, all missionaries were killed or expelled, and

Tokugawa Ieyasu:
Instructions to His Successor

Tokugawa Ieyasu was a careful planner, a good judge of men, and one who understood the virtue of patient waiting until the time was right for action. Here is one of the instructions he left to his successors.

> The strong manly ones in life are those who understand the meaning of the word patience. Patience means restraining one's inclinations. There are seven emotions: joy, anger, anxiety, love, grief, fear, and hate, and if a man does not give way to these he can be called patient. I am not as strong as I might be, but I have long known and practiced patience. And if my descendants wish to be as I am, they must study patience.

Source: A. L. Sadler, *The Maker of Modern Japan* (London: Allen and Unwin, 1937), pp. 389–390.

READING ACROSS CULTURES:

Japanese Overseas Trade in the Tokugawa Era

Heightened international trade and internal stability contributed to the prosperity of Japan's cities from 1570 to 1635. Japan's mines produced quantities of silver and gold that financed the flourishing overseas trade. Since Japan's ships were forbidden to trade directly with China, the exchange of Japanese bullion for Chinese silk and other goods had to take place in Southeast Asian ports—Hoi An in Vietnam, Manila in the Philippines, and Ayudhya in Siam.

During the transition to the Tokugawa shogunate, the Dutch displaced the Portuguese as the dominant Western traders in Japan's ports. To participate in the Japanese marketplace, Dutch merchants learned that they had to have ready access to silver coinage, most of which they acquired as the trade intermediaries for wealthy Spanish customers, who were willing to pay high prices for exotic and high quality Asian imports. The flow of Spanish silver from Spain and the Americas to Asia's marketplaces allowed Dutch merchants to build their working capital for the future and contributed to the further monetization of the Asian marketplace.

Despite the Tokugawa shogunate's curtailment of Japan's overseas trade in 1635, which prohibited Japanese from traveling abroad and restricted Japan's foreign trade to Nagasaki on Japan's southern periphery, its trade volume was impressive. Indeed, even after 1639, when the shogun barred all but the Dutch and Chinese from trading at Nagasaki, Japan's overseas trade volume continued to increase through the end of the seventeenth century. Japan's Tokugawa leadership took notice of the outflow of Japanese bullion that was fueling urban inflation and periodically tried to restrict it, but with little success. One consequence was that Tokugawa samurai-bureaucrats, wanting to sustain their standard of living against rising domestic prices, had to subsidize their fixed salaries by networking with Japanese merchants. These relationships were frequently formalized by marriage alliances, which enhanced the social and political stature of the otherwise disempowered merchant class.

Source: Robert Innes, "Door Ajar: Japan's Foreign Trade in the Seventeenth Century," PhD diss., University of Michigan, 1980.

---

converts were executed or forced to recant. The persecution culminated in the suppression of a rebellion by impoverished Christian peasants in the area of Nagasaki, which had been the chief port for trade with Westerners, in 1638. The survivors were slaughtered and many crucified, but a few escaped and kept Christianity alive on an underground basis until the reappearance of Western missionaries in the 1860s.

All Western traders were also expelled by 1638 and relations ended; Portuguese envoys who came in 1640 to ask for a reopening of relations were executed. Japanese were forbidden to go abroad, and no ships capable of overseas trade could be built. In order not to lose complete touch with what was happening in the rest of the world, one or sometimes two Dutch ships a year (because they showed no interest in Christian conversion and were there solely for trade) were permitted to come for trade, on the island of Deshima in Nagasaki Harbor, remote from the centers of Japanese population.

Culture and Urbanization

With such an array of controls over people's lives, the Tokugawa did indeed ensure peace and stability. For about two centuries they also largely succeeded in preventing most change, especially in social or political matters. Japan was still a poor country, and there were periodic peasant rebellions and urban-based revolts as expressions of economic distress, but they were easily put down. In larger terms, however, Japan continued to develop, and now, under the long Tokugawa peace, more rapidly than ever before. Production and internal trade grew, and with it an expanding merchant class. A truly national market system developed for many basic commodities, aided by the use of paper credits. This included even a futures market for rice. None of this fit well with the formally feudal arrangement of the social and political systems; it had the same disruptive effects on Japanese feudalism as the revival of trade, towns, and merchants had in late medieval Europe. As rich merchants began to lend money to needy or extravagant noblemen, and then to marry their daughters, they could no longer be treated as beneath the notice of daimyo and samurai. The cultural life of Tokugawa Japan was largely urban, and merchants came to dominate it as a new bourgeoisie. Towns grew around the many daimyo castles, which became trade centers. Most of modern Japan's cities began in this era as castle towns.

The amusement quarters in the cities, especially Edo, were supported mainly by merchants, "tired businessmen," with occasional samurai also as patrons, relaxing from the stiff conventions of aristocratic society. This was the great age of the geisha, who were not primarily prostitutes but entertainers who specialized in singing, dancing, and lively conversation with male patrons. Artists and novelists loved to depict geisha scenes, the highly popular puppet plays, and, from the seventeenth century, a new dramatic form, *Kabuki,* which is still popular in Japan. Kabuki catered to less refined tastes than the classical Noh theater and emphasized realism, comedy, and melodrama. Classical poetry on the Chinese model was reduced to three- or four-line miniatures, the *haiku,* which at their best were superb but which also attracted many literate amateurs. Painting became more flamboyant, splendidly

colorful, and on a grander scale, but still in keeping with the remarkable Japanese sense of good taste. Magnificent decorated screens and wall panels were produced for the palaces of the shogun and of noblemen, who wore gorgeous silk brocades and furnished their tables with beautiful lacquerware and porcelain. In time, much of this splendor could also be found in the houses of rich merchants, but popular art became more important and commoners' houses were more often decorated with woodblock prints. This is probably still the Japanese art best known abroad; it reached its high point in the last decades of the Tokugawa in the early nineteenth century.

A surprising amount of information about the outside world continued to filter in by way of the Dutch at Nagasaki, including Western advances in medicine, shipbuilding, and metalworking. A few Japanese scholars began to study Western science. They compared Dutch texts on anatomy with traditional Chinese medical texts, for example, and through their own dissection of the corpses of executed criminals demonstrated as early as 1771 that the Dutch version was accurate, whereas the Chinese was not. The Chinese rejected dissection, taboo in light of Confucian respect for the body. At the same time, Japanese acquired a new national

Tokugawa splendor: a view of the main audience hall at Nijo Castle in Kyoto. The superb screen paintings, beautifully set off by the plain *tatami* (rush mat) floor, are a fine example of early Tokugawa decorative art for the elite. (Anne Kirkup)

consciousness, thanks to the Tokugawa unification. They were able to adopt ideas and techniques from foreign sources, as they long had done from China, without in any way diluting their own cultural and national identity. Japan's separateness as an island further reinforced their feeling of uniqueness.

Together with a renewed interest in things foreign, late Tokugawa saw a revival of Shinto, the ancient Japanese worship of natural forces, primarily as a symbol of the new awareness of being Japanese. Buddhism, which had overshadowed and almost eliminated Shinto in earlier centuries, was after all a foreign import. Shinto legends and naive myths about the divine origin of the emperor, and through him of the Japanese people, now appealed more to popular nationalist attitudes, although Shinto never replaced Buddhism, or Confucianism for the upper classes and intellectuals, as the dominant religion. These and other changes were slowly transforming Japan, despite its unchanging surface, into a modern nation with a commercial economy and a society that would soon be ready to burst the artificial restraints imposed on it.

A CLOSER LOOK

Edo and the "Floating World"

By 1770, it is probable that Edo and its immediate environs had reached 1 million in population, rivaled or exceeded only by Beijing and larger than any city in Europe. This urban concentration in such a relatively small country (mid-Tokugawa Japan totaled about 25 million) resulted from a combination of administrative centralization under the shogunate and the rapid commercialization of the economy. Edo and Osaka were the major centers of a national trade system and the headquarters of large merchant groups. The requirement that all daimyo had to maintain households in Edo, where they left their wives and family members as hostages, further swelled the population, as did their regular formal visits with their large retinues. Daimyo family estates, the large court of the shogun, and rich merchant families employed very large numbers of servants and artisans, who provided them with luxurious furnishings and works of art. The heavy expense of daimyo travel with their servants and the maintenance of their Edo residences often left them financially dependent on loans from merchants and on marriage alliances with previously despised merchant families. The latter also profited from catering to the daimyo processions and their stopovers along the routes to Edo, a journey that might take many weeks. The longest stage for most daimyo was the route from Kyoto to Edo, known as the Tokaido.

Edo was also a major port, and much of Japan's coastal trade passed through it in addition to what came by land. Much of the site had originally been swampy or prone to flooding, and large new tracts were drained and reclaimed. Areas were set aside for daimyo and merchant residences and for shops, open-air markets, temples, and amusement quarters around the landward sides of the huge, new castle built by Ieyasu. Thousands of soldiers based in Edo added to the numbers, as did the even more numerous laborers and suppliers that maintained such a huge population.

Merchants dominated the bourgeois culture of Edo. Rich commoners wore forbidden silk under their plain outer clothing. The arts and amusements centered around what was called the Floating World of fugitive pleasures, an amusement quarter of theaters, restaurants, bathhouses, and geisha houses, lovingly portrayed in the woodblock prints that were produced in great volume. The main pleasure quarter was at the northern edge of the city, outside the official limits, a district known as Yoshiwara. Patrons there, sometimes including lesser aristocrats, retainers, or artisans as well as merchants, could enjoy Kabuki plays or an evening with favorite geishas. Except for the shogun's castle and a few daimyo mansions, Edo was built almost entirely of wood, like all Japanese cities of the time, and fires often could not be controlled. The city burned down almost completely several times, but each time it was rebuilt on an even larger and grander basis.

Literature, theater, and art were not necessarily vulgarized by their new bourgeois patrons, who in fact often insisted on high aesthetic standards in their prints, screens, clothing, porcelains, furnishings, books, and drama. It was a new urban age of great cultural vigor, reminiscent perhaps of Song dynasty Hangzhou but distinctly Japanese in its tastes. In Japan, as elsewhere, tastes and influence were passing increasingly into bourgeois hands in a new, urban-dominated world.

Under the long Tokugawa peace population increased, from about 18 million in 1600 to perhaps 26 million by 1720. The rise of castle towns meant major new demands for wood as the common building material and as firewood and charcoal. Many slopes were denuded, and floods and erosion became more common. The state realized, however, that their tax revenues depended on a productive agriculture, and, accordingly, they imposed strict regulations on forest cutting, which in general preserved most of Japan's vital forest cover. They also distributed pamphlets advising farmers how to increase their output through fertilization and irrigation and through conscientious hard work. In part as a result, population growth slowed after about 1720, but this was also attributable to the growing use of infanticide, especially of females, and to abortion, especially in the growing towns. Merchants increased and prospered with the growth of towns. Japanese society and economy developed well beyond the limits of a strictly feudal system. The country became an economic unit, with a

The Impact of Western Knowledge

Sugita Genpaku (1733–1817), a physician, recorded his reactions to the discovery of the accurate Dutch version of human anatomy.

> I was struck with admiration by the great difference between the knowledge of the West and that of the East. And I was inspired to come to the determination that I must learn and clarify the new revelation for applying it to actual healing and also for making it the seed of further discoveries among the general physicians of Japan.

Source: Conrad Totman, *Japan Before Perry* (Berkeley: University of California Press, 1981) p. 208.

new national market for many goods, especially rice and the sake made from it, centered in Osaka. The *sankin kotai* system not only helped to impoverish many of the daimyo but also helped to create a national economy and a national culture as the norms of Edo were spread more widely. The daimyo and samurai continued to feel that agriculture was the sole source of wealth, and indeed they measured their incomes in *koku* (about five bushels) of rice. The growing merchant class, however, was fast becoming more important, and as they began to marry their sons or daughters to the children of impoverished aristocrats and to lend money to them, often as part of a marriage contract, their status rose. Paper credits were used in most large transactions. Conglomerates like the Mitsui family became rich and prominent, but there was also a group of smaller entrepreneurs, many originally rural but moving to the towns and cities. More and more of farm output was sold, and many of the peasants became literate. None of these developments fit easily into the Tokugawa feudal structure and produced pressures for change.

A CLOSER LOOK

Hokusai, Master Artist

Probably the best known of Japanese woodblock print-makers under the Tokugawa was the man called Hokusai (not his real name, which remains unknown), who lived from 1760 to 1849. He was born in Edo to unknown parents and was adopted at age three by a craftsman named Nakijima, who made mirrors for the shogunate. The boy seems to have shown a talent for drawing by the time he was five, and by age thirteen he had been apprenticed to an engraver of woodblocks. Hoku-

sai was a devout Buddhist and chose the name by which he is known, which means "north studio," to honor a Buddhist saint who was thought to be an incarnation of the North Star. His early work centered on book illustration, and he also made many portraits of contemporary actors. His prints are very Japanese in style but became enormously popular in the West even before the end of Japan's seclusion policy. Trade had continued, even though most foreigners were excluded, and increased substantially after 1800. Japanese artisans began to copy the Chinese blue-and-white porcelainware that had proved so popular with Westerners and that became, together with silk and tea later, an important Japanese export.

It did not occur to the Japanese that Westerners would find their art desirable, and in any case woodblock prints were turned out in large numbers, sold very cheaply, and easily duplicated from the original block. But the freshness, color, and simple lines of Hokusai's work and that of many of his contemporaries appealed strongly to a Europe already impressed and influenced by Chinese art. The European craze for chinoiserie in the late eighteenth and early nineteenth centuries was joined by an enthusiasm for "japonoiserie." Many Japanese prints in fact arrived in Europe as wastepaper, used for wrapping porcelain and other export goods, but they soon became prized. Return trade to Japan brought among other things the color and materials for Prussian blue, which was soon used by Hokusai and others to further brighten and enliven their work.

Perhaps the best known in the West of Hokusai's prints is his *Thirty-six Views of Mount Fuji*. His style and that of his contemporaries had a great influence on Western artists, especially the impressionists in France, and the American James Whistler, although most of Hokusai's influence came after his death. Most of the impressionists acknowledged their debt to him,

Hokusai, *The Great Wave at Kanagawa,* from *Thirty-six Views of Mount Fuji,* perhaps the woodblock print best known outside Japan. Mount Fuji shows clearly in the background. (The Metropolitan Museum of Art, Henry L. Phillips Collection, bequest of Henry L. Phillips, 1939. [JP 2972] Photograph, all rights reserved, The Metropolitan Museum of Art.)

and many of them painted pictures in an avowedly Japanese style during the craze for things Japanese after 1870. Vincent Van Gogh carefully copied prints by Hokusai's contemporary, Hiroshige (1797–1858). Thus, while Meiji Japan was busily adopting Western ways as fast as it could, Western artists were returning the compliment.

Foreign Pressures for Change

The political system controlled so tightly from Edo ran relatively smoothly through the first half of the nineteenth century, and there were few outward expressions of dissent, except for the periodic peasant rebellions. In time, the pressures building up within the feudal facade would probably have forced basic change, although it was not easy to challenge the overwhelming Tokugawa power and its secret police. As it happened, an outside force provided the impetus that destroyed the

shogun's power and, hence, opened wide the floodgates that had held Japan in confinement for so long. It is not surprising that, having been so long suppressed, change then took place on a truly revolutionary scale.

Among the outsiders from the late eighteenth century, the Americans were most anxious to open Japanese ports to foreign trade. First American whalers, then clipper ships plying the China trade, then early steamships in need of coal supplies sought permission to obtain provisions in Japan and better treatment for sailors shipwrecked on its shores, who were often roughly handled. American, British, and Russian expeditions after 1800 were repelled by Edo, and their requests rejected. Finally, the American government took matters in its own hands and sent a small but powerful naval force under Commodore Matthew Perry in 1853 with a letter to the shogun demanding trade relations and better treatment of foreign castaways.

The government in Edo was not only bewildered but also impressed by the size and the guns of the Americans' steam-powered "black ships," against which they

Japanese Women:
An Outsider's View

From the early accounts of the Dutch at Deshima, some American authors in 1841 compiled this account of the state of women in Japan.

The position of women in Japan is apparently unlike that of the sex in all other parts of the East, and approaches more nearly their European condition. The Japanese women are subjected to no jealous seclusion, hold a fair station in society, and share in all the innocent recreations of their fathers and husbands. The minds of the women are cultivated with as much care as those of men; and amongst the most admired Japanese historians, moralists, and poets are found several female names. The Japanese ladies are described as being generally lively and agreeable companions, and the ease and elegance of their manners have been highly extolled. But, though permitted thus to enjoy and adorn society, they are, on the other hand, during their whole lives, kept in a state of tutelage: that is, of complete dependence on their husbands, sons, or other relatives. They have no legal rights, and their evidence is not admitted in a court of justice. Not only may the husband introduce as many unwedded helpmates as he pleases into the mansion over which his wife presides but he also has the power of divorce, which may be considered unlimited, since he is restrained only by considerations of expediency. The Japanese husband, however, is obliged to support his repudiated wife according to his own station, unless he can allege grounds for the divorce satisfactory to the proper tribunal; among which, the misfortune of being without children takes from the unhappy wife all claim to maintenance. Under no circumstances whatever can a wife demand to be separated from her husband. At home, the wife is the mistress of the family; but in other respects she is treated rather as a toy for her husband's amusement, than as the rational, confidential partner of his life. She is expected to please him by her accomplishments, and to cheer him with her lively conversation, but never suffered to share his more serious thoughts, or to relieve by participation his anxieties and cares. She is, indeed, kept in profound ignorance of his business affairs; and so much as a question from her in relation to them would be resented as an act of unpardonable presumption.

Source: P. F. Siebold, *Manners and Customs of the Japanese in the Nineteenth Century* (London: Murray, 1852), pp. 122–124.

realized Japan was defenseless. Perry's squadron had anchored in Tokyo Bay in full view of Edo for precisely this reason. Ten years earlier, the British had made the same point with China in the Opium War. Like the Chinese, the Japanese first tried to stall. Conservative forces, which dominated the Tokugawa, urged that the foreigners be refused and ejected. But when Perry returned the next year, the government saw that it really had no choice. It signed a treaty at Kanagawa, on the south shore of Tokyo Bay near Kamakura, opening two ports and allowing a limited amount of regulated trade. Similar treaties followed with European powers, and in 1858 a set of more detailed commercial treaties.

Foreigners could now reside in five ports as well as Osaka and Edo and could trade with whomever they liked. But this had all been agreed to at the point of a gun. Most Japanese still believed strongly that the barbarians must be expelled before they further sullied the sacred soil of Japan. The man who had signed the treaties was assassinated by conservative elements in

Crisis in 1853

The Tokugawa government issued a decree in 1853 after the visit of Perry's ships and a similar visit by Russian ships to Tokyo Bay only a month later with the same purpose. The decree read in part:

> Everyone has pointed out that we are without a navy and that our coasts are undefended. Meanwhile the Americans will be back next year. Our policy shall be to evade any definite answer to their request, while at the same time keeping a peaceful demeanor. It may be they will have recourse to violence. For that we must be prepared, lest the country suffer disgrace.

Source: R. Storry, *A History of Modern Japan,* rev. ed. (New York: 1982), p. 90.

1860. Other extreme nationalists murdered an Englishman near Yokohama, a former fishing village on the western shore of Tokyo Bay that had become the main foreign settlement and was soon to develop into one of the world's largest ports. There were, of course, reprisals, and the Tokugawa government was caught in a dilemma. It still tried to resist all foreign pressures but was unable to act, or even to control its own subjects, who increasingly believed that their government had failed them and that its weakness was revealed. The outer daimyo domains in western Japan, especially Satsuma in Kyushu and Choshu in western Honshu, had always been restless under Tokugawa domination and now saw their chance to challenge it. They and others began to intrigue at the court in Kyoto and finally confronted Edo's forces militarily.

When the emperor died in 1867, the shogun, sensing a growing popular desire to return to imperial rule, formally handed over power to the new boy emperor, Meiji, and his advisers, among whom samurai from rebellious western Japan had a prominent place. A little over a year later, they persuaded the outer daimyo to offer their domains to the emperor, and feudal lords in the rest of Japan followed suit. The emperor moved to more modern Edo, which thus became Tokyo ("eastern capital"). This largely nonviolent revolution in 1868 and 1869 is known as the Meiji Restoration, but it was a revolution nevertheless, and it brought to power a new government bent on radical and rapid change. The daimyo were compensated for their surrendered lands, and some remained as governors and other officials of the new government, but this was the sudden though peaceful end of feudalism in Japan. The way was clear for the wholesale remaking of Japan as a modern industrial power.

After 1869, the rapid growth of cities, trade, and merchants and the rise of a strong centralized government helped to make it possible for Japan to modernize rapidly along Western lines while China floundered. Tokugawa rule was profoundly conservative, even hidebound in its feudal forms, but despite its efforts to prevent change, Japan was being transformed economically. Tokugawa Japan has often been compared with late medieval Europe, where similar changes were taking place beneath the feudal exterior and central governments were building up their power. Antiquated though the feudal forms seemed, late Tokugawa Japan, like late medieval Europe, was ready to break out of those forms with new energy and purpose.

In China late Qing rule was also conservative, but its central administrative control, never strong given the immense size of the country, weakened further after 1800. The economy remained dominated by peasant agriculture, and although trade, cities, and merchants all increased, they never became more than a small part of this huge and basically agrarian system. China was just too big to be quickly affected by new trends. The inherent conservatism of both the peasants and their rulers worked against change, especially anything of foreign (barbarian) origin. But none of this was clear in 1860 or 1870. Most foreigners looked on China as the dominant force in the East Asian economy, and Japan as a far smaller, less developed, and poorer second. However, China's fortunes were on a steep downslope and Japan's were starting the equally steep rise that would soon far outdistance those of her traditional superior and teacher.

Qing China, under the last of the dynasties, tended to conform strictly to long-established Chinese tradition. The Qing knew of course that theirs was a dynasty of conquest and were anxious to follow faithfully Chinese ways on all things. At the same time, Manchu women were freer of restraints than their Chinese contemporaries, and, of course, the chief figure of the last decades of the Qing was the forceful Empress

Dowager Cixi, who plotted her way to the throne and became the second woman ruler of China, after the Empress Wu of the Tang. Nevertheless, Chinese women, though formally subjugated, were often the real powers within the family and managed the household money; as was said, "once the door is closed, the woman takes over." In Tokugawa Japan, women remained possibly still more subjugated, although there too they tended to take over management of the household once the door was closed. In both countries it seems likely that the geishas and their Chinese origin, the flower boat women, were the freest of their sex, literate, and well educated, who entertained their customers with music, dance, and capping classical quotations.

Questions

1. Describe the Sino-Manchu dyarchy, as it has been called.

2. What explains the tripling of China's population under the Qing?

3. How did the Qing reinforce Chinese ethnocentrism?

4. How do the reigns of Kangxi and Qianlong contribute to and demonstrate China's stability in the late eighteenth century? What changed between then and the Opium Wars in the 1840s?

5. How did Qing China's bureaucratic meritocracy contrast with the Tokugawa political system that was based in family alliances? What were the consequences of each, relative to the potentials for commercial development and the way families interacted with the Chinese and Japanese political systems? How did this also shape Chinese and Japanese reaction to the increasing Western threat?

6. In what ways did the Tokugawa shogunate develop Japan's political, social, economic, and educational infrastructures that were the foundations for Japan's rapid modernization after 1869? How did the Japanese move from their prior feudal order to a more mobile society?

7. In what ways did the first Opium War result in and reflect a changed Western relationship with Asia?

Notes

1. R. Fortune, *Three Years' Wanderings in the Northern Provinces of China* (London: Murray, 1853), p. 196.

2. J. K. Fairbank, E. O. Reischauer, and A. Craig, *East Asia: Tradition and Transformation* (Boston: Houghton Mifflin, 1978), p. 228.

3. J. L. Cranmer-Byng, ed., *An Embassy to China* (London: Longman, 1962), pp. 212–213.

4. G. Stanton, *Notes of Proceedings During the British Embassy to Peking in 1816* (London: Murray, 1824), pp. 153–225.

Suggested Web Sites

Qing (Manchu) Dynasty China

http://www-chaos.umd.edu/history/imperial3.html
http://www.mnsu.edu/emuseum/prehistory/china/ later_imperial_china/qing.html
Useful Web sites on the Qing dynasty, along with artwork: economy and social life, culture, science, technology, and political history.

Tokugawa Japan

http://www.wsu.edu:8000/~dee/TOKJAPAN/ SHOGUN.HTM
Textual information about Tokugawa Japan, 1603–1868.

Hokusai

http://www.monks.demon.co.uk/hocus.htm
Background information and beautiful images from Hokusai, the master Japanese artist (1760–1849).

Emergence of Modern China, the Opium War

http://www.wsu.edu:8000/~dee/CHING/OPIUM.HTM
The causes and essential players in the Opium War, 1839–1842.

Suggestions for Further Reading

China

Crossley, P. K. *The Manchus.* Oxford: Blackwell, 1997.

Elliott, M. *The Manchu Way.* Stanford:_Stanford University Press, 2001.

Elman, B., and Woodside, A., eds. *Education and Society in Late Imperial China.* Berkeley: University of California Press, 1994.

Elvin, M. *The Retreat of the Elephants.* New Haven: Yale University Press, 2004.

Entatsu, Y. *Banner Legacy.* Ann Arbor: Center for Chinese Studies, 2004.

Fairbank, J. K., ed. *The Cambridge History of China,* vol. 10: *Late Ch'ing.* Cambridge, England: Cambridge University Press, 1978.

Fay, P. W. *The Opium War.* Cambridge, England: Cambridge University Press, 1975.

Greenberg, M. *British Trade and the Opening of China, 1800–1953.* Cambridge, England: Cambridge University Press, 1951.

Ho, P. T. *Studies on the Population of China, 1368–1953.* Cambridge: Harvard University Press, 1959.

Kahn, H. L. *Monarchy in the Emperor's Eyes: Image and Reality in the Ch'ien Lung Reign.* Cambridge: Harvard University Press, 1971.

Ko, D. *Teachers of the Inner Chambers: Women and Culture in Seventeenth Century China.* Stanford: Stanford University Press, 1994.

Lach, D. *Asia in the Making of Europe,* 2 vols. Chicago: University of Chicago Press, 1965, 1978.

Metzger, T. *The Internal Organization of Ch'ing Bureaucracy.* Cambridge: Harvard University Press, 1973.

Miyazaki, I. *China's Examination Hell: The Civil Service Examinations in Imperial China,* trans. C. Shirokauer. New York: Weatherhill, 1976.

Naquin, S. *Peking: Temples and City Life.* Berkeley: University of California Press, 2000.

Naquin, S., and Rawski, E. S. *Chinese Society in the Eighteenth Century.* New Haven: Yale University Press, 1988.

Perkins, D. *Agricultural Development in China,* 1368–1968. Chicago: University of Chicago Press, 1969.

Polachek, J. M. *The Inner Opium War.* Cambridge: Harvard University Press, 1992.

Rawski, E. *Education and Popular Literature in Ch'ing China.* Ann Arbor: University of Michigan Press, 1978.

———. *The Last Emperors.* Berkeley: University of California Press, 1998.

Rawski, T. G., and Li, L. M., eds. *Chinese History in Economic Perspective.* Berkeley: University of California Press, 1991.

Reed, B. W. *Talons and Teeth: County Clerks and Runners in the Qing Dynasty.* Stanford: Stanford University Press, 2001.

Rozman, G. *Urban Networks in Ch'ing China and Tokugawa Japan.* Princeton: Princeton University Press, 1973.

Smith, R. J. *China's Cultural Heritage: The Qing Dynasty.* Boulder, CO: Westview, 1994.

Spence, J. *Ts'ao Yin and the K'ang Hsi Emperor.* New Haven: Yale University Press, 1988.

Van der Sprenkel, S. *Legal Institutions in Manchu China.* London: University of London Press, 1962.

Wakeman, F. *The Great Enterprise: The Manchu Reconstruction of Imperial Order in Seventeenth-Century China.* Berkeley: University of California Press, 1985.

Will, P. E. *Bureaucracy and Famine in Eighteenth Century China.* Stanford: Stanford University Press, 1990.

Wong, R. B., Will, P. E., and Lee, J. *State Granaries and the Food Supply of China,* 1650–1850. Ann Arbor: University of Michigan Press, 1992.

Japan

Barr, P. *The Coming of the Barbarians.* London: Macmillan, 1967.

Beasley, W. G. *The Rise of Modern Japan.* New York: St. Martin's Press, 1990.

Berry, N. E. *Hideyoshi.* Cambridge: Harvard University Press, 1986.

Bix, H. P. *Peasant Protest in Japan,* 1590–1884. New Haven: Yale University Press, 1986.

Bolitho, H. *Treasures Among Men: The Feudal Daimyo in Tokugawa Japan.* New Haven: Yale University Press, 1974.

Earle, J. *Splendors of Imperial Japan: Arts of the Meiji Period from the Khalili Collection.* London:Palgrave/Macmillan, 2005.

Elison, G., and Smith, B. *Warlords, Artists, and Commoners: Japan in the Sixteenth Century.* Honolulu: University Press of Hawaii, 1981.

Gerstle, C. A., ed. *Eighteenth-Century Japan: Culture and Society.* New York: HarperCollins, 1990.

Hall, J. W., ed. *The Cambridge History of Early Modern Japan,* vol. 3. Cambridge, England: Cambridge University Press, 1991.

Hane, M. *Peasants, Rebels, Women, and Outcasts.* Lanham, MD: Rowan and Littlefield, 2003.

Harrington, A. M. *Japan's Hidden Christians.* Chicago: Loyola University Press, 1993.

Hibbett, H. *The Floating World.* Rutland, VT: Tuttle, 1975.

Jansen, M. B. *China in the Tokugawa World.* Cambridge: Harvard University Press, 2000.

Koschmann, J. V. *The Mito Ideology in Late Tokugawa Japan.* Berkeley: University of California Press, 1987.

Leupp, G. P. *Servants, Shopkeepers, and Laborers in the Cities of Tokugawa Japan.* Princeton: Princeton University Press, 1995.

Matsunosuke, N. *Edo Culture.* Honolulu: University of Hawaii Press, 1992.

Michener, J. A. *The Floating World.* Honolulu: University Press of Hawaii, 1983.

Nakane, C., and Oishi, S., eds. *Tokugawa Japan,* trans. C. Totman. Tokyo: University of Tokyo Press, 1991.

Seigle, C. S. *Yoshiwara: The Glittering World of the Japanese Courtesan.* Honolulu: University of Hawaii Press, 1993.

Storry, R. *Tokugawa Ieyasu: Shogun.* San Francisco: Heian, 1983.

Totman, C. *Politics in the Tokugawa Bakufu,* 1600–1843. Cambridge: Harvard University Press, 1967.

Walthall, A. *Peasant Uprisings in Japan.* Chicago: University of Chicago Press, 1991.

Vlastos, S. *Peasant Protests and Uprisings in Tokugawa Japan.* Berkeley: University of California Press, 1986.

14

The Rise of British Power in India

This chapter surveys the chaotic state of India in the early eighteenth century as the Mughal order collapsed; the origins of the English trade in India; the founding of Madras in 1639, Bombay in 1687, and Calcutta in 1690; and the beginnings of wider territorial acquisitions with the conquest of Bengal by Robert Clive in 1757. Indian collaborators and the rise of the British "Orientalists," including Sir William Jones and Ram Mohun Roy in the Bengal Renaissance centered in Calcutta, the colonial capital, are then considered. But power corrupts, and as the British gained power in India and then rode the wave of the industrial revolution at home, arrogance and racism replaced the earlier tolerance and provoked the Indian revolt of 1857. Most Indians, however, supported the British, and such collaborators remained in the majority, especially in trade and the professions, until the twentieth century.

The collapse of Mughal power in India after 1707 was not followed by the rise of a new Indian order. The subcontinent's great cultural diversity and legacy of intergroup and interregional rivalry worked against unity, as in the similar context in Europe; there was no single effective successor to the Mughals. In this confused setting, the English East India Company began to extend its position, first to protect its merchants, Indian trade partners, and goods against banditry and civil war and then increasingly to take on the functions of government. By about 1800 the Company's power was uppermost, and it had become the real sovereign over most of India. In the course of the next half century, a combination of military campaigns, more peaceful takeovers, and treaties with local Indian rulers left the Company as the direct administrator of about half of the subcontinent and, indirectly through Indian princes, the dominant power in the rest of this huge area. Although it was

a development that rested to a large degree on Indian collaboration, alien rule is never popular. In 1857 dissidents joined forces in supporting a mutiny by some of the Indian troops in the Company's army. This was put down after much bloodshed, and the earlier fruitful mixing of Indian and Western cultures gave way to the arrogance of imperialism.

The Mughal Collapse

India was left in chaos at the death of Aurangzeb in 1707. His military campaigns in the south and his continued persecution of Hindus and Sikhs had exhausted the treasury and brought most of the country to rebellion. His successors on the throne at Delhi were far weaker men. His three sons fought each other in the usual battles of the Mughal succession. After two and a half years of civil war, the victor was then virtually besieged by a Sikh uprising that swept the Punjab and by guerrilla warfare to the west and south. His death in 1712 brought on another struggle for the throne among his sons. They were outmaneuvered by a cousin, who captured the Sikh leader and slowly tortured him to death; but then he was poisoned by his own courtiers in 1719.

The authority of the once-great Mughals was by now irretrievably lost, and it no longer mattered to most people what feckless creature sat on the Peacock Throne, dreaming away his days in the imperial harem and the pleasures of the *hookah* (a pipe for smoking marijuana). But even Aurangzeb could never have reestablished control over Rajasthan, Maharashtra, Gujarat, or

CHRONOLOGY

Bengal, let alone the Deccan or Afghanistan. All these areas became independent of Mughal power, as did most of the Punjab and the central Ganges Valley, leaving only a remnant of the former empire around Delhi and Agra. Unfortunately, this did not bring peace, and most of the rest of India continued to be torn by factional fighting, civil war, local banditry, and widespread raiding by Maratha cavalry all over the Deccan, along the east coast, and into the north.

Aurangzeb's immediate successors had accepted reality by officially recognizing the Maratha confederacy (so called, although it never really achieved unity) and its extensive conquests in Mysore and on the southeast coast. The Marathas were made nominally tributary al-

lies of the Mughals but controlled their own growing territories and large revenues. They were in effect given both the means and the license to extend their raids or conquests into still more of central, southern, and eastern India, whose revenues could further augment their power. They continued to nibble away at the remaining shreds of Mughal authority in the north and Hindustan, ultimately raiding even as far as Agra and Delhi itself as well as deep into Bengal and as far as Calcutta, though English defenses kept them out of the city.

For a time it looked as if the Marathas might inherit the former Mughal position, but they proved bitterly and incurably divided into contending factions, and no outstanding leader emerged who might have welded them into a coalition. The Maratha cavalry operated more and more as bandits and plunderers, rarely even attempting to set up any administration in the areas they swept for loot and then left in chaos. Their by now traditional role as spoilers and harriers of the Mughal drive into the Deccan had perhaps spoiled them too for any more constructive approaches. In the south, Hyderabad became a large and wealthy kingdom independent of both the Mughals and the Marathas, while in the central Ganges Valley the independent kingdom of Oudh (Awadh) with its capital at Lucknow also emerged from the breakup of the once great Mughal Empire. In many parts of India cultivated areas were abandoned by peasants because they were unable to defend their crops or their homes against raiders and bandits. Trade dwindled in many areas, famine increased, and much of India slipped further into mass poverty. At the same time there was a revival of trade in other areas, especially in the north, with the collapse of Mughal control.

The last shreds of Mughal power were swept away when the Persian army sacked and looted Delhi in 1739, massacred its inhabitants, and took back with them the famous Peacock Throne. Iran was in a period of revived strength under its new ruler, Nadir Shah (1688–1747), a powerful general who had repulsed an Afghani invasion and seized the Persian throne in 1736. He then asked for Mughal help to crush Afghanistan, formerly a part of the Mughal Empire, but the Mughals were by now hard-pressed to defend even Delhi against Maratha raiders. In 1738 Nadir Shah, acting alone, first conquered Afghanistan and then went on to Lahore and Delhi, which he left in smoldering ruins in 1739. The dynasty continued in name, and successive Mughal emperors sat in state in Delhi's Red Fort until 1858, when the last of them, an old man, was banished by the British.

Suprisingly, the once-brilliant aura of the Mughals continued to be acknowledged by most other Indian rulers after 1739 with ceremonial gifts and recognition of Mughal authority, at least ritually. Even the British followed suit until well into the nineteenth century. But

India in Turmoil

The Muslim Indian historian Khafi Khan, writing in the 1720s, gives a vivid picture of the chaos following the death of Aurangzeb in 1707.

> It is clear to the wise and experienced that . . . thoughtfulness in managing the affairs of state and protecting the peasantry . . . have all departed. Revenue collectors have become a scourge for the peasantry. . . . Many townships which used to yield full revenue have, owing to the oppression of officials, been so far ruined and devastated that they have become forests infested by tigers and lions, and the villages are so utterly ruined and desolate that there is no sign of habitation on the routes.

This is matched by English description of late seventeenth-century Bengal, which had broken away from Mughal control.

> Bengal is at present in a very bad condition by means of the great exactions on the people. . . . There are no ways of extortion omitted . . . [which] makes merchants' business very troublesome. . . . The king's governor has little more than the name, and for the most part sits still while others oppress the people and monopolize most commodities, even as low as grass for beasts. . . . Nor do they want ways to oppress people of all sorts who trade, whether natives or strangers.

Sources: I. Habib, *The Agrarian System of Mughal India* (New York: Asia Publishing House, 1963), p. 186; H. Yule, ed., *Diary of William Hedges,* vol. 2 (London: Barlow, 1887), pp. 237, 239.

after 1739, few people in India or elsewhere took the Mughals seriously. This was the harvest of Aurangzeb's cruel reign, which had condemned most of India to chronic civil war, local disorder, and impoverishment. Unfortunately, Rajputs, Marathas, Sikhs, Gujaratis, Bengalis, and other regional groups who had fought against the Mughals saw each other as rivals and indeed as enemies rather than as joint Indian inheritors of power. Their languages, though related like those of Europe, were different, and they differed culturally as well. They were comparable to the separate European cultures and states in size as well. Their divisions now made it possible for the first time for the Portuguese, Dutch, English, and French to make a place for themselves and increase their leverage.

Westerners in India

The story of the Portuguese arrival in India and the establishment of their major base at Goa on the west coast has been briefly told in Chapter 12. For about a century after Vasco da Gama's voyage to Calicut in 1498 the Portuguese dominated Western trade with India, as well as with Southeast Asia, China, and Japan. In India they competed with Indian and Arab traders and, increasingly after the end of the sixteenth century, with Dutch and English merchants and their ships. But no Westerners even thought about contending for political power in India for another 250 years, until the latter half of the eighteenth century. Although the Portuguese arrived well before the establishment of the Mughal Empire in 1526, they were a tiny handful with no effective means of confronting any of the Indian states of the south. They were also largely powerless against the Mughals when the latter took over the north, although Portuguese ships and their guns became a major force at sea and on the coasts, at times and places of their own choosing.

Westerners fought among themselves for control of the sea routes, but their objectives in India were purely commercial, except for the early Portuguese interest in winning converts to Catholicism. In their competition for trade, the Europeans commonly sought agreements with local rulers, offering them guns and naval help for their conflicts with other Indian states as well as a share of trade profits, in exchange for commercial privileges

India

With the collapse of the Mughal order, and in the ensuing chaos, the recently founded English trading bases slowly expanded their control over surrounding areas, collecting revenue and keeping order while at the same time defending themselves. After the battle of Plassey in 1757, their control rapidly spread, in time to include the whole of the subcontinent.

or the use of a port. Different Europeans might involve themselves on opposite sides of such inter-Indian conflicts, seeking to ally themselves with the winning side as well as with those who had the most desirable concessions to give or were most amenable as partners or patrons. Once the Mughals became the dominant Indian power, permission to trade at ports and in areas

they controlled was sought too by each European group, in competition with one another but as the humblest of petitioners before the Peacock Throne, whose power was so much greater than their own.

The Portuguese were first in India and, hence, obtained the largest number and geographical spread of bases, or more properly in most cases (except for Goa) trading arrangements and permission for warehouses and residences. These included several small ports on both east and west coasts, as well as commercial sites inland in Bengal, which was the source of the finest cotton textiles wanted by all the European traders and was thought to be the richest and biggest market. By the early seventeenth century, however, the Portuguese were rapidly losing ground to Dutch and English traders. Their ships were being outclassed in size, speed, maneuverability, firepower, and numbers, and their poor and tiny home base could no longer maintain an overextended commercial empire. The Dutch and later the English were able to move into the Indian market by making their own agreements with local rulers or with the Mughals and to begin to establish their own trade bases.

It must be remembered that India was the size of Europe and with at least equal cultural and political diversity; the north was in a strong Mughal grip, but the south was divided among many large and small kingdoms. Vijayanagara, for example, actively sought Portuguese help in its efforts to fight off its ultimate conquest by a coalition of Muslim sultanates in the northern Deccan. The Portuguese had earlier provided Vijayanagara with imported horses and cannon and had benefited commercially from their association with this dominant state of the south, but the ruler's urgent request for more aid in his greatest hour of need was shortsightedly refused. After the defeat of Vijayanagara in 1565, Portuguese trade and their position in India rapidly declined.

Dutch interest in Asia was from the beginning centered on the spice trade and its Southeast Asian sources in the Indonesian archipelago, but they established several bases in small ports along the east coast of India, retaining many of them until late in the eighteenth century and giving first the Portuguese and then the English vigorous competition. Their involvement in Ceylon was far more extensive. The Portuguese had fortified a base at Colombo some years after arriving there in 1502 and controlled large parts of the lowland west coast of the island, including the profitable trade in cinnamon bark from the Colombo area. Their efforts to extend their control inland were repelled by the Sinhalese kingdom of Kandy in the central highlands, which had become the chief power in a divided Ceylon after the late thirteenth-century collapse of the classical and medieval state based at Anuradhapura and Polonaruwa (see Chapter 4)*. But the Portuguese did succeed in converting many of the west coast Sinhalese to Catholicism, often originally by force, and Portuguese surnames

such as daSilva or Perera remain widespread there, as in those parts of Southeast Asia where the Portuguese established trade bases.

The Dutch drove out the Portuguese between 1640 and 1658 and established their own more extensive position in Ceylon, including bases on the east and west coasts. Although they too failed in several attempts to conquer the mountain-girt Kandyan kingdom, they made Ceylon an even more profitable commercial enterprise and began the plantation system there, first for coconuts and later for coffee, brought in from their territories in Java. Like the Portuguese, they often intermarried with the Sinhalese, producing a Eurasian group still known as "Burghers." By the 1630s Dutch ships dominated the Indian Ocean and its approaches and were even able to blockade Goa. Ceylon was an obvious prize, both for its trade profits and for its strategic role along the route eastward from India, in sight of the southern tip of the subcontinent and only three or four days' sail from Goa. The Dutch were to maintain their control of the trade of Ceylon from their several coastal bases until the Napoleonic Wars, when the British took over the island and in 1815 finally conquered the Kandyan kingdom.

The Early English Presence

To summarize briefly material presented in Chapter 12, the English, like other European trading nations, learned about and envied Portuguese profits earned in India and began explorations for a northeast passage to India by sea around Russia and Siberia in 1553. A later effort to run the Portuguese blockade in 1583 in the ship *Tiger* ended in Portuguese capture of the vessel, but one of the English merchants aboard, Ralph Fitch, escaped and went on to India, where he visited Akbar's capitals at Agra and Fatehpur Sikri as well as Goa, returning to London in 1591 with firsthand accounts of India's wealth. Portugal was united with Spain in 1580, but this tended to weaken rather than strengthen the Portuguese effort in Asia, and, with the defeat of the Spanish Armada in 1588, the way eastward was more open to England.

The first two ventures of the English East India Company, founded in 1600, were aimed at the spice trade in Southeast Asia, but the third went to India and reached Surat, the major port of Gujarat on the west coast, in 1608. Gujarat had been absorbed into the Mughal Empire in 1573, and Captain William Hawkins, who commanded the fleet of three English ships, carried presents and a letter from King James I to the Mughal emperor, Jahangir, requesting a trade treaty. Hawkins claimed that the Portuguese, especially the Jesuits who

---

*The Sinhalese (Singhalese) are the dominant inhabitants of Ceylon (Sri Lanka), having invaded and settled the island, probably from northern India, in the sixth century B.C.E.

were already ensconced at the Mughal court, conspired against him, but in any case he was kept waiting for over two years and was finally obliged to return home empty-handed. A second English envoy reached Agra in 1612 but was sent away even more summarily after the Jesuits urged the emperor not to deal with him.

However, later in 1612 a single English ship defeated and dispersed four Portuguese galleons and a number of frigates off Surat, in full view of the people on shore, a feat that was repeated in 1615. Indians now saw that the English were more valuable clients than the Portuguese and better able to defend Indian shipping and coasts from pirates and from rival Europeans (sometimes one and the same, especially with the Portuguese, who had been characteristically aggressive and ruthless whenever they had the opportunity). The Indian market, and the Mughals, had little or no interest in trade with England and were not impressed by the samples of goods they were offered from what was, after all, a much less advanced economy, which accordingly sought to buy Indian goods but had little that was attractive to exchange for them. The same problem hampered English, European, and American trade with China and the rest of Asia until well into the nineteenth century.

However, the Mughals had no navy and had to depend on foreigners for protection against piracy; of these, it now seemed clear, the English were the least troublesome and the most effective. In 1616, King James sent another ambassador, Sir Thomas Roe, who finally won permission from Jahangir for the East India Company to build a "factory" (warehouse; "factor" is an old word for "merchant") in Surat. Seven years later the Dutch tortured and then murdered ten English merchants who had been sharing in the spice trade of eastern Indonesia, signaling the end of Dutch willingness to allow any European competition in what thus became their private preserve. The English were obliged to abandon their effort to penetrate Dutch territory and to concentrate their attention on India.

Territorial Bases

From Surat, English ships completed the elimination of Portuguese power at sea, and English merchants became the principal traders in the port. But they still sought bases on the east coast and in Bengal, where they could buy the finest-quality cottons more directly as well as the indigo and saltpeter (for gunpowder) produced in the lower Ganges Valley, which was considered to be the finest quality in the world. (Later English military successes in Europe against Louis XIV of France and Napoleon were attributed in part to their superior gunpowder, made with Bengal saltpeter.) After their early attempts to penetrate Bengal had been driven off by the Dutch from their already established east coast

Bombay about 1790—Western sea power and one of its early beachheads. Note the fortification, the ship in the foreground firing a salute, and the western-style architecture of the buildings, including the church in the center. (Reproduced from R. Murphey, *The Outsiders: The Western Experience.* The University of Michigan Press, 1977, p. 177. Reprinted with permission.)

bases, the English in 1639 negotiated with a small local ruler to the south to buy land near the village of Mandaraz around a small lagoon at the mouth of the tiny Coum River. This later became Madras, where they soon built what they called Fort St. George, named for England's patron saint.

From Madras as their chief base in eastern India, which also gave access to south Indian cottons and other goods, they made repeated efforts to trade directly in Bengal and finally established a "factory" (a base for "factors," or merchants) upriver near the provincial capital. They found, however, that such proximity to the Mughal and Bengali authorities exposed them to arbitrary taxation and even sometimes expropriation of their goods; on at least one occasion the Company's agent was publicly whipped and expelled. Accordingly, they sought a more secure position. They had traded periodically at a small market called Sutanuti ("a hank of cotton") a day's sail up the Hooghly River, one of the lesser mouths of the Ganges, that was occupied only on market days. In 1690 they decided to make a settlement there where they thought their ships could protect or rescue them if needed and where they were more on the fringes of Indian authority. Shortly thereafter, they received permission to build a fort, and the new settlement was called Fort William (after William III, who had come to the English throne in the Glorious Revolution of 1688), soon to be known instead as Calcutta. The name probably came from the nearby shrine of the goddess Kali at Kalighat (*ghat* is a set of steps descending to a river) or from the adjoining village of Kalikata.

At Surat the English were only one among many merchant groups and were dependent on the fickle pleasure of Mughal and Gujarati powers. But Bombay, originally a chain of small islands enclosed in a large bay, was ceded to the English crown by Portugal in 1661 as part of the marriage contract of the Portuguese princess Catherine of Braganza and Charles II. The Portuguese had built no settlement there and used it only occasionally, since it was highly exposed to piracy, was cut off from landward access to markets by the rampaging Marathas, and had a harbor that was really too big for the small ships of the time. But the quite different drawbacks of Surat and the attractions of a more nearly independent and protected base, as at Madras and (later) Calcutta, led the East India Company to move its western India headquarters to Bombay in 1687. Several of their Indian trade partners at Surat, including Parsee firms, moved with them.

With the founding of Calcutta in 1690, they now had three small territorial footholds, well placed to tap the trade of India in each of its major segments, west, south, and east. But the English, like all other foreigners in India, remained petitioners, still dependent on the favors of the Mughal state or of local rulers and still liable to be driven out, expropriated, or denied trading privileges. No one, certainly not the English, realized at the time what was happening to Indian power after the death of Aurangzeb as the country as a whole slid ever more deeply into chaos.

The Company sent an embassy to the by then virtually powerless Mughal emperor in 1714. The embassy's leader prostrated himself before the throne as "the smallest particle of sand" giving "the reverence due from a slave." He asked first for additional trade privileges and then, more significantly, for the right to collect revenues in the immediate areas around Madras and Calcutta, where the Company was by now the de facto government. The embassy was largely ignored and would probably never even have been acknowledged if the emperor had not fallen ill and asked for treatment from the embassy's English doctor, Walter Hamilton. His success, probably just as much a stroke of luck as the emperor's illness, led to the embassy's reception, and in 1717 all their requests were granted. The Mughals, like many premodern states, were used to such arrangements with a variety of groups or individuals to whom they in effect farmed out the collection of taxes and the administration of local areas that the taxes supported. In their view the English were little different from scores of others who had long been granted such rights, equivalent to the Mughal jagir or zamindari, and Delhi attached little importance to the 1717 concession. Indeed, it seems important now only because we know what followed and can recognize it as the first step toward English territorial sovereignty in India.

The Mughal and Post-Mughal Contexts

Part of the context of the times was that since the death of Aurangzeb neither the Mughals nor the local or provincial administrations had been able to keep order. The East India Company was able to carry out this basic function of government in its small but fortified bases and, with the help of small private armies that they developed, in the areas immediately around their bases. The embassy to Delhi in 1714 had to fight off large bands of armed robbers even on the imperial road from Agra. Most of the rest of India was in even worse disorder. The Company could survive and prosper only if it could create security for trade goods in storage and in transit and offer similar security to its Indian trade partners. Areas of production could generate trade commodities only if they could be kept orderly. Hence, the main consequence of the fading of Mughal power was not that the English were seen or saw themselves as rising political powers in India but that they were driven increasingly to provide their own defense, policing, revenue collection to pay the costs, and local government. They did this well enough to survive, as well as to attract Indian merchants to deal with them and even become residents of the English bases, where their profits and property could also be secure.

Within a few years Madras, Calcutta, and Bombay were overwhelmingly Indian in population, home to many laborers and servants as well as merchants, artisans, bankers, and agents, all having decided that the still-tiny, English-dominated world of the fortified ports was more attractive than any Indian alternative. Apart from the Mughals, who after 1707 counted for almost nothing, local states and rulers were also often willing, as at Madras, to have the Company manage trade, collect taxes, and keep order—things they were usually unable to do themselves but that they realized were desirable for their own interests. Civil order and healthy conditions for trade, which the English offered, were more than enough to ensure the cooperation of most Indians.

The Company prospered, and Indian cottons became so popular in England that in 1701 Parliament, feeling the need to protect English textiles, prohibited their import. When that ban was ignored, a parliamentary ruling in 1720 prohibited their use or wear, but reexport to the continent continued, and even domestic consumption could not be prevented. Indian cottons were clearly superior, the finest of them never surpassed even now. A widely repeated story told how the emperor Shah Jahan had reproved his daughter for appearing naked in court, to which she is said to have replied that she was wearing seven thicknesses of Dacca muslin. (Dacca in east Bengal, now Bangladesh, was the source of the filmiest cottons; "muslin" is, of course, derived from "Muslim.")

But it was not only the Company that prospered. At every period, from the first "factory" at Surat to Indian independence in 1947, Indians found new employment, new scope, and new wealth in the expanding economy of colonial ports and inland trading posts, as well as in the colonial bureaucracy. They greatly outnumbered the English and Scots who prospered from the same system. However, most of the biggest gainers were British; most Indians remained poor, while those who prospered did so as junior partners and, especially after about 1830, despite British economic and social discrimination against them.

For the rural areas the spread of Company rule meant protection against banditry or Maratha raids and a growing new market open to them, within India and abroad, for commercial crops. Commercialization of agriculture was ruinous to some but profitable to many, a process greatly accelerated with the coming of the railways after 1850. The East India Company could never have succeeded without extensive and willing Indian collaboration. The connections into domestic trade networks and producing areas that Indian merchants, agents, and bankers could provide were in any case essential. All were dependent on the Company's ability to keep order so that trade could flow and profits accumulate securely for every party.

Anglo-French Rivalry and the Conquest of Bengal

The French had also been active contenders for the trade of India since the rather belated founding of the French East India Company in 1664. It had established a "factory" at Surat, an east coast base at Pondicherry south of Madras, and another "factory" just upriver from Calcutta. The French in India had the advantage of superb leadership under Joseph Dupleix (1697–1764) and of equally outstanding military and naval commanders. Their forces captured Madras in 1746 and went on to defeat the local Indian ruler of the southeast, becoming the dominant power in the whole of southern India. Unfortunately for them, they got little support from home, and the Treaty of Aix-la-Chapelle in 1748 restored Madras to the English. Two years later Robert Clive defeated both the French and their southern Indian allies with only a small force of Indian and British troops. When the Seven Years War (1756–1763) erupted in Europe, fighting spread to the French and British holdings overseas, in India as in North America, and the home governments took a more direct hand in providing troops and ships. Now deprived of Dupleix's leadership—he had been called home for spending too much of the French company's resources in "unprofitable adventures"—the French lost out in this struggle, which was fought mainly by Indian troops in the service of both sides as well as by independent but client Indian groups.

A major lesson of all this fighting was that very small numbers of European troops, operating with somewhat larger numbers of Indian soldiers trained in Western methods, could repeatedly defeat enormously larger Indian armies. Those on the European sides were disciplined to fire regular volleys on command and to plan and coordinate their actions. Their guns and cannons were better, but it was organization and leadership that made them more effective, as well as the morale that flowed from regular pay, uniforms, and esprit de corps, all of which their Indian opponents lacked.

Western military power was, however, tested most severely in a Bengali challenge to the growing English position in and around Calcutta. As their local authority increased, the English became less deferential to the still technically sovereign rulers of Bengal, now independent of the Mughals. No longer humble petitioners who had regularly kissed the feet of the *nawab* (ruler) of Bengal, their independent behavior and their addition to the fortifications of Fort William offended the new nawab, Siraj-ud-Dowlah, who came to the throne in 1756. In a last flash of imperial fire, his army and war elephants overwhelmed Calcutta and its relative handful of defenders in June 1756. Some escaped in boats and fled to Madras, but about 60 were left behind, to be thrown into the fort's tiny, airless dungeon and spend a hot night in this steamy climate. The next morning all but about 20 were dead of suffocation. The incident of the "Black Hole of Calcutta" became infamous. It seemed the end of the English position in Bengal, but appearances were deceiving. Within four months an expedition sailed from Madras under the same Robert Clive who had earlier ousted the French from the south. In January 1757 he retook Calcutta and then drove the French from their remaining bases in Bengal. With support from Indian groups, he then defeated the huge army of the nawab at the Battle of Plassey, some 75 miles northwest of Calcutta.

Although no one seemed fully to realize it at the time, the English were now masters of Bengal, in the absence of any effective rivals or even viable alternatives. Their military victory was, however, due in large part to Indian collaboration, including perhaps most importantly bankers who had lent money to both sides and who calculated, like most Indians, that an English victory was more desirable on practical grounds. The English paid their debts, as the nawab did not (nor did he pay his troops regularly), and as a merchant group the English East India Company furthered trade rather than preying on it. The leading Indian banker in fact paid very large sums to troops on the nawab's side to persuade them not to fight; the reserves that were to have swept the field at Plassey when the battle hung in the balance never came. The traditional Indian armies of the day were usually composed of different groups who were often rivals and were rarely effectively generalled or used as a concerted force according to tactical planning. Contingents often deserted or failed to appear when they decided to throw in their lot with another side or to sit out the battle.

Robert Clive and the Beginnings of British India

Robert Clive (1725–1774) had shipped out to Madras as an East India Company clerk, but he soon developed a reputation as an adventurer. He found his clerk's job so boring that he tried unsuccessfully to kill himself with a pistol that misfired. Adventure soon came when the French captured Fort St. George in 1746 and he was taken prisoner. He escaped and took a commission in the Company's small army. His first military expedition, against a powerful southern kingdom allied with the French, was won by brilliant strategy even though his opponents outnumbered him 20 to 1. Clive was acclaimed as a hero; he then repeated his successes by driving out the French and their Indian allies in the major Deccan kingdom of Hyderabad. Still only 27 years old, he was praised as a deliverer and granted two years' home leave. Sent out again with the rank of colonel in 1756, he reached Madras just as Calcutta was being overwhelmed by the armies of the nawab of Bengal.

Already known to Indians as "He Who Is Daring in War," Clive sailed north with a small force. He recaptured Calcutta, defeated the vastly superior army that tried to stop him just north of the city, and, four months later, met the main Bengali contingent at Plassey. By this time he had just over 1,000 British troops and about 2,000 Indians under his command. The Bengali army totaled 18,000 cavalry and 50,000 foot soldiers, as well as over 50 field guns managed by French artillerymen. Again Clive's tactical genius won the day, confusing, outmaneuvering, and finally routing the enemy. He then marched on to the Bengali capital, where he installed his own Indian client and ally as ruler. Clive and his English and Indian colleagues helped themselves to the provincial treasury, and the Company too was richly repaid in reparations and new revenues now under its control. After consolidating his conquests with further victories against Indian and French efforts to recoup their losses, he devoted his enormous energy to strengthening the Company's army, refortifying Calcutta, and administering the new domains. Four years of incessant activity broke his health, and he spent five years in England but was sent back to India in 1765 to try to check the plundering excesses of his successors and reorganize what now amounted to East India Company government in Bengal.

Two years later he was back in England to face charges in Parliament that he had defrauded the Company and enriched himself by extortion, accusations brought by people whom he had tried to restrain from exactly those things and who were jealous of his unbroken string of successes. Although in the end he was cleared, he brooded over his grievances, and, still suffering from poor health, he shot himself in 1774 at age 49. The same mercurial temperament that made him try suicide as a young man and then carried him to the heights of success proved to be his undoing. More than any one person, he began the process that was to end in British rule in India. He was far more than a brilliant field commander and was concerned about larger

 ## British Life in India

The English who succeeded in trade or in the higher administration of the East India Company lived luxuriously and affected an extravagant style. Here are some sample accounts, the first describing the governor's entourage in Madras about 1710.

> The Governor seldom goes abroad with less than three or four score peons armed; besides the English guards to attend him he has two union flags carried before him. . . . He is a man of great parts, respected as a Prince by the Rajahs of the country, and is in every way as great.

The secretary to a high Company official in Calcutta in the mid–1770s complained:

> The cursed examples of parade and extravagance they [the Indian servants] are holding up forever to us. "Master must have this. Master must do that." A councillor never appears in the street with a train of less than twenty fellows, nor walks from one room to another in his house unless preceded by four silver staves. . . . What improvement India may make in my affairs I know not, but it has already ruined my temper.

Things were much the same at Bombay, according to a visiting English lady in 1812, who might have been describing pretentious expatriate society anywhere and at any time, including the present.

> With regard to the Europeans in Bombay, the manners of the inhabitants of a foreign colony are in general so well represented by those of a country town at home that it is hopeless to attempt making a description of them very interesting. The ladies are underbred and over-dressed, ignorant, and vulgar. The civil servants are young men taken up with their own imaginary importance.

Caste Hindus, and most Muslims, could not normally receive Westerners in their homes, according to traditional rules. Even the well-intentioned British often felt isolated. There were some more imaginative ones among them who took the initiative in seeking out Indian friends or acquaintances, but Lord William Bentinck, later to be governor-general, spoke in 1807 for most of the colonial rulers, especially those of higher status.

> We do not, we cannot, associate with the natives. We cannot see them in their houses and families. We are necessarily very much confined to our houses by the heat; all our wants and business which could create greater intercourse with the natives is done for us, and we are in fact strangers in the land.

Of course, before full colonial control was established British-Indian relations were much closer, and there was a good deal of mutual admiration, as in the following example.

> It certainly is curious, and highly entertaining to an inquisitive mind, to associate with people whose manners are more than three thousand years old, and to observe in them that attention and polished behavior which usually marks the most highly civilized state of society.

Sources: C. Lockyer, *An Account of the Trade of India* (London: Crouch, 1711), p. 24; B. Francis and E. Kean, eds., *Letters of Philip Francis,* vol. 1 (London: Murray, 1901), p. 219; J. T. Wheeler, *Early Records of British India* (Calcutta: Newman, 1878), p. 53; J. Forbes, *Oriental Memoirs,* vol. 1 (London: White, Cochrane, 1813), p. 42; J. Rosseli, *Lord William Bentinck* (Berkeley: University of California Press, 1974), p. 146; P. Pal and V. Dehejia, *From Merchants to Emperors: British Artists and India, 1857–1930* (Ithaca: Cornell University Press, 1986), p. 11.

Robert Clive accepting tribute from Mir Jaffar, the puppet whom he had placed on the throne of Bengal after the battle of Plassey, as depicted in an oil painting by Francis Hayman, c. 1760. (By courtesy of the National Portrait Gallery, London)

patterns of British policy in India. His immediate successors were more interested in personal enrichment.

The Establishment of British Rule

With Bengal now in their hands, many of the English turned to simple plunder as well as trade, extorting silver and jewels from the rich and demanding what amounted to "protection money." After a few years this brought severe criticism from home, parliamentary inquiries, and finally, in 1784, the India Act, which created a new Board of Control for India in London. By this time the worst of the plunder was over, although beyond Bengal, the rest of India remained in turmoil. Afghan armies repeatedly ravaged the northwest and looted Delhi again in 1757, slaughtering most of the inhabitants. A huge Maratha army gathered to repel yet another Afghan invasion in 1760 was crushed in a great battle near Delhi early in 1761, removing the only Indian power able to contest the English. The Afghans, having done their work, withdrew. Three years later, the surviving government of Bengal, still nominally in place, then made common cause with the remnants of Mughal power and raised a large army to drive out the English, now belatedly recognized as the most dangerous contenders. The much smaller force of Company troops beat them soundly in a battle at Buxar at the western edge of Bengal in 1764, surmounting the last serious challenge to their power in the north.

From Trading Company to Government

From then on the policy of both the East India Company and its London supervisors was to acquire no more territory, but to achieve their ends through alliances with Indian princes, offering them military protection in exchange for trading rights. In Bengal as in the smaller areas around Madras and Bombay, they continued to collect taxes and run the administration as nominal agents of the local or regional Indian rulers, not as a sovereign power. Administration was expensive and distracted from the Company's main business, trade. Collection of rural taxes was farmed out to Bengali agents or zamindars, a bad system but one that gave the zamindars a stake in British rule, especially as they also became landlords, with British approval, acquiring land from defaulting taxpayers. Calcutta was made the capital of all of British India, which by 1785 had settled down to a generally efficient and honest administration bent on promoting trade and revenues, and on attracting Indian collaboration, although all higher administrative and military posts were reserved for the British.

Official policy against taking over more areas of India yielded in the 1790s to the strategic pressures of the Napoleonic Wars. The French still had small footholds in southern India and a history, like the English, of alliances with various Indian rulers. Successive heads of state in Mysore had had some dealings with the French and had also periodically threatened Madras. The tensions of the war against Napoleon in Europe made Britain anxious to end the French threat in India. In 1799, Mysore was overwhelmed by Company troops. Half of it, including the commercially important coastal strip, was annexed outright, thus linking the Madras area to the west coast. Most of the rest of it was given to a loyal Indian ally, the neighboring state of Hyderabad, which was to remain nominally independent until 1947.

The peninsular south was now firmly under Company control, but the Marathas, despite their earlier defeat by the Afghans in 1761, remained a formidable power, and their home base in Maharashtra blocked Bombay's access to inland markets. Taking advantage of internal Maratha division, the Company signed a treaty with one side in 1802 promising military support in exchange for territorial rights. When the Maratha puppet the British had installed tried later to revive his power, the Company defeated his forces and took over all the Maratha domains in 1818, soon joining them to Bombay Presidency, the major British territory in western India.

Meanwhile in Bengal, Warren Hastings (1732–1818) had been appointed governor of Fort William in 1772 and was later confirmed as governor-general of British-run Bengal, Madras, and Bombay. Hastings had long experience working for the Company and, like so many of the English who went out to India, had become fascinated by the rich Indian tradition; he was a scholar of Persian and Urdu and had many Indian friends. This gave him valuable insight into Indian customs and attitudes but also encouraged him to play the role of absolute ruler, in the Indian tradition. He largely checked the extortion and corruption by Company officials that had been widespread earlier and made sure that the official revenue collections got to his government rather than into private pockets. Hastings reduced the nawab of Bengal even more to a British client and stopped the annual tribute that was still being paid to the Mughal emperor. But he also began the British strategy of intervention in the faction fighting within the Maratha confederacy, partly to forestall the French, but also partly to strengthen the overall British position in India and meet the still-serious threat of Maratha power. Hastings began the first moves against the ruler of Mysore and sent a Company army south to defend Madras. All this cost money, and Hastings was driven to extort funds from several of his Indian "tributary states" to support the "pacification of India," which, he argued, was in everyone's interest. Jealous rivals at home engineered impeachment proceedings against him, and when the

new India Act of 1784 was passed setting up the Board of Control in London, he felt further threatened. He resigned in 1785 and left India for good.

He was succeeded as governor-general by Lord Cornwallis, the same man who had surrendered the British forces to the Americans and French at Yorktown. Cornwallis had a reputation for honesty and integrity and cracked down still more on extortion and corruption, but in 1793 he confirmed the landowning rights of the Indians, mainly Bengalis, who had been made zamindars, in what was called "The Permanent Settlement," thus strengthening an exploitative system that became still more so in subsequent years. Cornwallis, anxious not to be responsible for losing another colony, further pursued the campaign against Mysore and issued a new administrative code for all the British territories, establishing rules for all services, courts, and revenue systems and empowering British district magistrates to administer legal justice. In 1798, Richard Wellesley, elder brother of the future duke of Wellington who was to become the hero of Waterloo and who had also campaigned in southern India, succeeded to the governor-generalship as the Napoleonic Wars were in full spate. He completed the conquest of Mysore in 1799 and subsequently added still more territory in the south to British control, while in 1801 he reached up the Ganges Valley to force British "protection" on the Indian state of Oudh. It is generally thought that Britain's Indian empire, and attendant imperialist attitudes and actions, first took coherent shape under Wellesley, who remained until 1805.

Because India's major trade route ran through the central Ganges Valley west of Bengal, it was too important commercially to be left to periodic disorder. The ruler of the state of Oudh (Awadh) with its capital at Lucknow was forced to accept British protection, although he was promised that his own formal sovereignty would remain, as a Company ally. The same arrangement was made with the still-reigning Mughal emperor for his domains in the Delhi-Agra area. Southern Gujarat, including the commercially important port of Surat, was also brought under Company control. Only Rajasthan, the Indus valley and Sindh, Kashmir, and Punjab remained outside the British sphere, although much of what the British controlled was nominally ruled by Indian princes as allies.

Fear of the still-live French threat during the Napoleonic Wars and the memory of French naval successes in the Bay of Bengal 50 years earlier prompted the British to move on Dutch-held Ceylon after Napoleon occupied Holland. Their first concern was to take over the fine natural harbor of Trincomalee on the east coast of Ceylon, where they could base their naval vessels. There were no harbors safe to enter or leave during the northeast monsoon of winter anywhere on the Indian east coast, nor were any of them large enough for the fleet, which had to be withdrawn to winter haven in distant Bombay. Trincomalee filled this urgent need, and the British occupied it in 1795, subsequently taking over all of the other Dutch holdings in Ceylon.

With the fading of the French threat, British attention shifted to the far more productive southwestern lowlands of Ceylon, and the colonial capital was fixed at Colombo. From there roads were built crisscrossing the island and, after the final conquest of the Kandyan kingdom in 1815, into the central highlands, followed by railways after 1858. Coffee plantations spread rapidly with this improved access to export markets, as did coconut production, and by midcentury Ceylon had largely developed the plantation economy that it retained until

after independence. Tea replaced coffee after a disastrous coffee blight in the 1870s, and rubber was added at the end of the century, second only to tea. Tamil laborers were brought in from overpopulated south India to build roads and railways and to provide labor for coffee, tea, and rubber plantations. They had relatively little in common with the Tamils who had been living as farmers in the northern fifth of the island for some 2,000 years, but the Tamil minority as a whole was to become an explosive issue after independence. Ceylon was designated a Crown Colony, not part of British India, and was administered separately despite its long and close Indian connections. Coffee and tea from the highlands, coconut products, and later rubber all flowed by road and rail routes focused on Colombo, which grew as the major port and service center for Ceylon's expanding commercial sector.

Sound Advice

The first half of the nineteenth century saw several large-minded and intelligent British officials serving in India. Here is Sir Thomas Munro, governor of Madras.

> It ought to be our aim to give the younger servants [i.e., British recruits to the company's service] the best opinion of the natives, in order that they may be better qualified to govern them hereafter. We can never be qualified to govern men against whom we are prejudiced. If we entertain a prejudice at all, it ought to be rather in their favor than against them. We ought to know their character, but especially the favorable side of it. . . . We shall never have much accurate knowledge of the resources of the country, or of the causes by which they are raised or depressed until we learn to treat the higher classes of natives as gentlemen.

Here is Mountstuart Elphinstone from Maharashtra.

> We must not dream of perpetual possession, but must apply ourselves to bring the natives into a state that will admit of their governing themselves in a manner that may be beneficial to our interest as well as their own and that of the rest of the world. . . . It is not enough to give new laws, or even good courts; you must take people along with you, and give them a share in your feelings, which can be done by sharing theirs.

Finally, here is Charles Metcalfe, British resident at Delhi.

> The real dangers of a free press in India are, I think, in its enabling the natives to throw off our yoke. . . . The advantages are in the spread of knowledge, which it seems wrong to obstruct for any temporary or selfish purpose.

Source: P. Mudford, *Birds of a Different Plumage* (London: Collins, 1974), pp. 120–125.)

The Reasons for British Hegemony

This relatively sudden rush of land grab and the rise of the East India Company could not have happened without a great deal of Indian (and Sinhalese) support. Factional divisions fatally weakened what efforts there were at Indian resistance. Most people accepted Company control either because they benefited from it as merchants, bankers, collaborators, agents, or employees or because they saw it as preferable to control by the Mughals, the Marathas, or any of the local rulers, whose records were not attractive. Most contemporary Indian states were oppressive, taxing merchants and peasants unmercifully and often arbitrarily while at the same time failing to keep order, suppress banditry, maintain roads and basic services, or administer justice acceptably. Revenues went disproportionately to support court extravagances and armies, which spent their energy more in interregional conflict than in genuine defense. This was partly the legacy of the Delhi sultanate, and particularly of the Mughals. It became clear to most Indians that in fact only the British were both willing and able to protect them from banditry, to ensure the security of life and property, and to foster conditions under which trade and agriculture could again prosper. That was enough to win their support.

Although the British were foreigners and subscribed to a foreign religion, this was nothing new to most Indians and did not provoke widespread resistance on that account. For their part, after their early rapacity in Bengal, the Company tried in general to avoid displacing or offending Indians as much as possible or disrupting Indian customs (except for slavery and widow burning, which they tried to suppress); with Indian help, they tried to run an honest, efficient, and humane administration. That was also official policy in London, as illustrated in this letter from the directors to the Company offices in Bombay in 1784:

> By the exercise of a mild and good government people from other parts may be induced to come and reside under our protection. Let there be entire justice exercised to all persons without distinction, and open trade allowed to all.[1]

Such a plan reflected the original exclusive aim of trade profits, as succinctly stated in a letter almost a century earlier: "Merchants desire no enemies, and would create none."[2]

The Orientalists and the Bengal Renaissance

As British administration was extended, more and more Company employees were not merchants or clerks but officials and magistrates. English and Indian

William Jones, the pioneer Orientalist. (Peter Mudford, *Birds of a Different Plumage*)

merchants had obvious common interests, and many even appreciated each others' culture. Some Company traders and officials, such as Sir William Jones (1746–1794), found themselves fascinated by the rich variety of the Indian tradition. Jones, a judge in late eighteenth-century Bengal, had received the usual classical education in England and then learned Persian (still used for Mughal law), Sanskrit (the classical language of India and of Hindu texts, which were often cited in cases), and the modern languages of northern India spoken by those who appeared in court: Bengali, Hindi, and so on. He began to realize the close connections among them and between them and Greek, Latin, and the languages of modern Europe (like any educated person, he knew not only Greek and Latin but French, German, and Italian). In 1786 he published a paper that convincingly made the case for an Indo-European language family and earned himself the nickname "Oriental Jones."

Other Englishmen studied and translated the Indian classics, the great religious and artistic traditions, and the historical record, including archaeological work of great importance such as the later "rediscovery" of Harappa and Mohenjo Daro, the Mauryan Empire, Ashoka, and many of the great artistic and architectural monuments of the past. British scholars of Indian cul-

The British Indicted

In 1772, one of the early Orientalists, Alexander Dow, criticized the English.

> Posterity will perhaps find fault with the British for not investigating the learning and religious opinions which prevail in those countries in Asia into which either they or their commerce or their arms have penetrated. The Brahmins of the East possessed in ancient times some reputation for knowledge, but we have never had the curiosity to examine whether there was any truth in the reports of antiquity upon that head. . . . Literary inquiries are by no means a capital object to many of our adventures in Asia.

But William Jones was soon to join Dow and others. This is what he wrote in 1783.

> It gave me inexpressible pleasure to find myself . . . almost encircled by the vast regions of Asia, which has ever been esteemed the nurse of science, the inventress of delightful and useful arts, the scene of glorious actions, fertile in the production of human genius . . . abounding in natural wonders, and infinitely diversified in the forms of religion and government, in the laws, manners, customs, and languages as well as in the features and complexions of men. . . . [Later he wrote] It was my desire to discharge my public duties with unremitted attention, and to recreate myself at leisure with the literature of this interesting country. . . . I am no Hindu, but I hold the doctrine of the Hindus concerning a future state to be incomparably more rational, more pious, and more likely to deter men from vice than the horrid opinions inculcated by Christians on punishments without end.

Sources: A. Dow, *History of Hindoostan* (1772), p. 107; P. Mudford, *Birds of a Different Plumage* (London: Collins, 1974) pp. 88–90.

ture and history founded the Asiatic Society of Bengal in Calcutta in 1784; the society's *Journal* published Jones's paper and many others on a wide variety of Indian topics. Most of the members and contributors were employees or officials of the East India Company and pursued their research on the side, but some found their Indian studies so engrossing that they retired to devote all their time to what was now known as Indology. Many took Indian wives, though few brought them home in retirement.

These British Orientalists, as they were called, were matched by Indian scholars who learned perfect English, studied Latin and Greek, wrote in the English literary and academic tradition, and produced what is known as both the Hindu Renaissance and the Bengal Renaissance, begun primarily by the work of the Bengali Ram Mohun Roy (1772–1833). Having first mastered the English world, Roy and others who followed him, many of them also employees of the Company and others private scholars, turned their attention to the In-

dian and Hindu tradition, where they sought successfully for their own cultural identity and helped to restore the pride of educated Indians in their rich religious, philosophical, and literary heritage.

Roy founded a society in Calcutta to pursue these efforts, which made a deep impact on successive generations of Bengalis and Indians everywhere. Members of the society and like-minded Indians studied India's classical texts; this led to a revival of interest in the power and virtue of the Indian cultural tradition. H. L. Derozio (1809–1831), of mixed Indian and British parentage, became in his short life a brilliant teacher and poet, inspiring young Bengalis to pursue learning in both the Indian and the Western traditions, like the Orientalists among the British. Another prominent member of the society was Dwarkanath Tagore (1794–1846), an outstanding Western-style entrepreneur, banker, merchant, and industrialist who became, like Roy and many others, at least as much English as Indian and proud to be a part of both traditions.

These Western and Eastern synthesizers of the two cultures worked together, especially in Calcutta, to promote the similar education of young upper-class Indians, founding schools and libraries and publishing jointly a number of journals and books. It was a fruitful time of vigorous hybridization, enthusiastically pursued by both sides. Their efforts foreshadowed the full-scale emergence later in the nineteenth century of the Westernized Indian middle class of intellectuals and businesspeople, including Tagore's grandson Rabindranath Tagore (1861–1941), India's greatest modern literary figure, who devoted most of his life to bridging East and West. The Hindu Renaissance was also concerned to reform what in the perspective of the nineteenth century had come to seem less desirable aspects of Hinduism, such as *sati* (suttee, or widow-burning), and child marriage, and in time to make Hinduism an appropriate vehicle for modern Indian nationalism, especially in the work of Mohandas K. Gandhi (1869–1948).

A CLOSER LOOK

Calcutta, Colonial Capital

By 1810 Calcutta's population had reached 1 million, and it was already being labeled "the second city of the British Empire," a title it retained until Indian independence in 1947. It was also known as "the city of palaces," adorned not only with government buildings and the governor's residence but also with the mansions of rich English and Indian merchants, especially in an imposing facade along the river. Rudyard Kipling was later to call Calcutta "the City of Dreadful Night" for its hot, humid climate and its vast slums and shanty settlements set back from the river. From the beginning, it was overwhelmingly Indian in population, but British residents found its tropical environment a trial as well as a serious health problem, the more so because fashion required them to wear the woolen outfits expected of a gentleman at home, to overeat, and to consume large quantities of wine and whiskey. Anyone who aspired to a position in society had to keep a carriage, dress in fashion, and entertain lavishly.

Westerners also had no immunity to regional diseases, and the death rate among them was shockingly high until well into the twentieth century. It became the custom among Westerners to meet each year in November, when the cool season began, to congratulate each other on having survived another year. Probably less than half of the English and Scots who came out to Calcutta during its first century or so survived to return home. Malaria, dysentery, typhoid, and cholera were the major killers. It was in Calcutta in 1899 that Sir Ronald Ross first proved the theory that malaria was carried by mosquitoes and began preventive measures. Home leave was not common until after the opening of the Suez Canal in 1869, but the seat of government, which remained in Calcutta for all of India until 1912, moved up to the cool foothills of the Himalayas for the hottest summer months.

Calcutta was picked in 1690 for the site of the Company's trading base in Bengal because the Hooghly River, one of the many mouths of the Ganges, widened a little there and formed a deep pool where the ships of the time could anchor. There was a tiny intermittent trading village where Indian merchants periodically brought their goods, but Calcutta probably took its name from the nearby shrine to the goddess Kali at Kalighat, as mentioned earlier, or from the village of Kalikata close by. It prospered from the start and became the predominant trading center first for Bengal and then for all of eastern India, thanks to its position in the Ganges delta and its access to the easiest routes inland, by water and through the Ganges Valley as well as by coastal shipping. After 1850 railways were built with Calcutta as the major hub, and textile and metalworking factories rose beside the Hooghly, joined by the end of the century by a wide range of industrial enterprises. The biggest single manufacturing industry

Government House, Calcutta, in 1826: all very Western in style, although the sedan chair was a traditional Asian institution, too. (By permission of the British Library)

was the weaving of jute, a coarse fiber grown along the muddy banks of delta streams and made into gunny-sacking and twine. Calcutta had a near world monopoly. The city became the largest industrial center in India, as well as its biggest city. Kipling wrote a short poem about it in 1905 that caught it well:[3]

> Me the sea captain loved, the river built,
> Wealth sought and kings adventured life to hold.
> Hail England! I am Asia, power on silt;
> Death in my hands, but gold!*

Calcutta after 1760 was the major base for the English plunder of Bengal, and many fortunes made in those chaotic years were reflected in the splendid houses along the river. This was the extravagant culture of the people called "nabobs" (a corruption of the Indian title *nawab,* "ruler"), who had "shaken the pagoda tree" in India and used their new wealth in conspicuous display. Most of the British aimed to make a quick fortune and then retire to England or Scotland, where they could acquire gentry respectability by buying land and building ostentatious houses, often in semi-Indian style. But as the city grew, it attracted immigrants of all sorts and began to industrialize; it was no longer mainly a city of palaces but one of dingy warehouses, factories, and slums. However, Calcutta was also the scene of the Bengal Renaissance, that remarkable flowering of the blend between English and Indian cultures. The city remains India's most lively literary, intellectual, and cultural center. Western visitors find its grimy slums depressing, like those of any crowded city. It is still, as for all of its short history, an immensely vigorous and creative place.

From Tolerance to Arrogance

Until well into the nineteenth century, British rule in India, much of it indirect through the formal sovereignty of the so-called Princely States and their Indian rulers under loose British oversight, was becoming more and more an Indian government through its variety of adjustments to, acceptances of, and collaborations with, Indians and Indian ways. Even in recently conquered Maharashtra, as elsewhere, the British attracted support by their suppression of banditry and furthering of production and trade. Most Indians who had any dealings with them were content with their new rulers, and many were enthusiastic. Peasants who had been accustomed to the harsh exactions of the variety of Indian

Cultural blending in colonial India: an Indian ruler in British uniform, by an Indian artist. (Victoria and Albert Museum, London/Art Resource, NY)

states had come to distrust all governments but were little if any touched by this latest *raj* (ruler); most were only dimly if at all aware that a new group of foreigners now dominated the political scene, especially since local administration was left largely in Indian hands. Indirectly, peasant welfare became increasingly affected by the spread of exploitative zamindar landlordism encouraged by the British and by the expansion of commercial crops and market forces. Freedom from banditry and from arbitrary or excessive taxation were important gains, but there was a significant rise in tenancy and a decline in net economic well-being for many who lost their land or were exploited by new commercialization, such as the notorious indigo plantation system, which ruined thousands of Indian peasants, and the many more who suffered under oppressive zamindars.

Just as they worked largely through native rulers, the British at first left most of the structure of Indian society intact. They did feel compelled to suppress sati, banditry (including the cult of *thugee,* from which comes our word *thug*), and slavery. The thugs were members of a secret cult of the goddess Kali who waylaid travelers and then ritually strangled them as offerings to Kali, the "goddess of destruction." Thugee, as the cult was called,

---

*Jute was often referred to in Calcutta as "gold on silt."

was finally wiped out in the 1850s, and the last of its members executed. Otherwise the British did not tamper with Indian customs. Even Christian missionaries, who had been excluded as "disruptive" by the Company until 1813, were limited for some time under Company pressure after 1813 to running schools; these schools were popular with many young Indians and their families as a way of learning English and Western culture, an obvious means of upward mobility in this colonial society, leading for many to employment in the colonial system. The booming Indian commercial middle class made money in the expanding trade promoted by the British order, and they too founded or joined as partners in new Western-style banks, corporations, agency houses, and joint-stock companies, all instruments of Western capitalist enterprise with considerable Indian ownership, management, or participation. In 1833 Parliament abolished the East India Company's previous monopoly on all trade in and with India, as part of a commitment to free trade in general, and India was opened to all kinds of private enterprise.

But as the nineteenth century wore on, industrialization and advances in science and technology at home gave first Britain and then other Western nations new power, confidence, and wealth. Their growing conviction that they were the appropriate leaders of the world in all things began to change the earlier interest in Indian culture and Indian ways and substitute for it a new ethnocentric arrogance. Machine-made cloth from the mills of Lancashire ended most of the Indian cotton exports to the West that had for so long been the chief basis of trade. English cloth even invaded the Indian market, throwing millions of Indian hand spinners of cotton out of work, although raw cotton continued to be shipped to supply looms in Britain. Imported machine-spun yarn did help to keep traditional Indian weavers viable, as did yarn from Indian mills in Bombay after the 1850s. British policymakers for India and a series of governors-general, beginning with William Bentinck in 1828, who were followers of the new British school of utilitarian liberalism thought that it was the chief duty of government to "civilize" and "improve" Indians in the British mold as much as possible.

It was decided in 1835 that English and Western learning should be the main objects of education, in order "to form a class who may be interpreters between us and the millions whom we govern, a class of persons Indian in blood and color, but English in taste, in opinions, in morals, and in intellect."[4] The views of the Orientalists and their admiration of Indian civilization were largely set aside; Indians were now to be educated along British lines. A new law code was devised for all of British India, incorporating many aspects of Indian law but bearing the unmistakable stamp of its English authorship. Fewer Englishmen or Scots now bothered to

learn Sanskrit or study the Indian classics, although from 1809 all British recruits to the Company and later to the Indian Civil Service were required to learn at least one Indian language and something of the country's history and culture.

But racial and cultural arrogance were already asserting themselves as Britain attempted to solidify its new power and its self-appointed role as the vanguard of "progress," leading the way for more "backward" peoples in the rest of the world. Britain planned to extend to India "the three great engines of social improvement which the sagacity and science of recent times have given to the Western nations: railways, uniform postage, and the electric telegraph."[5] The first rail lines were begun in 1850, reaching inland from Calcutta and from Bombay. By 1855 all of India's major cities had been linked by telegraph, and by postal service down to the village level. Railways and telegraph service were soon to be of vital importance to the British in suppressing the revolt of 1857, but their primary use was to haul raw materials and agricultural goods to the rapidly expanding urban markets. Many had doubted that caste-conscious Hindus would crowd together on trains, but they were popular from the start and, indeed, showed the flexibility of caste in a changing environment.

At the same time, British ambition faced potential competition. They worried about a Russian invasion of India as they watched with growing concern the successive Russian takeovers of the independent kingdoms of Central Asia. Soon only Afghanistan stood between the two empires. To block Russian influence there the British foolishly sent an expedition to Kabul in 1839, taking over the lower Indus Valley (the province of Sind) along the way. Afghan guerrilla resistance finally forced the British to retreat in 1841 through the wild mountain and gorge country along the route to India, a natural setting for a devastating ambush. Only one British survivor of the nearly 20,000-man army of the Indus reached safety. Fierce Afghan tribal warriors had humbled yet another proud empire, but Sind was brutally reconquered in 1843 as "strategic territory."

The Sikhs of Punjab had refused passage to the ill-fated expedition to Afghanistan and now challenged the British as the only part of India not under their direct or indirect control. Factional conflicts over the political succession gave the British a chance to intervene in 1845–1846. The British ultimately defeated the Sikhs and absorbed Punjab and Kashmir, although they were nearly beaten by these tough fighters and had to mount a second campaign before the matter was finally settled in 1849. Having won the war, the British, appreciating the military skills of the Sikhs, offered them a prominent place in their army. This was the beginning of a long and happy partnership, which

A drawing by C. F. Atkinson, *Repulse of a Sortie,* depicting an incident in the Revolt of 1857.
(By permission of the British Library)

paid an early dividend in Sikh support for the British in the Revolt of 1857.

The Revolt of 1857

The indirect arrangement that left Indian princes in formal control of more than half of India, although under British supervision, was in many cases unsatisfactory to the new imperialist mind. Using the pretext that disputes over succession were disruptive (as they often were), the East India Company took over direct sovereignty in several central Indian states in the 1850s; in 1856, despite earlier treaty promises, they annexed the rich kingdom of Oudh in the central Ganges and deposed its nawab. Mounting British arrogance and racism had already provoked some discontent and even some mutiny among Indian troops. Now British land grabs had created new and potentially powerful enemies, who made common cause with disgruntled sol-

diers. The hereditary aristocracy saw not only that they had been displaced as rulers by the British but that their place in Indian society was being taken by upstarts, the collaborators and the rising commercial and Westernized Indian middle classes. Many of the troops were incensed at being required to accept service overseas, including the campaigns in Burma; caste Hindus were forbidden to leave India by "crossing the dark water." Lower Burma was nevertheless defeated in 1826, and British territory there expanded in 1852 with Indian troops under British officers (see Chapter 15).

Early in 1857 an improved rifle was introduced. It was rumored that the cartridges were coated in lard and animal fat and had to be bitten off before loading. That had been true originally, but the rumor persisted even after the cartridges had been changed. The outcry of protest from deeply offended vegetarian Hindus and pork-avoiding Muslims was met by rigid insistence on following orders. Those who refused were dishonorably discharged, many of them men from Oudh. Several regiments mutinied and killed their British officers. The mutineers captured Delhi and "restored" the last surviving Mughal emperor Bahadur Shah, now an old man, who had never been formally removed by the Company. Mutineers on the rampage slaughtered the British population of Delhi and of outlying districts there and in Oudh, massacred those who had surrendered from their encampment in the city of Cawnpore, and besieged the somewhat larger group of men, women, and children, including loyal Indians, who had fortified themselves in the grounds of the British residency at Lucknow, the capital of Oudh. Most of the rest of India either took no part in the struggle or stood by the British, who regained complete control within a year. Most army units remained loyal, and after the initial shock the outcome was never in doubt. But the mutiny worked a change in the relationship between India and the British, who thereafter were seen, and saw themselves, more and more as an occupying power.

The British repaid in kind the atrocities they had suffered. Captured rebel soldiers were strapped to cannons and blown away, and entire villages were put to the torch. The remarkable Rani of Jhansi, who had joined the revolt when the British took over her small central Indian state on her husband's death because they were unwilling to recognize a female ruler, was hunted down and died fighting on her horse, after leading probably the most effective campaign of all against the British. Bahadur Shah died in exile in Burma in 1858, and a British captain named Hodson murdered his two sons in cold blood when the British retook Delhi. Despite their continued reliance on Indian elites, including the native princes left in control over nearly half of the country, fraternization greatly decreased. Earlier friendship and even intermarriage gave way to mutual dislike, the British as oppressive conquerors, the Indians as inferiors. Such attitudes were far from universal on either side; the ideals of the Orientalists never completely died, and most Indians remained collaborators, while those who were educated enthusiastically patterned themselves on British models and indeed took pride in being members of the British Empire, the greatest show on earth until well into the twentieth century. Both individual Englishmen and successive governors-general also followed more positive and constructive policies and attitudes. But the dream of an equal Anglo-Indian partnership was largely over.

The Consolidation of the British Empire in India

It is tempting to look into the past for the seeds of the present—to look back, for example, to Sir Thomas Roe's mission in 1616, the founding of Madras

in 1639 or of Calcutta in 1690 as the beginning of Britain's Indian empire. But until the nineteenth century, the British were very far from seeing themselves as conquerors; nor did they expect or plan to become the government of India. Clive's victory at Plassey in Bengal in 1757, although it was not fought for that purpose, brought the East India Company much of the responsibility for administration in that area, but their chief role was still seen as furthering and profiting from trade. Administrative responsibility was to be avoided as much as possible so as to devote their energies to their major purpose, although in the wake of Plassey the energies of many Company officials and merchants were diverted to plundering a chaotic and defenseless Bengal from 1758 to about 1773, when controls on such rapacious behavior began to be imposed. Until 1757 and despite the Company's tiny footholds at Madras, Bombay, and Calcutta, the English position in India was marginal and precarious, as Siraj-ud-Dowlah demonstrated when he captured Calcutta in 1756. No one in the Company thought of taking over power elsewhere, still less of an Indian empire.

Rivalry with the French in the 1740s and 1750s spurred the English East India Company to seek further alliances with regional Indian rulers and then during the Napoleonic era to expand into large-scale takeovers of Indian states, first in the south (where the French were already active) and then in Maharashtra, while kingdoms in the north beyond Bengal, such as Oudh and Gujarat, were placed under British "protection." Ceylon was taken over in the 1790s originally as a base against the French. By 1800 the British were dominant in India, and went on subsequently to round out their holdings and construct a true Indian empire. But until then there was no concerted plan of all-India conquest, and even after 1857 half of the country remained at least nominally in Indian hands under indirect rule through hereditary Indian princes.

Having acquired an Indian empire, the British then had to decide what to do with it. Part of the debate that ensued, in England and India, centered on what sort of education and legal system would best serve the new dominions and serve British interests. The Orientalists argued that young Indians under British tutelage should be educated in their own culture and its great tradition. They should learn Sanskrit, the Indian equivalent of Latin and Greek, and study the classical Indian texts, much as educated Britons were immersed in the Western classics and the study of ancient history and philosophy as the best general preparation for adult life and its responsibilities. The followers of utilitarianism, who in the end became the dominant voice in the British government of India, argued that Britain had "a moral duty to perform," in the words of Lord Ellenborough, president of the East India Company's Board of Control in

London, in "civilizing" India according to the modern British model. This meant that English would replace Sanskrit and that the new Western subjects of science, mathematics, and Western history and literature would replace the traditional Indian curriculum.

The Orientalists saw the study of the Hindu cultural and religious legacy not only as valuable for its own sake, one of the great civilizations of the world, but also as a guide to proper social behavior. One of the British members of the Asiatic Society of Bengal wrote:

> Hinduism little needs the ameliorating hand of Christianity to render its votaries a sufficiently correct and moral people for all the useful purposes of a civilized society. . . . In the vast region of Hindu mythology I discover piety in the garb of allegory, I see morality at every turn blended with every tale. . . . It appears the most complete and ample system of moral allegory that the world has ever produced.[6]

Governor-General William Bentinck, himself a disciple of Jeremy Bentham's utilitarianism, chose a fellow Benthamite, Thomas Babington Macaulay, newly arrived in India in 1834, to preside over the education committee that was attempting to resolve the debate between the two sides and to plan British India's education system. Macaulay asserted that "a single shelf of a good European library is worth the whole native literature of India," and Governor Bentinck in the end declared that "the great object of the British government ought to be the promotion of European literature and science among the natives of India." The education system that grew in the course of the nineteenth century from such official designs and that involved most ambitious and higher-income Indians was strongly English in character and content, although most upper-class Indians continued to study also their own culture and linguistic tradition. Macaulay, a brilliant and widely read young man despite his prejudices and blind spots, also drafted virtually single-handed a new penal code of law for British India that produced for the first time uniformity throughout India, and a great variety of provisions to ensure impartial and scrupulous justice. Almost every possible offense was covered, and punishments according to the new code were in many cases less severe than under the English law of the time. Indian judges, trained in both Indian and Western-style law, were included in the system and by the end of the colonial period were in the great majority.

English-style education and law made a lasting impact on India. Both have been retained with relatively little change, as Indians made them their own. Between them, they helped to create successive generations of Indians who saw themselves as legitimate members of the British system. Most educated Indians were as familiar with English literature and history, as well as with

An East India Company official studying an Indian language with a *munshi* (teacher) about 1813. Especially after 1800, the Company required all of its officials to learn at least one Indian language fluently, an obvious necessity for those who dispensed justice and managed administration. (By permission of the British Library)

its language, as were educated Englishmen. Many of the Indian upper classes went on to British universities, where they competed successfully with English students and often outdistanced them. The Hindu Renaissance saw to it that most Indians also learned about their own cultural tradition and retained a sense of pride in it. Racist arrogance on the part of the British, and their denigration of Indian culture as well as their position as conquerors and rulers, understandably stimulated educated Indians to search their own tradition not only to explain how and why they had "failed" but also to restore their pride in their cultural identity, as the heirs of greatness, including many centuries of sophisticated development when Britain and Europe were still a primitive wilderness.

Indian restored pride, together with the railways and the spread of a uniform political system of colonial control over most of the country, created the necessary conditions as well as the breeding grounds for the rise of Indian nationalism. Educated Indians learned more than Shakespeare and Milton; they learned about the English traditions of democracy and justice, and they admired the strength of English nationalism. It was inevitable that in time they would develop the same values

The Charter Act, 1833

The rise of humanitarianism and liberalism in Britain led to a new Charter Act for India in 1833 when the Company's monopoly was removed. This was often cited later by Indian nationalists as showing the hypocrisy of British rule, but it stated a principle that many, if not all, colonial administrators into the twentieth century at least made an effort to follow.

No native [of India], nor any natural-born subject of His Majesty resident therein, shall by reason of his religion, place of birth, descent, color, or any of the above, be disabled from holding any place, office, or employment under the Company. . . . On a large view of the state of Indian legislation, and of the improvements possible in it, it is recognized as an indisputable principle that the interests of the native subjects are to be consulted in preference to those of Europeans whenever the two come in competition, and that therefore the laws ought to be adapted to the feelings and habits of the natives rather than to those of Europeans.

Source: From *A New History of India, Sixth Edition* by Stanley Wolpert, copyright © 1997 by Oxford University Press, Inc. Used by permission of Oxford University Press, Inc.

and goals and would demand their freedom from alien colonial control. India had never been effectively unified politically or culturally in the past. The British accomplished this, at least at the level of the educated elite, and greatly strengthened national integration through modern means of transport. Before the nineteenth century the strength of Indian regionalism had resulted in part from the great difficulty of communication among its parts, given its size, mountains, deserts, and the absence of navigable rivers in more than a small part of the country. Even the Ganges and the Indus were usable only by small boats over most of their courses, and the rivers of central and southern India were essentially unnavigable.

The rail and road system built under the British tied India together for the first time and brought most Indians into contact with one another, with English as their common language and the colonial-founded ports of Calcutta, Bombay, and Madras as their chief centers of new intellectual ferment. In these and other growing cities there was a vigorous press in both English and various regional languages, of high quality and widely read by educated Indians. The press was a forum for emerging Indian nationalism, especially among professional and educated people. Thanks in part to British efforts in education, this became a substantial segment of the population, including many thousands of lawyers trained in English law and its Indian version. Lawyers and others who had had an English-style education became the leaders of the movement for Indian independence.

Indian women in this period were, as before, subjugated, but with some exceptions, especially in the south, where they approached equality or even dominance, a survival of an originally matriarchal society in the Dravidian areas. The British launched an ultimately successful campaign against *sati,* the practice of burning widows on their husbands' funeral pyres, although it had never been widespread. Come the Revolt of 1857, one of the leading figures on the revolters' side was the remarkable Rani (Queen) of Jhansi, who rode a horse like a man and harried the British and loyalist Indian troops. The British had refused to recognize her as the ruler of Jhansi, a Princely state, solely because she was a woman, and she took to the field against them, finally to be killed in battle. The early origins of women's liberation began after the suppression of the revolt, signaled by the start of education for women and by legislative measures against child marriage.

The more far-sighted Britons recognized early what must happen. Charles Trevelyan, a secretary in the political department of the government in Calcutta, wrote in 1838, soon after the new education system and law code had been inaugurated:

The existing connection between two such distant countries as England and India cannot in the nature of things be permanent; no effect of policy can prevent the natives from ultimately regaining their independence. But there are two ways of arriving at this point. . . . One must end in the complete alienation of mind and separation of interests between ourselves and the natives; the other in a permanent alliance, founded on mutual benefit and goodwill.[7]

One may say that relations between Britain and independent India since 1947 have followed the happier of these two ways for the most part. But for much of the final century of British rule, beginning in 1857 but with its roots in the arrogance and racism that had begun to grow soon after 1800, the first way seemed all too likely an outcome.

Nevertheless, the beginnings of full colonial rule held considerable promise, and in the end much of that promise was realized and continued after 1947. Charles Metcalfe (1785–1846), British resident from 1813 at the still-preserved though tattered Mughal court at Delhi, wrote in 1835:

> Our dominion in India is by conquest; it is naturally disgusting to the inhabitants and can only be maintained by military force. It is our positive duty to render them justice, to respect and protect their rights, and to study their happiness. By the performance of this duty, we may allay and keep dormant their innate dissatisfaction.[8]

French visitors to India, not likely to see much good in the English, especially at this period, confirmed such an assessment. Here is only one sample, from the Abbé Dubois in 1823:

> The justice and prudence which the present rulers display in endeavouring to make these people less unhappy than they have been hitherto; the anxiety which they manifest in increasing their material comfort; the inviolable respect they constantly show for the customs and religious beliefs of the country; and the protection they afford to the weak as well as to the strong. . . . all these have contributed more to the consolidation of their power than even their victories and conquests.[9]

Ram Mohun Roy, the major figure of the Hindu Renaissance, was one of the first of many Indians who found their new rulers admirable. He wrote in 1833:

> Finding them generally more intelligent, more steady and moderate in their conduct, I gave up my prejudices against them and became inclined in their favor, feeling that their rule, though a foreign yoke, would lead most speedily and surely to the amelioration of the native inhabitants.[10]

Whether British rule did or did not accomplish this after Roy's time, it did clearly lead to a new Indian sense of national identity, to massive Western influences, and finally to an independent India that still preserves, by its own choice, basic elements first introduced in this early period of colonial control. The growth of Indian nationalism, later to blossom into an independence movement, was nourished by Westernization and then fed by British racist arrogance, especially after the mutiny of 1857, and by their authoritarian rule. British India was administered by the Indian Civil Service, until the end of the nineteenth century staffed exclusively by British although necessarily dependent on thousands of Indians in subordinate roles. The ICS proper totaled only about 900 men, including local district agents who also held court, often on circuit through the countryside, and dispensed justice.

It was understandable that they should see themselves as a superior elite and should be tempted to play god to the hundreds of millions of Indians over whom they had absolute power. They lived, with their families if they were married, in areas separate from the Indians, usually in a part of the town removed from the Indian quarter and the bazaar and separated by a barrier of open ground and trees. The British area was called the Civil Lines and included that center of social life, the British Club, where no Indians were admitted except as servants. Houses in the Civil Lines were in Anglo-Indian style, adapted to the climate with wide, shaded verandas, thick walls, and large lawns with trees, all tended by Indian servants. Otherwise there was little interaction with Indians, especially after about 1800, and they rarely met socially.

When British wives and families became the norm, especially after the opening of the Suez Canal in 1869, they constituted a further barrier against Indo-British social interaction. Most British became even more aloof from India. Although there were some notable exceptions, most British lived in considerable luxury and were detached from the poverty and squalor of most Indians. In the great heat of summer British families moved up to the lower ranges of the Himalayas to hill stations like Simla, Darjeeling, Dehra Dun, Mussoori, or Naini Tal or in the south up into the Nilgiri Hills to Ootacamund or Kodai Kanal. Higher officials conducted the government from Darjeeling or Simla during the long, hot months; husbands in lower-order jobs sweated it out on the plains. Many British who were born in India over the long period of colonialism came to love it, but few lived in the real India.

In the so-called Princely States, nominally independent but under the eye of a British resident, traditional court life continued, and in most there was little change. A few of the hereditary rulers, anxious to prevent a British takeover, promoted a degree of modernization: telegraph lines, railways, some Western-style education, and some public health measures. But most of the native states remained relatively backward, out of the main stream of change centered in the colonial port cities and along the major rail lines, and clinging to their hereditary privileges. Their largely peasant subjects were often oppressed, both by the rulers and by the large landholders whom they supported or with whom they were involved in feudal-like arrangements, survivals of or similar to the Mughal system of jagirs and their jagirdars. There, and in British northern India, women continued to be subjugated and kept in purdah, restricted to the household and its women's quarters and veiled when they infrequently left the house. The princely state of Kashmir was a qualified exception, where at least the Hindu women and many of the Muslims were not subjected to purdah and enjoyed a greater degree of equality. Most Kashmiris (including the ancestors of the Nehru family) mixed freely across caste lines and prided themselves on their distinction from most other Indians, especially in the north.

British power seemed complete, and most educated Indians followed British ways in many respects and with genuine conviction that this was the best path for India's own development. It was not the kinds of traditional groups and forces represented in the Revolt of 1857 but the new group of English-educated and professionals that was to question, and ultimately to demand its freedom from, British rule. This dominant group of modern India was being created in the very fabric and institutions of colonial rule, and at least in part by British design, especially in the educational system that it fostered. In that sense, the success of British colonialism and its sharpening edge of arrogance sowed the seeds of its eventual downfall.

Questions

1. How did the pattern of British behavior in India change from their first encounters with Indian cotton producers through the nineteenth century?

2. Why did the British attempt to rule through local power elites instead of directly?

3. Why did the Indian population fail to unite against British expansion? What did the British offer that the previous system did not?

4. How and why did the British eliminate French power in India? What were the consequences relative to the transition in the British East India Company's presence in India?

5. How did the development of Orientalism affect early British colonial experiences in India? In contrast, how did this colonial presence begin to change Indian society? What impact did British Utilitarianism have in the development of the British colonial administration?

6. What were the causes of the 1857 Sepoy Mutiny and why the choice of 1857? Why did it fail? How did the Mutiny mark a transition in the British relationship with India?

7. How did British rule of India subsequently contribute to the negation of prior Indian regionalism that was foundational to the development of a sense of national identity?

Notes

1. From Company records, quoted in S. N. Edwardes, *By-Ways of Bombay* (Bombay: Tara Poreuala, 1912), pp. 170–171.

2. From Company records, reproduced in C. R. Wilson, ed., *Old Fort William,* vol. 1 (London: Murray, 1906), p. 33.

3. R. Kipling, "Song of the Cities," *The Five Nations and the Seven Seas* (New York: Doubleday, 1915), p. 183.

4. From T. B. Macaulay's "Minute on Education," in S. Wolpert, *A New History of India* (New York: Oxford University Press, 1982), p. 215.

5. From a minute by Governor-General Dalhousie in 1856, in S. Wolpert, *A New History of India* (New York: Oxford University Press, 1982), p. 228.

6. G. Moorhouse, *India Britannica* (New York: Harper Row, 1983), p. 89.

7. Ibid., p. 97.

8. Ibid., p. 84.

9. Ibid., p. 85.

10. Ibid., p. 86.

Suggested Websites

British India

http://www.sscnet.ucla.edu/southasia/HISTORY/British/ BrIndia.html
Information and images about British India, the East India Company, the Black Hole of Calcutta, and Robert Clive.

http://www.fordham.edu/halsail/india/indiasbook .html#The%20Western%20Intrusion
Indian history sourcebook from Fordham University discusses European/British imperialism.

The Indian Revolt of 1857

http//www.english.emory.edu/Bahri/Mutiny.html

http://www.historyofindia.com/mutiny.html

http://www.indiasurvived.com/java/revolt.htm

http://www.indhistory.com/ 1857-war-of-independence.html
Information on the Sepoy Mutiny/Revolt of 1857.

Suggestions for Further Reading

Arnold, D. *Colonizing the Body: Medicine and Epidemic Disease in Nineteenth Century India.* Berkeley: University of California Press, 1991.

Bayly, C. A. *Indian Society and the Making of the British Empire.* Cambridge, England: Cambridge University Press, 1988.

Bearce, G. D. *British Attitudes Towards India, 1784–1858.* Oxford: Oxford University Press, 1961.

Broehl, W. G. *Crisis of the Raj: 1857 Through British Eyes.* Hanover, NH: University Press of New England, 1986.

Cannon, G. *The Life and Mind of Oriental Jones.* Cambridge, England: Cambridge University Press, 1990.

Cassels, N. E. *Orientalism, Evangelicalism and the Military Cantonment.* New York: Mellen, 1991.

Chandra, B. *Nationalism and Colonialism in Modern India.* New Delhi: Orient Longmans, 1989.

Chaudhuri, K. N. *The Trading World of Asia and the East India Company, 1600–1760.* Cambridge, England: Cambridge University Press, 1978.

Chaudhuri, S., ed. *Calcutta: The Living City.* 2 vols. Oxford: Oxford University Press, 1990.

Cohn, B. S. *The British in India.* Princeton: Princeton University Press, 1996.

Cooper, G. S. *The Anglo Maratha Campaigns.* Cambridge, England: Cambridge University Press, 2004.

Das Gupta, A. *Malabar in Asian Trade, 1740–1800.* Cambridge, England: Cambridge University Press, 1967.

Farrell, J. G. *The Siege at Krishnapur.* London: Weidonfeld and Nicolson, 1973. (A lively novel of India in 1857.)

Furber, H. *Bombay Presidency in the Mid-Eighteenth Century.* New York: Asia Publishing House, 1965.

———. *Rival Empires of Trade in the Orient, 1600–1800.* Minneapolis: University of Minnesota Press, 1976.

Goalen, P. *India From Mughal Empire to British Raj.* Cambridge, England: Cambridge University Press, 1993.

Grewal, J. S. *The Sikhs of the Punjab.* Cambridge, England: Cambridge University Press, 1990.

Hibbett, C. *The Great Mutiny: India 1857.* New York: Viking, 1978.

Kincaid, D. *British Social Life in India, 1608–1937.* London: Routledge and Kegan Paul, 1973.

Kling, B. *The Blue Mutiny: The I...* Philadelphia: University of Pennsy...

———. *Partner in Empire: Dwarkanath... terprise in Eastern India.* Berkeley: U... Press, 1976.

Kling, B., and Pearson, M. N., eds. *The Age o... olulu: University Press of Hawaii, 1979.

Kopf, D. *British Orientalism and the Bengal... 1773–1835.* Berkeley: University of California Pres...

Laird, M. A. *Missionaries and Education in Bengal, 1...* Oxford: Clarendon Press, 1972.

Marshall, P. J. *Bengal, The British Bridgehead.* Cambridge,... land: Cambridge University Press, 1988.

———. *East Indian Fortunes: The British in Bengal in the Eigh... teenth Century.* Oxford: Clarendon Press, 1976.

———, ed. *Problems of Empire: Britain and India, 1757–1813.* New York: Barnes and Noble Books, 1968.

Moon, P. *The British Conquest and Dominion of India.* London: Duckworth, 1989.

Mudford, P. *Birds of a Different Plumage: A Study of British and Indian Relations from Akbar to Curzon.* London: Collins, 1974.

Mukherjee, S. N. *Sir William Jones: A Study in Eighteenth Century British Attitudes to India.* Cambridge, England: Cambridge University Press, 1968.

Murphey, R. *The Outsiders: The Western Experience in India and China.* Ann Arbor: University of Michigan Press, 1977.

Robertson, B. C. *Raja Rammohan Ray.* Oxford: Oxford University Press, 1996.

Rothermund, D. *The Economic History of India.* London: Croom Helm, 1988.

Sinha, D. P. *The Educational Policy of the East India Company in Bengal to 1854.* Calcutta: Punthi Pustaic, 1964.

Spear, P. *The Nabobs: A Study of the Social Life of the English in Eighteenth Century India.* London: Thames and Hudson, 1963.

———. *Twilight of the Mughals.* Cambridge, England: Cambridge University Press, 1951.

Stokes, E. *The Peasant Armed: The Indian Rebellion of 1857.* Cambridge, England: Cambridge University Press, 1986.

Trautmann, T. *The Aryans and British India.* Berkeley: University of California Press, 1997.

Waller, J. H. *Beyond the Khyber Pass: The Road to British Disaster in the First Afghan War.* New York: Random House, 1991.

Indigo Disturbances in Bengal.
vania Press, 1966.
Tagore and the Age of En-
niversity of California
Partnership. Hon-
Renaissance,
s, 1969.
793–1837.
Eng-

15

The Triumph of Imperialism in Asia

After a brief general discussion of imperialism, this chapter covers the British empire in India after 1857, the building of railways and the beginnings of industrialization, the spread of English-style education and law, the role of the civil service, and the building of New Delhi as the new colonial capital. The extension of British control to Burma and Malaya is then considered, followed by the French conquest of Vietnam, the Dutch rule in Indonesia, and the American acquisition of the Philippines. Siam (Thailand since 1932) remained independent as a buffer zone between French Vietnam (plus Cambodia and Laos) and British Burma and Malaya.

China was increasingly invaded by Western traders and missionaries and wracked by the devastating Taiping Rebellion (1850–1864), but the Manchu government finally put it down, although its efforts at needed reforms were stymied by the archconservative empress dowager Cixi, who finally made common cause with the Boxers in their effort to rid China of all foreigners. They besieged the foreign legations in Beijing in the summer of 1900 but were finally defeated by an allied foreign expedition, and the Manchu dynasty fell in 1911. Japan responded more constructively to foreign pressures led by the new reformist government from 1869. The Meiji reforms included much Westernization and built a strong modern economy and military, which defeated China in a war over the status of Korea (1894–1895) and also took over the island of Taiwan. Japan then attacked the Russians in Manchuria in 1904 and became the dominant power there from 1905. Finally the chapter considers the American role in Asia, and attitudes toward Asians.

In the course of the nineteenth century, between 1800 and 1900, a handful of countries imposed their domination over large portions of the globe. In that brief period England, France, Germany, the United States, Japan, and to a lesser extent Italy and Belgium, took control of perhaps one-quarter of the earth's land surface and one-quarter of its entire population while becoming dominant over another quarter. Russia continued to push its borders eastward into Asia, while the United States and Japan both extended their presence into the Pacific region. One result of this grab for overseas power was the establishment of complex forms of interdependency among world civilizations that still profoundly shape our lives. This first major phase in the creation of a "global village" as the product of imperialism is the background of the contemporary age.

The New Imperialism

The new imperialism was the work of advanced industrial-capitalist nations rather than of mercantilist economies that were prominent in the centuries before 1800. It involved the commitment of significant financial investment as well as the deliberate exploitation of the material and human resources of the colonial areas. These economic functions led in turn to the establishment of direct political control over colonies, administered through elaborate colonial bureaucracies. By the opening of the twentieth century, therefore, a new and direct relationship of unequal exchange had been established among the civilizations of the world, one marked by a vast difference between the industrial and technological power of the West and the relative weakness of the less technologically developed cultures.

CHRONOLOGY

India

1869 ■ Opening of the Suez Canal

1877 ■ Queen Victoria adopts title of Empress of India

1878–1880 ■ Second Afghan war

1885 ■ Indian National Congress

1900 ■ Rail network completed

1911–1930 ■ Capital moves from Calcutta to Delhi

1919 ■ Amritsar massacre

Southeast Asia

1755 ■ Division of Mataram court into Surabaya- and Yogyakarta-based sultanates

1782 ■ Bangkok founded; Chakri dynasty

1786 ■ Penang becomes the principle British factory in Southeast Asia

1802 ■ Hue-based Nyugen rulers consolidate their Vietnam monarchy by annexing the Hanoi-based north

1819 ■ Singapore founded

1825–1830 ■ Java wars

1826, 1852, 1886 ■ British take Burma

1830–1900 ■ Culture (Cultivation) System in Java

1830–1920 ■ Chinese and Tamil labor migrations to Malaya

1851–1868 ■ King Mongkut of Siam

1862–1885 ■ French take Vietnam, Laos, and Cambodia and consolidate their colonial authority in French Indochina

1867 ■ Straits Settlements becomes a British Crown Colony

1871 ■ Federated Malay States established, with Kuala Lumpur as their capital

1890–1969 ■ Ho Chi Minh

1898–1902 ■ United States takes the Philippines

1906 ■ Young Men's Buddhist Association in Burma

1906 ■ Dutch consolidate their control over all of Indonesia

1909 ■ Unfederated Malay states

1932 ■ Overthrow of Thai monarchy by Thai military

China

1850–1864 ■ Taiping Rebellion

1858–1860 ■ Second Anglo-Chinese Opium War
■ Treaty of Tianjin

1860–1905 ■ Russia in Manchuria

1864–1894 ■ Self-Strengthening Movement

1882, 1905 ■ Oriental Exclusion Acts (U.S.)

1861–1908 ■ Empress dowager Cixi

1900 ■ Boxer Rebellion

Japan

1868–1912 ■ Meiji Era

1870–1940 ■ Westernization and industrialization

1895 ■ Japan defeats China, takes Korea and Taiwan

1904–1905 ■ Russo-Japanese war

1905–1945 ■ Japan in Manchuria

1910 ■ Japan adds Korea to its empire

Conflicting Interpretations

Scholars continue to debate imperialism's causes and consequences. Some have argued that all states are predisposed to aggression and dominance as a result of culturally inherited atavistic attitudes. The misapplication of Charles Darwin's theory of evolution to human behavior, an approach known as social Darwinism, was certainly atavistic in its stress on "the survival of the fittest" and the consequent justification or even glorification of aggression, with strong racist overtones about who was "fittest" and who "inferior." Others have stressed strategic motives. But perhaps the most basic aspect of the drive for territorial control was simply national

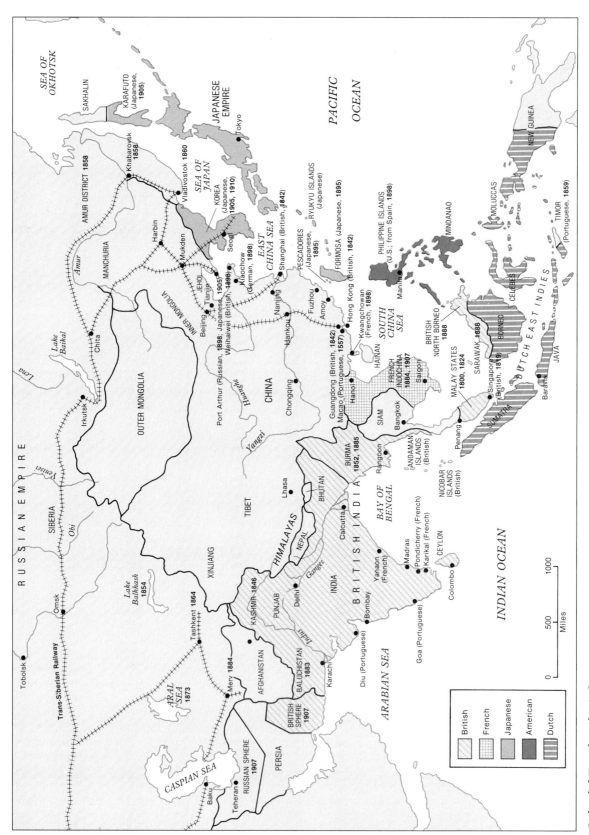

Colonial Empires in Asia

All of India and most of Southeast Asia, with the sole exception of Siam (Thailand) succumbed to colonialism, while China and Japan had their sovereignty compromised by the so-called "Unequal Treaties."

pride and the aggressive ambition of national states, in the West and then in Japan. The creation of new nation-states in Germany and Italy in the second half of the nineteenth century heightened the spirit of aggressive national rivalry on the international scene. Great-power status was increasingly equated with the possession of overseas colonies, so empire became a matter of national honor. Policymakers often used economic arguments to explain the necessity for expansion, but imperialism had significant support among all classes, including workers, and even trade union leaders and some socialists were enthusiastic about colonial expansion.

Economics and Empire

Economic rivalry between older industrial states like England and France and newly industrializing states such as Germany and the United States added to the competition for colonies, especially because tariff barriers tended to restrict European markets. The unprecedented material prosperity and military-industrial power produced by the Industrial Revolution and the rapid advances in science, technology, and industrial organization gave Westerners a new sense of overwhelming self-confidence in the superiority of their civilization. This generated a drive for cultural dominance and supported a belief in each country's "civilizing mission." Industrialization also led to a new search for markets for manufactured goods and for sources of raw materials. The steady abandonment of free trade after 1860 was already limiting the general European market. This growing competition prompted some to argue in favor of creating "sheltered" markets in overseas colonies, from which the products of other nations would be excluded in favor of monopoly trade with the home country. Industrial economies developed huge appetites for raw materials unavailable in Europe, especially rubber, cotton, jute, tin, and petroleum, as well as foodstuffs such as coconut, coffee, and tea, all produced in Asia. Not only were these materials increasingly necessary, but their value was enhanced because cheap labor in the colonies made mining, extraction, and agriculture especially profitable.

These economic trends and conditions clearly contributed to the origins of imperialism, but there is a continuing debate on the issue of accumulated surplus capital. This argument, which later became the major interpretation of Marxist writers, states that capitalism suffered from underconsumption; wealth in capitalist societies was poorly distributed as a result of overaccumulation by the rich. The business and financial interests that accumulated such surplus capital soon discovered that it could be more profitably invested in overseas

areas, where the availability of cheap labor and the raw materials demanded by Europeans made possible a significantly greater return. Imperialism, according to this argument, resulted from the inability of large capitalists to find investment outlets for the surplus wealth that they were not able to use effectively at home.

In 1916, Vladimir Ilyich Lenin (1870–1924), the future Communist leader of the Russian Revolution, wrote the classic Marxist analysis of the subject, *Imperialism: The Highest Stage of Capitalism*. The scramble for colonies, Lenin noted, coincided with the change in Europe's economy from a phase of free competition to one of intense and ever-increasing monopoly through combines, trusts, and the control of finance capital. Imperialism emerged from this last and "highest" stage of capitalism when business and financial interests in each country extended their monopolies overseas in the search for ever-greater profits. Imperialism was, therefore, an inevitable and predictable response to the "internal contradictions" of capitalism in its monopolistic stage. For Lenin, imperialism would result in the crisis and breakdown of the entire capitalist system.

Lenin was at least partially correct. Between 1860 and 1900, the value of British capital invested abroad grew from $7 billion to $20 billion. By the eve of World War I, one-fifth of the foreign investments of France and Germany were in colonial regions, while about 40 percent of England's overseas investments were in the colonial world. There were, however, many instances in which foreign rulers needed and requested Western capital, and financial investment hardly explained the imperialist expansion of less developed nations such as Italy and Russia, which had little surplus capital of their own. Nor does colonialism explain the even larger British investments in noncolonial areas, such as Latin America and the United States. Finally, it should be remembered that while some colonial possessions were profitable, the military and bureaucratic costs of occupation nearly always exceeded the financial return.

However important the economic motives behind imperialism, it is also true that imperialism caught the imagination of the European mind and responded to a popular thirst for the strange and exotic. The exploits of European explorers, recounted in best-selling travel books and the mass circulation press, provided excitement and entertainment. Scientists, missionaries, hunters, and mercenary adventurers poured into Africa and Asia in the late nineteenth century. Yet even the humanitarian instincts of the missionaries, intent on bringing Christianity and modern medicine to "savages," implied a conviction about the superiority of their own civilization. When the British writer Rudyard Kipling spoke of the "White Man's Burden," he reflected the view of many Europeans that the civilizing mission was a sacred duty of more advanced races. Imperialism was economically irrational and is perhaps best seen as a disease, highly contagious and reaching fever pitch in the last years of the nineteenth century, as a prelude to World War I.

Imperialism in Asia and Asian Responses

India, Ceylon, Burma, Malaya, Indochina, Indonesia, and the Philippines became outright colonies, and foreigners extorted special privileges in China, Japan, and Siam (Thailand). Much of traditional Asian culture survived (and remains) vigorous, most importantly not only the family system but also many, perhaps most, traditional values. At the same time, many Asian institutions were remade under Western influence or were augmented by new ones introduced by Westerners.

The arrogance as well as the success of Western imperialism was galling to most Asians, especially given their own cultural arrogance and pride in their ancient traditions of greatness. Western colonialism, and the unequal treaties forced on Siam, China, and Japan, stimulated a revival of the several national Asian traditions and an effort to make them relevant to a world dominated by the West and its standards. Thus in India there was the Hindu Renaissance and related movements to eliminate or restrict institutions now seen as "backward," such as sati and child marriage. There were similar movements in China against foot-binding, chaste widowhood, and concubinage and in Japan against premarital promiscuity, class-based restrictions on clothing, and more or less open pornography. Western imperialists looked down on all non-Westerners, a role reversal that was deeply disturbing to Asians. Now more than ever they needed to hold their heads up, convinced that to be Indian or Chinese or Japanese or Southeast Asian was something of which to be proud. Many persuaded themselves that while the West might be temporarily ahead in material things, the East was still superior spiritually and in the arts of civilization.

Rudyard Kipling caught the attitude of many Westerners in Asia in his poem "Mandalay":

> Ship me somewhere east of Suez, where the best is like the
> worst,
> Where there ain't no Ten Commandments, an' a man can
> raise a thirst.[1]

Westerners were often a law unto themselves, no longer bound by the mores of "home" and yet not part of Asian society and its mores. This was particularly true in the earlier period of adventurers, but such attitudes remained until the end of Asian colonialism. Most colonial officials, diplomats, and foreign merchants lived in Asia like kings, waited upon by innumerable servants in luxurious quarters and behaving often like "little tin gods," as they were called. It was an attractive life for many, especially by comparison with their circumstances or opportunities at home. Partly for this reason, but partly also because many of them found Asia fascinating, many Westerners developed a genuine attachment to the areas or cultures where they served, and to the people. Although Western (and later Japanese) racial arrogance became more and more prominent, "the call of the East" as Westerners labeled it, was strong, even for the common soldier, as Kipling says in "Mandalay":

> If you've 'eard the East a-callin'
> You won't never heed naught else,
> No you won't heed nothin' else,
> But them spicy garlic smells
> An' the sunshine and the palm trees
> An' the tinkly temple bells,
> On the road to Mandalay . . .
> Tho I walks with fifty housemaids
> Outa Chelsea to the Strand
> An' they talk a lot o' lovin'
> But what do they understand?
> Beefy face and grubby 'and—
> Lord what do they understand?
> I've a neater, sweeter maiden
> In a cleaner, greener land,
> On the road to Mandalay . . .

Industrialization was in time vigorously pursued, first in India, then in Japan, and finally in China, all by Asians as well as by Westerners, although such developments lagged in Southeast Asia. At least as important as technological change were the commercial and industrial institutions from the nineteenth-century West such as banking and joint-stock companies, which changed the face of Asia and ultimately helped to destroy colonialism. More important was the growing sense of national identity, which counterposed itself to the colonial masters. The great Asian empires and states of the past were cultural and bureaucratic structures different from the nation-states of modern Europe, whose national coherence and drive Asians rightly saw as a source of strength that they lacked but that they must have if they were again to be masters in their own houses.

British Imperial India

A divided and weakened India had progressively fallen under the domination of the English East India Company, as described in Chapter 14, and by 1857 most of it was being administered, directly or indirectly, as a unit. Most Indians exposed to or educated in it admired the new British model of order and Western-style progress, but in the longer run the experience of a people politically united for the first time and yet being treated as second-class citizens in their own country led to the emergence of Indian nationalism. The Rebellion (mutiny) of 1857 by some Indian troops was not yet a war of independence and involved only a tiny fraction of the population, but it marked the beginnings of Indian response to a foreign control now increasingly tinged with arrogance. The efforts of traditional conservatives to regain their lost position, in alliance with some rebellious troops, attracted little support from other Indians, most of whom still saw British rule as more desirable than any Indian alternatives then available, and certainly more so than a restoration of the Mughals. In the aftermath of the revolt's suppression, the English East India Company was dissolved, and the government in London was made both the real and the official sovereign. The revolt marks a watershed between the earlier stages of gradual colonialism under the Company, which saw considerable cultural and racial mixing, and the ascendancy of full-blown imperialism. British victory heightened the racism and arrogance that had begun to grow earlier, and such attitudes destroyed the chance that a genuine partnership with Indians might emerge.

Later in the nineteenth century and still more in the twentieth, many Indians joined the colonial civil service and in time filled a wide range of responsible positions in all fields, but the earlier honeymoon was largely over. To mark the change from Company rule to direct British government rule, Queen Victoria adopted the title "empress of India" in 1877. She took a special interest in her new dominions, which her prime minister, Benjamin Disraeli, called "the brightest jewel in the crown," and is said to have prayed nightly for her Indian subjects. Although she never went there, she was revered by millions of Indians as their own empress, accepted as part of the long Indian imperial tradition, and her picture was widely displayed.

The British were careful not to displace any more of the remaining Indian rulers of the "Princely States" or to take over any more territory, a policy held to until Indian independence in 1947. British residents were placed in each of the hundreds of small and a few large Indian-ruled states, but intervention or threats were rarely needed to keep the roughly half of India still formally in native hands in line with British policy. The army remained largely Indian, but the proportion of British officers and troops was increased. Military service and pride in their regiments became an attractive career for Sikhs, Rajputs, Gurkhas (from Nepal), and other Indians.

Modern Growth

The opening of the Suez Canal in 1869, the shift to steam navigation, and the rapid spread of railways brought India much closer to Europe, greatly accelerating the commercialization of the economy. India was now under far closer imperial control, and the Suez link tightened Britain's grip on its leading position throughout Asia. By the end of the century India had by far the largest rail network (25,000 miles) in all of Asia, on a par with many European countries although on a much bigger scale. British women could now join their husbands more easily in India, roughly two weeks from England by steamship via Suez on the ships of the Peninsular and Oriental Line (the P. and O.), and raise their families there, thus, creating another wedge of separation between the races and cultures. In each city or town colonial social life centered in the buildings and grounds of the British Club from which Indians were excluded.

Meanwhile, Indians who were quick to respond to new economic opportunities increased their role in commerce and began the industrialization of their country, first in machine-made textiles in Bombay and Calcutta and then in a widening range of other manufacturing. Railways speeded up such changes and stimulated the growing commercialization of agriculture, especially in industrial crops like jute, cotton, indigo, and new plantation production of tea, grown mainly in the rainy hills of Assam, which captured most of the world market. New irrigation projects, especially in the semiarid Punjab and the Indus Valley, opened new and productive farming areas to feed India's booming cities and increased output elsewhere. By 1900 India had the world's largest irrigation system.

Calcutta remained the largest city, closely followed by Bombay and then by Madras. Bombay, with its magnificent harbor and its closeness to cotton areas in Gujarat and Maharashtra, became the premier port and the chief center of Indian-owned textile manufacturing. These had all been founded as colonial ports, but large new industrial cities also arose inland as the railway linked most of the country in a single market: Ahmadabad in Gujarat, Lucknow, Kanpur, and Allahabad in the central Ganges, Salem and Coimbatore in the south, and many more. Karachi grew as the export center for irrigated cotton and wheat from the Indus Valley. British industrial and commercial investors, managers, and traders made money and sold goods in this vast new market, but Indians became increasingly prominent in the growing modern sector. Indians also entered and in time dominated the new Western-style professions such as law, medicine, and education. By 1900 India had the world's fourth-largest textile industry, and by 1920 the biggest steel plant in the British Empire; both, like many other industries were owned and managed largely by Indians.

The White Man's Burden

Rudyard Kipling, sometimes called "the bard of imperialism" wrote "The White Man's Burden" in 1899 for the Americans on the occasion of their conquest of the Philippines. It was widely quoted to justify imperialism's "civilizing mission."

Take up the White Man's burden,
Send forth the best ye breed;
Go bind your sons to exile
To serve your captives' need,
To wait in heavy harness
On fluttered folk and wild,
Your new-caught sullen peoples,
Half devil and half child.

Take up the White Man's burden
In Patience to abide,
To veil the threat of terror
And check the show of pride;
By open speech and simple
A hundred times made plain,
To seek another's profit
And work another's gain.

Take up the White Man's burden,
End savage wars, bring peace;
Fill full the mouth of famine
And bid the sickness cease.
And when your goal is nearest,
The end for others sought,
Watch sloth and heathen folly
Bring all you hope to naught.

Take up the White Man's burden,
Not tawdry rule of kings,
But toil of serf and sweeper,
A tale of common things:
The roads ye shall not tread—
The ports ye shall not enter,
Go make them with your living
And mark them with your dead.

Take up the White Man's burden
And reap his old reward:
The blame of those ye better,
The hate of those ye guard,
The cry of hosts ye humour
So slowly toward the light:
"Why brought ye us from bondage,
Our loved Egyptian night?"

Take up the White Man's burden,
Have done with childish days,
The lightly proffered laurel,
The easy ungrudged praise.
Come now and search your manhood
Through all the thankless years,
Cold, edged with dear-bought wisdom,
The judgement of your peers.

Source: Rudyard Kipling's Verses (New York: Doubleday, 1943), pp. 321–323.

The Colonial System

The British saw themselves as the bringers of order and "civilization" to India, as to the other parts of their empire, a role that many of them likened to that of the Romans 2,000 years earlier in Europe. Britain was the greatest power in the world from the mid-eighteenth century to the early twentieth. It was also the original home of industrialization, railways, and many modern political and commercial institutions. All this bred an understandable pride and a sense of greatness. Britons were fond of saying that the sun never set on the British Empire, since it stretched almost around the entire globe. Indians, they believed, should be grateful to be included, and indeed many were.

British-style education, in English, continued to shape most Indian intellectuals and literate people to a large degree in the British image. The law of British India, based on English common law, was practiced overwhelmingly by Indians themselves, and most of the teachers, engineers, physicians, lower-level administrators, writers, and journalists were Indian.

The prestigious Indian Civil Service (ICS), staffed until the twentieth century almost entirely by Britons trained in Indian affairs, long remained an exclusive supervisory group under the viceroy, the effective head of state in India appointed by London. The ICS was referred to proudly as the "steel framework" whose roughly 900 members ensured the smooth operation of the colonial government. But despite undoubted achievements, given such small numbers, in the generally even-handed administration of justice and the promotion of irrigation, agriculture, public health, education, and transportation, most Indians remained poor, illiterate, and powerless. Occasional regional famine continued, as in China. Tenancy and landlessness grew

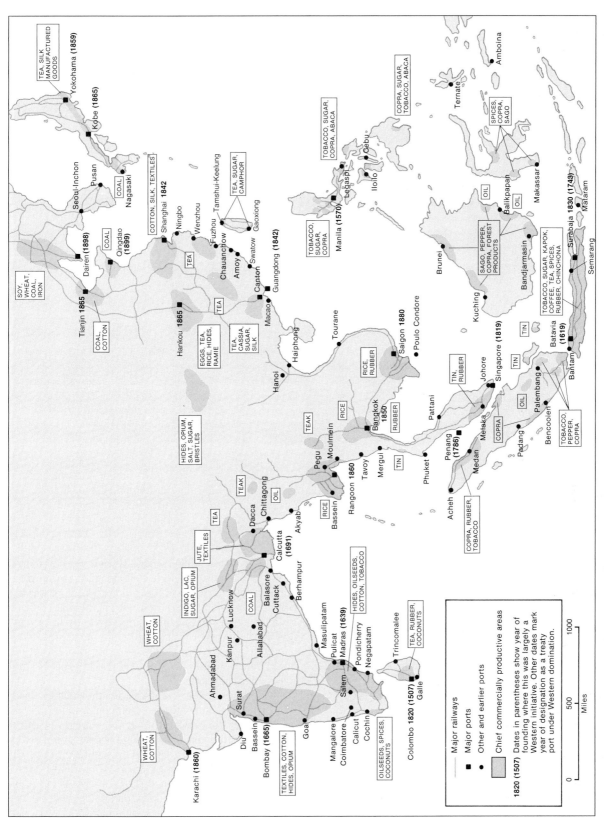

TEA, SILK MANUFACTURED GOODS — Yokohama (1859)
Kōbe (1865)
Seoul-Inchon
Pusan
COAL — Nagasaki
COTTON, SILK, TEXTILES — Shanghai **1842**
Ningbo
Wenzhou
Fuzhou Tamshui-Keelung
Chauanchow Gaoxiong
Amoy Swatow
TEA, SUGAR, CAMPHOR
Canton
Guangdong (**1842**)
Macao
TEA
Dairen (**1898**) COAL
Qingdao (**1899**)
SOY, WHEAT, COAL, IRON
Tianjin **1865** COAL
COAL, COTTON
Hankou **1865**
EGGS, TEA, RICE, HIDES, RAMIE
TEA, CASSIA, SUGAR, SILK
TEA
Hong Kong Haiphong
Hanoi
Tourane
RICE, RUBBER Saigon **1880**
Poulo Condore
HIDES, OPIUM, SALT, SUGAR, BRISTLES
TEAK Moulmein RICE
Pegu RICE
Bangkok **1850** RUBBER
TEAK
TEA Dacca
Chittagong OIL
Akyab RICE
Bassein Rangoon **1860**
Tavoy Mergui TIN
Phuket Pattani TIN, RUBBER
JUTE, TEXTILES
Calcutta (**1691**)
INDIGO, LAC, SUGAR, OPIUM
Berhampur
Balasore Cuttack
Lucknow COAL
Kanpur Allahabad
WHEAT, COTTON
Masulipatam
Pulicat
Madras (**1639**)
Pondicherry Negapatam
HIDES, OILSEEDS, COTTON, TOBACCO
Trincomalee
TEA, RUBBER, COCONUTS
Salem
Ahmadabad
Surat Goa
Bassein Mangalore Calicut Cochin
Diu Coimbatore
Colombo **1820** (**1507**) Galle
WHEAT, COTTON
Karachi (**1860**)
TEXTILES, COTTON, HIDES, OPIUM
OILSEEDS, SPICES, COCONUTS

TOBACCO, SUGAR, COPRA, ABACA Ternate
Legaspi Cebu
Iloilo
Manila (**1570**)
TOBACCO, SUGAR, COPRA
Amboina
SPICES, COPRA, SAGO
Brunei
OIL Balikpapan OIL Makassar
Surabaia **1830** (**1749**) Mataram
Semarang
SAGO, PEPPER, COPRA, FOREST PRODUCTS
Bandjarmasin
Kuching
TOBACCO, SUGAR, KAPOK, COFFEE, TEA, SPICES, RUBBER, CHINCHONA
Batavia (**1619**)
Bantam
Palembang OIL
Bencoolen
Johore TIN
Singapore (**1819**) TIN
COPRA Melaka
Medan Padang
Penang (**1786**)
Acheh
COPRA, RUBBER, TOBACCO
TOBACCO, PEPPER, COPRA

Major Ports and Commercially Productive Areas in East Asia, 1600–1940
Note the clustering of commercially productive areas in the hinterlands of the major ports, effectively drained by railways.

Legend:
— Major railways
■ Major ports
● Other and earlier ports
Chief commercially productive areas
1820 (**1507**) Dates in parentheses show year of founding where this was largely a Western initiative. Other dates mark year of designation as a treaty port under Western domination.

0   500   1000 Miles

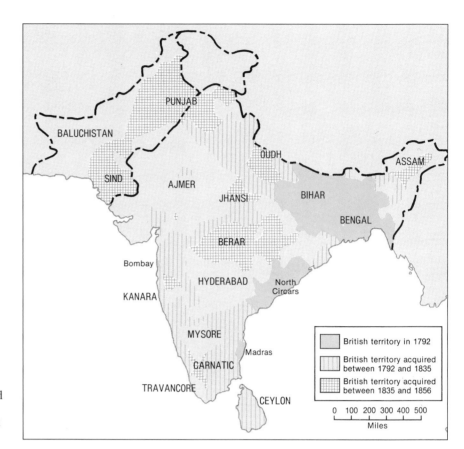

Growth of the British Empire in India

Starting with Bengal (then a larger area) in 1757, British control spread to engulf the whole of the subcontinent, including Ceylon (Sri Lanka).

with increasing commercialization of agriculture, and industrial growth, largely an Indian enterprise, was far too slow to absorb or produce adequately for the still-rising population.

The increase in numbers was in itself a sign that the colonial system was accompanied by greater economic opportunity. From 1800, a convenient date for the beginnings of British rule, to independence in 1947, the total population at least doubled, although that is a very modest rate of growth. One of the colonial government's outstanding achievements was the establishment of an efficient modern census, but the count did not become reasonably complete until 1881, after which it showed more or less continuous growth and a falling death rate. But overall economic growth was probably little greater and was in any case unbalanced. There was little margin for improved living standards, although some groups rose to wealth while others sank deeper into poverty. India remained poor because it was poor to begin with after the extravagances, exploitation, and collapse of the Mughals, who had left it torn and bleeding. Industrialization and commercialization impoverished some groups and benefited others, as happened in the West too, but overall their net impact on the Indian economy was to create more jobs and more productivity.

The major criticism of colonial rule in India is that it did not do enough. The government was chronically pinched for funds, and London insisted that all expenses, including the army, must be covered from Indian revenues. The colonial government was reluctant to extract more revenue from a still overwhelmingly peasant population; the army took much of it, and there was little to spare. While private British entrepreneurs, and many Indians, did well economically, the government barely broke even or lost money. Planning was difficult, and problems were met with inadequate ad hoc solutions. Reformers accused the government of playing the role of night watchman while most Indians remained in poverty. But despite growing racial discrimination, most Indians saw no preferable alternative until the twentieth century.

It would have been impossible for the relative handful of British to control the subcontinent and its 350 million people by the 1930s without the support or active help of most Indians. The British officer contingent in the Indian army reached 40,000 only in the special circumstances of World Wars I and II. Total British members of all levels and branches of the civil service, including district officers, judges, and police, were never more than 12,000. In short, colonial India was run

Social life in the hill stations: a fete at Simla, in a glade nostalgically named "Annandale," painted by A. E. Scott, c. 1845. (By permission of the British Library)

mainly by Indians, who until late in the day willingly supported the British raj (government). By 1910, for example, the police force comprised about 5,000 Britons and over 600,000 Indians. The rest of the civil service employed also about 600,000 Indians with only some 5,000 Britons, and the army consisted of 150,000 native troops and approximately 25,000 British officers.

The higher echelons of government remained a British preserve, and almost as if to show their degree of detachment from the country they ruled, they governed in the blazing hot months of summer from hill stations in the Himalayan foothills, first at Darjeeling in northernmost Bengal, and later from Simla, north of Delhi. From both they enjoyed spectacular views of the snow-covered mountains, the cool, bracing air, Western-style lodges and cottages that reminded them of home, and a round of parties, picnics, and receptions. As more of the British in India were expected to marry, young women came or were sent out to India to find husbands, an annual migration at the beginning of the cool weather in autumn irreverently referred to as "the arrival of the fishing fleet." Those who remained unspoken for by the time the hot weather arrived in mid-March, after a long round of introductions, receptions, and dances, often went back to England as "returned empties."

As the British community grew, many families had lived in India for several generations and thought of it as home. They called themselves Anglo-Indians, and lived, except for the top officials in summer, in separate residential areas built for them some distance from the Indian town where they worked. These areas were known as "civil lines" or sometimes as "cantonments," since many of them had begun as quarters for troops or garrisons. Each household was waited on by clouds of Indian servants. Another group was also known as Anglo-Indians; these were the descendants of British-Indian marriages that were common in the eighteenth and early nineteenth centuries and still occasionally took place in later years. They were an unfortunate group, rejected by both the Indian and British communities but usually trying to "pass" as English and talking wistfully of "home," meaning an England that most of them never saw. Many of them became Christians in an effort to upgrade their status, as did many Untouchables, who had the same motives. Missionary efforts made few converts otherwise; many Indians believed that they had themselves invented religion and needed no help, but in any case the religious ground was already fully occupied. However, mission schools remained an important means to Western education for many non-Christians as well as for the few faithful.

A CLOSER LOOK

New Delhi: Indian Summer of the Raj

Calcutta had long seemed inappropriate as the capital of a British India that had expanded to cover the subcontinent, thousands of miles from Bengal. Although a thoroughly Indian city, it had been an alien foundation with no previous indigenous roots, and like all ports it faced outward to the sea rather than inward. As the colonial capital, it emphasized the foreignness of

British rule. For several years after 1900 various alternative capital sites were considered, and Delhi won out. Although it was hardly central and was awkwardly far from the south, the logic of past empires, including the Mughals, whose capital it had been for many centuries, was too strong. At the head of the Ganges Valley, Delhi controlled routes east and south to the heart of India, at a defensible crossing place over the Jumna River (a Ganges tributary) where hills stretched to the southwest, funneling passage through Delhi. Successive invaders had to hold Delhi first, mounting their campaigns and ruling their empires from there. At the height of its power and pride, in 1911, the British raj moved to Delhi to put itself in line with the Indian imperial tradition, a symbolic effort to legitimate its rule.

Delhi was at least a major rail and road hub and much closer to India's center of population and economic activity than to its geographical center. It was decided to build a new planned city as an imperial statement, adjacent to the old city and with open space around it but still well within sight of Shah Jahan's Red Fort. The remains of other imperial Delhis of the past also showed on the skyline. An artificial hill was built as the setting for the monumental residence and gardens of the viceroy, flanked on each side by two large and stately government buildings known as the Secretariat. From this low rise, broad boulevards and wide vistas led to other buildings and monuments to empire, including the neoclassic parliament house, which by the 1920s was filled with mainly Indian members.

Like Paris and Washington, New Delhi was planned before the age of mass transit and the automobile. It was built in a star-shaped pattern with broad, tree-lined streets intersecting at angles and punctuated by circles of green around which traffic had to move. The plan included a large, separate commercial and shopping district, with buildings in neoclassical and Anglo-Indian styles, grouped around its own immense circle still called Connaught Circus (like Piccadilly Circus in London), with related enterprises along all the streets leading into it at various angles. Pleasant, shaded avenues with British names occupied most of the rest of the new planned city, most of them filled with gracious residences and beautiful gardens for civil servants, Indian princes (most of whom maintained extensive establishments in New Delhi), and other members of the upper classes. Workers and servants commuted the mile or so from Old Delhi, mainly by bicycle, or were housed in the unplanned developments that soon grew around the edges of New Delhi.

The ambitious building plans of 1911 and 1912 were greatly delayed by the disruptions of World War I, but by 1930 the new imperial capital was complete. The architects of New Delhi were of course British, but they made a generally successful effort to combine Western and Indian monumental and imperial traditions, consciously using the same red sandstone of which the Red Fort had been built and creating buildings that fit their Indian setting and role far better than the earlier Victorian extravaganzas in Calcutta and Bombay. Old Delhi remains a traditional Indian city, grouped around the Red Fort and including a confusing maze of tiny streets and alleys in the bazaar near Shah Jahan's great mosque, the Jama Masjid. The large, unbuilt area in front of the Red Fort remains a vast open-air market and a frequent scene of political rallies.

New Delhi became almost automatically the capital of independent India, with no sense of inappropriateness for the world's largest parliamentary democracy. Since independence Delhi has become a major industrial center as well. But Old and New Delhi represent different strands in India's varied past and now also show the two faces of contemporary India, traditional and modern.

An example of colonial architecture in India: Victoria Station in Bombay, with a statue of Queen Victoria on the top of its dome. (R. Murphey)

 An Indian View
of the British

The British raj was slow to admit Indians to power but did not lack Indian admirers never-theless. Here is a sample of Bengali opinion in the 1860s and 1870s, written originally in English.

Day by day is the dominion of mind extending over matter, and the secrets of nature are brought to the light to evolve the powers of the soil and make nations depend on their own resources. The railway turns the courses of men, merchandise, and mind all into new channels.

Progress is the law of God, and cannot be arrested by the puny efforts of man. As knowledge is acquired, facts accumulate and generalization is practiced; skepticism arises and engenders a spirit of inquiry, resulting in the triumph of truth. The final cause of the advent of the English in India is to forward the progress of mankind toward perfection. They are the destined instrument in the hand of Providence for this great work. . . . The march of civilization throughout the world is forward. . . . Progress is a necessary condition of creation, [and] the course of nature is perpetual development.

Source: R. Murphey, *The Outsiders: The Western Experience in India and China* (Ann Arbor: University of Michigan Press, 1977), p. 149.

The Rise of Indian Nationalism

British-educated Indians, including those successful in business or the professions, became increasingly resentful of the racial discrimination to which they were subject. Many began to ask themselves and their colonial masters whose country India was and demanded a larger role in its government. Gradually a movement for independence developed, encouraged by a great many Englishmen, at home and in India, who agreed with Indian critics that alien rule, without adequate Indian participation, was in fact contrary to the British tradition of representative government and political freedom. Gestures toward increasing the scope for Indians in the administration of civil service and the beginnings of elections for some officials and advisers came too slowly to satisfy either Indian or British critics.

The Indian National Congress, which was to become the core of the independence movement, was actually founded by an Englishman, Allan David Hume, in 1885. Indian political leaders made nationalist appeals to cultural pride in the great tradition of their country; among them were highly effective and articulate figures like M. G. Ranade (1842–1901), B. G. Tilak (1856–1920), G. K. Gokhale (1866–1915), and Motilal Nehru (1861–1931), the father of Jawaharlal Nehru (1889–1964), independent India's first prime minister. Their language, culture, and education were as much English as Indian, and they could speak convincingly of the "un-Britishness" of one-sided colonial rule of their country.

Meanwhile, paranoia about the still-expanding Russian empire in Central Asia prompted yet another disastrous invasion of Afghanistan in 1878 to install a British puppet on the throne of Kabul. The Afghan resisters finally murdered the British resident and his entire staff and military escort within a year; and guerrilla fighters stalemated the reinvasion and brutal retaliation until it was finally withdrawn in 1880 and the Afghans were again "permitted" to choose their own ruler. Opinion in Britain was outraged by both the brutality and the cost of this futile military adventure, and the Disraeli government in London fell as a result.

In addition to the three-stage conquest of Burma the government of India launched an armed reconnaissance to Lhasa, capital of Tibet, in 1903–1904, to forestall supposed Russian influence there. Russian influence proved to be illusory, but the mission showed the flag and obtained an agreement about the frontier.

While all this imperial posturing occupied the government, poverty in India remained largely unaddressed. There was severe economic distress in many areas and for many groups, which Indian nationalists now blamed on colonial rule. Boycotts of British imports were begun as a political weapon, cutting their value by a quarter between 1904 and 1908. The government's response was often repressive, including the jailing of many political leaders. There were still many British in government

The Amritsar Massacre of April 1919 was followed by further repression in the wake of new protests and demonstrations. Here British police officers in Amritsar watch while their Indian assistants search a demonstrator.
(Hulton/Archive/Getty Images)

with more liberal ideas, and many more outside government, who strove to reduce racial discrimination and urged Indian self-government as Britain's ultimate goal. In 1883, for example, it was agreed that Indian judges could preside over cases involving Europeans. But imperialist attitudes and bureaucratic inertia retarded the process of giving Indians a larger and more appropriate role in their own government.

Over 1 million Indian troops and noncombatants served the Allied effort in World War I in Europe and the Middle East, and many hoped that this would speed progress toward self-government. When change did not move fast enough after the war, civil disobedience movements spread, now led by Mahatma Gandhi (1869–1948) among others, only to be met by more government repression. In 1919, Indian troops under British command, called in to put down rioting in Amritsar near Lahore, fired on a peaceful and unarmed crowd celebrating a festival, leaving 400 dead. This massacre was a watershed in Anglo-Indian relations. It turned most Indians away from the idea of reform and toward the goal of full independence, creating almost overnight a greatly expanded nationalist movement. In 1907 Parliament in London had

declared that independence was Britain's objective in India. This was restated by the British government in 1917 and in 1921, but the colonial administration remained slow to move even toward full self-government. Although the electoral system was greatly widened in the 1920s and 1930s and Indian legislatures and officials were given far more power and responsibility, it was too little, too late. Time had run out for British rule in India.

One may wonder whether the imposition of British rule had ever been worth it, given its heavy costs. Imperial control was not needed for British goods to penetrate Indian markets. They managed fine elsewhere in Asia without such control, as they did in Europe and Latin America. India would have sold Britian her raw materials, and later her manufactured goods, as in world markets generally, without colonial control. Individual British merchants and companies profited from the Indian empire, but the British government lost substantially. Education and the system of law and courts were clear improvements of the raj, but they too might have been furthered without colonialism.

Colonial Regimes in Southeast Asia

 ### The British in Burma and Malaya

British interest in Southeast Asia, and their expulsion by the Dutch in the seventeenth century, was incidental to their concerns in India and their efforts to break into the China market. They first tried to found bases on the edges of Dutch power in Malaya and made a settlement at Penang on the northwest Malay coast in 1786, where they hoped to attract Chinese traders. This effort was only moderately successful, and they established what soon became their major Southeast Asian trade base at Singapore in 1819. They had taken over Melaka from the Dutch in 1795, symbolizing the new shift of power (as the Dutch capture of Melaka from the Portuguese had done in 1641), but its harbor was small and it no longer controlled trade through the straits. From the start, Singapore, with its large and excellent island-shielded harbor commanding the southern entrance to the straits, was a commercial center for all Southeast Asia and not just for Malaya, which remained largely undeveloped economically and thinly populated until the end of the nineteenth century.

Meanwhile, Burma was next door to India and under the rule of an antiquated monarchy that was nevertheless expanding westward. The Burmese king was too proud to deal with anyone, even the British, as an equal. His later successor conquered Arakan on Burma's west coast and again refused to deal with the British, who felt that Arakan was threateningly close to Bengal. It periodi-

Imperialist Arrogance

Winston Churchill as a young man served briefly as a newspaper correspondent and junior officer in the Boer War (1899–1902) against the Dutch settlers in South Africa. He also served briefly in the Indian Army. He early became a supporter of British imperialism and remained so all his life. According to him:

> The act [of colonial acquisition] is virtuous, the exercise invigorating, and the results often extremely profitable. . . . Besides, all the *vigorous* nations of the earth have sought and are seeking to conquer.

Missionary arrogance was apparent from the beginning of their effort in Asia. Here is a famous missionary hymn written by Reginald Heber, Anglican bishop of Calcutta, in 1819.

> From Greenland's icy mountains, from India's coral strand
> Where Africa's sunny fountains roll down their golden sand
> From many an ancient river, from many a palmy plain,
> They call us to deliver their land from error's chain.
>
> What though blow soft the breezes
> O'er Ceylon's spicy isle,
> Where every prospect pleases
> And only man is vile,
> In vain with lavish kindness
> The gifts of God are strewn;
> The heathen in his blindness
> Bows down to wood and stone.
>
> Can we whose souls are lighted with wisdom from on high,
> Can we to men benighted the lamp of life deny?
> Salvation, oh salvation! The joyful sound proclaim,
> Till each remotest nation has learnt Messiah's name.

Sources: W. Churchill, *The River War*, vol. 1 (London: Longman's Green, 1899), pp. 18–19; R. Heber, *Hymns Ancient and Modern* (Oxford, 1973, reprinted in Norwood, Mass: Plimpton Press, 1940), p. 254.

cally made difficulties for English merchants, appearing to flout British power. A brief war from 1824 to 1826 gave the East India Company special rights in the important coastal provinces of Burma and checked Burmese expansion. A treaty in 1826 ceded Arakan, Assam, and Tenasserim on the eastern borders of India to the British, gave them indemnity, and accepted a British Resident at the then capital at Ava, who shifted to Mandalay when the capital was moved there shortly thereafter.

Another war at British initiative, in 1852–1853, was followed by commercial treaties in 1861 and 1867, which included the British right to run steamers on the Irrawaddy. The new king, Mindon Min, in general a good ruler but tempted, like the contemporary kings of Siam, to try to play the British off against the French, signed a commercial treaty with the French in 1873. His successor, Thibaw, an old-style absolute monarch, continued to play "footsie" with the French, and in a two-week war in 1886, the British annexed all of Burma and exiled

Thibaw. Two more minor wars in 1852 and 1885–1886, largely provoked by the British, annexed both Lower Burma and the rest of the country. Burma was administered as a province of British India, with basically the same policies and results, until it was finally made a separate colony in 1937.

Burma and Malaya saw rapid commercialization after 1880 under British rule; railways were built and steam navigation was developed. The Irrawaddy delta in lower Burma, including much newly cultivated land, became a great exporter of rice, leading the world and yielding 75 percent of Burma's exports. Upper Burma produced timber, especially teak, and the central valley yielded oil from new wells drilled by the British. All these were exported from the port of Rangoon, which became a smaller-scale version of Calcutta and also served as the colonial capital. Rich deposits of tin were found in Malaya, a metal in great demand in the industrializing West, and toward the end of the century Malaya also became the world's major producer of plantation rubber. Labor for tin mining and rubber tapping had to be imported, since the local Malays, subsistence farmers, were not interested in such work. The gap was filled mainly by Chinese from overcrowded southern China, who soon became nearly half of the population of Malaya, including the colonial capital at Kuala Lumpur, originally a tin miners' camp.

In time many of these Chinese immigrants, who also entered the booming commercial economy of Singapore, became wealthy. Chinese dominated the money economy of Malaya, and there was growing resentment against them by Malays. Indians also came in, as laborers and as merchants, to the rapidly growing economies of Burma and Malaya. Chinese, Indians, and British dominated the commercial production and foreign trade of both countries. The colonial government, especially in Malaya where the locals had almost become a minority in their own country, tried to protect their culture and rights and ruled as much as possible through native sultans, but both countries were economically transformed under colonialism.

For most of the nineteenth century, Malaya was divided into the British-owned Straits Settlements: Penang, Melaka, and Singapore, founded in 1819, leaving the rest of Malaya in the hands of several local sultans, some with British residents. But in 1895 they formed what they called the Federated Malay States, incorporating the most important sultanates, mainly those on the tin- and rubber-producing west coast, under British control.

French, Dutch, and American Colonialism

Largely eliminated from India by the end of the eighteenth century, the French sought their own colonial sphere in Asia and used the persecution of French Catholic missionaries in Vietnam as a pretext for conquering the southern provinces in 1862, including the port of Saigon. Later they annexed Cambodia and Laos and, after defeating Chinese forces sent to protect their tributary state, took over northern Vietnam in 1885. Southern Vietnam also became a major exporter of rice and rubber grown in the delta of the Mekong River and exported through the chief port of Saigon, which was made the colonial capital. Cambodia and Laos remained little developed commercially. Northern Vietnam, the area around Hanoi, was already too densely populated on the Chinese model to have surpluses for export, but there was some small industrial growth there and in the northern port of Haiphong. The colonial administration tried to impose French culture on these territories, collectively called Indochina. Control was centralized in French

hands and traditional institutions were weakened. French rule was oppressive and often ruthless in squashing Vietnamese gestures toward political expression or participation, and was often brutal to workers. The army was augmented by special security forces and much of the apparatus of a police state, which executed, jailed, or drove into exile most Vietnamese leaders. These included the young Ho Chi Minh (1890–1969), later the head of the Vietnamese Communist party, who went to Europe in 1911 and later on to Moscow and Guangzhou.

The Dutch left most of Indonesia to native rulers until late in the nineteenth century, content with their control of trade from their major base at Batavia (now Jakarta), the colonial capital on the central island of Java. Tropical Java was richly productive of plantation crops promoted by the Dutch: sugar, coffee, tea, tobacco, and a variety of others. By the early 1900s, rubber production in Indonesia was second only to Malaya. Oil was also found and exploited. The discovery of more oil, as well as tin and prime land for rubber and tobacco, prompted the Dutch to increase their control first of Sumatra and then of the other islands of Borneo, Celebes (Sulawesi), the Moluccas, Bali, and the hundreds of smaller islands in the archipelago south of the Philippines. Tin and oil joined rubber as major exports, and new railways and ports were built to expedite trade.

Despite fierce resistance on some of the islands, especially in Sumatra, Dutch rule became absolute but never tried to penetrate effectively into the mountain and jungle interior of Borneo. The northern coast of Borneo was divided between British colonial administration and nominally independent sultanates run as private preserves by British entrepreneurs, the Brooke family. In time the Brooke empire included most of northern Borneo except for the tiny sultanate of Brunei, augmented in 1881 by the British North Borneo Company in Sabah. Dutch control outside Borneo became increasingly oppressive. Indonesians were excluded from participation in government and denied access to anything more than basic primary education or free expression. Protesters were jailed. Java was systematically exploited by forcing its peasants to grow export crops for Dutch profit. Production and population grew very rapidly, but living standards and quality of life declined.

In 1898 the United States won its war against Spain and acquired the Philippines as its first overseas colony. In the 43 years of American control, more impact was made on the culture and economy of the islands than in 400 years of Spanish rule. The new imperialists built roads, railroads, hospitals, and an education system up to the university level. Literacy and health levels became the highest in Asia after Japan. But the U. S. economic impact was exploitative. In partnership with rich Filipinos, it concentrated on growing commercial crops for export, especially sugar, and often neglected the basic needs of the people as a whole. Manila became a rapidly growing commercial center and colonial capital, and the chief base of the rising Filipino middle class and educated elite. The American colonists were more idealistic than the French or Dutch and saw their goal as conferring their own type of democracy on their new subjects.

To a degree this was successful, but Philippine politics were dominated by a small elite drawing support from those who profited from the American connection and paying little attention to the still predominantly rural and peasant population. The country had been subjugated only by a brutal war against Filipino nationalist resistance from 1899 to 1902 in which the Americans pursued policies that foreshadowed their later misadventures in Vietnam. In any case, free public education and free expression were not something most peasants were able to pursue. Nevertheless, the United States promised speedy independence and kept its promise in 1946, although on terms that diluted sovereignty economically and left huge American military bases in the Philippines.

Independent Siam

While the rest of Southeast Asia was being taken over by imperialist powers, the Thais kept their independence. Their country lay between the British in Burma and Malaya and the French in Indochina. Neither was willing to let the other dominate Siam. British preponderance in Thai foreign trade and investment was balanced by French annexation of Thai territory and claims in western Cambodia and Laos. British Malaya detached Siam's southern provinces. The Thais benefited from a series of shrewd and able kings who adroitly played the French off against the British and urged the advantages to both of leaving at least part of their country as a buffer state. They had to grant special trade, residence, and legal privileges to the colonialist powers, a system like that imposed on China, but there was no foreign effort to take over the government. Nevertheless the Thai economy developed along the same lines as colonial Southeast Asia, with a big new export trade in rice from the delta area in the valley of the Chao Praya, followed later by rubber, tin, and tropical hardwoods. Bangkok, the capital, grew rapidly as virtually the sole port for foreign trade and spreading commercialization. All of Southeast Asia was badly hurt by the world depression of the 1930s, since so much of its economy depended on exports to Western markets.

Overseas Chinese

Immigrant Chinese began to flood into all the commercially developed parts of Southeast Asia in growing numbers after 1870, as plantation and mining labor and as traders. They soon largely monopolized the retail trade in all the cities of Southeast Asia, although they shared it with immigrant Indians in Burma and Malaya. In Bangkok they became over half of the population and, as in Vietnam, controlled most of the large export trade in rice. They were understandably resented by Southeast Asians, especially since they also served as moneylenders and owned most of the shops. But they were often welcomed by the colonialists as useful labor and commercial agents. In Siam, unlike the rest of Southeast Asia, most Chinese were quickly assimilated into Thai society through intermarriage and acculturation. Elsewhere, Chinese immigrants tended to stick to their own culture and residential areas and were discriminated against by the local people. Altogether, Chinese settlers in Southeast Asia, almost all in the cities, totaled about 15 million by the outbreak of World War II.

China Besieged

The Opium War of 1839–1842 in which the British demolished the Chinese forces was ended by the Treaty of Nanjing, which granted to Britain most of its demands. Hong Kong was ceded outright and five mainland ports, including Shanghai and Guangzhou, were opened to British trade and residence. Other Western powers, including the United States, negotiated similar treaties the following year, including the provision of extraterritoriality whereby foreign nationals in China were immune from Chinese jurisdiction and were dealt with according to their own laws. The war had finally cracked China's proud isolation.

Foreign trade immediately began a rapid increase that continued until the world depression of the 1930s. Tea and silk remained the dominant exports and opium the main import, although it was overtaken after 1870 by cotton yarn, textiles, kerosene, and a variety of other foreign manufactured goods. The treaties further impinged on China's sovereignty by limiting import tariffs to 5 percent, opening the vast China market to Western goods. Although in fact China continued to provide for most of its own needs, and imports never became proportionately important, the "unequal treaties," as the Chinese nationalists later called them, reduced the country to semicolonial status. Beijing's reluctance to comply with these terms led to a second war from 1858 to 1860, when British and French troops captured Tianjin and Beijing and burned the imperial summer palace in retaliation for what they saw as Chinese "treachery." The Chinese had fired on British forces, imprisoned the representative sent to negotiate under a flag of truce, broken successive agreements to observe earlier treaties, and refused to receive an ambassador in Beijing. Lord Elgin, the commanding British general, said

Opium

The imperial commissioner, Lin Zexu, sent to Guangzhou in 1839 to stop the opium trade, wrote a letter in the same year to the young Queen Victoria that read in part as follows:

> Magnificently our great Emperor soothes and pacifies China and the foreign countries. . . . But there appear among the crowd of barbarians both good and bad persons, unevenly. . . . There are barbarian ships that come here for trade to make a great profit. But by what right do they in return use the poisonous drug [opium] to injure the Chinese people? . . . Of all China's exports to foreign countries, there is not a single thing which is not beneficial. . . . On the other hand, articles coming from outside China can only be used as toys; they are not needed by China. Nevertheless, our Celestial Court lets tea, silk, and other goods be shipped without limit. This is for no other reason than to share the benefit with the people of the whole world.

Source: S. Y. Teng and J. K. Fairbank, *China's Response to the West* (Cambridge: Harvard University Press, 1963), pp. 24–26.

he had no wish to harm the Chinese people but chose instead to burn the summer palace as a symbol of Qing government elitism and arrogance.

Traders and Missionaries

The Treaty of Tianjin, which ended the second war, opened still more ports to residence and trade and allowed foreigners, including missionaries, free movement and enterprise anywhere in the country. Missionaries, the largest number of them Americans, often served as a forward wave for imperialism, building churches and preaching the gospel in the interior and then demanding protection from their home governments against Chinese protest or riots. Trouble encountered by missionaries or foreign traders might be answered by sending a gunboat to the nearest coastal or river port to threaten or shell the inhabitants, a practice known as "gunboat diplomacy." When missionaries or their converts were killed by angry antiforeign mobs, Western governments often used this as a pretext for extracting still more concessions from the weakening Qing regime. Most Chinese were not interested in the Christian message, especially in the evangelical and intolerant form of most mission preaching, and resented foreigners with special privileges and protection encroaching on their country. They did not understand the missionary practice of buying or adopting orphans for charitable and religious purposes and assumed the worst of these strange barbarians. Stories circulated that missionaries ate babies or gouged out their eyes for medicine.

In 1870 a mob destroyed a French Catholic mission in Tianjin and killed 10 nuns and 11 other foreigners; gun-

boats and heavy reparations followed. Unlike the British, the French had no important trade with China and often used protection of their missionaries as a means of increasing their influence. In 1883 they went to war with China over Vietnam when Chinese troops crossed the border to eject them. The French destroyed part of the brand new Western-style Chinese navy and the dockyards at Fuzhou on the south China coast, which they had earlier helped to build. China was humbled again.

The Taiping Rebellion

Meanwhile, the greatest of all uprisings against the Qing governments, the Taiping Rebellion, erupted in 1850. Westerners tend to overemphasize their own role in China as the major influence on events after 1840. China was huge, Westerners were few, and their activities were sharply limited to the tiny dots of the treaty ports and outlying mission stations. China continued to respond primarily to its own long-standing internal problems, most importantly a population that had now long outgrown production and was falling into poverty and distress in many areas. The Taiping leader, Hong Xiuquan, was a frustrated scholar who had failed the rigid imperial examinations several times and then adopted a strange version of Christianity picked up from missionaries. He had religious visions in which he saw himself as the younger brother of Jesus Christ. Hong became the head of a largely peasant group from the poor mountainous areas of south China, which had been excluded from the new commercial opportunities in the treaty ports. The rebels, now armed with a "Christian" ideology, were devoted to the overthrow of the Manchus as

Through Each Other's Eyes

After the Opium War, foreign arrogance increased. Here is a sample from 1858.

> It is impossible that our merchants and missionaries can course up and down the inland waters of this great region and traffic in their cities and preach in their villages without wearing away at the crust of the Chinaman's stoical and skeptical conceit. The whole present system in China is a hollow thing, with a hard brittle surface. . . . Some day a happy blow will shiver it [and] it will all go together.

But the Chinese returned the compliment.

> It is monstrous in barbarians to attempt to improve the inhabitants of the Celestial Empire when they are so miserably deficient themselves. Thus, introducing a poisonous drug for their own benefit and to the injury of others, they are deficient in benevolence. Sending their fleets and armies to rob other nations, they can make no pretense to rectitude. . . . How can they expect to renovate others? They allow the rich and noble to enter office without passing through any literary examinations, and do not open the road to advancement to the poorest and meanest in the land. From this it appears that foreigners are inferior to the Chinese and therefore must be unfit to instruct them.

Sources: G. W. Cooke, *China: Being the Times Special Correspondence from China in the Years 1857–58* (London: Routledge, 1858), p. v; "A Chinese Tract of the Mid-Nineteenth Century," in E. P. Boardman, *Christian Influence on the Ideology of the Taiping Rebellion* (Madison: University of Wisconsin Press, 1952), p. 129.

an alien dynasty of conquest. They picked up massive support as they moved north and captured Nanjing in 1853. A northern expedition from there was turned back later that year near Tianjin, but their forces won at least a foothold in sixteen of China's eighteen provinces and dominated the rich Yangzi Valley.

Taiping efforts at government were relatively feeble, but their system was primarily a traditional Chinese one. Factions grew among the Taiping leadership, and the court at Nanjing was disorganized and increasingly given over to riotous living. Large-scale fighting against the imperial forces continued nevertheless without significant breaks until, in 1864, it was finally suppressed with horrendous destruction and loss of life. As many as 40 million people died as a result of the Taiping Rebellion, and much of the productive lower Yangzi region was laid waste. During the same period, the Qing also managed finally to put down three other mass uprisings, in the north, the southwest, and the northwest, the last two mainly Muslim rebellions against Qing rule that were not finally defeated until 1873. As one Qing official pointed out, these several revolts were a disease of China's vital organs, while the Western barbarians were a marginal affliction only of the extremities.

Attempts at Reform

One foreign power was still advancing by land: the Russians. Sensing China's weakness and internal problems, they penetrated the Amur Valley in northern Manchuria from which they had been excluded by the Treaty of Nerchinsk in 1689. In the treaties following the war of 1858–1860 the Russians detached the maritime provinces of eastern Manchuria and added them to their empire, including the port of Vladivostok, which they had earlier founded on the Pacific coast. Muslim rebellion in the northwest after 1862 led to Russian intervention in northern Xinjiang just across their own border, and their support of rebel Muslim leaders. The Qing government decided that this threat must be met head-on, raised an army under a highly effective general, marched it 2,500 miles from its base in eastern China, and, to everyone's surprise, defeated both the rebels and the Russians by 1878.

Suppression of the Taiping and other rebellions showed that even in its last decades the Qing were still capable of successful action. They still refused to accept or deal with foreigners as equals, but they had learned that adopting foreign military technology was essential if they were to defend themselves at all. After 1860 they began what they called "self-strengthening," including the establishment of new Western-style arsenals, gun foundries, and shipyards. These and other efforts to modernize were handicapped by government red tape and cross-purposes, but they made some slow progress. Several outstanding senior officials who realized the need for some changes and more effective management rose to power, helped by the victories over the rebels and the now-undeniable threat posed by foreigners. For a decade or two, the Qing seemed to have a new lease on life and to show surprising vigor.

Unfortunately, it was not to last; nor were the reforms ever fundamental enough to be equal to China's problems. They never won full support from the arch-conservative throne or from most of the people. Both remained basically antiforeign and opposed adopting barbarian ways even to fight barbarians. In 1862 a weak boy emperor came to the throne, dominated by his scheming mother, Cixi, originally an imperial concubine who plotted her way to the top. When the emperor died in 1875 at age 19 (many said he was poisoned by his mother), Cixi put her 4-year-old nephew in his place, retaining all real power for herself as the empress dowager until her death in 1908. She was clever and politically masterful, but narrow-minded and deeply conservative, the opposite of the leadership China so badly needed. She had no understanding of what China required to enable it to deal successfully with foreign powers, whom she continued to see as unruly and hateful barbarians. China's first tentative efforts at change were thus mainly aborted. The Confucian reactionaries, who now again dominated the government with few exceptions, grudgingly acknowledged that the barbarians had a few tricks (weapons) that China might find useful, but there could be no thought of abandoning or even altering traditional Chinese culture or view of the world.

Treaty Ports and Mission Schools

Meanwhile the treaty ports, which numbered over 100 by 1910, grew rapidly, attracting Chinese as merchants, partners, and laborers. Shanghai became the largest treaty port, as well as China's biggest city, followed in size by Tianjin, Nanjing, Hankou, and Guangzhou, respectively. Among major cities, only Beijing remained outside the treaty-port system, but it too was dominated by the foreign presence and foreign privilege. These Western-dominated cities, although foreign residents were a relative handful in number, were an example of Euro-American-style "progress." Manufacturing also began to grow in the treaty ports and increased especially rapidly after 1895 when the Japanese, who had defeated China in a war over the status of Korea, imposed

A powerful and unscrupulous ruler, the empress dowager Cixi (1835–1908), in keeping with the degeneracy of the late Qing period, favored an overornate style for decorating many rooms in the imperial palace in Beijing. It is perhaps no more so than late Victorian styles in the West. (Tzu-hsi, Empress Dowager of China, 1835–1908, Photographs Freer Gallery of Art and Arthur M. Sackler Gallery Archives Smithsonian Institution, Photographer: Hsun-ling)

a new treaty that permitted foreign-owned factories in the ports, producing mainly textiles and other consumer goods. This was the real beginning of modern industrialization in China and was soon joined by Chinese entrepreneurs and industrialists, including many who had been blocked or discouraged by the conservative government until they entered the more enterprising world of the treaty ports.

As elsewhere in Asia, however, imperialist arrogance was growing, and Chinese found that they were excluded from foreign clubs and parks and treated as second-class citizens. Given their ancient cultural pride, this was a bitter pill, but it fed the first stirring of modern Chinese nationalism and a determination to purge China of its century of humiliation. Such sentiments as yet affected only the few who lived in the treaty ports or encountered missionaries, and by no means all of them. Many treaty-port Chinese, like their Indian parallels in colonial Calcutta and Bombay, saw the Western way as the best for China and followed it increasingly in their own lives and careers.

But they were the tiniest fraction of the Chinese people. Most Chinese never saw a foreigner, and most of those who did still dismissed them as weird barbarians.

More influential than the treaty ports and their Western economic systems were the missionaries. The total of Chinese Christians remained discouragingly small, probably about 1 million at most, out of a total population of some 450 million by 1910. Most of them attended church for handouts rather than from sincere religious faith—"rice Christians" as they were called. But many of the missions saw that education and medical help were more attractive than Christian doctrine and might be a better path to the goal of conversion. Mission-run schools and hospitals spread rapidly. The schools drew many, in time most, of the young Chinese who wanted to study English and Western learning or science. They also got exposure to Christianity, but most graduates did not become converts, although they adopted Western ways of thinking in many respects, and Western-style nationalism as a source of the strength that China lacked. Most twentieth-century Chinese nationalists were influenced by mission schools, and most of China's universities before 1949 were founded by missionaries.

New government schools that included Western learning were also established, and in 1905, to mark the passing of an era, the traditional examination system was abolished. Missionaries and others translated a wide range of Western works, which were avidly read by the new generation of Chinese intellectuals. Many of them began to press for radical change and for the overthrow of the Qing. Ironically, they had to use the treaty ports, notably Shanghai, as their base, where they were protected from Qing repression by living under foreign law. It was in the treaty ports, which were both an irritating humiliation and an instructive model, that the first stirrings of revolution began.

The Boxer Rebellion

Missionaries in rural areas continued to provoke antiforeign riots as their activities spread. In the late 1890s, the empress dowager adroitly turned an anti-Qing group of impoverished bandits and rebels in Shandong Province against a different target—missionaries, and ultimately all foreigners, who were to be killed or driven into the sea. By early 1900 this group, known to foreigners as the Boxers (a crude translation of their name for themselves, "the fists of righteous harmony"), went on a rampage, burning mission establishments and killing missionaries and Chinese converts. Converts had always been resented because they often used foreign help, and sometimes gunboat diplomacy, to intervene in their disputes with other Chinese. The imperial court not only favored the Boxers but saw them as the final solution to the barbarian question. By June 1900, with covert imperial support, they besieged the foreign legations in Beijing, which barely held

out until relieved by a multinational expedition in mid-August. Having earlier declared war officially against all the foreign powers, the court fled to Xi'an.

After brutal reprisals, the foreigners (now including a large Japanese contingent) withdrew, and a peace was patched up a year later. China was saddled with a staggering indemnity on top of the one already extracted by Japan in 1895, but leaving the empress dowager and her reactionary councillors still in power. The Qing dynasty was almost dead, but no workable alternative was to emerge for many more years. China had still to learn the lessons of national unity and shared political purpose, which had been unnecessary in the past when the empire controlled "all under Heaven" and China had no rivals. The government finally fell in 1911, more from its own weight and incompetence than because of the small, weak, and disorganized group of revolutionaries whose mistimed uprising was joined by disgruntled troops. The fall of the Qing was hardly a revolution, but it ended the dynastic rule by which China had been governed for more than 2,000 years and opened the way for fundamental change in the years ahead.

Japan Among the Powers

Directed Change

In contrast to China, the Meiji Restoration in Japan, which replaced the Tokugawa rule in 1868, ushered in a period of rapid change and Westernization. The Tokugawa feudal order had long been undermined by the rise of merchants and by the growing restlessness of the outer daimyo, who were also incensed at Tokugawa weakness in the face of the foreign challenge. "Restoration" of the emperor was made a patriotic rallying cry against the decaying Tokugawa shogunate (see Chapter 13). Meiji was the reign title of the young emperor, who now moved to Tokyo ("eastern capital") as the restored head of state, although his role remained formal and symbolic only. He and his successors, though they were largely figureheads, served as a focus for new nationalist sentiment and most Japanese took inspiration from the fact that their country was once again formally under imperial rule.

The goal of the new government was to strengthen and modernize Japan so that it could get rid of the "unequal treaties" and win equality with other nations. As in China, loss of control over their own tariffs, the treaty-port system, and special privileges for foreigners, including extraterritoriality, were galling to the Japanese, who were accustomed to thinking of themselves as superior, with no history of foreign conquest. On the other hand, they had long understood the wisdom of adopting ideas and techniques from other countries, as they had done from China. To China, change meant disorder; to

Directions

In 1868 the boy emperor Meiji was given by the new reformers a document to sign that became known as the Charter Oath. Although its five articles are rather general, they do fit the mood of the new Japan and the course it took.

Article 1. Deliberative assemblies shall be widely established and all matters decided by public discussion.

Article 2. All classes, high and low, shall unite vigorously in carrying out the administration of the affairs of state.

Article 3. The common people, no less than the civil and military officials, shall each be allowed to pursue his own calling so that there may be no discontent.

Article 4. Evil customs of the past shall be broken off and everything based upon the just laws of Nature.

Article 5. Knowledge shall be sought throughout the world so as to strengthen the foundation of imperial rule.

Perhaps the best one-line statement of the mood of early Meiji is the reply given to a German physician who visited Japan in the mid-1870s and asked a Japanese friend about the country's history. He replied:

We have no history. Our history begins today!

Source: From R. Storry, *A History of Modern Japan* (London: Penguin, 1982), p. 105; W. W. Lockwood, "Japan's Response to the West," *World Politics,* Vol. 9 (1956), p. 32.

Japan, it meant the chance of improvement. Japanese pride rested not so much in their culture as in their sense of themselves as a people.

In any case, they were quick to realize that if Japan was not to become a colony or semicolony like the rest of Asia, it would have to adopt Western technology. In sharp contrast to the Chinese, and in part because of China's dismal experience, Japan also saw that military technology could not be separated from overall industrialization or the institutional structures that had produced and accompanied it in the West. Where cultural pride often blinded the Chinese to this truth, Japan showed little hesitation after 1869 in transforming or abolishing traditional institutions in favor of those that could give the country the modern strength it needed to survive. Many Japanese urged wholesale Westernization, arguing, "If we use it, that will make it Japanese." Some radical enthusiasts in the early years of Meiji actually tried to destroy traditional temples, to sweep away the old and make way for the new Japan. Although change was largely bloodless and accompanied by relatively minor political reorganization, Meiji Japan produced in many ways a real revolution.

Economy and Government

The first priority was rapid industrialization, especially in heavy industries and armaments. Foreign advisers from appropriate countries were hired to expedite this growth—from Britain for a modern navy, from Germany for a modern army and armaments industry, and so on. Railways were rapidly built to link the major cities, and new ports and facilities were created. The machinery of government and law was wholly remade, modeled on a judicious combination of Western systems. A constitution was adopted in 1889, but with very limited voting rights. In balance, it was a modified constitutional monarchy with a parliament and a largely Western-derived legal system. Such change was important also to demonstrate that Japan was a "civilized" country where foreigners did not need extraterritoriality to protect them. But all Western institutions, even the details of Western culture such as dress and diet, were seen as sources of strength. Samurai discarded their swords and picturesque garb, put on Western business suits, learned to waltz, and dominated the new bureaucracy. Some samurai found careers as officers in the new army, but most soldiers were now peasant conscripts and war was no longer a gentlemen's preserve. Other samurai went into business or manufacturing in the rapidly expanding economy.

Change was centrally directed, but succeeded in mobilizing most Japanese toward the announced goal of "a rich country and a strong army." The Japanese were used to direction from daimyo, samurai, or other hierarchical superiors, and most came to share the national objectives with genuine enthusiasm. Japan's almost ready-made nationalism as an island country with a long history of separateness was a strong asset, again in sharp contrast with China. Its people were also racially and culturally homogeneous (as the Chinese or Indians were not), and the country was small and easily integrated as a unit. In area and population, approximately 50 million by 1910, it was about the size of one of China's larger provinces. But some 90 percent of the Japanese lived in the area between greater Tokyo and greater Osaka. What was decided in Tokyo was quickly carried out everywhere as national policy.

Farm output doubled and then tripled between 1870 and 1940 with the use of new Western technology as well as hard work. In many ways it was the latter that was the basis of Meiji Japan's astounding success. But the costs of such forced draft development were high. Taxation was heavy, and most of the burden was borne by the peasantry, still the largest sector of the Japanese population. Rice riots became frequent, and peasant welfare was also affected by the new military conscription of a largely peasant army.

Japanese Imperialism

By the 1890s Japan had a modern navy and army and a fast-growing industrial base to support it. Japanese steamships had won a major place in East Asian trade, and its merchants had acquired a rising share of the China market. Exports to the West now included silk and tea, where Japanese efficiency and quality control had captured much of the market from a more disorganized China. In 1894 Britain agreed to relinquish the unequal clauses of the old treaty by 1899, and other nations soon followed suit.

As it had followed the Western lead in modern development, Japan now joined the other imperialist powers in colonial conquests. According to the Western example, this was part of being one of the "powers," but Japanese had long sought a special role for themselves on the mainland. Korea was the handiest target, and in brief campaigns in 1894–1895 the new Japanese fleet and army demolished the poorly led Chinese forces sent to protect their tributary dependency. The peace treaty made Japan dominant in a still nominally independent Korea; the Chinese also ceded to them the island of Taiwan (Formosa), a huge indemnity, and the right to operate factories in the China treaty ports.

The Russians were still extending their influence, railways, and concession areas in Manchuria, leasing its southern tip from China and developing the port of Dairen there. The Japanese saw this as a threat to their position in Korea, but in any case they had their own plans for Manchuria. As in 1895 in Korea, and 1941 at Pearl Harbor, they struck in 1904 before declaring war. To everyone's surprise, they won a series of land and naval battles against Russia, then the world's largest military power, by a combination of sneak attack, dash, and willingness to take heavy casualties. The Russians were

far from their home base and inadequately prepared; in time, their much greater resources would have won out, but the Japanese wanted to quit while they were ahead and agreed to a peace arranged by the Americans under President Theodore Roosevelt that was signed at Portsmouth, New Hampshire, in 1905. The Russians were concerned by then with the first stirrings of revolution at home, and the war was expensive and unpopular. Japan inherited the Russian position in Manchuria and tightened its grip on Korea, which in 1910 became an outright colony, part of the now-extensive Japanese Empire.

There was widespread British, American, and German support for Japan in this period, as an apt pupil who made all the proper moves but also as a counterweight against Russia and China. Japan had been encouraged to attack Russia by the Anglo-Japanese treaty of alliance and friendship signed in 1902, which was welcomed in Japan also as a mark of international equality with Western powers. Theodore Roosevelt saw the Japanese as promising allies, "bully fighters" as he called them. The Russo-Japanese War of 1904–1905 inaugurated a period of new pride, confidence, and continued economic progress.

Japan joined the Allies in World War I, ostensibly as an equal partner, although it took no part in the fighting in Europe apart from sending a few destroyers to join the British Mediterranean fleet. The opportunity was instead used to take over the German concession areas in China, centered in the province of Shandong in eastern north China. In 1915 Japan presented a list of Twenty-one Demands, including the stationing of troops and of Japanese "advisers" to the Chinese government, that would have made China in effect a Japanese colony. By such greedy and bullying tactics, Japan quickly lost the admiration and goodwill built up by its progress since 1869. The demands also infuriated Chinese patriots and more than any other event sparked the rise of genuine Chinese nationalism on a widening basis. Japan had begun a policy in China, and in the acquisition of empire, that was to lead it into what Japanese call "the dark valley," the fateful years leading to the military takeover of Manchuria in 1931 and to the bombing of Pearl Harbor in 1941. The demands were rejected, although Japan hung on to the German concessions in Shandong. Meanwhile, attention was centered on the further development of Taiwan, Korea, and Manchuria.

Taiwan offered rice, sugar, and tropical crops to feed Japan's booming and increasingly urban population. Korea had rich resources of coal, iron ore, and timber, which were exploited for export to Japan. Korea was drained of everything exportable, including food crops, to support Japanese growth. Koreans were reduced to menial occupations and denied even elementary education. They were forced to adopt Japanese names and were forbidden to teach or use their own language in public. Manchuria, still formally part of China but in

The first modern Japanese embassy abroad, sent by the Tokugawa to Washington and shown here in a navy yard in 1860 with their American hosts. Note that the Japanese are all dressed in samurai outfits, complete with swords. (Corbis)

effect a Japanese sphere of control, was a storehouse of coal, ores, timber, productive agricultural land, and potential hydroelectric power. All these resources were put to work with heavy investment of Japanese capital in railways, mines, irrigation, fertilizers, dams, port facilities, and colonial administration. Even in Korea, railways, mines, factories, and roads were built and basic economic growth was begun, although for Japanese benefit. In Taiwan, the infrastructure for economic development was also laid, primarily in agriculture, and there was new prosperity.

Japanese policy in Taiwan and Manchuria was more constructive than in Korea, where anti-Korean prejudice marred the Japanese record and impoverished most Koreans. Taiwan's successful economic growth after 1950 rested on Japanese foundations in irrigation, fertilizer, rail and road systems, power supplies, coal mines, education, and industry. In Manchuria the Japanese built the largest single industrial complex in Asia, including closely integrated mines and factories in the Mukden (Shenyang) area centered on heavy manufacturing, a dense rail net, and a highly productive commercialized agriculture generating large surpluses of wheat and soybeans for export to Japan and to world markets through the port of Dairen. Large power dams were built on Manchuria's rivers. The population increased by nearly 1 million a year from 1900 to the outbreak of the Pacific War in 1941, consisting al-

most entirely of Chinese who migrated from a disordered and impoverished north China seeking new economic opportunity. Japan's huge investment in Manchuria, which never paid off in net terms for the Japanese, laid the essential basis for China's industrialization after Japan's defeat in 1945. But Japan's record as a colonial power, despite the constructive achievements, was marred by a basically exploitative approach to the areas it controlled and by a disregard for local interests or aspirations.

A CLOSER LOOK

Ito Hirobumi: Meiji Statesman

Ito Hirobumi, the leading statesman of Meiji Japan and a typical figure of the period, was born in one of the outer daimyo domains in southwestern Japan in 1841. His career encapsulates the successive stages of Meiji attitudes and actions. As a youth he wanted passionately to save his country from the foreign threat, and at age 21 he tried to burn the newly established British embassy in Tokyo. But when he visited Britain next year, he realized that it was impossible to drive the Westerners out and returned to work for Japan's modernization. After the Meiji Restoration, he went with government missions to Europe and America to learn how to make his country strong, and in 1881 he became Japan's first prime minister under the new Western-style government. A later mission to Prussia convinced him that the Prussian constitutional monarchy was best suited to Japan. Ito was the chief architect of the new constitution proclaimed by the emperor in 1889, which contained many Prussian ideas. He understood, however, that constitutional government and the cooperation of the new parliament could not be made to work without political organization and popular support. In 1898 he left office to form a political party for that purpose, which was dominant until 1941.

After the Russo-Japanese War in 1905, Ito became the first Japanese resident-general in Korea. Japanese domination and occupation were deeply resented by patriotic Koreans, the more so as Ito increased pressure for further Japanese influence. He saw such a policy as preferable to a complete military takeover, which was urged by powerful voices at home, and hoped against the odds that he could win Korean goodwill and cooperation in modernizing their country under Japanese tutelage. In 1909 he was assassinated by a Korean patriot while on a visit to northern Manchuria; this ended the career of a man who might have played a vital moderating role in subsequent Japanese policies.

Ito was an enthusiastic modernizer, especially after his visits to the West, but he also understood the need for compromise in politics and for adapting Western ways to Japanese traditions, circumstances, and values. In some ways he remained at least as traditional as he was modern. His objective was the preservation and development of his country, not its Westernization. He saw the need for many foreign ideas, but never at the expense of a strong Japanese identity. He believed deeply in the restoration of the emperor's personal rule and aimed to accomplish his ends by working through the throne, but he also understood the rising interest in a less authoritarian form of government, the need for political parties, a constitution, and a parliament. He was both an enthusiast and a realist, a radical reformer and a traditional conservative, a promoter of change and a practical compromiser—in other words, a true statesman who served his country well and who never let personal ambition or power cloud his judgment or dedication to the public welfare.

Imperialism and Americans in Asia

Americans entered the trade with China early, and several merchant families in Boston, Salem, Philadelphia, and Baltimore grew rich on it. In 1784 the American ship *Empress of China* sailed from Brooklyn for Guangzhou; it was followed over the years up to the 1850s by clipper ships bringing back tea, silk, porcelains, and other luxury goods. American ship designers had perfected the clipper ship, and their captains held records for the fastest voyages, although they were soon copied by the British. American ships also traded to Calcutta, Madras, and Bombay, bringing back Indian cottons, spices, and handicrafts. It was hard to find Asian markets for American goods. For some years ice cut on New England ponds and packed in sawdust in the holds of ships was sold profitably in Calcutta and then in Guangzhou, after necessarily crossing the equator twice. Furs were another export to China, including sea otter from the American northwest coast. In time, American oil and kerosene became our leading exports to Asia, marketed by the Standard Oil Company, and later some American machinery and minerals.

Apart from the Philippines after 1900, U.S. trade with Asia was never very large, as part of U.S. or Asian foreign trade as a whole, and remained a small fraction of Britain's and later, Japan's, although Japanese silk exports after 1875 found their largest market in the United States. In the missionary field, however, Americans outnumbered those from any other country in China, Japan, Korea, and the Philippines; Britons dominated the missionary enterprise in India, Burma, and Malaya, and French and Dutch missions dominated Indochina and Indonesia. With its lure of 400 million potential converts and the absence, or so the missionaries thought, of any proper religious tradition, China drew by far the largest number of missionaries, 8000 at its 1920's peak, from a great variety of Protestant sects and Catholic orders.

The dominant foreign power in China was Britain, both in terms of its trade, investments, and concessions and through its role in the wars of 1839–1842, 1858–1860, and other lesser skirmishes. It was the British who as a result of these wars had extracted the unequal treaties, although the Americans were quick to obtain their own treaty in 1843, following the Treaty of Nanjing, which was the first to establish rights of extraterritoriality whereby they would not be subject to Chinese law. But Americans took no part in any of these wars. Until their contingent joined the allied expedition against the Boxers in 1900, they were content to let the British and to a smaller degree the French do the fighting to "open" China to traders and missionaries. It was the British navy that maintained the foreign position in China until the end of the century. In the late 1890s, China seemed about to break up into colonial concessions and at the same time the United States was expanding across the Pacific and conquering the Philippines. The British in particular were concerned that China not be divided up among the colonial powers, and especially that the Russians not be given an opportunity for further expansion, a concern that the American government shared.

A Japanese woodblock print of about 1860, showing an American ship in the harbor of Yokohama. (Chadbourne Collection, Library of Congress)

It was originally a British idea to oppose new concessions and to press for an "Open Door" for trade by all nations. The Americans, in consultation with the British, circulated a note to that effect to all the powers involved in China in September 1899 and again, prompted by the Russian occupation of Manchuria after the Boxer Rebellion, in July 1900, supporting China's "territorial integrity." As the Americans pointed out, they had no concession areas in China (although they had one in Shanghai earlier that was later merged into an International Concession) and claimed to be acting only in China's best interest. Cynics pointed out that the Open Door policy was merely an attempt to keep China open to exploitation by all nations. In any case, the other powers paid little attention to the Open Door notes.

American motives in Asia were mixed almost from the beginning: the search for commercial profits and Christian converts, but also as the nineteenth century progressed a genuine desire on the part of many to help Asians to "modernize" and to improve their material lot.

American missionaries were in the forefront of modern medical work in Asia and the establishment of hospitals and medical schools, as they were in education as a whole, including the founding of many of Asia's modern universities. American missionaries also led the way in mounting famine-relief programs and road building in the disastrous flood, drought, famine, and warlord decade of the 1920s in northern China. The foreign powers imposed a huge indemnity on China in 1901, supposedly to cover the costs of the allied expedition against the Boxers. In 1908, the United States followed the British lead in using the indemnity payments to finance Chinese students studying in each country, certainly a positive gesture but with an aspect of paternalism, as if China's hope lay in becoming "like us," i.e., "civilized." People who are poor and weak are seldom as grateful for help from outsiders as the stronger and richer donors think they ought to be, a basic aspect of human nature that has often clouded the American relationship with Asia.

Asians also had difficulty seeing American (or French or British) behavior in Asia as part of the Western tradition of freedom and democracy. There was little evidence of liberty, equality, and fraternity in French Indochina, the ideas of John Stuart Mill's *On Liberty* in late colonial India, or the ideals of the American Revolution among Americans in the treaty ports, the behavior of U.S. Marines garrisoned in China after 1900, or the American gunboats on the Yangzi, supporting America's "treaty rights," still less in the Philippines. Yet all of these Western ideals were an inspiration to Asia's emerging nationalists. The growing affluence and power of the United States were also attractive models of success in the modern world. Indian nationalists hoped that the Americans, who had fought for and won their own independence from Britain, would support them in their similar struggle. But the United States treated India as a British preserve and did not wish to interfere with another great power, whom they depended on in China.

Asians were most deeply hurt, however, by the series of so-called Oriental Exclusion Acts passed by the U.S. Congress in 1882 originally against Chinese immigrants, and elaborated in successive years into the 1920s. Japanese were specifically excluded in 1908, but all Asians faced discrimination. By an ironic coincidence, the Statue of Liberty, erected in New York harbor in 1886 as a gift from France bore the well-known poem by Emma Lazarus that read in part: "Give me your tired, your poor/your huddled masses yearning to breathe free/I lift my lamp beside the golden door." Asians, especially Chinese, Japanese, and Filipinos, had begun to flock to America in the wake of the California gold rush of 1849; they worked as miners, cooks, and manual laborers and provided most of the labor for the building of the western sections of the transcontinental railroads. By 1880 some 8 percent of California's population were Chinese; many Asians were killed in anti-Chinese riots there and in other western states in the 1870s and 1880s where these unwelcome immigrants were seen as competitors as well as being rejected on racist grounds; some Japanese, Koreans, and Filipinos who were often ignorantly mistaken for them were victims, too. But the new laws against Asian immigration reflected American racism as a whole, which was exhibited by individual Americans in Asia and at home as well as by their government and its military and diplomatic personnel.

A few American intellectuals knew something of and admired Asian culture; Emerson, Thoreau, and the Transcendentalists in nineteenth-century New England openly acknowledged the Indian source of many of their ideas, and Rabindranath Tagore attracted enthusiastic crowds on the American parts of his lecture tours, as had the Hindu revivalist Swami Vivekananda earlier. By the twentieth century many educated Americans were also reading Lafcadio Hearn's romantic and admiring accounts of Japan, and then Lin Yutang's books, which gave an idealized picture of the virtues and appealing qualities of traditional Confucian China. But the Asian immigrants who came to California and to east coast ports, where they were also obliged to live in ghettos, rioted against, and killed, were not easy to associate with the elite view of Asian culture. These were peasants and laborers, driven by poverty and overcrowding to emigrate, as they were doing at the same time to Southeast Asia. They themselves knew little about the elite cultures of their homelands; they were more like Emma Lazarus's "refuse of your teeming shore."

But the Exclusion Acts, aimed specifically at Asians, were perceived by Asians as a humiliating insult—as indeed they were. Nearly all Asian countries were noted, one might almost say notorious, for their pride, and for understandable reasons. To be treated by an upstart new Western nation as inferior and "undesirable" was a bitter pill to swallow, especially when no Asian government was yet able to stand up to the West and to demand equal treatment. Even Asians from upper classes were discriminated against and humiliated when they visited the United States. When Congress added new clauses to the Oriental Exclusion Acts in 1905, political activists and patriotic merchants in China organized a boycott of American goods that was effective both symbolically and economically, especially in Guangzhou and Shanghai.

Asian Women in the New Imperialist Age

In every country engulfed by colonialism, the Western example was accompanied by the beginnings of education for women, while the new colonial ports

began to offer an escape for women as well as men from their traditional constraints, as factory workers or simply as servants, in a world divorced from the otherwise deeply conservative Asian society. Western wives began to come out to join their husbands, especially after the opening of the Suez Canal in 1869, and made a significant impact. Western women brought the Victorian ideals of late nineteenth-century society with them. Married women demanded their husbands' commitment to the sanctity of the family unit, based in upholding Christian ethics, which began with spousal fidelity. This effectively eliminated the common practice among earlier male colonial administrators and merchants of taking local wives and fathering a second Asian family. The expectations of European wives who were now on-site carried over into the larger social fabric and began to establish a definitive social and cultural distance between Westerners and Asians. This new social ethic reinforced the new imperialist political and economic agendas, which mandated a clear division between the "superior" Europeans and their inferior Asian subjects. Christian missionaries, many of whom were women, criticized some of the social practices of the Asian societies, and thus began the process of women's liberation. In China they worked against foot-binding and in India against *sati*, and in every country they opened their schools to girls and their universities to women.

The new imperialism also had a major impact on the labor practices of Asian women. Southeast Asian women spun and wove cloth in almost every household in the early nineteenth century. During that century, however, the enormous growth in peasant consumption of cheap European manufactured textiles changed this. Potential textile producers reacted to the reality of the marketplace. Women found their production of native textiles to be overly costly in personal time. In turn, they chose to purchase the cheap European cloth in the market rather than to weave cloth in their own homes. Sumatran, Malay, and Vietnamese women dropped household weaving to work in the developing rubber industry. In Java, the value of imported textiles rose from 3.8 million guilders in 1830 to 13.1 million in 1840; in Burma three-fourths of the country's textiles were imported by 1930; in Thailand the nominal value of cotton manufacture imports rose seven times between 1864 and 1910.

Against this trend toward the import displacement of the indigenous textile industry is the case of Java, where local producers modified their production technique sufficiently to remain cost competitive. Dutch, Swiss, and English textile imports of machine-printed imitation batik sold more cheaply than traditionally produced batik, and, even more, the colors of these imports were brighter and more diverse than native dyes would allow. To retain a place in the marketplace, local craftspeople responded by developing a new method of cloth production that displaced time-consuming free-hand wax design methods.

Commonly, the new method made production quality more consistent, and synthetic dyes allowed new color schemes and resolved long-standing consumer complaints over the impermanence and dullness of traditional batik.

In India, China, and Japan many women won a degree of liberation from traditional subjugation by finding jobs in the growing industrial cities. Pay was low and they were often abused in company-owned dormitories. Battered women were free of the restraint traditionally imposed on them. A few found places in the entertainment world, including night clubs, dance halls, and prostitution.

The Legacy of Western Control

The age of Western domination saw Western powers take control of most of India and Southeast Asia, while exercising heavy influence and enjoying special rights in Thailand, China, and Japan. The Japanese, taking a lesson from their Western teachers, created their own colonial empire in Korea, Taiwan, and Manchuria. The wave of imperialism and colonial control transformed all of the cultures and societies that it touched. Control by a foreign power is easy to condemn, especially when it has been won by forcible conquest and has resulted in massive injustice and exploitation in the name of empire. Much that was desirable and valuable about traditional cultures was destroyed or weakened. But imperialism and colonial control also forced or stimulated all of the societies involved to break the mold of the past and start down the long road to modern development. The imperialists or their pupils (Japan) built railways, mines, and factories, revolutionized and commercialized the agricultural system, and began effective measures of public health. They built hospitals and schools, created or transformed educational systems in the Western mode, and spread not only their own technology but their values and many of their economic and political institutions. New or altered commercial-industrial cities and ports grew rapidly and soon became the largest in each country despite their Western nature.

All of these changes were disruptive to the indigenous cultures and societies and to traditional values. The suffering was far worse because the chief agents of change were foreign rulers or foreign pressures. Some of the changes had positive aspects in the long run, but any process of change, including the transformation of the West in preceding centuries, disrupts, destroys or harms some things of value and some groups in the process. Imperialism remains hard to accept because it clearly involved forced exploitation by outsiders for their own benefit, ambition, or pride. The injustice of imperialism, however, and the model of strength that it offered were largely responsible for the emergence of modern nationalism in all of the areas affected by it. Asians became determined to free their countries by united effort and build their own versions of strength and development based on many aspects of the Western model. The modern world thus begins with the spread of Western influence over most of the globe and the diverse responses evoked by it.

Questions

1. Define and explain the concept of imperialism in the hands of the British, French, Dutch, and Americans. What were their attitudes toward and policies enforcing imperialism? Did this imperialism advance or hinder the development of local cultures and economies?

2. How do Kipling's poems "The White Man's Burden" and "Mandalay" reflect late nineteenth-century Western romantic visions of their imperial mission?

3. Why did the British move their capital from Calcutta to Delhi? Was this a good choice? What were its consequences? How did New Delhi embody the ideal of the colonial metropole, in contrast to neighboring old Delhi?

4. What differing factors and ambitions contributed to the British takeover of Burma, the French in Vietnam, the Dutch in Indonesia, and the Americans in the Philippines?

5. What is "gunboat diplomacy"? How does the Treaty of Tianjin, which ended the second Opium War, fulfill gunboat diplomacy goals? How did this war, as well as the British seizure of Burma, the French annexation of southern Vietnam, and the American conquest of the Philippines each demonstrate the use of gunboat diplomacy as a means to further the partnerships of Western merchants and missionaries?

6. How did the Boxer Rebellion represent the final failure of nineteenth-century Chinese efforts to respond to the incursive policies of the Europeans? What were its consequences, in terms of increased Western presence in China as well as the Chinese reactions?

7. How did the achievements of Meiji Japan counter the Western imperialist characterizations of Asians? How and why did Japan follow the lead of the West in becoming an imperialist power? What was the nature of Japanese imperialism in Korea and Taiwan?

Note

1. R. Kipling, *Complete Verse* (New York: Doubleday, 1939), p. 417.

Suggested Web Sites

Imperialism

http://www.fordham.edu/halsail/mod/modsbook34.html
Detailed information on analyses, motives, attitudes, celebrations, and objections regarding imperialism in China, India, and Japan.

The Taiping Rebellion

http://www.wsu.edu:8080/~dee/ching/taiping.htm

http://www~chaos.umd.edu/history/modern2.html
Textual documents about the emergence of modern China and the Taiping Rebellion (1850–1864).

http://web.jjay.cuny.edu/~jobrien/reference/ob32.html
Three fascinating primary source selections on self-strengthening.

The Boxer Rebellion

http://www.fordham.edu/halsail/mod/1900Fei-boxers.html
Features an article by Fei Ch'i-hao, a Chinese Christian, from *The Modern History Sourcebook*, in which he recounts the activities of the "Boxers" in the Boxer Rebellion of 1900.

White Man's Burden

http://www.boondocksnet.com//ai/kipling/
The American anti-imperialist attack on Kipling's famous poem on race and empire, including sublinks to photos, responses, and the work itself.

Suggestions for Further Reading

India

Ballhatchett, K. *Race, Sex, and Class Under the Raj.* New York: St. Martin's Press, 1980.
Copland, I. *The Burden of Empire.* Oxford: Oxford University Press, 1996.
Davis, L. E., and Huttenback, R. A. *Mammon and the Pursuit of Empire.* Cambridge, England: Cambridge University Press, 1988.
Hopkirk, P. *The Great Game.* Tokyo: U.N. University Press, 1992.
Irving, R. G. *Indian Summer: Imperial Delhi.* New Haven: Yale University Press, 1983.
Kennedy, D. *Magic Mountains: Hill Stations of the British Raj.* Berkeley: University of California Press, 1996.
Mason, P. *The Men Who Ruled India,* rev. ed. London: Jonathan Cape, 1985.
Neill, S. A. *A History of Christianity in India.* Cambridge, England: Cambridge University Press, 1985.
Seal, A. *The Emergence of Indian Nationalism.* Cambridge, England: Cambridge University Press, 1968.

Southeast Asia

Harrison, B. *Modern Southeast Asia.* London: Macmillan, 1975.
Reid, A. *Southeast Asia: The Early Modern Era.* Ithaca: Cornell University Press, 1993.
Stanley, P. W. *Reappraising an Empire: The American Impact on the Philippines.* Cambridge: Harvard University Press, 1984.
Steinberg, D. J., ed. *In Search of Southeast Asia.* Honolulu: University Press of Hawaii, 1987.

China

Bays, D. *Christianity in China.* Stanford: Stanford University Press, 1996.

Cohen, P. *China and Christianity.* Cambridge: Harvard University Press, 1963.
———. *History in Three Keys: The Boxers.* New York: Columbia University Press, 1997.
Cohen, W. *The Asian American Century.* Cambridge: Harvard University Press, 2004.
Esherick, J. *The Origins of the Boxer Uprising.* Berkeley: University of California Press, 1987.
Fairbank, J. K. *The Missionary Enterprise in China and America.* Cambridge: Harvard University Press, 1974.
Gasster, M. *China's Struggle to Modernize.* New York: Knopf, 1982.
Gernet, J. *China and the Christian Impact.* Cambridge, England: Cambridge University Press, 1985.
Hao, Y. P. *The Commercial Revolution in Nineteenth Century China: Sino-Western Capitalism.* Berkeley: University of California Press, 1986.
Hsu, I. *The Rise of Modern China.* Oxford: Oxford University Press, 1989.
Murphey, R. *Shanghai: Key to Modern China.* Cambridge: Harvard University Press, 1953.
Peyrefitte, A. *The Immobile Empire.* New York: Knopf, 1993.
Schmid, A. *Korea Between Empires.* New York: Columbia University Press, 2002.
Schrecker, J. *Imperialism and Chinese Nationalism.* Cambridge: Harvard University Press, 1971.
Seagrave, S. *Dragon Lady: The Life and Legend of the Last Empress.* New York: Vintage, 1993.
Sutter, R. G., *The United States and East Asia.* Lanham, MD: Rowan and Littlefield, 2004.

Japan and Korea

Beasley, W. G. *The Rise of Modern Japan.* New York: St. Martin's Press, 1995.
Borton, H. *Japanese Imperialism, 1894–1945.* Oxford: Clarendon, 1987.
———. *Japan's Modern Century.* New York: Ronald Press, 1955.
Calman, D. *The Nature and Origins of Japanese Imperialism.* London: Routledge, 1992.
Chandra, V. *Imperialism, Resistance, and Reform in Late Nineteenth Century Korea.* Berkeley: University of California Press, 1988.
Duus, P. *The Abacus and the Sword.* Berkeley: University of California Press, 1995.
Harashima, Y. *Meiji Japan Through Woodblock Prints.* Tokyo: University of Tokyo Press, 1990.
Henthorn, W. E. *A History of Korea.* New York: Free Press, 1971.
Huber, T. M. *The Revolutionary Origins of Modern Japan.* Stanford: Stanford University Press, 1981.
Hunter, J. C. *The Emergence of Modern Japan.* London: Longmans, 1989.
Jansen, M. ed. *The Emergence of Meiji Japan.* Cambridge, England: Cambridge University Press, 1995.
Myers, R. et al. *The Japanese Colonial Empire.* Stanford: Stanford University Press, 1984.
Nish, I. H. *The Origins of the Russo-Japanese War.* London: Longmans, 1985.
Samuels, R. J. *Rich Nation, Strong Army.* Ithaca, New York: Cornell University Press, 1995.
Wilson, G. M. *Patriots and Redeemers in Japan.* Chicago: University of Chicago Press, 1992.

16

Subjugation, Nationalism, and Revolution in China and India

This chapter deals first with China's abortive struggle to reform, as Meiji Japan had done, to meet the threat of foreign encroachment. The Taipings and other rebellions were suppressed, but "self-strengthening" came to little under the rule of the scheming empress dowager Cixi. Defeat by Japan in 1894 was a crushing humiliation, and Western and now Japanese domination in the treaty ports increased. After a brief effort at reform by Kang Youwei in 1898, the dynasty was finally overthrown in 1911. The new leader, Sun Yat-sen, was politically inept, and power fell to a general, Yuan Shikai, until his death in 1916, the first of the regional warlords who ravaged China for some 15 years. Chinese nationalism surged in an angry response to the Japanese takeover of Shandong Province in demonstrations on May 4, 1919. This May Fourth movement spawned a new radical literature, including the bitter indictments of the old society by the great writer, Lu Xun.

In colonial India, railways aided new industrial growth and the commercialization of agriculture, including new crops such as tea and jute and the expansion of wheat and cotton growing, much of it for export. The flourishing ports of Calcutta, Bombay, and Madras generated a rising new middle class of Indians, including those in Western-style professions, but most Indians remained poor, despite large new British investments in irrigation. Indian nationalism began to grow and in 1885 the Indian National Congress was founded. British arrogance grew, and after World War I, in which Indian troops served, a peaceful, unarmed crowd at Amritsar in Punjab was fired on in April 1919; more than 400 were killed. This massacre fed the fires

of nationalism further, and M. K. Gandhi began his campaigns.

Chapter 15 looked at the nineteenth and early twentieth centuries in Asia from the perspective of foreign imperialism. We now need to examine the same period from the Asian point of view.

Upheaval in China grew slowly, out of a long period of pent-up problems with which the Qing government was increasingly unable to deal. Over a century passed between the disastrous Opium War of 1839–1842, which sharply revealed the inadequacies of the Qing, and the final triumph of the Chinese Revolution in 1949. Pressures for change built up and then were blocked or diverted in a series of failed "reforms," efforts at revolution, and betrayal by reactionary leaders. This long delay and the pressures that found too little outlet undoubtedly helped to make the finally successful revolution in 1949 more radical than it might otherwise have been. The success of the Russian Revolution in 1917 was a beacon to those working for radical change everywhere, including both China and India. The Russian model and Russian advisers were important in both countries. But the final success of the Chinese Revolution and its later development after 1949 were far more an indigenous phenomenon than a response to the Russian experience.

India's winning of independence cannot properly be called a revolution. Political power was handed over peacefully by Britain to two new governments, India and Pakistan, although not until after World War II, in 1947. The drive for Indian independence began late, among a handful of intellectuals. It was transformed after World

CHRONOLOGY

China

1842–1949	Establishment of over 100 treaty ports; missionaries and their schools appear
1864	Final defeat of Taipings
1864–1890	Self-Strengthening Movement; building of military arsenals (with the assistance of Western advisors)
1861–1908	Empress dowager Cixi
1881–1936	Lu Xun; Hu Shi
1884	Initial nationalist uprisings in Korea
1895	Defeated by Japan in Sino-Japanese War
1896–1911	Western scramble for concession territories
1898	The 100 Days
1900	Boxer Rebellion
1911	Fall of the Manchu dynasty; beginning of the Chinese Revolution
1912–1916	Yuan Shikai
1916–1927	Warlord years; founding of the Guomindang
1919–1923	May Fourth Movement
1921	Chinese Communist Party founded
1926	Death of Sun Yat-sen; transition to Chiang Kai-shek

India

1850–1910	Industrialization of many cities
1870–1941	Rise of Indian middle class, as well as mass poverty
1860–1915	Ranade; Gokhale; Tilak; Tagore
1869–1948	M. K. Gandhi, in India from 1914
1885	Indian National Congress founded
1905–1911	Partition of Bengal
1909	Indian Councils Act
1917	Parliamentary Declaration (committing the British to eventual Indian independence)
1919	Rowlatt Acts; Amritsar massacre

War I, primarily under the leadership of Mahatma Gandhi, into a mass movement involving, as in China and Russia, peasants and workers under the direction of political organizers. But there was little effort at radical restructuring of Indian society or its values, and Gandhi in particular emphasized nonviolence. In general the independence movement was limited to the goal of political freedom from colonialism. In other respects it was reformist rather than revolutionary. Nevertheless, the changes that took place in India were in some ways revolutionary, if only in the awakening of mass nationalism, the end of the largest colonial system in the world, the transfer of power over some 400 million members of the world's oldest living civilization, and the beginning of planned development.

Revolution in China began almost tentatively, sputtered and apparently died after a few years, and finally broke out in full force only after nearly 50 years of false starts and setbacks. There were perhaps revolutionary aspects to the Taiping Rebellion from 1850 to 1864; there was a brief, abortive effort at change from the top by a few far-sighted officials in the last half of the nineteenth century. All revolutions have their antecedents, but China's was particularly slow in the making. China had first to develop a national political consciousness and a political organization that could pursue revolutionary change rather than just another phase in the dynastic cycle. Radical change was something that most Chinese feared and distrusted, but by the twentieth-century the traditional model had lost its ability to deal with the now-overwhelming problems of mass poverty, technological backwardness, and political weakness.

In India, the pressures for political change were more narrowly concentrated on winning freedom from colonial rule. India too suffered from mass poverty, technological backwardness, and hurt pride. Indian nationalists tended to blame colonial oppression for their problems. But as in China, a new national consciousness had first to be developed and a political organization built. India had seldom functioned in its long and glorious past as a national unit, but rather, like China, as a cultural tradition. It took time to get Indians or Chinese to work together for a common political goal.

China in Decay

The account of the Qing dynasty in Chapter 13 ended, it will be recalled, with the Opium War and the Treaty of Nanjing in 1842, while Chapter 15 focused on foreign imperialism in China in the nineteenth century. Here we must pick up the thread of Chinese history itself after 1842. The Qing tried to ignore its defeat by the

British in the Opium War and to continue, as it had in the past, to refuse to deal with foreigners as equals or to establish what the British regarded as normal diplomatic relations. The Chinese had lost a skirmish with the Western barbarians but saw no reason why this should change their position, their attitudes, or their traditional ways of doing things. The official accounts of the Opium War said that the sea barbarians had been driven off, with the implication that China would now return to dealing with its internal administration as usual. Many of the terms of the Treaty of Nanjing were largely ignored, and difficulties were placed in the way of the Westerners, who nevertheless finally established their settlements at Shanghai, Ningbo, Fuzhou, Xiamen, and Guangzhou. British diplomatic representation and residence in Beijing were refused. It was almost as if nothing had happened in 1842.

Foreign impatience, now including the French and the Americans, grew, and a series of incidents culminated in an undeclared war in 1856. Chinese officials stopped a small, Chinese-owned, local ship wearing by special registration a British flag. Twelve of the Chinese crew were arrested on suspicion of smuggling and piracy, and the British flag was hauled down. British protests and Chinese intransigence led to hostilities, which spread to a British siege of Guangzhou and then to an Anglo-French expedition to Tianjin, the port of Beijing. In 1858 they extracted a new treaty confirming and expanding the terms of 1842 and opening ten new ports to foreign residence and trade. Many of the terms of the Treaty of Tianjin were also ignored by the Chinese, and in 1860 another Anglo-French expedition entered Beijing and burned the Summer Palace in retaliation. The Qing now had no choice but to accept foreign ambassadors at Beijing and to deal with them formally as equals. The foreign grip on China had tightened. Hong Kong, ceded outright in 1841, had been settled promptly and was flourishing as a trade entrepôt for the whole China coast. Its success attracted large numbers of adventurous Chinese eager for business Western-style and beyond the control of the bureaucratic state, as they were also in the coastal treaty ports. In 1860 the peninsula of Kowloon on the mainland just across the harbor from the island of Hong Kong was also ceded to Britain to accommodate the swelling number of immigrants and port functions.

From the Chinese point of view, these were still minor or even marginal matters, which the Qing continued largely to ignore. With the beginning of the Taiping Rebellion in 1850 they also had other and, from their perspective, far more urgent problems, including the later Russian infiltration in Xinjiang, the Muslim rebellions of the 1870s in the northwest and southwest, and a series of large and small rebellions that peppered the last half of the nineteenth century. It is understandable that the Qing gave these problems top priority and were

The wreckage left after Anglo-French forces stormed the forts at Dagu guarding the approaches to Tianjin and Beijing in 1860. The guns had been made in China's early efforts to copy modern Western armament, but they were no match for those of the Westerners. (Mansell/Time and Life Picture Collection/Getty Images)

slow to recognize that the Westerners, a relative handful easily kept at arm's length in the past, had become the major threat to the country because of their superior technology and aggressive policies. One must remember that China was an immense country in both area and population and that even a more open-minded government would have considered it proper to put domestic concerns first.

Westerners have tended consistently to exaggerate the importance of their role in China, from the time of Matteo Ricci to the present. Most Chinese remained at best vaguely aware of their presence, if at all, and little if any affected by their activities, most of which were heavily concentrated in a few coastal and Yangzi River ports or at the capital in Beijing. China was an overwhelmingly peasant country; comparatively few of its people lived in or near the cities, to which the foreigners were largely limited. Even the mission stations in what the foreigners called "the interior" were necessarily in towns or small cities. The foreigners thought that their example of "progress" Western-style would encourage China to follow a similar path, but the treaty ports made only the smallest impact on the main body of the country and its people. They did stimulate the growth of a new group, the Westernized treaty-port Chinese—originally agents for foreign firms, then merchants and industrialists in their own right, and in time Western-influenced intellectuals. But all told they were a tiny handful in this huge country and its masses of people and they, like the treaty-port foreigners, were often cut off from close contact with the real China of rural peasants. Certainly they did not represent it or understand its problems and needs.

Foreigners have always dreamed about the profits to be won by selling to the huge China market, that pot of gold at the end of the rainbow, and multiplied what they could make from selling even a pair of socks by 400 million, or a billion, people. Sir Henry Pottinger, chief British negotiator at the Treaty of Nanjing, remarked, "The treaty has opened to trade a market so vast that all the mills of Lancashire could not make stocking stuff enough for one of China's provinces."[1] This goal has remained elusive since China has continued to supply most of its own needs, either through traditional production methods or by importing foreign technology and machinery to build its own modern industry. The treaty ports remained tiny isolated dots on the edges of China. China's total foreign trade probably about doubled, but it remained a minuscule proportion of the Chinese economy. It transformed the treaty ports, but touched the rest of the country hardly at all; most of the imports were consumed in the treaty ports themselves by Westernized Chinese as well as by foreigners, who remained a very small though privileged minority of treaty-port populations.

The major foreign impact was in the ideas transmitted through mission-run schools and colleges. They conveyed a message of the benefits of modern Western national states, technology, industrialization, the values of free enterprise, and the modern Western legacy of individualism, free expression, and democratic forms of government. Especially after 1917, the influence of Marxism and Russian Leninism became newly compelling, appealing to many patriotic Chinese as a better model of strength and success, but in any case a preferable alternative to their own traditional system, which they saw as having failed on all counts.

But it took much time for the lessons of China's humiliation to be absorbed and for any substantial number of people with new ideas to emerge. The Chinese had been used to leading the world for 2,000 years or more. Their view of themselves and of the appropriate response to the outside world could not change quickly, even though it seemed obvious to Westerners that the world outside China had changed drastically and Chinese responses had become disastrously, even maddeningly, out-of-date. In any case, it was hard to move a mass as immense as China and its peasant millions in an area larger than the United States. Even its small educated group, still schooled in the Confucian classics and still proud to the point of arrogance, found anything foreign to be barbaric and distasteful if not contemptible. The new Western military technology was dismissed as "a few monkey tricks," which China need not stoop to copy. But slowly the message began to get through, even to some of the archconservative officials who dominated the Qing government.

"Self-Strengthening" and Restoration

The final suppression of the Taipings was supervised by a dedicated scholar-official, Zeng Guofan, (1811–1872), who began by organizing a militia-style army to chase

The treaty-port style. Its Anglo-Indian origins are apparent: thick walls, deep verandas on all sides, and vaguely Corinthian style, but open to whatever breezes can help to ease the hot climate. This is the office of an American firm in Guangzhou. (From Arnold Wright, *Twentieth Century Impressions,* London, 1908, p. 792)

Self-Strengthening

Li Hongzhang (1823–1901) was the chief architect of "self-strengthening" and made the case for it repeatedly.

> The present situation is one in which, externally, it is necessary for us to be harmonious with the barbarians after China's humiliating defeats in 1840–42, 1860, and 1885, and internally, it is necessary for us to reform our institutions. If we remain conservative, without making any change, the national will be daily reduced and weakened. . . . Now all the foreign countries are having one reform after another, and progressing every day like the ascending of steam. Only China continues to preserve her traditional institutions so cautiously that even though she be ruined and extinguished, the conservatives will not regret it. Oh heaven and man! How can we understand the cause of it? . . . The Westerners particularly rely upon the excellence and efficacy of their guns, cannons, and steamships, and so they can overrun China. . . . To live today and still say "reject the barbarians" and "drive them out of our territory" is certainly superficial and absurd talk. . . . How can we get along for one day without weapons and techniques? The method of self-strengthening lies in learning what they can do, and in taking over what they rely upon.

Source: S. Y. Teng and J. K. Fairbank, *China's Response to the West: A Documentary Survey* (Cambridge: Harvard University Press, 1954), pp. 87, 109.

the rebels out of Hunan, his native province. He taught his Hunan army discipline, built their morale, and made them into the government's major striking force, which took the offensive in many areas of central China. In 1860 Zeng was put in charge of all the middle and lower Yangzi provinces, where the imperial forces began slowly to wear down the Taiping rebels. He encouraged his young protégé Li Hongzhang, (1823–1901) to build up a provincial army in Anhui on the model of the Hunan army. Li and Zeng bought foreign arms and established Western-style arsenals, with Western advisers, to make Western guns and steamships. An American adventurer from Salem, Massachusetts, F. T. Ward, organized a volunteer corps of foreigners to defend Shanghai from rebel attacks, soon joined by a larger Chinese contingent trained in Western arms and tactics. When Ward was killed in 1862, he was succeeded by Charles Gordon, known in the West as "Chinese Gordon," on loan from the British army. Like Ward, he was given Chinese military rank under Li Hongzhang, by now governor of Jiangsu Province, where both Shanghai and Nanjing are located. Ward and Gordon won a number of engagements, but their contribution to the ultimate Qing victory was slight. Nanjing was retaken from the Taipings in 1864 with no foreign help, nor was any used in the

subsequent suppression of other rebellions. But the value of Western military technology had become clear.

A striking paradox of those years was that while the foreigners were assaulting Tianjin and Beijing in 1858–1860, they were fighting on the government's side in central China against the Taipings. Different Chinese government factions were in fact involved, and the foreign humiliation of the court in 1860 meant the defeat of that very conservative and antiforeign group, which in turn meant more scope for reformers like Zeng and Li. The foreigners did not understand this clearly at the time; they were merely defending themselves and their trade at Shanghai and nearby Ningbo while dealing separately with what they saw as an intolerable set of bad relations with the government in Beijing. After 1860 the foreigners increasingly saw that their best interests would be served by keeping the weakened Qing dynasty in power, propping it up as a client state that was unable to resist them and would do their bidding. The emperor fled from the Anglo-French forces that invaded the capital, and his brother, Prince Kong, concluded the final treaty settlement, which he saw as essential to save the dynasty. When the emperor died in 1861, Prince Kong took over as regent for the new boy emperor, whose reign title was Tongzhi, although he was obliged

Cixi's infamous marble boat, resting in the mud at her newly built and lavishly rococco summer palace outside Beijing. (R. Murphey)

to share power with the boy's scheming mother, the young empress dowager Cixi. Together they supervised the execution of rival antiforeign princes and lent support to Zeng and Li in their anti-Taiping campaigns.

This was the beginning of the "self-strengthening" movement, which consciously sought to adopt Western military technology, barbarian tricks to save China from the barbarians. The reign of the new emperor, from 1862 to 1875, was called the Tongzhi Restoration, and China seemed to be at last on the right track. A new school to train Chinese interpreters in Western languages was established and something like a foreign office to manage diplomatic relations. More effort was put into building arsenals for modern weapons and ships outside the foreign concession areas at Nanjing, Tianjin, Shanghai, and, with French help, at Fuzhou, including a naval dockyard.

But this was not Meiji Japan, despite the above similarities. China was still fundamentally conservative; the Manchu government was in its last half century and almost by definition had lost both the will and the ability to pursue changes, while as an alien dynasty it felt obliged to maintain the traditional Chinese way in all things. Like most Chinese, the Qing had a basic mistrust or even hatred of everything foreign and of change of almost any kind, except to spruce up the Confucian

tradition, which in effect is what the Tongzhi Restoration primarily aimed to do. In addition, the dynasty had been fundamentally weakened by the Taiping Rebellion and the enormous effort of its suppression—nor were such drains on the state's resources to cease until it finally collapsed in 1911.

Rebellions multiplied, and even the brilliant campaigns against the Muslim rebels in the west and the Russian schemes in Xinjiang under the able general Zuo Zongtang won only a brief respite, while exhausting the treasury. Revenues could not keep up with expenditures, even with the help of new taxes on trade. The growth of regional armies begun in the Taiping years signaled a trend toward regional diffusion of government authority and foreshadowed the warlordism that was to consume the first decades of the twentieth century. In the face of such problems, the government could only repeat the Confucian formulas: respect for superiors, deference to authority, and hence the maintenance of harmony. Even Zong Guofan criticized what he saw as the money-grubbing merchants in the treaty ports and believed that railways and the telegraph would disrupt the Chinese system and should be kept out.

The Tongzhi emperor died in 1875, possibly "assisted" by Cixi as he was only 19. She then had her own nephew, a boy of four, made emperor as Guangxu but kept real power for herself, and in 1884 removed Prince Kong from office. Some modernization projects continued, such as those promoted by Li Hongzhang, who became a governor-general, built up the arsenals, and promoted a number of other Western-style ventures. These included a highly successful steamship company, a modern-style coal mine, a telegraph company, and several modern textile mills. But they were insignificant ripples on the vast sea of the largely unchanged traditional economy, and most of the enterprises ran into financial trouble, in part because Li and many others siphoned off too many of the profits. They were supposed to be government-supervised and merchant-operated, but they became largely inefficient bureaucratic operations, with a few exceptions. Li's coal mine at Kaiping, north of Tianjin, had a short railway line by 1883 to haul the coal to a port that was improved to handle bigger ships; the rail line was slowly extended to Tianjin, and even to the outskirts of Beijing by 1896, but railway building elsewhere was even slower and often met with strong local resistance. A British firm in Shanghai built a short line to the outer harbor in 1876, but local opposition was so intense, especially after a man was run over, that the governor-general of the province in Nanjing bought the line in 1877 and had it torn up and the rails shipped to lie rusting on a beach in Taiwan.

A few Chinese began to go abroad to study, helped by missionaries, but an educational mission that sent 120 college-age boys to Hartford, Connecticut, in 1872 was withdrawn in 1881, and on their return the students were treated with suspicion, as were all new things or change in any form, especially where there was a foreign connection. Those few official Chinese who urged Westernization, as the Meiji Japanese were doing full speed, were criticized or forced into retirement. Li Hongzhang was basically a conservative in his views; although he recognized the need for some change, he had to move cautiously, especially with the empress dowager. The same was true of another prominent governor-general who agreed that reforms were essential, Zhang Zhidong; but he was outspokenly antiforeign. His formula was widely repeated: use Chinese ways for fundamentals, and Western ways only as tools. Like most Chinese of his time, he failed to understand that the whole of the traditional Chinese system, especially its "fundamentals," had to be changed if China were to escape from backwardness, poverty, and humiliation.

It was typical of the last decades of the Qing that when Li tried to rebuild a fleet after the disastrous war with the French in 1885, much of the funds he needed were diverted by the empress dowager to build a garish new summer palace northwest of Beijing at mammoth expense. Eunuchs and other courtiers grew even richer on this new source of graft, and the new palace included an ornate, two-tiered boat built of solid marble on the edge of a big lake; it became common knowledge that this was Cixi's little joke—a marble boat for her instead of an adequate new navy for China.

When the new Japanese navy at a peak of efficiency attacked in 1894 the Chinese admiral had no notion of modern naval tactics, many of the Chinese guns were supplied with the wrong size shells, and many of the shells proved to have been filled with sand by corrupt contractors. At the peace negotiations for the Treaty of Shiminoseki in 1895, Li, who was head of the Chinese delegation, said to Ito Hirobumi, his Japanese counterpart:

"China and Japan are the closest neighbors, and moreover we have the same writing system. How can we be enemies? . . . We ought to establish perpetual peace and harmony between us, so that our Asiatic yellow race will not be encroached upon by the white race of Europe." Ito replied: "Ten years ago I talked with you about reform. Why is it that not a single thing has been changed or reformed?," to which Li could only say: "Affairs in my country have been so confined by tradition that I could not accomplish what I desired. . . . I am ashamed of having excessive wishes and lacking the power to fulfill them."[2]

New Humiliations

The defeat by Japan was shattering to Chinese pride. Western powers were one thing, but Japan was almost like a younger member of the family, for centuries a patronized tributary state that had learned all the arts of civilization from China. Many conservatives, still in the great majority, repeated the phrase "Back to the Western Han!" as the cure for China's modern disaster. The Western Han was long enough ago that people tended to remember only the good things about it, as an age of brilliant accomplishment and imperial glory when China ruled the world. It was typically Chinese to look to the past for guidance rather than to the present, and to try to make themselves feel better by remembering their ancient greatness. As the nineteenth century drew to a close, the Western powers, including Russia, seemed to be closing in for the kill, extracting new concessions, naval bases, leased territories, and "spheres of influence." What saved China from a complete colonial takeover was primarily the rivalry among the powers, including Japan; none of them were willing to see any one country become dominant in China, and it made no sense for often bitter rivals to try to run it collectively. In any case it would have been a colossal administrative headache, and even at the height of the imperialist fever few countries really wanted to take that on.

The scramble for new concessions included a relatively sudden rush for loans to and contracts with the Chinese government to build railways, mainly by private foreign companies, although some had foreign government connections. A few major lines were completed in a process that extended into the 1930s, although after 1930 the Nationalist Guomindang government tried to keep control over all new lines. Railways were clearly a step forward, and badly needed for better national integration; even the Qing government built and financed a few new lines. But the foreign involvement further increased their control and was much resented by many, as well as saddling successive Chinese regimes with new debt burdens. The Russians made Manchuria into their special sphere and began extensive railway building and mining operations there.

The Russian position and activities were taken over by the Japanese after their victory in the Russo-Japanese war of 1904–1905. Under their direction Manchuria acquired a highly developed rail net and a major mining and industrial complex, but at the cost of any real Chinese authority there. Foreigners saw railway investment as profitable but also as a way of facilitating the supply of exports and the flow of imports to and from the treaty ports. In the Treaty of Tianjin in 1860 foreigners had extracted the right to operate their own steamships and carry cargo on the extensive Chinese inland waterways, especially the Yangzi and its tributaries, and they became the major carriers there and along the coastal routes. Foreign naval vessels were anchored prominently off the waterfront in every major treaty port and patrolled the inland waters as well, to "safeguard foreign interests." Foreign banks dominated the financing of China's foreign trade and the highly profitable insurance business, an idea new to China but soon popular with many Chinese merchants.

Efforts at Reform

Some officials, scholars, and gentry urged that the Treaty of Shiminoseki be rejected, especially since the huge indemnity it imposed, three times China's annual revenues, would complete the utter ruin of the government's finances. Kang Youwei, a vigorous Cantonese, became the leader of a group of graduates urging radical reforms; he was joined by his fellow Cantonese intellectual, Liang Qichao. No longer troubled by the apparent dilemma of how to save China by Westernizing it, they had made the resolution reached a generation

 ## Reform

Liang Qichao (1873–1929), a student and associate of Kang Youwei, was a tireless advocate of reform; he had this to say about China's situation in 1896, just after its crushing defeat by Japan.

Those who insist that there is no need for reform still say "Let us follow the ancients, follow the ancients." They coldly sit and watch everything being laid to waste by following tradition, and there is no concern in their hearts. . . . Now there is a big mansion which has lasted a thousand years. The tiles and bricks are decayed and the beams and rafters are broken up. It is still a magnificently big thing, but when wind and rain suddenly come up, its fall is foredoomed. Yet the people in the house are still happily playing or soundly sleeping. Even some who have noted the danger know only how to weep bitterly, folding their arms and waiting for death without thinking of any remedy. Sometimes there are people a little better off who try to repair the cracks, seal up the leaks, and patch up the ant holes in order to be able to go on living there in peace, even temporarily, in the hope that something better may turn up. [Liang means here the "self-strengtheners," still sticking to the old system.] These three types of people use their minds differently, but when a hurricane comes they will die together. . . . A nation is also like this.

Source: S. Y. Teng and J. K. Fairbank, *China's Response to the West: A Documentary Survey* (Cambridge: Harvard University Press, 1954), p. 155.

earlier by the Meiji reformers in Japan: at least in technology, education, and much of government, the Western way was the best way to promote national strength and prosperity. Kang reinterpreted Confucius as a reformer, someone who preached "the right of rebellion" against unfit rulers and who sanctioned change.

In late 1897 Kang was recommended as a tutor to Emperor Guangxu, and in 1898 he presented a long list of reform proposals, including a national assembly and a constitution. From June 11 to September 21, 1898, prompted by Kang and Liang Qichao, the emperor issued over forty edicts in what came to be called the Hundred Days of Reform, which aimed to remake the entire system of education, economy, and government. There was of course violent opposition from the official establishment. The empress dowager, who had temporarily retired at age 63, soon realized that Kang had gone too far to win the support of most Chinese and that her reactionary views still represented a majority of the political elite. She engineered a coup on September 21, seized the emperor and forced him into seclusion, and executed six of the reformers, though Kang and Liang escaped to Japan. When Cixi finally died in 1908 she had managed to ensure that the emperor, presumably poisoned, died one day earlier; she arranged as his successor her three-year-old nephew, Puyi, who "reigned" until the dynasty officially ended in 1912.

A few of the more moderate reforms begun in the Hundred Days were retained, including the establishment of modern schools, and in 1905 the imperial examinations were abolished, ending an ancient institution that had outlived its time. The government moved slowly to create provincial and national "consultative assemblies" and promised a parliament by 1913, but it was too slow and too late to deflect the mounting pressures for change. The chief effort of the reformers, to create a revolution from the top, failed primarily because most Chinese were not ready for such radical change despite the lessons of the years since 1842. Cixi's answer to the foreign threat to China was to support the Boxers in their hopeless attempt to kill or drive away all foreigners. She and her government were lucky to survive that disaster, only because the foreign powers—now including Japan—saw no alternative, did not want to take on the job of administering China themselves, and had grown used to propping up the moribund dynasty as a compliant stooge.

For the most part, the efforts at reform, including the "self-strengtheners" of the Tongzhi Restoration, were traditional answers to traditional problems. There was no significant industrialization, except on a relatively small scale in the treaty ports, most of it by foreigners, and little willingness to abandon institutions grown incapable of dealing with contemporary problems. China

 ## The Hundred Days

On June 11, 1898, the Guangxu emperor, inspired by Kang Youwei's ideas as well as by the example of Meiji Japan, issued a famous decree, inaugurating what came to be known as the Hundred Days of Reform. It reads in part as follows:

Those who claim to be conservative patriots consider that all the old customs should be upheld and the new ideas repudiated without compromise. Such querulous opinions are worthless. Consider the needs of the times and the weakness of our Empire! If we continue to drift with an army untrained, our revenues disorganized, our scholars ignorant, and our artisans without technical training, how can we possibly hope to hold our own among the nations. . . . The virtuous rulers of remote antiquity did not cling obstinately to existing ways, but were ready to accept change, even as one wears grass-cloth garments in summer and furs in winter.

We now issue this special Decree so that all our subjects, from the Imperial family downward, may hereafter exert themselves in the cause of reform.

Source: J. O. P. Bland and E. Backhouse, *China Under the Empress Dowager* (London: Heinemann, 1910), p. 186.

was still the Middle Kingdom, too successful in the past for too long to recognize the need for change or learn from barbarians. No effective answer emerged to the dilemma of how to preserve the Chinese essence if that meant, as it clearly did, adoption of foreign technology *and* institutions. Yet the pride in being Chinese was never lost; nor was it to be when finally, after many false starts, failures, and betrayals, revolution came from the bottom up. The long Chinese sense of membership in a common culture had first to be augmented by a new sense of nationalism, irrelevant during the centuries when China was the empire that ruled "all under Heaven" and only lesser people had "states." Now China had to learn the hard lesson that it too must become a modern state if it was to regain not its old superiority but an equal footing in competition with other states. Modern nationalism was to be the key to success, but political coherence was slow to grow beyond a few of the intellectual elite.

Chaos and Warlordism

The Qing dynasty collapsed in 1911 with the gentlest of shoves from a small and poorly organized group of revolutionaries. The end of Manchu rule is called a revolution because the government was overthrown by people who called themselves revolutionaries and had some new and radical ideas. But they were too few and too politically inexperienced to establish an effective government of their own, and to make matters worse they were split into factions. The leading organization was the Guomindang, or Nationalist party, founded in an earlier form around the turn of the century and led by Sun Yat-sen (1866–1925), an idealist with great personal charisma but little sense of practical politics.

Sun Yat-sen and Yuan Shikai

Sun was born to a peasant family near Guangzhou, traditionally a hotbed of separatism and political ferment. At age 13, like so many Cantonese, he joined his older brother in Honolulu, where he went to a church boarding school and became a Christian. At 16 he returned to study in Hong Kong and finished a medical degree there in 1892 at a British mission hospital. He tried to practice briefly in Macao but was forced out because he had no diploma from Portugal.

Sun still agonized over China's humiliation by foreign powers, and he soon founded a secret society, in the old Cantonese tradition, to overthrow the Manchus, who had failed his people and who were themselves a foreign

dynasty of conquest. He drew support also from overseas Chinese and quickly became wanted by the Qing police. When his plot to seize the Guangzhou government offices in 1895 was discovered and several of his fellow conspirators executed, Sun fled to Japan. From there he made repeated trips to build Chinese contacts in Hawaii, Britain, France, and North America. He was pursued by Qing government agents even abroad and had some narrow escapes; on one occasion he was rescued by his old Hong Kong medical teacher when he was kidnapped and imprisoned in the Chinese legation in London in 1896, before being sent back to China for execution.

Meanwhile, other radical leaders and groups in China were also active, and there were several joint and separate attempts to seize power, all of which failed and were marked by confusion and lack of coordination. Mounting peasant poverty led to rice riots, and in 1911 there was a gentry-led revolt in Sichuan protesting the government's plan to build railways there with foreign capital. The finally successful uprising at Wuchang (now part of Wuhan in the central Yangzi Valley) began as another comedy of errors. Some students and soldiers, not part of any of the previous revolutionary groups, had planned locally to seize power. Their plot was discovered on October 9, and they were forced to act when a dog barked in the night and a bomb they had made was found. Fortunately, they were joined by a few additional troops from the garrison there on October 10, the date celebrated as the Revolution of 1911. Wuchang fell to the rebels, who attracted a good deal of popular support and triggered uprisings here and there over the whole country.

From 1900, coincident to the rise of Chinese nationalism, the Chinese living abroad—primarily the residents of urban Chinatowns—were the target of distant Chinese reformers, revolutionaries, and conservatives who offered to recognize them as Chinese citizens as well as to grant them titles and government positions. The Chinese government began to use the term "Overseas Chinese" as a way to emphasize their continuing bond, to maintain the loyalty and support of those of Chinese descent who lived outside China. Sun Yat-sen and others received the funding for the 1911 revolution from Overseas Chinese, although all Overseas Chinese were not sympathetic to the revolution, and China's politics divided Chinatown residents.

By December most of China except the provinces around the capital at Beijing had declared their independence of Manchu rule, with very little fighting. A provisional government was set up at Nanjing. Sun Yat-sen was in the United States at the time trying to raise money among Chinese there to support the revolutionary effort. He read an account of the Wuchang revolt in a Denver newspaper, where he was living in the YMCA, and then went on to England to seek more help. He was sent a coded message from the revolutionaries saying that he should return to China as its first president, but he had lost his codebook and took some time to decipher the message. He was finally inaugurated at Nanjing in January of 1912.

Sun was a moving speaker and inspired many thousands of Chinese with his vision of a new China, but he was a failure as a political organizer. His blueprints for the future were fuzzy documents never very clearly laid out and included some quite impractical ideas, such as building railways into Tibet. He was also out of touch with China, especially peasant China, the great majority of the country. He had not lived there (as opposed to visiting) since he was 13 years old. His impressionable adolescence and his subsequent time as a student were spent in Hawaii, Hong Kong, and Macao, after which he lived almost entirely abroad, including for a time in Hanoi in French-controlled Vietnam. He was a genuine nationalist of deep and sincere conviction, but his perspective was more that of a highly educated, Westernized overseas Chinese than that of most of his countrymen.

Song Qingling, the woman Sun was to marry in 1915, was the daughter of a Chinese emigrant returned from the United States who had done well in treaty-port Shanghai and sent his children to American colleges. She heard the news of the 1911 revolution in Macon, Georgia, where she was a student at Wesleyan College, and wrote:

Sun Yat-sen and his young U.S.-educated wife Song Qingling in 1924. (Bettman/Corbis)

> The emancipation of 400 million souls from the thralldom of an absolute monarchy. . . . The Revolution has established in China Liberty and Equality . . . Fraternity is the as yet unrealized ideal of humanity. . . . It may be for China, the oldest of nations, to point the way to this fraternity.[3]

She exaggerated the success and the impact of 1911, but her remarks expressed views that were shared by many young Chinese intellectuals and at the same time showed the depth of Western influence on their thinking. The events at Wuchang were hardly a revolution, but they fired the spread of a genuine Chinese nationalism in the modern sense for the first time.

China was still hopelessly divided, and even Sun saw that he could not provide the unity and strong central government needed. He agreed to step down as president in favor of Yuan Shikai (1859–1916), a leading Qing military man who had thrown his lot in with the republicans. Sun had earlier put together a vague set of guidelines for a new government called the Three Principles of the People. These were nationalism, democracy, and the people's livelihood, none of them very clearly defined. Nationalism in the modern sense was still a new idea to most Chinese, but they could at least make common cause against the Manchus in the name of Chinese self-determination. Sun's idea of democracy, heavily influenced by Western models, implied but did not spell out social and political equality, a notable departure from Confucian forms, reflecting his Western education and his time in the United States. This was to be assured by a constitution largely on an American pattern, while "livelihood"—a partial redistribution of wealth on behalf of the poorer peasantry—was to be achieved through tax reforms.

There were no true political parties as yet, only a variety of elite or intellectual groups, divided among themselves. When the new Guomindang won national elections in 1913, Yuan Shikai, who had busily concentrated real power in his own hands, arranged the assassination of the leading Guomindang organizer, who had pressed for constitutional government. Sun again fled to Japan, while Yuan further tightened his grip as military dictator by force, bribery, and intimidation. In 1915 he had himself declared president for life and took to riding around in an armored car for fear of attack by frustrated revolutionaries. Meanwhile, he dared not confront foreign imperialism in China because he needed—and got—foreign support as a strongman who could keep order and would not threaten "special interests." The revolution had been betrayed.

Several southern and western provinces, where disgruntled military men and revolutionaries were active, broke away from Yuan's control. In 1916 he died suddenly after failing to get himself declared emperor. Political and ideological change had gone much too far to permit any return to such traditional forms, but there was still neither a consensus on what should succeed them nor a semblance of national unity.

For the next 12 years China dissolved into virtual anarchy, divided among a number of regionally based warlords and other local military leaders. The Guomindang and the early revolutionaries had a political ideology of a sort but no army; the warlords had armies but little or no political ideology, except to contest with each other for supreme power. Their troops marched around the countryside like a scourge on the peasants, while a bewildering variety of short-lived regimes or political cliques succeeded each other in Beijing as the nominal government of China.

In 1917 Sun returned to Guangzhou, formed a rival government, and began building a more effective political organization. He complained that trying to get the Chinese people to work together was like trying to make a rope out of sand. One can understand his frustration, but although he tried to arouse mass support he appealed mainly to intellectuals and those few who were as yet politically conscious. What began to spark Chinese nationalism more effectively was new imperialist moves and spontaneous popular protests against them.

The May Fourth Movement

Japan's Twenty-one Demands on China in 1915 (see Chapter 15) provoked immediate protests from patriotic Chinese, especially after Yuan Shikai accepted most of them. China joined the Allied side in the war in 1917, sent a 200,000-man labor battalion to the western front in Europe, and hoped thus to get a hearing at the peace conference. But although Japan did not join the fighting in Europe, it secretly obtained prior Allied agreement to keep the former German concessions that it had taken in Shandong Province. It soon became evident that President Woodrow Wilson's lofty talk about self-determination and open diplomacy did not apply to Asia: Japan was represented at the Versailles peace conference, while

China, despite its efforts, was not. The Western powers later confirmed Japan's "rights" in China; in fact, Japan's special position in Shandong did not end until 1923, after belated Allied intervention.

When news broke that the warlord government in Beijing had signed secret agreements with Japan, mass demonstrations erupted on May 4, 1919. Chinese nationalism boiled over in what came to be called the May Fourth movement. A new and increasingly radical generation of students from government and mission schools and universities were imbued with Western ideas and dedicated to building a new China. Student protesters beat up a pro-Japanese official and burned a cabinet minister's house. They went on to organize a union and to seek wider support from among Westernized businessmen, industrialists, and shopkeepers in the treaty ports. Strikes and boycotts of Japanese goods attracted widespread support. The cabinet resigned, and China refused to sign the Versailles Treaty.

The May Fourth Movement stimulated renewed intellectual ferment as well, especially in Beijing and Shanghai, where hundreds of new political and literary periodicals attacked traditional culture, deplored China's weakness, and advocated a variety of more or less radical solutions. The model of the Confucian scholar steeped in the classics gave way to that of "progressive" thinkers who wrote in the vernacular and tried to appeal not only to fellow scholars or intellectuals but also to the people as a whole. Parental and family tyranny, arranged marriages, and the subjugation of women and the young became targets of attack. Women, especially students, played a prominent part in the May Fourth Movement; they and their male colleagues urged full-scale female emancipation and an end to the rigidity of the traditional system as a whole.

The promise and enthusiasm of the May Fourth Movement were not to last. Its Western-style aims and ideals had relatively little to do with the urgent needs of the peasant majority, and its message never reached more than the tiny group of intellectuals, students, and treaty-port Chinese. It had no effective political organization and was not a contender for power. Its idealistic adherents, some of whom joined one or the other of the two political parties, the Guomindang or the Communists, were in the end absorbed by them and most of their goals subverted. There was too little basis in China for the middle ground that they represented or for their Western-derived ideals or models. The long contest for political power and for the leadership of the new China took place between the Guomindang and the Communists, a battle in some sense between two opposite extremes of the political right and left. Neither had much to do with the ideals of May Fourth. The story of that struggle, which lasted from the early 1920s to 1949, is resumed in Chapter 17.

A CLOSER LOOK

Prominent Figures in the May Fourth Movement

Lu Xun (1881–1936), the greatest of modern Chinese writers, voiced the ideas of his time among the May Fourth group in his bitter indictments of the old society, whose supposed "benevolence" and "virtue" were hypocritical masks for cruel oppression and exploitation. Foreign imperialism was deeply resented, but the May Fourth writers saw it as the result of China's weakness rather than as the cause. China had to be changed from the ground up if it were to regain its strength and pride. The example of Meiji Japan was much admired, despite the later corruption of Japanese imperialism in China. Like the Meiji leaders, China's new voices called for a clean slate and a new pattern that welcomed Western ideas as a source of strength.

Lu Xun made his character Ah Q famous as a personification of all that was wrong with China: cultural pride in its long tradition, which blinded it to the advantages of learning new ways, especially from foreigners; its consequent backwardness in the modern world; and its growing poverty. Lu Xun blamed all this on the outmoded and, as he saw it, hypocritical values of the Confucian scholar-gentry. He was painfully aware of his country's weakness and humiliation at the hands of Westerners and Japanese but saw China as its own worst enemy. He was especially bitter about the oppres-

sion of women and about the heartless, selfish, and cynical attitude of most of his countrymen. He was a consistent pessimist, but he lived during the worst years of China's history. Not only was it humiliated repeatedly by foreigners as a semicolony, but its own political and social system was falling apart and slipping into chaos. Drought, famine, and flood accompanied and followed the warlord era, especially in the 1920s, and added to the destruction of civil war.

Like so many young Chinese who sought modern technology as a cure for China's weakness, Lu Xun had been a medical student in Japan in the early years of the century. His father had died young, and Lu Xun believed that he could have been saved by Western medicine, which was taught in Japan after 1870 as part of the Japanese drive for modernization. In Japan Lu Xun saw a newsfilm showing Japanese troops in Manchuria at the time of the Russo-Japanese War. They had caught a Chinese accused of spying for the Russians. "Many others of my countrymen stood around him. They were all strong fellows but appeared completely apathetic. . . . The one with his hands bound . . . was to have his head cut off . . . as a warning to others, while the Chinese beside him had come to enjoy the spectacle."[4] After this experience, he left Japan and abandoned his medical studies, believing that what the Chinese people needed was not physical healing but "to change their spirit." He aimed to do this through his stories and political essays, published in the many new magazines of the May Fourth era, which brilliantly satirized what he saw as the failings of the old China.

Cosmopolitanism in Shanghai, 1933. From left to right, the American journalist Agnes Smedley, the playwright George Bernard Shaw, Madam Sun Yat-sen, Cai Yuanpei (a leading intellectual), and Lu Xun. Shaw was on a visit to China and is being welcomed here by the founders of the China League for Civil Rights. (Sovfoto/Eastfoto)

Radical Change

Chen Duxiu issued a "Call to Youth" in 1915.

> Chinese compliment others by saying "He acts like an old man although still young." Englishmen and Americans encourage one another by saying "Keep young while growing old." . . . Youth is like early spring, like the rising sun, like trees and grass in bud, like a newly sharpened blade. . . . I place my plea before the young and vital youth, in the hope that they will achieve self-awareness and begin to struggle. . . . It is the old and rotten that fills society. One cannot find even a bit of fresh and vital air to comfort those of us who are suffocating in despair. [But] *All Men are equal. Be independent, not servile. Be progressive, not conservative. Be aggressive, not retiring. Be cosmopolitan, not isolationist. Be utilitarian, not formalistic.*

Source: S. Y. Teng and J. K. Fairbank, *China's Response to the West: A Documentary Survey* (Cambridge: Harvard University Press, 1954), pp. 240–244.

Other prominent figures in the May Fourth Movement included Hu Shi, who had studied the classics in China and then gone on to study philosophy at Cornell and Columbia. Hu was the principal leader of what he called the Chinese Renaissance, which stressed the new literature aimed at a mass audience and written, supposedly, in the vernacular rather than the classical language of the scholar-elite. But the May Fourth writers had all been classically educated, and all were by definition intellectuals. Their stories and magazines reached other intellectuals almost exclusively, not the predominantly illiterate peasants and common people at whom they were theoretically aimed. Other May Fourth leaders were Cai Yuanpei, who became chancelor of Beijing National University, and Chen Duxiu, both of whom had been educated abroad as well as in China.

Like Lu Xun, Chen blamed China's decline on Confucianism. Chen became editor of the magazine New Youth, which called on the Chinese to be "independent, not servile . . . progressive, not conservative."[5] Chen joined Hu Shi and Cai Yuanpei at Beijing University, along with others of like mind. Chen urged that China badly needed the help of "Mr. Science" and "Mr. Democracy," as he put it: "Only these two gentlemen can cure the dark maladies in Chinese politics, morality, learning, and thought."[6] After May 4, 1919, the university became the chief center of the movement; it was quickly joined by a similar group of intellectuals and students in Shanghai, including Lu Xun, Li Dazhao, and Chen Duxiu, the chief founder of the Chinese Communist party in 1921.

India Under Colonial Rule

Here too we must pick up the thread of Indian history after the Revolt of 1857, discussed in Chapter 15. British policy for India now abandoned the earlier efforts of the Utilitarians like Governor-General Bentinck to push for changes in Indian society such as the abolition of *sati* and child marriage. Indian culture as a whole was to be left alone, and Indian religions protected against Western interference. Most Western missionaries now confined themselves largely to serving those few already converted, to studying and translating Indian texts, and to founding and running schools.

The British Indian army had grown out of troops originally formed to defend the main East India Company bases in Madras, Bombay, and Calcutta. Now it was reorganized under stronger central British control, and the proportion of British officers and troops was increased. The insurrection of 1857 began in a Bengali regiment barracks on the edge of Calcutta; after 1857 Bengalis were excluded from the army, as were Marathas and men from Bihar, many of whom had joined the mutineers. The Sikhs, who had stood by the British, the Gurkhas of Nepal, the Rajputs, and a few other groups were designated as "martial races" and specially recruited into the military, although all of them volunteered and made it an attractive career, in effect as mercenary soldiers but with great pride in their regiments.

Economic Change

Railway building had begun early in the 1850s and was resumed after 1858 with new speed and energy. By 1869, when the Suez Canal opened, India had 5,000 miles of lines, and 25,000 by the end of the century. Telegraph lines wove an even denser net. Jute mills and a variety of smaller industries grew rapidly in Calcutta; cotton mills, shipyards, and other manufacturing plants developed in Bombay, in the latter case predominantly under Indian ownership and management. Modern coal mines with mechanical equipment had been started as Bengali enterprises early in the century, notably by Dwarkanath Tagore, who also had a fleet of steamships and promoted Western-style banking and manufacturing methods. Acreage under cotton multiplied, mainly in the drier western parts of Punjab and the Indus Valley and in the semiarid Deccan. Raw cotton, jute from Bengal, and tea from Assam became the leading exports. While much of the cotton exports went to feed the mills of Lancashire, an increasing amount went to Japan's rapidly growing cotton textile industry and China's treaty-port cotton mills. Much of the jute went to mills in Scotland, where it was spun and woven into twine and burlap and reexported worldwide or used in Britain. Wheat became another major export, mainly from the same fertile soils of Punjab and the Indus, aided by new irrigation.

Tea was a new crop, stimulated by the previous Chinese monopoly. The East India Company had sent a botanist, Robert Fortune, to China in 1843 to smuggle out seeds and cuttings of the tea shrub and start a plantation industry in India, thus breaking the Chinese monopoly. Disguised as a Chinese but with the connivance of his guides, Fortune succeeded; he grew tea plants in tubs on the sea voyage back to England (around Africa with two crossings of the equator) and established a collection at Kew Gardens outside London. These were then shipped out to India and Ceylon, by the same long route, where they did well.

Ironically, however, the Indian tea plantation industry was ultimately based on a variety of tea shrub found growing wild in the hills of Assam, which was better suited to local conditions and more vigorous. As in China, tea preferred a cool, wet climate and good drainage on slopes. Large areas of Assam and northernmost Bengal, around the summer colonial capital of Darjeeling in the Himalayan foothills, became covered with tea plantations and curing and packing plants. Local labor was insufficient, and a stream of migrants flowed into the tea areas from overcrowded Bengal and elsewhere. Roads and some railways were built into this mountainous country, with its torrential rainstorms during the summer monsoon, to bring the tea out for export from the port of Calcutta, although it also became a universal drink in India. Tea was also grown in the hills of southernmost India, the Cardamoms and Nilgiris, where conditions were similar at higher elevations, and was shipped out from Madras and within the Indian market. The tea of India and Ceylon makes a reddish-brown drink, while most Chinese and Japanese tea is green; the difference is not in the plants but in curing—roasting and tinting. Tobacco, originally from the New World, also became an important commercial crop, especially in the south, where fine cigars were made, as at Trichinopoly, and mass-produced cigarettes, known in South India as *beedies*.

All these changes in agriculture and their support systems—ports, railways, processing plants—created new jobs and new opportunities. This was also true of the booming factory-based cotton textile and shipbuilding industries of Bombay and Ahmedabad in Gujarat, which became by the end of the nineteenth century the chief consumers of Indian-grown cotton, and of the equally rapid growth of jute mills and other manufacturing in Calcutta. New industrial cities grew in the Ganges Valley or added manufacturing to their traditional functions: Patna, Kanpur (Cawnpore), Lucknow, Allahabad, and even the old imperial capital of Agra, which became famous for locks and hardware. In the south, Madras, Salem, and Coimbatore also became industrial centers, although on a smaller scale, while Nagpur in central India grew into a major railway junction and textile producer. In addition to Calcutta, Madras, and Bombay, the once-small provincial town of Karachi developed as a major port for Punjab and Indus exports of cotton and wheat. All these enterprises demanded labor, and slowly an experienced Indian industrial labor force grew. They also needed capital. Some of it was British, and some, especially for building the railways, came from Indian tax revenues. But most of it was Indian capital from new entrepreneurs operating in the Western mode. Workers were poorly paid and often exploited, but a new kind of India was beginning to emerge.

All the major rail lines focused on or radiated out from the main ports and served the booming inland cities, bringing out primarily raw materials for export and hauling in imports of machinery and manufactured goods. It has been described as "a drainage economy," and to a large extent that was true. But the railways, originally planned for military uses, laid the essential groundwork for economic change and ultimately industrialization.

The scale of Indian railway building between 1860 and 1914 was paralleled only by the growth of U.S. railways in the same period and by the similar developments in European Russia. It was very expensive, and

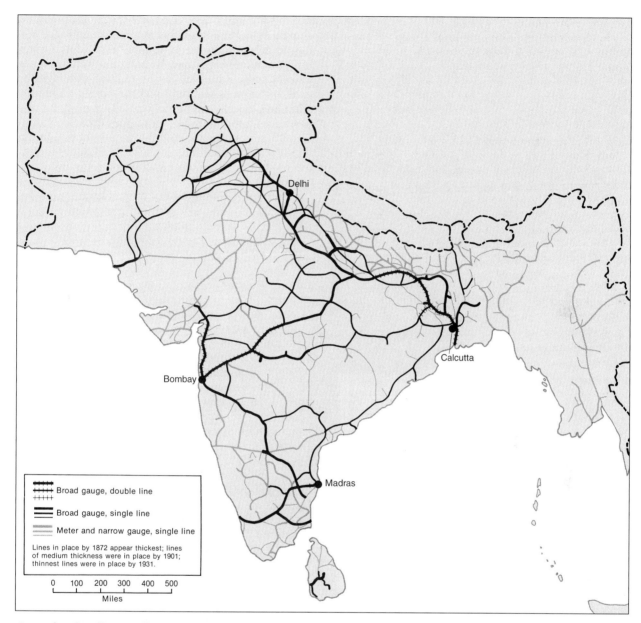

Growth of India's Railway Network

India's rail net was one of the most important of many British projects, greatly accelerating the process of commercialization and "modernization." In its early phase it helped the British to defeat the 1857 revolt, and then fed the boom growth of Bombay, Calcutta, Madras, and Delhi.

there were some complaints not only that Indian revenues paid most of the bills but that all the rolling stock and engines were made in Britain. The costs of the army were relatively small, given India's size and numbers, but they were met entirely from Indian revenues. Many Indians thought it was unjust for them to pay the bill for an army of occupation. Indian revenues also paid for the extensive harbor improvements that became necessary

as the size of the most economic ocean carriers continued to rise in the age of steam and steel. Constant dredging was needed to keep open the Hooghly River at the port of Calcutta. The original harbors of Madras, Karachi, and Colombo were tiny, shallow lagoons, just usable by the ships of the seventeenth century. For some time most larger vessels had to anchor off the beach and load or unload their cargoes by small boats or lighters. Finally in the 1880s breakwaters were begun to create largely artificial harbors at all three, with concrete docks, cranes, and storage facilities. Bombay was more fortunate, since it was originally a chain of several small islands that could be joined by landfill to provide shelter in a large, deep bay behind them, more than enough for the heavy volume of larger shipping that used it and the new docks.

In 1853 rail lines crossed the Western Ghats, which hemmed in Bombay to landward, giving it access to the Deccan with its cotton and wheat, and soon to the rest of India. With these new access routes by land and by sea, each of the port cities grew very rapidly, primarily by immigration from rural areas, and at the same time became processing and manufacturing centers. Already by 1850 Calcutta, Bombay, and Madras were the three biggest Indian cities, dwarfing the traditional inland centers; in fact, since about 1800 Calcutta had been second only to London. The British remained a handful of each city's population, although they dominated much of the new commercial-industrial economy as well as the government.

The New Middle Class

Although most of the new urban Indians were underpaid factory hands, servants, or menial workers who lived under appalling conditions in the sprawling slums, there was also a rising group of Indian entrepreneurs, including bankers and industrialists, and a rapidly growing professional class of Western-style lawyers, doctors, engineers, scholars, journalists, civil servants, teachers, and writers. Until late in the nineteenth century, most of this new Indian middle class, concentrated in the British-founded port cities, eagerly pursued Western ways, flourished in the British-style education system of colonial India, and saw such a path as best not only for themselves but for India. More and more of the well-to-do sent their sons abroad to study or learn a profession in England; they were not upset when their sons came back highly Westernized. Many of the wealthy Indians in the colonial ports owed their wealth to landowning in the rural areas. These absentee landlords were often descendants of the zamindars who had served as agents or allies of the British in the eighteenth century. They too became Westernized but, particularly in Calcutta, retained their active membership in Bengali culture and continued to be part of the ongoing Bengal Renaissance and the vigorous output of literature.

Whereas in China most treaty-port Chinese became divorced from their rural or national origins as they followed Western ways, in India there was little or no such split. Nor did other Indians regard them as "traitors," as Chinese came to regard the "running dogs of the foreigners" in the treaty ports. The major Indian response was to want to become a part of this expanding and exciting new world, even if that meant starting at the bottom as a laborer or street vendor, from which only a lucky few were able to rise. But India, like China, was the size of Europe, with even greater regional and linguistic variety, and most of it remained rural and agricultural. Like the Chinese under semicolonialism, many Indians never saw a foreigner or were affected by their presence. A survey taken soon after independence, in the mid-1950s, asked peasants in the central Ganges region, where the British influence was strong and railway traffic extensive, "Are things better for you now than under the British?" A common reply was "Who are/were the British?" The great majority of Indians remained in peasant villages, largely untouched by the momentous changes and developments centered in the cities.

The principal exceptions were in the areas close to rail lines and those where the new irrigation projects were concentrated. Many peasants with access to rail shipment began to change their cropping patterns to include a larger proportion of commercial crops for sale to the big city markets or for export. This did not by any means always yield a net gain, since such dependence on the market made producers subject to its fluctuations. Many farmers were drawn into the money economy in this way and were ruined or periodically impoverished. The same was true for those who sought work on the relatively few plantations, notably indigo (the name comes of course from "India") in the central Ganges Valley. In general and except for the tea areas in Assam and the south, most of which had never been cultivated, India had long been densely settled. Except for the areas brought under new irrigation, most cultivable land was already being farmed. In the central Ganges, indigo displaced food crops, bad enough in itself since the population was still growing. The largely British owners made handsome profits exporting indigo to the West for use as a dye, but the Indian plantation workers and those encouraged or pressured to grow indigo were often cruelly exploited, just as many of those growing opium in western Bengal and Malwa (just east of Gujarat) had earlier been. In 1859–1860 indigo workers went on strike in protest, a movement known as "the Blue Mutiny," the first workers' strike against the British. When fighting broke out, the government appointed a commission, which ended by supporting the peasants' demands.

Mass Welfare

In balance and despite suffering by many, it seems clear that most Indian peasants benefited more than they suffered from the increased commercialization of agriculture and their growing involvement in the market. The great expansion of the market created by railways, steamships (on Indian rivers and along the coasts), ports, and new safer overseas links by large, fast carriers giving improved access to foreign buyers and suppliers quickened the pace of economic development and change and benefited nearly everyone, although the British and a few Indians benefited most. The widening of the market helped to create new jobs, new economic opportunities, new diversification and regional specialization, and new manufacturing: the universal building blocks of economic development, which rest on the extension of the market. Some economic sectors, and many individuals, are hurt by any economic change, a process clearly demonstrated by the Industrial Revolution in the West, which created a new class of exploited and impoverished urban workers and ruined many traditional craft workers, while squeezing the livelihood of many farmers. This was a process repeated in most respects everywhere industrialization spread. India was no exception.

But further impoverishment was the lot of probably a minority, although most Indians stayed poor. We cannot measure their material welfare accurately, but it seems in general clear that most Indians were better off by the end of colonial rule than they had been in 1800, a reasonable if arbitrary date to use for the beginning of that era, or in 1860, when the pace of economic change began to accelerate. The major problem in India, as in China, was that population continued to increase, and overall economic growth probably barely kept pace with it. Nevertheless, most Chinese were almost certainly worse off in 1949 than they had been in 1842, thanks primarily to unaddressed internal problems, a decaying

government, the massive destruction of rebellions, banditry, and civil war, lack of significant economic development, the devastating Japanese invasion from 1931, and, far down on the list, Western and Japanese exploitation under the "unequal treaties." Indeed, most modern scholars agree that the net results of the foreign presence in a semicolonial China were in balance more positive than negative. It was the foreign example in the treaty ports, as well as the goad of humiliation by foreigners, that stimulated nearly all of what development there was in China, and almost all of the modern industry, banking, commerce, and education was in the treaty ports or in Japanese-controlled Manchuria. The comparison with British-run India is instructive, both in terms of the foreign role and in terms of what was happening to most people in each country.

In India the census showed a falling death rate as the means of livelihood expanded, railways reduced famine deaths, and public health measures began. In both countries, imports, and later domestic production, of machine-made textiles hurt many domestic traditional producers, especially the hand spinners of cotton, who had also been destroyed in the West over the preceding century by the spread of enormously cheaper and more productive machine spinning. But many of the Chinese and Indian weavers benefited from being able to use more even and cheaper machine-spun yarn; they had also improved their traditional looms by adopting Western technology just short of factory-based, power-driven machinery. Right up to the outbreak of the Pacific War in 1941, which sounded the death knell of colonialism, hand weavers in each

How the British lived in India: Notice the wide veranda, the shutters to ease the heat, and the two servants, one fanning and the other giving a pedicure, while the British colonialist in the chair reads his papers. (Hulton/Archive/Getty Images)

country, using improved hand looms and mainly machine-spun thread, mixed with some that was hand-spun, continued to sell the largest share of cloth to the domestic markets in both countries despite both foreign and domestic factory competition. A governor-general's report in the mid-1850s in India, supposedly quoting Karl Marx (although the remark is nowhere to be found in Marx's published writings), included the comment that "The bones of the weavers lie bleaching on the plains of Hindustan." Certainly the less efficient or less enterprising weavers were hurt, as they had been earlier in the West, but most of them survived and even prospered. The Indian Census, one of the great monuments of British colonial rule, recorded more hand weavers in 1941 than in 1871 or 1881, when its records began.

Agriculture and Population

In addition to the spread of railways and the introduction of new crops such as tea, the biggest colonial impact on Indian agriculture was new irrigation. There the major single enterprise was the building of dams and aqueducts or canals in the arid Indus valley and in semiarid Punjab. In many cases this opened up large areas of new land to cultivation; in others it greatly increased yields and preserved them even in years when the monsoon rains were inadequate. Like most desert or semiarid areas, the Indus Valley and Punjab had highly fertile soils that could be made very productive if they were given adequate water. New irrigation canals fed "canal colonies," which, like the tea districts of Assam, had been little if at all settled before, new frontiers for both people and economic growth. Like the contemporary settlement and development of Manchuria, the Great Plains of North America, the Argentine pampa, and the Australian wheat belt, agriculture on these new frontiers concentrated on commercial crops like wheat and cotton, to be shipped out for export or to the distant domestic market by the new rail nets. As in other frontier areas of this period, Punjab and the Indus Valley produced a new kind of Indian, the commercial farmer and entrepreneur, whose living standards and diet were better than those of most other Indian peasants and whose economy rested on a far greater use of new technology.

The cumulatively huge investments in new irrigation included the restoration and extension of the traditional tank (pond) system of the south to store the monsoon rains, new dams on many of the major southern rivers, and the spread of deeper drilled wells and power-driven pumps. But despite all of these improvements and some use of chemical fertilizers, increased supplies of food seem to have been little more than enough to feed the growing population. The agricultural data we have are not conclusive, but other evidence makes it clear that

there was little if any impact on the poverty and frequent malnutrition of the lower third or even half of the population; the prosperity of newly irrigated areas or those along rail lines affected only a minority, and the commercial and professional groups who did well out of the changes after 1860, mainly in the cities, were an even smaller proportion of the population. Agriculture was booming, but much of the increase was in nonfood crops—tea, opium, cotton, indigo, jute—and much of the wheat from newly irrigated areas was exported.

In any case, the Indian agricultural base overall was inadequate to the needs of the immense population, especially as it grew after 1800. The total amount of cultivated land was precariously small in this context, and much of it was marginal: soils of low productivity, areas in slope, others subject to flooding. But the major problem was inadequate moisture (much of the subcontinent is desert or close to it) and the frequent failures of the monsoon. The great heat of summer dries out the soil quickly, and if, as often happens, the rains are long delayed unirrigated crops die in the fields. Sometimes the monsoon produces destructive flooding, which drowns both people and crops. But apart from the shortcomings of its climate, India had and still has only about one-tenth the cultivated land per capita as the United States, and only about half of that for China. This unfavorable ratio between people and productive agricultural land remains a basic root cause of India's poverty.

Unfortunately, it was not so unfavorable as to prevent the further growth of an already large population, which compounded or perpetuated the problem. New land brought under cultivation after 1860, and some increases in per acre yields, were not enough to make a major dent, although the spread of railways greatly reduced famine deaths resulting from crop failure after the 1870s; the death rate from all causes continued to fall, and per capita income and consumption for the growing numbers thus rose relatively little. Averages for any large area or population, and especially for India, are almost meaningless, however; there was certainly substantial economic growth, but the benefits were too much limited to a few groups and areas, while most Indians remained poor. That is the most important criticism of the colonial government—that it did too little to attack this basic problem. On the other hand, the problem was and remains immense, and it is not easy to see how the colonial government, with its limited resources and its self-appointed role as a referee or keeper of order, could have done much about it.

Some Comparisons

To the extent that the modern West and Japan have "solved" the problem of mass poverty (far from completely in the West), the solution has come about through mass industrialization and technological change, which have made agriculture enormously more productive and at the same time created new non-farm jobs for over 90 percent of the population. Manufacturing and service industries based mainly in cities turn out a vast stream of consumer goods and services that most people can afford. That process did not succeed in Britain until some time in the early twentieth century, not long before the end of British control in India. Even then India had about eight times the number of people for which to provide. Indian industrialization was not a colonial goal, partly because some feared competition for British industry, but mainly because no governments of that period outside Meiji Japan saw their involvement in industry as either appropriate or needed. It was left largely to farsighted Indian entrepreneurs to promote this basic change, although some private British capital also went into manufacturing in India from its beginnings in Calcutta and Bombay. Meanwhile 70 to 80 percent of Indians remained rural peasants, as they still do. The figures for China are much the same.

The Beginnings of Indian Nationalism

Among the new Indian middle classes there slowly grew a sense of the injustice of British rule, as an alien power that allowed only token representation by Indians (apart from their labor and their manning of most of the civil service, the professions, the railways, and the army). After 1861 the viceroy appointed a few Indians to his advisory council, selected for their political loyalty. But there was no thought of admitting Indians, no matter how thoroughly educated along British lines or in Britain itself, to positions of real political responsibility or power. Examinations for admission to the prestigious Indian Civil Service (ICS) (see Chapter 15) were held only in London until 1923, but even the brilliant Bengali Surendranath Banerjea (1848–1926), who outdid most of his British competitors on the exam in 1869, was kept out of the ICS on various pretexts. On his return to Calcutta Banerjea organized a nationalist association to match what had been begun a few years earlier in Bombay by M. G. Ranade (1842–1901).

Ranade graduated from Bombay University in its first class, studied law, and became a judge, but he continued to be discriminated against by the British power holders. Like Banerjea and others who followed, Ranade argued that British rule of India was counter to British traditions of democracy and justice. He and his associates worked for reform rather than revolution, appealing to the better side of the British and using reason rather

than violence. Ranade's chief disciple, G. K. Gokhale (1866–1915), continued this work, and, like Ranade, he stressed the need for Indians to reform their own society and its values in the pursuit of justice and the building of a truly national community, overcoming the disunity created by the often-antagonistic social, regional, and religious groups that divided India. As in China, these reformers attacked the subjugation of women, the plight of widows, and religious hypocrisy; the caste system was also a consistent target, seen not only as unjust but as hampering India in its urgent need to modernize and to overcome its internal divisions if it were to regain its freedom.

Reformers spread these and other ideas through their speeches, publications, and associations and began to influence growing numbers of literate Indians. From the beginning the Indian response to foreign domination had a reformist and nonviolent character, later built on so effectively by M. K. Gandhi (1869–1948) but foreshadowed in part also by the work and writings of B. G. Tilak (1856–1920), who, like Gandhi, drew on the popular appeal of Hindu tradition to build Indian nationalism. Banerjea and his associates and successors in Bengal combined efforts at reform with similar appeals, mainly through a new literary blossoming, to what may be called cultural nationalism. The chief Bengali figures after Banerjea were Arabinda Ghosh (1872–1950), later canonized as Shri Aurobindo, and the cosmopolitan poet, dramatist, novelist, and essayist Rabindranath Tagore (1861–1941). In Madras too, the Westernized world of the colonial ports stimulated the rise of an Indian nationalist response, the founding of successive associations, and the rise of a vigorous press and literary movement.

The new nationalists everywhere wrote in both English and their regional languages—Bengali, Gujarati, Marathi, Tamil, and so on—and all increasingly turned to aspects of the Indian tradition, especially Hinduism, as a rallying ground for national pride and a counter to alien rule. These movements overlooked or ignored the large Muslim minority in India, about a fifth of the population. A few of the Muslim leaders, such as Sayyid Ahmad Khan (1817–1898) of Delhi, a loyal supporter of the British raj, tried to organize Muslims and founded a Muslim college (later university) at Aligarh near Agra to train a new, Westernized Muslim leadership.

In 1885 a large group of these new Indian nationalists, with the help of the ex-ICS Englishman A. D. Hume, founded the Indian National Congress, which as a political party dominated Indian politics for a century. Its first meeting took place in Bombay, always a more thoroughly Indian city than Calcutta (which continued to serve as the colonial and imperial capital until 1912). It was attended by seventy-three men representing every province of British India, although only two were Muslims. By the third annual meeting in Madras,

Rise Up!

The Bengali nationalist Brahmabandhab Upadhyay wrote a fiery editorial in his weekly Calcutta paper in 1907. For this declaration he was arrested and died in prison.

> We have said over and over again that we are not Swadeshi [for Indian self-sufficiency] only so far as salt and sugar are concerned. Our aspirations are higher than the Himalayas. Our pain is as intense as if we had a volcano in us. What we want is the emancipation of India. Our aim is that India may be free, that the stranger may be driven from our homes. . . . The fire of desire has been kindled within our bosom. Heaven we do not want. Deliverance we seek not. Let us be born again in India till our chains fall off. First let the Mother [i.e., India] be free, and then shall come our own release from worldly bonds. . . . Are we afraid of your cannon and guns? Arm brothers, arm! The day of deliverance is near. We have heard the voice and we cannot fail to see the chains of India removed before we die.

Source: W. T. de Bary, ed., *Sources of Indian Traditions,* vol. 2 (New York: Columbia University Press, 1958), pp. 185–186.

attended by some 600 delegates, eighty-three were Muslims; but the Congress remained dominated by high-caste, English-educated Hindus, nearly all from the professions, although there were a few merchants and landowners as well as many Englishmen who shared the Indian nationalist cause. Congress began as a reformist group, officially supporting the British raj but urging that Indians should have a greater role in their own governance. They pressed for more Indians to be admitted to the ICS, among other grievances, and for the reduction of military expenses, which consumed about 40 percent of Indian revenues by 1885. The colonial government dismissed Congress as a "microscopic minority" and continued to believe that it was the best judge of what was good for India and its people.

This arrogantly paternalistic attitude, increasingly characteristic of the colonial establishment as a whole, was of course galling to the growing group of Indian nationalists. But it was unfortunately true that they were still a tiny fraction of the Indian people, most of whom remained peasants, and that they did not have a strong claim to represent them. As with the May Fourth group in China, the Indian nationalists were a relative handful of Westernized intellectuals, largely limited to the colonial ports and with few cultural connections with the rural countryside. They talked, wrote, and interacted largely with each other, not with the mass of Indians, and their verbal sparring with the colonial government was very much in the British mode. Nor did their mount-ing tide of "resolutions" make any discernible impact on the raj, except perhaps for a slow and reluctant lowering of the bar against Indians in the ICS toward the end of the century and some increase in the number of "safely reliable" Indians on the viceroy's council. By 1895 even some of the new nationalists were elected, by a cumbersome indirect process, to seats on the council and its regional equivalents in Madras, Bombay, and Bengal.

The peak of imperial arrogance was reached by George Curzon, who served as viceroy from 1899 to 1905. In 1905 Curzon sent a British expedition to Tibet (see Chapter 15), but what enraged Indians most of all was his effort in 1905 to partition Bengal, on the grounds that it was too large and populous (85 million at that time) to be administered effectively as a unit. Bengalis believed that it was really an effort to weaken their major role in the nationalist movement and to sow discord by separating predominantly Muslim eastern Bengal from the Hindu western half. There was a prolonged outburst of protest, joined by all Indian nationalists from other areas, including Gokhale, by now president of Congress. A largely spontaneous movement arose to boycott British goods, joined as in China by merchants as well as intellectuals and students. The British answer was police repression, but by 1908 there was a 25 percent drop in British imports to India. At last a broad-based nationalist movement was underway. Muslims took little part in the protests. Still playing the part of loyal supporters of the raj, they petitioned the new

The first meeting of the Indian National Congress in Bombay, 1885; note the British co-founders in the picture, the most conspicuous of whom is Annie Besant (1847–1933), the only woman, seated in the front row center in all white. Besant was a passionate theosophist who believed that Indian tradition had much to offer the West, and would serve as the Congress president in 1917. (By permission of the British Library)

viceroy for separate representation, and in 1906 they founded the All-India Muslim League.

At the same time, Congress split between the older gradualist liberal reformers and the new group of more radical activists who were willing to use boycotts and strikes to make their point and ensure a response. Their activities only increased government repression, and many of their spokesmen were arrested, jailed, or deported. In response, some younger Indians, mainly Bengalis, turned to anti-British terrorism and were jailed in droves without trial. John Morley, who became viceroy in 1905, was in fact liberal-minded, understood the problem, and sided with the moderates in the Congress. Finding their demands reasonable, he worked away at the strong opposition to any changes within the colonial establishment. In 1909 he pushed through an Indian Councils Act, following the advice of Gokhale and his Congress colleague from Bengal, R. C. Dutt. In the elections of 1910, 135 Indian representatives, voted to office by their own Indian constituencies, became legislators on the central and provincial councils. In 1911 the partition of Bengal was rescinded, although its western and southern parts were detached, on reasonable linguistic grounds, to form the two new provinces of Bihar and Orissa, leaving Bengalis once again united and without linguistic or cultural minorities. This did not end Indian grievances, and the pace of change was too slow to satisfy many, but the trend was at last in the right direction.

World War I

When Britain declared war on Germany in August 1914, India was notified that it was automatically at war as well, as part of the empire. Indeed, most Indian nationalists, including Gandhi, supported the war, hoping that India's share in a British victory would hasten their own freedom. Both moderate and radical Congress leaders declared their support, as did nearly all of the native princes. Several of the Princely States sent volunteer detachments. The first wave reached France in September 1914. The New York *World* commented on September 26, "What an army! Its 'native' contingent belongs to a civilization that was old when Germany was a forest and early Britons stained their naked bodies blue."[7] Indians took heavy casualties at Ypres and the Somme and won high praise for their valor. When the Ottoman Empire joined the Central Powers (Germany and Austria) in November 1914, the British Indian Army sent an expeditionary force to the Persian Gulf in Iraq. It nearly reached Baghdad before it was driven back by Turkish forces and finally obliged to surrender after losing most of its men. Another Indian expeditionary force served in Egypt to guard the Suez Canal and later took part in the victorious Middle East campaign. Altogether over 1 million Indian troops and support personnel fought with the British army against Germany and its allies.

During the war the British-educated Muslim leader Muhammad Ali Jinnah (1876–1949), who had earlier joined Congress as a disciple of Gokhale and became his apparent successor as Congress president, worked with other Congress leaders to bring Congress and the Muslim League together. The agreement in the Lucknow Pact of 1916 provided for Muslim representatives on all legislative councils in proportion to the numbers of Muslims in each province. Congress and the League were to work together in demanding a more rapid pace of reform, more representation for Indians, and treatment equal to that given to all British subjects. The parliamentary declaration of 1917 that self-government for India was Britain's objective seemed to be an appropriate response. But the colonial government in India itself remained divided, and its bureaucratic machinery slowed or prevented effective change. Efforts in the India Office in London to push for "complete popular (i.e., Indian) control" at the local level "with the aim of complete responsibility as soon as conditions permit" were sabotaged on the spot by an arrogantly entrenched colonial system unwilling to see its power reduced.

Enter Gandhi

Meanwhile Gandhi, who had returned from South Africa in 1914, began to build the political strategy that was ultimately to prove successful. After organizing a volunteer corps to help in the war effort, he established a base in his native Gujarat where he further developed the techniques of passive resistance and nonviolent protest against injustice that he had first worked out in South Africa on behalf of the large Indian community there. Gandhi shed his Western ways and clothing, acquired during his years of legal training in London, dressed like a poor peasant, and adopted the lifestyle of an Indian sadhu, or holy man. He traveled widely in India, spreading his message of mass protest against oppression, and used his great personal charisma to build a mass following, drawing

on traditional Hindu symbols and values (which included nonviolence, or ahimsa) to create a national Indian response to alien tyranny. In 1916 he answered a call for help from indigo workers in Bihar, still suffering from gross exploitation, and within the year his tactics of passive resistance and mass protest had led to success, a feat soon repeated in Gujarat, where he won wage increases for textile workers in Ahmadabad and a reduction in taxes for peasants further impoverished by crop failures.

As in China, and the funding of Sun's political efforts, the funding for Gandhi's early nationalist activities received substantial subsidy from "Overseas Indians," a group generally linked to what is called "diasporic nationalism." The major difference between the Overseas Chinese and the Overseas South Asians was that the Chinese did not usually repatriate to China. They considered their overseas residence their permanent home. In contrast, in the period from 1830 to 1950, 90 percent of South Asians who left India were "temporary migrants" who believed they were not physically separated from their South Asian "home" long-term and considered themselves as "circulating" rather than migrating.

The war greatly accelerated the pace of change among all Indians who were aware of it: those who served abroad and saw the world and those whose British-style education had taught them the ideas of liberty and justice, which they now saw being flouted or denied in colonial India. Gandhi's recognition that he was an Indian and not simply a British subject, and his use of native traditional symbols to create a common national ground, was the beginning of a belated reassessment by all politically conscious Indians, to be followed successively by the leaders of the movement for independence. Despite their British training and their admiration of the British model, they were to realize, as Gandhi reminded them, that the colonial government was a different matter, and that their Indianness would have to be rediscovered and asserted if they were to win freedom.

Postwar Repression

Ironically, but perhaps inevitably, the colonial government, stimulated in part by the Russian Revolution of 1917 and the hysteria of the subsequent "Red scare" that spread over the capitalist world, decided to prolong the wartime martial law and muzzling of the press. When the repressive Rowlatt Acts embodying these and other control measures were passed in 1919, there were widespread protests and demonstrations. Gandhi urged Indians to refuse to obey the new laws and planned a na-

Nehru on Gandhi

Nehru describes how Gandhi changed his life and that of most other Indian nationalists.

And then Gandhi came. He was like a powerful current of fresh air that made us stretch ourselves and take deep breaths, like a beam of light that pierced the darkness and removed the scales from our eyes, like a whirlwind that upset many things but most of all the working of peoples' minds. He did not descend from the top. He seemed to emerge from the millions of India. . . . Political freedom took new shape then, and acquired a new content. . . . The essence of his teaching was fearlessness and truth, and action allied to these, always keeping the welfare of the masses in view. . . . I became wholly absorbed and caught up in the movement. I lived in offices and committee meetings and crowds. 'Go to the villages' was the slogan, and we trudged many a mile across fields and visited distant villages. . . . I learned to like the thrill of mass feeling.

Source: J. Nehru, *An Autobiography* (London: Chatto & Windus, 1942), p. 9.

tional strike against them. Sikh leaders in Amritsar in southern Punjab responded to Gandhi's call by holding meetings. When the chief organizers were arrested and deported on grounds that all political action was forbidden, their followers marched on the British district commissioner's house to protest and present a petition. When troops fired on them and killed several, the angry survivors burned some British banks and attacked British men and women, killing several people. There were rumors of an Afghan invasion, to be joined by Indians, and some British feared a repeat of the 1857 revolt. General Dyer was called in to restore order and banned all public meetings as part of his mandate. When Dyer learned that a meeting was nevertheless planned for the afternoon of Sunday, April 13, in a place called Jallianwala Bagh, a walled, open space near the edge of the city, he took his troops there and opened fire. The "meeting" was, in fact, a largely peasant gathering from neighboring villages, including many women and children, all unarmed, who had come to celebrate a Hindu festival, as Dyer could have discovered if he had inquired. Despite the lack of resistance, Dyer's troops kept firing for 10 minutes, killing some 400 people and wounding another 1,200.

A Parliamentary Commission of Inquiry censured Dyer, and at the viceroy's insistence he was sent back to England—where conservatives and the colonial establishment welcomed him as a hero. Savage repression continued in the Punjab, where Indians were flogged and forced to grovel in the dust to British officers. What

many Indians saw as the true face of the colonial government as it had become was revealed in the Amritsar Massacre. It marked the end of efforts at compromise and accommodation, at gradual reform within the colonial system, and the true beginning of a mass movement for independence. Even Rabindranath Tagore, who had remained largely outside politics, resigned his British knighthood, awarded to him in 1913 after he had won the Nobel Prize for literature.

While Japan was able to throw off the semicolonial control imposed on it in 1857, China failed, or refused, to adopt Western ways even to save itself from foreign domination. When revolution finally toppled the moribund Qing government in 1911, the revolutionaries were disorganized; they had no mass following and were unable to form an effective government. China was taken over by a military dictator and then by contending warlords and their armies. The disclosure of Japan's Twenty-one Demands and the unwillingness of the Western powers to defend China's interests at Versailles led to the formation of the May Fourth Movement in 1919, which began for the first time to build a popular base for Chinese nationalism and push for reforms in the outmoded traditional system of Confucian values. However, the May Fourth Movement was largely limited to Westernized intellectuals and a few merchants.

In India, nationalists pressed for similar reforms in traditional Hindu values. But those who worked for change were mainly a small group of British-educated

The Secretariat in New Delhi, consciously designed by two British architects to blend Indian and Western styles (note the Mughal-style cupolas) and built of the same red sandstone used for Shah Jahan's Red Fort. (AP/Wide World Photos)

intellectuals striving for reforms in the colonial system rather than its overthrow, and without a mass base. After the apparent promise of India's participation in World War I, colonial repression increased. It was to take another generation before a full-scale nationalist movement, led by Gandhi and Nehru, won independence for India. In China, the Guomindang government that took power in 1927 had some promise and seemed to share some of the May Fourth ideas, but became fearful of popular participation or radical change. Finally, it was overwhelmed by the Japanese invasion. Thus in both countries the rise of an effective national response to the challenges of imperialism and mounting domestic problems was long delayed—in India until 1947 and in China until 1949. The final resolution in both countries was also greatly delayed by World War II, as well as being shaped by it. The post-1920 course of events in China and India, as well as those in Southeast Asia and Japan, is described in Chapter 17, together with an account of the most destructive war in history.

Chinese nationalism, modern style, is said to have begun in the May Fourth Movement of 1919, and a prominent part in that movement was played by women, some of whom became martyrs. Lu Xun, modern China's greatest writer, devoted much of his bitter writing to the plight of women, and their liberation became a prominent part of the reforms that followed May 4, 1919. Women increasingly attended university and cut or bobbed their hair, while in many cases adopting West-

ern dress. In India many of the same trends were apparent, although Indian women stuck to their traditional saris or Punjabi trousers and jackets. Indian women became prominent in the Congress Party and in the movement for independence.

Questions

1. What were the goals of the Chinese "self-strengthening movement" and why did they ultimately fail in their efforts to reform China? How did the victory of Tseng Guofan over the Taipings begin a new military presence in determining China's future? How did this also threaten the political authority of the Chinese Confucian aristocracy?

2. Sun Yat-sen is hailed as China's "man of ideas" and Yuan Shikai representative of China's "men of guns." What was Sun Yat-sen's vision of China's future? How did Yuan Shikai block his ambition, following their brief cooperation in trying to establish a new Chinese government after the Qing dynasty fell in 1911, and with what consequence to China's immediate political future? How did Sun Yat-sen respond in his attempts to construct a functional government?

3. What was the May Fourth Movement, and what were its goals? What did it achieve in the short run,

and how did it lead to the eventual resolution of China's century of revolution?

4. Lu Xun was the most prominent among the May Fourth Movement authors. How did his character Ah Q personify what was wrong with China? In what ways did his views of the Chinese peasantry, the Confucian scholar-gentry, the plight of Chinese women, and Western technology shape the subsequent nationalist debate?

5. How does the map showing the growth of India's railway network (p. 345) illustrate the text's assertions that these lines were built to support "a drainage economy" as well as to reinforce British military interests in India? Is the Indian nationalist critique valid, that this railroad network reinforced the development of a new regionalization of India, centered on the three British urban centers at Bombay, Madras, and Calcutta, rather than providing the infrastructure for a new national political economy?

6. What were the economic changes that took place under the British raj, and how were these both beneficial and detrimental to India's future?

7. How did Gandhi bring together the division between the gradual liberal reformer and the radical activist factions of the Indian National Congress? How did his tactics of passive resistance and mass protest change the Nationalist Movement from one populated by the urban educated to one of mass participation? What was his broader impact on other Asian nationalist movements?

Notes

1. R. Murphey, *Shanghai: Key to Modern China* (Cambridge: Harvard University Press, 1953), p. 57.
2. J. K. Fairbank, *The Great Chinese Revolution* (New York: Harper and Row, 1986), p. 119.
3. *China Reconstructs,* January 1988, p. 26.
4. Lu Xun, *Preface to a Call to Arms* (Peking: Foreign Languages Press, 1954), p. 11.
5. J. K. Fairbank et al., *East Asia: Tradition and Transformation* (Boston: Houghton Mifflin, 1973), p. 767.
6. Ibid., p. 769.
7. S. Wolpert, *A New History of India* (New York: Oxford University Press, 1982), p. 289.

Suggested Web Sites

The May Fourth Movement

http://afe.easia.columbia.edu/menu_pages/time/
    20th_century.htm

From the Columbia University East Asian Curriculum Project. Of-

fers an introduction and primary source documents about the May Fourth Movement.

http://www.marxists.org/reference/archive/mao/
    selected-works/volume-2/mswv2_13.htm

Mao's reflection on the May Fourth Movement in a 1939 speech.

Indian Nationalism

http://fordham.edu/halsail/india/indiasbook
    .html#Indian%20Nationalism

Indian nationalism, with links to speeches and primary source documents.

Sun Yat-sen

http://www.wsu.edu/~dee/MODCHINA/SUN.HTM

http://acc6.its.brooklyn.cuny.edu/~phalsail/texts/
    sunyat.html

Detailed sites that provide materials and documents related to Sun Yat-sen.

Suggestions for Further Reading

China

Chang, H. *Chinese Intellectuals in Crisis.* Berkeley: University of California Press, 1987.

Chang, K. C., and Chu, S. *Li Hung-chang.* Armonk, NY: M. E. Sharpe, 1994.

Chang, S. H., and Gordon, L. *All Under Heaven: Sun Yat-sen and His Revolutionary Thought.* Palo Alto, CA: Hoover Institution, 1991.

Chen, J. T. *The May Fourth Movement.* Leiden: Brill, 1971.

Chesneaux, J., et al. *China from the Opium War to the 1911 Revolution.* New York: Pantheon, 1976.

Cohen, P., and Schrecker, J., eds. *Reform in Nineteenth Century China.* Cambridge: Harvard University Press, 1976.

Grieder, J. *Intellectuals and the State in Modern China.* Glencoe, IL: Free Press, 1981.

Hsu, I. C. Y. *The Rise of Modern China.* New York: Oxford University Press, 1995.

Kazuko, O., and Fogel, J., eds. *Chinese Women in a Century of Revolution.* Stanford: Stanford University Press, 1989.

Kim, H., *Holy War in China: The Muslim Rebellion*, Stanford: Stanford University Press, 2004.

Kuhn, P. Q. *Rebellion and Its Enemies.* Cambridge: Harvard University Press, 1970.

Li, L. *Student Nationalism in China.* Albany: SUNY Press, 1994.

MacKinnon, S. R. *Power and Politics in Late Imperial China.* Berkeley: University of California Press, 1980.

Perry, E. J. *Rebels and Revolutionaries in North China, 1845–1945.* Stanford: Stanford University Press, 1980.

Pruitt, I., ed. *Daughter of Han.* New Haven: Yale University Press, 1945.

Schiffrin, H. Z. *Sun Yat-sen: Reluctant Revolutionary.* Boston: Little, Brown, 1980.

Schrecker, J. E. *The Chinese Revolution in Historical Perspective.* New York: Praeger, 1991.

Sheridan, J. *China in Disintegration.* Glencoe, IL: Free Press, 1975.

Wakeman, F. *The Fall of Imperial China.* New York: Free Press, 1981.

Wright, M. C., ed. *China in Revolution: The First Phase, 1900–1913*. New Haven: Yale University Press, 1968.

———. *The Last Stand of Chinese Conservatism*. Stanford: Stanford University Press, 1957.

India

Brown, J. *Gandhi: Prisoner of Hope*. New Haven: Yale University Press, 1994.

———. *Modern India*. New York: Oxford University Press, 1985.

Dalton, D. *Mahatma Gandhi*. New York: Columbia University Press, 1994.

Ellinwood, D. C., and Pradhan, S. D., eds. *India and World War I*. Delhi: Manohar, 1978.

Gopal, S. *British Policy in India, 1858–1905*. Cambridge, England: Cambridge University Press, 1965.

Greenberger, A. J. *The British Image of India*. Oxford: Oxford University Press, 1969.

Iyer, R. *The Moral and Political Thought of Mahatma Gandhi*. Oxford: Oxford University Press, 1986.

Low, D. A., ed. *Congress and the Raj*. Columbia: University of Missouri Press, 1977.

McLane, J. R. *Indian Nationalism and the Early Congress*. Princeton: Princeton University Press, 1977.

Mehta, V., ed. *Mahatma Gandhi and His Apostles*. New York: Penguin, 1977.

Nanda, B. R. G. *The Indian Moderates and the British Raj*. Princeton: Princeton University Press, 1977.

Seal, A. *The Emergence of Indian Nationalism*. Cambridge, England: Cambridge University Press, 1968.

Sisson, R., and Wolpert, S., eds. *Congress and Indian Nationalism*. Berkeley: University of California Press, 1988.

Steger, M. B. *Gandhi's Dilemma*. New York: St. Martin's Press, 2000.

Tandon, P. *Punjabi Century, 1857–1947*. Berkeley: University of California Press, 1968.

Visram, R. *Women in India and Pakistan: The Struggle for Independence*. Cambridge, England: Cambridge University Press, 1992.

Wolpert, S. *Nehru*. Oxford: Oxford University Press, 1996.

17

The Struggle for Asia, 1920-1945

This chapter begins with a review of colonialism in Southeast Asia and the belated rise of nationalism. In India, M. K. Gandhi and Jawaharlal Nehru gave new impetus to Indian nationalism through passive resistance, which made a big impact, but imperialist sentiment blocked any change with the outbreak of World War II. China staggered through the warlord years from 1912 to 1927 as most Chinese became even poorer, wracked by famine and flood. The foreign-controlled treaty ports prospered and, despite the masses of urban poor, offered a model of modern technology and national strength, while also sheltering radical revolutionaries, including the new Communist Party. Chiang Kai-shek with his new Communist allies under Russian direction defeated most of the warlords in 1926–1927 and then tried to wipe out the Communists, but a few, including Mao Zedong, escaped and finally broke out in the Long March of 1934–1935 to found a new base in the isolated northwest at Yan'an. Chiang's Guomindang (Nationalist) regime with its new capital at Nanjing made some modernizing steps but had facist leanings and did nothing for peasants, the vast majority of Chinese.

Japan had prospered in World War I without Western competition, and saw a brief period of liberalization, but fell under the control of an aggressive military, who in 1931 created an "incident" in Manchuria and took over that rich area. In late 1936 they signed a pact with Nazi Germany and in 1941 a neutrality pact with the Russians; the way was then open for Japan in Southeast Asia. After their attack on the U.S. Pacific fleet at Pearl Harbor on December 7, 1941, they overran Malaya, Singapore, the Philippines, Burma, and Indonesia. They also took most of east China in heavy fighting from July 1937. Chiang moved his capital west to Chongqing while in the north Communist guerrillas fought the Japanese and captured the leadership of Chinese nationalism.

The Japanese were ruthless, guilty of even more atrocities than the Nazis, but were finally overwhelmed when the United States dropped the atom bomb. Japan surrendered on August 15, 1945.

Colonialism in Southeast Asia

Compared with India or even with treaty-port China, full colonialism came late to most of Southeast Asia. Dutch sovereignty over all of what is now Indonesia was not complete until the early twentieth century, more or less contemporary with the American conquest of the Philippines, from a loose Spanish control. Burma was not fully absorbed by the British until 1886, while they ruled Malaya indirectly through the traditional Malay sultans, who remained titular heads of the several small Malay states. The British resident at each Malay sultan's court slowly took over more and more administrative responsibility, and in 1985 the Malay states most important to the British were grouped into a federation under a British resident-general in what, thus, became the colonial capital of Kuala Lumpur. From this central location the British administered the economically important west coastal regions, where most of the tin and rubber were produced. The remaining and economically less important Malay states were to a greater degree left alone; they came under British "protection" as the unfederated states in 1909 but were allowed considerable autonomy, overseen by British advisers rather than by residents. Penang, Melaka, and Singapore, the straits settlements, remained under direct British administration.

It took time for most Southeast Asians to develop a national response to colonialism. Indeed it was not yet

CHRONOLOGY

Southeast Asia

1851–1910	Mongkut and Chalalongkorn in Siam
1889–1964	Jawarlahal Nehru
1890–1969	Ho Chi Minh
1901–1970	Sukarno
1930	Gandhi's salt march
1937	Indian national elections

China

1916–1927	Warlords
1921	Chinese Communist party founded
1926	Death of Sun Yat-sen; transition to Chiang Kai-shek
1927–1937	Nanjing Decade
1927, 1930–1934	Chiang Kai-shek attacks the Communists
1934–1935	Long March
1931–1945	Japanese invasions
1941	United Front with Guomindang ends as Chiang Kai-shek attacks the Fourth Route Army

Japan

1910–1945	Japan in Korea, Taiwan, Manchuria
1919–1926	Brief liberalization under parliamentary rule during Taisho democracy, then militarization
1925	Peace Preservation Law
1931	Japanese forced takeover of Manchuria
1936	Anti-Communist Pact
1937	Rape of Nanjing
1937–1945	Mao at Yanan: guerrilla attacks against Japanese
1938–1945	Chongqing, wartime capital
1940	Tripartite Pact with Nazis and Italy
1941	Neutrality pact with Russia
	U.S. embargo and subsequent attack on Pearl Harbor
1942–1945	Japan conquers Southeast Asia, and "liberates" nationalist governments, to join the Greater East Asia Co-Prosperity Sphere
1942	Battle of Midway; Japan loses
1945	Atom bombs; Japan surrenders

fully formed or well organized in most areas outside the Philippines by the outbreak of the Pacific War in 1941, which marked the end of colonialism in Asia, a scant half-century or less after it had been established in most of Southeast Asia. Outside Vietnam and Thailand, Western colonialism unified areas in much of Southeast Asia that had never been unified before, politically or culturally. Most were still composed of numerous different languages and culture groups with no tradition of living or working together and in many cases with a history of mutual antagonism. Under these circumstances, it is not surprising that modern nationalism and common effort were late and slow to grow. As in India, some Southeast Asians found the colonial system attractive and personally rewarding; the new Filipino commercial and political elite profitably collaborated with the Americans, and there were fewer numbers of similar collaborators in the rest of Southeast Asia. Many of the minority groups included in the new colonial domains found that the British were especially concerned to protect them against pressures and exploitation by the dominant majority, as in the long conflict between the majority low-

land Burmans and the Shans, Karens, and Kachins, quite different peoples of the Burmese hills and mountains. Even the French and Dutch used ethnic minorities in Vietnam and Indonesia as makeweights against the dominant, and resented, Vietnamese and Javanese.

Malays saw the British, quite accurately, as their protectors against the Chinese who immigrated into their country, threatened to dominate it numerically, and monopolized its booming commercial sector. The British admired traditional Malay culture and tried to preserve it as well as its people; Chinese were forbidden to own land and hence did not intrude into the traditional agricultural economy except as plantation workers, while Malays were encouraged to preserve their own customs and follow their traditional forms of law. Dutch policy in Indonesia was similar, based also on the belief that if the Indonesians remained fixed in their own traditional cultures and all outsiders were forbidden to own land, the locals would remain more docile and less likely to unite against the colonial powers or catch the germs of nationalism and protest. Many Dutch also admired the traditional Indonesian cultures—and they were indeed, as throughout

Imperialist Designs

British impatience and ambition over upper Burma, in the face of supposed French rivalry and the Burmese monarchy's resistance to British demands, are clearly revealed in this passage from a letter by Sir Owen Burne, undersecretary of state for India, to the British Foreign Office in the fall of 1885.

I feel quite sure that some far more absolute action than we are yet aware of must be taken. I say unhesitatingly that we should now get any pretext to annex or make Burma into a protected state. King Theebaw's sins are many and great and I feel quite sure your able pen, aided by a few snarls from myself, could formulate a Bill of Indictment against him that would make every old woman in London weep.

Source: H. Aung, *The Stricken Peacock* (The Hague: Nijhoff, 1965), p. 9.

Southeast Asia, very appealing to romantic-minded Europeans. Unlike Indians, and in time Burmese and Filipinos, most Malays, Vietnamese, and Indonesians had extremely limited access to Western-style education, in Vietnam and Indonesia by explicit French and Dutch policy (see Chapter 15). All of these several factors helped to retard the growth of nationalism and resistance to colonial control, despite its frequent ruthlessness.

Thailand (called Siam until 1932) is a separate case, since it never became a colony, thanks in part to Anglo-French rivalry and their tacit agreement to leave it as a neutral buffer zone between British Burma and French Indochina. Its independence was also due in part to a fortunate series of able Thai kings, most importantly Mongkut (r. 1857–1868) and Chulalongkorn (r. 1868–1910), who adroitly played the British and the French off against each other and at the same time promoted the modernization of their country. (Readers may recognize Mongkut as the ruler portrayed in *Anna and the King of Siam,* later the basis of the musical *The King and I.*) Nevertheless, in the late 1850s Siam had to submit to the same set of unequal treaties and special privileges for foreigners as were imposed on China and Japan and was obliged to cede territory to British Burma and Malaya on the west and south and to French Indochina in Cambodia and Laos on the east. Siam was, however, almost homogenous in culture and language, especially once it had been forced to give up these areas. Because of the relative recency of Thai occupation of the country, and of the Thai monarchy, most Thais shared a common sense of their culture, history, and identity and a common reaction to foreign pressures, although here too many Thais profited from the commercialization after 1850.

Chinese might have become an important minority in Siam. They were resented and were even the periodic target of riots as they came to dominate the new commercial economy, especially the export trade in rice, rubber, and hardwoods. But in Siam, unlike in most of the rest of Southeast Asia, the Chinese merged relatively peacefully with Thai society, married Thai women, took Thai names, and within a generation or less were no longer easily discernible as a minority. In the Philippines the many immigrant Chinese before 1850 were almost as easily assimilated by the same process, although later arrivals suffered from discrimination.

The Plantation System

Colonial Southeast Asia became the world's major center of plantation agriculture, which in turn accounted for most of the economic development that took place. In this tropical area with its year-long growing season and generally adequate and reliable rainfall, crops in great demand in the West could be profitably grown for export, drawing on local low-wage labor or the streams of immigrant Chinese and Indians. Colonialism took over Southeast Asia after industrialization was well established in the West and had begun to generate an enormous appetite for tropical products such as rubber, sugar, palm and coconut oil, kapok, quinine, tea, and other crops. Rice, another major export (though mainly to the rest of Asia), was generally grown by peasants on individual farms in the Irrawaddy, Chao Praya, and Mekong deltas (in Burma, Siam, and Indochina, respectively) rather than on plantations, while teak and other tropical hardwoods were cut in existing forests. Tobacco and sugar also became important plantation crops, especially in Indonesia and the Philippines. Hemp (abaca) was a staple Philippine export grown mainly by small landholders. Tin (west coast Malay and

Rubber plantation, Malaya. The tree is cut to let the latex (sap) run down for collection in buckets, which then are taken to a processing station on the plantation where the latex is concentrated into sheets or balls for export. (Culver Pictures, Inc.)

northwestern Indonesia) and oil (central Burma and Indonesia) were additional major exports; their existence was unknown until late in the nineteenth century, just when Western markets began to enormously increase their demand for both, as the age of the automobile opened. Rubber plantations mushroomed in Malaya, Indonesia, and southern Thailand and Vietnam. And from the time of the Portuguese on, the spice trade remained an important Southeast Asian export.

A plantation is a large unit of land under single ownership. Labor is hired to grow a single commercial crop for sale or export, and there are usually some processing facilities on the premises: preliminary or final sorting, curing, refining, and packing for shipment. It is run for profit only and usually grows no food crops for local consumption. The total amount of land occupied by plantations in Southeast Asia was never very large, but it was disproportionately productive. In most cases plantations did not displace food crops but made use of areas not previously cultivated. Many of the plantations concentrated on tree or bush crops that did well on slopes and did not need fertile soil: rubber, palms, kapok, quinine (from the cinchona tree, used for treating malaria), tea, and most spices. Rubber, a tree of the tropical rain forest, was introduced from Brazil where it had been gathered in the wild, but in Southeast Asia rubber trees were grown far more efficiently on plantations, where it was also easier to recruit low-wage labor, mainly immigrant Chinese and Indians. Southeast Asian rubber plantations soon destroyed Brazilian competition and dominated the booming world market, coagulating the

milky sap tapped from the trees into sheets and shipping them out through the ports of Singapore, Batavia (the Dutch colonial capital of Indonesia, now Jakarta), Surabaya in eastern Java, Bangkok, and Saigon, the French colonial capital of Vietnam.

Sugar was sometimes a plantation crop in the Philippines, but mainly it was grown there and in Java, the other major commercial producer, by individual peasant farmers, often as part of a crop rotation with rice; the deep, rich volcanic soil of Java made this possible and gave both sugar and rice the nutrients they needed even under continuous cultivation; conditions on the island of Negros and in central Luzon in the Philippines, the major sugar producers there, were similar. The delta rice lands of lower Burma, Siam, and Vietnam were for the most part newly opened to cultivation by clearing and drainage, and were thus very productive but without taking land from existing food crops. In Java, the much larger population—approximately 30 million by 1900—and the concentration on export crops, meant that, increasingly, rice to feed the people had to be imported, up to half of total consumption by the twentieth century. Rice was also imported to feed the booming port cities and coastal areas of India, China, and Japan.

The Rise of Southeast Asian Nationalism

Vietnamese resistance to the French conquest and subsequent rule has already been mentioned, but national-

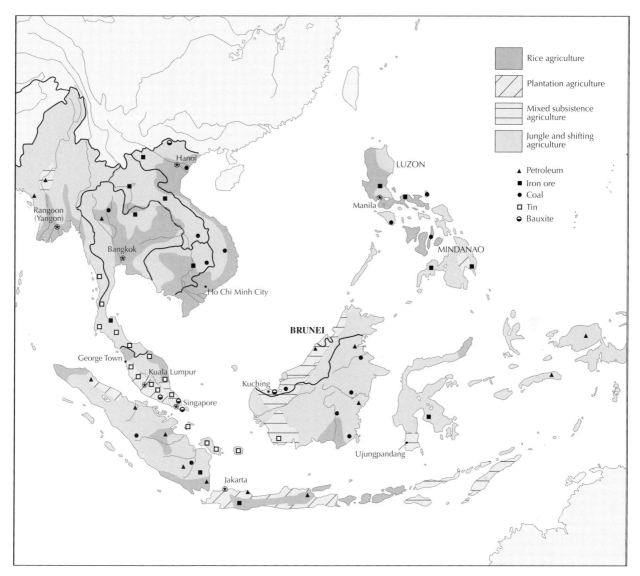

Rice agriculture

Plantation agriculture

Mixed subsistence agriculture

Jungle and shifting agriculture

▲ Petroleum
■ Iron ore
● Coal
□ Tin
◒ Bauxite

Minerals and Economic Patterns in Southeast Asia

Southeast Asia supports a plural economy: the small dots of plantations, the larger areas of rice growing, and the shifting cultivation, or slash and burn, which occupies the widest area of mountain and jungle—in fact, the major land use in the entire area. Mineral resources, mainly oil, tin, and iron (in the Philippines) are of course distributed in no relation to these land use patterns.

ism was nothing new to Vietnam. The first stirrings of anticolonial nationalism took place in the Philippines, where colonialism had a longer history than anywhere in the world. Three centuries of Spanish rule had spread a common language and religion among the national elite, and there was an emerging middle class of educated people, the *ilustrados,* who were increasingly

resentful of foreign rule. When their demands for reform in the 1870s were met by harsh repression, they were first supplanted by and then joined outright revolutionaries led by Emilio Aguinaldo, who mobilized widespread popular support and declared an independent republic in 1898. This would certainly have succeeded, making the Philippines the first Asian country

American Imperialism I

American senator Henry Cabot Lodge probably spoke for most of his countrymen when he tried in 1899 to justify to the Senate the American takeover of the Philippines.

> Duty and interest alike, duty of the highest kind and interest of the highest and best kind, impose upon us the retention of the Philippines, the development of the islands, and the expansion of our Eastern commerce.

Source: U. Mahajani, *Philippine Nationalism* (Brisbane: University of Queensland Press, 1971), p. 225.

to win its independence, if the Americans had not almost immediately intervened as part of their war against Spain.

Having promised the infant Philippine Republic its freedom in exchange for collaboration against the Spanish, the Americans then, once the Spanish had surrendered, turned on their Philippine allies and brutally suppressed Aguinaldo's forces in a long antiguerrilla war. The ruthless American military tactics were similar to those used in Vietnam 50 years later. Bitterness over this betrayal faded relatively soon among the ilustrados; most of them made their profitable peace with the Americans as collaborators in the full-scale commercialization of the Philippines and the Americanization of its economic, legal, political, and educational systems. Increasing scope was provided for elective Filipino representation by the U. S. Tydings-McDuffie Act of 1934, which also made a commitment to grant Philippine independence in ten years, and Manuel Quezon was elected the first president of the Philippine Commonwealth in 1935, under an American high commissioner. But the needs of the peasants, still the great majority of the population, remained largely unaddressed.

Elsewhere in Southeast Asia the colonial experience and the recently created political units were too new to allow similar developments. Most of the intellectuals who were troubled by foreign dominance began by reasserting their own traditional cultural identities, as in the General Council of Buddhist Associations in Burma, its Islamic parallels in Indonesia, and the Young Men's Buddhist Association (YMBA), which was a political group especially after 1910. Both became qualified mass movements, led by Westernized or Western-educated intellectuals, but they moved very slowly to form viable political programs and demands for representation or independence. In Burma a former monk, Saya San, led a failed rebellion from 1930 to 1932. In Vietnam, the Chinese Revolution of 1911 was an inspiration to many and led to the founding of the Vietnamese Nationalist party, based on the ideas of Sun Yat-sen and his strong influence on Ho Chi Minh (see Chapter 15). The party attacked the French colonial government in 1929 and the early 1930s but was completely destroyed, leaving the field to the newly founded Indochinese Communist party led by Ho Chi Minh. In Malaya there was little or no resistance to colonialism,

American Imperialism II

The American general Shafter, in charge of the military campaign against the Philippine patriots under Aguinaldo in central Luzon, added this in 1900.

> It may be necessary to kill half the Filipinos in order that the remaining half may be advanced to a higher plane of life than their present semi-barbarous state affords.

Source: F. Luzviminda, "The First Vietnam: The Philippine-American War," *Bulletin of Concerned Asian Scholars,* December 1973, p. 4.

and the growing sense of Malay nationalism had far more to do with preservation of their Islamic religion and traditional Malay culture against what they saw as the threat from millions of immigrant Chinese and Indians. Even in independent Siam there was a renewed interest in Buddhism, and in southern Vietnam a new sect, the Cao Dai, combined elements of traditional animism, Buddhism, and French-introduced Catholic Christianity. The Russian Revolution of 1917, the rise of Japan as an Asian power, and Gandhi's successes in building a mass movement against colonialism in India struck responsive chords among most educated Southeast Asians. World War I had revealed that Western civilization was deeply flawed and far from invincible. More and more Southeast Asian students now studied in Europe, India, and Japan, as well as at Rangoon University in Burma and a few at Hanoi and Batavia. Everywhere they went, these students learned the gospels of nationalism, which they brought home with them, including the organizational powers of modern political parties and the need for modernization in all aspects of life as conditions for the independence many of them now aimed for. But there was still nothing approaching a mass base for such changes, nor was one to develop until after the Japanese defeat of Western colonialism in Asia from 1941 to 1945. The Indonesian Communist party was founded in the early 1920s, but it remained a small and largely ineffective organization, especially given the ruthlessness of Dutch police control, which decimated it in several poorly prepared uprisings in 1926 and 1927. This happened also in Vietnam to both the Nationalist and Communist parties there, but under Ho's better organization and strategy and with help from China, the Communists survived. In Burma, nationalist groups were divided between the traditionalists and the more modern reformers; partly for that reason, Burma never matched the effectiveness of the Indian independence movement under Gandhi and the Congress.

Apart from Ho Chi Minh and the quite different group of ilustrado politicians in the Philippines, only one other figure emerged in the 1920s as a recognized nationalist leader, the man known as Sukarno (1901–1970; Indonesians usually use only one name). He was Dutch-educated in Java as an engineering student at Bandung University and picked up many Western ideas but developed a personal and political mixture of Western, traditional Javanese, Islamic, and Marxist notions, which he blended under the heading of Indonesian nationalism. Like Ho and Sun, he had great personal magnetism and was an accomplished orator, although his trueconvictions were often clouded by a Messiah complex and love of the limelight. He founded and headed the new Indonesian Nationalist party, but once in that prominent position he was an im-

mediate target for the Dutch, who arrested and jailed him in 1929, and finally exiled him from Java; he did not return until the end of Dutch rule (see Chapter 19). Other Indonesian nationalist leaders were also banished or imprisoned, and the movement broke up into self-defeating factionalism.

In Burma, belated British concessions resulted in more Burmese representation in the colonial administration, and, until the eve of World War II, collaborators outnumbered those urging independence. However, in the 1920s and 1930s, growing sympathy for the Burmese peasantry, who were losing their property to Rangoon-based Indian absentee landlords, began to raise concerns related to the long-term consequences of British rule. At that time a new generation of radical nationalists at British-founded Rangoon University won over most politically conscious Burmese to the side of freedom—only then to be exploited and betrayed by the Japanese. In independent Siam, modernization had included a foreign-style education system, civil service, and military, but access to all these was limited to members of the widespread royal family and some of the court nobility. By the late 1920s this was no longer acceptable to the rest of the educated elite, including those who had studied abroad. In 1932, a group of army reformers forced the king to accept a constitution and changed the country's name to Thailand, which thereafter came under a militarized autocracy with the traditional monarchy retained as a national symbol.

In twentieth-century Indonesia, Indonesian nationalists found memories of the fourteenth- and fifteenth-century Majapahit polity useful in their reconstructions of an Indonesian past (Chapter 7). The Budi Utomo—Indonesia's earliest nationalist organization, founded in 1908—drew heavily upon the Majapahit legacy as the inspiration for nationalism, initially for Java and then for the region as a whole. Indonesian nationalists projected the model of one Indonesia free and united like the "great" Majapahit. The "real" Majapahit had just been brought back to life, coincidentally with the Netherlands Indies. In the minds of the early Indonesian nationalists, *Nusantara* was inclusive of the "islands between two continents."

Muhammad Yamin, who was head of the Japanese occupation era's propaganda agency (*sendenhan*) in the 1940s, wrote a popular biography of Gajah Mada that reinforced this notion of an Indonesian empire, which was then dominated by the Japanese. In 1945, Yamin conceived the Indonesian political nation, including the Islamic populations living in British Malaya and southern Thailand.

In the rest of Southeast Asia, the colonial orders seemed secure on the eve of the Pacific War. Philippine independence had been promised for 1946 and the British had begun the movement toward self-government

Gandhi

Gandhi wrote Hind Swaraj *(Indian Home Rule) in 1909, and, in later editions, he said he had seen no reason to alter it. Here is a sample:*

> You English, who have come to India, are not good specimens of the English nation, nor can we, almost half-Anglicized Indians, be considered good specimens of the real Indian nation. If the English nation were to know all that you have done, it would oppose many of your actions. The mass of the Indians have had few dealings with you. If you will abandon your so-called civilization and search into your own scriptures, you will find that our demands are just. Only on condition of our demands being fully satisfied may you remain in India; and if you remain under those conditions, we shall learn several things from you and you will learn many from us. So doing we shall benefit each other and the world. But that will happen only when the root of our relationship is sunk in a religious soil.

Source: W. T. de Bary, *Sources of Indian Traditions,* vol. 2 (New York: Columbia University Press, 1964), p. 266.

in Burma and in India. But the French and Dutch colonial regimes held firm and seemed impossible to dislodge. Their destruction would be accomplished by the Japanese.

India Moves Toward Independence

India's progress toward freedom is in large part the story of the careers of two men: Mohandas K. Gandhi (often called Mahatma, "great soul") and Jawaharlal Nehru. Gandhi (1869–1948) gave the independence movement what it had not yet had—mass appeal and a mass following. Nehru (1889–1964), in close cooperation with Gandhi within the Congress party, gave vision and leadership on a different level but acknowledged the power of Gandhi's example. In the years following World War I, the Congress was transformed under Gandhi's direction from a small group of elite intellectuals to a truly national party representing a wide range of regional interest groups and mobilizing millions of Indians. Gandhi proved adept at using aspects of the Indian tradition as vehicles and symbols for protest against British imperialism and as rallying grounds for nationalist sentiment and organization.

Gandhi and Mass Action

The son of a minor official in commercial Gujarat, Gandhi followed the path of many upwardly mobile Indians in a rapidly changing society. When he was 19, he went to London to study law and there became thoroughly Westernized. Soon after his return to India, he took a job with an Indian law firm in South Africa, where he spent the next 20 years defending Indian merchants and other immigrants against racist oppression and developing tactics of nonviolent protest and noncooperation. He returned home in 1914 and soon began to organize among his countrymen.

The British secretary of state for India announced in 1917 that the government's policy was "the gradual development of self-governing institutions" and an increase of Indians in responsible positions, but with the end of the war it became clear that such change would be painfully slow. Meanwhile, peasant economic suffering and distress among exploited industrial workers and farmers were growing. Gandhi organized successful strikes and protest movements, using nonviolent methods with great effect. When these and other signs of ferment began to concern reactionaries in the government as "seditious conspiracy," repression replaced the slow movement toward self-government, culminating in the Amritsar Massacre of 1919 (see Chapter 16).

From then on, few Indians saw accommodation to colonialism as acceptable. The Congress party began to

Gandhi the ascetic spinning cotton yarn. He made it a point to spin 200 yards of yarn every day as a symbolic act, no matter how busy he was, and urged others to do the same. (Hulton/Archive/ Getty Images)

press for independence, and Gandhi's mass weapon of nonviolent protest and noncooperation attracted more and more followers. It was based on the ancient Hindu idea of *ahimsa,* or reverence for life, and drew, as Gandhi insisted, on the redemptive power of love to convert even brutal opponents by its "soul force," or *satyagraha.* Traditional Indian values stressed the avoidance of conflict and the importance of self-control, seeking resolution through compromise and consensus. Nonviolent action was also the only practical means for unarmed and powerless people to confront an oppressive state. As Martin Luther King Jr. was later to demonstrate, it worked, both to build a dedicated following and to make its protest against injustice effective.

Gandhi organized fresh boycotts of British imported goods, an action that, as in China, caught the popular imagination and helped build a larger following. He urged Indians to wear only their own traditional handmade cottons (khadi), and wherever possible to spin and weave the cotton themselves. The spinning wheel became a nationalist symbol, linked to 5,000 years of India's history. Some of the Congress party's intellectual elite were scornful of Gandhi's methods and personal style of a traditional sadhu, or holy man, his embracing of the poor, and his ascetic lifestyle. But as both an astute politician and a genuine saint he attracted more support and got more results than the Congress had ever done. He simply used traditional methods and symbols to appeal to the Indian people, most of whom were not

intellectuals, giving them a sense of pride in their national identity and inspiring them to action. He succeeded where others had failed in attracting Muslims, Sikhs, Christians, and agnostics to his cause, which he made India's cause, the first truly national movement. He urged Indians to "get rid of our helplessness" and to stand together. Nehru said, "He has given us back our courage, and our pride." Strikes, boycotts, and demonstrations spread in the early 1920s, but with millions of people now involved, Gandhi could not always ensure nonviolence. Thousands were jailed, there was violence on both sides, and in 1922 Gandhi was sentenced to prison for six years. He was released for medical reasons after two years but did not resume political agitation until 1930, distressed that his nonviolent campaign had gone astray.

Hindus and Muslims: Protest and Elections

Meanwhile, the government, affected by Gandhi's achievements, began to implement many of the reforms previously demanded by Congress, increasing the number of Indian officers in the civil service and the army and moving toward abolishing the tax on cotton. Nehru became mayor of his home city of Allahabad. At the same time, rioting between Muslims and Hindus broke out in many areas, a symptom not only of the general

Gandhi's Character

Gandhi's personal qualities are well brought out in Nehru's remarks about him.

> I have never met any man more utterly honest, more transparently sincere, less given to egotism, self-conscious pride, opportunism, and ambition. . . . It has been the greatest privilege of our lives to work with him and under him for a great cause. To us he has represented the spirit and honor of India.

Source: J. Nehru, "Mahatma Gandhi," *L'Europe*, February 1936, p. 21.

atmosphere of turmoil but also of the efforts of special groups to ensure a better place for themselves in the independent India that was clearly coming. When Gandhi's program was overwhelmingly endorsed by Congress in 1920, Mohammad Ali Jinnah, who had expected to head the party and was openly scornful of Gandhi and his satyagraha, resigned in disgust. Hindus and Muslims had worked together for many years in the Congress party. Now, especially under Jinnah, Muslims were being told they had to safeguard their interest against the Hindu majority and that their own party, the Muslim League, was their only sure protector. Jinnah pressed for separate votes for Muslim candidates for the new offices being opened to Indians and Indian voters. Meanwhile, Nehru, who like Jinnah had been educated in England and was highly Westernized, increased his control of the Congress party but maintained his loyalty to Gandhi as India's spiritual and symbolic leader. Nehru insisted that Congress was the party of all Indians, including Muslims, and that the independence movement would be weakened by factionalism. He was proved tragically right.

The world depression beginning in 1929, which bore heavily on India, greatly increased economic distress. When Gandhi resumed political action in 1930, he chose as his target the tax imposed by the government on salt, and the official ban on private or small-scale salt making from the sea, arguing that the tax especially hurt the poor. He led a protest march on foot across India to a beach on the coast, where he purposely courted arrest by picking up a lump of natural salt and urging Indians to do likewise, as many thousands did. Gandhi, Nehru, and many others were jailed, and there was a new wave of strikes. Gandhi had again touched the conscience of the nation. After eight months in prison, he was released to meet with the viceroy in the colonial capital at New Delhi. An agreement was reached to discontinue civil disobedience. In return, the government approved of the movement to promote the use of Indian-made goods and invited Gandhi to a London conference on India

later in 1931, together with Jinnah as a representative of the Muslims.

The conference ended in stalemate, and Gandhi was taken back to jail a week after his return. Boycotts, strikes, and violent demonstrations erupted again without the Mahatma to restrain them. Meanwhile, economic distress deepened as world markets for India's exports shrank and a new, more conservative viceroy was appointed. In England, however, popular and parliamentary opinion was turning more and more toward self-government for India, the issue that Gandhi had so successfully dramatized. In 1935 a new constitution for India was announced, followed by nationwide elections in 1937 in which nearly 40 million Indians voted. Congress candidates swept the election, and the Muslim League did not even win most of the seats designated for Muslims. The new constitution reserved "safeguard" powers to the colonial government, but Congress ministries took over the provinces. Jinnah was outraged and devoted the next 10 years until his death to building first an effective party for Muslims and finally a separate state. Nehru pointed out that Congress was a national party rather than a special-interest party and that over 100,000 Muslims belonged to it.

By the outbreak of war in 1939, India was well along the road to self-government, but the war changed everything. The proimperialist Winston Churchill came to power in England, and all talk of independence was postponed until the threat of fascism could be met and defeated in Europe and Asia. Indians were informed that they were automatically at war with Germany, and later with Italy and Japan. Neither Congress nor other Indian leaders were consulted. Nationalists of all sorts felt betrayed once again. The Congress provincial ministries all resigned in protest, leaving the political field to Jinnah and his Muslim League. A British offer, brought by Sir Stafford Cripps in 1942 but reduced at Churchill's insistence from independence to dominion status once the war was over, was rejected. Gandhi called it "a post-dated check on a failing bank." He began a series of nonviolent campaigns, culminating in the "Quit India" movement of 1942, with that slogan scrawled on walls all over the country and shouted at British people. Nehru spent most of the war in jail, while Gandhi was in and out. Jinnah, now with the political field to himself, could not believe his good fortune and increased his determination to have a separate state for Muslims, to be called Pakistan. Independence would come too late to avoid the bloody tragedy of partition.

Retrospect

What spoiled the British record most was the long delay in giving India its freedom. The terrible consequences that followed might have been avoided if independence had come earlier, as it should have, but for the opposition of a few conservatives, notably Winston Churchill, and the intervention of two world wars. As it was, the subcontinent paid a dreadful price. Nevertheless, there is little bitterness against the British, unlike most of the rest of Asia, which underwent a harsher colonial rule under the Japanese, French, or Dutch. Many originally British institutions are now firmly a part of South Asian civilization. Independent India has much in common with the United States and Canada as joint inheritors of many aspects of a common culture.

China in the 1920s and 1930s

China was still politically disorganized and without an effective central government. A succession of warlords and short-lived political cliques alternated as the "government" in Beijing, but none were able to control more than a small area around the city. Most of the country was divided into the domains of contending warlords and their peasant armies. Many of the warlord domains were more or less coterminous with provinces, whose limits usually coincided with mountain or river barrier boundaries; others centered on important economic regions such as the Guangzhou delta, the Liao River plain of southern Manchuria, or the rich lower Yangzi Valley. Regionalism was an old phenomenon in China, given its size and consequent regional differences, but such internal struggles kept China weak in its efforts to escape from foreign domination and made national development impossible. Few of the warlords had any rational program beyond the struggle for power, and their campaigns further impoverished the countryside. Most of them had begun as bandits or common soldiers, but by their time, after the death of Yuan Shikai in 1916, none thought of trying to become emperor; it was too late for that, but the warlords had no alternative system of government in mind. Sun Yat-sen tried to work with them and use them to spread his revolutionary ideas, but he met with little success. In 1922, after building connections with one of the southern warlords, Sun tried to move north with an army to unify China by force, but the campaign soon fizzled.

Meanwhile, China was slipping ever deeper into poverty, worsened by civil war and the absence of real central government. Northern China in particular suffered a series of disastrous famine years in the 1920s, made worse by massive flooding of the Yellow River, whose dikes had been neglected during the long years of government ineptitude. Drought, famine, floods, warlord armies, and bandits created streams of refugees, many of whom went to relatively uncrowded and nearby Manchuria, overland or often by open boat from the tip of Shandong. Southern Manchuria, the valley and floodplain of the Liao River, became a new agricultural and settlement frontier. Manchuria's population grew by about 1 million a year from 1910 to 1940, almost entirely peasants from poverty-stricken northern China, thus strengthening the Chinese claim to the area despite its Japanese control. The major new commercial crops of Manchuria were wheat and soybeans, largely exported to or through Japan via the Japanese-developed port of Dairen (now called Luda), served by a rapidly growing and extensive rail net. The often virgin soils of southern Manchuria, previously closed to Chinese settlement by the Manchus, were very productive; drought-tolerant millet and sorghum occupied the less favorable areas and provided food for local consumption. The Japanese, who replaced the Russians after 1905, continued the Russian development of mining and manufacturing, including the world's largest open-pit coal mine at Fushun northeast of Mukden (now Shenyang) and the biggest iron and steel complex in East Asia at Anyang, south of Mukden. Mukden and Dairen became major manufacturing and processing centers.

In the treaty ports of China proper, led by Shanghai, Tianjin, and Wuhan, Chinese-owned and managed factories became more numerous than those owned by foreigners (mainly Japanese and British), although most of the largest were foreign and all industry was dominated by consumer goods (textiles, flour, cigarettes, matches). Apart from Japanese-controlled Manchuria, Chinese industrialization was still tiny, and on the scale of the country as a whole and its needs, much more so even than in India. But the new urban factories and the larger economy of the treaty ports did offer some escape from both traditional peasant and traditional elite worlds and from the tyranny of the family. Nevertheless, the total number of industrial workers remained small, 1 million by the most generous definition, hardly an adequate base for the Russian model of revolution based on an urban,

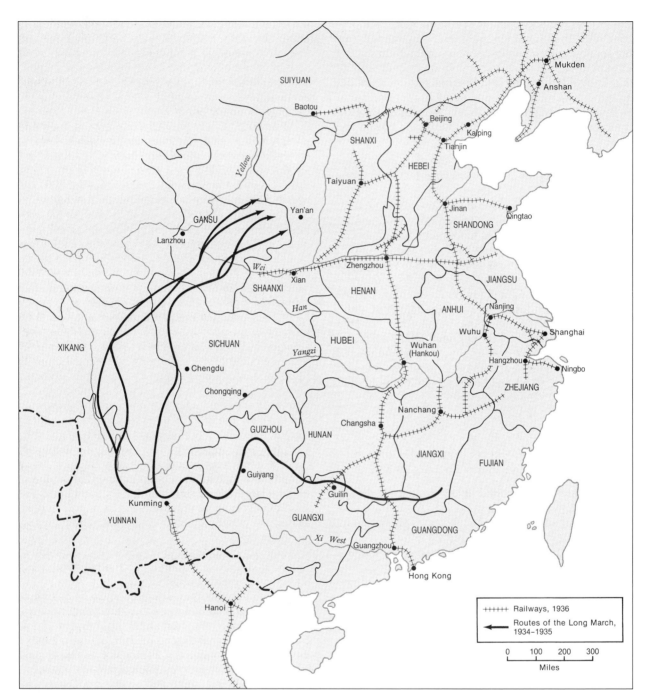

China in the 1930s

Many routes are shown for the Long March since several groups were involved, including one from Hubei to Yanan which is not shown.

industrial proletariat. China was still an overwhelmingly peasant country.

Marxism and Soviet Help

The May Fourth movement had stressed Western liberal notions of democracy, but especially after the success of the Russian Revolution of 1917, Marxism and Leninism were also appealing. Russia had been a relatively backward country of poor peasants that now embraced "progress" through Communist political organization and collective effort and rejected imperialism. To some this Soviet formula seemed to fit China's circumstances better than did Western democracy, as Marx himself had said in the 1850s. Marx wrote about "the toiling masses of the East," but he and his later followers seem not to have understood that India and China, seen as ripe for Communist revolution, were peasant countries whose context was very different from Europe's or Russia's. Nevertheless, a small group of intellectuals, including Chen Duxiu and Li Dazhao (Mao Zedong (1893–1976), then a young library assistant at Beijing University, also attended) founded the Chinese Communist party in Shanghai in 1921. The Guomindang (Nationalist) party was still a revolutionary group too, and it recognized that it needed help in building a stronger political organization to enable it to seize power from the warlords and build a larger base of support. Representatives from the Communist International (Comintern), including the Russian Michael Borodin, helped both parties, and from 1923 to 1927 they worked together under Comintern direction in a United Front against warlordism and for the building of national unity. During this period Mao and other Communist leaders worked with and for the Guomindang, the senior party still headed by Sun Yat-sen, the unquestioned leader of all Chinese nationalists. Sun's military assistant, Chiang Kai-shek (1887–1975) was sent to Moscow to study Soviet methods. But the Communist party remained tiny, mainly intellectuals, and without a mass base as yet.

Party dictatorship was seen as necessary in the early stages of national unification, but the vague Three Principles of the People and some form of representative government were reasserted by the united front as the ultimate goal. Sun may have been moving somewhat in the direction of socialism in his last years, but he died suddenly in 1925, and party control passed to Chiang Kai-shek, a far more conservative figure. Especially with his military background, Chiang saw China's first priority as national unity, by force if necessary, a goal that he never reached. However, he began promisingly by mounting a United Front military and political campaign with Communist help. Moving north from the Guomindang base in Guangzhou, with political agents in the advance wave to win support, the Northern Expedition defeated successive warlords in 1926 and 1927. Chiang finally established a new national capital at Nanjing in 1927, more centrally located than Beijing and free of both its dynastic and warlord associations.

Meanwhile a sense of Chinese nationalism continued to grow. After the demonstrations and riots of 1905 in Guangzhou and Shanghai aimed at American discrimination against Asian immigration, the focus shifted to Great Britain, the main imperialist country and, together with Japan, the dominant power in the treaty ports and in China's modern banking, shipping, industry, and foreign trade. Student demonstrations on May 30 and June 23, 1925, in Shanghai and Guangzhou, respectively, were met with violence by the foreign-controlled police of both treaty ports. Several of the marchers were killed. Patriotic Chinese, including many merchants, boycotted British goods until 1927, paralleling the contemporary Indian efforts. In response the British restored to China their concession areas at Hankou and Jiujiang on the Yangzi, but when the Northern Expedition reached Nanjing in March of 1927, foreigners there were attacked, and several were killed. British and American gunboats shelled the city in retaliation and killed many more Chinese while evacuating the remaining foreigners.

The Nanjing Decade

Chiang never completely eliminated warlord power in several of the outlying provinces, and although he dominated the Guomindang by repressive tactics, he led it far from its radical origins and progressively lost much support. He tried to wipe out his Communist allies in a military coup in Shanghai, still their major base, in 1927, using victorious troops from the Northern Expedition, and again in a series of campaigns from 1930 to 1934. Some of the Communists, including Mao, were not in Shanghai (where many were slaughtered) at the time of the coup but were trying unsuccessfully to organize peasant rebellion. After 1927 they retreated with their small remaining forces to a mountain stronghold in the southeast. Chiang's forces finally drove them out in 1934, forcing them into a retreat known as the Long March. An increasingly ragged column of Communists dodged ahead of Chiang's troops in a zigzag route across western China. At a conference along the way at Zunyi in Guizhou in January 1935, out of touch with Moscow and its directives, Mao was named party leader and his strategy based on the peasants, the countryside, and guerrilla warfare won out. Zhou Enlai (1898–1976), became his second-in-command, and Zhu De the military commander. The precariously few survivors finally reached a new base area in the remote and mountainous northwest, centered from 1936 on the small town of Yanan. Relatively safe from Chiang's efforts to eliminate

Mao on Revolution

Mao Zedong made a study of rural conditions in Hunan Province in 1927 (and thus escaped Chiang's coup in Shanghai). His report, though still somewhat premature, showed his conviction that peasants could become the vanguard of revolution.

The present upsurge of the peasant movement is a colossal event. In a very short time, in China's central, southern, and northern provinces, several hundred million peasants will rise like a mighty storm, like a hurricane, a force so swift and violent that no power, however great, will be able to hold it back. . . . They will sweep all the imperialists, warlords, corrupt officials, local tyrants, and evil gentry into their graves.

Source: Mao Zedong, "Report on an Investigation of the Peasant Movement in Hunan," in M. J. Coye, J. Livingston, and J. Highland, *China* (New York: Bantam, 1984), pp. 213–214.

---

them, they slowly extended their support base and pursued land-reform policies in this border area, from which they were to erupt after the anti-Japanese war in 1945 to lead in the end a victorious revolution.

The decade of the Nanjing government between 1927 and 1937, when the Japanese attacked China and sacked Nanjing, was in many respects, however, a constructive time. Chiang permitted no genuine democracy, with the excuse that order and unity must come first. But the forms at least of constitutional government took shape and there was considerable economic modernization. A central banking system was developed on Western lines by Chinese who had been trained abroad, and a national railway system was begun, although it was very limited outside Japanese-controlled Manchuria. Only in 1936 was the first north-south line through Wuhan completed, and total mileage remained far below India's. There was also some industrial growth, still almost entirely in the treaty ports but now increasingly with Chinese capital and management.

Although Chiang himself became increasingly a Confucian-style traditionalist, he married Soong Qingling's sister, Song Mei-ling, treaty port–raised and then educated at Wellesley College near Boston. She was highly Westernized, became Christian, and persuaded Chiang to be baptized as a Methodist. Her brother, T. V. Song (Harvard class of 1915), became finance minister from 1928 to 1933; he was succeeded by H. H. Kong, who had married another Soong sister, Soong Ai-ling. Together they extorted funds from the Shanghai business group of Chinese, issued bonds, and took control of the modern-style Bank of China, which obliged the foreign banks to cooperate and thus regained considerable control over China's foreign exchange. But taxes remained high, and the burden fell disproportionately on the merchant and industrialist group as well as on the peasants,

for whom little or nothing was done, while government officials became rich.

Chiang set up a secret police network that tried to enforce "thought control" and root out "Communist sympathizers," which in practice meant anyone who departed from the Guomindang party line. People were encouraged to inform on each other, and the press was strictly controlled, while many thousands of Chinese were jailed and tortured or executed. Chiang himself was attracted to many of the ideas of Italian and German fascism; he founded a group of Blue Shirts, a fascist-style secret society of his personal followers, and a New Life movement dedicated to the promotion of "moral virtues," all part of an attempted totalitarian approach to what he saw as China's problems, with a generally Confucian and authoritarian emphasis. Crack units of the Guomindang army were trained by officers from Nazi Germany, which also supplied Chiang with modern weapons.

All these developments, however, were tiny compared to the size and needs of the country and had little or no impact on most of it, or on its still predominantly peasant population. Rural poverty grew, accentuated by landlordism, but the Guomindang political base had become a coalition of businessmen from the treaty ports as well as rural power holders and landlords, and it feared rural change or the rise of a politicized peasantry. That was to be the ultimate route to power of the Communist party, but until the Japanese attack, the Communists barely managed to stay alive in their small base in the northwest, waiting their time. The Japanese had invaded Manchuria in 1931 and annexed it outright. They watched with concern as Chiang made progress toward national unification and the beginnings of some military strength. The militarists in control of Japan after 1930 saw their hopes for dominance in China and East Asia threatened, and launched a full-scale assault in 1937, attacking first at Beijing in July and then in August at Shanghai. With its new capital at Nanjing in flames, the Guomindang retreated up the Yangzi, largely to sit out the rest of the war, while the Communists in the north perfected their guerrilla strategy against the invaders and captured the leadership of Chinese nationalism.

A CLOSER LOOK

Shanghai: The Model Treaty Port

While the Communists retreated to remote Yanan behind its mountain barriers and began to work out their program for a new China under the leadership of Mao Zedong, Shanghai remained a bastion of foreign privilege and Chinese collaborators. But it also harbored a growing group of Chinese dissidents, radicals, and revolutionaries, who lived there under the protection of foreign law. Chinese police could not pursue suspects in the foreign settlements, which were ruled by a foreign-dominated municipal council and its own police. The Chinese Communist party had been founded there in 1921 for that reason by a small group of revolutionaries and writers who were part of the much larger numbers of such people living in Shanghai or using it as a refuge, many of them periodically hounded or captured and executed by the Guomindang secret police. Chiang Kai-shek's military coup in 1927 killed many of them and drove some of the survivors out, but many remained underground and continued to produce a long series of short-lived literary and political magazines with titles like *New China, New Youth,* and *New Dawn,* avidly read by intellectuals in the rest of China. After Shanghai passed Beijing as China's largest city about 1910, it became the country's chief center of literature, publishing, and cultural and political ferment. The May Fourth movement spread immediately from Beijing to Shanghai; student organizers persuaded many Shanghai merchants to boycott Japanese and later British goods. Shanghai joined Beijing as a major base for the New Culture movement, sometimes called the Chinese Renaissance, and its efforts to remake Chinese society. Lu Xun and many other New Culture writers lived in Shanghai.

At the same time, Shanghai remained by far the largest port and commercial center in China, through which over half of its foreign trade passed and which also contained over half of its modern industry. Chinese entrepreneurs, both traditional and Westernized, competed and collaborated with foreigners in trade, banking, and manufacturing, and many of them adopted a Western lifestyle. The foreign settlements at Shanghai were replicas of modern Western cities, and looked physically like Manchester or Chicago. The muddy foreshores of the Hwangpu River, a Yangzi tributary that ran along one edge of the city and constituted the harbor, were covered in the nineteenth century by an embankment known as the Bund. It became Shanghai's main thoroughfare, lined with imposing Western banks and hotels. Nanjing Road, the main shopping street, ran at right angles to it away from the river, and there were extensive residential areas with Western-style houses.

Shanghai was famous as "sin city." The Shanghai Club boasted "the longest bar in the world"; Chinese were not admitted except as servants. With its wide-open prostitution, gambling, bars, and cosmopolitan glitter, a mix of nearly all the world's nationalities away from their normal bases, it was a sort of moral no-man's land, even for its Chinese inhabitants, most of whom were recent immigrants. The foreign population peaked at about 60,000 in the 1930s, in a city that by then totaled about 4 million, many of whom lived outside the foreign concession areas in sprawling slums or in the walled Chinese city next to the concessions.

The vast majority were poor, clinging to survival as underpaid factory workers, coolies, rickshaw pullers, servants, dock workers, or transporters. In 1935 the Shanghai Municipal Council, staffed by foreigners with five Chinese members by 1931, collected 5,590 exposed corpses from the streets of the International Settlement alone, most of them refugees; in 1937, the first year of the full-scale anti-Japanese war, the total reached 20,746.

But the commercial and industrial heart of Shanghai was largely run by foreigners (Japanese edged out the British as the majority by the 1930s), and they built it in the Western image. They were proud of Shanghai's impressive economic success in the "modern" mode, and saw it as a beacon of "progress" in a vast Chinese sea of "backwardness."

Shanghai was described as "in China but not of it." They were two different worlds. The city drew most of its exports (silk, tea, and other agricultural goods) from the Chinese hinterland and sent there some of its imports (metals, machinery, and manufactured goods), but Shanghai's economic example made relatively little impact, except in the other treaty ports. Unlike the Indian experience, it was largely rejected as alien and unsuited to China. The Communists labeled Chinese collaborators in Shanghai and the other treaty ports "running dogs" of the imperialists and were contemptuous of their departure from Chinese ways in favor of Westernization.

Shanghai and the other treaty ports cut a deep wound of humiliation in the Chinese psyche but also offered an example of the kind of strength that China must have. Shanghai played a major role in stimulating as a reaction the rise of modern Chinese nationalism and a determination to rid the country of its foreign oppressors. The foreign way was rejected, but its technological and industrial achievements were to be adapted to serve Chinese needs in a Chinese way. Those who lived in Shanghai under foreign domination and protection were of course the most affected by its example, and it was primarily there that China's modern revolution began. Shanghai foreigners called it The Model Settlement and were convinced that its example of "progress" would transform China. In the end, it and all foreign privileges were swept away by the revolution, but Shanghai remains China's largest city and most advanced industrial and technological center. Shanghai's example thus survived the expulsion of the foreigners and shaped basic aspects of the new China.

Japan from 1920 to 1941

In addition to acquiring the former German concessions in Shandong and further developing its holdings in Manchuria, Japan benefited greatly from World War I, which removed Western industrial competition and thus gave Japanese industry a further major boost. Japanese exports and ocean shipping completed their dominance of Asian markets and built new economic strength at home. The British and Americans, meeting in Washington in 1922, obliged the Japanese to limit their navy, now seen as a threat, to a proportion of three capital ships to the British five and the American five; and in 1923, the Allies forced Japan to give up some of its concessions in Shandong. But economically the war and postwar years were a period of great prosperity and general confidence.

In 1910 Japan had taken over Korea as an integral part of its empire, and its grip on the country tightened. As mentioned in Chapter 15, there was development of minerals and industries, and a national rail net was built, but Koreans were treated, at best, as second-class Japanese. Nearly all administrative jobs were filled by Japanese, including even locomotive drivers. By the 1920s the Korean language could no longer be taught in the schools and all Koreans were forced to adopt Japanese names. Coal and iron mined in Korea was either exported to Japan or used to make pig iron and steel, which were similarly exported. Most of the forests in this mountainous country were removed to feed the Japanese appetite for wood, while Japan's own forests were largely preserved. Korean farm output was increased with Japanese technological help—irrigation and fertilization—but nearly all the rice was shipped to Japan, and Koreans were obliged to subsist on lesser grains such as millet and sorghum; altogether Korean grain consumption was greatly reduced. The port of Pusan, the major center for trade with Japan, was further developed, but in general Koreans were reduced to poverty and almost to the status of a slave population.

The Japanese impact on Taiwan was more positive; they also built there railway and industries and a greatly modernized agriculture, although much of the rice and sugar (Taiwan's main crops) went to Japan. But there was less Japanese prejudice against Taiwanese than against Koreans, and on the whole the Japanese interlude there was more constructive. After the Japanese surrender and the exploitative policies of the Guomindang when they reoccupied Taiwan, many Taiwanese said they would prefer to have the Japanese back. In Manchuria the Japanese built the largest industrial complex in East Asia, tied together by a dense rail net, which also served a largely new commercial agricultural system feeding huge amounts of wheat and soybeans to Japan, with some also for world markets through the port of Dairen(Dalian). The heavy Japanese investment in the development of Manchuria was never repaid, since it returned to China in 1945 and became the main base for China's industrialization.

In part because of this prosperity and confidence and in part as a symptom of Japan's growing Westernization since early Meiji, the 1920s saw a blossoming of parliamentary government and free expression such as Japan had not known before. Although there was no female suffrage until 1947 under the American occupation after the Pacific War, and less than 6 percent of the adult males could vote until the election of 1928, this was a considerable change from the first Japanese constitution in 1889 when only about 1 percent were enfranchised. Powers previously reserved to the emperor and his advisers were slowly being taken over by the lower house of parliament, or Diet, including a degree of control over the military. Unfortunately, the 1889 constitution provided that the minister of war in the cabinet must be a serving officer, and the constitution was after all modeled quite consciously on that of Prussia, a military-dominated state. Meiji Japan had seen its principal need as building strength against the foreign threat of dominance, and such a policy had been rewarded in Japan's dramatic victories against Russia in 1904–1905. The chief army leader of that war, General Nogi, became Japan's greatest national hero, closely followed by Admiral Togo, the victor in the battle of Tsushima against the Russian Pacific fleet. Japan had become a great power and was now treated as an equal; it is understandable that nearly all Japanese welcomed this military dominance and believed that the military must still be supported.

Nevertheless there was some reaction against excessive militarism, largely as a result of World War I and its

Militarism in Japan

Japanese militarism had deep roots. Fukuzawa Yukichi, one of the chief Meiji reformers, observed, well before Japan's war on China of 1894–1895:

> One hundred volumes of International Law are not the equal of a few cannon; a handful of treaties of friendship are not worth a basket of gunpowder. Cannon and gunpowder are not aids for the enforcement of given moral principles; they are the implements for the creation of morality where none exists.

Source: J. K. Fairbank, E. O. Reischauer, and A. M. Craig, *East Asia: The Modern Transformation* (Boston: Houghton Mifflin, 1965), p. 566.

bloody carnage. Even though Japan's forces suffered very few casualties, most Japanese still admired the Western model on which they had drawn so heavily since 1869; they saw the tragedy inflicted by Western armies on each other and tended to take the Allied side in its struggle against German militarism. When the Allies won, their cause of "liberty" seemed vindicated; Japanese have always admired success. Japan sent troops to Siberia in 1918, along with others of the Allies including the United States, to try to fight against the new revolutionary government of Russia. They stayed in Siberia until 1922, long after the other Allied forces had withdrawn, at great expense and at the further cost of growing resentment among most Japanese, especially since this intervention came to nothing. An emphasis on what was called internationalism began to replace the earlier stress on militarism and conquest.

Such sentiments were largely limited to students, intellectuals, and writers and a few journalists, liberal-minded politicians, and labor leaders. At the same time, however, there was a growing movement to extend the vote to all adult males, supported by most of the new white-collar middle class. The movement failed in 1920, but after the election of 1924 the new government passed an electoral law in 1925 creating universal adult male suffrage for those over 25 years old, increasing the electorate from 3 million to more than 12 million, although this was not exercised until the elections of 1928. There was still concern in Japan, as in the West, about the spread of "bolshevism," in the wake of the Russian Revolution of 1917 and the activities of the Communist International. The Japanese Communist party was founded in 1922, and many students found its message appealing, but the government was alarmed, and in 1925, while broadening the electorate, it also passed a Peace Preservation Law, which included strong "anti-

subversive" measures. In keeping with the general liberalized spirit of these years, the 1920s saw a rapid growth of new literature, Western-style art and music, and a mushrooming of new periodicals. This period as a whole is called Taisho democracy, from the reign title of the emperor who came to the throne in 1912 and ruled until 1926.

Growing Influence of the Military

But military training was now required for all males beyond elementary grades, including local training units for those who did not continue their education, and the government's position in China and Manchuria remained as aggressive as before. Anti-Japanese protests there continued, and in 1928 Japanese officers in Manchuria assassinated Chinese warlord Zhang Zuolin, hoping to use his son as a more obliging puppet. The new electorate in the election of 1928 disappointed many of those who had hoped for a new emphasis on Western-style democracy by voting strongly for conservative candidates, as they did again in 1930 and 1932. The Japanese government remained dominated by conservative elite groups in alliance with the big industrial and banking firms (combines known as *zaibatsu*), supported by rural landlords. It was still a civilian government, but its control over the military was often weak and the power balance between them was precarious.

The Great Depression, beginning in the United States in 1929 and spreading from there around the world, reached Japan by 1930 and severely damaged its economy. Exports dropped by half, real wages fell steeply, unemployment soared, and there was massive individual suffering. As elsewhere, however unreasonably, the government was blamed. There was a renewal of support for the military, and considerable admiration for German and Italian fascism, which had come to power under similar circumstances of economic disaster. The Japanese General Staff occupied a position directly under the emperor, and its officers in the field often acted independently, as in Manchuria in 1928. Manchuria was seen as important to Japan as a buffer against Russian power; such feelings were strengthened after the Russian Revolution of 1917 and the rise of a Communist state there. Japanese trade and investment in Manchuria were very large, and some 100,000 Japanese had moved there, mainly as officials and managers. Japan was busily developing Manchuria's extensive resources and building it up as a major industrial complex.

The Japanese government watched with growing concern the qualified unification of China under the Guomindang, the success of the Northern Expedition, and the support won by the new government at Nanjing, all of which was seen as a threat to the Japanese position in Manchuria. On September 18, 1931, a bomb exploded on the Japanese railway north of Mukden (Shenyang). It seems clearly to have been a Japanese plot to provoke an incident; the commanding officer on the spot had told the General Staff that was his intention, and there was no objection. In any case, the entire Japanese army in Manchuria launched a full-scale attack on Chinese troops. The still civilian cabinet in Tokyo tried fruitlessly to stop the army, but by early 1932 all of Manchuria had been taken over and was proclaimed an independent state, nominally under Henry Puyi, the pretender to the Qing throne who as a small boy had become the last emperor when the empress dowager Cixi died in 1908. Puyi was never more than a Japanese puppet, but his new "kingdom" was called Manchukuo (country of the Manchus), and his role was designed to give some sort of legitimacy to the Japanese takeover. The League of Nations condemned Japan as an aggressor; the Japanese delegation ostentatiously walked out, and Japan's connection with the League was severed. Japanese troops moved on to occupy large parts of adjacent Inner Mongolia.

The ruling party in the Diet now appointed as prime minister a navy admiral; he was followed in 1934 by another admiral, and civilian control over the military was irretrievably lost until Japan's defeat in 1945. The mood of internationalism went into eclipse, and most Japanese began to close ranks behind the military, who were to lead them into what the Japanese now call "the dark valley," which ended at Hiroshima and Nagasaki. Young superpatriot firebrands took to assassinating both politicians and military officers accused of something less than full support of the new expansionist policy. There were some divided opinions within the army, but when discipline and unity were reestablished by 1936 it was

under the principal leadership of General Tojo, who later led Japan into World War II. Those accused of leftism or "liberalism" were persecuted or jailed, and some were executed. The nominally civilian government, though with a cabinet now dominated by military men, increased measures for the control of "dangerous thoughts" and continued to raise the military budget. Diet and cabinet lined up in support of the army and its foreign policy, which now called for the neutralization of China's five northern provinces. At the end of 1936, Japan signed an Anti-Comintern Pact with Nazi Germany, aimed of course at Russia but giving the Japanese a further link with European fascism.

The developments in Japan were significantly different from German or Italian fascism, despite some obvious similarities. There was no one-man rule or dictatorship until General Tojo assumed some of that role with the outbreak of the Pacific War. Japan continued to be ruled collectively by a coalition of military and compliant civilian officials. There was no scapegoat group such as the Jews (although Koreans in both Korea and Japan were treated very badly), and no groups comparable to Mussolini's Brown Shirts, Hitler's Storm Troopers, or Chiang's Blue Shirts emerged. Thought control and police terror were prominent, but Japanese ideology was not revolutionized, as Germany's and Italy's had been. Veneration of the emperor was intensified, and schoolchildren were indoctrinated still more obsessively with the creed of Japanese nationalism. Racism is unfortunately universal and is always intensified in wartime; in Japan, belief in the superiority of the Yamato race, as it was called, was both officially promulgated and generally accepted, with dreadful consequences for Japan's victims once the wider war came, as the Chinese already knew.

But for most Japanese, the change from the qualified openness of the 1920s to the militarized Japan of the 1930s was not very abrupt and did not represent any major departure from familiar values or institutions. Nor did the ideas of parliamentary democracy completely disappear. Courageous members of the Diet periodically spoke against the army's interference in government and against the "forward policy" in China, and in the elections of 1936 a "prodemocracy" group won the largest bloc of seats, and various opposition groups collectively dominated the Diet. Unfortunately the Diet no longer controlled foreign policy.

Japan on the Eve of World War II

In August 1939 Hitler signed a nonaggression pact with the Soviet Union, thus freeing Germany to attack westward (though he was later to invade Russia as well). This was a heavy blow to the Japanese, who had counted on the Germans to help contain Russian power. Even before the pact, during the summer of 1939 and continuing into September, Japanese troops had probed further into Mongolia and become involved in a major though undeclared war with several Soviet/Mongol divisions. The Japanese were routed, and now Russia had freed itself for the present from German pressures in the West and could take a stronger position in the East. The Nazi victories in Europe beginning in the spring of 1940 made a German connection seem even more valuable to Japan, especially since the Americans were growing increasingly concerned about Japanese actions in China and unwilling to accept any of the Japanese claims. In September 1940, on the heels of the Nazi-Soviet nonaggression agreement, Japan signed a tripartite pact with Germany and Italy that provided that any power attacking any of the three states would be attacked by the other two. In April 1941, the Japanese negotiated a pact of neutrality with the Soviet Union; Russia feared a Nazi invasion and was willing to trade stabilization in the East for a stronger defense in the West.

Japan had managed to neutralize its most feared opponent, Russia, and to link up with a conquering Germany, which many Japanese thought represented the wave of the future for the West. Only the British, now standing alone against the Nazis and soon perhaps to be overwhelmed, and the United States, far away and not until now much involved, stood in the way of Japan's larger plans. Most Americans, like their government, disliked Japan's aggression in Manchuria and China but were unwilling to do anything about it, such as impose sanctions or stop the flow of oil and scrap iron needed by the Japanese military. Americans knew that their raw materials were being used to kill Chinese, and most took the Chinese side. But the government was reluctant to provoke a militaristic Japan, so close to the Philippines. The tripartite pact with Germany and Italy sharpened American opposition to Japan's policies by associating them with the fascists and their European record of aggression and oppression, while seeming also to add to Japanese strength, as did the nonaggression pact with the Russians. American opinion began to turn more sharply against Japan. Finally in the summer of 1941 Congress agreed to forbid the export of oil and scrap iron; this was done in part as a reaction to the Japanese move into French Indochina and the tightening of their control there after the fall of France in 1940, with bases in easy range of the Philippines.

The U.S. embargo put the Japanese in a dilemma, since they were almost totally dependent on these imports, which were essential to their military forces. Their objectives in China were never very clearly defined, their plan being not to take over the whole country but to turn it into some kind of protectorate where Japanese advisers would guide policy. China's resources would flow out to Japan, but Japanese investments and technical expertise would accelerate China's own development, as in Manchuria. During talks in Washington in the fall of 1941, the Japanese offered to withdraw their forces from Indochina in exchange for oil, but the Americans refused and insisted on a complete Japanese withdrawal also from China. Soon afterward, on December 7, 1941, and with the discussions supposedly still going on in Washington, the Japanese attacked Pearl Harbor. They knew they could not maintain their position in China without oil, scrap iron, and other vital imports, and their militarist government would not back down. In fact it would have been hard for any government to have done so, to admit that the "China Incident" had become a morass, that there was nothing to show for the mounting Japanese casualties, and the effort to dominate China was a failure. Too much had already been invested, and too much remained at stake, including, perhaps most importantly, Japanese national pride. To replace American oil, scrap iron, and other materials of war, the Japanese planned to conquer Southeast Asia, where these and other essential resources including tin and rubber were available: oil in Indonesia and central Burma, iron ore in the Philippines and Malaya, rubber in Thailand, southern Vietnam, Malaya, and Indonesia, and so on.

Some Japanese realized that in taking on the Americans and British, with their vastly superior resources, they were sealing Japan's fate. Admiral Yamamoto, who planned and executed the brilliant attack on Pearl Harbor, was one such; he had urged against waking "a sleeping tiger" and told the government he could give Japan a year, after which it would be overwhelmed. His plane was shot down in the South Pacific theater in 1944, but already by then his prediction was coming true. Others urged that the Americans were soft and would not fight, that the British had their backs to the wall and faced a Nazi invasion, and that both would come to terms quickly. There was enormous confidence in the Japanese military and its record of repeated successes (except for China), and in the Yamato people as disciplined and unbeatable, especially by "effete" Westerners.

The War in China

Japan never declared war on China; officially it was referred to as the "China Incident," while the "Manchu State" was formally declared to be a part of the Japanese Empire. The war, however, began for China in 1931. Japanese troops in Manchuria and China were

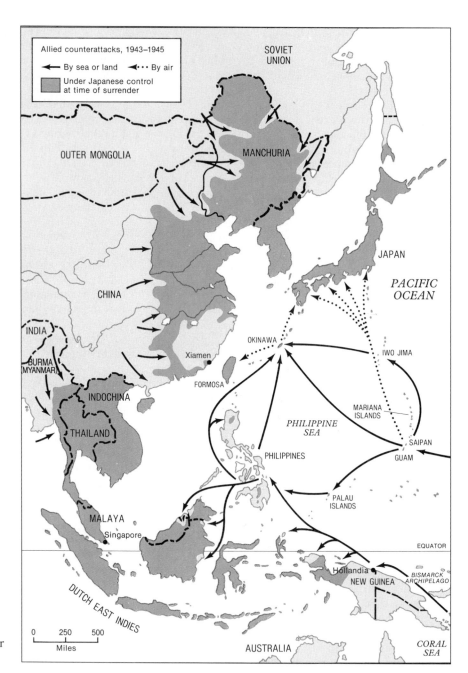

World War II in Eastern Asia

Japan's conquests were very widespread, if relatively brief. Japan's forces soon became overextended, and as the Allies continued to sink its navy and merchant marine it could no longer maintain its overseas positions.

relentlessly built up, and there were brushes with Chinese troops, especially around Beijing and in the area between there and Manchuria. Japan began to claim special rights in that part of north China and acted accordingly, asserting that Japanese troops were necessary to safeguard Japan's interests. Small-scale fighting with Chinese troops, as well as with Chinese guerrillas in Manchuria and in the mountains of northern China, increased as Japanese troops continued to behave like an army of occupation. Patriotic Chinese still bitterly re-

sented Japan's conquest of Manchuria, and in China proper they were clearly seen as the enemy.

The Failure of the United Front and the Fall of Nanjing

In August 1935 the Comintern and the Chinese Communist party called for nationwide resistance and a new United Front with the Guomindang. Chiang Kai-shek

This famous news photo, which conveys the aftermath of the Japanese bombing of Shanghai in 1937 was widely used to raise money and to lobby for military support of the ravaged Chinese. (Bettmann/Corbis)

refused, but in December 1936 Chinese troops who had withdrawn from Manchuria under their warlord commander Zhang Xueliang—the son of the murdered Zhang Zuolin—and were eager to continue to fight against the Japanese kidnapped Chiang at a hot springs resort outside Xi'an and tried to force him to agree to a United Front. Zhou Enlai, Mao's second-in-command, soon negotiated Chiang's release, on Comintern orders, believing that he had become too valuable as a symbol of national resistance. But Chiang still refused to take military action against the Japanese, fearing their strength, and ignored the demand for a United Front.

On July 7, 1937, a skirmish in the Beijing area at the Marco Polo Bridge (so-called because it had been described by Polo in the thirteenth century) between Chi-

nese and Japanese troops finally led to the outbreak of full hostilities, though still without a Japanese war declaration. The United Front was reestablished (although it was to fall apart in January 1941 when Guomindang troops attacked the Communist Fourth Route Army, claiming it was operating in territory south of the Yangzi where it should not have been). Japanese forces easily overran the Beijing area, bringing troops in from Manchuria; they advanced southward and westward along the rail lines and occupied Shandong and Shanxi provinces.

Nanjing, the Guomindang capital, was a major objective, and on August 14, 1937, the Japanese navy and air force bombarded Shanghai (trying to avoid the foreign concessions) to secure a landing of another army and

Mao at Yanan in 1935, writing and working out his strategy. (Culver Pictures, Inc.)

complete the pincer movement on Nanjing. Chiang committed most of his best German-trained troops, equipment, and tiny air force to the battle for Shanghai and the campaign from there to Nanjing. He might better have held at least some of this in reserve, since the Japanese superiority in men and equipment was overwhelming and largely destroyed the Chinese forces. But Chinese resistance did delay the Japanese timetable, which perhaps helps to explain their brutality when they finally took Nanjing in December. Japanese troops, with the full knowledge of their commanders, went on an orgy of torture, rape, and murder, vowing to "punish" the Chinese and using terror to persuade the Guomindang to surrender. Probably as many as 300,000 innocent civilians, including women and children, died in the "Rape of Nanjing." Survivors described horrifying sights of raped women impaled on stakes and children burned to death or sliced in half.

Mao's Guerrilla Strategy

Chiang, his government, and the remnants of his army retreated briefly to Hankou, and then when that too fell, to Chongqing in October of 1938 in mountain-girdled Sichuan, where the Guomindang (GMD) largely sat out the rest of the war. Its war effort was mainly spent, most of its best troops and equipment gone. New conscription drives in the western provinces brought the army to some 5 million men, but they were poorly clothed, often virtually starved, and disease-ridden; tyrannized by their officers, they had few or no weapons and very poor morale. The Japanese invasion was stalled by the mountains of western China, by their own overextended supply lines, and by the guerrilla resistance of the Communists in the north and northwest, who pinned down a million enemy troops and were never eliminated. The guerrilla strategy of Mao and Zhu De was further refined by experience and became a model of its kind. Unlike the Guomindang, Communist troops were trained to fraternize with and help their fellow peasants. It was a new kind of army in Chinese history, where soldiers had been feared and hated as little better than locusts or bandits, especially in the twentieth century and the warlord years. Communist troops actually paid for the food and other supplies provided by the peasants and helped the households where they were quartered in a variety of tasks, as well as defending them against the cruel Japanese. As they themselves put it, "We are the fish, the people are the water," paraphrasing the philosopher Xunzi (c. 300–235 B.C.E.), who said "The people are the water and the ruler is the boat; the water can support the boat but can also sink it!"[1]

Such policies ensured wide popular support—essential for the success of any guerrilla movement—avoided the need for cumbersome supply systems, and greatly increased troop mobility. The Communists also depended on peasants for information about Japanese forces and used them to help with sabotage operations. There were savage Japanese reprisals, but such tactics merely increased the already established role of the Communist party as the defenders of China against the hated invaders and as the true leaders of Chinese nationalism. Many intellectuals, survivors and heirs of the heady days of 1911 and the May Fourth movement, disillusioned with the GMD, were also attracted to the Communists. By the war's end the areas they controlled, the so-called "Liberated Areas," included as many as 90 million people. The Communist program was purposely moderate and avoided land confiscation or opposition to private ownership. It became known as "agrarian reform" from its emphasis on rent reduction, cooperatives, and concern for peasant welfare. Patriotic resistance against the Japanese held it all together. The Communist party seemed to be the true heir of Sun Yat-sen and his Three Principles, which they paraphrased as "national independence, democratic liberty, and the people's welfare."

There was no further stress on class warfare, the urban proletariat (not present in this generally poor and agricultural area in any case), or party dictatorship, although such ideas were still clearly part of Chinese Communist ideology and were to surface again once they won power in 1949. Their troops attempted some direct attacks on Japanese forces in north China and damaged them heavily, but they came to see that their advantage lay in avoiding fixed battles as much as possible in favor of hit-and-run attacks, night raids, strikes against isolated forces or outposts, and disruption of transport lines, usually by explosives set under cover of darkness. They had no air force, tanks, or heavy artillery, and most of their equipment was homemade, including crude grenades, or captured from the enemy. They used tunnel warfare and planted mines, both to defend themselves and to keep the element of surprise. All of these tactics were later to be employed, consciously following the Chinese model, by the Vietnamese in their long war against the superior forces first of the French and then of the Americans.

Meanwhile, Mao promoted a peasant and proletarian theme in art and literature, declaring that "art must serve politics" and "art must serve the masses," an aspect of what he called "the mass line," which was to be supported by intellectuals and all others who could not claim worker or peasant origins. These "bourgeois" groups were to be accepted, at least for the present, as part of what Mao called "The New Democracy," leaving their future, in what he indicated would be a later "socialist revolution," ambiguous. For the time being, it was to be a united front of all classes working together, a coalition against Japanese aggression and for building a new China once the invaders were defeated.

The radical nature of what was to happen after 1949 was inherent in the Chinese Communist party, but not yet made clear. Though Mao was not an original thinker and nearly all of his ideas had been stated earlier by others, he put them together in what purported to be a new doctrine, a development beyond Marxism-Leninism that was fitted to the particular circumstances of China. Maoism became a cult, and loyalty to him and his line was required and enforced for all, including the intellectuals who had grown up under the influence of Western liberalism and now were disciplined, "reformed," or expelled. Most politically conscious Chinese realized that the coming struggle would be between the Communists and the Guomindang for the future of China, and the Communists were building their strength.

From bases in French Indochina and east China, Japanese planes bombed the cities remaining under Chinese control in the west, largely GMD controlled, almost at will. There was almost no Chinese air force left after 1937, and the raids killed thousands of civilians but had little or no effect on the war. There were a few small battles, ineffective retreating actions by demoralized and poorly led Chinese forces easily brushed aside by Japanese armored columns probing westward, as in the capture of Changsha and Guilin and the advance toward Guiyang later in 1944, stopped again by mountains and fuel shortages rather than by Chinese resistance. Near the Burma border in the far southwest there were periodic artillery duels across the gorge of the Salween River but no real battles. In the north a different kind of war hurt the Japanese far more. Communist guerrillas controlled most of the countryside at night, especially west of the coastal plain, blowing up bridges, roads, and rail lines and ambushing Japanese patrols. They confined the invaders to the cities and towns, while they too depended on mountains and distance to limit the areas of enemy occupation to urban centers in the east. When Japan surrendered in August 1945, its armies still held most of the eastern half of China proper, from which the Chinese had never had the strength to drive them.

Although there were only skirmishes rather than major battles after 1937, over 21 million Chinese died at Japanese hands from 1937 to 1945, most of them civilians. The occupying army was at least as ruthless as the Nazis in Europe, exterminating whole villages as part of a policy of terror and slaughtering noncombatants indiscriminately. Their slogan formula, with official approval, was "Kill all, burn all, loot all!" and in many areas they carried it out. Chinese in the occupied territories were forced to bow or kneel to Japanese officers and were beaten or shot if they were not sufficiently deferential. The Japanese record in the rest of Asia was equally bad, but in China they began much earlier, and they made no effort to win Chinese support. Especially in Manchuria they conducted hideous medical experiments on Chinese prisoners, and elsewhere as well used them as live targets for bayonet practice. The Japanese were the only belligerents to use biological warfare, dropping germs of bubonic plague and other epidemic diseases by air onto Chinese cities. Japanese brutality stemmed also from their conviction of their own cultural and racial superiority, like the Nazis, and their contempt for those whom they conquered. It was a black period in the history of East Asia. At war's end the Guomindang had been fatally weakened, while the Communists had grown from a tiny and hunted band to a major military presence in the north. Their effectiveness against the Japanese had won them a broad base of popular support even among many in the Guomindang-controlled areas, and by mid-1945 they were the real government in much of the north.

A CLOSER LOOK

Chongqing: Beleaguered Wartime Capital

Just before the fall of Hankou on the central Yangzi in October 1938, China's capital moved farther up river to Chongqing, where it remained for the rest of the war. Chongqing sprawled over steep hills at the junction of

Japanese troops entering a town in eastern China, where they followed their general formula of "Kill all, burn all, loot all." (Hulton/Archive/Getty Images)

the Jialing River and the Yangzi near the center of the generally hilly Red Basin of Sichuan, which was in turn surrounded on all sides by mountains. The steep and narrow gorges of the Yangzi about halfway between Hankou and Chongqing along the provincial border were easily blocked by a boom. These natural defenses kept Chongqing secure from the Japanese army, but it had few defenses against air attack, and Japanese bombing caused great destruction and loss of life. By 1941, before Pearl Harbor, an unofficial private Ameri-

Guomindang army supply train on the Burma Road inside China. The road was Nationalist China's wartime surface link with the outside world, but the Guomindang soldiers were undernourished, diseased, maltreated by their officers, and with very poor morale. (R. Murphey)

can group, the Flying Tigers, paid by the Chinese but with their own fighter planes, had greatly reduced the bombing raids. Chinese morale was high for the first two or three Chongqing years, and the wartime capital was a symbol of patriotic resistance. Whole arsenals and factories had been disassembled and carried on the backs of workers to Chongqing and elsewhere in Sichuan, Guizhou, and Yunnan to escape the Japanese; university faculties and students made the same journey, carrying what they could of their libraries and laboratories. America's entry into the war against Japan late in 1941 gave morale another boost.

But disillusionment spread as the Guomindang army largely sat out the war and the increasingly corrupt government of Chiang Kai-shek and his cronies stockpiled arms for use against the Communists. Chongqing was also notorious for its gray, cloudy weather and drizzle, suffocatingly hot in summer, cold and damp in winter. The city was painfully crowded; over 1 million people from all parts of China, including officials and army personnel, were added to the originally smaller local population and there were too few additions to housing, water supply, and other basics. Fires set by Japanese bombs often burned out of control, and air-raid shelters were grossly inadequate. Chongqing's main link with the outside world was the extension of the Burma Road through mountainous southwest China and, after the Japanese took Burma, the American airlift from India over the "hump" of the Himalayas. The principal airport was a sandbank in the Yangzi hemmed in by steep hills on both sides, flooded every spring and summer by rising river levels, and obscured most of the time by heavy, low clouds. The summer airport was on the edge of a cliff above the river, which was equally dangerous. There were no railways anywhere in Sichuan. People understandably felt isolated. Prices for everything skyrocketed as a result of wartime shortages, government ineptitude, and a swollen population. The Sichuanese blamed it on "downriver people," who in turn were contemptuous of "ignorant provincials."

Tight "thought control" and the secret police suppressed all free political expression; many with "dangerous thoughts" or "improper" books were jailed or executed. Those with money and connections lived luxuriously in guarded villas with American-made limousines, but most people in Chongqing lived in poverty, mud, and squalor. By 1940 inflation began to rise at about 10 percent per month, accelerating wildly after 1943. Currency might lose half or more of its value between morning and afternoon. The government printed more notes of larger denominations, while its finance minister, H. H. Kong, brother-in-law of Chiang Kai-shek, obtained gold from the United States for his own accounts in overseas banks, as did other Guomindang officials. Salaries and wages fell hopelessly behind inflation, and there was widespread mal-

Chiang Kai-shek and Madame Chiang with the American general Joseph Stilwell in 1942. Stilwell was sent by President Roosevelt to try to reorganize the huge Chinese army and convince them to fight the Japanese, but Chiang deeply resented Stilwell and had him dismissed in 1944. (Hulton/Archives/Getty Images)

nutrition, tuberculosis, and other diseases of poverty. Furniture, clothing, books, and heirlooms were sold in a vain effort to stay afloat. Nearly all officials succumbed to bribery and other forms of corruption, whatever their original principles, if only to save their families. By the end of the war there was universal demoralization and a loss of faith in the Guomindang. The Chongqing years were the death of Guomindang hopes to remain the government of a China now sick of its ineffectiveness, corruption, and reaction.

Japan in the Pacific and Southeast Asia

Early on Sunday, December 7, 1941, without a declaration of war, as in 1895, 1904, and 1937, Japanese carrier planes bombed and sank most of the U.S. Pacific Fleet at Pearl Harbor in Hawaii. The Americans declared war on the Axis (Japan and Germany), as did the British, now no longer alone since the surrender of France. The whirlwind Japanese conquests of Malaya, Burma, Indonesia, and the Philippines followed. In 1940, the Vichy government of France, a Nazi collaborator regime, had agreed to Japanese use of bases in French Indochina, which were vital to the assault on Southeast Asia. Japanese occupation replaced French, although a facade of nominal French control was preserved. Thailand was forced to become an official ally of Japan and permit the use of additional vital bases for the invasions of Malaya and Burma. The rapid Japanese triumphs resulted from their well-planned campaigns, which were laid out well in advance. Pushing through jungle trails, often on bicycles, the Japanese attacked unprepared and thinly staffed British positions in Burma and Malaya, including Singapore, from their undefended rear. Japanese dive bombers knocked out the major capital ships of the British Asian Fleet off Singapore. Japanese troops moved south from bases in Thailand with amazing speed, capturing Kuala Lumpur on January 11, 1942, and accepting the surrender of the outmaneuvered garrison at Singapore on February 15. British and Indian forces fought a more effective rearguard action in Burma, but the Japanese took Rangoon in early March and Mandalay in early May, diverting some forces from their quick Malayan victory. Most, however, were diverted to the invasion of Indonesia, where they soon demolished the tiny Dutch naval and land forces, who surrendered on March 8.

The Philippines were invaded two days after Pearl Harbor, but the Americans now lacked the navy to defend or supply the Philippines; much of their air force had been destroyed on the ground a few hours after the attack on Pearl Harbor and despite that obvious warning. There was, nevertheless, heavy fighting until Manila surrendered on January 2, 1942. Filipino and American units retreated to the peninsula of Bataan on the south shore of Manila Bay, where they held out in the island fortress of Corregidor until mid-April. The commanding American general, Douglas MacArthur, fled by submarine to Australia well before Corregidor's surrender, but the captured survivors of his army were treated with inhuman brutality by the Japanese; many were beaten, bayoneted, or driven to their deaths in the infamous Bataan Death March, where from 5,000 to 10,000 Filipino troops (the exact number remains uncertain) and over 600 Americans died. The few who survived prison camp did so only as emaciated skeletons, with dreadful tales to tell. Their horror was matched by Westerners imprisoned by the Japanese in Java and Singapore, among other notorious prison camps, and by the British and Indian soldiers who were beaten, starved, and forced to work until they dropped on building a (never finished) rail line between Burma and Thailand through mountains and tropical jungles; 16,000 died in a nightmarish experience, well portrayed in the film *Bridge on the River Kwai.*

For the Japanese, this brutality was an expression of their own "racial superiority," their hatred for their former Western masters, and their contempt for soldiers who surrendered even when their position was hopeless. Japanese soldiers were taught that surrender was disgrace, and that they themselves were instead to fight to the last man, as they often did. Japanese behavior to both Western and Asian civilians was equally horrendous and was part of official policy. All armies are brutal in war, but the Japanese record in World War II is rivaled (but probably not equaled) only by that of the Nazis in Europe. "A man away from home has no neighbors," says a traditional Japanese proverb, and the Japanese army acted that out. In addition, it operated as a tightly controlled unit, not as a group of individuals, many of whom after the war freely acknowledged their gross immorality. The Japanese military was also very conscious of the traditional Japanese creed of *bushido,* the way of the warrior. Almost to a man they were proud to die for their emperor, and they saw their behavior abroad as glorifying him, while tolerating no dissent internally or resistance externally. They boasted of their flouting of the Geneva Convention on the treatment of war prisoners, which they saw as a contemptible Western notion that had no validity for soldiers of the Yamato "race."

The Japanese had developed late in the 1930s a light, fast, maneuverable fighter plane, the Zero, which proved superior to any opponent until later in the war. The Japanese navy was technically the equal of the Americans or British and had the great advantage of surprise and of brilliant leadership. In addition to their conquests described above, they had occupied all of the smaller islands of the western Pacific by early 1942 and even installed a garrison in the western Aleutians off Alaska. They probably had no intention of invading the United States itself, but the West Coast was alarmed; war hysteria and continued American racism and misguided policies led to the internment of nearly all of the many Japanese on the West Coast, over 100,000 in all, including U.S. citizens born there, who were kept in desert camps surrounded by barbed wire until the end of the war. Americans feared a long war as they began to build up their shattered Pacific fleet and to fight on two fronts, against Germany and against Japan.

Japanese expansion had long been planned, growing out of the Japanese position in China and their conquest of Manchuria. They spoke of a Greater East Asia Co-Prosperity sphere, under Japanese direction but theoretically in the mutual interests of the other countries in the area (not including Korea and Taiwan, which were seen as integral parts of Japan). The idea had considerable merit since it proposed to combine Japanese technological, industrial, and organizational skills with the labor power and resources of China and Southeast Asia. Japan was poor in natural resources, especially oil, and in agricultural land; its supposed partners could fill those gaps: oil, rubber, tin, sugar, and rice from Southeast Asia, and iron ore and coal from China and the

Philippines. The benefits to the partners were never spelled out, but one could certainly argue that they needed the kind of experience, technology, and direction the Japanese had for themselves, and their development could, thus, be assisted: raw materials in exchange for expertise. Such benefits flowed back to them only on the smallest scale and were more than made up for by Japanese exploitation. Japan also ignored and was clearly opposed to the rising force of Asian nationalism, first in China and then in her Southeast Asian conquests. Almost from the beginning and with very few exceptions, racist arrogance and brutality made a mockery of "co-prosperity" and earned the Japanese bitter hatred everywhere, while feeding still further the fires of Chinese and Southeast Asian nationalism. Japan was now master of Asia, and all other peoples must bow to it, accepting an inferior position.

Soon after its early sweeping victories, the tide turned against Japan. The naval battle of Midway in June 1942 was won mainly by U.S. aircraft carriers that had been out on patrol when Pearl Harbor was bombed. The Americans had broken the Japanese code, and now had the help of British-invented radar; both were critical at Midway. Then followed the long, "island-hopping" American and Australian campaign to retake one by one the fiercely defended islands of the western Pacific. There were bloody battles in the jungles of New Guinea, the adjacent Solomon Islands, and the Bismarck Archipelago; the war moved slowly northward, with hand-to-hand fighting and heavy losses on both sides. The Allies captured Saipan, within bombing range of all Japan's big cities, in June 1944. The Philippines were retaken with massive naval support by early 1945, and in June Okinawa, part of Japanese home territory, fell to the Allies. Fanatical Japanese defenders often fought to the last man. Their dwindling air force began to use what they called *kamikaze* attacks (see Chapter 9) by planes loaded with bombs and purposely crashed into U.S. and Allied ships. Allied losses were severe but were soon replaced. By now the Japanese fleet and supply ships were nearly all sunk, many by submarines, and the air force was largely gone. Indonesia was cut off from Japanese supply lines by Allied naval power and safely ignored.

Burma and India

The other major land campaign of the war was the battle for Burma; first the Japanese routing of ill-prepared British and Indian forces in 1942; then the Japanese drive aimed at the invasion of India, which was turned back with heavy losses on both sides at Imphal just inside the Indian border early in 1944; and finally the successful reconquest by Indian and British troops.

The Japanese seemed to have mastered the art of jungle fighting, but in time the British learned from bitter experience, and after Imphal they began to send commando raiding units in hit-and-run attacks to throw the Japanese off balance and remind them that a new British army was coming. British morale, shattered by their earlier defeat, began to build again. By late spring of 1944 large detachments of Indian troops under British command crossed the border from India and pushed steadily southward through the downpours and mud of the monsoon, capturing first north Burma, where they were joined by Chinese and American forces, then Mandalay, the old Burmese capital, and finally Rangoon in May 1945. The reconquest of Malaya was soon ready to begin, but the Japanese surrender in August 1945 made it unnecessary.

India was only marginally involved in the war on its own territory, although 2 million Indian troops fought under British command in several theaters; over 100,000 died, and India itself became a major military base and supply center for the Allied war effort in Asia. The Fourteenth Army in Burma was over 90 percent Indian, and Indians were a large part of the Eighth Army in the North African campaign against the Germans under Rommel. A few Japanese bombs fell on Calcutta, but the big push through northwestern Burma was stopped by British and Indian troops at Imphal (see above) in early 1944. A frustrated Bengali and Indian nationalist, Subhas Chandra Bose, who had been passed over for the leadership of the Congress party, saw his chance for power in alliance with the Japanese. He escaped from British arrest in 1941, made his way to Berlin, and in 1943 went by German submarine around Africa to Singapore, where the Japanese gave him command of 60,000 Indian prisoners of war. He called them the Indian National Army for the "liberation" of their homeland, but they were used as coolies, or as cannon fodder in the advance wave of the bloody and fruitless assault on Imphal. Bose escaped and was later killed in an air crash, but he remained a national hero to some Indians. Ceylon (Sri Lanka) also served as a major Allied base and became the headquarters of Southeast Asia Command which, under Lord Louis Mountbatten, directed the reconquest of Burma and Malaya.

Japan was ready to surrender by early 1945 and had begun feelers through the still-neutral Russians, and later through a neutral Sweden and the Vatican who had signed a nonaggression pact with Japan in 1941. U.S. bombers had destroyed nearly all of Japan's cities. Incendiary bombs were used to start giant firestorms, which in one horrible night in Tokyo killed an estimated 120,000 people, nearly twice the total killed in air raids throughout the war in England. Much of the surviving population there and in the other gutted cities was starving. The Japanese fleet and air force were destroyed,

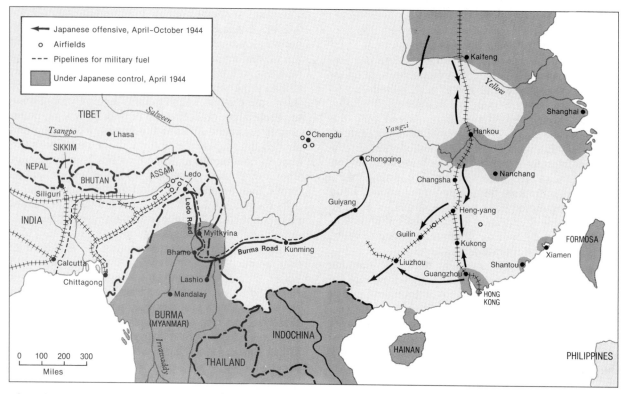

Legend:
- → Japanese offensive, April–October 1944
- ○ Airfields
- - - - Pipelines for military fuel
- Under Japanese control, April 1944

The China-Burma-India Theater in World War II

This shows the situation about a year and a half before the Japanese surrender. A British-Indian army had begun to drive the Japanese south in Burma, and Chinese guerillas continued to harass Japanese forces in northern China.

and U.S. planes bombed at will around the clock. One minor target remained: Hiroshima, a medium-sized city and army base.

U.S., British, and European scientists (the Europeans were refugees) had developed a primitive atom bomb and tested it in the New Mexico desert on July 16, 1945. In February 1945 at Yalta, Stalin had promised to attack Japan within three months after the defeat of Germany, which had come in May. Anxious to forestall the Russians and to show this awesome new power, the new American president Harry Truman decided to drop an atom bomb on Hiroshima on August 6, obliterating the city and killing over 100,000 people, nearly all civilians. Truman called it "the greatest thing in history." Russia declared war on August 8 and invaded Japanese-held Manchuria. The next day the Americans dropped a second atom bomb, which destroyed the city of Nagasaki; over 65,000 died. On August 15 the emperor announced Japan's surrender. The army in Japan was still in good order and would certainly have fought fiercely against an invasion, supported by many Japanese in guerrilla actions. Casualties on both sides would have been heavy, an argument that was of course used to justify using the

atom bombs. Patriotic Japanese diehards were appalled at the emperor's decision but obeyed his call, broadcast throughout the Japanese Empire by radio.

A total of 2.5 million Japanese military personnel had died in the war and nearly 1 million civilians had perished in air raids. But Japan's defeat of Western colonial regimes early in the Pacific War had broken forever the myth of Western invincibility, while its own brutality had further fed the fires of Asian nationalism.

Chinese and Indian women continued in this period to move further toward liberation, and as war erupted with the Japanese invasion of China in 1931 and 1937 and then involved India in 1942, women played an active part on the home front and in China in joining the guerilla resistance to the Japanese, as did women in Southeast Asia. In Japan, women worked in munitions and uniform factories and managed their families while their husbands were away fighting. One of the worst blots on the Japanese record was their forced recruitment of so-called "comfort girls" to provide sex for their troops, not only heavily from subject Korea but also from China and Southeast Asia. Such revolting slavery was deeply resented, but Japan has yet to pay any compensation.

Hiroshima after the bomb, 1945.
(Bettmann/Corbis)

Questions

1. Why was nationalism late to develop in Southeast Asia? How did the assorted Southeast Asian nationalist movements differ from those of India and China?

2. How did Gandhi's political and social goals draw upon India's philosophical and religious traditions?

3. Did Gandhi's efforts actually defeat the British and his political opponents or was it something else that helped to drive out the British and create an independent India? If Gandhi's actions were responsible, specifically how did his concept of nonviolence achieve this?

4. What were the achievements and the failures of the Nanjing decade? What were the successes and failures of Chiang Kai-shek's Guomindang government? What was the fate of the Chinese Communist party, and how and why did it change its strategy after 1927? How does one explain Chiang Kai-shek's actions against the Communists in the face of Japanese invasion?

5. Trace the rise of Japanese militarism in the post–World War I era. How did this counter the successes of Taisho democracy in the 1920s and early 1930s? What role did Manchuria assume in these transitions?

6. How did Japanese fascism differ from that of Germany and Italy? Was a Japanese war against the United States inevitable?

7. What were the broad consequences of Japan's World War II military aggression relative to shaping Asia's postwar future? How did Japanese rule alienate other Asians?

Note

1. J. K. Fairbank, *The United States and China* (Cambridge: Harvard University Press, 1979), p. 292.

Suggested Web Sites

Mahatma Gandhi

http://www.mkgandhi.org/

http://www.mahatma.org.in/

http://www.sscnet.ucla.edu/southasia/History/Gandhi/ gandhi.html

Detailed sites on the life and works of Gandhi, as well as a vast pictorial view of his life.

Modern India

http://ww.indhistory.com/modern-india-history.html

http://www.doindiago.com/history/modern.htm
Overviews of modern India's history.

Japan—Militarism and World War II

http://www.japan-guide.com/e/e2129.html
Some basic information on Japan from World War I to 1945, with sublinks to photograph archives and textual information.

http://afe.easia.columbia.edu/japan/japanworkbook/
modernhist/wwii.html
Useful Columbia University East Asia Project curriculum resources Web site, with links to classroom activity suggestions.

China's Republican Era (1912–1949)

http://afe.easia.columbia.edu

http://plaza.ufl.edu/jwweaver/Bibliography/China.html
Good source sites for materials and commentary on the Republican era.

http://newton.uor.edu/Departments&Programs/
AsianStudiesDept/china-mod.html
An annotated directory of internet resouces on East and Southeast Asia.

Suggestions for Further Reading

Southeast Asia

Adams, C. *Sukarno: An Autobiography.* Indianapolis: Bobbs Merrill, 1965.
Elson, R. E. *Javanese Peasants and the Colonial Sugar Industry.* Oxford: Oxford University Press, 1984.
Frederick, W. H. *Visions and Heat: The Making of the Indonesian Revolution.* Columbus: Ohio University Press, 1989.
McCoy, A., ed. *Southeast Asia Under Japanese Occupation.* New Haven: Yale University Press, 1985.
Osborne, M. *Southeast Asia: An Introductory History.* New York: HarperCollins, 1995.
Purcell, V. *The Chinese in Southeast Asia.* Oxford: Oxford University Press, 1965.
Ricklefs, M. C. *A History of Modern Indonesia.* Bloomington: Indiana University Press, 1981.
Steinberg, D. J., ed. *In Search of Southeast Asia.* Honolulu: University of Hawaii Press, 1987.
Tate, D. J. M. *The Making of Modern Southeast Asia,* 2 vols. Oxford: Oxford University Press, 1971, 1979.
Wyatt, D. K. *Thailand: A Short History.* New Haven: Yale University Press, 1984.

India

Brown, J. *Gandhi and Civil Disobedience.* Cambridge, England: Cambridge University Press, 1977.
———. *Gandhi's Rise to Power.* Cambridge, England: Cambridge University Press, 1972.
Fay, P. *The Forgotten Army.* Ann Arbor: University of Michigan Press, 1996.
Mehta, V. *Mahatma Gandhi and his Apostles.* New Haven: Yale University Press, 1993.
Nehru, J. *Toward Freedom.* New York: John Day, 1941.
Pandey, B. N. *Nehru.* New York: Stein and Day, 1976.
Wolpert, S. *Nehru.* Oxford: Oxford University Press, 1996.

China

Averill, S. *Revolution in the Highlands: Jingganshan.* Lanham, MD: Rowan and Littlefield, 2003.
Bergère, M. C. *Sun Yat Sen.* Stanford: Stanford University Press, 1999.
Bianco, L. *Origins of the Chinese Revolution.* Stanford: Stanford University Press, 1971.
Coble, P. M. *Facing Japan, 1931–1937.* Cambridge: Harvard University Press, 1992.
Dirlik, A. *The Origins of Chinese Communism.* Oxford: Oxford University Press, 1989.
Eastman, L. *The Nationalist Era in China, 1927–1949.* Cambridge, England: Cambridge University Press, 1990.
Fogel, J., ed. *The Nanjing Massacre.* Berkeley: University of California Press, 2000.
Gasster, M. *Chinese Intellectuals and the Revolution of 1911.* Seattle: University of Washington Press, 1989.
Grieder, J. B. *Hu Shih and the Chinese Renaissance.* Cambridge: Harvard University Press, 1970.
Hung, E. T. *War and Popular Culture.* Berkeley: University of California Press, 1994.
Nathan, A. *Peking Politics, 1918–1923.* Berkeley: University of California Press, 1976.
Martin, B. G. *The Shanghai Green Gang.* Berkeley: University of California Press, 1995.
Wilbur, C. M. *Sun Yat-sen: Frustrated Patriot.* New York: Columbia University Press, 1976.

Japan

Agawa, H. *The Reluctant Admiral: Yamamoto.* Tokyo: Kodansha, 2001.
Arima, T. *The Failure of Freedom.* Cambridge: Harvard University Press, 1969.
Beasley, W. G. *Japanese Imperialism, 1894–1945.* Oxford: Oxford University Press, 1991.
Bix, H. *Hirohito.* New York: Harper Collins, 2000.
Duus, P., et al., eds. *The Cambridge History of Japan: The Twentieth Century.* Cambridge, England: Cambridge University Press, 1988.
———. *The Japanese Informal Empire in China, 1895–1941.* New York: Columbia University Press, 1989.
Havens, T. *The Valley of Darkness.* New York: Norton, 1978.
Iriye, A. *The Origins of the Second World War in Asia.* New York: Longman, 1987.
Ka, C. M. *Japanese Colonialism in Taiwan.* Boulder, CO: Westview Press, 1995.
Kim, R. E. *Lost Names.* Berkeley: University of California Press, 1998.
Lebra, J., ed. *Japan's Greater East Asia Co-Prosperity Sphere.* Oxford, England: Oxford University Press, 1975.
MacPherson, W. J. *The Economic Development of Japan, 1868–1941.* London: Macmillan, 1987.

Matsuoka, Y. T. *The Making of Japanese Manchuria*. Cambridge: Harvard University Press, 2003.

Smith, K. *A Time of Crisis*. Cambridge: Harvard University Press, 2004.

Tipton J. *The Japanese Police State: The Tokku in Inter-War Japan*. Honolulu: University of Hawaii Press, 1990.

World War II

Boyle, J. H. *China and Japan at War, 1937–1945*. Stanford: Stanford University Press, 1972.

Chang, I. *The Rape of Nanking*. New York: Penguin Putnam, 1998.

Ch'i H. S. *Nationalist China at War*. Ann Arbor: University of Michigan Press, 1982.

Conroy, H., and Wray, H., eds. *Pearl Harbor Re-examined*. Honolulu: University of Hawaii, 1990.

Dower, J. *War Without Mercy*. New York: Pantheon, 1986.

Goodman, G., ed. *Japanese Cultural Policies in Southeast Asia During World War II*. New York: St. Martin's, 1991.

Harris, S. H. *Factories of Death*. London: Routledge, 1995.

Henson, M. R. *Comfort Women*. Lanham, MD, Rowan and Littlefield, 2003.

Hicks, G. *The Comfort Women*. New York: Columbia University Press, 1995.

Hsiung, J., and Levine, S. I. *China's Bitter Victory*. Armonk, NY: M. E. Sharpe, 1992.

Iritani, T. *Group Psychology of the Japanese in Wartime*. London: Kegan Paul, 1992.

Selden, K., and Selden, M., eds. *The Atomic Bomb: Voices from Hiroshima and Nagasaki*. Armonk, NY: M. E. Sharpe, 1992.

Sherwin, M. J. *A World Destroyed: Hiroshima and the Origins of the Arms Race*. New York: Viking, 1987.

Spector, D. H. *Eagle Against the Sun*. New York: Free Press, 1989.

Tanaka, Y. *Hidden Horrors: Japanese War Crimes in World War II*. Boulder, CO: Westview Press, 1996.

Tsuneishi, K. *Unit 731*. Lanham, MD: Rowan and Littlefield, 2003.

White, T., and Jacoby, A. *Thunder Out of China*. New York: Sloan Associates, 1946.

Williams, P., and Wallace, D. *Unit 731: Japan's Secret Biological Warfare in World War II*. New York: Free Press, 1989.

Wint, G., Calvocoressi, P., and Pritchard, J. *Total War*. New York: Random House, 1991.

Yoshiaki Y. *Comfort Women*. New York: Columbia University Press, 2000.

18

Revival and Revolution in Japan and China

Much of Asia was devastated by World War II, and no part of it was uninvolved. There were more war casualties in Asia than in all of the rest of the world. The heavy human and economic losses were, however, accompanied by the end of colonial or semicolonial rule and Western dominance in Asia. The Japanese conquest of Southeast Asia destroyed the image of Western superiority, while the war in Europe weakened both the power and the desire of the Western powers to resume their former positions in Asia. The Japanese economy was destroyed by the war, and almost all of its cities bombed to rubble. Japan lived under American military occupation from 1945 to 1952, but by 1950 the damage to the economy had been largely repaired and rapid new growth that would continue for decades had begun. By 1965 Japan had become the world's third industrial power, after the United States and the Soviet Union, and in the 1970s and 1980s it won a leading position in world markets for its manufactured exports.

In China long pent-up pressures for change built up still further during the anti-Japanese war, which also helped to weaken the Guomindang government and to strengthen the Communist guerrilla forces. The end of the war was shortly followed by civil war, from which the Communists emerged as victors in 1949 with massive popular support. War damages were quickly repaired by the new revolutionary government, but in 1957 Mao Zedong, the Communist leader, launched the Great Leap Forward, a radical campaign that ended by plunging the country into mass starvation. It was followed in 1966 by the Cultural Revolution, a destructive effort to revive flagging revolutionary ardor that ended only with Mao's death in 1976. China began to reopen its contacts with the West in the 1970s and to pursue economic growth rather than ideology.

The Revival of Japan

Japan, especially its cities, had been more completely destroyed by the war than any of the other belligerents. In addition to Hiroshima and Nagasaki, which had been leveled by the first atomic bombs, virtually all of Japan's cities, especially Tokyo and Yokohama, had been flattened and burned by massive conventional and incendiary bombing. A notable exception was Kyoto, the old imperial capital, which had been preserved by the intervention of American art historians. The government and what remained of the army in the home islands were still, however, in good order, and there was a smooth transfer of power to the American military government of occupation under General Douglas MacArthur. Japan had surrendered to the Allied forces, including Britain, China, Australia, Canada, New Zealand, and the Soviet Union, all of which had contributed to Japan's defeat. But MacArthur permitted only token representation from each of the other allies in his Supreme Commander Allied Powers (SCAP) regime of occupation, over which he presided like a virtual emperor in control of a wholly American enterprise.

With very few exceptions, the Japanese people, including officials, officers, and troops as well as other civilians, accepted Emperor Hirohito's pronouncement of surrender and his call to "endure the unendurable." Japan had never known defeat in war by foreigners, and for many it was a bitter experience. But most felt relief that the disastrous war was over. They soon found that the occupying Americans were not the devils some had feared and vented their bitterness on the now-discredited military leaders who had so nearly destroyed the nation they were sworn to serve. In general, the years of

CHRONOLOGY

Japan

1945–1952	U.S. occupation under Supreme Commander Allied Powers (SCAP)
1950s	Liberal Democratic Party (LDP); Japanese Self-Defense Force
1950–1990	The "economic miracle"
1956	Japan joins the United Nations
1969–1980	Pollution and controls
2001	Koizumi Junichiro becomes prime minister

China

1947–1949	Civil war; Communist victory
1952–Present	Economy booms in Taiwan and Hong Kong
1958–1959	Great Leap Forward
1959	Split with Russia
1966–1976	Cultural Revolution; fall of Liu Xiaoqi
1972	Nixon visit
1976	Deaths of Zhou Enlai and Mao Zedong; Gang of Four failed coup
1978–1997	Deng Xiaoping; "Four Modernizations"
1989	Tiananmen Square massacre in Beijing
1997	Hong Kong returns to China
1999	Macao returns to China
2003	Hu Jintao

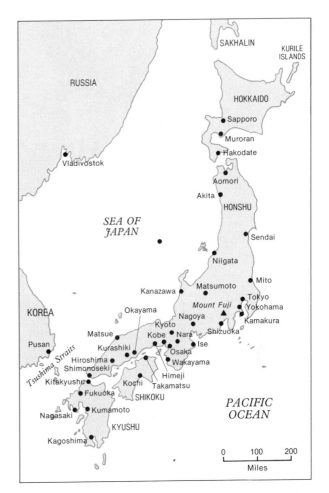

Modern Japan

Note the clustering of cities along the narrow coastal plains, where the great majority of Japanese have always lived.

the occupation, which lasted from late August 1945 to late April 1952, was a period of peaceful reconstruction, with the Japanese doing most of the work of government under American supervision, except at the highest level. Very few Americans knew the Japanese language and were thus far more dependent on the conquered people than in the occupation of Germany.

Occupation and Americanization

Relief on finding the occupying forces bent on reconstruction rather than revenge was soon joined by gratitude for American aid. Most Japanese had lived at best on an austerity diet during the last years of the war, and many were half-starved, living in makeshift shelters in the bombed-out cities. The winter of 1945–1946 would have been more difficult if the Americans had not flown in emergency supplies of food and repaired the main rail lines to again transport fuel and essential building supplies. Having expected far worse from their new rulers, the Japanese were pleasantly surprised. Many were even enthusiastic about the institutional changes that SCAP began to decree to root out the remnants of militarism and implant American-style democracy.

The big prewar industrial combines (zaibatsu firms) were broken up, although they were revived after the occupation. Thousands of political prisoners who had been accused of "dangerous thoughts" and jailed by the military-controlled government of the 1930s and 1940s were released. About 200,000 Japanese who were identified—sometimes wrongly—as too closely associated

General MacArthur with Emperor Hirohito of Japan at the U.S. Embassy in Tokyo in 1945. (Bettmann/Corbis)

with the Japanese version of fascism or with armed expansion abroad were removed from their posts, including a number of senior officials; most reentered public life after the occupation ended. Several hundred other Japanese were identified as suspected "war criminals," and most were tried by a special tribunal in Tokyo that included Allied representatives. Seven were executed, including the wartime prime minister, Tojo, and 18 others were sentenced to prison terms. Nearly 1,000 minor war criminals in Japan and Southeast Asia, largely military men, were executed for gross cruelty to prisoners or to inhabitants of conquered countries. This prompted charges of racism because it contrasted with the far more lenient treatment and in some cases even protection of all but the top Nazi leaders by the United States and its allies in Europe.

A victor's justice in the aftermath of a bitter war is easily criticized, but most Japanese accepted the tribunal's verdict as inevitable and perhaps even appropriate punishment. Most blamed their failed leaders rather

than their new masters. The national ability to accept what cannot be helped, and to change direction in keeping with new circumstances, had been demonstrated often before, most recently in the sweeping changes carried out after Japan had been forced by Western powers to open its doors in the 1850s. But it impressed the Americans, who had expected a sullen and resentful populace and found instead that they were both liked and admired—not only because they had won and not only because their relief and reconstruction efforts were welcome, but because their moves toward democratization were generally popular. The Japanese people had suffered terribly from militarism and its police state and were ready to follow new paths. American ways were sought after by many uncritically, but the basic political reforms of the occupation struck a deeper responsive chord.

Most of the changes were reaffirmed after the occupation ended, except for the zaibatsu dissolution, and have struck firm roots in contemporary Japan, or perhaps more accurately, were grafted onto earlier Japanese efforts to adopt institutions of government, law, education, and culture which had been in eclipse during the years from 1931 to 1945. In addition to a revitalization of electoral and party democracy, government was decentralized by giving more power to local organs. Public education, formerly supervised closely by the central government, was also decentralized and freed as much as possible from bureaucratic control. One of the most successful and permanent changes was the SCAP-directed program of land reform, which compensated the owners of large properties that were expropriated and provided for the selling of it to former tenants, in a way the last blow to the surviving traces of Tokugawa feudalism. Japanese society began to move rapidly toward its present very considerable social equality, where status results from achievement rather than from birth.

The new constitution drafted by SCAP officials retained the emperor as a figurehead but vested all real power in a legislature and prime minister elected by universal suffrage. The constitution, adopted by the Diet in 1946, stated that sovereignty resided not with the emperor but with the people of Japan. The emperor was defined as a symbol of the state—a limited monarchy similar to British or Scandinavian patterns. There was a detailed bill of rights for the protection of individuals against arbitrary state power. Article 9 of the constitution forbade Japan to have any armed forces except for police and denied it the right to go to war. To most Japanese this was not only reasonable but welcome, given the ruin that arms and warfare had brought on them; Japan, many believed, should set an example to the rest of the world of the folly of war. More than anything else, what soured the occupation was the shift in American policy beginning in 1948, as the Cold War

MacArthur: An Assessment

Most observers described General MacArthur as a vain man, ever conscious of his public image. Here is a leading Western historian's assessment of MacArthur in his role as the head of SCAP from 1945 to 1951.

A tendency toward complacent self-dramatization was encouraged by the adulation of a devoted wartime staff that he took with him to Japan. . . . They took almost ludicrous care that only the rosiest reports of the occupation should reach the outside world. In their debased opinion the slightest criticism of SCAP amounted to something approaching sacrilege. MacArthur took up residence in the United States Embassy in Tokyo. Each day at the same hour he was driven to his office in a large building facing the palace moat; at the same hour each day he was driven home again. . . . He never toured Japan to see things for himself. . . . The irreverent were heard to say that if a man rose early in the morning he might catch a glimpse of the Supreme Commander walking on the waters of the palace moat. There is no doubt that this aloofness impressed Japanese of the conservative type. . . . But it may well be doubted whether this kind of awed respect was compatible with the healthy growth of democratic sentiment. . . . The Japanese perhaps learned more about democracy from MacArthur's dismissal than from anything he himself ever did or said.

Source: From R. Storry, *A History of Modern Japan* (London: Penguin, 1960), pp. 240–241.

intensified, toward rebuilding Japan's military capacity and using it as a base of American military operation.

The goal of making Japan a Cold War ally of the United States soon became more important than reform. The Berlin blockade, the final Communist victory in China in 1949, and the Korean War all further hardened the American line. Although MacArthur was fired by President Truman in 1951 for his irresponsible management of the Korean War, Cold War considerations continued to dominate American policy, and when the occupation ended in 1952 Japan was bound to the United States by a security treaty that permitted the buildup of a Japanese "self-defense force," the stationing of American troops, and their use of several major bases in Japan. American pressures for Japanese rearmament have continued, and the bases remain, but Article 9 of the constitution still has the support of most Japanese.

Economic and Social Development

Whatever the political shifts and the change in attitudes as the occupation wore on, economic reconstruction was almost miraculously rapid. By 1950 the shattered cities, factories, and rail lines had been largely rebuilt. By the end of 1951 industrial production was about equal to what it had been in 1931, now from new and more efficient plants. The Korean War added an additional boost as Japan became the chief base and supplier for American forces in Korea. Prime Minister Yoshida Shigeru said that the Korean War was "a gift from the Gods." By 1953, with reconstruction complete, personal incomes had recovered to their prewar levels, and Japan was entering a new period of boom development. Some credit is due to American aid in the difficult years immediately after the war, but "the Japanese economic miracle," as it is called, was overwhelmingly the result of their own hard work, organization, and national pursuit of success through group effort, no longer military but economic and corporate. The growth of production and income in Japan from 1950 (the first "normal" postwar year) to 1975 was faster than has been measured in any country at any time; in those 25 years, output and incomes roughly tripled. Yet the Japanese continued to maintain a very high rate of personal savings, much of it invested in various forms in economic growth, demonstrating again the close relationship between the level of saving and economic growth rates.

At the same time, production quality also rose impressively, and in many respects Japanese goods, notably cars, cameras, sound reproduction equipment, optics, and many electronics, became the best in the world

Schoolchildren in front of the Heian Shrine in Kyoto. Japanese students wear uniforms, the boys' in military style and dating from Meiji times. (Steve Elmore)

market. This was a tribute to advanced Japanese technology and design, as well as to the efficiency of an industrial plant that was almost entirely new. The same factors were active in the postwar recovery of Germany, while the victorious Allies were saddled with their older and less efficient plants. After 1953 Japan dominated world shipbuilding, although it gave ground increasingly to South Korea in the 1980s. By 1964 Japan had become the world's third-largest producer of steel, and by 1980 it had overtaken both the USSR and the United States in steel output while also becoming a major producer and exporter of automobiles. Japan also invaded European and American markets on a large scale with its high-tech and industrial goods and became the largest trade partner of the People's Republic of China.

Japanese democracy, American-style, has retained a healthy growth, although politics continued to be dominated by a conservative coalition with no effective rival parties. High school education is virtually universal, and literacy is the highest in the world. The press has remained of high quality and is avidly read by a public that also buys and reads more books than in any other country (about ten times as many as Americans). Over half of

young Japanese continue with postsecondary education in a great variety of colleges, universities, and other institutions. The Japanese are now probably the best-educated population in the world.

Investment in education continues to be a major basis for Japan's spectacular economic success. Economic growth also largely eliminated poverty and unemployment, the only major country in the world to be virtually free of these scourges. With the postwar disappearance of what aristocratic survivals remained from Tokugawa and Meiji times, Japan became a nation of prosperous, middle-class people in an orderly society largely free of slums, violent crime, and social despair. Japan's murder rate is less than one two-hundredth that of the United States. The very low rate of crime, especially interpersonal violence, results from the absence of poverty and from the sense of group responsibility; individuals are unwilling to bring shame or disgrace to their families or work groups by antisocial or reprehensible behavior. As another measure of well-being, since 1980 Japan has had the world's longest life expectancy.

Japan has been largely unencumbered by the crushing economic burden of maintaining the huge military establishment undertaken by most other large countries in the postwar world. This has paid off handsomely. Money has been invested instead in economic growth, new technology, full employment, education, and a wide range of social services. Japan is virtually alone in the world in having escaped from most of the cankerous problems that breed in poverty, such as violence, hopelessness, and drugs. (There is a small gangster group, the Yakusa, that, like the Mafia in the U.S., controls most illegal or "detrimental" activity, but they use violence only on each other.) The national ethics of work, achievement, and high standards, now in the service of personal and group goals of economic advancement rather than imperial ambition, have produced a new and more constructive conquest.

But no society is free of problems. Japanese society is generally high-pressure, and the drive for achievement exacts a toll on schoolchildren as well as on adults. Pressures begin even for admission to the "right" kindergarten so that one can move on to the "right" elementary school, middle school, and college or university, all of which are carefully status-ranked. Each stage of schooling is accompanied by fiercely competitive examinations. Childhood, after the age of five, is a stressful time for most Japanese (although the juvenile suicide rate is in fact higher in the United States). Extreme urban crowding and cramped living space add further burdens. Population density in the urban corridor from Tokyo to Hiroshima, which contains three-quarters of the Japanese people, is the highest in the world. Commuting time for those who work in downtown Tokyo *averages* nearly two hours each way and is only some-

Rush hour at Shinjuku station, a major Tokyo junction. (David Madison/Bruce Coleman Inc.)

Apart from the very small group of urban poor, many of them dropouts from society, two minority communities in Japan still face severe discrimination: the *eta* or *burakumin* group of "untouchables" and the sizable Korean minority. *Eta* form more than 2 percent of the population and are ethnically indistinguishable from other Japanese, but they still are looked down on. They are avoided as neighbors, employees, and, most of all, as marriage partners because of their traditional occupations, and they live in segregated ghettos. In the dominantly Buddhist society of traditional Japan, the eta disposed of dead animals, cured the hides, made leather goods, and butchered and ate animals, all forbidden by Buddhism. As with untouchables in India, these practices made them "unclean." Such religiously based distinctions are long gone, but Japanese prejudice and discrimination remain.

About half a million Koreans live in Japan. Many migrated to Japan to escape the forced poverty and repression at home under Japanese domination from 1895, and many more were taken to Japan as forced laborers.

A mobile computer bus stopped at a Tokyo kindergarten, with children learning how to operate personal computers. (Reuters NewMedia Inc./Corbis)

what less for other big Japanese cities. Parks and recreation facilities are extremely limited. Housing is fearfully expensive, and most urban Japanese, over 80 percent of the population now, live in tiny apartments with minimal amenities. As one of the best-informed and widely traveled people in the world, most Japanese know that they are generally very well-off, but they also know that they are very cramped by comparison with others elsewhere. There seems no prospect that most Japanese will ever have adequate living space, privacy, or the kinds of comforts and elbow room that middle-class people in Western countries take for granted. Subway commuters crammed into overloaded cars are pressed against ads promoting various products using a backdrop of an alpine meadow, a country lawn, or a beach, all empty except for one or two lone figures—things that most Japanese can see only abroad.

Japanese prejudice against Koreans as an "inferior" people grew with Japanese imperialism, and those who lived in Japan were badly treated. Many of them drifted into illegal or shady activities, which strengthened Japanese prejudice against them. It is still very hard for anyone of Korean ancestry to obtain citizenship in Japan (as it is for all foreigners), or to receive anything approaching equal treatment.

Japanese society has always been strongly hierarchical. Given the postwar openness to the West and the other changes at work in the society, this now strikes many Japanese as onerous, especially the subordinate status of women. Younger people in particular believe that deference to superiors or elders and of all women to men is stultifying. The coming generation of Japanese may well reshape their society on somewhat freer lines, but most would agree that it will be a long time before women achieve anything close to equality. In the offices most women serve in subordinate or service roles, as secretaries, receptionists, or teamakers, collectively known as "OLs"—office ladies. Meanwhile married women are often the real powers within the family and household. They usually have control of the family finances and have

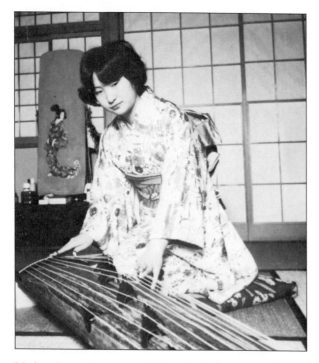

Modern Japanese women still learn traditional arts, such as playing the *koto*. Koto players must wear kimonos, and usually practice in a thoroughly traditional setting, such as that shown here, kneeling on a tatami in a traditional-style room. (Shashinka Photo, Inc.)

the preponderant role in the upbringing of children, since most fathers work long hours and commuting time means that they usually get home only after the children are in bed. Nevertheless, more than half of adult Japanese women work outside the house, close to the current American figure, although this often entails managing a small family business or neighborhood store. Equality in the professions remains a distant goal. Nearly half of Japanese women get some form of post–high school education; much of it is vocational, and relatively few attend the prestigious universities. Many women attend college for reasons of social status or to find husbands.

Japan's International Role

Japan's rising sun now extends economically more widely than its former military successes, but despite their major global stature, the Japanese have been reluctant to function as a world power in other terms, a role that has brought them such tragedy in the past. They have often been uncomfortably aware of this inconsistency between their technological and economic power and their more hesitant posture abroad in political terms. On several occasions they have felt that their interests were ignored in the maneuverings of Cold War diplomacy, especially by the abrupt American reversal of policy toward China in 1971. As an American client and bulwark against neighboring Communist states, Japan was dumbfounded when in 1971 Washington suddenly renewed contact with China without informing Tokyo in advance. The Japanese still refer to that event as "Nixon shock," and there have since been many other events like it when the Japanese felt slighted or ignored by the big countries in their power games.

It seems likely that in time Japan will come to play an international diplomatic role more in keeping with its economic role; this has already begun to happen, but most Japanese continue to hope that this can take place without their having to add new military power. As with many issues, there are cross-currents, and some Japanese openly favor rearmament so that Japan can occupy a more "appropriate" place in a world unfortunately now dominated by nations with the greatest military power. If that should happen, Japan's neighbors and former victims of her imperialist adventures would be deeply concerned. And although the Americans have pressed for it, a rearmed Japan would no longer be their client, which is indeed why some Japanese favor it. More positively, by 1988 Japan had become the world's largest donor of foreign aid, far outdistancing the much larger and richer United States. Japanese aid is also entirely economic rather than military.

One other way in which modern Japan has led the world is its success in the 1970s in limiting industrial pollution. Japan is small, and most of its population, cities, and industry are crowded into a narrow coastal corridor only about 400 miles long. Industrial concentration is higher there than anywhere in the world, and, hence, Japan was the first to notice the lethal effects of air and water pollution as one consequence of its postwar industrial growth. Many deaths and many more health casualties derived from heavy metal toxins and air pollution, all traced to specific plants or industrial operations and their poisonous discharges into water bodies or the atmosphere. Once this became clear and public opinion had been mobilized, national and municipal governments quickly passed stringent legislation to control emissions, beginning in 1969 with the city of Tokyo. Controls were strictly enforced with the help of new technology designed to limit emissions and effluents from coal and oil power plants, industry, and vehicles. As in the United States, the big car-making companies were reluctant to change, but the Japanese government was firm in enforcing the new controls. The car companies designed cleaner engines, and everyone benefited; Japanese cars, which are now both low in emissions and fuel-efficient, went on to dominate world markets.

As industrial growth continues, concentration and crowding will go on generating the same problems as elsewhere in the world; pollution levels are building up again, while controls have remained incomplete or in some cases relaxed. But Japanese organization, efficiency, and technology have demonstrated that the problems can be managed, given the willingness to confront them. The technology needed to control or even eliminate pollution was quickly developed, and the added cost involved in pollution controls was extremely modest, estimated at between 1 and 2 percent of total production costs.

Japan has also led the way in reducing energy use through more efficient plants and better-designed engines, reacting both to world energy shortages and price rises and to its own determination to reduce pollution. Nearly all Japanese trains are electrified, including the heavily used high-speed line that connects Tokyo with major Japanese cities to the south and southwest and Hokkaido to the north. Trains leave Tokyo every 15 minutes for Osaka, making the 310-mile trip in three hours, including stops at Nagoya and Kyoto, and running at speeds up to 140 miles per hour.

Population increase has been sharply reduced by personal and family choice and is below stabilization. As with high-income and better-educated groups in other countries, couples prefer to limit the number of children so as to better provide for them. Urbanization is higher in Japan than anywhere else in the world, and the coastal area from Tokyo to Osaka and on to northern Kyushu is rapidly becoming one vast urban-industrial zone. Although the rural Japanese landscape is very beautiful, especially the mountains that cover most of the country, most of it is increasingly empty as people have flocked to the cities in search of wider economic and cultural opportunities. On weekends and holidays urbanites rush to natural beauty spots, temples or shrines, and resorts nearest the big cities, which are often overrun by excessive crowding. Then there is the long journey back, crammed onto overloaded trains or buses, where most passengers must stand for hours, while others are

 ## Changes in Japan

Ogura Kazuo, Director of Cultural Affairs at the Japanese Foreign Ministry, offered the following observations in 1991:

> People sense that the old pattern has yet to change. Those on the U.S. side are still leaning heavily on Japan, never reflecting on their own country's shortcomings, and those on the Japanese side are still bowing before the American demands, as if doing so was Japan's fate. For many Japanese the concepts of freedom, democracy, and the market economy do not have a home-grown feeling. Although they have taken deep root in Japan, they give us a vaguely unsettling sensation, as if we were wearing a new suit of Western clothes. The consequence is that it is very difficult for the Japanese to believe that fighting to the death for these concepts is their natural duty as Japanese.

Source: Ogura Kazuo, *New York Times*, November 24, 1991 p. 21.

locked into gigantic traffic jams on the highways. Much of traditional Japanese culture has been lost or discarded in this avalanche of modern change. Although many Japanese regret such a price for development, their sense of national identity has remained strong, bound together with many symbolic survivals of traditional culture: the sharply distinctive Japanese food, clothing, many houses, or at least rooms, in traditional style, gardens, shrines and temples, the keen Japanese aesthetic sensitivity, and the commitment to order, self-discipline, and group effort in the pursuit of excellence.

A CLOSER LOOK

Tokyo and the Modern World

By about 1965 Tokyo had become the world's largest city and a symbol of Japan's new economic leadership. The urban area had grown outward to merge with that of previously separate cities in the same lowland basin, including Kawasaki and Yokohama. By 1990 this vast, unbroken conglomeration of dense settlement, commerce, industry, and government measured 50 miles across and included over 30 million people linked by the world's largest and most efficient subway system. Almost nothing is left of the Edo described in Chapter 13, most of which had been in any case periodically destroyed by fires. Modern Tokyo was also largely ruined by a catastrophic earthquake in 1923, and then again by American bombs and firestorms in 1944 and 1945.

The only part of the city that has survived all of these cataclysms unscathed is Tokugawa Ieyasu's massive shogunal castle, surrounded by its moats and stone walls, originally built in the early seventeenth century and since 1869 used as the imperial palace. In the middle of a huge and strikingly modern city of glass, steel, skyscrapers, and expressways, with urban traffic flowing around it, the palace still stands as a symbol of Japan's traditional past, both as a Tokugawa monument and as the home of a still-enthroned emperor whose lineage and ceremonial functions date back to before the dawn of Japanese written history. The death of the aged emperor Hirohito in 1989 and the accession of his son Akihito to the throne, with all the traditional rituals, signaled no change and reaffirmed Japan's commitment to its past and to its distinctively Japanese tradition.

Among Japan's many big cities, Tokyo still plays the role of the brash modernist, the focus of change, the center of everything new, but even in Tokyo Japanese do not forget their past. The palace is an anachronism, but it is nevertheless an appropriate focal point for the capital of Japan, more than the parliament or other government buildings, more than the banks, offices, sky-

Tradition meets modernity: At a bus stop in Tokyo, women dressed in traditional kimono. (Ira Kuschenbaum/Stock, Boston)

scrapers, factories, and other symbols of Tokyo's Western-style modernity. For all its apparent focus on the streamlined or frantic present and future, Tokyo is also a city of the traditional Japanese style.

That aspect of the city's character becomes clear beyond the immediate downtown and government areas. Except for the industrial clusters around the fringes of each originally separate municipality, Tokyo is primarily a vast collection of neighborhoods. Many are grouped around a surviving or rebuilt temple, shrine, former daimyo estate, or parklike garden. Wandering through the back streets and alleys of these neighborhoods, it is easy to imagine oneself in Tokugawa Edo. In the evening after work clouds of steam escape from public bathhouses, enveloping patrons dressed in traditional kimonos and walking in wooden clogs. Inside countless tiny restaurants and teahouses with their tatami straw mats, low tables, and scrolls on the wall, little seems to have changed since Ieyasu's time, including much of the food. Many of the tiny houses or apartments maintain miniature Japanese-style gardens the size of a small tabletop or lovingly tend potted plants set out to catch the sun by the doorway or on small balconies. Street vendors with their traditional chants peddle roasted sweet potatoes, chestnuts, or *yakitori* (Japanese shish kebab).

Crowds of kimono-clad worshippers, or people simply on an outing, throng the courtyards of traditionally rebuilt temples and shrines, especially on festival days. Similar crowds fill the narrow streets and patronize street vendors or shops selling traditional as well as modern goods: fans both manual and electric, silks and nylons, horoscopes and stock market guides, tea and beer, lacquer and plastic, scrolls and comic books. Like Japan itself, Tokyo is both very modern and very traditional, very Japanese and very Western. Few people seem to be torn by this dichotomy. The Japanese sense of national and cultural identity rides serenely through it all.

Japan's Relations with Its Former Enemies

Japan and Russia never signed a peace treaty primarily because the Russians continue to occupy the Kurile Islands, which stretch northeast from Hokkaido, as well as the southern half of Sakhalin Island, which the Japanese captured from Russia in 1905. Japan has been willing to let southern Sakhalin go, but not the Kuriles, which are of major importance to the Japanese fishing industry. A new Russia of the twenty-first century may return the Kuriles.

Anti-American feeling, which had grown during the later years of the occupation, peaked again in 1954, just after the signing of a U.S.-Japan Mutual Security Treaty, when a Japanese fishing vessel named *Lucky Dragon* was heavily contaminated by fallout from the American nuclear testing on Bikini Atoll in the western Pacific. The catch of tuna had already entered the market when the boat and its crew were found to be dangerously radioactive; some of the crew later died. Japan panicked, especially since fish, including tuna, were so important a part of their diet, but panic was mixed with anger. Hadn't the Japanese suffered enough at American hands, the only people in the world (until the Bikini tests) victimized by nuclear weapons?

Meanwhile successive conservative governments pursued what was called a "reverse course," undoing many of the democratic reforms of the occupation and building up the "Japan Self-Defense Force," really a cover for rearmament. This did not represent the views of many, perhaps most, Japanese, and the Socialist party

won more votes, but remained a largely powerless minority politically. The conservatives of the ruling Liberal Democratic party (LDP) had built a strong coalition of business and landed interests, including most farmers, who benefited from the high government price supports for rice. This was clearly against the interests of urban dwellers, the vast majority, but the LDP political machine proved hard to challenge.

National morale was boosted when Japan was admitted to the United Nations in 1956, where it slowly began to play a role, though still not commensurate with its new economic stature even by the 1980s. The U.S.-Japan Mutual Security Treaty, first signed in 1954, was renegotiated in 1960 and extended for another ten years. The huge American bases in Japan were retained. President Eisenhower was to visit Japan, but when ratification of the new treaty was forced through the Diet by strong-arm tactics, mass demonstrations erupted, and there was widespread violence and attacks on and by police. Eisenhower's visit was canceled after his secretary and the U.S. ambassador were trapped in a car at Tokyo's airport and rocked by an angry mob. Bitterness remained, but the violence faded. Attention shifted to the Olympic Games, held for the first time in Japan in 1964 in Tokyo, and to a World's Fair in Osaka in 1970, when with relatively little discussion or public protest the security treaty with the United States was renewed for another ten years. Growing affluence for most Japanese had made them more complacent and more inclined to support the conservative LDP, despite a long series of scandals involving successive prime ministers accused, with ample evidence, of taking bribes and other financial and moral corruption.

A longstanding grievance surfaced in the 1990's: Korean complaints, and those from other East Asian countries, that the Japanese during the war had requisitioned women to serve as "comfort girls" for their troops, a dreadful form of sex slavery that was deeply resented. But the Japanese government offered no adequate recompense. This heightened the already severe tension with Korea and with China and the countries of Southeast Asia.

Textbooks for use in schools were now approved by the national Ministry of Education, and periodically revised editions were published. Part of the changing times was changing Japanese attitudes, about themselves and about their role in World War II. There were vigorous protests from South Korea and China when successive editions in the 1980s and into the twenty-first century progressively toned down earlier critical statements about past Japanese actions in both countries. As for domestic affairs, the sordid history of pollution was also toned down; officially, the pollution problem was now "solved." The Chisso Chemical Company, which had been responsible for the worst offenses, including mercury and cadmium poisoning at Minamata and Ni-igata, was successful in having its name removed from the textbook accounts. The Keidanren, or Japanese Businessmen and Industrialists' Association, was anxious to project a positive image of the Japanese economic miracle and to favor the big corporations that had played such a large part in that success.

In general, the Japanese became more confident and more assertive as they became richer and as Japan became a major economic power in the world. People grew more conservative and more willing to support the LDP despite continuing financial and even sex scandals that forced several prime ministers and cabinet ministers to resign. In these and perhaps other respects, Japan was becoming more and more like the contemporary United States, on which its political system had, after all, been modeled. But despite such considerations, and despite the continuing whirlwind of Westernization in so many aspects of Japanese culture and life, the Japanese clung to their identity and to their national pride. The LDP was finally defeated in the elections of 1993 by a coalition of opposition parties, and in 1994 formed an alliance with the Socialist party, resulting in the Socialist Murayama Tomichi actually becoming prime minister, although there was little real change in government policies.

In early 1996 the LPD figure Hashimoto Ryotaro succeeded Murayama as prime minister in a coalition government, but voter dissatisfaction with the continuing recession led to the election in 1998 of Obuchi Keizo, the former LPD foreign minister. Obuchi promised economic reforms, but many were skeptical. When he suddenly died in 2001, the LDP chose as his successor Koizumi Junichiro, a determined reformer, who also broke tradition by choosing a woman as his Foreign Minister.

Perhaps as part of continuing Americanization, the divorce rate recently rose to about 25 percent, and the use of drugs has found a foothold with some of the young. With the economic downturn since 1991, there has also been a rise in unemployment, but it is still lower than in Europe or the United States. Japan is unlikely to resume the economic growth rates of the 1980s, but in the long run their national ethics of hard work and group effort, and their high technological level should certainly revive the economy.

China in Revolution

The cataclysmic changes that transformed twentieth-century China constitute the largest revolution in human history, measured by the number of people in-volved and the radicalness and speed of the changes. Although the events of 1911 leading to the overthrow of the Manchu dynasty are called a revolution, the pace of change was slow for many years, and the dominant political party, the Guomindang, became in time largely a supporter of the status quo rather than a force for radical reform. The Chinese Communist party barely survived Guomindang efforts to eliminate it, but during the anti-Japanese war from 1937 to 1945 it rapidly gained strength and support in the course of its guerrilla resistance to the hated invaders. The final contest between the two parties ended in Communist victory in 1949, and fundamental revolution began under a radically new set of ideas.

Communist Strength and Guomindang Weakness

The Japanese invasion and occupation of China from 1931 to 1945 ended in the Allied defeat of Japan but also fatally eroded the power and popular support of the Guomindang government of Chiang Kai-shek. Buttressed by massive American military and economic support, it hung on while American representatives under General George Marshall tried to arrange a coalition with the Communist party. With the predictable failure of this effort in 1947, China was torn by full-scale civil war. The Guomindang had vast superiority in number and weapons and held all the major cities, but its corruption and ineffectiveness had lost it the support of most Chinese. Runaway inflation, uncontrolled by the government, which ruined most urbanites, was accompanied by rural repression and predatory policies of confiscation or heavy taxation of most businessmen as the government reoccupied the areas in the east previously held by the Japanese. Critics were jailed or executed, and everyone outside the government went in fear of the secret police. As a result of all these factors, the Guomindang largely lost the support of the middle class and most business and professional people, as well as most peasants. Meanwhile, the Communist forces in their long fight against the Japanese had perfected a guerrilla strategy and attracted millions of Chinese by their defense of the nation and their program of peasant-oriented reform.

Their leader, Mao Zedong (1893–1976), offered a return to the simple virtues of hard work and self-sacrifice in order to build a new China, free from foreign influence and humiliation and from the now-discredited and reactionary elitism of Confucianism and the old order it represented. In their remote frontier base at Yan'an in the northwest, where they were centered from 1934 to 1947, the Communists under Mao's direction had

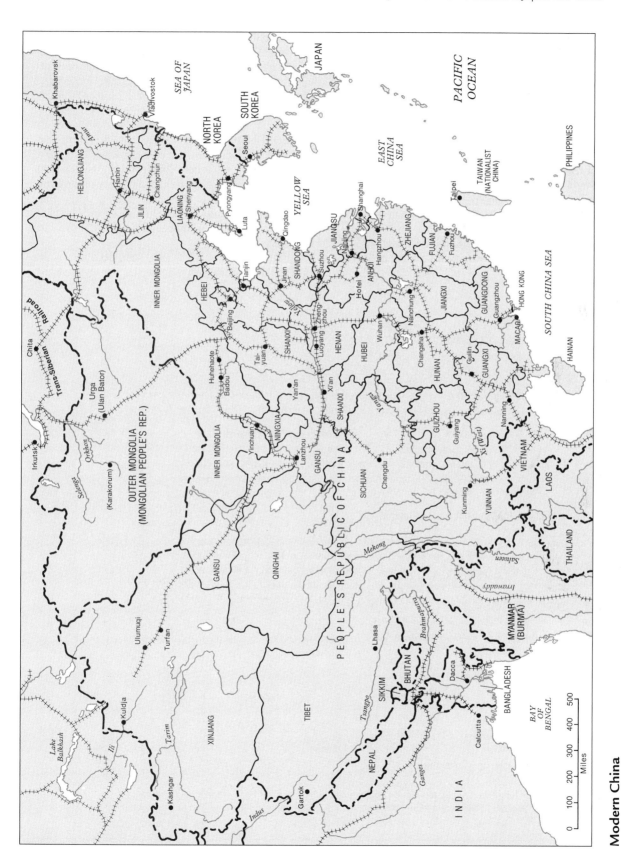

Modern China

China now incorporates all of the empires of the past, except for the brief Han-Tang control of North Korea and North Vietnam. Railways have linked every province with the national net.

worked out a number of ideas for China's regeneration, while at the same time appealing broadly to the masses.

Mao and several of the other Communist leaders came from peasant origins, and their program emphasized peasant welfare and virtues, overlooked or ignored by the Guomindang. Landlordism and oppression of the peasantry were popular issues in the face of widespread rural poverty and mass suffering. Chinese who collaborated with foreign businessmen in the treaty ports prospered. The cities, nearly all of which were foreign-dominated treaty ports as well as centers of Guomindang strength and the home of "running dogs" (collaborators with the foreigners), were obvious targets for a peasant-oriented revolutionary movement.

Success depended, however, on building a mass support base. This was achieved through land reform in the areas the Communists controlled—most of the north—

accompanied by campaigns to politicize the peasants and organize them into action. Intellectuals were also involved in an effort to create a new ideology and a new literature and art that could appeal to peasants and inspire them to work for the new goals. Mao himself, though the son of a rich peasant turned grain merchant and, hence, familiar with the countryside, was primarily an intellectual. His prescriptions for art and literature that would "serve politics" and "serve the masses" attracted growing numbers of fellow intellectuals disillusioned with the corruption and spiritual bankruptcy of the Guomindang. In organizing peasant rebellion, Mao consciously followed an old Chinese tradition, with himself playing the role of the urban-based intellectual theorist and organizer.

The civil war from 1947 to 1949 soon became a rout, despite major American support for the already superior

Mao: The Revolutionary Vision

The Communist revolution in China was in large part a peasant-based movement against the vested power of the cities. In 1939 Mao Zedong put it dramatically.

> Since China's key cities have long been occupied by the powerful imperialists and their reactionary Chinese allies, it is imperative for the revolutionary ranks to turn the backward villages into advanced consolidated base areas . . . bastions of the revolution from which to fight their vicious enemies.

Here is an equally famous statement made by Mao.

> China's 600 million people have two remarkable peculiarities; they are first of all poor, and secondly blank. That may seem like a bad thing, but it is really a good thing. Poor people want change, want to do things, want revolution. A clean sheet of paper has no blotches, and so the newest and most beautiful words can be written on it, the newest and most beautiful pictures painted on it.

Still driven by his revolutionary vision, Mao the poet wrote in 1963, in traditional classic verse:

> So many deeds cry out to be done,
> And always urgently.
> The world rolls on,
> Time passes.
> Ten thousand years are too long;
> Seize the day, seize the hour,
> Our force is irresistible.

Sources: Mao Zedong, *The Chinese Revolution and the Chinese Communist Party* (Peking: Foreign Languages Press, 1954), p. 17 (written in 1939); *Red Flag*, June 1, 1958, pp. 3–4; "Reply to Kuo Moruo" (dated February 5, 1963), in *China Reconstructs*, 16 (March 1967): 2.

forces of the Guomindang. The Communists had few weapons except what they could capture from their opponents or make themselves, but their strength quickly multiplied as growing numbers of Guomindang troops and officers surrendered, bringing with them their largely American equipment. Sometimes they were outmaneuvered by superior strategy, but often they were attracted to the promise and euphoria of the Communist cause. The close American connection with the Guomindang troubled many patriots, probably weakened rather than strengthened its fight against the Communists, and left a legacy of anti-American bitterness when the civil war ended. On October 1, 1949, Mao announced the inauguration of the People's Republic of China from a rostrum at Tian An Men ("Gate of Heavenly Peace") in front of the Forbidden City in Beijing, conscious, as always, of the tradition of China's imperial greatness to which he was now the heir. "China has stood up," he said, and the great majority of Chinese responded with enthusiasm.

The revolution had been long delayed, beginning with the fumbling series of misadventures in 1911, when the old Qing dynasty was overthrown. Many Chinese felt the need for radical change, only to see it aborted or betrayed by warlord regimes and then by the increasingly reactionary Guomindang under Chiang Kai-shek after 1927. It had been a revolutionary effort led and joined almost exclusively by intellectuals, a tiny handful of the population. Now the Communists had finally succeeded in creating a mass base, with a peasant army forged in the fires of the anti-Japanese war and a politicized people. They called their program "the mass line," no longer an elite affair but one that had its principal roots in the peasant countryside, where over 80 percent of the Chinese people lived.

Reconstruction and Politicization

Chiang Kai-shek and the remnants of the Guomindang government and army fled, with American assistance, to the offshore island of Taiwan (Formosa), where American aid helped them in time to rebuild a prosperous economy and gain firm control. Both Chinese governments claimed sole legitimacy, Taiwan as the Republic of China. The United States continued to support the Guomindang on Taiwan until the pressures of reality and the desire to exploit the 1959 Sino-Soviet split led belatedly to official American recognition of the government in Beijing in 1979, although unofficial ties with Taipei (the Taiwan capital) remained. On the mainland, the new government moved quickly to repair the physical damage of the long years of war and to extend its land reform and political education programs into the newly conquered south and southwest. All over the

country what was still called land reform became more violent as party organizers, in an effort to create "class consciousness," encouraged peasants to "speak bitterness" and to identify their landlord-oppressors. Many thousands were killed by angry mobs, and their land was distributed among the poorer peasants.

Firm central-government control was reestablished in all of the former empire, including Manchuria (now called simply "the northeast," given its troubled recent history), southern or "Inner" Mongolia, Xinjiang, and Tibet, and a major program of industrialization begun. Outer Mongolia had declared its independence in 1921 as the Mongolian People's Republic. Undeclared war with the United States in Korea from late 1950 to mid-1953 and an American-sponsored embargo on trade with China not only slowed these efforts at economic development but also helped to further radicalize the country and to strengthen its dedication to the goals of self-reliance and reconstruction. By 1956 Mao judged that support for the new government was wide and deep enough to invite criticism. In a famous speech, he declared: "Let a hundred flowers bloom; let a hundred schools of thought contend." But he probably also intended this as a move to smoke out and then punish opposition. Many intellectuals, and others, including many of China's ethnic minorities such as Tibetans and Muslims, responded with a torrent of criticism. Most of it was pronounced "destructive" and counterrevolutionary, and many of the critics were punished, jailed, or even executed. Mass campaigns identified many thousands as "rightists" or "counterrevolutionaries," who were also imprisoned or killed.

The Great Leap Forward

Despite the evidence of dissent, Mao still felt secure enough in the support and radical fervor of the majority of his people that he moved swiftly to collectivize all land. By 1958 he moved beyond the Soviet model of collectivization and organized most land into new communes; private ownership was abolished, and all enterprises were managed collectively. Communes varied widely in area and population but averaged about 15,000 to 25,000 people and incorporated large numbers of previously separate villages. Several villages made up a "production team," several teams constituted a "production brigade," and several brigades made a commune. Communes were supposed to include manufacturing enterprises also to bring industrialization to the rural areas. Communes were also set up in the cities but added little to existing factories, departments, or offices, so they did not last.

Mao announced that 1958 would be the year of the "Great Leap Forward" in which China would overtake

Tiananmen square, in front of the main gate to the Forbidden City. This is where the massacre of June 4, 1989, took place. Shown here a parade marks the tenth anniversary of the People's Republic on October 1, 1959. (Bettmann/Corbis)

Britain in industrial output by the united efforts of a galvanized people. This would be the mass line in action. Communal dining halls were set up so that families need not lose work time by preparing meals. Backyard steel furnaces sprang up all over the rural landscape, using local iron ore and coal or other fuel. Communes were given quotas for production of specific agricultural and industrial goods, but too little attention was paid to the nature of local resources or to overall rational organization. Peasants were shifted arbitrarily from farming to manufacturing, and communes were told to grow crops that were physically impossible for them to raise.

The Great Leap was a dismal failure, and the country collapsed into economic chaos in 1959. Peasants had been driven to exhaustion in pursuit of unrealistic goals and inefficient combinations of tasks and resources. Nearly all of the iron and steel from the backyard furnaces was of unusable quality and had to be thrown out, as did much of the other industrial output. Crops were neglected or failed as labor was shifted to different tasks, and for at least three years there were massive food shortages and widespread famine. Probably at least 30 million people died of starvation or malnutrition. It was the worst famine in world history. Mao's radical policies had brought disaster, and for several years other more

pragmatic measures and more moderate leaders such as Zhou Enlai (1898–1976) and Liu Xiaoqi (1894–1971) had a greater role and for the time being eclipsed Mao, although he remained the party chairman.

The Sino-Soviet Split

The Russians were alarmed by what they saw as the radical excesses of the Great Leap and its departure from the Soviet pattern. They were annoyed also by Mao's assertion that his version of socialism was superior to theirs, his continued support of Stalinist policies after they had been discredited in the USSR, and his accusations that Russia had now become ideologically impure, or "revisionist." The Russians saw Mao's bellicose stand on the reconquest of Taiwan, for which he requested Soviet nuclear aid, as a threat to world peace, and inevitable tensions arose out of the large-scale Soviet aid program and Soviet advisers in China. In 1959 the Russians withdrew their aid and advisers and moved toward a more antagonistic relationship with China. The next 15 years saw revived territorial disputes and armed border clashes between the two former allies on the long frontier that divides them, especially in the Amur region of northern Manchuria and along the northern border of Xinjiang.

Each claimed to be the true heir of Marx and Lenin and of the correct path to socialism. Long-standing substantive conflicts between them surfaced. These dated back to the early Czarist expansion into northeast Asia and to Russia's exploitation of Manchuria and its role as one of the Western imperialist powers during China's years of political weakness. On the other side, Russia was alarmed by China's billion people, next door to thinly settled Siberia and the Soviet maritime provinces and driven as they seemed to be by radical fanaticism. The rhetoric of mutual accusation mounted on both sides, and troops were stationed along the frontiers. But China could not stand alone against the world, and its leaders began indirect overtures to the United States. More than a decade later, with the end of their misadventure in Vietnam in sight, the Americans finally responded. Late in 1971, a cautious restoration of contact began when President Nixon visited Beijing. This slowly led to the establishment of diplomatic relations, with full U.S. recognition and the exchange of ambassadors in 1979.

The Cultural Revolution

From 1966 to 1976 China passed through the Great Proletarian Cultural Revolution, as Mao called it, perhaps the greatest cataclysm in world history, measured by the hundreds of millions of people involved in mass persecution and suffering. The failure of the Great Leap had necessitated more moderate policies and a period of recovery from economic disaster. By 1966 Mao judged recovery complete and launched a new campaign to renew a revolution that he saw as slipping into "revisionism," complacency, opportunism, and self-seeking on the part of party officials, managers, and all people in positions of authority. Mao remarked that he felt like "an ancestor at his own funeral and at the burial of his hopes." Basically, his message was the old one of "serve the people," with its clear echoes of Confucian responsibility, but the methods employed by the Cultural Revolution had devastating results. Mao was also carrying out a power play to eliminate rivals and their policies. The chief targets were the elite: party officials, teachers, writers, all intellectuals, all those who were "tainted" by foreign influence or "bourgeois" lifestyles, and all whose class origins were not poor peasant or manual worker.

Millions of officials, managers, writers, and teachers were hounded out of their jobs. Artists and musicians who showed any interest in Western styles were attacked. Many of the intellectuals and others who were labeled counterrevolutionary were beaten or killed; others were jailed, sent to corrective labor camps, or assigned to the lowest menial tasks, as both punishment and reeducation. Opera stars and concert violinists were set to cleaning latrines. All foreign music, art, literature, and ideas (except for Marxism-Leninism and Stalinism) were banned, and even Chinese books disappeared or were burned, except for the ever-present works of Mao himself and the so-called *Little Red Book* of his sayings. Those who had studied abroad, especially valuable for China's efforts at national reconstruction, were particular targets. People were encouraged to inform on friends, colleagues, and even family members, causing immense bitterness, separation, and suffering.

Those accused, often without evidence, of "rightist" or bourgeois tendencies were jailed, sentenced to corrective labor, or driven to suicide. Few had the courage to try to help them, for fear that they themselves would meet the same fate. Teachers were attacked and beaten by their students in a brutal reversal of traditional respect for learning; musicians and artists had their fingers broken. The official line was that it was "better to be Red than expert"; most of China's relatively small group of urgently needed professionals (that is, "experts") in most fields were hounded, jailed, or killed. Almost no one in this immense country beyond the age of one escaped the turmoil, which wrecked the lives of hundreds of millions of people and directly killed unknown numbers, probably at least 1 million. The rural communes were not exempt, and there too there were repeated radical campaigns and terror.

All universities and colleges were closed for several years, considered breeding grounds for a new elite. When they slowly began to reopen it was only to the children of peasants, workers, and party faithfuls still in power, but with a curriculum that concentrated on "political study." Most high school graduates in the decade after 1966, and in the big cities practically all, were assigned to "productive labor in the countryside," where they were told to "strike roots permanently." This was partly a leveling alternative to the now-closed or restricted universities, partly a means to ease unemployment and housing shortages in the cities, and partly a way to reeducate those too young to have shared the early Yanan years of hardship and sacrifice. Now they would learn from the peasants the meaning of hard work instead of following the upwardly mobile path that education had always meant to Chinese, which led to becoming both elite and bourgeois "experts."

Some 17 million young people were sent down to the countryside in this program, until it was largely discontinued in the late 1970s. Most saw it as ruinous to their own ambitions and career plans, for which their urban origins and education had prepared them. And most of them were not very helpful in rural agricultural or other development work. Their training was not very relevant, and indeed it had tended, as in China's past, to make them think of themselves as an educated elite who looked down on peasants and manual labor. The

The leaders of Communist China in 1965, on the eve of the Cultural Revolution. From left to right, Zhou Enlai, Zhu De, Mao Zedong, and Liu Xiaoqi. (Sovfoto/Eastfoto)

program was understandably unpopular with peasants too, since they had to feed and house disgruntled city youth who, despite their higher level of education, were both incompetent and uninterested in farmwork. All white-collar workers were also required to spend at least two months each year doing manual labor, mainly in the countryside, a far more sensible idea but one that, not surprisingly, also met with resistance from professionals and others.

Mao called on teenagers and students to serve as shock troops for the Cultural Revolution. Like young people everywhere, they had little stake in the status quo, were filled with idealism, and were easily diverted from their studies. They welcomed their exciting new role as a chance to exercise authority over their elders. Mao called them "Red Guards" and permitted them to abandon their families, jobs, and studies to roam the country ferreting out "rightists" (often including their own family members, another especially harsh denial of long-standing Chinese values) and harassing everyone in responsible positions. Red Guards invaded the homes of all people suspected of "bourgeois tendencies," destroyed books and art works, and beat up the residents. Millions of boys and girls rode free or commandeered trains and buses to Beijing, where cheering crowds of Red Guards were addressed by Mao at mass rallies, and to other cities, bastions of the elite. For a time the Red Guards even took over the Foreign Ministry and tried

to direct China's foreign policy. Mao and those supporting him promoted the even more extreme spread of a personality cult; huge pictures and statues of "The Great Helmsman" and copies of his *Little Red Book* mushroomed everywhere. Rival warring factions quickly emerged among the Red Guards, each claiming to be following the true line and pursuing what amounted to gang warfare. Groups and individuals welcomed the opportunity to pay off old grudges and denounce others or accuse them anonymously. There was uncontrolled violence, including large-scale street warfare, in many cities.

To prevent continued chaos, Zhou Enlai finally prevailed on Mao to call in the army in 1968 and put down the Red Guards, thus creating a new embittered group who felt they had been betrayed, a "lost generation." But the nightmare went on even after the Red Guards had been sent to the countryside. Even those at the top, except for Mao himself, were attacked for alleged "deviations" from the correct line, which changed unpredictably and was involved with political power plays. Liu Xiaoqi, originally picked by Mao as his successor, and an old revolutionary comrade, was accused of "rightist revisionism" because of his efforts to rebuild the economy after the disaster of the Great Leap Forward and died as a prisoner after public humiliations and beatings. Other high officials suffered similar fates. Professionals in all fields were scrutinized for their political views and activism. Absence from or silence during the endless daily political meetings was evidence of "counterrevolutionary tendencies." No one at any level felt safe or free to say what they really thought.

The Chinese revolution remained ostensibly a peasant movement, a Chinese rather than a Western answer to China's problems. This was appealing also on nationalist grounds, especially since nearly all the cities had been tainted by semicolonial foreign dominance while the great bulk of the country's people remained in the agricultural countryside. What little industrialization there was before 1949 was almost entirely in the cities, particularly in the foreign-run treaty ports or in Japanese-controlled Manchuria. There was thus both a pronounced antiurban bias to the revolution and a determination to exalt the countryside, to put the peasants in charge and concentrate efforts at development in the rural areas, the supposed source of all revolutionary values.

This was the theme of both the Great Leap Forward and the Cultural Revolution, and both included ambitious plans to bring the benefits of industrialization to the countryside. Since the mid-1950s, all movement of people was controlled, especially to the cities, where housing and ration books for food and household supplies were allocated only to those who were assigned jobs there. Individuals could not choose jobs; they worked where the state sent them. In the 1970s and 1980s a growing number of illegal migrants to the cities lived underground or on forged papers. Most of them are still there, their numbers apparently greatly increased; urban unemployment has become a major problem. Despite the official denigration of cities, they remained the places where most people, seeking wider opportunities for personal advancement as well as the excitement of any city, wanted to be. This was all disapproved of as "bourgeois" or even counterrevolutionary but is understandable enough and indeed has been the common experience of all modern societies.

In the countryside, each commune was designed to be as self-sufficient as possible. Under the Cultural Revolution there was considerable growth of small-scale rural industry, especially in what were labeled the "five smalls": iron and steel, cement, fertilizer, agricultural goods (including tools, machinery, and irrigation equipment), and electric power. There was also much production of light consumer goods for local use. Manufacturing in each area, using only local resources, reduced the load on an already overburdened road and rail system and saved transport costs while providing employment and experience to the masses of rural people. But in most cases the resulting product was considerably more expensive and of poorer quality than in larger-scale and better-equipped urban-based plants. Decentralized industry has been thought about by many in the West and in India as an ideally preferable alternative to the crowding, pollution, and dehumanization of industrial cities since the eighteenth century. But the economies of scale ("the bigger the cheaper") have meant that it is seldom fully practical. Like his other policies, it was part of Mao's utopian vision, appealing in many ways but pursued at dreadful cost, while China lagged still farther behind the rest of the world in technology and education.

Mao had said that the major goals of the revolution should be to eliminate the distinctions between city and countryside, between mental and manual workers, and between elites and peasants or workers; all three goals were of course closely related. In pursuit of these aims, workers or janitors became plant managers and university officials; poor peasants were elevated to power in commune "revolutionary committees"; professors, technicians, and skilled managers were humiliated or reduced to the lowest menial jobs. Even peasants who had been better off in the past and had been labeled "rich peasants" became targets. All those with any claim to expertise were suspect and often were hounded out of their positions in angry "struggle meetings"; those who refused to join in the denunciations were themselves denounced. The moral virtue and practical wisdom of the peasants and the countryside were extolled.

This was all in large part a reaction against the strongly hierarchical and elitist structure and values of traditional Chinese society and stemmed from a desire to realize the egalitarian ideals of Communism. The revolution had been based largely in the peasant countryside and was in any case aimed against the old established order and the cities. Nevertheless, Mao drew heavily on traditional ideas in emphasizing the duty of those in positions of power and responsibility to serve the masses, and he, like the Confucians, used moral example, slogans, and simplified philosophical sayings to inspire and mold group behavior in the common interest. As an intellectual himself, in the long Chinese tradition, he was a noted poet and calligrapher, like many emperors before him; in many ways he played the role of a new emperor. But he also relied on the new technique of what were called mass campaigns to galvanize people into action in the service of revolutionary goals. Some were constructive, like the campaigns to eliminate rats and flies or to build new dams and irrigation canals. But most were more politically inspired and were aimed at "rightists" and "counterrevolutionaries." The Cultural Revolution was the last and the most devastating of these campaigns. Most revolutions go through an extreme radical phase, like the Reign of Terror in Paris in the 1790s. The Chinese revolution's radical phase lasted longer and went to greater extremes than any other, but in time it too faded, if only because the Chinese people were exhausted by constant political campaigns and by

Trial by Mob

At the height of the Cultural Revolution in 1967 Red Guards often took it on themselves to attack, or "struggle with" as they called it, people identified as rightists. Sometimes they carried to extremes orders originating higher up. Here is part of an account of the mob arrest and trial of Liu Xiaoqi's wife, Wang Guangmei; her clothes and "bourgeois lifestyle" made her a target.

More and more big character posters, cartoons, and slogans appeared [on the campus of Tsinghua University in Beijing] attacking Liu Xiaoqi's wife Wang Guangmei. . . . With material on Liu himself far too scanty, the central authorities had granted the Red Guards permission to check all the files on Liu's visits to foreign countries. . . . It was here that a hole in [his] armor was found: his wife was a capitalist-class member. . . . "Wang Guangmei is caught in the net!" The news spread swiftly. . . . Using the only loudspeaker still under their control, the Headquarters announced a mass meeting . . . to struggle with "capitalist element Wang Guangmei."

. . . Wang's daughter . . . was taken by surprise in a classroom and forced by the Red Guards to accompany them to the Beijing Medical College, where she called her father's home . . . and was made to tell her mother that she had been seriously injured. . . . Because of her deep love for her daughter, Wang rushed to the hospital . . . and was captured—as easily as that. . . . [At the mass meeting] The chairman [said] "Drag out capitalist-class element Wang Guangmei to face the people!" Instantly a deafening roar of slogan shouting began. . . . She was in a blue cadre uniform, modest and plain. . . . There was a trace of a smile on her pale face. She was guarded by four girl Red Guards who walked her . . . across the stage several times so that everyone could have a good look at her. From time to time the Guards tugged at her hair, making her lower her head. . . . Wang lowered her head and confessed her crime and apologized . . . in a barely audible voice. . . . She admitted . . . that her awareness had been poor. . . . The chairman cut her short, denouncing her poor attitude. . . . There were shouts from the audience: "Let her show off her ugly look. Make her put on the [dress] she wore in Indonesia! We want to see this stinking woman's pose!" . . . She stood shivering in her bright silk dress, her head shrunk in her shoulders . . . the collar of the dress was yanked open . . . her hair was tousled like a mop. . . . We heard her sobbing voice: "Did Chairman Mao ask you to do this? . . ." [The chairman pronounced sentence.] The party central authorities [should] immediately dismiss her from all her posts. In addition she should undergo reform-through-labor in earnest and further expose the crimes of her husband in order to redeem her own crimes. . . . But no one was listening any longer to her reply.

Source: From K. Ling, *The Revenge of Heaven: Journal of a Young Chinese,* pp. 198–214. Copyright © 1972 (New York: Putnam). Reprinted by permission of SII/Sterling Lord Literistic, Inc. Copyright by Ivan London.

The mass line in action: some of the 100,000 people involved in building, largely by hand, a new irrigation dam outside Beijing. This is in fact an ancient system; similar armies of mass labor built the Great Wall, the Grand Canal, and other monumental public works in the long past. (R. Murphey)

the terror itself. Mao's death removed the chief obstacle to a return to more normal conditions, and China turned away with relief from its long ordeal.

A CLOSER LOOK

Jiang Qing and the Gang of Four

Many Chinese have long been quick to stereotype women with access to political power as dangerous, selfish, and an omen of degeneracy, or even of the inglorious end of a dynasty. Among others they remember the Tang emperor Xuanzong's favorite consort, Yang Guifei, who supposedly brought about the decline of the Tang through her "evil influence"; the notorious empress Wu, who usurped the throne earlier in the Tang dynasty; and the truly evil empress dowager Cixi. Jiang Qing, Mao's third wife, had been a minor movie star before she married him in Yanan in 1939. This gave her, she believed, a role in shaping party cultural policy, and with the Cultural Revolution in 1966 she emerged publicly as a member of the party's Central Committee in charge of cultural affairs. She was personally responsible for the persecution of writers and artists and for decreeing what was acceptable in music, art, literature, and drama. It was said that she used her power to pay off old scores against profes-

sional rivals and that she increasingly ignored or countermanded her husband's advice. She was often vituperative and spiteful in her personal style and ruthless in carrying out the line she favored. Both traditional and foreign works were banned in favor of a new and rigid socialist realism—art with a heavy political message designed to appeal to the masses of peasants and workers.

During Mao's last years, when ill health and senility obliged him to withdraw from the day-to-day management of affairs, Jiang and her radical colleagues increased their power and were probably the chief architects of the Cultural Revolution after about 1968. At her trial she insisted that she alone had been faithful to Mao's vision, but most Chinese had come to fear and hate her. She is still seen as the archvillain of China's dark years.

China After Mao

As Mao lay dying in 1976, a few months after Zhou Enlai had died of overwork and exhaustion while trying to hold the country together, the radical faction led by Mao's widow, Jiang Qing, tried to continue his extreme policies. But the country was sick of radical politics. In 1978 a new, more moderate leadership emerged under Hua Guofeng, whom Mao had designated as his successor. Jiang Qing and three of her associates, the so-called Gang of Four, were tried and convicted of "crimes against the people" and sentenced to jail. China began to emerge from its nightmare. Cautiously it resumed interchange with the rest of the world after 30 years of isolation that had cost it dearly, especially in technology. The universities and their curricula were slowly restored, and students now had to pass entrance examinations rather than merely to demonstrate proper "class origins." Efforts were made to provide somewhat greater freedom for intellectuals, writers, teachers, and managers.

The new mood in the country continued to move away from the madness of the period from 1957 to 1976. In 1981 Hua Guofeng was peacefully replaced by the old party pragmatist, Deng Xiaoping (born 1904) who returned to power as the real head of state and chief policymaker. Most of Mao's policies were progressively dismantled. The new government acknowledged that China was still poor and technically backward, that it needed foreign technology and investment, and that to encourage production its people needed material incentives rather than political harangues and "rectification campaigns."

The communes were quietly dissolved in all but name. Agriculture, still by far the largest sector of the economy, was largely organized into a "responsibility system" whereby individual families grew, on land still nominally owned by the commune, the crops that they judged most profitable in an economy that was now market-oriented. The state still took its tax share of farm output, but peasants were free to sell the rest in a free market that was encouraged as rewarding those who performed best. Those who did well under this system, and urban entrepreneurs who prospered in the small private businesses now permitted, felt free once again to display their new wealth. Expensive homes with television aerials sprouted here and there in the countryside, and in the cities motor scooters, tape recorders, washing machines, televisions, and refrigerators became more common. The new rich and even party officials began to indulge their personal tastes in clothing, including colors and Western-style or even high-fashion outfits instead of the drab uniform wear decreed in earlier years.

Some rural industry remained where it was economically rational, but renewed emphasis was placed on large-scale, urban-based industrial production and on catching up with world advances in technology to make up for the lost years. Many factory and office managers and workers were now rewarded on the basis of productivity and profitability. Technological, managerial, and educational elites also reappeared, and with them the bourgeois lifestyles so feared by Mao as the antithesis of revolutionary socialism. In earlier debates during the Cultural Revolution Deng Xiaoping had said, "I don't care if a cat is red [socialist] or white [capitalist] as long as it catches mice," and he now put this dictum into practice. He insisted, however, that although performance should be central, China was still a socialist country under a Communist government that planned and managed the economy and aimed to provide social justice. All too soon, after 1986, he was to suppress the growing movement by students and intellectuals for freer expression and what they rather vaguely called "democracy," something of which they understood little.

There has been no decline in government control over people's lives, direct and indirect, and the system in other respects, including the at least nominal state ownership of most means of production, is certainly social-

 ## Mao's Regrets

Toward the end of his life Mao wrote a poem to the dying Zhou Enlai in 1975 that looked back over the past 40 years and anticipated his own end:

> Loyal parents who sacrificed so much for the nation
> Never feared the ultimate fate.
> Now that the country has become Red
> Who will be the guardians?
> Our mission, unfinished, may take a thousand years;
> The struggle tires us, and our hair is grey.
> You and I, old friend,
> Can we just watch our efforts being washed away?

Source: Reprinted with permission of The Free Press, a Division of Simon & Shuster Adult Publishing Group from *Mao's China: A History of the People's Republic* by Maurice Meisner, pp. 180–181. Copyright © 1977 by The Free Press. All rights reserved.

ist. For a time it was no longer as highly politicized or ideological and became flexible enough to include, especially in economic matters, provision of individual incentives as an aid to production and some other patterns that one may call capitalist, though one could argue that such things have long existed in nearly all economies, of varying political stripes. In any case, China's revolutionary fervor and the utopian madness of 1966–1976 finally cooled, as all revolutions have in time. It was acknowledged that although Mao had been a great revolutionary leader before 1957 (some said before 1949), he made major mistakes later on that set the country back many years. He too largely ignored economic development and the basic need for "modernization," which were sacrificed to ideology, or as Mao put it, "politics in command." The dilemma remained how to "modernize" and yet retain the country's strongly held sense of distinctive Chinese pride and identity.

Most Chinese were weary of politics and ideology; those who had survived or were still redeemable wanted to get on with their lives and their careers, make up for what they called "the wasted years," and help to further China's aborted development. Despite the overdose of Maoist rhetoric, most Chinese still cared about their country and wanted it to catch up and perhaps, one day, again lead the world as it had for so long in its glorious past. Most Chinese are phenomenally hardworking people. Under a more rationally organized system, perhaps Mao will be proved right after all, that over a billion Chinese, over one-fifth of the world, can indeed move mountains.

Achievements and the Future

The years from 1949 to 1978 were by no means all chaos, and in fact the mass line, together with revolutionary fervor, national pride, organized group effort, and central direction, accomplished a great deal. China remained poor, but there was encouraging growth in agriculture (except for the years 1958–1964) owing to new irrigation, and later better seeds, and fertilization. Industry grew rapidly, if unevenly, from what had been a very small and limited base. In 1964 China tested a nuclear bomb and thereby joined the ranks of the major powers. Thousands of miles of new railways and roads were built, and China became a major industrial power. As in India, where similar developments were taking place in these years, gains in production, especially in agriculture, were only a little greater than continued increases in population. One of China's greatest successes was in delivering basic health care to most of its people, including for several years the system of "barefoot doctors" who traveled even to remote villages and the clinics established in every commune.

As in India, this greatly reduced the death rate, while the birthrate remained high. The population grew rapidly, nearly doubling from 1949 to the first real census in 1982. In the 1970s, China belatedly realized that this was perhaps its greatest problem in terms of the per capita welfare by which real economic growth must be measured. Mao had declared that any talk of overpopulation was counterrevolutionary and anti-Chinese, but from 1983 families were severely discouraged from having more than a single child, an extreme policy that was seen as necessary for perhaps a generation if China was to escape from poverty. One-child families were rewarded, and those who had more were punished with economic sanctions. The task of providing enough basic necessities, let alone amenities, for the well over a billion Chinese already born is dismaying, let alone for future population increases. The population growth rate has been slowed, but over 20 million babies are still born every year.

Meanwhile, there have been some substantial economic gains. Poverty at the bottom has been reduced, though far from eliminated, by increased production, better distribution, and the collective welfare system of communes and factories. Health levels, thanks in part to better nutrition and medical care, have been greatly improved. Literacy has more than doubled, and about half the population now get as far as the early high school grades, although there are places for only about 3 percent in the universities.

Living standards in the cities have risen far more rapidly and substantially, except for the overcrowded and inadequate housing, than in most rural areas. The growing division between urban and rural lifestyles and attitudes is a worrying problem for the heirs of a rural and peasant revolution, although it is shared by the rest of the developing world. Poor soil, mountainous, semi-arid, and remote areas lagged far behind the more productive ones, and in some of them there was widespread malnutrition. China's cities are not yet disfigured by masses of visibly homeless or unemployed, as are cities elsewhere in the developing world, but only because rigid controls on all movement and employment until recently still prevented most rural people from moving to the cities, as most of them clearly would like to do, despite the rhetoric of the Maoist vision. The cities are dangerously polluted, as bad as any in the world; the air is a choking mixture of smoke and gases the Chinese call "Yellow Dragon" and the rivers and wells are full of chemicals and heavy metals—the price of rapid industrialization. There was wide criticism, in China and abroad, of the decision to go ahead with the Three Gorges dam, above Yichang on the middle Yangzi. This immense project, by far the world's biggest dam, scheduled for completion early in the twenty-first century, will flood the famous Yangzi gorges, require the removal of millions of people who now live in the areas to be flooded, and do severe damage to the fauna of the river. It is argued that smaller dams on the tributaries would be much less destructive, but the ever-increasing demand for electric power and the attractions of flood prevention plus deep-draught navagation on the upper river were apparently more compelling. The unprecedented floods during the summer of 1998 on the Yangzi were a further argument for the dam, but the even more convincing argument was to stop the clearcutting of trees in the watershed—and in the basin of the Songhua River in northern Manchuria, which also suffered massive flooding. Progress in other respects has been won at the cost of state and collective social controls and the suppression of personal choices. This is not as disturbing to most Chinese as it might be to most Westerners, since the subordination of individualism to group effort and group welfare has long been central to Chinese tradition.

China's past achievements and its revolutionary progress were due in large part to the primacy of responsibility and the pursuit of common goals over privilege and self-interest. Nevertheless, there have been protests and even demonstrations against the continuing controls on free expression and choice of employment. As China opened its doors to more normal interchange with the rest of the world, more Chinese have come to see their political system as repressive. Many would argue that it has other important virtues and that some controls remain necessary. But China needs to make up for the years of isolation and destructive ideological aberrations, rebuild its educational and technological systems, and move ahead with what it now calls modernization, recognizing that this must include a large infusion of foreign technology and foreign ideas—and perhaps also greater scope for individual creativity.

The liberation of women, one of the goals of the revolution, is still relatively far from attainment, although there has been considerable progress. Women are no longer as oppressed as they were under the old society, but they are still far from equal, even less so than in the contemporary United States. The new marriage law of 1950 gave them equality with men in marriage rights, divorce, and the ownership of property—a major step forward, and Mao declared "women hold up half the sky." The traditional extended family—three generations living under one roof—is largely gone, especially in the cities, and with it the authority of the oldest surviving grandparents. A grandmother, and sometimes a grandfather, may live with a son's family but now serves more commonly as baby-sitter, shopper, and general household help, representing the family on neighborhood committees while the daughter or wife goes out to work. Nearly all adult women in China have full-time jobs outside the home, but they are usually not paid equally with men, and at the end of the workday it is usually they who cook the meals, clean the house, and care for the children. On the other hand, employers or the state provide extensive child-care facilities for working mothers,

"Women hold up half the sky," as Mao said, and since 1950 women have entered many occupations previously reserved for men. ("China Reconstructs")

far more than in the United States. The top positions in government, business, industry, and education are held almost entirely by men, with occasional token female representation on committees. At the same time, just about all occupations and professions are open to women, and probably a higher proportion of women are professionals than in the United States. But most Chinese women work in lower-level or even menial jobs, and despite government efforts to persuade people that daughters are as good as sons, most families still give sons the first priority, since only they will continue the family line and provide some security for aged parents. Daughters still become members of their husband's family at marriage.

There are considerable differences between city and countryside in all these respects, with the rural areas clinging more to traditional values and patterns—including the production of more children in the hope of having a son. Nearly all urban and now most rural women do at least keep their own names after marriage, and there is in general a major change from the old society in the status of and attitudes toward women. But China, like Japan, and like most of the rest of Asia outside the southeast, still has a long way to go before women are truly equal members of society.

Renewed Demands for Liberalization

In 1987, 1988, and 1989 the government under Deng Xiaoping became increasingly repressive in its response to growing disaffection and protests against "thought control." Meanwhile, inflation mounted, badly damaging most people, and there was widespread and bitter resentment of the unchecked corruption of party officials and those, especially businessmen, who had "connections" to them. In May 1989, remembering May 4, 1919, crowds of students began to demonstrate in Tiananmen Square in Beijing, Communist China's chief parade ground and ceremonial center where Mao had once addressed a million cheering followers waving his *Little Red Book*. Now the students were asking instead for "democracy" and eventually even built a cardboard statue of "The Goddess of Liberty," modeled on the statue in New York harbor. Their demands were vague, and there were few attempts to make them more specific, but they were clearly inspired by the recent increases in contact with the rest of the world, especially with the United States, as well as reflecting unhappiness with censorship, controlled job assignment, inflation, corruption, and political dictatorship. Communist China's 25 *million* officials, or more, had become a terrible burden, hated by most people as well as resented, as China had become the most closely controlled society in world history. The traditional saying "Become an official and get rich" was once again widely quoted. The student demonstrations, briefly joined by a few of the local population, were never violent, but the government regarded them as a threat, and after some two weeks of hesitation, as different responses were debated, the hard-liners in the government won out. On the night of June 4, 1989, and the following day, the army and its tanks moved in to crush the demonstrators, killing perhaps as many as 1,000 unarmed students.

The demonstrators had challenged an all-powerful state, and the state responded as it had so often before. China has never had parliamentary democracy, free expression, or the rule of Western-style law—nor have Western states responded very differently in the past to similar direct challenges. But the brutality of what soon came to be called "The Beijing Massacre," enacted in front of the world's television cameras, sent shock waves around the globe, as the Soviet Union and eastern Europe were entering an exciting new phase of liberation. China stood out as isolated and condemned, except for continued U.S. support. In the wake of June 4, the government imprisoned many of the surviving demonstrators, as well as many thousands of "liberals," executed several, and vigorously resumed its earlier policies of censorship, suppression, the apparatus of the police state, and strident denunciations of all forms of Western influence and lifestyles. Meanwhile, it continued its brutal suppression of protests in Tibet against Chinese efforts to stamp out expressions of Tibetan identity and requests for a more genuine role in the administration of their supposedly "Autonomous" Area.

Some 94 percent of the population of the People's Republic are Han Chinese, and the remainder are divided among a great number of cultures and languages. In some areas, such as parts of the mountainous south and southwest, these minorities have not yet been overrun or crowded out in the long southern expansion of Chinese settlement; their existence was officially recognized after 1949 by declaring them "Autonomous Regions." Tibet, Xinjiang (home of the Turkish Uighurs and other Turkish groups), and Inner Mongolia became "Autonomous Areas." But in all of them the hand of the Chinese state was heavy, and "autonomy" was mainly window dressing. Chinese control was especially deeply resented in Tibet after its bitter reconquest in the 1950s and widespread allegations of genocide. The Dalai Lama, both spiritual and temporal ruler of Tibet, fled the advancing Chinese forces with a group of his followers and continued to maintain a government in exile.

Officially, all religions were tolerated in China after 1950, despite the Communist stance against religion. But Christianity, which survived for perhaps 1 million Chinese and minority adherents, was "purged" of its foreign connections; all foreign missionaries were expelled, and the church was put in charge of Chinese clergy, solely dependent on local financial support. After 1978, Christians and their churches became more acceptable and visible, as did Buddhists, Daoists, Muslims, and their temples or mosques, with qualified official approval. The approval was especially qualified in strongly Lamaist-Buddhist Tibet, where there had been earlier Chinese efforts to eradicate Buddhism as a badge of Tibetan separatism. Muslims remained by far the largest religious group, including Uighurs and the other Turkish groups and as many as 50 million Han Chinese, often indistinguishable from other Chinese except for their avoidance of pork.

More recently, official policy and action have turned more against religion. The peaceful eclectic sect of Falungong, a mixture of folk Buddhism and some aspects of Christianity and other folk religions, has been the object of numerous attacks and imprisonment by the state, although it is hard to see it as any threat.

Chinese Christians have also come under attack and churches have been razed. There are more Chinese Christians than ever in the past, perhaps as many as 20 million, but they are resented by the state, no doubt in part because they follow an originally alien religion, like the Buddhists.

As of late 2001 Mao's successors appeared to have consolidated their power firmly, under Jiang Zemin as president and Zhu Rongji as premier. The death of Deng Xiaoping in 1997 was not followed by a power struggle as far as one could tell, but the new rulers were relatively hard-line conservatives. They released a few prominent political prisoners in an effort to placate the Americans, but there was no major liberalization of the state controls. Deng's policies on greater scope for private entrepreneurs and on joint ventures with foreign companies were augmented, and there was continued scaling down or closing of many often inefficient state-owned enterprises. There was strong growth in the expanding private sector, and with it destructive inflation from the overheated economy. Unemployment, open and disguised, remained a major problem. There was a floating population of some 100 million construction and factory workers in the booming cities trucked in daily or weekly from the countryside, housed in shacks and poorly paid, but this was still more attractive than the limited opportunities and even lower pay in most of the rural sector. Unknown but very large numbers remained in the cities as illegal immigrants.

Exports soared as "market forces" triumphed everywhere, especially in the new free trade zones in and around several coastal cities. Southeast Guangdong, adjacent to Hong Kong, became one of the fastest-growing economic areas in the modern world, along with Hong Kong itself. But some of the exports also came from prison labor, and there were said to be at least 20 million prisoners in China, many of them political. Figures that show the growth rate of the Chinese economy as the world's highest are thus somewhat misleading and do not adequately reflect the bulk of the country or its population, which remains rural-agricultural and includes major pockets of genuine poverty. There is now rapidly growing income inequality, perhaps as great as in the United States.

Meanwhile the "free market" policies continue to spawn vast corruption, a huge illegal underground economy, and more "bourgeois elements." There were discos, nightclubs, and beauty parlors in most cities and even a nightclub owned by the People's Liberation Army in Guangzhou. Mao would be horrified. China joined the World Trade Organization in late 2001, as did Taiwan. China had long wanted this, but it has meant a lot of new competition in world markets. Already China has high unemployment, about 20 percent. By now controls have been lifted on migration to the cities, part of the "free market" policies, and urban populations have boomed. In 2003 Jiang Zemin announced his retirement, though implying that he would retain some power behind the scenes, especially over the military. He designated as his successor Hu Jintao, a party faithful, who so far has appeared to continue Jiang's policies.

The Chinese people have suffered terribly under successive regimes: the last decades of the deteriorating Qing dynasty, the warlord years after its collapse in 1911, the reactionary, oppressive, and ineffective Guomindang, and the long nightmare of Maoism, some of which was revived after 1986; "foreign influences" were again reviled, "bourgeois" and "rightist" tendencies were declaimed against, and from 1989 "political study" was again required of all students. Controls over personal life have softened; people can now choose their own jobs for the most part, and the old "neighborhood committees" that once spied out "irregularities" in people's lives have largely disappeared. Incomes have continued to rise for most, and something like a middle class and attendant consumption patterns have begun to emerge. Obviously, most Chinese welcome this, and the new regime is generally popular. But overriding all is the remarkable vitality of the Chinese people.

Taiwan

The original inhabitants of the island were a Neolithic people whose origins are complex but who were progressively displaced or killed off by immigrants from the mainland, largely since the seventeenth century, and are now a dwindling minority of fewer than 200,000 people. The island was settled mainly by Chinese from Fujian Province, just across the narrow strait that separates it from the mainland. They retained their Chinese culture but developed some separate regional feeling, especially under Japanese control; their language, known as Taiwanese, is in fact coastal Fujianese and is not mutually intelligible with standard Chinese. The language difference, the geographic separation, and the relatively frontier circumstances of the island compared to overcrowded southern China all heightened the Taiwanese feelings of difference, especially since they were under very loose and often ineffective control from distant Beijing.

The island of Formosa (Taiwan) was taken over by the Japanese in 1895 as part of their colonial empire, but with Japan's defeat in 1945 it was returned to Chinese sovereignty. In 1949 Taiwan became the sole remaining base for the defeated Guomindang; the American military defended it against the Communist mainland, using the U.S. Seventh Fleet to patrol the Taiwan Strait. Some 2 million mainland Chinese, including units of the Guo-

An urban public housing complex Taipei, Taiwan. High-rise housing complexes in Asia's cities accommodated the region's rapid post–World War II urbanization. The initial publicly financed and managed housing projects are now being replaced by privately owned apartment and condominium developments that are more appropriate to the demands of Asia's upwardly mobile urban society. (Kenneth Hall)

mindang army and government, fled to Taiwan. Taiwanese had fought underground against Japanese rule and welcomed the mainlanders in 1945, hoping to work with them in forming an administration for the island, now again a Chinese province. But after the Guomindang brutally repressed them in 1947 and massacred most of their political leaders, they came to regard their new masters as worse oppressors than the Japanese. The mass influx of 1949 tightened Guomindang control and excluded indigenous Taiwanese from power, as "carpetbaggers" from the mainland dominated the scene.

Nevertheless, Taiwan in the 1950s began a period of rapid economic growth, at first with heavy American aid and then, by the early 1960s, on its own. An American-directed land-reform program, ignored by the Guomindang while it was in power on the mainland, gave farmers new incentives as well as increased supplies of fertilizer, new crop strains, and new irrigation. Growing rural prosperity was matched and, by the 1970s, exceeded by boom industrial growth as Taiwan experienced a small-scale version of the Japanese "economic miracle." Taiwan's path was much the same, including its technological achievements and both light and heavy manufacturing, beginning with textiles and other consumer goods and moving rapidly into electronics, high-tech products, shipbuilding, and industrial goods. As in Japan earlier, many components were made on a small-

scale or even household basis and brought new prosperity to rural as well as urban areas. Living standards rose sharply, and most Taiwanese became relatively affluent as well as well educated. As elsewhere, the two were causally linked. This was some recompense for their lack of political voice, but slowly Guomindang domination became less rigid, and Taiwanese began to play a fuller part in the political life of the island. Industrial development exacted a price in dangerous pollution; the capital, Taipei, lying in a basin surrounded by hills, became one of the world's most polluted cities by the 1980s.

Taiwan's trade with the rest of the world quickly exceeded that of vastly larger mainland China, and Taiwan is now, despite its small size, the fourteenth largest trading economy in the world. Taipei became a huge, overcrowded city and was joined by other rapidly growing industrial and port centers. By the 1980s prosperity, wider relations with the rest of the world, and an unspoken acceptance of political realities in China and East Asia began to soften somewhat the harsher aspects of control by the Guomindang, who finally relinquished earlier goals to reconquer the mainland. The Maoist economic disaster, contrasting so dramatically with Taiwan's new prosperity, bolstered confidence. More representation and more positions were offered to the Taiwanese, and the beginnings of more freedom of expression developed. These trends accelerated after the death of Chiang Kai-shek in 1975, and under his son Chiang Ching-kuo, who succeeded him as president, until his death in 1988. The vice president, Li Teng-hui, then became president, as the first native-born Taiwanese to do so, and was later confirmed by the Guomindang party. He was inaugurated in 1990 as the head of what was becoming a multiparty democracy with an active political opposition, which won a substantial number of legislative seats in the first islandwide and largely free elections of 1986. Li supported continuing liberalization within the Guomindang and encouraged the further growth of private and interpersonal travel and economic contacts with the mainland; indirect trade with the People's Republic, via Hong Kong, continued to increase. Reunification has remained a distant goal, but both sides began to make formal and informal overtures to each other. Taiwan was shocked by the brutal crackdown in China in June 1989 and after, and moves toward some qualified reconciliation were abruptly slowed. Much will depend on what happens to Hong Kong under Chinese rule. In 2000 Li was succeeded by another native Taiwanese, Chen Shuibian.

Hong Kong

The tiny, mountainous island of Hong Kong, just off the mouth of the West River, which leads to Guangzhou, had been ceded in perpetuity to the British in 1841. Adjacent Kowloon, on the mainland peninsula across the harbor, was also ceded permanently in 1860 at the Treaty of Tianjin. In 1898, additional adjoining territory on the mainland, the so-called New Territories, was leased for 99 years to supply Hong Kong with food and water and to provide some room for expansion. Although it was a British Crown Colony, Hong Kong remained an overwhelmingly Chinese city like the coastal treaty ports, peopled by immigrants from overcrowded southern China who brought with them their interest and skill in commerce and their capacity for hard work. Hong Kong flourished mainly as a trade entrepôt, a duty-free port serving all of the China coast, and as a center for international banking, finance, and insurance. With the Communist victory in China, Hong Kong was isolated from its major market, for which it had served as a leading foreign trade port. At the same time, it was flooded by waves of refugees from the mainland.

The city and its resourceful people survived the crisis by developing a highly successful array of light manufacturing industries, first in cotton textiles and then in a wide range of electronics and high-tech consumer goods. All these were necessarily dependent on imported raw materials but were made profitable by low-wage labor, efficient factories, and the advantages of a duty-free port for imports and exports. Hong Kong also continued to serve as an international shipping, banking, and financial center, and despite the great decline in direct trade with China indirectly handled about half of China's foreign trade. It also served as China's major window on the rest of the world, and through the stream of refugees provided much information about the catastrophic events of the years after 1949. The city's swollen population was housed over time, more or less adequately in both government and private apartment blocks, often one or more families per room; Hong Kong became probably the most densely crowded city in the world. At the same time, with virtually full employment, it joined Japan, Taiwan, and South Korea as one of the fastest growing economies in the world. Like them, it also put great stress on education.

Hong Kong became even more prosperous than it had been before World War II, and as China began to resume trade outside the Communist bloc, Hong Kong regained its former role as a major shipping, distribution, commercial, and financial center for the mainland, a function that it also performed for much of Southeast Asia. By 1998 the city and its adjacent small territories had a population of 6.5 million. But the Chinese government announced, and Britain perforce agreed in 1985, that when the lease of the New Territories expired in 1997, they and all of Hong Kong would be reclaimed. It remains to be seen how this citadel of capitalism will be integrated with the socialist system of the People's Republic of China. Hong Kong had flourished as a kind of "alternate China," a base for revolutionaries or dissidents, and an arena where Cantonese entrepreneurial talents have found a free field unhampered by traditional government, Confucian restrictions or prejudice, or Communist controls. The events of June 1989 shocked Hong Kong even more than they did Taiwan. As the date for its reabsorption into China approached, there were repeated anti-Beijing demonstrations. Business confidence in the future sagged, and some people began to emigrate. But Hong Kong has been highly profitable to China and is also an outstanding example of the kind of economic success that China truly needs. Beijing may realize that it has much to learn from Hong Kong's example and make a fuller place for it within an evolving Chinese system. As of 2005 China has kept its promise to leave Hong Kong largely alone under the formula of "one country, two systems," but its municipal government is, naturally enough, run by people who were in effect appointed by Beijing, and recently Falungong has been persecuted there as well. It is possible, however, that Hong Kong may change China at least as much as China changes Hong Kong.

Hong Kong in 2004. (Gareth Brown/CORBIS)

China, Taiwan, and Overseas Chinese

Hostility toward Overseas Chinese appeared in many Southeast Asian countries in the post–1950 era. Resentment of Chinese success and fear of Chinese competition were two economic reasons. Chinese cultural remoteness, and even cultural aversion, encouraged local politicians to target unpopular Chinese minorities. Major anti-Chinese policies have been common in almost every newly independent Southeast Asian society.

Feeling alienated, rootless Overseas Chinese debated the appropriateness of assimilating or integrating with local populations while still retaining the essence of being Chinese. Larger cultural questions became more complicated by the changing and contradictory definitions of Chinese culture that derived from the debates taking place in both China and Taiwan.

After 1978, the reopening of investment, technical aid, and other commercial opportunities in the People's Republic provided new opportunities for Overseas Chinese—the majority of whom were now born in Southeast Asia rather than China—as well as China's reciprocal willingness to promote the renewal of Overseas Chinese contact with their family clans. Partnerships between wealthy Overseas Chinese and their Chinese in-laws have been foundational to family-based international business empires that have especially flourished since the late 1990s, when the People's Republic began to phase out state corporations in favor of private ownership. Perhaps one of the most interesting developments has been the competition between the People's Republic and Taiwan to solicit partnerships with Southeast Asia–based Overseas Chinese, by stressing their shared ethnic heritage. From a Southeast Asian perspective, these renewals jeopardize the attempts of Overseas Chinese to acculturate into full membership in Southeast Asian societies, while also posing the threat that powerful Chinese family-based international corporate enterprises will dominate local economies, to the detriment of developing national enterprises as well as limiting the opportunities for Japanese corporate and other international competitors. The broader implication is that these Southeast Asian corporate linkages will reinforce China's prominence in the region with political as well as economic implications, and perhaps lead to China's reemergence as the preeminent force in Asia.

Questions

1. Evaluate the American occupation of Japan, and how this shaped Japan's future. How did America reform the Japanese political system but fall short in making radical transformations in Japan's

economic and political process? How did the Cold War change America's interests in postwar Japan?

2. What were the reasons for Japan's economic success between 1950 and 1990? What contributed to Japan's economic stagnation in the 1990s?

3. Postwar Japan is always cited as the model for a non-Western society's successful transformation from traditional to modern. Is Japan modern in the Western sense of the word, or is it still a nation loyal to its traditions of the past? How has the Confucian ideal contributed to but also inhibited Japan's modernization?

4. Describe democracy in postwar Japan, as it was shaped by the one-party political system that was dominated by the Liberal Democratic Party (LDP). What was the agenda of the LDP and how did the LDP maintain its political control of Japan's parliament?

5. Why were the Communist forces successful in replacing the Guomindang as China's rulers in 1949? Compare China in 1949 to China in 2005.

6. How did the Great Leap Forward, the Sino-Soviet split, and the Cultural Revolution contribute to the development of the new Chinese state? Which aspects of Mao's policies were successful and which were not—and why? How has China changed since Mao's death, first during the tenure of Deng Xiaoping, and then in the post-Deng era?

7. Why did Taiwan and Hong Kong do so much better economically between 1950 and 1990? How have the governments of both changed since 1990, and with what consequences?

Suggested Web Sites

People's Republic of China

http://www-chaos.umd.edu/history/prc2.html

http://afe.easia.columbia.edu

http://museums.cnd.org/fairbank/prc.html

http://mtholyoke.edu/courses/sgabriel/economic/
    china-essays/4.html
Useful resources on contemporary China.

Modern Japan

http://www.japan-guide.com/

http://afe.easia.columbia.edu

http://lcweb2.loc.gov/frd/cs/jptoc.html
Useful resources on contemporary Japan.

Suggestions for Further Reading

Japan

Allinson, G. *Japan's Postwar History.* Ithaca, NY: Cornell University Press, 1998.

Brinton, M. C. *Women and the Economic Miracle in Postwar Japan.* Berkeley: University of California Press, 1993.

Broadbent, J. *Environmental Politics in Japan.* Cambridge, England: Cambridge University Press, 1998.

Cohen, T. *Remaking Japan: The American Occupation as New Deal.* New York, Free Press, 1987.

Dore, R. *City Life in Japan: A Study of a Tokyo Ward.* Berkeley: University of California Press, 1994.

Fuess, H. *Divorce in Japan.* Stanford: Stanford University Press, 2004.

George, T. S. *Minamata.* Cambridge: Harvard University Press, 2002.

Gordon, A. *Postwar Japan as History.* Berkeley: University of California Press, 1993.

Hendry, J. *Understanding Japanese Society.* London: Routledge, 1988.

Hideke, R. *The Price of Affluence: Dilemmas of Contemporary Japan.* Tokyo: Kodansha, 1985.

Imamura, H. E. *Urban Japanese Housewives.* Honolulu: University Press of Hawaii, 1986.

Lebra, T. S. *Japanese Women: Constraint and Fulfillment.* Honolulu: University Press of Hawaii, 1984.

Liddle, J., and Nakajima, S. *Rising Sun, Rising Daughters.* New York: St. Martin's, 2001.

Lynn, R. *Educational Achievement in Japan.* Armonk, NY: M. E. Sharpe, 1988.

Minear, R. *Victor's Justice.* Princeton: Princeton University Press, 1971.

Ogasawara, Y. *Office Ladies and Salaried Men.* Berkeley: University of California Press, 1998.

Reischauer, E., Jansen, M. *The Japanese Today.* Cambridge: Harvard University Press, 1995.

Ryana, S. *Koreans in Japan.* New York: Routledge, 2000.

Saso, M. *Women in the Japanese Workplace.* London: Hilary Shipman, 1990.

Schaller, M. *The American Occupation of Japan.* Oxford, England: Oxford University Press, 1985.

Schonberger, H. B. *Aftermath of War, 1945–1952.* Kent, OH: Kent State University Press, 1989.

Sugimoto, Y. *An Introduction to Japanese Society.* Cambridge, England: Cambridge University Press, 1997.

Sumiko, I. *The Japanese Woman.* New York: Free Press, 1993.

Ui, J. *Industrial Pollution in Japan.* Tokyo: U. N. University Press, 1992.

Weiner, M., ed. *Japan's Minorities: The Illusion of Homogeneity.* London: Routledge, 1996.

Woronoff, J. *Asia's "Miracle" Economies.* Armonk, NY: M. E. Sharpe, 1992.

Zinn, R. B. *Winners in Peace.* Berkeley: University of California Press, 1992.

China

Chan, M., and So, A. *Crisis and Transformation in Hong Kong.* Armonk, NY: M. E. Sharpe, 2002.

Cheng, C. Y. *Behind the Tienanmen Massacre.* Boulder, CO: Westview, 1990.

Dietrich, C. *People's China: A Brief History.* New York: Oxford University Press, 1994.

Dikotter, F. *Crime, Punishment, and Prison in Modern China.* New York: Columbia University Press, 2002.

———. *The Discourse of Race in Modern China.* Stanford: Stanford University Press, 1992.

Ding, Y. *Chinese Democracy After Tienanmen.* Vancouver: University of British Columbia, 2001.

Economy, E. C., *The River Runs Black.* Ithaca, NY: Cornell University Press, 2005.

Fairbank, J. K. *The Great Chinese Revolution.* Cambridge: Harvard University Press, 1986.

Fairbank, J. K., et al., eds. *The Cambridge History of China: Vol. 14, 1949–79.* Cambridge, England: Cambridge University Press, 1987.

Garnaut, R., and Ligong, S., eds. *The Rise of the Private Economy in China.* London: Routledge, 2004.

Goldstein, M. C. *A History of Modern Tibet.* Berkeley: University of California Press, 1989.

Harding, H. *China's Second Revolution: Reform After Mao.* Washington DC: Brookings Institution, 1987.

He, B. *China on the Edge: The Crisis of Ecology.* San Francisco: China Books, 1992.

He, L. *Mr. China's Son.* Boulder, CO: Westview, 1992.

Hsu, I. C. Y. *China Since Mao.* New York: Oxford University Press, 1990.

Keith, R.C., and Lin, Z. *Law and Justice in China's New Marketplace.* New York: St. Martin's Press, 2001.

Lardy, N. *China in the World Economy.* Washington DC: Institute for International Economics, 1994.

Liang, H., and Shapiro, J. *Son of the Revolution.* New York: Knopf, 1984.

Liu, B. *China's Crisis, China's Hope.* Cambridge: Harvard University Press, 1990.

Long, S. *Taiwan: China's Last Frontier.* New York: St. Martin's Press, 1991.

Lu, X. B. *Cadres and Corruption.* S〔 〕 Press, 2000.

Meisner, M. *Mao's China and After.* New〔 〕

Mei Zhang. *China's Poor Regions.* London: R〔 〕

Nathan, A. *China's Crisis: Dilemmas of Refor〔 〕 Democracy.* New York: Columbia University Pr〔 〕

Ownby, P. *Falungang and China's Future.* Lanhan〔 〕 and Littlefield, 2003.

Philips, S. E. *Between Assimilation and Independence i〔 〕* Stanford: Stanford University Press, 2003.

Schram, S. *Mao Tse-tung: A Preliminary Reassessment.* New〔 〕 Simon and Schuster, 1984.

Schreker, J. E. *The Chinese Revolution in Historical Perspective.〔 〕* New York: Praeger, 1991.

Shapiro, J. *Mao's War Against Nature.* Cambridge, England: Cambridge University Press, 2001.

Simon, D. F., and Kau, Y. M. *Taiwan: Beyond the Economic Miracle.* Armonk, NY: M. E. Sharpe, 1992.

Smil, V. *China's Environmental Crisis.* Armonk, NY: M. E. Sharpe, 1993.

Smith, W. *Tibetan Nation.* Boulder, CO: Westview, 1996.

Spence, J. *Mao Zedong.* New York: Penguin, 2000.

Sutter, R. G. *Taiwan: Entering the Twenty-first Century.* New York: University Press of America, 1989.

Thurston, A. *The Ordeal of the Intellectuals in China's Great Cultural Revolution.* Cambridge: Harvard University Press, 1988.

Ts'ai, I. F. *Hong Kong in Chinese History.* Berkeley: University of California Press, 1993.

Vogel, E. *The Four Little Dragons.* Cambridge: Harvard University Press, 1992.

Watson, R. S., and Ebrey, P. B., eds. *Marriage and Inequality in Chinese Society.* Berkeley: University of California Press, 1991.

Wolf, M. *Revolution Postponed: Women in Contemporary China.* Stanford: Stanford University Press, 1985.

Wu, H. H., and Wakeman, C. *Bitter Winds.* New York: Wiley, 1993.

Yahuda, M. *Hong Kong: China's Opportunity.* London: Routledge, 1996.

19

orea and Southeast Asia in the Modern World

This chapter begins with a survey of Korea under the Yi dynasty (1392–1910) and its decline after the sixteenth century. Foreign pressures to open the country to trade ended with the forcible Japanese opening in 1876 and then a Japanese takeover; their rule was exploitative and oppressive. Independence in 1945 was quickly marred by a split between the Communist north and a dictatorship in the south. In 1950 northern forces invaded the south but were finally driven back, as were the Chinese "volunteers" who came to their aid. The war was devastating to both sides; the south had largely recovered by 1970 and had strong economic growth, while the north lagged as tension between the two halves hardened. The election of Kim Dae Jong as southern president in late 1997 promised to reduce tension and begin the path to reunification.

Under oppressive French rule, Vietnam suffered, and its Communist party under Ho Chi Minh became the main political force in its struggle for independence. The French tried to regain control in 1945 but admitted failure in 1954. The United States, in the grip of Cold War rhetoric, replaced the French and fought on a major scale from 1964 to 1973 against the Vietnamese national drive for independence; Vietnam was reunited under a Communist government in 1975 but is still recovering from the immense destruction of war. Cambodia and Laos were part of colonial French Indochina and were drawn into the war by heavy U.S. bombing. Thailand served as a major U.S. base, while Burma came under a military dictatorship from 1962. Malaya became Malaysia in 1963, adding former British areas in north Borneo. Singapore, a mainly Chinese city, remained separate. Indonesia won independence from the Dutch in 1949 but came under a dictatorship, first under Sukarno and then from 1965 under Suharto, who was

forced to resign in 1998 in favor of B. J. Habibie, who promised new elections in 1999. Independence came to the Philippines in 1946, from 1965 under the dictatorship of Ferdinand Marcos, ended by the election of Corazon Aquino in 1986, replaced in 1992 by Fidel Ramos, succeeded in 1998 by Joseph Estrada, who promised reforms.

Yi Dynasty Korea in Decline

We must first pick up the thread of Korean history since the founding of the Yi dynasty as recounted in Chapter 9, and present a background necessary to understand what has happened to Korea in the modern era. Under Yi rule from 1392 Korea preserved a correct tributary relationship with China, which was often referred to by Koreans as "elder brother." Chinese influence strengthened throughout this long period, including new emphasis on Confucianism and the adoption of the Chinese examination system based on mastery of Confucian scholarship, philosophy, and morality. For a century or more Korea experienced a lively cultural growth on the Chinese model, printing encyclopedias and extensive histories. The capital was fixed at Seoul, and the country was divided into eight provinces, subdivided into counties following the Chinese pattern, and administered by a scholar-elite class chosen from those who had passed the examinations.

Although the system was supposedly based on merit, or in practice on conformity with the often rigid Confucian code, Korean society remained sharply hierarchical, based on hereditary class distinctions as in Japan. All those who served as military or civil officials came from the yangban, or gentry group. The unity and vigor provided by the Yi dynasty in its first centuries could not be maintained, and its authority was progressively weakened by chronic conflicts among rival bureaucratic and court factions. At the end of the sixteenth century, Korea was devastated by the invasion of the Japanese warlord Hideyoshi. It was subsequently invaded by the Manchus in 1636 in preparation for their assault on Ming China. The government became more and more ineffective, while the economy and culture stagnated and declined. Thus, Korea was especially poorly prepared to meet the challenge posed by Western and then Japanese imperialists in the nineteenth century.

Rejection of Foreign Ideas

The Korean establishment and government were rigidly opposed to any and all foreign influences or presences and had no interest in adopting Western technology even in self-defense. Catholic missionaries from China reached Korea late, at the end of the eighteenth century, but they and their converts were soon persecuted as both foreign and heretical—that is, anti-Confucian—and Christianity was driven underground. Unfortunately for Korea, its position between the larger and more powerful states of China and later Japan on the one hand and in the later nineteenth century an expansionist Russia on the other exposed it to overwhelming forces that it could not permanently resist and made it a battleground of competing foreign interests. It should be remembered, however, that Korea has the same geographic size and population as many European states, with a far older, more sophisticated culture, a major civilization in its own right, though deeply in the shadow of China. Because of its seclusionist and antiforeign attitude, Korea was called by Westerners the Hermit Kingdom, but this merely increased foreign curiosity and determination to "open" the country to trade. The Korean government's response to mounting foreign pressures after 1860 was in effect to pull the covers over its head and hope the foreigners would go away. Shipwrecked mariners were treated roughly and expelled, while the Koreans fired on and drove off foreign ships that tried to establish contact.

To the alarm of the government, Christianity did spread despite persecution, and with it some of the Western learning and ideas that Jesuits and other missionaries had introduced into China and Japan. Followers in Korea called it "practical learning," and some began to urge fundamental change. There was a predictable backlash on the part of others who saw Western ideas as a threat to Korean values and identity. Bands of armed men called "tiger hunters" attacked foreigners and took part in the efforts to repel the still small-scale foreign expeditions. In 1862 and 1863, there was a major peasant revolt in the southeast in protest against mounting poverty and the ineffective government response, but it also had xenophobic overtones. In the 1860s a new religious cult arose that was violently opposed to Western learning and all foreign influences. Called Tonghak, or "Eastern Learning," it was founded by a poor village scholar, Ch'oe Che-u (1824–1864), who had repeatedly failed the official examinations. Much like Hong Xiuchuan, founder of the Taipings in China (see Chapter 15), Ch'oe claimed to have had divine instructions to lead a new movement. His religion combined elements from Confucian, Buddhist, Taoist, Catholic, and indigenous Korean beliefs, including more than a touch of magic, but centered on the creation of a new "way" that would conquer the Westerners and restore Korea to its ancient glory. He attracted widespread support from impoverished peasants, as with the Taipings, and there were renewed revolts. Ch'oe was arrested and executed in 1864 as a subversive, but after his death the Tonghak movement spread even more widely, for the time being on a more passive basis.

The government thus faced both domestic rebellion and foreign challenge. An official known as the Taewongun ("Grand Prince") served as regent for his son from 1864 to 1873. He instituted a series of conservative reforms aimed at restoring the golden age of the Yi dynasty nearly five centuries earlier. In a parallel to the Tongzhi restoration in China during the same years (see Chapter 16), there was an effort to reduce corruption, strengthen the central administration, build new forts, and introduce a few modern arms, but the government's basically reactionary and exclusionist emphasis did not change. The government executed some French Catholic priests, thus provoking a French naval attack in 1866. The Koreans managed to drive them off, and the commander lectured them in Confucian style, "How can you tell us to abandon the teachings of our forefathers and accept those of others?" Persecution of Christians was greatly increased, but the Koreans seem not to have realized even yet the potential or actual power of the Westerners and continued to insist that their foreign relations be managed only through Beijing, of which they remained a tributary state. In effect, they went on saying to foreigners who pressed for redress, or for admission and trade, "talk to my lawyer." Korea counted on China to protect it but failed to understand China's growing weakness or the West's strength and determination, soon to be supplemented by a resurgent Japan.

Foreign Contention for Korea

Japanese had continued to trade at the southeast port of Pusan, by special permission, rather like the Dutch trade at Nagasaki under the Tokugawa. With the Meiji Restoration of 1868, Japan began to acquire new strength and new ambition. The Japanese had had a

CHRONOLOGY

Korea

1860–1995	Korea as Hermit Kingdom
1894	Tonghak Revolution
1895	Japan takes Korea and plunders its raw materials and agricultural production
1910	Korea annexed into Japanese Empire
1945	Korea divided at 38th parallel
1950–1953	North invades the South and is pushed back; stalemate armistice, again at the 38th parallel
1960–1987	Both Koreas under military dictators
1992	Popular election of Kim Young Sam in South Korea
1994	Death of Kim Il Sung; son Kim Jong Il succeeds in North Korea
1997	Election of Kim Dae Jong as new president of South Korea; attempts to open communication between the two Koreas
1998–	North Korea experiments with production of nuclear weapons, while also facing massive food shortages

Southeast Asia

1941	Foundation of Viet Minh
1945	Ho Chi Minh declares Vietnamese independence
1945–1949	Indonesian guerrillas defeat the Dutch; declare independence
1946	French bombard Haiphong
1947	Murder of Aung San in Burma; U Nu becomes new head of state; alternate military and civilian governments in Thailand
1953–1957	Ramon Magsaysay leads Philippines
1954	French surrender at Dien Bien Phu; Geneva Peace Conference/Geneva Accords
1954–1963	South under Ngo Dinh Diem
1957	Malaysia and Singapore independent
1959	"Strategic Hamlet Program"; United States and Hanoi escalate involvement in South Vietnam warfare
1964	Gulf of Tonkin Resolution
1965	Operation Rolling Thunder; Search and Destroy
1949–1967	Sukarno president of Indonesia
1959	Lee Kuan Yew and the People's Action Party (PAP) assume leadership in Singapore
1962–2002	Military dictatorship under Ne Win in Burma
1964–1968	15,000–600,000 U.S. troops in Vietnam

long history of interaction with nearby Korea, and had even maintained footholds on the southeast coast in the past (see Chapter 9). Now they saw it as their first foreign opportunity to demonstrate their new power. But it was, after all, the Americans who had first succeeded in "opening" Japan in 1853, and in the growing rivalry over who would manage to do the same for Korea, the U.S. minister to China went in 1871 with five warships to the mouth of the Han River and sent his surveyors up river toward Seoul. The Koreans fired on them, wounding two. The Americans demanded an apology, and when none was forthcoming, destroyed five forts by gunfire and killed some 250 Koreans. But the government refused to deal with them and finally they had to sail away, leaving the Koreans sure that they had won a victory.

Japanese samurai soon decided to try to provoke a war with Korea and to detach it from the Chinese sphere into their own. Their first plan was stopped by the still-cautious Meiji government, but in 1875 Japanese who landed from warships to survey the Korean coast were fired on, and the Tokyo government determined to use this as a pretext for demanding that Korea open its doors. A Japanese fleet anchored off Inchon, the port of Seoul, in early 1876, and forced the government to sign an "unequal treaty" patterned on those imposed earlier on China and Japan by the West. The treaty opened the ports of Pusan, Inchon, and Wonsan to Japanese trade and declared Korea an "independent state."

The Taewongun, now formally out of power, nevertheless promoted an antiforeign riot in 1882, and a mob at-

1965 ■ GESTAPU (Indonesia); split of Malaysia and Singapore, ending the Federation of Malaysia	1986–1992 ■ Corazon Aquino "People Power" in Philippines
1965–1998 ■ Suharto controls Indonesian government under a military dictatorship	1990 ■ Election of Aung San Ssu Kyi in Myanmar (Burma)
1965–1986 ■ Ferdinand Marcos and Imelda govern the Philippines (martial law, 1972–1981)	1990s ■ Fidel Ramos, Joseph Estrada, Gloria Arroyo (takes over when Estrada was impeached in 2001; reelected 2004) in the Philippines; ongoing negotiations with New People's Army (NPA) and Moro Liberation Front (MLF)
1967 ■ ASEAN founded	
1968 ■ Tet offensive; My Lai	
1970 ■ King Norodan Sihanouk deposed by Lon Nol in Cambodia	1993 ■ UN supervised election establishes coalition government in Cambodia
1975–1978 ■ Khmer Rouge control Kampuchia	1997–1998 ■ Economic crisis in Asia
1974 ■ Carpet bombing of Cambodia; UMNO established in Malaysia	1998 ■ Indonesian REFORMASI; Habibie, Wahid, and Magawatti Sukarno follow as presidents of a civilian constitutional government
1975 ■ Final U.S. evacuation; Vietnamese victory	
■ Rise of Pol Pot and Khmer Rouge	
1976 ■ Indonesian military annexes Portuguese East Timor	2001 ■ Taksin Chinnawat elected prime minister of Thailand
1979 ■ Brief border war between China and Vietnam	2002 ■ East Timor becomes independent; SARS epidemic
1978–1990 ■ Vietnamese occupy Cambodia; Hun Sen head of state	2004 ■ Susilo Bambang Yudhoyono elected president of Indonesia; Gloria Arroyo reelected in the Philippines; Abdullah Ahmad Badawi elected prime minister of Malaysia
1981–2004 ■ Mahathir Muhammed UMNO prime minister of Malaysia	2005 ■ Postwar Cambodia begins stabilization

tacked the Japanese legation. Both China, still regarding itself as the ultimate legitimate authority, and Japan sent troops. Japan received an indemnity, and China removed the Taewongun and held him in China for the next three years. Li Hongzhang took control of relations with and for Korea and tried to foster "self-strengthening" measures there. Li saw it was best for Korea to develop some counters to the overwhelming Japanese presence and ambitions and urged trade and diplomatic treaties with the Western powers. Such treaties were negotiated between 1882 and 1886, first with the United States, but the efforts at self-strengthening were blocked by Korean conservatism and by continuing factional conflict. With the removal of the Taewongun, the archconservative Min family came to power; under the leadership of

Queen Min, the few feeble efforts at rational change were largely undone. Nevertheless, foreign influences increased, including those brought by a new flood of mainly American missionaries, and a Korean diplomatic mission was established in Washington in 1888.

But the major influence was still from Japan, whose example of modern development and strength since 1869 inspired most Korean patriots and reformers. They welcomed a larger role for Japan in Korea's overdue development, and when the Min faction at court blocked their efforts, they tried to stage a coup in 1884. In Japanese style, they assassinated several conservative ministers and seized the king. This was all done with the knowledge of the Japanese legation, but their coup failed when the young Chinese commander in Korea, Yuan Shikai, defeated the guards of the Japanese legation and rescued the king. The affair was settled in 1885 by an agreement between Li Hongzhang and Ito Hirobumi of Japan—known as the Li-Ito Convention. Both powers agreed to withdraw their troops and military advisers and to notify each other before sending them back. Li proceeded to push for Korea's modernization, including the creation of a customs service, telegraph lines, and new military training. But the Tonghak movement was still very much alive, and in 1894 it rose in rebellion, once again against unaddressed poverty, governmental ineffectiveness, and foreign influences. China and Japan once more intervened, but now Japan was clearly superior militarily. In the brief undeclared war between the two, with China still attempting to act as Korea's protector, Japanese naval and ground forces won a quick and decisive victory. Korea was declared independent of China, but from 1895 it became in effect a Japanese sphere.

Korea would clearly have done better if it had followed the Meiji pattern, or even that of post-1860 China or Siam (Thailand), letting in all foreign nations in order to balance each other out while pursuing its own modernization along Western lines. As it was, Korea became Japanese property and suffered terribly. Russian ambitions in Korea were ended with the Japanese victory over the Czarist empire in 1905, when Korea was officially declared to be a Japanese protectorate. The weak Korean king, successor to Queen Min (who had been murdered by the Japanese in 1895), was left nominally in power, but when he complained to the Western powers about Japanese domination, Tokyo forced him to abdicate and turn over the throne to his feeble-minded son. Japanese now filled most official posts, and the Korean army was disbanded. Japan brutally suppressed all efforts at protest, which they labeled "riots," killing over 12,000 people. Ito, from 1905 the Japanese resident-general, was assassinated by a Korean patriot late in 1909, and Korea was officially annexed to the Japanese Empire the following year as Chosen Province.

Korea Under Japanese Rule

Korea was perhaps more brutally exploited than any colonial country in the world, under an exceptionally harsh Japanese rule from 1910 to 1945. Living standards, already dangerously low, fell sharply during this period as Japan milked Korea of much of its raw materials and food. Modern mines, railways, roads, postal service, and factories were built for the first time, but most of the coal, iron, and food crops were shipped to Japan, and the forests were stripped. Public health measures and an enforced civil order led to a substantial population increase, but the people were increasingly impover-

ished. Koreans were obliged to take Japanese names; their language could not be used publicly or taught in schools. Most Koreans were denied even elementary education. Most nonmenial jobs, including even engine drivers, were filled by Japanese, while Koreans labored as near-slaves. A few found lower-level positions in the colonial bureaucracy, but Korean efforts at self-expression and movement for political reform and representation were ruthlessly suppressed; their supporters were jailed, killed, or driven out as refugees. By 1945, there were too few Koreans with the education or administrative experience to form a viable government.

A mass demonstration of nationalist feelings and grievances took place on March 1, 1919, designed to make a point with the Western statesmen then meeting at the Versailles Conference and appealing to U.S. president Wilson's calls for self-determination of nations. Over 1 million Koreans marched peacefully in Seoul. They were met by a brutal Japanese force; over 20,000 were killed or injured and a similar number were jailed. A few private schools continued to teach Korean subjects, but by 1929 they were forced to use only Japanese textbooks and language. Under all these conditions it is understandable that Korean nationalism flourished as never before. Japanese regarded Koreans as second-class Japanese, but in any case as inferior, and hence as proper subjects for exploitation. Cultural differences in diet, dress, speech, and behavior were cited as evidence of Korean "inferiority." Japanese spoke of them as "dirty" and as smelling of garlic. But they were now a conquered people and could be abused with impunity, forgetting Japanese civilization's heavy debt to Korea (see Chapter 9), which more and more Japanese came to deny. Koreans who fled to Japan in hope of a better material life, and the many others who went as forced labor, were crudely discriminated against, as they still are.

Western missionaries, mainly American, hung on in Korea and now began to make many new converts, who found the Christian message with its Western connections both an antidote to the Japanese and a consolation. In time, Korea became second to the Philippines as the Asian country with the largest Christian proportion of its population, nearly one-fifth by 1950. Missionaries also founded schools and hospitals, as in China and elsewhere in Asia, and were periodically in trouble with the Japanese authorities, as were of course their converts. Many Korean nationalists, including the first postwar president, Syngman Rhee (Yi Sung-man, 1875–1965), began their education in mission schools, although most, like Rhee, were later imprisoned and tortured by the Japanese and then forced to flee. Marxist ideas appealed to other Korean nationalists, and Russia was an obvious counter to Japan. The Korean Communist party was founded in 1925 but was kept ineffective by the Japanese police and their agents.

The Korean landscape. Note the largely bare hills, legacy of massive deforestation by the Japanese. Here, the exploding suburbs of booming Seoul have largely filled the lowland basin. (Cameramann International, Ltd.)

Division and War

In the frenzied weeks after the formal Japanese surrender in 1945, what was thought of as a temporary arrangement among the victorious allies left Russian troops to accept the Japanese surrender and administratively occupy the northern half of the country above the 38th parallel, pending a more permanent settlement. American troops did the same for the southern half. The deepening Cold War from 1945 led to a hardening of this artificial division, and the emergence of rival Korean political regimes. Extremists on both sides, fed by Cold War ideology, eliminated the few moderates. A Soviet-dominated Communist government ruled the north from its capital at Pyongyang, and a U.S. client government, strongly anticommunist, ruled the south, with its capital at Seoul. The American-educated, archconservative émigré, Korean politician Syngman Rhee, became the first president of the Republic of South Korea, while the Communist leader Kim Il Sung headed the Democratic People's Republic of North Korea. Both were puppets of the now bitterly rival superpowers, and Korea once again became a battleground. Korea has been called "the anvil of East Asia" and it has indeed received repeated hammer blows, being fought over by China, Japan, Russia, and the United States. Korea has reaped from this international rivalry only massive destruction and bitter, self-destructive internal division.

In June 1950, North Korean forces with their Soviet equipment (Soviet troops had withdrawn by 1949) invaded South Korea and made rapid progress. It seems clear that South Korea, with its American arms (Ameri-

can troops had also withdrawn in 1949), had been planning a similar strike northward. At a hastily called special session of the United Nations Security Council, which the Soviet Union was boycotting in protest against the seating of Guomindang China, the United States pushed through a resolution condemning North Korea as an aggressor. The United Nations agreed to send an expeditionary force to support the south under American command headed by General MacArthur, then supreme commander of the Allied powers in charge of the occupation of Japan. There was relatively small representation from several of the Allies, about 40,000 out of the total of U.N. and South Korean troops of about a million, but the nominally U.N. force was largely American. South Korea provided over half of the ground forces. The North Korean drive was finally halted deep in southern territory, just short of the major port of Pusan on the southeast coast. Strong reinforcements soon arrived via Japan. The North Korean forces were driven back in heavy fighting through bomb-shattered Seoul, across the 38th parallel, and nearly to the Chinese border.

MacArthur pressed on, and as his forces approached the border with China he made public statements about the possible need to bomb potential refugee or supply bases on the Chinese side, including power stations and military and industrial centers in Manchuria. American planes began flying survey missions over the area. The Chinese government repeatedly signaled its alarm at this approach of a clearly hostile force so close to its borders and its vital Manchurian industrial centers. But MacArthur ignored or dismissed these warnings and the clear Chinese threat to intervene. Finally, in October

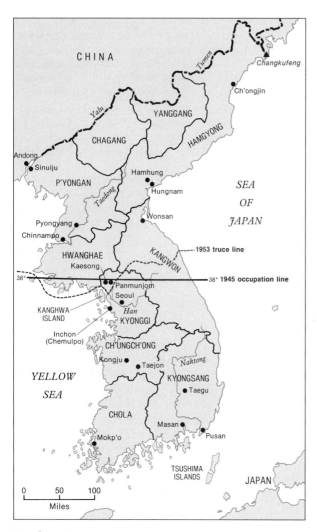

Modern Korea

Most of the good farmland is in the south, and most of the minerals and hydro power are in the north. The arbitrary partition line along the 38th parallel has also divided a unitary Korean culture, language, and sense of identity.

1950 Chinese "volunteer" troops poured into Korea across the Yalu River that forms the boundary, reaching a total of over one million. Together with North Korean troops, they drove the UN-U.S.-South Korean forces back through devastated Seoul and deep into the south. Slowly the UN-U.S.-South Korean troops fought their way north again, over country and cities already destroyed three times. They were now under a new American commander, General Matthew Ridgeway, President Truman having fired MacArthur for insubordination. They finally established a stalemate roughly along the 38th parallel just north of Seoul. A truce was ultimately arranged in October 1953, leaving the division of Korea as it was before June 1950 when the fighting began.

The war caused enormous destruction in both halves of the divided country and greatly set back Korean economic growth; in all, about 800,000 North and South Korean combatants, nearly 800,000 Chinese, and about 56,000 UN troops—mainly Americans—perished. The war also left a legacy of heightened North-South bitterness, tension, and mutual paranoia. There were streams of displaced refugees; over 3 million were driven from their homes, and there were uncounted but enormous civilian casualties, probably about 4 million killed or wounded. Both sides continued to build up their military strength, with fresh support from the two superpowers. If the United States and the United Nations had not intervened, there seems little doubt that Korea would have been united under northern direction as a Communist state. In the Cold War rhetoric of the 1950s, that was unthinkable, but one may legitimately wonder if the sacrifices and losses were worth it, especially since both Koreas continued as repressive police states. The United States has belatedly come to accept a Communist government in China. It is not easy to argue that a unified Communist Korea would have been worse for Koreans than the massive destruction they suffered and the legacy of division and tension.

Korea Since 1960

Korean culture, language, and national consciousness have remained unitary—a fact that serves to underscore the tragedy of the country's artificial division. The diversion of scarce resources into two large military establishments has meant great sacrifice in both countries, but especially in the less developed North. Most of the best agricultural land and most of the newer industry are located in the South, while Korea's industrial raw materials are in the area controlled by Pyongyang, developed under the Japanese. By the 1960s the South had begun to recover from the war, and by the 1970s it had leaped ahead economically, following the same path of rapid industrial development as Japan and Taiwan. In the North, economic growth was severely handicapped by a rigid Communist ideology and a faithfulness to the irrational Maoist policies of China. China had largely supplanted Russia as the North's Big Brother, especially after the valiant Chinese effort to defend the North against the Allied invasion. North Korea with its government-controlled press remained almost entirely closed to outsiders, but there was some modest economic growth after 1980.

In South Korea, Syngman Rhee was forced to resign as president in 1960, after his dictatorial style had alienated not only his rivals but many of his supporters. He makes an interesting parallel with Sun Yat-sen. Both were American-educated, both became Christians, and both lived for several years in Hawaii. But where Western influence tended to make Sun a radical reformer and democratic revolutionary, Rhee became a staunch conservative, a supporter of the status quo, and a domineering ruler who was willing to use terror tactics to enforce his way, ruthlessly beating down all who opposed him. As a result of the war, the South became determined to build its military strength with American arms aid and to press for order and anticommunism rather than for democracy and civil rights. Increasingly, the government became a military autocracy. A year after Rhee's forced retirement, a group of young military officers led by General Park Chung-hee seized power. Park was subsequently confirmed as president in the elections of 1963 and ruled until 1979, when he was assassinated by the Korean Central Intelligence Agency, a feared and hated secret military police that he had helped build. Another military group, led by General Chun Doo-hwan, then seized control. There were widespread protests and demonstrations against this sorry denial of responsible government, and the army and police killed many hundreds of demonstrators.

There was a judiciary and an elected legislature, or National Assembly, more or less on the American pattern, but from the beginning both were largely ignored by the authoritarian executive. The president appointed all cabinet ministers, judges, governors, and public university heads, while the military carried out his orders. Most cabinet posts were given to military men or arch-conservative economists and bureaucrats. Government took a leading role in promoting the economic develop-

ment and industrialization of the South on the Meiji Japanese pattern. This proved to be very successful as South Korean industry and commerce prospered and multiplied. There was a vocal political opposition, but when it garnered too much of the popular vote, it was subjected to severe government harassment; Kim Dae-jung, the main opposition figure, was repeatedly arrested and jailed. Student protests and demonstrations, which also continued against governmental authoritarian policies, were routinely met by riot police, clubs, and tear gas.

But there was also a growing urban middle class, professionals and businesspeople whose numbers and stake in society were stimulated still further by the economic boom of the 1970s and 1980s. Many who had begun as workers or even poor peasants moved into the middle class, especially as they acquired education, always a Korean priority. As in Taiwan, the benefits of South Korean economic growth were in time fairly well shared but to a lesser degree; most industrial workers were poorly paid, and mass protest demonstrations for better working conditions were often met with violence. Increasingly, both workers and middle-class people moved toward support for some alternative to the militarized authoritarian government, more responsiveness to people's needs, more respectful of human rights, and a more democratically responsible rule.

For the first time the elections of 1987 offered people the chance to vote directly for the president. Unfortunately, the opposition parties remained divided, and the presidency was won by a minority candidate, Roh Tae-woo. He was the first president in nearly 30 years to

Korean nativity scene, by Hye Ch'on Kim Hak-soo, a modern Korean Christian artist. The human figures are wearing traditional Korean clothing, including the black "stovepipe" hats and the dresses of the women. (Hye Cho'on Kim Hak-soo/Yonsei University Collection, Seoul; courtesy of the United Board for Christian Higher Education in Asia, New York)

A Korean Story

Here are some passages from a short story, "Bird of Passage," by the noted Korean writer O Yongsu, first published in 1958 and set in the years just after the Korean War. The story captures some of the hardship and pathos of that time.

Minu had been teaching at W. Middle School in Pusan, where he stayed until the recapture of Seoul. They called it a school, but it was a makeshift affair, just a group of tents. All kinds of peddlers came there, but the shoeshine boys were the worst. . . . To Minu, whose responsibility it was to keep the campus in order, fell the futile task of ejecting the shoeshine boys, only to have them reappear once his back was turned. . . . One day one of the shoeshine boys [Kuch'iri] held out his stool and said . . . "There are too many shoeshine boys here. . . . I'll shine all the teachers' shoes for just twenty hwan, if you will make it so that I'm the only one allowed to shine shoes here." . . . it made sense. . . . The other boys protested: "Aren't we all refugees together here?" . . . Minu managed to quiet the boys. Yet he could not help feeling moved when they said they were all refugees together, for Minu himself was a refugee school teacher who had left his home in the North. . . . When a new principal was appointed Minu left the school and went to Seoul. He forgot about Kuch'iri [But Kuch'iri turned up later in Seoul and found him]. . . . One day Kuch'iri said, "Teacher, your shoes are all worn out, [but] don't buy any. I'll get you some high-quality American ones from a guy I know. . . . It's okay if they're second-hand, isn't it?" . . . After that Kuch'iri worried about his offer each time he shined Minu's shoes. "I saw the guy yesterday and he says he'll get them soon"—and then mutter something to himself. [But then he disappeared, and another boy took over the spot who told him that Kuch'iri had gone with some other boys to an American army base up near the DMZ demilitarized zone along the 38th parallel]. . . . It would be autumn before they returned. . . . One day as leaves were beginning to fall Minu glanced up as a flock of geese flew by in a neat V. . . . "Kuch'iri too will be coming back soon," he thought.

Source: P. H. Lee, ed., *Flowers of Fire: Twentieth Century Korean Stories* (Honolulu: University of Hawaii Press, 1986), pp. 191–204.

---

enter office by vote rather than military coup, although there was widespread voting fraud and the other two opposition candidates together won a majority. Roh said he would work with them, and South Korea began to move toward a more democratic order. These trends were reinforced by the new wave of material prosperity. Economic development followed the Japanese model, first in light consumer goods using low-wage labor and then increasingly in heavy industry and high-tech products: shipbuilding, steel, electronics, and automobiles, all of which became competitive in world markets. Big business was closely tied to government and dependent on various forms of subsidy. Vertical conglomerates such as Hyundai and Samsung emerged; these were similar to the Japanese zaibatsu firms. New consumer goods spread widely among a now generally prosperous population, and many South Koreans even owned cars. Life expectancy rose almost to the Japanese level. Literacy was virtually universal. It was a replication of the Japanese "economic miracle" twenty years earlier and rested on the same basis: hard work, a national drive to succeed, and a high priority on education. And as in Japan, the middle class became the chief bulwark of a more democratic society and polity. After 1995 the Korean economy lagged, along with Japan and Southeast Asia, but the Korean pattern of hard work and group action should keep it on the road to recovery.

Violent clashes between students or workers and riot police continued, while Seoul, grown to giant size as an industrial center as well as political capital, became one of the most badly polluted cities in the world. Like Taipei, it lies in a lowland basin surrounded by hills, but it is far larger and more overcrowded, despite some government efforts at dispersal. As the Cold War began to thaw elsewhere, there were some signs of hope for a qualified reconciliation between North and South; a few of the U.S. troops still stationed in the South were withdrawn. But the goal of unity, which nearly all Koreans continued to want, remained elusive.

New tension with the North increasingly preoccupied Kim Young Sam, the president elected in late 1992 in an increasingly democratic system. Kim Il Sung, the dictator of the Communist North, created a world crisis in 1994 by putting obstacles in the way of inspection of his nuclear facilities, but finally he agreed to long-overdue talks with the South. In July 1994 he suddenly died and was succeeded by his son, Kim Jong il. The talks

were postponed and tension remained. It began to ease with the election in December 1997 of former dissident Kim Dae Jong as president of South Korea. He sent emergency food to the North as famine relief and maintained a conciliatory posture. The long dream of reunification, which nearly all Koreans want, is moving significantly toward realization. While Korea remains divided between two hostile governments supported by external power rivalries, the peace of this chronically troubled part of the world will continue at risk, and the welfare of its people will suffer. Continued talks between North and South suggested that moves toward reunification would gather force.

As the twenty-first century opened, North Korea greatly increased tensions in Korea and the world as a whole by experimenting with the production of nuclear weapons, presumably as a bargaining point with the

South Korea Indicted

Kim Dae-Jung, the most prominent of the minority politicians in South Korea and the chief spokesman for Western democracy, was a prominent critic of the military dictatorship of the 1960s, 1970s, and early 1980s. In a speech delivered at the University of Michigan on November 18, 1983, he had this to say:

The United States has maintained a close relationship with my country for over 100 years. Christianity first came to Korea from America; the United States liberated Korea from Japanese colonialism in 1945; it came to the rescue of the Korean people during the Korean War; and it supported the April 19, 1960, Student Revolution which ushered in a brief period of democratic expression. But with the advent of the Park Chung Hee dictatorship, the United States used the pretext of security as the rationale for ignoring popular aspirations for democracy. . . . Following his assassination, General Chun Doo Hwan was allowed to . . . massacre Kwangju citizens and suppress popular democratic aspirations. These slain patriots had advocated American-style democracy. . . . Some American leaders have supported the South Korean government's argument that democratic development will have to yield to the imperatives of economic growth. But [despite our new prosperity] we enjoy none of the democratic freedoms. . . . A recent national survey revealed that 80 per cent of the South Korean people desire democratic development even if it would mean slowing down economic growth. President Reagan's recent visit to Korea has disappointed the South Korean people. Though he expressed the importance of democracy and human rights, his visit did not bring the release of political prisoners, the relaxation of suppression of the mass media, nor a lift on the ban on many politicians. . . . Even though hundreds of democratic figures were put under house arrest because of his visit, he didn't make sufficient effort to have them freed. . . . I worry that Mr. Reagan's visit may result in fanning the flames of anti-American sentiment now smoldering among our people.

United States. The Americans asked the Chinese to try to dissuade the North Koreans, but the tensions continued. Kim Dae Jong's successor in 2003, Roh Moo Hyun, continues his policies of rapprochement with North Korea, but in 2002 South Korea said it too had nuclear capability.

Southeast Asia Since World War II

China's revolutionary resurgence sent shock waves through Southeast Asia, where there were also some 15 million permanent Chinese residents. The Japanese had helped to destroy European colonialism in Asia, but China now offered to many a different and more appealing model. In neighboring Vietnam the Chinese example encouraged the Communist party under Ho Chi Minh (1890–1969) in its struggle first against French colonialism and then against an American invasion in support of a U.S.-linked government in the south. In the Philippines there was a peasant Communist uprising among the Hukbalahaps (Huks), remnants and off-shoots of which still continue as the basis for today's New Peoples' Army (NPA). In 1965 the Indonesian military, with American CIA support, killed more than half a million innocent Indonesian Chinese and suspected Communists in retaliation for an alleged plot against the government. In Malaya from 1943 to 1957, a small group of Chinese residents led an insurrection, using Mao's example of guerrilla warfare. It was aimed first at the Japanese occupiers and then at the restored British colonial government. It was finally put down as virtually the last act of the colonial government when most Malayan Chinese, who had done well in the flourishing commercial economy of the country, refused to join it, and help from China did not materialize. In Burma there were major Communist-led revolts from 1948 to 1950.

Neighboring Thailand was wary, but there was no rebel effort by Thai Chinese, who had assimilated into Thai society much more successfully than in any other Southeast Asian country except perhaps the Philippines, where Chinese settlement and intermarriage with the locals are also long-standing and widespread. In Burma, chronic tension existed between the majority

Southeast Asia

Now consisting of ten separate states (including the city-state of Singapore), Southeast Asia has never been either a political or even a cultural unity, although some specifically Southeast Asian cultural traits, such as the high status of women, are universal.

Burmans of the Irrawaddy Valley and the numerous minority groups in the surrounding uplands and mountains, as well as between Rangoon-based Indian merchant/moneylenders and absentee landlords, who dominated Burma's rice export market. Most of the small Chinese minority in Rangoon had been expelled when Burma won its independence from Britain in 1947. The military government that came to power in 1962 under General Ne Win (1911–2002) followed the Chinese example by cutting nearly all of Burma's ties with the rest of the world and attempting to promote domestic development along "the Burmese way to socialism," which initially included repatriating large numbers of the Rangoon-based Indian merchant class to India.

In most of Southeast Asia colonial rule left too few educated people to form a stable political base and too few with any political experience. Parliamentary government was tried in Indonesia and Burma, but the lack of an adequate base and the political inexperience and ineptitude of leaders led to its collapse and a takeover by the military. Nowhere in Southeast Asia has Western-style democracy flourished, and in nearly every country power is exercised to varying degrees by a police state, a military-dominated government, or a Communist regime.

Vietnam

Here too, we must pick up the threads of the brief accounts given in Chapters 15 and 17. Indochina, a term reflecting Indian and later Chinese influences on the area, consists of Vietnam, Laos, and Cambodia. Like Korea, Vietnam has long been under the shadow of adjacent China. It was conquered and incorporated into the Qin empire in the third century B.C.E., and again under the Han. With the collapse of the Han dynasty it broke away but was overrun again by the armies of the Tang in the seventh century C.E. The Song wisely left Vietnam as a formal tributary state only, and the Vietnamese then, amazingly enough, repelled three successive Mongol efforts at conquest as well as later Ming and Qing attempts to reincorporate them into the Chinese Empire. Despite this history of bitter conflict and consequent Vietnamese fear and mistrust of China, they, like the Koreans, adopted most of Chinese literate culture, including the writing system, Confucianism and Daoism, a state bureaucracy and examination system, classical literature, an imperial censorate and administration on the Chinese model, public granaries, and a system of imperial roads. Though even more closely related than the Koreans to the Chinese racially, culturally, and linguistically, especially to the Cantonese of neighboring southern China, the Vietnamese nevertheless retained a strong sense of separate identity.

They had much in common with the rest of Southeast Asia, including the relatively high and free status of women and associated inheritance patterns, and the strong influence in their culture of originally Indian art forms and law, traceable to the early spread of Buddhism into Southeast Asia from India. As in Korea, Chinese forms and culture tended to be concentrated in the elite and the political realm, while culture at the village level remained clearly Southeast Asian, with Indian admixtures. Interaction with China continued, but Vietnam was at least equally involved in interaction with its neighboring Southeast Asian peoples and cultures.

While holding the Mongols and Chinese at bay, an amazing feat in itself, the Vietnamese continued their own expansion southward, incorporating most of Annam by the fifteenth century and reaching the Mekong Delta by about 1670, at the expense of the earlier inhabitants, primarily Chams and Khmers. French Catholic missionaries had been active in Vietnam since the seventeenth century and had made more converts there than in all of China. The new conservative Confucianist government that came to power in Vietnam in the 1850s, was opposed to foreign influences and especially to Christianity and its aggressive missionaries especially because these were the political allies of the French, who had their own ambitions to annex the Cochin China region. In the mid-1850s, when they became alarmed at the growth of converts and mission efforts as well as local efforts to seek French military intervention, they began a persecution of both, killing many priests and as many as 30,000 converts. This was the pretext for which the French had been waiting. They captured Saigon, the southern capital, in 1859 and began to take over the surrounding southern provinces. A treaty in 1862 ceded the south to France, which then took over neighboring Cambodia as well. But French ambitions were not satisfied, and in 1882 they seized Hanoi, the northern capital, provoking a war with China, which sent troops to protect its tributary state. The Sino-Vietnamese war against the French lasted from 1883 to 1885 and left the French in firm control; in 1893 they added Laos, formerly a Siamese (Thai) dependency.

The harsh French colonial rule was exploitative, and aimed to impose French culture on the elite of Vietnam, while providing few educational opportunities for the population. France drained resources from Vietnam rather than developing the economy or preparing Vietnamese to play a role in the administration, education, or modernization of their country. In addition, the French period saw a rapid growth of landlordism and sharecropping; living standards for Vietnamese fell. The French brutally suppressed all political expression, and many of the leaders of Vietnamese nationalism were jailed, executed, or forced to flee. These included the young Ho Chi Minh (Nguyen Ai Quoc), who in 1911 went to France.

Ho helped found the French Communist party in 1920, studied in Moscow, and then worked in Guangzhou with Sun Yat-sen and Michael Borodin, the Comintern agent. Like other colonialists, the French developed a public health system, with the result that the population increased faster than the food supply, especially as much of the rice was exported. Most Vietnamese landholdings were small, but about half the cultivated land was owned by the French or their Vietnamese collaborators. In the south there were many large estates or plantations where peasants worked as underpaid laborers, including rubber plantations. Railways and port facilities were built to serve this new commercial economy. Immigrant Chinese dominated the export trade, especially in rice, and became a major part of the population of Saigon, in the district known as Cholon. Although the French ran Vietnam as a police state, with the help of secret police, educated Vietnamese acquired much of French culture, learning about the French revolution and the ideals of liberty, equality, and fraternity. But Vietnam under France offered no chance for reformist change. In the end, Communist revolution became the chief vehicle of Viet-

namese nationalism and the independence struggle and was spurred on by the role that Vietnamese Communists played in the resistance to the Japanese after 1940.

From his base in Guangzhou, Ho organized the Communist party of Vietnam in 1930, with support from the Comintern. The world depression and drought-induced famine were causing great suffering in Vietnam, and there was a military uprising later in the same year. After the bloody French suppression of the mutiny, and the virtual destruction of the Nationalist party, the Communist movement spread among impoverished peasants. The French called on their Foreign Legion, broke the Communist organization, and killed, executed, or exiled many thousands. Ho fled to Hong Kong, but the Communists continued organizing underground. The French were an obvious and hated target, uniting most politically conscious Vietnamese against them, and Marxism-Leninism provided an appealing anti-imperialist rationale. Political, religious, and literary activity rose to the surface between 1936 and 1939, during the era of the French socialist Popular Front government, which released political dissidents and allowed them the opportunity to openly express their views, as well as to openly recruit opposition to the French colonial government. When the Japanese moved into Vietnam in 1940,

 ## Declaration of Independence

The Vietnamese declaration of independence on September 2, 1945, was consciously modeled on that of the United States. Here are some sample sentences:

All men are created equal. . . . They are endowed by their Creator with certain inalienable rights. . . . Nevertheless for more than eighty years the French imperialists, abusing their "liberty, equality, and fraternity," have violated the land of our ancestors. . . . They have deprived us of all our liberties. They have imposed upon us inhuman laws. . . . They have built more prisons than schools. They have acted without mercy toward our patriots. . . . They have despoiled our ricelands, our mines, our forests. . . . They have invented hundreds of unjustified taxes, condemning our countrymen to extreme poverty. . . . [But] we seized our independence from the hands of the Japanese and not from the hands of the French. . . . A people which has obstinately opposed French domination for more than eighty years. . . . who ranged themselves on the side of the Allies to fight against Fascism, this people has the right to be free. . . . All the people of Vietnam are determined to mobilize all their spiritual and material strength, to sacrifice their lives and property, to safeguard their right to liberty and independence.

Source: H. J. Benda and J. Larkin, *The World of Southeast Asia* (New York: Harper and Row, 1967), pp. 270–273.

they ran the country, as well as Cambodia and Laos, through the Vichy French officials and police until just before the end of the war, when they took over complete control. Thus, French rule was ended by the Japanese conquest, as elsewhere in colonial Southeast Asia.

Vietnam's 30 Years of War

When the war ended in 1945, Ho and his followers were ready to take over the government. They had been organizing from bases in southern China since 1941, where they set up a united front with other Vietnamese nationalists called the Viet Minh, or League for the Independence of Vietnam, supported by the American wartime OSS, the forerunner of the CIA. By 1944 the Viet Minh had infiltrated much of the northern part of the country and was mounting guerrilla resistance to the Japanese. Their commander, General Vo Nguyen Giap, entered Hanoi with his troops soon after the Japanese surrender, and in September of 1945 Ho proclaimed the independent Democratic Republic of Vietnam. In 1944 and 1945 a great famine in the north had the effect of building Communist strength. Ho's government controlled most of the north and tried to extend its support southward, but its dominantly Marxist line, while appealing to poor peasants, was resisted by many of the wealthier and more educated. Ho dissolved the Communist party in November and brought into the Viet Minh and the government in Hanoi many more non-Communists, hoping to broaden his appeal.

Meanwhile, the French returned with British and American arms and support and occupied Saigon in September 1945. By the end of the year they had reoccupied most of the south. Protracted talks with Ho and the Viet Minh ended in stalemate. In November 1946, French naval units bombarded Haiphong, the port of Hanoi, killing as many as 10,000 civilians, and landed troops. What has been called the "endless war" had begun. General Charles de Gaulle, now president of France, mindful of his country's humiliation by Germany and of the long French tradition of *la gloire*, declared that "France's sword shall shine again." But France, prostrate after the war, now operated necessarily with American-supplied arms. Cold War pressures had convinced the Americans that communism must be fought even halfway around the world in Vietnam, and that the French were a useful ally. Neither France nor the United States appeared to realize that colonialism in Asia was dead and that the struggle was for Vietnamese independence.

With their superior American equipment, the French reconquered all of the cities by early 1947. The Viet Minh, taking a leaf from the book of the Chinese Communists and following the same guerrilla strategy against a superior enemy, took to the countryside, from which they harried the French positions, especially at night, and disrupted road and rail traffic, while at the same time extending their political support against the hated foreign enemy. It was very like the Chinese Communist strategy against the Japanese, and a few of the more far-seeing observers realized that it would have the same ultimate outcome. In an effort to bolster their legitimacy, the French installed the former Vietnamese "emperor" Bao Dai in 1950, just as the Japanese had used Puyi in Manchuria. Cambodia and Laos were reincorporated as "associated states" within the French Union of Indochina. For most politically conscious Vietnamese, Ho Chi Minh remained the prime symbol and leader of their national strivings. After 1949, China sent economic aid, training, and arms to the Viet Minh.

 ## A Warning to France

As it became clear that France intended to reestablish its colonial rule of Vietnam, Bao Dai, whom the French had earlier installed as their puppet, appealed to General de Gaulle on behalf of Vietnamese nationalism, in part as follows:

> You would understand better if you could see what is happening here, if you could feel the desire for independence which is in everyone's heart and which no human force can any longer restrain. Even if you come to re-establish a French administration here, it will no longer be obeyed; each village will be a nest of resistance, each former collaborator an enemy, and your officials and colonists will themselves ask to leave this atmosphere which they will be unable to breathe.

Source: E. Hammer, *The Struggle for Indochina* (Stanford: Stanford University Press, 1954), p. 102.

China's revolutionary success and the pressures of the anti-French war strengthened the Communist leadership of the Viet Minh. The French foolishly diverted a major part of their forces to a large base in the mountains of the northwest at Dien Bien Phu to try to hamper a Communist invasion of Laos. This gave the Viet Minh a great opportunity to pick them off. General Giap and his troops hauled siege equipment to this remote mountain bastion, much of it by human labor, and strategically placed artillery above the fortified French compound in late 1953. In May 1954, the besieged French garrison had no choice but to surrender, and 10,000 prisoners were taken by the Viet Minh.

At the Geneva Conference of 1954, where China, India, and the major Western powers were represented, the French agreed to give up their struggle. Vietnam was temporarily partitioned between north and south along the 17th parallel just north of the old capital at Hue, with the Bao Dai government in the south, led by Ngo Dinh Diem as premier. The Geneva agreements called for the withdrawal of all foreign troops and for nationwide elections to be held the following year, but Diem and his American supporters refused to allow the elections, fearing that the Viet Minh would win hands down. Diem deposed Bao Dai in 1955 and declared himself president of the Republic of Vietnam; he was supported by many, including Vietnamese Catholics who had fled from the Communist-dominated north. But there were even more supporters of Hanoi in the south, and Diem attempted to suppress them.

Without significant Hanoi support initially, the opponents organized the National Liberation Front (NLF) to meet this threat. At that time the Hanoi regime was devoting its resources to the redevelopment of the war-ravaged north, emphasizing land reform and the political education of the Vietnamese population. Their first necessity, as Ho Chi Minh saw it, was to establish a solid base for what his regime believed was their inevitable annexation of the south, rather than to irrationally commit their meager resources to a full-fledged war against the Diem regime and their American allies. Clandestine guerrilla warfare spread in the south, and the United States began to send weapons and military advisors, as did Hanoi's government in response by the late 1950s. Despite growing American help, Diem's forces increasingly lost out in the struggle against the NLF, in large part because of massive corruption in Diem's regime and the unwillingness of the southern Vietnamese elite to accept land reform.

In 1963 Diem was assassinated by a military clique, with American CIA collusion. American ground troops began to augment the South Vietnamese forces more openly; there were 75,000 American troops by 1965 and over half a million by the end of 1968. Successive military regimes proved both ineffective and unpopular, and the United States became the real power in the south.

At the end of January 1968, during Tet (Vietnamese New Year), North Vietnamese forces mounted a surprise attack on fifteen cities in the south, fighting together with the NLF. The counterattack by southern and U.S. troops hurt the NLF badly, and from then on they and the northerners returned to a guerrilla strategy. But it had become a very bloody and ruthless war on both sides. Southern and U.S. forces tried to wipe out NLF and Viet Minh supporters, a guerrilla group known as the Viet Cong, often by killing villagers suspected of aiding them; other villagers were forced to live in fortified encampments called "strategic hamlets," where they could have no contact with the guerrillas. These hamlets forcefully alienated the rural populations from their lands and traditional communities as well as from their ancestral spirits, whom they could worship only in their traditional habitat. This strategic initiative thus had the unintentional result of offending and creating psychological havoc among those who were subjected to the cultural insensitivities of the Americans.

The NLF, Viet Minh, and Viet Cong forces also used terror tactics against those they suspected of collaborating with the other side. Much of the American actions were shown on U.S. television, and news leaked out of the massacre of an entire village at My Lai by American troops, only one incident of many. American public opinion began to turn strongly against a war that seemed to violate so much of American values and ideals and that increasingly seemed impossible to win. By 1969, the United States began slowly to reduce American forces in Vietnam, even though the tide had by no means turned in their favor. At the same time, the Americans bombed Hanoi almost to rubble, mined the harbor of Haiphong, and spread the war into Cambodia in an effort to prevent its use by northern forces as a refuge, or as part of their supply route to the south, the so-called Ho Chi Minh Trail.

Ho died in 1969, still short of his goal of Vietnamese unification and independence, but the United States was growing weary of this "endless war" and the terrible price it exacted. Peace talks had begun with the North Vietnamese in Paris in 1968; the bombings of Hanoi and Cambodia were designed to "put pressure" on the north and weaken their negotiating position. The agreements finally signed in Paris early in 1973 were limited to provisions for the safe withdrawal of the remaining American troops, who deserted their erstwhile southern allies and their civilian collaborators. The final evacuation of the last U.S. diplomatic personnel in 1975 by helicopter from the roof of the American embassy in Saigon—with frantic Vietnamese collaborators and their dependents fighting to get aboard—was an unedifying spectacle viewed by millions of Americans on their television sets. The NLF and northern forces overwhelmed the south. Saigon fell in 1975, and in 1976 the country was formally

Refugees in Vietnam being forcibly evacuated from their village by U.S. forces for resettlement in a guarded camp. Such village areas were then defoliated, thus denying the rice crop to the Viet Cong who had infiltrated the area. (UNIPIX)

reunited as the Socialist Republic of Vietnam, with its capital at Hanoi; Saigon was renamed Ho Chi Minh City. The Americans had tried to replace the French as a new foreign power, attempting to deny the unity and independence of Vietnam, an injustice that many Americans were uncomfortable with despite the prevailing crusade against Communism. Although they had vast superiority in high-tech weapons and firepower, the Americans were unable to defeat guerrilla-based nationalism, as the Japanese had found earlier in China. In the course of the long struggle, the Vietnamese Communists became the true leaders of their country's fight for independence.

In the American phase of the war, beginning in 1964, U.S. forces lost nearly 58,000 dead and some 300,000 wounded, in a conflict whose purpose and meaning were understood by very few Americans, including those in Vietnam. In an effort to use firepower rather than men, the United States dropped more bombs—some say twice the tonnage—on Vietnam alone than the Allies dropped on all fronts in World War II. But the losses were overwhelmingly greater on the Vietnamese side. From the beginning of the war in 1945 to its end in 1975, they lost nearly 2 million dead, mainly military personnel but including very large numbers of civilians; about 4 million soldiers and civilians were wounded or maimed, and there were well over 1 million refugees, driven from their homes by the fighting. Longer-run effects included the massive devastation of many of the cities and much

of the countryside, and the American defoliation of the forests with the herbicide Agent Orange, to deny the shelter of their leaves to guerrilla forces. While Agent Orange has caused human casualties among Americans, its consequences for Vietnam and its people were enormously more serious and longer-lasting; both the soil and the people have been poisoned.

It was part of an American strategy reflected in the much-quoted remark of a junior officer, "We had to destroy the village in order to save it." Like the village's inhabitants, who were also destroyed, the "saving" of Vietnam from Communism by a power from the other side of the world with no stake in Vietnam otherwise came to seem at best inappropriate. This was especially so given the terrible costs of that effort, and it became increasingly clear that it was in any case futile. Guerrilla-based nationalism had proven its power in the 2,000-year Vietnamese struggle against the might of the Chinese Empire, and now it had humbled the greatest power of the modern world. American policymakers would have done better to study Vietnamese history, and to try to understand the true force of Vietnamese nationalism. The fact that the nationalists were dominated by Communists, who predictably became more hard-line as the war progressed, was far less important to most Vietnamese and to the outcome of the war. China and the Soviet Union supplied arms to the north, but no troops. It was a Vietnamese victory, and perhaps only incidentally a Communist one.

The police chief of South Vietnam executing a Viet Cong suspect on a Saigon street. This and other similar pictures were widely circulated abroad and helped to build opposition to the war in the United States and elsewhere. (AP/Wide World Photos)

Politically also, the war exacted a high price. One can rarely safely predict, but it seems at least possible that if Vietnam had been given its independence, like nearly all of the rest of Asia, after the end of World War II, a Communist regime under Ho Chi Minh might have developed more openly, less rigidly, and with greater freedom for non-Communists than it became after 30 years of struggle much as it has in the past two decades. The long and bitter war for independence, which became in effect a civil war, divided northerners and southerners, Communists and non-Communists, into opposing camps of mutual suspicion and hatred, much of which still remain. Vietnam after 1976 was politically rigid, tolerating no opposition or divergent views. In part because of its doctrinaire policies, and suffering from a U.S.-led international trade and aid boycott, economic development lagged far behind most of the rest of Asia, and the devastating destruction of the 30-year-long war was still not fully made up by 2005.

The Americans were slow to accept their defeat. They imposed an embargo on impoverished Vietnam, refused to pay reparations or send urgently needed food, and blocked its access to the United Nations and to the rest of the world except for China and Russia. Negotiations for a peace treaty were stalled by American insistence on a full accounting and the return of the remains of their military personnel missing in action, the so-called MIAs. However much one may sympathize with the American families concerned, the number of men at issue was far smaller than in any modern war, including both world wars, estimated by the Americans at some 2

percent of their forces. Nearly 20 percent of U.S. forces were missing in action in World War II, and 30 percent in World War I, another reminder of the terrible chaos and human tragedy of warfare; 300,000 Vietnamese are still MIA. Vietnam's recovery from its unprecedented devastation continued to be slowed by its isolation from normal trade and interchange with the rest of the world, though by 1991 the U.S. position was softening somewhat and U.S. recognition finally came in 1995.

Meanwhile, doctrinaire economic policies in Vietnam were changing to follow the Chinese path of a supervised "free market," and since the mid-1990s economic growth has accelerated, as the U.S. embargo faded in response to the successful resolution of lingering MIA issues as well as the end of the Cold War; the United States and other countries now trade with and invest profitably in Vietnam.

Bloody Cambodia

The French reoccupied Cambodia in 1945 and presided over a series of ineffective puppet governments. At the Geneva Conference of 1954, Cambodia was granted its independence, and the country came under the rule of Prince Norodom Sihanouk, its former king. There was also a small Cambodian Communist party. Sihanouk's rule was largely benign, and Cambodia was for the present spared the ordeal of Vietnam, enjoying a modest prosperity and considerable foreign

READING ACROSS CULTURES

The Rediscovery and Restoration of Angkor

The spectacular temple and court complex at Angkor was the political and religious center of the Khmer Empire of early Cambodia. Jayavarman II (802–850) sponsored the initial building projects, and successive Khmer kings added their own monuments to it (see Chapter 7). Suryavarman II constructed Angkor Wat, the most magnificent of the Angkor temples during the height of the Khmer Empire in the early twelfth century, and Jayavarman VII added the adjacent Angkor Thom Buddhist complex with its serene bodhisattva heads at the end of that century. When the Thai invaded in 1431, the Khmer abandoned the city and much of Angkor and most of its temples fell into ruin.

Early in the nineteenth century, Vietnam's monarchs asserted their territorial interests to take control of Cambodia and reasserted their claims to Vietnam's southernmost regions. These claims put them into direct conflict with the French, who thought of the region as an unclaimed political frontier ripe for French taking, to provide a base for French commerce with China. The Franco-Vietnamese treaties of 1862 and 1874 gave the French authority over southern Vietnam and the remains of the Angkor complex.

Angkor was largely unknown in the West until 1857 when the French missionary, Father Charles-Emile Bouilleveaux, brought the existence of the abandoned city to the attention of the Western public with his publication of *Travels in Indochina 1848–1856, the Annam and Cambodia*. Angkor's beauty was revealed by the naturalist Henri Mohout, whose notes and drawings appeared in the widely distributed magazine *Le Tour du Monde* in 1863. To the French Angkor stood as a positive symbol of an Asian classical age, in some ways parallel to ancient Greece, to be celebrated, romanticized—and plundered for French museums and exhibitions. Recovery and documentation, if not the restoration, of Angkor civilization by the French became the centerpiece and stated purpose of French colonialism.

French archaeologists continued to control the Angkor complex until warfare made it impossible in the 1970s, but others have asserted their right to the city and its temples. Cambodia has used Angkor as the site for proclamations of political legitimacy since the end of World War II. Norodom Sihanouk, who became the ruler of Cambodia when the country became independent in 1954, asserted that he was the sole heir to Angkor's monarchs, and thus the only rightful spokesperson for the Khmer people.

Deposed by the Cambodian military under Lon Nol in 1970, Sihanouk was allowed to reclaim his position as the Khmer monarch in the 1990s during the government of Prime Minister Hun Sen. In exchange, Sihanouk had to perform a traditional Khmer ritual, including an investiture ceremony in which he bestowed a ritual name on the secular ruler—who in theory acts in the monarch's name to administer daily affairs. This ritual can only be performed by a Khmer monarch who is the acknowledged successor to Angkor's kings.

The Khmer Rouge under Pol Pot, who overthrew the government and took control of Cambodia in 1975, also saw themselves as heirs to Angkor. They initiated a new order under a revised ritualized ideology of Marxism and undertook projects throughout the region. Renaming their new nation-state Kampuchea to distinguish it from French colonial Cambodia, they modified the state flag by adding the Marxist star to the projection of Angkor Wat on a red background. The state flag of today's Khmer Republic continues to acknowledge its Angkor roots: it is a red flag with Angkor Wat as its centerpiece, minus the Marxist star.

During the 1990s, Indonesians, Japanese, Americans, French, and other Europeans participated in Angkor's restoration. Continuing the colonial-era theory of Javanese influence in Angkor, the Ecole Francaise maintains an active branch in Jakarta, Indonesia, and emphasizes the maritime and cultural relationship between island and mainland civilizations.

Today, Angkor stands as a symbol of Cambodia's successful past. Visited by people from around the world, it has also become a source for valuable international tourist dollars. It is also still an important point of reference in the histories of neighboring Thailand, Laos, and Vietnam. Along with other archaeological treasures of the region, such as Borobudor and Myanmar's Pagan Buddhist complex, Angkor represents the glory of Southeast Asia's past and potential for the renewal of the crosscultural relations and sharing of ideas that were common among precolonial Southeast Asian societies.

development aid. After 1965, Cambodia sold rice to North Vietnam and transported Soviet and Chinese arms from its port of Sihanoukville on the Gulf of Siam. A peasant uprising in 1967 was savagely repressed, and Sihanouk's popularity began to wane; he began to spend much of his time producing and starring in films and traveling abroad. In 1969, the Americans began their so-called secret bombing of Cambodia, in an effort to block the flow of supplies from North to South Vietnam and to disrupt troop sanctuaries. While Sihanouk was out of the country in early 1970, he was deposed by his own army, with American assistance. A new military regime under General Lon Nol took over Cambodia, and in May of that year American and South Vietnamese forces invaded the country and laid waste the border area with Vietnam. Despite these attacks and the repressive efforts of the Lon Nol government, Cambodian Communist insurgents, based in Cambodia's west and north, controlled about two-thirds of the country by the end of 1972.

As the United States began to withdraw from Vietnam in 1973, Cambodia became their target, in a campaign of "carpet-bombing" that in eight months (until it was stopped by Congress) dropped twice the explosive tonnage that was dropped on Japan in the whole of World War II—this on a country with which the United States was not even at war. Phnom Penh, the capital, was hopelessly overcrowded with perhaps 2 million refugees from the bombings. The civilian casualties were enormous, but the effect of the bombing was to further strengthen the Communists, as might have been predicted from experience in Germany and in Vietnam, and to help them recruit more support among the embittered survivors. In 1975, the country was taken over by the Communists, under the leadership of the man who called himself Pol Pot; as Saloth Sar he had given up teaching school at age thirty-two and became a high official in the Cambodian Communist party. His forces, soon to be known around the world as the Khmer Rouge, ordered almost the entire population of Phnom Penh and of the second city, Battambang, probably about 3.5 million altogether, to leave their homes and work indefinitely in the countryside. This was a distorted version of Mao Zedong's antiurban gospel. Maoist and Chinese influences were strong with Pol Pot and the Khmer Rouge.

There was indescribable suffering on the part of these newly created refugees, and mass murder of middle class, professional, and educated people, accurately portrayed in the films *The Killing Fields* and *Swimming to Cambodia,* although they told only a small part of the horror. Others were driven or worked until they died of exhaustion and starvation. Perhaps as many as 4 million Cambodians died in this holocaust in 1975 and four following years, about half of the total population. Cambodia was cut off from all foreign connections or influences, except for China, and cars, libraries, and other "alien" symbols were destroyed. Cambodia too announced a "Great Leap Forward," with much the same consequences in human suffering and economic chaos as in China a decade earlier. Pol Pot's agents continued to torture and murder many thousands, including especially teachers and alleged "counterrevolutionaries" and political opponents whom the paranoid Pol Pot saw everywhere.

By 1978 there was growing opposition to these hideous policies, especially in the eastern areas and with some Vietnamese support. Early in 1979 the Vietnamese army intervened, meeting no resistance outside of the retreating Khmer Rouge forces, which holed up in forest sanctuaries along the north and west Thai border. A pro-Vietnamese government was installed at Phnom Penh as the People's Republic of Kampuchea. The United States, China, and Thailand, all implacable enemies of Vietnam, recognized, supported, and continued to send arms to the Khmer Rouge and Pol Pot, on the theory that "the enemy of my enemy is my friend." Pol Pot's murderous government continued to represent Cambodia, or Kampuchea, in the United Nations. Under these circumstances and with sanctuaries across the Thai border, the Khmer Rouge held on and could not be eliminated by the Vietnamese. Under international pressure, and with the hope of restoring relations with the United States in particular, the Vietnamese withdrew their forces in 1989. American policy began slowly to move away from total anti-Vietnam hostility and vindictiveness, but China especially remained adamant.

In 1979, to "punish" Vietnam for its intervention in Cambodia, China had invaded its northern provinces in a brief campaign in which the Vietnamese again proved their ability to defeat their ancient antagonist, and without pulling troops back from Cambodia. There were heavy losses on both sides, but the Chinese soon withdrew. After the Vietnamese left Cambodia in 1989, the Khmer Rouge greatly expanded the area it controlled and even threatened the cities, still abetted and supplied primarily by China and, some say, covertly by the U.S. CIA. For nearly two decades Cambodia was a bloody battleground, and its future remained dark while it continued to be used as a pawn in wider power struggles. But by 1991 official American opinion was at last edging away from support of Pol Pot, who announced his official "retirement." In July 1991, at a meeting in Beijing, the Chinese, Vietnamese, and the Cambodian factions finally agreed to a Cambodian National Council headed by Sihanouk that would organize national elections in which the Khmer Rouge would take part together with the other Cambodian factions. The United Nations was to supervise a cease-fire and try to stop arms shipments. For the first time since 1973, Cambodia's long nightmare seemed to be approaching its end, but the Khmer Rouge remained an important player. As of 2005 there are hopeful signs that Cambodia's political future will finally stabilize. In late 2004, longtime king Norodom Sihanouk retired in favor of his son Norodom Sihamoni and a coalition government formed in 2003 following UN-sanctioned national elections and headed by Communist Prime Minister Hun Sen, who originally came to power after the Vietnamese invasion of 1978 deposed the Khmer Rouge.

Laos: The Forgotten Country

In tiny, mountainous, and isolated Laos too there has been little peace since 1945. After the end of the Japanese occupation, chronic internal struggles ended in the emergence of a Communist government in 1975, still with its capital at the old base of Vientiane. American aid to non-Communist groups in the 1950s and 1960s had little effect, and successive governments largely ignored the problems of the rural areas, where most Lao lived. By 1963, Laos was engulfed in a bloody civil war. Vietnamese support for the Communists and their use of Lao territory along the frontier as part of their supply route to the south led to massive and immensely destructive American bombing of Laos, producing uncounted casualties and nearly 1 million refugees. Communists in the then coalition government in Vientiane gained new strength from this example of "capitalist-imperialist aggression" and took over in 1975. The Vietnamese were confirmed as an ally, with a strong influence on Laos. Many Lao, especially the educated elite, and many minority tribespeople such as the Hmong, fled to Thailand or the West to escape collectivization and "reeducation," although the government's policies were far from being as severe as in Cambodia. But Laos, a poor country to begin with, still suffered from the destruction of chronic warfare and from its use as a pawn in contests between outside powers. Currently, however, as a member of the Association of Southeast Asian Nations (ASEAN), Laos is beginning to emerge from its dormancy and has been the focus of Chinese as well as Thai interest in building dams in the Mekong River basin and in the Laos highlands, which could provide vital hydroelectric power to the adjacent regions of Southeast Asia and southern China.

Burma, Thailand, Malaya, and Singapore

The rest of mainland Southeast Asia has had a varied history since 1945. Only Burma has failed to win internal order or benefit from rapid economic growth, while Thailand, Malaysia, and Singapore have been among the most rapidly growing economies in the world.

Burma

The Japanese at first used a few Burmese anticolonialists in their campaign against the Indian and British troops and allowed the organization of a small Burma Independence Army. But once the campaign was over, it was largely demobilized in July 1942, and the remnant was referred to simply as a defense force. The Japanese permitted a show of participation in administration by Burmese, but that did not prevent the drafting of forced labor. Underground resistance spread, and as Indian and British troops advanced south in 1944 and 1945, many Burmese cooperated with them and fought the Japanese. Many politically conscious Burmese had joined an Anti-Fascist People's Freedom League (AFPFL), led by Aung San. The British effort to resume colonial control and delay the granting of independence led to demonstrations and strikes organized by the AFPFL, and it was finally agreed that independence would follow national elections. The AFPFL dominated the voting, and Burma won its independence in January 1948, six months after India.

Meanwhile, Aung San, the chief Burmese political figure, was assassinated by conservative opponents in mid-1947, together with seven of his close associates; the AFPFL vice president U Nu became the first independent premier in 1948. But the death of Aung San had removed the only figure who could command the support of most Burmese and of the non-Burman minority groups who lived in the hills and mountains surrounding the Irrawaddy Plain, most importantly Shans, Karens, and Kachins. The colonial government had protected these major ethnic minorities, who feared a reassertion of Burman dominance when the British withdrew, and many of them were Christians. Communist groups also opposed the U Nu government, and chronic rebellion soon broke out. By 1949 the government controlled only the cities, and fighting often occurred in the suburbs of Rangoon. Slowly the government gained the ascendancy, holding new elections in 1951, but it was never able to put down rebellion in the remoter mountain districts. Both the AFPFL and the varied opposition groups were split; Burma made little or no economic progress as the central government was increasingly paralyzed by divisions and bureaucratic ineptitude. U Nu was an interesting charismatic figure, a devout Buddhist who disliked both violent and nonviolent conflict and who periodically retired to a monastery "to keep his vision clear." His wing of the AFPFL, the Union party, won a strong majority in the elections of 1960, but his authority and that of the government continued to deteriorate because it lacked an institutional or adequate political base. In 1962, the army general Ne Win seized power. U Nu fled into exile, and Ne Win suspended the constitution and imprisoned most of the remaining political opponents under the auspices of a "revolutionary council," staffed mainly by military men.

Under the banner of "the Burmese way to socialism," the council nationalized all foreign and major domestic firms, expelled the several thousand Indians remaining in the country, monopolized all internal and external trade, and progressively cut Burma's ties with the outside world. The "Burmese way" was a strange mixture of Marxism-Leninism, Buddhism, and Burmese traditionalism, which condemned greed and claimed to further the cultivation of spiritual values. In fact, Burma became a police state; student and worker demonstrations were harshly suppressed, and troops fired on unarmed demonstrators. Education at all levels was suspect and declining, and foreign or even domestic books were hard to find. The economy slowed even more, and there was much unemployment, especially among educated groups. Armed rebellion continued in the north, especially among the Karens and the Kachins, the latter periodically allied with the Burma Communist party. The Shan states were virtually autonomous, financed by their control of the lucrative opium and heroin trade in Burma's northeast, which comprises a significant sector of what is called the Asian "Golden Triangle," including sections of northern Thailand and China's Yunnan province.

It was reasonable for Burma to avoid alignments with any of the major powers and hence to avoid being drawn into wider conflicts, but in other terms its self-imposed isolation from the rest of the world, including its refusal to allow foreign investment and imported goods and technology, cost it dearly economically and further weakened its schools and universities. A vigorous black market in imported goods developed, basic services deteriorated, especially in increasingly tattered Rangoon, and tourist visas for foreigners were limited to one week. The patient, gentle Burmese still smiled, and of course there were nonmaterial rewards in preserving tradition against the avalanche of modernization elsewhere in the world, but life was hard for many. Burma turned its back on "progress," a path that pluses and minuses. Peasants were less severely affected and, where the civil war did not spread, were able to preserve their traditional way of life, but the slow or stagnant pace of agricultural development left them little if any better off, and there were occasional food shortages as the population continued to grow. Ne Win hung onto power despite cosmetic gestures about retiring, and in 1989 the military government changed the spelling of the country's name to Myanmar, linguistically and phonetically equivalent to Burma. In May 1990 elections in which opposition parties were permitted to compete produced a sweeping victory for the National League for Democracy, a socialist party headed by Aung San's daughter, Suu Kyi, who had been under house arrest for the previous year. The government was clearly taken aback by the vote; in early 1991 it outlawed the National League.

Buddhist Burma: a monk with shaved head and yellow robe in the courtyard of the Shwedagon pagoda in Rangoon. (Jean-Claude Lejeune)

But in October Suu Kyi was awarded the Nobel Peace prize; the government continued to stall and kept her still a prisoner, despite Ne Win's death in 2002. The military government stayed in power, as what they called the State Law and Order Committee (SLORC), and continued its all-out war against the Karens in the hilly northeast, while turning a blind eye to, and profiting from the opium trade in the Golden Triangle between Burma and northeast Thailand, a business from which the Thais also profited.

Thailand

The Thais were fortunate in having few ethnic minorities within their borders except for the Chinese immigrants, who for the most part had peacefully assimilated into the larger society. Forced collaboration with the

Japanese had saved the country from the destruction suffered by most of the rest of Southeast Asia, but the immediate postwar government proved ineffective and unpopular. A military group seized power in 1947 with a generally conservative policy, sending troops to fight in the Korean War and attempting to build American favor and support. The growing success of the Viet Minh in Vietnam helped to ensure such an outcome as Thailand became an American supply base, but the military government's repressive domestic actions led to its overthrow in a 1957 coup. For a brief period there was a parliamentary government, but the army found it "indecisive," and military rule was reimposed in 1958. Once again opposition groups were suppressed, but the new government, under General Sarit, built wide political support by effectively promoting economic development and education.

Thailand remained at least nominally a monarchy despite the reforms of 1932, but General Sarit encouraged the king to play a more active role in public life, and the monarchy became a popular focus for Thai nationalism. Sarit died prematurely in 1963, but by then the Vietnam War had become the country's major concern. Thailand gradually became an increasingly open ally of the United States in its effort to defeat the Viet Cong. Vietnam was feared for its past history of expansion and its ambition to dominate Cambodia and Laos, Thailand's immediate neighbors, which had been detached from the Thai sphere by the French. Thai troops fought under the Americans in Vietnam, and U.S. air bases in Thailand were of major importance. A total of 40,000 American military personnel were stationed in Thailand, which was heavily used for troops on leave. With the influx of American dollars, the economy prospered, much as Japan had benefited from being used as a supply base in the Korean War. Bangkok was the chief beneficiary, but there were also U.S. bases upcountry; provincial towns grew too, and national economic growth soared. The government sponsored extensive development projects in the northeast, in the provinces bordering Laos and Cambodia. But there were rebellions there, fueled by poverty and organized by the small Thai Communist party. After a brief revival in 1968, the constitution was again abrogated in 1971 by a military coup. Protests and demonstrations against the government mounted, especially among students in Bangkok. Due to the intervention of the Thai monarch Phumiphon Adunyadet, the first instance that a Thai king had taken a direct role in Thai politics since the absolute monarchy was deposed in 1932, in 1973 General Thanom was forced to flee the country, and a civilian government came to power.

But it proved difficult to satisfy all of the now vocal and periodically violent protestors, demonstrating for a more genuinely democratic government. In 1976 troops, police, and vigilantes went on a veritable orgy of violence against rioters at Thammasat University in Bangkok, lynching, beating, burning, and shooting scores of protesting students. Shortly thereafter the army moved in again, and the military ruled the country for most of the ensuing decade. A brief period of elected government in the 1980s was ended by another military coup early in 1991. Dissent was repressed, but Thai society had been transformed by economic development. Bangkok had become a huge, overcrowded city of industry and trade, with a burgeoning new middle class. Elsewhere, development meant that by 1990 most Thais were no longer farmers but industrial or transport workers, bureaucrats, or businesspeople. Successive government investments in education had also created a very large new group of well-educated people, including 2 million university graduates. Subsequently a new civilian constitutional government took power in the 1990s and the Thai economy boomed, until 1998 when the Asia-wide financial crisis hit Thailand especially hard, due to substantial overspeculation in real estate and other opportunistic developmental schemes. Since 2001, when Prime Minister Thaksin Chinnawat took office, Thailand has significantly rebounded under a civilian government that has broad popular support. Above all, Thaksin's direct involvement in managing Thai monetary policy has allowed him to balance the interests of Thailand's traditionally uncompromising rural and urban political factions. But Thailand's prime minister has been less successful in negating the terrorist attacks of rural Islamic fundamentalists living in southern Thailand, who feel isolated from and threatened by Thailand's rapid secularization.

Malaya and Singapore

Malaya, like Burma, had suffered brutal Japanese invasion and occupation. The Chinese of Malaya especially joined the underground resistance, while many Malays became collaborators, in part because the Japanese were not as brutal to them as to the Chinese. Chinese were nearly two-fifths of the total population, not counting dominantly Chinese Singapore, and the arrangements for the independence of Malaya, which all parties agreed was appropriate, were long delayed as Malay and Chinese groups worked out their compromises. Meanwhile, the Malay Communist party, largely Chinese, resorted to armed insurrection in mid-1948. The battle of the colonial government against what was called The Emergency lasted nearly ten years. The Communist guerrillas holed up in the jungles saw their numbers and support dwindle after 1950, in part because general prosperity deprived their somewhat vague radical program of much of its appeal. The

Emergency heightened anti-Chinese feeling; many Chinese were forcibly resettled in fortified villages so they could not support the guerrillas, and about 10,000 Chinese were deported to China.

The most effective counter to the guerrilla opposition was, however, speedy progress toward independence and general prosperity. A coalition of Malay and Chinese political organizations won nearly all the seats in a Legislative Council elected in 1955 and worked out the details of an independence agreement with the British that took effect in August of 1957. Malays were given the dominant position in the new state, including a virtual monopoly of political office, the civil service, and university education, while the Chinese were to continue their dominance of the economy. A group of wealthy Chinese then founded a Chinese university in Penang. Efforts were made to rediscover and revitalize traditional Malay culture, long in eclipse under colonial influence, but entrepreneurial activity had never been an important part of that culture, and foreigners, including Portuguese, Indians, Indonesians, Arabs, and British, as well as Chinese, had for centuries managed most of Malaya's trade and commercial sectors. The new government also made successful efforts to diversify an economy that was too heavily dependent on exports of rubber and tin and developed important production of palm oil and timber for world markets.

Singapore had been left out of the new Malayan state, mainly because the Malays feared to add still more to the Chinese share of the population, which would then have been almost equally balanced between Chinese and Malay. But the economic logic of union was powerful, and in 1963 Singapore joined Malaya, only to be ejected again by the Malayan government in 1965 on the same old communal grounds. The brief union with Singapore also included the former British colonial territories along the north coast of Borneo, never controlled by the Dutch and, hence, not part of Indonesia. (The tiny sultanate of Brunei became independent and rocketed to wealth when rich oil deposits were discovered there.) There had been heavy Chinese settlement in north Borneo too, especially in Sarawak and Sabah and in the commercial towns and cities on the coast, but they remained a large minority, outnumbered by a great variety of indigenous peoples. There were also many Malays, so that in balance incorporating these areas into what was now called the state of Malaysia would strengthen the Malay and non-Chinese share of the total population.

Nevertheless, bitterness and periodic conflict continued to divide Malays and Chinese, and there were outbreaks of violence in which hundreds, mainly Chinese, were killed. Chinese were about 32 percent of the Malaysian population, Malays about 47 percent, and the balance was split among Indians and other smaller ethnic groups. Although only about 60 percent of the people were Muslims, Islam was the official state religion, and now it became even more a Malay nationalist and communal badge. In the later 1980s the government began to put pressure on non-Muslims and to press for an orthodox Islamic line in all things, attempting to limit or emasculate even traditional Malay art, literature, and music. Although there continued to be violent Malay-Chinese clashes, Malaysia did very well economically, and the parliamentary system, with minimal Chinese representation, proved stable, unlike those in Thailand or Burma. The one-party-dominant leadership of the United Malay National Organization (UMNO) has been in power since 1974. Under the long-time leadership UMNO Prime Minister Mahathir Mohammad (1981–2004), the UMNO was able to create a middle-of-the road "civil Islamic state," which has neutralized eastern Malaysia's rural fundamentalists while defending the secularism necessary to allow Malaysia's west coast-centered economy to prosper. By the 1990s, Malaysia had an expansive industrial sector that specialized in the assembly of high-tech electronic products and other consumer goods, and those of Malay ethnicity began to balance Chinese entrepreneurs. Perhaps the most spectacular statements of Malaysia's modernity are the twin Petronas Towers, modern skyscrapers that provide a striking contrast to Kuala Lumpur's elegant colonial architecture. Mahathir Mohammad's hand-picked successor, Abdullah Ahmad Badawi won by a landslide in March 2004.

Singapore became a striking success story economically, thanks largely to its dominantly Chinese population and the entrepreneurial skills of its Indian minority, as well as its duty-free port status as a small city-state, a parallel to Hong Kong. Separated from Malaysia in 1965, it went on to achieve a very high economic growth rate, serving as an entrepôt, processing, servicing, and financial center for much of Malaysia and Indonesia. The forms of parliamentary democracy and courts were preserved, but the government remained dominated by its vigorous and strongly conservative British-educated prime minister, Lee Kuan Yew. He tolerated no opposition or criticism, censored the press, and enforced law and order according to his own views. There was no significant political opposition in what became a one-party—i.e., the People's Action Party (PAP)—as well as virtually a one-man state. Under longtime prime minister Lee Kuan Yew's paternalistic leadership, electronics and other light manufacturing joined earlier processing industries, and Singapore became a major banking as well as trade center. Most Singaporeans were prosperous, and indeed their living standards were second in Asia only to Japan, far ahead of the rest of Southeast Asia. The government also invested in public housing and maintained an enviable range of social services as well as a highly developed education system, a traditional Chinese priority. It was a bargain that most Singaporeans found attractive, economic security for nearly all, affluence for many, in exchange for some losses in free expression and personal liberties. In 2003 Lee made a gesture of "retiring" but by late 2004 his son and successor Lee Hsien Loong began to loosen some of the earlier authoritarian restrictions.

Indonesia

The East Indies, and Java especially, had suffered under a harsh Japanese occupation, but their invasion had destroyed the Dutch colonial order. The chief Indonesian leaders, Achmed Sukarno and Mohammed Hatta, had actively collaborated with the Japanese but were ineffective in moderating Japanese brutality or preventing the conscription of slave labor, most of whom were worked to their deaths. Sukarno and Hatta announced Indonesia's independence as a republic two days after the Japanese surrender, naming themselves as president and vice president, respectively. But there was no mass base, no organized government, and few Indonesians with any education or administrative experience, thanks to repressive Dutch colonial policies in the past. The Dutch, with British and American support, ill-advisedly tried to reestablish their colonial control. Negotiations with the Indonesian leaders were accompanied by Dutch reoccupation and a "police action," and by 1948 they had regained most of the area of In-

donesia and captured Sukarno and Hatta. But the Indonesians had put together an army, and patriotic youths flocked to it. Their guerrilla actions against the Dutch were increasingly successful. The Americans and the United Nations withdrew their support for the Dutch, and at the end of 1949 the Dutch were obliged to grant full independence.

The former Dutch East Indies, now called Indonesia for the first time, was a hodgepodge of different ethnic, religious, and linguistic groups with no common tradition except oppression by the Dutch and no experience of working together, still less of sharing a state. The territory was scattered over some 3,000 separate islands stretched along more than 3,000 miles. About 3 percent of the population was Chinese, concentrated in the cities and dominating the commercial sector and the export trade. In the rural areas, local hereditary elites and village chiefs retained their power and often ignored the dictates of the new central government based in Jakarta, the former Dutch colonial capital of Batavia. There was also deep resentment in the outer islands against the dominance of Java, traditionally the major power center as well as the richest and by far the most populous area. Christianity had spread widely in many of the outer islands, promoted both by Portuguese and Dutch missionaries, and this increased resentment of largely Muslim Java; Bali remained Hindu and Buddhist, a survival of earlier Indian influence that had also covered most of Java until the seventeenth century.

The Javanese language was foreign to the rest of the new Indonesia, which contained a great variety of other tongues. The new government created a new national

Indonesian rice fields, Sumatra. Rice remains the major crop of lowland Southeast Asia, and much of Java and Bali resemble this scene, as do the lowland rice-growing areas of Burma, Thailand, Vietnam, Malaysia, and the Philippines. (Henri Cartier-Bresson/Magnum Photos)

Indonesian Nationalism

Sutan Sjahrir (1909–1966) was one of the major leaders of the Indonesian nationalist movement. He studied for a time in Holland and married a Dutch woman. Here are some passages from his book, Out of Exile, *written after the Dutch had banished him and exiled him to New Guinea.*

> The number of intellectuals in my country is very small, and the few there are do not share a single outlook or culture. They are only beginning to seek a form and unity. . . . There has been no spiritual or cultural life, and no intellectual progress for centuries. . . . A feudal culture cannot possibly provide a dynamic fulcrum for people of the twentieth century. . . . In substance, we can never accept the essential difference between the East and the West, because for our spiritual needs we are in general dependent on the West, not only scientifically but culturally. We intellectuals here are much closer to Europe or America than we are to Borobodur or [the] Mahabharata or to the primitive Islamic culture of Java and Sumatra. Which is our basis: the West, or the rudiments of feudal culture that are still to be found in our Eastern society?

Source: S. Sjahrir and C. Wolf, *Out of Exile* (New York, John Day, 1949), pp. 66–68.

language, Bahasa Indonesian, based largely on Malay, which had long been a widespread trade language and lingua franca. It differed basically from Javanese and from the other languages of the outer areas but was taught in all schools and used in all government business so that most Indonesians slowly became bilingual, retaining their own local languages among themselves. In time, the Indonesian language-based education system and the preference for the language in the public sector was important in linking Indonesia's diverse populations, and today's generation regards Indonesian as their primary language.

The new government understandably had trouble establishing its authority and managing the economy after the devastation caused by both the Japanese and the Dutch. As the Dutch withdrew, there were far too few Indonesians who had the technical competence or experience to administer the basic infrastructure of transport, industry, and finance. By 1957 the effort to establish parliamentary rule collapsed, and there was widespread rebellion. The army took power, and in 1959 Sukarno reemerged as head of state in alliance with the Indonesian Communist party and the army under the banner of "guided democracy." To divert attention from the seriously deteriorating economy and runaway inflation, Sukarno campaigned successfully to recover the western half of New Guinea, which he renamed West Irian, from Dutch control. He then engaged in a con-

frontation with the new state of Malaysia over the status of several small islands that lay between them. His Communist allies began to push radical land reform and rent reduction, alarming many of the traditional local elites. Then in 1965 a group of junior officers assassinated six senior generals in an attempted coup, claiming Sukarno's leadership. The coup was officially interpreted as a Communist plot to seize power, although the evidence for that is poor. It was quickly suppressed by General Suharto. The army, aided by bands of youths and local mobs and supported by the American CIA, then went on to wipe out the Indonesian Communist party and all who were suspected of sympathy with it. The victims included many thousands of Chinese, who were suspected because China had gone Communist, but were also turned on as targets for long-standing ethnic resentment against them as alien exploiters. In this horrendous bloodbath, anywhere from 500,000 to 1 million unresisting people were killed. Sukarno was forced into retirement, and General Suharto took over.

Suharto's New Order regime successfully sought foreign economic aid and investments, and slowly began to rebuild the shattered economy. In 1968 he was elected president and confirmed with respectable majorities in subsequent stage-managed elections in which it was predetermined that he would win, and that the candidates of Suharto's Golkar party would win a legislative majority. Despite this show of democratic procedures,

Sukarno, in a characteristic pose, announcing the end of the struggle against the Dutch, in 1950. (UN/DPI)

Indonesia remained a police state under Suharto, suppressing free expression, jailing or torturing dissidents, including even major writers, and operating a brutal police system. Suharto ruled virtually as a dictator. He also invaded East Timor, an island in easternmost Indonesia, when the Portuguese withdrew in 1977 and cruelly suppressed the nationalist movement there. Bloody repression in East Timor continued, with police and army units killing many thousands of unarmed demonstrators, some say well over 200,000. Finally, in 2002, East Timor became independent, as the newest world nation, its viability strengthened by recently discovered oil under the East Timor Sea. Suharto built further close ties with the United States and Japan, encouraged investment by multinationals, and eased the way for large Indonesian-Chinese businesses by providing Indonesian "partners" with payoffs. Bribery became even more widespread, but the economy began to recover, and in many years it posted very high growth rates. Indonesian Chinese were still resented, and the government forbade the use of Chinese language or even the import of books in Chinese. While profiting from Chinese commercial skills, the government continued to discriminate against them and prevent their assimilation into what was already a multiethnic society. The Chinese had little choice but to stick to their own communities and to retain their traditional culture. A new bureaucratic, if not commercial, Indonesian middle class began to grow, nourished by the huge government bureaucracy and by considerable corruption, and there began to be a number of Indonesian professionals as well. Oil production from Java, Sumatra, and South Borneo (Kalimantan) was increased under the government monopoly firm Pertamina, providing an augmented boost to the economy.

But most Indonesians remained poor as population continued to grow rapidly. After about 1970 economic growth was substantial, but it was not equitably distributed. This was especially evident in the burgeoning urban slums and squatter towns and among the poor peasants, still the great rural majority, while landowners enjoyed relative prosperity. Public health measures became more effective and widespread, but this lowered the death rate and added more mouths to feed each year. Education was strictly controlled, but the level and extent of literacy gradually rose. Java had become dependent on food imports under the Dutch plantation system centered on cash and nonfood crops, but in the 1980s there were determined government efforts to increase rice production using better seeds and high-yielding crop strains. However, such measures also required heavy investment in fertilizers and irrigation, which only the richer peasants or landowners could afford. Many poor and landless peasants migrated to the already overcrowded cities, especially Jakarta, to seek work as scavengers, street vendors, or prostitutes. Vast urban squatter encampments mushroomed at the outskirts. But the disastrous decline of the Sukarno years was reversed, and as economic growth continued there was some hope that the rising tide might in time lift all boats, or at least most of them, and that this might also bring new support for a return to a more democratic system.

Widespread riots in 1998 led to the resignation of President Suharto, who was succeeded by his vice president B. J. Habibie; he agreed to hold elections in the following year, as Indonesians hoped that genuine democracy would emerge. Meanwhile the Indonesian economy was in deep trouble and corruption reached new heights, with Suharto and his family heading the list.

The elections brought in Abdurrahman Wahid as president and Megawatti Sukarno (Sukarno's daughter) as vice-president, but increasingly in 2001 Wahid was under fire for corruption and incompetence, and civil order was rapidly deteriorating. In July of 2001 Wahid was impeached and Megawatti Sukarno became president. There were attacks on Christians and their churches in eastern Indonesia and some counterviolence. In general, this vast country, so split by regional cultural differences, seemed to be on the verge of falling apart. Under Megawati's leadership, the situation stabilized, but she was widely perceived to be a figurehead rather than the embodiment of her father, as she allowed bureaucratic, commercial, and military supporters and their international business partners the opportunity to consolidate their special interests. The 2004 elections were notable in that they were universally peaceful, with the absence of paramilitary groups that had been highly visible participants in the 1999 general elections. Running a campaign that focused on Megawati's failure to fulfill Indonesians' expectations for the post-Suharto era, Susilo Bambang Yudhoyono (popularly referred to as SBY), a charismatic retired Indonesian army general, was elected Indonesia's new president in October 2004.

The Philippines

During the war most Filipino politicians collaborated with the Japanese, but most Filipinos supported or joined the resistance forces, and many died in guerrilla actions or at the hands of the Japanese military police. Anti-Japanese struggles were also mixed with peasant struggles against the rampant landlordism that had thrived under American colonialism. The Hukbalahap (People's Anti-Japanese Army) was involved with both, mainly in central Luzon, the main island of the Philippine archipelago, where they benefited from the disruption of the war and occupation and attracted many supporters. Most of the politicians who had collaborated with the Japanese had returned to public life and public office by 1948. The granting of independence in 1946, as promised before the war, was welcome, but Filipino gratitude was heavily mixed with resentment about the niggardly American aid, the special American property and trade concessions, and the huge military bases at Clark Field and Subic Bay. As Communism triumphed in China and Vietnam and appeared to threaten Malaya, Cambodia, and Laos, the Americans became fearful for the Philippines and lined up in support of successive conservative governments after 1946, no longer troubled that the people in power were in many cases the same as those who had welcomed the Japanese. Filipinos admired and copied much of American culture, including baseball, and blended it with their Spanish colonial heritage to make a kind of Latin American parallel. As one often-quoted remark states, Philippine culture was the result of 350 years in a Catholic convent and half a century in Hollywood.

Corruption became a trademark of Philippine politics, and the government was unable to control destructive inflation, rebuild the shattered economy, or defeat the Huks. By 1950 the country was in crisis on all these fronts. But the elections of 1953 brought to power a different kind of politician, Ramon Magsaysay, who as secretary of defense had earlier reorganized the army. He assembled around him a group of intelligent and dedicated younger men. In a relatively short time he put down the Huk rebellion and began land reform in the areas of their earlier support, thus easing the burdens of tenancy and helping to cut the ground out from under Communist appeals. Unfortunately, he was killed in a plane crash in 1957; some said it was not an accident. Successive members of the old conservative political elite restored the former oligarchy, which was dependent on family ties, corruption, and even violence; economic development for the masses languished while the few at the top earned new wealth. Magsaysay's early efforts at land reform were shelved, especially as rich landowners were an important political support for those in power. Multinationals were encouraged to invest in the Philippines, and there was some new economic growth, but its benefits were not widely shared. Manila boomed, American style, but its slums and shanty towns grew at least as fast.

Ferdinand Marcos, a former senator, was elected president in 1965 and reelected in 1969. By now the flow of new American investment had begun to create a period of prosperity for a few, but Marcos thought that democracy was inefficient, wasteful, and in the Philippine case especially, corrupt. He pushed instead for what he called "constitutional authoritarianism" and in 1972 declared martial law, but without making it very clear on what grounds. It soon became clear that his aim was to wipe out all forms of opposition and dissent. The press was controlled, many thousands were arrested, jailed, and tortured, normal legal procedures were suspended, and the army was built up, all because of the danger of a "Communist takeover." Marcos's power was already being challenged by other members of the old oligarchy, especially the Lopez family, owners of the daily *Manila Chronicle* and television stations. In 1973 Marcos pushed through a new constitution, rigged the courts, and proclaimed the New Society. An engineered referendum authorized him to continue indefinitely as president, and another to be both president and prime minister. An election in 1978, with widespread fraud, voted in a compliant national assembly that rubber-stamped his actions. Government became even more

Revolutionary Filipino Ideas

Louis Taruc (born 1913) became a Communist and then the head of the Hukbalahap, a guerrilla group that fought against the Japanese occupation and, after the war, against the independent Filipino government. Here are some passages from his Born of the People.

For over half a century the Philippines has become largely the private landed estate of a handful of big business men who live ten thousand miles away in the United States. . . . To guarantee their profits, American imperialism has kept us a backward, colonial people, with the majority living in the misery of poverty and ignorance. . . . It has claimed that it trained us in the ways of democratic government, but today [1949] the most corrupt regime in our history, with American approval, massacres the people. . . . The Filipino moves about in an American-made world. The clothes he wears, the cigarettes he smokes, the canned food he eats, the music he hears, the news of the world he reads are all American. . . . The Americans solved their problem by getting Filipinos to rule for them . . . the landlord-*ilustrado* class, the landed gentry . . . they were an integral part of the new American pattern of rule.

Source: L. Taruc, *Born of the People* (Manila: International Publishers, 1953), pp. 265–271, 274–275.

dominated by cronyism and associated corruption, most of all by Marcos and his wife, Imelda.

All of these flagrant abuses, and the neglect of rural areas and the worsening plight of most Filipinos, understandably provoked both resentment and rebellion. The Philippines are predominantly Catholic, but in the southern island of Mindanao, the Muslim Moro people joined an armed rebellion. Marcos was able to buy off some of the leaders and the rebellion remained relatively small and local. Elsewhere, a reorganized Communist party formed a radical guerrilla wing called the New People's Army, which attracted growing numbers of supporters especially in Luzon, which included the old Huk territory. In 1981 Marcos made a pretense of ending martial law, in deference to worldwide criticism. But his policies and actions remained largely unchanged, except that he now permitted a somewhat freer press and pointed to it as evidence that he presided over a genuine democracy. In fact his power over all dissent was as great as ever, and many of those who spoke out or tried to oppose him continued to be jailed, tortured, or shot, or they simply disappeared. In 1983 this included his chief political opponent, Benigno Aquino, who had been released from jail and exiled to the United States, and was shot down as he disembarked from his plane at the Manila Airport when he

tried to return. This blatant action began to turn Filipino opinion against Marcos and his wife, Imelda, whom many feared would succeed him. Many wealthy Filipinos fled the country, taking their capital with them; this contributed to a general economic collapse and uncontrolled inflation. Despite extensive vote buying, intimidation, and other fraud, the elections of 1986, called by an overconfident Marcos, ended in his defeat and the victory of Corazon Aquino, Benigno's widow. Marcos claimed that he had won and clearly intended to hang on, but a faction of the army deserted his cause and refused to fire on the crowds of demonstrators demanding that he leave, in what was popularly called the People's Power movement. In the United States, the Reagan administration, having long supported Marcos and even praised him as a "great democrat," now persuaded him to emigrate to the United States, where he died in 1989.

Aquino inherited an impoverished, ravished, and bankrupt country, still dominated by a few rich and powerful families and their political networks and by a large and powerful army. She was not able to break her ties with either of these groups and, indeed, depended on them. She herself came from a rich, landed family, the great-granddaughter of a Chinese immigrant who had prospered as a trader and sugar grower, and she necessarily operated as president in the long Filipino

Ayala Triangle in Manila, a scene typical of developing urban Southeast Asia. (Jose Fuste Raga/CORBIS)

tradition of family politics. She survived six army rebellions, the most serious in 1989, but was unable or perhaps in part unwilling to push for the kinds of basic change the Philippines needed if it were to escape from mass poverty for most, corrupt privilege and wealth for a few, and a political system notorious for its cronyism and inefficiency. She chose not to run for reelection in 1992, when Fidel Ramos succeeded her. By 1995, Ramos had made commendable progress in containing rebellion and attacking corruption and had begun to stimulate healthier economic growth. Ramos was defeated in the elections of 1998 by former film star Joseph Estrada, but there was no marked change as a result. He was jailed for corruption, and succeeded by Gloria Arroyo—yet another woman assuming power in a Southeast Asian country. For most Filipinos, gross inequality and poverty remain the major problems for the future.

In 1991 Mt. Pintatubo erupted in a violent explosion that engulfed the American bases at Clark Field and Subic Bay with dense clouds of ash and lava flows. This brought the abandonment of both bases, which most Filipinos welcomed. But most Filipinos remained poor, as the government remained in the hands of a small elite. It is notable that both Indonesia, by far the largest Southeast Asian country, and the Philippines,

the second largest, have been now ruled by women, a reaffirmation of longstanding Southeast Asian values.

Regional Cooperation in ASEAN

The Association of Southeast Asian Nations (ASEAN) was born as the Southeast Asian anti-communist and anti-China alternative to the U.S. dominated SEATO (Southeast Asian Treaty Organization) in 1967. Thailand, Malaysia, Singapore, Indonesia, and the Philippines were charter members; Brunei joined in 1984 after its independence from Britain. From its inception, ASEAN has been more an association than an alliance, whose members meet annually to discuss the politics of the region and the potential for cooperation in promoting regional culture and economics.

From 1978, China's and ASEAN's strategic interests converged. Both pressured the Vietnamese to withdraw their troops from Kampuchea, and ASEAN proposed that thereafter the Cambodian people would determine their political fate in an election supervised by the United Nations. This put ASEAN's membership in the less than desired position of leading the diplomatic offensive to retain the Khmer Rouge government's seat in the United Nations against the Vietnam-backed Phnom Penh-based government. ASEAN's continuing attempts to peacefully resolve the Cambodian question eventually brought a resolution in the 1990s. Subsequently, Vietnam joined ASEAN in 1995, Laos and Burma in 1997, and Cambodia in 1999.

ASEAN's greatest asset is its collective strength to assert Southeast Asia's interests in the global community. During the past decade ASEAN has more aggressively promoted regional economic cooperation. In 1993, its members created the ASEAN Free Trade Area (AFTA), in which all its members would eventually eliminate tariffs on regionally manufactured goods. To enhance ASEAN's position as a competitive production base geared toward servicing the global market, ASEAN countries are encouraged to enhance intraregional trade, pursue national specialties, and collectively solicit capital investments from the outside. To accomplish this, ASEAN has created special Dialogue Partnerships with major Western and Asian nations, including the United States, and maintains advocacy offices in each of these.

ASEAN has also been a major facilitator of cultural and intellectual exchanges, and funds cooperative resource centers that promote the Southeast Asian agenda. It also organizes strategic summit meetings that confront common problems as they occur. A 2002 convocation addressed regional response to the SARS epidemic; 2004 forums developed a policy to combat the spread of a poultry virus among member nations and to solicit member cooperation in an effort to end piracy and smuggling networks in the Straits of Melaka region.

Questions

1. Why was the Korean Yi dynasty so resistant to foreign influences? How did these policies encourage Korean reformers to seek Japanese assistance in the late 1800s? What were the consequences?

2. Why was Japanese rule of Korea so oppressive? What was Japan's specific interest in Korea? How did Japanese rule contribute to the development of a modern Korean economic and social infrastructure? How did Japanese occupation of Korea differ from its rule over Taiwan in the pre-World War II era?

3. Was the Korean War necessary? What has been its legacy in Korea since 1953? Compare and contrast the evolution of South Korea's democracy to that of Communist rule in North Korea. In what ways did Korean society radically change in the 1980s and 1990s? What have been the consequences of the transition from Kim Il Sung to his son Kim Jong Il in North Korea since 1994? What are the prospects of the resolution of hostilities between the two Koreas today?

4. Was the war in Vietnam an international war, a war for independence, or a civil war? Why did the French and then the Americans return to Vietnam after World War II? How has Communist rule of Vietnam changed during the postwar era?

5. Explain the origins of Pol Pot and the Khmer Rouge. Why did the Vietnamese intervene in the late 1970s? What is the aftermath of thirty years of conflict in contemporary Cambodia?

6. Compare and contrast the differences in the development of Burma, Thailand, and Singapore in the post–World War II era. Why has Burma retained its military government while Thailand's democracy has stabilized since the 1990s? How does Singapore's democracy differ from that of the United States? In what ways do all three countries have to respond to clashes or potential clashes between differing ethnic groups?

7. What have been the similarities and differences in the development of Indonesia and the Philippines since World War II? How do both demonstrate the difficulties of ruling over numerous islands that are inhabited by diverse ethnic groups? Is there a case to be made that big, multicultural nation-states—in

contrast to smaller, single-ethnic nation-states—are not necessarily the source of global stability?

Suggested Web Sites

Vietnam

http://www.historyplace.com/unitedstates/vietnam/
A comprehensive site retelling the events leading up to and through the end of the Vietnam War, with a complete timetable, slide show, and a number of links to this period in history.

http://newton.uor.edu/Departments&Programs/ AsianStudiesDept/
Annotated directory of resources on Southeast Asia and Korea.

Country Studies—Southeast Asia and Korea

http://lcweb2.loc.gov/frd/cs/khtoc.html

http://lcweb2.loc.gov/frd/cs/vntoc.html

http://lcweb2.loc.gov/frd/cs/latoc.html

http://lcweb2.loc.gov/frd/cs/thtoc.html

http://lcweb2.loc.gov/frd/cs/kptoc.html

http://lcweb2.loc.gov/frd/cs/krtoc.html

Maps

http://www.lib.utexas.edu/maps/korea.html
This site also accesses maps of other countries of Asia; originally produced by the CIA, from the Perry-Castaneda Library Map Collection.

Suggestions for Further Reading

Korea

Amsden, A. *Asia's New Giant: South Korea and Late Industrialization.* New York: Oxford University Press, 1992.

Bedeski, R. *The Transformation of South Korea.* New York: Routledge, 1994.

Cotton, J., and Neary, I. *The Korean War in History.* London: Humanities Press, 1989.

Cumings, B. *The Origins of the Korean War,* 2 vols. New Haven: Princeton University Press, 1981, 1991.

Cumings, B., and Halliday, J. *Korea: The Unknown War.* New York: Columbia East Asia Institute, 1983.

Deuchler, M. *The Confucian Transformation of Korea.* Cambridge: Harvard University Press, 1993.

Diamond, L., and Kim, B. K. *Consolidating Democracy in South Korea.* Boulder, CO: Lynn Reiner, 2000.

Duus, P. *The Abacus and the Sword: Japanese Penetration of Korea.* Berkeley: University of California Press, 1995.

Eckert, C. J. *Offspring of Empire: The Colonial Origins of Korean Capitalism.* Seattle: University of Washington Press, 1993.

Foot, R. *The Wrong War.* Ithaca, NY: Cornell University Press, 1990.

Gragert, E. H. *Landownership Under Colonial Rule.* Honolulu: University of Hawaii, 1994.

Grinker, R. *Korea and its Futures.* New York: St. Martin's, 1998.

Kim, E. M. *Big Business, Strong State.* Albany: SUNY Press, 2000.

Kim, S. *Korea's Democratization*. Cambridge, England: Cambridge University Press, 2003.

Kong, T. Y. *The Politics of Economic Reform in South Korea*. New York: Routledge, 2000.

Lett, D. P. *In Pursuit of Status: South Korea's New Urban Middle Class*. Cambridge: Harvard University Press, 1998.

Lowe, P. *The Origins of the Korean War*. London: Longmans, 1986.

Macdonald, D. S. *The Koreans*. Boulder, CO: Westview, 1990.

McNamara, D. L. *The Colonial Origins of Korean Enterprise, 1910–1945*. Cambridge, England: Cambridge University Press, 1990.

Nelson, L. C. *Measured Excess: Status, Gender, and Consumer Nationalism in South Korea*. New York: Columbia University Press, 2000.

Palais, J. B. *Politics and Policy in Traditional Korea*. Cambridge: Harvard University Press, 1991.

Stueck, W., *Rethinking the Korean War*. Princeton University Press, 2003.

———. *The Korean War*. Princeton: Princeton University Press, 1996.

Whelan, R. *Drawing the Line: The Korean War, 1950–1953*. New York: Faber and Faber, 1991.

Southeast Asia

Ablin, D. A., and Hood, M., eds. *The Cambodian Agony*. Armonk, NY: M. E. Sharpe, 1987.

Afurza, Z. *Renovating Politics in Contemporary Vietnam*. Boulder, CO: Lynn Reiner, 2001.

Alpert, W. T. *The Vietnamese Economy*. Armonk, NY: M. E. Sharpe, 2004.

Andaya, A. *A History of Malaysia*. London: Macmillan, 1982.

Atkinson, J. M., and Errington, S. *Power and Differences: Gender in Island Southeast Asia*. Stanford: Stanford University Press, 1990.

Bertrand, J. *Nationalism and Ethnic Conflict in Indonesia*. Cambridge, England: Cambridge University Press, 2004.

Broad, R., and Cavanagh, J. *Plundering Paradise: The Struggle for the Environment in the Philippines*. Berkeley: University of California Press, 1993.

Chandler, D. *A History of Cambodia*. Boulder, CO: Westview, 1996.

———. *Voices From S21: Terror and History in Pol Pot's Secret Prison*. Berkeley: University of California Press, 2000.

Flak, C. *Living Silence: Burma Under Military Rule*. New York: St. Martin's, 2001.

Friend, T. *Indonesian Destinies*. Cambridge: Havard University Press, 2003.

Gottesman, E. R. *Cambodia After the Khmer Rouge*. New Haven: Yale University Press, 2003.

Harper, T. *The End of Empire and the Making of Malaya*. Cambridge, England: Cambridge University Press, 1998.

Hawes, G. *The Philippine State and the Marcos Regime*. Ithaca, NY: Cornell University Press, 1988.

Hayslip, L. *When Heaven and Earth Changed Places*. New York: Doubleday, 1989.

Huff, W. G. *The Economic Growth of Singapore*. Cambridge, England: Cambridge University Press, 1995.

Jackson, K. D. *Cambodia, 1975–1978: Rendezvous with Death*. Princeton: Princeton University Press, 1989.

Karnow, S. *In Our Own Image: America's Empire in the Philippines*. New York: Random House, 1989.

Kerkvliet, B. *The Huk Rebellion*. Lanham, MD: Rowan and Littlefield, 2004.

King, D.Y. *Half-Hearted Reform in Indonesia*. Westport, CT: Praeger, 2002.

Kolko, G. *Anatomy of a War*. New York: Random House, 1990.

Larkin, J. *Sugar and the Origins of Modern Philippine Society*. Berkeley: University of California Press, 1993.

Lintner, B. *Burma in Revolt*. Seattle: University of Washington Press, 2000.

Manning, C. and Van Diemen, S. *Indonesia in Tranisition*. New York: St. Martin's, 2000.

Martin, A. *Cambodia*. Berkeley: University of California Press, 1994.

Maung, M. *The Burmese Road to Poverty*. New York: Praeger, 1991.

Osborne, M. *Southeast Asia: An Introductory History*. New York: HarperCollins, 1999.

Owen, N., ed., *The Emergence of Modern Southeast Asia*. Honolulu: University of Hawaii Press, 2005.

Patti, A. L. *Why Vietnam?* Berkeley: University of California Press, 1990.

Pelley, P. M. *Postcolonial Vietnam*. Durham, NC: Duke University Press, 2002.

Regnier, P. *Singapore*. Honolulu: University of Hawaii Press, 1992.

Ricklefs, M. C. *A History of Modern Indonesia*. Stanford: Stanford University Press, 2002.

SarDesai, D. R. *Southeast Asia Past and Present*. Boulder, CO: Westview, 1997.

Sheehan, N. *A Bright Shining Lie*. New York: Random House, 1988.

Steinberg, D. *The Philippines*. Boulder, CO: Westview, 1994.

Tarling, N., ed. *The Cambridge History of Southeast Asia.*, vol. 2. Cambridge, England: Cambridge University Press, 1992.

———. *Nations and States in Southeast Asia*. Cambridge, England: Cambridge University Press, 1998.

Taylor, J. G. *East Timor*. New York: St. Martin's, 2000.

Verma, V. *Malaysia*. Boulder, CO: Lynne Reiner, 2002.

Warner, R. *Shooting at the Moon: America's Clandestine War in Laos*. New York: Steerforth Press, 1997.

Wijeyewardene, G. *Ethnic Groups Across National Boundaries in Mainland Southeast Asia*. Singapore: Institute of Southeast Asian Studies, 1990.

20

South Asia: Independence, Political Division, and Development

The partition of India in 1947 with the creation of Pakistan cost the lives of more than 1 million people and left the Himalayan state of Kashmir as a source of chronic tension. Bangladesh in east Bengal was created in 1971 as a separate Muslim state. In what remained of Pakistan, in the west, military dictatorship alternated with corrupt politics, although there was some economic growth. Sri Lanka (Ceylon until 1975) won independence in 1948 and has done well economically but has been torn by violent terrorism by a Tamil minority and the counteractions of the army. India too has been marred by violence among Hindus, Muslims, and Sikhs. Nehru, India's first prime minister, arranged the federal division of the country into 16 language-based states and saw strong economic growth but was involved in a border conflict with China before his death in 1964.

Nehru's daughter Indira became prime minister and saw India become self-suffcent in food production thanks to the Green Revolution and continued industrial growth, but she mortally offended the Sikhs and was killed by her Sikh guards in 1984. Her son Rajiv succeeded her, but he too was killed by Tamil terrorists. India's war against poverty continues while the growing new middle class prospers. More than half the population live in villages, but even there change is spreading. India has become a world leader in computer technology, and high economic growth rates continue, but its population growth continues too and has overtaken China's. In 1998 the fundamentalist Hindu party of Bharatiya Janata (B.J.P.) won a plurality and kept its pledge to test India's nuclear weapons, to which Pakistan responded in kind, but the B.J.P.'s hold on power was fragile.

Partition and Independence

The Indian subcontinent, known since 1947 as South Asia, is composed of the separate states of Pakistan, India, Bangladesh, Nepal, and Sri Lanka and contains well over 1 billion people, one-fifth of the world's population. Most of it had been administered as a unit by the British, but colonialism died in the ashes of World War II and the British were in any case unwilling to continue their rule of an India determined to regain its freedom. Gandhi, Nehru, and other Indian political leaders had spent most of the war years in jail after they had refused to support the war without a promise of independence. Their example inspired many new followers, and by 1945 the independence movement was clearly too strong to be denied by a Britain now both weakened and weary of colonialism. Churchill, the arch-conservative wartime leader who had been rigidly opposed to Indian independence, was voted out of office. Earlier in the war he had declared "I was not made His Majesty's first minister in order to preside over the liquidation of the British Empire," and he was contemptuous of Gandhi. Lord Wavell, military commander in India and the first postwar viceroy, wrote in his diary: "Churchill hates India and everything to do with it. He

CHRONOLOGY

1947 ■ Jinnah and "direct action"

1947 ■ August 14—Indian independence and partition

1948 ■ Murder of Gandhi

1956 ■ Election of S. W. R. D. Bandaranaike in Sri Lanka

1958–1969 ■ Military takeover in Pakistan

1959 ■ Murder of Bandaranaike; his widow Sirimavo succeeds

1960–2003 ■ Tamil rebels in Sri Lanka; armistice 2003

1962–1964 ■ Brief India-China war over border

1964 ■ Death of Nehru

1971 ■ Independence of Bangladesh

1979 ■ Execution of Z. A. Bhutto in Pakistan

1984 ■ Murder of Indira Gandhi by her Sikh bodyguards

1991 ■ Murder of Rajiv Gandhi by Tamil nationalists

1998 ■ Election of the fundamentalist Hindu Bharatiya Janata party (BJP) in India

1999 ■ Pervez Musharraf takes power in Pakistan

2004 ■ Reelection of Congress party in India; M. M. Singh becomes prime minister

Mohammad Ali Jinnah in 1946. Notice his totally Western dress. (By permission of the British Library)

knows as much of the Indian problem as George III did of the American colonies. . . . He sent me a peevish telegram to ask why Gandhi hadn't died yet."

The new Labour government under Clement Attlee that won the British elections in 1945 moved quickly toward giving India its freedom. Elections were held in India early in 1946, but by then it had become clear that support for a separate state for Muslims had gained strength during and immediately following the war. The Muslim League, the chief vehicle for this movement, had been founded in 1906, but until 1945 it was supported by only a few Muslims, most of whom remained willing to work with and for the Indian National Congress as the main agent of politically conscious Indians. The Muslim League's president, Mohammad Ali Jinnah (1876–1948), had earlier been a member of Congress and was even for a time its president. He and a few other Muslim leaders became dissatisfied with the Congress

plans for a secular independent state that deemphasized religious identity and with the Congress leaders' unwillingness to reserve what Jinnah regarded as adequate positions and representation for Muslims. Hindus and Muslims had lived together peacefully for most of nine centuries, even at the village level. Persian Muslim culture had blended in with indigenous elements to form modern Indian civilization. Both groups were longstanding parts of the Indian fabric. It was hard to see them as irreconcilable.

Jinnah, like Nehru, was British educated. In his earlier career as a British-trained lawyer, he had paid little attention to Islam, and he knew no Urdu, the language of Islam in India. He was contemptuous of the Islamic prohibitions of pork, alcohol, and smoking and the requirements for daily prayers, and lived like a Western-style elitist. He despised Gandhi and his appeal to the poor and downtrodden, across religious lines. But as he saw his political ambitions threatened by the mass success of Gandhi and Nehru, he shifted his allegiance to the Muslim League and began to use it to persuade Muslims that a Hindu-dominated India would never, as he put it, give them "justice." He found support among some of the communal-minded (those who put religious identity above national feeling) and also from Muslim businessmen, especially in the port

Nehru on Nehru

Nehru wrote this of himself while in prison in 1935 for political conspiracy:

> I have become a queer mixture of the East and the West, out of place
> everywhere, at home nowhere. Perhaps my thoughts and approach to life
> are more kin to what is called Western than Eastern, but India clings to me
> as she does to all her children, in innumerable ways. . . . I am a stranger
> and alien in the West. I cannot be of it. But in my own country also,
> sometimes I have an exile's feeling.

*The year after the Amritsar Massacre of 1919, he had visited the Indian countryside for
three days, and during his prison sentence of 1935 he wrote about that experience.*

> [I felt] shame at my own easy going and comfortable life, and our petty
> politics of the city which ignored this vast multitude of seminaked sons
> and daughters of India. . . . A new picture of India seemed to rise before
> me, naked, starving, crushed, and utterly miserable. And their faith in us
> casual visitors from the distant city embarrassed me and filled me with a
> new responsibility that frightened me.

Source: J. Nehru, *An Autobiography* (London: Bodley Head, 1989), pp. 552, 596.

city of Karachi, who saw a possible way of ridding themselves of Hindu competition. Nehru and others insisted that communalism had nothing to do with religion and that the exploitation of religious differences by a few politicians for their own ends fueled communal tensions.

Hindus were often more active and more successful in business than most Muslims. They were generally more educated, and as the great majority in undivided India they also dominated politics and the professions. But they did not generally discriminate against Muslim intellectuals or professionals. Many Muslims, such as Maulana Azad, who became Congress president for nearly six years, were prominent in the independence movement on the Congress side. Some other Muslim political figures, like Jinnah, saw greater opportunity for themselves if they could have their own state and supported the League in its campaign to convince Muslims that "Islam was in danger." When such relatively peaceful tactics did not produce enough result, Jinnah and the League began to promote terror and violence, which Jinnah called "direct action," urging Muslims to demonstrate and to attack Hindus in order to call attention to their cause.

Congress was slow to respond appropriately, or to offer Muslims or the League a larger share in an Indian future. Gandhi and Nehru in particular were reluctant even to consider partitioning India just as it was about to win freedom. This tended to increase the League's

fear of a Hindu threat to Muslims and its resort to tactics of violence. In the later stages of the long negotiations during 1946 and 1947 Jinnah offered to give up the demand for Pakistan (as the separate Muslim state was to be called) if he could be guaranteed the position of first prime minister of independent India. That demand was rejected on principle, and Jinnah remained adamant in insisting on a separate state, of which he could be the head. Successive British representatives tried to work out a solution in sessions with Congress and the League that would hand over independence to an undivided India. But Jinnah was intransigent. He knew by then that he had not long to live (he had been told he was fatally ill, and in fact he died the following year). No agreement was possible. Finally, in early 1947 London sent Lord Louis Mountbatten (1900–1979), the wartime supreme commander in Southeast Asia. He was appointed viceroy of India, with the sole charge of working out the terms for independence as quickly as this could be done.

If independence had been granted, as most Indians and most British at home had wanted, at any time before 1939, the issue of partition would not have arisen. Jinnah was able to use the war years, while the Congress leaders were much of the time in jail, to build his political base and then to spread the fear of cultural engulfment and oppression among his followers. Mountbatten had no power to dictate terms but only to find a workable formula for the handing over of government. Muslim-Hindu

Muslim Solidarity: Jinnah's Call

Jinnah made a number of speeches during World War II in his effort to promote Muslim solidarity and political action. Here are excerpts from a 1943 speech.

> The progress that Muslims, as a nation, have made during these [last] three years is a remarkable fact. . . . Never before has a nation, miscalled a minority, asserted itself so quickly and so effectively. . . . We have created a solidarity of opinion, a union of mind and thought. . . . Let us cooperate with and give all help to our leaders to work for our collective good. Let us make our organization stronger. . . . We, the Muslims, must rely mainly upon our own inherent qualities, our own natural potentialities, our own internal solidarity, and our own united will to face the future. . . . Train yourselves, equip yourselves for the task that lies before us. The final victory depends upon you and is within our grasp. You have performed wonders in the past. You are still capable of repeating history. You are not lacking in the great qualities and virtues in comparison with other nations. Only you have to be fully conscious of that fact and act with courage, faith, and unity.

Source: W. T. de Bary, ed., *Sources of Indian Traditions,* vol. 2 (New York: Columbia University Press, 1964), pp. 286–287.

violence, once stirred up by the Muslim League, acquired its own dreadful momentum on both sides, especially in regions that were nearly evenly divided between the two religious communities, such as Punjab and East Bengal. Mob riots and mass killing spread widely. India was in flames. Although Mountbatten, like Nehru and Gandhi, hoped to avoid handing over power to a divided India, by July he as well as the Congress leaders recognized that partition and the creation of Pakistan were inevitable. Nehru remarked bitterly that "by cutting off the head we will get rid of the headache," while Gandhi continued to regard it as "vivisection."

Partition

Lines were drawn by a British-appointed commission to mark off the predominantly Muslim northwest and western Punjab and the eastern half of Bengal as the two unequal halves of Pakistan, separated from each other by nearly 1,000 miles of Indian territory. At midnight on August 14, 1947, the Republic of India and the Islamic state of Pakistan officially won their independence. Gandhi boycotted the independence day celebrations in New Delhi, going instead to Calcutta to try to quell fresh outbreaks of mass violence there as refugees streamed in from eastern Bengal. The ceremonies in New Delhi and in Karachi, the Pakistan capital, and the

ensuing months were tragically overshadowed by perhaps the greatest mass refugee movement in history, more than 10 million people in 1947 alone. Hindus fled from Pakistan and Muslims from India; about 1 million were victims of mob massacre along the route, helpless pawns of the mass hatred sown by a few ambitious or narrow-minded men. When it was all over, 50 million Muslims continued to live in India much as before, and India still has more Muslims than Pakistan.

For those who chose to migrate to Pakistan, including further millions after 1947, life in the new state was hard in the first chaotic years as Pakistan struggled to cope with the flood of refugees. Hindus remaining in Pakistan soon found that they had little place in an Islamic state that explicitly discriminated against all non-Muslims, and within a few years most of them had migrated to India, depriving Pakistan of many of its more highly educated and experienced people. For the educated elite of both countries, including the army officers who soon faced each other across the new boundaries, partition divided former classmates, friends, and professional colleagues who had shared a common experience, training, and values. The partition lines also split the previously integrated cultural and economic regions of densely populated Punjab and Bengal and caused immense disruption. Since the division was by agreement based solely on religion, nothing was considered except to separate areas with a Muslim majority, often by a thin

Nehru and Mountbatten in New Delhi in 1947. The two men developed an immediate liking for each other, which greatly eased the transition to independence. (Bettmann/Corbis)

margin. Many districts, villages, and towns were nearly evenly balanced between the two religions, which were deeply intertwined over many centuries of coexistence. The partition cut through major road and rail links, divided rural areas from their urban centers, and bisected otherwise uniform regions of culture and language.

The Kashmir Conflict

The still nominally independent native states under their own Indian rulers, comprising nearly half of the subcontinent in area, were technically given the choice to join India or Pakistan, but there was really no choice for the few Muslim-ruled states or smaller Muslim-majority areas surrounded by Indian territory, which were absorbed or taken over, including the large state of Hyderabad in the Deccan, Muslim-ruled but with a Hindu majority. The Princely State of Kashmir, with a Muslim majority but under a Hindu ruler, lay geographically between the two rivals and also had its own hopes for independence. The ruler, Hari Singh, delayed his decision until his state was invaded by "volunteer" forces from Pakistan; he agreed to join India in return for military help. Indian paratroops arrived just in time to hold Srinagar, the capital, and the central valley, the only economically important and densely settled part of the state. The cease-fire line, which still stands, gave roughly the western quarter of Kashmir to Pakistan, but the larger issue of which country Kashmir should be-

long to has never been resolved. The Kashmir dispute has continued to poison relations between the two states and has sparked two brief but inconclusive wars. Violence flared repeatedly as Pakistan supplied Muslim guerrillas and "volunteers" with arms, and as India imposed often repressive police control.

Thus, to the tragedy of partition and the violence following it has been added chronic Indo-Pakistani tension instead of the cooperation that would be more appropriate between two developing nations born out of the same context and sharing both modern problems of the fight against poverty and a common cultural tradition. Mahatma Gandhi, who had prayed and labored so diligently to stop Hindu-Muslim violence, ironically became one of its victims when he was murdered on January 30, 1948, by one of the Hindu extremists who saw him as too tolerant of Muslims. Nehru saw his death as "the loss of India's soul" and commented, "The light has gone out of our lives and there is darkness everywhere."

Bangladesh and Pakistan

East Bengal, which became East Pakistan in 1947, was one of the subcontinent's poorest areas and had virtually no industry. It had been heavily dependent on Calcutta as its educational, cultural, commercial, industrial, and shipping center, through which its exports and imports moved and where nearly all transport lines were

India and the Sense of History

On the eve of independence, Nehru addressed the Constituent Assembly in 1946 with his characteristic eloquence, stressing the sense of history that many Indians share.

As I stand here, Sir [addressing the Speaker in British Parliamentary style], I feel the weight of all manner of things crowding upon me. We are at the end of an era and possibly very soon we shall embark upon a new age. My mind goes back to the great past of India, to the 5,000 years of India's history, from the very dawn of that history which might be considered almost the dawn of human history, until today. All that past crowds upon me and exhilarates me, and at the same time somewhat oppresses me. Am I worthy of that past? When I think also of the future, the greater future I hope, standing on this sword's edge of the present between the mighty past and the mightier future, I tremble a little and feel overwhelmed by this mighty task. We have come here at a strange moment in India's history. I do not know, but I do feel, that there is some magic in this moment of transition from the old to the new, something of that magic which one sees when the night turns into day and even though the day may be a cloudy one, it is day after all, for when the clouds move away, we can see the sun again. Because of all this I find a little difficulty in addressing this House and putting all my ideas before it, and I feel also that in this long succession of thousands of years, I see the mighty figures that have come and gone and I see also the long succession of our comrades who have labored for the freedom of India. And we stand now on the verge of this passing age, trying, laboring, to usher in the new. . . .

I think also of the various constituent assemblies that have gone before and of what took place at the making of the great American nation when the fathers of that nation met and fashioned a constitution which has stood the test for so many years. . . . [He then mentions the French and Russian revolution also.] We seek to learn from their success and to avoid their failures. Perhaps we may not be able to avoid failures, because some measure of failure is inherent in human effort. Nevertheless we shall advance, I am certain . . . and realize the dream that we have dreamed so long.

Source: W. T. de Bary, ed., *Sources of Indian Traditions,* 4th ed., vol. 1 (New York: Columbia University Press, 1964), pp. 350–352.

---

focused. East Pakistan contained over half of Pakistan's population and produced three-quarters of its exports abroad, mainly jute, but it was strikingly underrepresented in the national government. Only about 10 percent of national officials were Bengalis, and East Pakistan received only about 10 percent of the national budget. Even its language, Bengali, was not officially recognized.

Pakistan continued to be run by and for the small clique of Karachi and Punjabi businessmen and politicians who had pushed for its creation, although the faltering effort at parliamentary government was swept aside by a military dictatorship in Karachi after 1958. When elections, finally held in late 1970, produced a victory for the East Pakistan party on a platform of greater autonomy, the military government in West Pakistan responded by arresting the party's leader, Sheikh Mujibur Rahman, and then turning its army and tanks against demonstrators in East Pakistan in a mass slaughter. About 10 million refugees poured across the nearby Indian border by the end of 1971, mainly to already overcrowded Calcutta, a problem with which the Indian government found increasingly hard to cope. Guerrilla

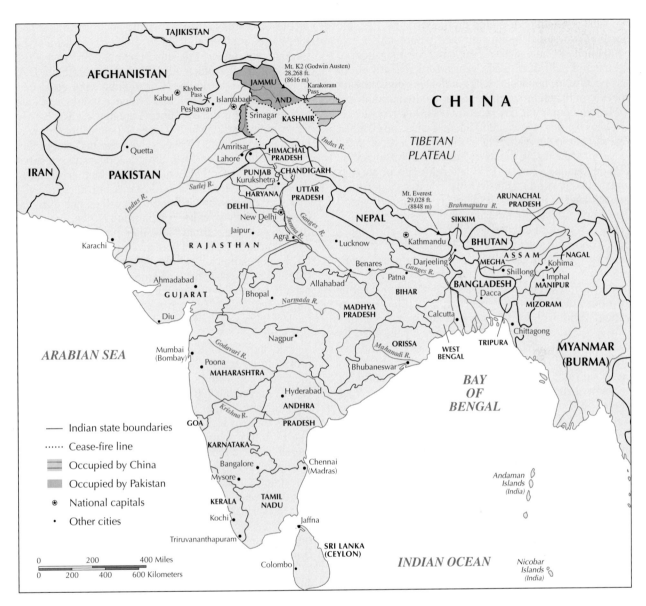

South Asia Today

Kashmir is still disputed between India and Pakistan, despite talks between the leaders of both countries in 2001. India itself is divided into nineteen states within a federal structure. Its border with China is still in dispute.

actions by Bengalis against the terrorism of the West Pakistani forces were finally joined by the Indian army, which in 10 days ended the slaughter.

With the Pakistani army defeated, East Pakistan declared itself the People's Republic of Bangladesh in December 1971. Sheikh Mujib, as he was called, became prime minister and the refugees returned home, but Bangladesh proved unable to achieve political stability or even effective government. Mujib was murdered by his own army in 1974, following charges of unbridled corruption and nepotism. His military successor was assassinated in 1981, and no clear or successful political order emerged. Bangladesh remains one of the world's poorest nations, despite the agricultural productivity of its delta and river valley rice lands. Population continued to grow at least as fast as agricultural output, indeed at one of the highest rates in the world, and efforts to limit it were impeded by poor planning, corruption, and widespread illiteracy. There was some industrial growth, but that too, like the economy as a whole, was hampered by the lack of effective planning and leadership. Periodic flooding, worsened by uncontrolled deforestation, has compounded Bangladesh's problems, resulting in crop destruction and death each year. More recently there has been more political stability, and some encouraging success in bringing down the birthrate. Remarkably for a Muslim country it has recently been headed successively by women as president: Sheik Hasina and Khaleda Zia, the latter the winner of elections in October 2001.

As for Pakistan, in the west, Jinnah died within a year of independence, and in 1958, after a series of corrupt and ineffective prime ministers, the country came under martial law, as it has been for many successive years. The huge military budget imposed by successive oppressive regimes has been largely paid for by the United States. The takeover by Field Marshal Ayub Khan in 1958 was peaceful, and there were few protests. Ayub was honest and efficient; he cracked down on the rampant corruption and restored some national morale. In an effort to break the connection with the "Karachi clique," Ayub had decided to move the capital in stages between 1961 and 1965 to a new planned site called Islamabad ("City of Islam"), about ten miles from the city of Rawalpindi in the northwest. The two cities operate as an urban unit, linked by commuting workers and civil servants. Lahore, an older and larger city and the chief center of Muslim culture, was more central, but it was thought to be too close to the Indian border to be safe. Pakistan lacks most industrial materials, except for the oil and gas found after partition, and it began in 1947 well below the all-Indian average economic level. Ayub Khan presided over the beginnings of some genuine national planning, including considerable industrialization, some modest land reform, and the exploitation of newly discovered oil and natural gas deposits. In more recent years impressive agricultural growth has been made possible by new irrigation works in the Punjab and Indus Valley, fertilizers, and improved seeds—the so-called green revolution. Although Pakistan has avoided major famine and built a basic industrial structure, as in India and China, its per capita economic gains continue to be retarded by a growing population. As an Islamic state, Pakistan has been reluctant to promote family planning or to limit the growth of its population. Islamic fundamentalism similar to that in Iran has won growing support in Pakistan.

Many politically active Pakistanis grew restless under Ayub's authoritarian hand and his bypassing of the political process, however effective and positive his rule. He was forced to resign in 1969, only to be succeeded after a brief interval of renewed political bickering by General Yahya Khan in another military coup. Yahya Khan proved to be a poor ruler and was largely responsible for the brutal response to the East Pakistan elections of 1970. When the Pakistan army was defeated in the east, Yahya Khan was driven from office, and there was another short-lived effort at parliamentary government under the unscrupulous, American-educated politician Zulfikar Ali Bhutto (who earned a B.A. in politics from Berkeley). Complaints about gross corruption under his regime and evidence that he had conspired in the murder of political opponents led in 1977 to a new military takeover by General Zia-ul-Huq, the army commander in chief. Zia dissolved the parliament and constitution and, in 1979, after a long trial, executed Bhutto for murder. Pakistan under Zia further strengthened its ties with the United States but became even more a police state. Economic development went increasingly into so-called glamor industries, including the international airline and other high-tech ventures, while too little attention was given to basic production for the population as a whole. Favoritism, cronyism, and corruption flourished, and American foreign aid was used to enrich the powerful few. There was also mounting evidence that Pakistan was working hard to make nuclear weapons and was stealing components from U.S. sources.

Pakistan also became deeply involved in aiding and providing refuge for the Afghan guerrilla resistance to the Soviet-supported government in Kabul, the Afghan capital, only about 100 miles from the Pakistani frontier. Such activity further strengthened Pakistan's role as a Cold War client of the United States and produced a new flow of American military supplies. But such aid had little relevance to Pakistan's domestic problems and again prompted Indian complaints that the arms were being stockpiled for use against India. The two states fought two small wars, in 1965 and 1971; in both, Pakistan's military power came virtually exclusively from U.S. equipment. Pakistan seemed useful to the United States as a regional anti-Communist bulwark against the Soviet Union and as a friend and intermediary with China. When China became a Soviet rival after 1959 instead of an ally and soon thereafter came in conflict with India over a border dispute in 1962, Pakistan took the Chinese side. American surveillance flights over the Soviet Union took off from bases in northwestern Pakistan, and in 1971 Washington used the Pakistan-China connection to respond to Chinese overtures, leading to President Nixon's visit to Beijing. But these international power games had little or nothing to do with Pakistan's people or their needs. Indeed they put the Pakistanis at serious risk both by exposing them to the threat of war, the suffering resulting from actual wars with India, and the massive diversion of the resources of a poor country away from urgently needed development into military expenditures and adventuring.

Pakistan is a highly diverse state, like India on a somewhat smaller scale. It includes a majority whose mother tongue, Urdu, is not the official national language, and many groups feel unrepresented, neglected, or oppressed by the military or military-dominated government. Outside the Indus Valley and western Punjab, where most of the national population is concentrated, Pakistan is mainly covered with arid mountains along its western and northern borders, inhabited by people like the Baluchis and Pathans whose cultures and histories have little in common with those of the lowlands. A truly national state that can include them as partners has not yet emerged. Pakistan has suffered from an especially poorly developed sense of common national purpose. Among both the elite and the masses, it is acknowledged that relatively few have believed in the idea of Pakistan in any public service sense. The partition has become a permanent fact of life, and the longer it lasts the more impossible it is to undo, but Pakistan has still to develop into a nation.

General Zia was killed in a plane crash in 1988, possibly not an accident. He had become widely hated and his death was regretted by few. In elections held in November 1988, Benazir Bhutto, the former prime minister Bhutto's daughter, won a surprising victory and seemed to offer hope for a revival of parliamentary democracy. But her regime was opposed by most of the military, by many of the big landlords of Punjab, and by the growing Islamic fundamentalist group, who were outraged to see a woman in power and declared that Pakistan had been cursed by Allah. Her political base remained precarious, and she was consequently unable to take any decisive action or pursue any significant new legislation. There were also increasing reports of gross corruption and nepotism in her government, growing violent ethnic conflict, and an alarming rise in drug abuse—especially disturbing to Islamic fundamentalists but linked to Pakistan's new Afghan connection. She did win much support in the United States and actively pursued the Pakistani role in providing sanctuary for and channeling U.S. arms to the Afghani guerrillas. But as the civil war in Afghanistan cooled with the withdrawal of Soviet forces in early 1989, unaddressed domestic problems and Bhutto's political failings became more prominent. Her survival as a leader was in question, while the risk of a new military takeover grew.

Benazir Bhutto, only 35 years old when she became prime minister, was initially very popular but lacked administrative experience and ran one of the most corrupt governments in even Pakistan's history. Earlier in 1990, perhaps in an effort to create a new diversion as well as to embarrass India, still the old enemy to many in Pakistan politics, her government gave much covert support to extremist Islamic groups among the Muslim majority in Indian Kashmir. India unwisely responded with a brutal crackdown, and communal violence mounted, for a time threatening a new outbreak of war between the two states, a suicidal course for Pakistan. The crisis

cooled later in 1990, but Kashmir remained a troubled area. Relations between India and Pakistan were once again embittered, just when there had begun to be some hope for a reduction in tension. In August 1990, after only 20 months in office, Bhutto was removed from office by the president of Pakistan, Ghulam Khan, with the tacit support of the army. Nawaz Sharif became the Pakistani prime minister in November 1990 following the October elections, and Pakistan tried once more to make parliamentary government work. But in April 1993 Sharif was removed from office by the Pakistani president for alleged corruption and subversion and replaced by an uneasy coalition under B. S. Mazari. New elections held in the fall made Benazir Bhutto the winner once more, but her campaign was marred by political and terrorist assassinations. In 1996 she was removed again to face charges of corruption, and was succeeded once more by Nawaz Sharif. Pakistan was still far from becoming a stable or democratic state.

Then in 1999 there was again a military takeover as General Pervez Musharraf made himself the ruler, and in June of 2001 declared himself President, though at the same time promising that he would return Pakistan to civilian rule in the elections scheduled for October, 2002; however, he also said that he would keep primary authority beyond that date. Pakistan has been under military rule for 24 of the 54 years of independence. Nawaz Sharif remained in exile in Saudi Arabia and Benazir Bhutto in London. It would seem that, despite its British legacy, Pakistan cannot make a real democracy work.

Afghanistan

Afghanistan is a semiarid mountainous state, as big as Pakistan but with only a little more than 20 million people. It was once a part of the Mughal Empire, but in the nineteenth century, with the rise of British power in India and the spread of the Russian Empire into adjacent Central Asia, it came to be regarded as a buffer zone between both powers. Two disastrous British efforts to install their client ruler in Kabul left the situation little changed, and both sides continued to jockey for influence there. Afghanistan remained an economically underdeveloped society where ancient tribal divisions still dominated, though they shared an Islamic faith and a fierce determination to resist outside control. Soviet influence slowly increased after 1950, and in 1973 the old traditional ruler was displaced by a Russian-sponsored government. Guerrilla resistance to this foreign-tainted regime mounted, with massive covert military aid from the United States, and in 1979 Russian troops and equipment moved in to support the government and to try to put down the guerrillas.

As the Americans discovered in Vietnam a few years earlier, conquering the guerrillas proved impossible, and the Russians withdrew in early 1989. The government nevertheless held on, despite continued American and Pakistani support to the guerrillas. There were bitter divisions among the many separate resistance groups, who had all along been unable to make common cause among themselves. Their traditional rivalries, further sharpened by fundamentalist Islamic disputes, were apparently more important than their common and equally traditional hatred of foreign influences. As always in any civil war, the people of Afghanistan suffered terribly, in a conflict that had far more to do with Cold War maneuvering by the superpowers and their stooges than with the pursuit of any Afghan interest. Having for so long been a zone of contention between rival foreign powers, it was understandable that Afghanistan wanted most of all to be left alone, but the chronic fighting, with the aid of U.S. and Soviet arms, drained the country's resources and perpetuated its fragmentation, and perpetuated also its grinding poverty. No effective national government emerged to provide the leadership for development that was so urgently needed.

From about 1995 a coalition of fundamentalist Islamic groups called the Taliban increased its control of the country to nearly 90 percent, although it was contested by a smaller coalition which came to be called the Northern Alliance. These changes were accompanied by a nearly unprecedented drought, which further increased the suffering of the people. Afghanistan is a semi-desert, dominated by high mountains which tend to shut out rain-bearing air masses, and most of its people are nomadic herders of sheep and goats. A few small rivers provide irrigation around Kandahar, the second city, and around Kabul, the capital. The country has produced opium for centuries, and although the Taliban attempted to ban production, Afghanistan accounted for over 70 percent of world supply in the year 2000, a means of revenue but also a response to problems of transport in this still low-tech economy by growing a crop of high value which could bear the cost of shipment to market. Then on September 11, 2001, terrorists, presumably on the orders of Osama bin-Laden (who as a Saudi had sought refuge in Afghanistan) drove two highjacked planes into the World Trade Center in New York and another into the Pentagon in Washington. The United States began a massive bombing campaign against the Taliban, who they presumed were sheltering Osama bin-Laden. It remained to be seen what sort of government might emerge. The fear was that in the longer run ethnic divisions in the population would threaten unity. Representatives of different groups in Afghanistan continued to meet in Germany in December of 2001, trying to agree on a new government for the country as the Taliban seemed about to lose all its control. But the fear was that in the longer run the country would break up again into warring factions, as so often in the past.

Sri Lanka

Ceylon, which in 1975 changed its name officially to Sri Lanka, an old precolonial name for the country, made a relatively easy transition to independence in 1948, primarily as a consequence of Indian independence rather than as the result of any strong nationalist movement on the island itself. No Ceylonese nationalists went to prison, and although there were some who pressed for self-government and independence, many, perhaps most, were content with colonial membership in the British Empire. The island had been under Western domination since the first Portuguese bases there early in the sixteenth century, and its small size and population were easily overwhelmed by foreign influences. Many of the elite were more British than Sinhalese (the majority of the inhabitants) in language and culture, and many regretted the end of their membership in the British Empire. But in the mid-1950s Ceylon was swept by what has been called "second-wave nationalism," a belated but emotional determination to rediscover and assert its own identity.

In the elections of 1956, self-serving politicians stirred up communal feelings among the dominant Sinhalese against the minority Tamils, originally immigrants from nearby south India, who form about a fifth of the population. Approximately half of them were descendants of people who had lived there, in the northern part of the island, nearly 2,000 years earlier, and were known as "Ceylon Tamils." But the other half were more recently arrived laborers recruited in overpopulated southern India after 1860 to work the tea plantations in the central highlands. Many of the Ceylon Tamils learned English, and with their tradition of hard work and ambition they came to occupy a disproportionate place in the colonial administration and in business. Most of the later arrivals, the so-called Indian Tamils, filled menial laboring jobs on the plantations, jobs that interested few Sinhalese. Most of the Indian Tamils remained poor tea and rubber estate workers, housed in shacks on the job. The Tamils are Hindu and speak primarily their own language, which has heightened their distinction from the Buddhist (or for the elite, nominally Buddhist) Sinhalese. They became a convenient scapegoat.

The tragic pattern of communal violence between Sinhalese and Tamils began with the 1956 election of S. W. R. D. Bandaranaike, on a platform of Sinhalese-only nationalism. Like Jinnah, he had been educated in Britain and was thoroughly Westernized; his personal ambition and his keen mind turned to communalism, until then of little interest to him, as a means of creating a new political base for himself. Like other Sinhalese leaders, his language was English and he spoke only a few words of "houseboy" Sinhalese; nevertheless, he decreed that Sinhalese would be the only language of government and education. Once called into existence by his campaign of discrimination, communal bitterness and violence could not be laid to rest, and Bandaranaike was assassinated in 1959 by a Sinhalese Buddhist extremist who thought he had not gone far enough.

His place was taken by his widow, Sirimavo Bandaranaike (born 1916), who continued most of his policies. Although she was succeeded by more middle-of-the-road leaders after 1977, they too were Sinhalese and did little or nothing to calm communal tensions.

Tamils felt increasingly excluded and oppressed and resorted to terrorism as a weapon, finally demanding a separate state. But Sri Lanka is a tiny country, and its Sinhalese government resisted partition and attempted to suppress what they referred to as insurrection. The government invited Indian troops in to restore peace in 1987, but they were predictably resented. Their mission failed and they were withdrawn at the end of 1989, while terrorist attacks and counterattacks continued. The Sri Lankan economy was disrupted by chronic fighting, which retarded its generally healthy growth after 1948.

Nevertheless the country became self-sufficient in rice production by the late 1970s, thanks to major investments in new irrigation and agricultural technology, and at the same time maintained its profitable plantation sector in tea, rubber, and coconuts, which dominated its exports until 1991, when new light manufactured goods, including computers and components produced mainly by foreign companies or on contract to them, outranked the old export staples. All exports and imports are funneled through the capital and major port of Colombo. Education, literacy, and public health were improved still further from the relatively high levels established under British colonial control, and per capita incomes remained somewhat higher than in any of the other South Asian states, thanks in part to the government's success in limiting population growth. But violence and terrorism on both sides, in an atmosphere close to civil war, eroded the British-inherited system of parliamentary government and the rule of law. Terrorism by the extremist Tamil Tigers and counteractions by the Sri Lankan army continued despite an earlier truce. As in Ulster and Lebanon, there seemed no easy solution to the hatred and violence created by a few extremists on each side. The old missionary hymn about Sri Lanka, "Where every prospect pleases / And only

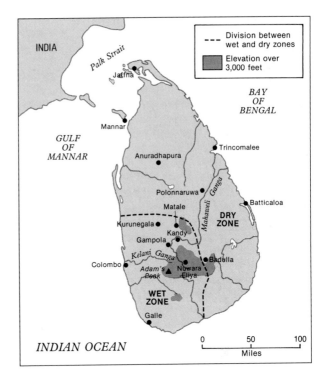

Sri Lanka

It is in the Wet Zone, that most modern economic development has centered: tea in the highlands, rubber and coconuts in the lowlands, and shipping and some manufacturing in the Colombo area.

man is vile," had come tragically true. There were outbreaks of terrorist violence even in Colombo, the capital, which included the bloody assassination of the president, Premadasa, in May of 1993. In late 2001, S. Wickramasinge was elected prime minister. Through a Norwegian negotiator, a cease-fire was agreed to, perhaps the end of violence.

Nepal

The small Himalayan kingdom of Nepal remained politically separate from India but became a British protectorate in 1816 after a brief war. The British were impressed by the fierce fighting skills of their Gurkha opponents and soon made a place for them in the British Indian Army. Under British oversight, Nepal remained dominated by its hereditary elite and monarchy and took little or no part in the modernization going

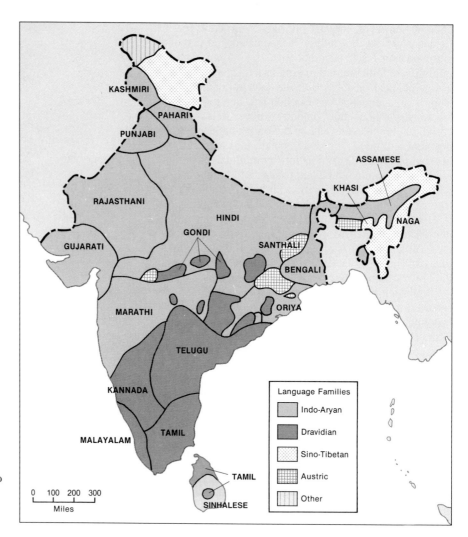

Major Languages of India

The map exaggerates the dominance of Hindi, which is in fact composed of several non-mutually intelligible dialects, but no other Indian language begins to rival it. The division of India into states was based largely on these language patterns.

on in colonial India. Motor roads were not built there, linking it with India, until the 1960s, although Nepal was given its independence in 1923. It remained one of the poorest countries on the globe, supported mainly by a low-yield, traditional agricultural system that had to contend with steep slopes in this mountainous region. Disastrous erosion was a growing problem after about 1965 as deforestation spread, aided by the coming of motor roads and fueled also by a population growing faster than its means of subsistence. The spectacular Himalayan views and hiking trails attracted more and more tourists, spawning new luxury hotels especially in Kathmandu, the capital, while most Nepalis continued in poverty. Tourism became Nepal's leading industry and source of foreign exchange, but this put further pressure on the fragile environment and brought in new foreign influences, not all of them beneficial.

Indian influence had always been strong. About 90 percent of Nepalis were Hindu, with some Buddhist admixtures (the Buddha had been born in what is now lowland Nepal), and most trade was with India. Nepali culture was a mix of Indian and Tibetan elements; many of its people originally migrated from Tibet. After the rise of Communist China, Nepal strengthened its ties with this powerful new neighbor, in part as a counter to Indian influences and in an effort to preserve Nepali freedom of action. A new constitution in 1951 reestablished the traditional Nepali monarchy, and in 1972 King Bihendra came to the throne, sharing power with a series of nominally parliamentary regimes.

In a dramatic episode in 2001, the crown prince murdered the king and most of his family, apparently after a dispute about the prince's choice of a wife; he then killed himself. The country was horrified, but the throne

Indian Independence

> *As midnight of August 14, 1947, approached, when Indian independence would begin, Jawaharlal Nehru spoke to the Constituent Assembly in New Delhi.*
>
> Long years ago we made a tryst with destiny, and now the time comes when we shall redeem our pledge, not wholly or in full measure [referring to the imminent partition of India] but very substantially. At the stroke of the midnight hour, when the world sleeps, India will wake to life and freedom. . . . We must take the pledge of dedication to the service of India and her people and to the still larger cause of humanity. . . . [But] the past clings to us still.
>
> *The following January 26, 1948, designated as Republic Day and celebrated ever since with parades and speeches, Nehru told the nation:*
>
> We are fortunate to witness the emergence of the Republic of India, and our successors may well envy us this day, but fortune is a hostage which has to be zealously guarded by our own good work and which has a tendency to slip away if we slacken in our efforts or if we look in wrong directions.
>
> *Nehru's will read in part:*
>
> My desire to have a handful of my ashes thrown into the Ganges has no religious significance, as far as I am concerned. . . . The Ganges especially is the river of India, a symbol of India's age-long culture and civilization, ever changing, ever flowing, and yet ever the same.
>
> *Source:* From *A New History of India, Sixth Edition* by Stanley Wolpert, copyright © 1977 by Oxford University Press, Inc. Used by permission of Oxford University Press, Inc.

passed to an uncle, Prince Gyanendra, who, thus, became the new king, although like all Nepali kings his functions are mainly ceremonial and real power remains with the parliament.

In 2004 demonstrations and much violence continued on the part of a fringe group of self-styled Maoists, who mustered a small army. They protested against Nepal's royal family and their determined resistance to all forms of change. Nepal remained in chaos, and the tourist trade suffered.

India After Independence

In the Republic of India, parliamentary democracy and British-style law have survived repeated tests and remain vigorous. Jawaharlal Nehru, who became prime minister at independence and served until his death in 1964, was a strong and revered leader who effectively dominated the new nation. He presided over the creation of sixteen new language-based states within a federal structure. Federalism was necessary in any case given India's size and diversity, and language was the single most obvious basis of regional differences. Nehru and others were reluctant to acknowledge the importance of language-based regionalism, given India's long history of separatism and their determination to build a new and united nation. But after several years of debate and negotiation it became clear that such a concession would have to be made. The states created by 1956 were the size of France, Germany, or Italy in population, and each coincided approximately with the distribution of what were officially declared to be "major" languages out of the many hundreds spoken. Each of these major languages had its own proud history and literary tradition, older, more extensive, and with more speakers than most European languages.

India's World Role

Nehru saw India as an emerging power in the modern world and as a major Asian leader. In the 1950s, he wrote about this and about East-West relations.

> One of the major questions of the day is the readjustment of the relations between Asia and Europe. . . . India, not because of any ambition but because of geography and history . . . inevitably has to play a very important part in Asia . . . [and is] a meeting ground between the East and the West. . . . The Middle East and Southeast Asia both are connected with India. . . . You cannot consider any question concerning the Far East without India. . . . In the past the West ignored Asia, or did not give her the weight that was due her. Asia was really given a back seat . . . and even the statesmen did not recognize the changes that were taking place. There is considerable recognition of these changes now, but it is not enough. . . . I do not mean to say that we in Asia are in any way superior, ethically or morally, to the people of Europe. In some ways, I imagine that we are worse. There is however a legacy of conflict in Europe. . . . We might note that the world progressively tends to become one. . . . [We should] direct [our] policy towards avoiding conflict. . . . The emergence of India in world affairs is something of major consequence in world history. We who happen to be in the government of India . . . are men of relatively small stature. But it has been given us to work at a time when India is growing into a great giant again.

Source: W. T. de Bary, ed., *Sources of Indian Traditions*, 4th ed., vol. 1 (New York: Columbia University Press, 1964), pp. 350–352.

Hindi, the language of the Delhi area and the upper Ganges Valley, was declared the official national language, to be used in the national government and taught to all Indians in every region, while leaving each state its own regional language—Bengali, Tamil, and so on—in its schools and legislatures. English, familiar to educated people in all the states, was retained as an "associate language" at the national level and continued to be learned by all educated people. Indian English has more speakers than American English, although it too has diverged from its British origins. Hindi is the mother tongue of only about 30 percent of the population, and even so consists of several mutually unintelligible dialects. No other Indian language comes close; the largest can claim only about 9 percent. Hindi was therefore the obvious choice as the national medium, but for most Indians it remains a foreign tongue. It is resented especially by Dravidian-speaking southerners, with their own proud cultural heritage, as yet another example of "northern domination" and the "oppression of Delhi."

India Under Nehru

Nehru saw India well launched on the path of economic development, both agricultural and industrial, but he acknowledged the Gandhian legacy by providing special government support for handicraft production and for small-scale rural industries, especially the hand weaving of cotton cloth. As in China, these were often not economically rational, but symbolically they were important because of their long association with the nationalist movement, and they also offered employment in rural areas, where most Indians still lived. Traditional village councils were revitalized and used as channels for new rural development in agriculture as well as other village enterprises.

But the most rapid growth was in the expanding cities, where industry and new economic opportunity were concentrated for the fortunate and which attracted streams of rural immigrants. Housing and other basic human services such as water, sewers, electric power, education, health care, and urban transport could not

Grain being fed into a storage facility in New Delhi: one of the fruits of the green revolution. (Bettmann/Corbis)

keep up with a mushrooming population, which included many still unemployed, a problem familiar throughout the developing world. New immigrants took time to make a place for themselves and lived, or squatted, in slums or in the open air, but the wider opportunity offered by the cities continued to draw them despite the squalor and hardships with which most of them had to contend. Calcutta, Bombay, and Delhi–New Delhi, the three largest cities, are among the largest in the world, but like most, including big American cities, combine luxurious lifestyles for a few and ragged poverty for many.

Despite government efforts to slow it down, total Indian population continued to grow, primarily because of improved nutrition from agricultural gains and advances in public health that largely eliminated epidemic disease; life expectancy rose and death rates fell. But rising production, including new industrial output, more than kept pace, and per capita incomes began a slow and uninterrupted rise (unlike China with its radical ups and downs), which still continues. A third or more of the population, however, remained in severe poverty while the top third won new wealth.

The later Nehru years were sadly marred by a border dispute with China in the remote Himalayas, which erupted in brief hostilities in 1962. The Chinese, fresh from their armed reoccupation of Tibet, won a quick victory. They retained control of the small border area they had claimed, the Aksai Chin, which they needed for access into western Tibet, where a rebellion against Chinese rule was in progress. The Chinese had built a road through this area, and when an Indian border patrol belatedly noticed the road nearly two years later, they fired on the Chinese. India refused to discuss the Chinese claim, although in fact it had never been settled and the remote area concerned had never been adequately surveyed. On the advice of V. Krishna Menon, the foreign minister, India foolishly tried to eject the Chinese troops, an effort for which the Indian army was poorly prepared. Delhi panicked when its forces were overrun, fearing an invasion, but the Chinese did not advance beyond their claim line, some twenty miles southward across the alpine wasteland of the high Himalayas.

Nehru had attempted, with much success until then, to build pan-Asian friendship and cooperation in partnership with China as the other major power and to promote India as the leader of the nonaligned nations. Nehru played this role especially effectively from the time of the 1955 Conference of Asian Nations at Bandung (in Java), where he established firm ties with Zhou Enlai and asserted that "India and China are brothers." Nonalignment brought complaints and some pressure from the United States, which tended thereafter to favor Pakistan as a firmer Cold War client. American aid and military supplies flowed to Pakistan. In defense, India turned to a degree to freely offered Soviet sources, though retaining as much of an American connection as Washington permitted. Indians were anxious not to become a client of either superpower, but their commitment to Western democratic values, parliamentary government, a free press, and the rule of law was deep.

Nehru's death in 1964 was hastened by the failure of relations with China, which he took as a personal failure, calling it "a Himalayan blunder" (*Himalayan* is used in India to mean "enormous"). With his passing, most Indians felt they had been left leaderless and were fearful about finding an adequate successor. Nehru had been the symbol and architect of the new India and its

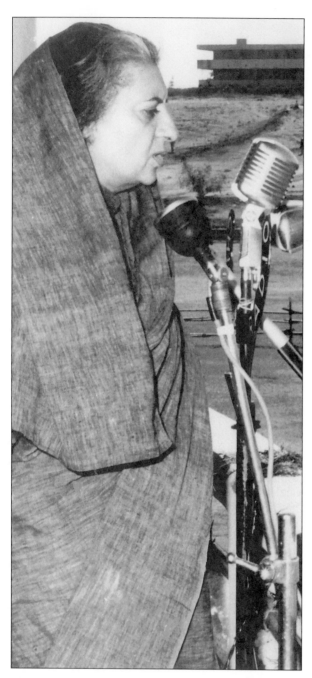

Indira Gandhi in 1972, addressing a crowd at Kolhapur, India. (Bettmann/Corbis)

(no relation to the Mahatma), who quickly established her firm leadership and vowed to continue Nehru's and Shastri's policies.

India Under Indira Gandhi

India had maintained its political stability and democratic system through successive crises, despite a still largely illiterate electorate and the multiple problems of new nationhood, wars, internal and external tensions, and poverty, a record matched by few other nations. Illiterate voters repeatedly demonstrated a surprising grasp of political issues, and a far higher proportion of those over eighteen voted there than in the United States. The Indian press remained freely critical of government shortcomings and offered an open forum for all opinions. Poverty and pressures for development have often been the enemies of democracy. India's faithfulness to the system that it inherited and has continued to cultivate stands in contrast to the failure of parliamentary democracy and the rise of totalitarianism, dictatorship, censorship, and the police state in so much of the rest of Asia and the world. American policy toward India has been slow to recognize the importance of this major democratic state, now larger than China in total population.

After lean years of drought in 1965 and 1966 that stopped short of famine deaths on any large scale but caused much suffering, India became one of the first countries to launch a major campaign in the green revolution, an agricultural policy that achieved higher yields with improved seeds and expanded irrigation and fertilizer production without which the higher yields from the new varieties of wheat and rice could not be maintained. By the end of the 1960s there was a real breakthrough in production, and by 1975 India was again self-sufficient in grains and had a surplus for export, a situation that has since continued as the green revolution spread to more farmers and more areas. Industrial growth also continued, but the gap between rich and poor widened. The green revolution benefited those with enough land and capital to use and pay for the new seeds, irrigation, and fertilizers. Farmers and areas without them sank further into relative poverty, and tenancy and landlessness rose. Upwardly mobile urban workers, managers, professionals, and technicians were matched by rising numbers of urban and rural poor. These growing pains were typical of economic development everywhere, including the nineteenth-century West.

Indira Gandhi (1917–1984) proved an able political manager, but although she dominated the scene, there was widespread dissatisfaction within and outside the Congress party and among many regional and communal groups who believed they remained disadvantaged. In part to quash charges of corruption and to weaken

dominant political figure for more than a generation. But the gap was filled through normal democratic processes by the old Congress party moderate Lal Bahadur Shastri as prime minister. His promising start, including an agreement with Pakistan to reduce tensions, was cut short by his death after only a year and a half. The party then chose Nehru's daughter, Indira Gandhi

Indian Democracy

In 1974 Indira Gandhi, despite her fortunately brief suppression of free expression under the "emergency," made a very true statement about India's tradition of democracy.

> India has not ever been an easy country to understand. Perhaps it is too deep, contradictory, and diverse, and few people in the contemporary world have the time or inclination to look beyond the obvious, especially because in our country we have the greatest scope for free expression of opinion and all differences are constantly being debated.

Source: From *A New History of India, Sixth Edition* by Stanley Wolpert, copyright © 1977 by Oxford University Press, Inc. Used by permission of Oxford University Press, Inc.

her political opposition, Indira Gandhi, in June 1975, proclaimed a state of national emergency in the name of "unity" and "reform." Civil rights were suspended, the press was controlled, opposition leaders and "trouble-makers" were jailed, the constitution was amended to keep the courts from challenging the government, and a series of measures were announced to control inflation, inefficiency, hoarding, and tax evasion. It seemed the end of India as the world's largest parliamentary democracy, but Gandhi miscalculated her people's judgment. When she finally permitted a national election in January 1977, she and her party were defeated, primarily on the issue of the "emergency" and its dictatorial character. The Indian democratic system and its tradition of free expression and a Western-style legal system were soundly vindicated, but the coalition government of non-Congress parties that emerged under Morarji Desai floundered badly, failed to make any headway with India's genuine problems, and finally dissolved into bickering, paving the way for Indira Gandhi's return to power in the elections of January 1980.

Although she made no effort to reestablish the "emergency," presumably having learned her lesson, Gandhi's response to tensions and protests by disaffected regions and groups became increasingly rigid and authoritarian. Meanwhile, economic growth continued in agriculture and industry. By 1983 over a third of India's exports were manufactured goods, many of them from high-tech industries that competed successfully on the world market. India had become a major industrial power, and its pool of trained scientists and technicians, products of the British-inherited education system, was exceeded only by those of the United States and the Soviet Union. In 1974 India's own scientists completed the first Indian nuclear test, though the government continued to insist it would not make nuclear weapons but would instead concentrate on the production of nuclear energy for peaceful purposes. Indian

satellites joined American and Russian ones in space, and Indian-made microchips began to revolutionize industry. In 1989 India test-fired an intermediate-range ballistic missile, aiming to keep up with China and ahead of Pakistan. By 1990 India had the world's second-largest stock exchange and was a major producer of nuclear energy. The rapidly growing urban middle class clogged city streets with their cars. Computerization in industry, business, and government was far advanced, and India led the world in use of solar energy. At the same time, many rural sectors remained in the bullock-cart age, and urban poor slept under bridges near the new luxury apartments of those who had done well in the rapidly growing economy.

The Sikhs

Of the many groups that felt disadvantaged, the most continuously and effectively organized were the Sikhs of Punjab. Ironically, Punjab had led the nation in agricultural progress under the green revolution, and while not all Sikhs were well-off, as a group they had prospered more than most others in the uneven growth characteristic of economic development everywhere. Sikhs had also done well in light industry and as imaginative entrepreneurs and financiers, following their traditional skills and experience. Even landless Punjabis shared in the new prosperity as demand for labor and wages both rose substantially.

Part of the Sikhs' discontent was no doubt related to the rising expectations that plague all periods of development. Once the process begins or acquires momentum, most people understandably want more; they are less content with what had been acceptable before and impatient with too slow an improvement. Having put the green revolution to work with their traditional entrepreneurial talents and hard work, the Sikhs grew increasingly angry at government controls on agricultural prices imposed by Gandhi's fight against inflation, which severely restricted farmers' profits. A religious community founded in the fifteenth century as a reformist offshoot from Hinduism, the Sikhs also wanted greater recognition, increased political status, more control of Punjab state (where they were in fact a minority), and greater provincial autonomy.

Sikhs comprised only about 2 percent of India's population, and Gandhi was reluctant to favor them or to make concessions on provincial autonomy when she had to confront so many similar demands from other discontented groups and protest movements. But her stance on the Sikhs was rigid to a fault; she met violence with more violence and then ordered the army to storm the Golden Temple in Amritsar, sacred to Sikhism, which a group of extremists had fortified. Four months later, in October 1984, she was gunned down by two of her Sikh guards in the name of Indian freedom. Many others had come to see her as corrupted by power.

Indira Gandhi's Successors

Again Indian democracy proved equal to the challenge as Indira Gandhi's son Rajiv (1944–1991) was chosen by the Congress party to succeed her, and in January 1985 he was overwhelmingly confirmed in a nationwide election. Rajiv Gandhi offered peace to the Sikhs, granted many of their more reasonable demands (including new borders for Punjab that created a state with a Sikh majority), and in other ways showed himself to be a sensitive and responsible leader.

As the grandson of Jawaharlal Nehru, Rajiv Gandhi had many of the same qualities of personal charm, ability, and diplomacy. He had never sought power and was accordingly trusted, but the reservoir of popular support for him began to decline as critics claimed that the Congress party under his leadership remained more interested in power brokering than in serving all the needs of the people. Many Indians thought that government was often insensitive to their wants and was excessively bureaucratic and corrupt. In the elections of 1989, Congress suffered heavy losses to a new Janata ("People's") National Front Coalition, whose leader Vishwanath Pratap Singh became prime minister. V. P. Singh had been minister of finance under Rajiv Gandhi and was largely responsible for the economic reforms and especially high growth rates beginning in 1985. He was, however, elected by a minority of the voters. The Congress party, though split, won most votes, especially in the Dravidian south, but no single Congress candidate emerged in a strong position. Singh soon showed a firm hand as premier, but Sikh and Hindu-Muslim tension and outbreaks of violence remained. In mid-1990 Muslim demonstrations for greater recognition or autonomy flared in Kashmir, with help from Pakistan. Brutally repressive Indian counterac-

tions were deeply resented but brought no resolution to the long-suppressed conflict over the status of Kashmir. India remained in a vulnerable position, refusing to hold a plebescite or acknowledge a greater role for the Kashmiri Muslim majority. India's old conflict with Pakistan helped to harden its line.

Since independence, as provided by the Indian constitution, Untouchables, who make up about a quarter of the population, have had 25 percent of government jobs and places in the universities reserved for them, in an effort to make up for past injustices (somewhat similar to equal opportunity hiring practices in the United States). Prime Minister Singh thought that the constitution did not go far enough and, late in 1990, he pressed for a quota of 50 percent for "depressed classes," including Untouchables, other lower castes, and "tribals," though this was not precisely defined. There was violent protest by others, especially by students and hopeful entrants into the job market; a few actually burned themselves to death to dramatize their case. V. P. Singh also took a firm line against the building of a Hindu temple on the site of a disused mosque in the town of Ayodhya in northern India. This had become a focus of Hindu-Muslim tensions and counterclaims, and there were violent clashes with police. Hindu-Muslim violence spread to other areas, and later even to Hyderabad in the Deccan. As prime minister, Singh attempted to calm communal tensions, which were clearly being used or even provoked by unscrupulous politicians for their own ends, but he was defeated in parliamentary voting. Chandra Shekar managed to form a government with a new coalition and became prime minister in November 1990, with some support from Rajiv Gandhi and the Congress party. Many observers anticipated a return to power by Rajiv Gandhi and Congress, but scattered communal violence continued. Chandra Shekar lost his parliamentary majority in April 1991, and as he began the new election campaign Rajiv Gandhi was assassinated by a Tamil terrorist in May near Madras. His Congress party won the elections, and P. V. Narasimha Rao became prime minister. The violent end to what some called the Nehru dynasty shocked the nation, and many hoped it would help to discredit violence. After 1992 Prime Minister Rao increasingly softened or removed many controls on the economy, including measures aimed to attract more foreign investment. This has had a strong positive effect as economic growth has accelerated and India has joined East Asia in the pace of its development.

In the national elections of 1998 the fundamentalist Hindu party of Bharatiya Janata ("Indian Peoples"), won a plurality, but short of a majority, and A. B. Vajpahee became prime minister. The BJP fulfilled their campaign pledge to test India's nuclear weapons, a gesture to which Pakistan soon replied in kind, to the condemnation of all the nuclear powers, which India had long claimed were hypocritical.

Elections in 2004 brought defeat for the BJP and a plurality for the Congress party, headed by Rajiv Gandhi's widow Sonya. She declined to serve as prime minister, deferring to Man Mohan Singh, former finance minister. He presided over a Congress-led coalition titled the United Progressive Alliance, with no representation of the BJP.

India Today

Three basic problems still resist solution: miserable poverty for the bottom third or more of India's people; a population that is still growing too rapidly (one root of poverty); and communal divisions within the highly diverse population. Caste distinctions and allegiances continue to weaken slowly, especially in the cities, but most Indians remain in traditional village worlds, where caste connections still serve a useful function. Higher or "dominant" castes, as they are often called, have resented and tried to suppress the rise of Untouchables. Hindus and Muslims fight one another in some areas, including Kashmir. Sikh terrorism and Hindu reprisals threaten to plunge Punjab and Delhi into a minor civil war. Other minority groups continue to press for greater recognition. There are no easy answers.

Nationalism grew among Indian intellectuals late in the nineteenth century, but it did not become a mass movement until the 1920s. Even Mahatma Gandhi and his message of strength through unity did not reach all Indians, and the country since independence in 1947 is still moving toward creating a single overriding sense of Indian identity that can take precedence over regional, religious, caste, and other group loyalties. India well illustrates the dictum of the British historian Lord Acton (1834–1902): "The nation is not the cause but the result of the state. It is the state which creates the nation, not the nation the state." To many—perhaps most—Indians it remains more important that they are Bengalis, Gujaratis, Marathas or Tamils, Hindus, Sikhs, or Muslims, Brahmins or Untouchables than that they are fellow Indians. It will take more time before such group loyalties can be merged into common "Indianness" through common experience in a single national state. This problem is shared with most new nations, many of which have difficulties comparable with India's. The difference is partly the scale of India's problem—more than a billion people with a diversity greater than all of Europe—and partly in the recency of its modern experience as a nation-state after 5,000 years of regional and group separatism. Since 1949 the traditional world of the village and its ties has expanded to include considerable integration with the modern world of the cities and with the larger world of regional states sharing a common language and culture.

Within India's federal political structure, central economic planning and an expanding national civil service also help to join people in mutual self-interest. Regular bus services on all-weather roads link every village with these wider worlds and with a national network. The sense of nationhood needs time to grow, but while it cannot come about in a single generation it is clearly the shape of India's future.

The war against poverty, as the government has called it, is of course related to communal and intercaste tensions and is the greatest challenge of all developing countries. India has done better economically than most of the so-called Third World, and probably overall better than China, whose record has been praised, often with inadequate data, by many in the West. Chinese performance has been hard to measure accurately, especially given the closed nature of the system and the deficiencies of Chinese statistics. It took, for example nearly 30 years for outsiders to figure out that 30 million people died of starvation between 1959 and 1964, a catastrophe far beyond anything India has encountered. But India's new wealth has not been well distributed. The hope is that as development, the "rising tide that lifts all boats," proceeds and as efforts to limit population growth succeed, the fight against poverty may make significant headway even for those thus far left out. This is the same path followed by the West a century earlier as the fruits of the Industrial Revolution eventually raised the economic level of most people, but that process took several generations.

The early and middle stages of development are hard for most people. The plight of the poor in the nineteenth-century West was almost certainly worse than in the currently developing world, as the novels of Charles Dickens remind us. We have reasonably accurate quantitative measures of welfare for most people in nineteenth-century Manchester or New York, as for western Europe and the United States as a whole, including such basics as disease, death rates, and life expectancy. The corresponding rates for Calcutta or Bombay and for India are considerably better, as are living conditions for most of their inhabitants, although in both the nineteenth-century West and contemporary India it is the misery of those at the bottom that attracts our attention.

Poverty is a relative notion, and it is relative deprivation that hurts when it is compared with what is available to one's more fortunate fellow citizens. The modern West has far from eliminated poverty, and its urban slums are probably breeders of more hopelessness than those of India, where most people are there because of the promise that the city offers them. In India, as in most of Asia, the economic trends are in fact strongly positive. Most of those who migrate to the cities eventually succeed or at least believe that they have given their children a more promising start than if they had remained in the limited world of the village. Every fifth person in the world is in the Indian subcontinent, and it will take time for development to provide adequately for all of them. Literacy is growing fast as universal free education spreads, and the pace of change is accelerating in all respects as India evolves from its peasant base into an urban, industrial, technological, and commercial world for most of its citizens.

A CLOSER LOOK

Female Leaders of South Asia

Like China and Japan, South Asia traditionally accorded women a relatively low status, especially during the centuries of Muslim domination in the north. There were exceptions, including female military figures and heads of state among the Marathas and other groups and dominant figures at court such as Nur Jahan. The Westernization that accompanied British control led to increasing education for women; many educated women were prominent in the independence movement and in government and the professions after 1947. However, this was a relatively small group, an intellectual and Westernized elite. Most South Asian women, especially in the villages, remained uneducated and subservient to their husbands to a degree that seemed extreme to Westerners. There were exceptions, of course, notably in south India and in the southern state of Kerala, where ancient matrilinear and matrilocal social forms persisted to some degree. Husbands there commonly walk behind wives and defer to them; property and family names often descend through the female line.

Elsewhere in South Asia some women have achieved great prominence in the national scene since independence. The world's first female prime minister was Sirimavo Bandaranaike (1916–), who succeeded her husband as prime minister of Sri Lanka (then called Ceylon) when he was assassinated in 1959 and ruled with a firm hand for two terms: 1960–1965 and 1970–1977. Like her husband, she was British-educated, sophisticated, and extremely able, showing a talent for both international and domestic diplomacy. Her authoritative rule restored order and relative stability at a time of domestic crisis.

Indira Gandhi (1917–1984) played a similar role in India after the unexpected death of Lal Bahadur Shastri in 1966. She too, like her famous father, Nehru, was British-educated and widely traveled. After her mother's death in 1936, she was her father's confidante and housekeeper, acting as hostess to streams of Indian and foreign visitors who sought Nehru's counsel or favors. She supported him throughout his long and arduous career for the first 17 years of India's independence. Indira Gandhi separated from her husband, Firoze, a journalist, a few years after their marriage and reared her two sons, Sanjay (1947–1980) and Rajiv (1944–1991) mainly in her father's house. She impressed all who knew her, including this writer, with her razor-sharp mental powers and keen grasp of political affairs, but during her father's lifetime she modestly eschewed any public role. After his death in 1964, she accepted the cabinet post of minister for information in Shastri's government. She was only one of many able women who held cabinet rank and who had been prominent earlier in the long struggle for independence.

The Ministry of Information gave Gandhi new public visibility, and when Shastri suddenly died she entered the contest for Congress party leadership, ending in her overwhelming victory and subsequent endorsement by the national electorate. During her years as prime minister from 1966 to 1977 and from 1980 to her death in 1984, she was a strong central figure, but her record was badly flawed by her assumption of dictatorial powers under the so-called emergency from 1975 to 1977 and by her rigid and heavy-handed response to Sikh demands and protests in the last year of her life. She was a consummate politician within the Congress party, but many accused her of becoming merely a power broker, without the charisma and deft diplomacy of her father. Congress was and remains a diverse coalition of political groups, divided into factions and including conservative, liberal, and radical wings.

Gandhi shared her father's commitment to Western values, but she drew her political strength mainly from left of center. When the United States adopted Pakistan as a client state in the Cold War and continued to supply it with arms, she was obliged to build relations with the Russians as a countervailing source of military supplies. India kept to a nonaligned stance in international politics despite its predominantly Western sympathies and character, but this too involved Gandhi in frequent disputes with the United States. Her handling of the Sikh problem cost her her life, but it is not reasonable to judge her career in terms of her last fatal error or to have her record overly clouded by her dictatorial mismanagement of the "emergency." She made mistakes, some of them big ones, but she learned from them. Future generations will surely see her as an outstanding though controversial leader. Meanwhile most South Asian women remain exploited and subjugated.

Indian and South Asian Achievements and Shortcomings

Despite the nagging problem of the gap between rich and poor, the Indian economy has done very well. Its average annual growth rate of over 3 percent (more from about 1985) was much higher than the annual U.S. rate of about 1 percent, or the wildly fluctuating Chinese

Bombay street scene, typical of most Indian and Pakistani cities in its mixture of traditional with modern and the wide use of English. (Soltan Frederic/Corbis Sygma)

growth rate that included years of sharp decline and mass famine. The economy is a mixed one, with a government-managed public sector in many industries and banking and a more vigorous private sector that in fact has led the process of economic growth. The private sector complained of excessive bureaucratic red tape and controls to a stifling degree, and this has clearly slowed the progress of the public sector still more. In principle, India has a planned economy, and controls are imposed especially on imports so as to make the best use of limited foreign exchange. Indian exports have boomed, but most oil and many other industrial components must be imported. It has made sense to depend wherever possible on domestic substitutes and to limit imports to essentials like oil, banning or restricting less essential consumer goods imports. Even imports for industrial use required special permits, often slowed by the bureaucratic control system and alleged to be more easily obtainable through bribery. Prime Minister Rao's reduction or removal of many of these controls was enthusiastically welcomed by most Indians.

Explorations continued to find some new sources of domestic oil, including offshore deposits near the west coast in the Bombay area and perhaps in the Bay of Bengal, but total domestic production covers only about half of national needs, especially as industrial expansion continues. Private cars and fuel for them are kept very expensive and, thus, are restricted to those who are well-off—a growing number, and in the cities perhaps half the urban population by 1990. There is a long waiting list, and nearly all of the cars are made domestically, mainly two uniform models stressing fuel and size economy. Others depend on bicycles and scooters or motorcycles, which dominate rush-hour traffic in the cities but are also widespread in rural areas, although there bullock carts still carry most local goods, leaving long-haul transport to trucks and to the extensive rail system. Businesspeople fight over limited space on the airplanes or travel by express train. India is now a world leader in computer technology and microchips and exports skilled workers in these and other fields. Indian space satellites circle the globe, and India has for some time been a nuclear power.

Changing Perceptions of Caste and Ethnicity

Industrial growth depends in part on India's rich deposits of iron ore, mainly in or near the Damodar Valley west of Calcutta, and on adjacent or nearby deposits of high-quality coking coal. This fortunate combination led to the creation of India's first modern steel plant at Jamshedpur, established in 1911 by the major Parsee firm of Tata and Company. Tata now dominates the private sector; it is a giant conglomerate involved in a great variety of industrial and transport enterprises. The Parsees were originally refugees from Persia (from which their name is derived). They retained their Zoroastrian religion, but like the Protestant sects of early modern Europe they also functioned as vigorous capitalists and became a very wealthy group. They settled in Gujarat and then moved with the East India Company to Bombay, where they prospered by trading

READING ACROSS CULTURE

India in the Global Marketplace: Bollywood and Outsourcing

While Westerners will flock to theaters to see their favorite action heros, the people of India are more concerned with tormented teenagers and young adults trying to find themselves and survive the anguish of love. These are the common themes of India's Bollywood, the informal name given to India's popular Bombay (Mumbai)-based film industry. In Bollywood films, there is never an on-screen kiss, and every time there might be the potential for one, the entire cast bursts into frantic song and dance routines. Indian audiences expect a three-hour extravaganza with an intermission, with songs and dances, love triangles, comedy, and daredevil thrills. Star-crossed lovers have to contend with angry parents, corrupt politicians, kidnappers, plotting villains, courtesans with hearts of gold, long-lost relatives and siblings separated by fate, dramatic reversals of fortune, and convenient coincidences. Melodramatic dialogues invoke God, family, mother, and self-sacrifice. Major stars are excellent dancers, but few are singers, and songs are generally prerecorded by professional playback singers with actors lip-synching the words, usually while dancing. Indian classical dance often blends with Western dance styles, as seen on Indian MTV.

Bollywood films are also referred to as "Hindi cinema," even though the language of the films is Hindustani, the colloquial dialect spoken in northern India and as Urdu in Pakistan; the songs use Hindi and Urdu vocabulary, with regular inclusion of English words and phrases in dialogues and songs. These films target young, affluent urban Indians who today are bilingual or trilingual but they have succeeded in reaching beyond this group: In 2002, *BusinessWeek* estimated that Bollywood films attracted an audience of approximately 3.6 billion people worldwide and accounted for $1.2 billion in revenues.

In addition to the film industry, Indian society is also focused on developing ways to increase revenue from the expansive Indian marketplace. Indian professionals, venture capitalists, and entrepreneurs have been especially successful in promoting India as an outsourcing destination. Although lower-cost Asian destinations are slowly catching up with India in outsourcing, it retains its edge because of the increasing influence and expertise of the Indian diaspora. Indian immigrants, many of whom were engineers who moved to the West in the 1960s, have promoted India to businesses engaged in or considering outsourcing, and continue to mentor Indian firms that provide contracted services, or frequently own their own Indian firms now that the Indian government has relaxed its foreign ownership restrictions.

Source for BusinessWeek *stat: BusinessWeek,* December 2, 2002. International cover story, Manjeet Kripalani and Ron Grover, "Bollywood: Can new money create a world-class film industry in India?"

---

with and for the Company and becoming major shipbuilders, using Indian and Burmese teak. A Parsee firm in Bombay built H.M.S. *Minden,* the British warship on which Francis Scott Key was imprisoned as he watched the bombardment of Fort McHenry in the harbor of Baltimore in 1812 and wrote "The Star-Spangled Banner." Many Parsee firms became prominent in the booming Bombay economy after 1850, and several became involved even before then in the opium trade to China.

Hinduism also provided a legitimate place for commercial gain, with the goddess Lakshmi as the patron of accumulation and wealth. Hindu merchants and entrepreneurs, especially Gujaratis, were far more numerous

than the Parsees. They were joined by the Sikhs, among others, in the expanding commercial economy of late colonial India and were a driving force for change and economic growth. Despite the otherworldly or mystical aspects of Hinduism, there was no shortage of Indian entrepreneurs. In independent India too they have been quick to pursue economic advantage wherever it could be found and needed few lessons from Western businessmen.

Many Western observers thought caste would exert a drag on economic growth and change. It is diminishing in importance, but even in the past it did not prevent caste groups from seeking their economic advantage, and indeed has continued to help that effort by providing the strength of group action. Caste distinctions have not impeded necessary economic interaction across caste lines or, for example, hampered the recruitment of an industrial labor force or the efficient operation of the workplace, where people from many castes or subcastes work together and even share common eating facilities. Economic opportunity has proved a more powerful motive than traditional culture in this as in so many other respects. Politically also, caste associations have become a powerful force—in some ways equivalent to political parties—and are used to further the interests of the groups so organized. This was especially true for the Untouchables and other lower-caste bodies, who have become major players on the political scene and have won significant benefits and advances for their members: reserved seats in parliament, government jobs, places in the universities, and other perquisites.

Caste is fading in importance in the cities, where much of the rest of traditional culture is of declining relevance. The new professions that dominate the modern world—engineering, law, business, and so on—are not connected with caste and not provided for by its rules. Westernization has also played a part in the discarding of caste rules and together with modernization more

generally has led to considerable intercaste marriage. Even in the traditional village world, still home to most Indians, these changes have begun to penetrate as the village is drawn in through new transport and commercial networks and as larger landholders and some others have acquired new wealth from the green revolution. Migrants to the cities keep their village ties and serve as transmission links for new ideas and values from urban to village worlds. Most of those at the bottom of the caste hierarchy are still severely disadvantaged, but what is called "the cake of custom" is beginning to crack. As one anthropologist's informant put it, "When I put on my shirt to go to my factory, I take off my caste."[1] Even in the villages, members of higher castes no longer refuse to eat with or take food and water from lower castes in many cases. They will even eat pork, though not in public.

Education has played an important role in these changes and will continue to do so. Elementary schooling is not compulsory, and many children either do not attend or drop out. Government resources tend to be concentrated on so-called higher education, which of course further accentuates social and economic distinctions and inequality. But at all levels, the emphasis is on modern rather than traditional values and skills. There

Female computer science students at Sioti College of Technology in Bangalore, India, in 2004. There are almost as many female as male students in postsecondary education in India. (Alamy Images)

are still not enough white-collar jobs for the many thousands of new college, university, or technical school graduates, and "educated unemployment" is a worrying problem. But the Indian reservoir of highly trained and educated men and women is potentially a strong asset and gives India an advantage over China, whose education system was so badly damaged for so many years and which still offers university-level training to only a tiny proportion of its college-age population. In India, about one-fifth of the population goes on to postsecondary education, most of them in state-supported institutions. Nearly as many women as men attend, a sound investment for the future and consistent with the traditional Indian emphasis on learning as the chief path to worldly success and economic growth.

Rural Development

In South Asia as a whole, the rural sector has continued to lag despite the major gains of the green revolution for many. Most of the poor are in the villages. Together with the urban poor, they constitute nearly half of the total population. The government has tried to reserve significant investment for rural development with some success. Average incomes have risen, many villages have radios and even motor scooters, and most have access to improved medical care, either in the nearest town clinic accessible by bus or through an extensive visiting nurse program. Some village boys and girls go to college or university. But the pace of change is still relatively slow, and by no means have all villagers benefited. Whole districts or even states remain poor, far below the national average, while many (often the same districts) continue to be plagued by landlordism, tenancy, and landlessness. Some of these regional disparities are related to differences in soil, climate, and the area in slope; most of the poorest areas are those officially labeled drought-prone, but government relief and work programs remain inadequate to the need.

South Asian agriculture's greatest single problem has long been moisture deficiencies. Agriculture is dependent on a fickle annual monsoon in a summer climate of great heat and high evaporation. The monsoon is late or inadequate nearly one year in three or four over much of the country, and drought is especially punishing in the normally dry or marginally dry areas such as much of the upper Ganges Valley, Punjab, Rajasthan, central India, and the Deccan. There were major government and government-assisted efforts to expand irrigation on a small, local scale through new drilled wells ("tube wells"), power-driven pumps, and storage reservoirs ("tanks"). On a larger scale, several very large, new dams have been built, most notably at

Bhakra Nangal on the Sutlej River in the Himalayan foothills north of Delhi, in Pakistan on the Indus at Tarbela and elsewhere, at Hirakud on the Mahanadi River in Orissa, on the Cauvery River south of Madras, plus many smaller dams elsewhere, and at Gal Oya in Sri Lanka. All are designed for hydroelectric power and flood control as well as irrigation. India and Pakistan more than doubled the supply of irrigation water from independence in 1947 to 1980, and from 1975 they have had a surplus of grain for export; Sri Lanka is now self-sufficient in rice production.

Critics maintained, with some justice, that too much of the new irrigation as well as the greatly increased supplies of chemical fertilizers and the new seeds of high-yield varieties of wheat and rice went to the richer farmers and landlords who could afford it. Successive Pakistani, Indian, and state governments avoided full-scale land reform, although in a few states there was substantial progress on some fronts. Landowners of large properties and those who had benefited most from the green revolution were too important as supporters of the major political parties and state political machines; even the Janata party did not push for radical rural reform. Land ownership became somewhat less inequitably distributed by gradual reform, however, and there is now a new and rising group of enterprising, hardworking farmers (no longer "peasants") who are using the land with great effectiveness. One sign of the new prosperity is the rapid increase in the number of tractors and other mechanical equipment at work in the fields.

These new farmers are, of course, far better off than the peasants—those who have remained subsistence farmers at the bottom, eking out a precarious living as tenants or landless laborers. Such people are close to a majority in many rural areas, but even their incomes have risen to some degree as rural wages rose. The big landlords and zamindars of the past have been largely eliminated, both by the gradual reforms and by new pressures of competition. Rural income distribution on a national average showed too wide a spread between top and bottom, but it is not substantially different from the national average-income distribution in the United States.

One rural problem that resisted change was the traditional veneration of cattle, an attitude as old as the Indus civilization. It is estimated that India has a quarter of the world's bovine population, most of them poorly nourished, giving little or no milk, and many unfit even for draft purposes. Hinduism forbids the slaughter or eating of cattle, and there is religious or traditional opposition to measures, often urged by people in government, including Mr. Nehru, to eliminate or sterilize useless animals. Cattle wander freely, even in the cities, eating what they can find and reproducing haphazardly, with little selective breeding or artificial insemination to upgrade breeds. Most cattle represent a drain on scarce resources rather than an asset, and their emaciated and miserable existence is not consistent with the Hindu emphasis on reverence for life. The cattle that are better fed and cared for are essential, especially to poorer peasants, as both draft animals and sources of milk and milk products like cheese or yoghurt, which are important parts of a diet otherwise short on protein. Nevertheless, since the late 1980s the more prosperous rural areas have been experiencing a "white revolution" of soaring milk production for urban and export markets (as milk powder) from high-bred cows kept on improved feed. Like the green revolution, only more well-to-do farmers have participated through milk cooperatives, and because of high prices, consumption is limited to higher-income groups.

Lentils, puréed as *dhal,* are another valuable source of protein, especially for those who keep to a vegetarian diet. Among other Indians, a growing majority, chickens, ducks, sheep, goats, and even pigs (in non-Muslim areas) are kept on a scavenger basis, as in China, and provide an increasing share of a generally improving diet. Rats and monkeys, the latter being sacred to traditional Hinduism and hence protected, are great destroyers of crops and of stored grain. Storage facilities were generally poor, and as much as a fifth of the stored grain in some areas spoiled or was eaten by pests. Many villages are still segregated along caste lines, with the dominant caste occupying the best land and the most dependable wells and the lower castes or Untouchables working the worst and least irrigated land. Indian law forbids such discrimination, but in traditional rural areas Untouchables are not permitted to use wells or other facilities used by the dominant castes.

Some Threats to Development

One menacing rural problem for all of South Asia is the progressive deforestation. As in China, this had been happening over many centuries as population cut away at the originally extensive tree cover. Wood was the predominant fuel and building material, and in South Asia grazing animals often prevented the regrowth of forests. But with the coming of railways and roads and the rapidly growing population, most of the forest stands on the plains and the Deccan of the south were destroyed. As cutting spread into the hills, especially in the heavy rain areas of the Himalayan foothills and Nepal, the problem has worsened. Soil erosion has multiplied, and floods have increased in number and size. Government efforts to restrict cutting and to replant are inadequate to the scale of the problem, but some private groups have

organized to protect trees and to promote reforestation. Given the acute shortage of fuel wood for cooking, most peasants use dried animal dung, which is carefully collected and dried in the sun as cakes and which burns with a slow, even heat. Unfortunately, this means that the manure does not get onto the fields in most cases. Soils are especially exhausted in much of South Asia outside the immediate river valleys and deltas after four millennia of use. With some exceptions, South Asians do not use ritually polluting human manure, and the soils suffer. Another drain on scarce wood resources is the Hindu practice of burning their dead on a funeral pyre.

In the cities, pollution of another sort, from industry and vehicles, has reached dangerous levels, especially in the largest cities; the air and water are as poisoned as in the rest of rapidly industrializing Asia outside Japan. There is growing realization of the menace this poses for all urban residents, but there are not yet any effective controls. Indians had a sharp reminder of the lethal effects of pollution in 1984 when workers at the Union Carbide plant at Bhopal in central India producing pesticides were negligent in their supervision of the operations and allowed a poisonous cloud of gas to escape, killing or disabling some 25,000 people and crippling or injuring many thousands more. There was a suit against Union Carbide, accused of providing inadequate safeguards, and token damages were finally paid to some of the sufferers, but the more general problem of urban pollution was not adequately addressed. As with all developing countries, South Asia was in a hurry and anxious also, like all poor countries, to minimize costs. Pollution controls were seen, despite the Japanese experience, as slowing growth and as imposing extra costs.

Continuing population growth acts as a drag on per capita economic improvement and of course contributes to deforestation, pollution, and crowding. The end of famine and epidemic and the improvements in diet and public health services were no doubt worth it, but they exacted a price. India has tried hard to bring down its birthrate as its death rate fell sharply, but with only limited results; it has come down below 2 percent, which is low for most developing countries, but that still adds about 15 million new people every year. The Indian government lacks, and would not choose to have, the absolute powers of the Chinese state in enforcing, for example, a one-child-per-family policy. India has offered free male sterilization and has set up clinics all over the country to give advice on family planning and hand out contraceptives. There is extensive publicity urging families to have no more than two children. But people everywhere make their family decisions on the basis of their perceived self-interest. In South Asia, as in the rest of the developing world, the state cannot provide

This is still a common sight in both rural and urban India. Bullock carts like this, largely unchanged for many centuries, continue to carry much of the short-haul freight. (AFP/Corbis)

adequate economic security in old age. People depend on their children for that, as well as their income contribution to the family as a whole.

Under these circumstances, most South Asians prefer to have more children, especially sons (daughters join their husbands' families on marriage). This is changing in the cities, a larger and larger proportion of the total population, where multiple children are often a burden and the emphasis is more commonly on providing well for a few, as in the modern West. Urban birthrates have remained lower than those in rural areas. For the South Asian peasant, economic security will have to be assured, as it still is not for most, before smaller families become the norm. The problem is well illustrated in the early responses of village women to a government family planning poster showing one family of two children living in plenty and another with five children living in squalor. Most village women commented, "Oh that poor family, only two children!" This is the same problem faced by efforts to bring down the birthrate in all developing countries around the world. Islamic Pakistan, moving further toward fundamentalism, has done much less to try to promote family planning, and such efforts have also been hampered in Muslim Bangladesh by bureaucratic ineptitude, while Sri Lanka has done much better than any South Asian state, thanks in part to its higher level of literacy, associated everywhere in the world with falling birthrates. Rising female literacy in the southern state of Tamilnadu, where girls were given free school lunches, was largely responsible for a 25 percent drop in the birth

rate by the time the schoolgirls began to marry in 1985. Even Bangladesh, generally poor and rural, has significantly reduced its birth rate through education. Female literacy may be the best key to family planning everywhere.

India presents a contrast between the relatively small number of educated women, who have played a prominent part in public life especially since independence, as in Indira Gandhi and Sirimavo Bandaranike, and the much larger number of peasant women, who have remained largely subjugated by their husbands, although spreading education and the growth of a national market in ideas are beginning to make an impact there. Pakistan, Bangladesh, and Afghanistan are fundamentalist Islamic states, which specifically degrade women, but even in Pakistan Benazir Bhutto, daughter of the executed Z. A. Bhutto, was elected prime minister for two relatively brief terms, although Muslim fundamentalists declared that Pakistan had been cursed by God in having a woman as head of state! In Bangladesh, despite its Muslim majority, the woman Kaleda Zia was again elected prime minister in 2001, over her rival, also a woman, Sheik Alasina, after a long period of military dictatorship.

It will take time for the development centered in the cities to trickle down to the rural areas and the poorer districts, just as it did in the West. Meanwhile, streams of migrants continue to pour in from the countryside, living in slums and shanty towns and hoping for some employment. There are no controls on movement, unlike China; India is a democracy and tries to avoid regimentation. As a result, foreign visitors often get a bad impression because, unlike China, everything in India is freely available for inspection. The uncontrolled Indian press is often sharply critical of the government's, and the country's, shortcomings, and in public relations terms is sometimes India's own worst enemy. Indira Gandhi's effort to muzzle the press was bitterly unpopular, and its exposés of corruption and mismanagement are avidly read.

It will take time for a fully developed sense of common Indian identity to emerge. In the early days of independence, a Calcutta lawyer is said to have remarked:

> Suppose all Europe could somehow be united under one government, with one parliament and one prime minister. Now take away three-quarters of its wealth, but leave all of its people. Let Spaniards speak Spanish and Bulgars speak Bulgarian. Let Italians mistrust Germans and Frenchmen bluster at Englishmen. What would you have? Why, my dear sir, you would have something very much like modern India.

That is still an apt description. Perhaps predictably, in all the South Asian states independence has also brought a resurgence of nativism, regionalism, traditionalism, and communalism among many groups and areas, such as Punjab and Kashmir. This too is a phenomenon familiar in all new nations, and can be observed, for example, in Africa and the Middle East, whereas in South Asia there is a split between urban and rural worlds, often an unhappy and hostile one. But as the common experience of nationhood continues, and as the development process proceeds, India will not break up into warring factions or regional conflict. Strains will certainly remain; poverty for many, and communal tensions are resistant problems that cannot be solved quickly, or perhaps ever wholly. South Asia, including India, is just too big, too diverse, and too fragmented culturally, religiously, and regionally to produce a uniform national mode or to mount a truly national effort to solve these and other worrying problems adequately. This is of course a matter of degree. No modern state, including our own, is free of similar problems. India's open and democratic system makes its problems more evident—and perhaps slower to solve. But India especially, with its extremely long history, is a society of great vigor and, hence, of promise.

Questions

1. Over what issues did India and Pakistan divide in 1947? What were the roles of Nehru, Gandhi, and Mohammad Ali Jinnah in this partition? What is the legacy of the partition, relative to continuing dis-agreements between the two nation-states—as in the example of Kashmir?

2. Why and how did Bangladesh declare its independence from Pakistan in 1971? What has happened in Pakistan's political system since then? Why is Pakistan currently under military rule—and how does this contribute to America's problems with neighboring Afghanistan? Why has America supported Pakistan's totalitarian governments rather than India's democracy?

3. What have been the major features of Sri Lanka and Nepal politics since the 1990s?

4. What have been the major transitions in Indian politics since its independence in 1947? What are the roles of caste and religion in contemporary Indian politics?

5. How do you explain India's remarkable economic growth since 1990? What problems persist in India? To what extent can India's rural sector share in the new prosperity?

6. Has India moved on the path that Mahatma Gandhi envisioned?

7. Why does the text conclude that "India will not break up into warring factions or regional conflict"? What contributes to this conclusion? What could be argued against it?

Note

1. R. Srinivas, "Modernization: Regional Implications," *Annals of the National Assoc. of Indian Geographers,* vol. 1, no. 1 (June 1981): 77.

Suggested Web sites

Partition of India

http://www.english.emory.edu/Bhari/Part.html
Assorted resources focusing on the partition of India, including a timetable, maps, and related links.

Jawaharlal Nehru

http://www.fordham.edu/halsail/mod/1941nehru.html
The life and works of Nehru (1889–1964), India's first prime minister and an important figure in the Indian Nationalist Movement and a leader in the linking of the newly independent non-aligned nations in the 1950s.

Indira Gandhi

http://ww.sscnet.ucla.edu/southasia/History/
    Independent/Indira.html

http://www.indiachild.com/indira_gandhi.htm

Resources about Indira Gandhi (1917–1984) as well as access to other materials of interest related to contemporary India.

Suggestions for Further Reading

Akbar, M. J. *Nehru: The Making of India.* New York: Penguin, 1989.

Alaudin, A., and Clement, A. *The Environment and Economic Development in South Asia.* New York: St. Martin's, 1998.

Bosse, S. *Kashmir.* Cambridge: Harvard University Press, 2004.

Brown, J. *Modern India: The Origins of an Asian Democracy.* New York: Oxford University Press, 1994.

———. *Nehru.* New Haven: Yale University Press, 2003.

Burki, S. J. *Pakistan.* Boulder, CO: Westview, 1997.

De Silva, K. M. *A History of Sri Lanka.* Berkeley: University of California Press, 1981.

Emadi, H. *State, Revolution, and Superpowers in Afghanistan.* New York: Praeger, 1990.

Embree, A. *Utopias in Conflict: Religion and Nationalism in Modern India.* Berkeley: University of California Press, 1990.

Farmer, B. H. *An Introduction to South Asia.* New York: Routledge, 1993.

Galanter, M. *Competing Equalities: Law and the Backward Classes in India.* New York: Oxford University Press, 1992.

Ganguly, S. *The Crisis in Kashmir.* Cambridge, England: Cambridge University Press, 1997.

Gauher, A. *Ayub Khan and Military Rule in Pakistan.* New York: St. Martin's, 1994.

Goodson, L. P. *Afghanistan's Endless War.* Seattle: University of Washington Press, 2001.

Jahan, R. *Bangladesh.* New York: St. Martin's, 2000.

Jalal, A. *The State of Martial Rule: Origins of Pakistan's Political Economy of Defense.* Cambridge, England: Cambridge University Press, 1990.

Jayakar, P. *Indira Gandhi.* New York: Vintage, 1993.

Joshi, R., and Rindle, J. *Daughters of Independence: Gender, Caste, and Class in India.* London: Zed Books, 1986.

King, R. D. *Nehru and the Language Politics of India.* Oxford, England: Oxford University Press, 1997.

Kohili, A., ed. *The Success of India's Democracy.* Cambridge, England: Cambridge University Press, 2001.

Kukreju, V. *Contemporary Pakistan.* Thousand Oaks, CA: Sage, 2002.

Kulke, H., and Rothermund, D. *A History of India.* London: Routledge, 1998.

Manor, J. *The Expedient Utopian: Bandaranaike and Ceylon.* Cambridge, England: Cambridge University Press, 1990.

McGrath, A. *The Destruction of Pakistan's Democracy.* Oxford, England: Oxford University Press, 1996.

Misra, B. B. *The Unification and Division of India.* Oxford, England: Oxford University Press, 1991.

Norman, O. *Pakistan: Political and Economic History Since 1947.* London: Kegan Paul, 1990.

Novak, J. J. *Bangladesh.* Bloomington: Indiana University Press, 1993.

Perkoveen, G. *India's Nuclear Bomb.* Berkeley: University of California Press, 1999.

Ragui, R. *Military, State, and Society in Pakistan.* New Haven: Yale University Press, 2000.

Rahman, M. *Divided Kashmir.* Boulder, CO: Lynne Riemer, 1997.

Rashid, A. *Taliban.* New Haven: Yale University Press, 2000.

Rose, L. E., and Sisson, R. *Pakistan, India, and the Creation of Bangladesh.* Berkeley: University of California Press, 1990.

Schofield, V. *Kashmir in Conflict.* New York: St. Martin's, 2000.

Stern, R. W. *Changing India.* Cambridge, England: Cambridge University Press, 2003.

Talbot, I. *Pakistan: A Modern History.* New York: St. Martin's, 1999.

Thapar, V. *Land of the Tiger: A Natural History of the Indian Subcontinent.* Berkeley: University of California Press, 1998.

Tharon, S. *From Midnight to Millennium.* New York: HarperCollins, 1998.

Thomas, R. G. *Perspectives on Kashmir.* Boulder, CO: Westview, 1992.

Tomlinson, B. R. *The Economy of Modern India.* Cambridge, England: Cambridge University Press, 1993.

Vanderveer, P. *Religious Nationalism: Hindus and Muslims in India.* Berkeley: University of California Press. 1994.

Varshney, A. *Democracy, Development, and the Countryside.* Cambridge, England: Cambridge University Press, 1995.

Whelpton, J. *A History of Nepal.* Cambridge, England: Cambridge University Press, 2005.

Wickramasinge, N. *Civil Society in Sri Lanka.* Thousand Oaks, CA: Sage, 2002.

Wilson, A. J. *The Breakup of Sri Lanka.* Cambridge, England: Cambridge University Press, 1988.

———. *Sri Lankan Tamil Nationalism.* Vancouver: University of British Columbia, 1999.

Wirsing, R. G. *India, Pakistan, and the Kashmir Dispute.* New York: St. Martin's, 1998.

Wiser, W., and Wiser, C. *Behind Mud Walls.* Berkeley: University of California Press, 2000.

Wolpert, S. *Gandhi's Passion.* New York: Oxford University Press, 2001.

Wolpert, S. *Jinnah of Pakistan.* New York: Oxford University Press, 1984.

———. *A New History of India.* Oxford, England: Oxford Press, 2003.

Cheng, C. Y. *Behind the Tienanmen Massacre.* Boulder, CO: Westview, 1990.

Dietrich, C. *People's China: A Brief History.* New York: Oxford University Press, 1994.

Dikotter, F. *Crime, Punishment, and Prison in Modern China.* New York: Columbia University Press, 2002.

———. *The Discourse of Race in Modern China.* Stanford: Stanford University Press, 1992.

Ding, Y. *Chinese Democracy After Tienanmen.* Vancouver: University of British Columbia, 2001.

Economy, E. C., *The River Runs Black.* Ithaca, NY: Cornell University Press, 2005.

Fairbank, J. K. *The Great Chinese Revolution.* Cambridge: Harvard University Press, 1986.

Fairbank, J. K., et al., eds. *The Cambridge History of China: Vol. 14, 1949–79.* Cambridge, England: Cambridge University Press, 1987.

Garnaut, R., and Ligong, S., eds. *The Rise of the Private Economy in China.* London: Routledge, 2004.

Goldstein, M. C. *A History of Modern Tibet.* Berkeley: University of California Press, 1989.

Harding, H. *China's Second Revolution: Reform After Mao.* Washington DC: Brookings Institution, 1987.

He, B. *China on the Edge: The Crisis of Ecology.* San Francisco: China Books, 1992.

He, L. *Mr. China's Son.* Boulder, CO: Westview, 1992.

Hsu, I. C. Y. *China Since Mao.* New York: Oxford University Press, 1990.

Keith, R.C., and Lin, Z. *Law and Justice in China's New Marketplace.* New York: St. Martin's Press, 2001.

Lardy, N. *China in the World Economy.* Washington DC: Institute for International Economics, 1994.

Liang, H., and Shapiro, J. *Son of the Revolution.* New York: Knopf, 1984.

Liu, B. *China's Crisis, China's Hope.* Cambridge: Harvard University Press, 1990.

Long, S. *Taiwan: China's Last Frontier.* New York: St. Martin's Press, 1991.

Lu, X. B. *Cadres and Corruption.* Stanford: Stanford University Press, 2000.

Meisner, M. *Mao's China and After.* New York: Free Press, 1999.

Mei Zhang. *China's Poor Regions.* London: Routledge, 2004.

Nathan, A. *China's Crisis: Dilemmas of Reform and Prospects for Democracy.* New York: Columbia University Press, 1990.

Ownby, P. *Falungang and China's Future.* Lanham, MD: Rowan and Littlefield, 2003.

Philips, S. E. *Between Assimilation and Independence in Taiwan.* Stanford: Stanford University Press, 2003.

Schram, S. *Mao Tse-tung: A Preliminary Reassessment.* New York: Simon and Schuster, 1984.

Schreker, J. E. *The Chinese Revolution in Historical Perspective.* New York: Praeger, 1991.

Shapiro, J. *Mao's War Against Nature.* Cambridge, England: Cambridge University Press, 2001.

Simon, D. F., and Kau, Y. M. *Taiwan: Beyond the Economic Miracle.* Armonk, NY: M. E. Sharpe, 1992.

Smil, V. *China's Environmental Crisis.* Armonk, NY: M. E. Sharpe, 1993.

Smith, W. *Tibetan Nation.* Boulder, CO: Westview, 1996.

Spence, J. *Mao Zedong.* New York: Penguin, 2000.

Sutter, R. G. *Taiwan: Entering the Twenty-first Century.* New York: University Press of America, 1989.

Thurston, A. *The Ordeal of the Intellectuals in China's Great Cultural Revolution.* Cambridge: Harvard University Press, 1988.

Ts'ai, I. F. *Hong Kong in Chinese History.* Berkeley: University of California Press, 1993.

Vogel, E. *The Four Little Dragons.* Cambridge: Harvard University Press, 1992.

Watson, R. S., and Ebrey, P. B., eds. *Marriage and Inequality in Chinese Society.* Berkeley: University of California Press, 1991.

Wolf, M. *Revolution Postponed: Women in Contemporary China.* Stanford: Stanford University Press, 1985.

Wu, H. H., and Wakeman, C. *Bitter Winds.* New York: Wiley, 1993.

Yahuda, M. *Hong Kong: China's Opportunity.* London: Routledge, 1996.

19

Korea and Southeast Asia in the Modern World

This chapter begins with a survey of Korea under the Yi dynasty (1392–1910) and its decline after the sixteenth century. Foreign pressures to open the country to trade ended with the forcible Japanese opening in 1876 and then a Japanese takeover; their rule was exploitative and oppressive. Independence in 1945 was quickly marred by a split between the Communist north and a dictatorship in the south. In 1950 northern forces invaded the south but were finally driven back, as were the Chinese "volunteers" who came to their aid. The war was devastating to both sides; the south had largely recovered by 1970 and had strong economic growth, while the north lagged as tension between the two halves hardened. The election of Kim Dae Jong as southern president in late 1997 promised to reduce tension and begin the path to reunification.

Under oppressive French rule, Vietnam suffered, and its Communist party under Ho Chi Minh became the main political force in its struggle for independence. The French tried to regain control in 1945 but admitted failure in 1954. The United States, in the grip of Cold War rhetoric, replaced the French and fought on a major scale from 1964 to 1973 against the Vietnamese national drive for independence; Vietnam was reunited under a Communist government in 1975 but is still recovering from the immense destruction of war. Cambodia and Laos were part of colonial French Indochina and were drawn into the war by heavy U.S. bombing. Thailand served as a major U.S. base, while Burma came under a military dictatorship from 1962. Malaya became Malaysia in 1963, adding former British areas in north Borneo. Singapore, a mainly Chinese city, remained separate. Indonesia won independence from the Dutch in 1949 but came under a dictatorship, first under Sukarno and then from 1965 under Suharto, who was forced to resign in 1998 in favor of B. J. Habibie, who promised new elections in 1999. Independence came to the Philippines in 1946, from 1965 under the dictatorship of Ferdinand Marcos, ended by the election of Corazon Aquino in 1986, replaced in 1992 by Fidel Ramos, succeeded in 1998 by Joseph Estrada, who promised reforms.

Yi Dynasty Korea in Decline

We must first pick up the thread of Korean history since the founding of the Yi dynasty as recounted in Chapter 9, and present a background necessary to understand what has happened to Korea in the modern era. Under Yi rule from 1392 Korea preserved a correct tributary relationship with China, which was often referred to by Koreans as "elder brother." Chinese influence strengthened throughout this long period, including new emphasis on Confucianism and the adoption of the Chinese examination system based on mastery of Confucian scholarship, philosophy, and morality. For a century or more Korea experienced a lively cultural growth on the Chinese model, printing encyclopedias and extensive histories. The capital was fixed at Seoul, and the country was divided into eight provinces, subdivided into counties following the Chinese pattern, and administered by a scholar-elite class chosen from those who had passed the examinations.

Although the system was supposedly based on merit, or in practice on conformity with the often rigid Confucian code, Korean society remained sharply hierarchical, based on hereditary class distinctions as in Japan. All those who served as military or civil officials came

Squatter slums in front of a new factory in Bombay. Such scenes can be duplicated in many Asian cities. (J. Nystuen)

and economic growth for most of its citizens. China's brutal repression in Tibet and its violent response to legitimate student protest have blackened its reputation abroad. Malaysia remains bitterly divided along racial and cultural lines. Vietnam still struggles to heal the wounds of its 30 years of war; north-south bitterness remains, and the legacy of Communism has been a drag on economic growth and on the emergence of more normal freedom of action.

A police-state government in Indonesia has had only small success in improving the welfare of most of its people, let alone in providing free expression; it continued its bloody repression of the people of East Timor. The Philippines have been torn by fighting, and the nominally democratic government has made little progress in ensuring a better life for most Filipinos while serving the few rich, and maintains its reputation for excessive corruption. North Korea, another surviving Communist state, has lagged far behind its southern neighbor in economic growth and still presides over a regimented society. Japan, and now South Korea, Taiwan, Hong Kong, and Singapore, are experiencing the different problems that come with affluence and with their preoccupation with "getting ahead." Thailand remains the only relatively prosperous Asian country where nearly half the people are still farmers, despite considerable industrial and commercial growth in Bangkok; it has also managed to avoid most violent conflict.

One can have too little perspective on one's own times to see them clearly. It is perhaps understandable that we are always preoccupied with dramatic events—most of them bad—rather than with the slower, more peaceful, and thus perhaps less noticeable, evolution of society, polity, economy, and culture. But if we look at Asia more carefully and compare the present with 10, 20, 40, or 100 years ago, the positive aspects of what has happened leap into prominence. There is no question that most Asians are far better off materially now than at any of these previous times, and probably more so than ever in the past. Several Asian countries led the postwar world in economic growth rates: Japan, South Korea, Taiwan, Hong Kong, Singapore, Malaysia, Thailand, and

In spring and early summer 2003, much of Asia's Pacific Basin faced the severe acute respiratory syndrome (SARS) epidemic, which infected over 8,000 and caused 774 deaths. The epidemic demononstrated the region's initial inability to counter a major disaster, but initiated regional cooperation and coordination that has been foundational to other linkages among the region's nations. (Kenneth Hall)

more recently China and India. In most, this rising tide has indeed lifted all boats, although in some, notably China and India, by far the largest, it is still a very uneven lifting and masses of poor, both relative and absolute, remain. Economists now rate the Chinese economy as the world's second largest, measured by gross domestic product (GDP).

The "free enterprise" or "capitalist" system as now practiced by most Asian countries does not necessarily lead to Western-style democracy. In most of them there are controls (as in the United States too), and "capitalist" is really a term that fits aspects of nearly all societies, past and present, where entrepreneurial efforts and the profit motive form part of basic human behavior. Representative parliamentary democracy, free expression, and Western-style law are vigorous only in India and Japan. Despite their British heritage these institutions are severely clouded or absent in Pakistan and Bangladesh and are badly tarnished by violence, counterviolence, and repression in Sri Lanka. The Philippines, Malaysia, and Singapore, Burma, and Indonesia are mainly dictatorships, while China, Vietnam, and North Korea remain wedded to Communist totalitarianism. Nevertheless, nearly everywhere most Asians are living better—and longer—and are beginning to enjoy some of the fruits of economic development. Cambodia, Laos, East Timor, and Burma are tragic exceptions. But even in Burma, as in a strife-torn India and a restless China, most people are not directly affected by the current violence, repression, and other problems that dominate the headlines. They get on with their lives, pursue education for their children as the traditionally Asian top priority, and look forward to even better years ahead.

Population Growth

Economic development everywhere exacts a price. Perhaps the greatest of these for most of Asia is the ironic one that as people live better they live longer and, hence, total population continues to grow. All Asian countries have long been crowded, not only in terms of people per square mile (where Japan and Java top the world list, together with tiny Belgium and Holland), but in relation to available resources. China, for example, has only about half of the good-quality cultivated land plus pasture area of the United States, but must somehow feed more than four times as many people. India has still less, to support a population now larger than China's. No Asian country begins to be as well endowed with agricultural land, industrial minerals, or forest resources as the United States, with its far smaller population.

Asian forests have been cut into progressively for thousands of years by huge populations; wood is in very short supply, soil is dangerously exposed to erosion, and unchecked runoff worsens floods and chokes rivers with silt. As population pressure has mounted and economic growth has generated a greatly increased appetite for wood, cutting has increasingly removed the tree cover on slopes, with disastrous consequences. So far this has been worst in China and India, the two biggest countries as well as those that have been longest inhabited by large populations. In both, most of the original forest cover has been destroyed, and attempts at reforestation are very far from keeping pace. The disastrous floods in central China in 1954, and again in 1991 and 1998, were a direct consequence of continued deforestation. In normally flood-prone Bangladesh and Assam, the scope and incidence of flooding, damage, and loss of life have increased for the same reason. Southeast Asia contains one of the world's major belts of tropical forest, which is thought to play a vital role in stabilizing world climate patterns. Since about 1950 it too has been heavily cut into, to help feed economic growth domestically and to earn foreign exchange as exports to pay for new imports. The results, in the age of the chain saw and logging truck, are alarming.

Population increases continue to press more and more heavily on limited natural resources everywhere in Asia. Except for China and Indonesia, all Asian countries must import oil to feed their growing industrialization and fuel the rising number of vehicles that are an aspect of economic development. Apart from the expense involved, oil is a vanishing resource that will disappear as the world uses it up in the course of the coming decades. Meanwhile, most of Asia, like most of the rest of the world, depends heavily on coal as its primary energy source. Coal supplies, though finite, will outlast oil, and China in particular has large reserves, but the effects of the rising use of these fossil fuels on the environment are worrisome. The continuing increase in population makes all of these problems more oppressive and slows the real—that is per capita—economic growth rate. It is a little like a fat man trying to chin himself while continuing to gain weight. Efforts to limit population growth rates have ranged from draconian state policies in China to provision of education and family planning in India to little or no official action. Birthrates have come down nearly everywhere, but, excluding Japan, Taiwan, and Singapore, they are still well above death rates, and hence population continues to grow.

The cumulative experience of all countries, including those in the West, makes it clear that birthrates come down only as incomes rise and people feel reasonably secure. Until that point is reached, infant mortality tends to be high (as it still is in most of the poor world),

Erosion in Shaanxi Province, northwest China. Removal of the original forest cover has opened the soil to disastrous erosion, which threatens to engulf the village. (Andrew Wong/Reuters/Getty Images)

and this encourages couples to have multiple children in the hope that some will survive. Sons are especially important, particularly in Asia. Except for Southeast Asia, daughters leave their parental families at marriage and join their husbands' families, so they cannot be counted as economic assets and may cost the family heavily in dowry. Sons and unmarried daughters contribute labor and provide the only economic security for parental old age, where in most of Asia the state still lacks adequate means to support the elderly or the sick. Sons can also continue the family name and line, which is still of basic importance to most Asians, and can perform the death and commemorative rituals for parents that are still considered vital. Families that produce only daughters continue to try for sons. As Mencius put it long ago, in fourth-century B.C.E. China, "Of all things that are unfilial, the greatest is to have no descendants."

Under these circumstances, efforts to persuade people to have fewer children are blunted. Individual self-interest will remain best served by having many children, especially sons, as long as they remain the family's chief security, sanctioned also by many centuries of cultural values. In the rapidly growing cities, large families are more likely to be an economic liability, and for most urbanites income has also risen. Housing, food, jobs, education, and consumer goods must be found for urban children, who make less contribution to family welfare than on the farm, where in any case redundant individuals can more easily be absorbed into and supported by family structures. Literacy is also higher in cities, and

literacy levels everywhere correlate with lower birthrates, perhaps because literate people acquire other values and goals beyond simple reproduction. Urban birthrates have come down nearly everywhere, but outside Japan, Taiwan, South Korea, Hong Kong, and Singapore most Asians are still villagers.

In Japan, economic development brought security to just about everyone in the 1950s, and birthrates came down sharply so that population since then has grown only minimally and now is below stability. This was the pattern somewhat earlier in Europe and North America, for the same reasons, and it is now being replicated in Taiwan, South Korea, Hong Kong, and Singapore. But in most of the rest of the Asian countries populations continue to grow, while per capita income shares grow more slowly as a result.

The twentieth century saw considerable progress in the liberation of women, especially in China. Even Mao Zedong declared that "Women hold up half the sky," although his behavior did not do much to support that idea. In Southeast Asia women continued their traditional equality to or even dominance over men, while in Japan one still finds pretty much the opposite, although a little slow change has begun. But despite the advances in China and in India, women in general (again apart from Southeast Asia) have not yet achieved the degree of equality characteristic of the United States. Much of this has to do with the Asian preference for sons and the fact of a patriarchal society, which also greatly retards the efforts to limit population growth, although in Japan the birth rate has come down to below replacement level, primarily as a result of new prosperity and economic security.

Pollution

Such problems are serious enough, but the steep rise in all forms of environmental pollution, flowing from economic growth and technological change, is equally alarming. It is not easy to be optimistic about the future in such terms. Anyone who has visited Seoul, Taipei, Hong Kong, Jakarta, Bangkok, or any of the cities of China or India recently can give a graphic description of the choking clouds of exhaust and the general atmospheric pollution that hang like a pall over nearly all Asian urban areas, as well as the constant din and fearsome congestion of motorized traffic, from scooters to cars to buses and trucks. There were fewer private cars in China, but the difference is more than made up for by the heavy use of soft coal as industrial and household fuel. Outside of Japan, South Korea, Hong Kong, Taiwan, and Singapore, bicycles outnumbered motor vehicles until very recently, as they used to in China. But as economic growth proceeds, the internal combustion engine increasingly takes over and makes a more and more major contribution to dangerous air pollution, as it has long done in the "developed," or rich, countries.

Americans were the first to be enslaved by the private car; as affluence has spread, even in poor countries like India, Indonesia, or the Philippines, private car ownership has mushroomed and has become an urban plague as well as a serious health menace. Now China has begun to join this trend as incomes have risen for many and a number of new factories have been built to produce cars as well as trucks. But what will crowded China be like with hundreds of millions of private cars? There are, of course, far better ways to deal with urban transport needs—better in that they are much more effective and faster as well as very much cheaper and less polluting, mainly subways and electric streetcars or buses. But the newly affluent everywhere prefer the status and ego building of a private car, however inefficient and antisocial. For them, as for most Americans, the car is a status symbol and an amusing toy. Its rise brings with it horrendous problems. Far from improving the quality of life in most Asian cities, the spread of the private car has greatly worsened it and threatens also to shorten it.

Just as serious is the deforestation that continues in every part of China, Korea, India, and Southeast Asia as demand for wood for these immense populations rises both with numbers of people and with economic growth. The unprecedented floods of the summer of 1998 on the

Tokyo billboard, which automatically prints out the parts per million (PPM) of sulfur dioxide, particulates, nitrous oxide, and an overall ambient air quality rating, changing as traffic changes. This proved one of several effective devices to alert people to what was happening to their environment.
(R. Murphey)

Yangzi and the Songhua were a direct result of devastating tree cutting. The upper and middle Yangzi used to run a clear jade green in the winter low water period; for many years now it has been a muddy brown at all seasons as tree cover no longer checks erosion. Deforestation is at least as severe in India, and in most of Southeast Asia, where continued inroads into the once extensive rainforest may well have a cumulative effect on global climate. Only in Japan have strict regulations kept tree cutting to a minimum, but the difference is made up by heavy imports of wood, mainly from already endangered Southeast Asia.

Equally serious is the pollution caused by industry, especially where it uses chemicals or large amounts of coal or oil, with wastes discharged both into the atmosphere and into water bodies. The "yellow dragon" of sulfurous smoke and haze produced from burning fossil fuels, mainly soft coal, that hangs over Chinese cities is duplicated in most urban areas outside Japan. In most Asian cities outside the charmed circle of the high-income countries, the water is also unsafe to drink and contains varying amounts of chemical toxins and heavy metals that have seeped into the water table or have been discharged into rivers or lakes. Piped water supplies, however unfit to drink, cannot keep up with booming urban populations, and taps often give out nothing but air or a rusty sludge. Water pollution, at least as menacing to human welfare as air pollution, is clearly the result of industrialization and especially of the use of chemicals and synthetics in many manufacturing processes. Here too economic development exacts a heavy price.

Industrial effluent discharging into Tokyo Bay. (R. Murphey)

Poisoned as they are, water tables in many large urban areas have been dangerously drawn down, and surface water bodies cannot keep up with surging demand for both industrial and household uses. The biggest cities compete with each other, and with smaller ones, in tapping more distant rivers to feed their water supply systems. In most cities outside the rich Asian countries—still the great majority—most households must draw and carry their water from an undependable tap or pump shared by many others in a courtyard or at the end of a lane. Urban housing is desperately inadequate in both quantity and quality, and the makeshift huts or tents of squatter colonies, in addition to clouds of street people and beggars, clutter the urban landscape. Despite all of these dismaying problems, people continue to flock to the cities from the countryside in search of wider economic opportunity.

Urbanization

For all their squalor (again excluding Japan), Asian cities are the chief growing points of industrializing economies and the chief centers of technological, cultural, and institutional change. They provide industry and commerce with the strongest cost and convenience advantages. They are also the seat of nearly all universities, the biggest national and regional bureaucracies, and the predominant if not the only cultural centers. Most of the cities are unable to keep up with the mass flow of immigrants; employment and resources do not grow fast enough. Delhi–New Delhi, for example, is said to receive 150,000 new rural immigrants each year. Most of them do ultimately succeed, enough at least to

ensure that there is very little return, or U-turn movement as it is called, and fresh recruits continue to pour in to live in makeshift slum shelters and eke out a hand-to-mouth existence. In the longer run, most of them manage to establish themselves and build a better life, if not for themselves, then for their children; by comparison, opportunities in the village are far more limited. Even for the urban poor, there is the multiple excitement of living on center stage: billboards, parades, shop fronts, markets, and the bustle of city life. In China, where movement was strictly controlled, rural people still seem clearly to prefer life in the cities, and more and more of them manage to evade the controls and gravitate to urban centers. Shanghai, for example, now has well over a million illegal residents drawn from the countryside.

Except for its larger scale, there is nothing about this process in Asia that differs significantly from the Western experience, including pollution, alienation, squalor, and the other urban ills with which we are familiar. In the West too, cities grew, especially in the earlier stages of the Industrial Revolution, more through migration than from natural increase, and there was serious unemployment, crowding, and squalor before employment and services began to catch up. Life for most people in the cities of nineteenth-century England and North America was a hard grind; such problems are by no means gone in our contemporary cities. Because of the far larger scale, it may take longer for urban life in Asia to reach minimum acceptable standards even in their own terms. But most new Asian urban migrants seem remarkably adaptable to squalor and even inventive, like their parallels in the slums of Latin American cities. They construct shelters out of waste or scrounge materials, sometimes forming whole cities in themselves—

fortunately in a climate in most of Asia with a mild winter or none at all—and they help each other in all of their activities, especially in the search for livelihood. New arrivals stay with people originally from the same rural areas, with whom they can share a regional language and customs. For them, urban ways are strange, and new urbanites need help and psychological support.

Population densities are extremely high, probably the highest in the world, topped by Hong Kong but little less in the big cities of China, Japan, Korea, India, and most of Southeast Asia. Much of the employment is casual and includes extensive begging, panhandling, hawking, selling of recycled items, or petty retailing, much of it from open-air pitches along the streets, sometimes sheltered from sun and rain by a tattered bit of cloth on bamboo supports. Five or ten people may share a single regular job. Probably about half of urban residents in Asia outside Japan were born elsewhere, most of them in rural areas. The city represents, as it has always done, the leading edge of social and cultural as well as economic change, cracking "the cake of custom" and pushing societies as a whole into a new world.

The speed and effectiveness of national economic and cultural change is largely a function of the speed and effectiveness of diffusion from the cities, sometimes referred to as "trickle-down." New urban migrants maintain close ties with their rural origins and thus help to expedite the diffusion of urban-generated change. There is a great deal of to-ing and fro-ing, active personal links between city and countryside, which helps to maintain the flow of migrants. Individuals periodically return to their native villages and spread the word about

Among the residents of Asia's older cities were businessmen and their families who lived in intensely settled commercial districts such as this one in Taiwan. These old urban districts are gradually being replaced by new urban housing and commercial developments. (Kenneth Hall)

the greater range of urban opportunities. Many send part of their earnings home to support family members in the village. Weddings, births, festivals, and funerals bring city people back to their village bases even after a generation has passed. Usually it is young adult males who go to the city first, bringing a wife from the village when they have established some base. Wives commonly return to the village to give birth and stay there until the child is a year or two old, depending on the support of family members.

Such links help to transmit the many urban-based changes, including changes in attitudes and values, to the rural areas. Despite their squalor for the poor, the cities appeal to most villagers as an opening to a wider world—and average urban wages, for those who manage to find jobs, are about double the rural average. Nor is everyone in the cities poor by any means. There is a rapidly growing middle class, who enjoy adequate or even luxurious housing and even such amenities as private cars. Urban shops are filled with a great variety of consumer goods: televisions, washing machines, videocassette recorders, and most of the goods found in the West. In most of these cities, half or more of the population are able to enjoy such things; it is understandable that the others, including sojourners from the village, want to be included.

Squalor, like beauty, is often in the eye of the beholder. What appalls Western observers in Bombay or Jakarta and their Asian parallels, the armies of street people and squatters, the piles of rubbish, the shanty towns—are for Indians or Javanese just part of the local scene and not all that disturbing. The cities are seen as places of hope, not of despair, hope for a better life. Few expect it to be easy or gracious, but rather a path won by sacrifice and hard work. Can one say the same about the slums of American cities now? It is harder to be poor in a rich country than in a poor one; again, it is relative deprivation that stings. In any case, how much better have the much richer Western countries done by their cities? For Asia, a more positive projection from the Western pattern of the past is that Asia's cities will go on generating economic growth and change and perhaps in the coming century transform the Delhis, Manilas, and Shanghais of today into something at least as successful as contemporary Western cities for most of their inhabitants, if not as prosperous and well organized as contemporary Tokyo.

The early stages of modern urban industrial growth are a miserable time for most people, as they were at that stage in our own history. It takes historical perspective to see the undoubtedly grave problems of the contemporary Asian city as merely the growing-pains of development—and one might say the same about pollution, slums, drugs, crime, and hopelessness of the bottom fifth in the cities of contemporary United States.

But data-based comparisons make it clear that Calcutta, the common worst-case example, already affords a better level of material welfare to most of its inhabitants than did its British or American counterparts of 1840 or 1880. Since World War II, Asian cities have avoided the major epidemics that killed so many Londoners or Philadelphians in the nineteenth century. Life expectancy rates, perhaps the single most basic measure of material welfare, are substantially higher in all Asian cities than they were in London 150 or New York 100 years ago. One must hope that despite the burden of huge numbers, the growing-pains stage will be shorter for them (as it was in Japan) than it was in the West. Technology is quickly transferred, and Asia has the usual latecomer's advantages. The trend is clearly positive, if one compares the present with even the recent past. It would be foolish to expect these cities, unlike the rest of life, to be without blemishes. They will do well to match the still-flawed Western experience of providing security or affluence for the top three-quarters of their populations. Meanwhile, the cities remain the chief engines of national and regional economic growth.

At the same time Asian cities are probably the most polluted in the world. If the Japanese and Western experiences are any guide, large numbers of people will have to die, as dramatically as possible (as at Bhopal), before anything substantial is done. Pollution control is seen (wrongly, given the Japanese record) as too expensive for poor countries, and as delaying the rapid industrialization that they need—a luxury for rich countries or, at worst, a Western plot to retard development in the poor world. Asian cities are in fact following the flawed Western model in this as in other respects and for the same reasons: the urban concentration essential to the speed and cheapness of industrialization, the drive for "better living through chemistry," and the reluctance to put long-term group welfare ahead of immediate gain. As pointed out in Chapter 18, the Japanese experience in fact demonstrated that pollution controls added only 1 to 2 percent to production costs, much of which was recovered in reuse of captured materials or in economies realized from cleaner and more efficient plants. As already mentioned, water pollution is as bad as air pollution in most Asian cities. Urban rivers are clogged with industrial wastes. The Huangpu at Shanghai and the Hooghly at Calcutta are just about biologically dead, a chemical cocktail in which nothing can live.

Ragged, overcrowded, squalid, and unhealthy as they may be, the cities are nevertheless where most Asians want to be. What development has taken place there is hard to see as "progress," but it is certainly there in the factories, workshops, universities, and other building blocks of development. The cities are also exciting places to be, socially, intellectually, politically, artistically, even for the nonelite, the street people,

and their throbbing, vital world, especially by comparison with the countryside. Much of urban life is in fact street life, and it is impressively rich, for all the squalor of its surroundings. Anyone who knows Calcutta, to take perhaps the most dramatic example, is well aware of its slums and street people, but will also attest that Calcutta is perhaps the most culturally vibrant city in the world, on both elite and mass levels: filmmaking, graphic arts, fiction, poetry, music, commentary of all sorts, festivals, and a vigorous street life. Those who live in Asia's cities, especially the biggest ones, know that they are where the action is. That in itself is enough for most of them to compensate for the grimness of current material conditions.

The cities are the womb of Asia's future, good and less good. The gestation period for the good parts will be long and painful, though perhaps not so much as it was for Western cities. Too much reliance on "trickle-down" may encounter the intolerance or violence of the millions affected by that revolution of rising expectations that the cities themselves generate. Unchecked squalor and pollution may sour, cripple, or kill too many Asian urbanites before something is done about them. But people are tough. The West demonstrated that by surviving the nineteenth century, and contemporary street dwellers demonstrate it daily in Bombay and its many Asian analogues. It seems unlikely that the next fifty years will see a major divergence from the Western experience that Asian cities have so far replicated. Both urban rich and urban poor will increase their standards of living, but the gap between them is more likely to widen than to narrow while at the same time the proportion of the reasonably well-off will continue to rise. Urban concentration will also continue, leaving most rural areas lagging behind in material terms, fueling more rural-to-urban migration to the bottom economic sector in the cities. There seems little likelihood of eliminating urban poverty, in the sense of relative deprivation, any more than we have managed to do so in our own cities. The same is probably true of pollution, overcrowding, alienation, aesthetic devastation, and the rest of the unlovely package now so widely regretted in the "successful" West and Japan.

In some ideal sense, one would like to see the present urban-centered development pattern continue, build up some surpluses, take care of the most urgent needs in the cities themselves, and then, when the basic infrastructure permits, begin to turn out the vast flow of consumer goods necessary to make a real impact for the better on most people's lives, including those in rural areas. But with development comes ambition for upward mobility and unavoidable discontent. Planners propose, but people dispose. A message found recently scrawled (in English) in the dust on the back of a battered bus in central India read "WE WANT A NEW

Aerial view of Kawasaki. Originally a separate city, Kawasaki is now engulfed in the expansion of Tokyo, which has become a vast industrial complex outside the old city of Edo. Note the smoke and the elevated highway. Both air and water are dangerously polluted, as in all Asian cities, although in Japan they have become much cleaner since the 1970s. (R. Murphey)

BUS." That is the voice of rising expectations—there was no bus at all for this remote area twenty or thirty years ago—but also a sign of change, ferment, and the gathering momentum of economic development, which is typical in varying degrees of all of Asia, even in cloistered Burma, and hopefully soon in battered Cambodia, Laos, and Vietnam.

This illustration makes it clear that ferment and change are spreading to the countryside too. Some areas and some farmers or entrepreneurs have won new prosperity on the tide of the green revolution, even though this has worsened the relative deprivation of disadvantaged areas and of people left out of the new rural affluence. Nevertheless, their average level of material well-being has risen too, if not as far or as fast. Famine has become a thing of the past in Asia, and rural areas have at least the beginnings of basic health care services and elementary education. Literacy rates and life expectancy are rising; these changes hold the best promise for bringing down birthrates as economic security grows for most people, although the pull of the cities will remain. Migrants usually move to a nearby smaller city or town as a first stage and only later to a big urban area. But more and more villagers have access to the wider urban world through regular bus services. Although it will be a long time, if ever, before the village can offer the goods or excitements of the city, its traditional world is beginning to change too.

Unfortunately, one aspect of that change is rural pollution, partly from new rural industries burning fossil fuels but mainly from the rapidly increasing use of chemical fertilizers and highly toxic pesticides. The con-

ditions at the Union Carbide plant in Bhopal were typical of many such plants throughout Asia, not to speak of the long-term effects of the indiscriminate use of pesticides and other toxic chemicals on an environment that must continue to sustain such dense concentrations of people. Rural air and water are no longer clean or safe. Technological change is very far from being cost-free. The Bhopal disaster helped to raise awareness of such risks for a time but has not yet led to anything like adequate controls or environmental legislation that could better protect air and water quality or the remaining forests, in any country outside Japan. Even there, as industrialization continues and as affluence spawns still more vehicles, the pollution-control legislation of the 1970s has been left basically unchanged rather than being adjusted to the growth of toxicants. Air and water quality have suffered, and Japan may have to confront more pollution disasters in the future.

Nevertheless, the Japanese example should encourage the other Asian countries to do something about pollution before many more people die. Controls are both technologically possible and inexpensive, especially when one considers what is at stake. Although such controls were strict in Japan and quickly enforced, they did not slow Japan's economic growth. Controls brought other rewards—relatively clean-burning car engines that went on to dominate world markets and the creation of a new industry making pollution-control devices. Unfortunately, people rarely learn from the mistakes of others, but only from their own. "Experience keeps a dear school, but fools will learn in no other," runs a nineteenth-century Western proverb. It seems likely that many more people elsewhere in a polluted Asia will have to die before their governments follow the Japanese example of the 1970s.

Economic Growth Rates

East Asia as a whole had the highest economic growth rates of any part of the world in the decades following World War II. Hong Kong, Taiwan, and South Korea, in that order chronologically, followed in the wake of Japanese economic success after the mid-1950s to produce their own very rapid development. Much of it was on the Japanese model, beginning in light industry and consumer goods and continuing into heavy manufacturing and precision goods. Singapore boomed as a close parallel to Hong Kong, both tiny Chinese city-states originally prospering as trade and financial centers and then moving into high-tech industrialization and processing. In China, despite the drag exerted by antiurbanism and irrational ideology and planning, there were also impressive industrial growth rates. However, it should be borne in mind that the data are unreliable and the original base was very small. It is easy to double or even triple a small number but progressively harder to produce equivalent rates as the base grows. And one must remember that China has to produce for a population now well over 1 billion, so that per capita shares have remained relatively small, although they are now growing more rapidly.

It is probably not a coincidence that all of these East Asian countries developed out of an originally Chinese tradition that emphasized disciplined hard work and organized group effort, as well as placing the highest value on education. Communist China's less impressive overall economic performance until about 1992 has been clearly related to its destructive education policies and perhaps to its effort to eradicate much else about the traditional system that it inherited. Japan has stressed the importance of education, especially since 1950 and to a great degree since 1870, and its modern achievement is closely related to that investment and to a national commitment to learning. South Korea, Taiwan, Hong Kong, and Singapore have been equally faithful to these aspects of their inherited Chinese tradition.

The system that has developed there and in Japan is sometimes loosely referred to as "Confucian capitalism," but it clearly has much less to do with Confucianism than with the common Chinese heritage in other respects: the value attached to hard work, and perhaps more importantly the unspoken commitment to group interest and group effort as opposed to individualism or, as the Chinese traditionally saw it, the anarchy of individual decisions and actions as against the order and the power of group decision and action. In each of these modern settings, the family has remained centrally important, and beyond that the work group. Loyalty to both and the pattern of working together in the common interest has supported the individual and minimized interindividual rivalry and competition, which tend to be subsumed within the group goals that all strive to advance.

Particularly in the Japanese case, the nation became, especially after 1870, an overriding group to which most Japanese gave their loyalty and their efforts. This pattern produced a powerful engine for national economic development, and it is still operative. Asians have always valued education as a means for upward mobility and as a conduit through which status and prestige are achieved. The learned man has traditionally been honored above all others. Japan, Taiwan, South Korea, Hong Kong, and Singapore have all continued this pattern to an outstanding degree and continue to produce a particularly highly educated citizenry. This has been a strong asset for economic growth, and has also enabled each country to keep abreast of the rapid technological changes that are characteristic of modern development. Education is perhaps the chief family priority in these countries, and each child's progress is treated as a family enterprise, in the realization that the family's welfare in the longer run, as well as its prestige, depend on it.

Fathers, mothers, and older siblings work with children to help them to excel, to a degree unknown in the United States, for example, as a recent psychological survey makes clear, based on interviews with parents in each society. If their child is not an outstanding student, far more American parents tend to blame the school, whereas East Asian parents blame themselves or the child's natural intelligence or diligence. Failure, like social deviance, brings shame on the family or other group, as success brings credit. In any case, East Asian children at virtually all levels outperform their American counterparts in every field of learning, and by a very large margin, as East Asian adults outperform them in the workplace. The two are obviously connected, not only through the societies' differing emphases on education but also through the East Asian consensus about the importance of diligent, conscientious work and loyalty in the service of group advancement.

This is not to imply that we in this country are necessarily wrong in the way we do things or that we should change our ways and become like the Japanese or Koreans. In any case, that would be impossible; our social patterns evolved out of very different circumstances, including far more living space, abundant resources, and a small population. We value individualism and individual freedom of action; we tend to dislike what we see as "regimentation" and do not have a highly developed sense of the primacy of the group. In general, we are willing to pay the price that such values tend to exact, and most of us would chafe under the kinds of constraints that Asian societies place on individuals. We may, however, soon have to accept more stringent environmental legislation in the common as well as individual interest of all, and to reexamine our attitudes toward and investment in education, not merely because East Asians are outperforming us but because it makes excellent sense to do so in our own interest.

Tradition in Modern Asia

The oldest living world traditions are in Asia, and the societies of modern Asia are probably the most historically conscious in the world. They are proud of the varied splendors of their Great Traditions, as they have been called, their long and rich record of achievement in culture, technology, and the arts, in the greatness, power, and wealth of their states, and in their leadership of the whole world until comparatively recently—a tradition that is currently being given new dimensions by the Japanese in the world of today and tomorrow. A further reason for the importance that Asians attach to their past is the blows to their pride inflicted by an aggressive imperialist West in the century and a half after 1800. The West had acknowledged Asia as its technological, economic, artistic, and political superior for many centuries. But Europeans suddenly drew new strength from the Industrial Revolution, and with it new arrogance. Their achievement of technological leadership was to some extent fortuitous, and indeed it is far more difficult to explain why the West produced the industrial and scientific revolutions than why Asia did not. Indians pioneered modern mathematics, medicine, and steelmaking 2,000 years ago. The catalog of Chinese discoveries in science and technology is overwhelming: paper, printing, cast iron, gunpowder, porcelain, and the compass centuries before the West, important discoveries in medicine, metal refining, canal locks, iron suspension bridges, and many others.

These and other early advances in Asia were not followed by the kind of transformation that remade Europe after 1800. The reasons are still being debated, but among them surely was the complacency bred in Asia by millennia of greatness, leadership, prosperity, and sophistication. There was less incentive, in an Asia that led the world, to pursue change or innovation than in a comparatively poor and backward Europe. It was Westerners who sought the routes to Asia, inspired by Marco Polo's accounts of the riches of China and India, not Asians who sought the West. Western observers after Polo, and as late as the 1840s, found Asia, especially China, still more prosperous, orderly, and in many ways more advanced than Europe. China fascinated them, and a stream of accounts sang its praises. In India, the British Orientalists were equally fascinated with the riches of the Indian Great Tradition, and many found it superior to their own. Such positive attitudes faded after 1850 as new Western wealth and power generated new cultural and racist arrogance, and as most of Asia entered a steepening decline, except for Japan after 1870. Even there, Japanese success under the Meiji oligarchs rested on the conscious pursuit of Western ways in all things.

The Victorian West saw itself as the new king of creation, riding the wave of its strength and prosperity from steam and steel while the rest of the world lagged behind. The nineteenth century witnessed the conquest or humiliation of every Asian country at the hands of aggressively expansionist Westerners. In the colonial areas of India and Southeast Asia and in the treaty ports and concession areas of China, Japan, and Korea, Westerners treated Asians as inferiors, criticized their cultures as backward, used gunboat diplomacy and other military force to keep them down, and lost sight of their earlier admiration of Asian achievements. Were they not now the lords of the universe? Given that, they were convinced they must also be virtuous and "civilized," with a mission to lead "backward" Asians to the light, including conversion to Christianity in its muscular and superconfident nineteenth-century version.

It is understandable that when colonialism died in the ashes of World War II, there was renewed pride in the Asian tradition. It is equally understandable that earlier, while the lash of Western arrogance was a bitter part of everyday life and the shame of Western conquest hurt Asian pride, there was a similar reassertion of the validity and greatness of the Asian way and efforts to revive it as something to cling to in the face of Western efforts to denigrate it. Asia was no Africa or Latin America, where the past was harder to make into a source of pride and where there was no literate Great Tradition. In response to Western assertions that their cultures were backward and useless, many Asians clung to them all the more fervently and indeed often asserted, not without reason, that their past achievements were superior even to those of the modern West, their cultures greater and richer. The West may have won an unaccustomed and temporary technical superiority, but Asia remained far more "civilized" in all other respects. To salve their wounded egos, many Asians maintained, again not wholly irrationally, that although the West had now become successful *materially,* Asia was still far ahead *spiritually,* which was what really mattered—cold comfort perhaps, and also more than a shadow of whistling in the dark, but for many people, balm for hurt minds.

Nevertheless, there were efforts to change aspects of the Asian tradition that were seen as less appropriate to a modern world, where the power and hence the moral values of the Victorian and post-Victorian West called the tune. In India, the Hindu revival beginning in the early nineteenth century attempted not only to restore the Indian tradition and pride in it but also to cleanse it of things like sati and child marriage, both shocking to the new Western masters. In China, later in the century, the movement against foot-binding and concubinage, and the ban on widow remarriage, began. In Japan, after its forceful "opening" by the West in 1853, but especially under the Meiji Restoration, there were efforts to suppress open premarital promiscuity, class-based restrictions on clothing, mixed nude bathing, and open pornography—the famous "spring pictures" (which seem pretty pale stuff these days!). Asians of course found Western criticisms of their traditional cultures disturbing but badly needed to feel good about their own heritages. Indeed, pride in their own cultural superiority had for centuries been a hallmark of every Asian country, and in most cases, notably China, had helped to blind them to the advantages of learning from these new "barbarians." No one foresaw, to begin with, that the Western "savages" would become the masters of Asia; they were accurately seen as crude, uncivilized, unruly, and smelly primitives with, as the Chinese put it, a "few monkey tricks"—such as better guns and ships.

It was small consolation that the West rose to power using Asian inventions: guns and gunpowder, oceangoing ships, and the compass, recording their profits on Chinese-invented paper. It was an Indian pilot who guided Vasco da Gama from East Africa to Calicut in 1498, along a route that both Indian and Chinese ships, far larger than anything in the West, had sailed for centuries. The Chinese, at least by da Gama's time, were less interested in the sea or in exploration than they had earlier been, after finding in their several probes westward nothing beyond India that they thought was worth the trouble of reaching or of trading with. Except for their trade with Southeast Asia, carried on almost entirely by a small minority of Cantonese and Fujianese in the southeast corner of the country, they were content to leave foreign trade to foreigners and were not concerned to find out much about them. Indeed, foreign trade and foreign merchants came to be confined to Guangzhou (where even so they were permitted to stay only for the trading season determined by the monsoonal winds), thus protecting the rest of China against their disturbing influences.

It took time for the early Western footholds established by the Portuguese, Dutch, and English to yield to the beginnings of territorial-based power in Asia. Nearly three centuries elapsed from Vasco da Gama's voyage in 1498 to the consolidation of British power in India and Dutch power in Java. China did not succumb to Western imperialism until after 1842, Japan until after 1853, most of Southeast Asia even later in the nineteenth century except for the Spanish Philippines. What happened was the result of a combination of factors: steeply rising Western strength, ambition, and military-industrial muscle on the one hand, and on the other the equally steep decline in the effectiveness and strength of the Asian domestic orders. India was in chaos with the end of substantial Mughal authority early in the eighteenth century, providing both opportunity and incentive for the English traders to move in and expand their control, filling a virtual vacuum. By 1842 China had entered its long downward slide as the Qing dynasty began its third century and lost its ability to deal with its mounting problems, domestic and foreign.

In Japan the Tokugawa shogunate was on its last legs by the 1850s and suffering from its self-imposed isolation as Europe surged ahead technologically. In Korea the feeble and ancient Yi dynasty was increasingly unable to cope with either domestic rebellion or foreign pressures. The situation in each Southeast Asian country outside of the Philippines was similar: antiquated monarchies, technological backwardness, and in many of them lack of effective political unity. Indonesia and Malaya were divided among many small and rival sultanates or traditional kingdoms. Thailand and Vietnam were qualified exceptions, but both were far too small and militarily ineffective to resist the Western pressures of the second half of the nineteenth century.

The relatively brief period of Western dominance—perhaps a century and a half in India, a scant hundred years in China, much less in Japan, Korea, and Southeast Asia (again except for the Philippines)—ended with World War II, and by the 1950s all of Asia was independent, each country once again master in its own house, though some of them, especially in Southeast Asia, were newly made from the wreck of former colonial empires. Each country or new nation then had to construct or reconstruct its own independent culture and sense of community. The aim was to preserve and emphasize each country's identity and to purge as much as possible of the Westernization imposed earlier; but they also wanted to encourage the growth of new technology and industrialization, originally Western innovations but now the only secure road to wealth and power in the modern world. Somehow these things had to be blended with distinctively Asian ways, and in a manner that did not harm the validity or stunt the growth of either. It would have been inconceivable for any newly independent Asian country to abandon its pride in its own cultural tradition, the basic stuff of nationalism and especially critical for peoples who had only recently escaped from alien domination. But each major culture worked out its own mix of tradition and modernization.

A Country-by-Country Survey

 India

India is the outstanding example, not only within Asia but in the world as a whole, of the use of traditional symbols and vehicles to expedite what is in fact radical modernization. This was a technique pioneered by Mahatma Gandhi in his struggle to create a national movement for independence from British colonialism. Educated Indians had been quick to follow Western ways in the nineteenth century, convinced that this was the best path for *Indian* development. Their language and much of their culture became English. Indian lawyers, engineers, teachers, civil servants, soldiers, industrialists, and businessmen followed British models, and with considerable success. Gandhi himself began as a British-style lawyer, complete with Western coat and tie and London education. In time many educated Indians wondered who they were, what culture they belonged to, or as Nehru later put it in his autobiography, queer sorts of persons, neither Western nor Eastern, out of touch with their own culture and its peasant masses. Nehru eloquently described his own discovery of India as he came to realize and to accept that, despite his Harrow and Cambridge education and consequent values, he was after all an Indian. He was merely an outstanding example of what was happening to more and more of his Westernized countrymen as they became Indian nationalists. Gandhi taught and inspired them to wear traditional Indian dress, as he did after about 1919, and to spend at least an hour each day at a traditional hand-driven spinning wheel, an Indian symbol and a source of spiritual peace.

But the greatest of Gandhi's inspirational adoptions of tradition to serve radical change was his technique of *satyagraha,* literally, "the power of truth": nonviolent resistance to oppression and injustice, based on traditional Hindu ideas and values. Satyagraha imbued Gandhi's followers with the courage and confidence, the patience and endurance, that come from the knowledge that they were on the side of justice and right. Many thousands of Indians learned to stand up to armed police and troops, to accept beatings, and to vanquish their opponents, as Martin Luther King Jr. was to do a generation later, consciously modeling his strategy and tactics on the Gandhian example. As Nehru put it for Indians, "Gandhi has given us back our courage, and our pride."

With the coming of independence, India has continued to use traditional symbols and vehicles to ease the way to modernization. The Indian flag displays the spin-ning wheel as a badge of India's freedom, and the government still subsidizes a range of cottage industries, including hand weavers. The Congress party uses the cow as its symbol. The radical changes taking place as India forges ahead with industrialization, urbanization, technological progress, the green revolution, and the so-called information age have been greatly expedited by clothing them in traditional symbols. The new Indian space missile is called *Agni,* the name of the ancient Hindu god of fire. Indian scientists, industrialists, and computer wizards, as well as politicians, wear cotton *khadi* jackets and Gandhi caps. Sophisticated women wear saris or Punjabi trousers—though this is no hardship or sacrifice in the name of nationalism, since saris especially are among the most graceful and attractive of garments anywhere in the world. Khadi is usually beautiful stuff too, nearly all handwoven cloth, but cotton was first grown and woven in India 5,000 years ago.

The institution of caste, so often cited by outsiders as a sign of hopeless backwardness and as a bar to change, has in fact not had that effect. Over and over again, caste has instead demonstrated its great flexibility, rarely if ever standing in the way of group and, hence, individual efforts to benefit from new or more promising circumstances. Caste has eased the process of change by helping people to retain a familiar cultural identity or anchor while assisting them to alter their lives in every other respect. Like other continuities with tradition, if only in symbolic form, caste makes people feel more comfortable with what would otherwise be disturbingly disruptive change. Groups have always both risen and fallen in the ranking hierarchy, as they still do. But the predominant means to upward mobility for the group, which of course brings with it upward mobility for individual members—indeed that is the essence and the reward of caste—is the featuring of traditional ritual and traditional behavior, as in the process called "Sanskritization." Caste associations are certainly traditional, and yet they have become in the modern world potent political action groups, using the power of ready-made organization and communality to push for the amelioration of group interests in a great variety of ways, from seats in Parliament to guaranteed places in the bureaucracy and universities to specific government financial and other measures designed to aid particular groups or to respond to their demands.

India is still changing rapidly, especially as modernization impinges on the previously separate world of the villages, but it remains at least as traditional as it is modern. Indeed the two are hard to sort out and in many cases are simply different faces of the same thing. There are of course some countercurrents. Independence has brought, as in all newly independent countries everywhere, tendencies toward what is labeled "nativism," including a reaction against things new or foreign and a clinging to tradition almost for its own sake. In some ways, India's great regional and linguistic diversity encourages such tendencies. Tamils in the south resist national pressures from northern Delhi, including the imposition of Hindi as the official language, Bengalis assert their own cultural, linguistic, and regional superiority, and so on. Religious minorities such as the Sikhs or the Muslims use tradition to defend and assert their sense of separate identity. But the long-term trends are clearly in the other direction, although it will take much time to forge a genuine nation from an area larger and more populous than Europe and far more diverse culturally, physically, and linguistically. Nevertheless, tradition and modernization have gone hand in hand, with tradition playing a basic enabling role.

China

China has had a far stormier and more violent history of interplay between tradition and modernization than has India. By the end of the nineteenth century, most Chinese intellectuals believed that their tradition had failed them. The bitterest among them, such as modern China's greatest writer, Lu Xun, rejected it completely and indeed blamed it, and not "foreign oppression," for China's collapse into impotence and deep humiliation at the hands of Westerners and Japanese. Lu Xun said that the old Confucian order masqueraded as benevolent but was in fact an "eater of men." China had become a nation of cowards, bullies, boasters, and losers, like his famous character Ah Q, who exemplified all these characteristics. Ah Q, who said that he "used to be more prosperous"—like China—was now reduced to begging, petty thieving, and being beaten up by everyone, still clinging to his tattered pride, while around him other Chinese followed a dog-eat-dog morality, trying simply to survive as the Great Tradition of order, splendor, and prosperity fell to pieces.

Lu Xun and others made it clear that the reason for all this was to be found not in foreign encroachments, conquests, and special privileges but in the rottenness of the Chinese tradition, once so proud and successful but now pathetically inept and morally bankrupt. It was notoriously inhumane to its own people, elitist, blind to the need for change, and scornful of everything "barbarian," even while these same barbarians—the supposed "monkeys"—were making monkeys out of China and Chinese. Chinese technology had become hopelessly antiquated, as was demonstrated in the series of nineteenth-century wars ending in total Chinese defeat and in Western and Japanese domination of Chinese shipping, railways, banking, factories, and foreign trade.

The traditional society was certainly elitist, but it did hold that the elite had a responsibility to lead and care for those below. By 1850 at least, such behavior had become exceptional. More and more local areas, where the imperial administration was at best superficial but had now largely disappeared in a swamp of corruption and ineffectiveness, were taken over by local parvenus, a new sort of gentry who lived not by learning and Confucian benevolence but by exploiting the peasantry; they were aided by their armed gangs of toughs in collecting rent and putting down protest or resistance. After the old Qing dynasty finally collapsed in 1911, China broke up into warlord domains, whose rival armies fought over the countryside like a scourge on the peasants.

The Guomindang government of Chiang Kai-shek established a measure of unity from 1927 to the Japanese invasion of the 1930s, but even at its height it controlled only about half of the country, and it made no significant progress toward addressing the by now crushing problems of mass poverty. Women had always been severely disadvantaged in the traditional system, but growing poverty was disproportionately hard on them, and in addition there was now a new group of working women who sought jobs in treaty-port factories, for minimal wages under sweatshop conditions. Lu Xun's bitterest stories deal with the inhuman cruelty of the old society toward women, especially those who had lost their husbands or had been sold into slavery at a young age, one of the results of mass poverty.

China took its humiliation at the hands of foreigners especially hard, because its traditional pride—even arrogance—was so great. China had led the world for so long that it was unbearably painful to acknowledge not only that this was no longer so but also that China had much to learn from "barbarians." Indians were far quicker to accept things from the West, even at the hands of their conquerors, and to take from them the idea of "progress" and its goals. The Indian state and its civil order had collapsed by the eighteenth century, well before Westerners gained the upper hand. Indians thought there was little to defend or be loyal to, especially not to the Mughals, themselves alien conquerors who had ruled most of India from 1526 to 1707 but ended with the cruel and exploitative reign of Aurangzeb. For China, the great model remained their own past, when they led the world. The imperial state hung on, badly shaken but still intact, and with it, Chinese pride and their contempt and growing hatred for all foreigners. The brutal Japanese invasion of Manchuria in 1931, which escalated to all-out war against China in 1937, increased the fear and loathing of outsiders.

It was China's misfortune that when at last it had freed itself of all invaders in 1945, the Communist revolution that soon followed in 1949 ejected all foreigners except Russian advisers; they also rejected all foreign ideas except for Marxism-Leninism and Stalinism, including of course many that could have been basically useful to China's urgent task of economic development. The rejection of Western influences was certainly understandable after the "century of humiliation," but China's consequent isolation amounted to throwing out the baby with the bathwater, in this case the baby of originally Western technology and industrialization. At the same time, the Chinese revolution also rejected Chinese tradition as "backward," "feudal," and exploitative—also an understandable reaction and one long urged by many intellectuals, but leaving the country with too little to guide its development. It was to be a new set of *Chinese* answers to the country's problems, but one that was to be purged of what was now seen as reactionary Confucianism and the trappings of an outmoded and unrepresentative elite culture. It was to draw instead on *peasant* values and use peasants and workers, the oppressed masses of the past, to chart a brave new world. The Guomindang government had been strongly traditionalist, making an effort at revival of a now-moribund Confucianism; this strengthened the Communist determination to wipe the slate clean once it had defeated Chiang Kai-shek, get rid of the burden of the past as well as of foreign ideas, and make a fresh start.

This was heady stuff for all patriotic Chinese, and it had understandable appeal—a new utopia in the bright sun of Chairman Mao, cheered by millions of glassy-eyed enthusiasts waving the *Little Red Book* of his sayings. Here was a new kind of Chinese pride, determined to once again lead the world under the banner of "The East Is Red." Chinese were, like all Asians, still very past-conscious but the past had to be sanitized and emasculated, put safely in a museum, to be acknowledged and admired but with its fangs drawn, no longer able to shape the present or the future as it had for so long in China's history.

But the revolution ran into mounting trouble economically. First came the Great Leap Forward of the later 1950s and the massive famine following it in which 30 million people starved to death. This was shortly followed by the nightmare of the Cultural Revolution from 1966 to the death of Mao in 1976. But there began to be a qualified revival of pride in China's glorious past, if only as an escape from the miserable present. Fanatic Red Guards vandalized or destroyed many traditional temples, books, and artworks, but there were stirrings of reassertion of traditional culture among the common people, especially the peasants, where such attitudes had merely gone underground during the dark years of hysterical ideological frenzy. New archaeological discoveries, many of them revealing splendors of the imperial past, also fed Chinese national pride and helped to soften the rejection of the Great Tradition. Common people, especially in rural areas, increasingly disregarded the official strictures on traditional practices, folk religion with its semimagical beliefs, and festivals. Traditional Chinese New Year began to be celebrated also in the cities; traditional Chinese music, old-fashioned storytellers, and gorgeously costumed opera reappeared. Slowly there grew an acknowledgment of the richness of the Chinese tradition and of the strength it could give to a nation struggling with the problems of modernization, made more difficult by what most Chinese recognized now as thirty years in the wilderness, three decades while ideological madness took the place of rational policies and cut China off from the rest of the world.

China is still struggling to find itself, to work out a viable combination of antiforeignism, new formulas for growth that must necessarily depend to a large degree on originally Western models in technology and organization, and traditional values. The Chinese are still proud of their identity and of their heritage, but they are now more fully aware that they have sadly fallen behind the rest of the world in the modern age and that they urgently need to catch up. It is not easy to keep one's pride, and one's cultural identity, while pursuing a path of catch-up based primarily on the foreign models that were until recently so bitterly rejected. Far too many young Chinese are pessimistic about their country and its future, especially after the ruthless massacre in Beijing in June 1989 and the continuing crackdown. But nearly all Chinese are proud to be so, and few think that their Chineseness is in question. In the longer run, the Chinese sense of their tradition seems likely to help give them the strength to confront their dismaying problems and to sustain them in their long ordeal as they struggle for development, an escape from poverty, freer expression, and the maintenance of their dignity.

Japan

Japan has often been seen as a paradox—so very modern-Western, and so very traditional-Japanese. This is not really paradoxical, in the sense that all societies, including our own, are a mix of traditional and modern. We are all products of our own past, and we all retain attitudes and aspects of behavior that come from our cultural tradition. Traditional and modern are hard to separate, since both are current and both coexist everywhere. The only thing notable about the Japanese, although it is something observable in every culture, is the extent to which traditional ways and symbols have been so consciously preserved and visibly retained in the midst of wholesale Westernization, which has gone further in Japan than anywhere else.

No doubt there is a causal connection. As in India, tradition has helped ease the enormous strains of Japan's uniquely rapid and radical transformation, almost in a single lifetime. From 1870 to the 1960s, a poor, isolated, feudalistic, agrarian society was remade into a world industrial and technological leader where just about everyone now belongs to a prosperous middle class. Japan has the world's highest literacy rate and life expectancy, and over 80 percent of the population lives in cities. Without the support of tradition, or parts of it, to buttress the Japanese sense of continuity and identity, Japanese would have been lost. The whirlwind of change that Japan experienced would have been impossible to tolerate and absorb without both individual and group breakdown.

In the early years of the Meiji Restoration after 1868, there were efforts to force the pace of change. Japanese were urged to give up their traditional clothing and wear Western dress. The traditional vegetarian (Buddhist) diet was abandoned in favor of meat, as the Westerners ate. Western music, art, and literature were promoted. There was even for a time an effort to persuade Japanese to marry Westerners, and some of the young radicals tried to destroy traditional temples. A German physician living in Japan in those years, when the Japanese brought in large numbers of Western experts to help them remake their country, reported an astonishing but typical conversation with a young Japanese. When asked to tell something about Japanese history, the friend replied, "We have no history! Our history begins today!" That is the clear voice of Meiji Japan, or of the early radical years of any revolution. But as the pace of change accelerated and Japanese found they were living in a world almost totally unrecognizable to their parents or even to themselves a decade or two earlier, aspects of the Japanese tradition were revived, and they are still prominent in the Japan of today.

Japanese girls, dressed in traditional kimono and obi, are taught the elaborate ritual of the tea ceremony and of flower arranging. Shinto shrines and Buddhist temples still draw millions of Japanese visitors and worshippers every year. The great shrine at Ise is lovingly and faithfully rebuilt every twenty years by traditional artisans precisely in its medieval form. Japan still preserves Tang period wooden temples, modeled on originals in Chang'an, which have long disappeared in China. Originally Chinese architecture adapted from China during the Tang has long become a part of Japanese tradition, and is more prominent and vital there than in its country of origin. Commuters on the world's most modern transport systems change into traditional kimonos and slippers when they get home, sit on tatami mats, and eat the highly distinctive traditional Japanese food, the more distinctive the better for its value in asserting and sustaining the sense of Japanese cultural identity. The traditional Japanese aesthetic sensitivity impresses all foreigners, resisting the mad rush of tasteless modernity or coexisting with it even in the exquisitely wrapped packages provided for purchases in the modern, Western-style department stores.

Tradition has helped to keep the Japanese sense of identity inviolate and enabled them to ride with remarkable serenity over the otherwise temptuous seas of change. The most "modern" of all countries in Asia, or perhaps in the world, owes much of its smooth success to its use of traditional culture to sustain it.

Southeast Asia and Korea

In Southeast Asia, it is hard to generalize about what are in fact at least eight sharply distinctive cultures, traditions, and countries. But in all of them, aspects of traditional culture have been brought to the fore to help build a sense of new nationhood and ease the strains imposed by rapid change or modernization. Economically, much of the colonial system has persisted or merely taken new forms. Western-based multinational corporations have expanded their operations in most Southeast Asian countries, taking advantage of cheap local labor to produce goods for export to the West or Japan. Most of Southeast Asia is still dependent to a disturbing degree on foreign capital and on foreign markets for its still dominantly agricultural, mineral, or forest products. Most advanced industrial goods are still imported from the West or Japan. Second-wave nationalism has been prominent in Southeast Asia in the decades following formal independence as each culture and nation has struggled to develop and assert its independent identity. This is most obvious in the revival of Islam in Malaysia and Indonesia as a badge of cultural nationalism and, especially in Malaysia, the efforts to canonize even older aspects of the traditional culture, as in the newly invented monumental architecture of the capital, university, and museum at Kuala Lumpur.

Burma has made perhaps the most sweeping move into its own past by cutting many of its ties with the outside world and reverting to a traditional, village-centered, Buddhist mode while at the same time coming under a military dictatorship. The Philippines continue to suffer perhaps most of all Asian countries from the strains of modernization, having lost most of what traditional culture they once possessed during the long centuries of Spanish control and then coming under American domination and influence. Nevertheless, Tagalog, not Spanish or English, has become the national language, and a rich literature is written in it. Filipinos strive to distance themselves from their colonial past and reassert their own cultural traditions. All of Southeast Asia shows the strains of rapid change and reaches for its own traditions to help sustain it.

Modern Korea has had a tragic history, a victim first of Western and then of Japanese imperialism, followed by a bitter civil war and a division of the country into two opposing halves as a result of Cold War pressures from the superpowers. Of all the peoples of Asia, Koreans may as a result be most anxious to retain and assert their distinctive identity and to use their own Great Tradition to buttress that sense and to separate them from the recent past of subjugation and humiliation. Traditional Korean culture is indeed distinctive, from diet to behavior norms, and it plays a basic role in maintaining the sense of Koreanness, to override the long years when that was forcibly eclipsed. Mongols and Tibetans, subjugated for even longer by China or under a Chinese or Russian shadow, show the same kind of response by reviving or newly asserting their traditional cultures: yurts and the veneration of Chinghis Khan among Mongols, Lamaistic Buddhism and the veneration of the Dalai Lama among Tibetans. For both, their traditional cultures, looked down on by Chinese and Russians, have become a badge of identity as well as a source of pride, in much the same way as for Koreans.

Nearly all Asian societies still put a higher priority on group rather than individual interest, and nearly all believe that effort, achievement, and responsibility are collective. Such attitudes are deeply rooted in the Asian tradition and are perhaps its most basic aspect. The Japanese, and now East Asian, economic miracle clearly rests on the greater Asian tradition of group effort in the pursuit of excellence. Thus, underlying Asia's rapid modernization is a strong foundation of traditional values and traditional modes. There can be no better demonstration of the centrality of tradition in a modernizing Asia.

The Nation-State in Contemporary Asia

An important contemporary debate among scholars and politicians also debate whether Asian countries can continue to exist in their current form as unitary states. Some see the potential for a reconfiguration into some less center-dominated form, perhaps a federalist system based in the development of stronger state governments that are less dependent on the center. At the extreme, some argue that in today's world the era of the large nation-states has passed, and that smaller regional polities are more representative and responsive to local needs as well as being better able to cope with the realities of a global society of the twenty-first century.

Questions

1. Since World War II, Asian nations have often been praised as the new economic forces in the world, especially post-1980. Is this a valid analysis?

2. What are the social, economic, political, cultural, and environmental problems still facing Asia? Address this question relative to the entire region as well as for individual countries.

3. Many Westerners think of Asia as a single homogeneous unit. Is this a valid representation? How does a common emphasis on families over individualism, continuing belief in societal hierarchy, celebration of traditional culture, and generalized support of education demonstrate this? What can be argued against this summation?

4. What is the reason for Asia's continuing relatively high birthrates, except in Singapore, Japan, South Korea, Hong Kong, and Taiwan?

5. How did the economic setbacks of the 1990s, the more recent SARS and tsunami crises, and the continuing ethnic clashes between Hindus and the Muslims in India, the Tamils and Sinhalese in Ceylon, and the Muslims and Christians in Indonesia demonstrate the vulnerabilities of Asia?

6. What has been Asia's evolving relationship with the United States and the West in the post–Cold War era? What initiatives have Asians made to promote their own interactions and interdependencies as alternatives to those with the West?

7. Some have proposed that China will become the most productive economy in the world by 2050. How has China's rise as an economic power had an impact on Japan's prior role in the Asian political-economy? What are the potential implications of China's prominence as related to the future of Asia?

Suggested Web Sites

Southeast Asia

http://www.iseas.edu.sg/
Resources provided by the Institute of Southeast Asian Studies, with information on modern Southeast Asia's politics as well as social and cultural developments.

**http://newton.uor.edu/Departments&Programs/
   AsianStudiesDept/**
Annotated references to useful information on Southeast Asia as well as East Asia.

Air Pollution in Asia

http.www.york.ac.uk/inst/sei/rapidc2/apma.html
Research-based site documenting regional air pollution in Asia.

Modern Asia

**http://www.isop.cula.edu/shenzhen/
   park**
An overview of modern Asia, featuring numerous photographs from China, Japan, Cambodia, India, Korea, Laos, Indonesia, Philippines, Taiwan, Myanmar, and Vietnam.

Acknowledgments

Page xxvi: Keeley, Edmund; C. P. Cavafy. Copyright © 1975 by Edmund Keeley and Philip Sherrard. Reprinted by permission of Princeton University Press.

Chapter 2

Pages 24–25, 27: A. L. Basham, *The Wonder That Was India, Third Edition.* Copyright © 1968. Reprinted by permission of Macmillan Publishers, Ltd.

Page 32: Reprinted by permission of Rhoads Murphey, after James Legge.

Page 36: From *Early Chinese Literature,* by Burton Watson, copyright © 1962 Columbia University Press. Reprinted by permission of the publisher.

Page 37: H. A. R. Gibb *Mohammedanism* (New York: Oxford University Press, 1962), p. 67.

Chapter 3

Page 50: A. L. Basham, *The Wonder That Was India, Third Edition.* Copyright © 1968. Reprinted by permission of Macmillan Publishers, Ltd.

Chapter 4

Pages 73, 75, 79, 84: A. L. Basham, *The Wonder That Was India, Third Edition.* Copyright © 1968. Reprinted by permission of Macmillan Publishers, Ltd.

Chapter 5

Page 96: After H. Maspero, *La Chine Antique* (Paris: Presses Universitaires de France, 1927), pp. 253–254.

Page 97: Excerpt from Hucker, Charles O., *China's Imperial Past,* copyright © 1975 by the Board of Trustees of the Leland Stanford Junior University. All rights reserved. Used with the permission of Stanford University Press, www.sup.org.

Chapter 6

Pages 116, 117: H. G. Rawlinson, *India: A Short Cultural History* (New York: Praeger, 1965).

Pages 118, 119, 123: From *Sources of Indian Traditions,* Wm. Theodore de Bary, ed., copyright © 1964 Columbia University Press. Reprinted by permission of the publisher.

Chapter 8

Pages 150, 151, 152: From *Sources of Chinese Traditions,* Wm. Theodore de Bary, ed., copyright © 1964 Columbia University Press. Reprinted with the permission of the publisher.

Page 158: Crump, J., trans. From *Songs from Xanadu.* Copyright © 1983 by Center for Chinese Studies, The University of Michigan.

Chapter 9

Page 179: Hall, John. Translations of three haiku from pages 254 and 257 of *Japan in the Muromachi Age* by Takeshi Toyoda, translated by John Hall. Copyright © 1977 The Regents of the University of California. Reprinted by permission.

Chapter 10

Page 188: Lach, Donald F. From *Asia on the Eve of Europe's Expansion* by Donald F. Lach and Carol Flaumenhaft. Englewood Cliffs, N.J.: Prentice-Hall, Inc., 1965. Courtesy of Donald F. Lach.

Page 200: M. Komroff, ed. *The Travels of Marco Polo* (New York: Doubleday, 1930), p. 95.

Chapter 11

Page 211: J. J. L. Duyvendak, "The True Dates of the Chinese Maritime Expeditions in the Early Fifteenth Century" *Toung Pao,* Vol. 24 (1938): 349–355.

Page 222: J. R. Davis, ed. *The Chinese,* Vol. 2 (London: Charles Knight, 1984), pp. 235–240.

Page 225: D. Lach, *Asia on the Eve of Europe's Expansion,* Prentice-Hall. Copyright © 1971. Reprinted by permission of the author.

Chapter 12

Page 233: M. Collis, *The Land of the Great Image* (New York: Knopf, 1943), p. 85.

Page 238: Reid, A. From *Southeast Asia in the Age of Commerce: The Lands Below the Winds.* Copyright © 1988 by Yale University. All rights reserved. Reprinted by permission of Yale University Press.

Chapter 13

Page 253: From Adam Smith, *The Wealth of Nations,* Vol. 2 (New York: Dutton, 1954).

Page 255: J. B. du Halde, *A Description of the Empire of China,* Vol. 2 (London: E. Cave, 1738).

Page 265: G. B. Sansom, *Japan: A Short Cultural History.* Copyright © 1931, 1943, and 1952 by G. B. Sansom. Reprinted with the permission of Stanford University Press, www.sup.org.

Page 267: A. L. Sadler, *The Maker of Modern Japan,* copyright © 1937. (London: Allen Unwin), pp. 389–390. Reprinted by permission of Routledge.

Page 271: Conrad Totman, *Japan Before Perry* (Berkeley: University of California Press, 1981) p. 208.

Page 273: P. F. Siebold, *Manners and Customs of the Japanese in the Nineteenth Century* (London: Murray, 1852), pp. 122–124.

Page 274: From *A History of Modern Japan* by R. Storry, p. 90, copyright © 1960 by Richard Storry (London, UK: Penguin Books). Reprinted by permission of the Estate of Richard Storry.

Chapter 14

Page 279: I. Habib, *The Agrarian System of Mughal India* (New York: Asia Publishing House, 1963); p. 186: H. Yule, ed. *Diary of William Hedges,* Vol. 2 (London: Barlow, 1887), pp. 237–239.

Page 286: C. Locker, *An Account of the Trade of India* (London: Crouch, 1711), p. 24; B. Francis and E. Kean, eds. *Letters of Phillip Francis,* vol. 1 (London: Murray, 1901), p. 219; J. T. Wheeler, *Early records of British India* (Calcutta: Newman, 1878), p. 53; J. Forbes, *Oriental Memoirs,* vol. 1 (London: White Cochane, 1813, p. 42; J. Rosseli Lord *William Bentinick* (Berkeley: University of California Press, 1974), p. 146; P. Pal and V. Deheja, *From Merchants to Emperors: British Artists and India, 1857–1930* (Ithaca: Cornell University Press, 1986), p. 11.

Page 289: P. Mudford, *Birds of a Different Plumage* (London: Collins, 1974).

Page 291: A. Dow, *History of Hindoostan* (1722), p. 107; P. Mudford, *Birds of a Different Plumage* (London: Collins, 1974), pp. 88–90.

Chapter 15

Page 308: From *Rudyard Kipling's Verses* (New York: Doubleday, 1943), pp. 321–323.

Page 313: R. Murphey, *The Outsiders: The Western Experience in India and China* (Ann Arbor: University of Michigan Press, 1977), p. 149.

Page 315: W. Churchill, *The River War,* Vol. 1 (London: Longman's Green, 1899), p. 18–19; R. Herber, Norwood, MA.: Plimpton Press, 1940, p. 254.

Page 318: Reprinted by permission of the publishers from *China's Response to the West: A Documentary Survey, 1839–1923,* by Ssu-yu Teng and John King Fairbank, pp. 24–26 (Cambridge, MA.: Harvard University Press). Copyright © 1954, 1979 by the President and Fellows of Harvard College. Copyright renewed 1982 by Ssu-yu Teng and John King Fairbank.

Page 319: G. W. Cooke, *China Being the Times, Special Correspondance from China in the Years 1857–58* (London: Routledge, 1958), p. v; "A Chinese Tract of the Mid-Nineteenth Century" in E. P. Boardman, *Christian Influence on the Ideology of the Taiping Rebellion* (Madison: University of Wisconsin Press, 1952), p. 129.

Chapter 16

Page 334: Reprinted by permission of the publishers from *China's Response to the West: A Documentary Survey, 1839-1923,* by Ssu-yu Teng and John King Fairbank, pp. 87, 109 (Cambridge, MA.: Harvard University Press). Copyright © 1954, 1979 by the President and Fellows of Harvard College. Copyright renewed 1982 by Ssu-yu Teng and John King Fairbank.

Page 337: Reprinted by permission of the publishers from *China's Response to the West: A Documentary Survey, 1839–1923,* by Ssu-yu Teng and John King Fairbank, pp. 155 (Cambridge, MA.: Harvard University Press). Copyright © 1954, 1979 by the President and Fellows of Harvard College. Copyright renewed 1982 by Ssu-yu Teng and John King Fairbank.

Page 338: J. O. P. Bland and E. Backhouse, *China Under Empress Dowager* (London: Heinemann, 1910).

Page 343: Reprinted by permission of the publishers from *China's Response to the West: A Documentary Survey, 1839–1923,* by Ssu-yu Teng and John King Fairbank, pp. 240–244 (Cambridge, MA.: Harvard University Press). Copyright © 1954, 1979 by the President and Fellows of Harvard College. Copyright renewed 1982 by Ssu-yu Teng and John King Fairbank.

Page 350: From *Sources of Indian Traditions,* Wm. Theodore de Bary, ed., copyright © 1964 Columbia University Press. Reprinted with the permission of the publisher.

Page 353: J. Nehru, *An Autobiography* (London: Chatto & Windus, 1942).

Chapter 17

Page 359: H. Aung, *The Stricken Peacock* (The Hague: Nijhoff, 1965), p. 9.

Page 362: U. Mahajani, *Philippine Nationalism* (Brisbane: University of Queensland Press, 1971), p. 225.

Page 362: F. Luzvimida, "The First Vietnam: The Philippine-American War," *Bulletin of Concerned Asian Scholars,* December 1973, p. 4.

Page 364: From *Sources of Indian Traditions,* Wm. Theodore de Bary, ed., copyright © 1964 Columbia University Press. Reprinted with the permission of the publisher.

Page 366: J. Nehru, "Mahatama Gandhi," *L'Europe,* February 1936, p. 21.

Page 370: From Mao Zedong, "Report on an Investigation of the Peasant Movement in Hunan," in M. J. Cove, J. Livingston, and J. Highland, *China* (New York: Bantam, 1984).

Page 373: J. K. Fairbank and E. O. Reischauer and A. M. Craig, *East Asia: The Modern Transformation* (Boston: Houghton Mifflin, 1965), p. 566.

Chapter 18

Page 391: From *A History of Modern Japan* by R. Storry, pp. 240–241, copyright © 1960 by Richard Storry (London, UK: Penguin Books). Reprinted by permission of the Estate of Richard Storry.

Page 395: Translated for publication in *The New York Times,* November 24, 1991, from the original Japanese language article published in "Gaiko Forum," June 1991. Reprinted by permission of Kazuo Ogoura.

Page 400: Mao Zedong, *The Chinese Revolution and the Chinese Communist Party* (Peking: Foreign Languages Press, 1954), p. 17 (written in 1939); *Red Flag,* June 1, 1958, pp. 3–4; "Reply to Kuo Mo-jo" (dated February 5, 1963), in *China Reconstructs,* 16 (March 1967), 2.

Chapter 19

Page 426: P. H. Lee, *Flowers if Fire: Twentieth Century Korean Stories* (Honolulu: University of Hawaii Press, 1986), pp. 191–204.

Page 430: H. J. Benda and J. Larkin, *The World of Southeast Asia* (New York: Harper & Row, 1967), pp. 270–273.

Page 431: Hammer, E. From *The Struggle for Indochina* (Stanford, CA: Stanford University Press, 1954). Reprinted courtesy of Stanford University Press.

Page 442: S. Sjahrir and C. Wolf, *Out of Exile* (New York: John Day, 1949), pp. 66–68.

Page 445: L. Taruc, *Born of the People* (Manila: International Publishers, 1953), pp. 265–271, 274–275.

Chapter 20

Page 451: J. Nehru, *An Autobiography* (London: The Bodley Head, 1989), pp. 552, 596.

Page 452: From *Sources of Indian Traditions,* Wm. Theodore de Bary, ed., copyright © 1964 Columbia University Press. Reprinted with the permission of the publisher.

Page 455: From *Sources of Indian Traditions,* Wm. Theodore de Bary, ed., copyright © 1964 Columbia University Press. Reprinted with the permission of the publisher.

Page 462: From *Sources of Indian Traditions,* Wm. Theodore de Bary, ed., copyright © 1964 Columbia University Press. Reprinted with the permission of the publisher.

Index